Encyclopedia of Human Evolution and Prehistory

Second edition

Garland Reference Library of the Humanities (Vol. 1845)

Encyclopedia of Human Evolution and Prehistory

Editors

Eric Delson
Lehman College, City University of New York
American Museum of Natural History

Ian Tattersall
American Museum of Natural History

John A. Van Couvering
American Museum of Natural History

Alison S. Brooks
George Washington University
National Museum of Natural History

Garland Publishing, Inc.
A member of the Taylor & Francis Group
New York & London, 2000

Published in 2000 by
Garland Publishing Inc.
A Member of the Taylor & Francis Group
19 Union Square West
New York, NY 10003

10 9 8 7 6 5 4 3 2 1

Library of Congress Cataloging-in-Publication Data

    Encyclopedia of human evolution and prehistory.--2nd ed./
       editors, Eric Delson... [et al.]
       p. cm.-- (Garland reference library of the humanities; vol. 1845)
       First ed. edited by Ian Tattersall, Eric Delson, and John Van Couvering.
       Includes bibliographical references and index.
       ISBN 0-8153-1696-8 (alk. paper)
       1. Human evolution--Encyclopedias. 2. Prehistoric peoples--
Encyclopedias. I. Delson, Eric. II. Tattersall, Ian. III. Van Couvering,
John A. IV. Series

    GN281 E53 1999
    599.93′8--dc21   99-045824

Printed on acid-free, 250 year-life paper
Manufactured in the United States of America

For
Bobbie, Jeanne, Enid, and John
and to the memory of Frank Spencer

Contents

Preface to the First Edition

The intense media coverage of new developments in human evolutionary studies testifies eloquently that to our egocentric species no subject is of greater interest than our own past. Yet up to now no comprehensive encyclopedia dealing with the evolution of humankind has been available. In the hope of providing such a source we have worked with our contributors and with Garland Publishing, Inc., to produce the present volume. We have defined human evolution in its broadest sense and so have covered such areas as systematics, evolutionary theory, genetics, primatology, primate paleontology, and Paleolithic archaeology in an attempt to provide the most complete context possible for the understanding of the human fossil record.

The contributions in this volume are written to be accessible to those with no prior knowledge of the subject, yet they contain sufficient detail to be of value as a resource to both students and professionals. The work should prove useful to the widest possible range of individuals interested in human evolution. Each entry has been prepared by a leading authority on its subject; and although every contributor was asked to represent all major points of view on the many topics that are the matter of dispute, each was left free to expound his or her preferred interpretation. The volume thus samples the heterogeneity of opinion that gives paleoanthropology so much of its liveliness, while remaining both authoritative and comprehensive.

We would like to thank our contributors for their efforts to ensure accuracy and comprehensiveness within the space limitations inevitable in a work of this kind. The project originated through the initiative of Gary Kuris, of Garland Publishing, whose enthusiasm and diligence were indispensable in seeing it through to completion. At Garland we would also like to thank Rita Quintas, Kennie Lyman, John M-Röblin, and Phyllis Korper. The late Nicholas Amorosi provided numerous clear renderings of fossils, artifacts, and prehistoric scenes and was responsible for a substantial part of the artwork in this volume. We are also indebted to the numerous other scientific illustrators who contributed to the visual qualities of the book. Jaymie Brauer helped with many editorial matters, as did David Dean; we are grateful to them both.

Preface to the Second Edition

The past decade has seen a wide variety of new fossil finds and theories relevant to human evolution. We are thus pleased to present a thoroughly revised, enlarged, and updated version of the Encyclopedia, incorporating a number of improvements in format based on experience with the first edition. We are especially pleased that Alison S. Brooks has joined the editorial team with primary responsibility for archaeological contributions. Once again, we are indebted to many individuals for their help. On the editorial side, we are most grateful to Ken Mowbray, Joanna Grand, Jaymie Brauer Hemphill, Roberta M. Delson, Steve Velasquez, Paula Lee, Rebecca Jabbour, Tara Peburn, and Haviva M. Goldman; many illustrations were produced or improved through the efforts of Diana Salles, Don McGranaghan, Lorraine Meeker, Chester Tarka, Haviva M. Goldman, John Krigbaum, Andrew Brown, Patricia Iorfino, Brian Stuart, Chet Sherwood, Caitlin M. Schrein and Katarina Harvati. At Garland, we have benefited once more from the inspiration of Gary Kuris and the technical organization of Marianne Lown, Earl Roy, Joanne Daniels, Richard Steins, Alexis Skinner, and their associates. And last but not least, our grateful thanks to all of our contributors.

Contributors

Peter Andrews [P.A.]
Department of Palaeontology
The Natural History Museum
London, England

Nancy Benco [N.B.]
Department of Anthropology
George Washington University
Washington, DC

Raymond L. Bernor [R.L.B.]
Department of Anatomy
Howard University College of Medicine
Washington, DC

Timothy G. Bromage [T.G.B.]
Department of Anthropology
Hunter College, City University of New York
New York, NY

Alison S. Brooks [A.S.B.]
Department of Anthropology
George Washington University
and Department of Anthropology
National Museum of Natural History
Smithsonian Institution
Washington, DC

Francis H. Brown [F.H.B.]
Department of Geology
University of Utah
Salt Lake City, UT

Bruce Byland [B.B.]
Department of Anthropology
Lehman College, City University of New York
Bronx, NY

Eric Delson [E.D.]
Department of Anthropology
Lehman College and the Graduate School
City University of New York
and Department of Vertebrate Paleontology
American Museum of Natural History
New York, NY

C. Jean de Rousseau* [C.J.D.]
Santa Barbara, CA

Daryl P. Domning* [D.P.D.]
Department of Anatomy
Howard University College of Medicine
Washington, DC

Niles Eldredge [N.E.]
Department of Invertebrates
American Museum of Natural History
New York, NY

John G. Fleagle* [J.G.F.]
Department of Anatomical Sciences
Health Sciences Center
State University of New York at Stony Brook
Stony Brook, NY

Frederick E. Grine [F.E.G.]
Department of Anthropology
State University of New York at Stony Brook
Stony Brook, NY

Katerina Harvati [K.H.]
Ph.D. Program in Anthropology
City University of New York
New York, NY

Andrew Hill* [A.H.]
Department of Anthropology
Yale University
New Haven, CT

Ralph L. Holloway [R.L.H.]
Department of Anthropology
Columbia University
New York, NY

Richard F. Kay [R.F.K.]
Department of Biological Anthropology and Anatomy
Duke University Medical Center
Durham, NC

William H. Kimbel [W.H.K.]
Institute of Human Origins
Arizona State University
Tempe, AZ

Carol Kramer* [C.K.]
Department of Anthropology
University of Arizona
Tucson, AZ

John Krigbaum [J.K.]
Department of Anthropology
New York University
New York, NY

George Kukla* [G.K.]
Lamont-Doherty Earth Observatory
Columbia University
Palisades, NY

Jeffrey T. Laitman [J.T.L.]
Department of Anatomy
Mt. Sinai School of Medicine
New York, NY

Susan G. Larson [S.G.L.]
Department of Anatomical Sciences
Health Sciences Center
State University of New York at Stony Brook
Stony Brook, NY

Leslie F. Marcus [L.F.M.]
Department of Biology
Queens College, City University of New York
and Department of Invertebrates
American Museum of Natural History
New York, NY

Jon Marks [J.M.]
Department of Anthropology
University of California
Berkeley, CA

Alexander Marshack [A.M.]
Peabody Museum
Harvard University
Cambridge, MA

John F. Oates [J.F.O.]
Department of Anthropology
Hunter College, City University of New York
New York, NY

John W. Olsen [J.W.O.]
Department of Anthropology
University of Arizona
Tucson, AZ

Todd R. Olson [T.R.O.]
Department of Anatomy and Structural Biology
Albert Einstein College of Medicine
Bronx, NY

Lorann S.A. Pendleton [L.S.A.P.]
Department of Anthropology
American Museum of Natural History
New York, NY

Geoffrey G. Pope [G.G.P.]
Anthropology Program
William Paterson College
Wayne, NJ

Richard Potts [R.P.]
Department of Anthropology
National Museum of Natural History
Washington, DC

G. Philip Rightmire [G.P.R.]
Department of Anthropology
State University of New York at Binghamton
Binghamton, NY

Alfred L. Rosenberger [A.L.R.]
National Museum of Natural History
Smithsonian Institution
Washington, DC

Kathy Schick [K.S.]
Department of Anthropology
Indiana University
Bloomington, IN

Henry P. Schwarcz [H.P.S.]
Department of Geology
McMaster University
Hamilton, Ontario CANADA

Jeffrey H. Schwartz [J.H.S.]
Department of Anthropology
University of Pittsburgh
Pittsburgh, PA

Brian T. Shea [B.T.S.]
Department of Cell Biology and Anatomy
Northwestern University
Chicago, IL

John J. Shea [J.J.S.]
Department of Anthropology
State University of New York at Stony Brook
Stony Brook, NY

Andrew Sillen [A.S.]
University of Cape Town
Cape Town, South Africa

Olga Soffer [D.S.]
Department of Anthropology
University of Illinois
Urbana, IL

Frank Spencer [F.S.]
Department of Anthropology
Queens College, City University of New York
Flushing, NY

Christopher B. Stringer [C.B.S.]
Department of Palaeontology
The Natural History Museum
London, ENGLAND

Gen Suwa [G.S.]
Department of Biological Science
University of Tokyo, JAPAN

Frederick S. Szalay [F.S.S.]
Department of Anthropology
Hunter College, City University of New York
New York, NY

Ian Tattersall [I.T.]
Department of Anthropology
American Museum of Natural History
New York, NY

David H. Thomas [D.H.T.]
Department of Anthropology
American Museum of Natural History
New York, NY

Alan Thorne [A.T.]
Department of Prehistory
Research School of Pacific Studies
Australian National University
Canberra, AUSTRALIA

Nick Toth [N.T.]
Department of Anthropology
Indiana University
Bloomington, IN

John A. Van Couvering [J.A.V.C.]
Micropaleontology Press
American Museum of Natural History
New York, NY

Robert C. Walter [R.C.W.]
Department of Geology
University of Toronto
Ontario, CANADA

Frances J. White* [F.J.W.]
Department of Biological Anthropology and Anatomy
Duke University Medical Center
Durham, NC

Tim D. White [T.D.W.]
Department of Integrative Biology
University of California
Berkeley, CA

Bernard A. Wood [B.A.W.]
Department of Anthropology
George Washington University
Washington, DC

*indicates authors who contributed to the first but not the second edition; some of their original work has been retained, as has their authorship.

How to Use this Book

The *Encyclopedia of Human Evolution and Prehistory* is alphabetically arranged with nearly 800 topic headings or entries varying from 50 to 9,000 words in length. This edition differs from the first in eliminating the in-text heading that simply cross-referenced to other entries. Instead, a concise index is provided.

As before, each entry supplies references to other articles in the volume that bear on the subject in question. Despite the unavoidable overlap among articles dealing with related subjects, readers should consult all entries thus indicated to be certain of obtaining full information.

Paleoanthropology is a science in which there is unanimity of opinion in few areas, and we have not tried to impose a common view upon our contributors. There are thus cases in which articles by different contributors put forward different views of the same questions; such cases are not examples of editorial inconsistency but rather reflect the fact that paleoanthropology harbors a legitimate variety of interpretations in virtually every one of its subfields. It is this variety, indeed, that lends the study of human evolution its particular fascination. Ours is also a fast-moving, ever-changing field, and we have tried to keep all entries up to the minute, including new references appearing into 1999.

The "Brief Introduction to Human Evolution and Prehistory" provides an alternative way of determining the headings under which information may be sought. This "Introduction" briefly surveys paleoanthropology and related fields, making reference to articles dealing with each topic as it arises. It is not a substitute for reading any of the articles it cites but simply points to and places in context the major entries that make up the bulk of the volume. The "Brief Introduction" does not attempt to refer to every short article; however, the "*See also*" references at the end of each main article cited in it point to other entries, long and short, that bear on the major subject involved. Additionally, all but the shortest entries are accompanied by suggestions for further reading. These reference lists are not exhaustive bibliographies but are pointers to (primarily) recent and easily accessible works to which readers can refer for more information. Each of these works contains a longer bibliography that serves as an entry point into the popular and technical literature on the subject.

A Brief Introduction to Human Evolution and Prehistory

The study of human evolution embraces many subject areas that at first glance appear only tangentially related. Yet one cannot hope to understand our past without reference to the biotic and physical context out of which, and within which, our evolution has taken place. Thus the articles in this volume deal at least as much with questions of geology, primatology, systematics, evolutionary theory, and genetics as with the fossil and archaeological records themselves. This brief discussion is meant simply to provide a context for each of the longer entries in this encyclopedia (these are cited in CAPITAL letters), and no attempt is made to refer to every entry. For the taxonomic entries, most references are to family or larger groups. Readers will find references to relevant shorter entries (or those of lower taxonomic rank) at the end of each of the longer articles cited below. Similarly, individual genera are given a separate entry only if they are of questionable or controversial allocation, except that all extinct genera of HOMINIDAE (in the larger sense discussed below) and species of HOMININ are discussed individually.

Human beings are PRIMATES. The living primates are our closest relatives in nature, and their study enables us to breathe life into our interpretations of the rapidly improving fossil record of prehuman and early human species. The related questions as to exactly which mammals deserve to be classified as primates, and which are the closest relatives of primates, have been a matter of debate (see ARCHONTA). Under current interpretation, those extant primates that most closely resemble the early ancestors of our order are the LOWER PRIMATES of the Old World, including MADAGASCAR (see CHEIROGALEIDAE; DAUBENTONIIDAE; GALAGIDAE; INDRIIDAE; LEMURIDAE; LEMURIFORMES; LORISIDAE; PROSIMIAN; STREPSIRHINI), which are closely related to several recently extinct forms from Madagascar (see ARCHAEOLEMURIDAE; LEPILEMURIDAE; PALAEOPROPITHECIDAE) and older forms from elsewhere (see GALAGIDAE; LORISIDAE).

The enigmatic *Tarsius* (see HAPLORHINI; TARSIIDAE; TARSIIFORMES) uneasily straddles the divide between these forms and the HIGHER PRIMATES, with which we ourselves are classified (see ANTHROPOIDEA; APE; HAPLORHINI; MONKEY). These latter include the New World monkeys of South America (see ATELIDAE; ATELOIDEA; CEBIDAE; PLATYRRHINI) and the Old World higher primates, or CATARRHINI, of Africa and Asia. Catarrhines embrace the Old World monkeys (see CERCOPITHECIDAE; CERCOPITHECOIDEA) as well as the greater and lesser apes (see APE; HOMINIDAE; HOMININAE; HOMINOIDEA; HYLOBATIDAE; PONGINAE).

Extant forms can be studied in a variety of ways that are useful in widening the scope of our interpretation of the fossil record. Study of the morphology of modern primates (see BONE BIOLOGY; BRAIN; MUSCULATURE; SKELETON; SKULL; TEETH) provides a base for interpretation of fossil morphology (see also ALLOMETRY; SEXUAL DIMORPHISM), as do correlated aspects of behavior (see BIOMECHANICS; DIET; EVOLUTIONARY MORPHOLOGY; FUNCTIONAL MORPHOLOGY; LOCOMOTION) and broader aspects of ecology and behavior in general (see PRIMATE ECOLOGY; PRIMATE SOCIETIES; SOCIOBIOLOGY). The traumas and developmental phenomena that occur to hard tissues during life (see PALEOPATHOLOGY) can yield valuable information about health and dietary factors in vanished populations; comparative studies of proteins and the genetic material have formed the basis not simply for hypotheses of relationship among primate and other species but also for calibrated phylogenies (see MOLECULAR ANTHROPOLOGY).

Interpretation of the fossil record clearly requires a grasp of the principles of EVOLUTION (see also EXTINCTION; GENETICS; PHYLOGENY; SPECIATION) and of the various approaches to the reconstruction of evolutionary histories and relationships (see CLADISTICS; EVOLUTIONARY SYSTEMATICS [DARWINIAN PHYLOGENETICS]; MOLECULAR "VS." MOR-

PHOLOGICAL APPROACHES TO SYSTEMATICS; NUMERICAL CLADISTICS; PALEOBIOLOGY; QUANTITATIVE METHODS; STRATOPHENETICS; SYSTEMATICS). It also requires an understanding of the processes used to name and classify living organisms (see CLASSIFICATION; NOMENCLATURE) and of the nature of SPECIES (see also SPECIATION), the basic systematic unit. Further, it is important to comprehend the nature of the FOSSIL record itself and the processes by which living organisms are transformed into fossils (see TAPHONOMY). This consideration brings us to the interface between PALEOANTHROPOLOGY and geology.

No fossil can be properly interpreted without reference to the geological context in which it occurs, and various aspects of geology converge on the interpretation of fossilized remains. Next to its morphology, the most important attribute of a fossil is its age. Traditionally, fossils were dated according to their relative position in the sequence of geological events (see TIME CHART), as reflected in their locality of discovery in local sedimentary sequences (see STRATIGRAPHY). Particular sedimentary strata are confined to local areas, and rocks laid down in different regions could formerly be correlated with one another only by comparing the fossil faunas they contained (see BIOCHRONOLOGY; LAND-MAMMAL AGES). In the past few decades, however, methods have been developed of assigning chronometric dates, in years, to certain types of rocks and young organic remains (see GEOCHRONOMETRY and individual dating methods). Additionally, the fact that the Earth's magnetic field changes polarity from time to time has been used, in conjunction with measurements of the remanent magnetism of iron-containing rocks, to provide an additional relative, but datable, time scale independent of fossils (see PALEOMAGNETISM).

The movement of the continents relative to each other (see PLATE TECTONICS) over the period of primate evolution has significantly affected the course of that evolution (see PALEOBIOGEOGRAPHY). More recently, the major geological process that has most profoundly affected human evolution has been the cyclical expansion of ice sheets in the higher latitudes (see GLACIATION; PLEISTOCENE) and the correlated fluctuation in sea levels worldwide (see CYCLOSTRATIGRAPHY; SEA-LEVEL CHANGE). The broader relationship between CLIMATE CHANGE and EVOLUTION is also a focus of active research. A series of entries describes the geological and biological history of each continent or major geographical region (see AFRICA; AFRICA, EAST; AFRICA, NORTH; AFRICA, SOUTHERN; AMERICAS; ASIA, EASTERN AND SOUTHERN; ASIA, WESTERN; AUSTRALIA; EUROPE; RUSSIA).

We first find primates in the fossil record ca. 65 Ma (millions of years ago; by contrast, the abbreviation Myr is used for time spans of millions of years—e.g., in the last 65 Myr). A substantial radiation of primates of archaic aspect took place in both North America and Europe during the PALEOCENE epoch (see ARCHONTA; PAROMOMYOIDEA; PLESIADAPIFORMES; PLESIADAPOIDEA; PRIMATES). In the succeeding EOCENE epoch, these forms were replaced by primates more modern in aspect. Some of these, the ADAPIDAE and the NOTHARCTIDAE (combined in the ADAPIFORMES), are considered to be related in a general way to the modern lorises and lemurs; the family OMOMYIDAE, which contains the subfamilies ANAPTOMORPHINAE, MICROCHOERINAE, and OMOMYINAE, is commonly classified within the TARSIIFORMES. Future studies may show this dichotomy among Eocene primates to be oversimplified.

At present, the higher primates, or ANTHROPOIDEA, appear to be first represented in Africa, despite claims for an Asian origin; for example, the newly discovered EOSIMIIDAE from CHINA is here included in the TARSIOIDEA. Some fragmentary jaws and teeth from the Eocene of North Africa may represent early members of ANTHROPOIDEA, but the only well-represented early anthropoid fauna comes from the FAYUM of Egypt, in the Late Eocene to Early Oligocene, dating to ca. 37–33 Ma. Apart from the enigmatic OLIGOPITHECIDAE and the tarsioid AFROTARSIUS, the Fayum haplorhines fall into two major groups. Of these, PROPLIOPITHECIDAE may be close to the origin of the later Old World anthropoids; PARAPITHECIDAE, although perhaps "monkey-like" in a broad sense, bears no close relationship to any extant anthropoid taxon.

The fossil record of New World monkeys goes back less far (to the latest OLIGOCENE, ca. 27 Ma) than that of the Old World higher primates, but even quite early forms generally appear to be allocable, with few exceptions (see BRANISELLINAE) to extant subfamilies (see ATELINAE; CALLITRICHINAE; CEBINAE; PITHECIINAE; PLATYRRHINI).

The MIOCENE epoch (see also NEOGENE) witnessed a substantial diversification of early CATARRHINI. Probably most closely affined to the propliopithecids of the Fayum was the family PLIOPITHECIDAE, a grouping of small, conservative Eurasian forms, often considered in the past to be related to the gibbons but now regarded simply as generalized early catarrhines. Their African (and Asian) contemporaries are less well understood, if somewhat more like modern forms, and are here placed in the paraphyletic "DENDROPITHECUS-GROUP." They may have been close to the ancestry of both the apes and the cercopithecoid monkeys, representatives of which also first turn up in the Miocene (see CATARRHINI; CERCOPITHECIDAE; CERCOPITHECOIDEA; MONKEY; VICTORIAPITHECINAE). The cercopithecids diversified considerably during the Pliocene in Africa and Eurasia (see CERCOPITHECINAE; COLOBINAE).

The Miocene (and latest Oligocene) of East Africa was the scene of the first documented radiation of hominoid primates (see HOMINOIDEA; PROCONSULIDAE), members of the superfamily containing apes and humans. In the period following ca. 20 Ma, the diversity of hominoid species reached its peak. The first surviving subgroup of Hominoidea to branch off in this period must have been the gibbons (see HYLOBATIDAE), but no known form can be considered a good candidate for gibbon ancestry. The first fossil hominoids that are reasonably placed within the family HOMINIDAE are the Early to Middle Miocene (20–12 Ma) African and Eurasian genera MOROTOPITHECUS, AFROPITHECUS, KENYAPITHECUS, and GRIPHOPITHECUS, included in the subfamily KENYAPITHECINAE. Somewhat more "modern" in morphology is the European Late Miocene DRYOPITHECUS (13–10 Ma), placed in the DRYOPITHECINAE; the enigmatic European OREOPITHECUS (9–7 Ma) may also be

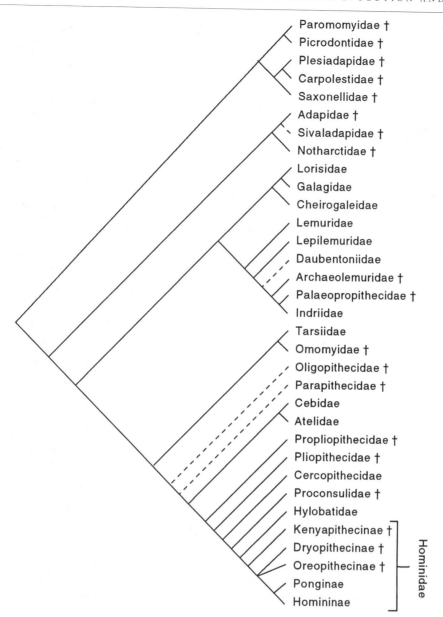

Paromomyidae †
Picrodontidae †
Plesiadapidae †
Carpolestidae †
Saxonellidae †
Adapidae †
Sivaladapidae †
Notharctidae †
Lorisidae
Galagidae
Cheirogaleidae
Lemuridae
Lepilemuridae
Daubentoniidae
Archaeolemuridae †
Palaeopropithecidae †
Indriidae
Tarsiidae
Omomyidae †
Oligopithecidae †
Parapithecidae †
Cebidae
Atelidae
Propliopithecidae †
Pliopithecidae †
Cercopithecidae
Proconsulidae †
Hylobatidae
Kenyapithecinae †
Dryopithecinae †
Oreopithecinae †
Ponginae
Homininae

Hominidae

Cladogram showing possible relationships among the various primate families, living and extinct. This "consensus" cladogram is not intended to be a definitive statement but rather to provide a framework within which the various discussions in this volume can be understood; not all authors will agree with all the relationships hypothesized here, some of which are highly tentative. The three subfamilies of Hominidae are represented separately at the far right. Daggers (†) indicate extinct taxa; dashed lines indicate especially tenuous hypotheses of relationship.

included here or in a subfamily of its own, despite past suggestions of cercopithecoid or hominin affinities. The first extinct catarrhine genus unequivocally related to a single extant genus is the Late Miocene (ca. 12–8 Ma) SIVAPITHECUS, already close in craniodental morphology to the modern orangutan, *Pongo* (*see* HOMINIDAE, in this volume interpreted to include both humans and the great apes; HOMINOIDEA; PONGINAE). This extinct genus also includes *Ramapithecus,* previously considered a potential ancestor of humans. Most authorities today consider that the two African-ape genera are more closely related to humans (*see* HOMININAE; MOLECULAR ANTHROPOLOGY) than are the orangutan and its fossil relatives, although the question is still debated. Despite the rich Miocene hominoid fossil record of East Africa, however, no convincing precursors of the

chimpanzee or gorilla are known, with the possible exception of the gorillalike form SAMBURUPITHECUS from Kenya. The European GRAECOPITHECUS (10–8 Ma), however, is argued by some to be close to the common ancestor of Homininae and is here included in this subfamily.

A virtually complete hiatus occurs in the African hominoid fossil record between ca. 13 and 5 Ma, and subsequent to that gap the record consists of early human relatives. The earliest form that can apparently be admitted to the human CLADE is ARDIPITHECUS RAMIDUS, known by a few fragments dated to ca. 4.4 Ma. Only the LOTHAGAM mandible (ca. 5 Ma) may be an earlier member of HOMININI. More extensive collections of early human fossils are referred to species of AUSTRALOPITHECUS. The first of these is AUSTRALOPITHECUS ANAMENSIS, represented by several jaws and postcranial elements from Kenya (ca. 4 Ma). AUSTRALO-PITHECUS AFARENSIS, known from PLIOCENE sites in Ethiopia and Tanzania in the 4–3 Ma range, is abundantly represented by a partial skeleton and numerous other elements (see also AFAR BASIN; AFRICA, EAST; HADAR; LAETOLI; MIDDLE AWASH). Members of this species were small-bodied upright walkers (although the extent to which they had relinquished their ancestral climbing abilities is debated), as revealed not only by their anatomy but also in the trackways dated to 3.5 Ma from the site of LAETOLI. The BRAIN remained small, but the chewing TEETH were relatively large compared with body size, and the face was rather projecting. Specimens recently discovered in Chad have been given the name AUSTRALOPITHECUS BAHRELGHAZALI, although there is as yet little agreement about the distinctiveness of this form or that of the Ethiopian AUSTRALOPITHECUS GARHI.

Australopithecus was first discovered in South Africa in 1924, when R.A. DART described the juvenile type specimen of AUSTRALOPITHECUS AFRICANUS from the site of TAUNG. Later discoveries at the sites of STERKFONTEIN and MAKAPANSGAT provided more substantial samples of this species, which is represented between ca. 3 and 2 Ma and which differed in numerous details from *A. afarensis*. No stone tools were made at this early stage of human evolution (see AFRICA, SOUTHERN).

Usually, if not entirely accurately, characterized as "gracile," or lightly built, these species of *Australopithecus* remain relatively generalized compared with the "robust" forms known as PARANTHROPUS. This genus differs from the "graciles" in numerous details of cranial architecture functionally linked to the relative expansion of the chewing teeth and diminution of the front teeth. PARANTHROPUS ROBUSTUS is known from the later South African sites of SWARTKRANS and KROMDRAAI (ca. 1.9–1.5 Ma). A related "hyperrobust" form from East Africa, PARANTHROPUS BOISEI, was first discovered by M.D. and L.S.B. LEAKEY at Tanzania's OLDUVAI GORGE in 1959; this form, with its even larger chewing teeth and yet more diminished front teeth compared with *P. robustus,* is now well known from sites in Kenya and Ethiopia ranging from ca. 2.3 to 1.4 Ma. Less abundant material from 2.7 to 2.3 Ma in the TURKANA BASIN represents yet a third species, PARANTHROPUS AETHIOPICUS.

Although the earliest stone tools, between 2.6 and 2 Ma, are not definitely associated with any particular hominin species, it is widely believed that they were an innovation on the part of the earliest members of our own genus, HOMO. With this innovation, the archaeological record begins. Understanding STONE-TOOL MAKING and the analysis of stone-tool assemblages in terms of LITHIC USE-WEAR and the RAW MATERIALS from which they are made form only a small part of the concerns of PALEOLITHIC (Old Stone Age) archaeologists. These specialists also study the nature of ARCHAEOLOGICAL SITES, which reflect the various SITE TYPES occupied by prehistoric people. These sites are located using a number of sampling techniques, and the information they contain is analyzed through the principles of TAPHONOMY. The goal is to reconstruct the PALEOLITHIC LIFEWAYS of vanished hominins.

The earliest species allocated to HOMO is HOMO RUDOLFENSIS, mainly known from the Lake Turkana region between 2 and 1.6 Ma, but specimens perhaps belonging to this species from HADAR, Ethiopia, the BARINGO BASIN TUGEN HILLS, Kenya and URAHA, Malawi, may be as old as 2.4 Myr. The smaller HOMO HABILIS was first described from OLDUVAI GORGE in 1961, in levels dated to slightly later than 2 Ma. Fossils ascribed to *Homo habilis* have been described from Kenya, Ethiopia, and perhaps South Africa as well, in the period between ca. 2 and 1.6 Ma. Fossils allocated to these two forms were previously included in a single species, but most workers now accept a division of the diverse assemblage of specimens involved. Distinctive features of this group appear to include a more modern body skeleton than that of *Australopithecus* (although a fragmentary skeleton from Olduvai Gorge is said to show archaic limb proportions), expansion of the BRAIN relative to body size, and reduction of the face. Accompanied by an OLDOWAN stone-tool kit (see also EARLY PALEOLITHIC; STONE-TOOL MAKING), early *Homo* may have been an opportunistic HUNTER-GATHERER that killed small animals while also scavenging the carcasses of bigger ones and gathering plant foods. We have no evidence clearly demonstrating that these early humans used FIRE or constructed shelters.

Potentially the longest-lived species of our genus was HOMO ERECTUS (see also HOMO). First described from INDONESIA, *Homo erectus* is known from ca. 1.9 Ma in East Africa and persisted in CHINA up to ca. 250 Ka (thousands of years ago; also Kyr for time spans of thousands of years). The earlier African specimens are, however, often separated into their own species, HOMO ERGASTER. These first *Homo erectus* made stone tools of Oldowan type, but these were rapidly succeeded by a more complex ACHEULEAN tool kit (see EARLY PALEOLITHIC) based on large bifacially flaked artifacts, such as handaxes and cleavers, although in eastern Asia this is only rarely the case. The "Turkana Boy" early African *Homo erectus* skeleton, dated to ca. 1.6 Ma, shows that these humans were slenderly built but nearly modern in postcranial anatomy. *Homo erectus* nevertheless was highly distinctive in its cranial structure, although with a yet shorter face and larger brain than *Homo habilis* or *H. rudolfensis*. This was apparently the first form of human to learn to control FIRE (although burnt bone from SWARTKRANS at ca. 1.6 Ma might have been the work of an earlier species) and spread beyond the confines of AFRICA (see also ASIA, EASTERN AND SOUTHERN; ASIA, WESTERN; CHINA; INDONESIA), and to live in caves as well as open sites (see ARCHAEOLOGICAL SITES). It is unclear whether *Homo erectus* ever occupied EUROPE; the earliest human remains (ca. 0.8 Ma and younger) from that region of the world do not belong to this species, but have recently been called a distinct form, HOMO ANTECESSOR.

The better-known early Europeans (ca. 0.5 Ma and younger) are usually classified as belonging to an archaic form of our own species, despite strong physical differences in cranial form from ourselves (see ARCHAIC HOMO SAPIENS). These differences are striking enough to lead an increasing number of paleoanthropologists to place them in their own

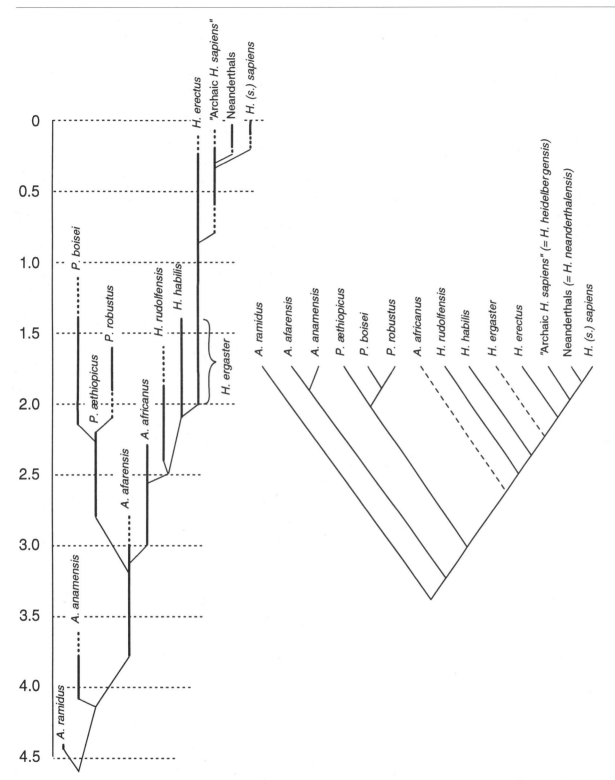

Two representations of relationships in the human fossil record. On the left, a family tree showing known ranges (solid vertical bars) and possible range extensions (broken bars) of the various species recognized; light oblique lines indicate possible paths of descent. On the right, a cladogram more formally expresses hypothesized relationships among the various species. Note: Australopithecus garhi was named too recently to be included here.

species, HOMO HEIDELBERGENSIS, that is also known from other parts of the world.

    Initially, stone-tool-making techniques continued more or less the same as among *Homo erectus,* but eventually a refinement was developed, leading the way to the development of the MIDDLE PALEOLITHIC stone industries. This was the

PREPARED-CORE technique, whereby a core was shaped from which a substantially completed tool could be struck with a single blow. These early humans also provide us with the first definite evidence for the construction of shelters at open sites. These were constructed using a framework of branches embedded in postholes on the ground and tied together at the top. The same period has yielded evidence for similarly advanced humans, with cranial capacities larger than those of *Homo erectus,* in other parts of the world, including AFRICA and Asia. Their PALEOLITHIC LIFEWAYS depended on the hunting of herd animals.

Perhaps the most famous of all extinct forms of human are the NEANDERTHALS, a European and western Asian group known from ca. 200 to 30 Ka. It is their western European representatives from the latest part of this period that show the morphological specializations of the Neanderthals in the most marked degree (*see also* ASIA, WESTERN; EUROPE). These archaic people employed a sophisticated stone-working tradition known as the MOUSTERIAN, a variety of the MIDDLE PALEOLITHIC, and were the earliest humans to bury their dead with RITUAL practices. They were unquestionably replaced in Europe by invading waves of modern people (*see* HOMO SAPIENS; NEANDERTHALS), but the transition from archaic to modern human types in other parts of the world is less clear (*see* ARCHAIC MODERNS). A special group of entries discusses this topic from various points of view (*see* MODERN HUMAN ORIGINS).

All modern HOMO SAPIENS share a distinctive skull anatomy, but the origin of this physical type remains a mystery. Sub-Saharan AFRICA provides the earliest hints of ARCHAIC MODERNS (more than 100 Ka), but in all cases either the fossils are fragmentary or the dating is insecure. More recently, North Africa and southwestern Asia have yielded remains in the 100 Ka range of individuals who were reasonably modern in appearance yet distinct from any surviving group; fully modern humans appear to have been present in eastern Asia by ca. 40 Ka also. The earliest modern humans brought with them the highly sophisticated blade-based stone-working industries of the LATE PALEOLITHIC (*see also* STONE-TOOL MAKING). This phase is most clearly documented in EUROPE, where it is termed the UPPER PALEOLITHIC and is accompanied by the earliest evidence for art, notation, music, and elaborate body ornamentation (*see* CLOTHING; PALEOLITHIC IMAGE; PALEOLITHIC LIFEWAYS; RITUAL). It was modern humans, too, who for the first time crossed into the New World (*see* AMERICAS; PALEOINDIAN) and traversed a substantial sea barrier to reach AUSTRALIA, where a series of highly interesting paleoanthropological finds has been made.

Following the end of the most recent glacial episode, ca. 10 Ka, the big-game-hunting cultures of the European UPPER PALEOLITHIC waned, yielding to the differently adapted societies of the MESOLITHIC period. It was perhaps first in the "Fertile Crescent" of southwest Asia that the next major economic and social developments occurred, with the growth in the NEOLITHIC period (New Stone Age) of settled village life and the DOMESTICATION of animals and plants. These developments paved the way toward COMPLEX SOCIETIES and the written word, and hence toward the end of the long period of human PREHISTORY.

Classification of the Primates

Primate classification is, and probably always will be, in a state of flux. This is because classifications, as the products of human minds rather than of nature itself, may legitimately reflect virtually any set of criteria, provided that those criteria are consistently applied (*see* CLASSIFICATION). Currently fashionable criteria range from the strict transliteration of phylogeny, as expressed in a cladogram (*see* CLADISTICS), to general expressions of overall resemblance. The first of these provides disputed and unstable classifications, because not all details (or in some cases major questions) of primate phylogeny have been definitively resolved. The second has much the same effect, because there exists no generally acceptable method of measuring such resemblance (but *see* EVOLUTIONARY SYSTEMATICS).

It was necessary, however, to settle upon a single classification for the purposes of organizing this volume. This is presented below. We wish to emphasize that we have not attempted to produce a "definitive" classification but rather the closest thing we could achieve to a "consensus" classification. No one, least of all the editors, will accept all of its details, and indeed some of our contributors inevitably take exception to parts of the classification in their entries; thus, each entry dealing with a family or a subfamily, depending upon the group involved, includes a classification of that group usually, but not always, equivalent to what follows. Yet most of it will be acceptable to most students of the primates, and it certainly serves as a coherent framework upon which to arrange the systematic contributions in this encyclopedia. For more details on authorship, synonymy, included species, and related topics, see *Evolutionary History of the Primates* by F.S. Szalay and E. Delson (Academic Press, 1979; second edition in prep). Our classification follows. (†denotes an extinct genus; ? indicates that allocation of a genus to a higher taxon, or a subgenus to a genus, is uncertain.)

Order Primates
  Semiorder Plesiadapiformes
      Superfamily Paromomyoidea
       Family Paromomyidae
         Subfamily Paromomyinae
           Tribe Purgatoriini
             †*Purgatorius*
           Tribe Paromomyini
             Subtribe Paromomyina
             †*Paromomys*
             †*Ignacius*
             †*Dillerlemur*
             †*Pulverflumen*
             †*Simpsonlemur*
             †*Phenacolemur* (including †*Elwynella* and †*Arcius*)
             Subtribe Palaechthonina
             †*Palaechthon*
             †*Plesiolestes*
             †*Palenochtha*
             †*Premnoides*
          Tribe Micromomyini
             †*Micromomys*
             †*Tinimomys*
             †*Chalicomomys*
             †*Myrmecomomys*
          Tribe Navajoviini
             †*Navajovius*
             †*Berruvius*
             †*Avenius*
       Family Picrodontidae
            †*Picrodus* (including †*Draconodus*)
            †*Zanycteris*
      Superfamily Plesiadapoidea

Family Plesiadapidae
 †*Pandemonium*
 †*Pronothodectes*
 †*Plesiadapis* (including
  †*Nannodectes*)
 †*Chiromyoides*
 †*Platychoerops*
Family Carpolestidae
 Subfamily Carpolestinae
  †*Elphidotarsius*
  †*Carpodaptes* (including
   †*Carpolestes*)
  †*Carpocristes*
 Subfamily Chronolestinae
  †*Chronolestes*
Family Saxonellidae
 †*Saxonella*
Semiorder Euprimates
Suborder Strepsirhini
Infraorder Adapiformes
Family Adapidae
 †*Adapis*
 †*Leptadapis*
 †*Simonsia*
 †*Paradapis*
 †*Cryptadapis*
 †*Alsatia*
Family Notharctidae
 Subfamily Notharctinae
  †*Notharctus*
  †*Cercamonius*
 Subfamily Protoadapinae
  Tribe Protoadapini
   †*Protoadapis*
   †*Mahgarita*
   †*Pronycticebus*
   †*Microadapis*
   †*Europolemur*
   †*Barnesia*
   †*Adapoides*
   †*Buxella*
   †*Periconodon*
   †*Huerzeleris*
  Tribe Pelycodontini
   †*Pelycodus*
   †*Cantius*
   †*Laurasia*
   †*Agerinia*
   †*Donrussellia*
   †*Copelemur*
   †*Anchomomys*
 Subfamily Sivaladapinae
  †*Sivaladapis*
  †*Sinoadapis*
  †*Smilodectes*
?Infraorder Adapiformes
 †*Caenopithecus*
 †*Lushius*

†*Azibius*
†*Panobius*
†*Djebelemur*
†*Wailekia*
†*Rencunius*
†*Pondaungia*
†*Amphipithecus*
†*Hoanghonius*
†*Chasselasia*
†*Fendantia*
†*Siamopithecus*
†*Shizarodon*
†*Omanodon*
Infraorder Lemuriformes
Superfamily Lemuroidea
Family Lemuridae
 Subfamily Lemurinae
  Varecia
  †*Pachylemur*
  Lemur
  Eulemur
 Subfamily Hapalemurinae
  Hapalemur
Superfamily Indrioidea
Family Indriidae
 Indri
 Propithecus
 Avahi
Family Palaeopropithecidae
 †*Palaeopropithecus*
 †*Archaeoindris*
 †*Mesopropithecus*
 †*Babakotia*
Family Archaeolemuridae
 †*Archaeolemur*
 †*Hadropithecus*
Family Lepilemuridae
 Subfamily Lepilemurinae
  Lepilemur
 Subfamily Megaladapinae
  †*Megaladapis*
Family Daubentoniidae
 Daubentonia
Superfamily Lorisoidea
Family Lorisidae
 Loris
 †*Indraloris*
 †*Mioeuoticus*
 Arctocebus
 Perodicticus
 Nycticebus
 †*Nycticeboides*
Family unspecified
 Pseudopotto
Family Galagidae
 Galago
  G. (*Galago*)
  G. (*Euoticus*)

Galagoides
    G. (*Galagoides*)
    G. (*Sciurocheirus*)
Otolemur
† *Komba*
Family indeterminate
  † *Progalago*
Family Cheirogaleidae
  Cheirogaleus
  Microcebus
  Mirza
  Allocebus
  Phaner
?Suborder Strepsirhini
  Superfamily Plesiopithecoidea
    † *Plesiopithecus*
Suborder Haplorhini
  Hyporder Tarsiiformes
    Superfamily Tarsioidea
      Family Tarsiidae
        Tarsius
        ?† *Afrotarsius*
        ?† *Xanthorhysis*
      Family Eosimiidae
        † *Eosimias*
    Superfamily Omomyoidea
      Family Omomyidae
        Subfamily Omomyinae
          Tribe Omomyini
            Subtribe Omomyina
            † *Omomys*
            † *Chumashius*
            Subtribe Mytoniina
            † *Ourayia* (including   † *Mytonius*)
            † *Macrotarsius*
          Tribe Uintaniini
            † *Steinius*
            † *Uintanius* (including † *Huerfanius*)
            † *Jemezius*
          Tribe Utahiini
            † *Utahia*
            † *Stockia*
            † *Asiomomys*
          Tribe Washakiini
            Subtribe Hemiacodontina (new)
            † *Loveina*
            † *Hemiacodon*
            Subtribe Washakiina
            † *Shoshonius*
            † *Washakius*
            † *Dyseolemur*
            Subtribe Rooneyiina (new rank)
            † *Rooneyia*
         Subfamily Ekgmowechashalinae
          † *Ekgmowechashala*
        Subfamily Anaptomorphinae
          Tribe Teilhardinini
            † *Teilhardina*

† *Chlororhysis*
  Tribe Trogolemurini
    † *Trogolemur*
    † *Anemorhysis*   (including
      † *Tetonoides* and † *Uintalacus*)
    † *Arapahovius*
  Tribe Tetoniini
    † *Tetonius*   (including
        † *Pseudotetonius* and
      † *Mckennamorphus*)
    † *Absarokius* (including † *Aycrossia*
      and † *Strigorhysis*)
  Tribe Anaptomorphini
    † *Anaptomorphus*   (including
      † *Gazinius*)
  Tribe Altaniini (new)
    † *Altanius*
  Subfamily Microchoerinae
    † *Nannopithex*
    † *Pseudoloris* (including † *Pivetonia*)
    † *Necrolemur*
    † *Microchoerus*
Family Omomyidae, indeterminate
  † *Decoredon*
  † *Kohatius*
  † *Altiatlasius*
Hyporder Anthropoidea
  Infraorder Platyrrhini
    Superfamily Ateloidea
      Family Atelidae
        Subfamily Atelinae
          Tribe Atelini
            Ateles
            Brachyteles
            Lagothrix
            † *Caipora*
          Tribe Alouattini
            Alouatta
            † *Stirtonia*
            † *Protopithecus*
            ?† *Paralouatta*
        Subfamily Pitheciinae
          Tribe Pitheciini
            Proteropithecia
            Chiropotes
            Cacajao
            † *Cebupithecia*
            † *Soriacebus*
          Tribe Homunculini
            Aotus
            Callicebus
            † *Tremacebus*
            † *Homunculus*
        Subfamily Pitheciinae, incertae sedis
          † *Carlocebus*
          † *Lagonimico*
          ?† *Xenothrix*
          ?† *Nuciruptor*

P. (Rhinopithecus)

Nasalis

   N. (Nasalis)

   N. (Simias)

Subfamily Colobinae, incertae sedis

   † *Mesopithecus*

   † *Dolichopithecus* (?including

      † *Parapresbytis)*

Subfamily Victoriapithecinae

   † *Victoriapithecus*

   † *Prohylobates*

Parvorder Eocatarrhini

   "*Dendropithecus*-Group"

      † *Dendropithecus*

      † *Micropithecus*

      † *Simiolus*

      † *Kalepithecus*

      ?† *Mabokopithecus*

      ?† *Nyanzapithecus*

      ?† *Turkanapithecus*

Family Pliopithecidae

   Subfamily Pliopithecinae

      † *Pliopithecus*

   Subfamily Crouzelinae

      † *Plesiopliopithecus* (including

         † *Crouzelia)*

      † *Anapithecus*

      † *Laccopithecus*

Subfamily indeterminate

   † *Dionysopithecus*

   † *Platodontopithecus*

Family Propliopithecidae

   † *Propliopithecus* (including

      † *Aegyptopithecus* and

      † *Moeripithecus)*

Infraorder Paracatarrhini

Family Parapithecidae

   Subfamily Parapithecinae

      † *Apidium*

      † *Parapithecus* (including

         † *Simonsius)*

   Subfamily Qatraniinae

      † *Qatrania*

      † *Serapia*

      ?† *Arsinoea*

   Subfamily indeterminate

      ?† *Biretia*

      ?† *Algeripithecus*

      ?† *Tabelia*

Family Oligopithecidae

   † *Oligopithecus*

   † *Catopithecus*

?Hyporder Anthropoidea, incertae sedis

   † *Proteopithecus*

Primates, incertae sedis

   † *Petrolemur*

Time Chart

Ma	PALEOMAG CHRONS	EPOCHS		GLOBAL STANDARD STAGES	Other Europ. Stages	WESTERN EUROPE		PARATETHYS MARINE STAGES	
						ZONE	MAMMAL AGE	CENTRAL	EASTERN
0	C1	PLEIST	L. / M. / E.	0.02 TYRRHENIAN / 0.9 IONIAN / 1.8 CALABRIAN		MQ 3 / 2 / 1	0.4 OLDENBURGIAN / 1.6 BIHARIAN	ROMANIAN	MOLDAVIAN / 2.0 ASHERONIAN
1.77 / 2.58	C2	PLIO-CENE	A / L. / M.	2.5 GELASIAN / 3.4 PIACENZIAN	Astian	MN 17 / 16	VILLAFRANCHIAN / 3.4		AKCHAGYLIAN / 4.2
4.18	C3		E.	ZANCLEAN / 5.2		15 / 14	RUSCINIAN / 5.2	4.8 DACIAN / 5.6	KIMMERIAN / 5.4
5 / 5.89	A			MESSINIAN / 7.1		13	TUROLIAN	PONTIAN / 7.1	PONTIAN
6.93 / 7.43	B		LATE		Pontian	12			
8.69	C4 / A			TORTONIAN		11 / 9.0	VALLESIAN	PANNONIAN s.s.	MAEOTIAN / 9.8
9.74 / 10	C5	MIOCENE		11.2		10 / 9 / 11.2		PANNONIAN s.l. / 11.5	KHERSONIAN / 11.0
11.93	A		MEDIAL	SERRAVALLIAN	Vindobonian	8 / 7	ASTARACIAN	SARMATIAN s.s. / 13.6	BESSARABIAN / 12.2 / VOLHYNIAN / 13.6
14.80	B			14.8 / LANGHIAN		6 / 15.2 / 5	(ARAGONIAN) 16.5	BADENIAN	KONKIAN / TSCHOKRAKIAN
16.01	C			16.4				16.5	
17.27	D			BURDIGALIAN	Bormidian	4b / 4a / 3b / 3a	ORLEANIAN	KARPATIAN / OTTANGIAN	TARCHANIAN / KOZACHURIAN
19.04	C6		EARLY	20.5			20.5	EGGEN-BURGIAN	SAKARAULIAN
20.51	A			AQUITANIAN		2b / 2a / MN 1	(RAMBLIAN) AGENIAN		22.0
22.58 / 23.35	B / C			23.8			23.8	EGERIAN	CAUCASIAN
24.73 / 25 / 25.49 / 25.82	C7		LATE	CHATTIAN	Stampian	MP 30 / 29 / 28	ARVERNIAN		
27.02	C8 / C9			28.5		27 / 26 / 28.5	28.5		
28.28	C10					24-25			
29.40	C11	OLIGOCENE	EARLY	RUPELIAN	Tongrian	23 / 22 / 21	SUEVIAN		
30.48	C12								
33.06	C13/14			33.7	Lattorfian	20 / 19 / 18 / 17	33.7 HEADONIAN		
34.66 / 35 / 35.34	C15		LATE	PRIABONIAN			36.9		
36.62	C16			36.9					
	C17					16			
38.43	C18			BARTONIAN		15			
40 / 41.26	C19		MEDIAL	41.3	Biarritzian	14	RHENANIAN		
42.53	C20	EOCENE		LUTETIAN		13 / 12			
45 / 46.26	C21					11			
49.03	C22			49.0		10 / 50.3	50.3		
50 / 50.78	C23		EARLY	YPRESIAN	Cuisian	9 / 8	NEUSTRIAN		
52.36	C24			54.5 / 55.6	Sparnacian / Ilerdian	7 / 54.8	54.8		
55 / 55.90	C25			THANETIAN					
57.55	C26		LATE	57.9 / SELANDIAN	Landenian	6	CERNAYSIAN		
60 / 60.92	C27	PALEOCENE		60.9	Montian		60.9		
62.50	C28		EARLY	DANIAN		MP 1-5	DANO-MONTIAN		
63.98	C29			65.0					
65 / 65.58		MAASTRICHTIAN							
67.74	C30								

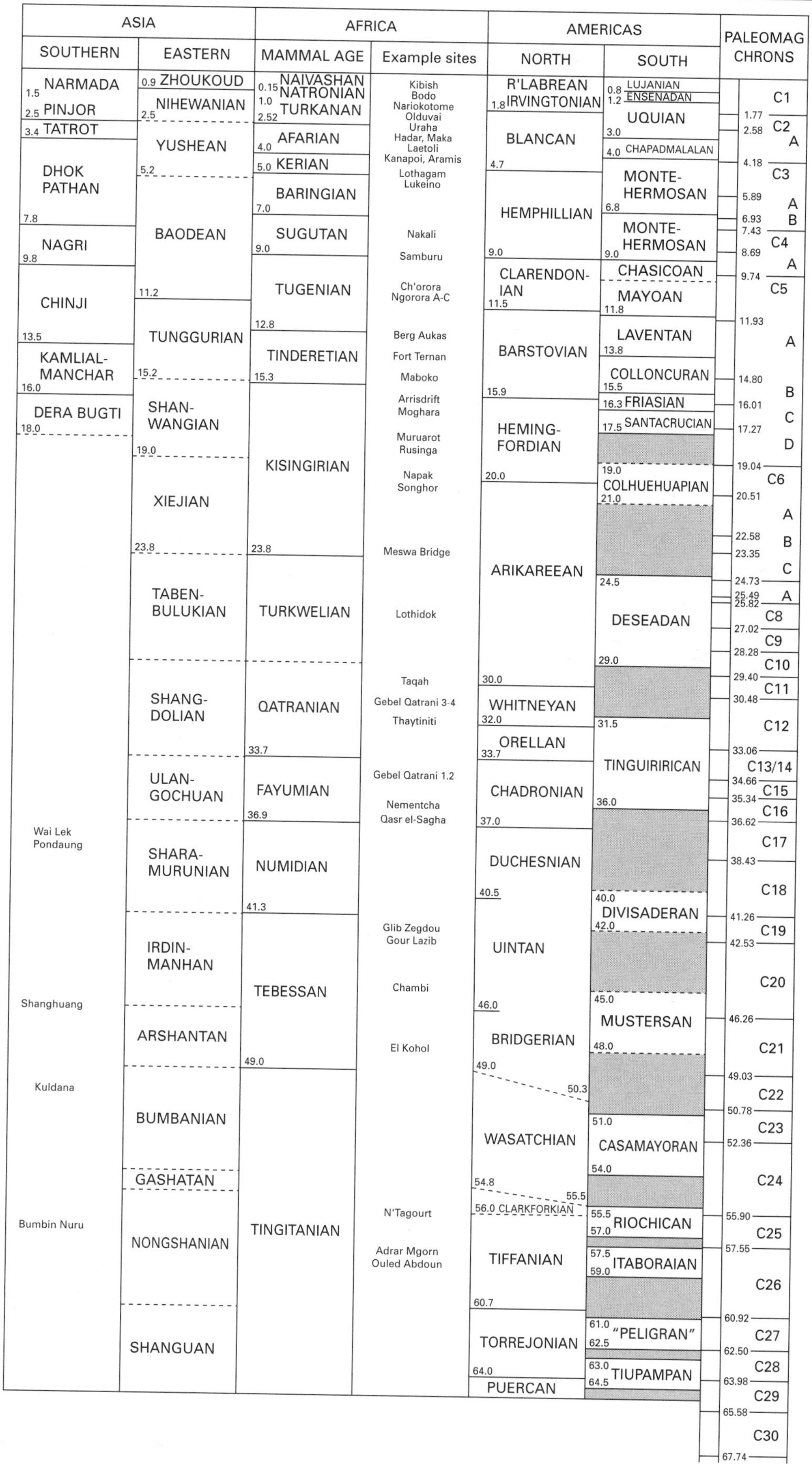

ASIA		AFRICA		AMERICAS		PALEOMAG CHRONS
SOUTHERN	EASTERN	MAMMAL AGE	Example sites	NORTH	SOUTH	

ASIA — SOUTHERN:
1.5 NARMADA · 2.5 PINJOR · 3.4 TATROT · DHOK PATHAN · 7.8 · NAGRI · 9.8 · CHINJI · 13.5 · KAMLIAL-MANCHAR · 16.0 · DERA BUGTI · 18.0 · Wai Lek Pondaung · Shanghuang · Kuldana · Bumbin Nuru

ASIA — EASTERN:
0.9 ZHOUKOUD · NIHEWANIAN · 2.5 · YUSHEAN · 5.2 · BAODEAN · 11.2 · TUNGGURIAN · 15.2 · SHAN-WANGIAN · 19.0 · XIEJIAN · 23.8 · TABEN-BULUKIAN · SHANG-DOLIAN · 33.7 · ULAN-GOCHUAN · 36.9 · SHARA-MURUNIAN · 41.3 · IRDIN-MANHAN · ARSHANTAN · 49.0 · BUMBANIAN · GASHATAN · NONGSHANIAN · SHANGUAN

AFRICA — MAMMAL AGE:
0.15 NAIVASHAN · 1.0 NATRONIAN · 2.52 TURKANAN · 4.0 AFARIAN · 5.0 KERIAN · BARINGIAN · 7.0 · SUGUTAN · 9.0 · TUGENIAN · 12.8 · TINDERETIAN · 15.3 · KISINGIRIAN · 23.8 · TURKWELIAN · QATRANIAN · 33.7 · FAYUMIAN · 36.9 · NUMIDIAN · 41.3 · TEBESSAN · TINGITANIAN

AFRICA — Example sites:
Kibish, Bodo, Nariokotome, Olduvai, Uraha, Hadar, Maka, Laetoli, Kanapoi, Aramis, Lothagam, Lukeino · Nakali · Samburu · Ch'orora, Ngorora A-C · Berg Aukas, Fort Ternan · Maboko · Arrisdrift, Moghara · Muruarot, Rusinga · Napak, Songhor · Meswa Bridge · Lothidok · Taqah, Gebel Qatrani 3-4, Thaytiniti · Gebel Qatrani 1.2, Nementcha, Qasr el-Sagha · Glib Zegdou, Gour Lazib · Chambi · El Kohol · N'Tagourt · Adrar Mgorn, Ouled Abdoun

AMERICAS — NORTH:
R'LABREAN · 1.8 IRVINGTONIAN · BLANCAN · 4.7 · HEMPHILLIAN · 9.0 · CLARENDON-IAN · 11.5 · BARSTOVIAN · 15.9 · HEMING-FORDIAN · 20.0 · ARIKAREEAN · 24.5 · 30.0 WHITNEYAN · 32.0 ORELLAN · 33.7 · CHADRONIAN · 37.0 · DUCHESNIAN · 40.5 · UINTAN · 46.0 · BRIDGERIAN · 49.0 · WASATCHIAN · 54.8 · 55.5 — 56.0 CLARKFORKIAN · TIFFANIAN · 60.7 · 61.0 / 62.5 TORREJONIAN · 64.0 PUERCAN

AMERICAS — SOUTH:
0.8 LUJANIAN · 1.2 ENSENADAN · UQUIAN · 3.0 · 4.0 CHAPADMALALAN · MONTE-HERMOSAN · 6.8 · MONTE-HERMOSAN · 9.0 · CHASICOAN · MAYOAN · 11.8 · LAVENTAN · 13.8 · COLLONCURAN · 15.5 FRIASIAN · 16.3 · 17.5 SANTACRUCIAN · 19.0 COLHUEHUAPIAN · 21.0 · DESEADAN · 29.0 · 31.5 · TINGUIRIRICAN · 36.0 · DIVISADERAN · 40.0 / 42.0 · MUSTERSAN · 45.0 · 48.0 · 50.3 · 51.0 CASAMAYORAN · 54.0 · 55.5 RIOCHICAN · 57.0 · 57.5 ITABORAIAN · 59.0 · 61.0 "PELIGRAN" · 62.5 · 63.0 TIUPAMPAN · 64.5

PALEOMAG CHRONS (top to bottom):
C1 · 1.77 · 2.58 — C2 A · C3 · 4.18 · 5.89 A · 6.93 B · 7.43 — C4 · 8.69 A · 9.74 — C5 · 11.93 A · 14.80 B · 16.01 C · 17.27 D · 19.04 — C6 · 20.51 A · 22.58 B · 23.35 C · 24.73 · 25.49 A · 25.82 C8 · 27.02 C9 · 28.28 C10 · 29.40 C11 · 30.48 · C12 · 33.06 · C13/14 · 34.66 C15 · 35.34 C16 · 36.62 · C17 · 38.43 · C18 · 41.26 C19 · 42.53 · C20 · 46.26 · C21 · 49.03 · C22 · 50.78 · C23 · 52.36 · C24 · 55.90 · C25 · 57.55 · C26 · 60.92 · C27 · 62.50 · 63.98 C28 · C29 · 65.58 · C30 · 67.74

Time scale used in this encyclopedia. The Global Standard Stages are formal subdivisions of Cenozoic epochs defined in western European stratotypes; vertically oriented terms refer to marine stage names used incorrectly (but often) in the literature as mammalian zones. The age-calibration of the stage boundaries and of the paleomagnetic record follows Berggren, W.A., Kent, D.V., Swisher, C.C., III. and Aubry, M.-P. 1995 (in W.A. Berggren, et al., eds., SEPM Society for Sedimentary Geology, Special Publication 54). Normal and reversed intervals within the paleomagnetic chrons are not indicated. The correlation of North American, South American, European, and (Eastern) Asian Land Mammal Ages to this time scale is that of M.C. McKenna and S.K. Bell, 1997, Classification of Mammals Above the Species Level, Columbia University Press. For Europe, the set of numbered MN (Mammalian Neogene) and MP (Mammalian Paleogene) zones subdivides the Cenozoic even more finely. Land Mammal Ages for Africa are based on characterizations summarized in the entry AFRICA. For Africa and the Paleogene of Southern Asia, specific sites with primates are shown as well. Oblique broken lines represent uncertainty as to the boundary between successive time units. Shaded intervals indicate gaps in the local stratigraphic record. The PLEISTOCENE time scale is shown in greater detail in that entry.

Summary of Major Subject Areas

ANTHROPOLOGICAL SUBDISCIPLINES

EVOLUTIONARY BIOLOGY
Basic Concepts
Models and Hypotheses
Behavioral Biology
Genetics
Numerical Approaches
Systematics

MORPHOLOGY
General Concepts
Bodily Systems

PRIMATE TAXA
Nonprimates, general terms, grades primates (including humans, arranged taxonomically)

GEOGRAPHIC REGIONS
Africa
Americas
Asia
Australia
Europe

GEOLOGY, PALEONTOLOGY, STRATIGRAPHY, GEOCHRONOLOGY
Geological Concepts
Paleontological Concepts
Time Intervals
Dating Methods

ARCHAEOLOGY
General terms and concepts
Tools, use and manufacture
Industries

ARCHAEOLOGICAL INDUSTRIES (BY AGE)
Early Paleolithic
Middle Paleolithic
Late Paleolithic
Epipaleolithic
Postpaleolithic
Paleoindian
Disputed or rejected industries

ARCHAEOLOGICAL INDUSTRIES (BY GEOGRAPHY)
Africa
Americas
Asia
Europe

LOCALITIES (BY AGE)
Paleogene
Miocene
Pliocene
Early Pleistocene
Middle Pleistocene
Late Pleistocene (and Holocene)

LOCALITIES (BY GEOGRAPHY)
Africa
Americas
Asia
Australia
Europe

BIOGRAPHICAL ENTRIES
NOTE: Centered headings in the preceding section may not appear as entries.

Detailed List of All Articles by Topic

Phenotype
Polytypic Variation
Population
Race (Human)

NUMERICAL APPROACHES
Morphometrics
Multivariate Analysis
Numerical Cladistics
Numerical Taxonomy
Quantitative Methods
Phenetics

SYSTEMATICS
aff.
cf.
Clade
Cladistics
Classification
Grade
Hypodigm
Incertae Sedis
Molecular "vs." Morphological Approaches to Systematics
Nomenclature
Priority
Synonym(y)
Systematics
Taxon
Taxonomy
  Order
  Semiorder
  Suborder
  Hyporder
  Infraorder
  Parvorder
  Superfamily
  Family
  Subfamily
  Tribe
  Subtribe
  Genus
  Subgenus
  Species
  Subspecies

MORPHOLOGY AND HUMAN BIOLOGY

GENERAL CONCEPTS
Allometry
Biomechanics
Bone Biology
Dwarfism
Forensic Anthropology
Gigantism
Morphology
Ontogeny
Paleopathology
Rules

Sexual Dimorphism
Speech (Origins of)
Stable Isotopes (in Biological Systems)

BODILY SYSTEMS
Brain
Diet
Ischial Callosities
Locomotion
Musculature
Skeleton
Skull
Tail
Teeth

GEOGRAPHIC REGIONS

AFRICA
Africa
  Africa, East
    Afar Basin
    Baringo Basin/Tugen Hills
    Djibouti
    Middle Awash
    Natron-Eyasi Basin
    Rift Valley
    Turkana Basin
    Western Rift
  Africa, North
  Africa, Southern
Madagascar

AMERICAS
Americas
  Patagonia

EURASIA
Asia, Eastern and Southern
  China
  Indonesia
  Siwaliks
Asia, Western
  Oman
Europe
  France
  Périgord
Russia

AUSTRALIA
Australia

PRIMATE TAXA

GENERAL TERMS, GRADES, NONPRIMATES
Apatemyidae
Ape
Archonta
Dermoptera
Higher Primates
Lower Primates

NOTE: *indet* refers to taxa which are of indeterminate position within the higher taxon that includes them; square brackets [ ] surround taxa that are monotypic (with only one member) and do not have entries separate from their included lower taxon. The sequence of taxa here differs slightly from that in the full classification on pages xxiii–xxvii to simplify and save space.

GEOLOGY, PALEONTOLOGY, STRATIGRAPHY, GEOCHRONOLOGY

ARCHAEOLOGY

Orangian
Pacitanian
Paleoindian
Perigordian
Pietersburg
Plano
Pre-Aurignacian
Protomagdalenian
Protosolutrean
Romanellian
Sandia
Sangoan
Sauveterrian
Second Intermediate
Smithfield
Soan
Solutrean
Stillbay
Szeletian
Tabunian
Tardenoisian
Tayacian
Tshitolian
Uluzzian
Upper Paleolithic
Wilton
Zhoukoudian

ARCHAEOLOGICAL INDUSTRIES (BY AGE)
EARLY PALEOLITHIC
Abbevillian
Acheulean
Buda Industry
Chopper-Chopping Tools
Clactonian
Early Paleolithic
Early Stone Age
Hope Fountain
Jabrudian
Karari
Levallois
Micoquian
Mugharan
Oldowan
Pacitanian
Sangoan
Soan
Tabunian
Tayacian
Zhoukoudian

MIDDLE PALEOLITHIC
Amudian
Aterian
Bambata
First Intermediate
Howieson's Poort

Lupemban
Middle Paleolithic
Middle Stone Age
Mousterian
Orangian
Pietersburg
Pre-Aurignacian
Sangoan
Second Intermediate
Stillbay

LATE PALEOLITHIC
Ahmarian
Antelian
Athlitian
Aurignacian
Badegoulian
Baradostian
Capsian
Chatelperronian
Dabban
Emiran
Gravettian
Kebaran
Late Paleolithic
Later Stone Age
Levantine Aurignacian
Magdalenian
Mushabian
Perigordian
Protomagdalenian
Protosolutrean
Solutrean
Szeletian
Tshitolian
Uluzzian
Upper Paleolithic

EPIPALEOLITHIC
Anyathian
Azilian
Creswellian
Epigravettian
Epipaleolithic
Hamburgian
Hoabinhian
Ibero-Maurusian
Maglemosian
Natufian
Pacitanian
Romanellian
Sauveterrian
Smithfield
Tardenoisian
Wilton

POSTPALEOLITHIC
Bronze Age

LOCALITIES (BY GEOGRAPHY)

BIOGRAPHICAL ENTRIES

Abbevillian

Term once used to refer to early Acheulean stone-tool assemblages in Europe. This "stage" of tool technology was distinguished by crude, thick handaxes made by hard-hammer percussion. It was named after Abbeville (France), where a Middle Pleistocene site in the 45-m terrace of the Somme River yielded roughly made handaxes.

See also Acheulean; Boucher de Perthes, Jacques; Early Paleolithic; Handaxe; St. Acheul; Stone-Tool Making. [R.P.]

Abri Pataud

Rockshelter with archaeological and human remains located on the left bank of the Vezère River in Les Eyzies, Dordogne, in southwestern France, dated by radiocarbon determinations between 34 and 20 Ka. With 14 major archaeological horizons, from Basal Aurignacian to Protomagdalenian and Solutrean, this site was excavated in the 1950s and 1960s by American prehistorian H.L. Movius, with emphasis on paleoecological reconstruction, horizontal exposure of minimal stratigraphic units or occupation horizons, and quantitative analysis of archaeological materials. The excavations prompted significant revisions in the classic Upper Paleolithic sequence of southwestern France and also yielded a series of human remains from the Protomagdalenian level.

See also Archaeological Sites; Aurignacian; Movius, Hallam L., Jr.; Paleoenvironment; Perigordian; Protomagdalenian; Solutrean; Upper Paleolithic. [A.S.B.]

Acheulean

Early Paleolithic industry characterized by handaxes and similar types of modified stone tools. Acheulean artifact assemblages are known from ca. 1.5 to 0.2 Ma and span Africa, Europe, and Asia. Based originally on numerous handaxes discovered at the site of St. Acheul (France), the term *Acheulean* is applied to stone assemblages with large bifacially flaked, ovoid tools. In an artifact assemblage, such tools must be abundant and/or finely made for the term to apply. In Africa, where the oldest Acheulean occurrences are known, handaxes and similar tools, such as cleavers and picks, are grouped under the term *bifaces*. Acheulean bifaces are highly standardized compared with flaked pieces of earlier non-Acheulean industries. It has been suggested that Acheulean sites in Africa are those where 40 percent or more of the intentionally flaked stones (i.e., tools or cores) are bifaces. However, sites where bifaces are fewer but are flaked carefully and symmetrically are also called Acheulean. In the view of some archaeologists, these criteria distinguish the Acheulean from other industries containing rare and crudely flaked bifaces, such as the Developed Oldowan or Clactonian. Still other researchers claim that, since the Acheulean is a tradition of tool manufacture involving the production of bifaces, any assemblage with such tools represents the Acheulean.

Preceded by the Oldowan and related core-flake tool kits, the Acheulean may have originated by gradual transition in the degree to which oval-shaped cobbles were flaked (chopper to protohandaxe to handaxe). Particularly in Europe, the idea of gradual refinement in tool manufacture from pre-Acheulean to Acheulean and throughout the Early Paleolithic period has been thought to involve a shift from using hammerstones in tool manufacture to "soft" hammers, such as bone or antler, which permit greater control over the transmission of force needed to remove a flake. It was suggested by G.L. Isaac, however, that the ability to remove large flakes (greater than 10 cm in length) was essential to the emergence of the Acheulean in Africa. This ability may have represented a threshold in tool manufacture, rapidly exploited as a starting point in the manufacture of bifaces. The rough oval shape of early bifaces is a natural extension of the original form of large flakes regardless of whether they had been further shaped intentionally into preconceived tools or simply used as cores for efficient production of sharp flakes. In Early Acheulean assemblages, such as those at Olduvai Gorge (Tanzania), it is nonetheless true that bifaces were sometimes made on cobbles and also on flakes smaller than 10 cm. Thus, it is still unclear whether the manufacture of

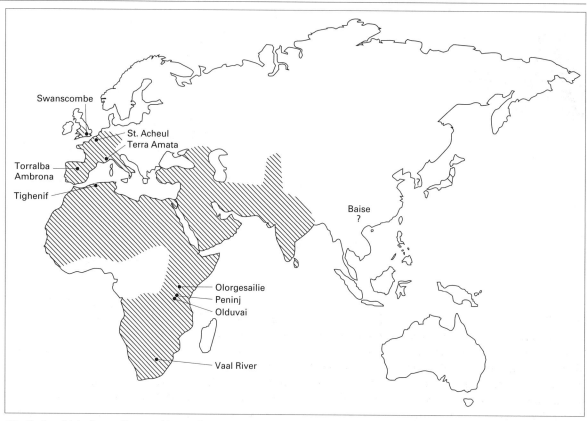

Distribution of Acheulean artifact assemblages and some important sites. Although bifaces are known from sites in China, Korea, and Japan, it is not clear whether the term Acheulean *is applicable to assemblages in eastern Asia.*

Acheulean bifaces came about by gradual refinement in the flaking of cobbles or by a technical refinement in the ability to produce large flakes.

Acheulean bifaces represent the distinctive product of early human technology during a period exceeding 1 Myr. Studies of sequences of sites from individual localities, such as Olorgesailie (Kenya), have shown that handaxe manufacture and the overall makeup of Acheulean assemblages are marked by conservative, nonprogressive variation over hundreds of thousands of years. Moreover, examples of bifaces from Africa, Europe, and Asia are remarkably similar to one another, despite the great distances between localities. Biface forms nevertheless did undergo refinement over the time span of the Acheulean. In the early Acheulean, handaxes and related tools were chunky in section, with one face flatter than the other. The striking platforms of large flakes and the cortex of large cobbles were not necessarily removed entirely, resulting in asymmetrical handaxes. By the end of the Acheulean, very sophisticated handaxes were often made; flat and symmetrical in shape, they required great skill to produce. Elaborate core-preparation (e.g., Levallois) techniques, characteristic of Middle Paleolithic industries, were employed in producing highly refined bifaces in the latest Acheulean. Although many Late Acheulean assemblages exhibit refined skills in toolmaking, others are characterized by crude bifaces and bold flaking, typical of the Early Acheulean. Indeed, many factors affected the degree of sophistication of bifaces, including the raw material used. Overall change in the Acheulean is reflected by the fact that

no Early Acheulean assemblage is known to be as refined as some Late Acheulean tool kits.

Lithic assemblages referred to as *chopper-chopping tool industries* are also known from the same time period throughout the Old World. These tool kits are typified by basic core-and-flake technology and tend to lack handaxes. Examples include the Clactonian in northern Europe, the Buda industry represented at Vértesszöllös (Hungary), and the Zhoukoudian industry in China. It is unknown whether these assemblages represent a distinct tradition of tool manufacture, geographic variants of the Acheulean, or, in some cases, an integral part of this industry. For example, it has been claimed that Clactonian assemblages reflect stages in the production of Acheulean tools. Other evidence suggests that biface and nonbiface assemblages are found in different habitats in the same area, as at Olorgesailie, and perhaps reflect different activities carried out by the same people. On the other hand, it is clear that assemblages in certain geographic regions, expecially in eastern Asia, simply are not characterized by bifaces.

At many Acheulean sites, bifaces occur in extremely dense concentrations in fluvial contexts. The behavioral interpretation of these sites is problematic due to the long time typically represented by fluvial strata and the possibility of winnowing of small flakes, leaving the heavier bifaces behind. While some Acheulean sites thus represent long periods of lag accumulation (similar to cobble bars in a stream), others appear to reflect the systematic deposition by hominids of handaxes near channels and of scraper-flake assem-

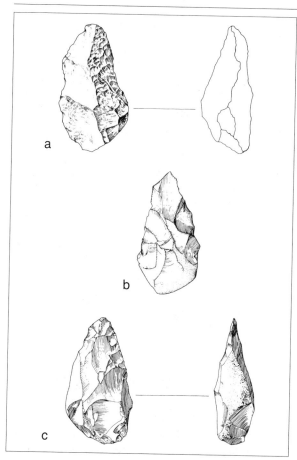

Acheulean handaxes from (a) Olduvai Gorge (Tanzania); (b) Lantian (China); (c) Combe-Grenal (France).

blages in floodplains away from the channel axis. The behavioral reasons for this pattern are unknown.

It is widely assumed that most Acheulean assemblages were manufactured by populations of *Homo erectus*. Fossils of *H. erectus*, however, are only rarely associated with Acheulean tools (e.g., at Tighenif [Algeria], Olduvai, and perhaps Swartkrans [South Africa]). In Africa, the oldest occurrences of the Acheulean (e.g., Konso and Olduvai middle Bed II) are in the time range of *H. erectus* (e.g., Olduvai Hominid 9). But after 700 Ka, they also occur at sites (e.g., Saldanha [South Africa], Ndutu [Tanzania], Bodo [Ethiopia]) yielding fossils often assigned to archaic *Homo sapiens*. In Europe, Acheulean assemblages first occur soon after 0.5 Ma. Acheulean tools persist alongside early *H. sapiens* populations in Europe (e.g., at Swanscombe) and Africa until they are succeeded by Middle Paleolithic tool kits ca. 250–150 Ka.

It is further assumed that these Acheulean toolmakers were hunter-gatherers who ranged widely for food. In fact, little is really known about the specific behavior and ecology of these hominids—for instance, whether they hunted big game or how they used their environments. Despite the prevalence of handaxes over an enormous time span, little is known about how they were used. One study of microscopic edge wear has shown that European handaxes were sometimes employed in butchery activities, and associated flakes also showed signs of working wood, hide, and bone. At other sites (e.g., an elephant skeleton and associated lithics exca-

vated at Olorgesailie), handaxes evidently served as the cores for sharp flakes used in butchery. Experimental studies have indicated that bifaces are excellent all-purpose tools; their widespread distribution over much of the Paleolithic appears to bear this out.

See also Africa; Africa, East; Africa, North; Africa, Southern; Archaic Homo sapiens; Asia, Eastern and Southern; Asia, Western; Boucher de Perthes, Jacques; Clactonian; Early Paleolithic; Europe; France; Homo erectus; Konso-Gardula; Lithic Use-Wear; Middle Awash; Middle Paleolithic; Movius's Line; Oldowan; Olduvai Gorge; Olorgesailie; Paleolithic Lifeways; Prepared-Core; Raw Materials; St. Acheul; Saldanha; Soleihac; Stone-Tool Making; Swanscombe; Swartkrans; Takamori; Tighenif; Vértesszöllös; Zhoukoudian. [R.P.]

Further Readings

Clark, J.D. (1994) The Acheulian industrial complex in Africa and elsewhere. In R.S. Corrucini and R.L. Ciochon (eds.): Integrative Paths to the Past: Paleoanthropological Advances in Honor of F. Clark Howell. Englewood Cliffs, N.J.: Prentice-Hall, pp. 451–469.

Gowlett, J. (1986) Culture and conceptualisation: The Oldowan-Acheulean gradient. In G. Bailey and P. Callow (eds.): Stone Age Prehistory. Cambridge: Cambridge University Press, pp. 243–260.

Isaac, G.L. (1975) Stratigraphy and cultural patterns in East Africa during the middle ranges of Pleistocene time. In K.W. Butzer and G.L. Isaac (eds.): After the Australopithecines. The Hague: Mouton, pp. 495–542.

Isaac, G.L. (1977) Olorgesailie: Archaeological Studies of a Middle Pleistocene Lake Basin in Kenya. Chicago: University of Chicago Press.

Keeley, L. (1980) Experimental Determination of Stone Tool Uses: A Microwear Analysis. Chicago: University of Chicago Press.

Schick, K. (1992) Geoarchaeological analysis of an Acheulean site at Kalambo Falls, Zambia. Geoarchaeology 7:1–26.

Villa, P. (1983) Terra Amata and the Middle Pleistocene Archaeological Record of Southern France. Berkeley: University of California Press.

Adapidae

Extinct primate family that has come to include a plethora of European Eocene primates ranging in size from as small as a mouse (*Anchomomys*) to as big as a large cat (*Leptadapis*). According to studies of body size and molar shearing-crest development, the larger forms (*Adapis, Leptadapis, Caenopithecus, Protoadapis, Europolemur*) were probably folivorous, whereas the smaller forms (e.g., *Periconodon, Anchomomys, Microadapis, Agerina*), and possibly *Pronycticebus* as well, were probably insectivorous, with the latter three taxa perhaps also including fruit in their diet. Although Adapidae is associated here with Notharctidae, it is only within the former group that the ancestry of modern strepsirhines has traditionally been sought.

History of Study

The genus *Adapis*, which gives its name to the family Adapidae as well as to taxa of other ranks, was described in 1821 by the French paleontologist G. Cuvier, who thought it might be either a pachyderm or an artiodactyl. Despite this "false start," *Adapis* claims the distinction of being the first fossil primate to be studied. Since its discovery, *Adapis* has become one of the best known of all European fossil primates: It is a particularly dominant mammal in collections from the limestone deposits of the Franco-Belgian Basin. The genus *Leptadapis*, the largest of the adapids, used to be included as a species of *Adapis* (*A. magnus*), but the genus *Adapis* is now reserved for the original form, *A. parisiensis*, and perhaps one other species of comparable size.

In 1912, the Swiss paleontologist H.G. Stehlin published a monographic study of *Adapis* (including "*Adapis*" *magnus*). In comparing it especially with the North American *Notharctus*, he concluded that, while the Old and New World taxa may somehow be related, differences warranted distinction at the family level between the groups they represented. This matter was addressed by the American paleontologist W.K. Gregory in his 1920 work on *Notharctus*, in which he argued that differences between *Adapis* and *Notharctus* in skull shape and particularly in dental elaboration (more in the latter taxon), while real, were no less profound than differences that existed among miacids, an assemblage of extinct but diverse carnivores that all paleontologists seemed to agree belonged in the same family. Thus, Gregory concluded that it was appropriate to group the European taxa in the subfamily Adapinae and the North American forms in Notharctinae and to subsume both in the family Adapidae.

The common ancestor of both adapid subfamilies was taken to be the Early Eocene *Pelycodus* (then known only from North America but subsequently also from Europe), from which Gregory believed that both the geologically younger *Adapis* and *Notharctus* could have evolved.

This basic phylogenetic scheme was not altered in the ensuing few decades, but largely through the studies of P. Robinson and C.L. Gazin in the 1950s, Stehlin's suggestion that the European and the North American taxa should be separated at the family level was revived. Thus, two alternative classificatory schemes have been applied to the family Adapidae: most recently, E.L. Simons and F.S. Szalay and E. Delson have preferred Gregory's subfamily divisions, while in this volume, for example, the distinctiveness of the two groups is maintained at the family level.

Phylogenetic Relationships

In addition to their ancientness (Middle-to-Late Eocene), adapids have been sought as potential ancestors of modern strepsirhines because of features that have been presumed to be primitive. Adapids lack a tooth comb of the sort seen in modern lemurs and lorises; they typically have a greater number of premolars (four as opposed to three in each quadrant of the jaw); and they have a "lemurlike" bulla, which, because it is similar to that in *Lemur*, was seen, almost by definition, as primitive. Aside from the occasional inconsis-

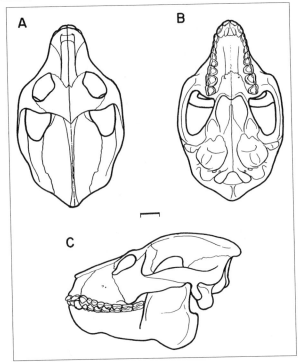

Three views of the cranium of Adapis parisiensis. *Scale is 1 cm. Courtesy of Frederick S. Szalay, from Szalay and Delson, 1979.*

tency, such as having a fused mandibular symphysis, *Adapis* especially could fulfill the role of ancestor to the modern strepsirhines. Gregory even argued that dental similarities between the fossil form and the extant Malagasy lemur, *Lepilemur*, demonstrated the primitiveness among the living taxa of *Lepilemur* and thus the descent from *Adapis* of other lemurs via *Lepilemur*. Just over 50 years later, P.D. Gingerich thought the dental similarities were greater between *Adapis* and the extant *Hapalemur* and thus suggested that this genus, rather than *Lepilemur*, was the link between the extinct taxon and the other modern strepsirhines, a view not accepted here. In 1979, J.H. Schwartz and I. Tattersall turned the argument around and suggested that the distinctiveness of the compressed cusps and shearing crests of the molars of *Adapis*, as well as *Hapalemur* and *Lepilemur*, indicated that these taxa were closely related and specialized members of Strepsirhini, forming a separate clade; these authors included the *Notharctus* group in Adapidae. Subsequently, Schwartz pointed out that there really are no features that would unite a *Notharctus* group with an *Adapis* group, and he and Tattersall presented dental and some cranial evidence suggesting a relationship between Adapidae, in the restricted sense of *Adapis* plus those few forms sharing derived characters with it, and a particular group of Malagasy primates, the indrioids.

During this latter review, Schwartz and Tattersall failed to discover any derived characters that would unite with *Adapis* those taxa traditionally placed into Adapidae. As Robinson had suggested about North American fossils included in the (primarily) Eocene family Omomyidae, it seemed that taxa had been placed in Adapidae because they were Eocene in age and European in location. An appraisal of the spectrum of so-called adapids led to the suggestion that some were actually related to *Notharctus* or *Pelycodus*, such as *Cercamonius* and *Protoadapis*, and *Pronycticebus* and *Agerinia*, respectively; others were linked to extant taxa, such as the fossil genus *Huerzeleris* to the living Malagasy primate, *Phaner*; and yet others were lorisoids of uncertain affinity, such as *Anchomomys* and *Periconodon*.

Adapidae seemed, therefore, to be a group of few members (*Adapis* and *Leptadapis*, as well as the recently proposed genera *Simonsia* and *Paradapis*) related to a small number of specialized extant primates. *Pelycodus* also emerged as sharing some potential derived features with *Notharctus*, as well as others with *Smilodectes*. Although not contributing to a resolution of its relationships, this does indicate that *Pelycodus* could not have been ancestral to both a *Notharctus* group and an *Adapis* group.

More recently, postcranial evidence has been brought to bear on the relationships of the *Adapis* group to the *Notharctus* group and of each of these groups to extant taxa. Studies by K.C. Beard and colleagues of wrist and ankle bones attributed to *Adapis, Notharctus, Cantius,* and *Smilodectes* indicated that there were distinct differences between *Adapis* and the three taxa representative of the *Notharctus* group. In a comparison with a diversity of extant primates, Beard et al. concluded that the *Adapis* group was more closely related to extant lemurs than to the *Notharctus* group because *Adapis* shared with extant lemurs a unique articulation between the ulna and the small pisiform bone of the wrist. This feature is not found in *Smilodectes* (the only taxon of the *Notharctus* group for which the appropriate bones are known) and is apparently not characteristic of the anthropoid primates analyzed. Thus, Beard et al. concluded that certain aspects of wrist morphology corroborated the interpretation based on craniodental features: The *Notharctus* group and the *Adapis* group are not sister taxa. Beard et al. did not, however, find support for the suggestion that *Adapis* may be closely related to only a few of the extant lemurs. Rather, these authors argued that another feature of the wrist—an os centrale that overlaps the capitate and makes contact with the hamate—is found uniquely in extant lemurs to the exclusion of *Adapis*. Although research being conducted by Schwartz and Yamada indicates that some features of wrist and ankle morphology require further documentation, it is apparent that the traditional phylogenetic and systematic schema involving Adapidae are in need of revision.

Family Adapidae
    Subfamily Adapinae
        †*Adapis*
        †*Leptadapis*
        †*Simonsia*
        †*Paradapis*
        †*Cryptadapis*
        †*Alsatia*
†extinct

See also Adapiformes; Diet; Indrioidea; Lemuriformes; Lemuroidea; Locomotion; Lorisoidea; Notharctidae; Skeleton; Strepsirhini; Teeth. [J.H.S.]

Further Readings
Beard, K.C., Dagosto, M., Gebo, D.L., and Godinot, M. (1988) Interrelationships among primate higher taxa. Nature 331:712–714.
Covert, H.H. (1986) Biology of the early Cenozoic primates. In D.R. Swindler (ed.): Comparative Primate Biology, Vol. 1: Systematics, Evolution, and Anatomy. New York: Liss, pp. 335–359.
Gregory, W.K. (1920) On the structure and relations of *Notharctus*, an American Eocene primate. Mem. Am. Mus. Nat. Hist. 3:49–243.
Schwartz, J.H. (1986) Primate systematics and a classification of the order. In D.R. Swindler (ed.): Comparative Primate Biology, Vol. 1: Systematics, Evolution, and Anatomy. New York: Liss, pp. 1–41.
Schwartz, J.H., and Tattersall, I. (1985) Evolutionary relationships of living lemurs and lorises (Mammalia, Primates) and their potential affinities with European Eocene Adapidae. Anthropol. Pap. Am. Mus. Nat. Hist. 60:1–100.
Szalay, F.S., and Delson, E. (1979) Evolutionary History of the Primates. New York: Academic.

Adapiformes
Primate infraorder including the mainly Eocene Adapidae and their close relatives, as distinguished from the living Lemuriformes. Together, Adapiformes and Lemuriformes form the Strepsirhini. Adapiformes was erected by F.S. Szalay and E. Delson to distinguish a collection of primarily Eocene primates from more recent and supposedly descendant strepsirhines. Adapiformes here subsumes the superfamily Adapoidea, which in turn contains the families Adapidae, Notharctidae, and perhaps Sivaladapidae. Adapoidea, when used previously, had included only the Holarctic family Notharctidae and the European family Adapidae and had been grouped with extant taxa in the infraorder Lemuriformes. Some researchers have thought that *Sivaladapis* and other southern Asian Miocene forms could be related to adapids and distinguished as the family Sivaladapidae, but it seems that this concept combines unrelated taxa whose phyletic links are to different strepsirhine groups (Notharctidae and Lorisidae); the family is no longer recognized here.

Szalay and Delson suggested that the adapiforms could be distinguished from all lemuriforms because they lack the derived tooth comb that characterizes the latter group. Here, however, it is argued that the only feature that distinguishes Adapiformes as a group apart from extant strepsirhines is its members' greater antiquity. There are no morphological features peculiar to adapiforms that would attest to their monophyly: The lack of a tooth comb is an ancestral condition that does not unify adapiforms or any other group; it is not even clear that the mere presence of *a* tooth comb unites all lemuriforms to the exclusion of any "adapiform."

Inasmuch as characteristics of Strepsirhini are based historically on aspects of soft-tissue morphology, the phylogenetic association of any adapiform with extant taxa must be based on fossilizable material. Traditionally, the association of adapiforms with extant taxa rested primarily on the sharing by various notharctids, adapids, and lemurs of the "lemurlike" bulla—i.e., an "inflated" auditory bulla whose lateral edge extends laterally beyond the inferior margin of the tympanic ring (the "free" tympanic ring). Recent studies of the wrist and ankle morphology of various extant primates and bones of these regions attributed to *Adapis, Leptadapis, Notharctus, Cantius, Caenopithecus,* and *Smilodectes* have concluded that certain features, while not uniting adapiforms as a group, are suggestive of the overall monophyly of "adapiform" and extant lemuriform taxa. These same studies of the postcranium, as well as earlier analyses based on craniodental morphology, came to the conclusion that Adapidae and Notharctidae, at least, were not sister taxa. Rather, the former taxon was more closely related to extant lemurs than was the latter.

To retain the overall pattern of primate phylogeny and classification laid out for this encyclopedia, Adapiformes is here utilized as a paraphyletic taxon. Genera previously included in a unitary family Adapidae have been allocated to the families Adapidae and Notharctidae or placed as possible adapiforms of uncertain relationship. Some of the latter have also been suggested as possible protoanthropoids and/or included in the adapid (or notharctid) subfamily Cercamoniinae (= ?Protoadapinae).

?Infraorder Adapiformes
    Family indeterminate
        † *Caenopithecus*
        † *Lushius*
        † *Azibius*
        † *Panobius*
        † *Djebelemur*
        † *Wailekia*
        † *Rencunius*
        † *Pondaungia*
        † *Hoanghonius*
†extinct

See also Adapidae; Anthropoidea; Lorisidae; Monophyly; Notharctidae; Skeleton; Skull; Strepsirhini; Teeth. [J.H.S.]

Further Readings

Beard, K.C., Dagosto, M., Gebo, D.L., and Godinot, M. (1988) Interrelationships among primate higher taxa. Nature 331:712–714.

Schwartz, J.H. (1986) Primate systematics and a classification of the order. In D.R. Swindler (ed.): Comparative Primate Biology, Vol. 1: Systematics, Evolution, and Anatomy. New York: Liss, pp. 1–41.

Schwartz, J.H., and Tattersall, I. (1985) Evolutionary relationships of living lemurs and lorises (Mammalia, Primates) and their potential affinities with European Eocene Adapidae. Anthropol. Pap. Am. Mus. Nat. Hist. 60:1–100.

Adaptation(s)

States of organismic phenotypes (an item of behavior, physiological process, or anatomical property) shaped by natural selection to perform a specific role. The evolutionary process of natural selection acting to shape, maintain, or modify such properties is also known as *adaptation.* The theory of adaptation is the evolutionary biological explanation for the design apparent in nature, whereby organisms appear to display a close fit to their environments. Adaptation is the central focus of Darwin's original formulation of evolutionary theory and of most modern formulations of the evolutionary process.

Much remains to be learned about the process of adaptation. On the one hand, theorists since Darwin have argued that selection should constantly improve the quality of adaptations or modify adaptations to keep pace with changing environments. According to this view of adaptation, constant, gradual change should be the norm. On the other hand, many species remain stable in most of their characteristics for long periods of their history (the phenomenon of stasis), and thus it is assumed that natural selection lends stability and conserves adaptations for large portions of a species' history. According to this "punctuational" view, adaptive change is relatively rare in evolution, is relatively rapid when it occurs, and is most often associated with speciation.

See also Adaptive Radiation; Darwin, Charles Robert; Evolution; Phenotype; Preadaptation; Speciation. [N.E.]

Further Readings

Bock, W.J., and von Wahlert, G. (1965) Adaptation and the form-function complex. Evolution 19:269–299.

Futuyma, D.J. (1986) Evolutionary Biology, 2nd ed. Sunderland, Mass.: Sinauer.

Lewontin, R.C. (1978) Adaptation. Sci. Am. 239:212–230.

Adaptive Radiation

Evolutionary diversification of a monophyletic lineage, whereby descendant species occupy a variety of environments representing an array of ecological niches. Such evolutionary events are typically rapid and commonly follow mass extinctions or reflect the invasion of underexploited habitats. A classic example is the diversification of marsupials in Australia.

See also Adaptation(s); Evolution; Phylogeny. [N.E.]

Afar Basin

Lowland region at the mouth of the Ethiopian Rift Valley where it meets the Red Sea Rift and the Gulf of Aden Rift in a triple junction. Roughly triangular in outline, the Afar is bounded by the sea to the east, the Somalia Plateau to the south, and the Ethiopian Plateau to the northwest. The Afar today is an equatorial desert stretching over nearly 200,000 km², with some areas up to 100 m below sea level, which is traversed by the lower Awash River. It is inhabited by the Afar people of Ethiopia, from whom the region takes its name. The paleontological and archaeological potential of the Afar was discovered by the geologist Maurice Taieb during geological reconnaissance of the Awash River Valley in the late 1960s, and paleontological and geological work

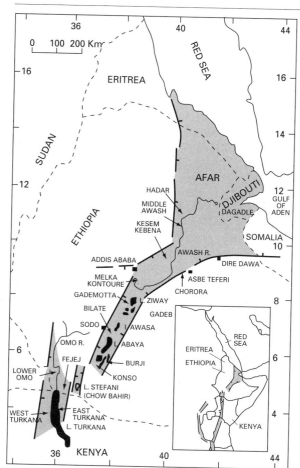

The Afar depression of Africa's horn is part of the eastern African rift system (inset). It includes Djibouti, Eritrea, and much of Ethiopia. Major sites of paleoanthropological interest in the Afar depression and the Main Ethiopian Rift to the south are shown on this map. Courtesy of Tim D. White.

since then has resulted in discovery and analysis of many highly productive sites by teams working in separate areas. The newest area of study is in the far northwestern corner of the Afar, around the Danakil Depression of Eritrea. In 1995, an Eritrean-Italian team found a partial human cranium preliminarily attributed to *Homo* cf. *erectus* in deposits, estimated to date to ca. 1 Ma, south of the Gulf of Zula, near Buia.

West-Central Basin

The most significant paleoanthropological discoveries have been made in the depression known as the West-Central Afar Basin, an elongate downfaulted structure adjacent and parallel to the Ethiopian Western Escarpment. Within this subsident basin, thick sequences of fluvial, deltaic, and lacustrine sediments have accumulated since Miocene times. Among the most signficant discoveries are those from the 200-m-thick Middle Pliocene Hadar Formation. Among the Hadar remains, the partial skeleton nicknamed "Lucy" and the remains of an associated group called the "First Family" are the best known. Based on more than 100 stratigraphic profiles, the Hadar Formation has been divided into four stratigraphic members. At the base, the Sidi Hakoma Member

(SH) yielded the 1973 hominid knee joint, several hominid mandibles, and the hominid palates. The Denen Dora Member (DD) contained the 13-plus hominid individuals sampled from the "First Family" Locality 333, and the lower Kada Hadar Member (KH) produced the "Lucy" specimen. New specimens, including an early *Homo*, have since been recovered in younger strata in the uppermost member, the Kada Hadar Member.

Radiometric dating has established the top of the main Hadar hominid-bearing succession (top of Middle Kada Hadar) at ca. 2.9 Ma. Dating for the lower units was initially controversial, with estimates from radiometric, biochronologic, and trace-element composition analysis ranging between 3.3 and 3.6 Ma. The correlation of tuff layers at Hadar with well-dated tuffs in the Turkana Basin, together with radiometric dating of the 3.4 Ma SHT/Tulu-Bor Tuff at the base of the Sidi Hakoma Member just below the lowest Hadar hominid fossil, has resolved this controversy.

The wealth of paleontological material at Hadar is due to the combination of low-energy sedimentation and a strongly mineralizing depositional environment in the West-Central Afar paleolake, resulting in an unusual taphonomic setting. Hadar beds are predominantly fine-grained mudstones, and the bones themselves are remarkably intact with many partially or wholly articulated skletons, indicating gentle currents and little postmortem transport.

The focal element of the Hadar landscape during Pliocene times was a marsh-rimmed lake fed by periodically flooding, silt-laden rivers from the Ethiopian Escarpment. Microfossils and pollen indicate that the site occupied an elevation much higher than it does today. The local environment was more humid and wooded than today, and fossils of hippopotamus and crocodile are indicative of relatively fresh, permanent water, at least in river pools if not in the lake itself. The Hadar vertebrate fauna and environment appear to have been dramatically distinct from those encountered at Laetoli in Tanzania, a Middle Pliocene site that has also yielded remains of the same early hominid found at Hadar, *Australopithecus afarensis*.

The adjacent Gona study area has yielded Oldowan tools that date to 2.6 Ma. One of the oldest well-dated specimens attributable to *Homo*, a maxilla (AL 666–1) from Makaamitalu, in the upper KH Member at Hadar, is dated to ca. 2.3 Ma. The fieldwork at Hadar and Gona since 1990 has resulted in large collections of hominid remains in the Middle and Late Pliocene and considerable refinement of the stratigraphy and dating of the Hadar sites.

Middle Awash

Unlike the extensive horizontal beds of Hadar, which are predominantly Pliocene in age, sediments outcropping in the Middle Awash from south of Gona to Gewane, along the central portion of the Awash River, are far more tectonically disturbed, with beds exposed in relatively small outcroppings. Despite the geological complexity, tephrostratigraphic and radiometric analysis of numerous volcanic layers has identified strata ranging from Middle and Lower Pleistocene down to Lower Pliocene levels predating those of the

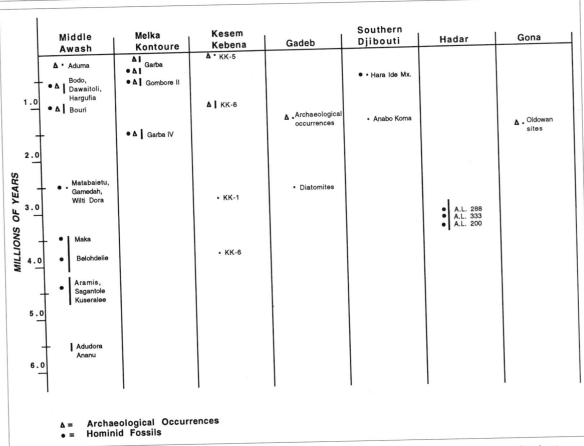

Temporal relationships among paleoanthropological areas of the Afar Basin and other sequences in northern and central Ethiopia and Djibouti. Courtesy of Tim D. White.

Hadar Formation. The most prolific levels are in the oldest and youngest parts of the section.

A partial hominid cranium and other remains from Bodo in the Middle Awash are associated with large numbers of Acheulean tools and an abundant Middle Pleistocene fauna. In the Maka area south of Bodo, Pliocene hominid remains have been recovered from below the SHT (Sidi Hakoma Tuff) layer dated at 3.4 Ma in the Maka area, and portions of a hominid cranial vault dated to ca. 3.8 Ma were found in 1981 at Belohdelie. Mandibles, teeth, and more hominid postcrania were recovered in 1981 and 1990 at Maka, along with a diverse fauna of large vertebrates. The still older Aramis localities (ca. 4.4 Ma) were prospected in the 1990s and produced at first a trickle and then a flood of fossil hominin and cercopithecid remains. *Ardipithecus* (previously *Australopithecus*) *ramidus* is represented by dental, cranial, and postcranial elements, including an as yet unpublished partial skeleton. Horizons even lower in the sequence have produced cercopithecid fossils, but no hominids have yet been recovered.

In addition to the fossil discoveries outlined above, several phases of the Oldowan and Acheulean, as well as Middle and Late Stone Age, archaeological sites with stone tools and fauna are known from other parts of the Middle Awash region of the Afar. Miocene beds, as well as the Pliocene and Pleistocene formations, have also yielded thousands of mammalian remains.

Southern Afar Region

Elsewhere in the Afar, near its southern edge at the town of Diré-Dawa, excavations in the Porc-Épic Cave yielded a Middle Stone Age assemblage with a fragmentary hominid mandible. In the headwaters of the Awash River is the site of Melka Kontouré, a stratified Plio-Pleistocene sequence some 30 m thick that ranges in age from ca. 1.7 to 0.1 Ma, according to K-Ar, paleomagnetic, and faunal correlations. The Melka Kontouré exposures stretch 5–6 km along both banks of the Awash River and contain abundant artifacts and faunal remains. More than 50 archaeological sites have been identified, and about 30 "living floors" have been excavated here, including fragmentary remains of *Homo erectus*.

The Gadeb site, above the southern escarpment, is actually in the drainage that flows toward Somalia instead of into the Afar. The exposures are of mid-Pliocene to mid-Pleistocene age and yield some vertebrate remains, with many Acheulean tools in the upper levels. At the southwestern corner of the Afar is the site of Ch'orora, a Middle-to-Late Miocene fossil locality that has not yielded primate fossils. Kesem-Kebena, a relatively new paleoanthropological study area located in 1992 by the Paleoanthropological Inventory Project of Ethiopia, lies north of the Awash River opposite Ch'orora, north of Gadeb, and southwest of the Middle Awash. Here the deposits have been radiometrically dated to 1.0 Ma and contain Early Acheulean assemblages and associated fauna. Mid-Pliocene sediments with fossil vertebrates are also known in this area. Far to the east, in the southern extension of the Afar occupied by the Djibouti Republic, sites near Barogali have yielded a vertebrate fauna containing a *Homo* partial maxilla that has been attributed to the late Middle Pleistocene. Other sites in the various formations in this area yield Early and Middle Pleistocene vertebrate faunas.

See also Africa, East; Ardipithecus ramidus; Australopithecus afarensis; Bodo; Dawaitoli; Djibouti; Hadar; Melka Kontouré; Middle Awash; Rift Valley. [T.D.W.]

Further Readings

Chavaillon, J., Chavaillon, N., Hours, F., and Piperno, M. (1979) From the Oldowan to the Middle Stone Age at Melka-Kunturé (Ethiopia). Quaternaria 21:87–114.

Johanson, D.C., Taieb, M., and Coppens, Y. (1982) Pliocene hominids from the Hadar Formation, Ethiopia (1973–1977): Stratigraphic, chronologic, and paleoenvironmental contexts, with notes on hominid morphology. Am. J. Phys. Anthropol. 57:373–402.

Kalb, J.E., Oswald, E.B., Tebedge, S., Mebrate, A., Tola, E., and Peak, D. (1982) Geology and stratigraphy of Neogene deposits, Middle Awash Valley, Ethiopia. Nature 298:17–25.

White, T.D., Suwa, G., Hart, W.K., Walter, R.C., Wolde-Gabriel, G., de Heinzelin, J., Clark, J.D., Asfaw, B., and Vrba, E. (1993) New discoveries of *Australopithecus* at Maka in Ethiopia. Nature 366:261–265.

WoldeGabriel, G., White, T., Suwa, G., Semaw, S., Beyene, Y., Asfaw, B., and Walter, R.C. (1992) Kesem-Kebena: A newly discovered paleoanthropological research area in Ethiopia. J. Field Archaeol. 19:471–493.

WoldeGabriel, G., White, T.D., Suwa, G., Renne, P., de Heinzelin, J., Hart, W.K., and Helken, G. (1994). Ecological and temporal placement of early Pliocene hominida at Aramis, Ethiopia. Nature 371:330–333.

aff.

From Latin *affinis*, related [to]. It is used to indicate the likely affinities of systematic materials, most commonly fossil, that are insufficient to permit exact determination of species or genus. Aff. generally implies somewhat more certainty of association than does cf., in that the unknown population is thought to be related to, rather than just to be compared with, the named taxon cited. A fragmentary fossil might be termed *Homo* cf. *erectus* if its identity were questionable, but *Homo* aff. *erectus* were it more clear that the fragment was similar to *H. erectus* but perhaps represented a different but related species.

See also cf.; Classification; Taxonomy. [E.D.]

Afontova Gora

A Late Paleolithic complex containing a number of stratified open-air sites (Afontova Gora I, II, III, IV) found along the right banks of the Yenisei River abutting the Afontova Mountain at the outskirts of the city of Krasnoyarsk in southern Siberia (Russia). The sites have yielded sparse hom-

inid remains consisting of teeth belonging to an adolescent as well as nasal and frontal bone fragments of an adult male. Lithic inventories, assigned to the Late Paleolithic Afontova culture, feature cobble wedge-shaped and disc cores used to produce an abundance of flake tools, including large bifacial side scrapers, as well as some microblades. Bone and antler tools, as well as items of personal adornment, have also been recovered. Faunal remains include mammoth, reindeer, sheep, horse, aurochs/bison, ibex, saiga antelope, red deer, hares, arctic foxes, and wolves. Inventories and features suggest the sites were temporary residential ones occupied from perhaps 20 to 12 Ka.

See also Late Paleolithic; Russia. [O.S.]

Africa

No other continent rivals Africa in its importance for human evolution and prehistory. Human evolution can be traced in the African fossil record from Paleocene euprimates to *Homo sapiens* (albeit with a frustrating pre-*Australopithecus* gap). Africa's role as evolutionary center for the higher primates is emphasized by the fact that only the Southeast Asian hylobatids and the South American platyrrhine monkeys have diversified outside of its bounds. Archaeological finds in Africa predate those in any other continent by at least 1 Myr, and a vast body of archaeological material is available to document progressive technological change on the continent from crudely chipped pebbles to iron and bronze casting. On the basis of fossils and tools, the continent would seem to have been the place of origin not only for genus *Homo,* but also, ca. 2.5 Myr later between 0.2 and 0.1 Ma, for modern humans as well.

Geology and Geography

The geology of Africa would seem to hold little promise for a notable Cenozoic vertebrate fossil record. The Afro-Arabian continent, segmented by the Red Sea stretch of the East African Rift system, is essentially a high plateau of Precambrian basement without significant Cenozoic deformation

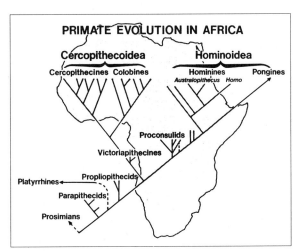

Primate evolution in Africa: diagram of the relationships of higher primates, most of which evolved and differentiated in Africa. Courtesy of John G. Fleagle.

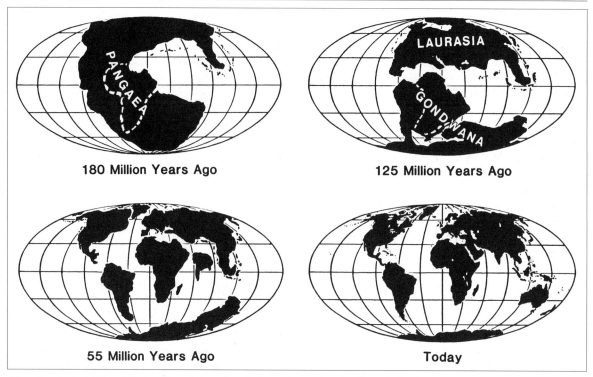

180 Million Years Ago

125 Million Years Ago

55 Million Years Ago

Today

Effect of continental drift on Africa's position relative to that of other continents. Courtesy of John G. Fleagle.

except in the Atlas and the East African Rift Valley. A sizable portion of the plateau is masked by Saharan, Arabian, and Kalahari dune sands, and even more by the "calcaire continental," indurated, unfossiliferous veneers of dune-base material cemented by limy groundwater. Favorable locations are thus of relatively limited extent, but, in compensation, some of the deposits have proven to be incredibly prolific.

Fossiliferous continental Cenozoic deposits in Afro-Arabia fall into four principal groups. The most important by far are the thick sections of Miocene-to-Recent lacustrine and fluvial beds and alkali volcanics that accumulated in the linear depressions formed by the East African Rift from Israel to Malawi, and in the paravolcanic basins of rift-shoulder volcanic complexes. Another cluster of fossil sites occurs in shoreward facies of Cenozoic coastal-plain deposits of North Africa and, to a lesser extent, in Southwest Africa and Arabia. A third source of fossils (with an unusually high proportion of anthropoid remains) is in Plio-Pleistocene (and some Miocene) cave deposits within the karstic limestones of southern Africa. Finally, seismic and drilling programs have shown many thousands of meters of Cenozoic strata in the intracontinental "sags," or passively subsiding basins, that underlie the Sudd of the upper Nile, Lake Chad, and the Etosha Pan of northern Namibia. However, these basins are not subject to uplift tectonics, and only the Plio-Pleistocene outer margin of the Chad Basin has been exposed by erosion.

The geological and faunal connections between Afro-Arabia and other continents have been a topic of debate for centuries. As soon as accurate maps came into existence, the parallelism of the Atlantic coasts of Africa and South America inspired speculation about continental drift, and we now know that Africa was at the center of the Gondwana super-

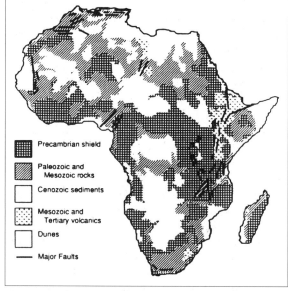

	Precambrian shield
	Paleozoic and Mesozoic rocks
	Cenozoic sediments
	Mesozoic and Tertiary volcanics
	Dunes
—	Major Faults

Geological framework of Africa: areas of outcrop of African rocks by age; note the relatively small area of Cenozoic sediments. From Cooke, H.B.S., in V.J. Maglio and H.B.S. Cooke, eds. 1978, Evolution of African Mammals. *Copyright © by the President and Fellows of Harvard College, reprinted by permission of Harvard University Press.*

continent ca. 225 Ma. This was the Permo-Triassic interval, when Afro-Arabia (together with Iran, Anatolia, and much of what is now Greece and Italy) was joined with South America, Antarctica, Australia, and the Indian subcontinent. During the Mesozoic, rift valleys evolved into ocean basins, and the Gondwana continents and subcontinents began to separate. Since Gondwana was also separated from the northern supercontinent, Laurasia, by the Tethys Ocean, all of the

Gondwana continents became islands. One by one, they have moved across the Tethys gap to join against Laurasia, so that Australia and Antarctica are the only ones still islands today. Although geologically isolated until the Miocene, Africa seems to have been open to intermittent and probably selective faunal exchange with the north throughout the Mesozoic (as indicated by clear relationships among dinosaurs) and at several times in the Early Cenozoic. One of the earliest exchanges, at ca. 55 Ma, brought omomyid primates into the continent, and for the next 40 Myr this lineage diversified in relative isolation from the rest of the world.

The African Fossil Record

Mammalian paleontology in Africa dates from nineteenth-century descriptions of Eocene sirenians and cetaceans in Egypt and Late Pleistocene large mammals in the coastal terraces of Algeria and Morocco. In the 1920s, the discoveries of *Australopithecus* at Taung (South Africa) and of *Proconsul* at Koru (Kenya), as well as recognition of uniquely primitive lithic industries throughout the sub-Saharan region, began the vindication of Charles Darwin's prediction that Africa would prove to be the cradle of human evolution. In the years since World War II, a steady stream of discoveries has made Africa the focus of the most advanced multidisciplinary programs in paleoanthropology (human paleontology and Paleolithic archaeology), with significant carryover in the allied fields of vertebrate paleontology, paleoenvironmental studies, and Cenozoic geochronology.

By 1998, well over 100 collecting areas had yielded diverse and well-preserved local faunas of fossil mammals to document the Cenozoic history of African mammals—approximately half with primate remains—and there are as many or more that are of significant archaeological interest. As noted above, most sites are confined to the Rift Valley, to the narrow coastal plains, and to scattered exposures of cave deposits in southern Africa.

Archaeological sites are only slightly less concentrated in these geologically favored regions. A significant number of the more recent discoveries, however, have been reported from hitherto lightly explored regions of Arabia, the Atlas, and Central Africa, suggesting that the fossil and artifact map will continue to fill in across the continent.

THE AFRO-ARABIAN PALEOBIOLOGICAL REGION
Mainland Africa, Arabia, and the Levant were a single continental unit until the Early Miocene. During this early period, the African faunal realm may also have extended into microcontinents that were structurally tangent to Afro-Arabia, such as the central massifs of Iberia, Apulia, Yugoslavia, Romania, northern Greece, Turkey, and Iran, all of which are now sutured to southern Eurasia. Eocene mammals from scattered occurrences in these regions have strong affinities to Africa and not to coeval faunas in the lands to the north. Fossils from the Eocene of Indo-Pakistan, Burma, and Thailand also suggest a degree of mid-Paleogene communication with Afro-Arabia, involving exchange of early rodents, tethytheres (sirenians, proboscideans), anthracotheres, and adapiform or tarsiiform primates (e.g., *Pondaungia* in Burma and the *Hoanghonius* and *Eosimias* associations in China, all of Middle Eocene age).

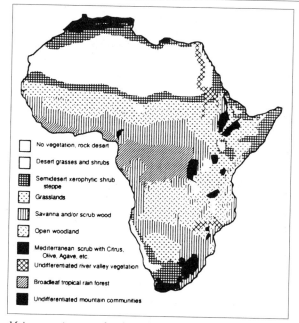

Major vegetation types of modern Africa. From Cooke, H.B.S., in V.J. Maglio and H.B.S. Cooke, eds. 1978, Evolution of African Mammals. *Copyright © by the President and Fellows of Harvard College, reprinted by permission of Harvard University Press.*

The Old World tropics was the only part of the world in which a diverse primate fauna survived the changing climates of the Oligocene. In the Late Eocene, the anthropoids and probably the strepsirhines were already present in Africa (including, presumably, lemuroids in Madagascar). From the Oligocene onward, seasonal and latitudinal differences intensified in Africa, but the primates, particularly the anthropoids (and lemurs), continued to thrive. Unfortunately, we know little or nothing of mammalian faunas outside of the coastal plains and the rift valley, and the paleoclimatic conditions and faunal assemblages of these regions are thus grossly overrepresented in the record.

REGIONAL SUBDIVISION
The latitude of the Afro-Arabian crustal plate changed very little during the Cenozoic, so that the present broad division into northern, equatorial, and southern environmental domains probably existed over the past 50 Myr. These domains have different environments and even more different fossil records due to regional taphonomic bias. The northern zone is equivalent to the Mediterranean coast and the great arid zone of the interior; for this work, we have selected its southern margin as a boundary that includes the Saharan Plateau, the Chad and Sudanese Basins, and the Arabian Peninsula save only Yemen. The 12° S parallel, which we have arbitrarily set as the boundary of the southern region from the west coast to the rift, lies slightly north of the known limit of the fossiliferous paleokarst, in southern Angola. The East African Rift ends at 15° S, not far below the environmentally transitional Pliocene faunas of Chiwondo in Malawi, and we have set the boundary of the southern Africa zone to angle towards this parallel from the rift to the east coast.

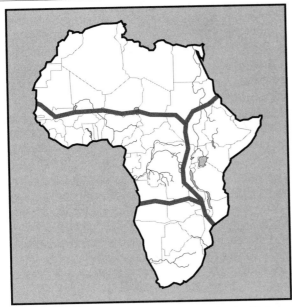

Eco-geographical regions of Africa as used in this encyclopedia. Clockwise from top, these are: North Africa, East Africa, Southern Africa, and West and Central Africa; of these, only the last is not treated in a separate entry. The boundaries of the first three regions are as discussed in their respective entries.

Between these two poleward zones lies the equatorial belt, here divided into eastern and West-Central Africa by the continental divide along the shoulder of the rift valley. East Africa is thus the region from the rift to the Indian Ocean between the 15th parallels. Unfortunately, so little is known of the paleontological history of the west-central region (and not much more of its earlier Paleolithic archaeology) that there is no separate encyclopedia entry for it.

CLIMATIC HISTORY

At ca. 35.5 Ma, at the end of the Eocene, exposure of significantly colder Antarctic bottom water in the upwelling cells along the west coasts of Africa and India initiated a major shift in prevailing winds and rainfall. Cold winds from the Namib and Senegal-Mauritania cells created arid low-pressure cells over adjacent parts of southern and northern Africa, while warm air from counterflowing Atlantic surface waters near the equator provided moisture for seasonal southwesterly monsoons in Central Africa, with most rainfall in the west. Given this general pattern, intensified by the north-south highland divide of the rift shoulders, the west half of Africa will always have been characterized by extreme contrasts between high precipitation near the equator and low precipitation to the north and south, while the eastern half will have had less average rainfall in the equatorial zone and, consequently, less conspicuous latitudinal variation.

Superimposed on this pattern were migrations of ecological zones under the influence of short-term climate changes, most notably in the Late Cenozoic in response to the orbitally forced cycles of Pliocene and Pleistocene climate. In the equatorial region, ecozone shifts were essentially vertical, in synchrony with retreats and advances of mountain glaciers and the declines and rises of pluvially controlled lakes. The presently extensive grasslands and xeric scrublands on the African high plains, for instance, were forced into coastal refugia during cold/pluvial events, and miombo and highland forests moved downslope from the mountainous regions to cover the plains. At higher latitudes, particularly in southern Africa, ecoplanes are tilted poleward, and the Late Cenozoic global climate cycles also involved notable lateral and altitudinal shifts.

REGIONAL TAPHONOMIC BIASES

In the African fossil record, the regional ecological differences have been exaggerated by regional taphonomic biases. The paleontology of the equatorial region in East Africa, the standard for African mammal biochronology, is completely dominated by material collected from the volcanic highlands and rift valleys. Throughout this area, the fossils are found in strata that accumulated in volcanically active, ecologically fragmented, and topographically varied terrain. In the peculiar geology of the rift, hyperalkaline volcanic ejecta created fossilizing environments resembling desert playas in the midst of tropical forest and brushland, in a process termed *mock aridity*. The number and diversity of fossils from such localities are exceptional; postmortem sorting is minimal; and the contribution from normally underrepresented (i.e., rapidly decomposed) forest communities is unusually high.

By contrast, Paleogene and Neogene paleofaunas in the northern zone are almost exclusively from low-relief coastal lowland settings. The exception is that part of the Mio-Pliocene small-mammal record recovered from karst fillings in the Atlas foothills. Aside from this, the northern sample represents swamp, forest, and interfluve savannah habitats on coastal plains, in which postmortem damage, sorting, and preservation under the influence of coastal sedimentary regimes are highly variable. Mammal remains from highland communities were normally too distant, except in the Israel Miocene sample, to have contributed.

Knowledge of the southern paleofaunal zone is again strongly biased, because here the great majority of material was preserved in cave deposits, with a much lesser amount from estuarine and aeolian sites. The cave-preserved assemblages built up under strongly selective conditions in which nocturnal small mammals (mainly in raptor middens), hyaenas, leopards, terrestrial cercopithecoids, hominoids, and small herbivores are consistently among the best-represented groups. In the cave sites, postmortem integrity of larger species is only moderate, but preservation tends to be good to excellent.

AFRICAN LAND-MAMMAL AGES

A stable biochronological framework for the growing volume of paleontological, stratigraphical, and archaeological data from Africa has long been needed. Much of the collected fossil material, however, has yet to be adequately described. On the other hand, geochronometry in East Africa is extremely well developed, and isochronous correlations, from magnetostratigraphy and tephrachronology, connect a large number of sites. In view of this, a recent approach has

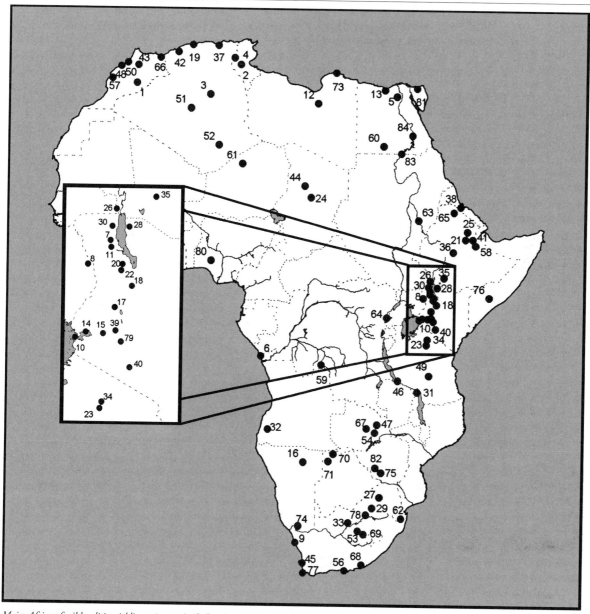

Major African fossil localities yielding primates (including hominins) and Paleolithic archaeological remains. Numbers represent site names (in approximate chronological order), as follows: 1, Adrar Mgorn 1; 2, Chambi; 3, Glib Zegdou; 4, Nementcha, Bir el Ater; 5, Fayum; 6, Malembe; 7, Lothidok; 8, Moroto; 9, Ryskop; 10, Rusinga; 11, Kalodirr; 12, Gebel Zelten; 13, Wadi Moghara; 14, Maboko; 15, Fort Ternan (also Koru, Songhor); 16, Berg Aukas; 17, Tugen Hills; 18, Samburu; 19, Menacer; 20, Lothagam; 21, Aramis; 22, Kanapoi; 23, Laetoli; 24, Bahr el Ghazal; 25, Hadar, Gona; 26, Omo (Usno, Shungura, Kibish); 27, Makapan, Cave of Hearths; 28, Koobi Fora; 29, Sterkfontein, Swartkrans, Kromdraai; 30, Nachukui (West Turkana); 31, Chiwondo (Uraha); 32, Leba; 33, Taung; 34, Olduvai Gorge; 35, Konso; 36, Melka Kontouré; 37, Ain Hanech; 38, Buia; 39, Kilombe; 40, Olorgesailie; 41, Bodo; 42, Tighenif; 43, Ain Maarouf; 44, Yayo (Koro-Toro); 45, Saldanha (Hopefield); 46, Kalambo Falls; 47, Kabwe; 48, Sidi Abderrahman, Thomas Quarries; 49, Isimila; 50, Salé; 51, Tachenghit; 52, Tihodaine; 53, Florisbad; 54, Twin Rivers; 56, Klasies River Mouth; 57, Jebel Irhoud; 58, Diré-Dawa; 59, Lupemba; 60, Bir Tarfawi; 61, Adrar Bous; 62, Border Cave; 63, Singa; 64, Katanda, Ishango; 65, Gobedra; 66, Taforalt; 67, Mumbwa; 68, Howieson's Poort; 69, Rose Cottage; 70, ≠Gi; 71, Tsodilo Hills; 73, Haua Fteah; 74, Apollo-11; 75, Pomongwe, Bambata; 76, GoGoshis Qabe; 77, Cape Flats, Fish Hoek; 78, Boskop; 79, Gamble's Cave; 80, Iwo Eleru; 81, Mushabi; 82, Khami; 83, Wadi Halfa, Khor Musa; 84, Wadi Kubbaniya, Kom Ombo. Site contents not indicated here—see detailed maps in regional entries; Note: sites 55 and 72 deleted.

been to group the East African local faunas according to external rather than internal criteria of age. The boundaries between these units are defined by the oldest site of each group, without primary reference to the presently known age limit of any included taxon. In this way, faunal range limits may continue to change with new finds and revisions without destabilizing the age or definition of unit boundaries. With regard to the most commonly observed fossils, a preliminary characterization of the units at the genus level can be proposed, and sites from northern and southern Africa can be assigned to the East Africa–defined regional land-mammal age units according to local geochronology and faunally based estimates of age.

(text continues on page 16)

KEY TAXA	EAST AFRICA	Age, Ma	OTHER AFRO-ARABIA	Age, Ma
Naivashan				
(◆) *Rusingoryx*	Naivasha Rockshelter	?0.01	Casablanca Soltanian *Morocco*	0.07
(↗) *Mustela, Nesokia, Sus*	OL Naisiusiu	~0.02	Melkbos; Swartklip *S. Afr.*	~0.06
(↙) *Megantereon, Praeomys, Paraethomys,*	Mumba Cave-V *Tanzania*	~0.02	Border Cave *S. Afr.*	~0.09
Pelorovis, Megalotragus, Rabaticerus,	ET Galana Boi	~0.10	Klasies River *S. Afr.*	0.12 - 0.09
Leptobos	Omo Kibish *Ethiopia*	?0.10		
	+Laetoli Ngaloba *Tanzania*	~0.15		
Natronian				
(↗) *Ursus, Leptobos, Capra, Connochaetes*	OL Ndutu Beds (upper)	~0.25	Casabl. Presoltanian *Morocco*	0.18 - 0.15
(↙) *Machairodus, Irhoudia, Hexaprotodon,*	Isimila *Tanzania*	~0.3	Jebel Irhoud *Morocco*	0.2 - 0.125
Kolpochoerus, Menelikia, Hipparion,	Lainyamok	0.36	Florisbad *S. Afr.*	~0.25
Elephas	OL Ndutu Beds (lower)	0.37	Salé; Thomas 1 *Morocco*	~0.28
	BA Kapthurin	0.3	Rabat *Morocco*	~0.3
	AW Melka Kunturé-5	0.6	Kabwe (Broken Hill) *Zambia*	~0.5
	AW Bodo	0.64	Saldanha (Hopefield) *S. Af.*	0.7 - 0.5
	Kariandusi	~0.8	Ternifine, Thomas "G" *Morocco*	~0.7
	SH Upper L; ET Silbo	1.0 - 0.74	Vaal River (upper) *S. Afr.*	?0.7-0.2
	AW Melka Kunture-3; -4	1.0 - 0.7	Namib-IV *Namibia*	~0.7
	OL Masek	1.0 - 0.9	Cornelia *S. Afr.*	?1.0
	+Olorgesailie 1-14	+0.99-0.49		
Late Turkanan				
(◆) *Gorgopithecus*	Kanam Rawi, Kanjera North.	?1.2	Djebel Ressas 568 *Tunisia*	~1.2
(↗) *Ourebia;* Georhychus, Meriones	OL Bed III / IV	1.4-1.0	An Nafud *Saudi Arabia*	~1.3
(↙) *Dinofelis, Homotherium, Chasmapor-*	SH-L; ET Chari	1.4-1.3	'Ubediya *Israel*	~1.4
thetes, **Rhinocolobus, Cercopithecoides,**	Konso (upper) *Ethiopia*	1.45-1.3	Kromdraai A, Swtkr. 2-3 *S. Afr.*	~1.5
Paranthropus, *Prolagus, Makapania,*	WT Nariokotome	1.33	Ain Hanech *Algeria*	~1.5
Deinotherium, Mammuthus, Anancus	Barogali *Djibouti*	1.5	Yayo *Chad*	~1.5
	AW-Melka Kunture-2/1	1.5-1.1	Humpata (Leba) *Angola*	~1.5
	Peninj *Tanzania*	1.5	Djebel Ressas 1 *Tunisia*	~1.6
	Gadeb *Ethiopia*	1.5	Irhoud Ocre *Morocco*	~1.6
	OL Bed II (upper)	1.6-1.4	Sterkfontein 5 *S. Afr.*	~1.6
	SH-J/K; ET Okote	1.64-1.4	Swartkrans I *S. Afr.*	~1.6
	BA Chesowanja (=Chemoigut)	~1.8	Kromdraai B *S. Afr.*	~1.8
	WR Nyabusosi	~1.8-1.3		
	ET Fejej-1	1.88		
	Konso (lower) *Ethiopia*	1.9		
	Anabo Koma *Djibouti*	1.9		
	OL Bed I, lower Bed II	1.9-1.6		
	+ET-KBS; SH-H	1.9-1.65		
Early Turkanan				
(◆) *Prototomys*	Kanjera South	?2.0	Swartkrans II, Bolt's 6 *S. Afr.*	~2.0
(↗) *Rhynchocyon, Erinaceus,* **Paranthro-**	ET Upper Burgi	2.0	Langebaan upper *S. Afr.*	~2.0
pus, Homo, *Vulpes, Lycaon, Otocyon,*	BA Chemeron (upper)	~2.4	Ouadi Derdemi, Koula *Algeria*	?2.0
Proteles, Alcelaphus	AW Matabaietu, K. Hadar (upp.)	2.5-2.3	Taung *S. Afr.*	~2.3
(↙) **Paracolobus, Parapapio, P. (Dino-**	WR Hohwa, Kaiso	2.5-2.0	Constantine, Ain Jourdel *Alger.*	~2.3
pithecus), *Paraxerus, Nyanzachoerus,*	Chiwondo 3A *Malawi*	~2.5	Ain Brimba *Tunisia*	~2.5
Notochoerus, Ancylotherium, Primelephas	Marsabit (Algas)	~2.5	Ahl al Oughlam *Morocco*	~2.5
	WT Lokalalei, Kalochoro	2.52-2.35		
	+SH-D/G	2.52-2.33		
Late Afarian				
(↗) *Crocidura, Elephantulus, Suncus,*	Laetoli Ndolanya *Tanzania*	~2.6	Sterkfontein-4 (main) *S. Afr.*	~2.6
Rhinocolobus, Cercopithecus, *Cerco-*	ET Hasuma; SH C	2.85-2.6	Ain Boucherit *Algeria*	?3.0
pithecoides, **Papio, P. (Dinopithecus),**	WR Kyeoro	~3.0-2.5	O. Fouarat, O. Akrech *Morocco*	?3.0
Steatomys, **Arvicanthus,** *Grammomys,*	Kesem-Kebena 1 *Ethiopia*	~3.0-2.5	Makapansgat-II / lwr. IV *S. Afr.*	~3.0
Equus, Phacochoerus, Camelus, Menelikia,	AW Kada Hadar (lower)	3.18-2.95	Gcwihaba *Botswana*	~3.0
Antidorcas	AW SHT/Denen D	3.39-3.2	Lac Ichkeul *Tunisia*	?3.5
(↙) **Australopithecus,** *Xenohystrix,*	WT Lomekwi	3.39-2.6	Bahr el-Gazal *Chad*	~3.5
Ugandax	ET Tulu Bor; SH B	3.39-2.9		
	AW Maka	3.4		
	WR Warwire	~3.5-3.0		
	+ET Lokochot; SH A	3.5-3.39		
Early Afarian				
(◆) *Praedamalis*	Karmosit	~3.6	Vaal River, Lower *S. Afr.*	?4.0-3.5
(↗) *Mungos, Ictonyx, Panthera, Chasma-*	Laetolil (upper) *Tanzania*	3.7-3.5		
porthetes, Canis, **Galago, Theropithecus,**	AW Belohdelie *Ethiopia*	3.8		
Serengetilagus, Pedetes, Xerus, Oenomys,	Ekora	3.8		
Thallomys, Notochoerus, Potamochoerus,	AW Sagantole *Ethiopia*	4.0-3.6		
Metridiochoerus, Pelorovis	+ET Moiti; Omo U-1	3.96-3.40		
(↙) *Miotragocerus, Stegodon*				

African Land Mammal Ages (LMAs). The time frame is based on the well-calibrated sequence of local faunas in East Africa (Kenya, except where noted). Many of the East African "local faunas" identified by site names (col. 2) were actually collected from many sub-sites in the same stratigraphic unit. Local faunas outside of East Africa (col. 4) are mostly not directly dated, and are positioned here according to faunal correlation. The age limits of each unit are set by the index fauna *at the base (marked with +), following the principle of "base defines boundary." Prior to the Fayum fauna, data are insufficient to justify setting firm boundaries, and names have been given to arbitrary spans of time that contain roughly comparable sites in North Africa. The range limits of* Key genera, *in the left side column, are selected from the known record because of their significance, either because they are abundant or because they are informative for diversity, habitat, or biogeography. Primates are shown in* **bold.** *In the pre-Fayumian sites, all identified genera are considered significant. The relationship of these LMAs to calibrated chronostratigraphy, magnetostratigraphy, and paleoclimatology, and to LMAs of other regions, is shown in the "Time Scale" section of the Introduction. Note that the upper and lower age range limits of the noted genera are not necessarily coincident with the upper or lower boundaries of the relevant mammal age.*

Key to notation			
(◆)	Characterizing taxon: apparently restricted to this time interval, in Africa	AW	Awash - *eastern Ethiopian Rift basin, Ethiopia*
(↗)	FAD: earliest known African occurrence of taxon is within this interval	BA	Baringo - *Lake Baringo basin & Tugen Hills, Kenya*
(↙)	LAD: last known African occurrence of taxon is within this interval	ET	East Turkana - *northeast Lake Turkana basin, Kenya-Ethiopia*
taxon	Known range includes East Africa during this interval	OL	Olduvai - *Eyasi basin, northern Tanzania*
taxon	Known range only in southern and/or northern Africa during this interval	SH	Shungura - *lower Omo River basin, southern Ethiopia*
?	Questionable date	WR	Western Rift - *Lake Albert basin, western Uganda, NE Zaire*
~	Approximate date	WT	West Turkana - *western Lake Turkana basin, Kenya*

KEY TAXA	EAST AFRICA	Age, Ma	OTHER AFRO-ARABIA	Age, Ma
Kerian (♦) *__Ardipithecus__, Stegodibelodon* (↗) *__Parapapio__, __Australopithecus__, Herpestes, Helogale, Mellivora, Torolutra, Lutra, Megantereon, Crocuta, Nyctereutes, Prolagus, Lepus, Tatera, Mastomys, Kolpochoerus, Syncerus, Redunca, Elephas, Loxodonta* (↙) *Agriotherium, Zramys, Progonomys, Brachypotherium, Dicerorhinus, Stegotetrabelodon*	Kanapoi Omo Mursi *Ethiopia* Aterir WT/ET Lonyumun AW Aramis Kanam Homa Chiwondo 2 (Uraha) *Malawi* BA Tabarin AW Kuseralee WR Ongoliba *Zaire* Manonga Kilolele *Tanzania* +Lothagam Apak	4.12 4.2?-4.0 4.2?-4.0 4.35-4.0 4.4 ~4.5 ?4.5 4.5 ~5.0-4.5 ~5.0 ~5.0 ~5.0-4.5	Hamada Damous *Morocco* Bochianga; Kolinga *Chad* Ain Guettara *Morocco* Argoub Kemellal *Algeria* Douaria *Tunisia* Amama-2 *Algeria* Kollé *Chad*	?4.5 ?4.5 ?4.5 ~4.5 ~4.5 ~4.5 ~4.5
Baringian (♦) *__Libypithecus__, Ailepus, Kanisamys, Cainotherium, Damalacra, Chemositia* (↗) *Civettictis, Agriotherium, Hyaena, Dinofelis, __Macaca__, Hystrix, Heterocephalus, Thryonomys, Mus, Rattus, Saccostomus, Ancylotherium, Sivatherium, Giraffa, Madoqua, Miotragocerus, Tragelaphus, Kobus, Aepyceros, Raphicerus, Primelephas, Mammuthus* (↙) *Sayimys, Africanomys, Myocricetodon, Libycosaurus*	Manonga Tinde *Tanzania* WR Nyawiega WR Nkondo Manonga Ibole *Tanzania* Lukeino Lothagam Nawata upper Kanam West Lothagam Nawata lower +BA Mpesida	~5.3 ~5.5 ~6.0 ~6.0 6.0 6.2-5.5 ~6.2 ~7.0-6.6 7.0-6.5	Langebaan "E" *S.Afr.* Sahabi *Libya* Wadi Natrun *Egypt* Hondeklip 30m *S. Afr.* Amama-1 *Algeria* Menacer (Marceau) *Morocco* Klein Zee *S. Afr.* Banyunah *Abu Dhabi*	~5.3 ~5.3 ~5.3 ?5.3 ~6.5 ?7 ?7 ~7
Sugutan (♦) *Indarctos, __Samburupithecus__, __Microcolobus__, Nakalimys, Kenyatherium* (↗) *Paraethomys, Hippopotamus, Hipparion Zygolophodon, Stegodon* (↙) *Paranomalurus, Tetralophodon*	Nakali BA Ngeringerowa +Namurungule (Baragoi)	?8.0 ~9.0 ~9.5	Khendek el-Ouaich *Algeria* Sidi Salem *Algeria* Dj. Krechem *Tunisia*	7.4 ~8.0 ~9
Tugenian (♦) *Vishnuonyx, Otavipithecus, Damalavus* (↗) *Canis, Mellivora, Progonomys, Nyanzachoerus, Miotragocerus, Prostrepsiceros, Paleotragus, Stegotetrabelodon* (↙) *Dissopsalis, __Victoriapithecus__, __Kenyapithecus__, Vulcanisciurus, Nguruwe, Nasus, Kenyapotamus, Dorcatherium, Canthumeryx, Chilotheridium, Prodeinotherium*	BA Ngorora D/E AW Ch'orora WR Kakara (Mohari) +BA Ngorora A/C	~11-10 10.6 ~12 12.8-11.6	Oued Zra *Algeria* Oued Mya *Algeria* Bou Hanifia *Algeria* Jebel Hamrin *Iraq* Beglia sup. *Tunisia* Hondeklip 50m *S. Afr.* Beglia inf. *Tunisia* Berg Aukas *Namibia*	9.7 ~10 ~10 ~10 ~10 ?12 ~12 ~12
Tinderetian (♦) *Paradiceros* (↗) *Genetta, Machairodus, Percrocuta, __Kenyapithecus__, Kenyapotamus, Climacoceras, Samotherium, Heterohyrax, Choerolophodon, Anancus* (↙) *Hyainailourous, Anasinopa, __Komba__, __Limnopithecus__, __Micropithecus__, __Proconsul__, __Simiolus__, Paraphiomys, Diamantomys, Myophiomys, Notocricetodon, Namachoerus, Libycochoerus, Eotragus, Aceratherium, Miorhynchocyon, Pachyhyrax*	BA Alengerr Kirimun Fort Ternan WR Kisegi Nyakach (Sondu) Nachola BA Muruyur, Kipsaramon +Maboko-Majiwa	13 13.5 14.0 ~14 ~15 15 ~15.5 15.3	Pataniak-6 *Algeria* Testour *Tunisia* Cherichera *Tunisia* Beni Mellal *Algeria* Hofuf *Saudi Arabia*	~13 ~13.5 ?13.5 ~14 ~15
Kisingirian (♦) *Afrocyon, Afrosmilus, Kichechia, Luogale, __Dendropithecus__, __Rangwapithecus__, __Prohylobates__, __Morotopithecus__, __Afropithecus__, __Turkanapithecus__, Kenyalagomys, Kenyamys, Kenyasus, Hyoboops, Prohyrax* (↗) *Hyainailourous, __Komba__, __Limnopithecus__, __Micropithecus__, __Proconsul__, __Victoriapithecus__, __Simiolus__, Paranomalurus, Megapedetes, Paraphiomys, Diamantomys, Myophiomys, Atlantoxerus, Vulcanisciurus, Notocricetodon, __Nasus__, Nguruwe, Namachoerus, Libycochoerus, Dorcatherium, Canthumeryx, Prolibytherium, Paleotragus, Eotragus, Gazella, Aceratherium, Brachypotherium, Miorhyncocyon, Gomphotherium* (↙) *Apterodon, Phiomys, Afromeryx, Eozygodon, Archaebelodon*	Ombo, Mariwa Rusinga Kulu, Uyoma Kajong (Mwiti) Loperot Kalodirr (Muruarot) Locherangan Rusinga Hiwegi, Karungu Bukwa *Uganda* Moroto *Uganda* Napak *Uganda* Songhor, Koru +Meswa	~16 16 ~17 17 17 17.5 17.8 ?18 ?18 ~19 ~19 ~20	Arrisdrift-Rooilepel *Namibia* Jebel Zelten; Siwa *Libya* Hadrukh - AsSarrar *Saudi Ar.* Huqf - Ghaba *Oman* Negev Rotem *Israel* Jebel Mrhila *Tunisia* Wadi Moghara *Egypt* Auchas *Namibia* Sperrgebiet *Namibia* Hondeklip 90m *S. Afr.* J. Midrash Shamali *Saudi Ar.*	~16 ~18 ~18 ~18 ~18 ~18 ?18 ~18 ~18 ~18 ?20

KEY TAXA	EAST AFRICA	Age, Ma	OTHER AFRO-ARABIA	Age, Ma
Turkwelian				
(◆) _Kamoyapithecus_	Lothidok	~26	Wadi Sabyah _Saudi Arabia_	?23
(➚) _Afromeryx, Prodeinotherium, Eozygodon, Archaebelodon_				
Qatranian				
(◆) Metapterodon, **Afrotarsius**, Omanodon, **Shizarodon, Parapithecus, Apidium, Propliopithecus**, Metoldobotes, Selenohyrax	(None)		Taqah _Oman_	~31
			Thaytiniti _Oman_	33
			Malembe _Angola (Cabinda)_	?33
			Zallah _Libya_	~33
(➚) Pachyhyrax			Gebel Qatrani-4 (I,M) _Egypt_	
(↙) **Qatrania**, Oligopithecus, Metaphiomys Megalohyrax, Titanohydrax, Saghatherium, Thyrohyrax, Bunohyrax, Barytherium, Paleomastodon			+Gebel Qatrani-3 (E,V) (_Egypt_	~33
				~34
Fayumian				
(◆) Ptolemaia, Hyaenodon, **Biretia, Aframonius, Anchomomys, Wadilemur, Plesiopithecus, Arsinoea, Serapia Catopithecus**, Nementchamys, Herodotius, Arsinoitherium, Moeritherium	(None)		Gebel Qatrani-2 (A,B,C) _Egypt_	~35
			Gebel Qatrani-1 (L-41) _Egypt_	~37
			Dur at-Talha _Libya_	~37-35
			Nementcha -Bir el Ater _Algeria_	?38
(➚) Apterodon, **Qatrania**, Oligopithecus, Phiomys, Metaphiomys, Bothriogenys, Thyrohyrax, Barytherium, Paleomastodon			In Tafidet _Mali_	?38
			+Qasr el-Sagha _Egypt_	~38
Numidian				
(◆) Azibius, **Algeripithecus, Tabelia**, Glibia, Glibemys, Zegdoumys, Microhyrax	(None)		M'Bodione Dadere _Senegal_	?44
			Gour Lazib-Glib Zegdou _Algeria_	?44
(➚) Megalohyrax				
(↙) Numidotherium				
Tebessan				
(◆) Kasserinotherium, Garatherium, **Koholia, Djebelemur**, Chambius, Seggeurius	(None)		Chambi (Kasserine) _Tunisia_	?46
			El Kohol _Algeria_	?50
(➚) Titanohyrax, Numidotherium				
Tingitanian				
(◆) Afrodon, Todralestes, Cimolestes, Palaeoryctes, Tachyoryctes, Khamsaconus, Abolytolestes, Adapisoriculus, **Altiatlasius**, Phosphatherium	(None)		N'Tagourt 2 _Morocco_	~54
			Adrar Mgorn 1 _Morocco_	~57
			Ouled Abdoun _Morocco_	~57

African Land Mammal Ages (LMAs). The time frame is based on the well-calibrated sequence of local faunas in East Africa (Kenya, except where noted). Many of the East African "local faunas" identified by site names (col. 2) were actually collected from many sub-sites in the same stratigraphic unit. Local faunas outside of East Africa (col. 4) are mostly not directly dated, and are positioned here according to faunal correlation. The age limits of each unit are set by the index fauna at the base (marked with +), following the principle of "base defines boundary." Prior to the Fayum fauna, data are insufficient to justify setting firm boundaries, and names have been given to arbitrary spans of time that contain roughly comparable sites in North Africa. The range limits of Key genera, in the left side column, are selected from the known record because of their significance, either because they are abundant or because they are informative for diversity, habitat, or biogeography. Primates are shown in **bold**. In the pre-Fayumian sites, all identified genera are considered significant. The relationship of these LMAs to calibrated chronostratigraphy, magnetostratigraphy, and paleoclimatology, and to LMAs of other regions, is shown in the "Time Scale" section of the Introduction. Note that the upper and lower age range limits of the noted genera are not necessarily coincident with the upper or lower boundaries of the relevant mammal age.

Key to notation				
(◆)	Characterizing taxon: apparently restricted to this time interval, in Africa	AW	Awash - _eastern Ethiopian Rift basin, Ethiopia_	
(➚)	FAD: earliest known African occurrence of taxon is within this interval	BA	Baringo - _Lake Baringo basin & Tugen Hills, Kenya_	
(↙)	LAD: last known African occurrence of taxon is within this interval	ET	East Turkana - _northeast Lake Turkana basin, Kenya-Ethiopia_	
taxon	Known range includes East Africa during this interval	OL	Olduvai - _Eyasi basin, northern Tanzania_	
taxon	Known range only in southern and/or northern Africa during this interval	SH	Shungura - _lower Omo River basin, southern Ethiopia_	
?	Questionable date	WR	Western Rift - _Lake Albert basin, western Uganda, NE Zaire_	
~	Approximate date	WT	West Turkana - _western Lake Turkana basin, Kenya_	

African Fossil Primates and Faunas

PALEOGENE

The early record of African primates begins with later Paleocene (Tingitanian) small-mammal faunas in Morocco that contain the indeterminate euprimate _Altiatlasius_, together with palaeoryctids and todralestids very close to Thanetian forms in western Europe. The earliest known proboscidean, _Phosphatherium_, is from this level as well. The adapiform status of _Djebelemur_, from the late Early Eocene (Tebessan) fauna of Chambi (Morocco), has been controversial, but recovery of an undoubted cercamoniine, _Aframonius_, from the Late Eocene (Fayumian) fauna in the lower part of the Fayum sequence, and the probable cercamoniines _Omanodon_ and _Shizarodon_ from the Early Oligocene (Qatranian) fauna of Oman, suggests that adapiforms may indeed have been a significant component of primate faunas in the Old World tropics. The two parapithecids from the late Middle Eocene (Numidian) fauna of Glib Zegdou in Algeria may be the oldest certain anthropoids.

The world's most diverse and well-documented Paleogene anthropoid fauna has been collected in the Jebel Qatrani Formation of Egypt. In the lower part of the sequence, sites assigned to the Fayumian contain a number of parapithecid and oligopithecid taxa. The degree to which these are replaced by propliopithecids in the Qatranian faunas from the upper part of the section is consistent with the passage of several million years at the observed replacement rate in the Miocene paleofaunas. While a Late Eocene (Priabonian) age is widely attributed to the Fayum sites, the correlation is broad enough to raise the question as to whether the upper Fayum (Qatranian) levels should also be dated to the later Priabonian or to the earliest Oligocene. The younger age is suggested by a preliminary magnetostratigraphic analysis; in addition, the Omani Thaytiniti and Taqah sites, which are faunally close, if not identically similar, to the Jebel Qatrani assemblages, are bracketed by Early Oligocene nummulite microfauna. A possible equivalent in sub-Saharan Africa is the Malembe faunule from Angola, with one debatable primate tooth.

The Middle-to-Late Oligocene is not well represented in Africa, and the first post-Fayum land mammal fauna is at Lothidok in East Africa (ca. 26 Ma). This small sample, the only one so far of Turkwelian age except for an even smaller collection from the Red Sea coast of Saudi Arabia, includes the earliest proconsulid, *Kamoyapithecus,* but none of the Fayum primate groups.

MIOCENE

Early Miocene Kisingirian localities provide the first pancontinental picture for Afro-Arabia, with fossil faunas from northern, equatorial, and southern regions. Evidence for a major post-Qatranian immigration and naturalization of Eurasian mammal lineages is apparent in the diversity of endemic genera of fissiped carnivores, sciurognath rodents, suids, ruminants (including the first known tragulids, bovids, and giraffids) and perissodactyls, none of which have ancestors in the Qatranian. A pronounced paleoecological difference between the tropical highlands and the pericontinental coastal environments is also evident in the Kisingirian faunas. Extremely well-preserved fossil mammal faunas (Koru, Songhor, Napak, Rusinga) from alkali-volcanic "mock arid" basins, in what were heavily forested volcanic highlands on the pre-rift Kenya Dome, contain abundant and largely arboreal proconsulids, archaic catarrhines (here included in the "*Dendropithecus*-group"), and strepsirhines, together with phyletically conservative, forest-adapted early ruminants, small carnivores, creodonts, hyraxes, rhinos, and proboscideans. A markedly different association has been sampled in the rift basin of northern Kenya, where the first hominid (*Afropithecus*) and the archaic catarrhine *Turkanapithecus* occur together with the first cercopithecoid (*Prohylobates*) in association with suids, ruminants, and carnivores that are clearly more advanced in their adaptations to open country. The nonprimate taxa correlate closely to Lower Miocene coastal-plain sites in Namibia, northern Africa, Israel, and the Persian Gulf (with *Heliopithecus*). None of the latter are closely dated, but the sites in North Africa, Israel, and Saudi Arabia are all well correlated to Late Burdigalian (ca. 17 Ma) marine strata. In Kenya, radiometric dates on the main "upland" sites range from 20 to 18 Ma, with

others known from ca. 16 Ma, while the "lowland" sites fall into the 18–17 Ma span. The radical differences between the two groups of Kenya Kisingirian local faunas have been attributed to evolutionary succession, but it seems preferable under the narrow time constraints to consider them as coeval ecofacies at different elevations. This grouping is entirely coincident with the paleotopography, so far as it is known, and the fact that the "upland" association continues to the end of the Kisingirian in the Kenya Dome cannot be ignored.

Beginning in the early Middle Miocene and continuing through the Late Miocene, the Tinderetian, Tugenian, Sugutan, and Baringan samples show less regional or environmental difference than in the Kisingirian. This may reflect the expansion of open-country habitat in the tropical highlands, as evidenced in the general, if not complete, replacement of the conservative forest-adapted genera in the Kisingirian with more advanced forms descended from the "lowlands" fauna (seen primarily in the rodents, bovids, giraffids, and proboscideans) together with new groups such as hyaenas, hippos, and (in the Tugenian) canids and equids. In the primate-bearing Tinderetian sites, whether on the dome (Maboko, Fort Ternan) or in the central rift (Muruyur, Alengerr, Nachola), *Kenyapithecus* is the sole hominid, together with the cercopithecoid *Victoriapithecus* and the last proconsulids. In Namibia, *Otavipithecus* may represent the local kenyapithecine. From 13 Ma until the end of the Miocene, however, primates are extremely rare. Hominids are virtually unknown, other than a partial maxilla of a potential hominine from Baragoi (Samburu Hills) and isolated teeth in the Tugen Hills sequence. By contrast, the open-country cercopithecids (i.e., *Macaca* but also more arboreal colobines) become more common at the end of the Miocene (Menacer in Algeria; Wadi Natrun in Egypt; Sahabi in Libya; Lothagam in Kenya), which suggests that the sampled environments may simply have been unsuitable for contemporaneous hominids. The latest Miocene (Baringian) interval, from ca. 7 to 5 Ma, was marked by an increase in the rate of apparent origination, with the earliest (or sole) records of at least 48 new genera, including the first true elephantids (*Primelephas, Mammuthus,* and *Loxodonta*) and, at Lothagam, indeterminate indications of what may be the earliest hominin.

PLIOCENE

The Pliocene begins with Kerian faunas in East Africa that show a continued sharp increase in the rate of diversification and the earliest well-documented record of hominines. There are no sites of this age in the southern region, and most, but not all, of the nine major Kerian sites in North Africa yield only small mammals. Even so, the appearance of *Australopithecus* and *Ardipithecus* in East Africa seems to document a hominid breakthrough into seasonally dry, open-country environments.

The Early Pliocene peak in generic origination rates contrasts with the termination rate, which showed a modest and regular increase until the Pleistocene. This is clear evidence for ecological fragmentation and niche diversification, at least in the open-country faunas that make up the known record.

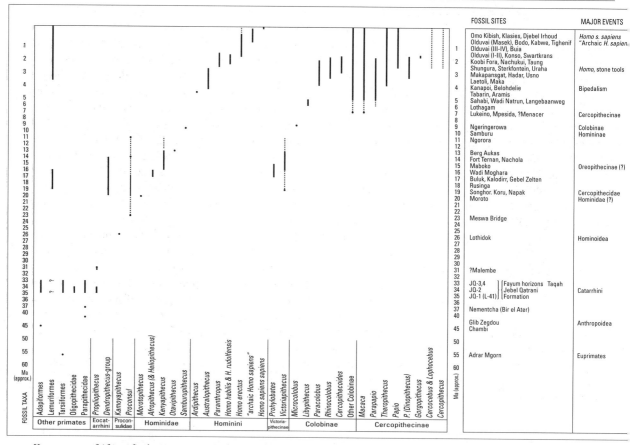

Known ranges of African fossil primate genera (and some higher taxa) and major sites and events in African primate and human evolution.

The African Pliocene is characterized by the evolutionary radiations of two major groups of higher primates, Old World monkeys and hominines. The rich Pliocene sites in Ethiopia, Kenya, Tanzania, and South Africa document a diversity of both colobines and cercopithecines, many of which were considerably larger than their extant relatives. *Parapapio* is known from the southern sites of Sterkfontein and Makapansgat, as well as from Hadar and the Turkana Basin. In eastern and southern Africa, fossil geladas (*Theropithecus*) were quite abundant, along with large colobines (*Cercopithecoides, Paracolobus,* and *Rhinopithecus*; the latter two are as yet known only from eastern African localities). The genus *Cercopithecus*, which is so successful in Africa today, is known from only a handful of fossils, and *Papio* also is generally not common, except in the latest Pliocene of the southern region.

Early Pliocene (ca. 4.4 Ma) fossils from Aramis in the Ethiopian Middle Awash Valley, named *Ardipithecus ramidus,* are the most conservative of any material assigned to Hominini. This form combines reduced canines and anteriorly positioned foramen magnum with "primitive" retentions such as apelike dP$_3$ morphology, as well as thin enamel on canines and molars, which may be conservative or secondarily reduced. It is not yet certain if this taxon represents a distant side branch or a twig on the "main line" of human evolution.

Slightly younger fossils from Kanapoi and Allia Bay, Kenya, have been assigned to *Australopithecus anamensis,* the

oldest species of that basal hominin genus. A mandible, a maxilla, and a tibia from Kanapoi date ca. 4.2 Ma, while other specimens may range up to 3.9 Ma or younger. They differ from *A. ramidus* in known features especially by having thicker dental enamel, while the more elongate and parallel-sided tooth rows help distinguish them from younger species.

The largest collections of mid-Pliocene hominins, all attributed to *Australopithecus afarensis,* have been recovered from sites in the Hadar Formation, the sites of Belohdelie and Maka in the Middle Awash, Fejej, the Usno Formation (all Ethiopia), the Koobi Fora Formation (Kenya), and the Laetolil Beds (Tanzania). These fossils span the period between ca. 3.8 and 2.95 Ma, while slightly younger fossils from Member B in the Shungura Formation (Ethiopia) have been tentatively assigned here as well. *A. afarensis* appears to have occupied both closed-forest and open-savannah habitats. Its postcranial skeleton attests to both bipedal and climbing locomotor repertoires, and it shows considerable sexual dimorphism. A partial mandible and an isolated tooth from the Koro-Toro area of Chad have been named *A. bahrelghazali*, which is distinguished from *A. afarensis* by several dental features. The Chad faunal assemblage is said to most closely resemble those from Hadar, suggesting a date of ca. 3.5–3 Ma.

The South African sites of Taung, Makapansgat, and Sterkfontein, which have been faunally dated to between ca. 3 and 2.3 Ma, contain fossils of *Australopithecus africanus.* There is as yet no convincing evidence for *A. africanus* in eastern Africa. Faunal evidence indicates a closed-brush-wood environment for *A. africanus.* This species is postcranially similar to *A. afarensis,* and it also shows evidence of strong sexual dimorphism. There are differences between the two taxa in vault roundness, forehead shape, mastoid projection, and developmemnt of the P_3 metaconid.

Two "robust australopith," or *Paranthropus,* species are known from the Pliocene of eastern Africa. *P. aethiopicus* is represented by a cranium from the Lomekwi Formation (Kenya) and a mandible and numerous isolated teeth from the Shungura Formation that are dated to ca. 2.7–2.3 Ma. *P. boisei,* which is better known in Pleistocene-age sediments from eastern Africa, is also represented in Pliocene deposits from the Shungura Formation, the Koobi Fora Formation, and Bed I of Olduvai Gorge. The earliest fossils attributed to *P. boisei* date to ca. 2.3 Ma, and this species appears to have occupied both open and closed habitats.

The earliest evidence for the genus *Homo* derives from Pliocene deposits in eastern Africa. The earliest representatives of this genus are presently attributed to the species *H. rudolfensis,* known from ca. 2.4 to 1.9 (perhaps to 1.6) Ma in the Omo Shungura Formation and perhaps at Hadar (Ethiopia), the Koobi Fora Formation and the upper Chemeron Formation (Kenya), and the Chiwondo Beds (Malawi). It is probably not coincidental that the earliest lithic artifacts date to ca. 2.6–2.3 Ma at sites in the Omo and Afar (Gona) regions of Ethiopia, at Lokalalei west of Lake Turkana, and possibly at Senga–5 in northern Zaire. These stone tools, like those from Olduvai Gorge and Koobi Fora (Karari), appear to represent the opportunistic flaking of small cobbles (Mode 1), and a small proportion of animal bones that are associated with these Oldowan artifacts show evidence of stone-tool cutmarks.

The very end of the Pliocene (ca. 1.9–1.8 Ma) saw the apparent coexistence of up to two additional species of *Homo* in eastern Africa. Both *H. habilis* and *H. erectus* may have their earliest records in the Turkana Basin about this time and both extended well into the Pleistocene. Considering the range of *H. rudolfensis* and *P. boisei,* the overlap of four hominin species for up to 250 Kyr is unexpected, to say the least. Perhaps the three species assigned to *Homo* were adapted to different microenvironments around Lake Turkana and seldom, if ever, occupied the same territory at any time.

PLEISTOCENE

The fossil record during the Pleistocene shows further evolutionary radiations of Old World monkeys (especially modern genera such as *Papio, Cercocebus, Cercopithecus,* and *Colobus,* as well as ever-larger *Theropithecus*) and hominins. The latter were characterized by increasing reliance on technology, resulting in an abundant archaeological record. Although the global definition of the Plio-Pleistocene boundary is fixed at ca. 1.8 Ma, there is little overall change in Africa at that precise horizon, even though it marked the end of at least two species of *Homo* and the succession of *H. erectus* as the dominant, and soon the only, representative of the genus.

Fossils of *Paranthropus boisei* are known from Early Pleistocene deposits in the Turkana Basin and the Olduvai Gorge, as well as from the Humbu Formation at Peninj (Tan-

zania) and Chemoigut Formation at Chesowanja (Kenya). *P. boisei* is not represented in the fossil record after ca. 1.4 Ma. In South Africa, *P. robustus* is known from the sites of Swartkrans and Kromdraai, dated to ca. 1.8–1.5 Ma, where it appears to have inhabited comparatively open environments.

Both species of *Paranthropus* appear to have coexisted with one or more species of *Homo.* A single fragment is assigned to *H. rudolfensis* from a 1.6 Ma horizon at Koobi Fora. *Homo habilis,* however, is relatively common at Olduvai between 1.8 and 1.6 Ma, though it is not definitively recognized in contemporaneous deposits in the Turkana Basin. Specimens of early *Homo erectus* (sometimes termed *H. ergaster*) are known from the Turkana Basin and the upper Bed II at Olduvai Gorge at ca. 1.8–1.5 Ma. Contemporaneous nonrobust fossils from Swartkrans Members 1–3 and Sterkfontein Member 5 are often allocated to *H. erectus* as well, but some recent studies have questioned these identifications. Most of the artifacts found alongside or coeval with these early *Homo* fossils are still part of Mode 1 assemblages, including the so-called Developed Oldowan A. The earliest Acheulean (proto)bifaces are known from sites dated to ca. 1.6–1.4 Ma, such as EF-HR at Olduvai (middle Bed II) and Konso (Ethiopia).

Younger human fossils from Olduvai (Beds III–IV), the upper Shungura Formation, Gomboré II at Melka Kontouré (Ethiopia), and perhaps Yayo (Chad) and Tighenif (Algeria) are generally regarded as representing later *H. erectus,* with greater similarity to East Asian members of that taxon. African *H. erectus* fossils thus span a considerable period of time, from ca. 1.9 to 0.7 Ma. Many of these fossils derive from deposits that contain lithic artifacts of the Acheulean tradition, and countless sites from this period throughout northern, eastern, and southern Africa preserve Acheulean artifacts and extensive fauna but no hominid remains (e.g., Olorgesailie). In contrast to the opportunistic flaking that appears to have been a feature of the Oldowan tradition, the Acheulean assemblages (Mode 2) are generally characterized by well-formed handaxes and cleavers, and there is evidence that a much wider landscape was being utilized by ca. 1.6 Ma than had been the case before. In a number of instances, the source rocks are located many kilometers from the Acheulean archaeological sites. Controversial studies may document controlled fire by 1.4 Ma.

Middle Pleistocene fossils of early (i.e., "archaic") *Homo sapiens* are known from such sites as Bodo (Ethiopia), Kabwe (Zambia), Ndutu (Tanzania), and Saldanha (South Africa). Moroccan specimens from Salé, Thomas Quarries, and Sidi Abderrahman probably also represent a similar population, and some have suggested that Tighenif is an early member as well. Most of these fossils probably date between 700 and 400 Ka. Moreover, it has been argued that somewhat younger specimens from Rabat (Morocco), Lake Eyasi (Tanzania), the Kapthurin Beds at Baringo (Kenya), and possibly the Cave of Hearths (South Africa) are referable to early *H. sapiens.* For the most part, these fossils are associated with Acheulean artifacts, with some indications of the use of the Levallois or a comparable technique of prepared-core flaking. In sub-Saharan Africa, industries of Acheulean or other

Mode 2 type are generally termed Early Stone Age, with local variants common in South and East Africa. For example, the Sangoan (ca. 300–200 Ka) includes finely made handaxes, prepared-core technology, and, in some cases, large blades struck from prismatic cores, foreshadowing Mode 4 assemblages. Dates for the youngest Acheulean/Mode 2 industries appear to span the period 200–150 Ka, as is also the case in Europe (although there the Micoquian may extend into the last interglacial).

By the Middle Paleolithic, regional differentiation becomes important in African archaeology and human paleontology. South of the Sahara, such specimens as those from Florisbad (South Africa) and Ngaloba at Laetoli (Tanzania) probably date to ca. 275–125 Ka. They may represent examples of a transition from "archaic" to the earliest "anatomically modern" *Homo sapiens*. Archaeological tool kits of this age are mainly of Mode 3 form and are broadly classed as Middle Stone Age (MSA). The earliest examples of MSA appear to date older (at ca. 250 Ka in South Africa, Zambia, Ethiopia, and perhaps Kenya) than the youngest Acheulean (ca. 250–175 Ka in South Africa, Tanzania, and Kenya), suggesting temporal overlap related to cultural differentiation and mosaic evolution of modern morphology.

Such South African MSA industries as the Pietersburg and Orangian typically include discoidal and Levallois-like cores, producing convergent flakes with faceted striking platforms, as well as flake blades, points, and side scrapers. Lupemban and Fauresmith assemblages also incorporate large bifacial tools, such as handaxes and picks, in some cases perhaps related to a woodworking, forest-dwelling adaptation. One of the most intriguing MSA variants is the South African Howieson's Poort, dated mainly between 80 and 65 Ka, which includes small blades struck from prismatic cores, similar to younger Mode 5 assemblages. In Zaire, a broadly contemporary industry at Katanda included barbed bone points (harpoons?), similar to those of the European Magdalenian at 15–10 Ka. Microlithic Mode 4–5 industries in Zaire and Tanzania also presage later European Upper Paleolithic developments. MSA industries continue until ca. 30 Ka, but they document a broader economic base (hunting of large game, fishing and shellfish collection, plant foods prepared with grindstones) than is common in the Eurasian Middle Paleolithic.

The earliest known representatives of "anatomically modern" *Homo sapiens* have been recovered from the Omo Kibish Formation (Ethiopia) and Klasies River Mouth Cave (South Africa). No tools were associated with the fossils in the former region, although a questionable date of 120 Ka was reported from levels older than the human remains. At Klasies (and the nearby Nelson Bay Cave, as well as Die Kelders [South Africa] and other sites), fragmentary human fossils are associated with MSA artifacts and dated to the Eemian (ca. 125–90 Ka) by geological inference. The Border Cave site in southern Africa has yielded a partial cranium and other remains of apparently African (rather than Eurasian or indeterminate) morphology, but the suggested age of 90 Ka has been questioned. Taken together, however, the southern African evidence is a strong indicator of the presence of anatomically modern humans by 100 Ka. It is tempting to

suggest a relationship with the Howieson's Poort industry and similar "precursors" of Mode 4 technology, but associations are unclear. As with the emergence of the genus *Homo*, southern Africa probably saw the origin of modern humans and some contemporaneous technological and economic advancements. In North Africa, Middle Paleolithic (Mode 3) Levallois-Mousterian and Aterian industries are known before, during, and after the Eemian interglacial. It does not appear that Neanderthals of European or Southwest Asian type ever occurred south of the Mediterranean, but human fossils older than 100 Ka are rare. Archaic varieties of "anatomically modern" *Homo sapiens* occur in northern Africa during the Weichselian, at such sites as Jebel Irhoud, Temara, and Mughuret el 'Aliya (Morocco), Haua Fteah (Libya), Singa (Sudan), and Diré-Dawa (Ethiopia). They are morphologically less comparable with the Neanderthals than with Levantine "archaic moderns" from Skhūl and Jebel Qafzeh.

No true Mode 4 (Late Paleolithic) industries are known well in west, central, or southern Africa, but they do appear after the Aterian in North Africa. At Haua Fteah, the Dabban is comparable with European blade-based industries of 40–20 Ka, and similar assemblages are known in Kenya, Ethiopia, and Somalia. The Ibero-Maurusian (or Oranian) occurs in western North Africa ca. 20–10 Ka, and the eastern Oranian of Libya is of similar age. Younger levels yield such industries as the Capsian in Tunisia. To the south, Later Stone Age (LSA) industries are characterized by microlithic technology and greater emphasis on fishing and hunting of large plains ungulates. The LSA begins before 40 Ka and continues into the Holocene, in some areas into the historic present.

See also Acheulean; Adapiformes; Afar Basin; Africa, East; Africa, North; Africa, Southern; Anthropoidea; Archaic Homo sapiens; Archaic Moderns; Ardipithecus ramidus; Asia, Western; Aterian; Australopithecus; Australopithecus afarensis; Australopithecus africanus; Australopithecus bahrelghazali; Bambata; Baringo Basin/Tugen Hills; Bone Tools; Border Cave; Bow and Arrow; Breccia Cave Formation; Broom, Robert; Catarrhini; Cave of Hearths; Cenozoic; Cercopithecidae; Cercopithecinae; Chiwondo Beds; Climate Change and Evolution; Colobinae; Dabban; "Dendropithecus-Group"; Early Paleolithic; Early Stone Age; Economy, Prehistoric; Eocene; Epipaleolithic; Fayum; Fire; First Intermediate; Florisbad; Haua Fteah; Hominidae; Homininae; Hominoidea; Homo; Homo erectus; Homo ergaster; Homo habilis; Homo rudolfensis; Homo sapiens; Howieson's Poort; Jebel Irhoud; Kabwe; Kalambo Falls; Karari; Kenyapithecinae; Klasies River Mouth; Kromdraai; Late Paleolithic; Later Stone Age; Lithic Use-Wear; Lupemban; Makapansgat; Man-Land Relationships; Mesolithic; Middle Awash; Middle Paleolithic; Middle Stone Age; Miocene; Modern Human Origins; Mousterian; Natron-Eyasi Basin; Oldowan; Olduvai Gorge; Oligocene; Oligopithecidae; Orangian; Paleoenvironment; Paleolithic; Paleolithic Lifeways; Paleomagnetism; Paranthropus; Paranthropus aethiopicus; Paranthropus boisei; Paranthropus robustus; Parapithecidae; Pietersburg; Plate Tectonics; Pleistocene; Pliocene; Pre-Aurignacian; Prepared-Core; Proconsulidae; Propliopithecidae; Raw Materials; Rift

Valley; Saldanha; Sangoan; Second Intermediate; Senga-5; Smithfield; Spear; Sterkfontein; Stillbay; Stone-Tool Making; Swartkrans; Taphonomy; Taung; Tshitolian; Turkana Basin; Victoriapithecinae; Western Rift; Wilton. [J.A.V.C., E.D., J.G.F., F.E.G., A.S.B.]

Further Readings

Fleagle, J.G., and Kay, R.F., eds. (1994) Anthropoid Origins. New York: Plenum.

Howell, F.C. (1978) Hominidae. In V.J. Maglio and H.B.S. Cooke (eds.): Evolution of African Mammals. Cambridge, Mass.: Harvard University Press, pp. 149–258.

Phillipson, D.W. (1993) African Archaeology, 2nd ed. Cambridge: Cambridge University Press.

Pickford, M. (1986) The geochronology of Miocene higher primate faunas of East Africa. In J.G. Else and P.C. Lee (eds.): Primate Evolution. Cambridge: Cambridge University Press, pp. 19–33.

Suwa, G., White, T.D., and Howell, F.C. (1996) Mandibular postcanine dentition from the Shungura Formation, Ethiopia: Crown morphology, taxonomic allocation, and Plio-Pleistocene hominid evolution. Am. J. Phys. Anthropol. 101:247–282.

Szalay, F.S., and Delson, E. (1979) Evolutionary History of the Primates. New York: Academic Press.

Vrba, E.S., Denton, G.H., Partridge, T.C., and Burckle, L.H., eds. (1995) Paleoclimate and Evolution, with Emphasis on Human Origins. New Haven: Yale University Press.

Wood, B.A. (1991). Koobi Fora Research Project, Vol. 4: Hominid Cranial Remains. Oxford: Oxford University Press.

Africa, East

A tropical region of distinctive topography and climate, extending from the Western Rift highlands (ca. 28–32° E longitude) to the Indian Ocean, between the north and south 15th parallels. This land is occupied by the nations of Ethiopia, Djibouti, Somalia, Uganda, Kenya, Tanzania, Rwanda, Burundi, and Malawi, together with northern Mozambique and the thin slice of easternmost Zaire that lies within the Western Rift. The dominant element in the geography of the African Plateau in this region is the East African Rift system, a chain of updomed highlands transected by enormous, volcanically active pull-apart grabens. The environment of the region is regulated by prevailing dry westerlies, punctuated by highly seasonal monsoonal rains. Ecotones are mostly open woodlands, gallery forests, and grassland, with thorn brush and xeric shrubland in the rainshadowed rift-valley basins. Higher precipitation on the isolated heights of rift highlands and volcanic massifs, on the other hand, support bamboo and deciduous rain forest, succeeded at the highest elevations by evergreen cloud forests and altiplano (equatorial-alpine) zones. A strip of deciduous forest also marks the narrow coastal plain.

The rift valleys of East Africa are characterized by heavily mineralized alkaline groundwater, subsiding closed basins, and active vulcanism and fault movement. These combine in conditions that are close to ideal for the accumulation, preservation, and later exposure of archaeological and paleontological remains. Mid-Miocene and younger paleoanthropological sites are therefore densely concentrated along the north-to-south strip that corresponds to the Eastern or Gregory Rift system from Afar to central Tanzania; other sites occur more sparsely in the Western Rift.

It must be noted, however, that climate and geological conditions were different in the Early Miocene, when the Kenya Dome was still rising and rifts had not developed. The earliest Miocene faunas are forest-adapted associations that were preserved in great volcanic massifs which built up on the flanks of the dome, including Tinderet, Kisingiri, Elgon, and Napak. After the dome ruptured, vulcanism and sedimentation shifted into the newly opened grabens, which lay in the rain shadow of the rift escarpments and were, in sharp contrast to the Early Miocene mountainsides, more arid than any other part of the landscape. The geological evolution of East Africa, in other words, distorted the paleoclimatic history: prior to 17 Ma, the fossil record is dominated by forest-adapted faunas from volcanic highlands, while after 14 Ma virtually all of the sample is from the rift basins, the driest part of the region. In the 17-to-14-Ma interval, both "highland" and "lowland" ecofaunas can be distinguished.

History of Paleoanthropological Discovery in East Africa

Fossil mammals and stone tools were known in East Africa for many years before significant primate remains were recovered. Probably the earliest collections were Plio-Pleistocene mammal fossils sent to Paris in 1902 from Count Teleki's exploration of the Lake Rudolf (Turkana) Basin, although these lay unknown until the French paleontologist Camille Arambourg came upon the unopened crates many years later. Arambourg's 1934 follow-up expedition also discovered Miocene fossils at Muruarot and Cretaceous dinosaurs at Lokitaung. The earliest known report of fossil mammals was in 1910, when G.R. Chesnaye, who was prospecting the Miocene formations around Lake Victoria for placer gold, sent word to the local authorities of fossil mammals he had found, first at Koru and shortly thereafter at Karungu. The famously unfortunate Mr. Piggott (who was eaten by crocodiles on his return trip) was sent out to collect at Karungu the following year by the district commissioner, C.W. Hobley. Piggot's collection survived to become the first fossil mammal fauna to be scientifically described from sub-Saharan Africa, prompting a full geological study by F. Oswald in 1911–1912. On his way out, Oswald found Plio-Pleistocene fossils, including the type of *Theropithecus oswaldi*, the first fossil primate from East Africa, at Kanjera (properly Kanjira) near the scene of Piggott's disaster. During the years 1912–1914, Hobley caused fossiliferous limestones on Rusinga Island to be mined for cement without noticing abundant bones of the deinothere, which had previously been named after him from nearby Karungu. It fell to Dr. H.L. Gordon, investigating his property at Koru in 1926, to discover the first hominoid remains from East Africa. These were assigned to the new genus and species

East African tuff horizons (*K-Ar dates, Ma)		Western Rift	West Turkana	East Turkana	Shungura, Omo	Awash, Hadar	Gulf of Aden
Kale	0.70	.	======	==( )==	.	.	.
Silbo	*0.74	.	.	==( )==	.	.	.
Gele	*1.25	.	.	==( )==	.	.	.
Nariokotome	*1.33	.	==( )==	.	.	.	.
Natoo	1.36	.	==( )==	.	=L-3=	.	.
Chari	*1.39	.	======	==( )==	=L=	.	======
L.Koobi Fora	1.63	=Kagusa=	======	==( )==	.	.	.
Okote	*1.64	.	.	==( )==	=J-7=	.	.
Morutot	*1.65	.	======	==( )==	=J-4=	.	.
Orange Tuff	?1.7	.	.	==( )==	======	.	.
Malbe	1.86	.	======	==( )==	=H-4=	.	.
KBS	1.87	=Hohwa=	======	==( )==	=H-2=	.	.
Kangaki	2.00	.	==( )==	.	.	.	.
Tuff G	*2.33	.	.	.	==( )==	=?BKT-3=	.
Ekalalei	2.35	.	==( )==	.	=F-1=	.	.
Kalochoro	*2.35	.	==( )==	.	=F=	.	.
Nalukuwoi	2.45	.	==( )==	.	=E-4=	.	.
Koikiselei	2.48	.	==( )==	.	=E=	.	.
Lokalalei	*2.52	.	==( )==	======	=D=	.	.
Burgi	2.58	.	.	==( )==	.	.	.
Emekwi	2.60	.	==( )==	.	=C-9=	.	.
Ingumwai	*2.75	.	======	==( )==	=C-4=	.	.
Hasuma	2.82	.	.	==( )==	=C=	.	.
Bouroukie BKT-2	*2.93	.	.	.	.	==( )==	.
Tuff B-10	*3.03	.	.	.	==( )==	.	.
Ninikaa	*3.10	.	.	==( )==	.	=?BKT-1=	.
Kada Hadar KHT	*3.18	.	.	.	.	==( )==	.
Triple Tuff-4	*3.22	.	.	.	.	==( )==	.
Waru	3.24	.	==( )==	======	.	.	.
Allia	3.25	.	.	==( )==	.	.	.
Toroto	*3.32	.	.	==( )==	.	.	.
Tulu Bor-b	3.35	.	======	==( )==	=B;U10=	==SHT==	======
Kaado	3.36	.	======	==( )==	.	.	.
Lokochot	*3.40	Kyampanga	======	==( )==	=A=	.	======
Loruth	3.42	.	======	==( )==	.	.	.
Lomugol	3.60	=Warwire=	==( )==	.	.	=Sagantole=	======
Topernawi	3.60	.	==( )==	======	.	.	.
Cindery Tuff	3.85	.	.	.	.	==( )==	.
Moiti	3.89	.	======	==( )==	=U-1=	=VT-1=	======
Gaala VTCf	4.40	.	.	.	.	==( )==	.

Tephrostratigraphic framework for Western Rift, Turkana, and Afar basins. The preferred nomenclature and dating for each tuff sheet are given at the left, with the type area indicated by parentheses. Commonly used alternative names in other basins are also shown (note that Sidi Hakoma Tuff or SHT in Hadar is called Maka Tuff in the Middle Awash Valley). Asterisks indicate radiometrically determined ages; other ages are interpolated from the dated horizons and from paleomagnetic reversals, according to estimated depositional rates. The identity of the tuff sheets in different basins has been determined by chemical-petrological fingerprinting. Sources: Western Rift—M. Pickford, et al., 1991, C. r. séances Acad. Sci. Paris, II, 313; West Turkana—J. M. Harris et al., 1988, Los Angeles County Museum, Contributions in Science, no. 399; East Turkana (Koobi Fora)—C. Feibel et al., 1989, Am. J. Phys. Anthropol., 78; Omo Shungura, Usno, etc.—B. Haileab and F. H. Brown, 1992, J. Hum. Evol., 22; Afar Basin (Middle Awash, Hadar—R. C. Walter, 1994, Geology, 22. Gulf of Aden (from deep-sea cores)—A. M. Sarna-Wojcicki et al., 1985, Nature, 313.

Proconsul africanus by British paleontologist A.T. Hopwood after he and Louis Leakey found numerous additional specimens at Koru and on Rusinga Island in 1931–1932. Leakey also revisited Kanjera and nearby Kanam at the end of the 1932 season and chanced to find modern burials in the fossil beds that he long held to be evidence for the antiquity of *Homo*. The skull cap from the Middle Pleistocene Kanjera deposits understandably caused much less of a stir than the mandible published as *Homo kanamensis* from the Lower Pliocene levels at Kanam.

The earliest report of stone tools associated with fossils may have been that of a lepidopterist named Kattwinkel, who described artifacts from Olduvai Gorge in 1911 (the story that he found the gorge by falling into it while chasing butterflies may be apocryphal). The collection made by German paleontologist H. Reck in 1913 (which included another rather sensationally misinterpreted human burial) led Louis Leakey and Swedish archaeologist L. Kohl-Larsen to mount separate expeditions to the region in 1931. Both

workers, as it happened, collected teeth of *Australopithecus afarensis* at Laetoli, which, although misdiagnosed at the time, were the first early hominin specimens to be found in East Africa. Kohl-Larsen also opened the Mumba Cave site (Tanzania), expanding on Leakey's discovery of a Paleolithic occupation at Gamble's Cave a few years before. In his 1919 monograph on the Rift Valley of Kenya, American geologist J.W. Gregory described abundant handaxes at Ol Gaselik, now known as Olorgesailie, a site that was not relocated until Louis and Mary Leakey found it again in 1942.

The 1930s through 1950s saw a focus on Asian and South African discoveries of *Homo erectus* and *Australopithecus*, respectively. However, the Leakeys persisted in eastern Africa, working at Olduvai, Olorgesailie, Kariandusi, Hyrax Hill, and other Pleistocene sites, as well as developing the Miocene primate record at Koru, Songhor, Maboko, and, above all, Rusinga. Their work was joined at various times by colleagues including Dorothea Bate, J. Desmond Clark, W.E. LeGros Clark, F. Clark Howell, Sonia Cole, and the geologists P.E.

Kent and R.M. Shackleton. During this period, the 1947 Wendell Phillips expedition, guided by H.B.S. Cooke, enlarged on Arambourg's pioneering work in the Turkana Basin with the discovery of remains from Lothidok now classified as *Kamoyapithecus*, which are dated to the late Oligocene and are thus the oldest known hominoid. In the late 1950s, W.W. "Bill" Bishop began work in Uganda on the Kanam-aged Kaiso beds of Lake Albert and the Early Miocene of Napak. In August 1959, however, the discovery of the robust australopith *Zinjanthropus* (now *Paranthropus*) *boisei* at Olduvai marked the beginning of the modern era of well-funded interdisciplinary research, which has raised East Africa to the preeminent place in human evolutionary studies that it now holds.

The number of known paleontological and archaeological sites in eastern Africa began to expand dramatically in the 1960s. Many of these discoveries came when researchers initially involved with the Leakeys began to look farther afield. During this decade, a generation of doctoral candidates in geology and paleontology were introduced to East Africa under the supervision of Leakey (Cambridge), Bishop and L.C. King (Bedford College, London), R.J.G. Savage (Bristol), Howell, J.D. Clark, G.L. Isaac, and G.H. Curtis (Chicago and Berkeley), and Bryan Patterson (Harvard). French students were also active under the guidance of Yves Coppens. The primary areas of new discoveries were the northern Turkana Basin (Omo Valley and Koobi Fora), where teams

under Coppens, Howell, Isaac, and R.E. Leakey developed a tremendously significant Plio-Pleistocene section; the comparably productive Afar region of Ethiopia, explored by groups led by J. Kalb, D.C. Johanson, and J.D. Clark; and the Miocene-Pliocene sequences exposed in the Central Kenya Rift west of Lakes Baringo and Hannington, which was studied intensively, first by students directed by Bishop and King and later by a successor group under D.R. Pilbeam. B. Patterson's expedition into the desolate region between the Tugen Hills and Lake Turkana located Kanapoi, Lothagam, Ekora, and Loperot. Archaeological work also went forward under Isaac's direction at Peninj, Olorgesailie, Eyasi, and Nakuru.

Since 1980, research has been productive in all parts of East Africa. Aside from important new discoveries from previously known areas such as Rusinga, Maboko, Chemeron, Kanapoi, and the Afar, material also came from new or neglected areas. West Turkana Plio-Pleistocene sites were developed by A. Walker and R.E. Leakey, and new Miocene sites at the southern end of the lake (Buluk, Kajong, Locherangan, Kalodirr) and in the Samburu Escarpment (Nachola) were also reported, the last by a Japanese team led by H. Ishida. Several locations with hominin remains and Acheulean tools were described by French workers in Djibouti, while exploration in Ethiopia uncovered promising sites outside the Afar at Gona, Kesem-Kebena, Burji, Fejej, and Konso. In the Western Rift, knowledge of Miocene,

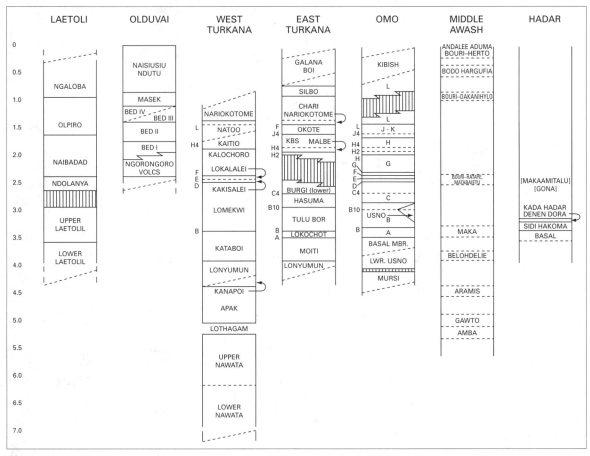

Correlation of major Miocene-Pleistocene sequences in East Africa. The units are dated according to radiometric ages on included lavas and tuffs. Some of the tuffs (indicated by letters to the left of the columns) have been traced over wide areas according to their trace element chemistry and mineral content, and by their relationship to paleontological and paleomagnetic data (see also accompanying table of tuffs and tephrostratigraphy).

Pliocene, and Pleistocene beds of the Lake Albert Basin and the Kazinga Channel was greatly expanded by American and French teams, respectively, and tephrostratigraphic analysis linked many of the index tuffs across huge distances from Uganda through the Turkana and Awash basins to the Red Sea. Another round of work on the Chiwondo beds brought the first hominin fossils to light in Malawi; new Mio-Pliocene fossil beds were reported from Manonga Valley in central Tanzania; and an Italian team recovered a fauna with a partial *Homo* cf. *erectus* skull at Buia in Eritrea (marginally within North Africa here), dated to ca. 1 Ma.

East Africa is central to several key themes in paleoanthropology, among which are the early history of hominoid diversity and adaptation, the origin of the human lineage, and the evolution of culture and human intelligence. These themes are chronologically sequential and depend on data coming mainly from the Miocene, Pliocene, and Pleistocene, respectively.

The Fossil Record

EVOLUTION OF HOMINOIDEA

Afro-Arabia in the Miocene is accepted by most workers as the center of diversity for the Catarrhini, including the endemic archaic catarrhines, victoriapithecines, and proconsulids; Afro-Eurasian taxa (colobines, cercopithecines, kenyapithecines, and hominines); and possible ancestors for extra-African lineages such as pliopithecids, dryopithecines, oreopithecines, hylobatids, and pongines. Documentation, however, is confined to the Miocene of East Africa with the exceptions of scanty remains from Namibia and the east coast of Arabia. Because of the Early Miocene bias toward tropical highland samples, the earliest part of the known record, from 23 to 17 Ma, is dominated by a wide diversity of small-to-medium-sized, presumably arboreal, archaic catarrhines (*Dendropithecus, Micropithecus, Kalepithecus* and *Limnopithecus*, loosely lumped as the "*Dendropithecus*-group") and proconsulids, such as *Kamoyapithecus, Proconsul,* and *Rangwapithecus,* in assemblages known from Lothidok, Koru, Songhor, Napak, Rusinga, Mfwangano, and ancillary sites. Monkeys and lorisoids are rare at these localities. The fact that catarrhines were also evolving in other ecosystems "out of sight" is signaled by a group of sites in the rift valley of northern Kenya dating to 17.5 Ma or slightly younger, including Buluk, Kajong, Locherangan, Loperot, Muruarot, and Kalodirr, which preserve a mammal fauna clearly more adapted to open

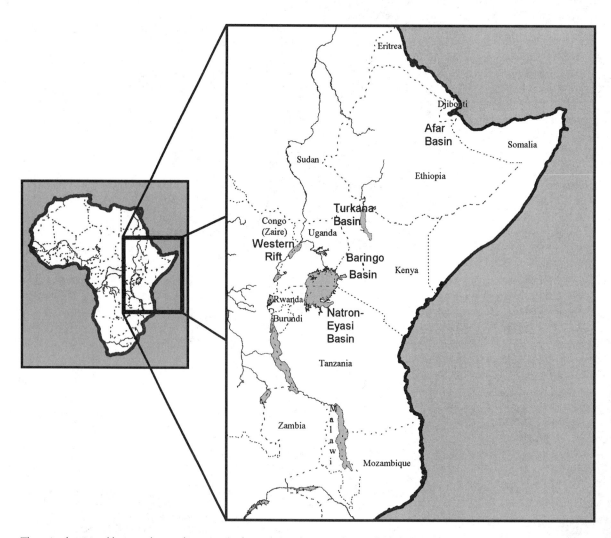

The major depositional basins and geographic regions (and countries) within East Africa, each of which is the subject of a separate entry.

conditions. In these sites, the earliest hominid, *Afropithecus,* as well as the probably "*Dendropithecus*-like" *Turkanapithecus* and *Simiolus* and the victoriapithecine monkey ?*Prohylobates,* are found with open-country bovids, giraffids, and suids, while proconsulids are rare. Mammal faunas of similar aspect and age have been found in coastal-plain sites in Namibia (Sperrgebiet, Auchas), Tunisia (Jebel Mrhila), Libya (Jebel Zelten), Egypt (Moghara), Israel (Rotem), and Arabia (Hadrukh), the latter with the kenyapithecine *Heliopithecus,* indicating that seasonally drier environments were widespread at lower elevations by this time. The Ugandan ?highland site of Moroto, with *Afropithecus*-like (kenyapithecine) fossils, may be of similar age or slightly younger.

Between 15 and 13 Ma, sampled environments were all open woodland, if not drier. Fossil mammal assemblages from Maboko Island and Fort Ternan in western Kenya were very like those of main-rift sites in central and northern Kenya such as Muruyur, Alengerr, Lothidok-Esha, and Na-

chola. In all of these sites, the kenyapithecine *Kenyapithecus* is the dominant hominoid, while early cercopithecids and the last proconsulids are much more rare (although *Victoriapithecus* is known from hundreds of specimens at the main Maboko horizons, by far the most common primate anywhere in the African Miocene). Unfortunately, the later Miocene history of hominoids in Africa is nearly unknown. Numerous fossil mammal faunas have been sampled from the time interval between 13 Ma and ca. 6 Ma, in both East and North Africa, without recovering any significant hominine remains (although monkeys are reasonably represented). Single teeth from the lower Ngorora Formation (ca. 12 Ma) and the Lukeino Formation (ca. 6 Ma) and a partial maxilla from the Samburu Hills (ca. 9 Ma) are still incompletely analyzed and hard to place phylogenetically, but they may represent rare traces of the Homininae or even the Hominini during the Late Miocene. The fact that all of these later Miocene mammal faunas appear to represent intensely seasonal and

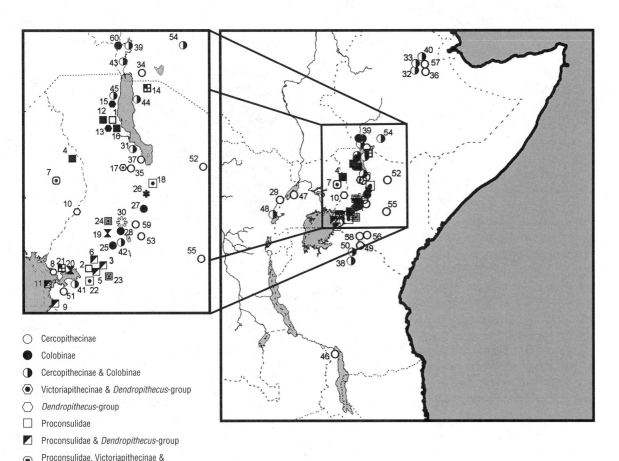

Main localities in East Africa yielding fossil non-hominin primates. Symbols indicate age and included primates, while numbers represent site names (in approximate chronological order), as follows: 1, Lothidok Hill; 2, Meswa Bridge; 3, Mteitei Valley; 4, Moroto; 5, Koru; 6, Songhor; 7, Napak; 8, Angulo; 9, Karungu; 10, Bukwa; 11, Rusinga, Mfwangano; 12, Moruarot; 13, Kalodirr; 14, Buluk; 15, Locherangan; 16, Esha Hill; 17, Loperot; 18, Nachola; 19, Kipsaramon; 20, Maboko; 21, Ombo, Bur-Siala, Majiwa, Kaloma; 22, Nyakach; 23, Fort Ternan; 24, Ngorora; 25, Ngeringerowa; 26, Samburu; 27, Nakali; 28, Mpesida; 29, Ongoliba; 30, Lukeino; 31, Lothagam; 32, Kuseralee; 33, Aramis, Maka, Matabaietu, Andalee; 34, Fejej; 35, Kanapoi; 36, Belohdelie; 37, Ekora; 38, Laetoli; 39, Omo Usno; 40, Hadar, Gona; 41, Kanam East; 42, Chemeron JM 90/91; 43, Omo Shungura; 44, Koobi Fora; 45, Nachukui (West Turkana); 46, Chiwondo Beds; 47, Kaiso Village; 48, Senga-5; 49, Peninj; 50, Olduvai Gorge; 51, Kanjera; 52, Marsabit; 53, Chesowanja; 54, Konso; 55, Nyeri; 56, Olorgesailie; 57, Bodo, Dawaitoli, Hargufia; 58, Lainyamok; 59, Kapthurin; 60, Omo Kibish.

open, not to say grasslands, environments suggests that most of the story of hominine evolution in Afro-Arabia during the Middle to Late Miocene may have been hidden in the trees.

EVOLUTION OF HOMININS AND CONTEMPORARY
CERCOPITHECIDS

As well as the oldest known hominids, East Africa has yielded the oldest remains of the human lineage recognized to date. A partial mandible from the lower part of the Apak Member of the Nachukui Formation at Lothagam (previously 1C, now dated just younger than 5 Ma), although still the subject of taxonomic debate, is the best candidate for the earliest known hominin.

The earliest identified hominin is *Ardipithecus ramidus*, known by fragmentary dental, cranial, and postcranial remains from the Aramis region in the Middle Awash of Ethiopia dated ca. 4.4 Ma. *Australopithecus anamensis* from Kanapoi and the lowest levels of the Koobi Fora sequence (and perhaps Tabarin, in the Tugen Hills) is slightly younger, at ca. 4.2–3.9 Ma. All East African hominins dating to the interval between 3.8 and 2.8 Ma are currently assigned to a single species, *Australopithecus afarensis*, and derive primarily from two regions: Laetoli, near Olduvai Gorge, and Hadar in the Awash drainage. The period 2.8–2 Ma is poor in fossil remains of hominins in East Africa, although extensive fossil beds of this age are found throughout the Turkana Basin, in the Gona region adjacent to Hadar in Ethiopia, and in the Chemeron Formation at Baringo. The hominins recovered to date suggest that the earliest members of the genus *Homo*, as well as the robust australopiths (*Paranthropus*), may have emerged during this interval, represented in material classified as cf. *Homo rudolfensis* from Chemeron, the Makaamitalu region at Hadar, and the Chiwondo beds of Malawi and rare specimens of *P. aethiopicus* from West Turkana and the lower levels of the Shungura sequence.

At the same time as this flowering of the human lineage, there was an even greater radiation of cercopithecid monkeys in eastern Africa. The dominant cercopithecine was *Theropithecus*, which appears to have split early into two lineages that can be recognized as subgenera. *T. (Theropithecus)* first appears in uppermost Lothagam sediments, in the Middle Awash sequence, and at Hadar, between 4 and 3 Ma, where it is represented by *T. (T.) oswaldi darti.* This is succeeded in the lower Shungura Formation and elsewhere by the subspecies *T. (T.) o. oswaldi*, which remained rare during the Pliocene but flourished in the Pleistocene. *T. (Omopithecus)* was initially common, as was *T. (O.) brumpti*, in the Turkana Basin later Pliocene and may have been preceded by *?T. (O.) baringensis* in the Tugen Hills and Koobi Fora regions ca. 3 Ma, but this clade appears to have become extinct before the end of the Pliocene. Other cercopithecines were rare, with only *Papio (Dinopithecus) quadratirostris* even moderately well represented, in the Shungura between 3.2 and 2 Ma. The colobines were represented by a still greater diversity of taxa over the Late Pliocene, especially around the Turkana Basin. *Rhinocolobus,* a large form (comparable to the largest modern baboons) known also at Hadar, seems to have been surprisingly arboreal for its size. Several species of

Paracolobus overlapped the range of modern *Papio* at Laetoli, Chemeron, and Turkana sites, apparently with mixed arboreal and terrestrial adaptations. The slightly smaller *Cercopithecoides* was represented at Koobi Fora and later Olduvai by two extremely terrestrial species. Rare specimens indicate the presence at many sites of one or more species comparable in size to living *Colobus*, while the enigmatic form known as Colobine species A was intermediate in size and terrestrial adaptations. Several of these taxa persisted into the earliest Pleistocene before becoming extinct. Unfortunately, there is as yet no evidence of the evolutionary history of the African apes.

Evolution of Human Culture and Modern Morphology
East Africa yields evidence that relates progressive changes in human toolmaking to human morphological evolution throughout the known time range of the genus *Homo*. Of particular interest are the 1990s discoveries of artifacts predating 2 Ma at several localities, the oldest being the Gona sites at ca. 2.6–2.5 Ma and the Lokalelei sites at West Turkana dating to 2.35 Ma. These artifacts, which overlap the known time range of *H. rudolfensis*, consist of simple flakes and pebble cores with a few removals, often made on lava cobbles. Some researchers argue that these constitute an Omo or "pre-Oldowan" stage of Mode 1 tool manufacture and reflect only minimal conceptual abilities consistent with a brain size not far removed from that of a chimpanzee, combined with a specialized manual dexterity. Others see these tools as reflecting the full range of cognitive capabilities seen in later Oldowan materials. In any case, the sites contain tools and cutmarked bones that are the earliest known signs of a new adaptation for both food procurement and land-use strategies by hominins in Africa. While human agency has been claimed for *eoliths* (to use a term denoting rocks with shapes or arrangements suggesting artificial modification) from equally ancient sites in many regions of the world, including France and Siberia, those in East Africa are distinguished by their systematic manufacture, their abundance relative to unmodified rocks, their fresh condition, and their location in fine-grained (low-energy) deposits well dated by potassium-argon and associated mammalian fossils. Indeed, there is little question as to their authenticity as human artifacts, and while the oldest artifacts in southern Africa are estimated to be slightly younger, from the base of Member 5 at Sterkfontein (close to 2 Ma), no inarguable evidence of human cultural activity occurs outside of Africa before 1.4 Ma.

The Oldowan (originally, Chellean) industries of East Africa, typified by simple flakes and chipped cobbles without other tools, are actually quite widespread, not only at Olduvai Gorge but also in the Turkana Basin, from levels with dates and faunas indicating ages between 2 and ca. 1.8 Ma, which is also the approximate time range of *Homo habilis* (but overlaps with both *H. rudolfensis* and *H. erectus*). Following this, a transition is seen in stratified sequences at Olduvai, Koobi Fora, Shungura, and Melka Kontouré, through a "mixed" interval to the typical Acheulean industry with bifaces, especially handaxes. Tools of this type, which have been found by the thousands at Olduvai upper Bed II through Bed IV,

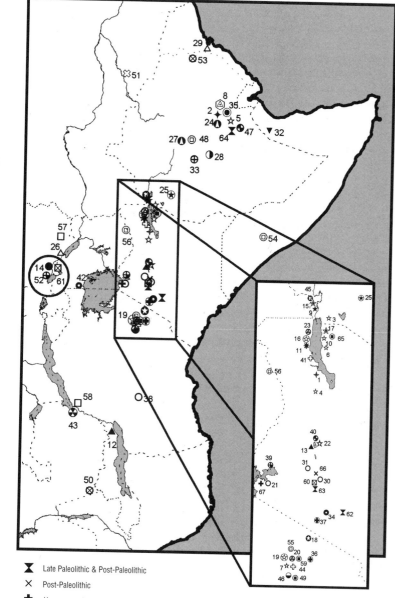

<table>
<tr><td>✢</td><td>cf. Australopithecus</td></tr>
<tr><td>◆</td><td>Ardipithecus</td></tr>
<tr><td>☆</td><td>Australopithecus</td></tr>
<tr><td>✳</td><td>? Australopithecus & Paranthropus</td></tr>
<tr><td>★</td><td>Paranthropus</td></tr>
<tr><td>✪</td><td>Paranthropus, Oldowan & Acheulean</td></tr>
<tr><td>✬</td><td>Paranthropus & Acheulean</td></tr>
<tr><td>◬</td><td>Australopithecus, cf. Homo sp. & Oldowan</td></tr>
<tr><td>●</td><td>Oldowan</td></tr>
<tr><td>▲</td><td>cf. Homo rudolfensis</td></tr>
<tr><td>✪</td><td>Paranthropus, Homo habilis (or H. rudolfensis) & Oldowan</td></tr>
<tr><td>○</td><td>Acheulean</td></tr>
<tr><td>★</td><td>Paranthropus, Homo habilis (&/or H. rudolfensis), H. erectus, Oldowan & Acheulean</td></tr>
<tr><td>★</td><td>Paranthropus, Homo erectus & Acheulean</td></tr>
<tr><td>◐</td><td>Homo habilis (&/or H. rudolfensis), H. erectus, Oldowan & Acheulean</td></tr>
<tr><td>◭</td><td>Homo erectus & Acheulean</td></tr>
<tr><td>△</td><td>cf. Homo erectus</td></tr>
<tr><td>◑</td><td>Oldowan, Acheulean & ?MSA</td></tr>
<tr><td>⊕</td><td>early "archaic Homo sapiens" & Acheulean</td></tr>
<tr><td>⊙</td><td>early "archaic Homo sapiens" Acheulean & MSA</td></tr>
<tr><td>⊖</td><td>early "archaic Homo sapiens" & Sangoan</td></tr>
<tr><td>⊕</td><td>MSA</td></tr>
<tr><td>◕</td><td>"archaic Homo sapiens," Acheulean, MSA, & early blade technology</td></tr>
<tr><td>✚</td><td>late "archaic Homo sapiens"</td></tr>
<tr><td>◎</td><td>Acheulean & MSA</td></tr>
<tr><td>☢</td><td>Acheulean, MSA & early blade technology</td></tr>
<tr><td>⊕</td><td>MSA & early blade technology</td></tr>
<tr><td>⊕</td><td>late "archaic Homo sapiens" & MSA</td></tr>
<tr><td>⊗</td><td>late "archaic Homo sapiens," early H. s. sapiens & MSA</td></tr>
<tr><td>◕</td><td>?early Homo s. sapiens & MSA</td></tr>
<tr><td>✗</td><td>early Homo s. sapiens</td></tr>
<tr><td>◉</td><td>Homo s. sapiens, MSA & LSA</td></tr>
<tr><td>▣</td><td>MSA & LSA</td></tr>
<tr><td>⊗</td><td>MSA, LSA & Post-Paleolithic</td></tr>
<tr><td>▼</td><td>Late Paleolithic & ?Acheulean</td></tr>
<tr><td>□</td><td>LSA</td></tr>
<tr><td>⊠</td><td>LSA & Post-Paleolithic</td></tr>
<tr><td>✘</td><td>Late Paleolithic & Post-Paleolithic</td></tr>
<tr><td>✕</td><td>Post-Paleolithic</td></tr>
<tr><td>✚</td><td>Homo s. sapiens in disturbed context & LSA if any archaeology</td></tr>
</table>

Main localities in East Africa yielding fossil hominins and Paleolithic archaeological remains. Symbols indicate age and included primates, while numbers represent site names (in approximate chronological order), as follows: 1, Lothagam; 2, Aramis; 3, Fejej; 4, Kanapoi; 5, Belohdelie, Maka; 6, Allia Bay; 7, Laetoli; 8, Hadar, Gona, Makaamitalu; 9, Omo Shungura older than 2.1 Ma; 10, Koobi Fora older than 2.1 Ma; 11, Nachukui (West Turkana) older than 2.1 Ma; 12, Uraha (Chiwondo); 13, Chemeron JM 85; 14, Senga-5; 15, Omo Shungura between 2.1–1.3 Ma; 16, Nachukui (West Turkana) between 2.1–1.6 Ma; 17, Koobi Fora between 2.1–1.3 Ma; 18, Peninj; 19, Olduvai Gorge Beds I-II (lower); 20, Olduvai Gorge Beds II(upper)-Masek; 21, Kanjera (main); 22, Chesowanja; 23, Nachukui (West Turkana) between 1.6–1.3 Ma; 24, Middle Awash horizons between 2–.07 Ma; 25, Konso; 26, Nyabusosi; 27, Melka Kontouré (earlier horizons); 28, Gadeb; 29, Buia; 30, Kariandusi; 31, Kilombe; 32, Hargeisa; 33, Gademotta; 34, Olorgesailie; 35, Bodo, Hargufia, Meadura, Andalee; 36, Lake Ndutu; 37, Lainyamok; 38, Isimila; 39, Muguruk; 40, Kapthurin; 41, Eliye Springs; 42, Sango Bay; 43, Kalambo Falls (earlier horizons); 44, Ngaloba (Laetoli); 45, Omo Kibish; 46, Eyasi; 47, Diré-Dawa (Porc-Epic); 48, Melka Kontouré (later horizons); 49, Mumba; 50, Kalemba; 51, Singa; 52, Katanda; 53, Gobedra Rock Shelter; 54, GoGoshis Qabe; 55, Apis Rock; 56, Magosi; 57, Matupi; 58, Kalambo Falls (later horizons); 59, Olduvai Gorge Ndutu-Naisiusiu Beds; 60, Gamble's Cave; 61, Ishango; 62, Lukenya Hill; 63, Nderit Drift; 64, Laga Oda; 65, Koobi Fora (later horizons); 66, Hyrax Hill; 67, Kanam, Kanjera (Leakey ?surface collections). Circle indicates 14, 52 and 61 essentially at same point, nearest to 52. Note that several other sets of points (2, 5, 24, 35; 9, 15; 10, 17, 65; 11, 16, 23; 19, 20, 59; 27, 48; 43, 58) are also effectively or actually coincident.

Olorgesailie, Kariandusi, Melka Kontouré, and at Bouri and Bodo in the Awash Valley, are comparable to those that have long been known from the Thames and Somme valleys in Europe. In East Africa, however, they can be dated in faunal and geological contexts to range in age from levels more than twice as old as those in Europe (i.e., 1.6 Ma or older) up to ca. 0.5 Ma, the general age of the European examples. This is ap-

proximately the same age range as the remains of *erectus*-grade humans in Africa, some of which may be classified as *Homo ergaster;* the youngest Acheulean assemblages may be associated with "archaic *Homo sapiens*" (= *H. heidelbergensis*), as at Bodo or Lake Ndutu. Acheulean sites are often (but not exclusively) located in stream channels, in contrast to the more usual location of Oldowan sites on or near lakeshores.

They also exhibit more careful work to prepare symmetrical bifacial tools, greater transport of raw materials (up to 11 km at Olduvai), repeated use of hammerstones resulting in spheroids, and more complex butchery of large animals, possibly implying earlier access to carcasses and thus a more successful defense mechanism against large predators. Contemporaneous with the biface industry, other sites with choppers and cleavers but without bifaces have been called "Developed Oldowan." In East Africa, as in southern Africa, evidence for controlled fire may first appear ca. 1.4–1.3 Ma at Chesowanja and FxJj 50 in Kenya. A wide variety of relatively modern cercopithecid and lorisid primates are found in Pleistocene sites, especially the large *Theropithecus oswaldi leakeyi*, which may have reached nearly 100 kg in mass and were probably hunted by Acheulean peoples, as at Olorgesailie.

In the Kapthurin Formation at Baringo, a late Acheulean industry contains large prismatic blades manufactured on blade cores similar to those from the Pre-Aurignacian of North Africa and the Levant. At the end of the Acheulean, ca. 300–200 Ka, a transitional, or Sangoan, period based on artifacts from Sango Bay in Uganda is evidenced in East Africa. It is characterized by sophisticated smaller handaxes and the introduction of prepared-core techniques, with picks and core axes. The Sangoan time interval is marked by indications of aridity in East Africa and the elimination from the fossil fauna of the few remaining mammalian taxa, including *Elephas*, which are not presently extant in Africa.

The Sangoan is succeeded by a variant of the MSA (Middle Stone Age), once termed "Kenya Stillbay," which occupies most of the rest of the Middle Pleistocene. By 200 Ka, at sites in Ethiopia such as Gademotta and Kukuleti, artifacts of true MSA technology with blades and highly standardized bifacial and unifacial points trimmed for hafting, together with Levallois and discoidal-core technologies, entirely replaced the Early Paleolithic tool forms. After ca. 80 Ka, toward the end of the MSA, these industries also include backed crescents and microliths. At the Katanda MSA sites in Zaire, even older barbed bone points were associated with fish remains that suggest seasonal hunting of large catfish, and in South Africa at Blonbos Cave, MSA levels also yielded both bone points and fish remains. After 40 Ka, East Africa produced a microlithic (mode 5) industry at sites like Matupi Cave in eastern Zaire, Mumba Cave in Tanzania, Twilight Cave in Kenya, and Ishango (Zaire) in contrast to the contemporaneous mode 4 industries of early Upper Paleolithic of Europe and the final MSA (mode 3) of South Africa. Both Mumba and Twilight caves have also yielded ostrich-eggshell beads dated to before 40 Ka.

The relationship of Middle and Late Pleistocene lithic industries to the human fossil record in East Africa is unclear. Specimens referred to the transitional grade of "archaic *Homo sapiens*," however, are generally found together with either Late Acheulean tools at Bodo, Ethiopia, and Ndutu, Tanzania, or with Sangoan tools at Eyasi and Kabwe, Tanzania. Both transitional and modern archaic forms are usually associated with MSA technology. This late Middle and early Late Pleistocene technology, although reminiscent to some extent of that in Europe at the same time, is not associated with human remains that could be called Neanderthal-like. On the contrary, from ca. 130 Ka onward, the human fossil remains in sites such as Mumba Cave (Tanzania), and Omo Kibish (skull 1) and Porc-Épic (Ethiopia) exhibit dental reduction, and in the case of Kibish angulation of the cranial base, a higher and more rounded cranial vault profile, and a reduction in prognathism, which is consistent with a minimal definition of *H. sapiens sapiens*.

Evolution of Modern Cultures in East Africa

Between 35 and 25 Ka, a Later Stone Age culture with microlithic debitage and some backed bladelets is found at several sites (Mumba, Nasera, Twilight Cave) in association with ostrich-eggshell beads. At Ishango, Uganda, on Lake Rutanzige (Edward), remains have been found of modern people with a very robust but tall and slender physique, associated with numerous small bone harpoons and microlithic debitage, as well as with a bone haft marked with incisions that may indicate an understanding of doubling, an early form of multiplication. Remains of deep-water-lake fishes suggest the presence of boats and nets. Other rich sites of this period with numerous backed bladelets are the lower levels at Lukenya Hill in Kenya and Kisese rockshelter in Tanzania. A fragmentary cranium from Lukenya Hill is comparable in frontal profile to several of the Ishango fossils. The earliest rock art in Tanzania could well date to this period.

During the Pleistocene-Holocene transition, a period of extreme aridity (corresponding to the cold-dry maximum of the final glacial phase) ca. 18 Ka may have reduced human population in the rift valleys, with all but the deepest rift lakes dried to ephemeral pools. One site dating to this period is Buvuma Island in Lake Victoria, Uganda. Following this arid interval, several sites such as Gamble's Cave and Nderit Drift in Kenya and Gobedra rockshelter near Axum in Ethiopia were occupied by people who left assemblages of large blades. In Kenya, these industries are known as the Eburran and contain many "Upper Paleolithic" tool types. At other sites in most East African countries—for instance, Laga Oda rockshelter in Ethiopia, QoQoshis Qabe in Somalia, and Lukenya Hill and Nasera in Kenya, microlithic industries of pointed backed bladelets and crescents are prevalent. By 10 Ka, most regions are characterized by microlithic technology. It is likely that these latest Paleolithic hunters were responsible for the rich corpus of rock art in Tanzania. Around the Lake Turkana Basin, the high lake shorelines dating to the Early Holocene have yielded not only microlithic industries and ostrich-eggshell beads but also numerous small bone harpoons and the abundant remains of fish, hippopotamus, and crocodile.

A succession of wet and dry intervals between 9.5 and 5.5 Ka apparently promoted interchanges and possibly migrations between east Africa and the Sahara region. By ca. 5 Ka (3000 BCE) remains of domesticated cattle, sheep, and goats, all nonindigenous species, are known from northern Kenya, and there is some evidence for semipermanent settlement and the intensive use of cereals. Agriculture, based on local plants such as millet, teff, and ensete, may have been independently developed in Ethiopia, but by the late 1990s the only evidence for this dated to between 2000 and 0 BCE.

The earliest state-level society in the region is the state of Axum in northern Ethiopia, whose origins date to ca. 500 BC and reflect strong influences from South Arabia. Historical inscriptions from Meroitic sites in Central Sudan indicate that the Nubian-Egyptian civilization had established trading and military outposts in the same region as far back as 1200 BC. Contact with Arabia was also important in the establishment of later East African states, such as those of the Swahili coast. The nature of this contact, however, and the extent to which it merged with already existing indigenous complex cultural systems, is the subject of several archaeological and historical investigations.

See also Acheulean; Afar Basin; Africa; Africa, North; Africa, Southern; Arambourg, Camille; Asia, Western; Australopithecus; Baringo Basin/Tugen Hills; Cercopithecinae; Clark, J. Desmond; Colobinae; "Dendropithecus-Group"; Early Paleolithic; Hominidae; Homininae; Hominoidea; Homo; Kenyapithecinae; Late Paleolithic; Later Stone Age; Leakey, Louis Seymour Bazett; Leakey, Mary Douglas; Middle Awash; Middle Paleolithic; Middle Stone Age; Modern Human Origins; Natron-Eyasi Basin; Oldowan; Olduvai Gorge; Paranthropus; Proconsulidae; Rift Valley; Sangoan; Second Intermediate; Senga-5; Turkana Basin; Victoriapithecinae; Western Rift. [A.S.B., J.A.V.C., E.D.]

Further Readings

Abbate E., Albianelli, A., Azzaroli, A., Benvenuti, E., Tesfamariam, B., Bruni, P., Cipriani, N., Clarke, R.J., Ficcarelli, G., Macchiarelli, R., Napoleone, G., Papini, M., Rook, L., Sagri, M., Tecle, T.M., Torre, D., and Villa, I. (1998) A one-million-year-old *Homo* cranium from the Danakil (Afar) Depression of Eritrea. Nature 393:458–460.

Bishop, W.W. (1971) The late Cenozoic history of East Africa in relation to hominoid evolution. In K.K. Turekian (ed.): The Late Cenozoic Glacial Ages. New Haven: Yale University Press, pp. 493–527.

Bishop, W.W., and Clark, J.D., eds. (1967) Background to Evolution in Africa. Chicago: University of Chicago Press.

Cole, S. (1975) Leakey's Luck: The Life of Louis Seymour Bazett Leakey, 1903–1972. New York: Harcourt, Brace Jovanovich.

Leakey, L.S.B. (1965) Olduvai Gorge, 1951–1961: Fauna and Background. Cambridge: Cambridge University Press.

Lewin, R. (1987) Bones of Contention. New York: Simon and Schuster.

McBrearty, S., Bishop, L.C., and Kingston, J.D. (1996) Variability in traces of Middle Pleistocene hominid behavior in the Kapthurin Formation, Baringo, Kenya. J. Hum. Evol. 30:563–580.

Phillipson, D.W. (1993) African Archaeology, 2nd ed. Cambridge: Cambridge University Press.

Reader, J. (1981) Missing Links. Boston: Little, Brown.

Roche, H., Delanges, A., Brugal, J.-P., Feibel, C., Kibunjia, M., Mourre, V. and Texier, P.-J. (1999) Early hominid stone-tool production and technical skill 2.34 Myr ago in West Turkana, Kenya. Nature 399:57–60.

Yellen, J.E., Brooks, A.S., Cornelissen, E., Mehlman, M.J., and Stewart, K. (1995) A middle Stone Age worked bone industry from Katanda, upper Semliki Valley, Zaire. Science 268:553–556.

Wood, B.A. (1992) Early hominid species and speciation. J. Hum. Evol. 22:351–365.

Africa, North

The northern part of Africa begins at the edge of the Sahel grasslands, along a line that closely follows the 15° N parallel from Dakar to Asmara. This region of Africa includes a narrow zone of Mediterranean ecology on the Mediterranean coast from Casablanca to Tunis, historically known as the Maghreb, and a continuation of arable drylands along the coast of Libya in Tripolitania and Cyrenaica. An interior band of brushy steppe and mountaintop deciduous forests in the high Atlas is known as the Rif. South of this is the Sahara, the Earth's largest desert, which extends across the Afro-Arabian continent from Mauritania to the Persian Gulf. In Africa, the Sahara proper also includes the outback of Morocco, Algeria, Libya, and Egypt, and the northern parts of Mali, Niger, and Chad. The Nile Valley and the Red Sea ranges to the east are demarcated as Nubia in southern Egypt and northern Sudan, and Misr (i.e., Egypt proper) in the lower reaches. The definition used here also includes Eritrea and northern Ethiopia. Major mountain ranges of northern Africa include the Atlas fold-belt, the Ahaggar and Tibesti granitic massifs in the southern Sahara, and the rifted highlands along the Red Sea. The only large river system is the Nile, which has been forced to flow north, constrained by rift highlands, since at least the Middle Miocene. Paleoclimatic and archaeological evidence suggests that, during the Pliocene and Pleistocene, periods of higher rainfall (coincident with cold-climate cycles at high latitudes) supported grasslands around the oases and evergreen forests (now a few relict groves) in the Tibesti and Ahaggar.

The Fossil Record

EARLY PRIMATES

North African sites yield nearly all known evidence for pre-Miocene mammalian evolution in Africa, with primate remains that appear to document the endemic origin of the Anthropoidea. The earliest known African primate is the indeterminate euprimate *Altiatlasius* from Adrar Mgorn 1 in the Ourzazate Basin of Algeria, which occurs in coastal-plain strata in association with insectivores (palaeoryctids and other lipotyphlans) indicating Late Paleocene (Thanetian) age, ca. 58–55 Ma. The site of Chambi in Central Tunisia contains the ?cercamoniine adapiform *Djebelemur* in a mammalian assemblage suggestive of later Ypresian (Early Eocene) age. *Algeripithecus* and *Tabelia*, from Glib Zegdou in Algeria, are considered to be of Lutetian or later Middle Eocene (Bartonian) age. These appear to be primitive parapithecids and thus among the earliest anthropoid primates. Some workers, however, arguing on morphological grounds, maintain that this material may be younger, even perhaps co-

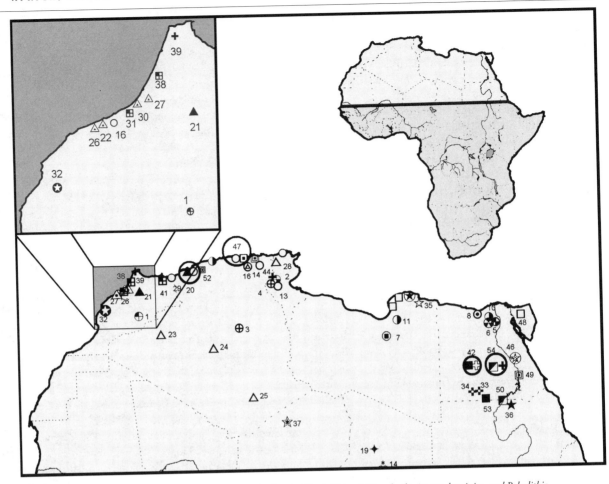

Main localities in North Africa yielding fossil primates, hominins, and Paleolithic archaeological remains. Symbols indicate site contents, while numbers represent site names (in approximate chronological order), as follows: 1, Adrar Mgorn 1; 2, Chambi; 3, Glib Zegdou; 4, Nementcha (Bir el Ater); 5, Fayum JQ 1–2 (Eocene); 6, Fayum JQ 3–4 (Oligocene); 7, Gebel Zelten; 8, Wadi Moghara; 9, Menacer (Marceau); 10, Wadi Natrun; 11, Sahabi; 12, Garaet Ichkeul; 13, Ain Brimba; 14, Bahr el Ghazal; 15, Ain Jourdel; 16, Ahl Al Oughlam; 17, Ain Hanech; 18, Buia; 19, Yayo (Koro-Toro); 20, Tighenif; 21, Ain Maarouf; 22, Sidi Abderrahman (Littorina Cave, Casablanca); 23, Tabelbala; 24, Tachenghit; 25, Tihodaine; 26, Thomas Quarries; 27, Salé; 28, Sidi Zin; 29, Ain Mefta; 30, Mifsud Giudice (Rabat); 31, Temara; 32, Jebel Irhoud; 33, Bir Tarfawi; 34, Bir Sahara; 35, Hajj Creiem; 36, Arkin; 37, Adrar Bous; 38, Dar es Soltane; 39, Mugharet el 'Aliya; 40, Hagfet et Dabba; 41, Taforalt; 42, Dakhla Oasis; 43, Hagfet et Tera; 44, Bir el Ater; 45, Haua Fteah; 46, Taramsa; 47, Tamar Hat; 48, Mushabi; 49, Wadi Kubbaniya, Kom Ombo; 50, Wadi Halfa, Khor Musa; 51, Afalou bou Rhummel; 52, Columnata; 53, Nabta Playa; 54, Kharga Oasis. Note that 4 & 44 and 5 & 6 are identical sites, separated due to contents.

Legend:

⊕ Adapiformes
⬤ ?Omomyoidea
⊕ Parapithecidae
✪ Parapithecidae, Oligopithecidae, Proteopithecus, Pleisopithecus, Adapiformes
◕ Propliopithecidae, Parapithecidae, Tarsiiformes & ?Lorisoidea
◉ Prohylobates & indet. eocatarrhine
▣ Prohylobates
○ Cercopithecinae
◑ Cercopithecinae & Colobinae
⚘ Australopithecus bahrelghazali
⬠ Oldowan & Acheulean
✦ Homo cf. erectus
▲ Homo ?erectus & Acheulean
△ Acheulean
⬘ Early "archaic Homo sapiens" & Acheulean
✪ "?Homo sapiens sapiens," Mousterian & "pre-Aurignacian"
✚ Aterian
⊹ Aterian & ?Acheulean
✜ Aterian, MSA (&? Acheulean)
★ Aterian &/or Mousterian
☆ Mousterian
✪ Early Homo sapiens sapiens? & Mousterian
✪ Homo sapiens ?sapiens & MSA
✬ Mousterian, Aterian & Post-Paleolithic
⊞ ?Homo sapiens sapiens, Aterian (& Late Paleolithic
⊡ Homo sapiens sapiens & Late Paleolithic
☐ Late Paleolithic
▣ H. s. sapiens, Late Paleolithic & Post-Paleolithic
◪ Late Paleolithic & Post-Paleolithic
■ Post-Paleolithic

eval with the earliest faunal levels of the Fayum. *Biretia*, a parapithecid from Nementcha (Bir el Ater) in Algeria, is poorly dated but is associated with other mammals that are consistent with a level of development equivalent to the lower Late Eocene (Priabonian) Qasr el-Sagha faunas in the Fayum.

Abundant and diverse primate fossils have been collected from the Jebel Qatrani Formation in the Fayum badlands of northern Egypt since 1961 by teams led by E.L. Simons. At least a dozen genera are known from four major faunal zones whose precise age and relationship to the global Eocene-Oligocene boundary are difficult to determine. The lower Jebel Qatrani beds, which conformably overlie the Qasr el-Sagha Formation (Lower Priabonian), seem clearly to belong within the Upper Eocene. The Priabonian, however, is 4.5 Myr in duration, and the age of the upper Jebel Qatrani with regard to the Eocene-Oligocene boundary is not obvious. Preliminary paleomagnetic results, and the appearance of a Fayum-like fauna in association with basal Oligocene marine microfauna in Oman, suggest that the upper two Fayum mammal zones could reasonably be considered to be of Early Oligocene age. The entire sequence would thus date between 37 and 33 Ma.

Rare Fayum remains of lower primates include possible omomyid and ?lorisid teeth, a possible tarsioid (or early anthropoid: *Afrotarsius*), and the distinctive tiny primate *Plesiopithecus*, the only representative of a new catarrhine family. Another rare taxon, *Proteopithecus*, is classified as Anthropoidea, incertae sedis. More abundant are parapithecids, including *Qatrania, Arsinoea, Serapia, Apidium,* and *Parapithecus* (= ? *Simonsius*); the oligopithecids *Catopithecus* and *Oligopithecus*; and the propliopithecid *Propliopithecus* (and *Aegyptopithecus*, considered by some to be a distinct genus). The wide diversity and clear record of anthropoids makes a strong case for the African origin of this group, in contrast to the rare and transitory occurrence of Middle Eocene forms, the anthropoid status of which is still debatable, in Burma and China.

OLD WORLD MONKEYS

North Africa has yielded the earliest well-known cercopithecid (victoriapithecine) monkey, *Prohylobates*, which is found at the late Early Miocene (c. 17 Ma) site of Jebel Zelten in Libya and in the faunally similar Wadi Moghara beds in Egypt; the genus has also been reported, provisionally, from coeval and ecologically similar sites of northern Kenya. The colobine *Libypithecus* comes from latest Miocene (or earliest Pliocene?) faunas at Wadi Natrun in northern Egypt and Sahabi in Libya, while the nearly indeterminate "?*Colobus*" *flandrini* is represented by somewhat older teeth from Menacer in Algeria. Macaques (or indeterminate cercopithecines tentatively assigned to that genus) are known from Menacer, Natrun, and a variety of Pliocene and Pleistocene sites (e.g., Garaet Ichkeul, Ain Brimba, Ain Mefta, and Tamar Hat), continuing into the living *M. sylvanus*, or "Barbary ape." *Theropithecus* is known rarely in the Pliocene of Algeria and Morocco (Ain Jourdel and Ahl Al Oughlam, respectively), and more abundantly at the later Middle Pleistocene archaeological sites of Tighenif in

Algeria and Thomas Quarries in Morocco. Interestingly, none of the scattered Miocene faunas of North Africa contains any representatives of early hominoids or eocatarrhines, except for a partial humerus from Moghara that resembles those of propliopithecids or pliopithecids. By comparison, East African contemporaneous assemblages produce abundant fossils of these taxa, and a kenyapithecine is known from both Namibia and Saudi Arabia, at comparable latitudes.

HUMAN FOSSILS

As yet, the only example of an early hominin from northern Africa is an *Australopithecus*, recently described from Bahr el-Ghazal in the Koro-Toro area of northern Chad in association with a faunal assemblage similar to those from Hadar (Ethiopia), and thus estimated to date between 3.5 and 3 Ma. A partial mandibular symphysis and an isolated tooth were allocated to the new species *A. bahrelghazali*, based on features that seem similar to those of *A. afarensis* in most respects. The incomplete Yayo cranium, recovered in the 1960s from the same general area, is associated with an Early Pleistocene fauna and has been attributed by most paleoanthropologists to early *Homo*, probably *H. erectus*. A skull of similar age and identity dated to ca. 1.0 Ma has also been reported in 1998 by an Italian team in Eritrea. Middle Pleistocene faunas, younger than 1.0 Ma, have been found with *H. erectus* or "archaic *H. sapiens*" remains in Morocco at Salé, the Thomas Quarries, and Sidi Abderrahman (Littorina Cave) near Casablanca and at Tighenif (ex-Ternifine) in Algeria.

Prehistoric sites with hominin fossils assigned to later "archaic *H. sapiens*" (or, in some cases, hesitantly to "early modern *H. sapiens*") include Rabat (= Kebibat), Mugharet el 'Aliya, Zouhrah Cave, Temara (Smuggler's Cave), and Jebel Irhoud in Morocco; Haua Fteah in Libya; and Singa in Sudan (dated at more than 130 Ka). The majority of these fossils are associated with Levalloiso-Mousterian or Aterian industries and are thought to date between 190 and 90 Ka. These finds may, in toto, represent different developmental stages in the precursors to anatomically modern humans, and, indeed, some researchers see evolutionary continuity in the assemblage of North African premodern *sapiens*.

Sites yielding Late Pleistocene remains assigned to early "anatomically modern *H. sapiens*" include Dar-es-Soltane in Morocco, where very robust cranial material in association with an Aterian industry may predate 40 Ka. Recently, a burial said to be of an anatomically modern adult female was TL-dated to ca. 40 Ka near Taramsa (Egypt), but only a preliminary report has yet been published. Later in time, Taforalt in Morocco, Afalou-Bou-Rhummel, and Columnata in Algeria, and Nazlet Khatr in Egypt have human fossils associated with Late Paleolithic industries. The majority of these are classified as the robust Mechta-Afalou physical type.

Paleolithic Archaeology

The earliest archaeological sites in North Africa belong to the Oldowan (or Mode 1) Industrial Complex, characterized by simple core forms and casually retouched flakes at the site of 'Ain Hanech in northeastern Algeria. Investigations here over the years have identified an industry of limestone cores, flaked spheroids, and retouched flint flakes. Provisional faunal correlations with East Africa would place this site equivalent to Olduvai Bed II, ca. 1.5 Ma.

North African Acheulean sites with handaxes and/or cleavers include Sidi Abderrahman and Thomas Quarry 2 in Morocco; Tighenif (Ternifine), Tihodaine, Tachenghit, and Tabalbalat in Algeria; Sidi Zin in Tunisia; Arkin in Nubia; and Bir Sahara and Dakhla Oasis in Egypt. At Tabelbala and Tachenghit in Algeria, large side-struck cleaver flakes were produced by an unusual prepared-core (Tachenghit, super-Levallois) technique from a thick, pointed bifacial core. As has been noted previously, *Homo* cf. *erectus* remains have been found at several of these sites.

The Middle Paleolithic, or Mousterian, of Northeast Africa exhibits some similarities with that of Europe and western Asia, particularly in the relatively high proportion of prepared Levallois cores and flakes detached from such cores. These industries, known as Levalloiso-Mousterian, are characterized by flake tools such as side scrapers, denticulates, and points. In many sites, however, points with basal trimming and other signs of hafting are considerably more numerous than in most classic Mousterian sites of Europe and southwest Asia. In Nubia, where points are particularly numerous, at least two types of specialized cores were used for their production. In addition, blades made on Levallois cores by working from alternate ends (bipolar platforms) across a flat upper face are a dominant blank type in many Middle Paleolithic sites of this region. With some exceptions, both blade technology and trimmed points are more characteristic of the African Middle Stone Age than of the classic Mousterian of Europe. Well-known sites with this industry include Jebel Irhoud in Morocco; Haua Fteah and Hajj Creiem in Libya; and Bir Tarfawi in Egypt. At the Haua Fteah Cave in Libya, an early blade-dominated industry with prismatic cores called the Pre-Aurignacian is found in strata below the Levalloiso-Mousterian.

In North Africa, particularly in the northwest in eastern Morocco, Algeria, and Tunisia, assemblages called Aterian (after the Algerian site of Bir el Ater) are relatively much more common than earlier industries. The Aterian appears to be a facies of the North African Middle Paleolithic and is characterized by tanged points and other tools; bifacial points are known from some Aterian sites, notably in the eastern and southern areas, such as Bir Tarfawi in Egypt and Adrar Bous in Niger. The emphasis on trimmed and carefully shaped points and the clear indications of hafting distinguish this facies from the classic Mousterian industries of Europe. The Aterian is found stratified above the Levalloiso-Mousterian at a few sites, including Adrar Bous in Niger and Bir Sahara in Egypt. Other Aterian sites include Taforalt, el 'Aliya, and Dar-es-Soltane in Morocco. Aterian industries disappear ca. 35 Ka with the onset of extreme aridity in North Africa. Other Middle Paleolithic variants include the Khormusan of the Nile Valley, characterized by blade elements and Middle Paleolithic types of prepared cores and dated older than 40 Ka.

In many parts of North Africa, there is a hiatus in human occupation between 40 and 20 Ka, coinciding with a period of "polar desert" hyperaridity at the climax of the last glacial age.

At the same time, Upper Paleolithic blade industries begin to appear in some parts of the North African coast and the Nile Valley, indicating that populations were shifting to the areas where water is found today. The Dabban complex, from sites such as Hagfet et Dabba and Haua Fteah in Libya, represent such an early Late Paleolithic industry in coastal areas; in the Nile Valley, Mousterian industries are replaced by Late Paleolithic industries beginning before 40 Ka with significant regional variability, including the Khormusan, characterized by blade elements and Middle Paleolithic types of prepared cores, and the Halfan, which began ca. 23 Ka with small blade industries in Wadi Halfa and other sites. At the Wadi Kubaniya in Egypt, Late Paleolithic populations dated to ca. 17 Ka used grindstones to process wild tubers and possibly wild cereal crops. Perhaps the most extraordinary site in the later Pleistocene Nile Valley is Nazlet Khater, where early Late Paleolithic mining for flint was carried out at ca. 40 Ka using picks to open up underground shafts and tunnels and then wooden props to support the mine roof. Ca. 15 Ka, a distinctive group of industries known as the Iberomaurusian, or Oranian, is found at Haua Fteah and other sites. These industries are characterized by smaller elements, especially backed bladelets. Well-known Iberomaurusian sites include Haua Fteah and Hagfet et Tera in Libya; Afalou bou Rhummel, Columnata, and Tamar Hat in Algeria; and Taforalt in Morocco. Large cemeteries with robust Mechta-Afalou populations are known from Afalou bou Rhummel, Columnata, and Taforalt.

Early Food Production in North Africa

At ca. 11 Ka, at the very beginning of postglacial time, a period of relatively wet climates began in North Africa. Some of the most desolate interior basins of the Sahara developed lakes, surrounded with open savannah and steppe vegetation. Lake Chad, for instance, expanded to cover an area of 1,100 km × 680 km, ca. 10 times its current size. In these areas, as well as along the Nile and in the nearby oases, groups of fisher-hunters with a distinctive tool kit involving bone harpoons, net or digging-stick weights, grindstones, mud-walled construction, and microlithic arrowheads spread out widely. By 8 Ka or even earlier in some regions, a distinctive pottery decorated with wavy lines was in common use, the world's second-oldest ceramics after Japanese Jomon sites.

Scholars have considered that the typical plants and animals exploited by modern North African farmers (e.g., wheat, barley, sheep, goats, and cattle) were introduced in their domesticated form from outside the continent, most likely from southwestern Asia. Evidence from Egypt and the Sahara, however, suggests that a degree of indigenous African domestication may have preceded the introduction of Eurasian domesticates. In particular, the evidence from Nabta Playa in the western desert of Egypt indicates that semisedentary populations were living there before 8 Ka and that they were collecting and storing wild sorghum with a possible selective effect in the direction of domestication. Furthermore, the predominance of cattle bones among the bones of gazelles and other animals adapted to semiarid savannah suggests that cattle were probably being kept or watered by humans, and thus the initial conditions of domestication were satisfied. Mitochondrial DNA studies confirm that African and Eurasian domestic cattle belong to separate races whose split predates the earliest possible dates for domestication in either region. On the other side of the Sahara, at Adrar Bous in northern Niger, the skeleton of a domestic short-horned ox was recovered from a relatively early context, dating to ca. 6.5 Ka.

Throughout the Sahara, rock paintings of variegated cattle and wild game attest to the lifeways of pastoralists. Although attempts have been made to date the paintings on stylistic grounds, their age remains uncertain. Their existence, however, is testimony to a way of life that disappeared some time close to 6 Ka, when the Sahara again began to dry up and settlements were once more concentrated on the permanent rivers and oases. In the Nile Valley, the increased intensity of settlement and the apparent cultural diversity reflected in the remains found at different oasis localities led initially to the formation of small states or chiefdoms. Agriculture and the specialized production of luxury goods (e.g., pottery and stone bowls) for export subsequently led to the establishment of thriving manufacturing towns (e.g., Hierakonpolis) and to the development of a trading class and the written signs of ownership similar to hieroglyphs in both Upper Egypt and Nubia. Ideas and goods entered Egypt via the Mediterranean littoral from the north and east, as well as from the south along the Nile corridor. By ca. 5.1 Ka, one of the most important of the southern states, whose symbol was the red crown of upper Egypt, had conquered the others and established the first Egyptian dynasty.

See also Adapiformes; Africa; Africa, East; Anthropoidea; Asia, Western; Aterian; Australopithecus; Bone Tools; Catarrhini; Cercopithecidae; Cercopithecinae; Colobinae; Domestication; Early Paleolithic; Fayum; Hominoidea; Homo; Late Paleolithic; Mesolithic; Middle Paleolithic; Neolithic; Oligopithecidae; Paleolithic; Parapithecidae; Propliopithecidae; Victoriapithecinae; Yayo. [N.T., K.S., A.S.B., J.A.V.C., E.D.]

Further Readings

Abbate, E., Albiane, A., Azzaroli, A., Benvenuti, M., Tesfanarian, B., Bruni, P., Cipriani, N., Clarke, R.J., Ficarelli, G., Macchiarelli, R., Napoleone, G., Papini, M., Rock, L., Sagri, M., Tacle, T.M., Torre, D., and Villa, I. (1998) A one-million-year-old *Homo* cranium from the Danakil (Afar) depression of Eritrea. Nature.

Bradley, D.G., MacHugh, D.E., Cunningham, P., and Loftus, R.T. (1996) Mitochondrial diversity and the origins of African and European cattle. Proc. Nat. Acad. Sci. of the U.S.A. 93:5131–5135.

Close, Angela, ed. (1987) Prehistory of Arid North Africa: Essays in Honor of Fred Wendorf. Dallas: Southern Methodist University Press.

Hublin, J.J. (1992) Recent human evolution in Northwestern Africa In M.J. Aitkin, C.B. Stringer and P.A. Mellars, (eds.) The Origin of Modern Humans and the impact of Chronometric Dating. Princeton: Princeton University Press.

McBurney, C.B.M. (1960) The Stone Age of Northern Africa. London: Penguin.

McDermott, F., Stringer, C., Grün, R., Williams, C.T., Din, V.K., and Hawkesworth, C.J. (1996) New Late-Pleistocene uranium-thorium and ESR dates for the Singa hominid (Sudan). J. Hum. Evol. 31:507–516.

Phillipson, D.W. (1993) African Archaeology, 2nd ed. Cambridge: Cambridge University Press.

Simons, E.L., and Rasmussen, D.T. (1994) A whole new world of ancestors: Eocene anthropoideans from Africa. Evol. Anthropol. 3:111–148.

Africa, Southern

For the purposes of this encyclopedia, southern Africa is considered to be the region below latitude 12° south, except for the area within the Rift Valley between 15° and 12° S, which is included in East Africa. This region encompasses the nations of South Africa, Namibia, Botswana, and Zimbabwe, along with parts of Angola, Zambia, and Mozambique. Climatically, there are several different zones across this region. The southern coast has a nearly Mediterranean climate, while the Namib-Kalahari Desert extends into the interior plateau from the west coast and occupies the large central basin. North of the arid zone, tropical savannah extends across the continent and down the eastern coast. A block of subtropical humid bushland lies in the interior of the eastern region, and the center of the region (the Great Karroo) is subtropical steppe, which extends south and east nearly to the Indian Ocean and west below the desert fringe to the Atlantic. Mountain highlands, notably in the Drakensberg and also in Swaziland and Natal, support ecological islands of temperate deciduous woodland. The Zambezi, Okavango, Limpopo, and Orange/Vaal rivers are the major (east-west) watercourses, and relief is generally moderate, although notable escarpments stand behind the narrow coastal plains in most of the region.

Pre-Pliocene Primates

No Paleogene sites have been reported in this region, although Malembe, in the Cabinda region of Angola (ca. 5° S), has yielded a Fayumlike probably Early Oligocene mammal fauna that includes one possible primate canine. Lower Miocene sites in paleoestuaries of the Diamond Desert, or Sperrgebiet, of Namibia were uncovered in the 1910 diamond rush, at Bogenfels in the Langental, Elisabethfeld, and in a water hole at Elisabeth Bay. Slightly younger faunas were later found in test pits along the lower Oranje River at Arrisdrift, Rooilepel, and Auchas. All of the Namib Early and Middle Miocene samples closely resemble those of coeval sites in Kenya, but as of 1998 none has yielded primate remains. In 1997, B. Senut and colleagues described a single upper molar of a gorilla-sized (proconsulid?) hominoid recovered from a stratified deposit at Ryskop on the western coast (Namaqualand), dated c. 18 Ma.

In the limestone hills of northern Namibia, the remains of a kenyapithecine, *Otavipithecus*, were discovered, along with thousands of small vertebrate specimens, in cave-breccia

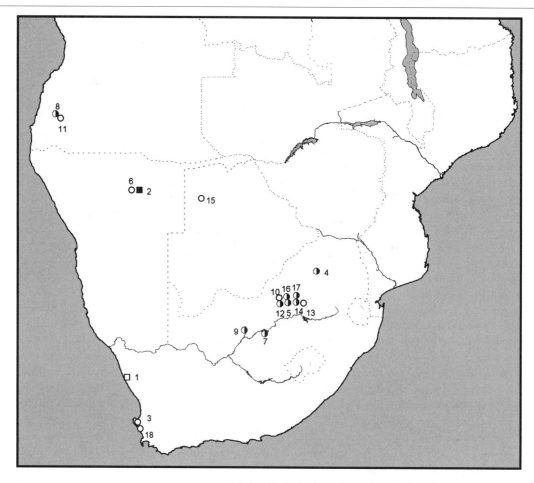

○ Cercopithecinae
◑ Cercopithecinae & Colobinae
□ Proconsulidae
■ *Otavipithecus*

Main localities in Southern Africa yielding fossil non-hominin primates. Symbols indicate site contents, while numbers represent site names (in approximate chronological order), as follows: 1, Ryskop; 2, Berg Aukas; 3, Langebaanweg; 4, Makapan; 5, Sterkfontein; 6, Jaegersquelle 1; 7, Haasgat; 8, Leba; 9, Taung; 10, Gladysvale; 11, Cangalongue, Malola Kiln; 12, Bolt's Farm; 13, Schurweburg; 14, Swartkrans; 15, Koanaka; 16, Kromdraai; 17, Coopers; 18, Saldanha (Hopefield).

fragments from the dump of the inactive Berg Aukas copper-vanadium mine. The presence of rodents similar to forms known in North Africa has suggested an age of 14–13 Ma. Teeth of later Miocene cercopithecids and remains of Plio-Pleistocene monkeys and strepsirhines have been informally reported from cave formations in this area as well. Several cercopithecine teeth are also known from the Early Pliocene deposits (ca. 5 Ma) of E Quarry at Langebaanweg, near Cape Town.

Plio-Pleistocene Humans and Other Primates

The fossiliferous cave deposits of Taung, Sterkfontein, Makapansgat, Kromdraai, Swartkrans, Gladysvale, Drimolen, Haasgaat, and Bolt's Farm in South Africa, and several sites on the Cangalongue Plateau near Leba, Angola, have yielded an abundance of cercopithecid fossils of later Pliocene and Early Pleistocene age. The earlier sites are dominated by species of the archaic cercopithecine *Parapapio*, with smaller numbers of *Theropithecus* and the colobine *Cer-*

copithecoides. At Taung and Bolt's Farm, *Papio* and *Parapapio* are roughly equal in frequency, while later sites yield mainly *P.* (*Papio*) and *P.* (*Dinopithecus*) alongside more derived forms of *Theropithecus* and *Cercopithecoides*.

With the exception of Bolt's Farm, Haasgaat, and the Angola sites, these faunas also contain australopiths. *Australopithecus africanus* was first recovered at Taung, but the most important sample is known from Sterkfontein Member 4, with fewer specimens from Makapansgat and perhaps Gladysvale and Drimolen. The type of *Paranthropus robustus* was found at Kromdraai, and the most extensive sample is from Swartkrans, especially Member 1 but also Members 2–3. Several specimens probably attributable to *Homo habilis* have been recovered from Member 5 of Sterkfontein, while specimens of *H.* cf. *habilis* and *H.* cf. *erectus* have been found in Members 1–2 (and 3?) at Swartkrans alongside *P. robustus*.

The oldest archaeological materials in southern Africa derive from the lowest part of Member 5 at Sterkfontein and date to ca. 2 Ma. The artifacts consist of ad hoc flakes and cores made by striking a core on an anvil or hard surface and selecting useful flakes. The toolmaker is obscure; it could be represented by Stw 53, an early *Homo* (or conceivably late *Australopithecus*) fossil. Arguments for older artifacts of bone, tooth, and horn (osteodontokeratic culture) associated with *A. africanus* have been invalidated by studies showing that the faunal assemblage features formerly considered as evidence of human activity are instead due to the actions of carnivores. Possible Oldowan finds are reported from surface localities and cave floors in northwest Botswana, but the age of these finds has not been precisely determined. Elsewhere in the region, Oldowan artifacts of Plio-Pleistocene age have been reported from the Chiwondo beds in Malawi, but there is some question about the *in situ* nature of these finds. A younger section of Sterkfontein Member 5 has yielded stone artifacts referable to the Acheulean, as has Member 3 at Swartkrans, the latter associated with both *Paranthropus* and early *Homo*. These horizons may date to ca. 1.5 Ma. The Member 3 assemblage at Swartkrans is particularly interesting because of the presence of burned bone, suggesting cooking and/or hominid use of fire, and the presence of bone tools, sharpened (probably by use-wear) as digging sticks, indicating early reliance on underground food sources, an important new and relatively uncontested niche for hominids. The faunal remains are distinguished from those of earlier australopith sites (e.g., Member 4 at Sterkfontein) by the presence of more immature herbivores and fewer primates among the victims, suggesting a possible transition from hunted to hunter.

Younger Acheulean occurrences of probable late Early to early Middle Pleistocene age are known from river gravels in South Africa (especially Vaal River), Botswana, and Zimbabwe (Zambezi). Between 700 and 400 Ka, Acheulean materials also appear in cave deposits at Cave of Hearths (Transvaal, South Africa) and Montagu Cave (Cape Province, South Africa). The latter site, together with open-air occurrences at Amanzi Springs (Uitenhage, Cape Province, South Africa) and Hopefield (Saldanha Bay, South Africa), are the earliest occupations of the winter rainfall zone at the southern tip of the continent. In both of the open-air sites, wooden artifacts are preserved. "Archaic *H. sapiens*" crania of Middle Pleistocene age are known from the sites of Kabwe (formerly Broken Hill) in Zambia and Elandsfontein (Hopefield, Saldanha) in South Africa, and a mandibular fragment has been recovered from Cave of Hearths. The latter two specimens are among the few hominins in association with Acheulean artifacts (also Tighenif in Algeria and perhaps Olduvai Bed IV), but no tools are definitely associated with the Kabwe fossil. These specimens probably all date between 700 and 400 Ka.

Farther to the north, one of the most important Acheulean localities in Africa is the site of Kalambo Falls (Zambia), excavated by J.D. Clark. Although fauna were not preserved, plant remains, including grass, worked wooden artifacts, seed pods, fruit remains, and pollen, were preserved in the multiple overlapping Acheulean horizons. Among the wooden artifacts was a partly charred object interpreted as a

fire paddle. A curved stone line suggested construction of a windbreak, while two hollows filled with grass indicated the location of possible sleeping areas. Pollen analysis indicates a swampy, gallery forest along the river, with savannah grassland beyond. The presence of present-day high-altitude species in the pollen diagram of the final Acheulean suggests a cooler and possibly wetter interval. Early dating efforts for the Acheulean at Kalambo Falls were unsatisfactory; the true age is probably in excess of the oldest published age of 190 Ka, based on amino-acid racemization.

The transition to the Middle Stone Age (MSA) is marked in southern Africa by the presence of very finely made handaxes, which can resemble large MSA points, and the advent of prepared-core technology. These handaxes and associated tools are known as the Fauresmith industry. A nonhandaxe industry, the Charaman, is known from Zimbabwe and Zambia, from such sites as Bambata, Kabwe and Pomongwe, among others. This industry is characterized by many small miscellaneous scrapers. While the Charaman was thought to be associated at Kabwe with a skull of "archaic *H. sapiens*," this assemblage may, in fact, represent a nonbiface facies of the Early Stone Age of much earlier date. Farther to the north in the region, at Kalambo Falls, the transition is marked, as in Central Africa and the western regions of East Africa, by the presence of large crude picks with a trihedral section at the tip, relatively crude bifaces or core axes, and a range of smaller tools. This industry, known as the Sangoan from the type area of Sango Bay in Uganda, was once thought to be associated with human penetration of the tropical forest ecozone. Newer evidence from East Africa (Simbi, Muguruk) and from Kamoa in Zaïre, however, has suggested that Sangoan sites are more likely to be associated with sandy lenses indicative of drier rather than wetter, forested conditions.

The Middle Stone Age of southern Africa is relatively well known compared to earlier periods. Indeed, the sequence of Middle Stone Age industries derived from deep cave deposits on the southern coast has been used as a model for this period throughout the continent, which is somewhat problematic as these sites lie in the cool, temperate winter-rainfall zone today and are not characteristic of environmental conditions in tropical Africa. The oldest MSA site in southern Africa may well be the spring eye at Florisbad, although the artifacts recovered here are generally undiagnostic. Associated with them is an incomplete cranium of late Middle Pleistocene age (260 ± 35 Ka) that is possibly an early antecedent of the modern human lineage. In most ways, it is reminiscent of the earlier Kabwe-Saldanha group, but the forehead is higher and the face broad, suggesting later premodern humans. Another recently reported early MSA industry with trimmed points comes from Twin Rivers in Zambia, where a speleothem overlying the archaeological layer yielded a uranium-series date of 230 ± 35 Ka.

The older MSA horizons in cave deposits at Cave of Hearths (Transvaal), Klasies River Mouth (Cape Province), and Border Cave (Natal Province) in South Africa have yielded Mode 3 industries on blades, dated to ca. 120 Ka or older. Typical tools include trimmed unifacial and bifacial points, many with basal thinning for hafting, scrapers, and

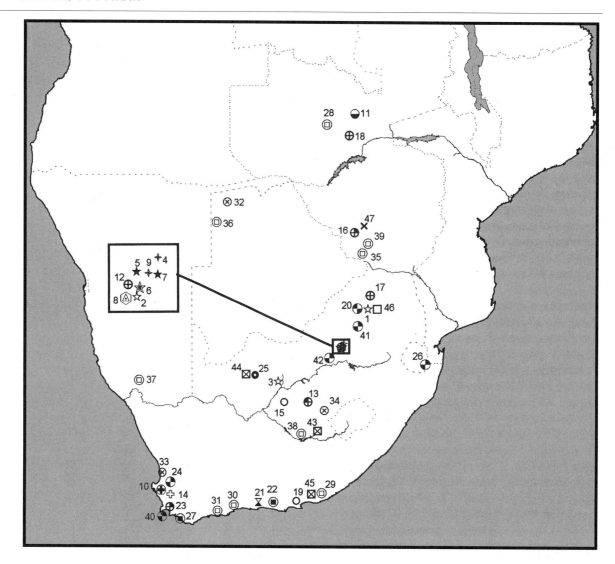

Main localities in Southern Africa yielding fossil hominins and Paleolithic archaeological remains. Symbols indicate site contents, while numbers represent site names (in approximate chronological order), as follows: 1, Makapan; 2, Sterkfontein, Mbr 1–4; 3, Taung; 4, Gladysvale; 5, Drimolen; 6, Swartkrans, Mbr 1–3; 7, Kromdraai; 8, Sterkfontein, Mbr 5; 9, Coopers; 10, Saldanha (Hopefield); 11, Kabwe; 12, Swartkrans, Mbr 4; 13, Florisbad; 14, Hoedjiespunt; 15, Rooidam; 16, Hope Fountain; 17, Kalkbank; 18, Twin Rivers; 19, Amanzi Springs; 20, Cave of Hearths (older levels); 21, Nelson's Bay Cave; 22, Klasies River Mouth Cave; 23, Stellenbosch; 24, Sea Harvest Cave; 25, Wonderwerk (older levels); 26, Border Cave; 27, Die Kelders; 28, Mumbwa; 29, Howieson's Poort; 30, Mossel Bay; 31, Stillbay, Blombos; 32, Tsodilo Hills; 33, Eland's Bay Cave; 34, Rose Cottage; 35, Bambata; 36, ≠Gi; 37, Apollo-11; 38, Orangia; 39, Pomongwe; 40, Cape Flats, Fish Hoek; 41, Tuinplaas (Springbok Flats); 42, Boskop; 43, Smithfield; 44, Wonderwerk (younger levels); 45, Wilton; 46, Cave of Hearths (younger levels); 47, Khami. The eight site units in the Sterkfontein (Blaauwbank) Valley have been expanded in their relative positions in the inset. Note that 20 & 46 and 25 & 44 are identical sites, separated due to contents.

burins. Layered strata at Klasies River Mouth yield incomplete human fossils in an MSA context, with an age inferred from geomorphological analysis of stream terraces to be between 120 and 95 Ka. These specimens are morphometrically within the range of modern human anatomical variation. The cranial remains of four individuals from the site of Border Cave, which have been attributed to a Middle Stone Age context of between ca. 110 and 85 Ka, are completely modern in appearance. However, a partial ulna appears more archaic, perhaps indicative of heavier musculature, as is also true of a comparable bone from Klasies. The stratigraphic-archaeological context and the age of the Border Cave specimens are matters of some dispute, and ESR (electron spin resonance) dating, while supportive, has not been conclusive. Moreover, a 1996 analysis of bone mineral crystallinity indicates that two of the cranial fragments are young and probably intrusive, while confirming an MSA age for the postcrania. Nevertheless, the evidence from Border Cave for the presence of anatomically modern humans in the late Middle to early Late Pleistocene of southern Africa gains some support from the more securely provenanced but fragmentary fossils from Klasies River Mouth, Die Kelders, and other sites. At ca. 80–65 Ka, particularly in the Cape Province, a cooler interval is associated with a very early Mode 5 industry that includes backed geometric forms made on small blades. This industry, the Howieson's Poort, is associated with greater use of exotic stone materials and an increase in the hunting of small game. Following the Howieson's Poort interval, MSA peoples once again made a variety of larger points, primarily on flake and flake-blade blanks.

In many ways, the Cape sites are quite different from the interior sites in what they indicate about economic sophistication in the MSA. In the Cape sites, evidence of hunting or remains of large, dangerous animals are rare; most animals tend to be the more docile species such as the blue antelope. But at open-air sites in Botswana (e.g., ≠Gi) and Namibia, remains of giant buffalo (Pelorovis), giant zebra (Equus capensis), and warthog suggest competent and regular hunting of these species, probably from ambush. On the Cape coast, shellfish were collected throughout the MSA, but fishing was not practiced at most sites, although large fish have been reported from "Stillbay" levels at Blombos in the eastern Cape. In the interior, however, at sites such as White Paintings shelter (Tsodilo Hills, Botswana), fish remains indicate that MSA people were fishing for catfish in freshwater rivers and lakes.

Symbolic activities are not well represented in the MSA. At Apollo-11 in Namibia, a Howieson's Poort–like industry (which could also represent an early Later Stone Age horizon) at the top of a long sequence of MSA industries dating to more than 100 Ka is associated with the oldest dated art on the continent: slabs with animal outlines in red ocher dated by radiocarbon on an overlying hearth to ca. 28 Ka. Other evidence of symbolic activity in the Middle Stone Age includes the presence of incised ostrich-eggshell fragments at Diepkloof, Elands Bay Cave, and Apollo-11, among others, and bone fragments with lateral notches from Klasies River Mouth. Grindstones stained with ocher were apparently used to process pigments at ≠Gi in the Kalahari (Botswana) and perforated and ground ochre plaques are known from Klasies and other sites. In northern Namibia, lanceolate stone points of Lupemban type, closer to Central than to southern Africa, are known from the site of Mirabib. Throughout Zimbabwe and in Botswana, the points have a particular triangular form and are frequently bifacial: These are known as the Bambata industry after the type site in Zimbabwe. Throughout the region, the MSA is distinguished by regionally specific point types, suggesting a patterning of styles more similar to the Late than to the Middle Paleolithic. In the final MSA, specular hematite was mined at Lion Cavern in Swaziland for transport elsewhere.

Following the MSA, early Later Stone Age microlithic industries appear very early, predating 40 Ka, at Border Cave (Natal Province), while in some other regions they do not appear until ca. 20 Ka. The Later Stone Age is characterized not only by microlithic (and some nonmicrolithic) technologies, but also by ostrich-eggshell beads, rock paintings, and evidence for increasing dependence on smaller-scale resources. Bone harpoons for fishing at White Paintings shelter (Tsodilo Hills, Botswana) may date to ca. 3730-Ka. Regionally distinct industries predating 12 Ka have been defined for many areas; these include the Tshangula of Zimbabwe, the Nachikufan 1 in Zambia, and the Robberg in the Cape Province. The latter is a nongeometric microlithic industry with small-backed points.

The number of Later Stone Age sites increases dramatically in the Holocene, and regional differences become more pronounced. Geometric forms such as lunates or crescents dominate many assemblages; these may have served as elements of projectiles, whether barbs or points, and the projectiles themselves may have delivered a fatal poison rather than an immediately fatal wound. Rock art is increasingly elaborate, and many of the older paintings on the Brandberg (Namibia) and the Drakensburg (South Africa) can be dated to the Pleistocene-Holocene transition. Many paintings may represent trance states and iconographic images that correspond to practices and beliefs of today's San peoples.

Skeletal remains suggest that these people were the ancestors of the modern-day Khoisan peoples of southern Africa and that their way of life was based on extensive utilization of plant foods and materials and on hunting. Craft production of beads and possibly of points for trade is a likely feature at many sites. Seasonally specific faunal remains suggest annual movement between summer and winter camps.

The end of the Later Stone Age in southern Africa can be arbitrarily set at ca. AD 0 when many local peoples appear to have adopted ceramic and sheep herding technology from farmers to the north. By 1200 Ka, central and east African people with iron metallurgy, cattle, and, presumably, Bantu language, began to filter into the area from the north. Stone-tool-using peoples, however, continued to live alongside Iron Age peoples in a variety of relationships, apparently into the nineteenth century in some areas. Some of these older inhabitants were entirely absorbed into the farming populations; others existed as clients or specialized castes of hunters or servants within farmer society; and others were relatively independent hunter-gatherers who may have traded their surplus for small amounts of metals and ceramics.

See also Acheulean; Africa; Africa, East; Apollo-11; Archaic *Homo sapiens;* Australopithecus; *Australopithecus africanus;* Bambata; Border Cave; Breccia Cave Formation; Broom, Robert; Cave of Hearths; Chiwondo Beds; Clark, J. Desmond; Dart, Raymond Arthur; Die Kelders; Drimolen; Early Stone Age; Florisbad; ≠ Gi; Gladysvale; Homo; *Homo erectus; Homo habilis;* Howieson's Poort; Kabwe; Kalambo Falls; Kenyapithecinae; Klasies River Mouth; Kromdraai; Later Stone Age; Makapansgat; Middle Stone Age; Modern Human Origins; Nelson Bay Cave; Paleolithic; *Paranthropus robustus;* Rose Cottage; Saldanha; Sea Harvest; Sterkfontein; Swartkrans; Taung; Tsodilo Sites; Wonderwerk. [E.D., A.S.B., J.A.V.C., F.E.G.]

Further Readings

Barham, L.S., and Smart, P.L. (1996) An early date for the Middle Stone Age of central Zambia. J. Hum. Evol. 30:287–290.

Brain, C.K. (1981) The Hunters or the Hunted? Chicago: University of Chicago Press.

Henshilwood C., and Sealy, J. (1997) Bone artifacts from the Middle Stone Age of Blombos Cave, southern Cape, South Africa. Curr. Anthrop. 38(5): 890–895.

Klein, R.G. (1994) Southern Africa before the Iron Age. In R.S. Corruccini and R.L. Ciochon (eds.): Integrative Paths to the Past. Englewood Cliffs, N.J.: Prentice-Hall, pp. 471–519.

Kuman, K. (1994) The archaeology of Sterkfontein—past and present. J. Hum. Evol. 27:471–495.

Phillipson, D.W. (1993) African Archaeology, 2nd ed. Cambridge: Cambridge University Press.

Sampson, C.G. (1974) The Stone Age Archaeology of Southern Africa. New York: Academic.

Sillen, A., and Morris, A. (1996) Diagenesis of bone from Border Cave: Implications for the age of Border Cave hominids. J. Hum. Evol. 31:499–506.

Singer, R., and Wymer, J. (1982) The Middle Stone Age at Klasies River Mouth in South Africa. Chicago: University of Chicago Press.

Afropithecus

Kenyan Miocene hominoid primate that may be the earliest known member of Hominidae. During the latest Early Miocene and the early part of the Middle Miocene, there appeared in Africa for the first time a type of hominoid with a radically different adaptation of its teeth. Up to this time, all hominoids had relatively thin dental enamel; with *Afropithecus,* thick enamel appeared, and this was to have far-reaching consequences for hominoid evolution. *Afropithecus turkanensis* was a large hominoid primate (males were the size of a female gorilla) known from two sites in northern Kenya, Kalodirr and Buluk, dated to ca. 17 Ma. The face of *Afropithecus* is long (and the teeth relatively small), but it appears

slightly upwardly flexed, suggesting relative airorhynchy, although not as strong as in Ponginae. In its premolar and molar morphology, it is similar to *Heliopithecus leakeyi* from Saudi Arabia. This similarity has led to the two genera either being synonymized or grouped together in the tribe Afropithecini of the hominid subfamily Kenyapithecinae. In 1997, the new genus *Morotopithecus* was proposed to receive both known and new fossils from Moroto, Uganda, which were dated at ca. 20 Ma, older than previously thought. The facial fragments had often been loosely included in *Afropithecus,* but they do differ somewhat (for example, Kalodirr specimens have an oblique and slightly constricted incisive canal as opposed to the vertical foramen in the Moroto palate), and the Moroto postcranium *may* present several character states derived in the direction of living hominids. It is still not clear whether this new genus is in fact distinct from *Afropithecus,* but that distinction is accepted here.

See also Africa, East; Buluk; Diet; Heliopithecus; Hominidae; Hominoidea; Kenyapithecinae; Morotopithecus; Ponginae; Proconsulidae; Skull; Teeth. [E.D., P.A.]

Further Readings

Leakey, M.[G.] and Walker A.[C.] (1997) *Afropithecus:* Function and phylogeny. In D.R. Begun, C.V. Ward, and M. Rose (eds.) Function, Phylogeny and Fossils: Miocene Hominoid Evolution and Adaptations. New York: Plenum, pp. 225–239.

Leakey, R.E., Leakey, M.G., and Walker, A.C. (1988). Morphology of *Afropithecus turkanensis* from Kenya. Am. J. Phys. Anthropol. 76:289–307.

Afrotarsius

Discovered in 1984, this is the only tarsiiform fossil found in Africa, which harbors no living tarsiers. *Afrotarsius chatrathi* is represented by a single lower-jaw fragment from deposits in the Upper Fossil Wood Zone of the Fayum Depression (Egypt), probably ca. 33 Ma. Like the microchoerine omomyid group of fossil tarsiiforms, it demonstrates the important fact that forms quite closely related to modern tarsiers were once widespread geographically. In fact, because it shares similarities with both living tarsiers and the Late Eocene microchoerine *Pseudoloris* of western Europe, *A. chatrathi* may clarify the affinities of the former. These points suggest the possibility that the direct ancestors of the living species arose far to the west of the Malay archipelago, where tarsiers are now confined. On the other hand, species more definitely included in Tarsiidae (if not in *Tarsius* itself) have been reported in the 1990s from the Eocene of China and the Miocene of Thailand. Resemblances to the molars of *Tarsius* in both size and occlusal function imply a similar diet of invertebrate and vertebrate prey. There is still some question as to whether it is best included in the Tarsiidae or placed in its own family (or incertae sedis). A minority view contends that this species is not a close relative of tarsiers but instead a conservative (proto)anthropoid.

In late 1998, D.T. Rasmussen and colleagues reported the find of a partial tibia (lower leg bone) attributed to *Afro-*

tarsius, which indicates that this animal shared with living tarsiers a fused tibia and fibula, thus supporting the relationship between these genera.

See also Anthropoidea; Asia, Eastern and Southern; Fayum; Microchoerinae; Omomyidae; Tarsiidae; Tarsiiformes; Tarsioidea. [A.L.R.]

Further Readings

Rasmussen, D.T., Conroy, G.C., and Simons, E.L. (1998). Tarsier-like locomotor specializations in the Oligocene primate *Afrotarsius.* Proc. Natl. Acad. Sci. USA 95:14848-14850.

Aggregation-Dispersal

Anthropological concept that refers to the differences in the number of people who live together in foraging societies in the course of a year. Ethnographic data on simple hunter-gatherer groups, those who directly forage for what nature provides and who do not store foods, indicate that their settlement systems feature seasonal pulsations in the size of the coresident groups. Information on such groups shows that small numbers of people (ca. 25 to 30 individuals or five to six nuclear families) live together during one part of the year and that these groups join similar groups during other seasons. During these relatively short periods of aggregation, population increases appreciably to 100 or more individuals (25 or more families). At these large gatherings, various forms of group ritual behavior are a common feature, as is exchange of information and of mates. Such seasonal fluctuation in the size of the coresident units is considered a universal feature of simple hunter-gatherer adaptations.

Data on past settlement systems of hunter-gatherers suggest that such aggregation-dispersal pulsations in group size may have been a feature of some Upper Paleolithic settlement systems as well. Such sites as Altamira and Lascaux have been interpreted as seasonal aggregation camps at which a number of groups dispersed during the rest of the year gathered and engaged in groupwide rituals that may have involved painting figurative and nonfigurative designs on cave walls.

Evidence from other Late Paleolithic regions, most notably from the Central Russian Plain, where no changes in group size have been found between the settlements occupied during different seasons, indicates that such changes in group size were not a universal feature of Late Paleolithic settlement systems.

See also Altamira; Lascaux; Ritual; Site types. [O.S.]

Further Readings

Conkey, M. (1980) The identification of prehistoric hunter-gatherer aggregation sites: The case of Altamira. Curr. Anthropol. 21:609–630.

Lee, R.B. (1979) The !Kung San. Cambridge: Cambridge University Press.

Soffer, O. (1985) The Upper Paleolithic of the Central Russian Plain. New York: Academic Press.

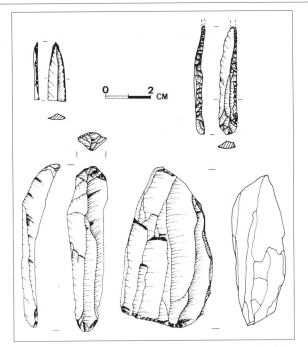

Ahmarian tools from the eastern Sinai, Egypt. Top row, pointed backed bladelets; bottom row, end-scraper and bladelet core. From I. Gilead, 1989, in O. Bar-Yosef and B. Vandermeersch, eds., Investigations in South Levantine Prehistory, *British Archaeological Reports, International Series, No. 497.*

Ahmarian

An early Late Paleolithic industry from the southern Levant dating to between 38 and 22 Ka. Unlike the Levantine Aurignacian, with which it is roughly contemporaneous, the Ahmarian features numerous blades, backed blades, and bladelets. Ahmarian occupations include Erq-el Ahmar D–F, Kebara E, Qafzeh 7–9, Boker A and Boker BE (Levels II–VII), and numerous sites near Lagama in the northern Sinai. The Ahmarian is one of several early Late Paleolithic industries from the eastern Mediterranean that are typologically distinct from the European early Upper Paleolithic Aurignacian industry.

See also Asia, Western; Upper Paleolithic. [J.J.S.]

'Ain Ghazal

One of the largest-known Neolithic sites in Southwest Asia, occupied for nearly 2,000 years (ca. 9.3–7.7 Ka). Located near Amman, Jordan, it was excavated between 1982 and 1989 by G. Rollefson and A. Simmons. The site produced impressive ritual and artistic objects, including small animal and human clay figurines, many with decapitated heads; human skulls with faces modeled in plaster; and large (up to 90 cm high) human statuary made of reeds and plaster. At its peak, the mudbrick settlement extended over 12 ha (30 acres) and had some 2,000 inhabitants; after 8 Ka it went into decline, and after 7.7 Ka it was sporadically occupied, probably by pastoralists.

See also Asia, Western; Jericho; Neolithic. [N.B.]

'Ain Hanech

An Early Paleolithic (Mode 1) locality near the town of Setif in northeastern Algeria, which may be the oldest evidence of hominid presence in North Africa. A rich Villafranchian fauna was recovered in the mid-twentieth century, as well as Oldowan-like limestone cores and flakes, including some flaked "stone balls," or spheroids. The fauna associated with the artifacts has been compared to that found in Bed II of Olduvai Gorge (Tanzania), which could place 'Ain Hanech at ca. 1.5 Ma. Renewed excavations by Sahnouni et al. have recovered Oldowan artifacts from fine-grained deposits, including a larger component made on limestone cobbles and a smaller component made on flint pebbles. Preliminary paleomagnetic analysis indicates normal polarity, which suggests correlation with the Olduvai Subchron (1.95–1.77 Ma). Acheulean handaxes are known from surface scatters at the locality and appear to have eroded out of later, overlying deposits.

See also Africa, North; Early Paleolithic; Oldowan. [N.T., K.S.]

Further Readings

Sahnouni, M. (1998) The Lower Paleolithic of the Maghreb: Excavations and analyses of Ain Hanech, Algeria. Cambridge Monographs in African Archaeology no. 42, BAR S689. Oxford: Archaeopress.

Allele

The ultimate source of genetic variation is *mutation,* the term applied to any alteration in a gene. Its effect is to create different variants of genes in a population: DNA segments responsible for identical functions but yielding slightly different products. Variant forms of a gene are known as alleles. Organisms with two identical alleles for the same gene are *homozygous;* organisms with two different alleles are *heterozygous.*

See also Gene; Genotype. [J.M.]

Allometry

Living organisms exhibit tremendous variation in overall size, ranging from single-celled creatures to the 100-ton blue whale, the largest known animal that has ever existed. Such variation in body size has major implications for the ways in which animals are constructed and function. The biological investigation of the morphological and physiological changes that are causally related to differences in body size is known as the study of allometry (from Greek roots meaning "of different measure or shape"). Allometric investigations are but one aspect of the broader study of scaling in biology, which focuses on not merely the morphological but also the ecological, life-historical, and even behavioral correlates of size change.

Early work in the field of allometry dates back at least to Galileo, who used physical principles to demonstrate the disproportionate changes in width or girth that long bones of larger animals must undergo if they are to function properly in their weight-bearing capacities. Just as in any physical

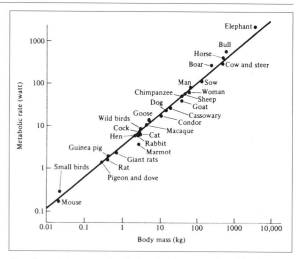

Plot of metabolic rate against body weight in mammals and birds, illustrating the strong correlation and exhibiting a slope of 0.74. After Schmidt-Nielsen, 1984. Courtesy of Brian T. Shea.

body, when animals enlarge in size, geometric similarity or isometry is maintained where lengths scale proportionally to lengths$^{1.0}$, areas$^{0.66}$, and volumes or weights$^{0.33}$. Since volumes in some real sense outrace surface areas and lengths, animals of roughly similar design but of significantly different overall size must frequently change their shape (i.e., scale allometrically rather than isometrically) if they are to function equivalently. For example, it has been determined that the weight of the skeleton in mammals scales allometrically (with a log regression slope significantly greater than 1.0) relative to overall body weight in order to support the rapidly increasing total mass. Large mammals thus have relatively as well as absolutely heavier skeletons than smaller mammals. Another excellent example is provided by metabolic rate in birds and mammals, which scales with body weight to approximately the 0.75 power (*see* figure). As a result of this negatively allometric relationship (a regression slope value significantly less than 1.0), larger mammals have relatively lower metabolic rates, while smaller mammals have relatively higher rates.

This negatively allometric pattern is presumably related at least in part to the progressively decreasing ratio of surface area to volume as mammals get larger. Without such an allometric scaling of metabolism, as M. Kleiber pointed out long ago, a steer with the relative metabolic rate of a mouse would have to maintain surface temperatures near the boiling point to dissipate heat adequately, while a mouse with the relative metabolic rate of a steer would require over 15 cm of insulating fur to maintain sufficient body temperatures. Countless other examples from both biology and engineering could be given to support the claim that the maintenance of functional equivalence often requires a regular alteration of shape as size changes.

Allometric relationships are also frequently examined within particular species, either in ontogenetic sequences or among adults of different size. Here progressive shape changes reflect differential growth, as in the general mam-

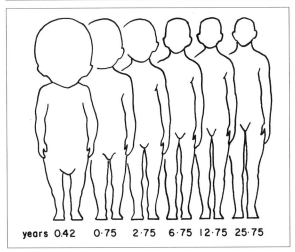

Graphic illustration of the progressive changes in shape during human ontogeny, made by scaling body shape at various growth stages to a common length. These shape changes reflect a positive allometry of hindlimb length and a negative allometry of skull size. After McMahon and Banner, 1983, and P. Medawar in W.E. LeGros Clark and P.B. Medawar, eds., Essays on Growth and Form, 1945, Oxford University Press; courtesy of Brian T. Shea.

malian postnatal pattern of positively allometric growth of the face relative to the brain or the relative lengthening of the hindlimbs during human ontogeny (*see* figure). These patterns of shape change result from shifts in the intrinsic and extrinsic controls of growth of various body regions, and we often discover a reasonable functional basis for these allometries as well.

Shape differences between adults of two or more species are thus determined to be allometric if they result either from the sharing and differential extension of common patterns of ontogenetic allometry (*see* figure), in which case we refer to the interspecific pattern as *ontogenetic scaling*, or from the need to maintain equivalence of some functional parameter or constraint as size changes (*see* figure), in which case we refer to the interspecific pattern as *biomechanical scaling*.

Allometric investigations are used in at least two important ways in studies of adaptation and phylogeny. Sometimes, our focus is on the general scaling relationship itself, as reflected in the slope of the regression line relating the two variables under consideration; at other times, our primary interest is in determining and explaining departures from such a best-fit line. Both of these related endeavors can be illustrated by classic analyses of brain/body allometry (*see* figure). Broad studies of interspecific scaling of the brain have demonstrated an allometric coefficient (regression slope) of somewhere between 0.66 and 0.75, or negative allometry. These empirical observations have led to important theoretical hypotheses concerning the physiological basis of such a pattern. Although these hypotheses have not been fully tested, the scaling pattern suggests possible control of brain size by body-surface areas, metabolic rates, or certain other factors. The placement of a particular species or group in relation to a general scaling pattern may also be informative, as, for example, when American paleoneurologist H. Jerison demonstrated that the relatively "peabrained" sauropod dinosaurs in fact had brain sizes in the range one would expect

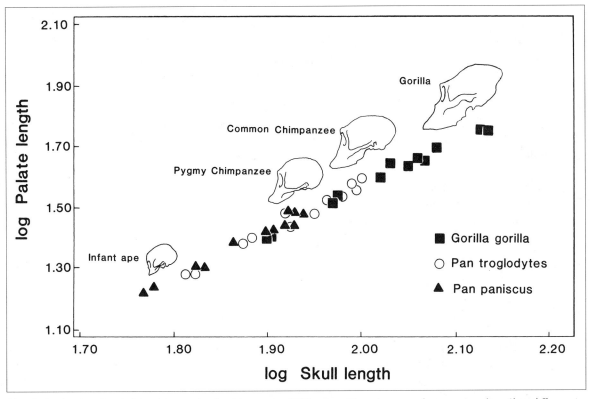

Plot of palate length against skull length in growth series of three species of African apes, illustrating a case of ontogenetic scaling. Shape differences in the skull (e.g., relatively longer palates) among adults of the three species result from the sharing and differential extension of common growth patterns of positive allometry; courtesy of Brian T. Shea.

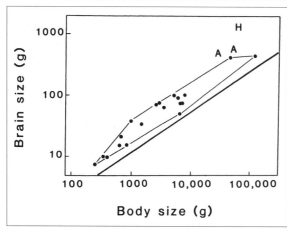

Plot of brain size against body size in haplorhine primates. The heavy solid line represents a regression line of $y = 0.12(x)3/4$ fit to extant mammals. The polygon enclosing these primates lies above this line, reflecting their relatively high encephalization. Modern humans (H) and australopiths (A, for Australopithecus africanus *and* P. boisei*) exhibit the strongest positive deviations from predicted values. After H.J. Jerison,* Evolution of the Brain and Intelligence, *Academic Press, 1973; courtesy of Brian T. Shea.*

for such giant reptiles. In other words, their brain/body ratios fell along an extension of the general allometric relationship for extant reptiles.

Deviations from such allometric baselines therefore require examination as possible cases of "special adaptations" unrelated to simple body-size differences. The large size of our own brain is one such positive deviation from expected values for mammals of our overall body size (*see* figure). Another example is the relative length of our hindlimbs: In plots of hindlimb length against total size for higher primates, humans are characterized by strong positive deviations from the general trend. This suggests a link to our peculiar pattern of bipedal locomotion and the fact that relatively long hindlimbs are functionally advantageous and not simply the result of our generally large size among primates. A third example from the human fossil record is the demonstration that the characteristic facial and dental proportions of robust australopiths do not merely reflect shape changes expected to maintain functional equivalence at larger overall size, as some have previously suggested, but rather apparently indicate divergent dietary adaptations, as argued by many others.

It is intriguing and even ironic that something as obvious as variation in overall size has proven to be such a productive and exciting field of morphological investigation. Biologists will continue to probe questions of allometry and scaling in morphology, physiology, ecology, and behavior and, in the process, increase our understanding of the form, function, and evolution of organisms.

See also Adaptation(s); Bone Biology; Dwarfism; Evolution; Functional Morphology; Gigantism; Ontogeny. [B.T.S.]

Further Readings

Gould, S.J. (1966) Allometry and size in ontogeny and phylogeny. Biol. Rev. 41:587–640.

Huxley, J.S. (1932) Problems of Relative Growth. London: MacVeagh.

Jungers, W.L., ed. (1985) Size and Scaling in Primate Biology. New York: Plenum.

McMahon, T.A., and Banner, J.T. (1983) On Size and Life. New York: Freeman.

Schmidt-Nielsen, K. (1984) Scaling: Why Is Animal Size So Important? Cambridge: Cambridge University Press.

Thompson, D.W. (1917) On Growth and Form. Cambridge: Cambridge University Press.

Altamira

Major Ice Age painted cave in northwestern Spain. Discovered in 1879, the famous painted ceiling of standing and lying bison was once considered a forgery. The polychrome red-and-black paintings were made in the Middle Magdalenian phase of the Upper Paleolithic, ca. 13.5 Ka, although there are also earlier Aurignacian bone engravings and wall markings, as well as animal engravings from the Solutrean, ca. 22 Ka. Excavation in the cave has recovered the bones of bison, horse, boar, and deer, in addition to the engraved and painted signs, symbols, and animals on the walls and ceilings.

See also Aurignacian; Europe; Magdalenian; Paleolithic Image; Solutrean; Upper Paleolithic. [A.M.]

Altamura

Cave site in southeastern Italy at which an apparently complete human skeleton, possibly dating to ca. 400 Ka, was discovered in 1993. Because it is enclosed in a hard calcareous matrix, this skeleton has not been fully excavated and cleaned. However, it has been described as that of a "preneanderthal," although informal reports suggest that it is not of typical Neanderthal morphology but comparable to contemporaneous "archaic *Homo sapiens*" (*H. heidelbergensis*).

See also Archaic Homo sapiens; Europe; Homo heidelbergensis; Neanderthal; Preneanderthal. [I.T.]

Altiatlasius

A small primate described by French paleontologist B. Sigé and collaborators as one of 23 species of the important Adrar Mgorn 1 fauna of approximately Late Paleocene age (ca. 56–55 Ma), from the foot of the Atlas Mountains in the Ouarzazate Basin of Morocco. This form, known from about ten isolated upper and lower teeth, was comparable in size to the Malagasy mouse lemur (50–100 g), and it is suggested by its original describers to be an early branch of the Omomyidae. The morphological traits of the molars put forward by the describers as evidence of omomyid ties are difficult to evaluate in the context of known early euprimates. The large protocone and somewhat bunodont cusps, the small conules and the virtual absence of either a nannopithex fold or any other manifestation of a hypocone at least on M[1] (a topographical designation on the tooth rather than a significant homology when comparing disparate groups of mammals) are probably primitive traits of the euprimates as the describers readily admit. While probably a euprimate, *Altiatlasius koulchii* lacks the characteristic approach of the paraconid to the metaconid on M_2 in contrast to M_1 as seen in the earliest Holarctic euprimates, or the buccal retraction of the paraconid seen in later omomyids such as Omomyinae. Besides the geographic provenance of the genus from Africa, the few teeth display no evidence of any sort that allows one to link them with the earliest known anthropoids. *Altiatlasius* is best regarded as an enigmatic probable euprimate.

See also Africa, North; Anthropoidea; Euprimates; Omomyidae; Paleocene; Tarsiiformes; Teeth. [F.S.S.]

Further Readings

Sigé, B., Jaeger, J.-J., Sudre, J., and Vianey-Liaud, M. (1990) *Altiatlasius koulchii* n. gen. et sp., primate omomyidé du Paléocène supérieur du Maroc, et les origines des euprimates. Palaeontographica Abt. A 214:31–56. (Partial English translation in Delson, E., Tattersall, I., and Van Couvering, J.A., eds. [1991] Paleoanthropology Annuals, Vol. 1. New York: Garland.)

Ambrona

Open-air archaeological site in northern Spain, faunally dated to later Middle Pleistocene (late Elster to early Saale), ca. 0.4–0.25 Ma. Although briefly surveyed by a Spanish nobleman in the late 1800s, Ambrona was scientifically excavated in the 1950s and 1960s by F.C. Howell and L. Freeman. A nearby "sister" site, Torralba, was further studied in the early 1980s. The two sites yielded an Acheulean industry with cleavers and a few possible bone and wood tools in association with scattered charcoal flecks. The partially articulated skeleton of an elephant (*Elephas antiquus*) and more fragmentary remains of other elephants, deer, horses, and aurochs are often cited as evidence for cooperative hunting of big game by *Homo erectus,* or more likely "archaic *Homo sapiens,*" but could also represent some carnivore predation and/or natural accumulation. No human remains were recovered.

See also Acheulean; Archaeological Sites; Cleaver; Early Paleolithic; Economy, Prehistoric; Europe; Fire; Handaxe; Man-Land Relationships; Paleolithic Lifeways; Site Types; Taphonomy. [A.S.B.]

Further Reading

Freeman, L.G. (1994) Toralba and Ambrona: A review of discoveries. In R.S. Corrucini and R.L. Ciochon (eds.): Integrative Paths to the Past: Paleoanthropological Advances in Honor of F. Clark Howell. Englewood Cliffs, N.J.: Prentice Hall, pp. 597–637.

Americas

The New World landmass measures 15,000 km from the Arctic to Cape Horn, both continents stretching 5,000 km across at their widest points. This immense territory (more than 42 million km²) covers more than one-quarter of the world's habitable surface.

The most impressive physiographic feature in North America is the western cordillera, running the length of the continent like a gigantic backbone. A more ancient mountain chain flanks eastern North America, reaching only half the height of its western counterpart. The vast area between the Appalachians and the Rockies includes the glaciated Canadian Shield to the north, the Great Plains in midcontinent, and the Mississippi Basin to the south. East of the Appalachians is a coastal plain, relatively narrow in the north but widening significantly as it approaches the Gulf of Mexico.

An equally impressive range of mountains, the Andes, runs the full length of the South American continent. Although narrower than the North American cordillera, the Andes are much higher, reaching over 7,000 m in places. Coastal lowlands, varying in width, border the Andes. The uplands of eastern South America are much older than the Andes, much more weathered, and considerably lower in elevation. The lowland plains of interior South America contain the Orinoco and Amazon drainage basins.

Primate History

NORTH AMERICAN EARLY PRIMATES

The first well-documented faunal assemblages containing primates occur in the Paleogene of western North America. Although the order may have originated in eastern Asia, fossils are rare there throughout the Cenozoic. Numerous localities yielding diverse mammalian faunas are known throughout the Paleocene and the Eocene of the Rocky Mountain region (then mainly lowland tropical forests), and primates are a common component of these faunas (*see* map). Plesiadapiform primates are the oldest widespread group, including a variety of archaic forms grouped into two superfamilies with five families.

Purgatorius, the oldest recognized primate, appears at the very end of the Mesozoic and continues into the earliest Cenozoic, ca. 66–64 Ma. It is usually included in the family Paromomyidae, which also includes a number of extremely small to small, mainly Paleocene taxa that are among the least-derived primates. Most of these are restricted to western North America, although two genera also occur in western Europe and the Arctic (Ellesmere Island). Most paromomyids were insectivorous, but larger forms, such as the speciose and widespread *Phenacolemur* (which persisted into the Middle Eocene), were partly frugivorous. The dentally batlike picrodontids were rare nectar feeders restricted to western North America and perhaps derived from paromomyids. These two families are loosely grouped into the superfamily Paromomyoidea.

A larger range of sizes characterized the Plesiadapoidea, a group of three families linked by the development of mitten-like prongs on the enlarged central upper incisor. The Plesiadapidae and the Carpolestidae range from Early Paleocene into Early Eocene in the American West, with some plesiadapids known also in Europe. Skulls and postcrania of plesiadapids are the best known among all the archaic primates, documenting a snouty face, the lack of a postorbital bar known in all other primates, and a semigrasping foot (presumably related to primate arboreality). Plesiadapids are known that were as large as living marmots or woodchucks, and they ate a variety of vegetable materials. The generally smaller carpolestids are known from less-complete remains, but they are characterized by an enlarged, bladelike P_4 and enlarged flattened and multi-cusped P^{3-4}, which probably helped shearing of a fibrous diet.

By the end of the Paleocene, the first members of the modern primates (the euprimates) may have evolved in Asia or perhaps in southern North America. Two groups of euprimates appear suddenly, through migration, in North America and Europe at the beginning of the Eocene (ca. 55 Ma): the strepsirhine Adapiformes and the haplorhine Omomyidae. The archaic primates soon disappeared, competed into extinction not only by later primates but also by the rapidly diversifying rodents. In the American West, the adapiforms are represented by the small-to-medium-sized Notharctidae, a mainly folivorous group similar in many ways to the living lemurs of Madagascar. Four genera of notharctids are known by a dozen species ranging into the Middle Eocene, while one adapiform of European affinity occurred in the Late Eocene of Texas. The generally small omomyids were much more diverse and long-lived, with perhaps two dozen mainly monospecific genera, placed in the subfamilies Anaptomorphinae, Ekgmowechashalinae, and Omomyinae, spanning the earliest Eocene to the latest Oligocene. Species range from the size of the smallest marmosets up to that of medium-bodied monkeys, at least in tooth-row length. Diets were similarly varied, with frugivores, folivores, and insectivores among the known species. Most taxa have enlarged lower incisors like those of less-derived archaic primates, but at least some species had incisors and certain foot bones more like those of the ancestral anthropoids. It seems likely that the protoanthropoid stock was derived from an omomyidlike ancestry. With climatic cooling through the Eocene, forested areas decreased in size, and most arboreal mammals were forced into competition for limited resources in the north or into the smaller geographic space of southern North America. Only one omomyid is known in the Late Eocene (ca. 36–34 Ma) of Montana, and another from the Late Oligocene (ca. 28 Ma) of Oregon and South Dakota (possible forest refuges?).

SOUTH AMERICAN PLATYRRHINES

Although the probable ancestry of the higher primates, or anthropoids, can be traced to near the tarsiiform omomyids, the nature of their dispersal into the southern continents is less clear. Early anthropoids arrived in South America by the Late Oligocene (27 Ma), when *Branisella* is known from Bolivia. The living New World primates, the platyrrhine monkeys, are divided here into two families, Cebidae and Atelidae, each with a long fossil history. In fact, *Branisella* can be included in the Cebidae, as can the Early Miocene (ca. 20 Ma) Patagonian *Dolichocebus* and Chilean *Chilecebus*, close relatives of the living squirrel monkey, *Saimiri*. Another Early Miocene genus, *Tremacebus*, is apparently a relative of the living nocturnal owl monkey, *Aotus*; both forms show enlargement of the eye sockets typical of nocturnal mammals, especially anthropoids. *Soriacebus* is probably the oldest known pitheciin. In the Middle Miocene (14–12 Ma) La Venta fauna of northern Colombia, at least nine genera continue to demonstrate the early diversification of the platyrrhines. *Micodon* and perhaps two other taxa are early callitrichines, *Neosaimiri* is little different from *Saimiri*, while *Aotus* is represented by an extinct species. *Stirtonia* is a large form close to the modern howler monkey, and three other genera represent early members of the atelid subfamily Pitheciinae. At least three further distinctive genera are known from Holocene deposits on Caribbean islands, suggesting a dispersal through that region from a probable Central American source. Two other very large ateline genera are known from the Late Pleistocene of eastern Brazil.

The modern platyrrhines have a wide range of diets, social behavior, and locomotor adaptations. As in the early primates, most genera can be distinguished by their dentitions. Yet, despite the presence of a widespread plains fauna in South America during the Miocene, no platyrrhine became terrestrial, in contrast to the multiple adaptations to ground life among Old World anthropoids. Instead, all New World monkeys are restricted to forested environments, and the rapid encroachment of humans on their habitats is driving several species toward extinction.

Humans in the New World

The New World was discovered at least three times. The most celebrated "discovery" is accorded Christopher Columbus, who landed on San Salvador in October 1492. But half a millennium earlier, Norsemen from Greenland and Iceland had already fished the waters of North America, shipping its timber back to their families on tree-barren Greenland. Although the New World adventures of Leif Eriksson were duly recorded in Norse epics, scholars debated the existence of a Norse New World settlement for nearly a millennium. The best archaeological evidence for their presence is at L'Anse aux Meadows (Newfoundland). Landing ca. AD 1020, the Vikings held onto their New World foothold for three decades before retreating. When the Vikings arrived at L'Anse aux Meadows, they encountered, and thoroughly alienated, the true first Americans, whom the Norse called *scraelings*. In fact, the first human footprints on New World soil belonged to the Asian people who were to become American Indians and the closely related Eskimo. The Americas were "discovered" and then populated from northeastern Asia by 20 Ka, perhaps as early as 30 Ka. People migrated into this New World as fully evolved *Homo sapiens sapiens*. Human beings did not evolve in the Americas.

The first Americans brought certain basic cultural skills: fire making, flint chipping, and serviceable means of procuring food, shelter, and clothing. These early immigrants must also have brought with them the rudiments of kin-group social organization and beliefs about magic and the supernatural. They certainly possessed forms of human language. When Columbus arrived, Native Americans of Alaska, Canada, and the U.S. mainland spoke about 2,000 mutually unintelligible languages; the linguistic complexity in South America was comparable. Although some degree of linguistic diversity may have been imported with the earliest New World settlers, much of the linguistic evolution took place as Native Americans adapted to their new environment.

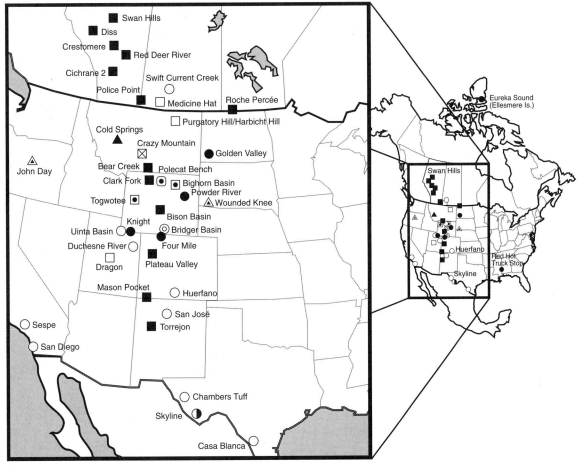

Selected North American fossil primate localities from Early Paleocene to Late Oligocene; inset shows sites east of the Mississippi. Age and included taxa are indicated according to the key at right.

★ Middle-Late Paleocene – Plesiadapiformes

● Early Eocene – Plesiadapiformes, Adapidae

⊙ Early Eocene – Plesiadapiformes, Adapidae, Anaptomorphinae

▣ Middle Eocene – Adapidae, Microchoerinae

■ Late Eocene – Adapidae, Microchoerinae

⊠ Early-Late Eocene – Adapidae, Microchoerinae

▲ ?Late Eocene – Adapidae

PALEOINDIAN OCCUPATIONS

The earliest well-defined archaeological assemblages in the Americas are termed *Paleoindian,* the earliest of which is the Clovis complex, dating sometime between 12 and 11 Ka. Despite decades of concerted research, no undisputed evidence of a pre-Clovis presence has been uncovered anywhere in the Western Hemisphere. But whether the Paleoindians were actually the First Americans is not known. Most archeologists still agree that the first Americans traveled from Asia sometime during the Late Pleistocene. Biology and language point to an Asian homeland; it is the timing and conditions surrounding their arrival that remain unknown. A few archeologists have suggested that the morphology and artifacts of the first Americans suggest very generalized, even Paleo-Eurasian or European ancestry rather than close relationships to East Asian ancestors.

Considerable nonarchaeological evidence also supports this position. In the 1980s, J. Greenberg's reanalysis of Amer-

ican Indian languages postulates three waves of migrants into the New World. This linguistic interpretation indicates that the earliest wave of migration took place ca. 12 Ka; they were the people of the Clovis complex. Independent correlations of dental traits and evidence from molecular biology can also be cited in support of the Clovis-first hypothesis.

But considerable controversy surrounds Greenberg's broad-brush linguistic reconstructions, and numerous skeptics question the relevance of the dental and genetic testimony relating to the first Americans. And, although still controversial, archaeological evidence is emerging from a number of sites suggesting that people arrived considerably before the well-documented Clovis complex. Many modern archaeologists have begun to acknowledge that people could readily have arrived in the New World as early as 40 Ka.

Numerous sites throughout North and South America offer tantalizing suggestions of pre-Clovis occupations, but none provides iron-clad proof acceptable to all archaeolo-

Selected South American fossil primate localities from Late Oligocene to Holocene. Age and included taxa are indicated according to the following key:

★   Late Pleistocene (<100 Ka) – Atelinae

✚   Late Miocene (ca. 10-6 Ma) – ?Atelinae, ?Cebinae

■   Early Middle Miocene (15-13 Ma) – Atelinae,
     ?Callitrichinae, Cebinae, Pitheciinae

▫   Earliest Middle Miocene (16-15 Ma) – new genus

●   Late Early Miocene (16.5 Ma) – Pitheciinae

⊙   Mid Early Miocene (20-18 Ma) – Cebinae,
     Pitheciinae

▲   Late Oligocene (27 Ma) – Branisellinae

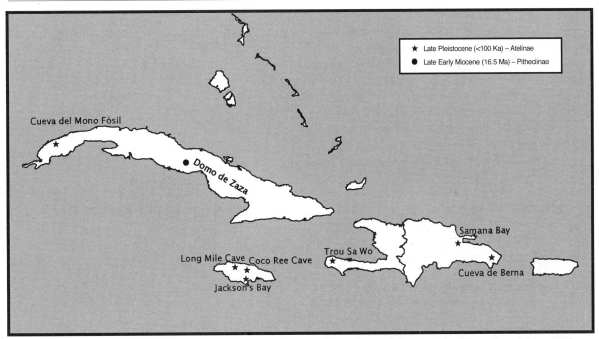

Caribbean fossil primate localities, all apparently of Holocene age, except Domo de Zaza (Miocene). Taxa located as follows: Cueva de Mono Fósil, Paralouatta; Long Mile Cave (and neighboring Sheep Pen cave, not shown) and Jackson's Bay sites, Xenothrix; Cueva de Berna and perhaps Trou Sa Wo and Samana Bay, Antillothrix; Coco Ree and Domo de Zaza, postcrania of uncertain identification.

gists. Some of the best evidence derives from excavations at Meadowcroft Shelter, a remarkably well-stratified site in southwestern Pennsylvania. J. Adovasio and his colleagues have documented a sequence of more than 40 radiocarbon dates, in near perfect stratigraphic order. The oldest cultural date is now thought to be slightly older than 15.9 Ka, and the oldest stone artifacts appear to date between 12.8 and 11.3 Ka. Evidence for early human occupation consists of occupation floors containing firepits, prismatic blades, biface-thinning flakes, flake knives, a wooden foreshaft, a piece of plaited basketry, and two human bone fragments.

Although many archaeologists consider the evidence from Meadowcroft to be conclusive, others remain unconvinced. The stone implements are rare, small, and relatively uninformative; they are disturbingly similar to much later artifacts. Extinct Pleistocene megafauna is surprisingly absent from the deposits, and the temperate character of the vegetation throughout the Meadowcroft sequence also seems anomalous, since, during a part of this time, the ice front should have been less than 75 km to the north. In 1998, however, new evidence from Cactus Hill near Pietersburg, VA, indicated a pre-Clovis horizon comparable to that at Meadowcroft with radiocarbon dates on charcoal of 15–16 Ka.

Another leading pre-Clovis candidate is Monte Verde, an open-air residential site in southern Chile. Excavator T. Dillehay and his colleagues have encountered four distinct zones of buried cultural remains. Nearly one dozen house foundations and fallen pole-frames of residential huts have been excavated, and fragments of skin (perhaps mastodon) still cling to the poles. Abundant botanical remains are associated with the archaeological deposits, as well as numerous shaped stone tools, including several grooved *bola* stones.

Dillehay argues that the upper layers contain "well-preserved and clear, conclusive evidence" of a human presence ca. 13 Ka. Even more controversial are the deep layers at Monte Verde that have produced two radiocarbon dates of 33 Ka, associated with possible cultural features and several fractured stones.

Selected North American archaeological sites. Age indicated by symbols as follows: Pre-Clovis ● (35–13 Ka); Paleoindian ■ (13–9 Ka); Viking ▼ landing (ca. AD 1000); Postclassic ▲. Note: Cactus Hill site, not shown here, is located just below 'a' in 'Meadowcroft'.

Not only do these controversial data suggest an earlier human presence in the New World, but their interpretation likewise theorizes that the earliest Americans did not employ the sophisticated big-game-hunting Clovis complex with its elegantly fashioned stone tools. The plant and animal remains from Monte Verde suggest a forest-adapted economy based primarily on the collection of wild plant foods and shellfish; only secondarily did the people rely on the scavenging and/or hunting of slow-moving game, paleollama, or mastodon.

Another candidate for pre-Clovis occupation in South America is the cave of Pedra Furada in Brazil. While ca. 12-11 Ka occupations are well documented both at this site and at the cave of Pedra Pintada (Brazil), the evidence for earlier occupation has been disputed. For Pedra Furada, the dispute concerns whether the charcoal and/or the "artifacts" result from human activities or natural processes.

Despite such evidence from Meadowcroft, Monte Verde, and numerous other sites, we have no unequivocal, indisputable archaeological documentation of a pre-Clovis occupation in the New World. The Clovis culture was firmly established in North America prior to 12 Ka. This widespread complex spans the width of North America and can be traced from northern Alaska to Guatemala. The Clovis, or Llano, complex comprises the oldest well-dated cultural material with clearly established association of humans and animals in North America. These sites, which lack established cultural antecedents, often contain choppers, cutting tools, a variety of bone tools, and (very rarely) milling stones, in addition to the diagnostic Clovis fluted points.

Despite technological similarities, the Paleoindian lifeway in eastern North America differed from the big-game-hunting pattern evident on the Plains. By 12 Ka, the floral and faunal resources in the Ohio Valley and far north into Wisconsin, Michigan, and Ontario were adequate to support scattered bands of hunters. Animal bones found in association with these Paleoindian sites are usually woodland caribou. Eastern Paleoindians concentrated their efforts on river-valley resources, in effect earning a head start toward the highly efficient gathering economies usually associated with later archaic periods.

Similar early hunting adaptations can be traced in South America. The diagnostic artifact of this tradition, fish-tail projectile points from El Inga and elsewhere, resembles the Clovis-derived points of North America. Established largely in Andean South America, this early hunting tradition spread to the southern tip of the continent and eastward into the Argentine Plains. Between 13 and 12 Ka, people in Central Colombia and southern Chile were collecting plants and hunting small game; there is no definite evidence that they hunted mastodons, as did contemporary El Jobo people in northern Venezuela. In southern Patagonia, people hunted horses and ground sloths ca. 11 Ka, but there is no evidence that people in Central and northern Brazil ever hunted such megamammals.

Later Developments
As the climate ameliorated, and an ever-thickening forest barrier formed between periglacial tundra and the temperate

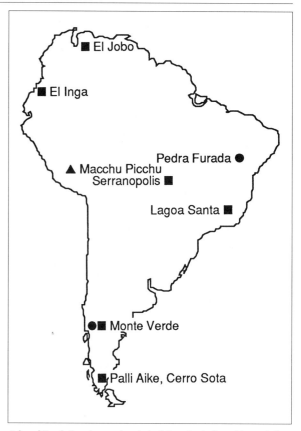

Selected South American archaeological sites. Age indicated by symbols as follows: Pre-Clovis ● (35–13 Ka); Paleoindian ■ (13–9 Ka); Postclassic ▲.

grasslands, different cultural orientations formed. In the far north, this archaic stage is a generalized, primary response to forest conditions emerging during this period of flux. Although this tradition arose from a Paleoindian substratum of big-game hunting, a series of regional modifications emerged. Caribou hunting remained the primary economic activity on the northern fringes of the forest, but to the south other large species (elk, moose, and deer) became mainstays. The regional density of seasonal hunting camps and more permanent settlements increased; migratory patterns involved smaller areas; and groups became increasingly sedentary. As a result, technological capacities improved and intensified.

In South America, the early hunting tradition gave rise to an Andean archaic pattern, a cultural tradition in which subsistence was provided by hunting deer and camelids and by collecting vegetable foods. A hallmark of this tradition was seasonal transhumance, shifting community residence as people pursued either highland hunting or coastal-lowland collecting. A distinctive tradition also developed along the Peruvian and Chilean coasts, where seasonal collecting camps began to be replaced by permanent villages whose inhabitants depended primarily upon marine foods, although, in Peru, plant gathering remained an important economic activity and provided the basis for the evolution of agriculture.

This full archaic stage of cultural development is evident throughout the New World, in general beginning with the climatic optimum, ca. 7 Ka and lasting in some places until 4 Ka. Pottery is found in a number of archaic-stage cultures, as among the Valdivia tradition in northwestern South America and the late archaic fiber-tempered ceramics in the southeastern United States. There are, of course, continuities of this stage into historic times in both North and South America, as, for example, in the later cultures of the California coast and the Northwest coast.

Throughout the archaic in Central and South America, interrelated developments ultimately brought about the emergence of settled village life based on full-time farming. Native American population grew beyond the limits that could be supported by a hunting-gathering economy. Under human selection, certain plants, notably maize, became larger and more productive, and it became increasingly cost-effective to clear away the wild vegetation in order to plant crops. As crops contributed more to the human diet, communities became increasingly sedentary. Improved farming technology increased productivity still further, and settlement patterns began to select for agricultural needs rather than for hunting and foraging.

The term *Formative* (or *Preclassic*) commonly designates the threshold of subsistence agriculture in the traditions of Mesoamerica, the American Southwest, the Mississippian, the Great Plains, and the Eastern Woodlands. In South America, this stage includes similar traditions in Peru, the South Andes, the Caribbean, and Amazonia. Of these, the latter two featured manioc (cassava) cultivation; all others were primarily maize based. In general, the Formative stage dates from ca. 4 Ka into the historic period (after AD 1600).

In Mesoamerica and Peru, the criterion of settled urban life is used to define a *Classic* stage, beginning about the opening of the Christian era. Regional expressions of the Mesoamerican Classic include Teotihuacan (Valley of Mexico), the Zapotec culture (Oaxaca), and the Maya (Guatemalan highlands and Yucatan lowlands). Classic Andean cultures include the Mochica and the Nazca kingdoms. How far the Classic can be extended into other areas is debatable, but it probably applies to the cultures of the Ecuadorian coast after 1 Ka.

The *Postclassic* is an epiphenomenon of the Classic, characterized by developments in urban living, an increase in large-scale warfare and empire building, and secularization of political control, in contrast to previously religious leadership. In Mesoamerica, the Postclassic began with the fall of the city of Teotihuacan (AD 730) and the rise of the militaristic Toltec empire and continued through the Aztec society encountered by the Spanish explorer Cortes in the sixteenth century AD. In Peru, this chronology corresponds to the time when the Tiahuanaco-Huari empire overran the Moche and the Nazca ca. 600 AD.

See also Adapiformes; Anaptomorphinae; Anthropoidea; Atelidae; Atelinae; Blackwater Draw; Branisellinae; Calico Hills; Callitrichinae; Carpolestidae; Cebidae; Cebinae; Cenozoic; Clovis; Diet; Domestication; Ekgmowechashalinae; Eocene; Euprimates; Extinction; Fells Cave; Folsom; Guitarrero Cave; La Venta; Llano Complex; Locomotion; Meadowcroft Shelter; Miocene; Monte Verde; Notharctidae; Old Crow; Oligocene; Omomyidae; Omomyinae; Paleobiogeography; Paleocene; Paleoindian; Paromomyidae; Pedra Furada; Picrodontidae; Pitheciinae; Plano; Platyrrhini; Plesiadapidae; Plesiadapiformes; Plesiadapoidea; Primates; Sandia; Tarsiiformes; Tlapacoya. [D.H.T., E.D.]

Further Readings

Adovisio, J.M., and Carlisle, R.C. (1984) An Indian hunter's camp for 20,000 years. Scien. Am. (May):130–136.

Adovisio, J.M., Donahue, J., Pedler, D.R., and Stuckenrath, R. (1998) Two decades of debate on Meadowcroft Rockshelter. North American Archaeologist. 19(4): 317–341.

Bonnichsen, R., and Turmire, K.L. (1991) Clovis: Origins and Adaptations. Corvallis: Oregon State University Center for the Study of the First Americans.

Bryan, A.L., ed. (1986) New Evidence for the Pleistocene Peopling of the Americas. Orono: University of Maine Center for Study of Early Man.

Carlisle, R., ed. (1988) Americans before Columbus: Ice Age Origins. (Ethnology Monographs No. 12). Pittsburgh: Department of Anthropology, University of Pittsburgh.

Dillehay, T.D., and Meltzer, D.J., eds. (1991) The First Americans: Search and Research. Boca Raton: CRC Press.

Fleagle, J.G., and Rosenberger, A.L., eds. (1990) The Platyrrhine Fossil Record. London: Academic.

Greenberg, J., Turner, C., and Zegura, S. (1986) The settlement of the Americas: A comparison of the linguistic, dental and genetic evidence. Cur. Anthrop. 17:477–497.

Guidon, N., Pessis, A.M., Parenti, F., Fontugue, M., and Guérin, C. (1996) Nature and age of the deposits in Pedra Furada, Brazil: reply to Meltzer, Adovisio and Dillehay. Antiquity 70:408–421.

Kay, R.F., Madden, R.H., Cifelli, R.L., and Flynn, J.J., eds. (1996) Vertebrate Paleontology in the Neotropics. Washington, D.C.: Smithsonian Institution Press.

Meltzer, D.J., Adovisio, J.M., and Dillehay, T.D. (1994) On a Pleistocene human occupation at Pedra Furada, Brazil. Antiquity 68:695–714.

Roosevelt, A.C. et al. (1996) Paleoindian Cave dwellers in the Amazon: the peopling of the Americas. Science 272:373–384.

Soffer, O., and Praslov, N.D., eds. (1993) From Kostenki to Clovis: Upper Paleolithic-Paleo-Indian Adaptations. New York: Plenum.

Stanford, D.J., and Day, J.S., eds. (1992) Ice Age Hunters of the Rockies. Boulder: University of Colorado Press.

Szalay, F.S., and Delson, E. (1979) Evolutionary History of the Primates. New York: Academic.

Amino-Acid Dating

A dating technique based on the rate of protein decomposition in mineralized tissues. Amino-acid geochronometry is an independent means to date organic material of Middle-to-Late Pleistocene age. The technique depends on the post-mortem racemization (random breakdown and reassembly) of the amino acids that make up the proteins in shell and bone. Amino acids are asymmetric organic crystals that all life-forms synthesize exclusively in the L (levorotary) isomer, meaning the form that rotates polarized light to the left, rather than the right-handed D (dextrorotary) isomer. After death, however, the bonds holding the amino acids together break down under the influence of water (hydrolysis), and the liberated amino acids begin to invert spontaneously and reversibly between the L and D isomers, about a single pivotal carbon atom. By the law of averages, this leads to a gradual increase in the proportion of the D-form over time, in a process known as *racemization*. Amino acids have been found preserved in shell and bone as old as the Cretaceous (135–65 Ka), but full racemization is usually attained, with stable D/L ratios near 1.0, by the time a sample is 1.0 Myr old.

In the special case of isoleucine, two pivotal carbons are present. *Epimerization*, or inversion about the alpha-carbon, results in the formation of D-alloisoleucene, which is not the mirror image of L-isoleucine but a separate amino acid. The reversible epimerization reaction progresses to an equilibrium D/L ratio of ca. 1.3, and the ease with which the structural difference of the two compounds can be resolved makes them a favorite tool of amino-acid dating.

Rates of racemization and epimerization are both strongly influenced by water and temperature, and epimerization rates vary by source taxon as well. The uncertainty introduced by uncontrolled short-term environmental changes, even in relatively well-insulated environments, tends to make "absolute" year-ages based solely on D/L ratios unreliable. Since the trends in climate, however variable, are nonetheless parallel over a wide area, samples that have the same degree of racemization will be close in age. As an example, amino-acid dating of fossil land snails is used with considerable success in time-correlation of the loess formations of Central Europe.

Amino-acid ratios can be used for "absolute" age determinations for Pleistocene levels down to the Brunhes-Matutyama boundary (0.78 Ma), with certain materials. Local groundwater leaching has strong and unpredictable effects on the racemization rate in porous biominerals such as bone and most mollusc and eggshell, but it is not as influential in nacreous (laminated) mollusc shells and least of all in the eggshell of ratites (ostrich, emu, rhea, cassowary, moa, elephant-bird). In such materials, long-term temperature trends are the only significant external influence on racemization rates. This can be factored out by radiocarbon calibration of D/L ratios in younger shell material. From the dated ratios, a correction curve can be projected into much older levels to give age values to more highly racemized samples.

Relatively reliable dates have been achieved through analysis of eggshells dating to the later Pleistocene before the glacial

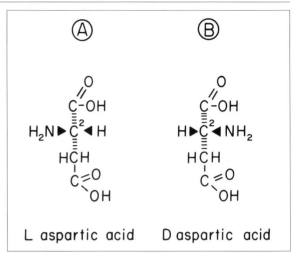

Three-dimensional representation of aspartic acid: A, L-aspartic acid; B, D-aspartic acid, resulting from detachment of the hydrogen atom on carbon 12 and its subsequent reattachment in a different position. From D. von Endt (1979), Techniques of amino acid dating. In R.L. Humphrey and D. Stanford, (eds.): Pre-Llano Cultures of the Americas: Paradoxes and Possibilities. *Courtesy of the Anthropological Society of Washington.*

maximum (ca. 35–20 Ka) by both radiocarbon and amino-acid dating. These results are then used to calibrate the ages of shells from the same or nearby sites that are up to two to three times the age of the calibration sample. The technique is particularly useful for sites in the time range between 200 and 40 Ka. The use of ostrich eggshells by prehistoric peoples for both ornamental and utilitarian functions (e.g., as water carriers) adds to the potential value of this technique in archaeological sites.

See also Geochronometry; Radiocarbon Dating; Radiometric Dating. [A.S.B., J.A.V.C.]

Further Readings

Bowen, D.Q., Hughes, S., Sykes, G.A., and Miller, G.H. (1989) Land-sea correlations in the Pleistocene based on isoleucine epimerization in non-marine molluscs. Nature 340:49–51.

Brooks, A.S., Hare, P.E., Kokis, J., Miller, G.H., Ernst, R.D., and Wendorf, F. (1990) Dating Pleistocene archaeological sites by protein diagenesis in ostrich eggshell. Science 248:60–64.

Murray-Wallace, C.V. (1993) A review of the application of the amino acid racemisation reaction to archaeological dating. Artefact (Australia) 16:19–26.

Rutter, N.W., and Blackwell, B. (1995) Amino acid racemization dating. In N.W. Rutter and N.R. Catto (eds.): Dating Methods for Quaternary Deposits, pp. 125–166. St. Johns, Newfoundland: Geol. Soc. Canada, Geotext 2.

Amud Cave

Israeli site excavated in the 1960s and the 1990s from which a large adult male Neanderthal and a neonate have been recovered in Level B. The adult Neanderthal is particularly tall (estimated stature ca. 179 cm), with a large cranial capacity (ca.

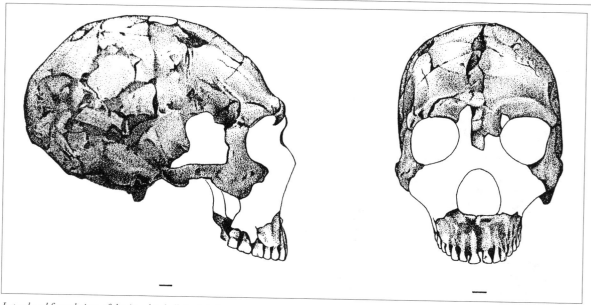

Lateral and frontal views of the Amud 1 skull. Scale is 1 cm.

1,740 ml) but relatively small teeth and a mandible with a slight chin development. Preliminary descriptions of the lithic industry indicate affinities with the Tabūn B variant of the Levantine Mousterian. Dating of this site has been plagued by intrusive pits from more recent archaeological cultures. Recent electron spin resonance assays date Amud B to 41.5 Ka.

See also Asia, Western; Mousterian; Neanderthals. [C.B.S., J.J.S.]

Amudian

Old name for a Late Paleolithic blade industry of the Levant (Israel, Syria, Lebanon), comparable with the Pre-Aurignacian. It was once dated to the end of the last interglacial (ca. 100 Ka) on stratigraphic grounds, but more recent radiometric ages have suggested dates in the range of 300–250 Ka. The Amudian was defined on the basis of Amud Level B but was better known from Tabūn and the Abri Zumoffen, where it was followed by a Jabrudian industry. Characteristic forms included blades with backing or "nibbled" retouch, burins, chamfered blades, and Levalloiso-Mousterian debitage, in contrast to the blade cores and Aurignacian-like carinate scrapers of the Pre-Aurignacian. It is now included in the Mugharan tradition.

See also Amud Cave; Jabrudian; Late Paleolithic; Middle Paleolithic; Modern Human Origins; Mugharan; Pre-Aurignacian; Stone-Tool Making; Tabūn. [A.S.B]

Anaptomorphinae

Subfamily of omomyids primarily known from North America and rarely Europe (*Teilhardina*) in the Eocene, but possibly also from the Late Paleocene of Asia (*Altanius* may be a primitive representative). Anaptomorphines, which are less diverse morphologically than the omomyines, mainly occur in the Early to Middle Eocene of North America and the Early Eocene of Europe. In general, the diagnostic combination of dental characters that may have been present in the last common ancestor of this subfamily (very likely to be the same for the family) appears to be a postprotocone fold on the upper molars coupled with a well-inflated base of the trigonid cusps on the lower molars. Anaptomorphines may be among the oldest known representatives of the family, and, based on some features of the earliest species included in this group, they may represent an earlier radiation of the tarsiiforms rather than the slightly younger diversification of the Omomyinae and Microchoerinae. It is also possible, of course, that equally ancient representatives of the omomyines simply have not been recovered as yet. Known stratigraphic precedence of a group before others does not automatically mean ancestor-descendant relationships, as some extreme practitioners of stratophenetics would imply in their work.

Anaptomorphines are classified into several tribes, but, with the exception of Teilhardinini that may represent the stem group for the subfamily, the precise relationship of the remaining tribes (Tetoniini, Trogolemurini, Anaptomorphini, and Altaniini) is difficult to contemplate on dental evidence alone.

The best-known and only undoubted teilhardinin is *Teilhardina belgica* from the Sparnacian (Early Eocene) of Europe, in many ways a good structural (if not actual) ancestor for the known Euroamerican members of the whole family. These small anaptomorphines retain the primitive euprimate dental formula of two incisors and a full complement of teeth behind them. The small incisors and sizable canines of *Teilhardina* are in sharp contrast to the earliest North American samples of *Anemorhysis* (which have been mistakenly called *Teilhardina*). *Anemorhysis, Arapahovius, Trogolemur, Tetonius,* and *Absarokius* share the enlargement (to varying degrees) of the lower central incisors to form a kind of robust spoon, along with the reduction of the relative size

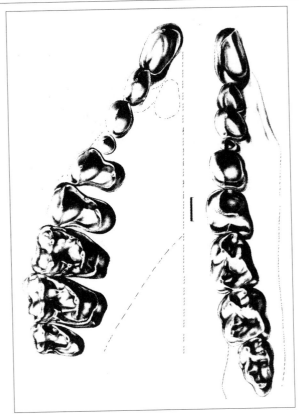

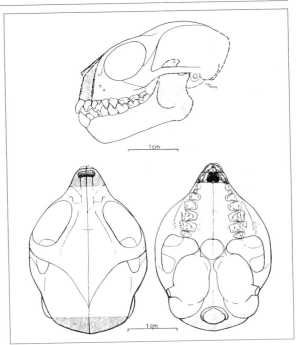

Reconstructed skull of the North American early Eocene anaptomporphine omomyid Tetonius homunculus. *Courtesy of Frederick S. Szalay, from Szalay and Delson, 1979.*

Upper and lower dentition of Tetonius homunculus. *Scale is 1 mm. Courtesy of Frederick S. Szalay, from Szalay and Delson, 1979.*

of the canines. It is this combination of characters that could diagnose the last common ancestor of the primarily Early Eocene (Wasatchian) anaptomorphines of North America vs. the European Teilhardinini.

The tribe Trogolemurini includes its type genus, the poorly known but fascinating small *Trogolemur*, recognized primarily from a deep and short lower jaw. *Trogolemur* was an animal whose estimated skull length (based on the jaw) was only ca. 2 cm. It had a relatively longer third lower molar than other anaptomorphines except *Altanius*, and it had an enormously enlarged central incisor, known, unfortunately, only from its root reaching under the molars. Gum and resins (scraped with the large incisors), nectar, and insects were the possible fare in this animal's diet. The older, possibly ancestral, *Anemorhysis* was probably primarily insectivorous, and the enlargement of incisors suggests possible exudate scraping habits. The highly wrinkled molars of the small, closely related *Arapahovius* suggest a possible specialization for nectar and gum or other resins, with insects perhaps being the bulk of the diet.

The somewhat larger *Tetonius* and *Absarokius* probably represent successful and probably speciose small radiations. Given their primitive tetoniin, but not anaptomorphin, incisor enlargement and their increasingly tall fourth premolars and relatively low and robust molars, they may have been adapted to a particular form of frugivory. This type of diet may have required an increasing reliance on crunching open hard fruits and nuts or perhaps hard seeds.

The Middle Eocene (Bridgerian) genus *Anaptomorphus* was perhaps the shortest-faced omomyid (all of which have an abbreviated muzzle) known, and it lacked the enlarged incisors of the tetoniins; this may well represent a phylogenetic reversal from a tetoniin rather than from a teilhardinin, as the canine in the known jaws is relatively small. This genus was probably composed of primarily fruit eaters, although its species undoubtedly consumed their fair share of insects as most small frugivores do.

Three poorly known genera are difficult to place within any of the recognized tribes: *Chlororhysis* from the Early Eocene of North America, the Early-to-Middle Eocene Pakistani *Kohatius*, and the Late Paleocene–Early Eocene Mongolian *Altanius*. *Kohatius*, known only by three fragmentary specimens, is barely identifiable as a small euprimate. *Altiatlasius* is also problematic—it may not be an omomyid.

As far as we can tell from the isolated but securely allocated postcranial remains of anaptomorphines (mostly foot bones and some upper arm bones), these small primates were not particularly different from such postcranially better known taxa as the omomyine *Hemiacodon* or *Shoshonius*. One important difference in the only good described skull of the anaptomorphine *Tetonius* from those of the omomyines *Shoshonius* (not a tarsiid) and *Rooneyia* lies in the construction of the region behind the ear, the petromastoid extension of the petrosal bone. In anaptomorphines and microchoerines, this part of the skull is greatly inflated; the bone is a huge latticework of small air cells. This highly evolved condition is in sharp contrast to that seen in *Shoshonius, Rooneyia,* and the living tarsiers, which have a less elaborate, and perhaps, therefore, more primitive, uninflated petromastoid section of the petrosal bone.

As there are so many genera in this subfamily, not all can be mentioned, so temporal and geographic ranges are given here.

Subfamily Anaptomorphinae
    Tribe Teilhardinini
        † *Teilhardina* (E. Eoc.; Eur.)
    Tribe Trogolemurini
        † *Trogolemur* (M. Eoc.; NA.)
        †*Anemorhysis* (including † *Tetonoides*
            and † *Uintalacus*; E. Eoc.;NA.)
        †*Arapahovius* (E. Eoc.; NA.)
    Tribe Tetoniini
        † *Tetonius* (including † *Pseudotetonius*
            and † *Mckennamorphus*; E. Eoc.; NA.)
        †*Absarokius* (including †*Aycrossia*
            and †*Strigorhysis*; E.-M. Eoc.;NA.)
    Tribe Anaptomorphini
        †*Anaptomorphus* (including † *Gazinius*; M.
        Eoc.; NA.)
    Tribe Altaniini (new)
        †*Altanius* (L. Paleo.-E. Eoc.; As.)
Subfamily Anaptomorphinae incertae sedis
        † *Tatmanius* (E. Eoc.; NA.)
        †*Steinius* (E. Eoc.; NA.)
        †*Chlororhysis* (E. Eoc.; NA.)
        †*Sphacorhysis* (E. Eoc.; NA.)
        †*Kohatius* (M. Eoc.; As.)
As. = Asia; Eur. = Europe; NA. = North America.

See also Microchoerinae; Omomyidae; Omomyinae; Shoshonius; Skull; Stratophenetics; Tarsiidae; Tarsiiformes; Teeth. [F.S.S.]

Further Readings

Bown, T.M., and Rose, K.D. (1987) Patterns of dental evolution in Early Eocene anaptomorphine primates (Omomyidae) from the Bighorn Basin, Wyoming. J. Paleontol., Suppl. 5, Mem. 23.
Szalay, F. S., and Delson, E. (1979) Evolutionary History of the Primates. New York: Academic.

Angles-sur-l'Anglin

Magdalenian III rock shelter, dated ca. 14.2 Ka, in the Vienne region of France. It has yielded bas-reliefs of bison, horse, ibex, chamois, lion, and four large human female torsos depicting the stomach, navel, and deeply incised vulvas. One of the females is carved upon the bas-relief of a bison, suggesting a symbolic relation between the two. The site remains to be fully published.

See also Late Paleolithic; Magdalenian; Paleolithic Image. [A.M.]

Further Readings

Saint-Mathurin, S. de. (1978) Les 'Vénus' pariétals et mobilières du Magdalénien d'Angles-sur-Anglin. Antiquités Nationales 10:15–22.

Ankarapithecus

A Late Miocene West Asian fossil ape, probably related to the orangutan. *Ankarapithecus* was first reported in 1957 from the site of Sinap Tepe, near the village of Yassioren, western Turkey, in beds that were later named the Sinap Formation. Recent studies have documented an age of 9.8 Ma by paleomagnetic correlation. The type specimen of *A. meteai* is a fragment of a large mandible. As it was little different morphologically from Siwalik fossil jaws, most researchers have considered the taxon as a species of *Sivapithecus*. In 1980, a partial maxilla and lower face found at Sinap Tepe was described as having the distinctive nasopalatine configuration of *Pongo*, an interpretation that was supported by the later description of a more complete face of *Sivapithecus* from Pakistan. In the mid-1990s, a third specimen was recovered from the same Turkish site, this time preserving even more of the face than the Siwalik individual. The upper face of the new Turkish individual is more conservative than that of *Sivapithecus* in presenting a relatively wider interorbital region and a better-developed brow ridge and glabella, and the orbit is less ovoid. Moreover, recent cleaning has revealed that the nasopalatine architecture of the first palate is more like that of a (conservative) gorilla than an orangutan. Overall, this suggests that *Ankarapithecus* may represent a less-derived member of the orangutan lineage than *Sivapithecus*, perhaps documenting an earlier stage in its evolution (although the known fossils are too young to be part of an actual ancestral population). Another possibility is that this taxon is (also?) related to the ancestry of *Dryopithecus*.

See also Ape; Dryopithecus; Hominidae; Ponginae; Sivapithecus; Siwaliks. [E.D.]

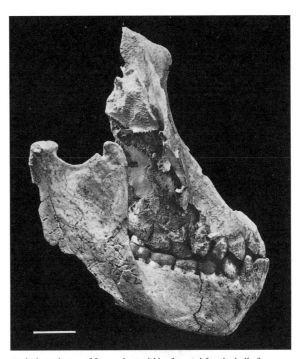

Right lateral view of face and mandible of partial female skull of Ankarapithecus meteai; *scale bar = 2 cm. Courtesy of Dr. Berna Alpagut and the Museum of Anatolian Civilization.*

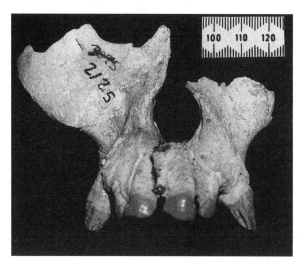

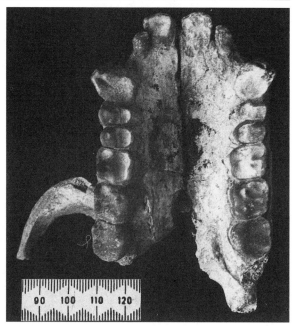

Face of male Ankarapithecus meteai *from late Miocene deposits at Sinap. Left, frontal view showing the nasal aperture and the lower outline of the right orbit and zygomatic process; right, occlusal view, showing the full dentition. Courtesy of Peter Andrews.*

Further Readings

Alpagut, B., Andrews, P., Fortelius, M., Kappelman, J., Temiszoy, I., Celebi, H., and Lindsay, W. (1996) A new specimen of *Ankarapithecus meteai* from the Sinap Formation of central Anatolia. Nature 382:349–351.

Begun, D.R., and Gülec, E. (1998) Restoration of the type and palate of *Ankarapithecus meteai:* Taxonomic and phylogenetic implications. Am. J. Phys. Anthropol. 105:279–314.

Antelian

Old term for Late Paleolithic industries of the Levant (Neuville Stages I–V), sometimes referred in part to the Aurignacian and represented at Ksar 'Akil (Wadi Antelias) in Lebanon, Jabrud Shelter III in Syria, and Mugharet el-Wad (Mount Carmel) in Israel. The industry was separated into a lower phase, with more Mousterian forms and Emireh points, and an upper phase, with Font-Yves points, nose-ended scrapers, and busked burins but fewer Mousterian types. The earlier phase is now regarded as a late development of the Mousterian, while the later phase is more commonly referred to as the Levantine Aurignacian.

See also Aurignacian; Emiran; Jabrud; Late Paleolithic; Mousterian; Stone-Tool Making; Upper Paleolithic. [A.S.B.]

Anteneanderthal

Term French workers use to identify European fossils that date from before the time that true Neanderthals appeared. The term is sometimes used distinctly from *preneanderthal,* which carries more connotations of direct ancestry. Nevertheless, many workers believe that anteneanderthals, such as the Mauer, Arago, and Atapuerca specimens, do represent probable ancestors for the Neanderthals.

See also Archaic Homo sapiens; Neanderthals. [C.B.S.]

Anthropogene

Final period and era of the Cenozoic in some usages, but not in this volume. It was formerly widely used, primarily in the former Soviet bloc, as a substitute for Quaternary when Paleogene and Neogene were substituted for Tertiary. While the term takes its meaning from the geological range of humanity, it cannot, as a standard chronostratigraphic unit, be defined on this ground. (The lack of agreement on the meaning of the term *humanity* would be another impediment.) The definition of Anthropogene, just as Quaternary, must be fixed in the chronostratigraphic hierarchy by the base of the Pleistocene epoch. In recent years, this has been established in the uppermost Olduvai Subchron, equivalent to isotope stage 64, at 1.8 Ma. Formerly, and for many years, Soviet workers placed the beginning of the Anthropogene at the level, ca. 0.9 Ma, when continental glaciation began in western Eurasia, followed by the earliest evidence of genus *Homo* in that region. The present revised base, as it happens, is approximately coincident with the earliest well-known *Homo erectus* in East Africa.

See also Homo; Pleistocene; Quaternary. [J.A.V.C.]

Further Readings

Nikiforova, I. (1996) N/Q boundary in the western C.S.S.R. In J.A. Van Couvering (ed.): The Pleistocene Boundary and the Beginning of the Quaternary. Cambridge: Cambridge University Press.

Anthropoidea

Higher primates, including platyrrhine (also called ateloid or previously ceboid) monkeys of the New World, and the catarrhine monkeys, apes, and humans of the Old World. Previously ranked taxonomically as a suborder of primates, they are here placed at the next lowest rank, hyporder, to retain subordinal rank for Haplorhini (including Anthropoidea and Tarsiiformes) and Strepsirhini. Anthropoids are the most successful surviors of the three major extant lineages of primates originating long ago in the Early Tertiary. The once-flourishing tarsiiform group is now represented by a single tiny genus, *Tarsius,* in the remote evolutionary outpost of the Philippines and Indonesia, and the remaining lemurloris strepsirhines of Madagascar, mainland Africa, and the Indian subcontinent are far less diverse than the anthropoids, taxonomically and adaptively. How the larger-bodied members of the strepsirhines and anthropoids would have compared during the Pleistocene, however, is another matter: We are only beginning to learn how many and what kinds suffered extinction as human populations expanded into their habitats in all areas of the world.

Geographical Background

The success of the anthropoids has been influenced by geography in a number of ways. Their history unfolded in two distinct theaters, in South America and in Afro-Eurasia—one large in area and the other relatively restricted. The occupation of four continents across two hemispheres makes their total areal distribution large. As a consequence, there have been many and varied opportunities for differentiation within and between regions, even to the extent of abandoning the tropical and subtropical habitats fundamental to the evolution of the order. Episodic mountain building, eustatic changes in sea level, continental collisions, and climatic gra-

dations have all contributed to the complex development and composition of the Old World faunas, which span an enormous part of the globe. For the platyrrhines, in contrast, continental quarantine has been a predominant long-term macroevolutionary factor, with but a few notable caveats.

The geographical separation of platyrrhines and catarrhines is a fundamental feature of the primate radiation, one about which we know little due to lack of fossils. It has been in effect ever since their common ancestral stock, wherever it lived, split into two or more lineages. The timing of this separation is important, for after the original ateloids became established in South America the oceans blocked or strongly filtered all primate migrations into or out of the continent until the Panamanian isthmus arose ca. 3 Ma. Thus, platyrrhines were permanently insulated from competition with nonplatyrrhine primates, at least for 27 Myr and perhaps for as long as 40 Myr. The complexion and balance of the current platyrrhine fauna may, therefore, reflect a homogeneity achieved over many epochs. One of the pressing questions is whether the living forms are samples of the first and only platyrrhine radiation or of a successor to an earlier division that was replaced. Some fossil evidence suggests that a significant degree of taxonomic and morphological stasis occurred among the ateloids, and this may reflect a general macroevolutionary pattern related to continental insularity.

The Old World situation presents a contrasting geography. There continents were less isolated from one another. Faunal turnovers were probably more common, as Africa, Europe, and Asia shifted their respective positions and points of contact, mixing their occupants. Their paleodistribution maps of extinct genera cross today's continental

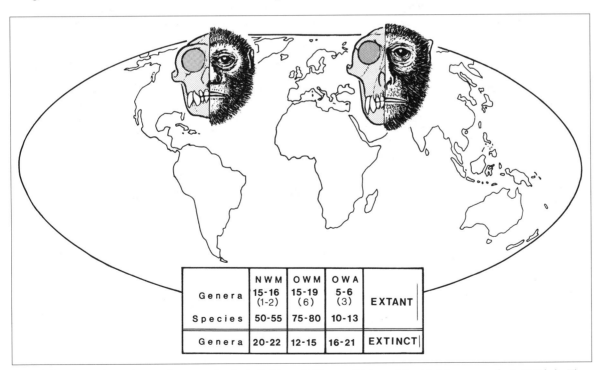

Genera	NWM 15-16 (1-2)	OWM 15-19 (6)	OWA 5-6 (3)	EXTANT
Species	50-55	75-80	10-13	
Genera	20-22	12-15	16-21	EXTINCT

Faces of platyrrhine and catarrhine monkeys, suggesting the similarities and differences of their cranial and facial structures, after A. H. Schultz, The Life of Primates. *Universe Books, 1969. The table shows the number of recognized genera and species of extinct and extant primates: the ranges reflect differences of opinion among researchers as to how many taxa should be accepted as distinct genera; the numbers in parentheses below extant genera indicate how many such genera have significant fossil records. (Abbreviations: NWM, New World monkey; OWM, Old World monkey; OWA, Old World ape, including humans.)*

boundaries for certain times during the Cenozoic, and the interruption of species ranges would have fostered speciation, differentiation, secondary contacts, competitive interactions, and replacement. Such conditions may have set an evolutionary premium on change rather than stasis and upon adaptive improvement, or novelties. The fossil evidence suggests that there have been a number of successive catarrhine radiations, each with its own character. Apes, for example, are now at their nadir, having been displaced by quite a different type of primate, the cercopithecoid monkeys, which are fairly new on the scene.

The summation of these continental effects produced an anthropoid radiation of tremendous variety and success. One might even speculate that some of the evolutionary parallelisms between platyrrhines and hominoids have resulted indirectly from their geographical separation—had they occurred together, competition would surely have driven them further apart anatomically and perhaps have pressured some forms into extinction. Geography, however, hardly explains the success of Anthropoidea or its real nature. Special adaptations set anthropoids apart from the other members of their order, and that foundation created the potential to exploit a broad spectrum of ecological niches, unsurpassed by any other group of primates during their 65-Myr history.

Morphology and Adaptation

The skull, more than any other part of the skeleton, embodies novel anthropoid characteristics. In the simplest terms, the outward appearance of the anthropoid head is human-like in aspect, having a relatively flat "face" with a vertical arrangement of eyes, nose, and mouth. Superficial structures, such as the external ears, lips, and nose, also tend to re-semble us in shape and proportion. If there is a singular feature that sets humans apart typologically from the universal design of the anthropoid head, it is our recently evolved, bloated forehead, although the little squirrel monkeys might even rival us there.

The major adaptive elements of this anatomical ensemble are the special senses of sight and smell, the cognitive functions of the brain, and the design of the masticatory apparatus. The anthropoid braincase is large and rounded, accommodating as much volume as possible within a small space. As a consequence, the foramen magnum is situated rather anteriorly within the skull base, which also makes head carriage more erect. The relatively small, close-set eye sockets face directly forward, maximizing stereoscopic vision. With the lower face tucked in beneath the eyes, facial bones tend to be short and deep, although snout length has increased secondarily in such forms as baboons and howler monkeys. The olfactory components, such as the size of the nasal cavity, the paper-thin scrolls inside it, and the endocranial space for the olfactory bulb, are all reduced, reflecting a diminished sense of smell. The mandible is fused solidly at the symphysis, and, like the premaxillary bone above, it supports and stabilizes a battery of broad, vertical incisors. The lower jaw is also hinged well above the tooth rows, giving the chewing muscles good leverage. The midline metopic suture between the frontal bones also fuses early in life. The premolars and the molars vary in shape, but they tend to be blunt rather than penetratingly sharp. The petrosal bone covering the middle-ear region has a tendency to develop many small cells and/or partitions within it, contrasting with the balloon-like capsule found commonly among nonanthropoids.

By comparison with strepsirhines, olfactory cues are less important to an anthropoid than are visual ones. Apart from having a small main olfactory bulb, the secondary olfactory

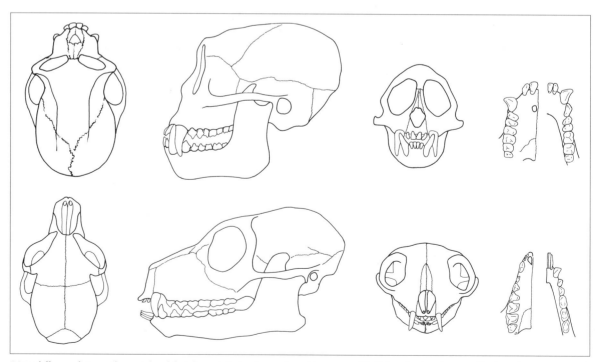

Main differences between the cranial and dental morphologies of an anthropoid, represented by Cebus *(top), and a generalized euprimate, represented by* Lemur *(bottom). After Rosenberger, 1986; courtesy of Alfred L. Rosenberger.*

bulb and its receptor element, the Organ of Jacobson, are also reduced. Whereas the former structure is an all-purpose mediator of scent, the latter is important in sexual contexts. Its reduction indicates that anthropoids have shifted to a more direct, "personal" system of intersexual and social communication, involving more elaborate bodily coloration and adornment, facial gestures, postural signals, vocalizations, and close-up, interactive displays. Although scent-producing glands still play a role in communication, especially among the platyrrhines, sensory input from the environment comes chiefly via the eyes and ears. As J. Eisenberg points out, like other mammals (such as felid carnivores) which have come to capitalize upon sight, both the eye and the brain have evolved specializations that make this possible. The feature most obvious to us is the enlargement in brain size.

This reliance upon vision is predicated on a critical adaptive shift achieved by the nearest relatives of the anthropoids, an earlier-evolving group that passed on its traits to the latter's ancestral species. That shift was the adoption of a diurnal lifestyle by the ancestral haplorhines, members of an umbrella taxonomic group whose existence we are able to recognize through two surviving descendant lineages: anthropoids and tarsiers. From the early haplorhines, anthropoids inherited structural preadaptations to enhance stereoscopic vision via a reorganized skull, a rod-and-cone system of photoreceptor cells in the eye attuned to good color vision, a dense packing of cells near the retinal fovea making the eye adept at pinpoint focusing, a complex network of crossover optical fibers within the brain that send nerve impulses to both sides for simultaneous processing, and enlarged visual centers of the brain.

This pattern may have been of great selective value to ancestral anthropoids not because of any particular advantages but because of its generality. A visually precise image of the environment is one filled with the discriminants of size, shape, pattern, texture, color, and distance. Nothing could better serve an animal in the highly complex fabric of an arboreal environment. Sight is far richer in information than

sound or taste. It also requires a complex system of memory storage, which in turn implies more storage space and higher cognitive functions to encode and decode the data. Thus, the world of the anthropoid is a complex world of learning and subtleties, where the hue of a fruit reveals its ripeness, the texture of a branch suggests flexibility, and the glint of an eye may spell trouble from a neighbor.

Anthropoids are the only mammals to have evolved a separate bony compartment housing the eyeball. This appeared with the development of the postorbital septum, a thin sheet of bone that forms the eye socket from behind, thereby also bridging the lateral bones of the face and the braincase. The origin of this adaptation, however, may have nothing to do with good eyesight. While it may safeguard the delicate eyeball from injury or shield it from the masticatory actions of muscles lying behind it, these may be only secondary benefits. The structure of this area of the skull suggests that the septum serves also as a mechanical brace to reinforce the connection between the face and the skull. This role is an elaboration of the original function of the postorbital bar, the ancestral structure from which the septum evolved.

The postorbital bar is a vertical branch of the zygomatic arch, a horizontal girder that supports chewing muscles under the cheek, spanning from the skull to the base of the mandible. It appeared first among the ancestral euprimates, ancestors of all the modern primates. There the bar served to stabilize the zygomatic arch and the tooth row against the pull of the masseter muscle and to minimize the shearing and twisting effects of chewing at the junction between braincase and face. As anthropoids tear and grab at food with their large incisors or chew tough foods with the cheek teeth, they are prone to generate relatively high levels of stress in the zygomatic arch and at the craniofacial junction. These loads may be acute in an anthropoid primate because the mandibular symphyseal joint is fused rather than mobile, as it is in most nonanthropoids. Hence, the symphysis does not convert into motion the muscular forces delivered, say, from the right side of the head as the animal chews on its left. Such

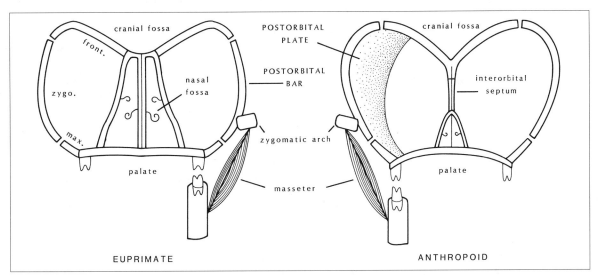

Mechanical model of the anthropoid postorbital plate (right), contrasted with the euprimate postorbital bar (left). The postorbital plate reinforces the connection between the facial and neurocranial parts of the skull in the absence of an enlarged nasal fossa and interorbital region, well developed in lower primates. Courtesy of Alfred L. Rosenberger.

internal stress is also difficult to balance or distribute within the head because of the shape of the anthropoid face. With their close-set eyes and reduced snouts, there is less centralized bony mass to take up the forces of mastication. This is where the septum provides additional support. It compensates by acting as a lateral pillar. In this position, the postorbital plate can also directly resist the tension of the powerful masseter muscle. Thus, one of the important innovations of the anthropoid head is associated with feeding. Whether its origin related to a new dietary preference or a revised mechanical approach to an existing feeding pattern is unclear. But since anthropoids also have a conspicuously enlarged set of incisor teeth, an obvious source for much of the mechanical stress the head is designed to endure, it is likely that the main dietary staple was originally fruit, perhaps species with resistant husks that had to be torn apart to access the nutritionally valuable content.

Among the other adaptations that make anthropoids unique, those pertaining to life-history strategies are probably the most important. As relatively large primates, anthropoids tend to have long gestation periods, lengthened phases of juvenile and adolescent dependency, and a long postreproductive life. Thus, intelligence, learning, socialization, and many other factors are major features of the anthropoid life cycle. The production of an offspring with a relatively large brain at birth is also possibly related to a novel prenatal development. The outer fetal membranes are attached to the wall of the uterus in an intimate way, so that fetal capillaries and maternal blood vessels exchange nutrients, immunogens, and waste materials very effectively. This hemochorial placenta is similar to the condition found in tarsiers. The anthropoid uterus is also an unusual bell-shaped chamber designed to accommodate one large fetus, whereas in other primates it tends to be Y-shaped, having a central cavity and two horns where multiple fetuses can attach.

Origins and Evolution: Hypotheses of Ancestry

Although primatologists now are confident that the characteristics shared by the anthropoids indicate that they are monophyletically related, this issue at times has been a matter of serious doubt and discussion. Even until the 1970s, some maintained that platyrrhines and catarrhines arose independently, meaning that the anthropoid "grade," or stage of evolution, was attained separately as each branch evolved from different lower primate ancestors. Geography figured importantly in this theory; the separation of the platyrrhines and the catarrhines does imply a complex history. In fact, the anthropoids were frequently cited as a model case illustrating the principle of parallelism. Such a theory was comfortable to nineteenth-century zoologists especially, who, influenced by the *scala naturae* doctrine and Victorian ideals of social progress, sought to epitomize adaptive improvement as the major driving force of the evolutionary machine. Then and thereafter, prominent researchers claimed that the transition to a higher-primate grade was a common phenomenon. Some reckoned it happened as many as four times, once among the platyrrhines, twice among the catarrhines, and once more among the Malagasy primates.

The puzzle of anthropoid origins has been a major focus of research for more than a century. During the 1990s, a wealth of new fossils from Africa and Asia, combined with new investigations of previously known forms, has sharpened interest in this question. Comparative morphological study of modern primates has revealed that anthropoids are most closely related to the tarsiers, with which they share derived features of vision (loss of tapetum lucidum, presence of retinal fovea, and at least partial postorbital closure), olfaction (reduction of various receptors and presence of dry circumnasal area with mobile upper lip), and placentation.

Unfortunately, most of these haplorhine characteristics are not discernable in fossils. Moreover, the great majority of primate fossil remains are dental, and the tarsier dentition is quite distinctive, not at all like that of anthropoids. Thus, the quest for understanding the origin and early evolution of anthropoids has been divided between studies of modern morphology and the search for extinct (or extant) groups that might be closely related to anthropoid ancestors. Three such groups have been widely advocated: the adapids and omomyids (both extinct) and the tarsiids, including the living tarsier and a few fossil allies. In the 1990s, the discovery of new, apparently unique fossils has led to a fourth hypothesis, that some of these extinct forms represented a nonadapid/nonomomyid ancestral stock for anthropoids. We will evaluate each of these views and then look more closely at some of the fossils that have been proposed as the earliest anthropoids, finishing with a survey of biogeographic models for anthropoid dispersal.

The adapid-anthropoid hypothesis is based largely on jointly shared features of the anterior dentition and mandible. This notion was first proposed in the nineteenth century, but P.D. Gingerich has given it new force. For example, he argued that both adapids and anthropoids have fused mandibular symphyses, vertical spatulate incisors, and interlocking and sexually dimorphic canines with canine/premolar honing. However, by restudying the anatomy and introducing functional reasoning to assess possible linking homologies, it has been shown that this entire suite of adapid-anthropoid similarities resulted from convergent evolution. A second prominent objection is that these adapids were possibly already strepsirhines phylogenetically rather than a formative euprimate stock ancestral to all of the modern groups. In their dentition, skull, and postcranial skeleton, adapids frequently display derived characteristics that align them with modern strepsirhines.

Above and beyond these difficulties, one specific subgroup of adapids that is becoming better represented as fossils, the Cercamoniinae (also termed Protoadapinae or Protoadapini by some researchers), has often been singled out as dentally most similar to early anthropoids. Newly discovered genera (and new fossils of known taxa) may include *Rencunius* and *Hoanghonius* from China (45–40 Ma), *Aframonius* from the Egyptian Fayum (Quarry L–41, ca. 36 Ma), and possibly *Djebelemur* from Morocco (ca. 45 Ma). Although these forms have been suggested by some authors as similar to the early anthropoid oligopithecids in their lower molars (usually with adjacent entoconid and hypoconulid) and canine-anterior pre-

Age (Ma)	Epoch	Afro-Arabian LOCALITIES and Primate Fossils [taxa in brackets are continued from the line above]	Asian & other LOCALITIES and Primate Fossils (A=Asia; E=Europe; S=South America)
26	OLIGOCENE	LOTHIDOK *Kamoyapithecus* (earliest Hominoidea)	
27			SALLA (S) *Branisella Szalatavus*
28			
29			
30			
31			
32		MALEMBE ?Propliopithecidae	
33			BOULDNOR & NEUSTADT (E) last *Adapis*
34		F JQ-4 *Propliopithecus Apidium Parapithecus Afrotarsius*	====GRANDE COUPURE=====
		A JQ-3 *Propliopithecus Apidium* ?*Parapithecus* [*Qatrania*]	TAQAH (A) "*Moeripithecus*" *Oligopithecus*
35	Late	Y JQ-2 *Oligopithecus Qatrania* ?omomyine	[*Shizarodon Omanodon*]
	Eocene	U JQ-1 *Catopithecus Qatrania Proteopithecus Serapia*	
36		M [*Arsinoea Plesiopithecus Wadilemur Aframonius Anchomomys*]	
37		NEMENTCHA (BIR EL ATER) *Biretia*	
38	Middle		
39			WAI LEK (A) *Wailekia Siamopithecus*
40	EOCENE		PONDAUNG (A) *Amphipithecus Pondaungia*
41			
42		GLIB ZEGDOU *Algeripithecus Tabelia*	
43			GONGLANGTOU (A) *Asiomomys*
44			
45		CHAMBI *Djebelemur*	HETI (A) *Eosimias Hoanghonius Rencunius*
46			SHANGHUANG (A) *Eosimias Tarsius* [*Adapoides Macrotarsius*]
47			LUSHI (A) *Lushius*
48			
49			
50			KULDANA Fm. (A) *Kohatius Panobius*
51	Early		
52			
53			
54	Eocene		SPARNACIAN (E) first Adapidae & Omomyidae
			WUTU (A) *Carpocristes Chronolestes*
55	PALEOCENE		BUMBIN NURU (A) *Altanius*
56		ADRAR MGORN 1 *Altiatlasius*	
57			
58			NANXIONG (A) *Petrolemur*
59			
60			WANGHUTUN Fm. (A) *Decoredon*
61			
62			

Stratigraphic and geographic occurrence of the earliest anthropoids and other primates which have figured in discussions of anthropoid (and primate) origins. All Afro-Arabian and Asian Paleogene primates are included, as these continents have been claimed by different authors as central to the origin and early evolution of anthropoids. In addition, the first New World anthropoids and selected European primates discussed in the text are indicated. The locations of many sites are shown on the map following. Note that when there is not enough space to list all of the taxa present at a given site, the list is continued on the line below, within square brackets [ ]. Note also that although the Arabian Peninsula formed part of Afro-Arabia into the Early Miocene, the Omani locality of Taqah is included in the Asia column for reasons of space.

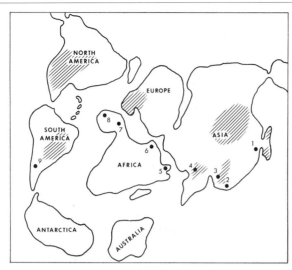

Reconstruction of the world's continents during the later Eocene. (After D.E. Savage and D.E. Russell, 1983, Mammalian Paleofaunas of the World, *Addison-Wesley.) Parallel lines indicate areas with significant fossil mammal assemblages. Numbers indicate major later Eocene and Oligocene sites on the southern continents yielding fossil primates discussed in the text: (1) Shanghuang (China); (2) Wai Lek (Thailand); (3) Pondaung (Burma); (4) Kohat (Pakistan); (5) Thaytiniti and Taqah (Oman); (6) Fayum (Egypt); (7) Chambi (Tunisia) and Nementcha (Algeria); (8) Adrar Mgorn and Glib Zegdou (Algeria); (9) Salla (Bolivia). By L. Meeker.*

molar complex (when known), they are still adapids in detail and thus probably not relevant to anthropoid origins.

Arguing that fossils are not highly informative here, M. Cartmill and coworkers have reasoned that the tarsier is the most likely sister group of anthropoids. While a still broader version of this hypothesis—that extinct relatives of the tarsiers are likely candidates—is supported by many, it seems unlikely that tarsiers themselves would be closer cladistically to anthropoids than their less-radical tarsiiform relatives. The tarsier lineage per se has always been too advanced anatomically to be the model of an anthropoid stock. The anatomies of the middle ear, postorbital septum, carotid arteries, and reproductive systems of tarsiers and anthropoids share important derived structural details, but these point to a more abstract taxonomic connection, via a group less bizarre adaptively than the tarsier. The unique particulars that could potentially link tarsiers more closely with anthropoids are probably parallelisms. For example, the postorbital wall of tarsiers most likely arose in relation to their fantastically large eyeballs, which is not the case in anthropoids, who have relatively small eyes. Hence, they are not uniquely derived features of phylogenetic value.

A third hypothesis (considered the most plausible by a majority of current researchers) is that anthropoids arose during the Eocene from a subgroup of omomyid primates that was widely distributed across North America and Eurasia. Omomyids are generally accepted as being closely related to tarsiers (together they are called tarsiiforms), and omomyids are well represented in the fossil record by many species, but the collections consist mostly of teeth and jaws. *Ourayia uintensis,* a form from the Late Eocene of Utah, is classified as an omomyid tarsiiform, but its dental anatomy

may be a good model for the protoanthropoid pattern, as E.L. Simons and others have pointed out. Unfortunately, it is still known only from dental elements. Given that the modern anthropoid head is so full of higher-primate novelties, the skulls of such protoanthropoids would be more telling. The known skulls of omomyids do, at least, indicate a significant morphological heterogeneity, including patterns that are much more primitive than the expected, tarsierlike departures. New evidence also demonstrates that some omomyids, known informally as necrolemurs, were close relatives of living tarsiers, as early workers had thought, and were also distributed broadly in Laurasia. This makes it all the more likely that another omomyid stock, ancestral to both the platyrrhines and the catarrhines, was widespread and sufficiently primitive to have evolved into the first anthropoids.

Recently, as a result of the discovery of new primate fossils (such as *Eosimias, Algeripithecus,* and others) from China and Northwest Africa, a fourth model has been suggested. Although the details vary among advocates, the underlying concept is that some of these new forms represent a previously unknown group of Eocene protoanthropoids, neither adapid nor omomyid. This "third major radiation" concept implies a more ancient origin for the anthropoids and requires further evaluation of the new fossils. However, it presents some significant difficulties. For example, it has yet to be clearly established that any number of the fossils motivating this hypothesis are definitely anthropoid rather than tarsiiform. One of the fossils in question, *Eosimias,* shows an extraordinary series of derived resemblances to tarsiers, and it is more likely to turn out to be a basal tarsioid instead of an ancestral anthropoid. If these fossils are indeed tarsiiforms, this concept simply restates the omomyid-anthropoid hypothesis in slightly different terms.

Origins and Evolution: Fossil Evidence

Four groups or classes of fossils are important in the attempt to understand the origin and early evolution of the anthropoids: (1) the earliest generally accepted anthropoids—the Parapithecidae and Propliopithecidae, mainly from the Early Oligocene Fayum deposits of Egypt (the first platyrrhines are too fragmentary to be of much help and, moreover, are later in time); (2) the Oligopithecidae, especially *Catopithecus* and *Oligopithecus,* two earlier Fayum fossils that researchers have argued are true anthropoids; (3) a variety of (mostly) newly discovered Eocene fossils from North Africa and eastern Asia; and (4) known Eocene tarsiiforms (omomyids) that may represent a "basal stock" for anthropoids.

Propliopithecus presents a suite of generalized anthropoid features, such as fusion of the mandibular symphysis and the frontal bones in the midline, full postorbital closure, spatulate, nearly vertical incisors, strongly expressed canine dimorphism, and lower molars with relatively flat crowns (trigonid and talonid of even height). Within Anthropoidea, the propliopithecids are clearly catarrhines, with such diagnostic dental features as loss of P_2, well-developed distal midline hypoconulids on lower molars, and general molar structure. But these derived states are combined with conservative anthropoid (platyrrhine-like) conditions, such as a ringlike ectotympanic (external ear opening) and several postcranial features.

The better-known parapithecids (*Parapithecus* and *Apidium*, especially) share the same typical anthropoid conditions as the propliopithecids. These are combined, however, with states more conservative than in catarrhines, such as a somewhat smaller hypoconulid and the retention of P_2, along with uniquely derived dental conditions (central cusp on upper premolars, tendency to extra cusps on molars, loss of lower incisors in some forms) and several postcranial states more "primitive" than those found in either platyrrhines or catarrhines. On that basis, parapithecids are now placed by most authors as the sister-taxon of all later anthropoids, thus among the most ancient *and* conservative members of the hyporder. It is with the parapithecids that other fossil groups putatively considered anthropoids must be compared.

From latest Eocene horizons in the Fayum come two genera that have also been placed within the Anthropoidea by many, but not all, researchers. *Catopithecus* is known from several partial skulls and lower jaws that present a remarkable mosaic of ancestral and derived character states. The frontal bone is solidly fused, and the orbit appears to show full closure, as expected in an anthropoid. Moreover, the upper incisors seem to be at least somewhat spatulate. But the mandibular symphysis appears to be unfused, and the molars are not anthropoidlike: The lowers have relatively high and long trigonids and a generally elongate shape more commonly found in lower primates; the upper molars also are less squared-up than in most anthropoids, with a small and low hypocone; premolars also do not look like those of anthropoids. *Catopithecus* shares some aspects of P_4 and molar shape (proximity of hypoconulid and entoconid, hypocone development) and lack of P_2 with *Oligopithecus*, which also has a P_3 with a large surface for honing, or sharpening, the upper canine, as do many catarrhines. Some authors place these forms close to propliopithecids (two premolars, with honing on the front one), while others think the conservative molars place them evolutionarily "below" the three-premolared parapithecids. Either molar shape or (more likely) premolar pattern must thus have evolved at least twice, in catarrhines and in some early anthropoids. Here the oligopithecids are considered less derived than the parapithecids, but still early anthropoids.

Proteopithecus, a contemporary of *Catopithecus*, was thought to be closely related but has since been distanced, as it preserves three premolars; it might provide a link of sorts between oligopithecids and less-derived parapithecids (see below). However, its molar morphology is exceedingly primitive, resembling tarsiiforms and other early euprimates, and it is likely not an anthropoid. *Catopithecus* and *Oligopithecus* may be late-surviving members of a true protoanthropoid stock, but they are too late in time as now known to be actual ancestors of later anthropoids. They suggest that the complex of features that is thought to characterize anthropoids did not all appear at one time, but in stages, as is often the case in evolution.

About a dozen genera of less well known fossil primates have been touted in the 1990s as protoanthropoids. *Algeri-*

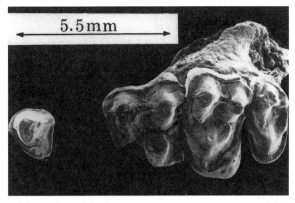

Occlusal view of P_4-M2 of Proteopithecus sylviae *from Fayum Quarry L-41. Courtesy of Elwyn L. Simons.*

pithecus and *Tabelia* are small forms whose isolated teeth have low rounded cusps like those of the parapithecid anthropoid *Apidium* and the omomyid *Microchoerus*; both of the former were discovered at the Middle Eocene site of Glib Zegdou (Algeria). Although originally suggested as close to propliopithecids, they now both appear to be provisionally referable to the Parapithecidae, as is *Biretia* from Bir el Ater (Algeria). The 42–36 Ma age of these forms significantly increases the time range of parapithecids, known in the Fayum from ca. 35–33 Ma. Slightly older (46–45 Ma?) are a lower jaw named *Djebelemur* and several isolated teeth perhaps representing other species from Chambi (Morocco). Some of these may be cercamoniine or similar adapiforms while the one upper molar is similar to *Algeripithecus* but even smaller. Two genera from the Early Oligocene of Oman (*Shizarodon* and *Omanodon*) were originally and probably correctly described as adapiforms, but they have also been mentioned as possible anthropoids, for which there is little evidence. The most ancient North African primate is *Altiatlasius*, from the Late Paleocene (ca. 58–55 Ma) of Adrar Mgorn 1 (Algeria). About a dozen isolated teeth of this genus reveal a conservative morphology: The hypocone is lacking on the upper molars although a cingulum extends entirely around the lingual edge, and the lower molar trigonid is large and, especially, tall compared to the talonid; however, the cusps are bunodont, as in the previous taxa. *Altiatlasius* is surely not an anthropoid, or probably even a protoanthropoid, and is best considered a euprimate of uncertain affinity. Nonetheless, it has some similarities to oligopithecids, which (*if* derived homologies) may indicate a source for that group.

In eastern Asia, the Late Eocene (ca. 40–39 Ma) Pondaung fauna of Burma yielded two primates early in the twentieth century, *Pondaungia* and *Amphipithecus*. Both were poorly known until the 1980s, when a few additional jaws were recovered. Each has been called an adapiform or an early anthropoid, but most authors accept the former designation for both. Of similar age in China are *Hoanghonius* and *Rencunius*, both noted above as probable cercamoniine adapiforms. The contemporaneous *Wailekia* from Thailand, although described as a possible oligopithecid, probably belongs with the same group. The most intriguing new Asian primate is *Eosimias*, known from two Middle Eocene localities in China, one the same age as *Hoanghonius*, the other slightly older (ca. 46–45 Ma). Most of the other Asian forms are moderately large, but *Eosimias* is tiny, comparable to *Algeripithecus*, and slightly larger than *Catopithecus*. The incisors and the canine of *Eosimias* are relatively vertical and broadly similar to those of some early anthropoids.

This condition and a selection of cheek-tooth features has led to some researchers suggesting that *Eosimias* is a basal anthropoid, representing an ancient protoanthropoid ancestry separate from both adapiforms and omomyids (see above). In some ways, this is analogous to the suggestion that perhaps *Altiatlasius* and especially the early ?parapithecids represented an equivalent stock in North Africa. But the morphology of these two putative protoanthropoid groups differs strongly, so only one (at most) could be reflective of actual anthropoid ancestry. In fact, the cheek teeth of *Eosimias* (especially the very tall trigonids and the strongly developed trigonid crests), and the tarsiiformlike postcrania known from the same site and assigned to this genus, suggest that it is better understood as an omomyid relative. Its exact placement is unclear within that complex, but, stripping away the tarsierlike features, *Eosimias* confirms a broadly omomyid-based ancestry for anthropoids by proving the existence of ancestral anthropoid features within this group (at least in the Asian Eocene). While waiting for additional fossil evidence of these Eocene protoanthropoids, the next question to examine is paleogeographic: How did early anthropoids disperse across the Paleogene world?

Origins and Evolution: Geography

Today, of course, the two main anthropoid groups, Platyrrhini and Catarrhini, occur in the geographically disjunct regions of the neotropics and the Old World, respectively. Platyrrhines have apparently always been restricted to the New World, while the earliest definite anthropoids are now seen to be (northern) African—only one possible tooth is known from an Oligocene site in Angola. There are, thus, two separate but related questions to ponder: How and when did the protoanthropoids reach Africa, and how did the protoplatyrrhines reach South America? Both were island continents in the Paleogene, with mainly distinctive faunas.

When the principles of plate tectonics and continental drift were first applied to primates during the mid-1960s, it was briefly argued that the ancestral stock of platyrrhines and catarrhines occupied a single great southern landmass that later rifted apart (as the South Atlantic Ocean grew), expanded to the north, and finally divided into South America and Africa during the early Cretaceous (ca. 130–110 Ma). Formative platyrrhines were thus passively separated from catarrhine forerunners, without crossing an oceanic water gap. This model led to the idea that the parapithecid primates of the Fayum Oligocene were direct platyrrhine ancestors, a notion that has been generally rejected on anatomic grounds. The dating of this event and the paleopositions of continents would also require, if this hypothesis were true, that anthropoid primates were in existence more than 30 Myr before the very first primates are documented in the fossil record.

In the face of counterevidence, modifications to this theory have been proposed. One postulates that tectonic mechanisms produced a system of east-west oceanic ridges or islands within the Atlantic. Nearly all of these are now submerged, but they could have been footholds for primates dispersing across the ocean. This stepping-stone hypothesis was also popular a century before continental drift was an established fact. Combined with floating on rafts of natural vegetation between islands, this idea is prominent in most late-twentieth-century views of platyrrhine origins. One series of problems relating to any oceanic raft-crossing refers to the dangers of exposure, lack of fresh water and food—*Microcebus*-like hibernation is unlikely in an early anthropoid. Moreover, neither the Fayum parapithecids nor, as some have suggested, the propliopithecids are morphologically reasonable as ancestors for platyrrhines. However, if the parapithecids indeed represent an archaic anthropoid group that now extends back to the Middle Eocene, it is conceivable that an as yet unknown (North)West African relative might have been a plausible Eocene protoplatyrrhine. A global recession of sea level, such as the one that occurred in the Late Eocene, might have narrowed the Atlantic gap sufficiently to permit a crossing.

A different idea proposes that an ancestral stock of omomyid-derived protoanthropoids occupied an assembly of northern continents, Laurasia, where Early Cenozoic primates were flourishing; contact between the Eastern and the Western hemispheres was possible at intervals across the Bering region. Spurred by a cooling of the Northern Hemisphere and the expansion of grasslands, most northern primates became extinct but some shifted their range to the south, possibly in both the Eastern and the Western hemispheres. Among these may have been the rare protoanthropoids, who found their way across the water barriers to reach the island continents of Africa and (later) South America during different regression episodes of low water. Passage into South America seems to have been the more remarkable one, for it may have involved few other mammals. The hystricomorph rodents, relatives of the modern porcupines, may have been the primates' only traveling companions. In fact, it is their geographic association that led such researchers as R.I. Hoffstetter to propose an African origin for platyrrhines in the first place: Both hystricomorphs and platyrrhines may have their closest living relatives in Africa.

Some would argue that possible East Asian (*Eosimias*) and North African (*Djebelemur, Algeripithecus*) protoanthropoids are of comparable Middle Eocene age, unless *Altiatlasius* is, indeed, related to this group. In the past, models of Asian ancestry for Fayum anthropoids depended upon interpretations of *Pondaungia* and *Amphipithecus*, but the proposed Early Eocene pathway around the southern margin of an Asia that had not yet collided with India is still plausible. If that collision occurred in the early to mid-Eocene, migration could even have proceeded across the contact zone at some point. What is most important to realize is that without acceptable morphological relatives (sister-taxa) in place, no paleozoogeographical hypothesis is worth formulating: It would be nothing but speculation, no matter how good the pathway.

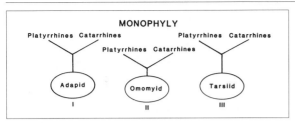

Three hypotheses of the ancestral stock from which anthropoids arose monophyletically. Courtesy of Alfred L. Rosenberger.

Macroevolutionary Patterns in Catarrhines and Platyrrhines

To comprehend and compare the evolutionary histories of the major divisions of the anthropoids, we will need many more fossils documenting changes in the taxonomic diversity, adaptations, and geographical distributions of the platyrrhines and the catarrhines. For the crucial Paleogene phase in the Old World, we have only the evidence from the Egyptian Fayum (36–33 Ma); and from La Salla, Bolivia (27 Ma), we have data at the Paleogene-Neogene boundary only, which means we know a bit about Africa and next to nothing about South America. Information on later epochs is even more biased in favor of the Old World. Therefore, reconstructions and comparisons must draw heavily upon the living forms for at least one side of the story. Nonetheless, as a start, E. Delson and A.L. Rosenberger began to examine the macroevolutionary histories of platyrrhines and catarrhines, concluding that each group experienced distinctly different patterns.

Among the catarrhines, both the fossil record and the extant forms indicate a dichotomization of adaptive zones into relatively nonoverlapping arboreal and terrestrial spheres. This is paralleled by an expansion out of the classical humid tropics into more xeric and even colder climates of the Old World. Terrestriality is also associated with the attainment of large body size in many catarrhines. Second, the terrestrial zone seems to be of recent vintage. The earliest catarrhines, ancestors of both the monkeys and the apes, all appear to be arboreally adapted. The ancestral Old World monkey stock shifted to a terrestrial habit, as indicated by their many ground-related postcranial adaptations, and this probably explains a large part of their geographic success. Among the apes, terrestriality seems to be superimposed upon an indelible arboreal heritage. Third, the morphology of the cercopithecoid radiation is fascinatingly simple; there is little variety other than in size and size-related features. The apes, on the other hand, are fairly diverse anatomically, given that they include a small number of taxa.

The New World monkeys present a contrasting picture. Abundant grasslands appeared in South America during the Cenozoic, but platyrrhines probably never evolved an open-country, terrestrial lineage. If they did, we seem to have no descendants of that group among the modern species. There is still no good explanation for the apparent absence of a terrestrial lineage, for these ancient savannahs supported large populations of herbivores, as in Africa and Asia where cercopithecoids eventually flourished. Perhaps the larger catarrhines were more formidable competitors vis-à-vis other

mammals than the platyrrhines; or maybe the grassland floras were quite different in the Old and the New worlds.

Rather than invade such an ecological terrain, platyrrhines flourished among the trees by finely dividing their microhabitats. This is what makes for their great intergeneric diversity, each genus evolving distinctive adaptations to permit coexistence with its close, sympatric relatives. A second factor contributing to their relative diversity is that platyrrhines radiated at the small end of the anthropoid body-size spectrum. This enabled some of them to utilize three feeding niches rarely (if at all) exploited by the larger catarrhines. One is the hard-fruit/seed-eating niche, occupied by a whole subfamily, the pitheciines. The second is the insectivore-frugivore (or animalivore-frugivore) niche, from which catarrhines are excluded due to their larger body size. A third, related paradigm is the gum-eating niche, central to the adaptations of the smallest marmosets.

Altogether unclear is what happened at the opposite end of the size spectrum, but hints are mounting that our notion of platyrrhine diversity and uniqueness will continue to change. New fossil discoveries in the Brazilian Late Pleistocene led C. Cartelle and W.C. Hartwig to determine that monkeys existed about twice as large as the biggest ones alive today. Does this foretell of other adaptive responses to arboreality? Or does it pave the way for realizing a terrestrial option, with baboon-sized platyrrhines milling about as giant ground sloths browsed? Another contrast between the radiations of platyrrhines and catarrhines is their temporal patterning. Lineage stasis has been a more common occurrence among platyrrhines than among catarrhines.

To properly evaluate this hypothesis, we need good biostratigraphic information over geological time, which is severely lacking, especially for the platyrrhines. In looking at the moderns and the fossils, however, it appears that generic lineages have a much longer duration in the New World. Among all of the Old World catarrhines, the macaques and orangs show the greatest geologic longevity. Specimens attributed to *Macaca* are known from deposits of 8–6 Ma, but there are few, if any, derived characters to clinch the identification. Congeners of *Pongo* go back only as far as the Pleistocene, but the craniofacial morphology that marks it as a generic entity is well developed in late *Sivapithecus* at 9 Ma, and these are preceded by dento-gnathic remains of probable congeners older than 12 Ma. In the Old World, these examples are the only two cases of anagenetic/taxonomic stasis from a fossil record that is strikingly rich by comparison with the South American data.

Among the modern New World monkeys, *Saimiri* is phylogenetically linked through a Colombian species classified either in the same genus or as *Neosaimiri,* at 14–12 Ma, to *Dolichocebus,* at ca. 21–19 Ma. The recently discovered *Chilecebus,* which may, in fact, be the same as *Dolichocebus,* is dated at 20 Ma and adds new evidence of a *Saimiri*-related stock. Equivalent in age to *Neosaimiri* is *Aotus dindensis,* the first recognized example of a living primate genus to occur deep in the fossil record. *Aotus* is also closely related to, if not a descendant of, the fossil genus *Tremacebus,* 21–19 Ma. *Alouatta* is probably a descendant, and at least a sister genus, of *Stirtonia,* at 14–12 Ma. In fact, it is difficult to distinguish the latter two at the generic level. Other fossils, such as *Soriacebus ameghinorum,* 18–16 Ma, and *Laventiana annectens, Cebupithecia sarmientoi,* and *Mohanamico hershkovitzi,* 14–12 Ma, indicate that major higher taxa such as subfamilies and tribes of platyrrhines also had remote origins.

See also Adapidae; Altiatlasius; Americas; Asia, Eastern and Southern; Atelidae; Branisellinae; Catarrhini; Cebidae; Cercopithecidae; Diet; Eosimiidae; Haplorhini; Hominoidea; Oligopithecidae; Omomyidae; Paleobiogeography; Parapithecidae; Pitheciinae; Plate Tectonics; Platyrrhini; Propliopithecidae; Skull; Tarsiiformes; Tarsioidea; Teeth. [A.L.R., E.D.]

Further Readings

Beard, K.C., Tong, Y., Dawson, M.R., Wang, J., and Huang, X. (1996) Earliest complete dentition of an anthropoid primate from the late Middle Eocene of Shanxi Province, China. Science 272:82–85.

Cartelle, C., and Hartwig, W.C. (1996) A new extinct primate among the Pleistocene megafauna of Bahia, Brazil. Proc. Nat. Acad. Sci. USA 93:6405–6409.

Clark, W.E. Le Gros (1959) The Antecedents of Man. Edinburgh: Edinburgh University Press.

Delson, E., and Rosenberger, A.L. (1984) Are there any anthropoid primate "living fossils"? In N. Eldredge and S. Stanley (eds.): Living Fossils. New York: Springer-Verlag, pp. 50–61.

Eisenberg, J. (1984) The Mammalian Radiations. Chicago: University of Chicago Press.

Fleagle, J.G., and Kay, R.F., eds. (1995) Anthropoid Origins. New York: Plenum.

Hoffstetter, R.I. (1981) Origin and deployment of New World monkeys emphasizing the southern continents route. In R.L. Ciochon and A.B. Chiarelli (eds.): Evolutionary Biology of the New World Monkeys and Continental Drift. New York: Plenum, pp. 103–122.

Rosenberger, A.L. (1986) Platyrrhines, catarrhines, and the anthropoid transition. In B.A. Wood, L. Martin, and P. Andrews (eds.): Major Topics in Human and Primate Evolution. Cambridge: Cambridge University Press, pp. 66–88.

Rosenberger, A.L., and Szalay, F.S. (1980) On the tarsiiform origins of Anthropoidea. In R.L. Ciochon and A.B. Chiarelli (eds.): Evolutionary Biology of the New World Monkeys and Continental Drift. New York: Plenum, pp. 139–157.

Ross, C. (1996) Adaptive explanation for the origins of the Anthropoidea (Primates). Am. J. Primatol. 40:205–230.

Simons, E.L., and Rasmussen, D.T. (1994) A whole new world of ancestors: Eocene anthropoideans from Africa. Evol. Anthropol. 3:111–148.

Szalay, F.S., and Delson, E. (1979) Evolutionary History of the Primates. New York: Academic.

Anthropology

Academic discipline concerned with the study of aspects of human (and other primate) culture and biology, past and present. The subject matter of anthropology ranges widely; to make the breadth of information and the diversity of approaches employed more manageable, the field is often divided into four subdisciplines: physical (or biological) anthropology, archaeology, cultural anthropology, and linguistics.

Physical anthropologists study the origins and evolution of primates (including humans), behavior of living primates, and human biology, which itself includes adaptation, variation, and genetics. Archaeologists study past human groups, focusing on the material evidence of behavior and adaptation, including both historical reconstructions of the past and processual studies of the mechanisms of change. Cultural anthropologists study all aspects of the community life of living human groups, encompassing social structure, political and economic relations, kinship and family life, religion and ideology, and even art and aesthetics. Anthropological linguists study human language and communication.

Taken together, these diverse fields make up an academic discipline with strong alliances to many other natural and social sciences, as well as to the humanities and the arts. In many ways, anthropology is the great integrative discipline.

See also Archaeology; Complex Societies; Cultural Anthropology; Culture; Paleoanthropology; Physical Anthropology; Primate Societies. [B.B.]

Further Readings

Harris, M. (1996) Culture, People, Nature: An Introduction to General Anthropology, 6th ed. New York: Harper and Row.

Anyathian

Paleolithic industry recognized in the 1930s from terraces of the Irrawaddy River (Burma). This industry consists of chopper-chopping tools manufactured from fossil wood, silicified tuff, quartzite, and quartz. Based on the stratigraphy of the terraces, the Anyathian was subdivided into Early and Late phases. The actual age of these artifacts can only be guessed at, since most of them (especially the Early Anyathian) are abraded and occur in secondary contexts. It also seems likely that at least some of these "tools" are the result of natural fracturing.

See also Asia, Eastern and Southern; Chopper-Chopping Tools. [G.G.P.]

Apatemyidae

A family of rare early Cenozoic mammals related to insectivorans, not primates as once thought, which occurs in both Europe and North America. In North America, its range is from the Paleocene well into the Oligocene, whereas in Europe they span the Eocene. These mammals are quite similar in some of their convergently attained adaptations to both the lemuriform primate *Daubentonia* (the aye-aye) and the phalangeriform marsupials *Dactylopsila* and *Dactylonax.* The robustness of the skull is related to the hypertrophied, rodentlike incisors, and new evidence from European Middle Eocene specimens (from Messel) show third and fourth hand-ray elongation, somewhat similar to the elongated third finger in *Daubentonia*. All of the evidence suggests an insect, grub-hunting, and possibly tree-gnawing, adaptive complex for apatemyids, one of the most striking of mammalian convergences of unrelated fossil mammals to living forms that themselves are convergent in their highly derived lifestyles. Paleocene dental evidence of apatemyids suggests their derivation from insectivorans that were quite unlike archaic primates. [F.S.S.]

Ape

Grade of primates most closely related to humans. It consists of the African apes—the two species of chimpanzee and one of gorilla—and the Asian apes—the orangutan and ten species of gibbon. Together with humans, these make up the superfamily Hominoidea, which can be distinguished from other primates by a number of characters.

As is true of all grades, there are no clear defining characters of the apes. They can be described as having relatively large brains (and, generally, bodies) and no tails, to distinguish them from the monkeys, but all of these are hominoid distinguishing marks shared also with humans, and the same goes for all of the other characters that are described for the Hominoidea. In fact, apes do not form a "natural" evolutionary group apart from humans: African apes and people are closely linked, with the orangutan the nearest relative of that unit, and the gibbons the sister of all larger apes, including humans.

There is an important historical element in the ways in which apes are referred to in scientific and popular literature. The apes are often seen as human "cousins," a group of closely related but distinct species. There is often an implication that humans are completely different from the brutish apes, and many attempts have been made to push back our evolutionary divergence from the apes into the remote past. None of this can be sustained, for, in evolutionary terms, there is no such thing as a group of nonhuman apes that is descended from a common ancestor not also ancestral to humans; in other words, the apes do not constitute a monophyletic group. It is, thus, an artificial, although still useful, group: artificial because it has no evolutionary meaning, but useful because it is a convenient term encompassing all nonhuman hominoids. It can be further subdivided into the lesser apes—the gibbons, or Hylobatidae—and the great apes—the orangutan of Asia and the gorilla and chimpanzees of Africa—which together with humans make up the Hominidae, the other family of extant Hominoidea.

Gibbons

Six to ten species of gibbon are included in a single genus, *Hylobates*. This is divided into three distinct groups, usually recognized by separate subgenera. The concolor group lives in Vietnam and Laos, the siamang group inhabits Malaysia and Sumatra, and the gibbons proper cover much of Southeast Asia. They are arboreal, highly active animals and are common wherever primary rain forest still exists. Their method of locomotion is varied, including four-footed hanging, bipedal walking (on large branches), and bimanual swinging from below branches. The last of these behaviors is *brachiation*, and the gibbon version of brachiation is unique in the animal kingdom.

The gibbons have a monogamous family system, which is unusual in primates. The sexes have equal roles in defending territory, and one of the results of the sharing of roles by males and females is the lack of size distinction (sexual dimorphism) between them (body weights range from 5 to 12 kg for all of the species; there is little difference between the sexes). They have also developed a complex system of vocalization that is related both to their social structure and to their environment: In the three-dimensional tree canopies of the forests, where visibility is poor but sound carries long distances, their wide range of vocalizations serves an important role in social interactions.

Orangutan

The orangutan, *Pongo pygmaeus*, is the only species of great ape in Asia. It is much larger than the gibbons, and its similarity in size to the African great apes has led in the past to all being included in the group called Pongidae. Most of the similarities, however, are due only to size, and the orangutan (along with its extinct relatives) is now put into its own hominid subfamily, the Ponginae. The orangutan is today confined to the rain forests of Sumatra and Borneo, where two distinct subspecies live, one to each island. It is arboreal, despite its large size (ranges of body weight are from 35 kg in females to 80 kg in males), and locomotion in the trees is by slow, cautious, four-handed climbing. Orangutans eat mainly fruit, often from high in the tree canopy. They are solitary animals or live in small groups centered on females, with male ranges overlapping those of females, and this has led to the marked sexual dimorphism so different from gibbons. Orangutans differ from gibbons also in being silent animals, with a low repertoire of calls.

Chimpanzees

Two species of chimpanzee are recognized, although the level of difference between them is in some ways less than that between the two subspecies of orangutan. As with the orangutan, the two types of chimpanzee have allopatric distributions, the pygmy chimpanzee (*Pan paniscus*) living south of the Zaire River and west of the Lualaba River, and the common chimpanzee (*Pan troglodytes*) spanning West and Central Africa and into East Africa in a broad belt north of the Zaire. Three subspecies are recognized, and recent molecular genetic studies have suggested that the westernmost variety may be especially distinct.

The pygmy chimpanzee, or bonobo, lives in swamp forests and is more arboreal than its slightly bigger relative. The common chimpanzee lives in a variety of habitats, spending much of its time on the ground, especially in more open or savannah habitats. Body weights are ca. 33 kg for female and 45 kg for male bonobos, while common chimpanzee mean weights range from slightly *less* than that to 45 and 60 kg, respectively. All are fruit eating, and all move about on the ground in a unique form of quadrupedal locomotion called knuckle-walking (shared only with gorillas). In this, the weight of the body is taken on the middle parts of the extended fingers, thus lengthening the already elongated

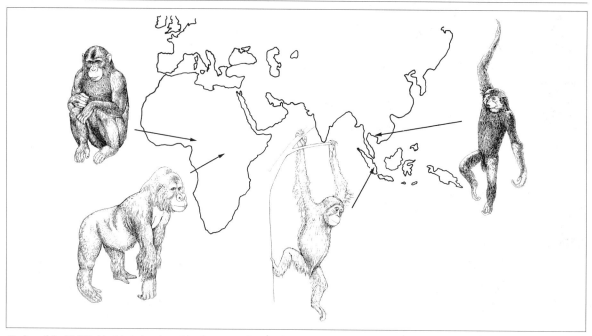

*Outline of the Old World with the location of the chimpanzee (*Pan troglodytes, *male, top left) and gorilla (*Gorilla gorilla, *male, bottom left) in Africa, the orangutan (*Pongo pygmaeus, *female, bottom) in Borneo and Sumatra, and the gibbons in Southeast Asia (*Hylobates hoolock, *male, right). Drawings not to scale; arrows point only to general regions of habitat.*

forearms. Social structure is complex, with large multimale groups occupying a large home range, but social structure can be varied according to need, and this fission-fusion fluidity is an important part of chimpanzee adaptation.

Gorilla

This is the largest of the great apes. Together with the chimpanzees and humans, it is grouped in the subfamily Homininae, but the exact relationships within this grouping are far from clear. The gorillas are also divided into three races or subspecies: a western form, an eastern form, and a rare subspecies found only on the mountains separating East from Central Africa. In all of these diverse regions, the gorilla is almost entirely terrestrial. It is restricted to forest habitats not so much because of the presence of trees as because these are the places where the lush ground vegetation on which gorillas depend grows. Its method of locomotion is knuckle-walking, identical to that of the chimpanzees, and, like chimps, it sleeps in "nests" built of loosely woven leaves and branches. Gorillas differ from chimpanzees in being much larger and more sexually dimorphic (mean body weights range from 70–100 kg for females to 160–180 kg for males, with almost no overlap between the sexes). Their greater terrestriality and their dependence on vegetable food as opposed to fruit are both related to this larger size. Gorillas live in multimale groups, as do the chimpanzees, but the groups are smaller and are age-graded. The oldest (and biggest) male is the dominant animal in the group, and, in all three subspecies, it develops a saddle of white hair on its back, so that this leading male is commonly known as a silverback.

See also Diet; Grade; Hominidae; Homininae; Hominoidea; Hylobatidae; Locomotion; Monkey; Monophyly; Ponginae;

Primate Ecology; Primate Societies; Scala Naturae; Sexual Dimorphism. [P.A.]

Further Readings

Chivers, D.J., Wood, B.A., and Bilsborough, A. (1984) Food Acquisition and Processing in Primates. New York: Plenum.

Fleagle, J.G. (1998) Primate Adaptation and Evolution. Second Edition San Diego: Academic Press.

Schwartz, J.H., ed. (1988) Orangutan Biology. Oxford: Oxford University Press.

Wrangham, R.W., McGrew, W.C., de Waal, F.B.B., and Heltne, P.G., eds. (1994) Chimpanzee Cultures. Cambridge, Mass.: Harvard University Press.

Apidima

Locality in the southern tip of the Mani peninsula, southern Peloponnese, Greece, yielding human fossils and artifacts. The site consists of four karstic caves eroded out of the Mesozoic limestone sea cliff face and containing fossiliferous brecciated deposits. Cave A has yielded two fossil hominin crania, Apidima I and II, which are thought to be possibly of Middle Pleistocene age, mainly on the basis of geomorphological considerations. Apidima II appears to be a relatively early member of the Neanderthal clade, perhaps a late "archaic *Homo sapiens*" in the sense of this Encyclopedia; it is a fairly well-preserved cranium with damage to the base, occiput, and dentition. Apidima I remains unprepared. A relatively complete early anatomically modern human skeleton has also been recovered from Cave B at the site. The lithic assemblages include Middle and Upper Paleolithic artifacts. The faunal remains are thought to represent a Late Pleistocene faunal assemblage,

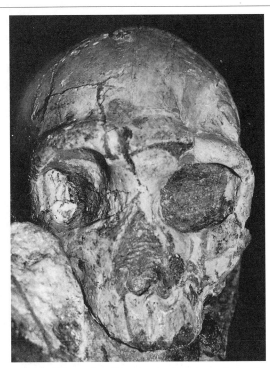

Frontal view of the Apidima II cranium (cast), resting on the breccia block from which it was removed.

perhaps indicating alternating forested and steppe-like paleoenvironments.

See also Archaic Homo sapiens; Europe; Middle Paleolithic; Neanderthals; Upper Paleolithic. (K.H.)

Further Readings

Harvati, K. and Delson, E. (1999) Conference report: Paleoanthropology of the Mani Peninsula (Greece). Journal of Human Evolution 36:343–348.

Apollo-11

Rockshelter site in the Orange River Valley of Namibia near the South African border. Excavated by W.E. Wendt from 1969 to 1972, the site is characterized by a long series of Middle Stone Age (Mode 3, 4) and Later Stone Age (Mode 5) industries, spanning the Late Pleistocene and the Holocene, ca. 130–6 Ka, and dated by both radiocarbon and amino-acid racemization. Industries include Middle Stone Age horizons based on both flake and blade technologies, possibly beginning as early as the last interglacial, ca. 130 Ka, and incorporating at least one layer of Howieson's Poort materials in association with pigments and incised ostrich-eggshell fragments. The uppermost Middle Stone Age horizon represents perhaps 20 Kyr of accumulation, dated by radiocarbon between 46.4 and 25.5 Ka, and incorporates at the top the oldest dated images in Africa: fragments of painted slabs with animal representations in red outline. Unlike many sites in interior southern Africa, the shelter was more or less continuously occupied or reoccupied between 20 and 6 Ka, and it preserves a long series, first, of nonmi-

crolithic Later Stone Age industries with ostrich-eggshell beads and then, by 10.4 Ka, of microlithic Wilton horizons.

See also Howieson's Poort; Klasies River Mouth; Later Stone Age; Middle Stone Age; Modern Human Origins; Paleolithic Image; Stone-Tool Making; Wilton. [A.S.B.]

Further Readings

Wendt, E. (1976) "Art mobilier" from Apollo 11 Cave, South West Africa: Africa's oldest dated works of art. S. Afr. Archeo. Bul. 31:5–11.

Arago

Cave near Tautavel in the French Pyrenees excavated since 1964. Deep Pleistocene sediments contain faunal remains, Early Paleolithic artifacts, and fossil hominids. The archaeological levels at Arago include Tayacian assemblages overlain by Acheulean assemblages. The Tayacian assemblage features large and small pebble-choppers and many small retouched tools, primarily simple scrapers, notches, Tayac points, denticulates, and becs (stubby perforators). Most tools are made of locally available materials, primarily quartz with small amounts of flint and quartzite. The Acheulean assemblage found in the uppermost levels, above the hominid fossils, is made mostly of schist. Oval and amygdaloid Acheulean handaxes are accompanied by flakes struck with the Levallois technique. The original dating of the main hominid finds was Rissian (late Middle Pleistocene), but this dating has been revised, and faunal and absolute dating methods are now claimed to place them as Mindelian (ca. 450 Ka). The relevant small-mammal faunas and certain other absolute

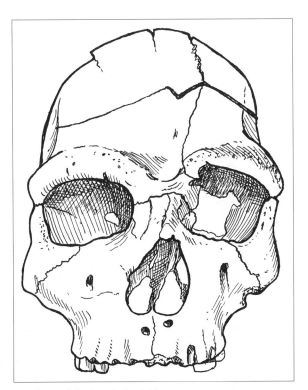

Facial view of the Arago 21 hominid.

dates, however, point to a somewhat younger age. The first significant hominid remains from Arago were two mandibles, Arago 2 and 13. Both are robust and chinless, but they contrast strongly in overall size and dental dimensions. This difference is probably a reflection of sexual dimorphism, with the smaller Arago 2 mandible deriving from a female. This mandible also appears more Neanderthal-like in the forward positioning of the dentition. The most complete Arago fossil hominid is the partial skull represented by a face and frontal bone (Arago 21) and a right parietal (Arago 47), which probably derive from the same individual. Fragmentary postcranial bones have also been discovered, including a robust innominate bone (Arago 44). The classification of the Arago hominids has been a source of some dispute. The main describers of the material favor assignment to *Homo erectus,* while others regard them as fossils of "archaic *Homo sapiens.*"

See also Archaic Homo sapiens; Early Paleolithic; Europe; Tayacian. [J.J.S., C.B.S.]

Arambourg, Camille (1885–1969)

French paleontologist. Born in Algeria, Arambourg conducted the first geological and paleontological survey of the Omo region (Ethiopia) in 1933. Some 34 years later, in 1967, Arambourg led a French contingent that joined efforts with groups from the United States (led by F.C. Howell) and from Kenya (directed by L.S.B. Leakey) to inaugurate modern work in the region. This combined effort resulted in the discovery of the remains of several hundred fossil hominids, recovered between 1967 and 1974. The major focus of Arambourg's work, however, was the prehistory of North Africa. During the 1950s he and R.I. Hoffstetter discovered, in a late Middle Pleistocene deposit at Ternifine (now known as Tighenif) near Oran (Algeria), the remains of a hominid that he later dubbed *Atlanthropus mauritanicus.* He was also responsible for describing the mandibular fragments found by P. Biberson at Sidi Abderrahman (Morocco) in 1954.

See also Africa, East; Biberson, Pierre; Sidi Abderrahman; Tighenif; Turkana Basin. [F.S.]

Archaeolemuridae

Recently extinct family of Indriiformes. The subfossil remains of archaeolemurids are known from marsh and cave deposits in southern, southwestern, central, northwestern, and northern Madagascar. Around the turn of the twentieth century, the archaeolemurids gave rise to the idea that "monkeylike" primates once existed in Madagascar, but there is no basis for this conclusion—although the expanded upper incisors of *Archaeolemur* may suggest that no superior labial tract was present and, thus, that these primates may not have retained the primitive "wet nose" characteristic of the highly olfactory surviving Malagasy lemurs.

Two genera are attributed to Archaeolemuridae: *Archaeolemur* and *Hadropithecus.* At least two species of *Archaeolemur* are known: the relatively robust *A. edwardsi* from the center of the island and the more gracile *A. majori* from

the south and southwest. Whether the new specimens of *Archaeolemur* described in the 1980s and 1990s from the northwest and the far north of Madagascar represent one or two additional species must await further study. A single species of *Hadropithecus, H. stenognathus,* has been described from sites in both the center and the south and southwest of Madagascar.

In size, the archaeolemurines are intermediate between the living indriids and the extinct palaeopropithecids, estimated body weights in all three species falling between ca. 15 and 25 kg. *Archaeolemur* is the less specialized of the two archaeolemurid genera, retaining a general conformation of the skull that is close to the indriid condition, although of much heavier build due to greater size. Alone among the large-bodied extinct lemurs, the archaeolemurids retain the primitive lemuriform inflated auditory bulla and the positioning of the eardrum at the outside of the skull. *A. edwardsi* is slightly larger and considerably more robust than is *A. majori* and characteristically shows a well-developed sagittal crest and heavy nuchal ridging. In both species, the mandible is robust, and the symphysis is fused and quite upright, in contrast to the oblique, unfused symphysis of the indriids.

The most striking skull specializations shown by *Archaeolemur* lie in the dentition. The premolars are compressed laterally to form a continuous longitudinal, scissor-like, shearing blade, and the molars are small and squared-off, with a cusp at each corner. The front and rear cusp pairs are joined transversely by continuous crests, known as lophs, producing a "bilophodont" condition otherwise seen in primates only among Old World monkeys. The central upper incisor is much enlarged, while the lower front teeth are relatively short and, in contrast to those of other lemuriforms, are not fully procumbent. The premolar blade represents an adaptation unmatched among extant primates, but the ensemble of dental characters suggests a diet preponderantly of fruit. All archaeolemurids retain a third premolar in each quadrant of the jaw that has been lost in the indriids and palaeopropithecids.

In its postcranial skeleton, *Archaeolemur* shows a set of adaptations very different from those of the families just mentioned. This lemur appears to have been a short-legged and powerfully built quadruped, with amazingly short extremities (the foot of *Archaeolemur* is shorter than that of its relative *Indri,* an animal only one-third its size) that suggest a substantial commitment to ground-dwelling.

Hadropithecus is yet more specialized in its dentition than *Archaeolemur.* Its front teeth are greatly reduced, and the lower ones are completely upright. The molars, in contrast, are hugely expanded, with high, rounded enamel folds, and the last premolar is enlarged and incorporated into this grinding row, although the two anterior premolars are reduced and still show some vestiges of an *Archaeolemur*-like shearing edge. The grinding battery of cheek teeth rapidly wore flat to produce a surface of alternating shearing edges of enamel and shallow basins of dentine. The skull of *Hadropithecus* is modified to accommodate this powerful and unusual dentition; it is extremely short-faced and heavily built to absorb great masticatory stresses, and it bears strong mus-

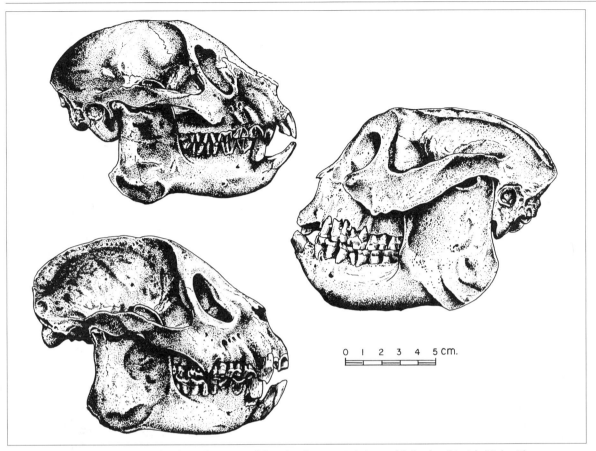

Crania, in lateral view, of the three archaeolemurid species. Top left: Archaeolemur majori; *bottom left:* A. edwardsi; *right:* Hadropithecus stenognathus.

cle markings, notably sagittal cresting. The postcranial skeleton of *Hadropithecus* is poorly known, but bones thought to belong to *H. stenognathus* are generally similar to those of *Archaeolemur* except in being more lightly built.

The contrasts between *Archaeolemur* and *Hadropithecus* have been likened to those between the close relatives *Papio*, the common baboon (a relatively adaptable denizen of both tree savannahs and more forested environments), and *Theropithecus*, the gelada. Like *Hadropithecus*, the latter displays reduction of the anterior dentition and enlargement and elaboration of a rapidly wearing posterior grinding battery, and—for a baboon—is short-faced. In contrast to *Papio*, essentially a woodland dweller, *Theropithecus* is adapted to an open, treeless habitat. Its sustenance comes entirely from terrestrial sources and consists largely of small, tough, and often gritty objects, such as the seeds, rhizomes, and blades of grasses, small bulbs, and arthropods. These objects are gathered by hand, obviating the necessity of cropping with the front teeth. In view of the detailed suite of dental similarities between the two, we may conclude that *Hadropithecus* was adapted to an ecological role similar to the gelada's: that of an open-country "manual grazer."

The postcranial adaptations of the archaeolemurids have proved to be the key to understanding how this family is related to the other indrioids (i.e., the indriids and the palaeopropithecids). The palaeopropithecids show a spectrum of suspensory adaptation culminating in the extraordinarily specialized sloth-like hanger *Palaeopropithecus*. However, the smaller, less apomorphic members of the family remain remarkably indriidlike in their skulls and dentitions; and all paleopropithecids and indriids, in contrast to the archaeolemurids, show the derived loss of one premolar in all dental quadrants. It appears that a craniodentally conservative and postcranially generalized indriiform ancestor with three premolar teeth gave rise, on the one hand, to the three-premolared terrestrial archaeolemurids and, on the other, to a two-premolared but still postcranially generalized lineage. The latter then split to produce the leaping (but still quite suspensory) indriids and the hanging palaeopropithecids. Archaeolemuridae, therefore, appears to be the sister of a single clade consisting of Indriidae plus Palaeopropithecidae. The question of how this should affect the classification of these taxa has yet to be formally addressed; when it is, it seems most likely that the superfamily Indrioidea will be seen to contain two families. Archaeolemuridae will contain the two genera that form the subjects of this entry, while the family Indriidae will contain the two subfamilies Indriinae and Palaeopropithecinae (each containing more genera than Archaeolemuridae).

The reconstruction of the archaolemurids as forms with a predominantly terrestrial specialization raises the question of the environment in which these lemurs lived. Until the 1980s, the feeling was that, on the advent of humans some 1,500 years ago, Madagascar was more or less completely forested. Scholars now realize that this was probably not the case. Madagascar has been as affected as any tropical area by the climatic oscillations that marked the Pleistocene epoch. Grasslands may have been a perennial feature of the Malagasy landscape, even if their extent fluctuated considerably; and if so, it is hardly surprising that the indrioids produced a branch adapted to such environments (with *Archaeolemur* perhaps having been a denizen of forest-edge environments, while *Hadropithecus* flourished in more completely open habitats). Further, if humans arrived while Madagascar was undergoing an unusually arid climatic regime, a high level of environmental stress may well explain why the large-bodied subfossil lemurs succumbed so rapidly to the impact of human activities, whether direct (hunting) or indirect (habitat destruction).

Family Archaeolemuridae
    †*Archaeolemur*
    †*Hadropithecus*

See also Indrioidea; Lemuriformes; Palaeopropithecidae; Teeth. [I.T.]

Further Readings

Mittermeier, R.A., Tattersall, I., Konstant, W.R., Meyers, D.M., and Mast, R.B. (1994) Lemurs of Madagascar (Tropical Field Guide No. 1). Washington, D.C.: Conservation International.

Tattersall, I. (1982) The Primates of Madagascar. New York: Columbia University Press.

Archaeological Sites

Places that contain evidence of past human activiy. This evidence consists of archaeological *inventories*—portable items like stone and bone tools or bones of animals hunted and eaten—and *features*—permanent objects like hearths, storage pits, burials, and dwellings.

Paleolithic sites vary in size from a handful of stone tools scattered over 1–2 m² to huge villages that cover areas of more than 10,000 m² and contain rich inventories and numerous features. The vast majority of the studied Pleistocene sites are found on land, although research indicates that some sites are today submerged under lakes and seas that expanded after the Late Pleistocene deglaciation. Archaeological sites contain information on an almost endless number of variables, including their location, the nature of the inventories and features they contain, and the geographic and geological context in which archaeological materials are found. Archaeologists use these variables to classify sites. Since their research questions involve only a few variables—those that provide the most suitable data—the resulting site classifications are not all-inclusive, nor are they valid when other variables are considered. The following are some of the more common ways of classifying Paleolithic sites.

Classification of Sites

CLASSIFICATION BY ARCHAEOLOGICAL CONTENTS

The oldest classificatory scheme used in archaeology, one that gave rise to the term *Paleolithic,* or *Old Stone Age,* grouped sites according to the archaeological materials found in them. We still use this classification: for example, Pleistocene sites containing predominantly simple choppers and unmodified flakes are Oldowan; those with bifacially worked handaxes and cleavers are Acheulean; those containing tools made on flakes are Middle Paleolithic; those with a predominance of blade tools are Late Paleolithic. This way of grouping sites emphasizes the chronological relationship among stone-working technologies and is used when questions about the relative chronology of a site are being asked.

CLASSIFICATION BY CONTEXT

The geological context in which prehistoric features and inventories are found is often used for site classification as well. This variable separates *surface finds,* or *scatters*—which consist of stone tools and sometimes faunal remains found lying uncovered on present-day surfaces—from *stratified* ones found buried in geologic strata devoid of human-made items. *Stratified layers* or *sites* can consist of either *single levels,* which resulted from discrete occupational episodes in the past, or *multiple layers* superimposed on one another and separated by sterile geologic deposits. The latter came about because the same location was repeatedly used by prehistoric people.

CLASSIFICATION BY CONDITION OF CULTURAL REMAINS

The condition in which features and inventories are discovered offers another way for classifying Paleolithic sites. If archaeological materials have remained where, and as, prehistoric groups left them, the sites are considered to be in *primary context* and are termed *in situ.* Often, however, post-depositional processes have severely affected the archaeological remains, redepositing them downslope, destroying some of them through erosion or weathering, and so on. Archaeological remains found in such a disturbed context are said to be in a *secondary, disturbed,* or *redeposited* state.

CLASSIFICATION BY SITE LOCATION

Another common way of classifying sites is by their geographic context or location. This scheme produces such types as *cave* and *rockshelter* (or *abri*) sites. The former usually refers to cases where cultural materials are found deep inside caverns; the latter two synonyms refer to materials found under rock overhangs. Human occupations that took place without the protection of such natural shelters are called *open-air* sites. Since most human settlements took place in well-defined geographic locations, these are sometimes used to define site types as well. In this scheme, archaeological remains found near present or past lakeshores are termed *lacustrine* sites, those near rivers or streams *fluviatile,* or *river valley,* sites, and so on.

CLASSIFICATION BY DURATION OF OCCUPATION

In some cases, especially when dealing with prehistoric settlement systems, the length of time a site was occupied is used for classificatory purposes. This parameter separates *seasonal camps* or *occupations* from *sedentary* ones occupied year-round. Sites that show evidence for brief occupation, a few hours at most, by a single person or a small number of individuals, are

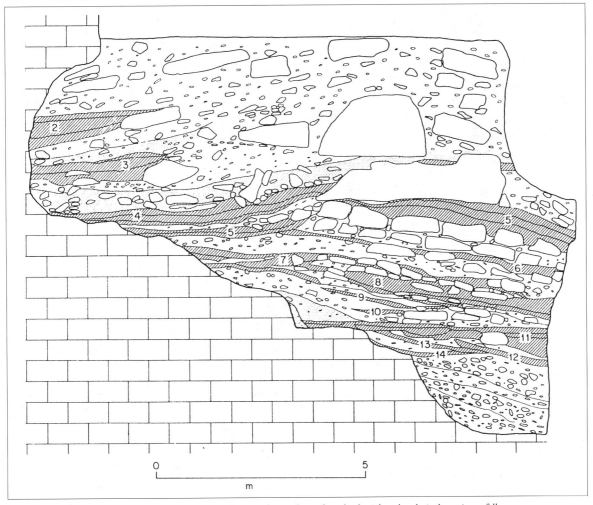

Stratified rockshelter site of Abri Pataud in southwestern France. The numbers refer to levels with archaeological remains as follows:

level 1: lower Solutrean

level 2: proto-Magdalenian

level 3: Perigordian VI

level 4: Perigordian Vc

level 5: Perigordian IV

level 6: evolved Aurignacian

level 7: intermediate Aurignacian

level 8, 9, 10: intermediate Aurignacian

level 11, 12: early Aurignacian

level 13, 14: basal Aurignacian

From T. Champion, C. Gamble, S. Shennan, and A. Whittle, Prehistoric Europe, *1984, by permission of the publisher, Academic Press Limited London.*

sometimes termed *locations* to distinguish them from *sites,* which in this scheme show a greater intensity of occupation.

CLASSIFICATION BY SITE FUNCTION

Archaeological remains often indicate the kind of prehistoric behavior that took place at a site, and so sites can be grouped according to the behavior that went on in them. Such a classificatory scheme separates *habitation,* or *living, sites* from *special-purpose sites* or *locations,* such as kill or butchery sites. Habitation sites occupied for relatively brief periods of time—say, one or two seasons—are called *base camps;* those inhabited year-round or nearly year-round are called *villages.* In later prehistory, settled villages were occupied for hundreds of years. As time went on and structures became dilapidated, were abandoned, and ultimately collapsed, new ones were built on top of them. In time, this produced huge mounds of old building debris, called *tells,* which are quite common in some parts of the Old World.

Lithic workshops, or *quarries,* are a type of task-specific site used by prehistoric groups to extract stone for toolmaking. *Middens,* found along seacoasts and rivers, contain sizable accumulations of shells, bones, and other cultural refuse. They occur where people routinely ate shellfish, snails, or goodly amounts of sea mammals and fish in prehistoric times. The resulting garbage dumps were sometimes used for burial of the dead but were rarely lived in.

A number of disparate sites where special types of nonutilitarian behavior took place in prehistory are known as *ceremonial sites.* When prehistoric burials took place outside of habitation sites, a special type of ceremonial site, the *bur-*

Enkapune ya Muto rockshelter site in Kenya. Courtesy of Stanley Ambrose.

ial site, resulted. In other cases, the painting of cave or rock-shelter walls during the Late Paleolithic and Mesolithic, possibly as a part of wider ritual practices, resulted in *cave-art sites.* Finally, some prehistoric groups, especially in the New World, constructed hillocks that they used for various purposes. Some of these earthen constructions, called *mounds,* were used as platforms for temples, others held burials, and still others were figurative in design and probably had some ritual or ideological significance for their builders.

See also Archaeology; Ritual; Site Types. [O.S.]

Further Readings

Fagan, B. (1997) In the Beginning: An Introduction to Archaeology. 9th ed. New York: HarperCollins.

Yudinovo Late Paleolithic open-air site under excavation. Courtesy of Olga Soffer.

Renfrew, C., and Bahn, P. (1996) Archaeology: Theory, Method, and Practice. Second edition. London: Thames and Hudson.

Archaeology

Recovery and study of material remains of past societies to gain insights into human history and prehistory. Modern archaeology also considers the association of these societies with one another (*man-man* relationships) and with the paleolandscape (*man-land relationships, archaeological context*). The goals of anthropological archaeology in particular include the reconstruction of cultural evolutionary sequences, the understanding of past lifeways, and the explanation of the natural and cultural processes that affect cultural systems and cause evolutionary shifts in human adaptations.

History of Archaeology

An interest in antiquities may be as old as *Homo sapiens.* Late Pleistocene fishing people at Ishango in eastern Zaire collected Pliocene fossils (e.g., *Stegodon kaisensis*); fossil shells were brought by Early Aurignacian people to Abri Pataud in southern France; and some of the earliest historical records suggest that the ancient Babylonians treasured the artifacts of their vanished predecessors and even conducted excavations to recover them. (The first recorded field archaeologist *cum* museum curator appears to have been En-nigaldi-Nanna, the daughter of King Nabonidus.)

It was not until the eighteenth century, however, with the excavations at Pompeii and Herculaneum in Italy, that field archaeology was established as a valid approach to the history of past civilizations. In European regions that were peripheral to the classical civilizations, such as Denmark and England, excavations of megalithic monuments led to speculation about prehistoric and pagan antecedents, to the study of Stonehenge in 1650–1670 (by J. Aubrey), and to the earliest recorded use of stratigraphy, archaeological context, and association to establish the age of a buried monument (by E. Lhwydd in 1699). At the end of the eighteenth century, British antiquarian John Frere identified handaxes from the Thames Valley site of Hoxne as "weapons of war, fabricated and used by a people who had not the use of metals" and correctly ascribed them to "a very remote period indeed, even beyond that of the present world." By the nineteenth century, archaeology was seen not only as a window into daily life in classical times, but also as the only access to a long expanse of prehistoric times, before written records.

In Denmark, during the late 1700s and early 1800s, the classification of Danish antiquities into three periods—Stone, Bronze, and Iron—provided the first relative chronology for archaeological sites. This three-age system was codified by Danish museum curators Thomsen and Worsaae in the exhibit halls and guidebook of the Danish National Museum during the period 1829–1843. The study of classical antiquities also became more systematic, through the decipherment of hieroglyphic (1822) and cuneiform (1837–1846) scripts.

By 1860, the existence of a very ancient age of "chipped stone" (redefined as the "Paleolithic Epoch" by Sir John Lubbock in 1865) was established by excavations in both England and France, especially by the work of J. Boucher de Perthes in the Somme gravels and E. Lartet at Aurignac. By the end of the 1860s, Paleolithic archaeology was firmly established by the excavation of ancient but recognizable *Homo sapiens* fossils in association with the bones of extinct animals in 1869 at Cro-Magnon in the Dordogne and by the beginnings of a biostratigraphic sequence for Paleolithic assemblages (E. Lartet and H. Christy, 1865–1875).

Important developments in twentieth-century archaeology include renewed emphasis in the period 1905–1920 on stratigraphy as the basis of relative chronologies; the development of regional sequences in most areas of the world between 1930 and 1970; a new focus beginning ca. 1940 on the reconstruction of paleoenvironments and paleoclimates; and a wide range of new techniques for the dating, recovery, and analysis of archaeological remains. Advances in data collection and analysis allowed later twentieth-century archaeologists to concentrate on questions concerning the processes of cultural evolution and the relationship between present and past cultures and the formation of the archaeological record.

Subfields of Archaeology

Since archaeology is simply a material approach to reconstructing the past, the questions asked by the archaeologist and the goals of archaeological investigations are determined by the particular historical discipline with which the archaeologist is affiliated.

Prehistorians study the archaeological remains of societies with no written records, and their training is often concentrated in geology and anthropology (ethnology). Depending on the prehistorian's training, the focus of inquiry varies from the reconstruction of cultural sequences through time, to paleoenvironmental reconstructions, to an understanding of past lifeways and the processes of change.

Classical archaeologists receive their primary training in art history, classics, or Near Eastern studies and have been concerned primarily with the documentation of art styles, the recovery and study of archives and inscriptions, the identification and description of particular monuments or sites of the ancient world known from historical records, and, more recently, the reconstruction of daily life in antiquity.

Biblical archaeologists are classical archaeologists whose training may involve divinity school and whose interests include verification and amplification of biblical history.

Historic archaeologists study the material remains of the recent antecedents of modern societies to provide an alternative view to that given by written records. Of particular interest to historic archaeologists are the ordinary lives of common people (e.g., workers, slaves, soldiers), who are often not well represented in archival materials, and changing settlement patterns, trade networks, economic strategies, and symbolic systems. In England, for instance, *Anglo-Saxon, medieval,* and *industrial archaeologists* share some of the historical archaeologists' goals and training. *Salvage archaeologists* (called cultural-resource managers in the United States), who may be trained in any archaeological specialty, conduct archaeological surveys and excavations for remains of any time period in areas threatened by construction or development.

Anthropological archaeologists, trained in anthropology, are the largest group of archaeologists, at least in the United States, where the connection between living Native Americans and the prehistoric past has led to greater expectations for the reconstruction of past lifeways. While early research in anthropological archaeology, as in other subfields, focused on the reconstruction of regional sequences, anthropological archaeologists have since the 1960s turned increasingly to questions concerning the processes responsible for cultural evolution and cultural adaptations to particular environments. More recent concerns of anthropological archaeologists include the reconstruction, or deconstruction, of prehistoric (or historic) philosophies or worldviews from material remains (*critical archaeology*), the understanding of emerging political and class relationships of domination; and the elucidation of past differences in gender roles and contributions to the archaeological record.

The new technologies of dating, data recovery, and analysis have led individuals trained in the physical, or natural, sciences to become interested in archaeological research questions. These scientists are known variously as *archaeometrists,* who handle dating techniques, human-bone biochemistry, physical and chemical analysis of artifacts, or prospection techniques; *archaeozoologists,* who study archaeologically recovered faunal remains to determine diet, subsistence patterns, and other aspects of past cultures; and *archaeobotanists,* who study archaeologically recovered plant remains, including fibers, phytoliths, pollen, seeds, and pottery or hardened mud impressions to determine human use of plants.

Formation of the Archaeological Record

Like the fossil record, the archaeological record is created through natural taphonomic processes resulting in concentration of remains in the landscape, differential preservation and burial, and postdepositional disturbances. Formation of the archaeological record, however, is also strongly affected by cultural rules concerning such factors as technology and raw-material use; activity placement; storage, discard, or "dumping"; long-distance trade or transport; and burial and reoccupation. Archaeological sites, or concentrations of artifacts, may be created primarily by the culturally defined discard patterns of a group of prehistoric occupants (*primary context*) or may result from the transport and concentration of discarded artifacts and noncultural remains by natural processes, such as erosion or stream action (secondary context). Interpretation of archaeological data depends on understanding both natural and cultural formation processes, as well as the symbolic aspects of artifact styles, use of space, and human relationship to the environment.

Although knowledge of ethnographic data from present-day societies, particularly in regard to cultural formation processes, is essential to the understanding of archaeological data, it can also be misleading. Human societies of the past, particularly societies of non-*sapiens* humans, often have no close or even distant parallels in the present. While some scholars disparage the use of ethnographic data, particularly from hunter-gatherers living in marginal environments at the fringes of modern national economies, others have developed transformational models that use the limited variability of modern societies (and/or experimental reenactments or simulations of past behaviors) to predict (or retrodict) how past societies would have operated under specified conditions. The expected archaeological correlates of these predictions can then be tested against the data recovered from survey and excavation, through the use of *middle-range theory*, which specifies the relationship between the ethnographic pattern and the archaeological one.

Recovery of Archaeological Data

Archaeological data consist of three main classes: (1) the actual artifacts, structures, and land-surface modifications; (2) physiographic, sedimentological, faunal, and botanical evidence bearing on past landscapes and environments; and (3) the contextual relationships among artifacts and between artifacts and the reconstructed landscape, region, and environment of the past. In recovering archaeological data through survey, surface collection, or excavation, the archaeologist interested in past lifeways should attempt to gather an adequate and representative sample of artifacts and structures, rather than just the most beautiful pots, gold jewelry, and temples. Collection of pollen and sediment samples, and recovery of microfaunal and microbotanical remains through sieving and flotation procedures, will allow a more complete description of the environmental context and an estimation of chronological age independent of that suggested by the artifacts. Finally, careful measurement and recording of finds in their landscape and stratigraphic context, as well as in three-dimensional space, will permit the eventual study of interrelationships within and among different classes of recovered data.

Although the archaeologist's eye is naturally drawn to large concentrations of artifacts and structures that are visible on the surface, the research design should ensure that a data sample is representative of the buried archaeological record in a given area. The first task is to define a region to be sampled, either with reference to a present environmental feature, such as a river valley, or a past one, such as a paleolakeshore. Definition of the sampling region often requires the archaeologist to envision the territory or range utilized by a past society, which may combine a group of environmental features, such as a lake, a river valley, and a mountain area.

After setting the boundaries of the sampling universe, the archaeologist chooses a sampling design. In rare cases, the archaeologist attempts to walk over the entire region, recording all surface artifacts and features, with the assumption that this is an adequate sample of the buried remains. More commonly, he or she divides the region into grid squares, circles, or transects and surveys the surface of a given percentage of these, chosen either entirely at random or at even intervals across the region (e.g., every tenth unit). The entire region may be treated equally, or greater emphasis or coverage may be given to those natural environmental subdivisions of the region judged most likely to yield archaeological remains (*stratified random survey*).

Since archaeological remains on the present land surface are often exposed through nonrandom processes of erosion and natural concentration (e.g., lag deposits, stream action, slopewash), the surface record may provide a poor picture of the buried record. There are several techniques for sampling the buried record, provided that the overburden is relatively shallow. These include deep plowing of selected grid units or transects, resistivity survey for magnetic anomalies in the soil, various forms of aerial remote sensing, and a posthole or auger sample at random or regular intervals. For more deeply buried remains, the archaeologist may elect to excavate one-meter-square or -diameter units at random or regular intervals, although this technique is costly for the information gained.

Once the surface or subsurface concentration of archaeological remains has been determined or estimated, the archaeologist may select several locations for more intensive exploration through excavation. Since modern excavation is an expensive and time-consuming procedure, sites are often chosen so as to yield the maximum information about the widest range of past activities. Unfortunately, this practice has resulted in a bias within regions toward areas in which certain past activities were concentrated (e.g., rockshelters, large towns) and away from loci where other activities may have been conducted in a more dispersed manner (homesteads, farms, gardens, low-density open-air patches of material). Strategies for correcting this bias through a deliberate emphasis on low-density sites are being developed in several archaeological research areas, from the Plio-Pleistocene of East Africa to the Upper Paleolithic of the Périgord region of France to the dispersed hamlets of ancient Mayan farmers.

Analysis of Data

One of the archaeologist's first tasks is to reconstruct chronological sequences. The age of buried remains may be determined through a combination of techniques, including geochronometry, biochronology, comparison with artifactual remains of known age (*cultural cross-dating*), or establishment of a putative regional sequence using site or assemblage similarity as a rough indicator of temporal proximity (*seriation*).

A second important task is the cataloging, description, and analysis of the recovered artifacts from a technological, functional, and stylistic perspective. Bones are identified as to species and examined for evidence of butchery or deliberate shaping; stone tools may be analyzed for the existence of scars from use or manufacture, of chemical residues, or of micropolishes indicative of function; ceramics, glasses, and metals can be studied in terms of design elements, chemical traces of raw-material sources, or physical traces of technological processes.

Other tasks are the reconstruction of the paleoenvironment and of the past diet and economy. Study of raw materials and their sources may provide information about trade routes, procurement practices, and economic organization; comparisons of technological practices, artifact styles, and differential access to materials may provide information about past social organizations. One question frequently asked of archaeological data, for example, concerns the relative abundance or poverty of grave or household goods for different segments of society (e.g., males vs. females, adults vs. children, leaders vs. the majority, and central settlements vs. outlying camps or villages) and the implications for the emergence of status or hierarchical differences. Finally, study of the symbolic aspects of the archaeological record can suggest clues to cognitive abilities, ritual practices, beliefs, and ideology.

See also Aggregation-Dispersal; Anthropology; Archaeological Sites; Biochronology; Bone Biology; Clothing; Complex Societies; Cultural Anthropology; Culture; Diet; Domestication; Economy, Prehistoric; Ethnoarchaeology; Exotics; Fire; Geochronometry; Hunter-Gatherers; Jewelry; Lithic Use-Wear; Man-Land Relationships; Musical Instruments; Paleoanthropology; Paleobiology; Paleoenvironment; Paleolithic; Paleolithic Lifeways; Paleomagnetism; Paleontology; Périgord; Physical Anthropology; Prehistory; Raw Materials; Ritual; Site Types; Stone-Tool Making; Storage; Taphonomy. [A.S.B.]

Further Readings

Bahn, P., ed. (1996) The Cambridge Illustrated History of Archaeology. Cambridge: Cambridge Univ. Press.

Binford, L.R. (1983) In Pursuit of the Past. London: Thames and Hudson.

Daniel, G. (1981) A Short History of Archaeology. London: Thames and Hudson.

Renfrew, C., and Bahn, P. (1991) Archaeology: Theory, Method, and Practice. London: Thames and Hudson.

Thomas, D.H. (1998) Archaeology. New York: Harcourt Brace.

Trigger, B.G. (1989) A History of Archeological Thought. Cambridge: Cambridge Univ. Press.

Willey, G.R., and Sabloff, J.A. (1993) A History of American Archaeology, 3rd ed. New York: Freeman.

Archaic Homo sapiens

The usage of the species name *Homo sapiens* has, since the early 1960s, often been extended to include such archaic fossil material as the European Neanderthals, the Broken Hill cranium from Zambia, and the Ngandong (Solo) specimens from Java, which many workers formerly regarded as representing species distinct from modern humans. My own view is that this wider usage of *Homo sapiens* has outlived its usefulness (see below). However, when used in this wide way, *Homo sapiens* consists of two main subgroups, "modern *Homo sapiens*" (living humans and closely related forms) and "archaic *Homo sapiens*" (Neanderthals and other nonmodern fossil forms). Although the Neanderthals in this reckoning must be considered as one type of "archaic *Homo sapiens*," they have their own special characters, and they are discussed separately in this volume. The Ngandong material has also been treated separately, as there is increasing evidence that these specimens, in fact, represent an evolved form of *Homo erectus* rather than "archaic *Homo sapiens*."

Determining which specimens actually belong in "archaic *Homo sapiens*" rather than *Homo erectus* is not always straightforward, as many fossils from the Middle Pleistocene display mosaic (mixed) features of the two species that are sometimes seen as reflecting a gradual evolutionary transition between the two groups. If a rapid punctuational evolutionary change had occurred between the two species *Homo erectus* and "archaic *Homo sapiens*," fossils with such mixed and apparently intermediate characteristics would not be expected in the meager fossil sample so far available.

Characteristics of "Archaic *Homo sapiens*"
Broadly speaking, it is possible to list the following characteristics that typify (but do not occur universally or exclusively in) the fossil specimens from Europe, Asia, and Africa that are sometimes grouped in "archaic *Homo sapiens*" (excluding the Neanderthals). Endocranial capacity ranges between ca. 1,000 and 1,400 ml, with the minimum figure similar to the mean of *Homo erectus* and the maximum figure comparable with the means of Neanderthal and modern samples. The face shows a reduced total prognathism (i.e., it juts out less from the cranial vault) compared with *Homo erectus* specimens, approximating the form of Neanderthal and some modern skulls in this respect. The upper face itself tends to be relatively broad, as in *Homo erectus*, but with a more pronounced midfacial projection, similar to the mean level found in modern *Homo sapiens* but less than in Neanderthals. On the base of the skull, the tympanic bone of the ear region is not strongly built and is nearly aligned with the adjoining petrous bone, both features being found in Neanderthal and modern humans but not in *Homo erectus*. As in the former groups also, the temporal bone is relatively short with an evenly curved upper edge. This feature is probably correlated with the increase in brain size and cranial height over most *Homo erectus*, as are a number of other changes in the shape and proportions of the cranial vault in "archaic *Homo sapiens*" fossils.

While the skull is still relatively long and low, the parietal bones tend to be longer and more curved, and the shape of the skull from behind does not show the upward narrowing found in *Homo erectus* specimens. Instead, the parietal bones are usually vertical, with some expansion in their upper regions, where *Homo erectus* skulls are poorly filled. At the back of the cranium, the occipital bone is higher and often less angled, and the occipital torus is reduced, especially at the sides. The nuchal (neck) musculature may still be strongly developed, but the nuchal area faces downward more. The cranial vaults of "archaic *Homo sapiens*" show a reduced robusticity compared with those of *Homo erectus*. Although the extent of this is variable, the reduced occipital torus development, the generally less thickened vault, and the reduced degree of midline keeling and overall buttressing (e.g., the less common occurrence of the bony swelling at the back of the parietal known as the angular torus) all reflect this. In general, the browridge is still strongly developed, but it may show a more curved form and internally may be lightened by the presence of large air spaces (sinuses), which are of uncertain significance.

Little is known of the rest of the skeleton of "archaic *Homo sapiens*" specimens, although a number of isolated finds have been made. Until the Atapuerca skeletons from

Spain and the Jinniushan skeleton from China have been fully published, however, there is little to compare with the more complete material available for *Homo erectus*, Neanderthals, and "modern *Homo sapiens*." Nevertheless, in the parts that are known, there is an overall robusticity like that found in *Homo erectus* and Neanderthals, and, of the three pelvic specimens so far described that may represent "archaic *Homo sapiens*," two show the presence of the strong iliac pillar above the hip joint that is known from early *Homo* pelves. The recently (1993) discovered Boxgrove tibia from the English Middle Pleistocene is perhaps the most massive fossil example known. Despite this, some skeletal parts do hint at a close approximation to the modern morphology in their overall shape.

Fossil Material of "Archaic Homo sapiens"

EUROPE

Europe and Africa have the best records of "archaic *Homo sapiens*" material. The European specimens include incomplete fossils, such as those from Mauer (Germany), Vértesszöl-lös (Hungary), and Bilzingsleben (Germany), that many workers would classify in *Homo erectus*, and it must be admitted that from their preserved parts it is difficult or impossible to resolve their taxonomic status. However, the inclusion of the Mauer mandible does provide the specific name *Homo heidelbergensis*, should a distinct taxon need to be recognized.

Where more complete material of comparable age is known from Europe, it is apparent that it cannot readily be referred to *Homo erectus*. The skull from Petralona (Greece) is a particularly fine example of such a fossil, and it is a pity that dispute about its age has clouded its significance. The cranium does display *Homo erectus*-like characters in its laterally thick browridge, broad face, interorbital region, palate, and base of the skull, centrally strong occipital torus, and thickened vault bones. Endocranial capacity is ca. 1,230 ml, overlapping the *Homo erectus* and late *Homo sapiens* ranges, and the endocranial cast is less flattened than in typical *Homo erectus* specimens. There are also, however, advanced (derived) characters that are shared with later Pleistocene (particularly Neanderthal) crania, and these include the reduced total facial prognathism but increased midfacial projection, the double curvature of the supraorbital torus, the prominent nasal bones, and the laterally reduced and lowered occipital torus. One particularly remarkable feature of the Petralona specimen is the degree of pneumatization of the maxillary, ethmoid, sphenoid, temporal, and frontal regions. While the maxillary sinuses are like those of Neanderthals, the frontal sinus development is even greater, since the pneumatization stretches right across the inside of the supraorbital torus. Such laterally developed sinuses are present also in the Broken Hill (Zambia), Bodo (Ethiopia), and Thomas 3 (Morocco) browridges, but variation is such that the Arago 21 specimen from France has a negligible development of the frontal sinus.

The Arago material has been classified as *Homo erectus* by some workers, mainly on the basis of primitive characteristics and the supposedly high antiquity of the specimens. When the material was thought to date from the Riss glacia-

tion (ca. 190 Ka?) of the late Middle Pleistocene, it was usually considered to represent a hominid population comparable with those from Steinheim (Germany) or Swanscombe (England) (i.e., an "archaic *Homo sapiens*" or an anteneanderthal). However, with the realization that the material was probably more ancient, supposedly dating from the "Mindel" glaciation, there was a greater emphasis on the primitive *Homo erectus*-like characteristics present in the material, such as the robusticity of the postcranial specimens (including an iliac buttress on the Arago 44 pelvis), the large size and robusticity of the Arago 13 mandible, and the strong development of the supraorbital and angular tori of the Arago 21 face and the Arago 47 parietal, respectively. The reconstruction of the Arago 21/47 skull also featured a high degree of facial prognathism, much greater than in the Petralona and Steinheim crania and comparable with that of true *Homo erectus* specimens. Yet, it is not clear whether this prognathism is, partly at least, an artifact of remaining distortion in the reconstruction. In other respects, the Arago specimens compare well with European fossils that are generally accepted as representing "archaic *Homo sapiens*," such as the Petralona, Steinheim, and Atapuerca material. Like some of those specimens, it is conceivable that the Arago sample derives from a population that was ancestral to the Neanderthals, and this is especially plausible in the case of the Arago 2 mandible.

Even more vexing than the classification of the Arago material is the assignment of the Bilzingsleben cranial fragments representing two or three individuals. These date from a Middle Pleistocene interglacial correlated with oxygen isotope stages 9 or 11, 300–400 Ka. They are the most *Homo erectus*-like of all the European cranial specimens in the strong supraorbital and occipital torus development and in occipital proportions and angulation. Yet the Bilzingsleben material lacks the areas that appear most *Homo sapiens*-like in the Petralona skull (although in the 1990s a temporal bone has been discovered) at Bilzingsleben, and the absent areas of the parietal region may well have been more "advanced." Even considering the *Homo erectus*-like occipital region, one should note that it is less robust than that of any of the Zhoukoudian (China) adults and is similar in proportions to that of the Saldanha (South Africa) skull, which is generally accepted as an African "archaic *Homo sapiens*."

The Steinheim skull is a puzzling specimen that is small brained and relatively large browed yet in other respects shows advanced characteristics in its thin vault and occipital shape. In certain respects, the occipital region resembles that of Swanscombe and the Neanderthals, yet the shape and proportions of the face seem distinctly primitive. This combination of a Neanderthal-like occiput and a primitive face is exactly the opposite of the situation in the Petralona skull. Even allowing that this variation in the expression of these characters may be partly related to sexual dimorphism, it is difficult to classify these fossils together or arrange them in an orderly morphological series from *Homo erectus*-like to Neanderthal-like specimens. It is apparent, however, that the Steinheim skull does not fit comfortably into the *Homo erectus* group and equally is not clearly an early Neanderthal.

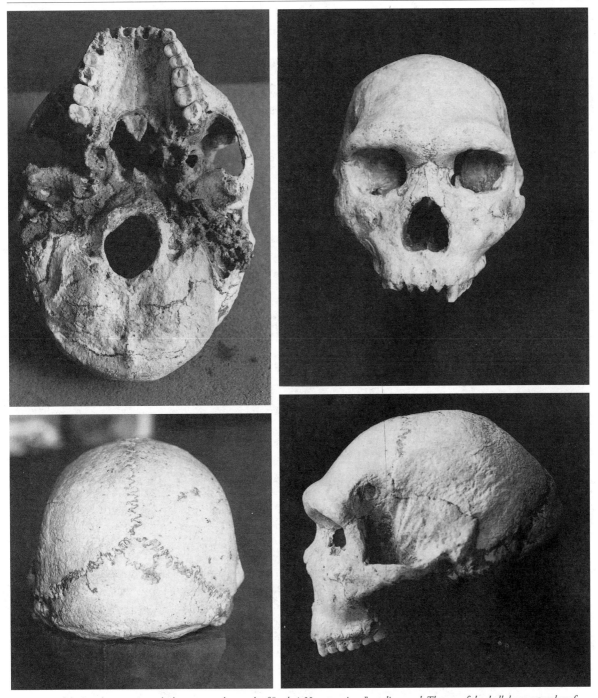

Four views of the Petralona cranium, the best-preserved example of "archaic Homo sapiens*" yet discovered. The rear of the skull shows a number of* Homo erectus *characteristics, but the parietal bones, skull base, and face show features found in later hominids. In particular the supraorbital torus and cheek region are reminiscent of those of Neanderthals. Not to scale. Courtesy of Chris Stringer.*

The extensive Atapuerca sample shows aspects of morphology found in many other European Middle Pleistocene hominids and some clear or incipient Neanderthal features. Its detailed study will greatly assist interpretation of many of the other isolated or incomplete specimens.

Several other European Middle Pleistocene fossil hominids are difficult to assign because of incomplete or conflicting data, and this is especially true of mandibular specimens, such as those from Mauer, Montmaurin, Arago, and Azych (the latter actually in Azerbaijan). Some of these do appear to show Neanderthal characteristics, but it seems premature to assign them to the Neanderthal group proper at present. Yet, by the later Middle Pleistocene, Europe was certainly populated by peoples who were closely related to the Neanderthals. The Swanscombe partial cranium probably belongs in this group, along with the Biache, the Fontéchevade, and the more ancient of the La Chaise fossils, all from France. Such specimens may more reasonably be referred to the species *Homo neanderthalensis* than to the "archaic *Homo sapiens*" grade (see below).

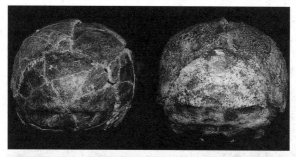

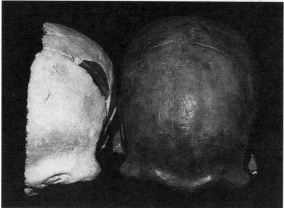

Above: rear (occipital) view comparing the specimens from Biache (left) and Swanscombe. The latter displays more primitive features, but both show Neanderthal characteristics. Below: comparison of the Irhoud 2 (left) and Pavlov 1 crania demonstrates the similarity in the region shown between a North African "archaic sapiens" specimen and a robust modern Homo sapiens *fossil from Europe. Courtesy of Chris Stringer.*

AFRICA

A number of North African fossil hominids from the Middle Pleistocene have been referred to *Homo erectus* on the basis of primitive characteristics. These include the Salé (Morocco) skull, with its cranial capacity of only 900 ml. However, such specimens as the Salé and the Thomas Quarries (Morocco) fossils do bear a general resemblance to European material discussed above under the category of "archaic *Homo sapiens*," and further study may establish this relationship, or classification as *Homo heidelbergensis*, on firmer grounds. Certainly, from evidence elsewhere in Africa, there are strong grounds for linking African and European hominids of the Middle Pleistocene in at least a general way to differentiate them from Asian *Homo erectus* fossils. In particular, there are close resemblances in overall cranial form and in certain anatomical details among the Broken Hill, Bodo, and Petralona crania. The Bodo specimen, however, while probably having the largest endocranial capacity, was also the most *Homo erectus*-like in such features as cranial thickness, keeling, and facial prognathism. So there is a real problem involved in determining whether these fundamentally similar specimens should be grouped together as "archaic *Homo sapiens*" or *Homo heidelbergensis* or whether the Bodo skull should be separated off as representing *Homo erectus*. Given recent chronometric dating of the Bodo site to the early Middle Pleistocene (ca 600 Ka), this latter point is certainly a real consideration. One additional aspect of interest here is the postcranial material that may be associated with the Broken Hill skull. Although several

individuals of both sexes are represented, it is apparent that the material combines archaic and modern features in a way that differs from that of *Homo erectus* and Neanderthal skeletons. While bone thickness in the tibia, femora, and at least one of the pelves is comparable with other nonmodern fossils, the inferred limb proportions indicate a relatively long tibia and tall stature, with femora of more modern shape than indicated for many archaic specimens.

Other African Middle Pleistocene specimens, such as Ndutu (Tanzania) and Saldanha, involve fewer problems concerning assignment to "archaic *Homo sapiens*" or *Homo heidelbergensis*, and, in the absence of clear Neanderthal or modern synapomorphies "archaic *Homo sapiens*" is usually extended to include such fossils as those from Eliye Springs (Kenya), Florisbad (South Africa), Jebel Irhoud (Morocco), and Ngaloba (Tanzania). When we arrive at the terminal Middle and early Late Pleistocene, probable synapomorphies with modern *Homo sapiens* begin to appear in such specimens as Omo Kibish 2 and Jebel Irhoud 2, and this marks the point at which the term "archaic *Homo sapiens*" loses the limited validity it possesses.

FAR EAST

The isolated skull from Narmada (India) is a candidate for assignment to "archaic *Homo sapiens*," although it was referred to *Homo erectus* in preliminary reports. While the specimen does appear to have a somewhat tented and keeled vault, it is also very high, with a rounded occipital region. More possible examples of "archaic *Homo sapiens*" are known from farther east, at Chinese sites like Maba, Dali, Jinniushan, and Yunxian. Only Maba is published in any detail, but the Jinniushan specimen consists of a partial skull and elements of the postcranial skeleton. It shows *Homo sapiens*-like characters, despite large brows and absolute age determinations of ca. 280–200 Kyr, in that the vault is thin and well expanded (capacity ca. 1,390 ml), and the face is rather gracile in preserved parts. It might have been considered as a female individual of the Dali group but for the fact that it is reportedly sexed as a male from the associated skeleton; and it has a considerably larger cranial capacity than the Dali skull. If the Jinniushan skeleton is correctly dated, it has important implications for human evolution in the Far East, particularly in the difficulty involved in deriving it from the possibly penecontemporaneous late *Homo erectus* populations known from Zhoukoudian and Hexian (China).

In Southeast Asia, the only plausible claimants for "archaic *Homo sapiens*" fossils are those from Ngandong (Solo) on the Indonesian island of Java. Many of the apparent *Homo sapiens*-like characteristics, however, may be reflections of endocranial expansion achieved in parallel with that of Middle Pleistocene specimens in Europe and Africa, for, in the majority of features, the Ngandong crania closely resemble their *Homo erectus* antecedents, with whom they are most reasonably classified.

Status of "Archaic Homo sapiens"

Although the characteristics of the group of extinct hominids usually referred to as "archaic *Homo sapiens*" were listed

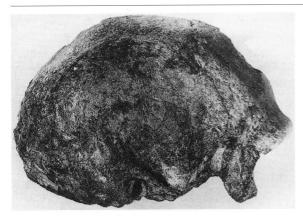

Lateral view of the cranium from the Narmada Valley (India).

the other group through synapomorphies. Thus, for example, while the Mauer mandible would represent *Homo heidelbergensis,* Swanscombe would be allocated to *Homo neanderthalensis,* and the Jebel Irhoud fossils to *Homo sapiens.*

See also Africa; Arago; Archaic Moderns; Asia, Eastern and Southern; Asia, Western; Atapuerca; Biache-St. Vaast; Bilzingsleben; Bodo; Boxgrove; Clade; Dali; Europe; Florisbad; Fontéchevade; Grade; Hexian; Homo sapiens; Jebel Irhoud; Jinniushan; Kabwe; La Chaise; Mauer; Montmaurin; Narmada; Ndutu; Neanderthals; Ngaloba; Petralona; Saldanha; Salé; Steinheim; Swanscombe; Thomas Quarries; Vértesszöllös; Yunxian; Zhoukoudian. [C.B.S.]

Further Readings
Kimbel, W.H., and Martin, L.B., eds. (1993) Species, Species Concepts, and Primate Evolution. New York: Plenum.

Kimbel, W.H., and Rak, Y. (1993) The importance of species taxa in Paleoanthropology and an argument for the phylogenetic concept of the species category. In W.H. Kimbel and L.B. Martin (eds.): Species, Species Concepts, and Primate Evolution. New York: Plenum, pp. 461–485.

Rightmire, G.P. (1998) Human evolution in the Middle Pleistocene: the role of *Homo heidelbergensis.* Evolutionary Anthropology 6(6): 218–227.

Smith, F.H., and Spencer, F. eds. (1984) The Origins of Modern Humans. New York: Liss.

Stringer, C.B. (1985) Middle Pleistocene hominid variability and the origin of Late Pleistocene humans. In E. Delson (ed.): Ancestors: The Hard Evidence. New York: Liss, pp. 289–295.

Stringer, C.B., Hublin, J-J., and Vandermeersch, B. (1984) The origin of anatomically modern humans in western Europe. In F.H. Smith and F. Spencer (eds.): The Origins of Modern Humans. New York: Liss, pp. 51–135.

Tattersall I. (1986) Species recognition in human paleontology. J. Hum. Evol. 15:165–175.

Tattersall I. (1992) Species concepts and species identification in human evolution. J. Hum. Evol. 22:341–349.

Turner A. (1986) Species, Speciation, and Human Evolution. Hum. Evol. 1:419–430.

at the beginning of this entry, the reality and utility of this term is not clear. Even under a conventional system of classification, it is apparent that the specimens assigned to this group show great variation and are most easily typified by characteristics belonging to other groups, such as *Homo erectus* and Neanderthals, rather than by their own characteristics. Under a cladistic system of classification, the meaning of the term "archaic *Homo sapiens*" becomes even less clear, since it is apparent that these specimens may have had different evolutionary origins and different evolutionary destinies. A separate, parallel transition may have occurred in different areas between local forms of *Homo erectus* and their "archaic *Homo sapiens*" descendants, and these distinct descendants could represent only an evolutionary grade rather than a clade. Furthermore, if the European "archaic *Homo sapiens*" specimens, such as Arago and Petralona, were, in fact, ancestral to Neanderthals, as many workers believe, and this could be demonstrated by the presence of synapomorphies, these specimens should more reasonably be classified with the Neanderthals. Equally, if African "archaic *Homo sapiens*" uniquely gave rise to modern *Homo sapiens,* the African specimens could justifiably be classified with modern humans.

Another problem with the term "archaic *Homo sapiens*" is that most specimens in this group show more similarities to *Homo erectus* or Neanderthal fossils than to anatomically modern *Homo sapiens,* so the justification for assigning them to *Homo sapiens* at all is unclear. If the difference between Neanderthals and modern *Homo sapiens* were once again elevated to the level of species, as some workers are suggesting, there would be more justification for extending the use of the taxon *Homo neanderthalensis* to include most of these specimens than for the current extended usage of the term *Homo sapiens.* Yet, given that the Neanderthals do display apomorphies not present in most "archaic *Homo sapiens*" fossils, it might instead be preferable to replace the term "archaic *Homo sapiens*" with a distinct species name, for which *Homo heidelbergensis* (from the Mauer mandible) or *Homo rhodesiensis* (from the Broken Hill skull) are the most appropriate. This species would then be considered as the probable last common ancestor for the *Homo neanderthalensis* and *Homo sapiens* groups, and specimens that clearly postdated the divergence of the two clades would be allocated to one or

Archaic Moderns

Various fossil hominids, while representing anatomically modern *Homo sapiens,* display certain archaic characteristics that appear to be primitive retentions. This is true for some specimens of the terminal Pleistocene, such as the Kow Swamp material from Australia, and even for living humans, but this discussion will restrict the use of the term *archaic moderns* to specimens that probably date to more than 35 Ka. Two geographical areas, Africa and Southwest Asia, contain fossils that fall into this category; there are only disputed examples from Europe or eastern Asia. It should be borne in mind, however, that the term *archaic moderns* is a contradiction in terms and may be confused with another unsatisfactory term, "archaic *Homo sapiens.*"

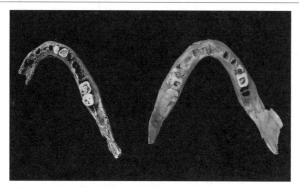

Klasies River Mouth 41815 (left) and Border Cave 5 mandibles.
Courtesy of Chris Stringer.

African Evidence

The African record of archaic moderns consists of specimens from the South African sites of Klasies River Mouth and Border Cave and the North African sites of Dar-es-Soltane and Omo Kibish. Ngaloba (Tanzania) and Jebel Irhoud (Morocco) also provide fossils that some workers include in the category, as well as other specimens whose age is uncertain, such as Guomde (Kenya). Because several of the specimens are fragmentary or derived from dubious contexts or ones where absolute dating is not a practical proposition, some workers do not accept these specimens as representing genuinely early records of a modern morphology from Africa.

The material from the Klasies River Mouth complex of caves is fragmentary and shows clear morphological variation. The specimens were believed by their excavators to date to more than 70 Ka, and they are all associated with Middle Stone Age (MSA) artifacts. However, although doubts had been expressed about the reliability of correlations used to date the Klasies material to the early Late Pleistocene, the results of recent excavations and the application of absolute dating techniques have supported the proposed antiquity of the hominid specimens and have produced new hominid specimens that can be dated at more than 100 Ka.

The MSA-associated material from Klasies consists of cranial, maxillary, mandibular, dental, and postcranial fragments. The cranial pieces include one (adult?) frontal fragment that displays a small, modern type of supraorbital torus and other fragments that suggest a rounded but perhaps low cranial vault. The mandibular pieces generally look modern, with small teeth, but there is much variation in size, robusticity, and chin development. The maxillary fragments are those found most recently at the site and are the oldest, and perhaps most robust, yet recovered. The few postcranial pieces appear to be small and relatively modern in morphology. One must assess the degree of modernity of the Klasies material with caution when the specimens are so fragmentary, but they are at least bordering on a modern human morphology well before comparable evidence is available from such areas as Europe. It is even possible that the specimens document an increase in gracility and modernity through the early Late Pleistocene sequence at Klasies.

While there may be doubts about the assignment of some of the Klasies material to modern *Homo sapiens*, the modernity of the MSA-associated fossil hominids from Border Cave is clear to most researchers. The specimens consist of a partial skull and possibly associated limb bones, the partial skeleton of an infant, and two mandibles. All seem to fall clearly into the overall range of modern humans, although the skull has a broad frontal bone and moderately strong browridge. However, since the skull, postcranial bones, and one (unassociated) mandible were not excavated systematically, while the infant's skeleton and the other mandible might have been intentionally buried in the MSA levels from which they were excavated, doubt has been expressed about claims that they all date to more than 70 Ka. Further work at the site is clearly needed to resolve some of these questions, but, given the evidence from Klasies of modern-looking hominids associated with the MSA, the Border Cave evidence may yet prove to be important.

The site of Omo Kibish in southern Ethiopia has produced two fossil hominids that may represent archaic moderns (Omo [Kibish] 1 and 3), as well as a third skull of nonmodern type (Omo [Kibish] 2). The Omo (Kibish) 3 skull fragments show only a slight brow development but are probably younger than the more complete and informative Omo (Kibish) 1 partial skeleton. This was found in beds that considerably predate 40 Ka, based on radiocarbon dates from higher levels, and that may date to 130 Ka according to uranium-series dating on mollusc shells (which tends to give a minimum age). The postcranial bones indicate a heavily built but anatomically modern individual, and the same can be said for the partial skull of Omo 1. It has a long and broad frontal bone with moderately strong brows, but the form of the rear of the skull and mandible appears entirely modern. If the specimen does derive from the oldest beds at Omo Kibish, it is a most important fossil hominid, one that documents the presence of essentially modern humans in northeastern Africa in the late Middle–early Late Pleistocene (although it would be premature to consider an age as much as 130 Ka as accurate without further confirmation).

Elsewhere in Africa are specimens of fossil hominids that, while certainly dating to more than 35 Ka, are difficult to classify as archaic moderns because they show so many archaic characters. There are also specimens that, while more certainly representing modern humans, do not definitely date to more than 35 Ka. Examples of the former category are the fossils from Ngaloba (Laetoli Hominid 18) and Jebel Irhoud, discussed elsewhere; examples of the latter category are the KNM-ER 999 femur and 3884 partial cranium from Guomde (Kenya) and the Springbok Flats cranial and postcranial material from South Africa. There is, however, one more African sample that probably represents an archaic form of modern *Homo sapiens*: the early material from Dar-es-Soltane (Morocco). Mostly unpublished, this material includes a robust partial cranium and mandible associated with the Middle Palaeolithic Aterian industry. It almost certainly dates to more than 40 Ka.

Western Asia

Western Asia has rich samples of archaic-modern skeletons from the Israeli sites of Skhūl (Mount Carmel) and Qafzeh, many of which derive from intentional burials. The extensive material from the former site was at first united with the

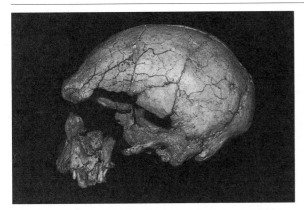

Lateral view of the Ngaloba-Laetoli H. 18 cranium. Courtesy of Chris Stringer.

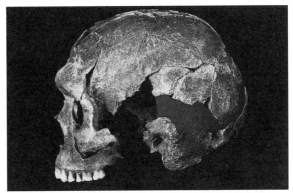

Lateral view of the Qafzeh 6 cranium. Courtesy of Chris Stringer.

Neanderthal material from the adjacent cave of Tabūn, but it is now regarded as archaic modern and is dated by TL (thermoluminescence) and ESR (electron spin resonance) techniques on associated materials to 120–80 Ka. However, uranium-series checks on the ESR dates suggest that some of the Skhūl material could be somewhat younger. The dating of the even larger Qafzeh sample of partial skeletons is better established, since the Middle Palaeolithic levels of Qafzeh have been dated by TL, ESR, and uranium series to 120–90 Ka, and the Qafzeh 6 cranium has been directly dated by gamma radiation to at least 80 Ka. The fossil material from Skhūl and Qafzeh consists of partial skeletons of adult males and females, as well as several children and subadults. The adult crania have, by the standards of living humans, large and prognathic faces with large teeth, well-developed supraorbital tori, and large cranial capacities. Yet, these and other features that have been used to link the specimens to the Neanderthals are not specifically Neanderthal-like, and details of facial morphology contrast strongly with those of Neanderthals. Similarly, in the rest of the skeleton, there is little of the robusticity and muscularity so typical of the Neanderthals (and of earlier humans generally), and details of pelvic structure are as in modern-day populations. Additionally, body proportions for the Skhūl and Qafzeh skeletons are unlike those of Neanderthals and instead specifically resemble those of modern-day tropical or subtropical populations. Overall, the morphology of these Israeli archaic moderns can be characterized as modern, but with some primitive features retained from Middle Pleistocene ancestors. Those ancestors, to judge from certain details of the fossils, may have been African contemporaries of the early Neanderthals. A later example of an early-modern hominid from the region is the Ksar 'Akil child's skull ("Egbert") from Lebanon. It is associated with an early Late Palaeolithic industry, dating from ca. 37 Ka.

Archaic Moderns from Other Areas

Elsewhere, claims for the occurrence of modern human skeletal materials that date from more than 35 Ka are rare and always controversial. In western Asia, archaic moderns possibly occur at such sites as Darra-i-Kur (Afghanistan) and Starosel'e (Ukraine), although the latter may represent an intrusive burial, while in Europe possible examples are found at such sites as Krapina (the child's skull labeled "A") and Bacho Kiro (Bulgaria). In eastern Asia, there is the burial of the modern-looking skeleton of a youth from the Niah Cave (Borneo, Malaysia), which may date to 40 Ka, and beyond that is the very robust skull (WLH 50) from the Willandra Lakes in southern Australia, which might be of comparable antiquity. Many of these finds, however, are isolated and have associated difficulties of dating or interpretation.

See also Africa; Asia, Western; Australia; Bacho Kiro; Border Cave; Dar-es-Soltane; Jebel Irhoud; Kibish; Klasies River Mouth; Krapina; Ksar 'Akil; Modern Human Origins; Ngaloba; Niah; Qafzeh; Skhūl. [C.B.S.]

Further Readings

Day, M.H., and Stringer, C.B. (1982) A reconsideration of the Omo Kibish remains and the *erectus-sapiens* transition. In de Lumley, H. (ed.): *L'Homo erectus* et la place de l'Homme de Tautavel parmi les hominidés fossiles. Nice: Centre National de la Recherche Scientifique/Louis-Jean Scientific and Literary Publications, pp. 814–846.

Day, M.H., and Stringer, C.B. (1991) Les restes crâniens d'Omo-Kibish et leur classification a l'interieur du genre *Homo*. L'Anthropologie 94:573–594.

Rak, Y. (1993) Morphological variation in *Homo neanderthalensis* and *Homo sapiens* in the Levant: A biogeographic model. In W.H. Kimbel and L.B. Martin

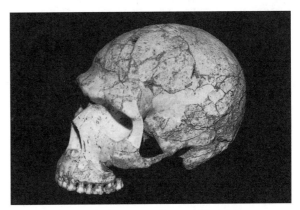

Lateral view of the Skhul 5 cranium. Courtesy of Chris Stringer.

(eds.): Species, Species Concepts, and Primate Evolution. New York: Plenum, pp. 523–536.

Smith, F.H., and Spencer, F., eds. (1984) The Origins of Modern Humans. New York: Liss.

Trinkaus E. (1992) Morphological contrasts between the Near Eastern Qafzeh-Skhūl and Late Archaic samples: Grounds for a behavioral difference. In T. Akazawa, K. Aoki, and T. Kimura (eds.): The Evolution and Dispersal of Modern Humans in Asia. Tokyo: Hokusen-Sha, pp. 277–294.

Vandermeersch, R. (1981) Les hommes fossiles de Qafzeh (Israel). Centre National du Recherche Scientifique, Paris.

Archonta

A controversial but research-stimulating cohort (a taxonomic rank above the order) of mammals that includes four living orders: Scandentia, Dermoptera, Primates, and Chiroptera, as well as a number of families of fossils (depending on the author) allied with any of the four living orders. Treeshrews and putative fossil relatives such as the Mixodectidae (scandentians) and the "flying lemurs," or colugos (dermopterans), were more widespread during the early Tertiary than they are today. Nevertheless, the affinities of the family Plagiomenidae of the Northern Hemisphere Paleocene-Eocene, previously widely accepted to be dermopteran, are again controversial.

Aspects of dental and cranial morphology mark the dermopterans as distinct early in their history when compared to archaic primates or primitive bats (chiropterans). Yet, features of elbow morphology, and particularly the details of foot form and function, strongly indicate that colugos share with the other archontans a common ancestor exclusive of any other group of mammals. This view is not shared by all students of these groups, and, largely as a result of numerical cladistic studies applied to a wide range of attributes, a general disagreement prevails concerning the phylogenetic reality of the concept *Archonta*. It is remarkable, however, that a number of apparently derived placental similarities (putatively synapomorphous but as yet not fully tested) exist among the inferred primitive stages of the taxa that are included in this cohort. For example, special similarity between the gliding membrane of colugos, in particular the membrane spread between the rays of the hand, and the finger-supported wing of bats suggests a uniquely shared advanced trait that is a differentially developed adaptation. The wing of bats may have had its origins similar to the finger-modulated gliding of colugos (as distinct from other therian gliders that do not use a membrane stretched between fingers in gliding). Similarly, the fusion of the carpal bones scaphoid, lunate, and centrale forms a scaphocentrale in Dermoptera and possibly Chiroptera, and these two taxa also share derived similarities of elbow mechanics. In turn, shared derived similarities in the tarsus and, to some degree, in the molars occur in the Paleogene family Mixodectidae and the modern Dermoptera. The plagiomenid dentition is most similar to that of Mixodectidae and Dermoptera, probably a synapomorphous similarity.

The morphological and molecular aspects of the relationships of the archaic primates (Plesiadapiformes) to colu-gos, tupaiids, and euprimates, as well as the problem of the closest relatives of bats, have been vigorously researched lately, but without any concensus. The last word on the reality of the Archonta is not in. There is increasing evidence that the protoplacentals began their distinctive radiation from an ancestry of opossumlike mammals with marsupial-type development and reproduction, but that these last common ancestors of the eutherian mammals were obligate terrestrial foragers. In turn, the last common ancestor of the Archonta (independent from the rodents) may have been among the first placental mammals that were fully committed to the trees, a way of life approximately retained by some of the tree-shrews, like *Ptilocercus*. Primates diversified primarily in an arboreal environment, whereas the colugos early became successful gliders and omnivore-herbivores, long before rodent gliders had a chance to displace them from that way of life. The earliest bats, of course, carried the (putative) ancestral (colugolike?) adaptations to the air, developed them to an extreme, and became, as far as we know, the only known true flyers among the mammals.

See also Dermoptera; Flying-Primate Hypothesis; Numerical Cladistics; Plesiadapiformes; Primates; Treeshrews. [F.S.S.]

Further Readings

MacPhee, R.D.E., ed. (1993) Primates and Their Relatives in Phylogenetic Perspective. New York: Plenum.

Szalay, F.S., and Lucas, S.G. (1996) The postcranial morphology of Paleocene *Chriacus* and *Mixodectes* and the phylogenetic relationships of archontan mammals. Bull. New Mex. Mus. Nat. Hist. Sci. 7:1–47.

Ardipithecus ramidus

Species of australopith named in 1994 to incorporate the early hominid fossils from the Ethiopian Middle Awash localities of the Aramis drainage. This species was originally named *Australopithecus ramidus* but later transferred to the new genus *Ardipithecus*; it was thought to be the ancestor of *Australopithecus afarensis*, but subsequent finds have placed this conclusion in some doubt.

By the early 1990s, the sites of Hadar (Ethiopia), Laetoli (Tanzania), and Maka (Ethiopia) yielded hominid fossils as old as 3.6 Myr that clearly belonged to *A. afarensis*. Some workers assigned fragments from the Ethiopian sites of Fejej and Belohdelie and from Koobi Fora (Kenya) to that species based on antiquity and primitive morphology. Until 1992, the only available possible hominids older than 4 Ma comprised a small collection of teeth and fragments of jaw and arm from the Kenyan sites of Lothagam, Tabarin, and Kanapoi. Again, on the basis of primitive characters, most of these fossils were referred to *A. afarensis*, and the search for the ancestor of this species intensified. On December 17, 1992, G. Suwa of the University of Tokyo discovered a hominid molar in the Aramis catchment of the Awash River. Suwa was a member of the team investigating the Middle Awash paleoanthropological research area. His discovery was followed, over the next two seasons of fieldwork, by the recovery of remains representing 17 hominid individuals from

Juvenile mandibular fragment of Ardipithecus ramidus *from Aramis, Middle Awash study area, Ethiopia. Photo by and courtesy of Tim D. White.*

Aramis. These fossils are placed stratigraphically just above the prominent Gàala Vitric Tuff Complex (GVTC), dated to 4.4 Ma. The series comprises dental, cranial, and postcranial specimens. Most of the fossils are highly fragmentary, and several individuals are represented by isolated teeth.

In 1994, T.D. White, Suwa, and B. Asfaw identified these 1992–1993 Aramis fossils as belonging to a new species of *Australopithecus, Australopithecus ramidus.* They chose the name *ramidus,* which means "root" in the Afar language, to honor the local Afar people who live in the Afar region today. For a type specimen, they chose a set of associated teeth from the available series.

G. WoldeGabriel and other Middle Awash team members provided radioisotopic dates for the Aramis sediments and sketched the taphonomic and environmental conditions that led to the hominid-bearing assemblage. The hominid remains are interpreted to have come from a habitat that was wooded at the time of deposition, with abundant colobine monkeys and kudus. In late 1994, the team recovered additional specimens at Aramis, including a damaged partial skeleton. In May 1995, a correction was published altering the generic name to *Ardipithecus,* with essentially the same diagnosis as the species.

A. ramidus is distinguished from other hominid species, including *A. afarensis,* by its relatively large upper and lower canines, its small, narrow, apelike dP_3, its flat temporal-bone articular surface, its absolutely and relatively thin canine and molar enamel, and its primitive premolars. The species *A. ramidus* is distinguished as a hominin from modern great apes and known elements of Miocene apes by relatively blunter, smaller, more incisiform canines, a more hominin-like canine/premolar complex, and a relatively short cranial base. The species does not show the expanded incisors and small, crenulated molars of chimpanzees, nor the large body size and specialized postcanine teeth of gorillas.

Evidence from the dP_3 is particularly striking. This tooth has been crucially important in studies of *Australopithecus* since the Taung (South Africa) discovery of 1924. It has been used frequently as a key character for sorting apes and hominids. The *A. ramidus* dP_3 is morphologically far closer to a chimpanzee than to any known hominid. It lacks the specialized hominin features seen in all *Australopithecus* species.

The *A. ramidus* permanent dentition is represented at most positions. The relatively thin enamel and large size of the *A. ramidus* canine, together with its primitive P_3 morphology, suggest a C/P_3 complex morphologically and functionally only slightly removed from the presumed ancestral ape condition. The limited available Aramis teeth are interpreted as indicating a single species with a postcanine dentition significantly smaller than in *A. afarensis.* The cranial fossils display a strikingly chimpanzeelike morphology.

Included in the published *A. ramidus* postcranial sample is a rare association of all three bones from the left arm of a single individual. In size, the specimen indicates a hominin larger than the A.L. 288–1 ("Lucy") *A. afarensis* from Hadar and smaller than other individuals of the same species. The arm displays a mosaic of characters usually attributed to hominins and/or great apes. A definitive appraisal of the locomotor habits of *A. ramidus* is not possible on the basis of the upper-limb fossils available.

A. ramidus shares a wide array of traits with *A. afarensis* but it differs in lacking some of the key traits that *A. afarensis* shares exclusively with all later hominids. In other words, *A. ramidus* is more "primitive." The Aramis remains display significant cranial, dental, and postcranial similarities to the chimpanzee condition. However, some or all of these features may be primitive retentions. Only further discoveries and comparisons may clarify which features actually define the chimp-human and/or African ape-human clades.

The Aramis fossils were originally placed in the genus *Australopithecus* because of their similarities to other dental and cranial fossils representing that taxon. It was noted that the anticipated recovery at Aramis of additional postcranial remains, particularly those of the lower limb and hip, might require future reassignment of these fossils at the genus and family level. The placement of this species into the new genus *Ardipithecus* was made in a brief note that merely indicated "as *ramidus* is likely to be the sister taxon of the remaining hominid clade, generic separation from *Australopithecus* is appropriate. We hereby make available a new generic nomen. . . ." The word *ardi* means ground or floor in Afar. At a higher taxonomic level, characters such as the modified C/P_3 complex, an anterior foramen magnum, and proximal ulnar morphology (shared with later *Australopithecus* species) suggest that the Aramis fossils belong to the hominin clade. On the other hand, it is worth noting that the ca 4.5 Ma mandible fragment (with M_{1-2}) from Tabarin (Baringo Basin, Kenya) has been formally named *Homo antiquus praegens* by W. Ferguson; if this specimen is conspecific with the Aramis fossils, the name *praegens* may have priority.

As of the late 1990s, *A. ramidus* was the earliest and most primitive hominin, but its role as an ancestor of later species has been questioned by several workers. Additional fossils and more detailed analyses and interpretations should help to clarify this question.

See also Afar Basin; Africa; Africa, East; Australopithecus; Baringo Basin/Tugen Hills; Belohdelie; Fejej; Hadar; Kanapoi; Laetoli; Lothagam; Middle Awash; Turkana Basin. [T.D.W.]

Further Readings

White, T.D., Suwa, G., and Asfaw, B. (1994) *Australopithecus ramidus,* a new species of early hominid from Aramis, Ethiopia. Nature 371:306–312.

White, T.D., Suwa, G., and Asfaw, B. (1995) *Australopithecus ramidus,* a new species of early hominid from Aramis, Ethiopia—Corrigendum. Nature 375:88.

WoldeGabriel, G., White, T.D., Suwa, G., Renne, P., de Heinzelin, J., Hart, W.K., and Heiken, G. (1994) Ecological and temporal placement of Early Pliocene hominids at Aramis, Ethiopia. Nature 371:330–333.

Asia, Eastern and Southern

Region of ca. 20 million km², which has yielded many important hominid and hominoid fossils and an archaeological sequence that, in some parts of the region, differs markedly from those of Europe, Africa, or southwestern Asia. For the purposes of this encyclopedia, the Eurasian continent has been divided into four geographical regions: Europe, west of the Caucasus; Russia (including Siberia); western Asia (including the area commonly referred to as the Middle East and the Central Asian republics of the former Soviet Union); and eastern and southern Asia, from Pakistan and China eastward and southward to the Pacific and Indian oceans, including Malaysia and Indonesia (but not Australasia). The most important fossiliferous areas of eastern and southern Asia are the Siwalik Hills of Pakistan and India, which have yielded an important collection of Miocene and Plio-Pleistocene fossil hominoids and cercopithecoids; China, where both hominins and nonhuman hominoids are known; and Java, which has yielded hominid fossils from throughout the Pleistocene. In mainland Southeast Asia (Burma, Thailand, Laos, Vietnam, Malaysia, and Cambodia), much archaeological evidence has been recovered, but hominin specimens earlier than the latest Pleistocene are limited to finds of individual teeth ascribed to both *Homo erectus* and "archaic *Homo sapiens.*" Fossils of *Pongo* and *Gigantopithecus* have also been recovered from this region.

The geography and geomorphology of Asia are best understood in terms of the continuing collision between the Indo-Burmese continent on the Indian plate and the Sino-Malaysian margin of Eurasia, beginning in the Early Cenozoic (or, in new interpretations, in latest Cretaceous). Together with smaller plates carrying the Anatolian and Iranian massifs northward at the same time, resulting in an unbroken mountain wall all across Asia, from the Taurides through the Elburz and the Tibetan Plateau to the Shan-Yunnan Massif. These highlands accentuate and, by and large, define a very sharp divide between tropical and subtropical habitats in the south, and much more seasonal and xeric (dry) conditions to the north. The complex tectonics of northern China and the archipelagos of the Southwest Pacific are also linked to subduction and transform faulting along this plate boundary.

Eocene continental sediments are found in northern India and Nepal with faunas that suggest a biogeographic connection with both Africa and Eurasia. Interestingly, nothing in the Indian Eocene fauna appears to represent a survivor from a postulated endemic population that likely would have inhabited the subcontinent during its passage across the Indian Ocean from Africa during the later Mesozoic. It has been suggested that ancestral strepsirhines might have boarded this "Noah's Ark" from Africa early in the Cenozoic, but there is no fossil evidence for this hypothesis, nor is it likely, given the deep-water isolation of the Indian plate.

Nonhuman Primate History in Eastern Asia

The earliest Asian primate is probably *Petrolemur,* a possible plesiadapiform of Early-to-Middle Paleogene age in South China. *Decoredon,* of comparable age, may be the earliest euprimate and suggests that omomyids, and perhaps adapiforms, might have entered North America from eastern Asia. *Altanius,* an omomyid from the Early Eocene of Mongolia, as well as new Chinese carpolestids, support this view of paleobiogeography. Middle-to-Late Eocene probable adapiforms from southern Asia include *Pondaungia* and *Amphipithecus* from Pondaung (Burma), *Kohatius* from Pakistan, *Hoanghonius* and *Rencunius* from China, some of which have been compared with the enigmatic *Oligopithecus* of Eocene-Oligocene age in the Fayum beds of Egypt. In the 1990s, a whole new suite of Middle Eocene primates has been described from fissure fillings and other sites in southeastern China. These include the adapiform *Adapoides,* the otherwise North American omomyid *Macrotarsius,* the tarsiid *Tarsius eocaenus,* and the probable tarsioid (claimed as an ancient anthropoid) *Eosimias.*

Fortunately for students of early hominoids, the Indo-Asian collision resulted in the uplift of the Potwar Plateau and the Salt Range in the foothills of the Himalayas, which exposed the famous Neogene fossil beds known as the Siwaliks. The most fossiliferous exposures crop out in Pakistan and India, but the beds also extend into Nepal and Bangladesh. The oldest Siwaliklike faunas of late Early and early Middle Miocene age, for example at Dera Bugti (Baluchistan), document the immigration of proboscideans and bovids, among other African groups, via the newly formed Mesopotamian land bridge.

The earliest Middle Miocene levels of the Kamlial beds (ca. 16.1 Ma) yielded a few teeth referred to *Dionysopithecus,* making them the earliest well-dated primates in eastern Asia. More complete specimens from Sihong (eastern China) occur alongside teeth of *Platodontopithecus;* both genera are included in the Pliopithecidae. *Pliopithecus* itself, otherwise known from several European species, has been described from Tongxin in North-Central China. The Siwalik Chinji fauna includes the first Asian hominoids, *Sivapithecus,* dated ca. 13–12 Ma. These are pongines, related to orangutans and perhaps to *Gigantopithecus.* Although fragmentary remains occur at 12.5 Ma in Pakistan and perhaps slightly older in India (Ramnagar) and Southeast China (Xiaolongtan, Yunnan Province), the diagnostic features of the palate are first

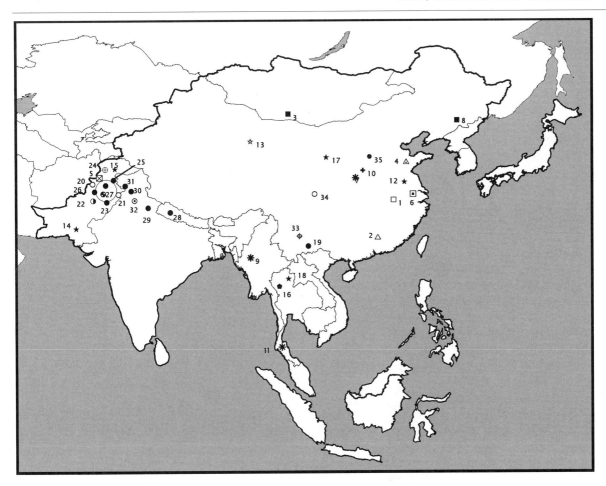

△ Late Paleocene: *Petrolemur*

◬ Early Eocene: Carpolestidae

✳ Middle-Late Eocene: ?Adapiformes

■ Early-Middle Eocene: Omomyidae

□ Middle Paleocene: *Decoredon*

⊠ Early Eocene: ?Adapiformes ?Omomyidae

✚ Middle Eocene: Adapiformes, Eosimiidae

▣ Middle Eocene: Adapiformes, Omomyidae, Eosimiidae, ?Tarsiidae

⬟ Middle Miiocene: ?Tarsiidae

★ Middle Miiocene: Pliopithecidae

☆ ?Early Miocene: ?Pliopithecidae

● Middle-Late Miocene: *Sivapithecus*

⊕ Late Miocene: Lorisidae, *Sivapithecus*

○ Middle-Late Miocene: Dryopithecinae

◑ Middle Miocene: Dryopithecinae, *Sivapithecus*

⊙ Late Miocene: "Sivaladapinae," *Gigantopithecus*, *Sivapithecus*

⊕ Late Miocene: "Sivaladapinae," Pliopithecidae, Dryopithecinae

◕ Late Miocene: Colobinae

● Late Miocene: Colobinae, ?*Macaca*

Map of Eastern and Southern Asia (heavy outline) showing major fossil localities with Paleocene-Miocene primates. Symbols indicate age and included primates, while numbers represent site names (in approximate chronological order), as follows: 1, Qian-Shan; 2, Nanxiong; 3, Naran Bulak; 4, Wutu; 5, Chorlakki; 6, Shanghuang; 7, Lushi; 8, Gonglangtou; 9, Pondaung; 10, Yuanqu Basin (incl. "River Section", Rencun, Heti); 11, Krabi; 12, Sihong; 13, Taben Buluk; 14, Manchar; 15, Kamlial; 16, Mae Long; 17, Maerzuizigou; 18, Ban San Khlang; 19, Xiaolongtan; 20, Chinji; 21, Domeli; 22, Kundal Nala; 23, Sethi Nagri; 24, Kaulial Kas; 25, Khaur; 26, Dhok Pathan; 27, Hasnot; 28, Tinau Khola; 29, Dhara; 30, Kangra; 31, Ramnagar; 32, Haritalyangar; 33, Shihueba; 34, Wudu; 35, Yushe. Sites 15 and 20–32 are representative of the Siwaliks; note that the density of Pakistan localities (15, 20–27) required that some site markers be moved to allow separation; Hasnot (site 27) is marked by two symbols inside the small circle, which corresponds to the actual Siwalik/Salt Range region.

documented ca. 12 Ma. Three time-successive species range through to ca. 8 Ma.

Also about 8 Ma, *Lufengpithecus* occurs in great quantity at Lufeng, also in Yunnan Province. Its cranial morphology is more conservative than that of *Sivapithecus*, and it is tentatively included in the Dryopithecinae. Other fossils in that subfamily occur in the Siwaliks ("*Sivapithecus*" *simonsi*, ca. 10 Ma) and western China (*Dryopithecus wuduensis* from Wudu, Gansu Province, ca. 8–6 Ma). Lufeng also yielded a pliopithecid and adapiforms, while adapiforms and a lorisid are known from the Siwaliks. The youngest Siwalik hominoid is *Gigantopithecus*, known by a mandible and an isolated tooth estimated at ca. 7–6 Ma. Numerous specimens of a younger species (*G. blacki*) are known from southern China between perhaps 2–0.5 Ma and from northern Vietnam ca. 0.5–0.3 Ma. It is generally assumed that *Gigantopithecus* is an offshoot of the pongine clade, but some *Lufengpithecus* specimens show striking similarities to the premolarized lower canines of the younger taxon. Another enigmatic hominoid occurs in supposedly Early Pliocene levels in Yuanmou County, Yunnan Province. The material has not been well described, but a juvenile face looks somewhat pongine, although the taxon has also been linked to *Lufengpithecus*.

The earliest cercopithecid monkeys in eastern Asia (teeth of a small colobine) appear in the Siwalik record ca. 7–6 Ma, coincident with other indications of faunal change. A few teeth from the latest Miocene of eastern China document a somewhat larger colobine and a macaque, the first Asian cercopithecine. Although the dating is unclear, the large terrestrial cercopithecine *Procynocephalus*, apparently a macaque derivative, appeared in Plio-Pleistocene deposits in the Siwaliks and in China. Its relationship to the generally similar *Paradolichopithecus*, which occurs mainly ca. 2 Ma from Spain to Tadzhikistan, is unclear. An even more enigmatic cercopithecine fossil is the single specimen of *Theropithecus oswaldi delsoni* from Mirzapur, India, perhaps dating to 1.5–0.9 Ma; other than one tooth from Spain, this genus is endemic to Africa. Fossils of the modern Asian genera *Macaca*, *Semnopithecus* (*Trachypithecus*), *Pygathrix* (*Rhinopithecus*), *Hylobates*, and *Pongo* are known from the Pleistocene of China, India, Indonesia, and Vietnam.

Human Paleontology and Archaeology

During the Early Pleistocene, early hominins almost certainly reached eastern Asia from Africa by first passing through southwestern Asia and then South Asia. What are perhaps the earliest fossil hominins in the region have been recovered from the island of Java and the Chinese sites of Gongwangling (at Lantian) and Longgupo (Wushan). In the past, Java and many other Indonesian islands were intermittently united with the mainland by exposure of the now-submerged Sunda Shelf, as the result of low sea levels during glacial periods, which provided dry-land migration routes for hominids and other Pleistocene mammals.

Although there is still no consensus as to how many hominin species are represented in Java, it is clear that the diversity of hominid taxa often has been overestimated. There is growing agreement that most of the adequately preserved speci-

mens, consisting of more than 50 individuals, represent a form of *H. erectus* that first reached Java well before 1 Ma; indeed, the earliest example may date to as much as 1.8–1.6 Ma, just younger than the oldest African specimens assigned to *H. erectus*. One form, *Meganthropus*, has occasionally been hypothesized to represent an Asian form of australopith, but little evidence supports this conjecture. In general, our interpretation of the Javanese forms has been hindered by the specimens' lack of accurate provenance, due in large part to the continuing practice of purchasing fossils from local collectors.

An assemblage of younger forms excavated apparently *in situ* in the 1930s, the so-called Solo hominids (also known as the Ngandong hominids), has remained controversial both because of the claim that they show evidence of cannibalism and because they appear to be morphologically intermediate between *H. erectus* and *H. sapiens*. There has been much debate not only about the species to which they belong, but also about whether they were ancestral to Australian aborigines. Moreover, a 1996 publication dates the Solo finds to 50–25 Ka, far younger than generally thought and contemporaneous with local anatomically modern humans. It is safe to say that much of the controversy that began with Dutch paleoanthropologist E. Dubois's original hominid finds of the 1890s continues unabated today.

Almost all of the other evidence for Early Pleistocene humans in East Asia comes from China, with the earliest and best-documented evidence of *H. erectus* from Lantian in Shanxi, North-Central China. Here a partial cranium (Gongwangling) and mandible (Chenjiawo) may date to the late Early Pleistocene (ca. 0.9–0.7 Ma). The cranium may be slightly older than the mandible, but this is no longer certain; some have even claimed that it dates to ca. 1.2 Ma. The cranium is small by comparison with later Chinese *H. erectus*, and the low cranial capacity, 780 ml, has been explained by its early date and by the interpretation of the specimen as a female; it is also badly crushed, with bones telescoped over one another.

A few other scattered finds from South China also offer tantalizing evidence of earlier Chinese hominids. Three teeth found in a karst cave in Hubei (Jian Shi) were at first thought by Chinese workers to represent a form of *Australopithecus*. At least two of these teeth are aberrant, however, and Chinese and Western workers now place these specimens in the genus *Homo*. The early age of the finds is also perhaps indicated by the fact that they were found in association with *Gigantopithecus*. The site of Longgupo in South China has also yielded fossils of *Homo* (or perhaps a pongine) and *Gigantopithecus* from the same stratigraphic unit. These are the only such association(s) known in China, but a similar association occurs in Vietnam at the cave sites of Lang Trang and Tham Khuyen.

Although two incisors from Yuanmou (Yunnan Province) were once thought, on the basis of associated fauna and paleomagnetic stratigraphy, to be older than 1.67 Ma, recent geological work and reanalysis of the paleomagnetic stratigraphy now place these specimens at well under 0.6 Ma. Researchers have always recognized that the morphology of the shovel-shaped incisors bears a strong resemblance to that of the Zhoukoudian specimens.

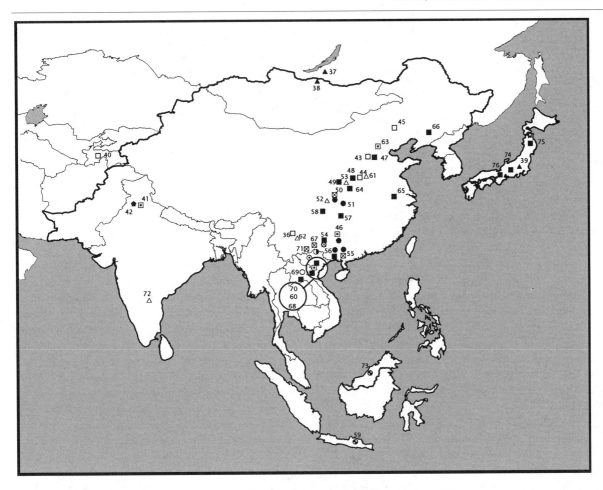

▲ Later Pliocene: *?Dolichopithecus*

□ Pliocene: *Procynocephalus*

■ Pleistocene: *Macaca*

▣ Late Pliocene-Pleistocene: *Macaca, Procynocephalus*

◓ Pleistocene: Colobinae, *Macaca, Hylobates, Pongo*

⬠ Pleistocene: *Theropithecus*

△ Pleistocene: Colobinae

⊠ Pleistocene: Colobinae, *Macaca*

● Early-Middle Pleistocene: *Gigantopithecus*

⊙ Pleistocene: *Hylobates*

⊗ Middle Pleistocene: *Hylobates, Gigantopithecus, Pongo*

◑ Middle Pleistocene: *Gigantopithecus, Pongo*

○ Middle Pleistocene: *Pongo*

Map of Eastern and Southern Asia (heavy outline) showing major fossil localities with Pliocene-Pleistocene primates. Symbols indicate age and included primates, while numbers represent site names (in approximate chronological order), as follows: 36, Hudieliangzi; 37, Udunga; 38, Shamar; 39, Atsugi; 40, Kuruksay* (taxon is* Paradolichopithecus, *not* Procynocephalus*); 41, Pinjor; 42, Mirzapur; 43, Gudi; 44, Xinan (Pliocene); 45, Dongcun; 46, Liucheng; 47, Chingshihling; 48, Mianchi; 49, Gongwangling; 50, Longgupo; 51, Longgudong; 52, Yenchingkou I; 53, Xishuidong; 54, Bama; 55, Heidong; 56, Wuming; 57, Dongpaoshan; 58, Koloshan; 59, Trinil and Sangiran; 60, Lang Trang; 61, Xinan (Mid Pleistocene); 62, Hoshangdong; 63, Zhoukoudian; 64, Dujiagou; 65, Longtandong (Hexian); 66, Miaohoushan; 67, Tham Khuyen, Tham Hai, Keo Leng; 68, Tham Om; 69, Tam Hang; 70, Tung Lang; 71, Hang Hum; 72, Karnul Caves; 73, Niah; 74, Ushikawa; 75, Shiriya; 76, Kanondo. Pairs of symbols stacked vertically with one number relate to a single site. * indicates locality outside geographic area, but included for comparison. Site numbering sequence continues from previous map of earlier primate localities.*

The oldest artifacts from stratified contexts in eastern Asia derive from China: in the north the Nihewan Basin (Hebei Province) and Lantian (Shanxi Province) and in the south, the Baise Basin (Guangxi Province). These simple assemblages of cores, chopper-chopping tools, and flakes may date to the Jaramillo Subchron, at ca. 1 Ma, or slightly older in the case of the earliest Nihewan sites. Work in the Nihewan Basin in the 1980s has confirmed that two localities (Xiaochangliang and Donggutuo) contain undoubted artifacts in a lakeside context in association with abundant fauna and chert artifacts, consisting mainly of simple flakes and cores.

Co-occurrence of *Hipparion* and *Equus* confirms the paleomagnetic correlation. The Donggutuo locality appears to be a colluvial deposit that does not document hominid occupation. The Xiaochangliang site is, on the other hand, a hominid-utilization site where cores, flakes, microdebitage and some surprisingly standardized artifact types are associated with a fauna, some of which exhibits signs of butchering. Bifacially worked, roughly pointed cores approximating crude protohandaxes as well as ovates unifacially shaped on large flakes have been reported from localities in the Baise Basin of South China dating to 740 Ka. Still older deposits apparently dating to ca. 2 Ma near Riwat, Pakistan, have produced chipped stones claimed as artifacts but questioned by some archaeologists.

In northern Thailand, a few sites offer archaeological evidence for hominins in mainland Southeast Asia during the late Early Pleistocene. Mae Tha and Ban Don Mun have yielded unifacially and bifacially worked quartzite cobbles that stratigraphically underlie basalts of reversed polarity. Another locality, Kao Pah Nam, has yielded artifacts and a hearth in association with fauna in a rockshelter. The locality remains undated, but the mammalian fauna strongly suggests a Middle Pleistocene age. The only early human fossils in Southeast Asia are a very few isolated teeth from the Vietnamese caves Tham Khuyen and Tham Hai. Two teeth and cranial fragments comparable to those of Chinese *H. erectus* were recovered from the late Early and early Middle Pleistocene contexts at Tan Hang Cave in northern Laos.

Zhoukoudian (formerly Chou-k'ou-tien) Locality 1 is the most famous of the Chinese Middle Pleistocene localities. This cave complex has yielded partial remains of more than 40 individuals from the excavation of more than 40 m of brecciated sediments. The cave, located ca. 45 km southwest of Beijing, has been worked on and off since a few teeth were first recovered in 1927. Unfortunately, the original collection was lost in late 1941, during World War II. The records of careful prewar excavation, accurate casts, precise descriptive analyses by German paleoanthropologist F. Weidenreich, and postwar Chinese work have all helped minimize the loss of information.

We are fairly confident that *H. erectus* occupied the cave intermittently between ca. 0.6 and 0.25 Ma, because of the agreement of a variety of modern dating techniques. Much evidence bearing on the behavior of these hominids has also been forthcoming over the years. Layers of charcoal and "ash" interspersed throughout the middle and upper layers suggested that Zhoukoudian hominids used fire on a regular basis, even if it cannot be shown that they knew how to make it. Chemical analysis in 1996 and 1997, however, showed that ash was not present in these gray-colored lenses, at least in the area of the remaining deposits. Burned hackberry seeds and the charred remains of large mammals like deer and horses have also been put forward as evidence for the diet of "Peking Man." The blackening on some bones may be a result of manganese staining but others are clearly burned. There has also been a renewed recognition of the role that carnivores, which also occupied the cave at times, must have played in the accumulation and modification of the bones that document the Zhoukoudian fauna. Nonetheless, some of the bones are indisputably worked by stone tools. There is much less evidence, however, for the existence of the bone-tool industry once postulated by early workers. The stone-tool industry from the cave consists mostly of simply flaked vein quartz and other substances that are poor natural materials from which to manufacture more standardized artifacts. The fossils of "Peking Man" have at times been taken to show evidence of cannibalism, but, again, this is far from certain. The cranial capacity of Zhoukoudian hominins probably increased through time (from ca. 0.5 to ca. 0.2 Ma), as did

the complexity and standardizations of their tool kits. Further study of this unique locality will enlarge our knowledge of hominid adaptation in the Pleistocene.

Additional cranial remains of Chinese *H. erectus* have been announced, but, as of the late 1990s, inadequately reported from Hexian (Anhui Province), Yunxian (Hubei Province), and Tangshan (near Nanjing, Anhui Province); other sites have yielded teeth. The Hexian cranium may document the latest known *H. erectus* in China. The Nanjing and Yunxian crania may present some morphological characters that recall those of early *H. sapiens*.

The nature and the antiquity of Asian archaeological assemblages continue to spark debate. A major point of contention has been the distributions of Acheulean assemblages and the so-called chopper-chopping tool complex. In 1940, American prehistorian H.L. Movius recognized a difference in the geographical distribution of these assemblages, with Acheulean assemblages occurring in central and southern parts of the Indian subcontinent and more crudely manufactured, nonbifacially worked assemblages occurring farther east. Local variations of the Mode 1 chopper-chopping tool complex have been given various names: Pacitanian (Indonesia), Anyathian (Burma), Fingnoian (Thailand), and Tampanian (Malaysia). Movius further suggested that a line, termed *Movius's line* by his colleague the American anthropologist C.S. Coon, could be drawn between the "cultural backwater" of eastern Asia and the "more developed" cultures of Africa, India, and Europe. Others have suggested that this line may actually reflect different adaptations to contrasting environments, with the East Asian assemblages reflecting the exploitation of decidedly more forested habitats. G.G. Pope has suggested that bamboo provided a versatile raw material that, to a large extent, supplanted a reliance on lithic raw materials.

Debate has been further complicated by the fact that the vast majority of Asian archaeological assemblages, especially outside of China, cannot be shown to be earlier than ca. 60 Ka. Some artifacts have been recovered from Middle Pleistocene contexts in Siberia, India, and Southeast Asia, but they tell us little about the nature and extent of variation of the Early Paleolithic in Asia. Apparently later Middle Pleistocene sites in India have long yielded assemblages with handaxes effectively identical to those from Europe and Africa. S. Mishra and colleagues reported that the Bori site near Pune (Maharashtra state) has yielded numerous flakes and several simple bifaces in association with tephra layers dated to 670 Ka by $^{39}Ar/^{40}Ar$. Younger Acheulean sites in South Asia have been dated less securely. Middle Paleolithic (Middle Stone Age) assemblages are also known in quantity.

As in Southeast Asia, no Acheulean or handaxe assemblages have yet been recognized in China. Chinese workers recognize two "tool traditions" in what is probably a highly oversimplified interpretation of the archaeological record there: a large-tool tradition including "protobifaces" and "choppers" and a small-tool tradition composed largely of undifferentiated flakes. Some assemblages, like those from Dingcun, are said to be composed of both traditions. A selection of artifacts from the Lantian region (but not the two sites yielding human remains), Dingcun, and a few other sites have been

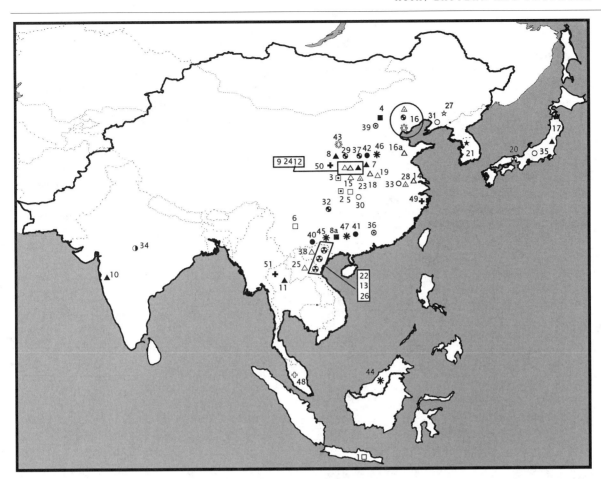

Early Pleistocene: *Homo erectus* (□)

Early Pleistocene: Early Paleolithic (■)

Early Pleistocene: *H. erectus* & Early Paleolithic (▣)

Middle Pleistocene: *Homo erectus* (△)

Middle Pleistocene: "archaic *Homo sapiens*" (○)

Middle Pleistocene: "archaic *H. sapiens*" (or *H. erectus*) (◉)

Middle Pleistocene: Early Paleolithic (▲)

Middle Pleistocene: Early or Middle Paleolithic (★)

Middle Pleistocene: *H. erectus* & Early Paleolithic (⧊)

Middle Pleistocene: "archaic *H. sapiens*" & Early or Middle Paleolithic (☆)

Middle Pleistocene: "archaic *H. sapiens*" & Middle Paleolithic (◓)

Late Middle or early Late Pleistocene: "archaic *H. sapiens*" & Early or Middle Paleolithic (◑)

Late Pleistocene: "archaic *Homo sapiens*" (●)

Late Pleistocene: "archaic *H. sapiens*" & Middle Paleolithic (◉)

Late Pleistocene: *Homo sapiens sapiens* (✳)

Late Pleistocene: *H. s. sapiens* & Late Paleolithic (❄)

?Late Pleistocene: Tampanian – probably post-Paleolithic (⊕)

Holocene: Neolithic or other post-Paleolithic (✚)

Map of Eastern and Southern Asia (heavy outline) showing major fossil hominin and archaeological localities. Symbols indicate age and included taxa and/or industries, while numbers represent site names (in approximate chronological order), as follows: *1, Mojokerto, Sangiran, Solo, Trinil, etc.; 2, Longgupo; 3, Gongwangling (Lantian); 4, Nihewan; 5, Longgudong (Jian Shi); 6, Yuanmou; 7, Xihoudu; 8, Xishuidong; 8a, Baise; 9, Chenchiawo (Lantian); 10, Bori; 11, Mae Tha, Ban Don Mun, Kao Pah Nam; 12, Kehe; 13, Lang Trang; 14, Huludong (Nanjing); 15, Yunxian (Quyuanhekou); 16, Zhoukoudian (note 3 symbols of different age); 16A, Qizianshan (Yiyuan); 17, Takamori; 18, Xinhuashan (Nanzhao); 19, Dujiagou (Yunxian); 20, Nishiyagi; 21, Chon-gok-ni; 22, Tham Khuyen, Tham Hai, Keo Leng; 23, Bailongdong (Yunxi); 24, Donghe (Luonan); 25, Tam Hang; 26, Tham Om; 27, Miaohoushan; 28, Longtandong (Hexian); 29, Dali; 30, Longdong (Changyang); 31, Jinniushan (Yinkou); 32, Tongzi (Tungtzu); 33, Yinshan (Chaoxian); 34, Hathnora (Narmada); 35, Ushikawa; 36, Maba; 37, Dingcun; 38, Hang Hum; 39, Xujiayao; 40, Xuanrendong (Xichou); 41, Shuiyen; 42, Xigou; 43, Salawusu; 44, Niah; 45, Jiulengshan; 46, Xiaonanhai; 47, Liujiang; 48, Kota Tampan; 49, Hemudu; 50, Banpo; 51, Spirit Cave. Numerous sites in southern Asia yielding only archaeological residues are not indicated. Two sets of symbols boxed because of insufficient space for site numbers, no special relationship implied.*

interpreted as bifaces, but they are either of uncertain prove-nance or younger than ca. 150 Ka. Well-made bifaces are also known from Chon-gok-ni in South Korea, which have been demonstrated to date to the final Middle or early Late Pleistocene. All of these are probably unrelated to the Acheulean tradition of Africa, Europe, Southwest Asia, and India. Clearly, much remains to be done to clarify and define the earlier Paleolithic in East Asia. In the 1990s, however, symmetrical pointed unifacial tools and partially flaked bifacial tools on large flakes have been recovered from the Baise basin in south China. These finds, which predate 0.732 ± 0.039 Ma, together with small well-made bifaces from Takamori in Japan dating to c. 500 Ka, begin to blur the distinctions made by Movius.

Several regions of mainland southern and eastern Asia have provided evidence about the later phases of human evolution. Crania from India (Narmada) and China (Dali, Xujiayao, Mapa, Jinniushan) testify to the presence of various forms of *Homo* morphologically intermediate between *H. erectus* and anatomically modern *H. sapiens*. Like the Ngandong hominids, the Dali specimen has been of particular interest, since its morphology has been claimed to bridge the gap between *H. erectus* and modern regional Asian populations while at the same time diverging from the morphology of the "archaic *Homo sapiens*" known from Africa and Europe. Other researchers consider that it is within the range of such Western fossils as Petralona and Kabwe. No true Neanderthals are known within the areal range of eastern and southern Asia, although they do extend eastward to the margins of western Central Asia (Uzbekistan).

The origin and antiquity of the modern races of Asia are poorly understood. Early workers, such as Weidenreich, discerned contemporaneous racial types—Esquimoid, Melanesian, and Ainu (related to Caucasian)—in a sample from the Upper Cave at Zhoukoudian. Other authors, such as C. Coon, M.H. Wolpoff, and A.T. Thorne, have suggested that even Middle Pleistocene Asian hominids show a regional continuity that allies them with recent and modern populations in the same areas of Asia. On the other hand, based on both paleontological and genetic analyses, it has been suggested that anatomically modern *H. sapiens* were the result of invading populations that replaced the descendants of *H. erectus*. These alternative models of modern human origins often focus on the South and East Asian fossil evidence. A variety of modern human remains discovered in the 1990s in China were reviewed in 1996 by D. Etler, and detailed studies of these should help to clarify the relationships of early East Asians.

Late Palaeolithic artifacts accompany anatomically modern people in eastern Asia, but the assemblages are characterized by a low frequency of blades. Microliths are also rare in China, except in the north, which also has wedge-shaped cores not unlike those found at a later date in Alaska. Bone needles and harpoons, elaborate jewelry, and grave goods were included with the burials at Zhoukoudian Upper Cave.

Early evidence of agriculture and domestication, established in Southwest Asia by 11 Ka, is also found somewhat later in northeastern Asia (Japan). Although dates as early as ca. 10 Ka have been claimed for horticultural practices at Spirit Cave in northern Thailand, most workers think that the evidence is equivocal and does not distinguish between food collecting and horticulture. At Jomon sites in Japan, with an economic pattern of sedentism apparently based on fishing, pottery is thought to antedate 12.5 Ka and is followed by the introduction of cereal grains by 9 Ka. By 5 Ka, rice farming was established in several areas, including Thailand and coastal China, where sites such as Hemudu (Zhejiang) suggest a mixture of hunting (deer, rhinoceros, elephant), rice cultivation, and animal husbandry (pigs and water buffalo). By 5000–2500 BP, the coastal Neolithic culture (Longshan) was also characterized by such classic Chinese crafts as jade carving, and scapulimancy (predicting the future from the patterning of cracks in burned animal bones, especially scapulae). Inland sites reflect a different line of Neolithic development: the Yangshao culture. At the site of Banpo near Xian in north China's Shanxi Province, dating to ca. 7000 BP, an elaborate system of defensive ditches and walls protected the settlement of farmers. A very large, centrally located structure and a specialized area set aside for the production of beautifully painted pottery also suggest the early development of economic and social complexity. Fishhooks and barbed points, together with the stylized fish designs on the pottery, suggest the importance of this resource as a supplement to an agricultural economy based on millet and pigs.

See also Acheulean; Adapiformes; Africa; Anthropoidea; Archaic Homo sapiens; Asia, Western; China; Dali; Decoredon; Dingcun; Dryopithecinae; Early Paleolithic; Eosimiidae; Europe; Gigantopithecus; Hexian; Homo; Homo erectus; Homo sapiens; Indonesia; Jinniushan; Lang Trang; Lantian; Longuppo; Lorisidae; Lufeng; Lufengpithecus; Meganthropus; Modern Human Origins; Narmada; Neolithic; Ngandong (Solo); Nihewan; Notharctidae; Omomyidae; Paleolithic; Paleolithic Lifeways; Petrolemur; Plesiadapiformes; Pliopithecidae; Pondaung; Ponginae; Raw Materials; Russia; Sivapithecus; Siwaliks; Stone-Tool Making; Xiaochangliang; Yuanmou; Zhoukoudian. [G.G.P., A.S.B., E.D.]

Further Readings

Akazawa, T., Aoki, K., and Kimura, T., eds. (1992) The Evolution and Dispersal of Modern Humans in Asia. Tokyo: Hokusen-Sha.

Andrews, P., and Franzen, J.L., eds. (1984) The early evolution of man, with special emphasis on Southeast Asia and Africa. Cour. Forsch. Inst. Senckenberg 69:1–277.

Barry, J.C. (1995) Faunal turnover and diversity in the terrestrial Neogene of Pakistan. In E.S. Vrba, G.H. Denton, T.C. Partridge, and L.H. Burckle (eds.): Paleoclimate and Evolution, with Emphasis on Human Origins. New Haven: Yale University Press, pp. 114–134.

Etler, D. (1996) The fossil evidence for human evolution in Asia. Ann. Rev. Anthropol. 25:275–301.

Franzen, J.L., ed. (1994) 100 Years of Pithecanthropus: The *Homo erectus* problem. Cour. Forsch. Inst. Senckenberg 171:1–361.

Harrison, T., Delson, E., and Guan, J. (1991) A new species of *Pliopithecus* from the Middle Miocene of China and its implications for early catarrhine zoogeography. J. Hum. Evol. 21:329–361.

Huang, W., and Hou, Y. (1997) Archaeological evidence for the first human colonisation of East Asia. Indo-Pacific Prehistory Association Bulletin 16(3):3–12.

Ikawa-Smith, F. (1978) Early Paleolithic in South and East Asia. The Hague: Mouton.

Mishra, S., Venkatesan, T.R., Rajaguru, S.N., and Somaya-julu, B.L.K. (1995) Earliest Acheulian industry from peninsular India. Curr. Anthropol. 36:847–851.

Olsen, J.W., and Miller-Antonio, S. (1992) The Paleolithic in Southern China. Asian Persp. 31(2):129–160.

Petraglia, M.D., and Korisettar, R. (eds.) (1998) Early Human Behavior in Global Context. London: Routledge.

Pope, G.G. (1992) The craniofacial evidence for the origin of modern humans in China. Yrbk. Phys. Anthropol. 35:243–298.

Pope, G.G. (1993) Ancient Asia's cutting edge. Nat. Hist. 102(5):55–59.

Pope, G.G., and Keates, S.G. (1994) The evolution of human cognition and cultural capacity: A view from the Far East. In R.S. Corruccini and R.L. Ciochon (eds.) Integrative Paths to the Past. Englewood Cliffs, N.J.: Prentice-Hall, pp. 531–567.

Russell, D.E., and Zhai, R. (1987) The Paleogene of Asia: Mammals and stratigraphy. Mém. Mus. Nat. Hist. Nat. (Paris) 52:1–488.

Schick, K.D., and Dong, Z.A. (1993) Early Paleolithic of China and Eastern Asia. Evol. Anthropol. 2:22–35.

Schwartz, J.H., Long, V.T., Cuong, N.L., Kha, L.T., and Tattersall, I. (1995) A review of the Pleistocene hominoid fauna of the Socialist Republic of Vietnam (excluding Hylobatidae). Anthropol. Pap. Am. Mus. Nat. Hist. 76:1–24.

Swisher, C.C., Rink, W.J., Anton, S.C., Schwarcz, H.P., Curtis, G.H., Suprijo, A., Widiasmoro (1996) Latest *Homo erectus* of Java: Potential contemporaneity with *Homo sapiens* in southeast Asia. Science 274:1870–1874.

Weiner, S., Xu, Q., Liu, J., Goldberg, P., and Bar-Yosef, O. (1998) Evidence for the use of fire at Zhoukoudian, China. Science. 281:251–253.

Wolpoff, M.H. (1996) Human Evolution, 1996–1997 edition. New York: McGraw-Hill.

Wu, R., and Olsen, J.W., eds. (1985) Paleoanthropology and Paleolithic Archaeology in the People's Republic of China. New York: Academic.

Wu, X., and Poirier, F.E. (1995) Human Evolution in China: A Metric Description of the Fossils and a Review of the Sites. New York: Oxford University Press.

Asia, Western

Geographic region extending from western Turkey to eastern Afghanistan and from the Arabian Peninsula and the Persian/Arabian Gulf to the Caucasian and Central Asian republics of the former Soviet Union; it includes what is sometimes referred to as the Near East, the Middle East, or Southwest Asia. Western Asia as used in this work is bounded on the north by Russia, on the east by Pakistan and China, and on the south and west by Europe and the Black, Mediterranean, Red, and Arabian seas. It shares many cultural and ecological features with North Africa (including Egypt), South Asia (Pakistan, India, and Sri Lanka), and southern Russia. Despite long and complex cultural and historical interactions among these areas, however, western Asia is sufficiently distinctive in its ecology and culture to be treated as a separate entity by historians, geographers, and social scientists. The rest of Asia is considered in the articles ASIA, EASTERN AND SOUTHERN and RUSSIA.

Western Asia encompasses a wide range of habitats—temperate, hyperarid, humid, desert, steppe, mountains—but it is generally characterized by long, hot, rainless summers and cooler, wetter winters. Linguistically and culturally diverse in the earliest historic periods five millennia ago, the area is dominated today by Muslims of various sects but is also home to Christians, Jews, Yazidis, and other religious minorities distributed among a range of ethnic groups. The region was the setting for most of the first successful experiments in plant cultivation and stock breeding, as well as the earliest civilizations, and current adaptations are marked by complex interactions among sedentary village agriculturalists, mobile pastoralists, and city dwellers.

Our understanding of prehistoric settlement patterns is distorted both by the history of archaeological investigation and by the burial of sites by late- and postglacial geomorphological processes. Some areas, like the Arabian Desert and Anatolia, are poorly known; others, especially the Levantine border of the eastern Mediterranean and the Zagros Mountains of Iraq and Iran, have been comparatively well explored. As further research is carried out in western Asia, our understanding of various prehistoric periods there, and of the area's place in the prehistoric world, will continue to improve. The archaeology of western Asia is best and most extensively documented for the Holocene, but there is scattered evidence of occupation earlier in the Pleistocene. Palynological analysis suggests that climatic regimes and vegetational successions during the later Pleistocene differed from one region to the next, but through much of the past 2 Myr the greater part of Southwest Asia was colder and drier than it is at present.

Primate Fossils

During the Paleogene, most of western Asia was effectively part of the Eurasian landmass and thus separated from the island continent of Afro-Arabia, although it was broken up into a number of small tectonic plates. By ca. 18 Ma, the Afro-Arabian plate made contact with Eurasia to its northeast, allowing the passage of terrestrial mammals, including primates, between the two areas. Central to this interchange was the western-most part of Asia, with important early fossils in both Saudi Arabia and Turkey in the Miocene. A hominoid jaw fragment and several teeth from Ad Dabtiyah (Saudi Arabia), named *Heliopithecus* and dated to ca. 17 Ma, document the continuity of the African catarrhine fauna across the Red Sea

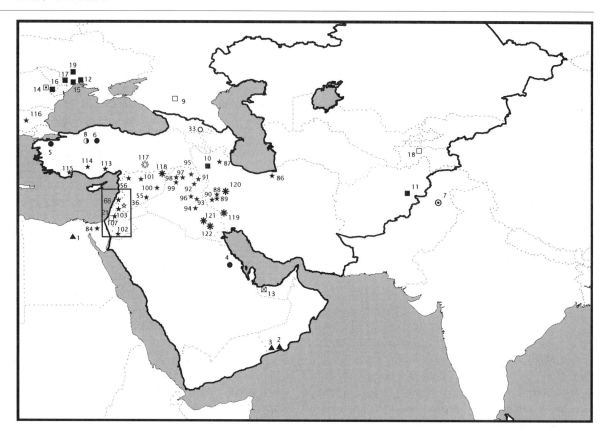

▲ Late Eocene-Early Oligocene: early Anthropoidea

⊠ Late Miocene: Cercopithecidae indeterminate

□ Pliocene-Pleistocene: Cercopithecinae

■ Pliocene: Colobinae

⊡ Pliocene: Cercopithecinae & Colobinae

◉ Miocene-Pleistocene: Adapiformes, Lorisidae, Cercopithecidae, Dryopithecinae, Ponginae

● Middle Miocene: *Kenyapithecinae*

○ Late Miocene: *Dryopithecus*

◑ Late Miocene: *Ankarapithecus*

★ Epi-Paleolithic and/or Neolithic

☆ ?Neolithic

✳ Post-Neolithic (cities)

✱ Neolithic & Post-Neolithic

Map of Western (and Central) Asia (heavy outline) showing major fossil localities with primates and post-Paleolithic archaeological sites. Symbols indicate age and included primates or cultural content, while numbers represent site names (in approximate chronological order), as follows: 1, Fayum*; 2, Taqah; 3, Thaytiniti; 4, Ad Dabtiyah; 5, Pasalar; 6, Candir; 7, Potwar Siwaliks*; 8, Sinap Tepe; 9, Udabno; 10, Maragheh; 11, Molayan; 12, Grebeniki*; 13, Djebel Dhanna 3 (Abu Dhabi); 14, Malusteni*; 15, Kuchurgan valley*; 16, Budey*; 17, Novopetrovka*; 18, Kuruksay; 19, Kotlovina*; 21, 'Ubeidiya; 32, El Kowm; 33, Kudaro*; 36, Jabrud; 55, Douara; 56, Dederiyeh; 68, Ksar-Akil; 84, Mushabi*; 85, Abu Hureyra; 86, Belt & Hotu Caves; 87, Sarab; 88, Ganj Dareh; 89, Ali Kosh; 90, Asiab; 91, Karim Shahir; 92, Jarmo; 93, Choga Mani; 94, Jemdet Nasr; 95, Zawi Chemi Shanidar; 96, Tell es-Sawwan; 97, M'lefaat; 98, Hassuna; 99, Umm Dabaghiyah; 100, Bouqras; 101, Mureybit; 102, Beidha; 103, 'Ain Ghazal; 107, Jericho; 113, Mersin; 114, Çatal Hüyük; 115, Hacilar; 116, Karanovo*; 117, Cayonnu; 118, Tell Brak; 119, Susa; 120, Godin Tepe; 121, Uruk; 122, Ur. * indicates locality outside geographic area, but included for comparison. Rectangle outlines Levantine region shown at larger scale in later illustration; a few sites in this region are shown for reference, while others fill the "gaps" in the number sequence.

Rift at this time. *Heliopithecus* is very similar to the contemporaneous *Afropithecus* from northern Kenya, and together these forms represent the earliest members of Hominidae.

The importance of this region as a migration corridor for higher primates during the Miocene is documented by the presence of several species of monkeys and apes. From Paşalar and Çandir, western Turkish sites dated at ca. 16–15 Ma, come a partial mandible and hundreds of isolated teeth that can be identified as the kenyapithecine *Griphopithecus*. Younger specimens from the Sinap beds (western Turkey, 9.8 Ma) were once termed *Sivapithecus* but are now recognized as *Ankarapithecus meteai*. This genus is similar to the pongine *Sivapithecus* from the Indo-Pakistani Siwaliks, but it is less *Pongo*-like in retaining the conservative broader interorbital region and stronger supraorbital torus. Two teeth originally

named *Udabnopithecus* but now included in *Dryopithecus* are known from the Georgian Republic on the northwestern margin of western Asia.

In the later Miocene, the southern European colobine monkey *Mesopithecus* is known from Maragheh (northwestern Iran) and Molayan, near Kabul (Afghanistan); similar colobines extend eastward into the Siwaliks. An isolated male canine not yet identifiable as to subfamily is known from one of several Late Miocene (ca. 8–6 Ma) localities in Abu Dhabi. Macaque monkeys probably also spread through the region in the Pliocene, but the earliest fossils are from the Early Pleistocene of 'Ubeidiya (Israel). The probable macaque relative *Paradolichopithecus* is known by a species in Tadzhikistan (at Kuruk, ca. 1.9 Ma), apparently different from that known in southern Europe.

Early Paleolithic

During the Paleolithic, western Asia exhibits evidence both of indigenous cultural development and of influences (probably including numerous migrations) from adjacent regions. The earliest documented hominin presence in western Asia occurs at 'Ubeidiya (Israel), which dates to at least the end of the Matuyama Chron (older than 780 Ka) and probably to ca. 1.4 Ma on biochronologic grounds. Claims of artifacts from the Pliocene Erq el-Ahmar Formation in the Jordan Valley have yet to be thoroughly investigated. While the Early Acheulean and Developed Oldowan archaeological residues at 'Ubeidiya are very similar to those found in East Africa (especially Olduvai Upper Bed II), palynological analysis and studies of fossils from this site indicate a temperate climate much like that found in southern Europe. It seems likely that 'Ubeidiya reflects early hominin exploration of temperate environments. Several human teeth have been queried as to provenance, but they may well represent *Homo erectus*. A mandible of that species from Dmanisi in the Georgian Republic is dated to 1.5–0.9 Ma; while technically located in southeasternmost Europe, it is presumably indicative of the earliest human populations of western Asia.

Archaeological sites of Middle Pleistocene age are known from open-air contexts, such as Latamne and other sites on the terraces of the Orontes River and from the El Kowm oasis in Syria; from Gesher Benot Ya'acov, Kissufim, Holon, Maayan Barukh, and the Evron Quarry in Israel; from Berekat Ram on the Golan Heights; and from numerous other localities throughout the region. Middle Pleistocene cave deposits are somewhat less common. Such sites include Umm Qatafa, Jabrud, Ras el-Kelb (Bezez and Zumoffen caves), Zuttiyeh, and Tabūn Cave Levels E-G. Very few verified occurrences of Early Paleolithic remains (e.g., Barda Balka in Iraq and the lower levels of Karain Cave in Turkey) have been recovered from the Taurus-Zagros Mountain ranges or the Iranian Plateau.

The lithic industrial succession in southwestern Asia is very similar to that seen in Europe and adjacent parts of North Africa. Early Paleolithic assemblages lacking handaxes, such as those found in the Fi Member at 'Ubeidiya, are often described as Developed Oldowan. Similar assemblages from caves (e.g., Tabūn Level G) are frequently called Tayacian or Tabunian. Early Acheulean assemblages, like those from 'Ubeidiya and Latamne, feature rather blocky bifaces and trihedral picks, generally made of basalt or flint. Somewhat later Acheulean assemblages feature more symmetrical bifaces and the use of Levallois prepared-core techniques (e.g., at Maayan Barukh in the Huleh Valley and Berekat Ram). One site in particular, Gesher Benot Ya'acov, features basalt cleavers made on large rectangular flakes struck from boulders. This technique is strongly reminiscent of the Tachengit/Tabalbalat technique from Morocco, where it is also used to produce cleavers, and its occurrence at Gesher Benot Ya'acov may hint at a cultural connection between the Levant and North Africa.

In the late Middle Pleistocene, unique regional variants of the Acheulean appear in the Levant and possibly in the Taurus Mountains. One of these variants, the Mugharan tradition (also known as the Acheulo-Jabrudian industry) is known from Tabūn E, Bezez C, El Kowm, Jabrud rockshelter 1a Levels 11–18, and Zuttiyeh. The Mugharan is marked by widely variable percentages of thin, symmetrical handaxes, thick and steeply retouched sidescrapers, and—in some levels—unusually high numbers of prismatic blades struck from simple unidirectional cores. The Levallois technique is generally absent from Mugharan sites on the Mediterranean coast, but it is present in Late Acheulean sites from the interior of the Levant, such as Maayan Barukh, Berekat Ram, and numerous sites in the El Kowm oasis. At several sites (Tabūn, Ras el-Kelb, Jabrud), Mugharan levels feature a precociously early blade industry generally known as the Pre-Aurignacian or the Amudian (after the Wadi Amud in the eastern Galilee).

Early Paleolithic hominin fossils from the Levant consist of a few isolated and highly fragmentary remains, such as the Zuttiyeh frontal, femoral diaphyseal fragments from Gesher Benot Ya'acov and Tabūn Ea, and a few isolated teeth (Tabūn Ea, 'Ubeidiya). While all of these remains are attributable to *Homo*, their fragmentary nature in most cases precludes any precise (i.e., species-level) assessment of their relationships to one another or to hominin populations in adjacent regions. The Zuttiyeh frontal has been interpreted as both pre-Neanderthal and premodern (on the basis of its seemingly high forehead), but it may best be considered comparable to the Florisbad (South Africa) face of similar age: an "archaic *Homo sapiens*" without Neanderthal features but possibly foreshadowing early moderns.

In most respects, the Early Paleolithic archaeological evidence from the Levant is similar to that seen in Middle Pleistocene Europe and during the Early to Middle Pleistocene of Africa. Patches of ashy sediments at Tabūn seem plausibly attributable to human control of fire. On the basis of their geographic position and/or their faunal associations, most Early Paleolithic sites probably were located within the Mediterranean woodland phytogeographic zone, which features a wide range of plant and small animal food sources. Apart from Tayacian occupations in the lower levels of Karain (Turkey), there is little evidence of sustained human presence in the montane zones or in the steppe-desert. Unfortunately, the quality of faunal preservation is so poor at most Early Paleolithic sites that it is difficult to obtain detailed information about hominin hunting or scavenging strategies.

In the eastern part of western Asia, numerous localities with predominantly Mode 1 (pebble-chopper) tools and flakes are known. The most secure lithic evidence comes from the stratified site Karatau I, found in a 90-m loess deposit in Tadzhikistan, thermoluminescence-dated to ca. 200 Ka. There a paleosol 64 m below the surface was excavated over an area of 500 m², yielding more than 600 artifacts (mainly flakes and fragments, with some 50 chopper cores). A more ancient assemblage was recovered from Kuldara, ca. 100 km to the east. There a sequence of 28 paleosols was excavated in a river gorge, with the artifact horizon in geomagnetically reversed layers between normal ones, suggesting a Late Matuyama age ca. 0.85 (between 0.97 and 0.78) Ma. In a surface of 40 m², at least 40 artifacts were recovered,

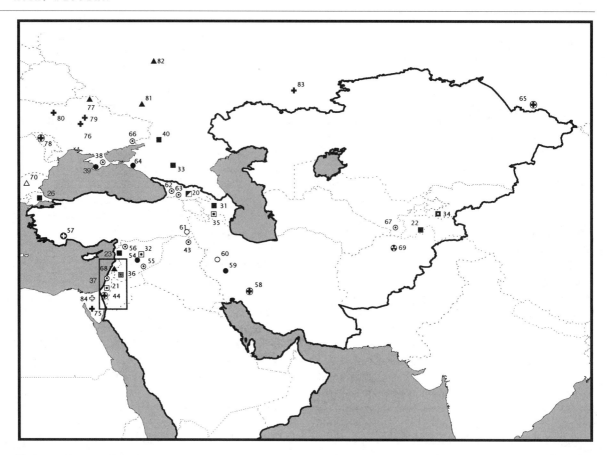

Legend

☐ Pliocene-Pleistocene: Ceropithecinae

◪ Early Paleolithic & Homo erectus

▣ Early Paleolithic &? Homo erectus

▣ Early Paleolithic & "archaic Homo sapiens"

▣ Early Paleolithic &? "archaic Homo sapiens"

■ Early Paleolithic

⊙ Early &? Middle Paleolithic

▣ Earlly, Middle & Upper Paleolithic

⊙ Middle Paleolithic & Neanderthal

◯ Middle Paleolithic &? Neanderthal

⊗ Middle Paleolithic & Neanderthal OR Homo sapiens sapiens

◑ Middle Paleolithic & Homo sapiens sapiens

◐ Middle & Upper Paleolithic & Neanderthal &? H. s. sapiens

△ Middle & Upper Paleolithic &? Neanderthal

⊕ Middle & Upper Paleolithic

✛ ?Middle & Upper Paleolithoic

● Middle Paleolithic

▲ Upper Paleolithic & Homo sapiens sapiens

✚ Upper Paleolithic

♱ ?Upper Paleolithic

Map of Western (and Central) Asia (heavy outline) showing major fossil hominin and Paleolithic archaeological localities. Symbols indicate age and included included taxa and/or industries, while numbers represent site names (in approximate chronological order), as follows: 20, Dmanisi; 21, 'Ubeidiya; 22, Kuldara; 23, Latamne; 24, Maayan Barukh; 25, Gesher Benot Ya'acov; 26, Yarimburgaz*; 27, Zuttiyeh; 28, Holon; 29, Kissufim; 30, Evron; 31, Barda Balka; 32, El Kowm; 33, Kudaro*; 34, Selungur; 35, Asych; 36, Jabrud; 37, Tabun; 38, Kiik-Koba*; 39, Starosel'je*; 40, Mikhailovskij Khutor*; 41, Djebel Qafzeh; 42, Skhul; 43, Shanidar; 44, Boker Tachtit; 45, Berekhat Ram; 46, Shovakh; 47, Nahal Aqev; 48, Quneitra; 49, Rosh Ein Mor; 50, Amud; 51, Kebarah; 52, Shukbah; 53, Ras-el-Kelb; 54, Jerf Ajla; 55, Douara; 56, Dederiyeh; 57, Karain; 58, Warwasi; 59, Kunji; 60, Bisitun; 61, Tamtama; 62, Sakhazia; 63, Dzhruchula; 64, Il'skaia*; 65, Strashnaya*; 66, Rozhok*; 67, Teshik-Tash; 68, Ksar-Akil; 69, Darra-i-Kur; 70, Bacho Kiro*; 71, Emireh; 72, El Wad; 73, Erq el Ahmar; 74, Sefunim; 75, Lagama; 76, Mezhirich*; 77, Mezin*; 78, Molodova*; 79, Dobranichevka*; 80, Radomysh'l*; 81, Kostienki-Borshevo*; 82, Sungir*; 83, Kapova*; 84, Mushabi. ** indicates locality outside geographic area, but included for comparison. Rectangle outlines Levantine region shown at larger scale in later illustration; a few sites in this region are shown for reference. Numbers missing from the sequence here are found on the preceding and following maps.

mainly flakes with some cores. At Selungur Cave, in Kyrgyzstan, Mode 1 artifacts and human remains said to be *H. erectus* were recovered below a travertine layer dated by uranium-series analysis to ca. 125 Ka. Industries with handaxes have been found in several localities in the Caucasus, again formally included in Europe. Azych (Azerbaijan) and Kudaro (Russia) are the least ambiguous sites, with moderate

lithic assemblages and, at Azych, a human mandible. Faunal and pollen data indicate that these upland sites were first occupied during a warm interglacial period, supposedly early (Stage 9 or 7) but perhaps only Eemian (Stage 5e). While the lowest layer at Azych contains Mode 1 tools in association with a Tiraspol fauna; the lowest deposits at Kudaro contain handaxe industries that are associated with hearths.

Middle Paleolithic

The chronology of the Early-Middle Paleolithic transition in the Levant is somewhat unclear, due to large standard errors of thermoluminescence (TL) and electron spin resonance (ESR) dates in excess of 100 Ka. Thus far, both the youngest Mugharan and the oldest Middle Paleolithic occurrences are between 200 and 150 Ka. Transitional assemblages have been identified in Unit X of A. Jelinek's Tabūn excavations and in the vicinity of El Kowm in Syria, where they are known as the Hummalian industry.

During the Middle Paleolithic, there is evidence of a sustained human presence in the Taurus-Zagros Mountains, but the record of this region differs significantly from that of the Levant. Montane sites like Karain (Turkey), Shanidar (Iraq), Bisitun, Kunji, and Warwasi (all in Iran) preserve assemblages with generally low Levallois indices, heavily retouched tools, and predominantly centripetal core preparation. Ibex figures prominently among the faunal remains from these sites, and the associated hominin fossils are Neanderthals. Shanidar (Level D) yielded nine Neanderthal skeletons, one of which was apparently buried with flowers, as reflected in very high frequencies of flower pollen over the skeleton relative to amounts of such pollen elsewhere in and around the site. Another individual evidently was cared for following a crippling injury to his right arm. The radiocarbon dates for the latest skeletal material at Shanidar (ca. 44 Ka) might best be regarded as infinite (minimum) dates.

In the Levant, the record is somewhat better documented, although occupations of the steppe-desert are still rare. The principal Middle Paleolithic industry is known as the Levantine Mousterian. Key Levantine Mousterian cave sites include Tabūn, Kebara, Amud, Qafzeh, Skhūl (all in Israel), Jerf 'Ajla (Syria), and Tor Faraj and Tor Sabiha (both in Jordan). Well-described open-air sites include Biqat Quneitra, Rosh Ein Mor, and Nahal Aqev (all in Israel). Levantine Mousterian assemblages, as a group, are made mainly on flint and feature high percentages of Levallois debitage. Blades are rather common in Levantine Mousterian assemblages, scrapers are generally lightly retouched, and, in contrast to European Mousterian assemblages, Levallois points are very common. Several technotypological variants of Levantine Mousterian have been recognized, and most assemblages are described in comparison to the assemblages from Tabūn Cave Levels B, C, or D. The most common animal remains found in Levantine Mousterian occupations include *Bos primigenius*, *Dama mesopotamica*, *Cervus elaphus*, *Sus scrofa*, *Gazella gazella*, and *Capra ibex*. Levantine Mousterian sites furnish evidence for the controlled use of fire, burial of the dead, and the use of mineral pigments (red ocher). Limited horizontal exposures at Kebara Cave and Rosh Ein Mor suggest a rather haphazard scattering of hearths and artifacts, presumably reflecting short-term occupations. Biqat Quneitra preserves numerous broken bones of large mammals, a unique flint industry, and numerous basalt pounding tools on the shores of an ancient lake on the Golan Heights.

Both Neanderthals and early modern humans occur in Levantine Mousterian contexts. Neanderthal fossils have been recovered from Amud, Tabūn, Dederiyeh (Syria), and Kebara. Early modern human fossils have been found at Skhūl and Qafzeh. TL and ESR dates place the Skhūl-Qafzeh fossils between 120 and 80 Ka, older than at least one of the Neanderthals (Kebara; probably also Amud and Dederiyeh). Moreover, it has been suggested that the mandible Tabūn 2 (from Layer C) fits with the slightly younger Skhūl-Qafzeh population, while the female Neanderthal skull Tabūn 1 might derive from either Layer C or the Skhūl-aged Layer B. It is thus possible that *no* local Neanderthal preceded the more modern population.

The new dates in the Levant challenge the longstanding hypothesis of archaic-modern human evolutionary continuity in this region, although some scholars continue to view all of these fossils as part of a single polymorphic population. Proponents of this latter hypothesis generally point to Neanderthals' and early modern humans' similar archaeological associations as signifying a close cultural connection between these hominins in the Levant. Others regard these associations as superficial reflections of behavior patterns shared broadly among most early Late Pleistocene humans. There is no evidence that both Neanderthals and early modern humans occupied the same site at the same time. The scarcity of hominin fossil material from the preceding Mugharan makes it difficult to evaluate whether the Levantine Neanderthals or the Skhūl-Qafzeh fossils bear the strongest resemblance to late Middle Pleistocene humans from western Asia.

Neanderthals are also known from the Teshik-Tash Cave in Uzbekistan (a juvenile burial with grave goods) and from the caves of Kiik Koba and Staroselye in Crimea (Ukraine, thus the edge of Europe). Other than Teshik-Tash, Early Mousterian assemblages are rare in Central Asia, but two "Loessic Paleolithic" sites at Lakhuti, near Kuldara in south Tadjikistan, may be relevant. Both are found in paleosols dated only by regional correlation to the last interglacial and just after (ca. 120–80 Ka), although alternative correlations place them older. The older site, Lakhuti I, produced 388 artifacts, including various types of scrapers and points, and both simple (pebble) and prepared (Levallois-like) cores. Some tools are said to resemble European Clactonian or Tayacian pieces, but the whole is thought by V. Ranov to be a local continuation of the Kuldara-Karatau tradition, rather than related to Western cultures, such as the Mousterian. The younger Lakhuti III (Obi-Mazar) assemblage is much smaller, with only 33 flakes and a few cores and wedges, but figured pieces resemble Mousterian scrapers and points. A variety of sites have been said to yield typologically Late Mousterian implements similar to those from farther west. The cave of Darra-i-Kur in Afghanistan also yields Mousterian, but the human fossil originally thought to be Neanderthal may instead relate to early modern humans.

Upper Paleolithic

The transition from Middle to Upper Paleolithic in the Levant was once linked to an Emiran industry that is now recognized as a geological conflation of separate Middle and Upper Paleolithic elements. *In situ* deposits of an early Upper Paleolithic transitional industry occur between 45 and 38 Ka at Ksar 'Akil and Boker Tachtit. These sites preserve sequences in which blanks for characteristically Upper Paleo-lithic tool types (endscrapers, burins) and some novel forms, such as the Emireh point, were initially made on Levallois blanks and later made on prismatic blades. The modern human fossils from Ksar 'Akil ("Egbert") and the Upper Paleolithic frontal bones from Qafzeh are probably associated with this industry.

Upper Paleolithic assemblages dating between 38 and 20 Ka in the Levant are generally assigned to one of two co-traditions. The earliest of these, the Ahmarian, is characterized by a well-developed blade/bladelet industry and is found throughout the Levant. The Ahmarian is represented at Ksar 'Akil, Kebara, Qafzeh, Erq el-Ahmar, Lagama, Boker BE, and Kadesh Barnea. The other industry, called Levantine Aurignacian, features a flake-based industry with lamellar retouch on carinated scrapers and burins. Small retouched bladelets (El Wad points) also occur in most assemblages. The oldest dates for the Levantine Aurignacian derive from Hayonim, where a split-base bone point provides a further stylistic linkage to the European Aurignacian. The date of 34 Ka, however, is at least 4–8 Kyr *younger* than the oldest Aurignacian sites in Europe (Bulgaria and Spain), negating in simplistic terms the old theory that anatomically modern humans bearing an Aurignacian culture moved into Europe from the Levant. Nonetheless, a Southwest Asian source for the European Aurignacian must still be considered a possibility.

The Levantine Aurignacian is known primarily from sites in the North-Central Levant, such as Ksar 'Akil, El Wad, Kebara, el-Khiam, Sefunim, and Hayonim. This northerly distribution is especially interesting in view of the (western) Aurignacian affinities noted in the Upper Paleolithic Baradostian industry of the Zagros region. Directly overlying the Mousterian at Shanidar without an intervening bladelet industry, the Baradostian is characterized by high percentages of burins, some with a distinctive nosed profile reminiscent of Aurignacian burins. The distinctive carinate scrapers and busked burins of the European and Levantine Aurignacian are present but rare. The Baradostian appears earlier than the Levantine Aurignacian, however; radiocarbon dates from Shanidar (Level C) and Yafteh Cave in western Iran fall between 38 and 35 Ka. D.I. Olszewski and H.L. Dibble discussed in 1994 the equivalent industry at Warwasi rockshelter (Iran), emphasizing the similarities to both Levantine and Central European Aurignacian (and Ahmarian) assemblages, including regional variation and the occurrence of typical European index-implements. They suggested that the Baradostian be renamed the Zagros Aurignacian to reflect its likely affinities.

In those sites in which horizontal exposures have been made, Upper Paleolithic levels have preserved discrete hearths and knapping areas. Ahmarian sites excavated in the Wadi Abu Noshra, however, may yield additional information about site structure. Ochre is often found in Upper Paleolithic sites, and ochre-grinding stones were found in Qafzeh Level 9. However, neither the Upper Paleolithic sites in the Zagros nor their counterparts in the Levant preserve mural or portable art comparable to that seen in the European Upper Paleolithic.

Upper Paleolithic sites farther north and east are rare. Kara Kamar (Afghanistan) provided radiocarbon dates in the 1950s that were probably beyond the range of the early technique; the assemblages may relate to the Zagros Aurignacian. On the other side of the Afghan-Tadzhik Depression, Shugnou produces blade tools and at least the upper layer may be quite late (10,700 BP). Within the city of Samarkand, an apparently early Upper Paleolithic assemblage is said to include pebble tools and to show continuity with the local Middle Paleolithic; this penchant for regional cultural continuity seems to characterize the Central Asian interpretive paradigm. Some high-altitude areas, such as the high Zagros and the Iranian and Anatolian plateaus, may have been abandoned around the time centering on the last glacial maximum (ca. 28–14 Ka). There seem to be gaps in the occupational histories of parts of the Zagros, in northern Afghanistan, and in Central Asia during this period.

Ca. 20–14 Ka, true microlithic blade industries occur in the Levant, where they are assigned to the Kebaran industry. The Kebaran, which is known from Kebara, El Wad, Ksar 'Akil, Ein Gev, and Hayonim, is characterized by obliquely truncated blades, bladelets, and microliths. Ground-stone mortars and pestles also occur at Kebaran sites, where they are believed to have been used to pulverize acorns and cereal grasses. Ein Gev I, a site near the foot of the Golan Heights in Israel, preserves a Kebaran occupation that consists of several small, circular, semisubterranean hut footings that appear to have been repeatedly, perhaps seasonally, occupied. The Kebaran probably reflects hunter-gatherers practicing a strategy of seasonal transhumance or circulating mobility between highland and lowland sites. Fallow deer are common in Kebaran sites, followed by ibex (in Lebanon and Syria) and gazelle (in the southern Levant). The waterlogged Kebaran site of Ohalo discovered in the 1990s on Lake Kinneret will probably yield important information about Kebaran plant use. Cold, arid conditions seem to have restricted Kebaran occupations mainly to areas near the Mediterranean coast and the northern shores of Lake Lisan, a freshwater lake that covered much of the Jordan valley. In the Zagros, the epipaleolithic Zarzian culture may reflect a similar adaptation.

In both the Levant and the Zagros, the number of sites and the diversity of ecological niches they occupied increased throughout the Late Weichselian, and faunal analyses suggest increasing local specializations involving the hunting of particular species. Regional and interregional movement, and perhaps long-distance exchange, are suggested by finds of ocher, marine shells, and obsidian in areas where they do not occur naturally. Toward the end of the Upper Paleolithic, several changes suggest the development of increasingly diversified subsistence strategies. Some sites in western Asia and the Levant have produced remains of molluscs, fish, and turtles; a few have abundant remains of land snails. The sample of avifauna is larger for this time range, although this may be partly a function of better preservation in more recent deposits.

The relatively humid interval of 14–12 Ka witnessed an expansion of settlement into the interior and highland zones (i.e., the Negev, Sinai, and southern Jordan). Two principal

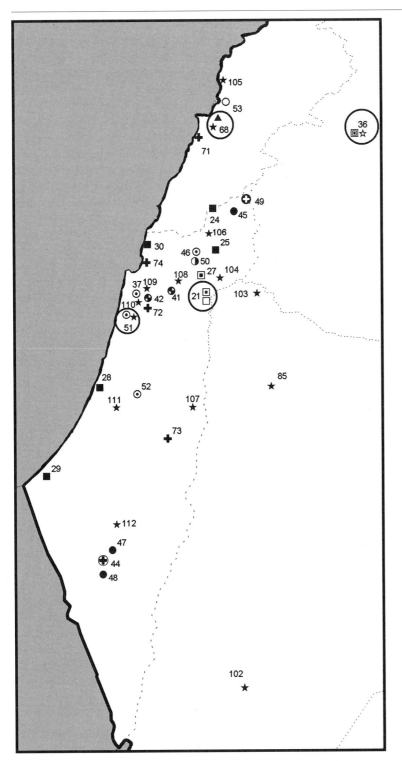

Pliocene-Pleistocene: Cercopithecinae

Early Paleolithic

?Homo erectus & Early Paleolithic

"Archaic Homo sapiens" & Early Paleolithic

Early & Middle & Upper Paleolithic

Middle Paleolithic

Neanderthal & Middle Paleolithic

?Neanderthal & Middle Paleolithic

Neanderthal & ?H. s. sapiens & Early & Middle Paleolithic

Homo sapiens sapiens & Middle Paleolithic

Middle & Upper Paleolithic

?Middle & Upper Paleolithic

Homo sapiens sapiens & Upper Paleolithic

Upper Paleolithic

?Neolithic

Epi-Paleolithic and/or Neolithic

Map of portion of Levant (Israel and Lebanon, plus parts of Syria and Jordan) with high concentration of localities yielding fossil primates, hominins, and archaeological remains. Symbols indicate age and included included taxa and/or industries, while numbers represent site names (in approximate chronological order), as follows: 21, 'Ubeidiya; 24, Maayan Barukh; 25, Gesher Benot Ya'acov; 27, Zuttiyeh; 28, Holon; 29, Kissufim; 30, Evron; 36, Jabrud; 37, Tabun; 41, Djebel Qafzeh; 42, Skhul; 44, Boker Tachtit; 45, Berekhat Ram; 46, Shovakh; 47, Nahal Aqev; 48, Rosh Ein Mor; 49, Quneitra; 50, Amud; 51, Kebarah; 52, Shukbah; 53, Ras-el-Kelb; 68, Ksar-Akil; 71, Emireh; 72, El Wad; 73, Erq el Ahmar; 74, Sefunim; 85, Abu Hureyra; 102, Beidha; 103, 'Ain Ghazal; 104, Ein Gev; 105, Byblos; 106, Ain Mallaha (Eynan); 107, Jericho; 108, Ohalo; 109, Nahal Oren; 110, Neveh David; 111, Hatoula; 112, Rosh Zin.

lithic cultures are known from this period, the Geometric Kebaran and the Mushabian. The Geometric Kebaran, as its name suggests, exhibits numerous technological and typological continuities with the Kebaran, differing mainly in featuring geometric microliths (chiefly trapezes). Geometric Kebaran sites vary widely in size, from substantial sites like Neveh David on Mount Carmel to smaller lithic scatters in the Sinai. A different industry, the Mushabian, is marked by steeply arched microliths and the frequent use of the microburin technique. The Mushabian is found exclusively in the arid interior southern Levant (e.g., Sinai), suggesting it could represent an arid-land adaptation. Some researchers have noted stylistic continuities between the Mushabian and the Ibero-Maurusian of North Africa, suggesting the Mushabian may represent a migration of African groups into the southern Levant.

In the Zagros, the earliest domesticate, the dog, is reported from a Zarzian site, Palegawra (Iraqi Kurdistan) dated to ca. 14 Ka. Oak wood suggests that acorns (and the often-associated pistachios) had become available for fall harvesting; wild cereal grasses, such as wheat and barley may have accompanied oak as it recolonized the area after 11 Ka. As in the Levant, a number of sites contained grindstones, which may have been multipurpose implements used to crush nuts, hard-husked grasses, and pigments.

Transition to Food Production and Village Life

Ca. 12–10 Ka, during a period of increasing aridity, the Levant witnesses the appearance of the Epipaleolithic Natufian culture. Natufian sites occur throughout the Levant, but the largest sites are located in the oak-pistachio forests in the coastal lowlands. Natufian sites include both caves (Kebara, Hayonim, Nahal Oren) and open-air localities (Ain Mallaha/Eynan, Hatoula, Rosh Zin). Natufian lithic assemblages feature numerous crescentic microliths produced with the microburin technique. Bone tools increased in number and sophistication and included harpoons, fishhooks, projectile points, awls, needles, and scrapers. Large ground-stone mortars and pestles are believed to have been used primarily for pounding nuts, but possibly cereal grasses as well. Rare backed blades with sickle polish, a wear pattern referable to prolonged cutting of cereal grasses, together with actual bone or antler sickle hafts with embedded backed microliths, may suggest incipient plant cultivation. Gazelle are the most abundant species at most Natufian sites. Several sites have also yielded skeletons of domesticated dog, among the earliest known occurrences of *Canis familiaris*. Unlike their Upper Paleolithic predecessors, Natufian groups carved elaborate bone and stone art objects, including both anthropomorphic and zoomorphic forms. *Dentalium* shells from the Mediterranean, perforated animal teeth, and perforated pieces of polished bone were also circulated widely among Natufian groups.

Burials occur at many sites and take a wide range of forms. Some burials have had their crania removed, a mortuary ritual seen in subsequent early Neolithic cultures. It has been suggested that because some individuals at Natufian sites were interred beneath large stone slabs, with comparatively elaborate personal ornaments, this period was marked by developing rank or status hierarchy.

Hayonim Terrace, Hatoula, and Ain Mallaha/Eynan are large open-air Natufian sites featuring semisubterranean hut foundations lined with stones. Similar structures also occur at the later Levantine sites of Mureybit (Syria) and Abu Hureyra (Jordan). Natufian groups undoubtedly practiced a wide range of subsistence adaptations, but some of the larger sites with substantial architecture and multiple superimposed occupation floors hint at prolonged occupations, possibly year-round sedentism in some areas. The hypothesis of Natufian multiseasonal sedentism has been supported by season-of-death determinations based on the analysis of cementum annulli in gazelle teeth. Rapid population growth, a likely consequence of prolonged sedentism, and the availability of cereal grasses were probably major factors in the origins of agriculture in the Levant. Natufian occupations occur beneath early preceramic Neolithic levels at Jericho, Beidha, Nahal Oren, and the early Neolithic rockshelter of Iraq ed-Dub (Jordan).

In the Zagros, a parallel but somewhat different development is evident at sites such as Zawi Chemi near Shanidar Cave, Karim Shahir, and Ganj Dareh (Iran). At Zawi Chemi, for example, round structures may indicate a sedentary or

seasonally redundant occupation. Interregional exchange is reflected in the presence of Anatolian obsidian at some Zagros sites, together with marine shells, ocher, and the bitumen used to haft stone tools. Ground-stone objects include pendants, bangles, beads, and palettes. At several sites, including Karim Shahir and Ganj Dareh, experimentation with clay is suggested by the presence of lightly baked clay figurines and other objects. Some lumps of clay carry impressions of matting and basketry. Farther east and north, Mesolithic or Epipaleolithic sites have been described from northern Iran (Belt and Hotu caves), western Turkmenistan, southern Tadzhikistan, and the mountains of eastern Tadzhikistan and Kirghizia.

While both the Levant and the Zagros provide evidence for increasing use of small-scale protein resources (land snails, mussels, clams, nuts, fish, and the like), there is somewhat more evidence in the Zagros for incipient domestication of food resources. At Zawi Chemi, ca. 10,500 BP, humans were possibly beginning to exercise some degree of control over sheep, as shown by a disproportionately large number of juveniles' bones. Better-dated evidence from such slightly later sites as Cayonnu (Turkey) and Ganj Dareh (Iran), however, suggests that in these areas plants were domesticated before animals.

The so-called Pre-Pottery Neolithic (PPN) witnessed an increase in the number and diversity of sites, some of considerable size and duration. Sites in this time range (ca. 10.5–8.5 Ka) include Abu Hureyra, Mureybit, and Bouqras (Syria), 'Ain Ghazal and Beidha (Jordan), and Jericho (Israel). North of the Taurus Mountains and east of the Euphrates River, lithic technology and food resources were somewhat different; sites of the same period include Cayonnu and Çatal Hüyük (Turkey), Ganj Dareh, Asiab, Sarab, Guran, and Ali Kosh (Iran), and Jarmo and M'lefaat (Iraq). Gazelle, deer, ox, onager, boar, sheep, and goat were hunted in the tenth and ninth millennia but domesticated forms had appeared at a number of sites throughout Southwest Asia by 9500 BP. The earliest domesticated plants, evident in the tenth and ninth millennia BP, were wheat and barley, accompanied by lentil, chickpea, vetch, and others. Several sites dating to the ninth millennium BP have yielded pottery, and many have substantial rectilinear, multiroomed structures with hearths, ovens, and, in a few cases, painted walls and other internal ornamentation. Çatal Hüyük produced a large assemblage of sculpted figures, wall paintings, and combinations of cattle horns and plaster arranged in benches and platforms and on walls. Elsewhere, representational figures were carved on bone, and small figures of animals and humans were molded in clay, as was a wide range of geometric shapes considered by some to have served as counting devices. A few late-ninth-millennium BP sites, including Jericho, 'Ain Ghazal, and Tell Ramad, have produced human skulls covered with molded plaster, and some of these also yielded large anthropomorphic statues of plaster molded over reed cores.

As in earlier times, interregional exchange in Red Sea cowries and Anatolian obsidian was carried out; such exchange is best monitored by analyzing raw materials whose

Reconstruction of room at Çatal Hüyük. After J. Mellaart, Çatal Hüyük: A Neolithic Town in Anatolia, *1967, Academic Press.*

origins can be traced, because their chemical or mineralogical composition is idiosyncratic (they are "fingerprinted" by such techniques as X-ray spectroscopy and neutron activation). The period 12–8 Ka saw populations becoming increasingly sedentary, with the development of villages as a settlement type, increasing interregional interaction in the form of exchange for exotic materials (evidently including, in a few cases, plants and animals), increasing regionalism, and growing diversification in the subsistence base and control over an ever-widening range of domesticates. Both at Jericho and at Çatal Hüyük, there is substantial evidence that not all interregional or intraregional contacts were peaceful. At Jericho, the evidence takes the form of substantial defensive walls dating to 8500 BP, while at Çatal Hüyük the contiguous houses were built without ground-level entrances, so as to present a solid wall to the outside (presumably they were entered via retractable ladders to an upper story or the roof). In addition, a relatively large proportion of the male skeletons from Çatal Hüyük had suffered transverse fractures of the left forearm—the shield arm for a right-handed person. The Çatal Hüyük skeletons also exhibit substantial evidence for the development of genetic anemias related to malarial resistance, and thus, indirectly, for the emergence of this disease as a consequence of sedentism and incipient agriculture. In general, the dead from this period, often buried intramurally, provide some evidence for social differentiation; burials were not standardized, and some were accompanied by comparatively elaborate, exotic, and, therefore, presumably costly grave goods.

Many sites were occupied for several generations; some, for centuries. The absence of large burial populations at some sites suggests the early use of specialized disposal grounds, but there are no substantial cemeteries yet known from this early time range.

The Development of Complex Societies

Throughout Southwest Asia, the Neolithic period in the eighth and seventh millennia BP represents a period of regional consolidation and growing interregional differentiation. Villages like Hajji Firuz and Guran (Iran), Yarim Tepe, Umm Dabaghiyah, Hassuna, Halaf, and Tell es-Sawwan (Iraq), Hacilar and Mersin (Turkey), Ghassoul (Jordan), Munhata (Israel), and Byblos (Syria) were based largely on plant cultivation and stock breeding; their inhabitants lived in agglutinated, multiroomed, rectilinear structures, some with courtyards and upper stories; they made ceramics, textiles, basketry, metal objects, and personal ornaments, as well as a range of stone, bone, and wooden utilitarian objects. It was on this broad foundation that increasing social differentiation and occupational specialization developed. Pottery, whose manufacture was presumably at first a cottage industry, varied stylistically from one region to another. Eventually, the ceramic craft, which requires special clays and abundant fuel, came to be controlled by a small number of specialists whose wares were needed by, and distributed among, a larger population. Other early specialties may have included copper metallurgy, in which early experiments had been undertaken at Cayonnu; the carving of stone and bone seals, possibly used as signets or as stamps for painting textiles; and the sculpting of stone into amulets, ornaments, and representational figures. A few settlements, such as Hacilar and Tell es-Sawwan (Iraq), were surrounded by large walls, perhaps defensive in nature. Others had structures provisionally identified as shrines. At a few sites of the seventh millennium BP Ubaid period of Mesopotamia, there is some evidence pointing to the development of irrigation canals (e.g., Choga Mani), suggesting the concomitant rise of organizational principles by which decisions governing allocation of scarce water might be made, conflicts resolved,

Aerial view of excavation in progress at Jarmo. Courtesy of the Oriental Institute, University of Chicago.

and canal-digging and -cleaning tasks assigned. At the same time, these modifications in the landscape imply the growing need to intensify agrarian production, although whether to meet the needs of an expanding population, the whims of a burgeoning elite, or the desire for a surplus to exchange for skills, labor, or exotic materials is unclear. During this period, settlements became increasingly diverse in location, size, and function. Some sites, such as Tepe Tula'i (Iran), may be the ephemeral remains of early specialized pastoral nomads; others may have served as regional centers of trade, transport, production, and administration.

By the end of the sixth millennium BP, some centers had become quite large, with areas of ten or more hectares implying populations exceeding 1,000. A number of these sites, not only in Mesopotamia proper (Ur, Uruk, Jemdet Nasr) but also in northern Syria (Tell Brak, Habuba Kabira) and western Iran (Godin Tepe, Susa, Choga Mani), have yielded clear evidence of the world's earliest writing: clay tablets inscribed in cuneiform in the unrelated languages Sumerian, Proto-Elamite, and Akkadian. Deciphering of the texts has added immeasurably to our understanding of the ancient Near East, since it permits us to read the records of administrative transactions, lists of kings, letters, poems, marriage and divorce contracts, ledgers, schoolboys' exercises, myths, religious and omen texts, pharmaceutical recipes, legal codes, historical narratives, city archives, travel itineraries, trade documents, accounts of sales of land, slaves, and animals, and bilingual dictionaries left by the thousands at scores of sites over a period exceeding 3,000 years. From such texts, king-lists have been compiled, relations between cities and between nations have been reconstructed, and many aspects of daily life in this earliest civilization have been fleshed out. There is rich evidence for complex division of labor, marked status differentiation (with social groups ranging from royalty to slaves), a polytheistic religion associated with specialist officials and elaborate temples and ritual, sprawling and internally differentiated cities, abundant and representational art that sometimes depicts military activities, and hierarchical bureaucracies. *Civilization,* a term much abused, is not discussed here, but it is fair to say that it would not have been possible without the developments of the Late Pleistocene and Early Holocene.

See also Acheulean; Ahmarian; 'Ain ghazal; Amud Cave; Amudian; Ankarapithecus; Archaic Homo sapiens; Archaic Moderns; Beidha; Boker Tachtit; Broad-Spectrum Revolution; Çandir; Çatal Hüyük; Cercopithecinae; Colobinae; Complex Societies; Domestication; Dryopithecinae; El Wad;

Emiran; Emireh Point; Ethnoarchaeology; Exotics; Florisbad; Geochronometry; Gesher Benot Ya'Acov; Griphopithecus; Hayonim; Heliopithecus; Hominidae; Homo sapiens; Jabrud; Jarmo; Jerf 'Ajila; Jericho; Karain; Kebara; Kebaran; Kenyapithecinae; Ksar 'Akil; Late Paleolithic; Levantine-Aurignacian; Levallois; Middle Paleolithic; Modern Human Origins; Mousterian; Mugharan; Mushabi; Mushabian; Natufian; Neanderthals; Neolithic; Paşalar; Ponginae; Pre-Aurignacian; Prepared-Core; Qafzeh; Shanidar; Siwaliks; Skhūl; Tabūn; Tabunian; Takamori; Tayacian; Teshik-Tash; 'Ubeidiya; Zuttiyeh. [N.B., A.S.B., E.D., C.K., J.J.S.]

Further Readings

Akazawa, T., Aoki, K., and Bar-Yosef, O. (eds.) (1998) Neanderthals and Modern Humans in Western Asia. New York: Plenum.

Andrews, P., Harrison, T., Delson, E., Martin, L.B., and Bernor, R.L. (1996) Systematics and biochronology of European and Southwest Asian Miocene catarrhines. In R.L. Bernor, V. Fahlbusch, and H.W. Mittmann (eds.): Evolution of Western Eurasian Late Neogene Mammal Faunas. New York: Columbia University Press, pp. 168–207.

Bar-Yosef, O. (1980) Prehistory of the Levant. Ann. Rev. Anthropol. 9:101–133.

Bintliff, J.L., and Van Zeist, W., eds. (1982) Paleoclimates, Palaeoenvironments, and Human Communities in the Eastern Mediterranean Region in Later Prehistory (BAR International Series 133 [i and ii]). Oxford: Archaeopress.

Braidwood, L.S., Braidwood, R.J., Howe, B., Reed, C.A., and Watson, P. (1983) Prehistoric Archeology along the Zagros Flanks (Oriental Institute Publication No. 105). Chicago: University of Chicago Press (Oriental Institute).

Braidwood, R.J., and Howe, B., eds. (1960) Prehistoric Investigations in Iraqi Kurdistan (Studies in Ancient Oriental Culture No. 31). Chicago: University of Chicago Press (Oriental Institute).

Brice, W.C., ed. (1978) The Environmental History of the Near and Middle East since the Last Ice Age. New York: Academic.

Curtis, J., ed. (1982) Fifty Years of Mesopotamian Discovery. London: British School of Archaeology in Iraq.

Davis, R.S. (1987) Regional perspectives on the Soviet Central Asian Paleolithic. In O Soffer (ed.): The Pleistocene Old World: Regional Perspectives. New York: Plenum, pp. 121–133.

Flannery, K.V. (1969) Origins and ecological effects of early domestication in Iran and the Near East. In P.J. Ucko and G.W. Dimhleby (eds.): The Domestication and Exploitation of Plants and Animals. London: Duckworth, pp. 73–100.

Klein, R.G. (1996) Neanderthals and modern humans in West Asia: A conference summary. Evol. Anthropol. 4:187–193.

Lloyd, S. (1978) The Archaeology of Mesopotamia. London: Thames and Hudson.

Nissen, H.J. (1988) The Early History of the Ancient Near East 9000–2000 BC. Chicago: University of Chicago Press.

Olszewski, D.I., and Dibble, H.L. (1994) The Zagros Aurignacian. Curr. Anthropol. 35:68–75.

Postgate, J.N. (1992) Early Mesopotamia: Society and Economy at the Dawn of History. New York: Routledge.

Ranov, V. (1995) The "Loessic Paleolithic" in South Tadjikistan, Central Asia: Its industries, chronology and correlation. Quatern. Sci. Rev. 14:731–745.

Ranov, V., Carbonell, E., and Rodríguez, X.P. (1995) Kuldara: Earliest human occupation in Central Asia in its Afro-Asian context. Curr. Anthropol. 36:337–346.

Smith, P.E.L. (1986) Palaeolithic Archaeology in Iran (American Institute of Iranian Studies Monograph No. 1). Philadelphia: University Museum, University of Pennsylvania.

Atapuerca

Range of limestone hills (the Sierra de Atapuerca) lying ca. 20 km east of Burgos in northern Spain. Earlier in the twentieth century, cavers discovered a small chamber deep within a long cave system, which was packed with the remains of Pleistocene cave bears. This chamber became known as the Sima de los Huesos (Pit of the Bones), and cavers quarried it to extract the beautifully fossilized cave-bear teeth. It was in one of their dumps that a paleontologist discovered fossil human bones in 1976. Spanish workers then began an ambitious program of excavations at a number of sites in the Atapuerca region, which have produced a wealth of information about Spanish Middle Pleistocene faunas and environments. These sites, mainly fissure fillings or cave chambers now opened by erosion, span various periods as far back as the Brunhes-Matuyama boundary (780 Ka) and contain artifacts (including handaxes and cleavers) on flint or quartzite, as well as remains of large and small mammals and other small vertebrates.

The Sima de los Huesos itself has produced a remarkable collection of more than 1,300 fossil human bones and teeth, representing the jumbled remains of at least 25 individuals. Taphonomic conclusions vary, but it seems likely that the hominids died elsewhere and their bones worked down to the sima, falling or sliding in mud flows through now sealed passages. There is no evidence that any of the early humans lived in the remote darkness of the pit, since there are no signs of ancient fires or artifacts alongside the bones. They may have died in an ancient disaster or epidemic, or their bodies were perhaps left elsewhere in the cave by animals or other humans. The remains come from adults and children, with a preponderance of adolescents or young adults, and will provide an unprecedentedly detailed picture of the whole skeleton of these ancient Europeans. Already we know that they had brains within the Neanderthal and modern range, but on average they were perhaps not as large bodied or large toothed as some other archaic humans, even including many Neanderthals who came after them.

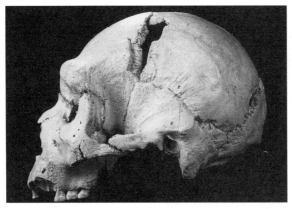

Lateral view of Cranium 5 from Atapuerca, Spain. Courtesy of J.L. Arsuaga; photo by J. Trueba.

As of the late 1990s, postcranial material was mainly still undescribed, but it shows clear resemblances to Neanderthals in features such as the morphology of the pubic ramus and distal phalanges. The cranial material includes a small adult (female?) with an endocranial volume of 1,125 ml and a face showing evident resemblances to Petralona (Greece) and Arago 21 (France). However, the midfacial region shows much more pronounced projection, like that of Neanderthals. A large facial fragment, in contrast, shows a flatter face with a moderate canine fossa. Other cranial material includes a much larger, and especially broad, vault, with an endocranial volume of 1,390 ml. At least one immature Atapuerca temporal bone resembles Neanderthal examples, but older specimens show larger mastoid processes and relatively small juxtamastoid eminences. However, all the preserved midoccipital regions foreshadow those of Neanderthals in displaying an incipient suprainiac fossa. The cranial profile viewed from behind lacks the spherical shape of late Neanderthals and more closely resembles that of specimens like Petralona, Swanscombe (England), and Ehringsdorf (Germany). The Atapuerca mandibles show features of both Neanderthals and earlier European specimens, such as Mauer (Germany), Arago, and Montmaurin (France), and the teeth are comparable to the smaller sample from Pontnewydd (Wales).

Classification of the Atapuerca material is difficult unless we take a wide view of the application of the species names *Homo neanderthalensis* or *Homo sapiens*. The lack of the typical cranial superstructures and robusticity found in *Homo erectus* certainly precludes assignment to that taxon, and the Atapuerca material as a whole seems to show more Neanderthal features than the early European fossils often assigned to *Homo heidelbergensis* (e.g., Mauer, Arago, Petralona, Bilzingsleben [Germany]). C.B. Stringer prefers to give priority to the presence of Neanderthal-derived features and to recognize the Atapuerca material as a primitive form of *H. neanderthalensis*, but the status of *H. heidelbergensis* as a separate species may need reassessment as the growing sample of hominids from the Sima de los Huesos is described. As of the late 1990s, the age of the hominid sample had not been established definitively, but a late Middle Pleistocene age seems probable. The relevance of a published uranium-series date older than 300 Kyr on a speleothem overlying the hominids is doubtful, as the dated material appears to have been redeposited.

Another Atapuerca site, Gran Dolina, has produced several fragmentary cranial, dental, and postcranial hominid fossils since 1994. This site includes 18 m of section exposed by an old railway trench. Discovery of a geomagnetic polarity reversal within this part of the sequence suggests that the material from the TD6, or Aurora, horizon may date to the Late Matuyama Chron (end of the Early Pleistocene, ca. 0.8 Ma) and represent the oldest known European population. This material has been named *Homo antecessor* by Bermúdez de Castro and colleagues in 1997. Associated artifacts are of Mode 1 technology made on quartzite, limestone, and flint. An even older horizon, TD4, yields similar artifacts and fauna.

See also Arago; Archaic Homo sapiens; Bilzingsleben; Early Paleolithic; Europe; Homo antecessor; Homo heidelbergensis; Homo sapiens; Mauer; Montmaurin; Neanderthals; Petralona; Pontnewydd; Swanscombe; Vértesszöllös. [C.B.S., J.J.S.]

Further Readings

Arsuaga, J.L., Martinez, I., Gracia, A., Carretero, J.-M., and Carbonell, E. (1993) Three new human skulls from the Sima de los Huesos Middle Pleistocene site in Sierra de Atapuerca, Spain. Nature 362:534–537.

Arsuaga, J.L., Bermúdez de Castro, J.M., and Carbonell, E., eds. (1997) The Sima de los Huesos Hominid Site. J. Hum. Evol. 33:105–421 (special issue).

Bermúdez de Castro, J., Arsuaga, J., Carbonell, E., Rosas, A., Martinez, I., and Mosquera, M. (1997) A hominid from the Lower Pleistocene of Atapuerca, Spain: Possible ancestor to Neandertals and modern humans. Science 276:1392–1395.

Carbonell, E., Bermúdez de Castro, J.M., Arsuaga, J.L., Diez, J.C., Rosas, A., Cuenca-Bescós, G., Sala, R., Mosquera, M., and Rodríguez, X.P. (1995) Lower Pleistocene hominids and artifacts from Atapuerca-TD6 (Spain). Science 269:826–830.

Carbonell, E., and Rodríguez, X.P. (1994) Early Middle Pleistocene deposits and artefacts in the Gran Dolina Site (TD4) of the "Sierra de Atapuerca" (Burgos, Spain). J. Hum. Evol. 26:291–311.

Parés, J.M., and Pérez-González, A. (1995) Paleomagnetic age for hominid fossils at Atapuerca archaeological site, Spain. Science 269:830–832.

Atelidae

Family of New World platyrrhine monkeys including the subfamilies Atelinae and Pitheciinae and their fossil relatives. The atelid common ancestor was typified by a derived masticatory system, including moderate-to-large fourth cusps on the first and second upper molars, a posteriorly enlarged mandible, robust bony attachments on the zygomatic and pterygoid bones, and a deep temporomandibular joint surface where the mandible articulates with the skull. This pattern implies powerful chewing and a specialized use of the pterygoid and masseter muscles, which are often well developed in mammalian herbivores. Apart from these traits, atelids are highly varied morphologically, a reflection of the divergent ecological adaptations of the two descendant subfamilies. The term *Atelidae* was reintroduced by A.L. Rosenberger to promote a taxonomically and conceptually balanced classification of the ateloids. It is meant to represent the unique common origins of the pitheciine and ateline branches of the radiation and alleviate the adaptively diffuse and genealogically heterogeneous composition of the traditional cornerstone taxon of the platyrrhines, the Cebidae. The hypothesis of atelid monophyly is supported by complementary morphological and molecular evidence.

See also Atelinae; Ateloidea; Cebidae; Pitheciinae. [A.L.R.]

Further Readings

Rosenberger, A.L. (1981) Systematics: The higher taxa. In A.F. Coimbra-Filho and R.A. Mittermeier (eds.): Ecology and Behavior of Neotropical Primates, Vol. 1. Rio de Janeiro: Academia Brasiliera de Ciencias, pp. 19–26.

Rosenberger, A.L. (1992) Evolution of feeding niches in New World monkeys. Am. J. Phys. Anthropol. 88:525–562.

Szalay, F.S., and Delson, E. (1979) Evolutionary History of the Primates. New York: Academic.

Atelinae

Subfamily of atelid platyrrhine monkeys including the tribes Alouattini and Atelini (see classification below). Physically the largest platyrrhines, atelines are noteworthy for their prehensile tails and suspensory positional behaviors, which many regard as apelike. During feeding, they may hang by forelimb, hindlimb, and/or tail, and the more acrobatic spider (*Ateles*) and woolly spider (*Brachyteles*) monkeys can move swiftly through the forest canopy in a bimanual fashion analogous to brachiation. Howler (*Alouatta*) and woolly (*Lagothrix*) monkeys tend to move more cautiously, quadrupedally. The anatomical complex underlying the prehensile tail includes a specialized gripping pad near its tip and an enlargement of the areas of the brain that control tail function. These unique ateline attributes do not occur in the capuchin monkeys (*Cebus*) and the squirrel monkeys (*Saimiri*), which have evolved semiprehensile tails in parallel. Atelines are frugivore-folivores with a spectrum of dietary habits, ranging from *Alouatta*, the most highly folivorous of the platyrrhines, to *Ateles*, one of the most exclusive ripe-fruit specialists among the primates. *Brachyteles* is the largest, and one of the most interesting, of the living New World monkeys. Although it is most closely related to *Ateles*, *Brachyteles* converges upon howlers in its dentition and reliance upon a leafy diet. In their skeleton and social organization, however, woolly monkeys resemble spiders. They are a monotypic

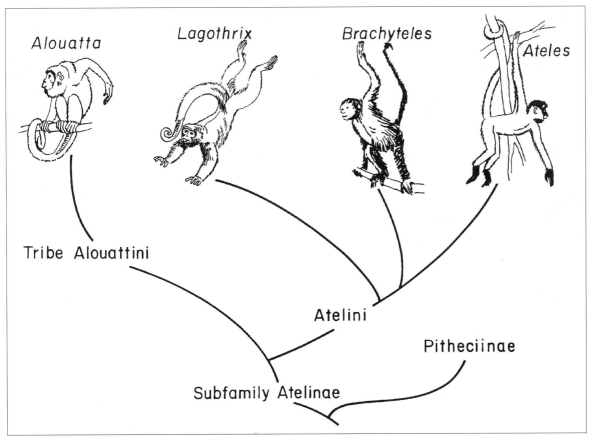

Classification and interrelationships of ateline platyrrhine monkeys. Courtesy of Alfred L. Rosenberger.

form restricted to the southern portions of the Atlantic coastal forest of Brazil. This area has been severely disturbed by human population growth and industrialization during the twentieth century. Consequently, the woolly spider monkey, which has become the conservation symbol for all of Brazil, survives in small numbers in a handful of remnant forests. It is one of the most severely threatened of all Neotropical mammals.

Atelines are first represented in the fossil record by two species of *Stirtonia* of the La Venta Middle Miocene (14–12 Ma), an *Alouatta*-like form that may be more properly classified in the same genus as the howler. There is an intriguing group of Late Pleistocene (sub)fossils whose scope is just becoming clear. *Protopithecus* from eastern Brazil has an *Alouatta*-like skull but atelin postcranium; its contemporary *Caipora* appears more typically *Ateles*-like in skull and skeleton; both forms are now known to have been nearly twice as large as the largest living genus. In the Caribbean, the Cuban *Paralouatta* also has an alouattin skull but distinctive dentition.

Atelinae
    Alouattini
        Alouatta
        †*Stirtonia*
        †*Caipora*
        ?†*Paralouatta*
    Atelini
        Ateles
        Brachyteles
        Lagothrix
        †*Protopithecus*
†extinct

See also Americas; Atelidae; Ateloidea; Cebinae; Diet; Locomotion; Tail; Teeth. [A.L.R.]

Further Readings

Hartwig, W.C., and Cartelle, C. (1996) A complete skeleton of the giant South American primate *Protopithecus*. Nature 381:307–311.

Rosenberger, A.L. (1983) Tale of tails: Parallelism and prehensility. Am. J. Phys. Anthropol. 60:103–107.

Rosenberger, A.L., and Strier, K.B. (1989) Adaptive radiation of the ateline primates. J. Hum. Evol. 18:717–750.

Strier, K.B. (1992) Ateline adaptations: Behavioral strategies and ecological constraints. Am. J. Phys. Anthropol. 88:515–524.

Ateloidea

Primates of South and Central America, including Cebidae and Atelidae; also known as the New World monkeys, or platyrrhines, in reference to their pug-nosed faces. They were previously termed Ceboidea, but taxonomic priority demands that the earlier name based on *Ateles* be substituted. Among the anatomical features that distinguish them from the living (but not all of the Oligocene) catarrhines are: generally smaller size; 2.1.3.3 dental formula (except in derived callitrichines with 2.1.3.2); eye-socket wall completed by su-

tural contact of the zygomatic with the parietal bone of the braincase; and eardrum supported by a ring-shaped ectotympanic bone fused to the skull. The diversified, strictly arboreal ateloid radiation is represented by some 60 living species but by fewer than 20 fossil genera. Although termed *monkeys,* ateloids tend to resemble living apes and their ancestors anatomically, rather than the cercopithecoid monkeys of the Old World.

See also Americas; Atelidae; Atelinae; Callitrichinae; Cebidae; Cebinae; Monkey; Pitheciinae, Platyrrhini. [A.L.R.]

Further Readings

Biegert, J. (1963) The evaluation of characteristics of the skull, hands, and feet for primate taxonomy. In S.L. Washburn (ed.): Classification and Human Evolution. Chicago: Aldine.

Fleagle, J.G., Kay, R.F., and Anthony, M.R.L. (1997) Fossil New World monkeys. In R.F. Kay, R.H. Madden, R.L. Cifelli, and J.J. Flynn (eds.): Vertebrate Paleontology in the Neotropics. Washington, D.C.: Smithsonian Institution Press, pp. 473–495.

Horovitz, I., and Meyer, A. (1997) Evolutionary trends in the ecology of New World monkeys inferred from a combined phylogenetic analysis of nuclear, mitochondrial, and morphological data. In T.J. Givnish and K.J. Sytsma (eds.): Molecular Evolution and Adaptive Radiation. Cambridge: Cambridge University Press, pp. 189–224.

Kinzey, W.G. (1986) Primate field studies: What's in it for anthropology. Ann. Rev. Anthropol. 13:121–148.

Rosenberger, A.L. (1992) Evolution of feeding niches in New World monkeys. Am. J. Phys. Anthropol. 88:525–562.

Aterian

Late Pleistocene industry of North Africa, named after the type site of Bir el Ater (Algeria) and dated from as early as ca. 100 Ka on stratigraphic grounds to at least 30 Ka, with some radiocarbon ages as late as 21 Ka. Concentrated in the coastal regions from Mediterranean Morocco to Tunisia but extending over much of the Sahara and as far east as the western desert of Egypt, the industry is characterized by Levallois technology, discoidal and tortoise cores, flake scrapers with and without tangs, and small tanged bifacial (Aterian) points. Associated human remains at such sites as Dar-es-Soltane (Morocco) are primarily of Mechtoid anatomically modern type. In western and central North Africa, the Aterian succeeds a more generalized Levalloiso-Mousterian industry with small cordiform handaxes. Blades and blade tools appear in later Aterian sites, in a possible parallel to the development of the Dabban industry in Cyrenaican Libya.

The maximum extent of the Aterian industry appears to have occurred during a wetter interval corresponding to the early phases of the Weichsel glaciation of higher latitudes. Associated faunal remains indicate that both sub-Saharan and Mediterranean faunas extended at the time into

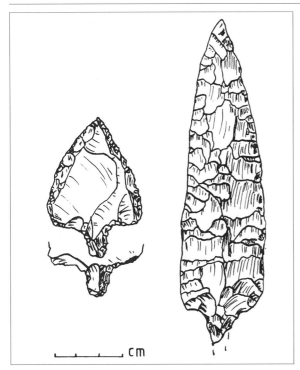

Typical Aterian points (note tang at base) from Bir el Ater (Algeria, left) and Adrar Bous (Niger). From Phillipson, 1993, with permission of Cambridge University Press.

present-day desert areas. By 30 Ka, a period of increasing desiccation in the Sahara led to the abandonment of most Aterian sites.

See also Africa, North; Dabban; Dar-es-Soltane; Haua Fteah; Ibero-Maurusian; Late Paleolithic; Levallois; Middle Stone age; Mousterian; Prepared-Core; Sea-Level Change; Stone-Tool Making. [A.S.B.]

Further Readings

Kleindienst, M.R. (1994) What is the Aterian? The view from Dakhleh Oasis and the Western Desert, Egypt. In Marlow, (ed.): Proceedings of the First Dakleh Oasis Project Seminar. Oxford: Oxbow Press.

Athlitian

Old name for a Late Paleolithic (Neuville Stage V) industry of the Levant, defined at Mugharet el-Wad (Mount Carmel) in Israel and characterized by polyhedric burins on tabular flint, steep and carinate scrapers, lamelles Dufour, and numerous backed points of Chatelperronian/Audi type. Retouch is much finer than in the preceding Aurignacian industry. Attribution of these industries to a later stage has been complicated by the small-backed points (Ahmarian) now known from very early contexts in the Levant, before the Levantine Aurignacian. Thus, materials once designated Athlitian may now be variously attributed to the Ahmarian, Levantine Aurignacian, or early Kebaran stages.

See also Ahmarian; Aurignacian; Blade; Burin; Chatelperronian; Kebaran; Late Paleolithic; Levantine Aurignacian; Scraper; Stone-Tool Making. [A.S.B.]

Aurignac

Late Pleistocene cave in the Pyrenees (Haute Garonne) region of southwestern France; type site of Aurignacian industry. E. Lartet's excavation of this site in 1860 formed the basis for his landmark 1861 paper establishing the coexistence of humans and extinct Late Pleistocene mammals ("l'Age du Grand Ours des Cavernes"), although the human skeletal material later proved to be modern and intrusive.

See also Aurignacian; Lartet, Edouard; Upper Paleolithic. [A.S.B.]

Aurignacian

Early Upper Paleolithic industrial complex, dating to ca. 40–29 Ka, and extending over much of Europe although rare or absent in Russia, Greece, peninsular Italy, and western Iberia. A comparable industry often termed *Aurignacian* occurs in the Levant at many sites, such as Ksar 'Akil (Lebanon), Jabrud (Syria), Hayonim (Israel), and Mount Carmel (Israel). A few early Upper Paleolithic assemblages of Aurignacian type are found in Britain (e.g., Kent's Cavern and Efynnon Beuno). The Aurignacian is the oldest Upper Paleolithic industry of Europe definitely associated with modern humans.

The Aurignacian is clearly distinguished from Middle Paleolithic industries by a strong emphasis on blade technology and on bone and antler working. This distinction, together with the large geographical area in which the Aurignacian is found, has been used to argue for an invasion of Europe at this time by modern humans with an advanced culture and technology. In the early stages, blades are often large and irregular and bear heavy invasive marginal retouch on both sides. Lamellar removals are used to create carinate and nose-ended scrapers on thick flakes or chunks, as well as thick-edged carinate and busked burins or gouges, although the latter are rare in eastern Europe. Bladelets with semi-abrupt inverse-obverse retouch on one or both edges (Dufour bladelets) or narrow-pointed blades and bladelets with semi-abrupt to abrupt retouch on both edges (Font-Yves/Krems Points) are associated with certain Aurignacian industries.

Named after the type site of Aurignac in the Haute Garonne (France), the Aurignacian as defined by French paleontologist E. Lartet and English prehistorian H. Christy, as well as by French archaeologist H. Breuil, originally included all early Upper Paleolithic industries ("first epoch of the reindeer age") and was extended to encompass initial blade industries from as far away as Kenya. In 1933, French schoolteacher D. Peyrony separated the Aurignacian *sensu stricto*, or Breuil's "middle" Aurignacian, with bone points and lamellar retouch on thick blanks, from early Upper Paleolithic industries with backing or abrupt retouch (Breuil's "lower" and "upper" Aurignacian), which he termed Perigordian. These two complexes, each with five successive phases, were interpreted as expressions of two distinct ethnic groups, or "phyla," who coexisted with little admixture over a period of ca. 15 Kyr. On the basis of four levels at La Ferrassie (France), Peyrony distinguished four successive Aurignacian phases and added a fifth phase on the basis of a single assemblage from Laugerie Haute (France). The four stages were

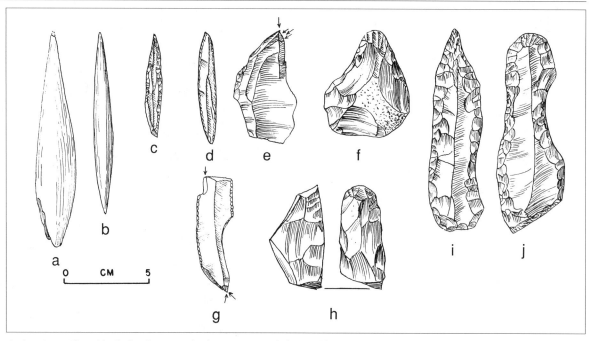

Aurignacian artifacts: (a) split-base bone point (Early Aurignacian); (b) biconical bone point (Evolved Aurignacian); (c) Krems point (Eastern Aurignacian); (d) Font-Yves point (?all stages); (e) busked burin (Intermediate to Evolved Aurignacian); (f) nose-ended scraper (all stages, but especially Intermediate); (g) perforator on heavily retouched blade (Basal to Early Aurignacian); (h) end-scraper on "strangled" blade (Basal to Early Aurignacian); (i) double burin (Intermediate to Evolved Aurignacian); (j) carinate scraper (all stages).

distinguished by changes in bone-point manufacture as follows: Aurignacian I, split-base bone points, heavily retouched blades (La Ferrassie F); Aurignacian II, lozenge points with flattened section, diminished marginal retouch, abundant nose-ended scrapers and busked burins (La Ferrassie H); Aurignacian III, lozenge points with oval section, fewer busked burins and nose-ended scrapers (La Ferrassie H'; and Aurignacian IV, biconical points, burins on retouched truncations and a few pieces with heavy marginal or lamellar retouch (La Ferrassie H").

The Aurignacian V, stratified *above* the Perigordian III (now VI) at Laugerie Haute and known from few other sites, is much later (ca. 20 Ka) and is characterized by thick, denticulate carinate scrapers, created by broader removals than in Stages I–IV, and biconical bone points. The relationship between this stage and the other four is poorly understood and probably does not reflect cultural or ethnic continuity.

In some French sites, split-base bone points and marginal retouch, both possibly indicative of a simpler technology, may be associated with earlier Aurignacian horizons, while busked burins and nose-ended scrapers are more numerous in later assemblages. In general, however, the details of Peyrony's Aurignacian scheme have not been widely supported by evidence from most sites. In particular, each stage is, in reality, highly variable from site to site, with no exact counterparts to the Aurignacian III and IV at any site, apart from a generalized "evolved" Aurignacian. The overall synchrony of Aurignacian and Perigordian traditions is also disputed and has been generally replaced by a separation of the Perigordian into the Chatelperronian (which overlaps with Early Aurignacian and is associated with Neanderthal remains) and the Perigoridian or Gravettian (which separates Aurignacian 0–IV from V).

Aurignacian sites are associated initially with evidence of very cold, dry conditions and are dominated by remains of large, cold-adapted herd animals, such as reindeer, mammoth, woolly rhinoceros, steppe horse, and bison. Figurative carvings, especially in ivory and including a male figure as well as a range of animals, are known from several very early German sites (e.g., Geissenklösterle, Vogelherd, Höhlenstein-Stadel). In 1995, the oldest figurative paintings in newly discovered Chauvet Cave in eastern France were directly dated to ca. 31 Ka, within the Aurignacian time range. In addition, a funerary complex at Cueva Morin (Spain), plaques with punctations interpreted by A. Marshack as calendars, an abundance of perforated objects, musical instruments (Istállöskö, Isturitz), and widespread evidence of long-distance trade in stone, ivory, and fossil and marine shells attest to the social and cognitive complexity of Aurignacian adaptations to a much greater extent than in either the Mousterian or the Chatelperronian. Burials at Grimaldi and Cavillon on the Italian Riviera are robust but fully modern in physical type, comparable to the five individuals from Cro-Magnon (Les Eyzies), who are thought to be associated with Aurignacian industries. Other Aurignacian human remains from eastern Europe (e.g., Mladeč, Vindija) may preserve more archaic traits.

See also Abri Pataud; Antelian; Athlitian; Aurignac; Bacho Kiro; Chatelperronian; Chauvet Cave; Cro-Magnon; Cueva Morin; Europe; Gravettian; Grimaldi; Hayonim; Homo sapiens; Istállöskö; Jabrud; Jewelry; Ksar 'Akil; Kent's Cavern; La Ferrassie; Late Paleolithic; Laugerie Sites; Middle Paleolithic; Mladeč; Mousterian; Musical Instruments; Paleolithic Calendar; Paleolithic Image; Paleolithic Lifeways; Perigordian; Skhūl; Stone-Tool Making; Szeletian; Tabūn; Upper Paleolithic. [A.S.B.]

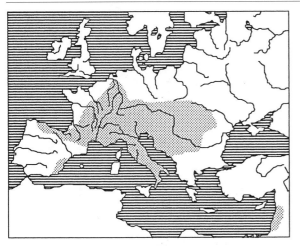

Distribution map of Aurignacian sites.

Further Readings

Chauvet, J.M., Deschamps, E.B., and Hillaire, C. (1996) Chauvet Cave: The Discovery of the World's Oldest Paintings. London: Thames and Hudson.

Gamble, C. (1986) The Palaeolithic Settlement of Europe. Cambridge: Cambridge University Press.

Laville, H., Rigaud, J.P., and Sackett, J.R. (1980) Rock Shelters of the Périgord. New York: Academic.

Marshack, A. (1991) The Roots of Civilization: The Cognitive Beginnings of Man's First Art, Symbol, and Notation. Revised and Expanded. Mount Kisco, N.Y.: Moyer Bell Ltd.

Wymer, J. (1982) The Palaeolithic Age. New York: St. Martin's.

Australia

Island-continent of ca. 8 million km², with a history of human settlement stretching back some 60 Kyr. Recent studies have provided considerable insight into the prehistory of the Australian Aborigines, but many aspects of their past remain unknown. When they first arrived, how they came, where they came from, or why they left their original homes are questions that remain at the heart of investigations of Australian prehistory and paleoanthropology.

The continent of Australia, together with the islands of New Guinea and Tasmania, once constituted the landmass of Greater Australia. This is an important relationship, which emphasizes that for most of human prehistory these landmasses were united as a single larger continent. Greater Australia, part of the region called Sahul, has always been separate from the main landmass of Southeast Asia and most of Indonesia, an area known as Sundaland. Between the two areas is a collection of smaller islands known as Wallacea, so named to honor the great British biologist A.R. Wallace, who in 1860 was the first to recognize the area as a faunal boundary zone between the two larger landmasses.

The independent histories of the Sunda and Sahul landmasses have been a key element in determining the uniqueness of the fauna, particularly the mammals, of the present islands of New Guinea and Tasmania, as well as Aus-

tralia. The water barrier between Sunda and Sahul enabled the marsupial mammals of Sahul to evolve largely independently of the placental forms of the Asian mainland. The sea also served to keep humans from reaching Greater Australia for more than 1.5 Myr after their presence can first be identified in areas of Southeast Asia.

Earliest Inhabitants

The occupation of Greater Australia is a relatively recent event in the human past. Paleogeographic data suggest that the initial migration to the region took place during a period when sea levels were much lower than they are today. Archaeological and skeletal evidence may indicate human presence before 60 Ka, although the evidence is scanty, restricted to the north, and very controversial. The earliest site is Malakunanja in western Arnhem Land, where polished peices of red ocher are dated by thermoluminescence (TL) to 60–50 Ka. As this site was 1,000 km from the northern coast of Greater Australia at the time, it is reasonable to see the initial colonization of the continent as having taken place some time before 60 Ka. Other early discoveries include sites on the Huon Peninsula of Papua New Guinea containing *waisted blades,* large flaked-stone implements of unknown function. Occupation of the entire continent, including the arid core, was established before 35 Ka, based on excavations of Puritjarra in Central Australia.

TL dating published in late 1996 of the lower levels of the Jinmium site in the western Northern Territory suggest initial occupation there as early as 175 Ka. While there may be bedrock contamination associated with these samples, presence of people at the site at 120 Ka is more probable but has been strongly questioned. A date of 75 Ka for ocher staining and a fallen piece of engraved wall surface indicates very early painted and engraved wall art in the region, extending back in time the known ocher pieces from Arnhem Land.

The arrival of human colonists in the Greater Australian region represents the earliest evidence of sea travel. Given the shallow seas of Southeast Asia, where a land area the size of modern Europe was exposed at extreme low sea levels, many islands were enlarged, fused, or appeared intermittently over at least the last 100 Kyr. It is generally agreed that this highly dynamic paleogeography, the often dramatic impact of volcanic activity in the area, and the many social reasons for migration all came together to produce the eastward maritime movement that resulted in the settlement of Sahulland. While no early remains are known, it is likely that rafts, possibly of bamboo and perhaps with simple sails, were the vehicles involved. After reaching the Sahul continent by 60 Ka, further eastward movements brought people to New Ireland (and probably the Solomon Islands) by 30 Ka and to Manus Island in the Admiralty Group before 15 Ka. The Manus settlement represents the extreme example of human maritime traveling in the Pleistocene epoch.

Among the most important of all early occupation sites in Australia are those at Lake Mungo, located in the western part of the state of New South Wales in the southeastern part of the continent. Lake Mungo is part of the Willandra Lakes region, a series of interconnected lake basins that have been dry for at least the last 15 Kyr. Prior to this, they were fresh-

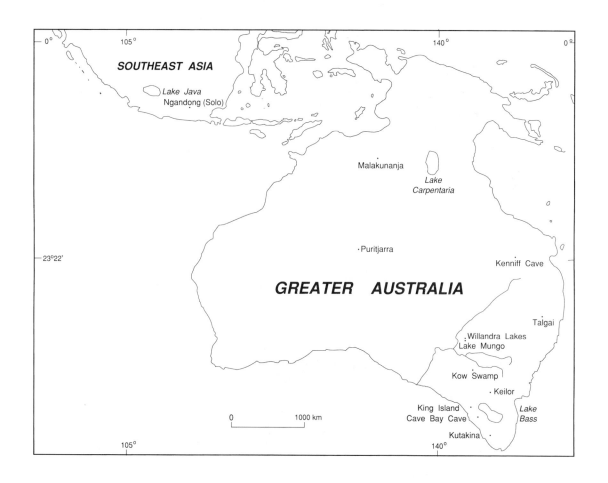

SOUTHEAST ASIA

Lake Java
Ngandong (Solo)

Malakunanja

Lake
Carpentaria

·Puritjarra

Kenniff Cave

GREATER AUSTRALIA

Talgai

·Willandra Lakes
Lake Mungo

Kow Swamp

·Keilor

King Island
Cave Bay Cave

Lake
Bass

Kutakina ·

0   1000 km
23°22'

105°

140°

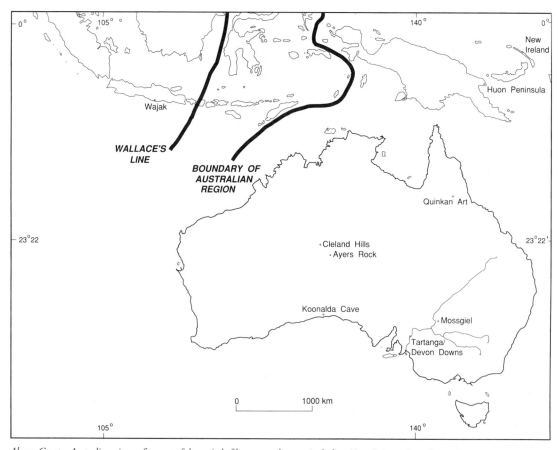

New
Ireland

Huon Peninsula

Wajak

WALLACE'S
LINE

BOUNDARY OF
AUSTRALIAN
REGION

Quinkan Art

23°22'

·Cleland Hills
·Ayers Rock

Koonalda Cave

·Mossgiel

Tartanga/
Devon Downs

0   1000 km

105°

140°

Above: Greater Australia as it was for most of the period of human settlement, including New Guinea, Australia, and Tasmania. Sundaland, the fused Southeast Asian landmass, was always separate from the Australian region.

Below: Australasia today, showing the major biogeographic boundaries that distinguish the Asian and Australian regions. Wallacea, between the major lines, is an area of overlap. Courtesy of Alan Thorne.

water lakes. The sites at Lake Mungo appear during erosion of the lake's lunette, a crescent-shaped dune formed on the shore of the lake when it was full. Early sites have been dated at between 45 and 9 Ka.

Lake Mungo had yielded the oldest human skeletal remains yet found in Australia. One individual, known as Lake Mungo 1, is a slender young adult female estimated by radiocarbon dating to be more than 30 Kyr old. The individual had been ritually cremated, and the remains were heavily fragmented when discovered. This is the earliest evidence of human cremation yet found anywhere in the world.

Nearby, another burial site was discovered, containing the remains of an adult male dated at ca. 35 Ka. The body of this individual, known as Lake Mungo 3, was placed in a shallow grave lying on his back with his hands folded together. Once placed in his grave, he was covered with powdered red ocher. The cremation of Mungo 1 and the postmortem red-ocher adornment of Mungo 3 illustrate the occurrence of complex ritual burials in Australia by at least 35 Ka.

These individuals from Lake Mungo, along with some others, such as the complete cranium from Keilor in Victoria (dated to before 13 Ka), show cranial features that have been described as very *gracile* or modern. For example, these fossil specimens are generally lightly built, with thin vault bones, well-rounded foreheads, weak or moderate browridge formation, and relatively small palates, mandibles, and teeth. Fossil Australian skeletons that show these characteristics have often been categorized together as representing a gracile type of Australian ancestor.

Standing in contrast to the gracile Lake Mungo specimens are a group of individuals whose skeletal remains are much more *robust*. These fossils are typified by remains from the shores of Kow Swamp in the northern part of the state of Victoria. Fossil remains of more than 40 individuals, including infants, juveniles, and adults, have been found at the site. These have been dated to between 14 and 5 Ka, making them appreciably younger than the remains from Lake Mungo. Although found at a different time, the cranium from Cohuna, near the northwestern edge of Know Swamp, is considered part of the Kow Swamp population and is of similar age.

The Kow Swamp population, best exemplified by the near intact crania of Kow Swamp (KS) 1 and KS 5 and the Cohuna cranium, exhibit characteristics that contrast sharply with the gracile specimens from Lake Mungo or Keilor. The robust Kow Swamp specimens are characterized by thicker bone; large, wide, often projecting faces; prominent browridges; flat, sloping foreheads; and large palates, mandibles, and teeth. Specimens exhibiting this morphology are frequently said to be *archaic* in appearance. Often assigned to this group on the basis of these robust cranial features are remains from nearby Lake Nitchie and Mossgiel (both earlier than 7 Ka), Cossack (ca. 6.5 Ka), and the heavily fragmented Talgai cranium from southeast Queensland (ca. 12 Ka). Crania from a large but undated sample from Coobool Creek in southern New South Wales also exhibit a number of these robust traits.

Analysis of rock and portable art motifs, particularly that of the Rainbow Serpent that is essential to much of north Australian Aboriginal religous belief even today, indicates that this element can be traced back at least 6 Kyr. This serpent is a symbol of unity, as well as of creation and destruction. Many features of the landscape are ascribed to the movement and behavior of the Dreamtime Rainbow Serpent. While it can be seen as the earliest known peace symbol, it makes clear that Aboriginal religion is demonstrably older than any other religious or philosophic tradition.

Theories on the Peopling of Australia

Who were the first inhabitants of Greater Australia, the ancestors of the modern Aborigines? While many theories have been offered to answer this question, they fall into two basic groups: (1) Aboriginal origins are the result of two or more migrations to Australia of people with different physical features; and (2) the present population is descended largely from a single migration.

One of the multiple-source theories, based entirely upon aspects of contemporary morphological variation, has suggested that three waves of ancestors arrived in Australia. This explanation, advanced by American anthropologist J.B. Birdsell, is known as the *tri-hybrid theory.* Birdsell theorized that a wave of Oceanic Negritos came to Australia first, followed by migrations of a group referred to as the Murrayians (the dominant group, possibly related to the Ainu people from northern Japan), and finally by a group known as the Carpentarians (whose geographic origins may be in India). The interbreeding of these three groups, according to this theory, has produced the extensive variability found among modern-day Aborigines.

A second multiorigin theory, the *dual-source hypothesis,* has received considerable attention in recent years. This explanation, proposed by A. Thorne, is based upon the comparison of fossil hominid material from Asia with that of Australia. This theory holds that the extreme disparities found between the gracile and the robust groups of ancient Australians are too great to indicate a single ancestral lineage. The differences are deemed to be inherited from separate parental populations. Proponents of this view suggest that the robust crania bear great similarities to fossil hominids from the island of Java (such as the Sangiran or Ngandong fossils), while the gracile individuals show many resemblances to material from ancient China (such as those from Liujiang or the Upper Cave at Zhoukoudian). Accordingly, it is suggested that the ancestors of the more robust Australians came from island Indonesia. The gracile and the robust groups eventually interbred, resulting in the variations found among modern Australian Aborigines.

The single-source theory, also known as the *homogeneity hypothesis,* disagrees with the rigid categorization of Australian fossil humans into discrete groups labeled gracile or robust. It was proposed around midcentury by the Australian anatomist A. Abbie. Adherents argue that the gracile and the robust fossils represent morphological extremes of a highly variable population rather than evidence of two completely separate lineages. This theory suggests that the modern-day variability among Aborigines is due to both genetic and cultural influences having acted on a small, founding

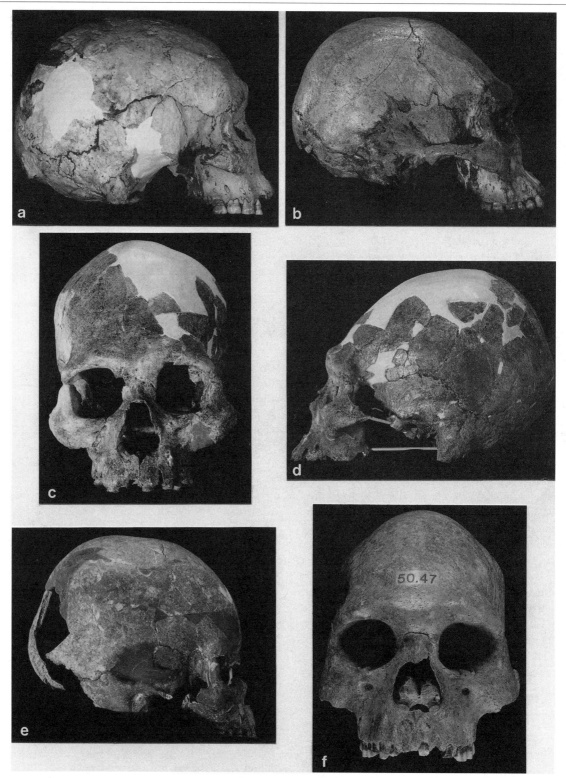

Examples of some early Australians: (a) the Keilor cranium; (b) Cohuna cranium, part of the Kow Swamp population; (c–d) an adult from Kow Swamp (KS 5); (e) a juvenile from Kow Swamp (KS 6); and (f) one of the Coobool Creek population. Keilor has often been described as an example of the "gracile" Australian population, while the others have been spoken of as representative of the "robust" type. Courtesy of Jeffrey T. Laitman.

population. This population came from a single homeland and gradually spread out to colonize the continent.

Both groups of theorists admit the general development of local adaptations to changing environments in Australia over the more than 50 Ka of occupation. Human remains from King Island in Bass Strait between Australia and Tas-

mania, dated to 14 Ka, suggest that southern Late Pleistocene populations were making high-latitude physical changes to adapt to extreme Australian environments.

While constrasting theories will undoubtedly remain for some time, recent finds are helping to clarify some potential relationships. For example, a fully opalized cal-

Evidence of early Australian presence and behavior is widespread: (a) Ayers Rock in central Australia, an area colonized by 35 Ka; (b) engraved face at Cleland Hills, northwest of Ayres Rock. Rock art in this area has been dated to ca. 30 Ka; (c) Quinkan Figures painted in caves in Cape York in northern Queensland. Painted art in this area is dated to before 20 Ka; (d) a waisted blade from the Huon Peninsula, Papua New Guinea. This artifact is dated to 40 Ka; (e) Toas, small "signposts" made by the Dieri people of South Australia to indicate travel directions. Much of Australian art is ephemeral; (f) aerial view of the dry bed of Lake Mungo in western New South Wales, with the sand lunette in foreground. Human remains older than 35 Ka have been found here. Courtesy of Alan Thorne.

varia discovered from a site near Lake Mungo in the Willandra Lakes (WLH 50) shows features that are extremely robust, more so than any previously discovered Australian skeleton. This specimen shows many similarities to some of the Ngandong material from Central Java that is thought to data to ca. 200 Ka. While WLH 50 had not been dated as of the late 1990s, estimates of its age suggest it is older than 30 Kyr. If this proves to be the case, this robust human may tell us what the earliest Australians were like and provide a direct link with the earlier Indonesian materials.

See also Archaeology; Asia, Eastern and Southern; Birdsell, Joseph B.; China; Homo sapiens; Keilor; Kow Swamp; Lake

Mungo; Modern Human Origins; Ngandong (Solo); Sangiran Dome; Talgai; Zhoukoudian. [J.T.L., A.T.]

Further Readings

Flood, J. (1995) Archeology of the Dreamtime. Sydney: Collins.

Fullager, R.L.K., Price, D.M., and Head, L.M. (1996) Early human occupation of northern Australia: Archaeology and thermoluminescence dating of Jinmium rockshelter, Northern Territory. Antiquity 70:751–773.

Kirk, R.L. (1981) Aboriginal Man Adapting. Sydney: Oxford.

Kirk, R.L., and Thorne, A.G., eds. (1976) The Origin of the Australians. Canberra: Australian Institute of Aboriginal Studies.

O'Connell, J.F., and Allen, J. (1998) When did humans first arrive in Greater Australia and why is it important to know? Evol. Anthropol. 6:132–146.

Thorne, A.G., and Raymond, R. (1989) Man on the Rim: The Peopling of the Pacific. Sydney: Angus and Robertson.

Thorne, A.G., and Wolpoff, M.H. (1981) Regional continuity in Australasian Pleistocene hominid evolution. Am. J. Phys. Anthropol. 55:337–349.

White, J.P., and O'Connell, J.F. (1982) A Prehistory of Australia, New Guinea, and Sahul. Sydney: Academic.

Australopithecus

Genus name many paleoanthropologists use in reference to Pliocene and Early Pleistocene hominid fossils from southern and eastern Africa that are not considered to belong to the genus *Homo*. The name *Australopithecus,* literally "southern ape," was coined by South African paleontologist R.A. Dart in 1925, when he described the juvenile hominid specimen from the site of Taung (South Africa) as belonging to the taxon *Australopithecus africanus.* In his analysis of the Taung skull, Dart perceived several distinctly hominin, or humanlike, features, such as the ventral position of its foramen magnum and its relatively small canines, together with several more primitive, or apelike, features, such as its small brain size and its relatively large snout. Dart recognized *Australopithecus* as a primitive human forebear, whose small brain excluded it from being recognized as a member of the genus *Homo,* but whose hominin features excluded it from being considered an ape. In fact, Dart suggested that his new species be placed in a new intermediate family called "Homo-Simiadae" (*Simia* then being one of several generic names used for apes), but this idea was biologically unacceptable as well as taxonomically incorrect: Any family name must be based on the valid and available name of a type genus, and of course no genus "Homo-Simia" existed.

In 1936, South African paleontologist R. Broom recovered Pliocene fossils from the site of Sterkfontein (South Africa) that he recognized as being similar to the Taung skull. He referred the Sterkfontein fossils to the genus *Australopithecus,* albeit to a separate species, *A. transvaalensis.* He later suggested that the Sterkfontein fossils might be attributable to a separate genus, for which he proposed the name *Plesianthropus.* In the

late 1940s, hominin fossils from Makapansgat (South Africa) were described by Dart, who attributed them to the genus *Australopithecus,* but to a separate species, *A. prometheus.* Most authorities now recognize all of these fossils as belonging to a single species, *Australopithecus africanus.* Subsequent discoveries of hominin remains from Members 2 and 4 at Sterkfontein and Members 3 and 4 at Makapansgat have greatly increased the *A. africanus* hypodigm. Hominin fossils discovered at the South African sites of Kromdraai and Swartkrans were attributed by Broom to the genus *Paranthropus* because they were considered to be distinct from the Taung and Sterkfontein specimens.

In 1959, L.S.B. Leakey attributed a large-toothed, heavily crested cranium from Bed I of Olduvai Gorge to a novel taxon, *Zinjanthropus boisei.* J.T. Robinson, however, recognized its close affinities to South African *Paranthropus,* and proposed that the Olduvai cranium be attributed to *P. boisei.* Broom and Robinson maintained that *Australopithecus* and *Paranthropus* represented separate phyletic lines of evolution and that their generic separation was therefore fully justified.

Subsequent studies, such as those by P.V. Tobias, C. Loring Brace, and M. Wolpoff, viewed all of these early hominins as making up a single evolutionary grade of organization, characterized primarily by comparatively small brain size. These studies, which minimized the differences between *Australopithecus* (termed the *gracile* species) and *Paranthropus* (the "robust" forms), influenced opinion such that most students and almost all textbooks of human evolution have come to regard *Paranthropus* as a junior synonym of *Australopithecus.*

Despite the overwhelming influence that this "grade" paradigm has had upon anthropologists, a strong body of evidence has accumulated indicating that specimens of *Paranthropus* possess a host of derived specializations that probably reflect significant evolutionary (i.e., functional and ecological) differences between them and other early hominin taxa. Most, but not all, of these specializations pertain to trophic (i.e., dietary) features, and they attest to the close evolutionary relationships among the different "robust" species. It is abundantly apparent that the species of *Paranthropus* form an independent phyletic clade of human evolution.

The grade view that African Plio-Pleistocene hominin fossils that are not attributable to the genus *Homo* are referable to the genus *Australopithecus* has had significant consequences, including the attribution of the Hadar (Ethiopia) and Laetoli (Tanzania) fossils by D.C. Johanson, T.D. White, and Y. Coppens to *Australopithecus afarensis.* Similarly, White, G. Suwa, and B. Asfaw originally attributed still earlier fossils from the Aramis region of the Middle Awash Valley to the taxon *Australopithecus ramidus,* and M.G. Leakey and her colleagues have attributed early hominin remains from the Kenyan sites of Allia Bay and Kanapoi to *Australopithecus anamensis.*

Even with the recognition of *Paranthropus* as a distinct genus, it is likely that *Australopithecus,* which comprises three (or four) currently (1999) recognized species—*A. afarensis, A. africanus, A. anamensis,* and perhaps *A. bahrelghazali*—is paraphyletic. The problem of paraphyly is exacerbated when the three generally recognized species of *Paranthropus*—*P. robus-*

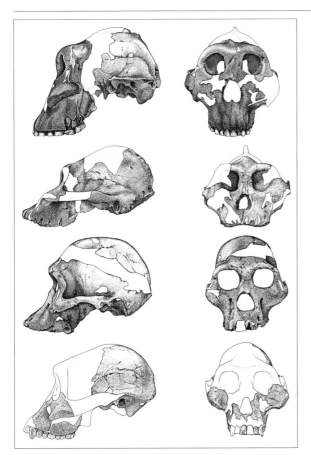

Lateral and facial views of (from top to bottom): Paranthropus boisei, P. robustus, Australopithecus africanus, *and* A. afarensis.

tus, P. boisei, and *P. aethiopicus*—are also considered by some researchers to be members of the genus *Australopithecus.*

The belief that all Plio-Pleistocene hominins that are not attributable to the genus *Homo* should be referred to the genus *Australopithecus* has also had the effect that the problematic term "australopithecine" has become firmly entrenched in the paleoanthropological literature. This term is a direct vernacular transliteration of the taxonomic subfamilial rank Australopithecinae; its use, therefore, denotes an implicit recognition that *Australopithecus* should be afforded subfamilial separation from *Homo,* although few (if any) authorities would still accept this level of distinction. Nevertheless, the term is unlikely to fall into disuse in the near future. Suffice it to say that when "australopithecine" is used, it is almost always taken to connote *Australopithecus* (sensu lato). Here, the taxonomically neutral, equivalent term "australopith" will be used for non-*Homo* hominins.

Thus, as of the late 1990s, there are three distinct species that are attributed to the genus *Paranthropus: P. robustus, P. boisei,* and *P. aethiopicus.* These are discussed in detail under their separate species entries, and together under the entry for *Paranthropus.* There are four (or five) distinct species that are generally (although not universally) attributed to the genus *Australopithecus: A. africanus, A. afarensis, A. anamensis, A. bahrelghazali,* and *A. ramidus,* although the latter formally has been transferred to a separate genus, *Ardipithecus.* The four species that are generally attributed to

the genus *Australopithecus,* and their possible phylogenetic relationships with *Homo* and *Paranthropus,* are discussed below.

Australopithecus

The cranial, dental, and postcranial features that serve to distinguish the genus *Australopithecus* from other hominin genera are difficult to enumerate because this is manifestly a paraphyletic genus. Thus, any morphological traits that these four species possess in common do not necessarily represent shared derived characters (i.e., synapomorphies). Compared to Miocene and modern apes, the canines of *Australopithecus* are somewhat reduced, although not to the extent that is expressed in *Homo* and *Paranthropus.* The foramen magnum is positioned at the bitympanic line; the nasoalveolar clivus is separated from the floor of the nasal cavity by a distinct step; and the incisive fossa is rather large. The petrous portion of the temporal bone is oriented intermediately between the more sagittal position in modern apes and the more coronal position of *Homo* and *Paranthropus.* Dental development—the calcification and eruption patterns of the permanent teeth—follows a primitive apelike pattern, compared to the precocious development of the incisors and canines in *Homo* and *Paranthropus.*

A. africanus

This is the type species of the genus *Australopithecus.* The holotype derives from the site of Taung; the hypodigm of this species is composed of specimens from Members 2 and 4 of the Sterkfontein Formation and from Members 3 and 4 of the Makapansgat Formation (South Africa). Recently discovered teeth from the South African site of Gladysvale have also been attributed to this taxon.

This species is characterized principally by a more globular and less pneumatized cranium than other species of *Australopithecus;* a calvaria that is hafted onto the facial skeleton at a high level (resulting in a high supraorbital height index); a deep mandibular fossa that is bounded anteriorly by a distinct articular eminence; a tympanic bone with a nearly vertical anterior face; moderate separation of the lambda and the inion; a slight angulation of the petrous pyramid to the sagittal plane; a pyriform aperture whose lateral margins are variably rounded by the presence of anterior pillars; P_3s that are bicuspid or nearly fully bicuspid; dP_3 not molarized, with a mesial marginal ridge delineating an anterior fovea that opens lingually; and incisors and canines that are humanlike in their proportions to the sizes of the premolars and molars. In a number of these features, *A. africanus* appears to be more derived than the other three species of *Australopithecus.* Endocranial-capacity estimates for *A. africanus* are on the order of 410–450 ml (with an average of ca. 440 ml), although one large cranium from Sterkfontein (Stw 505) may have a capacity that exceeds 500 ml. These values tend to be larger than those for *A. afarensis* and slightly smaller than those for specimens of *Homo* and *Paranthropus.*

A. africanus specimens from Sterkfontein and Makapansgat likely date to between ca. 3 and 2.5 Ma. Although the geochronological age of the Taung skull has long been a matter of dispute, the most reliable faunal estimates place it at ca. 2 Ma at the very youngest and most likely between 2.8 and 2.3 Ma.

Paleoenvironmental reconstructions for these South African sites suggest a predominance of wooded, closed conditions. The dentition of *A. africanus* suggests that it had a herbivorous diet, likely consisting of fruits and foliage. Postcranial remains indicate a hominin that employed bipedal locomotion on the ground—although the mode of bipedality almost certainly differed from that practiced by modern humans—that was equally well adapted to climbing. For example, the big toe is divergent and mobile; the finger bones are long and curved; and the shoulder girdle indicates enhanced mobility compared to modern humans. Estimates of body size suggest considerable size dimorphism between presumptive males and females, with an average of ca. 45 kg.

A. afarensis

The hypodigm of this species consists of specimens from the sites of Laetoli (Tanzania) and Hadar (Ethiopia), together with several referred specimens from the sites of Fejej, Maka, and Belohdelie (Ethiopia) and from the Tulu Bor Member (e.g., KNM-ER 2602) of the Koobi Fora Formation (Kenya). Fossils from the Usno Formation (Ethiopia) and Members B and C of the Shungura Formation (Ethiopia) also have been referred to this species, which appears to span the period between ca. 3.9 and 2.7 Ma. Two fragmentary mandibular corpora from the sites of Lothagam and Tabarin (Kenya) have been variously referred to this species, but their assignment to *A. afarensis, A. anamensis,* or *A. ramidus* remained questionable into the late 1990s. In 1996, a mandible fragment from site KT 12 in the Bahr el Ghazal region of central Chad, originally referred to *A. afarensis*, was named a new species, *A. bahrelghazali*, on the basis of several dental features such as three-rooted P_3. The distinction of this taxon is also unclear as yet.

A. afarensis is characterized principally by its possession of a suite of primitive craniodental characters, including strong facial prognathism; a flat cranial base; a flat glenoid fossa without a distinct articular eminence; a postglenoid process that is situated anterior to the tympanic; a tubular tympanic; an anteriorly shallow (flat) palate; sharp lateral margins of the pyriform aperture; a convex nasoalveolar clivus that is demarcated from the floor of the nose by a horizontal sill; maxillary lateral incisor roots that are lateral to the margins of the pyriform aperture; a strongly flared parietal mastoid angle together with an asterionic notch, large maxillary central incisors compared with lateral incisors, relatively large canines that wear primarily along the distal edge, and sectorial (unicuspid) to semisectorial (with small metaconid) mandibular P_3s. Endocranial-capacity estimates range between ca. 310 and 485 ml, with an average of ca. 400–410 ml for four Hadar specimens.

The postcranial skeleton of *A. afarensis*, together with the footprint trails at the site of Laetoli, indicate a hominin that was bipedal while on the ground, but whose mode of bipedality differed markedly from that employed by modern humans. In addition, a large number of discrete postcranial features indicate a hominin that was well adapted to climbing in the trees. These features are found primarily on the foot and the hand bones and in the shoulder girdle. *A. afarensis* likely spent a considerable amount of time in the trees both sleeping and feeding. Analysis of the knee joints from Hadar suggests that the smaller (presumptive female) and the larger (presumptive male) individuals differed in a manner indicative of different degrees of arboreality, such as is encountered today among orangutans. Body-size estimates for *A. afarensis* indicate a strong degree of sexual dimorphism, approximating or even exceeding that exhibited by modern gorillas, with females having a mass of ca. 30 kg and males a mass of ca. 65 kg.

Paleoenvironmental reconstructions indicate a diversity of habitats from well-watered and wooded conditions along lake margins (such as at Hadar) to savannah (or even denser) woodland conditions (such as at Laetoli). This suggests that *A. afarensis* had a fairly broad range of locomotor abilities. Analyses of the teeth suggest that *A. afarensis* was also a herbivore and that its diet likely consisted of fruits and foliage.

A. anamensis

This name has been applied by M.G. Leakey and her colleagues to East African hominin fossils that date between ca. 4.2 and 3.9 Ma from the Kenyan sites of Allia Bay and Kanapoi. These specimens display a number of primitive features, as well as several that appear to be unique. *A. anamensis* is characterized by a very small, elliptical external auditory meatus; a tubular tympanic bone that extends laterally only as far as the medial edge of the postglenoid process; mandibular corpora and tooth rows that are close together and nearly parallel; a marked postero-inferior slope to the mandibular symphysis, which extends back as far as the M_1; upper molars in which the mesial part of the crown (i.e., the trigon) is buccolingually much broader than the distal portion (i.e., the talon); and the least molarized dP_3 of any *Australopithecus* species. As in *A. afarensis*, the mandibular fossa of *A. anamensis* is very shallow, with a poorly developed articular process, but it appears to be more primitive in that the temporal bone is strongly pneumatized, with air cells extending into the squamous portion and into the root of the zygomatic arch.

A tibia from Kanapoi indicates a hominin that walked bipedally while on the ground. It is larger than the largest known tibia of *A. afarensis*, and the body weight of its owner has been estimated to be between 47 and 55 kg. Other features, such as the hamate from the Turkwel site, suggest the presence of large, strong flexor tendons of the hand, which would be consistent with a species that was like *A. afarensis* and *A. africanus* in its use of an arboreal milieu. *A. anamensis* was a bipedal species that was capable of, and probably heavily engaged in, tree climbing.

The paleoenvironments at Kanapoi and Allia Bay are consistent with the hypothesis that *A. anamensis* was a capable climber. There are fish and aquatic vertebrates associated with *A. anamensis* fossils at Kanapoi; there is also a considerable diversity of mammalian taxa. It is evident that at Kanapoi, *A. anamensis* occupied a woodland-bushland habitat along the banks of a large river. The Allia Bay fauna also appears to be associated with a gallery forest that would have fringed the large proto-Omo River.

A. ramidus

This name was applied by T.D. White and his colleagues in September 1994 to a collection of 17 hominin fossils from the Aramis region of Ethiopia. In May 1995, however, they made available the generic nomen *Ardipithecus*, noting that this species is likely the sister taxon of the hominin clade. This change was made in what was called a "corrigendum" to their original article, although it is difficult to give much credence to their explanation that this particular item did not appear in the original article because of an error. Indeed, it is clear from reports in the popular press at the time the original article was published that White believed that the attribution of the Aramis fossils to a novel genus was unwarranted. Rather, this particular corrigendum appears to have been motivated by the prospect that one of several other hominin paleontologists—some of whom were quoted in the popular press as considering that the Aramis fossils warranted separate generic status—might make available another name.

It is clear that the Aramis fossils are considerably more primitive in several features than specimens that have been attributed to *Australopithecus afarensis*, and probably to *A. anamensis*, and that these early Ethiopian fossils deserve separate generic rank.

The Aramis fossils derive from sediments between the Gàala Vitric Tuff and the Daam Aatu Basaltic Tuff, both of which have been dated to ca. 4.4 Ma. The associated fauna includes many specimens of several primates, especially a possibly semiterrestrial colobine monkey; the other large-mammal species and the presence of suids (members of the pig family), as well as paleobotanical remains, indicate that *A. ramidus* inhabited a woodland-forest environment.

A. ramidus is characterized principally by a suite of primitive cranial and dental features. These include canines larger than in other *Australopithecus* species; premolars and molars that tend to be smaller than in other *Australopithecus* species; a shallow glenoid fossa that lacks a definable articular eminence; a narrow, elongate dP_3 that lacks a fovea anterior; a tubular tympanic that extends to the lateral edge of the postglenoid tubercle; a weak entoglenoid process; molar teeth that are relatively narrow buccolingually; and permanent tooth enamel that is both absolutely thin and relatively thinner than in any other early hominin species.

Described postcranial elements are limited to those of the upper limb, although an as yet (1999) unpublished partial skeleton was discovered at the end of 1994. The forelimb possesses several features that are reminiscent of those expressed in *A. afarensis* or modern great apes, such as a strong angulation of the distal end of the radius and a strong lateral trochlear ridge together with a large lateral epicondyle of the humerus. These and other features are generally associated with arboreal climbing capabilities.

Other fossils from Ethiopia and especially Kenya that date to earlier than 4 Ma may be attributable to the same species as represented by the Aramis remains, or they may warrant inclusion in *A. anamensis*. In particular, the fragmentary mandibular corpus from Lothagam (Kenya) has been said to possess relatively thinner enamel than *A. afarensis* homologues, which may well serve to align it with the *A.*

ramidus specimens. The bit of mandibular corpus from Tabarin (Kenya) and some of the pieces of rather questionable age from Chemeron (Baringo Basin, Kenya) may be attributable to either *A. ramidus* or *A. anamensis*, depending upon the recovery of more elements that are definitely attributable to these two species and upon the thickness of the enamel of the teeth. The Tabarin specimen was formally named *Homo antiquus praegens* (the term *Homo antiquus* being used by W. Ferguson for some *A. afarensis* fossils), and the species name *praegens* may be a senior synonym of *ramidus* if the Aramis and the Tabarin fossils prove to be conspecific.

Evolutionary Relationships

There has been considerable controversy over the relationships among the species of *Australopithecus* and *Paranthropus* and between these taxa and the genus *Homo*. Almost all of the innumerable phylogenetic and taxonomic hypotheses that have been posited since the description of the Taung skull have been either rejected outright or substantially altered by ongoing research and new discoveries. Nevertheless, it is useful to review some of the more salient hypotheses because of the impact that they have had upon perceptions of the course of human evolution. As of the late 1990s, there was no clearly formulated hypothesis that incorporates the *A. anamensis* and the *A. ramidus* fossils, although T.D. White has been quoted in the popular press as claiming that there is simple unilineal evolution from *A. ramidus* through *A. anamensis* to *A. afarensis*. This anagenetic view of single-species evolution is easily incorporated into several of the other hypotheses that have been put forward (see figure on page 116).

Hypothesis 1 (advanced by T.D. White and D.C. Johanson in the late 1970s): *A. afarensis* represents the stem hominin from which both the *Homo* and the "robust australopithecine" lineages diverged. According to this hypothesis, *A. africanus* is more closely related to the robust species *P. robustus* and *P. boisei* than to any other hominin taxon. The discovery of KNM-WT 17000 and other reasonably well preserved specimens of *P. aethiopicus* has led to the almost universal rejection of this hypothesis.

Hypothesis 2 (advanced by R.R. Skelton, H.M. McHenry, and G.M. Drawhorn in the 1980s): *A. afarensis* represents the stem hominin from which *A. africanus* evolved, and *A. africanus* represents the last common ancestor of the *Homo* and the robust (*P. robustus* and *P. boisei*) lineages. The discovery of the KNM-WT 17000 cranium of *P. aethiopicus* has led many workers to reject this hypothesis, although, in a subsequent work, Skelton and McHenry argued that *P. aethiopicus* is more primitive than *A. africanus*, the other robust australopiths, and *Homo*. In this later study, *A. africanus* continued to be viewed as the sister of a robust australopith + *Homo* clade, and the species *aethiopicus* was a sister to that group; the genus *Paranthropus* was, therefore, found to be polyphyletic.

Hypothesis 3 (advocated originally by J.T. Robinson in the late 1960s): The robust australopiths (*P. robustus* and *P. boisei*) represent a distinct evolutionary lineage that diverged very early from the human (*Homo*) line. According to this

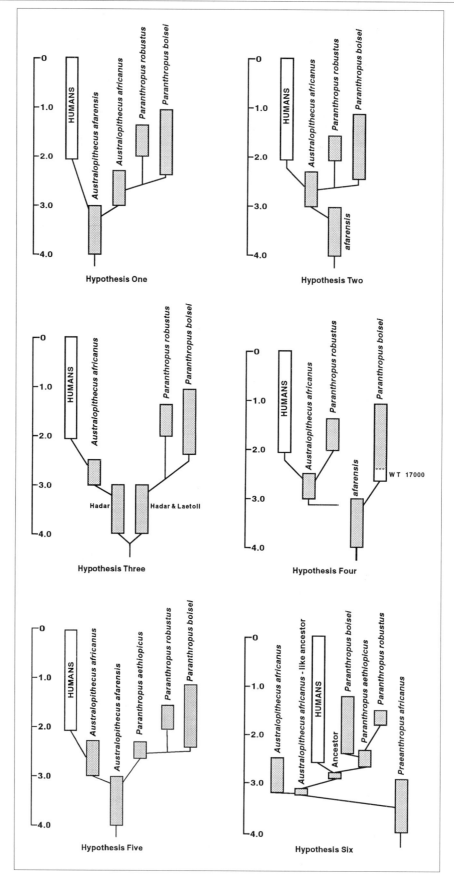

Six hypotheses of relationships among australopiths. See text. Courtesy of Frederick E. Grine.

hypothesis, since *P. robustus* and *P. boisei* make up a distinct evolutionary branch (clade), it is valid to view them as representing a genus that was distinct from those taxa on the *Homo* line. Robinson argued that, since *A. africanus* was part of the latter lineage, there was no valid reason to recognize *Australopithecus* as a distinct genus. The specimens from Taung, Sterkfontein, and Makapansgat could be accorded membership in the genus *Homo* as the species *H. transvaalensis* (there is already a species named *africanus* in the genus *Homo*). This hypothesis, put forward before the description of *A. afarensis,* was altered slightly by T.R. Olson, who argued that *afarensis* actually comprised two separate species, one of which was related to the *Paranthropus* lineage and the other to the *Homo* lineage. (It is of interest to note that while Robinson recognized the Garusi [Laetoli area] fossils to be part of the *Homo* line [i.e., *H. transvaalensis*], Olson interpreted them as being part of the *Paranthropus* lineage.) The phylogenetic diagram published here represents Olson's alterations to the scheme originally proposed by Robinson. This hypothesis (the presence of two parallel lineages) has been corroborated in part by the discovery of the KNM-WT 17000 cranium of *P. aethiopicus*, although there is a general consensus that the Laetoli and Hadar samples represent a single species, *A. afarensis.*

Hypothesis 4 (originally advocated by A. Walker and colleagues in their 1986 initial interpretation of KNM-WT 17000 from West Turkana): *A. afarensis* represents the common stem from which the eastern African "robust" lineage (comprising *P. aethiopicus* and *P. boisei*) emerged, together with another lineage that led ultimately to the South African "robust" form (*P. robustus*) and to *Homo* via their common ancestor, *A. africanus*. This hypothesis states that the morphological resemblances between the South and the East African "robust" forms arose through convergent evolution, primarily through convergent functional adaptations of the masticatory complex; thus, it interprets *Paranthropus* to be polyphyletic.

Hypothesis 5 (advocated originally in 1986 by E. Delson and F.E. Grine): This hypothesis is similar to Hypothesis 3 inasmuch as it recognizes the "robust" taxa from southern and eastern Africa—*P. robustus, P. boisei,* and *P. aethiopicus*—as consisting of a single evolutionary branch (clade). It differs from Hypothesis 3, however, in that a single species, *A. afarensis,* is recognized for the fossils from Hadar and Laetoli. *A. afarensis* is postulated as the last common ancestor of the *Paranthropus* clade and the lineage leading to humans; *A. africanus* or an *A. africanus*-like form is held to represent the forebear of *Homo*.

This hypothesis, which stemmed principally from an interpretation of the evolutionary relationships of *P. aethiopicus,* largely corroborated Robinson's arguments that the "robust" australopiths constitute a lineage distinct from that formed by *A. africanus* and *Homo,* with the result that the genus name *Paranthropus* can be legitimately applied to members of the former clade. In a strictly cladistic interpretation of the taxonomy of this phylogenetic hypothesis, the species "*A.*" *afarensis* (and also "*A.*" *anamensis*) should properly be placed in a distinct genus, with the result that the name *Australopithecus* would pertain only to *A. africanus*.

Hypothesis 6 (advocated by D.S. Strait, F.E. Grine, and M.A. Moniz in the mid-1990s): Cladistic analysis of early hominin relationships found strong evidence in support of two monophyletic clades, *Paranthropus* and *Homo*. It concluded, in common with Skelton and McHenry, that *A. africanus* was the sister of *Homo* and the "robust" australopiths, except that Skelton and McHenry posited that *P. aethiopicus* was not part of a "robust" clade. According to the analysis by Strait and his colleagues, which did not include the species *A. ramidus* and *A. anamensis, A. afarensis* is the sister of all other hominins. The two phyletic schemes that most closely approximate and, therefore, possibly explain the pattern of relationships hypothesized by the cladogram require the presence of at least two hypothetical ancestral species. These differ according to whether the primitive features of *P. aethiopicus* represent secondary reversals from a more derived condition, or whether some of the derived features of *A. africanus* represent parallel (i.e., nonhomologous) acquisitions. Various other studies of early hominin phylogeny have concluded that homoplasy (i.e., parallelism and convergence) is likely to be common among these taxa, which might suggest that *Australopithecus afarensis* gave rise to an *A. africanus*-like ancestor that retained a number of primitive features (e.g., a shallow glenoid fossa without a distinct articular tubercle). This, in turn, gave rise to *A. africanus* (which represents an evolutionary dead-end) and to a hypothetical last common ancestor of the *Paranthropus* and *Homo* clades. According to this scenario, *P. aethiopicus* retains its primitive cranial features from the two hypothetical ancestors and represents the common ancestor of *P. boisei* and *P. robustus*.

One of the consequences of this study is that the name *Australopithecus* will likely find use only in reference to *A. africanus,* because the genus *Australopithecus* is paraphyletic. The Hadar and Laetoli fossils are properly referred to under the nomen *Praeanthropus africanus*. The term *australopithecine* has little meaning, and it is hoped that the even more misleading sobriquets *gracile* and *robust* will fall into disuse.

See also Ardipithecus ramidus; Australopithecus afarensis; Australopithecus anamensis; Australopithecus bahrelghazali; Belohdelie; Broom, Robert; Clade; Classification; Dart, Raymond Arthur; Fejej; Gladysvale; Hadar; Kanapoi; Kromdraai; Laetoli; Leakey, Louis Seymour Bazett; Makapansgat; Olduvai Gorge; Paranthropus; Paranthropus aethiopicus; Paranthropus boisei; Paranthropus robustus; Robinson, John Talbot; Sterkfontein; Swartkrans; Taung. [F.E.G.]

Further Readings

Broom, R. (1950) The genera and species of the South African fossil ape-men. Am. J. Phys. Anthropol. 8:1–13.

Brunet, M., Beauvilain, A., Coppens, Y., Heintz, E., Moutaye, A.H.E., and Pilbeam, D. (1995) The first australopithecine 2,500 kilometres west of the rift valley (Chad). Nature 378:273–275.

Delson, E. (1986) Human phylogeny revised again. Nature 322:496–497.

Grine, F.E. (1981) Trophic differences between "gracile" and "robust" australopithecines: A scanning electron microscope analysis of occlusal events. S. Afr. J. Sci. 77:203–230.

Howell, F.C. (1978) Hominidae. In V.J. Maglio and H.B.S. Cooke (eds.): Evolution of African Mammals. Cambridge, Mass.: Harvard University Press, pp. 154–248.

Kimbel, W.H., White, T.D., and Johanson, D.C. (1988) Implications of KNM-WT 17000 for the evolution of "robust" *Australopithecus*. In F.E. Grine (ed.): Evolutionary History of the "Robust" Australopithecines. New York: Aldine de Gruyter, pp. 259–268.

Leakey, M.G., Feibel, C.S., McDougall, I., and Walker, A. (1995) New four-million-year-old hominid species from Kanapoi and Allia Bay, Kenya. Nature 376:565–571.

Olson, T.R. (1985) Cranial morphology and systematics of the Hadar Formation hominids and *"Australopithecus" afarensis*. In E. Delson (ed.): Ancestors: The Hard Evidence. New York: Liss, pp. 102–119.

Robinson, J.T. (1954) The genera and species of the Australopithecinae. Am. J. Phys. Anthropol. 12:181–200.

Skelton, R.R., and McHenry, H.M. (1992) Evolutionary relationships among early hominids. J. Hum. Evol. 23:309–349.

Skelton, R.R., McHenry, H.M., and Drawhorn, G.M. (1986) Phylogenetic analysis of early hominids. Curr. Anthropol. 27:21–35, 38–39.

Strait, D.S., Grine, F.E., and Moniz, M.A. (1997). A reappraisal of early hominid phylogeny. J. Hum. Evol. 32:17–82.

Walker, A.C., Leakey, R.E.F., Harris, J.M., and Brown, F.H. (1986) 2.5-Myr *Australopithecus boisei* from west of Lake Turkana, Kenya. Nature 322:517–522.

White, T.D., Johanson, D.C., and Kimbel, W.H. (1981) *Australopithecus africanus:* Its phyletic position reconsidered. S. Afr. J. Sci. 77:445–470.

White, T.D., Suwa, G., and Asfaw, B. (1994) *Australopithecus ramidus,* a new species of early hominid from Aramis, Ethiopia. Nature 371:306–312.

White, T.D., Suwa, G., and Asfaw, B. (1995) Corrigendum: *Australopithecus ramidus,* a new species of early hominid from Aramis, Ethiopia. Nature 375:88.

Australopithecus afarensis

Species of *Australopithecus* named in 1978 to incorporate the early hominid fossil material from the Tanzanian Laetolil Beds and the Hadar sites in Ethiopia. Additional fossils from Kenya, Ethiopia, and Chad have been referred to this taxon as well. This species is thought by many to be a common ancestor of all later hominid species in the genera *Homo, Paranthropus,* and *Australopithecus.*

The first specimens of *Australopithecus afarensis* were recovered in Tanzania during the 1930s. Because more abundant fossils of *Australopithecus africanus* were being recovered during the 1920s through 1940s in southern Africa, most authorities attributed the scanty material, consisting of a maxilla and a molar collected by F. Kohl-Larsen in the headwaters

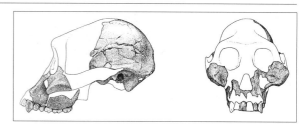

Front and side views of composite cranium reconstructed from fragments found at various Hadar localities.

of the Garusi River above Lake Eyasi (near Laetoli, Tanzania) to this taxon. A canine and an incisor recovered in 1932 by L.S.B. Leakey from nearby exposures of the same strata at Laetoli in the uppermost drainage of the Olduvai Side Gorge (Tanzania) went unrecognized until the 1970s. In the 1950s, the recognition by H. Weinert and S. Senyürek of primitive characters in the maxillary fragment led them to attribute the Garusi material to *Meganthropus africanus* and *Praeanthropus africanus*, respectively. Few agreed with these workers, and the Garusi maxilla, as it was called, continued to be considered a northern representative of *Australopithecus africanus.*

Between 1973 and 1977, fieldwork by M. Taieb, D.C. Johanson, and Y. Coppens in the Hadar Formation in the Afar region of Ethiopia led to the recovery of hundreds of hominid fossils dating between 3.4 and 3 Ma. These fossils included an intact knee joint, a partial skeleton nicknamed "Lucy," a sample of body parts from at least 13 individuals, and many isolated jaws and teeth. Almost simultaneously, between 1974 and 1978, M.D. Leakey and her colleagues recovered a smaller sample of hominid fossils dating to ca. 3.5 Ma in the Laetolil Beds, as well as footprints in a deposit of Laetoli ash.

The Laetoli hominids and part of the Hadar collection were at first considered to represent early *Homo* in eastern Africa. Other Hadar hominids, such as the "Lucy" partial skeleton, were attributed to gracile *Australopithecus*, while specimens of robust *Australopithecus* were also tentatively identified. The recovery of more fossils from Hadar and Laetoli, particularly from the Hadar 333 locality, led to a reassessment of these attributions by D.C. Johanson, who was studying the Afar material, and T.D. White, who was studying the Laetoli remains. They found no evidence for multiple hominid species in either the Hadar Formation or the Laetolil Beds, but rather a wide range of size and shape, which they attributed to individual and sexual dimorphism. Taking this variability into account, they agreed that the hominin fossils found at the two sites could be placed in a single species. At the same time, they found that many of the characters in the material from Ethiopia and Tanzania were more primitive than in *Australopithecus africanus* of southern Africa, and they concluded that the less-derived condition of the species from Laetoli and Hadar made it a suitable common ancestor for *A. africanus* and the earliest species of *Homo.*

Johanson and White considered that the Hadar and Laetoli hominin should still be placed in the genus *Australopithecus*, rather than *Homo*, because the fossils indicated bipedality but lacked the cranial expansion and facial reduction seen in *Homo*. This meant that the trivial name *africanus,* which had been applied by Weinert and Senyürek to the original Laetolil fossils, was unavailable, because this name had already been in use for the South African *Australopithecus* for decades before it was applied to the Garusi maxilla. For this reason, Johanson, White, and Coppens in 1978 named the material from Ethiopia and Tanzania *Australopithecus afarensis,* after the Afar region of Ethiopia where most of the remains had been found. To emphasize the similarities between the Hadar and the Laetoli material, they chose the adult mandible from Laetoli as the holotype specimen and emphasized variation in the new species by naming all of the hominines then known from the two sites as paratypes. This choice was later questioned by several authors who argued that, by including the Garusi maxilla in the hypodigm of *A. afarensis*, Johanson et al. were equating the two named species; in that case, the name *afarensis* could be used as a replacement for *africanus,* which was preoccupied in the genus *Australopithecus,* but (1) the type should remain Garusi and (2) if the species were placed in another genus (e.g., *Praeanthropus*), the species would be *africanus*. These views have not taken hold, although some workers have suggested using *Praeanthropus*.

Australopithecus afarensis, according to Johanson and White, represented the only hominin, indeed the only hominid species, known from Africa between 3.5 and 3 Ma. They later hypothesized that *Australopithecus afarensis,* not *A. africanus,* also gave rise to the robust lineage of *Paranthropus aethiopicus, P. robustus,* and *P. boisei,* as well as to the genus *Homo* as first represented by *Homo habilis.*

Australopithecus afarensis is characterized by a distinctive suite of primitive cranial and postcranial characteristics. In the cranium, the braincase is small, with a measured capacity of between 380 and 430 ml for the few specimens available. The molars and the premolars are large relative to body size but lack the molarization and extreme size seen in later *Australopithecus*. Palate and mandible shape are decidedly primitive, and incisors and canines are relatively large. The face is very prognathic. The base and posterior portions of the cranium are apelike in many features. Postcranially, *Australopithecus afarensis* shows many anatomical characteristics of the hip, knee, and foot that indicate that it habitually practiced bipedalism, while apelike curvature of the hand and foot phalanges, and extreme robusticity of these and other skeletal elements, show that the species differed from the modern human condition. Female body size was significantly smaller than male, and this sexual dimorphism is also seen in the cranial and dental remains.

The description of *Australopithecus afarensis* in 1978 and the 1979 Johanson and White interpretation of this species' phylogenetic status prompted considerable discussion and debate. Some workers suggested that the fossils should be retained in the genus *Praeanthropus,* as suggested by Weinert and Senyürek, whereas others advocated treating the fossils as northern representatives of a polytypic *Australopithecus africanus*. Several workers considered the Hadar and Laetoli fossils to be different and, therefore, questioned the choice of a Laetoli specimen as a holotype, and others

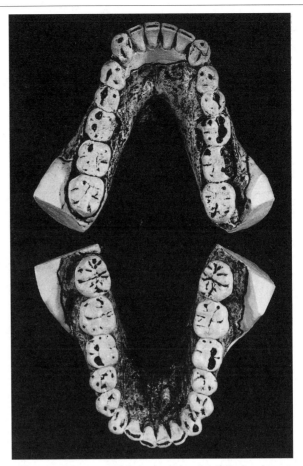

A comparison between casts of a lower jaw from Laetoli (top) and a lower jaw from Hadar, both of A. afarensis. *Photo by and courtesy of Tim D. White.*

continue to recognize more than one species among the Hadar and Laetoli remains although there is no agreement among these workers about which specimens belong to which taxon. For example, some view "Lucy" as a relict *Ramapithecus;* some view her as an early representative of *Homo;* and others place her in *Australopithecus africanus*. The larger Hadar fossils are thought by different authors to represent *Sivapithecus,* robust *Australopithecus,* or early *Homo*. W. Ferguson formally proposed the name *Homo antiquus* for "Lucy" and suggested that the larger specimens, including the Garusi maxilla, should be termed *Praeanthropus africanus* and interpreted as a "pongid" (i.e., an ape or nonhuman hominid).

Further debate has centered on the inferred locomotor activities and habitat of *Australopithecus afarensis*. J.T. Stern, R.L. Susman, and others have interpreted postcranial characters such as curved phalanges to indicate that the species spent large amounts of time climbing in trees. For these workers, *Australopithecus afarensis* is an intermediate between the pongine and the hominine conditions. C.O. Lovejoy has consistently maintained that this species was fully committed and adapted to existence as a habitually terrestrial biped.

The primitive characters seen in the cranial and dental anatomy of *Australopithecus afarensis* have been interpreted by some as evidence for a relatively recent divergence between the ape and the human lines and, therefore, as support for biochemically derived divergence dates of less than 6 Ma. Fossils from Fejej and Belohdelie (ca. 3.8 Ma), Tabarin (greater than 4 Ma), and Lothagam (ca. 6–5 Ma) have all been attributed to *Australopithecus afarensis*, although the identity of the older specimens is rendered questionable by recent finds (*A. anamensis* and *Ardipithecus ramidus*). Fragmentary remains, mostly teeth, from the Omo Usno and Shungura Formations (Ethiopia) and from Koobi Fora (Kenya) also have been tentatively allocated here. The presence of primitive characters in the relatively recent but definitively hominid fossils from Hadar and Laetoli contributed greatly to the climate of reassessment of the hominid status of the much earlier *Ramapithecus*, which was often heralded as a direct human ancestor until the 1980s.

The recognition of *Australopithecus afarensis* and *Australopithecus* (= *Paranthropus*) *aethiopicus* in the 1970s and 1980s led to new perspectives on early hominid phylogeny. The 1990s witnessed the recovery of large new samples of *Australopithecus afarensis* from the Ethiopian sites of Hadar and from Maka in the Middle Awash, culminating in the discovery of a large skull from the upper Kada Hadar member (ca. 3 Ma) announced in 1994. In the following years, two new, somewhat older species of australopith were described, *Ardipithecus ramidus* and *Australopithecus anamensis*. In addition, a mandible fragment from Chad was referred to this species on the basis of morphological similarity and comparable faunal association, vastly increasing its known geographic range. This specimen was later named *A. bahrelghazali*, distinguished from *A. afarensis* on relatively minor dental differences. All of these new fossils and their alternative interpretations continue to test the integrity and utility of the species *A. afarensis*, which has become the standard of comparison for Pliocene hominins.

See also Afar Basin; Africa, East; Ardipithecus ramidus; Australopithecus; Australopithecus africanus; Australopithecus anamensis; Australopithecus bahrelghazali; Baringo Bason/Tugen Hills; Belohdelie; Fejej; Hadar; Laetoli; Lothagam; Middle Awash; Paranthropus. [T.D.W.]

Further Readings

Delson, E., ed. (1985) Ancestors: The Hard Evidence. New York: Liss.

Johanson, D.C., ed. (1982) Pliocene hominid fossils from Hadar, Ethiopia. Am. J. Phys. Anthropol. 57:373–719.

Johanson, D.C., and Edey, M. (1981) Lucy: The Beginnings of Humankind. New York: Warner Books.

Johanson, D.C., and White, T.D. (1979) A systematic assessment of early African hominids. Science 202:321–330.

Kimbel, W.H., Johanson, D.C., and Rak, Y. (1994) The first skull and other new discoveries of *Australopithecus afarensis* at Hadar, Ethiopia. Nature 368:449–451.

Suwa, G., White, T.D., and Howell, F.C. (1996) Mandibular postcanine dentition from the Shungura Formation, Ethiopia: Crown morphology, taxonomic allocation, and Plio-Pleistocene hominid evolution. Am. J. Phys. Anthropol. 101:247–282.

Walter, R.C. (1994) Age of Lucy and the 1st family: Single-crystal Ar-^{40}/Ar-^{39} dating of the Denen Dora and lower Kada Hadar members of the Hadar Formation, Ethiopia. Geology 22:6–10.

White, T.D., Suwa, G., Hart, W.K., Walter, R.C., Wolde-Gabriel, G., de Heinzelin, J., Clark, J.D., Asfaw, B., and Vrba, E. (1993) New discoveries of *Australopithecus* at Maka in Ethiopia. Nature 366:261–265.

Australopithecus africanus

Type species of the genus *Australopithecus* and the taxonomic name that is commonly used in reference to the "gracile" australopith fossils from the South African sites of Taung, Sterkfontein, Makapansgat, and possibly Gladysvale.

The first specimen to be discovered was found at Taung in 1924. The fossil consists of a complete facial skeleton, a nearly complete mandible, and a hemi-endocast of a juvenile individual with a complete deciduous dentition. It was described by R.A. Dart in 1925. The name that Dart gave to the Taung skull, *Australopithecus africanus*, means literally "southern ape of Africa." The Taung skull was the first early hominin specimen to be recovered from ancient sediments in Africa, and Dart's pronouncement that *Australopithecus africanus* represented an intermediate between apes and humans was met with considerable resistance by the paleoanthropological community. The first adult specimen of *Australopithecus* was recovered 11 years later by R. Broom from the site of Sterkfontein. Broom described the Sterkfontein specimen in 1936, and because he was struck by the similarities between it and the Taung specimen he placed it into the same genus, albeit in a different species, *A. transvaalensis*. Further discoveries from Sterkfontein made in conjunction with the first hominin specimens to be recovered from Kromdraai (South Africa) caused Broom to refer the Sterkfontein fossils to a separate genus, *Plesianthropus*, whence the name "Mrs. Ples" for the supposedly female Sterkfontein cranium Sts 5. The first hominin specimen from Makapansgat was described in 1948 by Dart, who attributed it to a separate species of *Australopithecus*, *A. prometheus*. Thus, by the late 1940s three different taxonomic names had been applied to the fossils from Taung (*Australopithecus africanus*), Sterkfontein (*Plesianthropus transvaalensis*), and Makapansgat (*Australopithecus prometheus*). On the basis of detailed comparative studies of the specimens from these three sites, J.T. Robinson proposed in 1954 that they represented a single species, *A. africanus*. This has received almost universal support by workers in the field. By the late 1990s, the hypodigm of *A. africanus* comprised the Taung skull (the type specimen), fossils from Members 3 and 4 of the Makapansgat Formation, and those from Member 4 of the Sterkfontein Formation. Several associated foot bones purportedly from Member 2 of the Sterkfontein Formation may also be attributable to *A. africanus*, and several isolated teeth of questionable provenance recovered by renewed work at the site of Gladysvale (as well as an incisor from Coopers) may also be attributable to this species.

The fossils from Makapansgat Member 3, representing the vast bulk of the sample from that site, appear to date close to 3 Ma, while the Sterkfontein Member 4 specimens

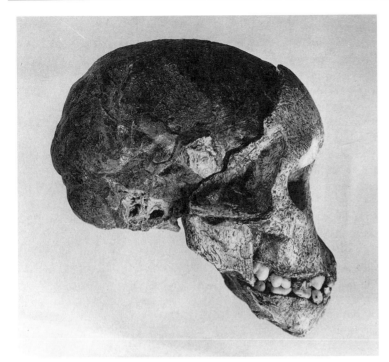
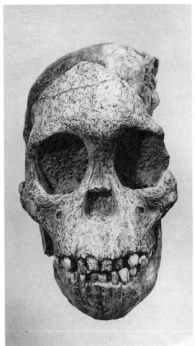

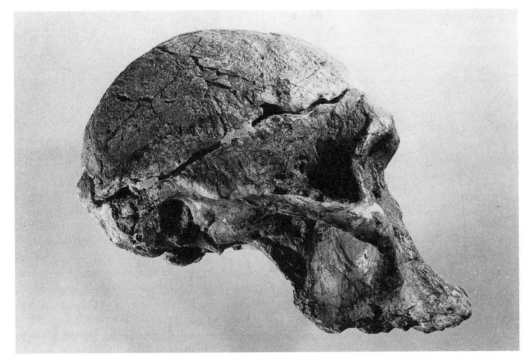

Frontal and lateral views of the Taung child face and brain cast (top), and the Sterkfontein 5 cranium. Courtesy of Frederick E. Grine.

are dated to ca. 2.5 Ma based upon faunal comparisons with radiometrically dated samples from eastern Africa. Although it has been claimed that the Sterkfontein Member 2 fossils may be older than 3 Ma, this is based solely upon geological inference. The geochronological dating of the Taung fossil has been a matter of dispute. An ill-founded attempt at geomorphological dating in the early 1970s suggested an age of less than 1 Ma, which prompted speculation that the skull may be that of a "robust" australopith, although analyses of

the faunal remains from the site suggest an age between 2.3 and 2 Myr. Moreover, the Taung specimen is morphologically similar to those from Makapansgat and Sterkfontein and quite distinctive from the *Paranthropus* fossils of Kromdraai and Swartkrans. As of the late 1990s, the fossils from Gladysvale remained undated. Thus, *A. africanus* appears to have existed in southern Africa between ca. 3 and 2 Ma. No fossil from eastern Africa has been demonstrated convincingly to represent this taxon.

Initial studies of the faunal remains associated with *A. africanus* led Dart to postulate that this hominin was a hunter. The faunal elements from Makapansgat were thought by him to represent not only the food remains, but also the implements of *A. africanus*. Dart referred to these purported bone, tooth, and horn tools as the Osteodontokeratic culture. Subsequent taphonomic studies by C.K. Brain, however, have demonstrated convincingly that, far from representing the tools and food remains of *A. africanus*, these faunal elements and, indeed, the hominins themselves probably represent the food remains of carnivores, such as leopards, and scavengers, such as hyenas. *A. africanus* appears to have been the hunted rather than the hunter! This interpretation agrees with analyses of the teeth of *A. africanus*, which suggest a herbivorous diet, and the details of wear on these dentitions indicate subsistence upon fruits and foliage.

The postcranial elements of *A. africanus*, including the structure of the shoulder girdle, the shape of the pelvis, the structure of the femur, the size and shape of the hand bones, and the morphology of the foot skeleton, are indicative of a creature that employed bipedal locomotion on the ground (although the mode of bipedality almost certainly differed from that practiced by modern humans), but one that was well adapted to climbing. There appears to have been considerable dimorphism in size between presumptive males and females as reflected by both craniodental and postcranial remains. Among the postcranial features that serve to characterize *A. africanus* are: metacarpals and phalanges moderately curved; os coxae with low ilium that is broad anteroposteriorly; iliac blade approximating coronal plane in its orientation; femoral head relatively small and femoral neck relatively long; hallux medially diverged (varus) and mobile.

Among the cranial and dental features that characterize *A. africanus* are: cranial vault globular and lacking ectocranial superstructures in both males and females; calvaria hafted to facial skeleton at a high level resulting in high supraorbital height index; slight forehead rise from glabella to bregma; cranium with moderate pneumatization of mastoid region; lambda and inion moderately separated; glenoid fossa deep with marked articular eminence; slight angulation of petrous to sagittal plane resulting in low petromedian angle; moderate to marked maxillary alveolar prognathism with nasoalveolar clivus delineated from floor of nasal cavity by distinct ridge; incisive canals opening into inclined surface of nasal floor as a capacious incisive fossa; anterior palate shelved; alveolar margins of maxillary canine and incisor sockets arranged in an anteriorly convex line; pyriform aperture set anterior to level of anterior surfaces of zygomatics; lateral margins of pyriform aperture rounded with variable presence of canine pillars; glabella prominent and situated at level of supraorbital margin; nasion located below glabella as a result of high glabella; incisors and canines harmoniously proportioned to sizes of cheek teeth; P3 tending to possess two roots; and dP_3 not "molarized" with anterior fovea lingually skewed and incompletely walled by mesial marginal ridge.

These and other features serve to distinguish the skull and dentition of *A. africanus* from the more primitive *A. ramidus*, *A. anamensis*, and *A. afarensis* and from the highly

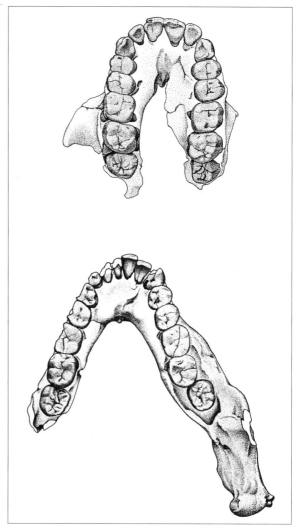

Australopithecus africanus maxilla Sts 52a (left) and mandible Sts 52b.

derived and specialized "robust" australopiths (*Paranthropus*). *A. africanus*, however, does not appear to possess any unique morphological features (autapomorphies) that would necessarily preclude it from being considered as the ancestor, or at least as the ancestral morph, from which *Homo* evolved. Indeed, a number of workers have argued that early specimens attributed to the genus *Homo* (e.g., *H. habilis*) are virtually indistinguishable from *A. africanus*.

Endocranial capacity estimates for *A. africanus* are on the order of 410–450 ml (with an average of ca. 440 ml), although a large cranium from Sterkfontein (Stw 505) may possess an endocranial capacity that exceeds 500 ml. The endocranial-volume estimates for *A. africanus* tend to be slightly larger than those for *A. afarensis*, and slightly smaller than those for *P. robustus* and *P. boisei*, but significantly smaller than those for most specimens of early *Homo*. As of the late 1990s, no identifiable stone artifacts had been found in the cave breccias that contain *A. africanus* remains.

Although there are very subtle differences in some of the postcranial elements of *A. afarensis* and *A. africanus*, their morphological configurations are remarkably similar. Body-weight estimates from long-bone shafts and articular surfaces range from ca. 35 kg to ca. 65 kg.

See also Ardipithecus ramidus; Australopithecus; Australopithecus afarensis; Australopithecus anamensis; Gladysvale; Makapansgat; Paranthropus; Paranthropus aethiopicus; Paranthropus boisei; Paranthropus robustus; Sterkfontein; Taung. [F.E.G.]

Further Readings

Berger, L., Keyser, A., and Tobias, P.V. (1993) Gladysvale: First early hominin site discovered in South Africa since 1948. Am. J. Phys. Anthropol. 92:107–111.

Clarke, R.J. (1985) *Australopithecus* and early *Homo* in southern Africa. In E. Delson (ed.): Ancestors: The Hard Evidence. New York: Liss, pp. 171–177.

Clarke, R.J., and Tobias, P.V. (1995) Sterkfontein Member 2 foot bones of the oldest South African hominid. Science 269:521–524.

Grine, F.E. (1981) Trophic differences between "gracile" and "robust" australopithecines: A scanning electron microscope analysis of occlusal events. S. Afr. J. Sci. 77:203–230.

Howell, F.C. (1978) Hominidae. In V.J. Maglio and H.B.S. Cooke (eds.): Evolution of African Mammals. Cambridge, Mass.: Harvard University Press, pp. 154–248.

Reed, K.E., Kitching, J.W., Grine, F.E., Jungers, W.L., and Sokoloff, L. (1993) Proximal femur of *Australopithecus africanus* from Member 4, Makapansgat, South Africa. Am. J. Phys. Anthropol. 92:1–15.

Robinson, J.T. (1954) The genera and species of the Australopithecinae. Am. J. Phys. Anthropol. 12:181–200.

White, T.D., Johanson, D.C., and Kimbel, W.H. (1981) *Australopithecus africanus:* Its phyletic position reconsidered. S. Afr. J. Sci. 77:445–470.

Wood, B.A. (1985) A review of the definition, distribution, and relationships of *Australopithecus africanus*. In P.V. Tobias (ed.): Hominid Evolution: Past, Present, and Future. New York: Liss, pp. 227–232.

Australopithecus anamensis

Taxonomic name that refers to East African hominid fossils that date between 4.2 and 3.9 Ma from the Kenyan sites of Allia Bay and Kanapoi. The species name, which means "lake" in the Turkana language, was applied by M.G. Leakey and her colleagues in 1995 to 21 fossils from these two sites in the vicinity of Lake Turkana. In 1998, they described over 30 more fossils and clarified the dating at Kanapoi.

The fossils that have been referred to *Australopithecus anamensis* display several primitive features, as well as a number that appear to be unique for this species. This species is diagnosed by: the external auditory meatus being very small and of an elliptical outline; a tubular tympanic bone that extends laterally only as far as the medial edge of the postglenoid process of the mandibular fossa; mandibular corpora and tooth rows that are nearly parallel and close together; a mandibular symphysis with a marked inferoposterior slope that extends back as far as the M1; upper molars in which the mesial part of the crown

(the trigon) is much broader buccolingually than the distal part of the crown (the talon) and a dP_3 intermediate in its degree of molarization between *A. ramidus* and *A. afarensis*. It differs from *Ardipithecus ramidus* principally in having thicker enamel on its tooth crowns. Like *Ardipithecus ramidus* and *Australopithecus afarensis*, the mandibular fossa is very shallow, with a poorly developed articular eminence, and, like the former, the temporal bone shows strong pneumatization that extends into the squamous portion and into the root of the zygomatic arch.

A tibia from Kanapoi shows features that are clearly indicative of bipedalism (e.g., both proximal articular surfaces are elongated anteroposteriorly, concave, and of approximately equal area). It is larger than the largest tibia of *Australopithecus afarensis* that has been recovered so far from the Hadar Formation (Ethiopia). The weight of this individual is estimated to have been between ca. 47 kg and 55 kg. A hamate (wrist bone) has a very long hook, which would have been associated with a deep carpal tunnel through which the tendons of large, powerful hand flexors would have run. This suggests that *Australopithecus anamensis*—like *Ardipithecus ramidus, Australopithecus afarensis*, and *Australopithecus africanus*—was a bipedal species that was capable of, and probably heavily engaged in, tree climbing. A capitate (another wrist bone) is highly distinctive in that its facet for the second metacarpal (palm bone) faces laterally as in apes, rather than obliquely as in later *Australopithecus* and *Homo* species.

Of the more than 20 specimens from Kanapoi, most (including the type specimen, which is a nearly complete, probably female mandible with a full adult dentition catalogued in the Kenya National Museums as KNM-KP 29281) derive from sediments between two tuffs that are dated to 4.16 and 4.07 Ma. These sediments are correlated with the presence of the Lonyumun Lake, which came into existence in the Turkana Basin ca. 4.2 Ma; this sedimentary phase is overlain by the Moiti Tuff, dated to ca. 3.9 Ma elsewhere in the basin. The hominids from Allia Bay derive from beneath or within the Moiti Tuff.

Reconstructions of the paleoecology at Kanapoi and Allia Bay are consistent with the hypothesis that *A. anamensis* was both a biped and a capable climber. At Kanapoi, the associated fossils include a number of fish and aquatic vertebrates and a considerable diversity of mammalian taxa. Kudu and impala are the dominant bovids. This suggests a woodland-bushland habitat along a large river at Kanapoi. The Allia Bay fauna appears to be associated with a gallery forest that would have lined the large proto-Omo River.

See also Africa, East; Ardipithecus ramidus; Australopithecus; Australopithecus afarensis; Australopithecus africanus; Hadar; Kanapoi; Turkana Basin. [F.E.G.]

Further Readings

Andrews, P. (1995) Ecological apes and ancestors. Nature 375:555–556.

Leakey, M.G. (1995) The dawn of humans: The farthest horizon. Nat. Geog. 188(3):38–51.

Leakey, M.G., Feibel, C.S., McDougall, I., and Walker, A. (1995) New four-million-year-old hominid species from Kanapoi and Allia Bay, Kenya. Nature 375:565–571.

Leakey, M.G., Feibel, C.S., McDougall, I., Ward, C., and Walker, A. (1998) New specimens and confirmation of an early age for *Australopithecus anamensis*. Nature 393:62–66.

Australopithecus bahrelghazali

Proposed new species of early hominin from Chad, Central Africa, dated to ca. 3.5–3 Ma. A 1995 report of this material, limited to a mandibular symphysis with both C_1-P_4 and one I_2, along with an isolated P^3, suggested that it was closely similar to *A. afarensis*, of comparable age. Further study, however, convinced M. Brunet and colleagues that the dentition and the anterior mandible are distinct enough to be considered a new species. Reaction from colleagues has been limited.

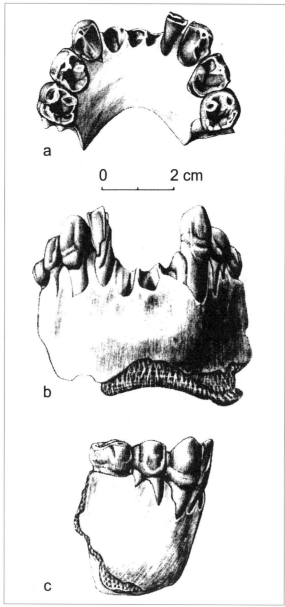

Three views of holotype mandibular symphysis with LC_1-P_4, $R I_2$-P_4. Courtesy of Michel Brunet.

The Koro Toro region of Chad first yielded fossil mammals in the 1960s, but the only hominin specimen recovered was a badly weathered facial fragment of ?Early Pleistocene age usually referred to *Homo* cf. *erectus*. After a hiatus of about 20 years, a new expedition surveyed the area and located a faunal assemblage said to be comparable in age to that from Hadar (Ethiopia), 2,500 km to the east. The species name derives from the classical Arabic for "River of the gazelles," the local name of the region.

A. bahrelghazali is distinguished especially by a more vertical symphysis than in other species of *Australopithecus* and by three- rather than two-rooted lower premolars. In other features, it is essentially similar to *A. afarensis*. It differs from *A. africanus* by a less-robust mandibular corpus and smaller anterior teeth, and from *A. anamensis* by a shorter planum alveolare, smaller inferior symphyseal transverse torus, and the presence of a strong P_3 metaconid. As with other *Australopithecus* species, the molar and canine enamel is thicker than in *Ardipithecus ramidus*, while the corpus is more gracile, the anterior teeth are larger, and P^3 is asymmetrical rather than oval as in *Paranthropus*. The obvious question is whether the extra premolar root (more conservative) and the flatter, more vertical symphyseal profile (derived?) are sufficient to merit species status by comparison to roughly contemporaneous species of *Australopithecus*. Only time and additional specimens from Central Africa will tell. But for now, this material greatly enlarges the known geographic range of early hominins and falsifies the hypothesis that they lived only to the east of the rift valley.

See also Africa; Ardipithecus ramidus; Australopithecus; Australopithecus afarensis; Australopithecus anamensis; Paranthropus. [E.D.]

Further Readings

Brunet, M., Beauvilain, A., Coppens, Y., Heintz, E., Moutaye, A.H.E., and Pilbeam, D. (1996) *Australopithecus bahrelghazali*, a new species of early hominid from Koro Toro region (Chad). C.R. Acad. Sci. (Paris), ser. 2a, 322:907–913 (French with long English summary).

Australopithecus garhi

A species of *Australopithecus* proposed in early 1999 for newly recovered specimens from deposits at Bouri (in the Middle Awash area of Ethiopia), dated ca. 2.5 Ma. B. Asfaw and colleagues described this species on the basis of a partial cranium and several additional fragmentary specimens. Among the claimed diagnostic features are large teeth with thick enamel, subnasal prognathism, incisor procumbency, low degree of premolar molarization, no anterior pillar or facial dishing, and probably at least some sagittal crest development. The combination of these features (and several others) is said to distinguish the new specimens from all known hominin species and to suggest some transition toward early *Homo*. On the other hand, one might also consider the possibilities that: 1) the new cranium is female rather than male and might possibly represent *Paranthropus aethiopicus*, which is known from the same time period in the Turkana Basin; or 2) is a late variant of *Australopithecus afarensis*.

From the same Bouri 12 locality, Asfaw and colleagues recovered a partial postcranial skeleton preserving the femur and three arm bones but no teeth or cranial parts. It was thus not possible to allocate this specimen to the same species as the cranium—they were separated by nearly 300 m on the ground. The forelimb elements are about the same length as those of "Lucy" (female *Australopithecus afarensis*), but the femur is significantly longer, suggesting that femoral elongation preceded forearm shortening (compared to humeral length) in human evolutionary history.

The late J. De Heinzelin and colleagues, in a companion article, described cutmarked horse and antelope bones from Bouri 12 and the nearby and contemporaneous Bouri 11. These reflect hominin activities such as removal of leg muscle and tongue meat, as well as marrow. No stone tools were recovered *in situ*, perhaps due to the scarcity of suitable raw materials on the then-featureless lake margin. Many such artifacts were recovered at Gona (near Hadar, some 100 km north and ca. 100 Kyr older), but only a few surface pieces were located at Bouri. As with the postcranium, it is not sure to whom these tools belong, whether *A. garhi* or another as yet unidentified taxon.

See also Afar Basin; Africa, East; Australopithecus; Australopithecus afarensis; Hadar; Middle Awash; Oldowan; Paranthropus aethiopicus; Raw Materials. [E.D.]

Further Readings

Asfaw, B. White, T., Lovejoy, O., Latimer, B., Simpson, S., and Suwa, G. (1999) *Australopithecus garhi*: a new species of early hominid from Ethiopia. Science 284: 629–635.

De Heinzelin, J., Clark, J.D., White, T., Hart, W., Renne, P., WoldeGabriel, G., Beyene, Y. and Vrba, E. (1999) Environment and behavior of 2.5-million-year-old Bouri hominids. Science 284:625–629.

Awl

Pointed boring tool made out of stone (sometimes called a perçoir, perforator, or borer) or bone, probably used for making holes in skins, wood, bone, antler, or other materials. Although some stone artifacts have been identified typologically as awls even at Early Paleolithic sites, such artifact forms become more common and more standardized in shape in tool assemblages in the Mousterian and the Late Paleolithic.

See also Clothing; Late Paleolithic; Mousterian. [N.T., K.S.]

Azilian

Epipaleolithic or Early Mesolithic industry of western Europe. The term was introduced by the French prehistorian E. Piette (1826–1906) in 1899 to describe a phase in the transition from the Paleolithic to the Neolithic. Specifically, Piette had discovered in the deposits of the Mas d'Azil cave (near Ariège in the Pyrenees region) a tool assemblage consisting of flat harpoons made of deer horn and a collection of varioussized and -shaped pebbles decorated with colored schematic designs. Although his interpretation of these artifacts was initially resisted, subsequent discoveries in other sites throughout France and elsewhere in northern Europe (e.g., H. Breuil found similar artifacts at the Ofnet Cave, near Bayern, Germany, in 1909) verified his original proposal. Today, the Azilian is generally acknowledged as representing an initial phase in the Mesolithic cultural sequence, which is dated to 11–9 Ka. [A.S.B.]

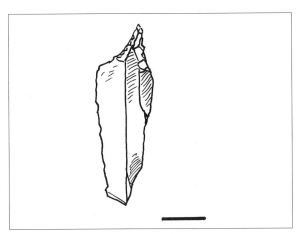

Typical stone awl. Scale is 1 cm.

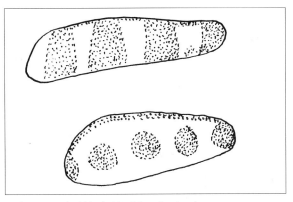

Azilian painted pebbles (originals in red and tan).

B

Bacho Kiro

Stratified cave site in the Balkan Mountains of Bulgaria with three Mousterian and 10 Upper Paleolithic layers. Layers 14 through 12 contained lithic inventories assigned to the Charentian and Typical Mousterian. Two fragments of bone from Layer 12 appear to have been intentionally engraved. The Upper Paleolithic layers contain numerous faunal remains of both herbivores and carnivores; blade-tool assemblages predominantly fashioned of nonlocal flint, basalt, and quartzite; bone tools, including bone points; and bone jewelry. Remains of hearths have been found in these layers as well. A series of radiocarbon dates for the different layers indicate that Upper Paleolithic inventories from Layer 11, dated to more than 43 Ka (and perhaps as old as 60–45 Ka), represent some of the earliest securely dated Late Paleolithic remains in Europe. Assemblages from Layers 11 on have been classified as Bachokirian, a regional variant of the Aurignacian. Hominid remains from the Upper Paleolithic layers, consisting of fragments of a neurocranium, two mandibles with teeth, and five single teeth, possess some primitive characteristics and may represent somewhat archaic modern humans or possibly forms transitional between the Neanderthals and fully modern *Homo sapiens.*

See also Aurignacian; Europe; Istállöskö; Late Paleolithic; Neanderthals; Upper Palaeolithic. [O.S.]

Badegoulian

Early Magdalenian-like industry of Central France, ca. 16 Ka, with a distribution from the Périgord east to the Auvergne and north to the Paris Basin. Sometimes referred to as Magdalenian "O" and "I," it differs from the classic Magdalenian in its emphasis on blades and burins, especially transverse burins on notches, the presence of *raclettes,* the rarity or absence of backed bladelets, and the simplicity of its bone industry reflected in a small number of simple beveled-bone spear points.

See also Blade; Burin; Harpoon; Magdalenian; Périgord; Sagaie; Stone-Tool Making; Upper Paleolithic. [A.S.B.]

Bambata

African Middle Stone Age industry of Zimbabwe and Botswana (probable age ca. 100–40 kyr) named after the Bambata Cave site in the Matopos Hills south of Bulawayo. The Bambata differs from the Stillbay, Pietersburg, Orangian, and other Middle Stone Age industries to the south in the relative rarity of blades, burins, perforators, endscrapers, and backed knives. Characteristic forms include discoidal cores and small unifacial and bifacial points and sidescrapers. Other major sites, all near Bulawayo, include Pomongwe and Tshangula caves and the Khami waterworks open site. The industry appears to extend as far as ≠Gi in the northwestern Kalahari Desert of Botswana.

See also Howieson's Poort; Levallois; Middle Stone Age; Orangian; Pietersburg; Stillbay; Stone-Tool Making. [A.S.B.]

Further Reading

Cooke, C.K. (1984) The industries of the Upper Pleistocene in Zimbabwe. Zimbabweia 1:23–27.

Baradostian

Late Paleolithic blade and burin industry defined by R. Solecki on the basis of Layer C at Shanidar Cave on Mount Baradost (Iraq), dated to 34–29 Ka by radiocarbon. Also found in western Iran, the industry differs from the Aurignacian in its high percentage of burins, some with a distinctive nosed profile, and in the lessened emphasis on carinate and nose-ended scrapers and busked burins. The presence of the latter, however, has led to a recent, but not universally accepted, attribution of the Baradostian to a more generalized Aurignacian tradition as the Zagros Aurignacian.

See also Asia, Western; Aurignacian; Blade; Burin; Late Paleolithic; Shanidar; Stone-Tool Making. [A.S.B.]

Further Readings

Olszewski, D.I., and Dibble, H.L. (1994) The Zagros Aurignacian. Curr. Anthropol. 35:68–75.

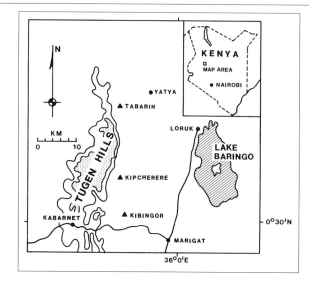

Map of the Lake Baringo area showing the location of the Tugen Hills and several neighboring fossil localities. Courtesy of Andrew Hill.

Solecki, R. (1971) Shanidar: The First Flower People. New York: Knopf.

Baringo Basin/Tugen Hills

Region of the Central Kenya Rift Valley exposing Late Neogene sediments and volcanics ranging in age from ca. 15.5 to 0.2 Ma. Paleontological and archaeological finds are numerous, including *Kenyapithecus*, indeterminate ?hominins, ?*Australopithecus, Paranthropus, Homo*, and prolific open and stratified Paleolithic sites. The main importance of this area for human evolution lies in the fact that the fossil record represented here includes sites that document the period from 12 to 4 Ma, which is otherwise extremely poorly known in sub-Saharan Africa. It was during this time that the Ethiopian fauna became established and humans and modern African apes diverged from their common ancestor.

Paleontological investigation of this region began in the 1930s, when expeditions by C. Arambourg and L.S.B. Leakey passed through en route to the Turkana Basin. The geologist H. Wayland had already made it the type area of the Kamasian pluvial, following initial geological studies by J. Thomson in the 1880s. The 20-km-long Lake Baringo, just north of the equator, is surrounded by badlands that yield abundant fossils of plants and animals. Isolated sites are found in the north, at Karmosit and Aterir, and to the east at the foot of the Laikipia Escarpment, at Alengerr and Chesowanja. Most of the Baringo sites, however, are found on the west of the lake in the Tugen Hills.

Tugen Hills Stratigraphy and Dating

The Tugen Hills, sometimes known as the Kamasia Range, extend ca. 75 km north-south along the rift on the west of Lake Baringo. The Tugen Hills are a complexly faulted, west-tilted horst (upthrust block) in which ca. 3,000 m of rift-floor deposits are exposed in scarps and foothills facing the lake. The strata are displaced by a crazy-quilt of large and small faults, including some that were already active during deposition of the beds, making stratigraphic correlation be-

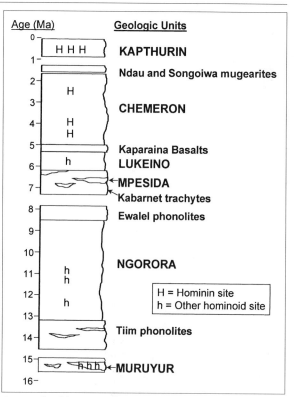

Stratigraphy of the Tugen Hills succession. The major geologic units are shown in an idealized stratigraphic column, with sedimentary formation names in capital letters, and the horizons of hominoid fossils indicated. Courtesy of Andrew Hill.

tween separate areas difficult. Despite this, the sediments have been placed in six main fossiliferous formations. From oldest to youngest these are the Muruyur Beds, the Ngorora Formation, the Mpesida Beds, and the Lukeino, Chemeron, and Kapthurin formations. They are, for the most part, separated from one another by volcanic horizons, including several thick lava sequences, and they also include numerous tuffaceous horizons. Radiometric dating on the volcanics, and paleomagnetic stratigraphy in the sedimentary succession, support a relatively detailed and fine-grained age calibration.

The Muruyur Beds span roughly 16–15 Ma and, while they are as yet little known, have yielded a diverse fauna from a number of sites, especially around Kipsaramon (ca. 15.5–15 Ma). The more widely exposed Ngorora Formation, which spans a lengthy time interval from 13 Ma to less than 9 Ma, is a fairly unbroken sequence up to 450 m thick. Most Ngorora fossils, however, come from sites dated between 12.7 and 10.5 Ma, with a few in outlying fault blocks that are most probably younger (e.g., Ngeringerowa, ca. 9 Ma or less). Most of the time interval between ca. 8.5 and 6 Ma is either not exposed or is known only by volcanic rocks. The exception is the Mpesida Beds, lenses of fossiliferous sediment within the very thick Kabarnet Trachyte that are dated at ca. 6.5 Ma. The extensive Lukeino lake beds and sands resting on the lavas have a number of sites that have been dated between ca. 6.3 and 5.6 Ma. The overlying Chemeron Formation is informally divided into three segments that span nearly all of the Pliocene, from ca. 5.6 to 1.6

Myr. Unconformably resting on Chemeron strata in the area close to Lake Baringo are the Kapthurin Beds, dated from ca. 0.8 to 0.25 Ma, an extensive blanket of sediments that contains important fossil sites.

In addition to fauna, many levels in the Baringo Basin sequence have yielded important collections of plant remains. An extensive macroflora, indicating forest conditions, is known from the Lower Ngorora Beds at 12.6 Ma.

Significant changes in the mammalian fauna can be detected throughout the sequence. The most noticeable faunal shift comes between the highest Ngorora faunal level and the Mpesida Beds and is even more apparent in the better-sampled Lukeino Formation above. This change documents a dramatic first step toward the modern Ethiopian fauna and the effective end of the archaic Miocene fauna of older sites.

Tugen Hills Hominoids and Other Primates

Fossils of hominoids have been found at several levels in the Tugen Hills sequence. The earliest are numerous specimens of *Kenyapithecus*, still largely undescribed but including a partial skeleton, from Kipsaramon. The cercopithecid *Victoriapithecus*, a large species of *Proconsul*, and the archaic catarrhine *Kalepithecus* also occur there. In the lower part of the Ngorora Formation, isolated hominoid teeth represent *Proconsul* and perhaps another genus; archaic catarrhines and the youngest known *Victoriapithecus* are also present, all ca. 12.5 Ma. The earliest African colobine, *Microcolobus*, comes from Ngeringerowa. Another isolated hominoid molar, from a site in the Lukeino Formation at ca. 6 Ma, is impossible to assign unequivocally to any known species, but it could have belonged to a hominin. If so, it would be the earliest so far known; recent study by P. Ungar and colleagues suggests similarities to *Australopithecus anamensis*, as well as to chimpanzees.

Of three hominid specimens from the Chemeron Formation, all most probably hominins, one derives from the older, Tabarin outcrops dated between 5 and 4.15 Ma. This specimen is one of the earliest well-documented hominins in the fossil record; only the specimens from Lothagam, near Lake Turkana, are a little older. The Tabarin specimen is a piece of right mandible with intact first and second molars. In its dental features and details of subocclusal and mandibular morphology, it closely resembles smaller specimens of *Australopithecus afarensis* and also (as A. Hill has pointed out) the more fragmentary material that has been assigned to *Australopithecus anamensis* and *Ardipithecus ramidus*. W. Ferguson has named the Tabarin jaw *Homo antiquus praegens*, which might have priority if this specimen is conspecific with either *anamensis* or *ramidus*. The other early Chemeron specimen, from a site some kilometers to the north of Tabarin, is a proximal fragment of a humerus that seems likely to represent the same species as that of the Tabarin mandible.

The third hominin, from the upper part of the Chemeron, is much younger than the other occurrences, dating close to 2.4 Ma. This is a temporal bone that comes from a site on the Kapthurin River near its mouth on Lake Baringo. After languishing as Hominidae indeterminate, it has been reanalyzed and identified as *Homo* sp. indet. (cf. *H.*

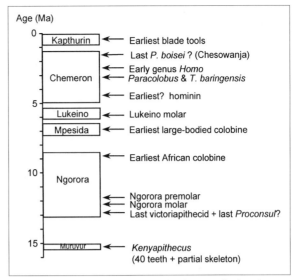

Important occurrences of primate (including hominin) fossils and stone tools in the Baringo Basin sequence. Courtesy of Andrew Hill.

rudolfensis?), one of the three earliest representatives of the genus *Homo*, the others being from Hadar (Ethiopia) and Uraha (Malawi). An older site, near the base of the Upper Chemeron, yielded a partial skeleton of *Paracolobus chemeroni* (the type) and a partial skull of ? *Theropithecus* (*Omopithecus*) *baringensis* (also the type); these fossils remained undated for many years, but they are now closely es-

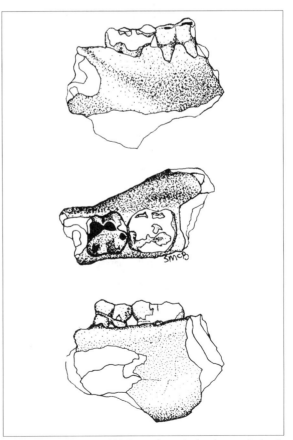

The partial hominin mandible from Tabarin (with right M1–2), dated between 5–4.15 Ma; from the top: buccal, occlusal, and lingual views. Courtesy of Andrew Hill.

timated to date to 3.1–3 Ma. Other sites in the much younger Kapthurin Beds (dated ca. 500 Ka in early 1999) have produced two hominin mandibles and several postcranial bones, as well as an important late Acheulean artifact assemblage featuring prepared-core technology and large blades.

The isolated Chesowanja site on the east side of the lake has yielded specimens of *Paranthropus boisei*, including a partial cranium, in association with a sequence of artifacts. The absence of a toolmaker (*Homo*), if the *Paranthropus* is excluded from consideration, is reminiscent of the situation in the Bed I sites at Olduvai Gorge (Tanzania) just prior to the discovery of *Homo habilis*.

See also Africa; Africa, East; Ardipithecus ramidus; Australopithecus afarensis; Australopithecus anamensis; Chesowanja; Hominidae; Homininae; Homo; Kapthurin; Rift Valley. [E.D., J.A.V.C., A.H.]

Further Readings

Hill, A. (1994) Late Miocene and Early Pliocene hominoids from Africa. In R.S. Corruccini and R.L. Ciochon (eds.): Integrative Paths to the Past. Englewood Cliffs, N.J.: Prentice-Hall, pp. 123–145.

Hill, A. (1995) Faunal and environmental change in the Neogene of East Africa: Evidence from the Tugen Hills sequence, Baringo District, Kenya. In E.S. Vrba, G.H. Denton, T.C. Partridge, and L.H. Burckle (eds.): Paleoclimate and Evolution, with Emphasis on Human Origins. New Haven: Yale University Press, pp. 178–193.

Hill, A., Behrensmeyer, A.K., Brown, B., Deino, A., Rose, M., Saunders, J., Ward, S., and Winkler, A. (1991) Kipsaramon, a Lower Miocene site in the Tugen Hills, Baringo District, Kenya. J. Hum. Evol. 20:67–76.

Hill, A., Drake, R., Tauxe, L., Monaghan, M., Barry, J.C., Behrensmeyer, A.K., Curtis, G., Jacobs, B.F., Jacobs, L., Johnson, N., and Pilbeam, D. (1985) Neogene paleontology and geochronology of the Baringo Basin, Kenya. J. Hum. Evol. 14:759–773.

Ungar, P., Walker, A., and Coffing, K. (1994) Reanalysis of the Lukeino molar (KNM-LU 335). Am. J. Phys. Anthropol. 94:165–173.

McBrearty, S., Bishop, L.C., and Kingston, J.D. (1996) Variability in traces of Middle Pleistocene hominid behavior in the Kapthurin Formation, Baringo, Kenya. J. Hum. Evol. 30:563–580.

Baton de Commandement

Characteristic artifact form of the European Paleolithic, especially the Magdalenian phase, made from antler (usually reindeer). It is usually perforated near the juncture of the main body and the two major branches of the antler. The function of these artifacts is not clear; suggestions have included spear-shaft straighteners, and thong softeners, as well as magical or symbolic devices (such as a sign of authority; thus, the name).

See also Magdalenian; Spear; Upper Paleolithic. [N.T., K.S.]

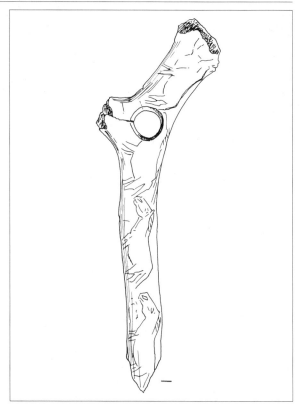

Baton de commandement. Scale is 1 cm.

Beidha

A preceramic village site in southern Jordan excavated in the 1950s–1960s by D. Kirkbride. The earliest levels at the site are a Natufian occupation consisting of a cluster of circular stone-lined hut foundations. These are followed by numerous Pre-Pottery Neolithic occupations dating to 9–8 ka. Throughout the Neolithic sequence, there is a gradual shift from round single-chamber semisubterranean dwellings to rectangular multichamber dwellings with plaster floors. Ornamental objects, such as perforated shells, bone, and stone beads, were common. Several flakes from Anatolian obsidian sources indicate connections with regional long-distance exchange routes. Burials of six adults and 20 juveniles were found within the site. Several bodies had been defleshed prior to burial. Two of the adults were missing their crania, a mortuary ritual also observed in Natufian sites. Numerous ground-stone querns (saddle-shaped grindstones) and mortars indicate the processing of cultivated cereal grasses, and impressions of barley have been found in clay and plaster from the site. Most of the flaked-stone tools are arrowheads, and the faunal remains from this site attest to the hunting of gazelle, ibex, and wild cattle. Remains of domesticated goat are also present.

See also Asia, Western; Natufian. [J.J.S.]

Belohdelie

A locality in the Middle Awash region in the Afar Rift of Ethiopia at which several fragments of a Pliocene hominid cranium were found in 1981. This fossil specimen (comprising three adjoining and four isolated fragments representing a large part of the right frontal), was found in the Sagantole

Formation ca. 11 m below a volcanic ash, the Cindery Tuff. This fossil, dated to ca. 3.9 Ma, has been provisionally assigned to *Australopithecus afarensis*. It appears to preserve a relatively primitive australopith cranial morphology.

See also Africa, East; Australopithecus afarensis; Middle Awash. [N.T., K.S.]

Beryllium and Aluminum Nuclide Dating

Age estimates for relatively young (latest Pleistocene and Holocene) geomorphic surfaces such as moraines and alluvial fans are obtained by determining the *in situ* production of the nuclides ^{26}Al and ^{10}Be in the surface of rocks subjected to cosmic-ray bombardment. The cosmogenic exposure age is calculated according to a model that incoporates the changing geomagnetic field strength, field strength and rigidity relationships, and latitude-longitude corrections for muon flux as it affects the production of the isotopes. The effect of geomagnetic field variations is highest at high altitudes and low latitudes.

See also Calcium-41 Dating; Geochronometry; Radiocarbon Dating. [J.A.V.C.]

Further Readings

Bierman, P.R., and Clapp, E.M. (1996) Estimating geologic age from cosmogenic nuclides: An update. Science 271:1606.

Biache-St. Vaast

Open-air site in northwestern France (Pas-de-Calais) located on a river terrace that has yielded both hominid fossils and an early Middle Paleolithic industry. The hominid occupation of Biache dates to 175 Ka by thermoluminescence (TL) and probably occurred during relatively warm phases in the penultimate (Saalian or Rissian) glaciation. The principal occupation floor, Level IIa, has been heavily faulted by tectonic pressure. Archaeological remains from Biache feature a Middle Paleolithic industry with abundant laminar Levallois debitage but no handaxes. Many of the Levallois tools are elongated points or pointed blades that wear studies suggest

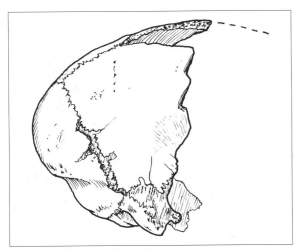

Lateral view of the Biache hominid.

were hafted. The Biache hominid consists of the back part of a skull and parts of the upper jaw and dentition; it is probable that the whole skull was fossilized, but the remaining parts were not recovered. The partial vault is thin but is derived from a subadult individual. Brain size was quite small, with an indicated capacity of ca. 1,200 ml. The overall cranial form is decidedly Neanderthal-like, with a spherical shape when viewed from behind and an occipital chignon, very reminiscent of the form of the later La Quina Neanderthal skull. In addition, there is a prominent occipitomastoid crest and a suprainiac fossa. There is little doubt that the specimen represents a member of an early Neanderthal population, and it also provides a morphological link between earlier specimens, such as Swanscombe, and the later Neanderthals.

See also Archaic Homo sapiens; La quina; Levallois; Neanderthals; Swanscombe. [C.B.S., J.J.S.]

Biberson, Pierre (1909–)

French geologist and archaeologist. Biberson's main contribution was a long series of papers, published during the 1950s and 1960s, relating stone-tool cultures to climate and sea-level changes in the North African Pleistocene. In 1954, at Sidi Abderrahman near Casablanca (Morocco), Biberson discovered fragments of an adult hominid mandible in a stratum dated as late Middle Pleistocene. In 1955, these fragments were described by C. Arambourg, who concluded that they belonged to a form of hominid closely related to the Tighenif *Homo erectus*. Biberson also described the stone tools recovered from the quarry at Sidi Abderrahman, belonging to the so-called Moroccan Pebble culture.

See also Arambourg, Camille; Sidi Abderrahman; Tighenif. [F.S.]

Biface

Strictly speaking, an artifact that is flaked on two different faces (surfaces) of a piece of stone, such as bifacial choppers, handaxes, or projectile points. The term is often used to describe the large Acheulean artifacts of the handaxe/pick/cleaver/knife variety made on nodules or large flakes. This can be something of a misnomer though, since in some typological systems unifacial picks or handaxes still go into the biface category; at present, however, there is no other generic term for describing these large Acheulean forms.

See also Acheulean; Cleaver; Handaxe; Stone-Tool Making; Takamori. [N.T., K.S.]

Bilzingsleben

Open-air site in eastern Germany near Erfurt containing travertine deposits from which fossils and archaeological residues have been recovered, primarily since 1973. The site, which sits on the edge of a lake and has been exceptionally well preserved by travertine deposits, dates from a Middle Pleistocene interglacial (Holsteinian?), and a date of ca. 280 Ka appears likely, although some determinations have suggested an age in excess of 400 Ka. Dense concentrations of boulders, animal bones, and stone tools occur in several patches at the site. Several of these concentrations have been interpreted as the foundations of structures, perhaps huts or windbreaks. Hearths and flint-working areas have also been identified. The lithic assemblage from Bilzingsleben features a few large flakes but is generally small and does not feature handaxes. Bilzingsleben contains many pieces of antler that appear to have been shaped into picks or digging tools, as well as preserved wooden artifacts. Smaller pieces of bone and ivory appear to have been shaped into pointed forms and then polished by use, while others bear incisions that some scholars see as intentional markings rather than the by-products of butchery and naturally caused damage.

The hominid specimens, consisting of ca. 25 cranial fragments and seven molar teeth, probably derive from two to three individuals. The main pieces are a fragment of strongly built browridge and an occipital bone that is small, thick, and angled, with a developed occipital torus. A temporal has not yet been described. Cranial capacity was probably less than 1,200 ml, and the hominid has been classified as a new subspecies: *Homo erectus bilzingslebenensis.* Yet, despite the absence of critical areas of the cranium (e.g., the parietal regions), it is apparent that the hominid fragments also resemble other Middle Pleistocene specimens from Europe and Africa, such as Saldanha, that many regard as representing "archaic *Homo sapiens.*"

See also Archaic Homo sapiens; Early Paleolithic; Europe; Homo erectus; Saldanha. [J.J.S., A.S.B., C.B.S.]

Biochronology

Geohistorical analysis that divides time according to sequences of reconstructed paleobiological events. The events in question are primarily the evolution or extinction of taxa or groups of taxa, but also include expansions and contractions in geographic range, which may be seen as immigration events and local extinction events, respectively. The fossil record provides the evidence on which these historical interpretations are based, but the accuracy by which fossil occurrences reflect actual events is reduced by every circumstance that prevents a fossil from being preserved, observed, and identified. In other words, the diachrony (time variation) in biostratigraphic correlation is always greater than the true diachrony of the causative event. Biochronology, being probabilistic and predictive rather than actualistic, is not so dependent on the limitations of the fossil record. This makes it more appropriate where fossils are scarce, as in continental vertebrate paleontology or in correlating between different biofacies.

In recognition of the inherent difference between the occurrence of fossils and the historical events that they suggest, stratigraphers have adopted the acronyms FAD (First Appearance Datum) and LAD (Last Appearance Datum), and variants thereon, for stratigraphic range limits. The intention is to end careless use of interpretive terms such as *evolution, immigration,* or *extinction* in objective descriptions of fossil distribution.

See also Extinction; Stratigraphy; Time Scale. [J.A.V.C.]

Further Readings

Berggren, W.A., and Van Couvering, J.A. (1978) Biochronology. In G.V. Cohee, M.F. Glaessner, and H.D. Hedberg (eds.): Contributions to the Geological Time Scale (Studies in Geology No. 6). Tulsa: American Association of Petroleum Geologists, pp. 39–56.

Biomechanics

The term *biomechanics* is often used as if synonymous with the study of functional morphology, but more properly it refers to the application of basic physics to biology—specifically, the study of forces and their effects in biological systems. In most anthropological cases, it concerns forces in the musculoskeletal system. Forces may be *external*—that is, outside of the structure, including gravity, air resistance, inertia, muscle action, or ground reaction forces (reaction of the ground equal and opposite to the foot pushing down on it). External forces are often referred to as loads. Forces also may be *internal,* such as the reaction of structures to externally applied loads and their resistance to those loads. Internal forces are usually referred to as *stresses.* The deformation of a structure in response to stress is called *strain.*

Forces have four characteristics: magnitude, direction, line of action, and point of application. As such, forces can be represented as mathematical vectors that have the same four characteristics. When two or more forces are acting in the same plane and on the same point, biomechanics provides methods for finding their combined effect as a single

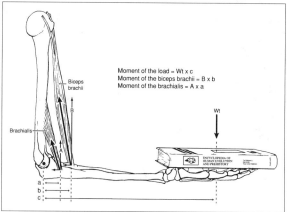

Model of a human forearm holding a load. The weight of the book held in the hand will tend to extend the elbow which is resisted by two elbow flexors, the biceps brachii and the brachialis. The thick arrows are vectors representing the force of each muscle. The four components of a force, magnitude, direction, line of action, and point of application, are represented by the length of the shaft, the head of the arrow, the orientation of the shaft, and the end of the arrow, respectively. Each vector has been resolved into a component acting parallel to the forearm bones, and one perpendicular to them (A and B). The parallel components tend to push the bones together at the elbow joint. Only the perpendicular components (A and B) can cause flexion (resist extension) and are therefore referred to as the effective components. The tendency for the book (load) to extend the elbow is called its moment or torque, and is equal to the weight of the book multiplied by the perpendicular distance to the pivot point (c = load arm). This is resisted by the muscle moments, which are equal to the effective components of the muscle forces (A and B) multipllied by their perpendicular distances to the pivot point (a and b = lever arms). Since b is longer than a, the biceps brachii is said to have better leverage to produce flexion at the elbow than the brachialis. Courtesy of S.G. Larson, by L. Betti.

force known as the *resultant*. It also includes methods for resolving a force into separate components acting in particular directions, such as the component of the ground reaction force that supports the body compared to the component that tends to accelerate the body forward. Often, resolution of forces into their components is done in order to find the overall resultant of those forces. A body is said to be in equilibrium when it remains at rest (static equilibrium) or is in motion with constant velocity (dynamic equilibrium). Statics is the study of the external effects of forces on a body in equilibrium. If two or more coplanar, nonparallel forces are acting on a rigid body, a force equal and opposite to their resultant must act on the body to maintain equilibrium. That force is known as the *equilibrant*. Dynamics is the study of the action of forces on bodies not in equilibrium. Included in dynamics are kinematics, which deals with a description of movement, and kinetics, which concerns the forces that act to produce motion. In dynamics, movement is defined as change of position (distance); speed is defined as the rate of change of position (distance over time); velocity is speed in a given direction; and acceleration is the rate of change of velocity.

In the musculoskeletal-linkage system, one is often concerned with the rotation of a limb segment at a joint, and, in this case, one must consider not linear velocity but angular velocity—that is, the rate of rotation of a segment around a pivot. Angular acceleration, then, refers to the rate of change of angular velocity. The tendency for a force to cause rotation of a segment around some pivot is called the *moment* or *torque* of a force and is equal to the magnitude of the force multiplied by its perpendicular distance to the pivot (lever arm). Muscles represent forces acting on limb segments to produce this rotation, and, since the moment they can produce is influenced by the length of their lever arms, the attachment sites of muscles vary in different taxa to alter the muscle's leverage at a joint.

See also Bone Biology; Evolutionary Morphology; Functional Morphology; Musculature; Skeleton; Skull; Teeth. [S.G.L.]

Further Readings

Biewener, A.A., ed. (1992) Biomechanics—Structures and Systems: A Practical Approach. Oxford: Oxford University Press.

Hildebrand, M. (1988) Analysis of Vertebrate Structure. 3rd ed. New York: Wiley, pp. 443–464.

Bipolar Technique

Technique of stone working in which the core is placed on an anvil stone and struck from above with a stone percussor. By this technique, flakes can be detached from either end of the core. These flakes tend to have thin or punctiform platforms and a subtle, flattened, or sheared bulb of percussion. The resultant core, sometimes called an *outil ecaille,* tends to be barrel shaped in planform and rather thin, with flakes usually removed from either end. This Paleolithic technique can be found from the Early Stone Age to modern times.

See also Stone-Tool Making. [N.T., K.S.]

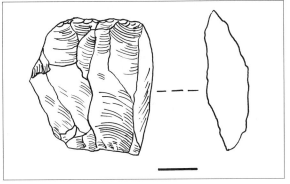

Bipolar core, or outil ecaillé *Scale is 1 cm.*

Birdsell, Joseph B. (1908–1994)

American anthropologist/human biologist and collaborator of N.B. Tindale. His Australian surveys of genetic and physiognomic variation resulted in the tri-hybrid theory of Australian origins, involving threefold migrations by Negritoid, Murrayian, and Carpentarian elements from Southeast Asia. He also made major contributions to modern notions of human microevolution and paleodemographic forces in human populations.

See also Australia; Tindale, N.B. [F.S.]

Bishop, Walter William (1931–1977)

British geologist. "Bill" Bishop was the leading authority on African Cenozoic geology, especially of the fossil-bearing sediments of the East African Rift Valley. A member of the Uganda Geological Survey and director of both the Uganda Museum (1962–1965) and the Yale Peabody Museum (1976–1977), Bishop also held academic positions in British universities. From 1956 to 1971, he was co-organizer of the East African Geological Research Unit, which put British doctoral students in the field to work out the geology of rift-valley strata. Bishop's students discovered many sites, including Chemeron, Chesowanja, Kapthurin, Lukeino, Ngorora, and Mpesida, in the Baringo Basin. His own work included valuable studies of fossils and stratigraphy at Kaiso, Moroto, Napak, Songhor, and Fort Ternan and the description of the Moroto *"Proconsul major"* (now *Morotopithecus bishopi*).

See also Baringo Basin/Tugen Hills; Chesowanja; Fort Ternan; Kapthurin; Napak; Songhor. [F.S.]

Black, Davidson (1884–1934)

Canadian anatomist and paleoanthropologist. Black began his career as a lecturer at (Case) Western Reserve University in 1909. In 1918, he was appointed professor of anatomy at the Peking Union Medical College; later he was given added responsibility as director of the Cenozoic Laboratory, Geological Survey of China. While he long harbored an interest in paleoanthropology, as well as a conviction that Central Asia had been the homeland of the genus *Homo,* it was not until 1927 that Black's paleoanthropological career was finally launched. At that time, a hominid lower molar was discovered at Zhoukoudian, near Beijing. From this single tooth, Black hypothesized the existence of a previously un-known hominid genus and species, which he called *Sinan-thropus pekinensis*. Between 1929 and 1932, he supervised a spectacular series of fossil discoveries at this site that essen-tially confirmed his original diagnosis, although the material is no longer considered as a species separate from *Homo erec-tus*. Further discoveries at this site were made shortly after his death.

See also Homo erectus; Weidenreich, Franz; Zhoukoudian. [F.S.]

Blackwater Draw

Stratified Paleoindian locality on the Llano Estacado (New Mexico). The site contained a series of seep springs, which formed a large, deep pond. The sediments that ultimately filled the spring and associated channel have yielded a strati-fied, three-part succession of Paleoindian cultures. The basal grey-sand level contained elephant remains and Llano arti-facts, including Clovis points, prismatic blades, and bone projectile-point tips. A brown-sand level separated these Clovis materials from diagnostic Folsom artifacts contained in a diatomaceous earth zone. The overlying carbonaceous silts yielded Plano-culture artifacts.

See also Americas; Clovis; Folsom; Llano Complex; Paleoin-dian; Plano. [D.H.T.]

Blade

Flake that is at least twice as long as it is wide, typically with straight, parallel sides and struck from a specially prepared blade core. Standardized blade cores often have a cylindrical or conical shape for the mass production of a quantity of blades, but they can take on a variety of shapes. Blades may be produced by hard-hammer percussion, soft-hammer per-cussion, indirect percussion (the punch technique), or pres-sure flaking. Blade (Mode 4) industries, especially character-istic of Late Paleolithic and many later technologies, were often produced with a punch technique. Blades can be used without further modification or may serve as blanks for pro-ducing such tool forms as endscrapers, burins, backed blades, and awls. In some areas, notably North America, the term *blade* has also been used for large, elongated, bifacially flaked projectile points or knives, which has led to some confusion.

See also Awl; Burin; Late Paleolithic; Prepared-Core; Scraper; Stone-Tool Making. [N.T., K.S.]

Blombos

Cave site on the South African coast ca. 240 km east of Cape Town containing Middle and Later Stone Age horizons. The Middle Stone Age horizons have yielded cylindrical bone points, drilled ocher slabs, incised bone fragments, and finely flaked bifacial Stillbay points. The associated fauna in-cludes large fish, suggesting greater economic and techno-logical sophistication than documented elsewhere for the MSA in South Africa. Dating of the site by several tech-niques (ESR, Uranium series, amino acid racemization) sug-gests that the Stillbay levels may be comparable in age or even older than the Howieson's Poort industry, which in turn is dated to ca. 80–65 Ka at most sites.

See also Bone Tools; Economy, Prehistoric; Katanda; Klasies River Mouth; Middle Stone Age; Modern Human Origins; Paleolithic Lifeways; Stillbay. [A.S.B.]

Further Readings

Henshilwood, C., and Sealy, J. (1997) Bone artifacts from the Middle Stone Age at Blombos Cave, Southern Cape, South Africa. Curr. Anthropol. 38:890–895.

Bodo

Stratified site in Central Ethiopia, spanning the Early Pliocene (4.5 Ma) to the Late Middle Pleistocene (ca. 0.2 Ma) according to K/Ar and fission-track dating combined with faunal analysis.

The Bodo Basin, on the eastern side of the Middle Awash study area in the the Afar Valley, exposes a strati-graphic sequence divided into Lower, Middle, and Upper units dated to the Early Pliocene, the Early Pleistocene, and the Middle to Late Pleistocene, respectively. While verte-brate fossils are abundant throughout the sequence and Oldowan-style tools have been recovered from the Middle Bodo Beds, the only hominid remains are from the Upper Bodo Beds in association with abundant archaeological ma-terial belonging to the Acheulean Industrial complex to-gether with small-tool occurrences that resemble the Devel-oped Oldowan. Possible traces of fire are reported to be associated with some of the archaeological occurrences.

In 1976, a massive, adult, presumably male, specimen with large face and thick cranial vault was recovered from the Upper Bodo Sand Unit in the lower part of the Upper Bodo Beds by A. Asfaw in a team led by J.E. Kalb. Contemporary fauna is Middle Pleistocene in age, which dates on underly-ing tephra confirm. The specimen was found resting on the surface of a sandy gravel layer containing abundant Acheulean tools. The cranium bears striking resemblances to

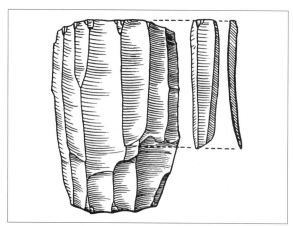

Upper Paleolithic prismatic blade core with front and side view of removed blade blank. From F. Bordes, The Old Stone Age, *1968, McGraw-Hill, with permission.*

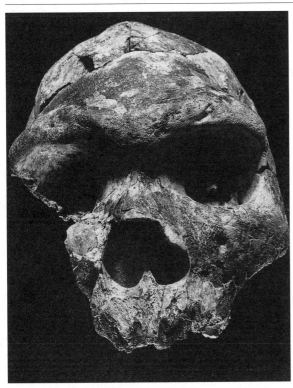

Facial view of the Bodo 1 human fossil from Middle Pleistocene deposits in the Middle Awash Valley, Ethiopia. Photo by and courtesy of Tim D. White.

the Kabwe (Broken Hill) specimen from Zambia, the Petralona specimen from Greece, and some of the Sima de los Huesos crania from Spain. In many morphologic features, the specimen is intermediate between advanced *Homo erectus* and "archaic *Homo sapiens*," and its taxonomic status is under debate. A second fossil, a fragment of parietal, was found in 1981 ca. 400 m from the original find, and additional postcranial remains were found in 1990. The latter represent a second (and possibly third) hominid individual. The 1976 Bodo cranium bears fine, artificial, perimortem striations on the face and the vault and within the orbit. These have been interpreted as cutmarks indicating an intentional defleshing by another hominid wielding a stone tool.

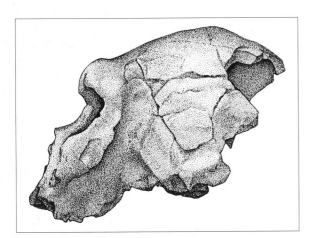

Lateral view of the Bodo partial cranium.

See also Acheulean; Afar Basin; Africa, East; Archaic Homo sapiens; Homo erectus; Kabwe; Middle Awash; Petralona. [T.D.W.]

Further Readings

Clark, J.D., Asfaw, B., Assefa, G., Harris, J.W.K., Kurashina, H., Walter, R.C., White, T.D., and Williams, M.A.J. (1984) Palaeoanthropological discoveries in the Middle Awash Valley, Ethiopia. Nature 307:423–428.

Conroy, G.C., Jolly, C.J., Cramer, D., and Kalb, J.E. (1978) Newly discovered fossil hominid skull from the Afar Depression, Ethiopia. Nature 275:67–70.

White, T.D. (1986) Cutmarks on the Bodo cranium: A case of prehistoric defleshing. Am. J. Phys. Anthropol. 69:503–509.

Boker Tachtit

An open-air site in the Central Negev, Israel, excavated in the late 1970s under the direction of A. Marks. Boker Tachtit dates to 47–35 Ka and consists of four main levels, each containing dense scatters of lithic debris around hearths. These levels, numbered 1–4 from bottom to top, contain a sequence spanning the Middle-Late Paleolithic transition. At the base of the sequence, stone tools are produced by primarily bidirectional flaking in a characteristically Middle Paleolithic technique. Through Levels 2–4, this production method is gradually replaced by unidirectional flaking, a characteristically Late Paleolithic technique. Throughout this sequence, the types of stone tools being produced remain largely the same. For example, Emireh points are made primarily on short triangular flakes in Level 1 and primarily on long pointed blades in Level 4. This pattern of technological change and typological continuity has been interpreted as evidence of cultural continuity across the Middle-Upper Paleolithic transition.

See also Asia, Western; Emiran; Emireh Point; Upper Paleolithic. [J.J.S.]

Bone Biology

The study of human evolution depends heavily on comparisons of bones and teeth, the hard tissues most commonly preserved as fossils. Traditionally, such comparisons have analyzed variation in the size and shape of anatomical structures in order to reconstruct past lifeways and evolutionary change. Another approach to the study of hard tissues emphasizes the cellular processes by which a bone is formed and remodeled rather than the resultant form itself. The following discussion summarizes what is known about these processes in human bone.

Bone Behavior

Three types of cells are involved in the formation and maintenance of bone: osteoblasts, osteocytes, and osteoclasts. *Osteoblasts* secrete collagen and organic matrix, which is then hardened, or mineralized, with calcium and phosphate salts to form bone tissue. These bone-forming cells are active during growth, maintenance, and repair of bone. At intervals

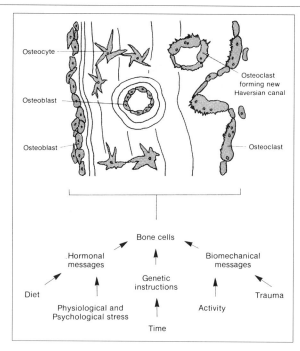

Bone cells form and remodel the skeleton. Although the structure and distribution of bone through the skeleton is undoubtedly outlined by genetic instructions, the final form will depend on the balance of messages sent to the cells by hormonal, biomechanical, and other factors.

that depend on the rate of bone growth and the location in the skeleton, these cells settle and surround themselves with their own products. These entombed cells are referred to as *osteocytes,* and the spaces they occupy are called *osteocyte lacunae.* All osteocytes within a bone are coupled to their nearest neighbors by slender processes forming an interconnected network of living cells throughout the hard extracellular matrix. It is likely that these cells monitor the integrity and strength of bone and communicate this information to the osteoblasts, which make any necessary adjustments to the properties of the bone such as its volume and geometry. Mineralized bone is resorbed by *osteoclasts,* which demineralize the bone surface and consume the organic components. In so doing, they create small pits called *osteoclast lacunae.* Osteoclasts are responsible for the wholesale removal of bone during the resizing and shaping of bones during growth; they ream out cylindrical shafts of bone for the incorporation of new blood vessels (Haversian systems); and they reduce bone volume when the customary functional strains are reduced. These bone-resorbing cells also tap the reservoir of calcium and phosphates stored in bone and release them into the bloodstream when levels are low.

The two processes, bone resorption and deposition, by their patterning over the surfaces of growing bones and their rates of activity, are responsible for the form and composition of the skeleton. It is clear from species-specific bony structures that these processes are guided by genetic instructions and epigenetic influences (controls exerted by the genetically determined growth and form of other tissues). It is equally clear from studies of bone physiology, however, that these processes respond quite readily to environmental conditions. Environmental circumstances are conveyed to the cells via at least two channels of communication: through hormonal messages that are themselves a response to circulating levels of calcium and phosphates in the bloodstream, and possibly through the generation and movement of electrical potentials between osteocytes when a bone is functionally strained. In the presence of disease, local immune and repair responses also influence the behavior of bone cells.

Bone Structure and Function

It has long been recognized that the shape and the internal structure of a given bone are well suited to the mechanical demands placed on it. This recognition has led to the search for "laws" that define the relationship between a bony structure and its function. One of the earliest statements of this kind, popularized as Wolff's Law, suggested that the trabeculi, or the internal struts within a bone, are oriented along the major pathways of stress acting on that bone. More generally, this principle has been stated as the tendency for bone to be laid down where it is needed mechanically and resorbed where it is not. This *trajectory theory* was supported by W. Roux's biomechanical analysis of a pathological knee, in which he showed that the observed pattern of trabeculi coincided with the amounts and distribution of abnormal stress caused by the pathology. Such theories of functional adaptation have been criticized for their failure to recognize the soft-tissue context of a bone and the dynamic nature of both bone and positional behavior.

More recently, F. Pauwels has used photoelastic techniques to test the trajectory theory. His work suggests that, overall, anatomical structures, including muscles and ligaments as well as the bones themselves, function to reduce bending stresses within bones. Furthermore, experimental work by L. Lanyon and others suggests that bone-cell behavior may be guided by several biomechanical characteristics, including not only stress distribution and magnitude but also the history of previous remodeling and the rates at which stresses change.

Bone As a Record of Life History

After certain critical stages of embryological development, the cells taken from a particular bone will assume the general form of that bone even when grown in culture or transplanted to another part of the body. This *canalization,* as well as species-specific patterns of overall growth and aging, indicate that genetic factors play an important part in the development of the functional skeleton. Yet, the final size and material properties of a bone depend also on dietary, hormonal, and biomechanical factors. Nutritional deprivation and other stresses affecting growth hormones can result in smaller body size and skeletal dimensions. If the stress is relieved before too long, then the body and the bones exhibit "catch-up growth" and attain their normal size. Use and disuse of bone lead to changes in the volume of bone that are consistent with the levels of functional strain. Consider the professional tennis player, for example, who exhibits a dramatic increase in the girth of the bones of the swinging arm in contrast to the balancing arm.

The potential impact of environment on bone form and size during adulthood may be considerably less than during the growth period, perhaps amounting to small adjustments in bone density and size assuming only minor changes in function. A susceptibility to the hormonal environment may return in later life, as when loss of estrogen production in postmenopausal females is associated with a reduced ability to maintain bone volume. This is called osteoporosis. At this time in the life cycle, dietary and/or biomechanical insults may result in pathological conditions rather than in adjustments in form.

In summary, bone structure and integrity can be seen as a record of life-history events. That record results from interactions between an underlying genetic program of development and aging, environmental stresses, and changes in function that occur throughout the life cycle.

Applications of Skeletal Biology

Two fields in particular have explored the implications of bone biology for human evolution and adaptation. One of these, bioarchaeology, concerns itself primarily with the study of prehistoric cemetery populations. It has used a largely statistical approach to document environmental perturbations in processes of growth and development and to describe the biological success and health of prehistoric populations. A few studies in this field have alternatively emphasized traits whose expression may be largely canalized and thus useful as measures of genetic distance. Combined with archaeological data, genetic distance measures, signs of growth disruption, disease, and dietary inadequacies have revealed much about recent human adaptations.

Another area of research explores the plasticity and biomechanical properties of primate bone subjected to functional stresses. It often includes the use of bone-histology techniques to monitor bone behavior after experimentation (muscle removal, dietary manipulation, implants). Other researchers study the relationship between form and function through analyses of how forces (e.g., muscle forces during chewing or locomotor forces) are transmitted through bones, through analyses of the cross-sectional geometry and mass distribution of bone material (bone shape and volume), and through the study of the density, elasticity, and orientation of the fibrous organic component (collagen) of bones. Physical anthropologists focus their research in these areas on practical orthopedic and orthodontic problems, working closely with medical and dental experts, and have contributed much basic research applicable to paleobiological reconstructions of fossil primates and hominids.

Skeletal Biology and Paleoanthropology

The cellular and tissue properties of fossil bones and teeth have become an important focus in paleoanthropology. The fossilized record of bone-cell behavior, combined with more traditional functional anatomy, offers the paleoanthropologist new insights into prehistoric lifeways. Studies using scanning electron microscopy of the pattern of bone-forming and -resorbing activities on fossil hominid bones has provided a dynamic view of their growth and development (ontogeny). These studies illustrate a certain taxonomic specificity to early hominid growth patterns and, as

such, may be used in phylogenetic analyses as ontogenetic *characters*. Differences in the timing of growth, development, and aging, as well as in the impact of environmental insults on developmental processes, have come from examinations of teeth, including various markers of incremental growth and hypoplasias.

See also Archaeology; Forensic Anthropology; Ontogeny; Paleopathology; Skeleton. [C.J.D., T.G.B.]

Further Readings
Bromage, T.G. (1989) Ontogeny of the early hominid face. J. Hum. Evol. 16:751–773.

Enlow, D.H. (1990) Facial Growth, 3rd ed. Philadelphia: Saunders.

Frankel, V.H., and Nordin, M. (1980) Basic Biomechanics of the Skeletal System. Philadelphia: Lea and Febiger.

Murray, P.D.F. (1936, 1985) Bones: A Study of the Development and Structure of the Vertebrate Skeleton. New York and London: Cambridge University Press.

Pauwels, F. (1980) Biomechanics of the Locomotor Apparatus. (Translated by P. Maquet and R. Furlong.) Berlin and New York: Springer-Verlag.

Shipman, P., Walker, A., and Bichell, D. (1985) The Human Skeleton. Cambridge, Mass.: Harvard University Press.

Wilson, F.C., ed. (1983) The Musculoskeletal System: Basic Processes and Disorders. Philadelphia: Lippincott.

Bone Tools

Bone is a softer, more resilient, and more flexible, material than stone, lending itself to the manufacture of tools that require strength, flexibility, and a sharp edge or point. Needles, points, and awls of bone are less likely to snap under the torsional stress of penetrating leather, skin, wood, and the like than similar objects of stone. Stone, however, especially glassy materials such as obsidian, can attain and retain a sharper edge, making it a preferred material for cutting implements.

The earliest bone tools have been a subject for much debate on every continent. When the early australopiths of South Africa did not appear to possess a lithic industry, R.A. Dart argued that the differential representation of various skeletal elements at the site of Makapansgat, together with the evidence of crushing and impact damage on many bones, suggested that australopiths used tools of bone, tooth, and horn instead, an *Osteodontokeratic* culture. These aspects of the faunal assemblage were later shown by C.K. Brain to be due to taphonomic effects, especially predation by hyenas, who had differentially broken and destroyed marrow-bearing bones and inflicted heavy damage on many bone fragments. Brain also noted the presence of two pointed implements from the later South African site of Swartkrans that could not be explained as hyena damage but were more likely the product of repeated use as digging sticks. Other bone tools, mostly modified by use rather than deliberate design, have been reported from Early Paleolithic sites in Africa and elsewhere. These include anvils, hammers or percussion implements, splintered pieces or wedges, and roughly pointed digging implements. A few pieces of large mammal bone show evidence of deliberate flaking; at least one biface in bone is known from the Early Paleolithic of Italy. Such artifacts seem to represent an attempt to transfer evolving lithic technologies to bone, rather than the invention of new technologies for this very different material.

The discovery of bone's unique properties during the Early Paleolithic is indirectly reflected in the development of soft-hammer percussion for flaking stone. Since bone (and wood) absorb some of the energy of the blow, the resultant flake is flatter, and the bulb of percussion less pronounced, than with hard-hammer percussion (stone-on-stone technique).

A few Middle Paleolithic sites in Europe, Africa, and western Asia contain roughly shaped bone awls for piercing. Earlier implements described as "awls" are not usually sufficiently pointed to have had a definite piercing function (e.g. those from Bilzingsleben in Germany). Most often, these Middle Paleolithic pieces retain an unmodified end, often the epiphysis, which served as a handle. In general, Middle Paleolithic bone tools reveal little of the careful shaping and polishing that is characteristic, indeed diagnostic, of the Upper or Late Paleolithic. The regular detachment of long-bone splinters by using a burin to incise parallel grooves in a long bone is also seen as an Upper or Late Paleolithic phenomenon.

Exceptions to the relative lack of carefully shaped bone tools in the Middle Paleolithic are found in Africa at several sites. Shaped bones with marginal notches are recorded from Klasies River mouth in southern Africa, while at Katanda in eastern Zaire three sites with Middle Stone Age industries dated to ca. 80–60 Ka yielded shaped and polished bone points with both barbs and basal shaping for hafting. At Blombos Cave in South Africa, cylindrical bone points are associated with fish remains, drilled ocher plaques, and Middle Stone Age points of the Stillbay industry.

In the Upper or Late Paleolithic, techniques for detaching and polishing bone splinters became widespread. Bone points with varying basal configurations—split base, bevel base, pointed base, ringed base, notched base—suggest experimentation with different kinds of hafted projectile technology. Bone also continues to be formed into piercing implements for hide-working, although Upper Paleolithic awls tend to be more carefully and thoroughly polished along much of their length than those of the Middle Paleolithic. Bone spatulas, lissoirs or smoothers, flat daggers, and perforated ornaments are also well documented. By 20 Ka, two new bone inventions reflect increasing technological innovation. One is the spear thrower, which extended the range over which projectile technology was effective. The other is the eyed needle, which made possible more elaborate clothing at a time when climatic deterioration was at a maximum. In Africa, innovation in bone technology also increases in the Late Paleolithic, reflected in the development of small bone linkshafts, which were fixed to a microlithic stone point but detachable from the arrow shaft. These indicate the early use of poison to increase the effectiveness of projectile technology. The detachable arrowhead remains in the animal, delivering a fatal dose of the poison; the animal's efforts to rub off the arrow only remove the shaft. In eastern Zaire, as in Botswana, small barbed points with basal shaping to retain a line suggest the development of harpoon technology, in which a detachable head remains in the animal (most often a fish) while the hunter/fisher holds it by a line connecting directly to the point until the animal tires and dies. Both of these developments in Africa are documented before 25 Ka.

The relative plasticity and softness of bone were also conducive to the depiction of images, whether by shaping the bone or by engraving outline figures on its surface. These are also characteristic of the Upper (or Late) Paleolithic.

During the final Paleolithic and the Mesolithic or Epipaleolithic, bone technology was particularly adapted to the utilization of aquatic resources, not only through the production of bone harpoons but also in the creation of hooks, leisters, and net weights.

See also Awl; Bilzingsleben; Burin; Dart, Raymond Arthur; Harpoon; Katanda; Klasies River Mouth; Modern Human Origins: Archaeology and Behavior; Paleolithic Image; Paleolithic Lifeways; Stone-Tool Making; Swartkrans; Tsodilo Sites. [A.S.B., N.T., K.S.]

Further Readings

Brain, C.K. (1981) The Hunters or the Hunted? Chicago: University of Chicago Press.

Brooks, A.S., Melgren, D.M., Cramer, J.S., Franklin, S., Hornyak, W., Keating, J.M., Klein, R.G., Rink, W.J., Schwarcz, H., Smith, J.N.L., Stewart K., Todd, N.E., Verniers, J., and Yellen, J. (1995) Dating and context of three Middle Stone Age sites with bonepoints in the Upper Senliki Valley, Zaire. Science 268:548–553.

Henshilwood, C., and ZSealy, J. (1997) Bone artifacts from the Middle Stone Age at Blombos Cave, southern Cape, South Africa. Curr. Anthropol. 38(5):890–895.

Knecht, H. (1993) Early Upper Paleolithic approaches to bone antler projectile technology. In G.L. Peterkin, H.M. Bricker, and P. Mellars, (eds.): Hunting and Animal Exploitation in the Later Paleolithic and Mesolithic of Eurasia. Archaeological Papers of the American Anthropological Association 4:33–47.

Yellen, J.E., Brooks, A.S., Cornelissen, E., Mehlman, M.J., and Stewart, K. (1995) A Middle Stone Age worked bone industry from Katanda, Upper Senliki Valley, Zaire. Science 268:553–556.

Border Cave

Middle Paleolithic cave site in the Natal Province of South Africa that has produced five important hominid specimens, found between 1940 and 1974. The cultural sequence contains an occurrence of an early prismatic blade industry, first classified as a local variant of the Pietersburg industry but later referred to the Howieson's Poort, stratified between more typical flake-based Middle Stone Age (MSA) assemblages. Early Late Stone Age occupations dated to 40–35 Ka

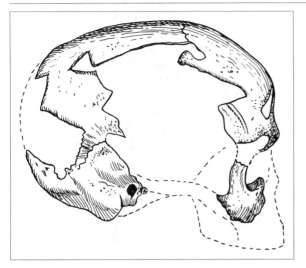

Lateral view of the anatomically modern Border Cave 1 cranium.

by radiocarbon cap this sequence. The anatomically modern human fossils from this site have excited great interest because of their possible early Late Pleistocene antiquity. The excavator, P. Beaumont, believes that they all derive from levels dated to 141–43 Ka by electron spin resonance (ESR) and amino-acid racemization of ostrich eggshell. However, some specimens were recovered in rubble from the early commercial guano-mining activities at the cave, while others (e.g., BC-3) are burials that might have been intrusive from more recent levels. None of the Border Cave specimens displays the robusticity seen in other African early Late Pleistocene fossils. Although the Border Cave 1 and 2 partial skull, mandible, and postcranial fragments were not found during controlled excavations, analysis of the attached matrix of BC-1 suggests that it may indeed derive from Middle Stone Age deposits. BC-3 (an infant burial) was excavated in 1941 from a shallow grave cut into the sediments underlying the Howieson's Poort horizon, while BC-5 (a mandible) was excavated in the 1970s from the base of the Howieson's Poort horizon. Analysis of bone-mineral features such as crystallinity by A. Sillen and A. Morris indicates that both of these specimens sort with younger faunal elements and are probably intrusive into the MSA. Two forelimb fragments recovered from slumped sediments were found to sort with the MSA fauna. Morphometric study of the ulna revealed that it is more robust than modern equivalents, perhaps suggesting the greater muscularity typical of archaic humans; the humerus showed no special features. BC-1 and BC-2 were also subjected to crystallinity analysis, but the results were equivocal, perhaps related to the sampling procedures. If these morphologically modern fossils are correctly associated with the Middle Stone Age horizons, the Border Cave specimens would document the earliest known occurrence of fully modern humans in southern Africa.

See also Africa, Southern; Archaic Moderns; Cave of Hearths; Homo sapiens; Klasies River Mouth; Later Stone Age; Middle Paleolithic; Middle Stone Age; Pietersburg. [J.J.S., A.S.B., C.B.S.]

Further Readings

Beaumont, P.B., de Villiers, H., and Vogel, J.C. (1978) Modern man in sub-Saharan Africa prior to 49,000 BP: A review and evaluation with particular reference to Border Cave. S. Afr. J. Sci. 74:409–419.

Miller, G.H., Beaumont, P.B., Joll, A.J.T., and Johnson, B. (1993) Pleistocene geochronology and Paaleothernometry from protein diagenesis in ostrich eggshells: Implications for the evolution of modern humans. In M.J. Aitken, C.B. Stringer, and P.A. Mellars, (eds.): The Origins of Modern Humans and the Impact of Chronometric Dating. Princeton: Princeton University Press, pp. 49–68.

Pearson, O.M., and Grine, F.E. (1996) Morphology of the Border Cave hominid ulna and humerus. S. Afr. J. Sci. 92:231–236.

Sillen, A., and Morris, A. (1996) Diagenesis of bone from Border Cave: Implications for the age of the Border Cave hominids. J. Hum. Evol. 31:499–506.

Bordes, François (1919–1981)

Noted French prehistorian who revolutionized European Early and Middle Paleolithic systematics in 1950 by creating a standard lithic typology consisting of 63 tool types and by focusing on the entire lithic assemblage, rather than just the most characteristic forms, or *fossiles directeurs*. His excavations at the multilayered sites of Combe Grenal and Pech de l'Azé (Dordogne, France) revealed that some of these tool types regularly occur together. He interpreted these statistically patterned associations as reflecting the existence of four distinct tool kits (Denticulate, Typical, Mousterian of Acheulean tradition, and Charentian with the Quina and Ferrassie subgroupings) and argued that they were made and used by different Mousterian tribes, each of whom had a distinct stone-tool-making tradition. This interpretation was subsequently challenged by scholars who argued that the variability that Bordes noted reflected not only stylistic differences but also functional and chronological ones and pointed out differences in the raw material used, as well as stages of the reduction sequences.

See also De Sonneville-Bordes, Denise; Europe; France; Middle Paleolithic; Mousterian; Pech de l'Azé; Périgord. [O.S.]

Boucher de Perthes, Jacques (1788–1868)

French prehistorian. Boucher de Perthes' interest in antiquarian studies was first aroused by the archaeological discoveries made by C. Picard (1806–1841), a physician and archivist of the local Société d'Emulation d'Abbeville, in the Somme River Valley during the early 1830s. Following his lead, Boucher de Perthes began his investigations in 1837. During the next decade, he recovered a series of Paleolithic artifacts, many of which were found in strata containing the remains of extinct fauna, which convinced him of their great antiquity. The results of this work were summarized in his book *Antiquités celtiques et antédiluviennes* (1847). Prior to publication, he sent a copy of this manuscript to the Académie de Sciences in Paris in the hope that they might endorse it, but his request was rejected. Aside from the ongoing resistance to the idea that human beings had been co-eval with extinct animals in antediluvian times, there were also technical objections. Not only did the artifacts illustrated in the book appear to be a bizarre mixture of recent Celtic material and natural stones, there were also apparent stratigraphic inconsistencies, not to mention the fact that he had couched his entire thesis in a form of catastrophism that was "far removed from the mainstream of mid-nineteenth century views" (Grayson 1983:129). Although he was not without his French supporters, such as E. Lartet (1801–1871) and I. Geoffroy Saint-Hilaire (1805–1861), it was from the English rather than the French scientific community that an endorsement of Boucher de Perthes' claims finally came. This movement was precipitated in 1858 by the paleontologist H. Falconer (1808–1865), who had been responsible for organizing the excavation of Brixham Cave (Devon) under the auspices of the Geological Society of London and the Royal Society. Recognizing the similarity between the artifacts illustrated in Boucher de Perthes' book and those recovered from Brixham Cave, Falconer had visited Boucher de Perthes in the autumn of 1858. This visit consolidated his conviction, and, as a result, he urged his skeptical colleague and much-respected geologist J. Prestwich (1812–1896) to make the trip to Abbeville and review the evidence for himself. The following spring, Prestwich made his now celebrated trip to Abbeville in the company of the archaeologist J. Evans (1823–1908). They returned to England as zealous converts to Boucher de Perthes' claims, which were further reinforced by a study of similar river terraces in Suffolk, including those where, at the turn of the century, J. Frere (1740–1807) had reportedly discovered antediluvian artifacts. The results of their work were summarized in Prestwich's landmark paper delivered to the Royal Society on May 26, 1859. The impact of this was, as Falconer's biographer C. Murchison (1830–1879) later noted, "a great and sudden revolution in modern opinion, respecting the probable existence of a former period of man and many extinct mammalia." While there remained pockets of resistance, by the early 1860s Boucher de Perthes was widely acclaimed as the founder of the new science of prehistory.

See also Archaeology; Frere, John; Lartet, Edouard; Paleolithic. [F.S.]

Further Readings

Grayson, D.K. (1983) The Establishment of Human Antiquity. New York: Academic.

Cohen, C., and Hublin, J.-J. (1989) Boucher de Perthes, 1788–1868: Les origines romantiques de la préhistoire. Paris: Belin.

Boule, [Pierre] Marcellin (1861–1942)

French paleontologist and geologist. For much of his career, Boule occupied the chair of paleontology at the Museum National d'Histoire Naturelle in Paris (1902–1936), and for many years he was also director of the Institut de Paleontologie Humaine, also in Paris, established in 1914. He served as editor of *L'Anthropologie* from 1893 to 1940. Although he was originally trained as a geologist and a paleontologist, and with important contributions to the geology of France to his credit, Boule became increasingly focused on human paleontology. He is perhaps best remembered for his comprehensive study of the first complete Neanderthal skeleton, found at La Chapelle-aux-Saints (France) in 1908, and for his book *Les Hommes fossiles* (1912). Boule was an early supporter of the *presapiens theory*, rejecting the proposition that the Neanderthals were the precursors of modern humans.

See also La Chapelle-aux-Saints; Neanderthals; Presapiens. [F.S.]

Bow and Arrow

Important technological innovation characteristic of many Stone Age groups since the last glaciation, suggesting a shift from spear hunting to archery. Archery allows the projectile to be propelled at higher velocities and at greater distances from the prey, thus increasing the chances of success. The smaller projectiles are often used ethnographically to deliver poison to the animal's bloodstream, also increasing the likelihood that a hit will result in death rather than escape. The earliest direct evidence for archery comes in the form of arrow shafts from Stellmoor (Germany), ca. 10.5 Ka; mesolithic bows from Scandinavia; and a bow stave from Gwisho Springs (Zambia), ca. 3.5 Ka, although small projectile points found in the Upper or Late Paleolithic have been considered candidates for arrowheads by some prehistorians. Arrowheads could have been made of wood, bone, antler, or stone.

See also Late Paleolithic; Later Stone Age; Mesolithic; Paleolithic Lifeways; Upper Paleolithic. [N.T., K.S., A.S.B.]

Further Readings

Bergman, C.A. (1993) The development of the bow in western Europe: A technological and functional perspective. In G.L. Peterkin, H.M. Bricker, and P. Mellars, (eds.): Hunting and Animal Exploitation in the Later Palaeolithic and Mesolithic of Eurasia (Anthropological Papers of the American Anthropological Association, No. 4). pp. 94–105.

Boxgrove

The open site of Boxgrove lies near the south coast of England and was occupied during a Middle Pleistocene interglacial prior to the Anglian glaciation. It may, therefore, date from ca. 500 Ka, about the same age as the Mauer (Heidelberg, Germany) site. Hominids used the chalk cliff cut by the interglacial high sea level to extract flint nodules, and preserved land surfaces contain finished handaxes and knapping debris, as well as fossil vertebrates, some showing butchery marks. In 1993, a massive human tibial shaft with thick walls was recovered from a stratified context. It has been assigned to *Homo* cf. *heidelbergensis* (= "archaic *Homo sapiens*").

See also Acheulean; Archaic Homo sapiens; Europe; Mauer. [C.B.S., J.J.S.]

Further Readings

Roberts, M., Stringer, C., and Parfitt, S. 1994. A hominid tibia from Middle Pleistocene sediments at Boxgrove, U.K. Nature 369:311–313.

Brain

The human brain is the largest brain among primates but not the largest in either absolute or relative terms among the mammals. Accounting for ca. 2 percent of total body weight, the human brain consumes ca. 20 percent of our metabolic resources at any given time. By all estimates, our brain is three times as large as would be expected for a primate of our body size, and that fact alone should suggest that our brain is an organ of exceptional importance, related to our unique cultural and symbolic behavioral adaptations. The brain is not a homogeneous mass, however, but a composite of hundreds of nuclear masses and several more hundreds of interconnecting fiber tracts. Our uniqueness as a species depends both on the size of our brain and on its organization. Trying to understand the evolutionary development of the human brain is a major challenge, as we have plenty of evidence regarding the size of our ancestors' brains but little about their organization or how they were used. Perhaps it is a tribute to our species that, despite our grim problems of adapting to the world, we alone in the animal kingdom can choose to study our own evolutionary development.

The brain is an extraordinarily complex organ. It has billions of parts, if one is simply talking about nerve cells. Basically, these are either firing or not and may be excitatory or inhibitory. Thus, there is a *digital* aspect to the functioning of so many components. Whether a nerve cell will fire, however, also depends on a summation process of thousands of inhibitory or facilitative connections with other nerve cells and the surrounding neuroglial cells. This is the *analogue* aspect to the brain. To make matters more complex, the brain also has both *parallel* and *serial* organizations to its many components, so that information about the external and the internal environments of the animal are evaluated both directly and indirectly. The brain is hierarchically organized, as between its most recent acquired mantle, the grey cerebral cortex (*neopallium*), and the underlying basal ganglia, limbic system, and olfactory lobes that make up the *telencephalon,* or forebrain. This division surrounds the underlying *diencephalon,* the "between brain," which includes the thalamus, the epithalamus, the hypothalamus, and the pineal gland or body. At a lower level there is the *mesencephalon,* or "midbrain," which is behaviorally a part of the brain stem, containing the *tectum* and the *tegmentum,* consisting principally of the inferior and the superior colliculi, which are auditory and visual in function, respectively. More ancient is the next level of structures making up the *metencephalon* and the *myelencephalon,* consisting of the cerebellum, the pons, the medulla, and the third and fourth ventricles, which are integrated with the spinal cord.

While it is not strictly true that all parts of the brain are connected with each other, the combination of parallel and serial, crossed and uncrossed fiber interconnections does mean that any complex volitional act involves most, if not all, of the brain working together. No one is certain how many genes control the development of the brain and its phenotypic expressions, but a rough estimate of 40,000 genes may, in fact, be conservative. This represents an enormous amount of potential genetic variability for natural selection to work upon. Many of these genes, however, must be very conservative, for it is an awesome fact that, despite all the variation in different animal species' behavioral repertoires (species-specific behaviors), almost all mammals, if not vertebrates, have the same components in their brains. The human animal does not possess any new structures in its brain compared with most other mammals. What seems to have occurred during evolution is that certain parts of the brain have become enlarged relative to others; in the mammals, particularly the higher primates, this has involved a dramatic increase in the cerebral cortex and the underlying thalamus, with which it has two-way connections. In the human animal, the cerebral cortex accounts for ca. 76 percent of total brain weight, the highest ratio among primates. In the chimpanzee, the cortex is 72 percent of brain weight, and in the gorilla, 68 percent. The amount of cortex in humans as well as in chimpanzees and macaques is exactly what would be expected allometrically for their respective brain weights.

Thus, one of the major challenges facing any scientist trying to understand the evolution of the brain is how to account for a complex mixture of conservative and new genetic expressions involved in all of the parts of the brain and how these relate to behavior, adaptation, and evolution. Much of our current scientific explanation focuses on brain size, as this is simple to measure. The more difficult task is to quantify the organization of the brain's components and to relate this information to evolutionary histories and dynamics among species.

Lines of Evidence

Three lines of evidence exist for understanding the evolution of the human brain. The first is *direct,* derived from the study of endocasts, and is called *paleoneurology.* Data about the once-living brain are provided by either natural or human-made casts of the interiors of fossil crania. Such data include brain size (volume), convolutional details, traces of the meningeal vessels, and overall morphological patterns that include shape and asymmetries of the cerebral cortices. In life, the brain is covered by three meningeal tissues that often prevent the cortical gyri and sulci from being completely imprinted on the internal table of bone: the *pia mater,* the *arachnoid mater* (including cerebrospinal fluid), and the thick *dura mater.* It is extraordinarily rare, at least in higher primates, for the cortical convolutions to be fully preserved on endocasts, and thus the volume of the brain and possible asymmetries of the cortices constitute the most reliable evidence.

The second line of evidence is *indirect* and is provided by comparative *neuroanatomy.* This studies the brains of *living* animals, each an end product of its own line of evolutionary development. In this case, quantitative studies are made of the brains of different primates, including the neural nuclei and fibers, as well as overall brain sizes, and these data are correlated with variations in behavior. Within this line of study, *allometry* is one of the most valuable tools of analysis.

A third line of evidence, even more indirect, is the study of the products once made by hominins, such as stone tools and different kinds of archaeological sites that preserve patterns of hominin behavior. In addition, one can use the skeletal remains of hominins to understand locomotor adaptations, such as bipedalism, or to study bone fragments of the hands to appreciate manipulatory behavior. These provide only the most indirect clues, but major patterns of locomotor adaptation cannot evolve without some reorganization of the central nervous system controlling musculoskeletal patterns. All three lines of evidence should be used together in the attempt to enlarge our knowledge of human brain evolution, as none of them alone is sufficient for such understanding.

Paleoneurology, or the Study of Endocasts

The accompanying table (table 1) provides a partial listing of the endocranial volumes determined for many of the earlier hominins and the methods used. The brain volume in our own modern species normally varies from ca. 1,000 to 2,000 ml, with an average volume of ca. 1,350 to 1,400 ml. No convincing relationship has ever been shown between brain volume and behavior, aside from pathological cases, such as microcephaly or hydroencephaly, in which behavior is often subnormal. Microcephaly is especially interesting, as there are recorded cases of human beings having brain volumes less than those of some pongids but nevertheless using articulate language. This suggests that, while brain size is important, the organization of the brain's components is a significant contributing factor toward species-specific behavior.

This range of normal variation, without any known behavioral correlates, is about the same as the total evolutionary change in brain size from our earliest hominin ancestors, *Australopithecus afarensis* (3 Ma) to our own species, *Homo sapiens*. With the exception of the large-bodied robust australopiths, which averaged ca. 525 ml in brain volume, the earliest hominins, such as *A. afarensis* and *A. africanus,* had brain volumes ranging from 375 ml to ca. 485 ml. When the genus *Homo* appears, currently dated at ca. 2–1.8 Ma, the brain volume increases dramatically to ca. 750 ml, as represented by the KNM-ER 1470 *Homo habilis* specimen. At this time, there is certain evidence for stone-tool making, hunting, and scavenging behavioral activities, and archaeological sites suggesting complex social activities. The endocasts show three interesting developments: volume increase to ca. 750 ml (and, one supposes, an increase in relative brain size), asymmetries of the cerebral cortex suggesting right-handedness, and a more complex humanlike pattern of the third inferior convolution, which includes the famous area of Broca that helps control the motor aspects of sound production. Unfortunately, the posterior portion of the endocast, which contains Wernicke's region and is associated with receptive sound functions and intermodal associations, seldom if ever shows convolutional details that would permit one to conclude that these hominins possessed language. Some of this increase in brain volume must surely have been related to

an increase in body size from the earlier smaller-bodied australopiths. Exactly how much was an allometric increase related to body size, and how much beyond that relationship, is simply unknown. From the time of *Homo erectus* on (i.e., at least 1.6 Ma), the endocasts of hominins do not show any primitive features, but rather a more or less constant growth in brain volume from ca. 800 ml to our present average of ca. 1,400 ml. This increase in brain size probably did not come about through allometry, as the body sizes of *Homo erectus*, at least as judged by the recent Nariokotome youth (KNM-WT 15000) found in Kenya, were already comparable to modern humans. Neanderthals had slightly larger brains than modern humans, but this curious fact is perhaps explained as a part of an allometric relationship to lean body mass and perhaps cold-adaptation. Thus, it appears that some of the increases in brain volume were allometric while other increases were not, and that the evolution of the human brain resulted through different selection pressures at different times, another example of complex mosaic evolution in hominin lines.

Evidence from Comparative Neuroanatomy

This line of indirect evidence is essential to our understanding of human brain evolution, a statement, incidentally, that could be made for any animal from aardvarks to zebras. While much is known about the naturalistic behavior of many species of animals, and each has a set of species-specific behavioral repertoires for adapting to its environment, the science of explaining species-specific behavior based on the structure and functioning of the brain is in its infancy. Consider the wide range of behavioral differences among living primates, such as lemurs, tarsiers, New and Old World monkeys, the chimpanzee, gorilla, orangutan, and gibbon: None of these behavioral differences can yet be related to respective brain organizations. As dog breeds are perhaps more familiar to us, it is interesting to reflect that, while enormous differences in breed behavior are known, none of the behavioral variation has been correlated with neuroanatomical differences. What are the magic variates that surely must link the two levels? Brain size, taken alone, has little explanatory power in this regard, yet it is obviously an important starting point. Indeed, considerable progress has been made through allometric studies that treat brain size as a dependent variable and in which relationships are then made to body weight, metabolism, gestation duration, longevity, and, in some cases, broad ecological domains relating to subsistence patterns such as folivory, frugivory, omnivory, and predation. But the brain is a complex organ, consisting of many different neural cell masses and interconnecting fiber tracts, many of which are differentially susceptible to hormonal secretions and environmental stimuli. Within Mammalia, it is a stark truism that all mammals have the same brain components: there are no new parts (nuclei or fiber systems) to distinguish among genera within orders or among orders. Thus, not only does brain size vary in animals, but so do the quantitative relationships among components of the brain and the ontogenetic, developmental sequences of DNA-RNA interactions that specify the development of different brain regions and

Table 1. Endocranial (brain) volumes of reconstructed hominins

Specimen	Taxon	Region	Volume (ml)	Method	Evaluation
AL 333–45	*A. afarensis*	E. Africa	485–500	C	2
AL 162–28	"	"	375–400	est.	2
AL 333–105	"	"	310–320	C	2
L 338y–6	*A. africanus ?*	"	427	C	2
Taung	*A. africanus*	S. Africa	440*	A	1
STS 60	"	"	428	A	1
STS 71	"	"	428	C	2–3
STS 19/58	"	"	436	B	2
STS 5	"	"	485	A	1
MLD 37/38	"	"	435	D	1
MLD 1	"	"	500–520	B	3
SK 1585	*P. robustus*	"	530	A	1
KNM-WT 17000	*P. aethiopicus?*	E. Africa	410	A	1
KNM-ER 13750	*P. boisei*	"	475	A	1
OH 5	"	"	530	A	1
KNM-ER 406	"	"	525	D	2
KNM-ER 407	"	"	510	A	1
KNM-ER 732	"	"	500	A	1
KNM-ER 1805	*H. ?*	"	582	A	1
KNM-ER 1813	*H. habilis*	"	510	A	1
KNM-ER 1470	*H. rudolfensis*	"	752	A	1
OH 7	*H. habilis*	"	687	B	1
OH 13	"	"	650	A	1
OH 24	"	"	590	A	2–3
KNM-ER 3732	"	"	600–650	est.	3
OH 9	*H. erectus ?*	"	1067	A	1
KNM-ER 1590	"	"	min. 800	est.	3
KNM-ER 3733	"	"	848	A	1
KNM-ER 3883	"	"	804	A	1
KNM-WT 15000	*H. erectus*	"	900	X	1
Trinil 1(1892)	"	Indonesia	953	A	1
Sangiran 1 (1937)	"	"	815	A	1
Sangiran 4 (1938)	"	"	900	C	2–3
Sangiran [ ] (1963) Pith 6	"	"	855	A	2
Sangiran 17 (1965)	"	"	1059	C	1–2
Sangiran [ ] (1969) Pith 8	"	"	1004	A	1
Sambungmachan 1	"	"	1035	X	2
Modjokerto 1 (child)	"	"	est. 550–575	A	1
Lantian 2	"	China	780	X	2
Zhoukoudian II	"	"	1030	X	2
Zhoukoudian III	"	"	915*	X	2
Zhoukoudian V	"	"	1140	X	2
Zhoukoudian VI	"	"	850	X	2
Zhoukoudian X	"	"	1225	X	2
Zhoukoudian XI	"	"	1015	X	2
Zhoukoudian XII	"	"	1030	X	2
Hexian	*H. erectus*	"	1025	X	3
Solo I	*H. erectus* (or? archaic *H. sap.*)	Indonesia	1172	A	1
Solo V	"	"	1250	A	1
Solo VI	"	"	1013	A	1
Solo IX	"	"	1135	X	3
Solo X	"	"	1231	A	1
Solo XI	"	"	1090	A	1
Kabwe (Rhodesian)	"Archaic *Homo sapiens?*"	S. Africa	1285	X	1

continues

Table 1. *Continued*

Specimen	Taxon	Region	Volume (ml)	Method	Evaluation
Sale	"	N. Africa	880	A	1
Laetoli 18	"Archaic *Homo sapiens*"	E. Africa	1367	X	1
Eyasi	"	"	1285	X	3
Lake Ndutu	"	"	1100	X	1
Saldhana	"	S. Africa	1225	X	3
Narmada	"	India	1200	X	3
Dali	"	China	1120	X	2
Yinkou	"	"	1390	X	3
Vértesszöllös II	"	Europe	1325	X	3
Reilingen	"	"	1430	A	2
Steinheim	"	"	1225	X	1
Swanscombe	"	"	1325	X	2
Fontachevade	"	"	1350	X	3
Ehringsdorf	"	"	1450	X	2
Biache	"	"	1200	X	3
Petralona	"	"	1230	X	2
Arago 21	"	"	1150	A	2
Monte Circeo I	*H. sapiens neanderthalensis?*	"	1552	X	2
Saccopastore I	"	"	1200	X	2
Saccopastore II	"	"	1300	X	2
Spy I	*H. sapiens neanderthalensis*	"	1553	A	1
Spy II	"	"	1305	A	1
LaChapelle	"	"	1625	X	1
La Ferassie I	"	"	1640	X	1
Neanderthal	"	"	1525	X	1
La Quina V	"	"	1172	X	1
Le Moustier	"	"	1352	X	2
Atapuerca 4	"	"	1390	X	2
Atapuerca 5	"	"	1125	X	2
Krapina B	"	"	1450	X	3
Krapina C	"	"	1200	X	3
Krapina D	"	"	1450	X	3
Gibraltar I	"	"	1200	X	1
Ganovce	"	"	1320	X	3
Jebel Irhoud I	"	S.W. Asia	1305	A	1
Tabun I	"	"	1271	X	2
Skuhl IV	" ?	"	1554	X	2
Skuhl V	" ?	"	1520	X	1
Skuhl IX	" ?	"	1590	X	2
Amud	*H. sapiens neanderthalensis*	"	1740	X	1
Shanidar I	"	"	1600	X	1
Cro-Magnon	*H. sapiens sapiens*	"	1590	X	1
Chancelade	"	"	1530	X	2
Oberkassel	"	"	1500	X	2
Predmosti III	"	"	1580	X	2
Predmosti IV	"	"	1250	X	2
Predmosti IX	"	"	1555	X	2
Predmosti X	"	"	1452	X	2
Brno I	"	"	1600	X	2
Qafzeh VI	"	M. East	1568	X	2
Border Cave	"	S. Africa	1510	X	3
Omo II	" ?	E. Africa	1435	X	2

Cranial capacities in ml for selected hominin crania. An asterisk (*) refers to estimated adult volume from a juvenile or child's endocast. The values were obtained by one of four methods: (A) direct water displacement of either a full or a hemiendocast with minimal distortion and plasticene reconstruction; (B) partial endocast determination as described by Tobias (1971); (C) extensive plasticene reconstruction amounting to half of total endocast; (D) volume calculated from regression formula or estimated on the basis of a few measurements. X refers to previously published values, either confirmed or not by the author. The reliability of these values is evaluated on a scale of 1 to 3, where 1 indicates the highest reliability, and 3 the lowest depending on endocast completeness, distortion, and methods.

Table 2. Selected primate brain and body weights and EQs (encephalization quotients)

Taxon	Mean Body Weight (g)	Mean Brain Weight (g)	EQ1 Homocentric—As % of *Homo*	EQ2—All Primates	EQ2—As % of *Homo*
Microcebus murinus	53.0	1.81	0.138	0.887	0.299
Cheirogaleus major	417.3	6.90	0.137	0.700	0.236
Lemur catta	1780.3	21.99	0.171	0.738	0.249
Eulemur mongoz	1653.8	23.68	0.193	0.841	0.284
Daubentonia madagascarensis	2203.5	44.05	0.298	1.257	0.424
Loris tardigradus	267.1	6.67	0.178	0.951	0.321
Perodicticus potto	932.8	13.23	0.156	0.727	0.246
Galago senegalensis	161.0	4.43	0.164	0.928	0.313
Tarsius spectrum	175.0	4.65	0.163	0.915	0.309
Saguinus oedipus	302.0	9.68	0.238	1.256	0.424
Cebus capucinus	2340.0	72.51	0.472	1.976	0.667
Saimiri sciureus	446.6	22.12	0.422	2.131	0.719
Aotus trivirgatus	706.5	16.69	0.236	1.133	0.382
Callicebus moloch	669.0	15.95	0.234	1.129	0.381
Ateles geoffroyi	7944.8	108.98	0.321	1.169	0.395
Macaca fascicularis	4332.8	69.72	0.304	1.188	0.401
Macaca mulatta	5688.2	91.34	0.334	1.265	0.427
Macaca nemestrina	6567.0	103.64	0.345	1.286	0.434
Cercocebus albigena	7064.3	99.76	0.317	1.171	0.395
Papio hamadryas anubis	24780.0	196.20	0.276	0.884	0.298
Papio hamadryas hamadryas	13833.3	175.67	0.361	1.235	0.417
Papio hamadryas ursinus	18294.5	175.27	0.300	0.996	0.336
Cercopithecus aethiops	3226.6	67.69	0.357	1.444	0.487
Miopithecus talapoin	1040.3	39.70	0.437	2.007	0.677
Erythrocebus patas	5350.0	97.33	0.370	1.412	0.483
Procolobus badius	6581.2	77.33	0.257	0.958	0.323
Hylobates agilis	5890.0	90.20	0.322	1.216	0.411
Hylobates lar	5698.4	102.16	0.373	1.412	0.477
Hylobates moloch	5915.1	93.37	0.333	1.255	0.424
Hylobates syndactylus	11684.5	132.63	0.304	1.061	0.358
Pongo pygmaeus	52140.4	346.46	0.301	0.886	0.299
Pan troglodytes	41250.6	378.00	0.382	1.155	0.523
Gorilla gorilla	93095.0	454.11	0.270	0.746	0.252
Homo sapiens	62772.2	1334.41	1.000	2.962	1.000

The regressions are based on 85 species including Homo sapiens *(data from H. Stephan). Two different approaches to EQ are used. The* homocentric *EQ1 values are calculated by using the equation,*

$$EQ_{HOMO} = \text{brain weight/body weight}^{0.64906}$$

in which the animal's body weight is raised to the 0.64906 power.

This exponent is derived from drawing a line connecting the average brain and body weight values for Homo *(1330, 65,000 g) and the origin (0,0) on a log base 10 graph. This makes the coefficient 1.0, and resulting EQ is expressed as a percent of the human value, which is the highest among all mammals.*

The EQ2 values were calculated using the equation,

$$EQ2 = .0091 \times \text{brain weight/body weight}^{0.76237}$$

The column "EQ2 as % of Homo" simply divides EQ2 by 2.962, the value for Homo. *As can be seen, these values are sometimes very much higher than the homocentric EQ1 values. These values show that the intervals between the values are arbitrary in the case of EQ2. There is no reason to believe that the squirrel monkey (Saimiri sciureus) should have an EQ that is 71.9% of Homo's. This illustrates well the "relativity of relative brain measures."*

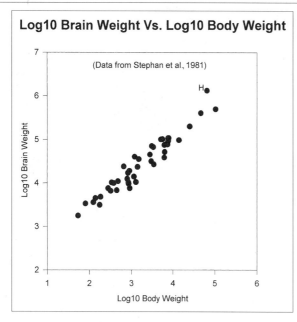

Log10 Brain Weight Vs. Log10 Body Weight

(Data from Stephan et al., 1981)

A log-log (base 10) plot of the mean brain and body weights for 85 species of primates, including Homo sapiens, *from data kindly provided by Dr. Heinz Stephan, Max Planck Institute for Brain Research. The H is the human value, and the closest three are chimpanzee, gorilla, and orangutan. The correlation coefficient without* Homo *is 0.97, and the human value for the brain is about three times higher than would be predicted for a primate of its body weight. The slope of the regression line is about 0.76 without* Homo. *This value suggests a metabolic constraint between body weight and the weight of the brain. It should be remembered that the points in this figure are for a large number of primate taxa. If these data points are plotted within different taxonomic categories (i.e., prosimians alone, New World monkeys alone, etc.) each group would scale somewhat differently, usually with a slope of about 0.66. This latter exponent suggests a geometric relationship between surface area and volume (i.e., the ratio 2/3). Thus, the calculated encephalization coefficients (EQs) are "relative," as each species value depends on the allometric equation used. Courtesy of Ralph Holloway.*

their underlying neurotransmitter substances. Humans are not the only animals that have asymmetrical brain regions: Almost all animals have asymmetries to varying degrees, and some, like certain birds, have a seasonal sensitivity to increases and reductions of certain nuclei related to song patterns. In the human case, however, it is probably both the kind and the degree of cortical asymmetries that are distinctive.

As mentioned above, in our own species the brain accounts for ca. 2 percent of our total body weight but uses close to 20 percent of our metabolism at any given moment. It is a voracious organ. Thanks to recent allometric studies, it appears that the relationship between brain and body size is constrained more strongly by metabolic factors than by surface-area/volume relationships as was once popularly believed. Thus, when the log (base 10) values of brain size and body weight are plotted together, the resulting slope is usually close to 0.75 rather than 0.66. This is for the order as a whole; in plotting the values for superfamilies or lower-level taxa (e.g., families), the slope is ca. 0.66. In general, the slope decreases as the taxonomic units become more specific, until, within a species such as ours, the slope is ca. 0.25.

Shown here is one such plot based on 85 species of primates from data kindly supplied by Dr. Heinz Stephan. The

human value is clearly an "outlier" in this plot and has a brain volume (or weight) roughly three times that expected for a primate of this body size. The gorilla value is lower than expected, and, indeed, one can go through the list of primates and find differences between predicted and observed values of greater than 100 percent. The point here is that the slope of 0.75, reflecting metabolic factors, is not a *law,* but a *constraint,* around which species vary. The picture becomes more complex when individual parts of the brain are plotted against brain weight for different species of primates, and such data provide a basis for understanding differences in brain organization among primate species.

Usually, brain components scale closely to total brain weight, and predicted and observed values differ by less than 10 percent. The cerebral cortex and the cerebellum are two good examples of this. The differences between expected and observed values are, for *Homo sapiens,* only 0.33 percent and 6.5 percent, respectively, when based on a sample of 44 primate species excluding *Homo.* There are, however, some extraordinary departures from predicted values for certain brain structures, and one of these in particular is important to a fuller understanding of human brain evolution and of the importance of certain key fossil hominin endocasts in showing *Homo*-like derived, rather than pongidlike retained, primitive characteristics. As the second plot shows, the volume of primary visual striate cortex (area 17 of Brodmann) is some 120 percent *less than expected* in the human primate with our brain size. Similarly, the lateral geniculate body of the epithalamus shows a reduction of 140 percent + from the predicted or expected volume of this nucleus based on allometry within the Anthropoidea. These deviations should make us wary that all size differences can be explained through allometry alone. Both the primary visual striate cortex and the lateral geniculate nucleus are important components of our visual system. This relative decrease in *Homo* probably meant that there was a relative *increase* in parietal association cortex during human evolution. The real question is, when did this occur?

The third figure shows a lateral view of chimpanzee and human brains. In the posterior part of the cerebral cortex is found the *lunate sulcus,* which represents the most anterior boundary of purely sensory cortex: the *primary visual striate cortex.* Anterior to this cortex is what we commonly call the *association cortex* of the parietal and temporal lobes, a region of complex intermodality association and cognitive functioning, which happens to include, at least in humans, Wernicke's area. Based on the same sample of 45 primate species, the human primary visual striate cortex subserving vision is roughly −121 percent less than expected for a primate of this brain size. This fact does not mean that our visual sense is functionally reduced but rather that there has been a compensatory increase in the relative amount of parietal and temporal-lobe association cortex. The ventricles of the brain, which in the fetal stages provide the neuroblasts that become part of the 10 billion neurons making up the adult cerebral cortex, are ca. 52 percent greater than expected on the basis of allometry. Some neural structures deviate from expected values by as much as 7,000 percent. These departures from

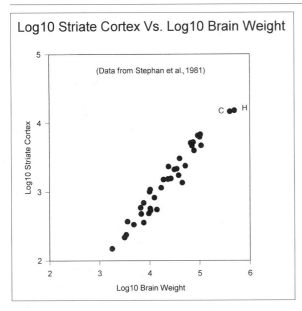

Log10 Striate Cortex Vs. Log10 Brain Weight

(Data from Stephan et al., 1981)

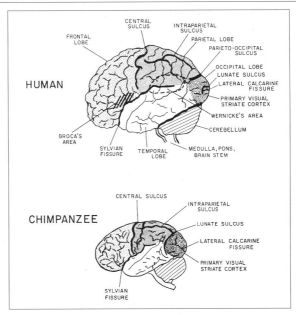

The figure shows the log-log (base 10) relationship between the volume of primate visual striate cortex, area 17 of Brodmann, against the mean weight of the brain for 37 species of primates, including Homo, shown as H. The regression has a correlation coefficient of about 0.97 without the human value. The human value is over 121 percent lower than would be predicted for a primate with its brain weight. Most other differences between observed and predicted values are around 10–25 percent, and are mostly explained by statistical error from small samples. The Homo difference, however, is quite large and is paralleled by the same result when the volume of the lateral geniculate nucleus of the thalamus is regressed against brain weight. In this case the human value is over 140 percent lower than would be predicted. The two neuroanatomical systems are intimately related. As the human primate has no loss of vision compared to other primates, these results suggest that during evolution there was either a relative reduction in primary visual striate cortex (area 17) in the human brain or a relative increase in parietal association cortex. The major question, of course, is when did the reduction occur in the course of hominoid evolution? Courtesy of Ralph Holloway.

The brains of chimpanzee (below) and human in lateral view. Although the human brain is some three to four times heavier than the chimpanzee brain, there is considerable similarity between the two species with regard to the convolutional details. The human brain has more convolutions and considerable variation of its gyri (hills) and sulci (valleys), particularly in the parietal and frontal lobes, but the primary and secondary gyri and sulci are the same between the two species. Of considerable interest to those studying the paleoneurology of our fossil ancestors are the sulci labeled the lunate, the intraparietal, the sylvian, and the lateral calcarine. In apes, such as the chimpanzee, the lunate sulcus is always present and is the anterior boundary of the primary visual striate cortex, which subserves visual functions. The intraparietal sulcus, in its posterior part, always terminates against the lunate sulcus and divides the parietal portion of the cerebral cortex into superior and inferior lobules. The calcarine fissure always runs medial to lateral but terminates before it reaches the lunate sulcus. When a lunate sulcus appears in the human brain, it is in a very posterior position, relative to where it can be found in other apes. As the figures for the volume of visual striate cortex discussed in the text indicate, the human brain has relatively less of this cortex making up its cerebrum than does the ape brain. This means that the relative amount of parietal "association" cortex has increased in the human species. The challenge is to document when such change took place in hominid evolution. Unfortunately endocasts seldom show the convolutions that existed in the brain. The central sulcus divides the frontal from the parietal lobe and functionally marks the separation between the mainly motor anterior gyrus and the posterior sensory gyrus. Both the inferior third frontal convolution (with Broca's area) and the posterior temporal and middle parietal lobes (containing Wernicke's area) appear more convoluted in the human species and have important relationships to both the motor and sensory (receptive) aspects of communication by language. These particular regions are seldom well preserved on fossil endocasts and are areas of considerable interpretive controversy among paleoneurologists. Courtesy of Ralph Holloway.

allometric expectations could very well provide interesting clues about which structures in the human brain might have undergone significant evolutionary change.

Comparative studies of the brain provide other clues about the evolution of our major organ of adaptation, of which three can be briefly mentioned: encephalization, asymmetries of cortical hemispheres, and sexual dimorphism of the brain.

Encephalization has two meanings in comparative neurology. First, it refers to evidence that in the course of evolution the cerebral cortex has taken on more functions and that the organization of the cortex is more susceptible to debilitating damage through injuries. A second, more recent meaning of encephalization refers to a ratio in which an animal's brain weight is divided by an allometric equation derived from a particular taxon. For example, the equation

$$EQ = .0991 \times \text{brain weight}/(\text{body weight})^{0.76237}$$

provides an *encephalization quotient* (EQ), in which the denominator is the allometric equation based on 88 species of primates. In this case, using an average brain weight for *Homo sapiens* of 1,300 gm, the EQ is 2.87. For the chimpanzee and the gorilla, the EQs are 1.14 and 0.75, respec-

tively. If an allometric equation for insectivores were used, the human, chimpanzee, and gorilla EQs would be 28.8, 11.3, and 6.67, respectively. The important points here are twofold: first, the human animal always has the highest EQ regardless of the denominator; second, the EQ values and their relative values among species can vary by as much as 20 percent. When these equations are applied to fossil hominins, their relative closeness to modern humans or to our ape cousins, such as chimpanzees, will vary depending on the basal equation chosen. This is known as the *relativity* of relative brain measures.

Since the human animal apparently has the highest EQ value among mammals, we can use a *homocentric* equation, in which *Homo sapiens* has the highest value of 1.0, or 100 percent. This equation appears as follows:

$$EQ_{HOMO} = \text{brain weight/body weight}^{0.64906}$$

This equation is derived by drawing a line through the average log (base 10) values of modern *Homo* to the origin point of zero brain and body weights. The advantage of this equation is that all other animal EQs are expressed as a direct percentage of the human value. For example, the chimpanzee EQ is 0.39 (39 percent) and the gorilla value 0.23 (23 percent). Unfortunately, it is a matter of taste as to which EQ equation one selects, or which groups or taxa one wishes to compare and discuss. To work out the EQs for particular hominin fossils requires an accurate knowledge of both brain and body weights, and the latter values must necessarily be guessed. A single EQ value for a particular fossil hominin tells us nothing about how the EQ varied within the species. In general, australopiths show slightly higher EQ values than do chimpanzees, but not by very much.

Asymmetries of the cerebral cortex, while existing in animals other than humans, do not show the *pattern* that is most often expressed in our own species. Humans are mostly right-handed (numbering up to ca. 87–90 percent of most populations), and both the motor and the sensory regions involved in symbolic language are dominant on the left side of the cerebral cortex. Evidence from the neurosciences shows that the left hemisphere controls symbolic parsing and cognitive tasks mediated by symbols. The right hemisphere appears to have more control over gestalt appreciation of visuospatial relationships, facial recognition, and emotions. While only sophisticated neurological examinations of the working brain show this, it is well known that the gross appearance of the cerebral hemispheres is highly correlated with handedness and thus with cerebral dominance. *Petalias* are extensions of parts of the cerebral cortex extending beyond their counterparts on the other side of the brain. For example, in most right-handers the classical petalial pattern is for a longer left occipital pole, a broader left parietal region, and a broader right frontal width. True left-handers and many mixed-handers show the opposite pattern. While other primates, particularly the gorilla, do show some asymmetries, they rarely show the combined torquelike petalial pattern described above for humans. There is also a lack of any clear-cut data demonstrating handedness (rather than preference) for other primates. It is thus an intriguing fact that fossil hominins show overwhelmingly the human petalial pattern, and N. Toth has discovered that many of the early stone tools were apparently made by right-handers. Some of the australopith fossil endocasts show a petalial pattern that suggests right-handedness, despite their pongidlike brain sizes. It is possible that the brain evolved some modernlike human patterns of organization early in hominin evolution before the great expansion of brain size, although this is a controversial area.

Sexual dimorphism of the human brain can be found in the anterior hypothalamus and in the corpus callosum, through which pass most of the fiber tracts that interconnect the two cerebral hemispheres. Females show a larger splenial portion (which integrates the two occipital, parietal, and temporal regions of the cortices) than do males, when both are corrected for brain size. The corpus callosum is the only brain structure to show a very different pattern between male and female brains. Almost all structures of the brain (i.e., the cerebellum, the septum, the hippocampus, the striatum, etc.) are larger in males than in females, and significantly so. The corpus callosum, however, is roughly equal in absolute size between the sexes. When these structures are related to brain weight, however, there are no significant differences between males and females, *except* in the corpus callosum, which is *relatively* larger in females, and the differences are usually statistically significant. Given the cultural variability of most modern societies, this small anatomical difference probably does not have much significance in different cognitive-task abilities between our two sexes. It is more interesting to consider these differences (which are apparent by 26 weeks prenatal) as evolutionary residua from past selection pressures that may have favored a complementary behavioral adaptation between males and females for the increased period of social and maternal nurturance of longer-growing offspring.

Summary

Summarizing all of the changes that may have taken place over 3–4 Myr of human brain evolution is a speculative matter. Table 3 provides but an outline of how these changes might have interdigitated. The earliest australopiths (e.g., Taung and the Hadar 162–28 *A. afarensis*) already show evidence for cerebral reorganization in that the lunate sulcus is in a posterior position, suggesting that the posterior parietal association cortex had increased beyond the ape level. Cerebral asymmetries are also present, but these are more strongly represented in early *Homo*, whose appearance coincides with a major expansion of brain size (to ca. 750 ml from 450 ml) at ca. 2 Ma. Coincident with these patterns are stone tools and evidence for hunting and scavenging. The remaining doubling of size, to ca. 1,400 ml, is perhaps best explained through a combination of allometric and nonallometric processes in which natural selection favored increased body size, longer periods of childhood growth, and, one assumes, more sophisticated brains capable of more sophisticated social behavior. While this basic scenario fits well within our popular conceptions of mosaic evolution, it would be wise to remember that there were mosaics within the mosaic, and the brain has always been an important part of human adaptation whatever its size at various phases of hominid evolution. It is pointless to say that bipedalism evolved first, then brains. A complex musculoskeletal set of such adjustments as attend bipedalism could not evolve in a nervous vacuum, nor does the structural adaptation hold much meaning without reference to behavioral function. Thus, the evolution of the brain can only be understood not just in the context of its size, the reorganization of its components, and its asymmetries but in the context of the total range of the ecological and behavioral record that is associated with the actual fossil hominin discoveries.

Table 3. Summary of reorganizational and size changes in the evolution of the hominin brain

Brain Changes, Specimens	Taxa	Time
(1) Reduction of volume of area 17, primary visual striate cortex; relative increase in posterior parietal association cortex. AL 162–28 has a posterior position of the lunate sulcus.	*A. afarensis*	by 3.5–3 Ma
(2) Small increase in brain size, probably allometric, to 400–450 ml.	*A. africanus*	3–2.5 Ma
(3)Reorganization of frontal lobe, increase in cerebral asymmetries. Major increase in brain size of 250–300 ml. KNM-ER 1470.	*H. habilis/ rudolfensis*	2.5–1.9 Ma
(4) Modest allometric increase in brain size, to 750–900 ml, and increase in cerebral asymmetries. *H. erectus* brain casts, incl. KNM-WT 15000 youth.	*H. erectus*	1.9–1.6 Ma
(5) Modest increase in brain size, 300 ml, *neanderthalensis* to 1200–1700 ml, and refinements in cortical organization to a modern *Homo* pattern. Archaic *Homo* endocasts.	*H. sapiens*	200–100 Ka
(6) Small allometric reduction in brain size among modern *Homo sapiens*. Modern range of cranial capacities.	*H. sapiens sapiens*	after 100 Ka

See also Allometry; Anthropoidea; Archaic Homo sapiens; Australopithecus; Hominoidea; Homo; Homo erectus; Homo sapiens; Neanderthals; Primates; Skull; Speech (Origins of). [R.L.H.]

Further Readings

Bryden, M.P. (1982) Laterality: Functional Asymmetry in the Intact Brain. New York: Academic.

Connolly, C.J. (1950) External Morphology of the Primate Brain. Springfield, Ill.: Thomas.

Damasio, A.R., and Geschwind, N. (1984) The neural basis for language. Ann. Rev. Neurosci. 7:127–147.

de Lacoste-Utamsing, M.C., and Holloway, R.L. (1982) Sexual dimorphism in the corpus callosum. Science 216:1431–1432.

Geschwind, N., and Galaburda, A.M., eds. (1984) Cerebral Dominance: The Biological Foundations. Cambridge, Mass.: Harvard University Press.

Holloway, R.L. (1975) The Role of Human Social Behavior in the Evolution of the Human Brain. Forty-third James Arthur Lecture. New York: American Museum of Natural History.

Holloway, R.L. (1978) The relevance of endocasts for studying primate brain evolution. In C.R. Noback (ed.): Sensory Systems in Primates. New York: Plenum, pp. 181–200.

Holloway, R.L., and de Lacoste-Lareymondie, M.C. (1982) Brain endocast asymmetry in pongids and hominids: Some preliminary findings on the paleontology of cerebral dominance. Am. J. Phys. Anthropol. 58:101–110.

Holloway, R.L., Anderson, P., Defidine, R., and Harper, C. (1994) Sexual dimorphism in the human corpus callosum from three independent autopsy samples: Relative size of the corpus callosum. Am. J. Phys. Anthropol. 92:481–498.

Kinsbourne, M., ed. (1978) Asymmetrical Function of the Brain. Cambridge: Cambridge University Press.

LeMay, M. (1976) Morphological asymmetries of modern man, fossil man, and nonhuman primates. Ann. N.Y. Acad. Sci. 280:349–366.

Martin, R.D. (1983) Human Evolution in an Ecological Context. Fifty-second James Arthur Lecture. New York: American Museum of Natural History.

Passingham, R.E. (1982) The Human Primate. Oxford: Freeman.

Radinsky, L.B. (1979) The Fossil Record of Primate Brain Evolution. Forty-seventh James Arthur Lecture. New York: American Museum of Natural History.

Stephan, H., Frahm, H., and Baron, G. (1981) New and revised data on volumes of brain structures in insectivores and primates. Folia Primatol. 35:1–29.

Tobias, P.V. (1971) The Brain in Hominid Evolution. New York: Columbia University Press.

Branisellinae

Extinct subfamily of cebid platyrrhine monkeys including *Branisella boliviana* and *Szalatavus attricuspis* (if the latter is a distinct taxon). These are the oldest and most archaic ateloid primates, known from the Late Oligocene Bolivian deposit at La Salla, which has been dated to ca. 27 Ma. Braniselline upper molars are in part morphologically conservative, although they do resemble those of the cebine *Saimiri*. The lower jaw is very shallow, as in the relatively primitive parapithecid anthropoids.

See also Anthropoidea; Cebidae; Parapithecidae; Platyrrhini. [A.L.R.]

Further Readings

Rosenberger, A.L., Hartwig, W., and Wolff, R. (1991) *Szalatavus attricuspis*, an early platyrrhine primate. Folia Primatol. 56:225–233.

Takai, M., and Anaya, F. (1996) New specimens of the oldest fossil platyrrhine, *Branisella boliviana*, from Salla, Bolivia. Am. J. Phys. Anthropol. 99:301–317.

Breccia Cave Formation

Breccia, as the Italian word suggests, refers to rocks composed of broken fragments that show little abrasion or rounding effects of transportation. The term is applied to all volcanic, metamorphic, and sedimentary deposits with this texture. The South African australopith-bearing deposits are examples of limestone breccias, consisting of angular chunks of limestone and interstitial sand, frozen into a solid mass by impregnations of limy cement. The deposits at the Transvaal sites of Kromdraai, Makapansgat, Sterkfontein, and Swartkrans are partially unroofed remnants of breccia-filled caves that formed in dolomitic limestone; the breccias at Taung (Botswana), however, were formed by cementation of a talus fan below a cliff in the dolomite of the Gaap (or Kaap) Escarpment along the

southeastern margin of the Kalahari Desert. Primate-bearing cave breccias are also known farther north at Gcwihaba and at Berg Aukas (Namibia) and Leba (Angola).

Generally speaking, breccia-filled caves begin with subterranean dissolution of susceptible formations. By far the most common of the cavern-forming rocks are carbonates (sedimentary limestones and dolomites, biogenic reef complexes, metamorphic marbles, hydrothermal tufas, igneous carbonatites), but cavernous salt and gypsum breccias are known as well. Cave formation usually begins with solution of the surrounding rock where infiltrating, relatively undersaturated surface water reaches the water table. When the water table drops (due to regional uplift, drought, or deepening incision of the landscape), surface cracks and sinkholes may admit circulating air to the empty chamber. This leads to the formation of stalactitic and/or stalagmitic travertines, or dripstones, through evaporation in the caves. When caves become more open to the surface through time, freshwater dissolution will be more active, and sands and other debris—including bones—may wash into deeper recesses and fissures, while blocks and smaller fragments will spall away from the weakened walls and ceilings to mix with the rest. Cementation of breccia bodies takes place wherever chemical conditions in this environment of constant solution and precipitation are favorable, and not necessarily in all parts of the cave.

It commonly happens that where breccias are solidifying, the growing mass may become so extensive as to choke the opening through which the talus of broken rock, sand, and debris was being washed in. As conditions change, a new solution channel may form a shaft through the limestone breccia, and a new cycle of deposition and calcification may begin. By the same token, as unroofing continues, vertical avenues may open, and younger, surface-derived material

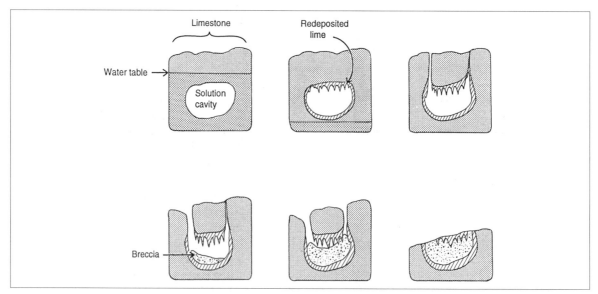

Sketch of successive stages (left to right, top then bottom) in the development of a breccia cave in limestone country rock, as in the australopith-yielding sites. A solution cavity forms below the local water table; when the water table falls, water filtering through the rock may form a lime crust on the exposed inner wall of the cavity. Joints and cracks in the limestone massif may open to the surface through solution and climatic effects, which allows sediment (including skeletal parts) to enter the cave; this mass becomes cemented as limy matrix is dissolved and redeposited. In some cases, the cave may fill in one or more cycles; more rarely, part of the fill may be eroded away and a new generation(s) breccia be deposited above, below, or alongside previous material (as at Swartkrans). The cave roof may collapse down on top of the breccia fill. Often the last stage will be erosion of the overlying limestone hill, exposing the filled cavity to excavators.

may build up layers on the original breccia mass. In the final stages of erosion of cavernous rocks, breccia-filled chambers and fissures are exposed at the surface as pits, and eventually only the floor of the cave may remain as a thin plastering of breccia on a hillside.

A complex succession of dissolution, filling, cementation, secondary decalcification, erosion, and re-cementation is possible in each cycle of breccia formation, and there may be several cycles in any given cave system. Variations in surface conditions, in the form of long-term climate and vegetational changes, or local geological events that might affect the chemistry and amount of percolating rainwater as well as the regional hydrology, have been cited in attempts to synchronize the succession of events preserved in the breccia formations, but accurate stratigraphic interpretation under such circumstances is always difficult.

See also Africa, Southern; Kromdraai; Makapansgat; Sterkfontein; Swartkrans; Taung. [F.E.G., J.A.V.C.]

Further Readings

Brain, C.K. (1958) The Transvaal ape-man-bearing cave deposits. Transvaal Mus. Mem. 11:1–131.

Brain, C.K. (1976) A re-interpretation of the Swartkrans site and its remains. S. Afr. J. Sci. 72:141–146.

Breuil, [Abbé] Henri [Edward Prosper] (1877–1961)

French archaeologist. Breuil became interested in Paleolithic art and prehistoric archaeology soon after being ordained in 1897 and rapidly established himself as a leading authority in both areas. He was a professor at the Muséum National d'Histoire Naturelle from 1910 and at the Collège de France from 1929 to 1947. Among his many contributions to the development of prehistoric archaeology was his enduring paper "Les Subdivisions du Paléolithique supérieur et leur signification" (1912), in which he elaborated on G. de Mortillet's earlier (coarse) division of the Upper Paleolithic into the Aurignacian, the Solutrean, and the Magdalenian. Breuil's name is also associated with a number of major European Paleolithic sites, including Altamira, Spain (1906) and Genista Cave, Gibraltar (1922). He was also associated briefly during the early 1930s with the excavations at Zhoukoudian; later, the Chinese archaeologist Bei Wenzhong (1904–1982) (also known as W.C. Pei) studied under him in Paris, receiving his Ph.D. in archaeology in 1938.

See also Altamira; Mortillet, Gabriel de; Paleolithic; Paleolithic Image; Zhoukoudian. [F.S.]

Further Readings

Broderick, A.H. (1963) Father of Prehistory: The Abbé Henri Breuil: His Life and Times. New York: Morrow.

Broad-Spectrum Revolution

Concept advanced by L.R. Binford and K.V. Flannery in the 1960s suggesting that late Upper Palaeolithic people gradually shifted their subsistence base from a reliance on large migratory animals to a broader spectrum of wild foods, including small game, fish, turtles, seasonal water fowl, invertebrates (crabs, mussels, snails), and plant foods (cereal grasses), starting ca. 20 Ka, a process that ultimately led to increased sedentism, population growth, and domestication in both southwestern Asia and Mesoamerica. Such a shift may have occurred because an ameliorating climate and rising sea levels made new resources more readily available to growing human populations and/or because large migratory species disappeared, either because of environmental changes or because of overexploitation by human beings.

Archaeological evidence in the 1980s and 1990s, however, suggests that the timing and the pace of the shift may have differed and that the basic diet did not actually broaden. The sudden appearance of plant remains and processing tools in the southern Levant during the Early Natufian (ca. 12–10.5 Ka) suggests that changes in food resources occurred several millennia later and more rapidly than previously thought. While a wider range of exploitable foods (e.g., molluscs, fish, waterfowl) appear at archaeological sites, faunal and botanical distributions suggest that people still got most of their daily protein needs from only one or two species (e.g., gazelle, wheat, barley). Instead of diversifying, then, Early Holocene collectors may have actually narrowed, and intensified, their subsistence base.

See also Asia, Western; Domestication; Natufian; Neolithic. [N.B.]

Further Readings

Binford, L.R. (1968) Post-Pleistocene adaptations. In S.R. Binford and L.R. Binford (eds.): New Perspectives in Archeology. Chicago: Aldine, pp. 313–341.

Flannery, K.V. (1969) Origins and ecological effects of early domestication in Iran and the Near East. In P.J. Ucko and G.W. Dimbleby (eds.): The Domestication and Exploitation of Plants and Animals. London: Duckworth, pp. 73–100.

Henry, D.O. (1989) From Foraging to Agriculture: The Levant at the End of the Ice Age. Philadelphia: University of Pennsylvania Press.

Broca, Pierre Paul (1824–1880)

French anatomist and physical anthropologist who made notable contributions to the fields of anatomy, pathology, surgery, and anthropology. Much of his anthropological research concerned the study of racial variations in crania and involved the invention of craniological techniques and instruments. He is also remembered for his comparative neuroanatomical studies. In 1861, he demonstrated the location of the speech center in the left frontal region of the brain, since known as *Broca's region*. Broca also made a number of significant contributions to the institutional development of French anthropology, involving the founding of the Société d'Anthropologie de Paris (1859), the Laboratoire d'Anthropologie of the Ecole Pratique des Hautes Etudes (1868), the Ecole d'Anthropologie (Paris) in 1876, and the journal *Revue d'Anthropologie* (1872). [F.S.]

Bronze Age

Second in the three-stage sequence of Stone Age, Bronze Age, Iron Age. This tripartite scheme was the first developmental framework widely adopted in the archaeology of Europe. It has since been extended to other regions where bronze metallurgy was developed. In any area, the scheme is based on the material used to produce cutting tools. Despite this simple technological definition, the Bronze Age has frequently been taken to refer to a period of broad-spectrum cultural advance.

The term first gained currency when employed by two early-nineteenth-century Danish archaeologists, C. Thomsen and J. Worsaae, in their efforts to order the prehistory of northern Europe. To these scholars, the three-stage system reflected a unilinear development of human culture from simple origins to progressively more complex conditions. The Bronze Age was thought of as the period of time (in any given part of the world) when copper or bronze metallurgy began, when settled villages dependent on agriculture became the rule, and when disparate social ranking of members of society first developed. These developments are each products of long-term processes of change that are not necessarily linked to one another. Hence, the simplistic unilineal development often implied in the term is not generally accepted today.

See also Archaeology; Broad-Spectrum Revolution; Complex Societies; Europe; Iron Age; Neolithic. [B.B.]

Further Readings

Coles, J., and Harding, A. (1979) The Bronze Age in Europe. New York: St. Martin's Press.
Redman, C. (1978) The Rise of Civilization. San Francisco: Freeman.

Broom, Robert (1866–1951)

South African (b. Scotland) physician and paleontologist. On receiving his M.D. at the University of Glasgow in 1895, Broom moved to Cape Town (South Africa), where in 1903 he was appointed professor of geology at Victoria College, Stellenbosch, and became famous for his studies of mammallike reptiles. Broom's interest in anthropology and more specifically paleoanthropology was heightened by the discovery of the Taung (infantile australopithecine) specimen in 1924, for which fellow South African paleontologist R.A. Dart had claimed hominid affinities—a conclusion Broom endorsed without reservation. In 1934, he joined the Transvaal Museum, Pretoria. This appointment coincided with his succession of spectacular finds of adult australopithecines at Sterkfontein and subsequently at Kromdraai and Swartkrans, all in South Africa. These discoveries essentially vindicated his support of Dart's earlier claims for the Taung specimen. The remainder of Broom's career was devoted to exploration of these sites and the interpretation of the many early hominid remains discovered there.

See also Australopithecus; Dart, Raymond Arthur; Kromdraai; Sterkfontein; Swartkrans; Taung. [F.S.]

Buda Industry

Diminutive-chopper-core industry of Middle Pleistocene (Biharian) age in Central Europe, probably ca. 0.6–0.4 Ma. First defined on the basis of a site at Budapest (Hungary), the industry is better known from the nearby site of Vértesszöllös. The small size of both flakes and cores is probably due to the use of river cobbles as the raw-material source rather than natural stone outcrops or quarries.

See also Chopper-Chopping Tools; Core; Early Paleolithic; Flake; Raw Materials; Vértesszöllös. [A.S.B.]

Buluk

Early Miocene site near the southern end of Lake Turkana in northern Kenya, dated to ca. 17 Ma. Four catarrhines, including a hominoid, two probable members of the "*Dendropithecus*-group," and one cercopithecid (cf. *Prohylobates*) have been found in a small but diverse fauna. The large hominoid, first assigned to *Sivapithecus,* was included in *Afropithecus turkanensis* when this taxon was erected for additional specimens from Kalodirr, a similar site to the northwest.

See also Africa, East; Afropithecus; "Dendropithecus-Group"; Hominoidea; Kalodirr; Sivapithecus; Victoriapithecinae. [P.A.]

Burin

Stone-tool class especially common during Late Paleolithic times (and after), with a sharp chisel-like edge produced by removing one or more narrow flakes (burin spalls) along the thickness of a flake or blade. The narrow surface from which the burin spalls are struck may be created by snapping the flake or blade in two, by relatively abrupt retouching or truncation of the edge or end, or by a series of prior burin-spall removals. The resulting edge, created by the intersection of two narrow planes, is both sharp and strong. Burins are thought to have been primary tools for engraving and shaping such materials as bone, antler, ivory, and probably wood.

See also Late Paleolithic; Stone-Tool Making; Upper Paleolithic. [N.T., K.S.]

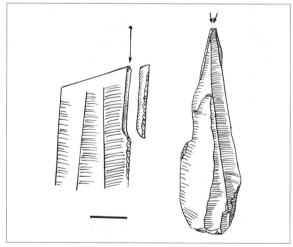

Left: close-up of burin (larger) and burin spall. Right: dihedral burin on a blade (spalls removed in two directions). Scale is 1 cm.

Calcium-41 Dating

Radiometric dating method dependent on the decay of a minor isotope of calcium. The great potential of this method, which is as yet not developed sufficiently for reliable application, is that calcium is a major component of animal bone. The isotope ^{41}Ca has a half-life of ca. 100 Kyr and would thus allow direct dating of specimens ranging in age from 10 Ka, or even less, to as much as 1 Ma. This range would extend the dating of Late and Middle Pleistocene archaeological and paleontological material beyond the current limits of radiocarbon, uranium-series, and trapped-charge methods, spanning the gap to the upper limits of typical K/Ar and Ar/Ar dating. There are, however, several major difficulties involved with this method, which, as of the late 1990s, had not been tested on ancient materials.

Calcium-41, like carbon-14, is produced naturally by cosmic radiation impact on ^{40}Ca, the common isotope of calcium. This process occurs through neutron capture in calcium in the upper meter of soil, with a production ratio of 10^{-14} to 10^{-15}. Radiocalcium is thus several hundred times as rare, compared to the parent isotope, as radiocarbon is to carbon-12. Its decay, to ^{41}K, involves the production of a neutrino, which is extremely hard to observe. Moreover, the "zeroing" of the dating clock is not at the death of the animal to be dated but upon its removal from cosmic neutron radiation by burial below several meters of soil or entombment in a cave.

R.E. Taylor has suggested that the state of the radiocalcium-dating method in the late 1990s is comparable to the situation with radiocarbon in the late 1940s. The half-life has been reasonably well estimated, if not closely determined; its origin and decay cycle is understood; and the technology for arriving at a date with this information is at least theoretically known. In the next decade, this may become an exciting new approach, or it may disappear as infeasible.

See also Bone Biology; ESR (Electron Spin Resonance) Dating; Geochronometry; Radiocarbon Dating; TL (Thermoluminescence) Dating; Uranium-Series Dating. [E.D.]

Further Readings

Taylor, R.E. (1987) Dating techniques in archaeology and paleoanthropology. Analyt. Chem. 59:317A–331A.

Calico Hills

Controversial archaeological site in an alluvial fan in San Bernardino County (California). Continuously excavated since 1964, it was given prominence by the involvement of L.S.B. Leakey. Although some claim that the earliest artifact-bearing deposits of the site due to 200 Ka, the geomorphological context and the presence of human workmanship on the artifacts from Calico remain the subject of considerable debate.

See also Paleoindian. [L.S.A.P., D.H.T]

Callitrichinae

Subfamily of cebid platyrrhine monkeys including the living tribes Callimiconini and Callitrichini and fossil allies. Informally termed *marmosets* (and for some *tamarins,* distinguished by low-crowned rather than high-crowned, marmosetlike incisors), there are more than 20 species, all of which exploit a canopy-subcanopy, frugivorous-insectivorous feeding niche, in which competition with the larger cebines is minimized.

Callitrichines are, on the whole, the smallest living anthropoids, characterized also by reduced posterior dentitions, nonopposable thumbs and big toes, and the occurrence of claws on all of the fingers except for the large toe. The callimiconin tribe is a primitive branch. They produce a single offspring per litter and retain third molars, whereas the more derived callitrichins lack third molars, have reduced second molars, and produce dizygotic twins, an unusual strategy for an anthropoid. Their mating system and social organization, which involve extensive paternal and sibling care of young offspring and, in some cases, polyandrous mating, may relate to the heavy reproductive load that females experience. Some species of *Callithrix,* and the monotypic *Cebuella,* are highly gumivorous, having evolved a modified dentition that permits them to gouge and scrape tree bark to promote the flow of secretions that the animals then harvest. Although they have rather unconvoluted brains, clawed fingertips, and morphologically simple molars (all resemblances to "primitive" mammals), callitrichines evolved this adaptive pattern secondarily, at least partially as an allometric consequence of small size. The golden-lion marmoset, *Leontopithecus,* literally on the brink of extinction in the 1980s, is the first mammal to have been captively bred and then reintroduced successfully into a park preserve within its native geographical range.

The poorly known *Micodon kiotensis* from the Middle Miocene (14–12 Ma) of La Venta, Colombia, is possibly a fossil marmoset. It is similar in size to the larger eastern Brazilian marmosets, but it does not have the highly reduced fourth upper-molar cusp (hypocone) that typifies the callitrichin tribe. Another La Venta species, *Mohanamico hershkovitzi,* is sometimes thought to be a pitheciine but is most likely a close relative of *Callimico.* A third genus, *Patasola,* was described in 1997 as a callitrichine. Together, they indicate a fairly ancient origin for the group. On the other hand, the recently described *Lagonimico conclucatus* was originally considered a giant tamarin but is probably better interpreted as a pitheciine.

Callitrichinae
    Callimiconini
        Callimico
      ?†*Mohanamico*
    Callitrichini
        Saguinus
        Leontopithecus
        Callithrix
        Cebuella
    incertae sedis
      ?†*Micodon*
      ?†*Patasola*
†extinct

See also Allometry; Americas; Ateloidea; Brain; Cebinae; Diet; Dwarfism; Teeth. [A.L.R.]

Further Readings
Hershkovitz, P. (1977) New World Monkeys (Platyrrhini), Vol. 1: Callitrichidae. Chicago: University of Chicago Press.

Leutenegger, W. (1980) Monogamy in callitrichids: A consequence of phyletic dwarfism? Int. J. Primatol. 1:95–98.

Rosenberger, A.L. (1984) Aspects of the systematics and evolution of the marmosets. In M.T. de Mello (ed.): A Primatologia no Brasil. Belo Horizonte: Universidade Federal de Minas Gerais, pp. 160–180.

Rosenberger, A.L., Setoguchi, T., and Hartwig, W.C. (1991) *Laventiana annectens,* new fossil evidence for the origins of callitrichine New World monkeys. Proc. Nat. Acad. Sci. USA 88:2137–2140.

Rosenberger, A.L., Setoguchi, T., and Shigehara, N. (1990) The fossil record of callitrichine primates. J Hum. Evol. 19:209–236.

Sussman, R.W., and Kinzey, W.G. (1984) The ecological role of the Callitrichidae. Am. J. Phys. Anthropol. 64:419–449.

Candelabra Model
Name that W.W. Howells used to represent F. Weidenreich and C.S. Coon's polyphyletic evolutionary schemes of several parallel local transitions from *Homo erectus* to *Homo sapiens* in different continents. However, while Coon's model of multiregional evolution did, indeed, feature separate evolutionary branches and could be accurately depicted as a candelabra, Weidenreich's scheme, like present versions of multiregional evolution, also emphasized interregional gene flow and could be more appropriately represented as a reticulate or an anastomosing network.

See also Coon, Carleton Stevens; Homo sapiens; Howells, William White; Modern Human Origins; Weidenreich, Franz. [C.B.S.]

Further Readings
Stringer, C.B. (1994) Out of Africa: A personal history. In M. Nitecki and D.V. Nitecki (eds.): Origins of Anatomically Modern Humans. New York: Plenum, pp. 149–172.

Capsian
Late Paleolithic industry of North Africa named for the type site of el-Mekta near Gafsa in southern Tunisia, of early Holocene age, ca. 10–6 Ka. The Capsian is characterized by large backed points and blades, truncation burins, microburins, and microliths, especially lunates or segments and gravettes in the early phase. In the more widespread Upper phase (actually contemporaneous or earlier), tools are smaller, and geometric microliths (especially trapezoids and triangles), along with bone awls, ostrich-eggshell beads, and polishing stones, are more common. Sites are often associated with large piles of snail shells, leading to the theory that snails formed a large, although seasonal, part of the Capsian diet. An earlier-to-contemporary, and probably unrelated backed-blade industry in Kenya, the Eburran, was originally termed the Kenya Capsian.

See also Economy, Prehistoric; Late Paleolithic; Later Stone Age; Mesolithic; Stone-Tool Making. [A.S.B.]

Carpolestidae
A family of primarily Paleocene archaic primates found in several North American localities and in the Early Eocene of China, but, interestingly (like the picrodontids), absent from the fossil record of Europe. The distribution of carpolestids points out some of the major gaps in our knowledge of archaic primates, but it also educates about the timing and nature of holarctic dispersal of primates in the Paleocene and Early Eocene. There are four recognized genera: The Carpolestinae consists of the Middle Paleocene North American *Elphidotarsius,* the Late Paleocene North American *Carpodaptes* (including *Carpolestes*), and the Late Paleocene-Early Eocene Chinese and North American *Carpocristes,* whereas

the long distinct and most primitive Early Eocene Chinese *Chronolestes* warrants its own subfamily, Chronolestinae.

The distribution of these primates points to some dispersal probabilities for archaic primates and other mammals across the Bering area between Asia and North America in the Paleocene-Eocene. In the ancestry of the North American *Elphidotarsius* lurks a chronolestine carpolestid. In light of early Plesiadapiformes in North America, this ancestry was likely North American, in spite of the fact that this subfamily is not as yet represented in America and that the representatives of these earliest chronolestine carpolestids dispersed to Asia in the Early Paleocene. In addition, the latest Paleocene-earliest Eocene also witnessed the arrival of many Asian forms into North America (including euprimates and rodents among other groups) but also gave access to Asia for North American lineages like *Carpocristes*.

Carpolestids display a specialization in their cheek teeth called plagiaulacoidy, a term coined for the similarity of some mammalian teeth to those of Jurassic multituberculate postcanine teeth. Plagiaulacoidy has been defined as a condition in which one or more of the cheek teeth are modified into compressed, bladelike structures with serrated cutting edges on the top. This specialization can be recognized in an incipient state in the oldest carpolestid genus, but it is even more rudimentary in the dentally most primitive, but youngest, Chinese *Chronolestes*. Both the more primitive and the more advanced species of carpolestines are characterized by a vertically semicircular bladelike enlargement of the fourth lower premolar and the equally enlarged but flattened and expanded upper third and fourth premolars. In advanced carpolestid upper premolars, these teeth become polycuspate, and the cusps are arranged into three mesiodistally aligned parallel rows.

In addition to this premolar specialization, carpolestids also display their heritage of enlarged incisors but seem to have evolved a reduced anterior dentition in the dentally more advanced Carpolestinae. The more advanced species of *Carpodaptes* drastically reduce the second incisors, the canines and the remaining second and third premolars above, and the third premolar below.

The incisors, the premolars, and the molars bear special similarity to the earliest well-known plesiadapid (*Pronothodectes*) and *Saxonella*. This is the reason carpolestids are considered close relatives of plesiadapids and the Saxonellidae and are included in the superfamily Plesiadapoidea.

The function and the biological roles of the plagiaulacoid dentition of carpolestids (we do not know the number of possible roles these teeth may have performed), along with those of the other plagiaulacoid forms, have been of great interest to students of mammalian evolution. Although emphasis is clearly on some cutting-sawing function by these independently evolved dental structures, the nature of the selective agents that molded this solution is not entirely clear. Advanced carpolestids, with their plagiaulacoid lower blades moving food across the rasplike and unique upper premolars, probably consumed some vegetable diet of high-fiber content. These foods could have been fruits, nuts, or even succulent shoots. These mouse-to-rat-sized primates might have exploited a relatively narrow adaptive zone due to the

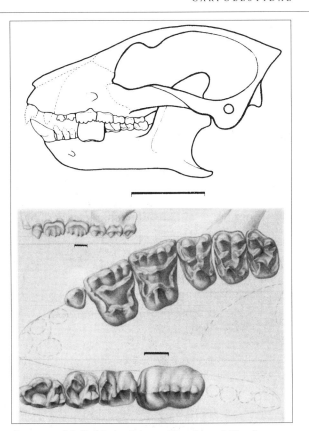

Reconstructed skull of the late Paleocene Carpodaptes dubius *from North American (above), and the partial upper and lower dentition of the late Paleocene* Carpodaptes hazelae. *Scale for the skull is 1 cm, and scales for the teeth, 1 mm. Courtesy of Frederick S. Szalay, from Szalay and Delson, 1979.*

special abilities of their premolar dentitions. The great similarity of their molar teeth strongly suggests that the differences between *Elphidotarsius, Carpodaptes,* and *Carpocristes* species were not due to significantly different diets but rather to the steady improvement in design for the same biological roles through the latter half of the Paleocene into the Eocene.

Carpolestids are not known to have given rise to any other group of primates. Their fossils, along with those of the primate family Plesiadapidae, are of particular value to paleontologists for the dating of Paleocene rocks in North America. These species were rapidly evolving but widespread, with the consequence that the individually recognized species were of short duration, and therefore, of great stratigraphic value.

Family Carpolestidae
    Subfamily Carpolestinae
        † *Elphidotarsius*
        † *Carpodaptes* (incl. † *Carpolestes*)
        † *Carpocristes*
    Subfamily Chronolestinae
        † *Chronolestes*
†extinct

See also Eocene; Paleocene; Plesiadapidae; Plesiadapiformes; Plesiadapoidea; Saxonellidae; Teeth. [F.S.S.]

Further Readings

Beard, K.C., and Wang, J. (1995) The first Asian plesi-adapoids (Mammalia, Primatomorpha). Ann. Carnegie Mus. 64:1–33.

Szalay, F.S., and Delson, E. (1979) Evolutionary History of the Primates. New York: Academic.

Cartailhac, Émile (1845–1921)

French prehistorian. During the 1860s, Cartailhac became associated with G. de Mortillet (1821–1898), and together they had an integral role in the founding of the International Congress of Anthropology and Prehistoric Archaeology, which held its inaugural meeting in Neuchâtel, Switzerland, in 1866. Soon thereafter, he became the owner of *Matériaux pour l'histoire naturelle et primitive de l'homme*, a journal founded by de Mortillet. Under Cartailhac's editorship, this journal became an influential vehicle for the promotion of anthropology and prehistory. In 1890, however, the journal was united with the *Revue d'Anthropologie* and the *Revue d'Ethnologie* to form *L'Anthropologie*—of which Cartailhac was coeditor until 1895, when M. Boule (1861–1942) took over the editorship. Along with his publishing activities, Cartailhac was also associated with the study of numerous European prehistoric sites (e.g., Altamira, La Ferrassie, Grimaldi). Among his most notable publications is the now classic survey *La France préhistorique* (1889).

See also Altamira; Boule, [Pierre] Marcellin; Grimaldi; La Ferrassie; Mortillet, Gabriel de. [F.S.]

Çatal Hüyük

Neolithic site 40 km southeast of Konya in Central Turkey, occupied for at least 1,000 years, from ca. 8.5 Ka. Excavations directed by J. Mellaart from 1961 to 1965 focused on the Neolithic 16-ha eastern mound and largely ignored the later 13-ha mound to the west. An unusually large site for its period, Çatal has yielded a wealth of organic materials, including baskets, textiles, and wooden objects; abundant ceramics and worked-stone artifacts; unique and well-preserved architecture with elaborate paintings and plaster reliefs, both geometric and representational; and almost 500 intramural burials. Analysis of the skeletal material by J.L. Angel suggested the prevalence of widespread anemias, possibly reflecting genetic responses to an increasing incidence of malaria as fields were cleared and watered for agriculture. He also noted an unusually high level of traumatic injuries to adult males, suggesting frequent intergroup or interpersonal conflict. New excavations at the site began in 1993.

See also Asia, Western; Complex Societies; Neolithic. [C.K., A.S.B.]

Further Reading

Hodder, I., (ed.) (1996) On the surface. Cambridge: McDonald Institute.

Mellart, J. (1967) Çatal Hüyük: A Neolithic Town in Anatolia. New York: Academic Press.

Catarrhini

Old World infraorder of Anthropoidea, including the families Propliopithecidae, Pliopithecidae, Cercopithecidae, Proconsulidae, Hylobatidae, and Hominidae, as well as Miocene forms included here in the "*Dendropithecus*-group." Of these seven sets of Afro-Eurasian higher primates, four are extinct (three African and one Eurasian), while one is extant in Asia and two are extant in both Africa and Asia, with extinct European representatives (other than the worldwide *Homo* and the relict or introduced Gibraltar macaque). The last three named families appear to form a monophyletic superfamily Hominoidea as they are understood here.

Catarrhine Characteristics

Defining the catarrhines by means of uniquely shared characters depends upon which taxa are considered when such a list is developed. If only the living forms are examined, the list of such characters is long and includes numerous features not determinable for any fossils, as well as others known only for a few extinct forms. Such a list, of course, can yield information only about the last common ancestor of the living forms, and still earlier catarrhines, or even earlier ancestors, might present a different mosaic of character states. Nonetheless, an abbreviated version of such a list does provide a starting point for a survey of catarrhine morphology and evolution.

Research in the 1980s and 1990s suggests that the ancestor of living catarrhines (Cercopithecoidea and Hominoidea, here termed the Eucatarrhini) would have been characterized by the following dental features, which are derived by comparison with those of an ancestral anthropoid and are not known to have evolved in parallel among platyrrhines: dental formula of 2–1–2–3; singlecusped, bilaterally compressed P_3, involved in honing C^1; and five-cusped lower molars with no paraconid, midline distal hypoconulid (not very large on M_3), talonid and trigonid of roughly equal height, and M_2 rather larger than M_1 but only slightly smaller than M_3. The presence of a wear facet (termed facet x) caused by Phase 2 contact between the distolingual surface of the protoconid and the mesiobuccal aspect of the protocone has also been used as a diagnostic catarrhine feature, but it now appears that this may have been developed in parallel in several anthropoid lineages. Cranially, such characters might include a moderately prominent glabella, separate from the supraorbital tori; a tubular external auditory meatus; a moderately developed mandibular inferior transverse torus; a long mandibular ramus with nearly vertical anterior margin; a U-shaped mandibular arcade; and very reduced olfactory lobes of the brain. Postcranially, characters of this type might include humerus with low deltopectoral and supinator crests, a narrow brachialis flange, and a deep olecranon fossa, but with no entepicondylar foramen or dorsal epitrochlear fossa; ulna with weak pronator crest and round head; ischium with expanded tuberosity (and callosities); and a synovial distal joint between the tibia and the fibula.

Relationships of Major Catarrhine Subgroups

If we now examine a variety of fossils, it is possible to see which of these characters they share and, thus, how strongly they are linked to the modern catarrhines. A number of Eocene and Oligocene Old World taxa have been previously included in the catarrhines, but, as discussed in ANTHROPOIDEA, few such referrals are accepted here. In brief, *Djebelemur, Pondaungia,* and *Amphipithecus* are best interpreted as adapiforms; *Eosimias* is a tarsioid; the oligopithecids are probably archaic anthropoids; and the parapithecids are likely advanced early anthropoids but probably not catarrhines. Only the last two of these taxa merit further discussion here.

The parapithecids include five genera from the Fayum Eo-Oligocene and probably three others from slightly earlier North African sites. E.L. Simons has long argued that they are the sister taxon to Cercopithecidae; E. Delson has considered them to be the sister of all other catarrhines and has formally termed them Paracatarrhini; R. Hoffstetter has proposed that they may be the African sister taxon of the platyrrhines; and in the late 1980s T. Harrison and then J.G. Fleagle and R.F. Kay suggested that parapithecids are the sister taxon to Platyrrhini plus Catarrhini, thus archaic anthropoids (the view accepted here). It is now widely agreed that parapithecids share no derived features with either cercopithecids or platyrrhines, the apparent similarities that do exist being best interpreted as parallelisms.

Of the list of catarrhine features noted above, parapithecids share a moderate glabella, molar trigonids and talonids of nearly equal height, and a well-developed midline distal hypoconulid with a generally large distal fovea. They are clearly less derived than any other catarrhine in the following

features (and conservative by comparison with platyrrhines in those marked with *): retention of P2 (which may show honing contact with the canine), molar paraconids (at least in some species), lingually open P_4 trigonid, small P_4 metaconid placed distolingual to protoconid*, a weak mandibular inferior torus, shallow corpus, short ramus with sloping anterior margin, narrow tibial shaft*, and a fibrous distal joint between the tibia and the fibula. They share with the propliopithecids (see below) an annular auditory meatus, large olfactory bulb*, and numerous conservative postcranial features, such as humerus with prominent deltopectoral crest, high supinator crest, elongate capitulum, shallow olecranon fossa, moderate brachialis flange, entepicondylar foramen, and dorsal epitrochlear fossa; and ulna with prominent pronator crest. Two conservative parapithecid features cannot be determined in propliopithecids: ulna with narrow head* and ischium with narrow tuberosity* (and presumably no callosities). Unique derived features shared by at least several parapithecids are apparently restricted to a central conule on the upper premolars and a sulcus separating the metaconid from the protoconid on P_4. Despite a few derived similarities with catarrhines, it now appears most likely that the parapithecid clade split away from a common anthropoid ancestral "stock" before the platyrrhines and the catarrhines diverged. This situation is even more true for the oligopithecids, now well represented by *Catopithecus.* Although Simons and D.T. Rasmussen have included this group as a subfamily of Propliopithecidae, only the two-premolared condition is a shared derived feature, but one that does not appear to be homologous. Dentally, cranially, and postcranially, oligopithecids are marginally acceptable as anthropoids, but the most primitive ones now known.

Eocatarrhini: The Archaic Catarrhines

The Oligocene and many Miocene catarrhines are not specially related to the modern eucatarrhines. Instead, they appear to form a "comb" of successive clades or radiations, each with a larger frequency of eucatarrhine character states. Of these, the Propliopithecidae includes only one genus with several species; the Pliopithecidae is a monophyletic group of six to eight genera; and the "*Dendropithecus*-group" is a paraphyletic group of six Early-to-Middle Miocene East African genera intermediate in morphology between pliopithecids and eucatarrhines.

Propliopithecus of the Fayum and Omani Early Oligocene is known by fragments of up to five species, but the most complete remains are those of *P. zeuxis,* sometimes placed in the genus *Aegyptopithecus.* This species, and presumably its congeners, is derived by comparison with the parapithecids in such features as having lost P2 and possessing a bilaterally compressed P_3 that hones C^1; P_4 with lingually closed trigonid and metaconid subequal in size to directly buccal protoconid; lower molars lacking paraconids but with facet x; inferior transverse torus of mandible moderately developed; long ramus with vertical anterior border; corpus deep under M_1; no contact between zygomatic and parietal bones in temporal fossa and clearly closed rear of orbit; and a moderately broad tibial shaft with synovial joint between tibia and fibula distally. A number of conservative conditions are shared with pliopithecids and listed below. It

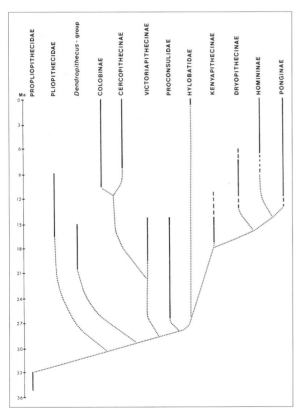

Diagram of evolutionary relationships and temporal ranges of the higher taxa of catarrhine primates. Solid vertical lines indicate known ranges, heavy dashed lines indicate probable range extensions, and dots represent phyletic relationships.

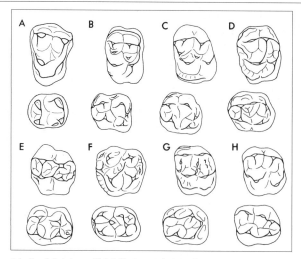

Idealized drawings of left M² above right M₂ of representative catarrhines and early anthropoids. (A) Catopithecus; (B) Parapithecus; (C) Propliopithecus; (D) Pliopithecus; (E) Victoriapithecus; (F) Oreopithecus; (G) Proconsul; (H) Sivapithecus.

is as yet unknown whether propliopithecids are derived compared with parapithecids in the shape of the ulnar head, development of the ischial tuberosity, size of the femoral lesser trochanter, or depth of the femoral distal condyles. If not, the derived state(s) would have been evolved independently in platyrrhines and later catarrhines; in turn, this would strengthen a parapithecid link to catarrhines. The Propliopithecidae now represent the most ancient known catarrhines and provide a tentative model for the eucatarrhine common ancestor.

Pliopithecus, known from several European Middle Miocene partial skeletons, is, in turn, further derived than *Propliopithecus* in having a P₄ somewhat longer than broad, a prominent glabellar region, and a hallux with a modified saddle joint, as well as having lost the dorsal epitrochlear fossa on the distal humerus. Both genera retain such ancestral anthropoid conditions as a ringlike external auditory meatus (partly tubular in *Pliopithecus,* as in juvenile eucatarrhines); distinct prehallux bone in the foot; humerus with entepicondylar foramen, moderately broad brachialis flange, high supinator crest, shallow olecranon fossa, and elongate capitulum; ulna with prominent pronator crest and narrow head; and narrow ischial tuberosity (the latter two are unknown in propliopithecids). The other genera of pliopithecids are less well known but agree with *Pliopithecus* in most of these conditions where determination is possible. Among the most fascinating aspects of the pliopithecids is their presence in the fossil record contemporaneous with, or younger than, a number of far more derived taxa; they must have diverged from propliopithecidlike ancestors by mid-Oligocene time and then remained relatively rare in some as yet unsampled region or habitat of Africa. When that island continent finally contacted Eurasia by ca. 19 Ma, pliopithecids were among the first mammals to leave, entering eastern Asia, whence they seem to have reached Europe perhaps twice.

The generally older Early-Middle Miocene small catarrhines from Africa are more derived than pliopithecids when character states can be observed. The best known of

these forms is *Dendropithecus,* whose humerus has low deltopectoral and supinator crests and a narrow bicipital groove and lacks an entepicondylar foramen, although the olecranon fossa is conservatively deep. *Simiolus* also presents postcranial elements that may place it closer to the last common ancestor of Hominoidea and Cercopithecoidea. *Micropithecus, Kalepithecus, Nyanzapithecus* (a possible *Oreopithecus* relative), *Limnopithecus,* and *Turkanapithecus* (the last two possibly proconsulids) are generally less fully preserved, but the last form may be the most derived of all. Most of these genera (especially the pliopithecids) have at various times been allied with the Hylobatidae, but that was mainly on the basis of small size and relatively gracile limb bones, rather than any sharing of the distinctive derived postcranial features of gibbons. Based on subjective considerations, it appears reasonable to suggest that *Dendropithecus* and any species monophyletically linked to it merit placement in a family distinct from any so far named, but that step is not taken here. Instead, the "*Dendropithecus*-group" is used as an informal cluster of taxa between the pliopithecids and the common eucatarrhine ancestor.

Eucatarrhini: The "Modern" Catarrhines

HOMINOIDEA

Recent finds have pushed the first occurrence of hominoid eucatarrhines back into the final Oligocene, where they are older than any other catarrhine but *Propliopithecus.* The hominoids comprise mainly the hylobatids and the hominids, the latter including *Pongo* and its extinct allies, African apes plus humans, and a group of mostly fragmentary Miocene taxa that share with later hominids such derived features as thick molar enamel, elongated premolars, robust P₃ and canines, spatulate I², subparallel tooth rows, deep mandibular symphysis with superior torus less pronounced than inferior, enlarged maxillary sinus, and/or prominent keels on humeral trochlea. The Early Miocene *Proconsul* appears to fall between this latter group and *Dendropithecus,* in that it presents such ancestral hominoid features as P₃ with low crown, upper premolars with reduced cusp heteromorphy, development of the maxillary jugum, frontal bone wider at bregma than anteriorly, strong humeral trochlear keels but without sulci bordering the lateral keel, humeral head medically oriented, rounded and larger than the femoral head, and scapula with elongated vertebral border and robust acromion (the last several not known for *Dendropithecus*). On this basis, the family Proconsulidae is included in the Hominoidea. In addition to several species of mainly Early Miocene *Proconsul* and the poorly known *Rangwapithecus,* the Oligocene *Kamoyapithecus* is also placed in the Proconsulidae.

By the end of the Early Miocene (ca. 17 Ma), the first hominoids appear with features that link them to the living hominids. *Afropithecus* has thick molar enamel and relatively large upper premolars compared to its molars. The slightly younger *Kenyapithecus* also had somewhat more modern postcranial elements. About the same time (ca. 15 Ma), the broadly similar *Griphopithecus* is found in Turkey and Central Europe. *Morotopithecus* (ca. 20 Myr old) may also differ from *Afropithecus* in its more advanced postcranium. These kenyapithecines represent an early radiation of archaic hominids not clearly linked to any living forms. Although there is no fossil record, it is likely that this time interval saw the divergence of the hylobatids from ancestral hominoids, perhaps in Eurasia.

The Middle-to-Late Miocene dryopithecines are on the border of relationship to the living great apes but still cannot be definitively included in either modern subfamily. *Dryopithecus* is known from Europe between ca. 13 and 8 Ma and is represented by crania in Hungary and Spain, the latter associated with a partial skeleton. Molar enamel is thin, but the subnasal region and the limb bones appear somewhat more like modern apes than those of the kenyapithecines. Some authors have suggested that *Dryopithecus* be included in Homininae and others in Ponginae, but both views appear overstated. Instead, the genus represents a reasonable approach to the last common ancestor of those later clades (although its thin enamel seems to be a reversal that sets it off from direct ancestry). *Oreopithecus* of the Italian Late Miocene is broadly similar to *Dryopithecus* postcranially, but its highly distinctive dentition leads to its continued placement in a separate subfamily. Its previously suggested affiliation with Cercopithecidae has been rejected.

Sivapithecus from the Siwaliks of Pakistan and India appears to be the first hominoid with derived similarities to a modern genus. In its narrow interorbital pillar, ovoid orbits, expanded and flattened zygomatic region, well-developed airorhynchy, lack of glabellar thickening or browridges, a rotated premaxilla giving a smooth floor to the nasal cavity, an extremely reduced incisive canal with no incisive fossa, and small upper lateral incisors very small relative to the central and relatively thick molar enamel, *Sivapithecus* presents a complex of character states otherwise found only in *Pongo*, the orangutan. Most of its postcranium is also rather modern, although the proximal humerus is more conservative than in any living hominoid (including hylobatids); this latter feature may reflect habitus more than heritage, however. *Sivapithecus* specimens with these diagnostic features appear as early as 12 Ma, providing a solid minimum age for the hominine-pongine divergence. *Ankarapithecus* (ca. 10 Ma in Turkey) may be a less-derived representative of Ponginae, with somewhat intermediate upper facial morphology and a conservative palate; it is too late to be an actual ancestor for *Sivapithecus* but (like *Pliopithecus*) presumably lasted well after its descendants became widespread.

The Homininae is perhaps the least well known hominoid clade in the Miocene. Cranially, hominines are relatively conservative, with a stepped premaxillary-maxillary contact in the subnasal area (a condition likely ancestral to the pongine state), wide interorbital pillar, and moderately sized I^2. The only diagnostic facial complex seems to be increased klinorhynchy, including well-developed browridges and glabella. Thus, recognition of early hominines requires relatively complete fossil material. As of the late 1990s, the only reasonable candidate for such a role was *Graecopithecus*, known from Greece between ca. 10 and 8 Ma. It also has extremely thick molar enamel and reduced canine height, as well as a rather gorillalike face. *Samburupithecus* from Kenya may be a contemporaneous African equivalent. The next several million years are nearly void of potential hominine fossils, although this is the very time that the molecular clock predicts divergence of the gorilla and then the chimpanzee clades from the early human lineage. During the Pliocene, the latter diversified into *Australopithecus*, *Ardipithecus*, *Paranthropus*, and eventually *Homo*. In turn, during the Pleistocene, *Homo* spread out of Africa and across the Old World, probably in several successive migrations, coming to dominate the natural environment through technology.

CERCOPITHECOIDEA

Views of Old World monkey evolutionary history generally agree that the postcranium and perhaps skull, as well as the teeth, of cercopithecoids are derived by comparison to the eucatarrhine morphotype. Previously, it was thought that monkeys were primitive, but detailed study demonstrated that in addition to the derived bilophodont dentition, the terrestrially adapted postcranium is about as different from the common ancestor as is that of the hominoids. B.R. Benefit and M.L. McCrossin have further argued that facial remains of early cercopithecoids share a relatively narrow interorbital pillar, frontal trigone (depression bounded by raised temporal lines), and elongated muzzle with faces of *Propliopithecus* and *Afropithecus*. They have suggested that this implies that such a pattern was ancestral for catarrhines, in opposition to the previous view that a relatively short face, widely spaced orbits, and rounded vault (as in colobines and gibbons and, to a lesser degree, humans, *Oreopithecus*, and *Pliopithecus*) were ancestral. This question has not been resolved.

The later Early and Middle Miocene African *Victoriapithecus* and *Prohylobates* document the earliest definite cercopithecoids, albeit less completely bilophodont than later monkeys. These forms present a variable expression of the hypoconulid on lower dP_4-M_2 (lost entirely in later cercopithecids) and an incomplete formation of the distal transverse loph combined with variable expression of a crista obliqua on upper molars. These and other features have led Benefit to place the two genera in the family Victoriapithecidae, but here this taxon is ranked as a subfamily.

The first occurrence of colobines is nearly contemporaneous in East Africa and Europe, ca. 10 Ma, but cercopithecines do not appear until several Myr later (North Africa). The European colobines form a terrestrial clade that may also extend into northern Asia in the Pliocene, while the numerous modern genera of southern Asian colobines are poorly represented in the fossil record. A variety of macaques and more terrestrial relatives occur across Eurasia. In Africa, there is a radiation of large colobines in the Pliocene, alongside a long-lived lineage of *Theropithecus* which shows continuing size increase into the Middle Pleistocene.

See also Africa; Afropithecus; Anthropoidea; Asia, Eastern and Southern; Australopithecus; Cercopithecidae; Cercopithecinae; Colobinae; "Dendropithecus-Group"; Diet; Dryopithecinae; Europe; Fayum; Griphopithecus; Hominidae; Homininae; Hominoidea; Homo; Kenyapithecinae; Kenyapithecus; Locomotion; Miocene; Molecular Clock; Morotopithecus; Oligocene; Oliogopithecidae; Oreopithecus; Paranthropus; Parapithecidae; Pleistocene; Pliocene;

Pliopithecidae; Ponginae; Proconsulidae; Propliopithecidae; Samburupithecus; Sivapithecus; Skeleton; Skull; Teeth; Victoriapithecinae. [E.D.]

Further Readings

Benefit, B.R. (1993) The permanent dentition and phylogenetic position of *Victoriapithecus* from Maboko Island, Kenya. J. Hum. Evol. 25:83–172.

Benefit, B.R., and McCrossin, M.L. (1993) Facial anatomy of *Victoriapithecus* and its relevance to the ancestral cranial morphology of Old World monkeys and apes. Am. J. Phys. Anthropol. 92:329–370.

Delson, E., and Andrews, P. (1975) Evolution and interrelationships of the catarrhine primates. In W.P. Luckett and F.S. Szalay (eds.): Phylogeny of the Primates: A Multidisciplinary Approach. New York: Plenum, pp. 405–446.

Fleagle, J.G., and Kay, R.F. (1988) The phyletic position of the Parapithecidae. J. Hum. Evol. 16:483–531.

Harrison, T. (1987) The phylogenetic relationships of the early catarrhine primates: A review of the current evidence. J. Hum. Evol. 16:41–79.

Szalay, F.S., and Delson, E. (1979) Evolutionary History of the Primates. New York: Academic.

Cation-Ratio Dating

A highly controversial method of dating, based on the progressive weathering of *desert varnish* films on rock surfaces of arid and semiarid regions. Desert varnish, which forms through biogeochemical weathering of diurnally heated rock, gradually becomes enriched in titanium (Ti^{4+}) relative to potassium (K^+) and calcium (Ca^{2+}) cations (a cation, or cat-ion, is a positively charged atomic fragment). The change in the cation ratio ($Ca^{2+}+K^+/Ti^{4+}$) with time is independent of the thickness or the extent of the varnish deposit, but it is influenced by changes in humidity and temperature. The effects of short-term climate swings are damped out by the slow rate of enrichment, but regional long-term climate change has an effect that must be controlled for the cation ratios to have a geochronometric value. It has been found that, in any local geomorphological surface or terrain, the desert varnish on all stabilized rocks usually has the same ratio of these cations, indicating a common starting age. Independent calibration of these terrains, through ^{14}C (carbon-14) or Th/U analysis of fossils or authigenic carbonate in younger surfaces, and K/Ar (potassium-argon) dating of volcanics associated with older surfaces, leads to a regional time/weathering curve to which the cation ratio in other varnishes from the region can be compared. In this way, open-air sites on terraces and malpais flats, and even surface finds removed from the field, can be given reasonably accurate year-ages.

The method, which is relatively new, has been criticized on several grounds. Extreme temperatures, from fire or lightning, may temporarily disrupt the structure of the varnish and expose it to differential leaching, as may submergence in a water body for any length of time or exposure to the chemical environment at the base of a transient sheet of vegetated soil. Burial also halts the formation, and presumably the Ti^{4+} enrichment, of the varnish. These potentially biasing events are, for the most part, impossible to reconstruct from the geological and geochemical analysis, and their effects on the cation ratio are difficult to control. In addition, the cation quantities must be determined with extreme accuracy, and the pioneering analytical method of dispersive x-ray emission (PIXE) has the potential, according to some critics, of confusing barium and titanium signals. In 1998, Beck and colleagues questioned the validity of the radiocarbon dating program used to calibrate R. Dorn's cation method.

See also Beryllium and Aluminum Nuclide Dating; Geochronometry; Obsidian Hydration; Radiocarbon Dating. [J.A.V.C.]

Further Readings

Beck, W., Donahue, P.J., Jull, A.J.T., Burr, G., Broecker, W.S., Bonani, G.S., Hajdas, I., and Malotki, E. (1998) Ambiguities in direct dating of rock surfaces using radio carbon measurements. Science 280:2132:2135. Reply by R. Dorn, pp. 2135–2139.

Bierman, P.R., and Gillespie, A.R. (1994) Evidence suggesting that methods of rock-varnish cation-ratio dating are neither comparable nor consistently reliable. Quatern. Res. 41:82–90.

Catto, N.R. (1995) Cation ratio dating. In N.W. Rutter and N.R. Catto (eds.): Dating Methods for Quaternary Deposits. St. Johns, Newfoundland: Geol. Soc. Canada, Geotext 2, pp. 199–200.

Cave of Hearths

South African (Transvaal) site excavated by R.J. Mason that has produced a long and deeply stratified, Early and Middle Paleolithic archaeological sequence and hominid fossil remains. The earliest levels of Cave of Hearths (Beds 1–3) are Acheulean and are associated with faunal remains of extinct mammals, such as *Archidiskodon broomi* (= *Elephas iolensis*), *Equus helmei*, *Alcelaphhus robustus*, and *Antidorcas* cf. *bondi*. A late Middle Pleistocene age is suggested. Several distinct hearths with burnt bone have been found in these levels. Following a stratigraphic break, several horizons of Middle Stone Age assemblages featuring large flake blades made of quartzite and relatively few retouched tools are deposited in Beds 4–5. These are followed by three horizons (Beds 6–8) with fewer blades, more radial core technology and increasing numbers of retouched tools, particularly trimmed unifacial and bifacial points that reach frequencies of 10 percent–12 percent of the assemblage, and sidescrapers that attain a frequency of ca. 15 percent. The uppermost Middle Paleolithic level (Bed 9) contains an even larger proportion of trimmed points and sidescrapers, with the addition of backed blades and crescents. This latter industry may be referred to the Howieson's Poort, which has been dated elsewhere in Southern Africa to ca. 80–60 Ka.

A fragmentary mandible of a subadult individual was recovered from the Acheulean levels in 1947. The mandible is robust and has a moderate development of a chin and three fairly large teeth. It is notable for the rare condition (in fossil hominids) of congenital absence of the third molar.

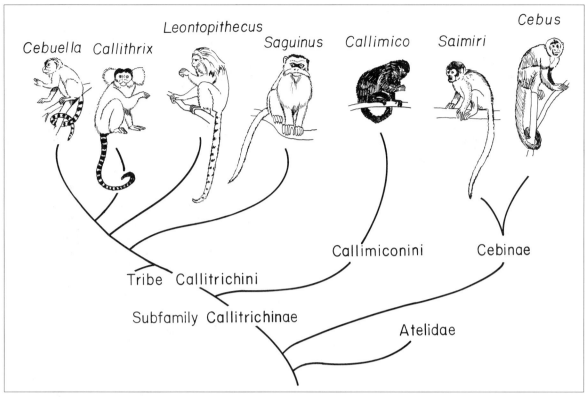

Classification and interrelationships of cebine and callitrichine platyrrhine monkeys.

See also Africa; Archaic Homo sapiens. [J.J.S., A.S.B., C.B.S.]

Cebidae

Family of New World platyrrhine monkeys including the subfamilies Cebinae and Callitrichinae, with their fossil allies, and the extinct subfamily Branisellinae. This taxonomic composition differs from most classifications. The traditional definition of the family dates to the middle 1800s. It was a gradistic concept designed to accommodate taxa thought to be separated by a chasm of morphological difference. The cebid group distinguished nonmarmosets (i.e., all platyrrhines bearing nailed digits) from the marmosets, which have claws and were judged to be diverse enough to warrant their own family, Callitrichidae or Hapalidae (occasionally the Callimiconidae was recognized as well). It is now known, however, that this arrangement tends to confuse both the phylogenetic and the adaptive relationships of various New World monkeys, particularly the cebines and callitrichines. The current concept of the Cebidae is based upon the hypothesis that callitrichines (marmosets) and cebines form a monophyletic unit and that their morphological differences relate to alternative lifestyles within a common frugivorous-insectivorous adaptive zone. The derived traits that these cebids display in common include reduced third molars; broad, large premolars; relatively large canines; and short faces. DNA sequencing confirms the cladistic relationship of cebines and callitrichines, although it suggests that owl monkeys (*Aotus*) are part of this group as well.

See also Atelidae; Branisellinae; Callitrichinae; Cebinae. [A.L.R.]

Further Readings

Hershkovitz, P. (1977) Living New World Monkeys (Platyrrhini), Vol. 1: Callitrichidae. Chicago: University of Chicago Press.

Napier, P.H. (1976) Catalogue of Primates in the British Museum (Natural History), Part 1: Families Callitrichidae and Cebidae. London: British Museum.

Rosenberger, A.L. (1981) Systematics: The higher taxa. In A.F. Coimbra-Filho and R.A. Mittermeier (eds.): Ecology and Behavior of Neotropical Primates. Rio de Janeiro: Academia Brasiliera de Ciencias, pp. 19–26.

Szalay, F.S., and Delson, E. (1979) Evolutionary History of the Primates. New York: Academic.

Cebinae

Subfamily of cebid platyrrhine monkeys including *Cebus* (capuchins), *Saimiri* (squirrel monkeys), and fossil allies. They make up a predaceous-frugivorous, large-brained radiation, which specializes in foraging concealed insects by extracting them from foliage and crevices and sorting through dead leaf batches and infestations at broken branch ends. Extinct members include a Holocene form from the Dominican Republic, *Antillothrix* (previously *"Saimiri"*) *bernensis;* a Middle Miocene (14–12 Ma) species from Colombia's La Venta, *Saimiri* (previously *Neosaimiri*) *fieldsi;* and two Early Miocene (21–19 Ma) species: *Dolichocebus gaimanensis* from Argentina and *Chilecebus carrascoensis* from Chile. The latter three may have very close, potentially ancestral, phylogenetic ties with *Saimiri*. *Laventiana annectens*, also from La Venta, is classified as a cebine but appears to be intermediate morphologically between cebines and callitrichines, emphasizing the close relationship of these two subfamilies; some researchers have synonymized it with *Neosaimiri*, however. Cebines share only primitive platyrrhine resemblances with the atelid pitheciines and atelines, with whom they have been traditionally classified. *Cebus* and *Saimiri* share homologous derived traits, such as an enlarged brain, a rounded braincase, centrally placed foramen magnum, close-set orbits, abbreviated faces, large sexually dimorphic canines, broad premolars, robust mandibles, and a semiprehensile tail. These characteristics are all interrelated facets of their foraging strategy.

Cebinae
    Cebus
   † *Antillothrix*
  (†)*Saimiri* (including †*Neosaimiri*)
   † *Dolichocebus*
   † *Chilecebus*
   † *Laventiana*
†extinct

See also Americas; Brain; Cebidae; Diet; La Venta; Locomotion; Patagonia; Skull; Teeth. [A.L.R.]

Further Readings

Delson, E., and Rosenberger, A.L. (1984) Are there any anthropoid primate "living fossils"? In N. Eldredge and S. Stanley (eds.): Living Fossils. New York: Springer-Verlag.

Flynn, J.J., Wyss, A.R., Charrier, R., and Swisher, C.C. (1995) An early Miocene anthropoid skull from the Chilean Andes. Nature 373:603–607.

Masanuru, T. (1994) New specimens of *Neosaimiri fieldsi* from La Venta, Colombia: A middle Miocene ancestor of the living squirrel monkeys. J. Hum. Evol. 27:329–360.

Rosenberger, A.L. (1979) Cranial anatomy and implication *of Dolichocebus gaimanensis.* Nature 279:416–418.

Rosenberger, A.L. (1983) Tale of tails: Parallelism and prehensility. Am. J. Phys. Anthropol. 60:103–107.

Rosenberger, A.L., Setoguchi, T., and Hartwig, W.C. (1991) *Laventiana annectens,* new fossil evidence for the origins of callitrichine New World monkeys. Proc. Nat. Acad. Sci. USA 88:2137–2140.

Szalay, F.S., and Delson, E. (1979) Evolutionary History of the Primates. New York: Academic.

Cenozoic

Youngest and briefest era in the geological time scale, encompassing the last 65 Myr from the end of the Cretaceous to the present. The Cenozoic inherited an ancient subdivision of the "post-Chalk" strata into two parts: the Tertiary for consolidated deposits, and the Quaternary for glacial drift and alluvium. In modern time scales, the Quaternary period is restricted to the last 1.8 Myr, with one epoch, and the Tertiary period covers all of the rest, with five epochs. Consensus is growing to replace the Tertiary with two periods, the Paleogene and the Neogene, and it has been suggested that the name *Quaternary* be suppressed as well, in favor of a term such as *Pleistogene* or *Anthropogene.*

The Cenozoic is popularly known as the Age of Mammals, but the mammalian orders that inherited the world at the end of the Cretaceous are no longer with us. The Eocene was a time of almost total tranformation, when most of the extant placental orders made their first appearance in faunas that also contained the last of the surviving lineages from the Cretaceous. The first euprimates and proboscideans, however, are known from the Late Paleocene of Africa, and many regard the plesiadapiform *Purgatorius,* from the latest Cretaceous of Montana, as a member of the primates.

In the Paleocene and the Eocene, global climate was stabilized by efficient transfer of equatorial heat to high latitudes, with a well-developed circumtropical current via the Tethys Ocean separating southern and northern continental regions. The Central Plateau of Antarctica probably had an ice cap even in the Early Cenozoic, but its controlling effect on world climate was not felt until the Oligocene. In the Paleocene, ventilation and convection in the deep seas were controlled by thermohaline overturn in the tropics, bringing warm saline water to the abyssal depths. Thermohaline circulation came to a dramatic end at the beginning of the Eocene, with the initiation of the present circulation driven by high-latitude advection of cold-water masses, but the oceans continued to be relatively warm during the Eocene. Thus, for the earliest third of the Cenozoic, seasons were relatively undifferentiated; warm and moist climates prevailed over most of the globe; and continental aridity was rare.

Gradually, however, northward motion of Gondwana plates pinched off the Tethys while opening up the seaways around Antarctica. With regard to the Tethys, diversion and narrowing of the equatorial circumglobal circulation began with the Early Cenozoic docking of the Anatolian, Iranian, and Indian landmasses along the Pontide-Elburz-Himalayan suture, and the Oligocene closing of the Mesogean straits of Central Europe in the Alpine-Carpathian suture. Total blockage came, first, in the Early Miocene contact of Afro-Arabia against the Anatolian and Iranian borderland and, subsequently, by the Pliocene closures of the inter-American and Australo-Malaysian deep channels in northern Colombia and the Flores Straits, respectively.

The northward motion of the Australian, African, and South American landmasses also increased the volume and influence of the Circum-Antarctic Current. This led to expansion of the Antarctic ice cap and its increasing contact with the sea. Beginning in the Oligocene, the cold, dense water masses produced by this contact drained ever more voluminously into the deep ocean basins, to well up in Coriolus cells along the west sides of the continents, with dramatic effects on continental climate. In this way, polar cold began to influence temperate regions, just as Tethys circulation, the basic agent in the transfer of equatorial warmth to higher latitudes, began to break down. Climatic feedback, in the form of colder winters, acclerated the trend, creating ice caps in the northern polar regions that became a new source of refrigerated deep water in the Pliocene. The world's oceans beneath the thermocline are now almost at freezing and colder than at any time since the Permian. It is probable that the oceans will remain cold for as long as the continents remain in their present configuration, anthropogenic influences notwithstanding. For this reaon, the instability of Late Cenozoic climates, with orbitally driven swings from glacial to interglacial, is likely to continue indefinitely.

The changes in continental geography and world climate during the Cenozoic appear to have been accompanied by a steady increase in the number of mammalian taxa. This trend seems intuitively unlikely, given the incorporation of formerly isolated continental faunas in Africa and South America and the waves of climate-driven extinction in the Pliocene and the Pleistocene. A continuous increase in mammalian diversity could, however, be related to an increasingly partitioned environment. Sharply widening geographic and annual extremes in climatic parameters such as temperature, rainfall, and seasonality, together with the rapidly increasing amplitude of variation in these parameters during the later Cenozoic, have resulted in the replacement of formerly extensive ecological regimes with far more complexly subdivided habitats.

Some notable milestones in the progressive diversification of continental environments in the Cenozoic were the initiation of temperate arid zones and of drought-tolerant tropical evergreen forests in the Oligocene; the expansion of fire-climax grass and conifer-dominated communities in the Late Miocene; and the spread of frost-tolerant deciduous forest in temperate high-rainfall regions during the Pliocene.

By the end of the Eocene, mammals had already reoccupied most of the niches formerly exploited by dinosaurs. The novel habitats that opened in the latter part of the Cenozoic, such as desert, steppe, tundra, deciduous forest, and polar ocean, called forth a second wave of adaptations among the mammals. Primates, a consistently conservative group perhaps more fundamentally dependent on tropical forest than any other major order, were not notably successful in coping with Cenozoic change. The Middle Miocene anthropoid expansion into Eurasia collapsed when temperate climates grew more seasonal, ca. 10 Ma. Today, the only primates able to survive outside of the tropics and subtropics are *Macaca* and *Homo*.

See also Climate Change and Evolution; Eocene; Grande Coupure; Miocene; Neogene; Oligocene; Paleocene; Plate Tectonics; Pleistocene; Pliocene; Primates; Quaternary; Tertiary; Time Scale. [J.A.V.C.]

Further Readings

Berggren, W.A., Kent, D.V., Aubry, M.P., and Hardenbol, J., eds. (1995) Geochronology, Time Scales, and Global Stratigraphic Correlation (Special Publication No. 54). Tulsa: Society for Sedimentary Geology.

Briskin, M., ed. (1983) Paleoclimatology and chronology of the Cenozoic. Palaeogeog., Palaeoclimatol., Palaeoecol. 42:1–209.

Prothero, D., and Berggren, W.A., eds. (1992) Eocene-Oligocene Climatic and Biotic Evolution. Princeton: Princeton University Press.

Savage, D.E., and Russell, D.E. (1983) Mammalian Paleofaunas of the World. Reading: Addison-Wesley.

Vrba, E.S., Denton, G.H., Partridge, T.C., and Burckle, L.H., eds. (1995) Paleoclimate and Evolution, with Emphasis on Human Origins. New Haven: Yale University Press.

Ceprano

Early Middle (or late Early) Pleistocene locality in Latium, Italy, southeast of Rome, dated older than 700 Ka by potassium-argon and faunal correlation, which has yielded a partial human cranium and stone tools. The site is located near the base of a thick (up to 50 m) section of later Pleistocene sediments, volcaniclastics, and basalts, the latter dated at a number of points and levels. Mousterian and later Acheulean artifacts have been recovered from the upper layers, with dates from ca. 400 to 100 Ka. Below that, there is an early Acheulean assemblage with bone tools, associated with a variety of mammal species. This horizon is correlated to the Ranuccio site in the Agnani Basin, ca. 37 km distant, where it is dated ca. 460 Ka. The human fossil derives from a still lower level, which is otherwise sterile and reconstructed as a paleosol on a slope leading down to a marshy pool. Below this is another horizon yielding older mammalian fossils and Mode 1 artifacts. Basalts dated to ca. 700 Ka are correlated to a level above the cranium. It has been suggested that the cranium might have been redeposited from the older faunal level and that it might date to more than 800 Ka, but this is not definite.

The human fossil is represented by most of a slightly crushed and warped braincase, lacking much of the base and all of the face. The parietals are heavily damaged and fragmentary. The vault is low but rounded, with thick bones; the occiput is moderately angular. The supraorbital torus is heavy and turns down slightly at glabella. There is no sagittal keeling on the frontal bone. The cranial capacity has been estimated ca. 1050 ml. The original describers attribute the specimen to "late *Homo erectus*" because of the low vault, strong brows, and occipital shape. However, in light of what is known about other early European hominins, such as those from Petralona, Bilzingsleben, Arago, and Atapuerca TD6, it appears more likely that this cranium represents a population more derived than those usually included in *H. erectus*. It would perhaps better be included in "archaic *Homo sapiens*" (= *Homo heidelbergensis*), albeit as an ancient and conservative member of that group. A. Ascenzi and colleagues note that such an interpretation is less likely due to the lack of fit between the Ceprano calvaria and the Mauer mandible (type of *Homo heidelbergensis*), adding that a better fit exists with the Tighenif 3 mandible. On the other hand, D. Dean has suggested that the Tighenif sample is better included in "archaic *Homo sapiens*" than in *Homo erectus*, while J.-J. Hublin has argued for the resuscitation of *H. mauritanicus* (with Tighenif as holotype) to replace *H. antecessor* as a Euro-African post-*erectus* taxon including Ceprano and Atapuerca TD6. In 1998 it was reported that a new reconstruction of Ceprano has been made by R.J. Clarke which resulted in an even more *Homo erectus*-like morphology. Further analysis of the calvaria and recovery of facial elements are awaited with great interest.

See also Acheulean; Archaic Homo sapiens; Atapuerca; Europe; Homo antecessor; Homo erectus; Homo heidelbergensis. [E.D.]

Further Readings

Ascenzi, A., Bidditu, I., Cassoli, P.F., Segre, A.G., and Segre-Naldini, E. (1996) A calvarium of late *Homo erectus* from Ceprano, Italy. J. Hum. Evol. 31:409–423.

Dean, D., and Delson, E. (1995) *Homo* at the gates of Europe. Nature 373:472–473.

Cercopithecidae

Family of living and extinct anthropoid primates, commonly known as the Old World monkeys. Cercopithecidae as recognized here is the only family in the superfamily Cercopithecoidea and includes three subfamilies: Cercopithecinae, Colobinae, and the extinct Victoriapithecinae. The diagnostic derived characters of at least modern cercopithecids include loss of the hypoconulid on dP_4- M_2, elongation of the cheek teeth, and realignment of the cusps into a bilophodont pattern with occluding upper and lower molars becoming mirror images of each other, an adaptation mainly for folding and slicing leaves or crushing hard food items like nuts (this complex of features is incomplete in Victoriapithecinae); flare or widening of cheek teeth from the cusp apexes to the cervix; extension of the P_3 mesial flange below the alveolar plane and extension of the C^1 mesial sulcus onto the root, both especially in males; shortened posterior calcaneal facet for the astragalus and divided anteromedial facet, which stabilizes the lower ankle joint; and restriction of the hallucal facet on the entocuneiform, again to stabilize the foot for terrestrial or cursorial locomotion. A high and narrow nasal aperture probably characterized the ancestral cercopithecid (re-

cently found also in *Victoriapithecus*) and was secondarily modified in the cercopithecine tribe Papionini.

This combination of features, along with conservative retentions from a catarrhine ancestry, like a narrow thorax, long ulnar olecranon and styloid processes, narrow ilium, strong ischial tuberosity (and callosities), and long tail, allow some reconstruction of the mode of life of the common ancestor of the cercopithecids. One of the major adaptations of the family was a shift to greater use of a terrestrial substrate, either in open country or on the forest floor. The dentition is modified to include more leaves in the diet, a shift from the more purely frugivorous diet of eocatarrhines. Perhaps this was to permit early monkeys to compete with contemporaneous pliopithecids and early hominoids in marginal or seasonally varying habitats, where fruits were sometimes scarce but leaves usually plentiful. This emphasis on lower-quality foods was increased in the colobines, where the dentition and the digestive system were further modified to facilitate a diet that in some species consists mainly of young leaves. Cercopithecines, on the other hand, emphasized a more varied diet, often in at least partly open habitats in which a variety of foodstuffs were available.

The early history of Cercopithecidae is entirely African, with the first entry to Eurasia probably in the earliest Late Miocene (ca. 11 Ma). The later Early Miocene and early Middle Miocene saw a variety of victoriapithecine species present in northern and eastern Africa, with the primate assemblage at the partly open woodland habitats of Maboko Island (Kenya) dominated by this group. Although the fossil record is scarce from 14 to 8 Ma, it is possible to suggest the following outline of cercopithecid diversification. The early colobines probably increased the proportion of leaves in their diet in a more arboreal habitat, as evidenced also by the be-

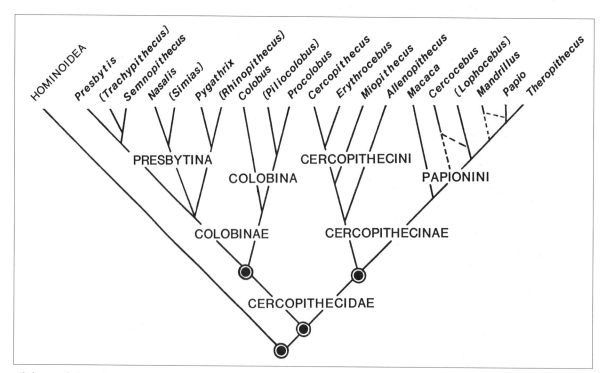

Cladogram of relationships among genera, and subgenera (in parentheses) of Cercopithecidae, with subfamilies, tribes, and subtribes indicated. Modified from Strasser and Delson, 1987.

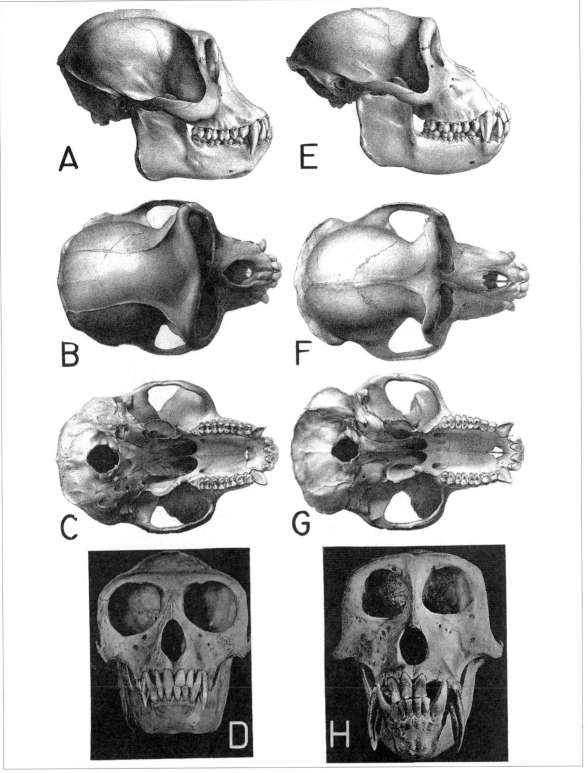

Crania of medium-sized male cercopithecids, illustrating the two major patterns seen in the family: on the left, Pygathrix, *a colobine; and on the right,* Macaca, *a cercopithecine. Views, top to bottom: right lateral, dorsal, basal, frontal. Drawings from H.M.D. de Blainville,* Ostéographie. I: Primates, *1839, Baillière.*

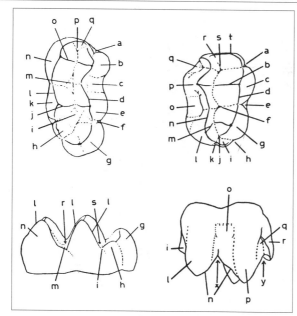

Upper and lower molar of Theropithecus *to illustrate cercopithecid morphology and terminology used in descriptions. Left: M₃ in lingual and occlusal views. Right: M³ in occlusal and buccal views. In all views, raised features indicated by solid line, depressed features by dotted line. For complete dentitions, see illustrations in articles on* CERCOPITHECINAE *and* COLOBINAE *Structures labeled on lower tooth: (a) mesial buccal cleft; (b) protoconid; (c) median buccal cleft; (d) buccal margin; (e) hypoconid; (f) distal buccal cleft; (g) hypoconulid; (h) 6th cusp (tuberculum sextum); (i) distal fovea; (j) hypolophid; (k) entoconid; (l) lingual margin; (m) talonid basin; (n) metaconid; (o) protolophid; (p) trigonid basin (mesial fovea); (q) mesial shelf; (r) median lingual notch; (s) distal lingual notch. Structures labeled on upper tooth: (a) mesial buccal cleft; (b) paraloph; (c) paracone; (d) buccal margin; (e) median buccal cleft; (f) trigon basin; (g) metacone; (h) distal buccal cleft; (i) distal shelf; (j) distal fovea (talon basin); (k) distal lingual cleft; (l) hypocone; (m) metaloph; (n) lingual maragin; (o) median lingual cleft; (p) protocone; (q) mesial lingual cleft; (r) mesial shelf; (s) mesial fovea; (t) mesial margin. From Szalay and Delson, 1979.*

ginning of thumb reduction even in the semiterrestrial *Mesopithecus*. This European Late Miocene colobine represents a clade that may have exited Africa to Eurasia via a partly forested corridor, presumably through southwest Asia. At the same time, early cercopithecines, with no fossil documentation at all, may have increased their adaptations to terrestriality, involving lengthened faces as well as postcranial changes; they appear also to have returned to a more frugivorous diet, perhaps as a result of competition with the colobines. In turn, they may have competed successfully with the frugivorous hominoids, which were forced to alter their mode(s) of locomotion radically to obtain food unavailable to the cercopithecines. Probably later during the Late Miocene, the cercopithecines (tribe Cercopithecini) reentered the forest, undergoing dental changes in parallel with colobines (flare reduction and M₃ hypoconulid loss) and perhaps diversifying through chromosomal fissioning. The larger-bodied papionins appear to have been divided into two major zoogeographic units by the expansion of the Sahara Desert barrier during the Late Miocene, with the macaque group eventually spreading into Eurasia from North Africa and the geladababoon-mandrill-mangabey lineage entering a broad range of habitats in sub-Saharan Africa.

See also Africa; Catarrhini; Cercopithecinae; Cercopithecoidea; Colobinae; Hominoidea; Miocene; Monkey; Primate Ecology; Primate Societies; Teeth; Victoriapithecinae. [E.D.]

Further Readings

Andrews, P. (1981) Species diversity and diet in monkeys and apes during the Miocene. In C.B. Stringer (ed.): Aspects of Human Evolution. London: Taylor and Francis, pp. 25–61.

Benefit, B.R., and McCrossin, M.L. (1993) The lacrimal fossa of Cercopithecoidea, with special reference to cladistic analysis of Old World monkey relationships. Folia primatol. 60:133–145.

Delson, E. (1992) Evolution of Old World monkeys. In R.D. Martin, D. Pilbeam, and J.S. Jones (eds.): Encyclopedia of Human Evolution. Cambridge: Cambridge University Press, pp. 217–222.

Ripley, S. (1979) Environmental grain, niche diversification, and positional behavior in Neogene primates: An evolutionary hypothesis. In M.E. Morbeck, H. Preuschoft, and N. Gomherg (eds.): Environment, Behavior, and Morphology: Dynamic Interactions in Primates. New York: Fischer, pp. 37–74.

Strasser, E., and Delson, E. (1987) Cladistic analysis of cercopithecid relationships. J. Hum. Evol. 16:81–99.

Szalay, F.S., and Delson, E. (1979) Evolutionary History of the Primates. New York: Academic.

Temerin, L.A., and Cant, J.G. (1980) The evolutionary divergence of Old World monkeys and apes. Am. Nat. 122:335–351.

Cercopithecinae

Subfamily of Old World monkeys including the cheek-pouched cercopithecids, such as guenons (*Cercopithecus* and allies), baboons (*Papio*), macaques (*Macaca*), and mangabeys (*Cercocebus*) and their extant and extinct relatives. The underlying adaptation of the cercopithecines appears to be their increased reliance on the terrestrial environment for feeding and social activities, although some members of the subfamily are highly arboreal. As part of a general increase in terrestriality by comparison with ancestral cercopithecids, the earliest cercopithecines apparently evolved several novel features that continue to characterize all of their descendants, whatever their current mode of life. The derived conditions of Cercopithecinae are essentially craniodental and include large pouches in the cheeks for temporary storage of food; relatively enlarged I²; loss of enamel on the lingual surfaces of both lower incisors; facial elongation, linked with narrow interorbital distance, long nasal bones, the lacrimal bone often extending beyond the anteroinferior border of the orbit with the lacrimal fossa wholly enclosed within that bone, the vomer expanded to form part of the medial wall of the orbit, and the ethmoid apparently expanded anteriorly; a low-vaulted and long neurocranium; mandibular corpus deepening mesially and symphysis with poorly developed inferior torus; brain modification involving rostral expansion of the occipital region and increase of the associa-

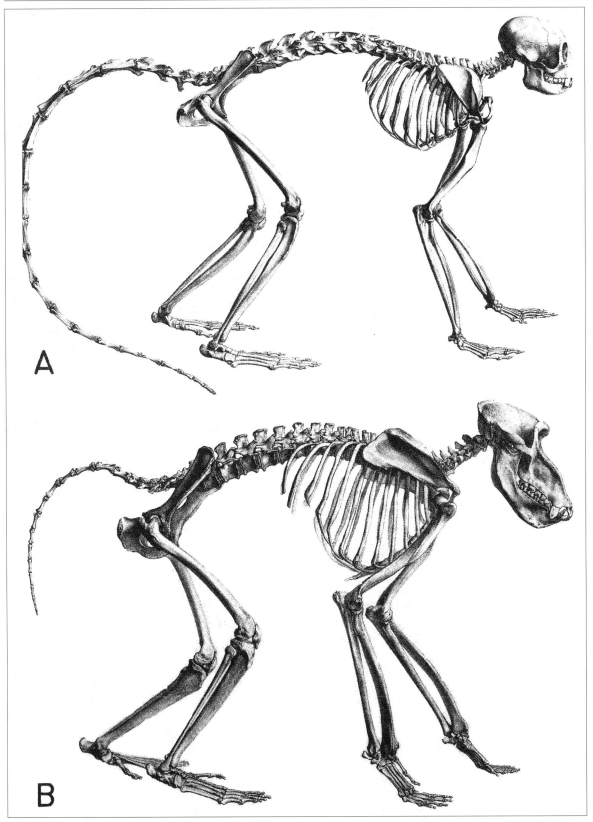

Skeletons of representative cercopithecids: above, arboreal Cercopithecus; *below, terrestrial* Papio. *From H.M.D. de Blainville,* Ostéographie. I: Primates, *1839, Baillière.*

tion and the visual cortex, documented on the surface by numerous sulcal modifications. Postcranially, cercopithecines differ from colobines in several consistent ways. The majority of these are conservative retentions from the common cercopithecid ancestor, while in others morphocline polarity is uncertain (e.g., robust and straight-shafted limbs, subequal supratrochlear and supracapitular fossae on the distal humerus, and doubled radial articular surface on the proximal ulna). Most of these locomotor-related features are probably retained from an increasingly terrestrial ancestral cercopithecine, which was also the interpretation offered for cheek pouches: filled with food while an animal was foraging terrestrially, then emptied if the animal fled to the security of upper branches. Carefully designed studies revealed, to the contrary, that terrestrial species have reduced pouches, implying less terrestriality at the origin of this feature. Cercopithecines have a varied diet, including fruit as its usual central focus, and their generally large incisors and especially the reduction of enamel on the lowers are adaptations for scraping and cutting the outer covering of tough fruits prior to reduction of pieces by the molars. Cercopithecine cheek teeth appear to be broadly conservative, with low relief compared with those of colobines, as well as greater flare, or basal broadening, and longer trigonids; the last feature may, in fact, be derived. It appears that this dentition was originally evolved for a mixed leaf-and-fruit diet, by comparison with the more frugivorous ancestral catarrhine diet, and that cercopithecines, especially the baboon-macaque group, hardly modified it subsequently.

Within the Cercopithecinae, there are two major subdivisions, or tribes, that each can be further divided into subtribes; the characters of these groups can be reviewed, although they are not emphasized here. The tribe Cercopithecini includes the mainly arboreal guenons (*Cercopithecus*) and talapoins (*Miopithecus*), the perhaps semiterrestrial swamp monkey *Allenopithecus*, and the very terrestrial patas (*Erythrocebus*). All of these share loss of the hypoconulid on M_3 (lost on anterior cheek teeth in ancestral cercopithecids) and an increase in chromosome number above 42.

Allenopithecus is conservative, and the other three genera derived, in having reduced molar flare and the male ischial callosities separated by a strip of hairy skin. *Cercopithecus* further presents a greatly increased diploid chromosome number over the 48 of *Allenopithecus* and the 54 seen in *Miopithecus* and *Erythrocebus,* and it shares with *Erythrocebus* loss of a roughly monthly cycle in its female sexual swellings. This suggests that *Allenopithecus* is most similar to the common ancestor of all cercopithecins and its lineage diverged first, followed, in turn, by those of talapoins, patas, and the many guenons. The swamp-living adaptations of the first two of these clades may suggest this as the original environment to which the tribe was adapted.

Patas monkeys live in open woodlands with acacia trees between the Sahara and the rain forests of Central Africa. Small troops led by a single adult male have large ranges. Different authorities recognize between one dozen and two dozen species within *Cercopithecus,* but there are only about six to eight ecological-behavioral patterns. *C. aethiops* and *C. lhoesti* are quite terrestrial, living in gallery forests along watercourses

or denser forest, respectively, but most other species are highly arboreal. Members of four to six species may inhabit a single grove of trees, at different canopy levels or concentrating on complementary foods. Multispecies associations are common in generally unimale troops. The fossil record of this tribe is scarce, but characteristic teeth are known from Kenyan and Ethiopian localities as far back as 3 Ma.

The second, far more diverse and widespread, cercopithecine tribe is Papionini, including the macaques of North Africa and eastern Asia and the baboons, mandrills (*Mandrillus*), mangabeys, and geladas (*Theropithecus*) of sub-Saharan Africa. There may be only one distinct derived character of this tribe, a secondary increase in the maximum width of the nasal aperture, but papionins are characterized by further development of such cercopithecine tendencies as increased molar flare, accessory cuspules in molar clefts, an elongated face, posterior inclination of the mandibular ramus, and a generally high degree of terrestriality. It has been suggested that the two geographic divisions of Papionini represent true clades, separated by the development of the Sahara Desert as an ecological barrier to continued north-south migration and gene flow during the Late Miocene (ca. 10–7 Ma). No clear and consistent morphological features characterize these two, but the African genera do share a steep drop in facial profile in front of the orbits and often hollows or fossae on the maxilla and the lateral surfaces of the mandible (facial fossae). Chromosome number is constant at 42, and the dentition of almost all papionins is identical, although some mangabeys have especially high flare, while geladas, which at times have been considered to represent a third subtribe, have uniquely derived dental and cranial form.

Macaques inhabit a wide range of environments, including rain forest, woodland, steppe, and snow-covered regions, and their diets are concomitantly varied. Some of the dozen or so recognized species are highly arboreal, others semiterrestrial; most live in multimale troops with female as well as male hierarchies and maternally inherited social status. Mangabeys are ecological equivalents of macaques in the African forests, with some species making much more use of the ground than others. Two groups are now often recognized as full genera, and some evidence suggests that they are not each other's closest relatives (i.e., that mangabeys as a group are paraphyletic). Savannah baboons form a single widespread species ranging from Guinea (West African coast) to Ethiopia and southern Saudi Arabia, down to South Africa and into Angola. At least six subgroups may be recognized; each used to be thought full species but have since been observed to interbreed in overlap zones, confirming the genetic unity of the species. Multimale troops are the rule, especially in open country, but in forest habitats the structured social hierarchies are less evident. Mandrills are deep-forest baboons, with brightly colored faces in the male to serve as signals in unimale troops. The living gelada is the last remnant of a once widespread lineage, now restricted to the dry uplands of Ethiopia. There *Theropithecus* individuals live in unimale harems, which may come together in associations of several hundred for sleeping on scattered cliffs and for feeding in certain seasons. They are the most terrestrially adapted of living monkeys, with short digits

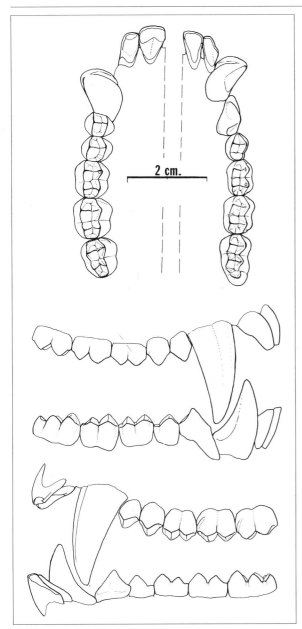

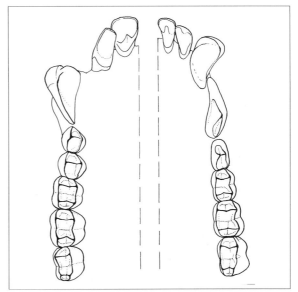

Dentition (right side) of male Erythrocebus, *in occlusal (upper on left, lower on right) view, for comparison with those of* Macaca *at the left. From Szalay and Delson, 1979.*

Dentition (right side) of male Macaca, *in occlusal (upper on left, lower on right), buccal, and lingual views. These teeth are typical for* Papionini. *From Szalay and Delson, 1979.*

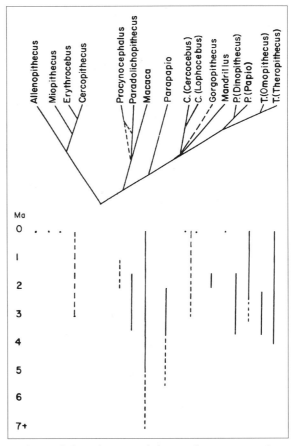

Cladogram of relationships among the living and extinct genera and subgenera (in parentheses) of Cercopithecinae. Dotted lines indicate uncertain links. Note that some molecular and new morphological data contradict this older morphological interpretation, suggesting instead that Theropithecus *and* Lophocebus *are farther removed. Below the cladogram are indicated the known time ranges of these genera; solid lines indicate well-preserved fossils, dotted lines indicate fragmentary remains, less clear allocations or dating uncertainty.*

for better walking and for manipulation of the grass blades and stems that form their dietary staple. Their teeth have converged on those of colobines in having high relief (deep notches and elevated cusp tips), but they also have thick enamel and a characteristic wear pattern to prolong tooth life while grinding up their low-quality gritty diet. Morphological and molecular studies of the relationships among the African genera have yielded conflicting views: Skull form suggests that mandrills might belong to the genus *Papio*, with *Theropithecus* close but derived and *Cercocebus* unified; DNA sequencing and other genetic evidence, on the other hand, indicates that *Theropithecus* and *Papio* are closest, with *Cercocebus* related, while *Mandrillus* and *Lophocebus* seem to form a separate clade. In 1999 J.G. Fleagle and W.S. McGraw described a complex of derived postcranial features (and one dental similarity) which link *Lophocebus* and *Mandrillus*, strongly supporting the genetic viewpoint.

The fossil record of Papionini is rich, especially in Africa. The earliest members of the tribe are known by teeth from North Africa and Kenya late in the Miocene (8–6 Ma), perhaps, from geological evidence, after the Sahara had formed an ecological barrier. In the Pliocene (4–2 Ma) of eastern and southern Africa, the conservative *Parapapio* is fairly common. It has a similar facial conformation to macaques and mangabeys (but may share some anteorbital deepening with *Papio*), and rare postcranial elements suggest a semiterrestrial adaptation. *Parapapio* may represent a form close to the common ancestor of later African papionins.

At least four varieties of *Theropithecus* are frequent, especially at waterside sites. Three of these form a lineage known across Africa, from southern South Africa to Morocco, from the Early Pliocene to the later Middle Pleistocene. They are characterized by a gradual size increase and anterior tooth reduction through time, and the late large forms (up to 70–100 kg) probably were hunted by Acheulean peoples, perhaps to extinction. There is controversy over taxonomic ranking, but here they are recognized as three subspecies of *T. oswaldi*. Several teeth suggest that this group also reached Spain and the Siwaliks of India ca. 2–1 Ma. The living *T. gelada* is more conservative than even the earliest fossil form (although it is placed in the same subgenus) and probably separated from them by 4–3.5 Myr. Another lineage (the subgenus *Omopithecus*) is represented only in the Lake Turkana region, at Koobi Fora (Kenya) and Omo (Ethiopia) between ca. 3.5 and 2 Ma: The moderately well known *T. brumpti* had *Papio*-like large incisors and a low, flat muzzle with typical gelada molars and flaring zygomatic arches, but its putative ancestor ?*T. baringensis* had smaller incisors and less-complex molars, suggesting that molar form evolved in parallel in the two lineages.

Mangabeys are poorly represented paleontologically, probably because forest soils are notoriously acid rich (bone thus deteriorates quickly), but some East African Pleistocene specimens have diagnostic facial features of the group. *Papio* is known by large-bodied populations probably referable to the living savannah baboon species in southern (and more rarely eastern) Africa after 3 Ma, but they were almost always less common than *Theropithecus*. It has been suggested that they were then more forest-fringe dwellers, while geladas were more successful in open country, the pattern changing only in the later Pleistocene. Small-bodied *Papio* is also known in South Africa between 2.5 and 1.5 Ma, and a very large form known as *P.* (*Dinopithecus*) is common at sites in South Africa, Angola, and Ethiopia from 3 to 1.5 Ma. Although this group has previously been given its own genus, it differs from *Papio* only in lacking facial fossae and is now considered a baboon subgenus, possibly related to the ancestors of mandrills. The large-bodied *Gorgopithecus* is represented only at one group of South African sites between 1.9 and 1.5 Ma, but its distinctive facial conformation, deep fossae, and reduced dental sexual dimorphism justify its generic identity.

Macaque fossils are known in North Africa and across Europe from Spain and Britain to Israel and the Caucasus

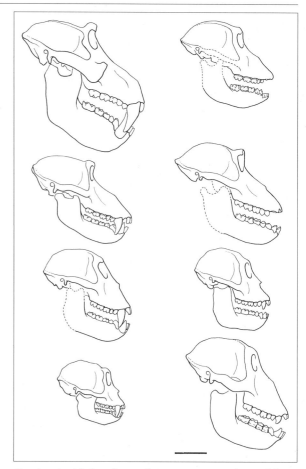

Drawings, in right lateral view, of representative cercopithecines; left column males, right column females. Top row: †Theropithecus (O.) brumpti, †T. (T.) oswaldi darti. *Second row:* Papio (P.) hamadryas, †P. (Dinopithecus) quadratirostris. *Third row:* †Parapapio broomi (both). *Bottom row:* Macaca fascicularis, †Paradolichopithecus senezensis. *Scale bar = 5 cm;* †indicates extinct species. By Lorraine Meeker.

throughout the Pliocene and the Pleistocene (5.5 Ma onward). The living "Barbary ape" (*Macaca sylvanus*) of Algeria and Gibraltar probably represents the remaining relic of this far wider distribution. Living macaques have been divided into four to six subgroups, all of which show independent reduction in tail length and have overlapping distributions in eastern Asia. Fossil teeth document their arrival in China by 5.5 Ma and India by ca. 2.5 Ma, and a variety of populations are known from the Pleistocene of China and Indonesia. The extinct *Paradolichopithecus* was larger bodied than any macaque (males ca. 35 kg), far more terrestrially adapted, and less sex-dimorphic in cranial size, but had similar facial morphology. It is known from Spain through Central Asia in the later Pliocene (ca. 3–1.8 Ma) and probably represents a baboonlike macaque derivative. A similar form, *Procynocephalus*, is represented by fragmentary remains from the later Pliocene of India and China; it is kept taxonomically distinct because its limb bones do not appear to present the reduced dimorphism of its western "cousin."

Subfamily Cercopithecinae
    Tribe Cercopithecini

Subtribe Allenopithecina
Allenopithecus
Subtribe Cercopithecina
Cercopithecus
Miopithecus
Erythrocebus
Tribe Papionini
Subtribe Papionina
Papio
P. (*Papio*)
† P. (*Dinopithecus*)
Mandrillus
Cercocebus
C. (*Cercocebus*)
? C. (*Lophocebus*)
† *Gorgopithecus*
Theropithecus
T. (*Theropithecus*)
† T. (*Omopithecus*)
† *Parapapio*
Subtribe Macacina
Macaca
† *Procynocephalus*
† *Paradolichopithecus*

†extinct

See also Africa; Asia, Eastern and Southern; Cercopithecidae; Colobinae; Diet; Europe; Extinction; Miocene; Molecular "vs." Morphological Approaches to Systematics; Monkey; Paleobiogeography; Pleistocene; Pliocene; Primate Ecology; Primate Societies; Skull; Teeth. [E.D.]

Further Readings

Benefit, B.R., and McCrossin, M.L. (1993) The lacrimal fossa of Cercopithecoidea, with special reference to cladistic analysis of Old World monkey relationships. Folia Primatol. 60:133–145.

Delson, E. (1984) Cercopithecid biochronology of the African Plio-Pleistocene: Correlation among eastern and southern hominid-bearing localities. Cour. Forsch. Inst. Senckenberg 69:199–218.

Disotell, T.R. (1994) Generic level relationships of the Papionini (Cercopithecoidea). Am. J. Phys. Anthropol. 94:47–57.

Fleagle, J.G. and McGraw, W.S. (1999) Skeletal and dental morphology supports diphyletic origin of baboons and mandrills. Proc. Natl. Acad. Sci. USA 96:1157–1161.

Gautier-Hion, A., Bourlière, F., Gautier, J.P., Kingdon, J. eds. (1988) A Primate Radiation: Evolutionary Biology of the African Guenons. New York: Cambridge University Press.

Jablonski, N., ed. (1993) *Theropithecus:* Rise and Fall of a Primate Genus. Cambridge: Cambridge University Press.

Jolly, C.J. (1993) Species, subspecies, and baboon systematics. In W.H. Kimbel and L.B. Martin (eds.): Species, Species Concepts, and Primate Evolution. New York: Plenum, pp. 67–107.

Lindburg, D.E., ed. (1980) The Macaques: Studies in Ecology, Behavior, and Evolution. New York: Van Nostrand.

Murray, P. (1975) The role of cheek pouches in cercopithecine monkey adaptive strategy. In R. Tuttle (ed.): Primate Functional Morphology and Evolution. The Hague: Mouton, pp. 151–194.

Rowell, T.E. (1985) Guenons, macaques, and baboons. In D. MacDonald (ed.): The Encyclopedia of Mammals. New York: Facts-on-File, pp. 370–381.

Shellis, R.P., and Hiiemae, K.M. (1986) Distribution of enamel on the incisors of Old World monkeys. Am. J. Phys. Anthropol. 71:103–113.

Strasser, E., and Delson, E. (1987) Cladistic analysis of cercopithecid relationships. J. Hum. Evol. 16:81–99.

Szalay, F.S., and Delson, E. (1979) Evolutionary History of the Primates. New York: Academic.

Cercopithecoidea

One of the two extant superfamilies of Old World anthropoids (Catarrhini), including the family Cercopithecidae (Old World monkeys). Although cercopithecoids are termed *monkeys,* they are not closely related to the platyrrhine monkeys of the New World but instead are the sister taxon of the Hominoidea (apes and humans). Together, the hominoids and the cercopithecoids form a monophyletic subgroup of the catarrhines, here termed eucatarrhines. The common ancestor of hominoids and cercopithecoids was probably an animal similar to the Oligocene Propliopithecidae or the Miocene Pliopithecidae. It was suggested previously that the Cercopithecoidea should also include the extinct Italian Miocene family Oreopithecidae, based on perceived similarities of the dentition to cercopithecids. This hypothesis has been rejected by more detailed analyses of the postcranium and skull (and, to some extent, the teeth) of *Oreopithecus,* now placed as a subfamily of Hominidae. Similarly, it has been suggested at times that the Eocene-Oligocene North African Parapithecidae were the direct ancestors of the Cercopithecidae. Although this group can be recognized as of monkey *grade* and may share a few morphological similarities with cercopithecids, the parapithecids are best interpreted as archaic anthropoids, the sister-taxon to Catarrhini plus Platyrrhini.

Since there is only one family recognized within Cercopithecoidea, this taxon is equivalent to Cercopithecidae, and the name rarely needs to be employed. Within Cercopithecidae, three subfamilies are usually recognized: Cercopithecinae (the cheek-pouched macaques, baboons, and relatives) Colobinae (leaf-eating colobus, langurs, and allies), and Victoriapithecinae (extinct archaic cercopithecids of the African Miocene). Some authors have argued that the last of these is the sister-taxon to the first two and should be ranked as the separate family Victoriapithecidae. This would give greater meaning to the concept Cercopithecoidea, with two included families, but here only subfamily rank is accepted.

See also Anthropoidea; Ape; Catarrhini; Cercopithecidae; Cercopithecinae; Colobinae; Eocatarrhini; Eucatarrhini;

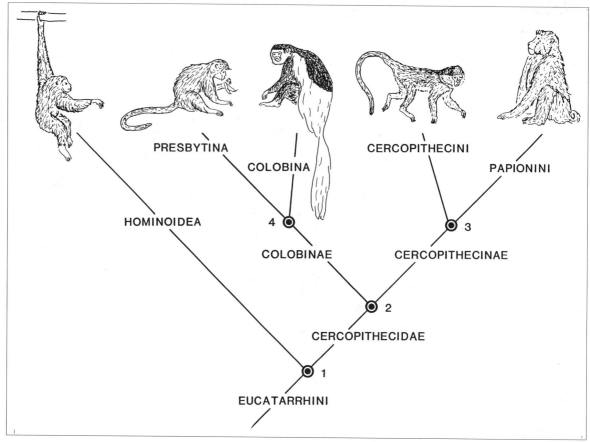

Cladogram of relationships among the higher taxa of Cercopithecoidea, with sketches of representative animals. Courtesy of E. Strasser.

Hominoidea; Monkey; Oreopithecus; Parapithecidae; Pliopithecidae; Primates; Propliopithecidae; Teeth; Victoriapithecinae. [E.D.]

Further Readings

Delson, E. (1992) Evolution of Old World monkeys. In R.D. Martin, D. Pilbeam, and J.S. Jones (eds.): Cambridge Encyclopedia of Human Evolution. Cambridge: Cambridge University Press, pp. 217–222.

cf.

From Latin *confer*, compare. Used to indicate the probable affinities of systematic materials, most commonly fossil, that are insufficient to permit exact determination of species or genus. Thus, a fragmentary Middle Pleistocene hominid fossil that most closely compares with *Homo erectus* but cannot certainly be established as a member of that species might be classified as *Homo* cf. *erectus*.

See also aff.; Classification; Taxonomy. [I.T.]

Châtelperronian

Earliest Upper Paleolithic or final Middle Paleolithic industry of central and southwestern France, extending to northeastern Spain, and dated to 35–32 ka. by radiocarbon, in association with sediments reflecting cold but fluctuating conditions at the end of a major Weichselian interstadial. Named after the Grotte des Fées at Châtelperron (Allier), the

Châtelperronian is characterized by some of the earliest bone, antler, and ivory objects (especially tubular beads) in Europe; by perforated teeth and shells and other pendants in stone and bone; by curved backed or abruptly retouched knives or points; and by the appearance of burins. Incised stone plaques have also been found at Châtelperronian sites. At the Grotte du Renne at Arcy-sur-Cure (Yonne), an arrangement of postholes, stone blocks, and artifacts was interpreted as a hut floor; traces of several smaller structures were reported from the open site of Les Tambourets (Haute Garonne). Faunal remains at most sites are dominated by reindeer, with numerous examples of horse, bovines, and woolly rhinoceros.

Initially denoted by H. Breuil, a French prehistorian, in 1906 as the earliest stage of the Aurignacian, the backing technique and dominance of burins led his colleague D. Peyrony in 1933 to classify the Châtelperronian industry, known from La Ferrassie E, as the first stage of the Perigordian tradition of southwestern France. Up to 50 percent of each Châtelperronian assemblage, however, is made up of Levallois flakes and cores, sidescrapers, and other tools of Mousterian type. The only clearly identifiable human skeletal material definitely associated with a Châtelperronian industry (excepting the material from Combe Capelle, which is of uncertain provenance) is that of a Neanderthal, discovered at Saint-Césaire (Charente-Maritime) in 1979. As in the early Upper Paleolithic leaf-shaped-point industries of central and eastern Europe, the flake technology and the

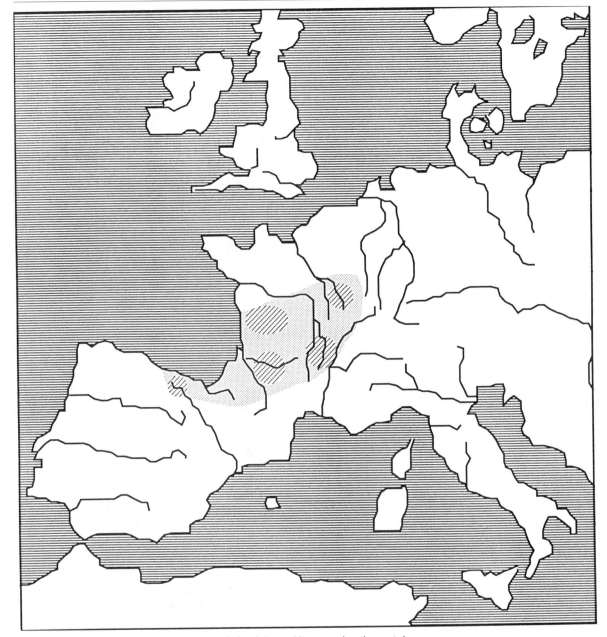

Distribution map of Châtelperronian sites. Areas marked with diagonal lines *most heavily occupied.*

skeletal associations of the Châtelperronian have been cited as evidence for an *in situ* development of Upper Paleolithic technology by humans of Neanderthal type.

At two sites in southwestern France, Roc de Combe (Lot) and Le Piage (Dordogne), the Châtelperronian is interstratified with the earliest Aurignacian industries, which are widespread in central and southern France by 32–30 Ka. This now-disputed interstratification has been used to support Peyrony's *parallel phyla hypothesis* of contemporaneous Aurignacian and Perigordian cultural traditions repeatedly replacing each other at certain sites in southwestern France, with little admixture or mutual influence, over a period of ca. 15 Kyr. Earlier dates closer to 40 Ka for the Aurignacian of both northeast Spain and central Europe, suggest that the Châtelperronian may represent a late accommodation by Neanderthals to the increasing presence of Upper Paleolithic

(Aurignacian) peoples and technologies. Most modern-day scholars do not recognize the similarities between Châtelperronian and later Perigordian assemblages as evidence of cultural continuity.

See also Aurignacian; Breuil, Henri; Jewelry; La Ferrassie; Late Paleolithic; Middle Paleolithic; Mousterian; Neanderthals, Modern Human Origins: Behavior; Paleolithic Image; Paleolithic Lifeways; Peyrony, Denis; Saint Césaire; Stone-Tool Making; Upper Paleolithic. [A.S.B.]

Further Readings

d'Errico, F., Zilhão, J., Julien, M., Baffier, D., and Pelegrin, J. (1998) Neanderthal acculturation in Western Europe: a critical review of the evidence and its interpretation. Current Anthropology 39 (supplement): S1–S44.

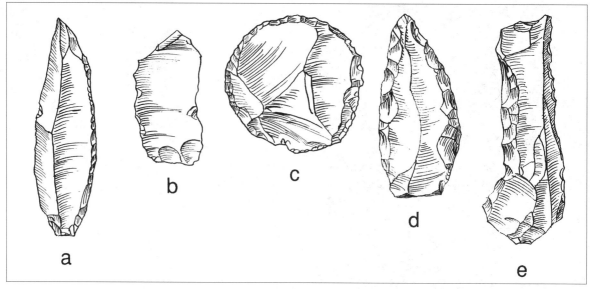

Châtelperronian lithic artifacts: (a) Châtelperronian knife; (b) burin; (c) circular scraper; (d) Mousterian point; (e) denticulate on truncated blade.

Klein, R. G. (1989) The Human Career. Chicago: University of Chicago Press.

Lévêque, F., Backer, A.M., and Guilbaud, M. (1993) Context of a Late Neanderthal: Implications of Multidisciplinary Research for the Transition to Upper Paleolithic Adaptations of Saint-Césaire, Charente-Maritime, Francis. (Monographs in World Archaeology No. 16). Madison, Wis.: Prehistory Press.

Mellars, P. (1995) The Neanderthal Legacy: An Archaeological Perspective from Western Europe. Princeton: Princeton University Press.

Wymer, J. (1982) The Palaeolithic Age. New York: St. Martin's.

Chauvet Cave

Site at Vallon-Pont-d'Arc (Ardèche, France), discovered in 1994, which has been proclaimed the oldest known painted and engraved Upper Paleolithic cave in Europe. Carbon dating of the paint of some of the animals has suggested dates ranging from ca. 32 to 30 Ka, with torch marks on the walls dated at ca. 27 Ka. The animal paintings would, therefore, fall within the period of the Aurignacian mammoth ivory carvings from Vogelherd and Höhlenstein-Stadel in Germany, the earliest known set of Upper Paleolithic carved animal depictions. This joint evidence suggests a sophistication in depiction and representation within the early Upper Paleolithic, even earlier than the Venus figurines of the Gravettian period.

The animals in Chauvet, representing the fauna of the middle Rhône Valley in that period, include woolly rhinoceros, lion, mammoth, reindeer, horse, aurochs, bear, ibex, one leopard, and an owl; there are also numerous handprints, signs, and sets of red dots. Of particular interest is evidence for the renewal or reuse of lion, reindeer, and rhino by the later addition of anatomical parts to the original animal (legs, heads, backs, horns, etc.), as well as a later outlining of an animal form or an overmarking with signs. These represent modes of image use found throughout the later West European Upper Paleolithic, modes of animal use that have been documented in France, Italy, Germany, and Spain. Some of the depicted animals at Chauvet were probably seasonally migratory (reindeer, bison); the bear spent the winter in hibernation; and other species are depicted in their summer pelage (rhino and horse).

Because of the apparent early date and the processual and referential complexity it contains, Chauvet, perhaps more than any Upper Paleolithic cave, offers an opportunity to investigate aspects of Upper Paleolithic symboling traditions (changes in style, the use of perspective, modes of image use and reuse, seasonality of depiction, and the like) that would continue to develop in the West European Upper Paleolithic over the succeeding 20 and more millennia.

See also Aurignacian; Late Paleolithic; Paleolithic Image. [A.M.]

Further Readings

Chauvet, J-M., Deschamps, E.B., and Hillaire, C. 1995. La Grotte Chauvet à Vallon-Pont-d'Arc. (Preface by J. Clottes.) Paris: Seuil.

Cheirogaleidae

Family of Lorisoidea that contains the Malagasy members of the superfamily. Five genera, all extant, are recognized (see below). All cheirogaleids are nocturnal in activity pattern and arboreal in habitat.

With body weights fluctuating seasonally around means of ca. 30–60 g, the three species of *Microcebus,* the mouse lemur, are the smallest primates in the world, rivaled only by the dwarf galago (*Galagoides demidoff,* averaging 70 g). Although mouse lemurs are active individually at night, they often sleep together in groups during the daylight hours, either in leaf nests or in tree hollows. Population nuclei of mouse lemurs, from which subordinate males appear to be peripheralized, contain a preponderance of females, the nightly ranges of several of which are overlapped by those of central males. In correlation with their small body size, mouse lemurs are the most insectivorous of the Malagasy primates, but fruit (and some flowers) seem to provide a large proportion of their diet, which is essentially opportunistic. Mouse lemurs (especially *M. rufus,* which has been been intensively studied) appear to concentrate heavily on a limited number of abundant local plant resources, taking advantage of new fruits when they become seasonally available. The fruits of certain epiphytic plants, shrubs, and lianas are frequently eaten. Coleopterans (beetles) are a favorite insect food, but a great variety of insects and spiders is consumed over the year.

Within a population of mouse lemurs, some mature adults develop extra fat deposits at the beginning of the dry season and commence a period of torpor (depressed metabolic activity) from which they may emerge in August or September, considerably lighter in weight. The period of torpor may not be continuous or even long (some individuals may enter torpor for a single day), nor does it involve all individuals in the population. In these ways, torpor in *Microcebus* differs from that in *Cheirogaleus,* but in both taxa it seems to be a means of coping with poor food availability.

Most closely related to *Microcebus,* but larger bodied at ca. 280 g, is *Mirza coquereli,* Coquerel's dwarf lemur. This lemur also constructs elaborate daytime sleeping nests and may exhibit a "loose pair bonding," although male and female nightly ranges, while overlapping, do not coincide. These ranges may be up to 25 acres in extent, but most time is spent in much smaller core areas. During the wet season, when resources are abundant, Coquerel's dwarf lemurs feed opportunistically, primarily on fruit, flowers, and insects. In the dry season, they subsist, at least regionally, mostly on larval secretions.

Allocebus, the hairy-eared dwarf lemur, and *Phaner,* the fork-marked lemur, form a group characterized by the presence of enlarged, caniniform anterior premolars; long, slender tooth combs; and strongly keeled nails. While *Phaner,* which weighs under 0.5 kg, has a widespread (if patchy) distribution in Madagascar, *Allocebus* is known only from two areas of the northeast of the island, and little is known about it other than that, unlike mouse lemurs, it favors forest habitats with large trees, eschewing the forest edge. *Phaner* often live in pairs, which vocalize frequently during the night to maintain contact while foraging. The females are apparently dominant over the males, having priority of access to feeding sites. Feeding itself is highly specialized, being largely on gums exuded from the bark of certain tree species. The keeled nails and the long tooth scraper seem to be adaptations related to a diet of this kind, facilitating movement on tree trunks and the prizing loose of gum deposits. Insects and, in the wet season, flowers and fruit also contribute to the fork-marked lemur's diet. Uniquely among cheirogaleids studied so far, *Phaner* does not appear to employ urine or fecal marking. Males, however, possess throat glands with which they mark their partners as well as trees.

Two species exist of the dwarf lemur, *Cheirogaleus:* the larger *C. major* (weighing ca. 450 g) in the wetter eastern part of Madagascar and the smaller *C. medius* (whose weight fluctuates seasonally around a mean of ca. 280 g) in the drier west. The latter, at least, is unusual in apparently undergoing a period of several weeks, or even months, of torpor during the dry season when resources are scarce. Storage of fat in the

Two cheirogaleids: Microcebus rufus *(above) and* Cheirogaleus major.

tail to help tide it over this dormant period has given this form its common name, the fat-tailed dwarf lemur. Little is known about the species of *Cheirogaleus* in the wild, but olfactory marking is known to be an important component of their social behavior, a caudally displaced and protuberant anus emphasizing the significance of fecal marking in this genus. Dwarf lemurs forage alone; insects do not appear to be an important food resource, but fruit, nectar, and pollen have been reported as significant items in a seasonally varying diet.

Family Cheirogaleidae
 Cheirogaleus
 Microcebus
 Mirza
 Allocebus
 Phaner

See also Diet; Galagidae; Lemuriformes; Locomotion; Lorisidae; Lorisoidea; Primate Societies; Primates; Strepsirhini; Teeth. [I.T.]

Further Readings

Atsalis, S., Schmid, J., and Kappeler, P.M. (1996) Metrical comparisons of three species of mouse lemur. J. Hum. Evol. 31:61–68.

Mittermeier, R.A., Tattersall, I., Konstant, W.R., Meyers, D.M., and Mast, R.B. (1994) Lemurs of Madagascar (Tropical Field Guide No. 1). Washington, D.C.: Conservation International.

Tattersall, I. (1982) The Primates of Madagascar. New York: Columbia University Press.

Tattersall, I. (1993) Madagascar's lemurs. Sci. Am. 268(1):110–117.

Chesowanja

Central Kenyan stratified sequence of early Pleistocene age, dated ca. 1.4 Ma by K/Ar (potassium-argon) dating of underlying basalt and faunal analysis. In this site west of Kenya's Lake Baringo, a partial *Paranthropus boisei* cranium was found in 1970, and an additional, more fragmentary specimen from the same taxon was recovered 1 km away in 1978. Systematic archaeological excavations began in 1978, and burnt clay lumps found *in situ* with Oldowan tools have been interpreted by some as evidence for early hominid control of fire.

See also Africa, East; Baringo Basin/Tugen Hills; Fire; Oldowan; Paranthropus boisei. [T.D.W.]

Childe, Vere Gordon (1892–1957)

Australian prehistorian. Trained in classical archaeology at Oxford University, Childe became an acknowledged leader of European prehistory in the early twentieth century. Throughout his life, he read extensively in many languages and visited dozens of European museums. In the 1920s, in *The Dawn of European Civilization* (1925), he proposed that early civilization had diffused from southwestern Asia into Europe. He attributed the development of a distinctive European culture to the Indo-European invasions of the Early Bronze Age (*The Aryans* 1926). His appointment in 1927 as Abercromby Professor of Archaeology at Edinburgh University prompted him to focus on Scottish and English prehistory, and he began excavations at Skara Brae, Orkney Islands. In the 1930s, he proposed the idea of two great revolutions in human history—the change from food gathering to food production (Neolithic Revolution) and the establishment of urban civilization (Urban Revolution)—in several books, including (*New Light on the Most Ancient East* (1934) and *Man Makes Himself* (1936). Inspired by Karl Marx, Childe framed most of his theories within a materialist conception of history. In 1946, Childe became director of the Institute of Archaeology, London University; after he retired in 1956, he returned to his native Australia, where he died the following year.

See also Asia, Western; Neolithic. [N.B.]

Chilhac

Open-air site in the Auvergne region of South-Central France on terraces of the Allier River. Excavations at Chilhac I-III since the 1870s have recovered a rich Villefranchian fauna, including *Anancus arvernensis*, *Rhinoceros etruscus*, and *Ursus etruscus*. Simple quartz choppers and flake tools have been recovered from many levels, although the assemblage most convincingly of human origin comes from younger strata at Chilhac III, Levels B–K. Chilhac I yielded an excellent specimen of *Anancus arvernensis*, but only five irregularly flaked pebbles from a slope area, four of which are in quartz. If Chilhac III is of the same age as Chilhac I, which dates to ca. 1.8 Ma by potassium-argon, it may be among the oldest archaeological sites in Europe. Questions persist, however, about the dating of this site.

See also Early Paleolithic; Europe; Soleihac. [A.S.B., J.J.S.]

China

East Asian country covering ca. 6 million km², with a long (if discontinuous) record of primate and human evolution. Chinese topography and climate are varied and complex, with the west and the southwest of the country dominated by highlands with a strongly continental climatic regime. The country is also divided into northern and southern portions by the east-west-running Qinling Shan (Mountains).

The oldest Chinese primate may be *Decoredon*, a possible Paleocene omomyid. A variety of early primates is known from the Chinese Eocene. *Hoanghonius* is probably an adapiform, while *Asiomomys* appears to represent a clade of the omomyid tarsiiforms also known in North America. Even more intriguing are the numerous new taxa recovered from the Shanghuang fissures in Jiangsu Province, dated to ca. 45 Ma. These include two adapiforms of European affinity (including *Adapoides*), a species of the North American omomyid *Macrotarsius*, a species attributed to the living *Tarsius* and *Eosimias*, a genus claimed to be an early anthropoid unrelated to the tarsiiforms. Additional material of *Eosimias* from Shaanxi Province near Heti suggests instead that *Eosimias* is a close relative of *Tarsius*, best placed in the tarsioid family Eosimiidae.

Miocene primates are also widespread in China. The earliest catarrhines are the pliopithecids *Dionysopithecus* and *Platodontopithecus* from Jiangsu Province and *Pliopithecus* from Ningxia (all dated to ca. 16–14 Ma). Specimens from Xiaolongtan (Yunnan Province, ca. 12 Ma) have been allocated to *Dryopithecus* but could possibly represent *Sivapithecus* instead; a fragmentary mandible of *Dryopithecus* is also known from Gansu, dated to ca. 9–6 Ma. The most extensive Miocene primate assemblage is known from Xihueba, Lufeng County, in Yunnan, dated ca. 8–7 Ma. From here, there are two species of the sivaladapid *Sinoadapis*, the crouzeliine pliopithecid *Laccopithecus* and hundreds of mostly dental specimens of the hominid *Lufengpithecus*. Originally, these fossils were identified as *Ramapithecus* and *Sivapithecus*, but they are probably not pongine, instead perhaps belonging to the Dryopithecinae. Similar material, as of the late 1990s incompletely published, is known from the Late Miocene or Early Pliocene at Hudielangzi and nearby sites, also in Yunnan (in Yuanmou County). Perhaps the most famous Chinese nonhuman primate is *Gigantopithecus*, whose dentition and jaws at least are far larger than those of gorillas; no skull or postcranial elements are yet known. *Gigantopithecus* has been recovered from about half a dozen small southern sites mainly of probable early Middle Pleistocene age (ca. 800–500 Ka) and especially from Liucheng

County (Guangxi Province), which yielded three mandibles and more than 1,000 teeth. This genus has been tentatively classified in the Ponginae because of similarities to *Sivapithecus*, but there are also possible links to *Lufengpithecus*. Various Pleistocene localities have also produced fossils of *Hylobates* and *Pongo*.

Cercopithecid fossils are moderately common in China as well. The latest Miocene Mahui Formation in the Yushe Basin (ca. 5.5 Ma) has yielded two teeth assigned to *Macaca* and one colobine referred to *Semnopithecus*. Macaques assigned to several species continue into the present. The large cercopithecine *Procynocephalus* is known at several localities dating to ca. 2–1.0 Ma, such as the *Gigantopithecus* cave in Guangxi, Longgupo in Sichuan, and sites in Honan and Nei Monggol (Inner Mongolia). The living colobine *Pygathrix* (*Rhinopithecus*) is known from several species in Middle Pleistocene sites such as Gongwangling (Lantian) and the Yanjinggou (ex-Yen-ching-kou) fissures in Sichuan and in Honan.

Both the extreme north and south, as well as the eastern coastal lowlands of China, were occupied by hominins since at least Middle Pleistocene times. The fossils from Lantian in Central Shaanxi may be the earliest known Chinese hominins, with a partial cranium dating to at least ca. 0.9–0.7 Ma. Other important *Homo erectus* finds include the famous fossils from Zhoukoudian (near Beijing), the Hexian hominid materials from the coastal province of Anhui, two crania from Yunxian, Hubei, and the cranium from Nanjing, Sichuan. No hominids of early antiquity have been recovered from the western highlands, but two incisors dated at perhaps 0.6 Ma have been recovered from Yuanmou in Yunnan Province. The site of Longgupo (Sichuan Province), dated tentatively at 1.8 Ma but perhaps younger, yielded an incisor and a mandible fragment originally identified as *Homo* cf. *erectus*; several workers have questioned the hominin nature of these fossils. Where present, archaeological residues are generally of Mode 1 technology ("choppers" and "chopping-tools"), although they are contemporary with Acheulean and other Mode 2 tool kits to the west of Movius' Line. The oldest Chinese artifacts are known from sites in the Nihewan region, some of which may date to ca. 1.0 Ma. The Xihoudu site has been claimed to be as old and to include traces of fire, but these claims are questioned. Bifacial and infacial tools on large flakes recovered from the Bose basin in south China and dating to more than 780 Ka are the closest analogue in China to Lower and Middle Pleistocene Acheulean industries of regions to the west.

The well-preserved material from Dali and Jinniushan document early forms of *Homo sapiens* that clearly diverge in morphology from African and European forms assigned to "archaic *Homo sapiens*." Other, more fragmentary finds have also been recovered at scattered localities of various ages in both the north and the south. The paleoanthropological and archaeological evidence from China suggests that early humans in the region were exploiting a wide variety of habitats, which included temperate as well as subtropical climatic regimes.

See also Acheulean; Adapidae; Anthropoidea; Asia, Eastern and Southern; Cercopithecinae; Colobinae; Dali; Decore-

don; Dragon Bones (and Teeth); Dryopithecinae; Early Paleolithic; Eosimiidae; Gigantopithecus; Hexian; Hoanghonius; Hominidae; Homo erectus; Jinniushan; Lantian; Liucheng; Longgupo; Lufengpithecus; Modes, Technological; Movius' Line; Nihewan; Omomyidae; Pliopithecidae; Ponginae; Xihoudu; Yuanmou; Yunxian; Zhoukoudian. [G.G.P., E.D.]

Further Readings
Chang, S., Gu, Y., Bao, Y., Shen, W., Wang, Z., Wang, C., and Du, Z. (1980) Atlas of Primitive Man in China. Beijing: Science Press.

Huang, W., Ciochon, R.L., Gu, Y., Larick, R., Fang, Q., Schwarcz, H.P., Yonge, C., de Vos, J., and Rink, W.J. (1995) Early *Homo* and associated artifacts from Asia. Nature 378: 275–278.

Olsen, J., and Miller-Antonio, S. (1993) The Paleolithic in southern China. Asian Perspectives 31(2):129–160.

Wu, R., and Olsen, J.W., eds. (1985) Paleoanthropology and Paleolithic Archaeology in the People's Republic of China. New York: Academic.

Wu, X., and Poirier, F.E. (1995) Human Evolution in China: A Metric Description of the Fossils and a Review of the Sites. New York: Oxford University Press.

Chiwondo Beds

Middle Pliocene to Early Pleistocene sediments exposed in the northernmost halfgraben of the Malawi Rift (Karonga Basin), northern Malawi, belonging to the western branch of the East African Rift system. There are two main fossil-bearing regions: one northerly near the town of Karonga, and one more southerly near the village of Uraha. The large-scale transgressive-regressive cycle of the Chiwondo Beds represents a highly dynamic depositional system in a nearshore to backshore position. Facies elements include fluviatile, paleosol, swamp, beach, and foreshore and offshore lacustrine deposits. Maximum thickness is 125 m, and five depositional sequences (Units 1–5) are limited by unconformities (paleosols, angular unconformities) reflecting lake-level changes and/or tectonic activity. Age estimates of somewhat older than 4 Ma (Unit 2) to ca. 1.5 Ma (Unit 3) rely on correlation with radiometrically dated biostratigraphical units in eastern Africa.

The first comprehensive surveys of the Chiwondo Beds were undertaken by J.D. Clark in the 1960s and 1970s, followed by T.G. Bromage and F. Schrenk from 1983 into the late 1990s. Research on the Malawi Rift and its paleofaunas, including an early hominid mandible, UR 501, recovered from Uraha and attributed to *Homo rudolfensis*, provides knowledge of the biogeographical context between the many tropical eastern and temperate southern African Plio-Pleistocene hominid-bearing sites. Situated between climatic regimes, the Chiwondo Beds region has been a meeting point, even a faunal boundary, for many northern and southern endemic faunas. The faunal assemblage also indicates, however, that southern African taxa transgressed this region when ecological extremes effected latitudinal shifts in their temperate vegetation zones. Latitudinal shifts likely began by ca. 2.8 Ma, when cooler and dryer conditions prevailed until these conditions peaked about 2.5 Ma, resulting in the shift toward the equator of dry grassland and woodland biomes reflected in the *habitat theory* of E.S. Vrba.

See also Africa; Climate Change and Evolution; Homo rudolfensis; Rift Valley; Uraha. [T.G.B.]

Further Readings

Betzler, C., and Ring, U. (1995) Geology of the Malawi Rift: Kinematic and tectonosedimentary background to the Chiwondo Beds, northern Malawi. J. Hum. Evol. 28:7–21.

Ring, U., and Betzler, C. (1995) Sedimentology of the Malawi Rift: Facies and stratigraphy of the Chiwondo Beds, northern Malawi. J. Hum. Evol. 28:23–35.

Chopper-Chopping Tools

Numerous and often poorly defined Mode 1 archaeological assemblages from east of Movius' Line in East and Southeast Asia. This line seems to mark the transition between Paleolithic assemblages to the west, in which handaxes and Levallois flakes are common, and assemblages to the east, in which these components are rare or absent. Artifacts were originally separated into unifacial "choppers" and bifacially worked "chopping tools." Early East Asian workers interpreted this distribution as an indication of what they called the cultural retardation of East Asian Paleolithic populations. More recent workers have sought ecological explanations that relate the geographic distribution of these assemblages to habitat types and the differential availability of raw materials. In spite of the implications of the term *chopper-chopping tools,* many of these artifacts appear to be unutilized cores. It is now apparent that a substantial number of East Asian Paleolithic assemblages contain small flakes as well as core tools. Despite decades of research, bifacially worked, formalized handaxes remain extremely rare in this part of the Old World, with the possible exceptions of poorly dated occurrences in the Baise basin of South China dated to more than 780 Ka, the Middle Pleistocene of Japan (Takamori), and the late Middle to Late Pleistocene of North China (Dingcun) and the Korean Peninsula (Chon-Gok-Ni). On the other hand, typologically similar Mode 1 assemblages without handaxes also occur west of Movius' Line, such as the Tayacian or the Clactonian of Europe.

See also Acheulean; Anyathian; Asia, Eastern and Southern; Clactonian; Europe; Levallois; Movius' Line; Pacitanian; Paleolithic; Soan; Tayacian. [G.G.P.]

Chromosome

Structure visible in the nucleus of a plant or animal cell during cell division. It is formed as a result of the coiling, folding, and condensation of the genetic material (DNA) with proteins. An individual has two sets of chromosomes in most cells, one set derived from each parent. A normal human cell has two sets of 23 chromosomes, for a total of 46 in the human karyotype; deviations usually result in congenital ab-

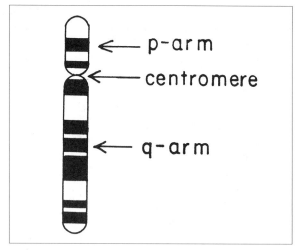

Human chromosomes can be stained to yield a distinctive pattern of bands. This is chromosome #5, showing the G-bands and major features, the centromere, p-arm, and q-arm. Courtesy of Jon Marks.

normalities. Any normal chromosome possesses a single constriction, the *centromere,* which divides the chromosome into a short arm (the p-arm) and a long arm (the q-arm).

See also Genetics; Molecular Anthropology. [J.M.]

Clacton

An open-air Middle Pleistocene site in southeastern England that has been excavated since the 1910s. Recent excavations suggest that a series of braided river channels flowed through the area depositing gravels in a series of terraces. Archaeological residues collected from the Clacton gravels include stone tools (mostly simple choppers and flakes), faunal remains, and wooden artifacts—most notably, a wooden spear tip. The Clacton site gives its name to the distinctive Clactonian industry.

See also Clactonian; Early Paleolithic; Europe. [J.J.S.]

Further Reading

Singer, R., Wymer, J.J., Gladfelter, B.G., and Wolff, R.O. (1973) Excavation of the Clactonian industry at the golf course, Clacton-on-Sea, Essex. Proc. Prehist. Soc. 39:6–74.

Clactonian

Early Paleolithic industry without handaxes found principally in Great Britain (Clacton-on-Sea, Hoxne, Swanscombe) and northern France (St. Colomban [Brittany]). The Clactonian is known primarily from interglacial contexts older than 250 Ka such as the early Hoxnian (Holstein, Elster-Saale) of Britain. Uranium-series dates of ca. 245 Ka are in agreement with this age. *In situ* Clactonian assemblages, such as those from the type site of Clacton-on-Sea and the lower loam at Swanscombe, are associated exclusively with stream-channel deposits. Associated fauna include a predominance of *Elephas antiquus*, the straight-tusked forest elephant, and *Dama clactoniana*, as well as remains of other large mammals such as horses, bovids, red deer, and rhinoceratids.

tries appear to have been made at around the same time as, or slightly earlier than, Acheulean assemblages but do not exhibit technological features indicating biface production.

Earlier hypotheses about the nature of the Clactonian-Acheulean relationship related the contrasts between these industries to different cultural traditions or to different groups of hominids. In the British case, the Clactonians were seen as indigenous Britons; the Acheuleans, as invaders from the south. More recent hypotheses have focused on possible functional, behavioral, and ecological sources for the unique features of the Clactonian and similar Middle Pleistocene industries. For example, at Barnham, British archaeologist N. Ashton and colleagues have recovered a large Clactonian assemblage around a channel margin estimated to date to ca. 400 Ka (climatostratigraphic correlation) and, 50 m along the same channel, a small collection of biface-manufacturing flakes typical of the Acheulean.

See also Acheulean; Buda Industry; Early Paleolithic; Early Stone Age; Europe; Hope Fountain; Hoxne; Kent's Cavern; Paleolithic; Paleolithic Lifeways; Přezletice; Stone-Tool Making; Stranská Skála; Swanscombe; Tabunian; Tayacian; Vallonnet. [J.J.S., A.S.B.]

Further Readings

Ashton, N., McNabb, J., Irving, B., Lewis, S., and Parfitt, S. (1994) Contemporaneity of Clactonian and Acheulian flint industries at Barnham, Suffolk. Antiquity 68:585–589.

Ohel, M. (1979) The Clactonian: An independent complex or an integral part of the Acheulean? Curr. Anthropol. 20:685–726.

Roe, D. (1981) The Lower and Middle Palaeolithic Periods in Britain. London: Routledge and Kegan Paul.

Wymer, J. (1982) The Palaeolithic Age. New York: St. Martin's.

Clade

A monophyletic group of species. The successive diversifying or splitting pattern of evolution, as one species gives rise to others through time, yields a picture that has long been compared to the branches of a tree. Even more than a tree, which exists in three dimensions, the multidimensional pattern of evolution is difficult to illustrate on a two-dimensional page. Branches may be separated or distinguished from their neighbors at any node or splitting point, whether or not the populations along the separate branch are distinguished from one another as sister-taxa, time-successive species, or just segments of an evolving lineage. Any such lineage segment, including subsidiary branches, may be termed a clade, with no implication of taxonomic rank.

See also Cladistics; Evolution; Monophyly; Phylogeny; Species. [E.D.]

Cladistics

Methodology for the reconstruction of phylogeny. First formulated explicitly in the 1950s by German entomologist W.

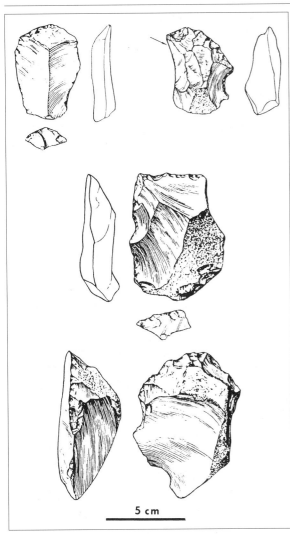

Flake tools from Clacton-on-Sea, England. From J. Wymer, The Palaeolithic Age, *1982. Reprinted with permission of St. Martin's Press, Inc.*

Although the Clactonian has often been considered the earliest Paleolithic industry of Britain, faunal and stratigraphic evidence from Kent's Cavern in Devon and from the earliest levels at Hoxne, Suffolk, may indicate that the Acheulean was as early or earlier here, based on the presence of micromammals that are extinct elsewhere by Hoxnian times.

Clactonian assemblages are made primarily on flint, which is common in these regions, and are characterized by thick flakes struck from simple pebble cores. Prominent bulbs of percussion reflect the use of direct hard-hammer, or hammer-and-anvil, technique. Double bulbs of percussion and complete cones of percussion are also common, perhaps reflecting relatively poor control over the flaking technique. The corresponding cores are large and crude, with deep negative flake scars. Retouched tools include endscrapers and sidescrapers, denticulates, becs, and a characteristic series of deeply notched flakes. In a broad sense, the Clactonian is similar to a number of other Middle Pleistocene Mode 1 pebble-core industries from western Eurasia and Africa (the Tayacian and the Evenosian of France, the Buda industry of Hungary, the Tabunian of the Levant, and the Hope Fountain of East Africa). These indus-

Hennig under the name *phylogenetic systematics,* cladistics is a branch of comparative biology in which taxa are defined and recognized exclusively by the possession of shared derived characteristics. Cladistics ranks with *numerical taxonomy* and *evolutionary systematics* as a methodology and school of thought in systematic biology. Since the 1970s, cladistics has become the dominant approach to classification and phylogeny reconstruction.

Hennig's formulation is strongly rooted in evolutionary biology. The recognition of lineages by joint possession of all descendants of one or more evolutionary novelties inherited from a common ancestral species is based entirely on the pattern of *descent with modification* envisioned by Darwin as the fundamental result of the evolutionary process. Thus, cladistics is the biological version of a more general methodology of genealogical reconstruction as developed in historical linguistics and in other fields.

The essence of reconstruction of any genealogical system is recognition of novelties introduced at a single point within a single lineage; descendant entities will inherit the novelty in its new, or a still further modified, form. Older known entities within the lineage of necessity lack the innovation, as do entities that are parts of collateral lineages. Joint possession of such novelties defines lineages from the point of origin of the novelty through the entire subsequent history of the lineage. For example, manuscripts copied by hand occasionally contain copying errors that themselves have been copied, thus forming a lineage of copies distinct from those not copied from the manuscript with the original introduced error.

As with manuscripts, so with organisms. Modifications introduced in due course as evolutionary novelties in one lineage but not in others automatically lead to a nested pattern of resemblance interlinking all members of the biota, past and present. This nested set of resemblances can be used to define and delineate taxa—one or more species—that belong to a genealogically coherent branch of the phylogenetic tree of life. Such taxa are monophyletic in the strictest cladistic sense: Monophyletic taxa consist of all those species descended from a single ancestral species.

In cladistic analysis, organismic characteristics are compared among a series of organisms of focal interest. Those characters that are invariant, and those that are unique to each specimen or basic taxon (be it species, genera, or other taxon being compared) are of no further use in the analysis. The analysis instead examines patterns of shared similarity that appear to link up two or more entities within the sample under study. Typically, conflicting patterns of shared similarity emerge, and the task becomes one of determining which similarities represent joint possession of uniquely derived (i.e., evolutionary) similarities, which represent joint retention of evolutionary novelties inherited from some more remote ancestor (and are thus actually primitive similarities in the sample under study), and which are the result of parallel or convergent evolution (i.e., the similarities are not actually homologies).

Methods of Character Analysis in Cladistics

Because each specifiable attribute of any organism has a point in evolutionary history when it was introduced, it follows that each such attribute has a finite distribution in the organic world. Some characteristics, such as fingerprint patterns, appear to be unique to a single organism; other characteristics, such as RNA (ribonucleic acid), are common to all known forms of life.

The vast majority of characters have a distribution somewhere between these two extremes. Mammary glands, placentation, and three middle-ear bones, for example, are some of the features shared by all placental mammals and are thus interpreted as shared evolutionary novelties inherited from a common ancestral species. Such sets of characters define taxa and are termed *shared derived characters* or, in Hennig's terminology, *synapomorphies.* Note that, within placental mammals, possession of a placenta becomes a primitive character: the placenta was present in the common ancestor; thus, the simple character "placenta present" is of no further significance in recognizing separate lines of descent within the placental mammals. The placenta is a synapomorphy of placental mammals but is a *symplesiomorphy* (shared primitive character) when two mammalian groups (e.g., Rodentia and Primates) are being compared.

Thus, the central analytic task of any cladistic analysis is the correct assessment of distribution of the characters observed to vary among the organisms or taxa under study. Two basic approaches are common to both the systematics of extant organisms and the study of fossils. The first is *outgroup comparison.* Most cladistic studies begin with some previously constructed hypothesis of affinity among the organisms under examination—including a hypothesis of the next-most-closely-related taxon outside the group under direct examination, the outgroup. If a character that is observed to link two or more study taxa is also observed in the outgroup, the character is judged to be primitive for the study group and of no significance in linking any two or more taxa within the study group. Outgroup comparison is essentially a mapping exercise to determine the actual distribution of a given character. The second approach is *ontogeny.* The development of an organism from a fertilized zygote to an adult involves complexification as well as modification of structure. Often, a character seems to be missing in adult form, found to be present only in early developmental stages—the classic example is pharyngeal gill slits of Vertebrata, present in adult form in various aquatic "fish" taxa but seen as well in developing embryos of tetrapods. Finally, because characters more widely distributed than the taxa within a particular study group are held to be *primitive* for that group, it is also commonly asserted that the order of appearance of characters in the fossil record may additionally serve as a direct form of inference in character analysis—a point that continues to be debated.

The results of a cladistic analysis are plotted on a *cladogram,* which depicts the relationships among the study taxa; the nodes joining the branches of such a diagram simply reflect joint possession of one or more synapomorphies. Evolutionary trees are more complex statements, specifying ancestral and descendant species in a reconstructed phylogeny. A single classification may be derived directly and unambiguously from a cladogram with a minimum of rules and conventions; however, a number of classifications may be consistent with any one evolutionary tree. Recently, quantitative methods have been developed for generating cladograms using various algorithms based on parsimony analysis. These are discussed in the entry on NUMERICAL CLADISTICS.

See also Classification; Evolution; Evolutionary Systematics (Darwinian Phylogenetics); Homology; Numerical Cladistics; Phylogeny; Quantitative Methods; Taxonomy. [N.E.]

Further Readings

Eldredge, N., and Cracraft, J. (1980) Phylogenetic Patterns and the Evolutionary Process. New York: Columbia University Press.

Hennig, W. (1966) Phylogenetic Systematics. Urbana: University of Illinois Press.

Platnick, N.I., and Cameron, H.D. (1977) Cladistic methods in textual, linguistic, and phylogenetic analysis. Syst. Zool. 26:380–385.

Wiley, E.O. (1981) Phylogenetics. New York: Wiley.

Clark, J[ohn] Desmond (1916–)

British-trained archaeologist. Professor emeritus at the University of California, Berkeley, Clark has been responsible for significant discoveries and has set directions and emphases in the study of African prehistory; he has also trained a large cohort of African archaeologists, both from the West and from Africa itself. His contributions, many in collaboration with international colleagues, include the initiation and leadership of the Pan-African Congress of Prehistory and Quaternary Studies; the definition of the basic Stone Age terminology for sub-Saharan Africa; an emphasis on behavioral and environmental reconstruction; the promotion of ethnoarchaeology as a tool for understanding the past; major excavations at Lunda (Angola), Kalambo Falls (Zambia), Mwanganda's Village (Malawi), and Latamne (Syria); and extensive surveys and excavations in Somalia, Ethiopia, and the Sudan, the latter relating to the origins of domestication.

See also Africa; Domestication; Early Stone Age; Ethnoarchaeology; First Intermediate; Kalambo Falls; Later Stone Age; Magosian; Middle Stone Age; Sangoan; Second Intermediate. [A.S.B.]

Clarke, [Sir] John Grahame Douglas (1908–1996)

English archaeologist. Clarke was one of the formative influences in British archaeology in the second half of the twentieth century. Based for his entire career in Cambridge, where he became Disney Professor and Master of Peterhouse College, Clarke played a major role in the development of economic archaeology. In doing so, he broadened the horizons of the subject from a preoccupation with stone-tool typology to a more general understanding of how earlier populations exploited their environments. This did not mean any lack of interest in technology, however; indeed, for many readers of this encyclopedia, his most important contribution was the Mode 1–5 classification of Paleolithic industries that freed such classification from local and regional connotations. The

author of several books on world and European prehistory, Clarke specialized in the Mesolithic period and was particularly well known for his excavations at the English Mesolithic site of Starr Carr.

See also Mesolithic; Modes, Technological; Starr Carr. [I.T.]

Further Readings

Clarke, J.G.D. (1952) Prehistoric Europe: The Economic Basics. London: Methuen.

Clarke, J.G.D. (1954) Excavations at Starr Carr. Cambridge: Cambridge University Press.

Clarke, J.G.D. (1957) Archaeology and Society. 3rd Edition. London: Methuen.

Clarke, J.G.D. (1972) Starr Carr: A Case Study in Archaeology. (Addison-Wesley Modular Publications, McCabe Module No. 10). Reading, MA: Addison-Wesley.

Classification

In biology, the arrangement of organisms into sets. The world contains millions of kinds of living organisms. Many more existed in the past but are now extinct. For us to understand and to communicate with one another about this extraordinary variety of organisms, it is essential that we classify them. But it is important to bear in mind that any classification we adopt is a product of our minds and not a property of nature. Rules exist for naming organisms, but organizing them in a classification is a less objective procedure.

Practice of Animal Classification

The system universally used today to classify animals and plants was devised by the eighteenth-century Swedish systematist Carolus Linnaeus. He expounded this system in his *Systema Naturae,* the definitive edition of which is taken to be the tenth, dated 1758. No names of organisms published before that date are recognized as valid, while all names of animals published subsequently must conform to the rules of the Linnaean system, codified today in the *International Code of Zoological Nomenclature* (hereinafter, "the Code").

The Linnaean approach to classification establishes an inclusive hierarchy of ranks, within which every living organism has its place. An inclusive hierarchy is one in which every rank includes all of those below it: All members of a subfamily, for example, belong also to a family. This contrasts with the exclusive, "military" type of hierarchy, in which an individual can belong to only one rank. The basic unit of the Linnaean system is the species, which is denoted by a *binomen,* or a combination of two names, each of which is written in latinized form and italicized. We, for example, belong to the species *Homo sapiens.* Species are grouped into genera, and the first component (*Homo*) of the double name is the name of the genus. In combination with the first, the second (specific) name (*sapiens*) identifies the species. Species belonging to different genera can share a specific name (e.g., *Proconsul africanus, Australopithecus africanus*); it is thus the combination of the genus and species names that is unique. Sometimes, one sees yet a third latinized, italicized name, as, for example, in *Eulemur fulvus rufus;* the last name denotes a subspecies, a category within the species itself. The name that must be used in referring to any species is the one first applied to it in accordance with the Code (in force at that point; the rules are amended from time to time). This is the name with *priority;* other names that may later have been given to the same organism are known as *junior synonyms.*

Categories in the Hierarchy of Classification

Because of the sheer vast numbers of living organisms, we are obliged to have many categories (ranks) in our classification, not all of which there is room to mention here. Continuing with *Homo sapiens* as an illustration, as animals we belong to the kingdom Animalia. This contains several phyla, ours being Chordata; within Chordata, we belong to the subphylum Vertebrata; within Vertebrata, to the class Mammalia. Within Mammalia, we are members of the order Primates; within Primates, we are classed as follows:

Order	Primates
Semiorder	Euprimates
Suborder	Haplorhini
Hyporder	Anthropoidea
Infraorder	Catarrhini
Parvorder	Eucatarrhini
Superfamily	Hominoidea
Family	Hominidae
Subfamily	Homininae
Tribe	Hominini
Genus	*Homo*
Species	*Homo sapiens*

As we ascend the classification, we share each successive rank with more and more relatives. Thus, among living forms we share the order Primates with the lemurs, lorises, tarsiers, Old and New World monkeys, and the greater and lesser apes, whereas besides ourselves the superfamily Hominoidea includes only the apes. Each category, at whatever level, is known as a *taxon* (plural *taxa*): Species are taxa, so are families, so are orders. From this, we derive the term *taxonomy,* which is the study of the theory and practice of classification. Note that the family and the subfamily names end in "-idae" and "-inae," respectively; this is required by the Code for taxa at those ranks. The Code also recommends the suffixes "-oidea" for superfamilies, "-ini" for tribes, and "-ina" for subtribes.

Principles of Classification

The only theoretical requirement of any classification is that it be consistent. We can use any criteria we like to construct the classification itself. Linnaeus's classification, in which he included *Homo* in Primates along with the apes, monkeys, and lemurs, predated the concept of evolution and was based purely on structural resemblance. Nowadays, elements of both structure and evolutionary relationship are often included in arriving at zoological classifications. However, since the only information that can actually be retrieved from (as opposed to put into) a classification is the inclusive sets of animals represented, and because the only attribute of nature to

which this structuring corresponds is the branching of lineages in phylogeny, it has been strongly argued that classifications should strictly reflect evolutionary relationships in the narrowest sense. While the point is well taken, such strict adherence to phylogeny makes classifications susceptible to constant change with advancing knowledge. Stability in classifications is essential if they are to serve as effective means of communication about groups of organisms; their potential instability, together with the large number of categories they tend to require, makes strict phylogenetic classifications impractical. No classification will ever be satisfactory for all purposes or remain useful forever, but those that are the most generally useful are likely to be based on phylogeny (and insisting on monophyly—i.e., that every group should contain all known descendants of the common ancestor of the group, and only them) but modified in the light of structural considerations to minimize the number of ranks.

See the front matter pg. xxiii for a complete generic classification of the primates.

See also Cladistics; Incertae Sedis; Nomenclature; Phylogeny; Priority; Species; Subspecies; Synonym(y); Systematics; Taxonomy. [I.T.]

Further Readings

Eldredge, N., and Cracraft, J. (1980) Phylogenetic Patterns and the Evolutionary Process. New York: Columbia University Press.

International Trust for Zoological Nomenclature (1985) International Code of Zoological Nomenclature, 3rd ed. Berkeley: University of California Press.

Mayr, E. (1969) Principles of Systematic Zoology. New York: McGraw-Hill.

Simpson, G.G. (1961) Principles of Animal Taxonomy. New York: Columbia University Press.

Cleaver

Large, usually bifacially flaked artifact with a straight, sharp-edged bit on one end, characteristic of the Acheulean technological stage and generally associated with handaxe industries (it can also be found in some Mousterian industries). Many cleavers, especially those in lava or quartzite, are made on large flakes with a natural flake-edge bit, while those of flint may also be shaped by bifacially flaking a

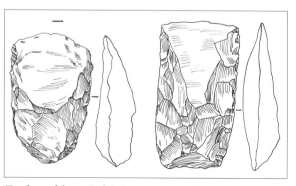

Two forms of cleaver. Scale is 1 cm.

straight-edged bit on the end of a large biface, or by a tranchet blow to create a sharp, regular bit-edge. Experiments indicate that these forms make excellent cutting tools in animal butchery and are also good woodworking tools.

See also Acheulean; Biface; Early Paleolithic; Handaxe; Mousterian; Raw Materials; Stone-Tool Making. [N.T., K.S.]

Climate Change and Evolution

Climate consists of prevailing annual patterns of near-surface atmospheric conditions in a given region, measured in terms of temperature, precipitation, and wind. In general, climate is the result of four factors: (1) the balance between incoming solar energy and the loss of energy from the Earth, known as the radiation balance; (2) wind-borne moisture and heat; (3) the influence of bodies of water that store and transport heat and moisture (ocean currents are of particular importance); and (4) the physical characteristics of the region and its surroundings. The latter include surface- and groundwater, soil cover, vegetation density and ecology, color and reflective properties of the ground surface, and topography. Hills, mountains, and seacoasts also channel winds and create local circulation patterns.

Long-term climate change has been linked to cyclical variations in the eccentricity of the Earth's orbit, the precession of the equinoxes around the elliptical orbit, and the wobble in the spin axis, together generally known as *Milankovitch cycles* after the Serbian geographer who published calculations of the variations in solar energy at the Earth's surface that would be caused by these cycles. These different cycles have major periodicities of ca. 100 Kyr, 40 Kyr, and 21.7 Kyr, respectively. Eccentricity also has longer cycles in amplitude variation at 410 Kyr and 1.3 Myr. The strength and the angle of incidence of the Earth's solar radiation, and therefore terrestrial temperatures, are affected by these astronomical cycles. The variations in the tilt of the Earth in relation to the sun also change the effective latitudinal position of the polar circles and the tropics by a few degrees.

Geological agencies contribute to climate change by affecting wind and ocean circulation patterns. Continental drift, mountain building, regional uplifts, rifting, vulcanism, and changes in sea level all influence the intensity and the path of prevailing winds and currents and, hence, the temperature and moisture content of local air masses. On a regional scale, the uplift of the Tibetan and the Colorado plateaus, as part of increased crustal movement in the later Cenzoic, appears to have intensified Pleistocene climate swings. On a local scale, evidence has been cited that changes in rainfall and sedimentation due to rift faulting were influential in the evolution and distribution of Plio-Pleistocene mammals, including hominids.

Long-Term Climate Trends

Continental drift is the underlying cause of the global change from equable, pantropical conditions of the later Mesozoic and Early Cenozoic to the unstable, highly seasonal, and geographically differentiated climates of the mod-

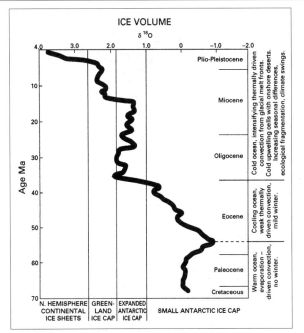

Global climate over the past 70 million years. Changes in the volume of ice on land, determined by variation in the "light" isotope of oxygen in sea water, is the best available indicator of Cenozoic climate. The curve shown here, from oxygen isotope ratios tracked in ten deep-sea drill cores in the Atlantic Ocean Basin, shows well-defined steps in global cooling that were reflected in sharp changes in continental environments. (The sharp peak while the ocean was stagnant in the early Eocene probably does not reflect ice melting or high temperature, but higher-than-normal concentration of freshened sea water in the ocean depths due to weakened circulation.)

ern world. The world oceans today (saving only the near-isolated Mediterranean) are colder than at any time since the Late Paleozoic ice ages, with the main water masses of the deep-ocean basins 4 to 10°C and a thin film of sun-warmed water on top. The deep waters are constantly replenished through the refrigeration of surface water in the polar regions, primarily around Antarctica, that results in plumes of dense cold water flowing down the continental slopes into the ocean depths. Added to this is the fact that the influence of equatorial winds and currents in distributing heat to high latitudes is weakened by the present north-south alignments of the continents, and the subduction-induced elevation of the Himalayas, the Andes, and the Colorado Plateau. Under the present cold-ocean conditions, the Milankovitch cycles have their greatest effect on world climate, because the thermal mass of the oceans is at a minimum.

In the Early Cenozoic, on the other hand, the advective circulation of seawater came instead from the sinking of warm, evaporatively concentrated water in the tropics, which filled the deep-ocean basins with water masses at an average temperature of ca. 28°C. Oceanographic studies indicate that the change from evaporative to refrigerative circulation, when sinking water zones shifted from the tropics to the poles, came at the end of the Paleocene. Deep-sea cores show a sharp, abnormal spike in dissolved CO_2 and a massive die-off in deep-water microfaunas, which was probably due to a brief, catastrophic stall in ocean advection. While evidence for pre-Oligocene ice fields in Antarctica is debatable, there is no question that, since the mid-Cretaceous, the polar continent had been steadily growing colder as the straits between Antarctica and the other Gondwana continents widened, thereby strengthening the massive Circum-Antarctic Current. The effect of this current, today the only circum-global oceanic circulation, is to thermally isolate the polar continent, with a direct effect on glacial ice buildup.

The climatic effects of a cold ocean were not felt, however, until the end of the Eocene. At this time, a marked change in climate, in the form of new extremes in seasonality, affected both marine and mammalian faunas in the temperate regions. One important consequence was the virtual extinction of the primate faunas of North America and Eurasia, so that the only remaining center of primate diversity was in Afro-Arabia. Coincident with this extinction event was a sharp drawdown in world sea level, which may have been triggered by a new advance in Antarctic ice and a massive wave of intercontinental migration, the Grande Coupure.

The tectonic joining of Afro-Arabia to Eurasia in the Early Miocene, the closure of deep-water passages between the Indian and the Pacific oceans during the Late Miocene and Early Pliocene, and, finally, the sealing of the Magdalena Straits in Colombia as South and North America pressed together in the Late Pliocene—all increased the breakdown of equatorial circulation and the dominance of refrigerative circulation. The effects of Milankovitch cycles intensified gradually, with major cold-climate spikes at 2.5 Ma, 1.8 Ma, 0.9 Ma, and 0.4 Ma. Each of the cold-climate steps was more severe than the one before, and each left a new imprint on the flora and fauna that was not erased during the intervening warmer climates. As a result, the world biota became steadily more fragmented and impoverished. The relevance of these steps to the definition of the base of the Pleistocene has long been debated; the international boundary is identified with the 1.8 Ma step, but the 2.5 Ma cooling had a major effect on terrestrial environments.

Short-Term Climate Influences

In the short term, large-scale volcanic activity alters climate by diminishing the transparency of the atmosphere. The aerosol of ejected microscopic particles and sulfuric acid (H_2SO_4) can form a veil of mist in the stratosphere. This partially intercepts the sun's short-wave radiation, while the long-wave radiation passes through unimpeded. This filter layer is warmed while the surface and lower atmospheric temperatures are somewhat reduced. The carbon dioxide content of the atmosphere also plays a major, perhaps critical, role in controlling air temperatures and may be one of the principal means by which orbitally driven insolation cycles influence climate. Atmospheric CO_2 content is regulated by changes in CO_2 solubility in ocean surface waters. This process is strongly temperature dependent, and slight changes in insolation can lead to major changes in the CO_2 effect on global temperature.

The reflective properties of the Earth's surface, or albedo, affect the amount of radiant energy absorbed. Glacial episodes are triggered by orbitally forced lower winter temperatures and begin with periods of increased winter precipitation (*pluvials* in the tropics) with deeper snow packs, so that the areas covered with permanent ice expand outside of the core areas of Antarctica and Greenland. At

some point, the growth of the reflective ice alters the radiation balance while, at the same time, the SST (sea surface temperature) is lowered by increased ice contact, so that precipitation declines sharply. The reduced cloud cover allows heat to be reflected back into space—a reverse of the greenhouse effect—resulting in further cooling. Another factor acting in the same direction is the depletion of surface water, which reduces vegetative cover and further increases reflectivity. Thus, all glacial-climate episodes of the later Cenozoic, whether mild or intense, normally begin with cool and wet conditions and climax with cold and dry; in higher latitudes, the climax is also known as the *polar desert* phase. Because they "make their own climate," the cold, highly reflective continental ice sheets of the Northern Hemisphere tend to persist well past the climax phase and then catastrophically collapse during the early part of the interglacial interval.

Climatic Influences on Hominid Evolution

In the context of the relatively highly developed state of geochronometry and paleontology in Africa, the Late Cenozoic cool-climate episodes appear to coincide with, and arguably to influence, major events in the cladogenesis of the Hominidae. Arguments based on the correlation of paleoclimate to changes in vegetation and pulses of faunal extinction and speciation have been outlined in the *habitat theory* of E.S. Vrba. Basic assumptions in this theory are that the fundamental adaptations for specific terrestrial vegetational habitats tend to be heritable and, thus, characteristic for clades, that terrestrial mammal biomes may be characterized by the gross vegetational physiognomy of their habitat, and that distribution movements (drift) occur primarily in the context of changes—above all, climate changes—in the physical environment.

It has long been recognized that the Late Miocene (Turolian or Clarendonian) of the temperate regions of Eurasia and the Americas was marked by a major climate change toward more seasonal, summer-dry conditions that dramatically affected terrestrial environments. Savannah biomes, dominated by grasses and deciduous trees, rapidly replaced forests and evergreen broadleaf woodlands over huge areas, and mammalian communities that were adapted to these conditions proliferated. This crucial interval, dated at ca. 10 Ma, is far less well documented in Africa, but there is somewhat equivocal evidence that this period saw a retreat of tropical forests in East Africa and an increase in wooded savannah and open grasslands, with increased habitat diversity. The global climate change may have been accentuated by active development of the African Rift system at this time, in which the fossilizing basins of the rift floor would lie increasingly in the rain shadow of the rising rift shoulders. The tectonic fragmentation of the environment may have facilitated a pulse of vicariant diversification and adaptation among Late Miocene hominids, similar to many other mammal groups (e.g., bovids, suids, and carnivores), but, in the absence of any fossil material, this is only speculative. It has been suggested, for instance, that the expansion of grasslands at this time might have favored the advent of hominid bipedalism. This adaptation is, of course, an energetically efficient means of locomotion in open country, available only to animals preadapted to prolonged semierect balancing, and has the added advantage of posture that allows for better vision in grassland even as it reduces the surface area exposed to radiation. At the dawn of the twenty-first century, however, we have no evidence for when this excellent innovation first appeared.

The most compelling, though still controversial, evidence for the relationship of climate change to human evolution is based on studies of the fossil evidence dated to, or slightly before, 2.5 Ma, the time of the global cooling event seen in deep-sea cores. At approximately this time, biome boundaries, grading from dry grasslands through open woodlands to tropical forests, shifted markedly toward the Congo Basin, with the result that the grassland vegetation and associated mammalian faunas expanded at all latitudes. The ca. 2.5 Ma fauna of the Chiwondo Beds in Malawi contains several mammal genera that today are limited to areas much farther south—most notably, bovids with preferences for open habitats. The same deposits also yield the earliest records in southern Africa of the Asian immigrants *Oryx* and *Equus*, further indicating the spread of open-grassland conditions. Supporting evidence for this shift comes from an increase of open-grassland pollen in both marine and terrestrial (particularly low-altitude basin) samples, although overall the regional environmental settings remained a mosaic of habitats. However, in 1997, A.K. Behrensmeyer and colleagues reviewed the record around this time in the Turkana Basin and questioned the degree of climatically induced faunal turnover, at least in that region.

The floral changes suggest a period of relatively xeric conditions and appear to correspond to a pulse of faunal extinctions and speciations in response to the relatively extensive and rapid environmental shifts. The selective pressures of this habitat change appear to have favored megadont adaptations for feeding on tougher, more fibrous fruit, leaves, and grass in the dry, open woodland-savannah environment. Among the megafauna, the bovids, suids, and elephantids with larger teeth and more robust jaws became more diverse and more abundant at this time, and this was also true for early hominines as well. In *Paranthropus robustus, P. boisei,* and *Homo rudolfensis,* all of which appear to have evolved ca. 2.5 Ma or soon after, the same tendency is seen to postcanine megadontia, heavily reinforced and massive facial skeletons supporting relatively large masticatory musculature, and relatively thick enamel.

See also Cenozoic; Cyclostratigraphy; Glaciation; Grande Coupure; Milankovitch, Milutin; Pleistocene; Stable Isotopes (in Biological Systems). [T.G.B., J.A.V.C.]

Further Readings

Behrensmeyer, A.K., Todd, N.E., Potts, R., and McBrinn, G.E. (1997) Late Pliocene faunal turnover in the Turkana Basin, Kenya and Ethiopia. Science 278:1589–1594.

Bromage, T.G., Schrenk, F., and Juwayeyi, Y.M. (1994) Palaeobiogeography of the Malawi Rift: Age and vertebrate palaeontology of the Chiwondo Beds, northern Malawi. J. Hum. Evol. 28:37–57.

Cerling, T.E., Harris, J.M., MacFadden, B.J., Leakey, M.G., Quade, J., Eisenmann, V., and Ehleringer, J.R. (1997)

Global vegetation change through the Miocene/Pliocene boundary. Nature 389:153–158.

Köhler, M., Moyà-Solà, S., and Agusti, J. (1998) Miocene/ Pliocene shift: One step or several? Nature 393:126–127.

Potts, R. (1998) Environmental hypotheses of hominin evolution. Yrbk. Phys. Anthropol. 41:93-136.

Turner, A., and Wood, B. (1993) Taxonomic and geographic diversity in robust australopithecines and other African Plio-Pleistocene larger mammals. J. Hum. Evol. 24:147–168.

Vrba, E.S., Denton, G.H., Partridge, T.C., and Burckle, L., eds. (1996) Paleoclimate and Evolution, with Emphasis on Human Origins. New Haven: Yale University Press.

Cline

Linear pattern of variation in one or more phenotypic organismic features within a species. Generally, such patterns adaptively match a linear range of variation of environmental features, such as altitude or mean annual temperature. Simpson termed such geographic clines *choroclines,* in contrast to *chronoclines,* which are linear, gradational patterns of phylogenetic change within a species through time. The two phenomena, however, are not strictly comparable, and use of these terms is to be discouraged.

See also Adaptation(s); Evolution; Phylogeny. [N.E.]

Clothing

As hominids spread to cooler, more temperate zones, it is likely that the need for clothing became an adaptive necessity, especially during winter months. The earliest forms of clothing were probably simple garments of skin or beaten vegetable material, draped over or tied around the body, perhaps with the aid of skin thongs or other forms of cordage.

Although the materials from which early clothing might have been made are perishable and do not survive in the Paleolithic record, several lines of evidence suggest the use of garments (e.g., in later Acheulean and, especially, Mousterian times). The prevalence of well-made sidescrapers may suggest a reliance upon hide working, an activity corroborated by the detection of microscopic hide-polish development on some of these scraper edges. The presence of pointed perçoirs (awls) in some of these assemblages may also suggest the perforation of hides for lacing with leather thongs.

By Aurignacian times in the Upper Paleolithic, bone awls are common, suggesting widespread use of these perforators in preparing hides for clothing and possibly for other purposes such as tents or containers. Bone and antler needles first appear in the Solutrean period of the Upper Paleolithic and suggest the sewing of hides with a thread made of sinew or vegetable material. Twine made from vegetable fibers is indicated in ceramic impressions at Dolni Vestoniče (Czech Republic) as early as 26 Ka. The high frequency of endscrapers found in Upper Paleolithic assemblages also suggests hide working, again corroborated by microwear analysis. Since many bone and antler needles may not have been strong enough to sew through hides by themselves, the use of

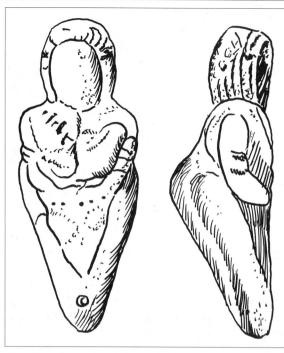

Carved-bone figurine from the Late Paleolithic site of Malt'a, Siberia (Russia), with apparent representation of clothing (ca. 6 cm tall).

perçoirs to initiate holes in material to be stitched is likely. At the Upper Paleolithic site of Sungir on the Russian Plain, each of three burials had thousands of associated bone beads, probably representing decorations sewn into garments.

Artwork from the later phases of the Paleolithic may portray human figures with clothing: Some of the figurines from the Upper Paleolithic appear to be wearing skirts, aprons, headdresses, or parkas.

See also Acheulean; Aurignacian; Awl; Europe; Mousterian; Paleolithic Image; Paleolithic Lifeways; Sungir; Upper Paleolithic. [N.T., K.S.]

Further Readings

Daumas A., ed. (1969) A History of Technology and Invention: Progress through the Ages, Vol. 1. New York: Crown.

Hodges, H. (1976) Artifacts: An Introduction to Early Materials and Technology. London: Baker.

Clovis

Distinctive, large, bifacially flaked lanceolate point manufactured by percussion flaking. The base is thinned by one or more fluting flakes, and the basal edge is dulled, presumably to facilitate hafting. First discovered at Clovis (New Mexico), such points have since been found throughout much of North America. They date to 11 Ka in the earliest layers of Blackwater Draw (New Mexico). Clovis points, typically associated with mammoth kills, belong to the earliest of the Paleoindian traditions.

See also Americas; Blackwater Draw; Llano Complex; Meadowcroft Shelter; Paleoindian; Sandia. [L.S.A.P., D.H.T.]

Colobinae

Subfamily of Old World monkeys including the leaf-eating cercopithecids, such as langurs (*Presbytis* and *Semnopithecus*), doucs (*Pygathrix*), proboscis monkeys (*Nasalis*), guerezas (*Colobus*), and their extant and extinct relatives. In adapting to the high proportion of leaves and other low-quality foods in their diet, colobines have evolved a number of derived conditions as compared with the cercopithecid morphotype.

These include extra chambers in the stomach to enhance fermentation and digestion of cellulose; increased cheek-tooth crown relief (between cusp tips and notch bases) but reduced flare and short lower molar trigonids (possibly conservative); reduction in incisor size (and greater frequency of underbite); a mandible with expanded gonial region but shallowing mesially. As part of their adaptation to arboreal running and leaping, colobines have relatively longer limbs, hands, and feet than do cercopithecines of similar weight. In addition, the external thumb is reduced in length, in some cases lost entirely, and the tarsal region is shortened; the latter is best seen in the cuboid-ectocuneiform contacts, where the distal facet is lengthened while the proximal is reduced or lost. Although in most catarrhines the major weight-bearing axis of the foot passes through the middle digit, which is longer than the fourth, in colobines these two are equal, signaling the shift of the axis of the foot to between these two rays. In concert with this, a number of related muscle functions have been modified and a groove developed on the proximal astragalus. Colobines generally have retained the ancestral cercopithecid conditions of a short, broad face with wide interorbital distance, short nasal bones, and a lacrimal fossa extending onto the maxilla; a relatively high-vaulted skull; fully enamel covered lower incisors; and a simple cerebral sulcal pattern.

Within the modern Colobinae, both morphological and (rare) molecular evidence suggests a division into subtaxa according to geography. Because the number of diagnostic features separating them is low, these groups have been ranked as subtribes rather than full tribes; they seem to be about as distinct from one another as the subtribes of the Cercopithecinae.

The African colobinans have completely lost the external thumb and the proximal cuboid-entocuneiform contact, while these features are only reduced in the Asian presbytinans. Two living genera are recognized in Africa: *Colobus* (the guerezas, or black-and-white colobus) with four species, characterized by the derived loss of female sexual swellings and the development of a large larynx and subhyoid sac; and *Procolobus* (for olive colobus and red or bay colobus) with perhaps three to four species, typified by a four-chambered stomach (other colobines have only three chambers), a sagittal crest (perhaps implying a relatively small brain), a male perineal organ, and discontinuous male ischial callosities (also in Asian *Pygathrix*). The Asian colobines are more numerous and their interrelationships more complex; in fact, it is possible that they may not form a natural (holophyletic) group. For the present, four genera are recognized, most with subgeneric divisions. *Semnopithecus* may be the most conservative, *Presbytis* intermediate

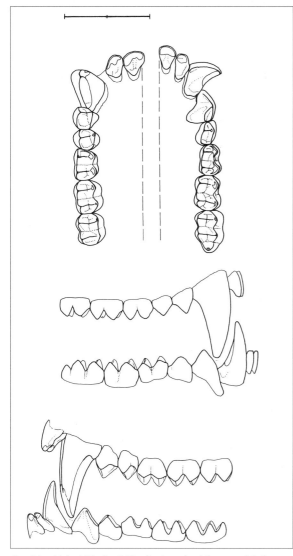

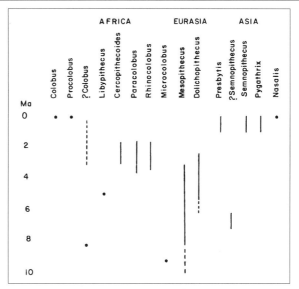

Known time ranges of colobine genera; solid lines indicate well-preserved fossils, dotted lines indicate fragmentary remains, less clear allocations, or dating uncertainty. The relationships among these taxa are still relatively unclear, and thus no attempt is made to present a cladogram, but see the diagram of living genera in the entry CERCOPITHECIDAE.

Dentition (right side) of male Nasalis, *in occlusal (upper on left, lower on right), buccal, and lingual views. Scale is 2 cm. From Szalay and Delson, 1979.*

(possibly dwarfed, according to N. Jablonski), and *Nasalis* and *Pygathrix* the most derived, at least in terms of facial shape.

The colobine diet includes not only leaves but a variety of fruits, flowers, buds, shoots, seeds, insects, gums, and earth (for minerals). Their enlarged stomach permits the ingestion of foods high in toxic substances (*secondary compounds*), which can be detoxified through the action of the same bacteria that break down the cellulose in leaves. Most living colobines are active arboreal leapers and runners, with only one species, *Semnopithecus entellus,* spending much time on the ground; several fossil colobines have independently become terrestrial, however. Group composition is mainly multimale, with troop sizes up to 100 (e.g., *Procolobus badius)* but more commonly 20–40. Some species live in small groups with a single adult male (most *Colobus* and *Presbytis,* among others), and at least *Presbytis potenziani* is apparently monogamous. In *S. entellus,* among other species, coalitions of peripheral males may attack the primary male of a troop and kill or expel him, at which time they, or a new leader, may attack and kill juveniles. Among colobines, juveniles are

often carried by females other than the mother—known as *aunting* behavior, this may serve to speed independence of the infant from its mother and protect it from infanticide during male takeovers. Home-range size averages ca. 30 ha but is variable both between species (e.g., 130 ha in *Nasalis larvatus*) and even within species, depending on environmental factors (e.g., from 5 to 1,300 ha in *S. entellus!*). Numerous species are endangered, often as the result of human hunting and expansion of cultivated land.

The fossil record of the colobines is quite good in both Africa and Europe but poor in Asia. The earliest African colobine, *Microcolobus,* is known by a single mandible from Ngeringerowa (Kenya), estimated to date to ca. 10–9 Ma. This is the smallest known colobine, slightly smaller in tooth size than *Procolobus verus* but larger than the cercopithecin *Miopithecus talapoin.* Tooth relief is low for a colobine, and the inferior transverse torus of the symphysis is poorly developed, as in cercopithecines but no other colobine. A larger colobine is known by isolated teeth from the Late Miocene (ca. 8 Ma) of Marceau (Algeria). Originally identified as a macaque, then termed "*Colobus*" in the sense of an African colobine, these teeth show some similarities to the Pliocene *Cercopithecoides.* Late Miocene sites in Libya and Egypt have yielded a nearly complete cranium, some teeth, and perhaps fragmentary limb bones of *Libypithecus,* a form broadly similar to the red colobus. The Pliocene of southern and especially eastern Africa saw a great flowering of colobine diversity. *Cercopithecoides* was long known by skulls and teeth in South African sites dating between 3 and 1.5 Ma (e.g., Makapansgat, Sterkfontein, Kromdraai), but an associated partial skeleton from Koobi Fora (Kenya) demonstrated that it was the most terrestrially adapted colobine known. Isolated limb bones of this 20–25 kg species (male estimate only) can be mistaken for those of *Theropithecus* baboons. The teeth of *Cercopithecoides* are often heavily worn, suggest-

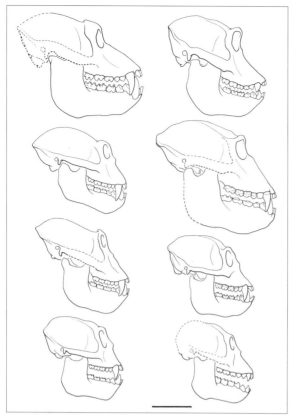

Drawings, in right lateral view, of representative colobines; M = male, F = female. Top row: †Paracolobus chemeroni *(M),* †Rhinocolobus turkanaensis *(F). Second row:* †Cercopithecoides williamsi*(M),* †C. kimeui *(M). Third row:* †Libypithecus markgrafi *(M),* Colobus guereza *(F—note large canine). Bottom row:* †Mesopithecus pentelicus *(M),* †Dolichopithecus ruscinensis *(F). Scale bar = 5 cm;* †*indicates extinct species. By Lorraine Meeker.*

ing that its diet included grit taken in with terrestrial foods and that enamel had not been thickened to prolong tooth life. Somewhat larger (at 43–50 kg for males) was *Paracolobus,* whose fossils span from 3.5 to 1.9 Ma at such East African sites as Laetoli (Tanzania), Koobi Fora (Kenya), and Omo (Ethiopia). A nearly complete skeleton reveals a forelimb that looks like those of more terrestrial monkeys, but a scapula and a foot that indicate a relatively arboreal adaptation. A third genus, *Rhinocolobus,* from Koobi Fora, Omo, and Hadar (Ethiopia) localities between 3.5 and perhaps 1.3 Ma, was intermediate in size, and fragmentary limb bones suggest a degree of arboreality comparable to that in living colobinans. This is unexpected for such a large-bodied species. A medium-sized colobine is known by a partial skull and skeleton from the Hadar region and from isolated teeth in other deposits, and small teeth of *Colobus* size have also been found at Laetoli, Omo, and Koobi Fora. Most of these species seem to have survived Late Pliocene climatic cooling but had disappeared by the start of the Pleistocene.

The earliest Eurasian colobine, *Mesopithecus pentelicus,* ranged over a wide area from Yugoslavian Macedonia to Afghanistan ca. 8–7 Ma, and a tooth from central Germany may date to 11–10 Ma. This species, known from dozens of skulls and numerous limb bones, was probably a semiterrestrial inhabitant of gallery forests bordering open steppe,

comparable in its morphological features to the modern *Semnopithecus entellus,* the Hanuman langur. Body size is estimated at ca. 11–15 kg for males, 7–10 kg for females. At the end of the Miocene, although southern Europe was rather arid, northern Central Europe retained forested regions, which may have served as a refuge for a flora that spread rapidly from Spain to Ukraine with the return of moist conditions at the start of the Pliocene.

Another terrestrial colobine, *Dolichopithecus,* is common in Early Pliocene sites over this wide range of monsoon forest. Larger than *Mesopithecus* (20–30 kg for males, 12–18 females), with a long face and numerous postcranial adaptations to life on the ground, *Dolichopithecus* was in some ways a colobine "mandrill" or forest baboon. It has been thought to be a direct descendant of *M. pentelicus,* but that view was somewhat weakened by the finding that, while the latter species has the derived African colobinelike loss of the proximal cuboid-entocuneiform contact, *Dolichopithecus* presents the less-derived small facet. This pattern is variable in the living species, however. A second, less terrestrial, species of *Mesopithecus* coexisted with *Dolichopithecus* through most of the Pliocene. A current problem in colobine systematics is the relationship of this group (if, indeed, it is a unified clade) to the eastern Asian species.

Asian colobine fossils are quite rare, but a number of teeth have been recovered from levels in the Pakistan Siwaliks dated ca. 7–6 Ma. These might represent a late extension eastward of *Mesopithecus,* but, as most colobine teeth are similar, it is difficult to make a comparison without cranial or postcranial material. An isolated M_3 from a latest Miocene level in the Yushe Basin of east-central China (ca. 5.5 Ma) represents the earliest colobine in eastern Asia. Several partial dentions, cranial fragments, and a partial elbow joint from Shamar (Mongolia) and Udunga (Siberian Russia), dated to ca. 3–2.5 Ma, have been named *Parapresbytis eohanuman,* but they might represent an East Asian species of *Dolichopithecus.* A colobine face from Atsugi, Japan (near Yokohama), estimated to date to 2.5 Ma, has only been announced in the popular press. It appears similar to the previous species, but also to some African forms. Fossils of the modern *Pygathrix* (*Rhinopithecus*) are known from several Pleistocene sites in China, while *Semnopithecus* and *Presbytis* species have been recovered in Java.

Subfamily Colobinae
  Tribe Colobini
    Subtribe Colobina
      Colobus
      Procolobus
        P. (*Procolobus*)
        P. (*Piliocolobus*)
      † *Libypithecus*
      † *Cercopithecoides*
      † *Paracolobus*
      † *Rhinocolobus*
      ?† *Microcolobus*
    Subtribe Presbytina
      Presbytis
      Semnopithecus

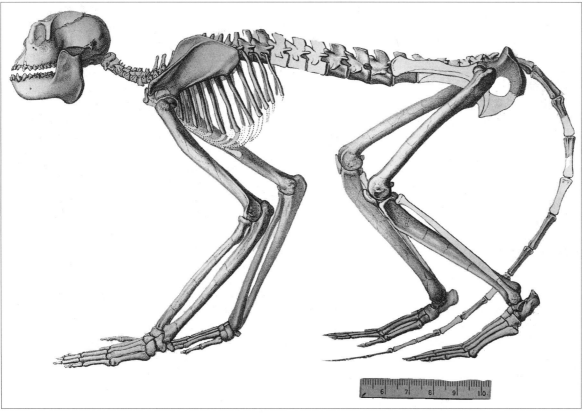

Reconstruction of female skeleton of Mesopithecus, *from Pikermi (Greece), ca. 8.5 Ma. A medium-sized, semi-terrestrial colobine,* Mesopithecus *is known from England through Afghanistan at times between 10 and 3 Ma. From A. Gaudry,* Animaux Fossiles et Géologie de l'Attique, *1862, F. Savy. Three cm on scale = 7cm of actual size.*

S. (*Semnopithecus*)
S. (*Trachypithecus*)
Pygathrix
P. (*Pygathrix*)
P. (*Rhinopithecus*)
Nasalis
N. (*Nasalis*)
N. (*Simias*)
Subfamily Colobinae, incertae sedis
†*Mesopithecus*
†*Dolichopithecus* (?including †*Parapresbytis*)
†extinct

See also Africa; Asia, Eastern and Southern; Cercopithecoids; Cercopithecinae; Diet; Europe; Hadar; Kromdraai; Laetoli; Makapansgat; Miocene; Monkey; Pliocene; Primate Ecology; Primate Societies; Siwaliks; Skull; Sociobiology; Sterkfontein; Teeth. [E.D.]

Further Readings

Benefit, B., and Pickford, M. (1986) Miocene fossil cercopithecoids from Kenya. Am. J. Phys. Anthropol. 69:441–464.

Brandon-Jones, D. (1985) *Colobus* and leaf-monkeys. In D. MacDonald (ed.): The Encyclopedia of Mammals. New York: Facts-on-File, pp. 398–408.

Delson, E. (1994) Evolutionary history of the colobine monkeys in palaeoenvironmental perspective. In G. Davies and J.F. Oates (eds.): Colobine Monkeys: Their Ecology, Behaviour, and Evolution. Cambridge: Cambridge University Press, pp. 11–43.

Groves, C.P. (1970) The forgotten leaf-eaters, and the phylogeny of the Colobinae. In J.R. Napier and P.H. Napier (eds.): Old World Monkeys. London: Academic, pp. 555–587.

Kalmykov, N.P., and Mashchenko, E.N. (1992) The northernmost Early Pliocene Cercopithecidae from Asia. Paleontol. J. (Moscow) 26:178–181.

Leakey, M.G. (1982) Extinct large colobines from the Plio-Pleistocene of Africa. Am. J. Phys. Anthropol. 58:153–172.

Strasser, E., and Delson, E. (1987) Cladistic analysis of cercopithecid relationships. J. Hum. Evol. 16:81–99.

Szalay, F.S., and Delson, E. (1979) Evolutionary History of the Primates. New York: Academic.

Complex Societies

Societies in which social stratification exists and access to real power is limited to members of the upper strata. The beginning of history is tied roughly to the emergence of complex societies in many parts of the world, a development that marks the close of the period of interest for this encyclopedia. Prehistory ends when writing begins, and, in many areas, this was about the time that city-states appeared on the landscape.

An examination of complex societies requires, first, a broad understanding of what is meant by the term. Just how is *complex society* to be defined, and how is it to be distinguished from *noncomplex* or *simple society?* Second, we must ask how complex societies came into being: the eternal question of origins.

Definition

Complex society has often been taken to be synonymous with *state* or *stratified society*, as those terms are used by such authors as American anthropologists E.R. Service and M. Fried. Service defined a state as a sociopolitical organization characterized by a centralized government with a ruling class that was clearly separated from the remainder of the community in that it was not bound by kinship ties to them; it had control of strategic goods and services; and it was able to enforce its will through the imposition of law and the force of sanction. Fried defined stratified societies by reference to their position on a scale of access to power. Stratified societies were those in which a class of people was defined in nonkinship terms to hold power over the other members of society. States, in his view, were political entities in which institutions had developed to hold and impose power. It is important to note that these views of complex society emphasize the relations of people within a society.

V.G. Childe had earlier tried to characterize the state in terms of a wide range of criteria. These have come to be seen as the traditional hallmarks of the state and civilization. His list included features like the aggregation of people into cities, the development of nonagricultural specialization of labor, the production and concentration of surpluses, the emergence of strictly defined class distinctions; and the creation of nonkin-based rules for membership in society. He also included the construction of monumental public works, such as temples or irrigation systems; the beginning of long-distance trade; the creation of an elite art style; and the development of writing and mathematics as abstract means of keeping records. Each of these characteristics might, indeed, be observable in a society that we might identify as complex, but they do not get at root variables that could define the abstract process of development of the complexity itself. Moreover, in some cases, several appear well before complex societies. To understand the process, we must appeal to more basic underlying ideas.

The definition of *complex society* requires a focus on the relations of people to the environment that supports them and to other people within that environment. The ability of individuals to influence the behavior of others rests on political and economic relationships, which Fried described in terms of *authority* and *power*. Authority is the ability to persuade others to comply with one's wishes. Power is the ability to require compliance under threat of sanction. He understood the source of power as control of the basic resources of society.

Any society can be characterized in these terms. Changes in those relations drive the development of complex societies. The origin of complexity in society can be reduced to the question: "Why do the relationships of people and environment change in the first place?"

A definition that focuses on this level of understanding is necessarily a socioecological one. The recognition that interhuman relations have some external causes implies a materialist view of the nature of human relations. Society must be seen as the result of a complex system of interactions between several domains: people and groups of people, the productive capacity of the environment, and the physical characteristics of the environment that affect communication. This sort of approach was pioneered by J. Steward and has since been followed by many American archaeologists, including R.M. Adams, C. Redman, and W. Sanders.

The outcome of this sort of view is one of gradation. When *complex society* is used as a term of relation, some societies are more complex than others because they have more marked development of institutions of power and authority and more structured control of the productive land. In more absolute terms, we can say that, when *complex society* refers to states, stratified society, civilization, or the like, it must be defined in terms of the organization of relations between people, or political and social institutions, and the centralization of control over the subsistence base of the society and the actual products generated by farmers and other specialists.

Development of Complex Society

Understanding how simple societies become more complex requires an examination of both the stresses that drive change and the processes by which complexity arises. Traditionally, archaeologists have tried to explain cultural evolution in terms of the response of a society to some single driving force for change, some *prime mover*. Recently, the various prime-mover explanations have come under heavy criticism for their oversimplification of a patently complex process. These explanations emphasize an initial stress without questioning the source of the initial condition that has been identified. When, for example, the rise of complex society is attributed to cultural responses to uncontrolled population growth, a host of effects of rising population may be identified but little attention is given to explaining why a population that has for many years been maintained at a relatively stable level has suddenly decided to grow. When warfare is seen as a prime mover, the question of why people fight is brushed aside in favor of a consideration of the consequences of conflict.

This sort of approach lacks rigor, and few active archaeologists still cling to such simple explanations. Instead, most theorists focus on a multiplicity of factors, combining several of the simpler explanatory frameworks generated over the past few decades. One can argue that such multiple-cause models are simply more tightly argued restatements and reorganizations of earlier constructions.

UNICAUSAL MODELS

A number of simple, unicausal explanations have been put forward. Childe proposed that the development of craft specialists, especially in metallurgy, changed the social order because such people had to be fed with food produced by others. For the first time, there were healthy, adult members of society who did not provide their own sustenance. The organization of the surplus production of farmers to support these specialists and the organization of means of redistributing their products led to a class of decision makers and hence to the state.

K. Wittfogel has argued that the development of intensive agricultural systems required the development of cooperative systems of planning and decision making. The creation of public utilities in the form of large-scale irrigation systems meant that some labor expended by members of society would benefit not only themselves but others. To regulate this cost and to ensure that the benefit from the utility was equitably apportioned, a central decision-making apparatus was required. Progressively greater investment in the public utility led to more and more responsibility being vested in the central body and ultimately to the development of political integration based on the economic advantages of intensive agriculture.

Similar proposals have been made by American archaeologist W. Rathje and others concerning the advantages of a central administrative structure to regulate long-distance trade for the acquisition of important scarce commodities. Scarce goods that can measurably improve the quality of life in a region constitute a sort of universal objective. The trading expeditions required to gather these goods become a public utility, since not everyone can leave the agricultural system to trek off to trade for them. The administration of investment in the trading mission, support of the traders, and redistribution of the products would have the same consequence as the irrigation-regulating commission hypothesized by Wittfogel. Again, the driving force of this formulation is the economic benefit derived from participation. Those who are party to the long-distance trade have an enhanced capacity to succeed; they have access to the products of the trade while nonparticipants do not.

Another broad set of unicausal proposals has been made by theorists who focus on population growth and resultant competition as the engines of change. R. Carneiro, for example, points out that any environment is limited in size. Areas of high productive capacity are necessarily circumscribed by areas of lesser potential. This is the case whatever the cultural means of extracting energy might be. In other words, the environment is patchy for any resource. Carneiro suggests that growing populations are faced with unreconcilable problems. The capacity of the land to support them is limited, but any nearby land to which they might emigrate is inferior and, thus, limited in its own way. Intensified use of the better land provides only a short-term solution. Ultimately, conflict increases between groups of people who all want to have access to the most productive land, leading to increased military organization; and military organization is seen as the root of political organization. The rise of military leaders represents the institutionalization of power within society, so the rise of complex society is a direct outgrowth of population growth in the context of circumscribed productive resources.

A model of the rise of complex societies based on competition between internal groups has been proposed by I. Diakonoff following Marx and Engels. He suggests that with the rise of intensive agriculture comes the ability of individuals to produce surplus energy, crops beyond the subsistence requirements of the producing families. The emergence of craft specialists is seen in this argument, as in Childe's, as the beginning of a class of people who do not directly provide for their own subsistence. Diakonoff's view is different from that of Childe in that he recognizes a divergence of self-interest between the agricultural producers and the craft producers. Craft producers are in a unique and novel position, because their sustenance depends on a system of exchange in which comparability of value is not evident. To the extent that they can overvalue their products they can concentrate wealth. Growing differences in economic status led to class consciousness and class conflict. Ultimately, conflict among members of a single society led to the formation of the state as a means of protecting the self-interest of the new economic ruling class. In this view, the growth of a market economy leads to the concentration of wealth, the emergence of classes, and the development of increasingly complex means of maintaining economic inequity.

Yet another approach to the question has been explored by R. Blanton for the particular case of Oaxaca (Mexico). Blanton's model is based on the same observations as Carneiro's. He suggests that, in a compartmentalized, or circumscribed, environment, some areas will be more productive than others. The division of the environment will lead to the development of separate self-identifying polities. The outcome is that less-productive areas, or polities, will compete with other polities in control of the more-productive areas. The model here diverges from Carneiro's. Blanton claims that the ultimate goal of the system is to reduce the costs of conflict rather than simply to dominate the entire social landscape. He suggests that one way to reduce these costs is for the wealthier groups to enter into an agreement for their mutual protection from the more hostile, poorer groups, the ones relegated to the least productive parts of the environment.

The unicausal models of the rise of complex societies, although very different from one another, all seem to have structural similarities in terms of the stresses that initiate the cultural processes. Many of them skirt the question, but each appeals to a certain class of variables to explain why the system starts to change. Those variables are biological ones that have to do with the structure of the environment in which the cultural process takes place, or the capacity of the environment to produce accessible energy, or the capacity of human populations to grow (although they generally do not explain why a population grows but merely assume that it does). What these environmental characteristics have in common is simply that they are biological and ecological rather than cultural.

MULTICAUSAL MODELS

Most of these models are idiosyncratic—that is, they were created to help explain a particular case of the emergence of the state. American Archaeologist K.V. Flannery, in 1972, made an important effort to generalize these and other theories through the application of systems theory. He suggested that the transition from simple to complex societies requires an explanation that identifies and explains the processes of cultural change, the mechanisms by which change occurs, and the stresses that motivate the change and select the mechanisms actually employed. These three aspects are requisite parts of an adequate systems explanation of any observed change. Flannery was striving for a single general explanation of the rise of the state in all cases. He identified two basic processes: *segregation,* the differentiation of subsystems within society, and *centralization,* the expansion of control by a central authority. The mechanisms that he identified were *promotion*, by which institutions expand their range of operation, and *linearization*, by which high-level authority takes direct control of low-level decisions. The systems approach has become almost universal among archaeologists studying the emergence of cultural complexity. Flannery's proposed processes and mechanisms have been far less widely adopted, because they seem to be more descriptive than explanatory. Segregation, centralization, promotion, and linearization each reflects aspects of the institutions of society rather than the relations of society that produce institutions.

All of the unicausal models can be described by two complementary cultural processes, in Flannery's terms. Each of these theories is based on one of two processes of social interaction, either *cooperation* or *competition,* between people. These two interactions may take place either within a single community or society or between two or more communities.

The socioenvironmental stresses that drive the cultural processes of cooperation and competition and the institutional processes proposed by Flannery are the subjects of the various unicausal models enumerated above. Agreement on the efficacy of the stresses that motivate change in any particular case has long been elusive. The precise mechanisms in operation in any given case are certainly idiosyncratic and vary depending on historical and ecological conditions.

The kind of multicausal theories proposed by Adams, Flannery, Redman, Sanders, and others seems to be creating a new cultural ecology with a renewed emphasis on culture. If explanation of the stresses that drive change in cultural systems relies on human interaction with environmental conditions, like ecological variability and biological capacities, then cultural ecology is still alive and vigorous, although somewhat modified from its traditional form. The weakness of cultural ecology has been a perception that it had a one-sided view that explained change in relation only to environmental variability. It has long been hard to distinguish this approach from environmental determinism. The new cultural ecology takes into account the variability introduced by cultural tradition. Processes of cooperation and competition may be implemented in various ways depending on the physical circumstances and historical tradition of a given case. A single causal network must not be seen as the only avenue to complexity. External stresses can be responded to in an unlimited variety of ways; the adoption of mechanisms to alleviate stresses is an interactive outcome of culture, history, and ecology. Articulating the detailed relations that give rise to a particular historical case remains the challenge that it has always been.

Complex Societies around the World

The operation of these stresses, mechanisms, and processes can be viewed archaeologically in many parts of the world.

The emergence of complexity in society has followed many pathways, virtually as many as there are cases. In some areas, pristine states have formed without benefit of communication with preexisting states; in others, the development of complexity never yielded the special institutions that characterize the state, giving rise instead to organizations of lesser scope; in still others, the state grew only in relation to earlier developments in neighboring areas as a secondary process.

Pristine, or largely pristine, states developed in only six regions: Mesopotamia, Egypt, the Indus Valley, China, Mesoamerica, and the Andes. The secondary development of the state occurred over a far wider range, including sub-Saharan Africa, India, Central Asia, Southeast Asia, Japan, northern South America, and Europe. The institutions of these states grew in relation to nearby, preexisting states. Communication between emerging elites at relatively similar levels of political integration allowed the less organized groups to emulate the characteristics of those that had already developed. This begs the question of just how the first states emerged, but articulating the mechanisms of cultural change in particular historical contexts is beyond the scope of this entry. Suffice it to say that a wide range of mechanisms, including those identified by Flannery, are available for selection.

In Mesoamerica, for example, the general pattern of development of complex society must be explained in these cultural and ecological terms. Within this region complexity arose in several areas: the Olmec civilization, the first influential group of chiefdoms, in the tropical lowlands of the Gulf Coast; the early Maya and, ultimately, the Classic and Postclassic Maya civilization in the eastern tropical forests of the Yucatan; the singularly important state at Teotihuacan and later the Aztec empire in the semiarid highland basin of Mexico; and the Zapotec state at Monte Alban in the semiarid highland valley of Oaxaca. In each case, environmental and cultural factors interacted in a specific process of cultural evolution. The course of events varied widely and led to different outcomes. We are not yet in a position to explain why, but it is instructive that, in such diverse circumstances, channels existed that promoted the development of complex society. In some areas, the course of change seems to have been almost continuously toward ever more complex organizations; in others, change led at times to more complex organizations and at other times to their dissolution. These changes depended not solely on the environments but equally on the cultural and historical contexts of each case. In any study of process, it is important to distinguish the underlying stresses from the operative mechanisms.

The Olmec rise to prominence in the lowlands of the Gulf Coast likely coincided with the rise of maize agriculture as a locally important food crop. Their swift rise to the status of a dominant, although diverse, chiefly organization is well documented archaeologically. Excavations, particularly at San Lorenzo, have revealed a social and political order in which access to exotic goods and special positions of power were held in the hands of only a few Olmec leaders. Their ability to generate surpluses beyond their subsistence needs provided the energetic basis for these cultural developments.

Pyramid of the Sun, "Avenue of the Dead," and neighboring structures in the Classic-phase city of Teotihuacan, Mexico. This city and its state were at their height ca. AD 500.

The richness of the fertile soils near the streams of the coastal plains would have given them an advantage over their highland neighbors, who lived in a riskier, less productive environment. They used religion to reinforce their right to rule locally, and both religion and economic interaction to extend their influence through much of the central highlands of Mexico. The great impact of the Olmec on the rising elites of the highlands has long been noted, but its nature is little understood. The cultural mechanisms are the most elusive part of the explanation of early Olmec ascendancy.

In the highlands, the rise of the complex societies centered on Teotihuacan and Monte Alban are similarly difficult to explain. Much ink has been expended in efforts to discover the stresses that promoted the centralization of political control so inarguably observed at these two great cities. Most agree that, in both cases, the economic foundation of the state was the ability of the emerging elites to control the most productive land. The surplus was needed to support the members of society who produced goods and services other than food. Clearly, there are complex interrelationships among environmental preconditions, human use of the landscape, and interactions of people within the environment, all of which affect the outcome of evolutionary processes. The operative mechanisms that produced the Pyramid of the Sun at Teotihuacan or Mound J at Monte Alban are hard to define. Just how Monte Alban extended its control over the valley of Oaxaca and surrounding areas and how Teotihuacan controlled the basin of Mexico and influenced so wide an area throughout highland Mesoamerica remain topics of inquiry.

Mesopotamia poses similar questions. In this region as well, most explanations of the rise of complex societies appeal to changing relations between human populations and their environment. The growth of early centers like Çatal Hüyük probably depended upon specially favored local resources, in the case of Çatal Hüyük perhaps the important nearby obsidian resource. Small centers like this one were the precursors of larger sites like Eridu and the later Ubaid-period cities of Uruk, Ur, and Umma. For these cities, the important environmental feature may have been agricultural fields and the irrigation systems constructed to ensure their productivity. Intergroup conflict arising in the context of limited high-quality farmland or the administrative requirements of public utilities that promote production strike familiar chords in the realm of culture process.

The emergence of complex society and its institutions has fascinated archaeologists for decades and will undoubtedly continue to do so. In the near future, the focus will likely be, as Flannery suggested, on the processes, mechanisms, and stresses by which change in cultural-environmental systems occurs. The recognition of the operative stresses as biological or ecological is rapidly emerging, even in the face of a resurgence in some quarters of a superorganic concept of culture divorced from the physical world. The processes themselves are coming to be seen as specifically cultural, whether one focuses on social processes like cooperation or competition or on institutional processes like promotion, linearization, segregation, and centralization. As a result, the area that promises the most excitement is the analysis of the mechanisms that link ecological stress with cultural process.

See also Americas; Archaeology; Asia, Western; Bronze Age; Çatal Hüyük; Culture; Domestication; Iron Age. [B.B.]

Further Readings

Adams, R.M. (1966) The Evolution of Urban Society. Chicago: Aldine.

Blanton, R.E. (1978) Monte Alban: Settlement Patterns of the Ancient Zapotec Capital. New York: Academic Press.

Carneiro, R. (1970) A theory of the origin of the state. Science 169:733–738.

Flannery, K.V. (1972) The cultural evolution of civilizations. Ann. Rev. Ecol. Syst. 3:399–426.

Fried, M. (1967) The Evolution of Political Society: An Essay in Political Anthropology. New York: Random House.

Rathje, W. (1975) The last tango in Mayapán: A tentative trajectory of production-distribution systems. In J.A. Sabloff and C.C. Lamberg-Karlovsky, (eds.): Ancient Civilization and Trade. Albuquerque: University of New Mexico Press, pp. 409–448.

Redman, C. (1978) The Rise of Civilization. San Francisco: Freeman.

Sanders, W., and Webster, D. (1978) Unilinealism, multilinealism, and the evolution of complex societies. In C. Redman et al. (eds.): Social Archaeology. New York: Academic, pp. 249–302.

Sanders, W., Parsons, J., and Santley, R. (1979) The Basin of Mexico: Ecological Processes in the Evolution of a Civilization. New York: Academic.

Service, E.R. (1962) Primitive Social Organization: An Evolutionary Perspective: New York: Random House.

Wright, H. (1977) Recent research on the origin of the state. Ann. Rev. Anthropol. 6:379–397.

Wright, H., and Johnson, G. (1978) Population, exchange, and early state formation in southwestern Iran. Am. Anthropol. 77:267–289.

Coon, Carleton Stevens (1904–1981)

American generalist anthropologist. Coon conducted extensive ethnographic, archaeological, and anthropometric studies in North Africa and Southwest Asia. One of Coon's major research interests was the origin of modern humans, which he pursued in excavations in North African and West Asian caves, including Bisitun, Belt, Hotu, Jerf 'Ajla, and Mugharet el-Aliya. In *The Origin of Races* (1962), he proposed an early model of multiregional continuity in the archaic-modern human transition.

See also Africa, North; Asia, Western; Candelabra Model; Jerf 'Ajla; Modern Human Origins. [J.J.S.]

Core

Block or nodule of stone from which flakes have been removed by deliberate flaking for further use or modification;

also termed a *nucleus*. Many cores may simply be waste products of flake or blade manufacture, while others are thought to have been used after flaking (as in some choppers, handaxes, or picks), and the term *core-tool* is sometimes used. If the flakes removed from the lithic piece are not considered to be useful, usually because they are too small, as in the case of scrapers or projectile points, the piece is usually referred to as a *retouched piece* rather than a core.

See also Biface; Prepared-Core; Stone-Tool Making. [N.T., K.S.]

Cosquer Cave

A partly submerged painted and engraved cave off Cap Margiou (Provence) east of Marseilles (France), whose entrance was found by underwater explorer Henri Cosquer in 1985. Chambers containing art were discovered in 1991 and were studied by French prehistorians J. Courtin and J. Clottes. The cave contains hand stencils with missing phalanges and fingers, dated at ca. 27,000 BP (Phase I), and later engravings and paintings depicting the fauna of the coastal ecology, dated at ca. 18,840 BP (Phase II): These include horses, bison, deer, ibex, seals, Megaceros, the Great Auk, jellyfish, and squid, with rare reindeer. Clottes has noted the depiction of seasonal characteristics among the different species.

See also Late Paleolithic; Paleolithic Image. [A.M.]

Further Readings

Clottes, J., and Courtin, J. (1994) La Grotte Cosquer: Peintures et Gravures de la Caverne Engloutie. Paris: Seuil.

View of Cosquer Cave, showing calcite "draperies" with painted hands and inundated floor. Courtesy of Ministère de la Culture, Direction du Patrimoine; photo by A. Chêné, Centre Camille Jullian (CNRS).

Creswellian

Final Upper Paleolithic industry of Britain, ca. 12–8 Ka, with similarities to contemporary industries of northwestern France and Belgium (e.g., final Magdalenian, Hamburgian). Named for type sites, such as Mother Grundy's Parlor, in the Creswell Crag area of Derbyshire, the Creswellian contains medium- to large-sized angular backed blades, hooked perforators (*zinken*), and shouldered points, together with uniserial and biserial harpoons of bone and antler. Faunas of Creswellian sites are dominated by horse remains but also include remains of reindeer, *Megaceros,* and other cold-adapted mammals as well as birds.

See also Epipaleolithic; Hamburgian; Late Paleolithic Maglemosian; Mesolithic; Paleolithic Lifeways; Stone-Tool Making. [A.S.B.]

Cro-Magnon

Rockshelter in Les Eyzies (Dordogne), France, that yielded several Upper Paleolithic crania, mandibles, and partial skeletons, along with artifacts and features, during the construction of a road in 1868. Subsequent excavations primarily in 1868–1869 but continuing sporadically through 1905 uncovered a number of horizons (A–L) containing the remains of cold-adapted mammals (e.g., mammoth and reindeer), as well as abundant cultural material. The latter included not only flint artifacts but also stone-lined hearths, split-based bone points, a bone fragment bearing a series of sequential notches, numerous (more than 300) perforated Atlantic marine shells, perforated teeth, and three perforated ivory plaques or pendants. The human remains, some stained with red ocher, are said to have derived from the uppermost cultural horizon (most likely K, but possibly J). Since all of the cultural material available in museums can be related to the Aurignacian (no diagnostic Perigordian or Solutrean pieces were recovered), it is likely that the five crania and associated postcrania represent Aurignacian burials, probably from a later phase of the Aurignacian in view of their presumed position in the stratigraphy. If the chronology of the Abri Pataud, a site with a similar stratigraphy ca. 200 m to the southeast, is taken as a guide, the probable age of the Cro-Magnon hominids is ca. 30 Ka.

Although strongly built and large headed, the specimens contrast markedly with the Neanderthals in their morphology and body proportions. The name *Cro-Magnon* has been generalized to refer to long-limbed, robust, but anatomically modern skeletons from other early Upper Paleolithic contexts in Europe. The Cro-Magnon site constituted the first widely accepted association between modern human remains and extinct fauna and was, thus, central to the establishment of human antiquity.

See also Abri Pataud; Aurignacian; Breuil, [Abbé] Henri [Edward Prosper]; Europe; Homo sapiens; Jewelry; Lartet, Edouard; Late Paleolithic; Neanderthals; Paleolithic Lifeways; Perigordian; Ritual; Upper Paleolithic. [C.B.S., A.S.B.]

Further Readings

Gambier, D. (1989) Fossil hominids from the early Upper Palaeolithic (Aurignacian) of France. In P. Mellars and C.B. Stringer (eds.): The Human Revolution. Edinburgh: Edinburgh University Press, pp. 194–211.

Movius, H.L. (1969) The Abri de Cro-Magnon, Les Eyzies (Dordogne), and the probable age of the contained burials on the basis of the evidence of the nearby Abri Pataud. Anuario de Estudios Atlanticos 15:323–324.

Movius, H.L. (1995) Inventaire analytique des sites aurignaciens et périgordiens de Dordogne: Abri de Cro-Magnon. In H.M. Bricker (ed.): Le Paléolithique Supérieur de l'Abri Pataud (Dordogne): Les Fouilles de H. L. Movius, Jr. (Documents d'Archéologie Française 50). Paris: Éditions de La Maison des Sciences de l'Homme, pp. 249–254.

Stringer, C.B., Hublin, J-J., and Vandermeersch, B. (1984) The origin of anatomically modern humans in western Europe. In F.H. Smith and F. Spencer (eds.): The Origins of Modern Humans. New York: Liss, pp. 51–135.

Cueva Morin

Archaeologically important cave located near Santander in northeastern Spain, dated to the later Late Pleistocene by faunal and archaeological correlations and radiocarbon ages. In the 1960s and 1970s, American archaeologist L. Freeman distinguished 16 archaeological levels at this site: nine Mousterian, one Chatelperronian, and six Aurignacian. One of the earliest levels in the latter group yielded a structural complex consisting of a rectangular subsurface depression interpreted as a hut floor, incorporating a hearth, a possible arrangement of small irregular elliptical holes interpreted as postholes, and four graves. Two graves had been destroyed in Aurignacian times; the other two contained *pseudormorphs,* or outlines of bodies with no associated skeletons.

See also Aurignacian; Châtelperronian; Middle Paleolithic; Mousterian; Ritual; Upper Paleolithic. [A.S.B.]

Further Readings

Freeman, L.G. (1983) More on the Mousterian: Flaked bone from Cueva Morin. Curr. Anthropol. 24:366–377.

Freeman, L.G., and González-Echegaray, J. (1970) Aurignacian structural features and burials at Cueva Morin (Santandere, Spain). Nature 226:722–726.

Cultural Anthropology

Branch of anthropology that studies living human groups as cultural entities. It includes *ethnography,* the effort to describe accurately the workings of human societies, and *ethnology,* the effort to explain those observations. The unifying concept of *culture,* the shared knowledge and patterns of behavior of human societies, is central to the practice of cultural anthropology.

See also Anthropology; Archaeology; Culture; Primate Societies. [B.B.]

Culture

Term traditionally used in prehistoric archaeology to define a specific collection of portable material objects, most often stone and bone tools, that exhibit similarity in a number of variables and that are found within a delimited region and time period (e.g., the Magdalenian, the Perigordian, or the Solutrean cultures). This use of the term is widespread in the literature that deals with the culture history of regions.

Shifts in research focus, especially evident in North American anthropological archaeology, have brought with them an expansion of this concept, and the term has acquired a broader meaning, more like that used in sociocultural anthropology. Numerous definitions of culture exist in anthropology. Perhaps the most inclusive is L. White's, which sees culture as referring to all human extrasomatic means of adaptation, including ideas and beliefs, behavior, and material results of that behavior.

Applying this all-encompassing concept in archaeology raises many problems. The archaeological record contains direct information about only some materials used in the past—those, like lithics, that preserve the best. These remains, which constitute a small fraction of what was originally used, thus carry direct information about only a limited range of past behavior, and this information may be ambiguous. Behavioral complexes without direct material expression are not preserved in the archaeological record and must be inferred indirectly through analogy.

There is an ongoing debate among archaeologists about just what similarities in the recovered artifacts reflect. Some argue that they mirror past ethnicity; others see the similarity originating from shared norms; still others see it reflecting the frequency of interactions. Research by ethnoarchaeologists has also shown that material culture can signal both individual identity and group identity, and that the imprinting of these identities is not a constant, but, rather, reflects ongoing social relationships. For example, in some situations it may be more advantageous to deemphasize one's differences by making objects more similar to those of one's neighbors, while in others it may be more advantageous to emphasize them.

Finally, *culture* also refers to a shared system of learned behaviors, passed on through several generations and thus characteristic of particular groups or communities. In this sense, there is considerable debate over whether humans are the only living primate species with culture, and, if so, when culture first appeared. At one extreme, only anatomically modern humans are considered to have possessed culture; at the other, chimpanzees and even certain species of cercepithecoid monkeys (macaques, baboons) are described as exhibiting culture in the form of long-term learned behavioral differences between populations.

See also Archaeology; Cultural Anthropology. [O.S., A.S.B.]

Further Readings

Trigger, B.G. (1989) A History of Archaeological Thought. Cambridge: Cambridge University Press.
White, L.A. (1959) The Evolutions of Culture. New York: McGraw-Hill.

Cyclostratigraphy

The analysis of rhythmic features in the stratigraphic record according to astronomical cycles and, in particular, the Earth-orbital cycles with periodicities between 0.1 and 1.0 Myr that support an orbital-forcing time scale (OFT). Precision in OFT dating does not decrease with increasing age because the cyclic effects are stratigraphic features that are directly observable in the rocks. The accuracy of OFT dates, which depends on the extrapolation of orbital and rotational cycles into the past, is also well controlled because the cycles are independent and can be cross-checked against one another, and because changes in the astronomical periodicities over time can be calculated with great confidence. Other appellations for this relatively new discipline include "*cosmostratigraphy*," "*orbital stratigraphy*," and *astrochronology*.

Milankovitch Cycles

The frequency spectrum of astronomical-motion periodicities ranges from pulsar spin, measured in milliseconds, through rotational and orbital periods of Earth, moon, and sun, to galactic cycles measured in tens of millions of years. Using the present sidereal year as the unit of measurement, this spectrum has been subdivided for convenience into frequency bands: calendar ($1/yrx10^{-3}$ to $1/yr$), solar ($1/yr$ to $1/yrx10^3$), Milankovitch ($1/yrx10^3$ to $1/yrx10^6$), and galactic ($1/yrx10^6$ to $1/yrx10^9$). The effects of calendar- and solar-frequency astronomical motion, such as tidal, seasonal, annual, and sunspot cycles, have long been recognized in growth stages of fossilized organisms and in fine-laminated sediments. At the turn of the twentieth century, G.K. Gilbert was proposing that such astronomical cycles might be useful in geochronology, but the known cycles were of too high frequency or, like cyclothems, were too episodic and noisy, to be of any practical use in this regard. M. Milankovitch, beginning in 1920, argued a direct relationship between the broad fluctuations of Pleistocene climate and the calculated variations of insolation (the flux of solar energy reaching the atmosphere at a given latitude) that could result from cyclic patterns in three different orbital motions—precession of the equinoxes, obliquity wobble, and eccentricity—and proposed that this could be used to determine the age of paleoclimatic features.

Milankovitch's calculations have been significantly extended and refined in massive computerized treatments that bring out the internal complexity of the orbital oscillations. It should be kept in mind that the numerical values used in general discussion are only convenient approximations or averages and that the effect of each cycle is different from the others in quality as well as timing. Over the duration of the Phanerozoic, the rotation of the Earth has slowed appreciably, and the moon's orbit has contracted, with effects on the computed orbital-forcing functions that must be incorporated. The obliquity wobble, for instance, is now 40 percent faster than in the Silurian. The resultant of the three Milankovitch cycles is projected as a family of latitude-dependent insolation curves, with that of 65°N considered as the standard.

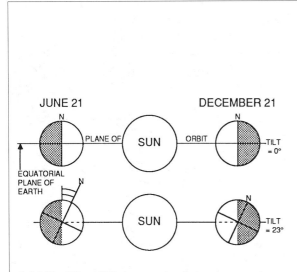

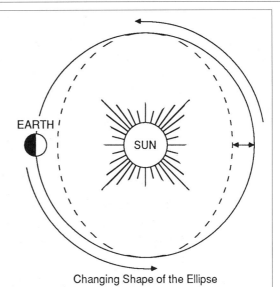

Axial tilt. When tilt is increased, polar regions receive more sunlight, since the summer sun is higher in the sky, while intensity of winter light is little changed. When tilt is low, regions close to the pole receive practically no sunlight the year round.

Orbital eccentricity. The shape of the earth's orbit changes from nearly circular to more elliptical, in cycles that repeat at irregular intervals concentrating around 100,000 and 400,000 years.

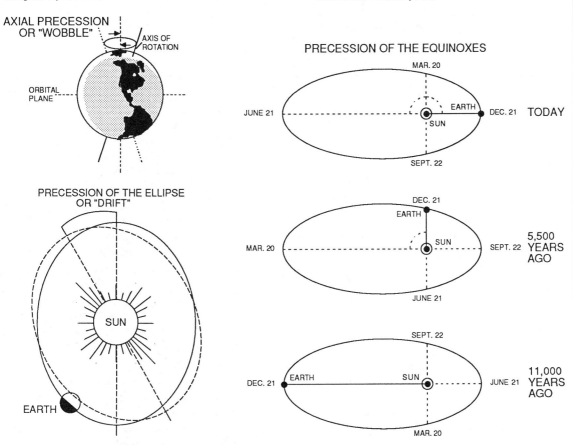

Precession of axial tilt and orbit. "Wobble" and "drift" together result in a cycle of 22,000 years in the timing of the seasons with regard to the orbit. Today the winter solstice in the northern hemisphere occurs when the Earth is near the sun; 11,000 years ago it occurred when the Earth was far from the sun.

PRECESSION

This refers to the shift of seasons with regard to the Earth's orbit, due to the combined effect of a 26-Kyr swing in the orientation of the Earth's rotational axis with regard to the orbit, and an independent, separate progression of the perihelion-aphelion nodes (nearest and farthest points in orbit) around the orbital path. This has the effect of causing the seasons to precess with respect to perihelion in periods of 19 and 23 Kyr, with an effective quasi period or average of insolation variation at 21.7 Kyr. The effects of precession are opposite in the Northern and Southern Hemispheres because aphelion (colder) winters and perihelion (warmer) summers in one hemisphere will be synchronous with perihelion winters and aphelion summers in the other hemisphere. At present, the Earth is approaching the peak of northern perihelion summers.

OBLIQUITY

Also known as *tilt*, this refers to the angle between the Earth's rotational axis and the plane of the ecliptic. Tilt variations have greatest effect at the poles, and higher obliquity means warmer summers and colder winters at high latitudes in both hemispheres. Currently, the tilt of the axis varies between 22° and 24°30′, with a major quasi periodicity of 41 Kyr and minor components at 29 and 54 Kyr. The present angle of tilt is 23°27′, and it is in decrease toward the minimum. In addition, the amplitude of the variation in tilt changes by almost 100 percent on a cycle of 1.3 Ma. Intervals of high-amplitude obliquity coincide with clusters of the most severe glacial phases, but the obliquity amplitude at present is close to a minimum.

ECCENTRICITY

This term refers to the degree of ellipticity (deviation from roundness) in the Earth's orbit. Eccentricity is caused by interactions with other planets, with major periods at 120, 100, and 95 Kyr, leading to a quasi period of insolation that varies around a mean of 100 Kyr. Eccentricity is declining from a recent maximum. The amplitude of eccentricity cycles also varies, with a major quasi period of 410 Kyr. Eccentricity significantly modulates the effects of both obliquity and precession.

Considering the entire year and integrating over the entire planet, the precession and tilt variations do not result in a change in total insolation, but only in its distribution. Only eccentricity cycles have an effect on total received insolation. Thus, eccentricity and precession dominate the signal at the equator, while obliquity is the primary influence on radiation received at the poles.

Stratigraphy and Cycles: Proxy Curves

The insolation of the past cannot be measured directly, of course, and cyclostratigraphy depends on sedimentary features whose variations are a proxy, or reflection, of the Milankovitch periods. None, however, of the various proxy curves in common use are completely faithful reproductions of the calculated net insolation curves. For one thing, the Milankovitch cycles probably affect insolation by only 5 to 10 percent and must be enhanced by feedback in climatic-oceanic systems in order to produce a sedimentary signal that is strong enough to be filtered from background variability. The amplification of the feedback, in turn, depends greatly on the degree of instability in the global climatic-oceanic system. The sedimentary imprint of Milankovitch cycles on Mesozoic and Lower Cenozoic strata is relatively muted because the warm oceans of that period buffered insolation-driven variations. In the later Cenozoic, however, the contrast between increasingly refrigerated ocean masses and the sun-warmed surfaces meant that global climates were much less stable, so that effects of the Milankovitch cycles were more influential. To make matters more complex, the climatic-oceanic system tends to respond independently to each of the three primary Milankovitch cycles.

Fortunately, the proxy curves, however distorted in amplitude, record insolation periodicities fairly well. The most detailed and reliable studies of Milankovitch cycles are based on proxy responses in three climate-sensitive systems: (1) stable isotopes of carbon and oxygen in the open ocean, (2) sapropels, and (3) marl-limestone rhythmites in sediments of protected basins.

STABLE-ISOTOPE RATIOS

Milankovitch's theories were taken lightly until the mid-1960s, when the micropaleontologist Cesare Emiliani at the University of Miami began to present evidence for global climate changes that corresponded with the Milankovitch predictions. Emiliani and his students had found that the ratio of the two most common isotopes of carbon, ^{12}C and ^{13}C, (written as $\delta^{13}C$), in the shells of the surface-floating planktonic foraminiferan *Globigerina* varied according to the temperature of the water in which the shells had formed. Looking at this ratio in the fossilized tests of this foraminifer in sea-floor cores, it was found that the $\delta^{13}C$ varied with depth below the ocean floor, indicating historical changes in water temperatures that synchronized with Milankovitch's calculations. The primitive state of core sampling and geochronometry at that time prevented Emiliani from conclusively identifying Milankovitch cycles below Upper Pleistocene levels. In the following years, data from the Deep Sea Drilling Project and concurrent advances in dating abundantly substantiated and extended these pioneer findings.

In addition to the carbon-isotope ratios, it was found that the ratio of the common oxygen isotopes ^{16}O to ^{18}O (written as $\delta^{18}O$) in the carbonate of the fossil shells also varied with geologic age in curves that closely (but not exactly) matched the carbon-isotope curves. There is no difference, however, between oxygen-isotope ratios in modern marine seas from the poles to the tropics, so the observed geologic variations in $\delta^{18}O$ cannot be a reflection of changes in local water temperature. Instead, oxygen isotopes in seawater are fractionated by surface evaporation that takes up the lighter isotope preferentially, making airborne water much lighter isotopically than seawater. Considering the size of the oceans, a perceptible long-term variation in the oxygen-isotope ratio of surface waters requires a significant change in the amount of fresh water that is held separate from the ocean. Calculations indicate that only the growth and melting of major continental ice sheets could affect the $\delta^{18}O$ of seawater with the extent and rapidity observed in the Late Cenozoic. In other words, the oxygen-isotope record of the ocean reflects worldwide variation in continental ice sheets, while the carbon-isotope record reflects variation in sea surface temperature (SST) in the sample area.

Since the mid-1960s, the undisturbed, microfossil-rich sediments in the abyssal basins have been probed by hundreds of deep-drilled cores (and thousands of gravity cores) all around the globe, providing a strongly reinforced record of ocean history in unprecedented detail and accuracy. Several sets of these cores have been analyzed to give a continuous, standardized stable-isotope curve that extends to the base of the Pliocene, where the abnormal conditions of the Messinian event remain to be bridged, at least in terms of this proxy if not in others (see below). Because SST is subject to large, unpredictable local biases, the temperature curve from carbon-isotope ratios in planktonic foraminifera is considered to be a less reliable indicator of global climate change than the ice-volume curve described by the oxygen-isotope ratios. By convention, the major stable-isotope peaks are numbered from the present, so that warm (ice-minimum) peaks have odd numbers, and cold (ice-maximum) peaks have even numbers. For instance, the base of the Pleistocene, in the Eburonian glacial advance, is identified with isotope peak 64.

SAPROPELS

Variations in the carbon content of laminated strata in certain marine and lacustrine sequences have been found to accurately proxy both the relative intensity and the duration of Milankovitch-forced climatic cycles. To consider sapropels first, these are distinct, fine-laminated layers found in certain deep basins, such as the Eastern Mediterranean, that have anomalously high amounts of unreduced organic carbon (2 percent or more by weight) compared to negligible amounts in enclosing strata. Individual sapropel beds can be traced over wide areas, and in diluted form (as *sapropelic laminites*) into areas of higher sedimentation, clearly as the result of events of regional or wider significance.

Characteristically, sapropels and laminites are rich in diatoms and contain undisturbed fish skeletons, indicating high surface productivity and anoxic bottom conditions. In outcrop, they tend to stand out as distinct soft, dark bands, sometimes with a white gypsiferous efflorescence from the weathering of pyrite.

The modern consensus is that sapropels and sapropelic laminites tend to form at perihelion summer peaks, termed precession minima, in the 21-Kyr precession cycle. Analysis of sapropels supports the contention that the transient change in the carbon cycle is associated with weaker winter storms and higher summer rainfall in temperate regions at such times. As a result, circulation is markedly slowed, at these latitudes, in semiclosed basins (such as the Balearic Basin and the eastern Mediterranean) where seasonal convection overturn is the primary source of oxygenated water to the depths. Simultaneously, even as ventilation of deep water is reduced or cut off completely, the supply of limiting nutrients such as iron, phosphate, and nitrogen into the surface waters may be increased through higher levels of summer erosion and runoff. Whether or not surface waters become more productive, an excess of unreduced carbon will accumulate in response to the stagnation during perihelion peaks.

CARBONATE CYCLES

Experiments in connection with *global warming* amply demonstrate the role of atmospheric CO_2 as a heat trap. That its variation amplifies orbital effects, and those of precession-driven cycles in particular, is indicated by geological observations. For example, it has been found that, in Antarctic ice cores, layers with elevated carbon-dioxide content appear to be synchronous with intervals in the $\delta^{18}O$ curve that represent reduced ice volume. Atmospheric CO_2 is, however, largely controlled by the much greater CO_2 content of oceanic surface water. This is, in turn, influenced by conditions in the atmosphere, in what appears to be a complex interplay of deep water upwelling in response to wind velocity, terrestrial biotic activity, sea surface temperature, and the areal extent of limestone deposition in reefs and shallows. In this system, the increase and decrease of atmospheric CO_2 appears to involve self-reinforcing feedback that is set in motion by insolation changes.

The higher summer temperatures of precession minima mean lowered solubility of calcium carbonate and CO_2 in surface waters. At these times, the boundary of carbonate-saturated water deepens, and more carbonate is precipitated (or less is dissolved) in shallow- and medium-depth sediments. In outcrops of strata that were deposited under the migrating boundary, the precession rhythm is clearly seen in the alternation of soft marls and harder, more limy strata. In some basins, where both oxygen and carbon dioxide were at sensitive levels, precession cycles are recorded by superimposed sapropel and carbonate signals, and the two-layered marl-limestone rhythmite is replaced by a four-layered marl-limestone-sapropel-limestone unit.

CYCLE GROUPS

In sections with well-developed cyclic lithology, groupings of stronger and weaker (or missing) precession-driven peaks are evident and bespeak the influence of longer-term orbital cycles. The 100-Kyr eccentricity cycle, which strongly moderates the amplitude of the 21.7-Kyr precession cycle, is presently the dominant overprint in the stable-isotope record; prior to the Elsterian glaciation peak, broadly centered at 450 Ka, the 41-Kyr obliquity cycle had more effect, suggesting that the Arctic climate was less stable (i.e., warmer during obliquity maxima) than today. Over longer intervals, the interaction of the 410-Kyr periodicity in eccentricity-amplitude and higher-frequency cycles produced beats widely recognized as "major cold-climate peaks" at 2.5, 1.8, 0.9, 0.6–0.45, and 0.1 Ma. The 1.3-Myr. cycle in obliquity amplitude appears to have augmented the Elster-

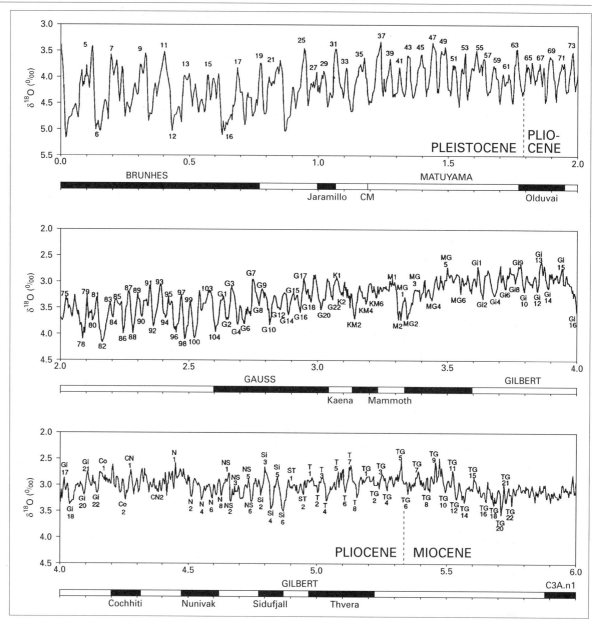

Standard oxygen isotope stages of the upper Cenozoic. The variation of the oxygen isotope ratio in the world ocean, due to changes in ice volume on land, show how orbital cycles have increased their influence as the ocean cooled and climate became increasingly sensitive to slight changes in annual insolation. Analysis of fine-layered marine deposits has shown that variation in carbonate and organic content, storm-related dust, and debris dropped from icebergs, all related to climate change, can be matched precisely to each isotopic peak and valley. The stratigraphic records of East African lakes, Chinese loess, and vegetational successions have also been closely matched to the cyclostratigraphic "time scale." Courtesy of N.J. Shackleton.

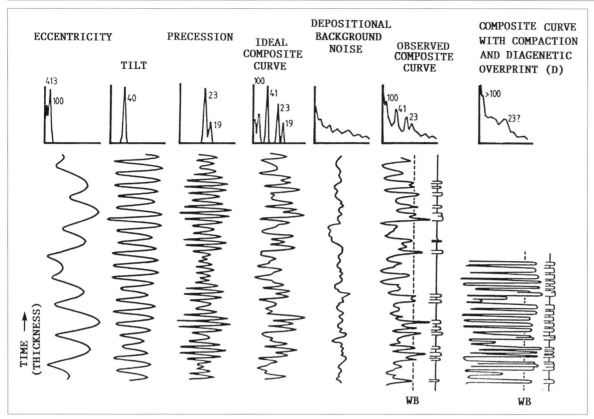

Relationship of orbital motion to the stratigraphic record. Computed variability of solar radiation due to orbital eccentricity, axial tilt (or obliquity), and equinoctial precession is indicated in the three left-hand columns, as are their cycle durations. The ideal composite insolation curve for a temperate latitude shows the 41 Kyr obliquity cycle as the dominant influence, as in the early Pleistocene. The insolation signal, although degraded by random variation in sedimentation ("background noise") and modified by CO_2 feedback (not considered here), is imprinted on receptive stratigraphic sequences as alternating bands of sediment reflecting cyclic climate change. The distorted signal is shown on the left and the resulting banding pattern on the right side of the observed composite column. Cutoff sensitivity of the depositional system to the orbitally forced climate shifts (line WB), and the effects of post-depositional change such as sediment compaction, cause further loss of orbital information in the resulting sedimentary sequence. After Einsele, G., Ricken, W., and Seilacher, A. (eds.), 1991. Cycles and Events in Stratigraphy. Berlin: Springer Verlag.

ian peak (0.45), and also the Eburonian peak (1.8) at the beginning of the Pleistocene. The overprint of the longer cycles is extremely useful in controlling the count of precession cycles.

CALIBRATION

The first successful correlation of the geological time scale to cyclostratigraphy produced some striking results. Recognition of the 21-Kyr precession cycles through the Pleistocene and into the Middle Pliocene was first achieved by oxygen-isotope analysis of microfossils in Pacific deep-sea cores obtained during the Ocean Drilling Program in the late 1980s. Direct counting of the cycles demonstrated that the exisiting radiometric calibration of the geomagnetic polarity reversals, as seen in the same cores, was from 2 to 7 percent too old. A series of high-resolution laser-fusion $^{40}Ar/^{39}Ar$ dates on key sections, including several containing the Brunhes-Matuyama boundary as well as the type section of the Olduvai Subchron, has since confirmed the orbitally corrected time scale. The extension of the OFT into the Miocene is proceeding, based on lithological cyclostratigraphy in the western Mediterranean region.

The larger and more persistent lake basins—those in rift basins, above all—may well contain sequences with use-

ful cyclostratigraphic data, in terms of stable-isotope variations or sedimentary patterns. In the African Rift basins, however, the detection of precession cycles may be complicated by the fact that, in the tropics, the opposite signals of precession in Northern and Southern hemispheres could be confused.

See also Climate Change and Evolution; Paleomagnetism; Pleistocene; Time Scale. [J.A.V.C.]

Further Readings

Hays, J.D, Imbrie, J., and Shackleton, N.J. (1976) Variations in the Earth's Orbit: Pacemaker of the Ice Ages. Science, v. 194, pp. 1121–1132.

Hilgen, F.J., Krijgsman, W., Langereis, C.G., Lourens, L.J., Santarelli, A., and Zachariasse, W.J. (1995) Extending the astronomical (polarity) time scale into the Miscene, Earth, and Planetary Sciences Newsletters, v. 136, pp. 495–510.

Wadleigh, M.A. (1995) Applications of oxygen isotopes to Quaternary chronology. In N.W. Rutter and N.R. Catto (eds.): Dating Methods for Quaternary Deposits. St. Johns, Newfoundland: Geological Society Canada, pp. 51–60.

D

Dabban

Early Late Paleolithic backed-blade and burin industry of Cyrenaica (Libya), defined at Haua Fteah and Hagfet ed-Dabba (Cave of the Hyena) by C.B.M. McBurney. The first appearance of the industry at ca. 40–32 Ka, sometimes compared with the Emiran at Abu Halka, is marked by chamfered blades, endscrapers, and a large component of backed blades. This is followed at Haua Fteah by a reappearance of Levalloiso-Mousterian and then by a second Dabban phase with more burins and endscrapers but *no* chamfered blades. The Dabban lasted until ca. 14 Ka, when it was replaced by an eastern Oranian industry with backed bladelets and microblade cores.

See also Blade; Burin; Emiran; Haua Fteah; Ibero-Maurusian; Late Paleolithic; Levallois; Mousterian; Stone-Tool Making. [A.S.B.]

Further Readings

McBurney, C.B.M. (1967) The Haua Fteah (Cyrenaica) and the Stone Age of the South-east Mediterranean. Cambridge: Cambridge University Press.

Dali

Archaeological and paleontological site in fluvial deposits overlain by loess (wind-blown silt) at T'ien-shui-kou in Dali County of Shaanxi Province (China) excavated since 1978. Level 3 of the site preserves a hominid skull associated with a lithic industry consisting of small irregular cores, numerous scrapers (69 percent of the assemblage), and other simple retouched tools. Uranium-series dating places Level 3 between 230 and 180 Ka, although the faunal assemblage may indicate a somewhat younger, early Late Pleistocene antiquity. The hominid cranium is well preserved with an endocranial capacity of less than 1,200 ml and a large supraorbital torus but a gracile and flat face. It is usually classified as a Chinese "archaic *Homo sapiens*," and several workers, particularly in China, regard it as morphologically intermediate between earlier *Homo erectus* and modern Chinese populations.

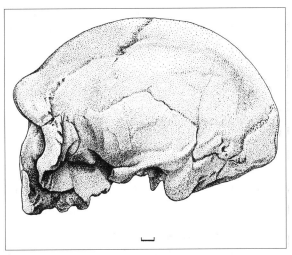

Lateral view of the Dali cranium. Scale is 1 cm.

See also Archaic Homo sapiens; China. [C.B.S., J.J.S.]

Dar-es-Soltane

Cave site in dunal sandstone near Rabat (Morocco) containing an archaeological succession from Middle Paleolithic to the Neolithic and hominid fossils associated with an Aterian industry. The dating of the Aterian level is uncertain, but it is probably more than 45 Ka. Most of the fossils have not been described, but they include the robustly built front of a skull and associated mandible. Although anatomically modern, this specimen is reminiscent of the earlier Jebel Irhoud crania from Morocco and may indicate local continuity in this area between nonmodern and modern populations.

See also Archaic Moderns. [C.B.S., J.J.S.]

Dart, Raymond Arthur (1893–1988)

South African (b. Australia) anatomist and paleontologist. Following completion of his medical training at the University of Sydney in 1917, Dart spent several years working with G.E. Smith (1871–1937) in England and R.J. Terry (1871–

1966) in the United States before receiving the chair of anatomy at the University of Witwatersrand in 1922, a position he held until his retirement in 1958. In 1925, he was catapulted to international fame by his description and interpretation of the fossil hominid infant skull from Taung, which he named *Australopithecus africanus.* Dart claimed that this apelike creature stood on the threshold of humanity and as such warranted a new family name: Homo-Simiadae. While these pronouncements instantly embroiled him in controversy, his insights were later confirmed and represented a major milestone in the history of paleoanthropology. Following World War II, Dart was responsible for the systematic excavation of the Makapansgat site, which yielded several dozen new australopithecine fossils along with an enormous accumulation of bone fragments from other animals. Dart concluded that the australopithecines inhabiting this site had been responsible for the bone accumulations and that they had fashioned and used some of these bones as primitive tools. To describe this tool making he coined the term *osteodontokeratic culture.* While the reaction to this hypothesis was largely negative, it had the positive effect of promoting the search for alternative explanations, a direct product of which was the incorporation of taphonomic research techniques in Paleolithic archaeological research. In addition to his paleoanthropological studies, Dart also played an active role in developing studies on living subequatorial human populations and contributed to the development of nonhuman primate behavioral studies through his establishment in 1958 of the Witwatersrand University Uganda Gorilla Research Unit.

See also Australopithecus; Australopithecus africanus; Makapansgat; Taung. [F.S.]

Darwin, Charles Robert (1809–1882)

British naturalist. Following a false start at Edinburgh as a medical student (1825–1827), Darwin went to Christ's College, Cambridge, where he earned a B.A. degree in 1831. At Cambridge, Darwin's interest in natural history was fostered by the geologist A. Sedgwick (1785–1873) and the botanist J.S. Henslow (1796–1861). It was Henslow who subsequently recommended him for the position of companion to the captain of the HMS *Beagle,* a vessel that had been commissioned to explore and survey the South American coastline and the islands of the South Pacific. During the *Beagle's* voyage, from December 1831 to October 1836, Darwin gathered an immense body of scientific data on the flora, fauna, and geology of the continents and islands he visited. All of Darwin's later work stemmed directly from the observations and collections made during this voyage. The immediate result was the publication in 1839 of a general account of the voyage, the *Journal of Researches into the Geology and Natural History of the Various Countries Visited by H.M.S. Beagle, 1832–36.* Three other books followed, in 1842, 1844, and 1846, respectively: *Structure and Distribution of Coral Reefs, Geological Observations on Volcanic Islands,* and *Geological Observations on South America.*

At this juncture, Darwin's concerns shifted progressively from geology to biology. From 1846 to 1854, he devoted his attention primarily to the study of living and fossil barnacles, which did much to clarify his ideas on classification, variation, and the origination of species. It was not until 1858, when he received a manuscript from the young naturalist A.R. Wallace (1823–1913) outlining similar ideas on natural selection and evolution, that Darwin was prompted to complete what he called an "abstract" of the full work he had been laboring on for years. This abstract was *On the Origin of Species,* which appeared on November 24, 1859. In this work, he painstakingly documented the evidence supporting the view that the Earth's diverse organic life had a common ancestry and presented a theory for the operation of the evolutionary process. The book was an immediate sensation and brought Darwin instant and enduring fame.

During the remaining years of his life, Darwin published three more books that amplified and extended the principles presented in *On the Origin of Species.* These were *The Variation of Animals and Plants under Domestication* (1868), *The Descent of Man and Selection in Relation to Sex* (1871), and *The Expression of the Emotions in Man and Animals* (1872). Although such honors as knighthood and the coveted Fellowship of the Royal Society eluded him in life, in death he received universal praise for having discovered the greatest general principle in biology. He died April 19, 1882, and was buried in Westminster Abbey.

See also Evolution; Haeckel, Ernst Heinrich; Huxley, Thomas Henry; Wallace, Alfred Russel. [F.S.]

Further Readings

Gillespie, N.C. (1979) Charles Darwin and the Problem of Creation. Chicago: University of Chicago Press.
Gruber, H. (1981) Darwin on Man: A Psychological Study of Scientific Creativity, 2nd ed. Chicago: University of Chicago Press.
Peckham, M. (1959) The Origin of Species by Charles Darwin: A Variorum Text. Philadelphia: University of Pennsylvania Press.

Daubentoniidae

Family of Lemuriformes that contains the aye-aye, *Daubentonia madagascariensis.* The only living member of its family, the aye-aye is a highly specialized form whose affinities appear to lie within Indrioidea but whose aspect is different from that of any other lemur. Sites in Madagascar's south and southwest have yielded subfossil bones that are significantly larger and more robust than those of the living aye-aye and have been assigned to a recently extinct species, *D. robusta.* This species was very robust and may have weighed three to five times as much as the living aye-aye, whose average weight is ca. 2.7 kg. No skull of the extinct form is known, but it almost possessed all of the diagnostic features of its genus.

Morphologically, the aye-aye is unusual in a variety of ways. Perhaps the most marked peculiarity of this lemur lies in its anterior dentition, which has been reduced in the adult to a single pair of incisor teeth in each of the upper and lower jaws. These teeth are enlarged, laterally compressed, and continuously growing, their open roots extending far back in

Daubentonia madagascariensis. *From R. Owen, 1866,* Trans. zool. Soc. London, *vol. 5.*

the jaws above or below the roots of the molar teeth, which are greatly reduced in size and simplified in morphology. A single tiny permanent premolar is present in the upper jaw. The anterior teeth are thus reminiscent of those of rodents and are adapted to a similar gnawing function. This function has affected the entire structure of the skull, which is flexed to help absorb gnawing stresses, giving it a globular appearance in side view.

The most striking character of the postcranial skeleton of the aye-aye may be the great elongation of the digits of the hand, particularly the middle one, which is thin and attenuated. When walking on a flat substrate, the aye-aye is obliged to hyperflex its wrist to clear the ground with these digits. This gives its terrestrial locomotion a stiff-armed appearance, even though the aye-aye is an animal of great agility in the trees. The digits of the aye-aye are tipped with highly compressed nails, or *pseudo-claws,* except in the case of the hallux, which is equipped with a flat nail. In the external characters of its soft anatomy, the aye-aye is likewise unusual, especially in the large size of its external ears and in the quality of its fur, which has a layer of long and coarse guard hairs that overlie the softer fur beneath. Uniquely for a primate, female aye-ayes have a single pair of mammae situated far back on the abdomen.

It is probable that the aye-aye was once distributed widely throughout the forests of Madagascar. Nowadays it is relatively rarely reported and probably does not occur in high density anywhere. Nonetheless, it retains a fairly ubiquitous distribution, possibly vicarious with its larger extinct congener. It is known throughout the eastern forest, in the Sambirano, in the northwest, and in the Ankarana Massif near Madagascar's northern tip. Still, the aye-aye is among the most critically endangered of all the lemurs, and its chances for survival are not helped by local beliefs that it is a harbinger of misfortune.

An arboreal quadruped, the aye-aye is nocturnal, and little is known about its behavior and ecology in the wild. Adults appear to range alone, with adult females accompanied by their immature offspring; olfactory marking is an important part of the behavioral repertoire and presumably helps maintain social relations between individuals with overlapping ranges. Aye-ayes build elaborate nests in which they sleep during the daytime; where they have been studied during their nightly ranging, they specialize in rather few food items. Insect larvae, *ramy* nuts, nectar (or larvae) from the traveler's tree *Ravenala madagascariensis,* fungi of various kinds, and a recurrent growth on species of *Intsia* compose the bulk of their diet on the island of Nosy Mangabe in the east. One of the aye-aye's most famous feeding behaviors involves gnawing through the tough fibrous husk of coconuts to feed on the flesh within; but the coconut palm is almost certainly a recent introduction to Madagascar. One type of feeding behavior uses a combination of many of the aye-aye's specialized traits. An individual will listen, with its large sensitive ears, for the sounds of insect larvae burrowing inside dead branches. The front teeth are then used to gnaw a hole in the dead wood, exposing the larval tunnels. The thin middle finger, equipped with a claw, is used to spear larvae inside the tunnels and withdraw them.

Because certain very early primates possessed much-enlarged front teeth, albeit ones that did not continuously grow, it has been suggested that a particular evolutionary relationship might exist between these forms and the aye-aye. Clearly, however, there is no basis for this conclusion, and the aye-aye has no known fossil record. The precise affinities of *Daubentonia* are hard to determine, because its anatomy is so highly modified in so many respects, but there is no question that it belongs in Lemuriformes, and various characters of the skull and dentition point, if weakly, toward a relationship with the indriids and their subfossil relatives.

See also Indrioidea; Lemuriformes; Skull; Teeth. [I.T.]

Further Readings

Mittermeier, R.A., Tattersall, I., Konstant, W.R., Meyers, D.M., and Mast, R.B. (1994) Lemurs of Madagascar (Tropical Field Guide No. 1). Washington, D.C.: Conservation International.

Simons, E.L. (1994) The giant aye-aye *Daubentonia robusta.* Folia Primatol. 62:14–21.

Sterling, E. (1993) Patterns of range use and social organization in aye-ayes. In P.M. Kappeler and J. Ganzhorn (eds.): Lemur Social Systems and Their Ecological Basis, pp. 1–10. New York: Plenum.

Tattersall, I. (1982) The Primates of Madagascar. New York: Columbia University Press.

Tattersall, I. (1993) Madagascar's lemurs. Sci. Am. 268 (1):110–117.

Dawaitoli

Drainage area in the eastern Middle Awash region in the Afar Rift (Ethiopia) that has yielded vertebrate fauna as well as sites with Early Stone Age artifacts, in alluvial deposits dated to the Middle Pleistocene. The earliest examples are simple Oldowan-type cores and flakes, dated to ca. 0.6–0.5 Ma and contemporary with sites yielding well-developed Acheulean implements elsewhere in Ethiopia and other parts of Africa. In the overlying sediments, which show a shift from alluvial floodplain to shifting fan deposits, Acheulean sites are prevalent.

See also Acheulean; Africa, East; Early Stone Age; Middle Awash. [N.T., K.S.]

De Sonneville-Bordes, Denise (1919–)

French prehistorian responsible, with J. Perrot, for the most widely used typology of the European Upper Paleolithic, as well as for the application (with her late husband, F. Bordes) of descriptive statistics to Upper Paleolithic industries. In addition, she has directed significant excavations at such Upper Paleolithic sites as Abri Caminade, has suggested important revisions to the Upper Paleolithic sequence of France, and has continued to stress stylistic and cultural (ethnic) distinctions among Upper Paleolithic industries.

See also Bordes, François; Upper Paleolithic. [A.S.B.]

Decoredon

Middle Paleocene small mammal of possible euprimate affinity from southern China. Until the mid-1980s, the two known specimens of the only known species, which in fact belong to the same individual animal, had been referred to two separate species of two genera, placed in two different orders. The poorly preserved teeth of the upper and lower dentition of this single species, however, show some striking special similarities to the earliest euprimates. The potential significance of *Decoredon* for primate evolutionary studies lies in its great antiquity in a region of the world that is just beginning to be explored paleontologically. *Decoredon*, along with the undoubted Mongolian omomyid *Altanius*, suggests that the immense southern forests of the Asian Paleocene may have been an important theater for the evolution of the euprimates before they appear in Euroamerica in the Early Eocene.

See also Asia, Eastern and Southern; Euprimates; Omomyidae; Primates. [F.S.S.]

Dendrochronology

Like so many of archaeology's dating techniques, *tree-ring dating* (dendrochronology) was developed by a nonarchaeologist, A.E. Douglass, an astronomer studying the effects of sunspots on the Earth's climate. Douglass knew that many tree species, especially conifers, grew through the addition of well-defined concentric growth rings. Because each ring represents a single year, it is, in theory, a simple matter to determine the age of a newly felled tree: Just count the rings.

Douglass took this relatively common knowledge one step further, reasoning that because tree rings vary in size they may preserve information about the environment in which they grew. These patterns of tree growth (i.e., ring width) for a particular area should fit into a long-term chronological sequence. Douglass began his tree-ring chronology with living specimens from Flagstaff and Prescott, Arizona. He would examine a stump (or a core from a living tree), count the rings, then overlap this sequence with a somewhat older set of rings from another tree. But the dead trees and surface snags went back only 500 years or so. To go further back, Douglass had to turn to beams and supports in the an-

cient archaeological sites of the American Southwest. Once the "gap" between modern and archaeological sequences was closed, the Southwestern dendrochronological sequence could be extended back for millennia. Many other areas (e.g. northwest Europe, the Aegean) have since constructed their own sequences.

Tree-ring dating can be applied to many, but not all, species of trees, but matching unknown specimens to the regional master key remains a slow, laborious process requiring an expert with years of experience. Gradually, more automated means such as correlation graphs have been devised, and computer programs have been attempted (based on the statistical theory of errors). But the skilled dendrochronologist can still date samples much faster than any computer today.

Dendrochronology also has potential for providing climatic data. Assuming that tree-ring width is controlled by environmental factors such as temperature and soil moisture, one should be able to reconstruct past environmental conditions by examining the band widths. But tree metabolism is complex, and ecological reconstruction has not provided as many answers as might be desired.

See also Geochronometry. [D.H.T.]

"Dendropithecus-Group"

Informal grouping of small Early-to-Middle Miocene East African and East Asian catarrhines apparently intermediate phyletically between Pliopithecidae and the modern catarrhine superfamilies. Nearly a dozen species of eight genera have been named to receive a wide variety of specimens ranging in age between 22 and 14 Ma, mainly from Kenya and Pakistan. They have also been discussed as "small-bodied apes" or nonhominoid/noncercopithecid catarrhines, and some authors have included them in the Pliopithecidae or Proconsulidae, depending upon the definition of those families. Pending the formal naming of a family to receive at least some of these taxa, they are here discussed together with reference to the best-known species, *Dendropithecus macinnesi*.

None of these forms unequivocally presents any features linking them to Hominoidea (or to Cercopithecoidea, for that matter), although many of them have in the past been termed hominoids. They are, however, more derived than *Pliopithecus* in such character states as the probable presence of a tubular external auditory meatus, slightly longer and narrower upper molars with less cingulum (but not subsquare as in hominoids), and lack of an entepicondylar foramen on the distal humerus. Most of these species are known mainly by teeth and jaws, with postcrania moderately well represented only in *Dendropithecus* and *Turkanapithecus* (the latter more derived, almost *Proconsul*-like) and only *Turkanapithecus* preserving much of the face. Variation among the genera involves proportions and shape of the incisors and molars, with implications for different dietary adaptations. It is reasonable to infer that the ancestors of both Hominoidea and Cercopithecoidea once resembled these forms, in the same sense that even earlier they resembled pliopithecids or propliopithecids. But as the earliest hominoid (*Kamoyapithecus*) predates them, and they are contemporaneous with both the hominoid proconsulids and the earliest cercopithecoids, it is unlikely that any known members of this group are closely related to the modern superfamilies. T. Harrison has argued, in fact, that *Proconsul* and allies are not significantly more derived than these taxa, and he has placed all of them in a greatly expanded Proconsulidae, but that view is not accepted here. It may be that, with greater knowledge of their morphology, some species could be transferred to the Proconsulidae or another family, and some may be shown to share derived features making at least part of this group truly monophyletic.

Catarrhini, incertae sedis
    † *Dendropithecus*
    † *Micropithecus*
    † *Simiolus*
    † *Kalepithecus*
    ?† *Turkanapithecus*
    ?† *Nyanzapithecus*
    ??† *Limnopithecus*

†extinct

See also Ape; Catarrhini; Cercopithecoidea; Hominoidea; Pliopithecidae; Proconsulidae; Propliopithecidae. [E.D.]

Further Readings

Andrews, P., and Simons, E. (1977) A new African Miocene gibbonlike genus, *Dendropithecus* (Hominoidea, Primates) with distinctive postcranial adaptations: Its significance to origin of Hylobatidae. Folia Primatol. 28:161–170.

Harrison, T. (1987) The phylogenetic relationships of the early catarrhine primates: A review of the current evidence. J. Hum. Evol. 16:41–80.

Harrison, T. (1988) A taxonomic revision of the small catarrhine primates from the Early Miocene of East Africa. Folia Primatol. 50:59–108.

Harrison, T. (1992) A reassessment of the taxonomic and phylogenetic affinities of the fossil catarrhines from Fort Ternan, Kenya. Primates 33:501–522.

Leakey, R.E.F., and Leakey, M.G. (1987) A new Miocene small-bodied ape from Kenya. J. Hum. Evol. 16:369–387.

Leakey, R.E., Leakey, M.G., and Walker, A.C. (1988) Morphology of *Turkanapithecus kalakolensis* from Kenya. Am. J. Phys. Anthropol. 76:277–288.

Rose, M.D., Leakey, M.G., Leakey, R.E.F., and Walker, A.C. (1992) Postcranial specimens of *Simiolus enjiessi* and other primitive catarrhines from the Early Miocene of Lake Turkana, Kenya. J. Hum. Evol. 22:171–237.

Denisova Cave

A multilayered cave along the banks of the Anui River in the northwestern part of the Mountainous (Gornyi) Altai in southern Siberia (Russia). The cave's interior gallery contains 14 Middle and Late Paleolithic layers; eight Holocene layers have been identified outside the cave's entrance. The Middle Paleolithic layers contain lithic inventories dominated by sidescrapers, denticulates, notches, and Levallois points, while the Late Paleolithic ones show the advent of blade technology and the production of typical Late Paleolithic tools, including microliths and bone tools. The Middle Paleolithic layers have yielded some teeth originally identified as Neanderthal, but it is unlikely that this group extended so far east; they are perhaps better identified as representing indeterminate premodern *H. sapiens*. Faunal remains are represented by such carnivores as hyenas, wolves, bears, and foxes. Herbivore remains include mammoths, woolly rhinoceroses, saiga antelopes, horses, ibex, hares, and pikas. Chronometric dates suggest that the earliest Late Paleolithic inventories here date to greater than 40 Ka.

See also Afontova Gora; Late Paleolithic; Middle Paleolithic; Mousterian; Neanderthals; Upper Paleolithic. [O.S.]

Dermoptera

A relict order of living (hand modulated) gliding mammals that were far more widely distributed in the past than their Southeast Asian range of today. There are two extant species of colugos, the primarily Malaysian *Galeopterus variegatus* and the Philippine *Galeopithecus volans*. These animals are small (weighing 1–1.75 kg) but impressive looking when in flight, mainly folivorous, and nocturnal to crepuscular. They have a stomach adapted for folivory and a cecum divided into compartments. Their cheek dentition is highly diagnostic, but the most striking dental specialization is in the incisors, which are as completely comblike as any known mammalian tooth. Their gliding membrane (patagium) extends from the tip of the tail all the way behind their ears. Other mammalian gliders (members of the rodent families Sciuridae and Anomaluridae and of the diprotodontian marsupial family Petauridae, with three independently attained genera of gliders) extend the patagium to various points of the forearm and wrist. The colugos, like the bats, have an intercheiridial (between-the-digits) patagium on their hands. Unlike in bats, however, the membrane is also present between the rays of the foot. The colugos' ability to "finger-glide," using their hands as spoilers and thus giving them considerable control during the flight, makes them more advanced in their aerial activities than other living gliding-adapted mammals. Their patagium has a ca. 15:1 gliding ratio, and they are known to cover 50–60 m during a glide. Their slow climbing on vertical substrates and their habitual underbranch climbing, probably without any significant ability for above-branch or terrestrial locomotion, are the apparent consequences of their extreme limb elongation linked to the relative size of their patagium. These living mammals may represent the group from which the bats (Chiroptera) evolved by building on their finger-modulated gliding abilities.

The Paleogene, largely North American, family Plagiomenidae has previously been widely acknowledged to represent this order because of its unique molar and incisor similarity to colugos. Studies on the ear region of the Early

Eocene *Plagiomene* (a form identical in cranial size and general conformation to colugos) have cast doubt on this association, although the comparative dental evidence remains a significant indicator of shared special similarities between these groups. Postcranial remains of plagiomenids would be needed to conclusively test the hypothesis that these archaic forms were dermopterans. Another family primarily from the Paleocene of North America, the Mixodectidae, shows special molar similarities to the Plagiomenidae and shares some significant unique traits in the tarsus with the colugos. In the early 1990s, C. Beard suggested that a third northern Paleogene group, the Paromoyoidea, is related to the dermopterans on the basis of similarly elongate manual phalanges. Closer scrutiny of the interpretation of the evidence for that hypothesis (the Primatomorpha hypothesis) fails to corroborate the special similarity of Plesiadapiformes to the Dermoptera in exclusion of other archontan groups.

See also Archonta; Paromomyoidea; Plesiadapiformes; Primates. [F.S.S.]

Devon Downs

Extensive shelter overlooking Murray River, South Australia. Devon Downs was the first modern archaeological excavation in Australia, by H.M. Hale and N.B. Tindale in 1929. This rockshelter, occupied at least 6 Ka, was the first to demonstrate change in resources used and in stone technology. It is important also as the first discovery in Australia of human remains in a scientific context.

See also Australia. [A.T.]

Die Kelders

South African cave site on the southwestern coast of the Cape Province (34°32′S, 19°22′E). Two contiguous caves (DK1 and DK2) were formed near present sea level at the base of a 12-m cliff of limestone, at the contact with underlying quartzitic sandstone. The larger cave (DK1) was excavated between 1969 and 1973 by F.R. Schweitzer, who concentrated on a rich Later Stone Age (LSA) shell midden. The LSA layers accumulated between 2 and 1.5 Ka, according to ^{14}C analyses on charcoal, during the time that pottery and domestic animals (e.g., sheep) were first being introduced in southern Africa, and the DK1 LSA levels contain potsherds and bones of domestic stock. These are associated with typical LSA stone and bone artifacts, the shells of marine invertebrates, and the bones of indigenous animals, especially birds, fish, tortoises, small bucks (*Raphicerus*), and dune molerats.

Excavations since 1990 at DK1 by F.E. Grine and colleagues concentrated on the underlying, thick Middle Stone Age (MSA) layers, separated from the overlying LSA deposits by archaeologically sterile sands. The MSA levels appear to document repeated cycles of human occupation, but the deposit is deeply leached and decalcified, and the abundant lithic artifacts are not accompanied by recognizable bone or shell artifacts. Paleontological material is also poorly represented. [F.E.G.]

Diet

Primate species exploit almost all of the possible food sources they find in their environments. Arboreal species eat fruits, flowers, leaves, bark, pith, seeds, tree gum, and nuts. Animal foods include eggs and small vertebrates and invertebrates. Ground-living primates eat many of the same things, as well as grasses, roots, and tubers. But primates do not simply eat anything that comes into their path that is tasty. Each species concentrates on a few kinds of foods, in relation to its energy needs, requirements for specific nutrients, constraints of the digestive system, degree of food clumping or dispersal, interspecific competition, and predation.

Categorizing Primate Foods

Primate adaptations for diet occur at two levels. First, food must be foraged for and/or captured and subdued. Behavioral adaptations for foraging are especially obvious among predators. Particularly important for nonhuman primates are specializations of the special senses and locomotor system for finding and capturing insects. Second, once the food is "in hand," it must be broken up in the mouth into suitable form for swallowing and then assimilated by the digestive tract. To understand dietary adaptations of the masticatory and digestive systems, knowledge about the physical and chemical structure of food is important. Keeping in mind food-acquiring, ingestive, and digestive aspects of dietary adaptation, primate dietary specializations are discussed here in three broad categories: animal foods (insects and other invertebrates, as well as vertebrates); plant materials high in structural carbohydrates, such as cellulose, hemicellulose, and lignin (usually leaves, bark, and pith); and plant materials high in nonstructural carbohydrates, such as simple sugars or starches (some roots, fruits, nuts, gum, and nectar). As a convenient shorthand, these categories are referred to by the most abundant food type within them: insects, leaves, and fruit, respectively.

A number of other aspects of potential foods are crucial for primate food choice. Primary considerations are physical location and availability. Some foods are preferred over others simply because they more easily reached. Many foods are available only at certain times of the year, so their potential consumers must find other foods, sometimes called *keystone resources,* when the preferred ones are scarce. Also, some foods are clumped in space, whereas others are more uniformly dispersed, so consumers must make decisions about the energetic costs of obtaining the food vs. the energetic or nutritive return for the effort.

To fulfill its nutritional needs, a primate must also select a diet containing adequate amounts of protein, carbohydrate, fat, and trace nutrients in a form that can be digested. For example, although fruit is a particularly good source of carbohydrate, it is often protein poor. Further, the consumer must be able to overcome various chemical defenses against being eaten. For example, many plants produce toxins in some of their parts and at various times during growth to avoid or reduce predator activity; likewise, many insect species have noxious tastes or smells, or mimic others that do have them, to discourage predation. Various physical proper-

DIET	INSECTIVORY	FRUGIVORY	FOLIVORY
CHEMISTRY			
PROTEIN	high	low	high
LIPIDS	high	low (seeds high)	low
CARBOHYDRATE			
NONSTRUCTURAL	moderate	high	moderate
STRUCTURAL	low (chitin)	low to moderate	high
TOXINS, DIGESTIVE INHIBITORS	low	low to moderate	high
G-I TRACT			
DETOXIFICATION ABILITY	low	low	high
INTESTINAL VILLI, FOLDING	many large villi few folds	many folds	few small villi
RELATIVE GUT DIMENSIONS	large	small	large
MECHANICAL PROPERTIES OF FOOD	brittle, hard (chitin)	deformable (except seeds, nuts)	tough, fibrous
DENTAL STRUCTURE			
PUNCTURING	well developed	poorly developed	moderate
SHEARING	well developed	weak	well developed
CRUSHING, GRINDING	weak	well developed	variable
ENAMEL THICKNESS	thin	moderate (thick for nut eaters)	thin

ties of foods also constrain the potential consumer: Some fruits have very hard exocarps (shells) that must be broken.

The table summarizes the physical and chemical properties of primate foods and some anatomical traits of the species that eat them.

Insectivory

Animal foods are very good sources of energy and protein, so it is not surprising that most primate species eat at least some insects, while some are strongly specialized for eating insects. Many prosimians (lower primates) are insectivorous. The roster of insectivores includes small nocturnal lemuroids, lorisoids (*Microcebus, Galago, Loris*), and tarsiers (*Tarsius*). Some of the small diurnal New World monkeys are also fairly insectivorous, especially *Saguinus* and *Saimiri*. Animals that eat other animals have special adaptations to capture and subdue prey. Methods of prey location and capture vary from species to species, but there are many similarities in feeding techniques of all primates as distinct from most other mammalian insectivores. Consider the similarities and differences in the foraging techniques of two very different primate insectivores, tarsiers and slow lorises, and how this contrasts with nonprimate insectivores.

Tarsiers live close to trees that have ripe fruit lying on the ground beneath them. They apparently are attracted to the insects and other animals that are attracted to the fruit. They capture most of their prey on the ground. According to M. Fogden:

> they would scan the forest floor from a perch a meter or more above the ground, and having located the prey (which is generally moving) leaped directly onto it, killing it by biting with tight shut eyes. Tarsiers were seen to catch in this way with leaps up to 2 meters, but most leaps were considerably shorter. The scanning phase of hunting sometimes lasted up to 10 minutes at a single perch, with the tarsier remaining more or less immobile; but more usually a failure to locate the prey at one perch resulted in it moving on after only a minute or two. Some observations suggest that hearing as well as sight plays a part in locating prey (Fogden, 1974:171).

Tarsiers also forage in the leaf litter with their hands. This hunting by touch also appears to be effective in causing cryptic insects to move so that they can be seen and pounced upon. The above description exemplifies the distinctness of small-primate hunting techniques: Prey detection is generally a visual and, to some extent, auditory procedure, and prey capture involves precise hand-eye coordination; the mouth is rarely involved in actual prey capture; olfactory and snout-tactile senses are little used. The highly insectivorous

Loris tardigradus has a different prey-capture technique, but there are important similarities with tarsiers. Unlike tarsiers, slender lorises are slow moving and stalk their cryptic, slow-moving insect prey with deliberation. Like tarsiers, however, lorises catch their prey in both hands or in one hand. Only when securely caught is the prey taken into the mouth to be crushed to stop its struggle.

The special reliance on stereoscopic vision in prey location and the enhanced importance of the hands for prey capture of both tarsiers and lorises are strikingly different from the way "primitive" mammalian insectivores locate and capture insects. In *Echinops*, a tenrec, prey is located with olfaction and by touch with the snout. Once the prey is located, its "capture involves orientation to the prey object . . . sniffing and seizing it with the mouth. There is little involvement of the fore-paws in the capture of prey . . ." (Eisenberg and Gould, 1970). This distinction helps explain the acquisition of stereoscopic vision, the reduction of the olfactory apparatus and of snout-tactile sense, and the augmentation of digital-tactile sense in the earliest primates, which were almost certainly insectivorous. The different feeding approach of slow lorises compared with tarsiers and bushbabies highlights a reliance on different sorts of insect prey. Lorises eat mainly caterpillars and ants, which can be obtained readily with a slow, deliberate form of prey stalking. Such slow-moving prey normally protect themselves by being cryptic, by producing noxious smells or tastes, or by having stinging hairs. Tarsiers and bushbabies are active leapers and can capture and eat quickly moving insects: beetles, nocturnal moths, and grasshoppers, for example.

Insect-eating species have a characteristic cheek-tooth structure reflecting common physical properties of the insects eaten. In their adult stages, insects have tough exoskeletons composed in part of chitin. Chitin is essentially the animal equivalent of plant fiber in its physical and chemical properties. To puncture and cut chitin into the size and consistency required for swallowing, insect eaters have molars with tall, pointed cusps and sharp, precisely interlocking crests. Cutting up chitin has the added effect of increasing its surface area exposed to digestive action. Digestion of chitin is effected by special chitinolitic enzymes in the stomach.

Another important structural adaptation of insectivorous primates is small body size. The invertebrate prey of primates are small and often do not have communal habits; they have to be located one by one. This places an important upper limit on body-size of primate insect predators, above which it is difficult to capture enough insects to meet energy needs. It is rare to find a primarily insectivorous primate with a body weight over ca. 300–500 g.

Many larger primates occasionally eat insects, and these may contribute significantly to their protein requirements. For example, *Cebus* (the capuchin monkey) and some Old World monkeys forage on the ground for insect prey. Chimpanzees use tools, such as stripped twigs or grass blades, to poke into termite hills for grubs. Overall, however, insects do not account for a particularly large part of the diet of these larger primates. Because of the small proportion of insects compared with fruits in the diets of these large species, structural modifications for insectivory in the teeth or digestive tracts are not apparent.

Plant Eating (Herbivory)

Plants are the essential food of most living primates, but all that is green is not edible. Many plant parts are composed principally of inedible woody materials. Other parts are protected from being eaten by poisonous secondary compounds or compounds like tannin that inhibit digestive processes. Thus, the feeding strategy of primate plant eaters includes not just the ability to find and reach the food source, but also the ability to prepare the foods adequately for rapid assimilation and to neutralize or avoid plant poisons. Prey capture is relatively unimportant, of course—you don't have to beat a banana over the head before eating it!

LEAF- AND GRASS-EATING PRIMATES

Eating leaves and woody materials presents special challenges for the digestive tract, but the primates that have solved these problems have a high return in nutrients for their investment. Foliage commonly contains high percentages of energy-rich carbohydrates. Comparatively little of the carbohydrate, however, is in readily digestible forms like starch or sugar; the major part of this material is in structural carbohydrates: cellulose, hemicellulose, and pectin. Such substances are not directly available to primates, because these animals lack the enzymes needed to digest them. Foliage is also the major, superabundant source of protein in plants, second in quality (digestibility) and quantity only to animal foods.

Folivory (feeding on leaves, bark, buds, and grasses) is common among primates. Species of the strepsirhine family Indriidae appear to concentrate on arboreal leaves, as do several species of lemurids. Arboreal leaf eating is also commonly practiced by the platyrrhines *Alouatta* and *Brachyteles*. Among catarrhines, the subfamily Colobinae, familiarly known as leaf monkeys, eat mainly tree leaves. Some of the terrestrial cercopithecines, such as *Papio*, *Erythrocebus*, and especially *Theropithecus*, eat considerable proportions of grasses in woodland-savannah environments.

Among the lesser apes, the siamang (*Hylobates syndactylus*) eats a large amount of leaves, as do the great apes *Pongo* and, especially, *Gorilla*. The latter forages on the ground for many foods high in structural carbohydrates, such as bamboo, bark, pith, and buds.

Leaf-eating species have enlarged, elaborate digestive tracts. Often either the stomach or the cecum, a blind pocket at the end of the large intestine, is greatly enlarged. Species that have enlarged stomachs are said to practice *foregut* fermentation, whereas those that have an enlarged cecum are *hindgut* fermentors. Either of these parts of the digestive tract is home for symbiotic microorganisms that can digest cellulose and other structural carbohydrates. Without these microorganisms mammals would be unable to digest structural carbohydrates, because they cannot produce the digestive enzymes for this process. The by-products of this breakdown, together with the remains of the dead microorganisms themselves, satisfy an important part of the nutritional re-

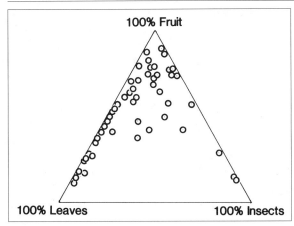

100% Fruit

100% Leaves

100% Insects

"Ternary" diagram illustrating the dietary behavior of some of the more fully studied primate species. Species that eat 100 percent leaves, insects, or fruit are plotted at the corners; a species that ate equal portions of all three would be in the middle. This highlights the fact that most primates concentrate on just a few or several dietary items. After Kay and Covert, 1984.

quirements of leaf eaters. Enlargement of certain parts of the gastrointestinal tract and elongation of the tract as a whole also slow the passage of food through the body. Since the breakdown and assimilation of structural carbohydrates is a relatively slow process, such slowing enhances digestibility. One benefit for foregut fermentors is that many toxins carried in leaves can be acted upon and neutralized by the microorganisms of the stomach before they reach a part of the gastrointestinal tract where they could be absorbed into the bloodstream. Another important adaptation to leaf eating may be a lowered basal metabolic rate.

Leaf-eating primates have elaborate cheek teeth with well-developed cutting edges that assist the digestive process. Carefully chewing these foods increases the surfaces exposed to digestive action and speeds the digestive process. Grass-eating species, such as some of the terrestrial Old World monkeys, have further specializations of the cheek teeth. Grass leaves contain large amounts of silica, making them extremely abrasive. A consequence of feeding on grasses is that the teeth wear down very fast. To counteract this, grass eaters like *Theropithecus* have high-crowned teeth. In this way, they can forestall the time when the teeth wear out.

FRUIT-EATING PRIMATES

A number of different feeding strategies are subsumed under the general heading of frugivory. Some species feed mainly on the pulp of ripe fruit, a particularly good source of readily metabolized simple sugars. These foods, however, are less nutritious in terms of protein, so species that feed on ripe fruits will often also eat either leaves or insects as a source of protein. Another specialization is for eating seeds. Many ripe-fruit eaters swallow the seeds of fruits whole, and the seeds pass through the gut in an undigested state. Others are seed predators that actually break open, chew up, and digest seeds. For them, seeds or nuts are extremely rich sources of lipids, a particularly high-energy nutrient.

Feeding on fruit pulp is the most common adaptive strategy among primates. Fruit eaters are found in practically all families of primates, with the exception of the Indriidae. The digestive system of most fruit eaters is fairly simple and relatively much shorter than that of leaf eaters. Fruit eaters have comparatively little fiber in their diets, so there is not the need for slowed food-passage time as in folivores. The cheek teeth of frugivorous species have low, rounded cusps with smooth contours. The most important aspect of the fruit-eating dentition is the reliance on crushing and grinding surfaces, which often are enlarged. Special anatomic changes accompany reliance on breaking open seeds. Seed-eating primates, such as the cercopithecine *Cercocebus* and the platyrrhines *Cebus* and members of the subfamily Pitheciinae, have tusklike canines for cracking open hard exocarps or seed pods, and/or thick cheek-tooth enamel to resist the stresses engendered by crushing seeds.

GUM-EATING PRIMATES

A feeding pattern that does not fit very well in the above scheme is gum eating. *Galago* and some other small strepsirhines, as well as some cheirogaleines and marmosets, are gummivores. *Galago* feeds especially on the gum of the acacia tree. Chemical analysis shows this to be an abundant source of carbohydrates and water and to contain small amounts of protein and minerals. One interesting point is the presence of large amounts of polymerized pentose and hexose sugar. It seems likely that *Galago* and other gum eaters may have symbiotic microorganisms in their digestive tracts (especially in the cecum) that enable them to use these complex carbohydrates. The front teeth of some gum eaters are specialized to allow them to cut into tree bark to promote gum flow and to scrape up the gum. *Phaner*, for example, has a sharp, projecting upper canine and upper front premolar, which it uses to dig into bark to accelerate gum flow. Gum is later collected from the damaged tree. The cheek teeth of gum eaters somewhat resemble those of frugivorous species.

Omnivory

A true omnivore eats a wide variety of food types, with each of the main forms contributing significantly to the total intake. Among mammals, pigs (and perhaps bears) are often considered the archetypal omnivores, and this class of dietary specialists is usually not thought to occur among nonhuman primates. But, in fact, the human lineage appears to have become specialized for an omnivorous diet early in its history, and the increased use of tools for foraging and food processing contributed greatly to the success of this striking human adaptation.

See also Atelidae; Cebidae; Cercopithecidae; Galagidae; Hominoidea; Indriidae; Lemuridae; Lorisidae; Paleodietary Analysis; Primate Ecology; Primates; Skull; Stable Isotopes (in Biological Systems); Teeth. [R.F.K.]

Further Readings

Chivers, D.J., and Hladik, C.M. (1984) Diet and gut morphology in primates. In D.J. Chivers, B.A. Wood, and A. Bilsborough (eds.): Food Acquisition and Processing in Primates. London: Plenum, pp. 213–230.

Chivers, D.J., and Langer, P., eds. (1994) The Digestive System in Mammals: Form and Function. Cambridge: Cambridge University Press.

Clutton-Brock, T.H., ed. (1977) Primate Ecology. London: Academic.

Davies, G., and Oates, J.F., eds. (1994) Colobine Monkeys: Their Ecology, Behaviour, and Evolution. Cambridge: Cambridge University Press.

Eisenberg, J.F., and Gould, I. (1970) The tenrecs: A study in mammalian behavior and evolution. Smith. Contrib. Zool. 27:1–137.

Fogden, M. (1974) A preliminary field study of the western tarsier, *Tarsius bancanus* Horsefield. In R.F. Martin, G.A. Doyle, and A.C. Walker (eds.): Prosimian Biology. London: Duckworth, pp. 151–166.

Kay, R.F., and Covert, H.H. (1984) Anatomy and behavior of extinct primates. In D.J. Chivers, B.A. Wood, and A. Bilsborough (eds.): Food Acquisition and Processing in Primates. New York: Plenum, pp. 467–508.

Parra, R. (1978) Comparison of foregut and hindgut fermentation in herbivores. In G.G. Montgomery (ed.): The Ecology of Arboreal Folivores. Washington, D.C.: Smithsonian Institution Press, pp. 205–230.

Waterhouse, P.G. (1984) Food acquisition and processing as a function of plant chemistry. In D.J. Chivers, B.A. Wood, and A. Bilsborough (eds.): Food Acquisition and Processing in Primates. New York: Plenum, pp. 177–212.

Whitten, A., and Widdowson, E.M. (1992) Foraging Strategies and Natural Diet of Monkeys, Apes, and Humans. Oxford: Clarendon.

Dingcun

Series of localities near Dingcun, on the Fen River in Shanxi Province (China), that have yielded both human remains and archaeological assemblages. The sites are probably of early Late Pleistocene or latest Middle Pleistocene age, based on faunal correlations and some uranium-series and amino-acid-racemization dates from low in the sequence. One adolescent human (represented by three teeth) and a separate parietal bone are known from Locality 54.100. In addition to human remains, thousands of artifacts are also known from primarily surface contexts at various localities at Dingcun, formerly known as Ting-t'sun. The Dingcun assemblage is unusual in comparison with most other Chinese assemblages in exhibiting a relatively high percentage of bifacially flaked chopping tools, as well as distinctive trihedral points, or *picks*. Dingcun-like assemblages have also been recovered from other nearby localities in Shanxi. Furthermore, it is possible that the Dingcun industries are somehow related to the so-called Chongok-Ni "industry" of Korea.

See also Asia, Eastern and Southern; China. [G.G.P.]

Djetis

Fossil-collecting area in eastern Java with a Late Pliocene or Early- to Middle-Pleistocene stratified sequence, on the basis of biostratigraphy and radiometric dates. The name *Djetis* (or *Jetis*), that of a village in the Sangiran area, was applied by G.H.R. von Koenigswald to vertebrate fossils supposedly derived from the Black Clays member of the Putjangan (now Pucangan) Formation of east-central Java. Originally, he thought that the presence of *Leptobos,* "primitive" proboscideans, and hippos indicated a Villeafranchian-equivalent (Late Pliocene), age for the formation and for the human fossils, which he believed to have been derived from the marine and fluviatile clays. Furthermore, he argued that the fauna showed affinities with Siwalik faunas of India and characterized it as having a "Siva-Malayan" character. He distinguished the Djetis Fauna from the later Middle Pleistocene Trinil Fauna, which he said showed "Sino-Malayan" affinities. Other workers argued that the vertebrates from the clays had been misidentified and really represented more progressive forms. Systematic recollections in the 1970s to 1990s and excavations of the Pucangan area have indicated that this highly endemic and impoverished fauna may be of little utility for dating the human fossils that supposedly derive from the Djetis Formation. The Djetis Fauna is thought to date to ca. 2–0.8 Ma. Fluorine studies have suggested that the majority of Djetis faunal elements and one or two of the human fossils from Java (Sangiran 5 and 6) may derive from the black clays of the uppermost portion of the formation.

In 1994, a date of of 1.8 Ma was suggested by Swisher and colleagues for the Modjokerto fossil site, based on a new ^{40}Ar/^{39}Ar analysis. A microprobe analysis of sediments adhering to the fossil cranial vault suggested that the fossil matrix was very similar in composition to the material dated. Questions remain, however, about the relationship of the date to the fossil specimens, as well as about the mixing of the Sangiran sediments with both older and younger sediments due to the action of mud volcanoes and lahars.

See also Asia, Eastern and Southern; Indonesia; Koenigswald, Gustav Heinrich Ralph von; Meganthropus; Trinil. [G.G.P.]

Further Readings

Hooijer, D.A. (1952) Fossil mammals and the Plio-Pleistocene boundary in Java. Proc. Kon. Nederl. Akad. van Weten. (Amsterdam), ser. B, 35:436–443.

Hooijer, D.A. (1983) Remarks on the Dubois collection of fossil mammals from Trinil and Kedungbrubrus in Java. Geol. Mijnbow 62:337–338.

Pope, G.G. (1983) Evidence on the age of the Asian Hominidae. Proc. Nat. Acad. Sci. USA 80:4988–4992.

Sémah, F., Sémah, A., and Djubiantono, T. (1990) They Discovered Java. Jakarta: PT Adiwarna Citra.

Swisher, C.C., Curtis, G.H., Jacob, T., Getty, A.G., and A. Suprijo and Widiasmoro (1994) Age of the earliest known hominids in Java, Indonesia. Science 263:1118–1121.

Djibouti

Plio-Pleistocene sites in the Republic of Djibouti occur in the southeastern extension of the Afar Depression, where it opens on the Gulf of Aden. The most important are several

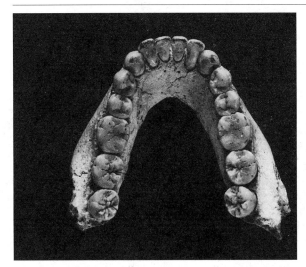
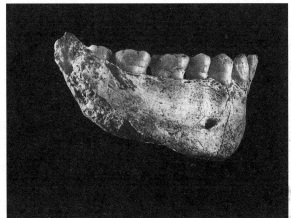

Lateral and occlusal views of the Dmanisi mandible. Courtesy of E. Delson and L. Gabunia.

sites in the valleys of the Dagadl and Chekheyti rivers near Barogali, dated to 1.5 Ma, with an Olduwan-Acheulean industry and vertebrate fauna, including remains attributed to *Homo erectus*. Younger levels are represented at Hara Ide, while a diverse large-mammal fauna at Anabo Koma is comparable to that of Olduvai Bed I, ca. 1.8 Ma.

See also Afar Basin; Africa, East. [J.A.V.C.]

Further Readings

Amosse, J., Boisaubert, J-L., Bouchez, R., Bruandet, J-F., Chavaillon, J., Faure, M., Guerin, C., Jeunet, A., Ma, J-L., Nickel, B. Piboule, M., Poupeau, G., Rey, P., and Warzawa, S.A. (1991) Le site de dépecage Pléistocène anciens à *Elephas recki* de Barogali (République de Djibouti): Chronologies relatives et datation par RPE et spectrométrie gamma d'émail dentaire. Cahiers de Quaternaire 16:379–399.

Bonis, L. de, Geraads, D., Jaeger, J-J., and Sen, S. (1988) Vertébrés du Pléistocene de Djibouti. Bull. Soc. Géol. Fr., ser. 8, 4:323–334.

Dmanisi

Locality in (ex-Soviet) Georgia where a mandible attributed to *Homo erectus* was discovered in 1991. Archaeologists excavating a medieval village found bones of Plio-Pleistocene mammals in the walls of underground storage pits. One pit yielded a human mandible as well. The specimen is well preserved, with complete dentition and most of the corpus (the base is broken), but lacking the rami. The size of the jaw and the teeth compare well with those of *H. erectus*, but the molars show greater front-to-back reduction in size (15–20 percent from M_1 to M_2 and from M_2 to M_3) than in other *H. erectus*. The Dmanisi mandible presents a mosaic mixture of conservative and derived features, and specific similarities are observed with a variety of African and Chinese specimens of the species. Associated artifacts are of broadly Mode 1 form. The age of the site is unexpectedly early: The associated fauna suggests a Late Villefranchian age, perhaps 2.1–1.4 Ma; an underlying basalt has been preliminarily

dated to ca. 1.8 Ma; and the basalt and sediments are said to present normal magnetic polarity, which in light of the two other indications could only represent the Olduvai Subchron at 1.77–1.95 Ma. Further chronometric dates and confirmation of the magnetic polarity are required, but, if the age of this fossil is indeed ca. 1.8 Ma, it would be one of the earliest-known human fossils outside Africa and among the oldest-known *H. erectus* anywhere. On the other hand, recent geochronological work suggests that the Dmanisi faunal and geological situation may be more complex than originally thought, raising the possibility that the jaw may better be estimated to date between 1.5 and 1.0 Ma.

See also Archaic Homo sapiens; Asia, Western; Homo erectus; Homo ergaster; Paleomagnetism. [E.D.]

Further Readings

Bräuer, G., and Schultz, M. (1996) The morphological affinities of the Plio-Pleistocene mandible from Dmanisi, Georgia. J. Hum. Evol. 30:445–481.

Dean, D., and Delson, E. (1995) *Homo* at the gates of Europe. Nature 373:472–473.

Gabunia, L., and Vekua, A. (1995) A Plio-Pleistocene hominid mandible from Dmanisi (East Georgia, Caucasus). Nature 373:509–512.

DNA Hybridization

A method of determining relationships among organisms by comparing the total similarity of the genetic material. DNA (deoxyribonucleic acid) is a two-stranded molecule, built from pairs of nucleotides. A nucleotide consists of a sugar molecule (deoxyribose), a phosphate molecule, and one of four bases: adenine (A), guanine (G), cytosine (C), and thymine (T). The nucleotide pairs that are the units of DNA consist of only two kinds: A-T and G-C. Thus, if the nucleotide sequence of one DNA strand is AGATTTCGAT, the other strand must be TCTAAAGCTA.

The bonds that hold the nucleotide pairs together, when summed over the entire DNA molecule, hold the two DNA strands together. Adding energy, in the form of heat,

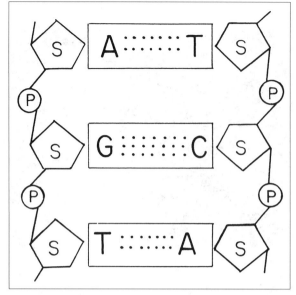

The two DNA strands are held together by weak bonds (dotted) joining the nucleotide pairs. S and P indicate the sugar and phosphate aspects, respectively, of the DNA molecule. Adenine (A) and Thymine (T) are joined by two bonds: Guanine (G) and Cytosine (C) are joined by three bonds. Heating breaks these bonds and leaves the DNA as two single strands. Courtesy of Jon Marks.

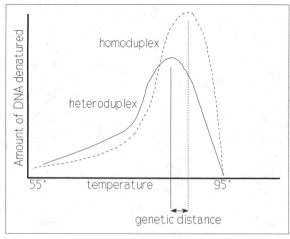

At low temperature (left), the hybrid DNA is completely double-stranded; as the temperature is raised, the DNA sample denatures into single strands. The melting temperature can be taken as that corresponding to the highest point on the curve. Heteroduplex DNA produces a melting curve that is lower, wider, and shifted to the left. The genetic distance between the two species under study is taken as a measure of how far to the left the curve is shifted. Courtesy of Jon Marks.

breaks these bonds and dissociates the two strands from each other. This is called *denaturing* (or melting) the DNA. Controlled cooling permits a single DNA strand to reattach to its complementary strand and to regain its stable two-stranded conformation (see figure). Much of the cellular DNA, however, consists of short sequences repeated many times: These sequences are able randomly to reattach to a complementary sequence much more easily than unique-sequence DNA can. DNA hybridization can, therefore, be used to estimate the degree of complexity of the genome of a species by providing a measure of what proportion of the genome reanneals very rapidly, rapidly, or slowly.

Different species have accumulated specific point mutations during their separate histories. If the unique-sequence DNA from one species is isolated, radioactively labeled, and denatured (the *tracer*), then mixed with a great excess of DNA from a different species (the *driver*), it is unlikely that the tracer DNA will be able to "find" its own complementary strand. Instead, it will bind imperfectly to the abundant, nearly complementary, strand from the other species.

This *heteroduplex,* or hybrid, DNA can be isolated and denatured again. This time, however, fewer bonds will be holding the DNA molecule together; less energy is required to break apart the DNA strands; and the molecule will, therefore, dissociate at a somewhat lower temperature than the original *homoduplex* DNA. As the dissociation of the DNA strands is a continuous process, the critical temperature is generally given as that at which 50 percent of the DNA being studied is single stranded. The difference in dissociation temperature between homoduplex and heteroduplex DNA is proportional to the amount of genetic mutation that has accumulated between the two species. It can, therefore, be used as a measure of *genetic distance* between the two species.

There are several different ways to measure the melting temperature of the DNA, however, some of which conflate base-pair differences (the structural integrity of the hybrids formed) with genome complexity (the mixture of redundant and unique DNA in the samples) or with the extent to which hybridization between the two species' genomes actually occurs. The first of these is the variable of greatest evolutionary interest. The result of an idealized experiment is shown in the figure: The amount of genetic difference between the DNA samples from the two species is estimated by the difference between the melting temperature of the homoduplex (say, chimp-chimp DNA hybrids) and heteroduplex (say, chimp-human DNA hybrids) DNA.

See also Genetics; Molecular Anthropology. [J.M.]

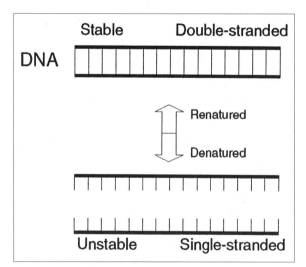

DNA hybridization exploits the double-stranded structure of DNA. The strands can be dissociated from one another by heating, and the process can be reversed by controlled cooling. Courtesy of Jon Marks.

Further Readings

Marks, J. (1991) What's old and new in molecular phylogenetics? Am. J. Phys. Anthropol. 85:207–219.

Dobzhansky, Theodosius (1900–1975)

American (b. Russia) geneticist. A former student of T.H. Morgan (1866–1945), Dobzhansky played a prominent role in the development of what J. Huxley called the "evolutionary synthesis," which combined Darwinian evolution and Mendelian genetics. Dobzhansky's book *Genetics and the Origin of Species* (1937) was the first major attempt at such a synthesis and marks the establishment of evolutionary genetics as an independent discipline. Among his many other notable and influential publications is *Mankind Evolving* (1962). Dobzhansky was an early and influential advocate of the "lumping" approach to hominid taxonomy, whereby the number of taxa is minimized.

See also Evolution; Genetics. [F.S.]

Dolni Věstonice

Complex of at least six open-air Late Paleolithic sites and a huge accumulation of mammoth bones from more than 100 individuals located on the slope of the Pavlov Hills ca. 35 km south of Brno (the Czech Republic). The features include hearths, small pits, surface bone accumulations, remains of round and oval dwellings, and a number of burials. Several important new burials, one with three probable teenagers, were excavated in 1986–1987. The rich lithic and bone inventories are assigned to the Pavlov industry and to the Eastern Gravettian technocomplex. A complete female "Venus" figurine, numerous small animals, and thousands of fragments of fired clay found at Dolni Věstonice, together with remains of two rudimentary kilns, are the earliest evidence for ceramic technology. Clay impressions of woven plant materials also provide the earliest-known evidence for matting or basketry technology. Chronometric estimates date the occupation to ca. 26 Ka.

See also Europe; Pavlov; Předmosti. [O.S.]

Further Reading

Svoboda, J., Ložek, V., and Vlček, E. (1996) Hunters Between East and West: The Paleolithic of Moravia. New York: Plenum.

Domestication

Controlled breeding of animal and plant species for human use (including some exclusively for livestock fodder). Many of these domesticated species are primarily food for the humans who breed them, but some provide us with clothing, containers, companionship, and protection; with raw energy for carrying heavy burdens or pulling carts, ploughs, or sleds; or with assistance in hunting, herding, and clean-up operations. Human beings have controlled plants and animals for only a tiny fraction of the 2–3 Myr of their history and prehistory. Before domesticates were developed as the result of human interference in other species' reproduction, people relied entirely on whatever plant and animal products they could gather, hunt, and scavenge. Because writing was not invented until a little over 5 Ka, prehistoric hunter-gatherers' use of such resources has been reconstructed primarily from the remains of kills and meals found by archaeologists. These reconstructions are refined and augmented by observations made among the few surviving hunting-and-gathering societies, whose people use and interact with wild plants and animals. Such people are generally mobile, following their prey—but they can rarely predict whether it will be young or old, male or female. Domestication, in contrast, has introduced the crucial elements of choice and control over precisely such matters.

Plants and animals were domesticated in many parts of the world, but in all known cases, with the apparent exception of the dog, this process occurred within the past 10 Kyr. The reasons for changing Holocene relationships between humans and other species were probably diverse. Humans were interested in different species for different qualities, such as the sheep's production of "harvestable" milk and wool, the camel's ability to survive on little water, and the storability of cereal grains like maize, wheat, and rice, which generally yield abundant surpluses and which are today the staple foods for three-quarters of the world's population.

The earliest animal domesticated was the dog (*Canis domesticus*), ca. 12 Ka in Iraqi Kurdistan and possibly earlier (ca. 14 Ka) in northern Europe. Sheep (*Ovis*) and goat (*Capra*) were domesticated in western Asia by ca. 9.5 Ka. They were joined within a millennium by cattle (*Bos*) in Anatolia (Çatal Hüyük) and in the eastern Sahara (Nabta Playa) and by pig (*Sus*) in Western Asia and southeastern Europe. Later Old World domesticates include donkey (*Equus asinus*), horse (*Equus caballus*), and camel (*Camelus* spp.), all domesticated by 4 Ka and perhaps substantially earlier. New World domesticates include turkey (*Meleagris gallopavo*), guinea pig (*Cavia porcellus*), and the meatier llama and alpaca (*Lama* spp.), valued for their strength and their wool, respectively. Far fewer animal species were domesticated in the Western Hemisphere; perhaps there were fewer wild species of medium- and large-sized gregarious herbivores native to the New World.

The earliest-known plant domesticates have been retrieved at southwest Asian sites; wheat (*Triticum*) and barley (*Hordeum*) dating to ca. 10.5 Ka are found at a growing number of sites in the Levant, along with legumes, such as lentils, peas, and chickpeas, which also may have been cultivated. Rice (*Oryza sativa*), another major Old World cereal, was domesticated as early as 7–6 Ka in the lower Yangtze delta of east China, where it is associated with bones of pig and water buffalo, both of which may have been domesticated in East Asia. Rice (*O. glaberrima*) was also independently domesticated in West Africa. Other species important in the tropics and subtropics of the Old World are millet and sorghum; grains of both species that are transitional between wild and domesticated forms have been found in the eastern Sahara (Nabta Playa) dating to 8–7 Ka. Other tropical species include a variety of root crops, such as yam and taro, whose history of domestication is poorly known, partly because of preservation problems. Some

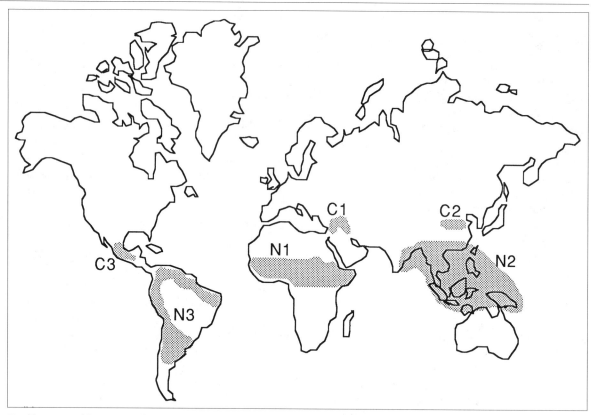

Possible centers and "noncenters" of plant domestication, as suggested by J.R. Harlan in 1971. In this model, each of three relatively restricted centers—(C1) Near East; (C2) North China; (C3) Mesoamerica—was associated with a more diffuse noncenter—(N1) central Africa; (N2) south and southeast Asia; (N3) coastal South America—where domestication took place over a broad area, in some cases perhaps, earlier than in the nearby center. Modified after J.R. Harlan, 1971, in Science, *vol. 174.*

plants, whose wild forms have a wide geographic distribution, may have been domesticated independently in both hemispheres; among these are the bottle gourd (*Lagenaria*) and cotton (*Gossypium*).

Although plant domestication in the New World has long been thought to have taken place substantially later than in the Eastern Hemisphere, research is beginning to refute this. The earliest evidence for cultivated squash (*Cucurbita pepo*) comes from deposits at Guila Naquitz dating to ca. 10 Ka, and domesticated maize (*Zea mays*) and beans (*Phaseolus vulgaris*) appear ca. 7 Ka in other parts of highland Mesoamerica. This triumvirate of plants (maize, beans, and squash), which is used today, frequently grows together in the wild and may have been domesticated as part of a mixed farming or intercropping strategy. Like *Zea, Triticum,* and *Hordeum,* many plants domesticated in various geographic areas are annuals, growing in dense stands of single or few species, comparatively easily harvested on a predictable basis. The root crops, in contrast, have the advantage of serving as subsoil bank accounts from which capital can be extracted through much of the year. Of these, the white potato (*Solanum*) and the yam (*Dioscorea*) are New and Old World domesticates, respectively. In North America, early farmers apparently domesticated indigenous forms of winter squash, or gourds, and *Chenopodium,* a wild grass, before adopting maize cultivation from the American tropics.

Because humans were interested in each species for its own distinctive features, each underwent changes over time in morphology and behavior resulting from human selection for particular traits chosen for transmission to future generations. Many domesticated-animal species, and their wild counterparts, are gregarious, and some tend to follow a leader. This animal behavior may have made it easier for prehistoric people to habituate herd animals to human companionship and the reproductive meddling that eventually accompanied it. A fundamental aspect of domestication is that humans decide which individuals in a particular population will transmit their genes to future generations. Thus, for example, if large pigs or bulls are particularly threatening or ferocious, they are more likely to be selected for the dinner table than left in the barnyard, and there will be fewer fierce piglets or calves in the next generation.

Benefits of Domestication

The appeal of many domesticated animals today, as it must have been in the Early Holocene past, is that they are more useful alive than dead. Many people who raise livestock eat far less meat than the average urban North American; some, but by no means all, consume more milk, cheese, and yogurt. Animals provide resources that can be collected, or they have qualities that can be exploited on a predictable, repeated, and long-term basis; examples are eggs, milk, hair and wool, and labor. Dried animal manure is an essential fuel in many of the world's deforested regions; it is also good fertilizer for cultivated fields. Pigs are scavengers; eating, they convert garbage into edible meat, and their value to humans increases. In some societies, dogs play a comparable role. Domesticated animals are capital on the hoof.

Domesticated plants are equally appealing. Weather and technology permitting, surpluses surpassing the quantities sown are the rule rather than the exception; in extreme cases, up to 40 or 50 times the quantity of seed planted can be harvested. Human selection of desirable and transmissible traits operates here, too, with humans playing an active role in deciding which plants to consume and which to store as seed grain. In sufficiently dry contexts, many plants preserve well and can be consumed or sown for more than a year following their harvest. Harvested surpluses can also be used to support those not producing their own food, such as craftsmen or religious leaders, or, like animals and their products, they can be offered in exchange for other goods.

Identification of Domesticates

The history and prehistory of domestication are reconstructed in greatest detail when nonperishable remains are recovered in archaeological contexts. For animals, reconstructions are based on bones, horns, and teeth. The best direct evidence of prehistoric plants and their use comes from seeds, pits, pollen, and impressions in mud or pottery. The domestication of some species, such as potatoes, tomatoes, and various forms of poultry, is not well documented, either because conditions of preservation in their native habitats are less than optimal (e.g., they are buried in acidic tropical soils) or because the elements routinely discarded by humans lack the hard parts that are generally most resistant to depredations of soil chemicals and bacteria. Circumstances of disposal and burial, and habitat ecology, affect the preservation of the botanical and zoological remains from which archaeologists reconstruct the history of human interaction with plants and animals. As a consequence, our understanding of this history is still biased in favor of temperate and arid zones and of mammals and grain plants (in contrast, for example, to problematical reconstructions for avian fauna having cartilaginous bones and root crops lacking hard shells or pits).

The archaeological record for most animal species' domestication reflects a long-term selection for reduced overall body size accompanied by increasingly shortened jaw and snout. Comparisons of wild and domestic members of the same genus can indicate which traits were subject to selective breeding. In the case of the pig, for example, tusks have been greatly reduced. The dog barks in a way that wild canids do not. Sheep generally have woolly fleece and reduced horns, and some subspecies also have economically useful fat tails.

In addition to morphological changes reflected in dentition and bones, domesticated animals and their transformations from wild forms have been reconstructed, in part, from other forms of evidence. These include representations (e.g., Neolithic clay figurines of domestic livestock at sites like Jarmo) and geographic distributions of bones (e.g., faunal remains found beyond the range of the current natural habitat zones of ancestral wild forms are potential candidates for identification as domesticates). In gregarious species, such as sheep and goat, comparison of the demographic

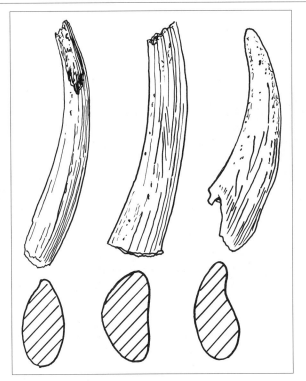

In the course of goat domestication in the Near East, the cross section of the horn changed, after many generations, from an oval shape (left), to flattened on one side, to indented on one side (right).

composition of wild herds may also reveal differences in age and sex ratios from those seen in domesticated flocks. It is also possible that the body parts of hunted wild animals found in archaeological sites will differ in kind and frequency from those of domesticated species killed and butchered nearer human habitations. A growing reliance on tamed animals may also be indicated by an increase in the relative abundance of certain domesticable species, such as sheep and goat.

Where morphological changes involve metric rather than nonmetric attributes, or where bones revealing nonmetric features are not available archaeologically, it may be difficult to pinpoint where in the trajectory of domestication a particular specimen should be placed. Sample size can be critical: Any species is characterized by a range of metric variability, and there may be overlaps between wild and domesticated forms. Before a given specimen can be characterized as either wild or domesticated, the zooarchaeologist must determine whether metric differences reflect intra- or interspecies variation.

Domesticated species also became increasingly tractable and dependent on humans. While some morphological changes occurred over a period of at least a millennium, the rate at which behavioral change associated with domestication occurred remains a matter for speculation; osteologically "wild" animals may have been behaviorally "domesticated." It has been suggested that taming and semi-domestication may have involved the imprinting of juveniles caught and kept as pets, the use of salt as a lure, and/or the attracting of herd animals by altering vegetation communities through burning, which in some areas probably increased the grass cover that is so appealing to many herbivorous domesticates and their wild counterparts.

Comparable methodological problems exist for plants, whose domestication in many cases entailed size increases, as in maize cob, and/or increases in numbers of edible elements (as was the case in the change from two-row to six-row barley). In several plant species, an important diagnostic nonmetric change involved selection for particular seed-dispersal and germ-protection mechanisms. For example, remains of wheat and barley reflect a shift from brittle to tough rachis and from tough to brittle glume. Humans evidently selected for plants that had stalks that neither snapped nor dropped grains immediately upon ripening (which a wild, brittle rachis allows) and for husks that could be crushed more readily than those that fell to the ground on ripening, protecting the enclosed seed until it could germinate months later (a nonshattering, tough glume, seen in wild forms). In addition to morphology, plant domestication has been reconstructed from representational art and from archaeological examples of distinctive technological items used today in processing domesticated plants (e.g., ceramic manioc graters in lowland South America). Some tools, such as flint sickles, identified from the sheen deposited on the edge of the flint blade, and such grinding implements as mortars and querns are problematical, since they can also be used to process wild plants; indeed, in southwest Asia and elsewhere they are sometimes associated with food-collecting economies of the Mesolithic.

Many plant species can be identified in prehistoric soil samples containing pollen. Datable pollen profiles are a vital source of information on the plant species in a particular area at a particular time and, hence, on options available to humans. They may also be used to reconstruct the history of land use, since they may reveal changes in vegetative cover (such as a sharp decrease in arboreal species followed by an increase in grasses, perhaps including edible cereals) and may have associated charcoal flecks (which can reflect slash-and-burn cultivation). Even in the absence of direct evidence for plant domestication, data on prehistoric pollen may be useful in developing hypotheses about the availability of ancestral wild forms and the transformation of the botanical landscape as plants were manipulated and domesticated. Finally, since some botanical species are consistently associated with one another, it is possible to use pollen profiles to pinpoint the presence or absence of wild ancestors at various times. In

Corn cobs enlarged greatly in size and number of rows of kernels, as a result of domestication in Mexico from wild antecedents (7000 BP) to fully modern form (2000 BP). Courtesy of R.S. Peabody Foundation for Archaeology, Phillips Academy, Andover, Mass.

the Late Pleistocene of southwest Asia, for example, oak pollen was absent in some areas where oak flourishes today; since wild wheat is often associated with oak forests, it is likely that when the oak disappeared because of extreme cold during the latter part of the Pleistocene, cereal grasses were also unavailable to foraging human populations using such areas on even a temporary basis. Palynology can suggest when and where some of the parameters permitting domestication might have existed.

Indirect evidence on the domestication of foods can also be obtained through studies of human skeletal remains. The adoption of agriculture in some parts of the world resulted in the appearance of new diseases; in the New World, for example, there is a proliferation of dental caries in human skeletal populations because of the high sugar content of maize. Certain prehistoric dietary changes are also reflected in the chemical composition of human bone collagen through various chemical techniques. Stable carbon isotope analysis, for example, identifies an individual's reliance on one of three plant groups (C_3, C_4, or CAM), each of which has a distinctive isotopic ratio ($^{13}C/^{12}C$ that remains indefinitely in bone collagen. Carbon isotope analysis has successfully traced the New World introduction of maize, a C_4 plant, into a long-term diet of temperate grasses, such as *Chenopodium,* which are C_3 plants. The technique has been less useful in southwest Asia, where most cultivatable plants belong to the C_3 group. Other chemical studies of bone collagen involve changes in nitrogen-isotope ($^{15}N/^{14}N$) ratios, which distinguish between a dietary preference for agricultural foods or marine resources, and strontium-calcium (Sr/Ca) ratios, which separate meat eaters from vegetarians. Such techniques can also be used to reconstruct the food preferences of wild ancestors of domesticated animals.

Origin of Domestication

Food collecting was the basic human subsistence adaptation for several million years preceding the beginning of agriculture and animal husbandry; domestication occurred comparatively rapidly, independently in many parts of the world, and in all known cases but one (the dog) in the ameliorating climate of the Holocene. Domesticates were imported into new areas (e.g., maize into North America) or, through processes of diffusion and imitation, were altered local species (e.g., rye in Europe). Several explanations of this fundamental and worldwide transformation in human lifeways have been offered. V.G. Childe noted that "post-Pleistocene" climatic change in northeast Africa and southeast Asia, the setting for the earliest domestication, involved increasing desiccation and perhaps encouraged humans and other species to aggregate at oases. Such concentration in limited localities resulted, he suggested, both in animals' increasing habituation to humans and in humans' increasing knowledge of the behavior of both plants and animals. In this propinquity hypothesis, familiarity bred appreciation rather than contempt. The degree to which Holocene climatic change affected spatial distribution and proximity of the key southwest Asia species remains a matter for investigation, but Childe's hypothesis has not been conclusively refuted. American archaeologist R.J. Braid-

wood was among the first to note that much of southwest Asia constitutes a "natural habitat zone" for the earliest domesticates: wheat, barley, dog, sheep, and goat. Geographer C. Sauer has noted that some of the domesticated plant species prefer disturbed soils (i.e., they are weedy "camp followers"), and he has suggested that wild ancestral forms left in the refuse at human camps might grow abundantly in the disturbed localities used repeatedly by nomadic hunter-gatherers, who would discover them during return visits.

American archaeologists L. Binford, K.V. Flannery, M. Cohen, and others have suggested that increasing population growth during the Pleistocene, resulting in population pressure by the Holocene, encouraged humans to experiment with new food sources. In such circumstances, dense stands of such readily harvestable plants as wild wheat and such potentially tractable gregarious herbivores as sheep may have appeared increasingly attractive. (With climatic change, they also may have been more available than they had been previously.) Where emigration was used as a solution to overpopulation, migrants to new regions may have taken familiar, wild, storable foods with them; such potential domesticates would thus have colonized new geographic areas. J. McCorriston and F. Hole suggested in 1991 that intensified seasonality (longer hot dry summers and shorter cool wet winters) in the Early Holocene may have prompted people to deliberately plant seeds to ensure sufficient year-round food supplies. The seasonality and predictability of certain plants, and the seasonal movements of herd animals, may have provided an important basis for humans' increasing familiarity with, and ultimate control over, the ancestors of today's domesticates. "Capital on the hoof" and plant surpluses provide a potential hedge against uneven environments in which drought, insect pests, and flooding are frequent events, and they may have made the extra work involved in food production appear worthwhile to Early Holocene hunter-gatherers.

Consequences of Domestication

Regardless of its causes in various world areas, domestication radically altered humans' relations to their environment and to one another. Food for stabled livestock must be grown and stored; fodder crops may compete with other plants for limited arable land. Where such animals as sheep, goats, and camels are able to forage freely, specialized forms of nomadic pastoralism have developed. Such nomads' livestock often graze on stubble in peasants' recently harvested fields, where their dung provides fertilizer for next season's crops. Complex economic, social, and political relations exist between pastoralists and the farmers with whom they exchange animal products for plant foods.

With domestication, fields and animals become new forms of wealth, critical in marital alliances and inheritance disputes. Some plants or parts of plants, such as maize pollen in the American Southwest, play key roles in religious activities. Some domesticated animals have also acquired ritual status, such as the cat in ancient Egypt, the bull in ancient Greece, cattle in Hindu India, and the pig in southwest Asia (where it is abhorred equally by Muslims and Jews). In both farming and pastoralist societies, larger families can be useful when livestock must be driven to distant pastures for weeks or months at a time and when dispersed fields require tending at the same time. Thus, it is probable that domestication affected the size and composition of human families, perhaps encouraging larger households because of increased demands for labor. The addition to the human diet of foods such as porridge from domestic grains and animal milk, which can easily be digested by children younger than 4 years old, provided the first successful substitute for human milk. This allowed women to wean their children at an earlier age and to reduce the interval between births, thus increasing the total number of children born.

In short, from its Neolithic origins, domestication impinged upon and altered a range of existing social conventions concerning wealth, inheritance, family structure, and labor. It was associated with an increasingly sedentary way of life, in which the temporary camps of hunter-gatherers have been replaced by permanent communities, villages, and towns, whose residents bring plants and animals to them rather than follow them through the landscape. Without domestication, the complex urban life of the Bronze Age and subsequent periods could not have developed.

See also Americas; Asia, Western; Bronze Age; Çatal Hüyük; Childe, Vere Gordon; Complex Societies; Economy, Prehistoric; Europe; Genetics; Jarmo; Mesolithic; Neolithic; Paleodietary Analysis; Phytolith Analysis; Pollen Analysis; Primate Societies; Stable Isotopes (in Biological Systems); Taphonomy; Zooarchaeology. [C.K., N.B.]

Further Readings

Braidwood, R.J. (1953) The earliest village communities of Southwestern Asia. J. of World Hist. 1:278–310.

Childe, V.G. (1934) New Light on the Most Ancient East: The Oriental Prelude to European Prehistory. London: Kegan Paul.

Clutton-Brock, J., ed. (1989) The Walking Larder: Patterns of Domestication, Pastoralism, and Predation. London: Unwin Hyman.

Cohen, M.N. (1977) The Food Crisis in Prehistory. New Haven: Yale University Press.

Cowan, C.W., and Watson, P.J., eds. (1992) The Origins of Agriculture: An International Perspective. Washington, D.C.: Smithsonian Institution Press.

Crabtree, P.J. (1993) Early animal domestication in the Middle East and Europe. In M.J. Schiffer (ed.): Archaeological Method and Theory, Vol. 5. New York: Academic, pp. 201–245.

Davis, S.J.M. (1987) The Archaeology of Animals. London: Batsford.

Flannery, K.V. (1973) The origins of agriculture. Ann. Rev. Anthropol. 2:271–310.

Flannery, K.V. (1986) Guila Naquitz: Archaic Foraging and Early Agriculture in Oaxaca, Mexico. New York: Academic.

Gebauer, A.B., and T. D. Price, eds. (1992) Transitions to Agriculture in Prehistory. Madison, Wisc.: Prehistory Press.

Harris, D.R., and Hillman, G.C. eds. (1987) Foraging and Farming: The Evolution of Plant Exploitation. London: Unwin Hyman.

McCorriston, J., and Hole, F. (1991) The ecology of seasonal stress and the origins of agriculture in the Near East. Am. Anthropol. 93(1):46–69.

Ucko, P.J., and Dimbleby, G.W., eds. (1969) The Domestication and Exploitation of Plants and Animals. London: Duckworth.

Donrussellia

Early Eocene European genus known from two species. The special significance of this group of primates lies in the fact that their only known morphology, their teeth, shows the two species to be extremely similar to both early adapiforms (particularly *Cantius* and *Pelycodus*) and early omomyids (particularly *Teilhardina*). This intermediacy is a signal that *Donrussellia* is not much evolved, at least dentally, from the last common ancestor of the known anaptomorphine omomyids and the adapiforms. Recent studies indicate, however, that in spite of overall similarities to both early groups of euprimates, the most recent phylogenetic ties of *Donrussellia* are with the adapid radiation.

See also Adapidae; Adapiformes; Euprimates; Omomyidae. [F.S.S]

Drachenloch

Cave in the Churfirsten Range in northeastern Switzerland where remains of more than 10 cave bears (*Ursus spelaeus*) have been found in a 3-m-thick deposit that also contained Mousterian stone tools. Dating of the bones indicates an age of ca. 49 Ka. The sorted distribution of the bear skeletal elements, the spatial association of the skulls with some sort of a stone cist, and the presence of Mousterian lithics led some researchers to associate all of the remains behaviorally and interpret them as evidence for Neanderthal bear cults. Taphonomic research by Tillet in the 1990s suggests that both the death of the bears and the spatial sorting of their bones may have resulted from natural geomorphological processes and not from hominid ritual behavior.

See also Mousterian; Neanderthal; Ritual. [O.S.]

Dragon Bones (and Teeth)

These objects—called *longgu* (dragon bones) and *longya* (dragon teeth), respectively, in Mandarin—are fossils that traditionally have been collected and sold in Chinese drugstores as ingredients for pharmaceuticals. Many of China's fossiliferous karst caves are referred to as Dragon Bone Caves (*longgudong*). According to legend, the land, as well as earthquakes, is associated with dragons that live in the Earth. Thus, many villagers have logically concluded that vertebrate fossils are the bones of dragons, and, since the dragon is a revered and powerful entity, it is not surprising that its bones are prized for their medicinal powers. One hominoid taxon, *Gigantopithecus blacki*, and two highly questionable hominin taxa, *Sinanthropus officinalis* and *Hemanthropus* (also *Hemianthropus*) *peii*, have been proposed solely on the basis of drugstore fossils.

See also Gigantopithecus; Hemanthropus (Hemianthropus); Liucheng; Zhoukoudian. [G.G.P.]

Drimolen

South African karst-cave breccia site in dolomitic limestone ca. 7 km northwest of the well-known Sterkfontein and Swartkrans sites, discovered in 1992 by A. Keyser. Early surveys reveal a comparatively rich fauna, including *Paranthropus robustus*. Ca. 12 hominin specimens have been recovered to date (1997) from an area of ca. 100 m², in which a number of pits were excavated during lime-mining operations in the early 1900s. Most of the hominin fossils derive from a breccia pinnacle and from decalcified breccia immediately below it in the main pit of the site.

See also Africa, Southern; Kromdraai; Paranthropus robustus; Sterkfontein; Swartkrans. [F.E.G.]

Dryopithecinae

Subfamily of Hominidae including species close to the common ancestors of the modern great apes and humans. The subfamily Dryopithecinae was originally named by W.K. Gregory and M. Hellman in 1939 to accommodate the then known Miocene apes. In a major revision in 1965, E.L. Simons and D.R. Pilbeam again used it as a catchall taxon to include the three main groups of Miocene ape that were recognized as subgenera of the single genus *Dryopithecus: D. (Proconsul), D. (Sivapithecus), and D. (Dryopithecus)*. At that time, the genus *Ramapithecus* was identified as a hominid and separated from *Sivapithecus*. *Ramapithecus* and *Sivapithecus* have since been synonymized and placed in the orangutan clade, Ponginae, while *Proconsul* and *Dryopithecus* have been placed in different families, Proconsulidae and Hominidae, respectively. In the early 1990s, Dryopithecinae was used yet again as a "dustbin" category to include three tribes: Afropithecini, Kenyapithecini, and Dryopithecini. The first two are very similar to each other, and they may form a monophyletic group, but it seems most likely that what was termed Dryopithecini is distinct and more closely related to the living great apes and humans than are the first two tribes. Therefore, it is here returned to subfamily rank, while the two other tribes are included in the more conservative Kenyapithecinae.

In this concept, the genus *Dryopithecus* remains central to the subfamily Dryopithecinae. Several species of this genus are now accepted in the Middle to Late Miocene (ca. 13–8? Ma) of Europe, from Spain through France, Germany, Austria, Hungary, and into Georgia. These forms share thin molar enamel and a rather conservative subnasal region (almost as in gibbons, Old World monkeys, and *Proconsul*, but with a slight angulation and narrowing of the incisive canal), combined with robust limb bones somewhat more derived in the direction of modern apes than those of kenyapithecines or earlier catarrhines. The browridge is not very well developed, although D. Begun has suggested that it is

stronger in some specimens, which may indicate moderate klinorhynchy (downward flexion of the face or the cranial base), foreshadowing the Homininae.

Some Asian fossils have been included in *Dryopithecus*, mainly on the basis of apparently thin molar enamel. It is not clear whether *D. wuduensis* from Gansu Province in China (ca. 9–6 Ma) or *D. simonsi* from the Pakistan Siwaliks (ca. 10–8 Ma) belong to this genus or to another, as no facial or postcranial remains are known. The name *Hylopithecus hysudricus* was given in 1927 to some dental fragments from the Siwaliks that may conceivably belong to a similar form, and this genus might be used for the Asian "*Dryopithecus*" if a new name should prove necessary.

Three other fairly well-known genera may also be included in the Dryopithecinae, depending upon interpretations of their phyletic position. *Graecopithecus freybergi* is a European form known from only four Greek Late Miocene localities, apparently dating between 10 and 8 Ma. It is represented by numerous jaws and parts of two male faces. These are robust, with strong browridges, prominent glabella, and squarish muzzles, in some ways reminiscent of gorillas. The subnasal region is also gorillalike, which may be ancestral for Homininae and perhaps Ponginae as well. The teeth have extremely thick molar enamel, and the male canines appear to be reduced in height if not diameter. *Graecopithecus* has been proposed variously as an ancestor or relative of *Australopithecus, Gorilla*, or all hominines, as well as the sister taxon of *Dryopithecus*. Several of these views may be mutually acceptable, if the taxon is slightly more derived than *Dryopithecus*, in the direction of Homininae. Direct links to *Gorilla* or *Australopithecus* are less likely, but ultimate ancestry is a possibility. Comparison with the *Samburupithecus* maxilla from Kenya might prove interesting as well, as these populations are roughly contemporaneous. Here, *Graecopithecus* is tentatively classified as the most conservative known member of Homininae, but it might easily be the most derived dryopithecine instead.

Another European species, *Oreopithecus bambolii*, is slightly younger and more autapomorphic. Known from a series of Late Miocene lignite deposits in Tuscany and Sardinia (Italy) dating to ca. 9–6 Ma, *Oreopithecus* combines highly distinctive teeth with a conservative but hominidlike skull and derived hominid postcrania. Although it has also been suggested to be either the sister taxon to Cercopithecoidea or a direct human ancestor, it now is broadly accepted to show strongest links to modern apes in its postcranium. It is, in fact, the most "modern" Miocene ape below the neck, with closest similarities to the postcranial elements of *Dryopithecus* reported from Spain in the mid-1990s. On the other hand, its lophodont dentition (adapted presumably to a leafy diet) and generally conservative skull (with a few possibly hominid features), as well as the badly crushed condition of most specimens, urge caution in proposing a close link to *Dryopithecus*. For the moment, it is placed in its own subfamily within Hominidae, but it could instead be included in the same subfamily as *Dryopithecus*, perhaps as a distinct tribe (in this case, the rules of priority would require the subfamily to be named *Oreopithecinae*).

Finally, the south Chinese Late Miocene *Lufengpithecus* (ca. 9–7 Ma) is also represented by mostly crushed cranial remains but lacks postcranial elements. It probably had thin molar enamel and a conservative skull (with wide interorbital distance, no clear frontal sinus, weak browridges, and fairly simple incisive canal complex); the lower anterior dentition is somewhat pitheciinlike, with tall incisors and heavy canines; the I^2 is quite small compared to I^1. The weak brow and small lateral incisor are ponginelike, but the other features are less derived. *Lufengpithecus* could conceivably be classified in the Dryopithecinae, Kenyapithecinae, or even Ponginae, once it becomes better known.

Dryopithecinae
>†*Dryopithecus*
>?†*Lufengpithecus*
>?†*Hylopithecus*
>??†*Oreopithecus*
>??†*Graecopithecus* (more probably in Homininae)
†extinct

See also Ape; Asia, Eastern and Southern; Asia, Western; Australopithecus; Dryopithecus; Europe; Graecopithecus; Griphopithecus; Hominidae; Hominoidea; Kenyapithecus; Lu-fengpithecus; Oreopithecus; Ponginae; Priority; Skull; Teeth. [E.D., P.A.]

Further Readings

Andrews, P. (1992) Evolution and environment in the Hominoidea. Nature 360:641–646.

Begun, D.R. (1994). Relations among the great apes and humans: New interpretations based on the fossil great ape *Dryopithecus*. Yrbk. Phys. Anthropol. 37:11–63.

Gregory, W.K., and Hellman, M. (1939) The dentition of the extinct South African man-ape *Australopithecus (Plesianthropus) transvaalensis* Broom: A comparative and phylogenetic study. Ann. Transvaal Mus. 19:339–373.

Moyà Solà, S., and Köhler, M. (1993) Recent discoveries of *Dryopithecus* shed new light on evolution of great apes. Nature 365:543–545.

Moyà Solà, S., and Köhler, M. (1996) A *Dryopithecus* skeleton and the origins of great-ape locomotion. Nature 379:156–159.

Simons, E.L., and Pilbeam, D.R. (1965) Preliminary revision of the Dryopithecinae (Pongidae, Anthropoidea). Folia Primatol. 3:81–152.

Dryopithecus

European Miocene hominid possibly close to the ancestry of Homininae. *Dryopithecus* species were small-to-moderate-sized hominid primates that lived during the Middle to Late Miocene, 13–9 (or 8) Ma. They had robust limb bones, similar to those of the living great apes, but in their thin-enameled teeth they were little advanced over Early Miocene *Proconsul*.

The first specimen of *Dryopithecus* that was found predated C. Darwin's *On the Origin of Species* (1859) by several

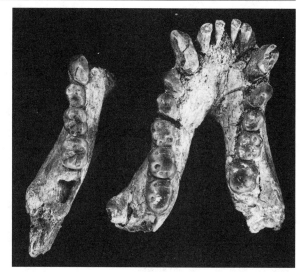

Occlusal view of two male mandibles of Dryopithecus fontani *from the late Middle Miocene of St. Gaudens, France. Left, the left corpus with P3-M2 of the subadult holotype; right, partly crushed but nearly complete adult.*

years. It was discovered near the village of St. Gaudens in southern France in 1855, and it was described the following year by E. Lartet as *Dryopithecus fontani* after its discoverer, M. Fontan. The material from this site consists of several mandibles and part of a humerus: Lartet recognized its great-ape affinities, a view still accepted.

More recent and much bigger collections of *Dryopithecus* have been made in Spain and Hungary. The Spanish specimens can be assigned to two species of *Dryopithecus*: *D. fontani* and *D. laietanus*, although a third species that may be valid has been described: *D. crusafonti*. On the basis of a skull described in 1993, phylogenetic affinity has been suggested between *Dryopithecus* and the orangutan, but this is perhaps more likely to be based on shared ancestral retentions. A partial skeleton, apparently of the same individual, described in 1996, confirms previous indications that the postcranium of *Dryopithecus* is morphologically intermediate between modern apes and kenyapithecines. The Hungarian material, from Rudábánya, which includes good cranial and fragmentary postcranial specimens, appears to fit within the limits of one species of *Dryopithecus*, although its specific name is disputed. Despite its great similarity to the Spanish material, evidence has been put forward by D.R. Begun purporting to show it to be closer to the African ape and human clade than other fossil hominids based on its proposed klinorhynchous state. This dispute has still to be resolved, but the most likely solution based on evidence current to the late 1990s is that *Dryopithecus* represents the latest divergence immediately preceding the split between the pongines and the hominines, so that it may have some characters retained in both descendant groups. On this basis, it is included here in a distinct subfamily, Dryopithecinae, possibly along with such other European Late Miocene genera as *Oreopithecus* and perhaps *Graecopithecus*.

The European *Dryopithecus* populations ranged between Spain and Georgia, although most sites other than those mentioned above have yielded only a few teeth or isolated bones. Several specimens from eastern Asia have also been referred to this genus, mostly on the basis of shared thin molar enamel. One mandible from Gansu Province in China has been termed *D. wuduensis*, while other jaws from the Siwaliks previously named *Sivapithecus simonsi* have been transferred to *Dryopithecus*. It is not clear whether these eastern taxa are congeneric with, or even closely related to, the European species.

See also Ape; Dryopithecinae; Europe; Hominidae; Homininae; Hominoidea; Kenyapithecinae; Miocene; Proconsulidae. [P.A.]

Further Readings

Begun, D.R. (1994) Relations among the great apes and humans: New interpretations based on the fossil great ape *Dryopithecus*. Yrbk. Phys. Anthropol. 37:11–63.

Kordos, L., and Begun, D.R. 1997. A new reconstruction of RUD77, a partial cranium of *Dryopithecus brancoi* from Rudabánya, Hungary. Am. J. Phys. Anthropol. 103:277–294.

Moyà Solà, S., and Köhler, M. (1995) New partial cranium of *Dryopithecus* Lartet, 1863 (Hominoidea, Primates) from the Upper Miocene of Can Llobateres, Barcelona, Spain. J. Hum. Evol. 29:101–139.

Dubois, Eugene (1858–1941)

Dutch physician and paleoanthropologist. In 1891, while serving as a military surgeon in the Dutch East Indies, Dubois discovered at Trinil (Java) the calotte and femur of a fossil hominin. The fauna found in association with these remains indicated a relatively great age, near the boundary between the Pliocene and Pleistocene as then reckoned. According to Dubois, the morphology of the skull cap suggested "pithecoid" (apelike) features, while the femur was essentially modern, implying that the creature was bipedal. Initially, he was convinced he had found the "missing link," and, in deference to E.H. Haeckel (to whom he had been an assistant at Jena University in 1880), Dubois fittingly dubbed the hominin *Pithecanthropus erectus*. Differences arose immediately in interpretation of the taxonomic status and phylogenetic significance of the fossil. Dubois withdrew from the debate in 1898 and remained silent on the issue until 1922. During this time, his ideas changed. Where originally he had supported the view that the fossil represented a form that was transitional from hominoid to hominin, he now contended that it was nothing more than an extinct giant gibbon, a view that had been championed by R. Virchow (1821–1902) during the mid-1890s. In 1922, Dubois also published accounts of two Late Pleistocene crania he had brought back from Java—namely the Wadjak I and II specimens—which he considered to have Australoid affinities.

See also Haeckel, Ernst Heinrich; Homo Erectus; Trinil; Virchow, Rudolph. [F.S.]

Dwarfism

Selection for smaller body size in an evolutionary lineage is most commonly observed in large mammals isolated on islands, where resources sufficient to maintain a breeding population are limited. The limitations may be sensed in different ways depending on the species, and a variety of selective pressures are involved. In other instances, isolation dwarfism may be nothing more than phenotypic response to poor nutrition. Anomalous dwarfism among individuals in a population is most often associated with achondroplasia.

See also Gigantism. [D.P.D., R.L.B.]

Dyuktai

Late Paleolithic archaeological industry of eastern Siberia (Russia) characterized by bifacially worked stone projectile points and knives, wedge-shaped cores, and microblades. Inventories assigned to this industry have been found at the Dyuktai Cave type site, at Ikhine and Ust-Mil' in the vicinity of the Aldan River, and at Ushki on Kamchatka. Although no radiocarbon dates older than ca. 15 Ka have been obtained for these sites, this industry may have existed from 30 to 11 Ka. The similarity of archaeological inventories from these Siberian sites, which are repeatedly found in association with bones of large herbivores, has led some researchers to see this industry as a part of the wider Paleoarctic tradition and a possible precursor to the Paleoindian industries in the New World.

See also Clovis; Paleoindian. [O.S.]

E

Early Paleolithic

Term describing the archaeological sites and the time interval of the Oldowan and Acheulean industries, as well as of the non-handaxe traditions of the Middle Pleistocene (e.g., the "chopper-chopping-tool" complexes of Asia). Grouping all of these sites and industries under the same rubric is primarily a function of the history of archaeology, in which divisions tended to be made in groups of three: Lower, Middle, and Upper. In the nineteenth century, handaxe industries were assigned to the Early Paleolithic and subdivided into the Chellean, Abbevillian, and Acheulean. The simple technologies of the Oldowan were subsequently also assigned to the Early Paleolithic (= African Early Stone Age) as research in Africa progressed.

There is probably no more similarity, in terms of technology, subsistence, and social behavior, between Oldowan and later Acheulean populations than there is between Acheulean and Mousterian (Middle Paleolithic) populations. At least 2 Myr of biological evolution and cultural development are documented during the Early Paleolithic, and it is likely that there were many profound biological, cognitive, and cultural changes during this time.

East Africa

The earliest evidence for stone tools comes from Africa. Some Paleolithic sites in the Omo Valley (Ethiopia) are dated to ca. 2.4 Ma, and tools from the Gona sites in the Hadar region of Ethiopia may be older (2.5 to 2.6 Ma). The site of Lokalalei on the west side of Lake Turkana (Kenya) is of broadly comparable age (ca. 2.3 Ma). Claims have also been made for anvil-like battered boulders in the Ndolanya Beds (ca. 2.5 Ma) at Laetoli. These early industries are normally assigned to the Oldowan industrial complex or termed *Mode 1* (as proposed by British prehistorian J.G.D. Clark), characterized by simple core forms, casually retouched pieces, débitage, battered stones, and manuports (unmodified but transported pieces of stone). Other Oldowan sites from East Africa include Melka Kontouré and Gadeb (Ethiopia), Koobi Fora (Kenya), and especially Olduvai Gorge (Tanzania). The latter sites all date to the Early Pleistocene and vary

enormously in the types of rock used for raw material and the assemblage composition of the artifacts. At Olduvai Gorge, such artifact classes as spheroids and a wide range of small retouched pieces tend to become more common through time and have been assigned to the Developed Oldowan. Similar nomenclature has been used in other parts of Africa. Stone artifacts recovered from Senga-5 in the Western Rift Valley of eastern Zaire are also believed to date to the Early Pleistocene or Late Pliocene.

Starting ca. 1.5 Ma, new artifact forms make their first appearance in Africa: large picks, handaxes, and cleavers (collectively called bifaces), often shaped from large flakes struck from boulder cores. They are first documented from such sites as Konso-Gardula (Ethiopia), Peninj (Tanzania), and Olduvai Gorge. These new forms, which are characteristic elements of the Early Acheulean industrial complex, or Mode 2, tend to become much more refined through time. Other important Acheulean sites from East Africa include Melka Kontouré, Gadeb, and the Middle Awash (Ethiopia); Kariandusi, Kilombe, Kapthurin, and Olorgesailie (Kenya); and Olduvai, Chesowanja, and Isimila (Tanzania).

At some localities in the Early and Middle Pleistocene, archaeological sites with handaxes are roughly contemporaneous with nonhandaxe sites; the latter are sometimes called *Hope Fountain* industries in Africa. The significance of these technological dichotomies is not yet understood; whether they represent contrasting functional activities, proximity to different types of raw material, distinct cultural norms, or other causes has not been adequately demonstrated.

Southern Africa

The earliest evidence for hominid tool making in central and South Africa is from the cave deposits of Sterkfontein and Swartkrans in the South African Transvaal. A range of simple artifact forms, primarily of Mode 1, have been found in these deposits, believed to date ca. 2–1.5 Ma. In Member 5 breccias at Sterkfontein, an Oldowan industry has been found along with a few early *Homo* specimens and other animal remains, estimated to date to 2–1.7 Ma. Overlying this infill

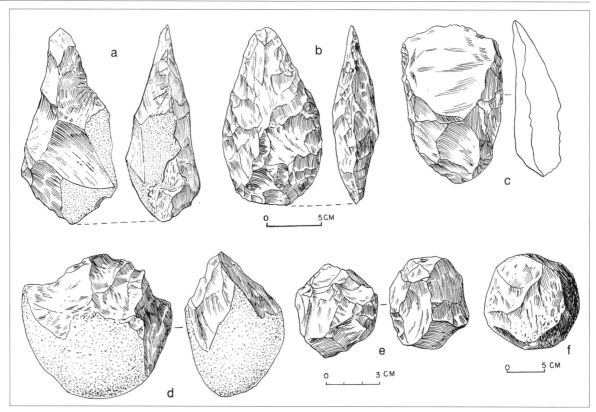

Representative Early Paleolithic lithic artifacts from Africa: (a) pointed handaxe; (b) ovate handaxe; (c) cleaver; (d) bifacial chopper; (e) polyhedron; (f) spheroid.

containing Oldowan artifacts is another breccia containing crude Acheulean artifacts. At Swartkrans (Members 1–3) stone and bone implements are known in association with early *Homo* cf. *erectus* and also *Paranthropus robustus*. It has been suggested that hand bones identified as those of the latter species appear capable of making these tools, but this has not been widely accepted.

Important Middle Pleistocene Acheulean sites from southern Africa include Victoria West, Cave of Hearths, and Saldanha (South Africa), and Kalambo Falls (Zambia). At Saldanha, the Acheulean may be contemporary with an early fossil attributed to "archaic *Homo sapiens*" rather than with *H. erectus*. Kalambo is noteworthy in yielding the preserved remains of plant and wood materials.

Central Africa

While finds of Oldowan and Acheulean type are known from surface and secondary context sites in many areas of Central Africa, dating and faunal associations are usually lacking, so that it is unclear if the finds in question are the bases of a similar cultural succession. Middle Pleistocene occurrences of Acheulean materials in fluvial sands and grounds at Kamoa, Zaire, at Nsongezi in Uganda, and in northeast Angola almost certainly are comparable to east and southern African samples.

North Africa

Several sites in North Africa have yielded materials that appear to be older than 1.0 Ma. These include possible Oldowan assemblages from the Casablanca marine-beach sequences in Morocco and the Algerian site of 'Ain Hanech.

Important Middle Pleistocene Acheulean sites from North Africa include Tighenif (ex-Ternifine, Algeria), Rabat (Morocco), Sidi Zin (Tunisia), and Arkin and Kharga Oasis (Egypt).

Southwest Asia

The obvious route of hominid migrations out of Africa would have been via southwest Asia, since southwestern Asia was joined with that continent to an extent dictated by the size of the Red Sea. It is no surprise, then, that the earliest evidence of hominin groups outside of Africa comes from this area. The site of 'Ubeidiya (Israel) is estimated to date between 1.4 and 1.0 Ma, based upon faunal correlations and paleomagnetism, and comprises superimposed cobble beaches from an ancient lakeshore containing fossil bones and stone artifacts. The industries consist of Early Acheulean and Oldowan-like artifact forms. Important Middle Pleistocene Acheulean sites from southwest Asia include Tabūn, Zuttiyeh, Gesher Benot Ya'acov, and Ma'ayan Barukh (Israel); Latamne (Syria); Jabrud (Lebanon); and Lion's Spring (Jordan).

Eastern and Southern Asia

The earliest definitive evidence for hominin occupation of eastern Asia comes from sites yielding *Homo erectus* fossils and stone artifacts. Interestingly, handaxe industries are all but absent from the whole of eastern Asia, as pointed out by H.L. Movius in the 1940s. Movius' line, separating Acheulean industries in Africa and western Eurasia from chopper-chopping-tool (Mode 1) industries to the east,

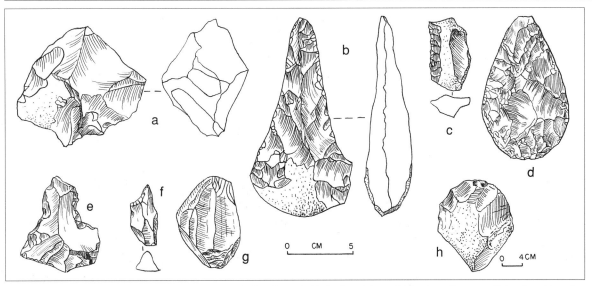

Representative Early Paleolithic lithic artifacts from Europe (a–f) and Asia (g–h): (a) discoidal core; (b) handaxe; (c) scraper; (d) handaxe; (e) notch; (f) Tayacian point; (g) bipolar core; (h) chopper.

shows an important technological dichotomy between these great geographical areas.

Exactly why there are no handaxe-cleaver industries to the east is not clear; certainly in these millions of square kilometers, hominins must have frequented raw-material sources adequate for the large bifacial forms characteristic of the Acheulean. There are three commonly forwarded explanations. The first theorizes that the cultural concepts of such handaxe-cleaver (Mode 2) technologies (although widespread from the tip of southern Africa through western Europe and as far east as Southwest Asia and parts of the Indian subcontinent) never spread as far as eastern Asia; these eastern Asian populations thus were geographically cut off from the rest of the Old World and their technological innovations. The second explanation suggests that other raw materials, such as bamboo, were used in many parts of eastern Asia, so there was much less emphasis on lithic materials for finished tools; stone served instead as a raw material for woodworking. The third view, now discredited, theorizes that the East Asian hominin populations had different, perhaps biologically determined, cognitive or cultural systems that were not shared by African or western Eurasian hominin groups. A fourth idea is that the earliest inhabitants of eastern Asia may have left Africa before the Acheulean was fully developed, thus bringing with them only a Mode 1 technology. Another curious pattern that has emerged is that most of the earliest European Paleolithic sites do not appear to have handaxe-cleaver industries, but the more casual Mode 1 technologies similar to the East Asian material. None of the explanations for the relative lack of large bifacial forms in East Asia appear entirely satisfactory, however, and more fieldwork and refined chronological control will be necessary to explain this technological dichotomy.

Stone tools have not been found in direct association with the *H. erectus* fossils of Java, but rather in separate sedimentary contexts. In the 1930s, finds of some crude stone tools in Java were attributed to a purported Early Paleolithic industry called the *Pacitanian,* but these are now believed to

be much more recent, probably from the Holocene. Similar Mode 1 industries composed of simple chopper cores and débitage were also identified elsewhere in Southeast Asia, though, again, they usually come from fluvial contexts or terraces in which secure chronological placement is impossible. These include the Soan industry of India, the Anyathian of Burma, the Tampanian of Malaysia, and the Fingnoian of Thailand; some of these industries are now thought to be of Late Pleistocene or Holocene age. Early Paleolithic industries in China—such as those found at the Lantian localities, at sites in the Nihewan Basin (e.g., Donggutuo, Cenjiawan, and Xiaochangliang), and at Zhoukoudian—consist of characteristically simple Mode 1 artifacts. A technological tradition involving large bifaces appears at a few sites in eastern Asia by late Middle to early Late Pleistocene times (e.g., Chongokni in Korea, and Dingcun in China), but this does not seem to be directly related to the Acheulean technological tradition observed in western Asia, Europe, and Africa. Most recently, however, survey and preliminary excavations in the Baise basin of south China in 1995–1996, have suggested that large, unifacial and bifacial ovate and pointed shaped tools may occur there in an Early Pleistocene context. Furthermore, the Takamori site in Japan, dated by electron spin resonance (ESR) to the early part of the Middle Pleistocene, appears to contain true bifaces in an array of raw materials grouped together in hollows or pits.

Europe

Establishing a chronology for the European Early Paleolithic is a formidable task, since most areas do not have volcanic rocks suitable for potassium-argon (K/Ar) and fission-track dates, and much of the biostratigraphic work cannot be tied to a reliably dated sequence.

Although there are claims for very early occupation of Europe (e.g., the sites of Chilhac and St. Eble in the French Massif Central, with reported K/Ar dates of ca. 1.8 Ma), the anthropological consensus sees little evidence of hominids in western Eurasia prior to 1.0 Ma. Hominid populations

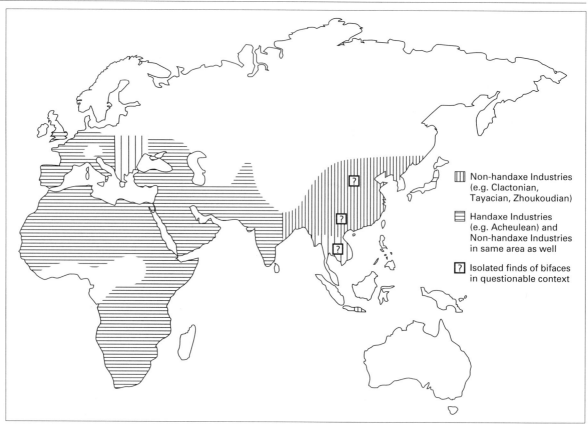

Distribution map of handaxe (Mode II) vs. non-handaxe (Mode I) Early Paleolithic industries during the Middle Pleistocene.

could have spread out of Africa and into Europe by a number of routes: from northeastern Africa via western Asia; across the short expanse of water of the Straits of Gibraltar from northwestern Africa to Iberia; and by island hopping in the Mediterranean during low sea levels, from North Africa via Sardinia to the Italian mainland. The early date suggested for 'Ubeidiya indicates a hominin expansion into southwestern Asia by at least 1.4 Ma. An *H. erectus* mandible recovered in 1991 at Dmanisi (Georgia) probably dates well over 1.0 Ma. Stone artifacts from this locality are of a non-Acheulean (Mode 1) nature, while those from 'Ubeidiya include both Mode 1 (Oldowan) and, in slightly later horizons, Mode 2 (Acheulean) forms.

The first strong evidence for hominin groups in Europe comes from several sites in the latest Early Pleistocene or just after (1.0–0.7 Ma), such as Atapuerca (Spain) and Isernia, Ceprano, and Notarchirico near Venosa (Italy), which have yielded human fossils and/or artifacts, generally of Mode 1 form (Notarchirico contains handaxes, however). An increasing number of sites with "archaic *Homo sapiens*" fossils and artifacts occurs through time: Boxgrove (England) and Mauer (Germany) ca. 500 Ka; Arago (France), Petralona (Greece), Vértesszöllös (Hungary), a younger level at Atapuerca, Swanscombe (England), and Steinheim (Germany) between 400 and 250 Ka. Sites representing the earliest occupations of Europe are characterized by lithic assemblages best described as Mode 1 technologies: casual cores, numerous retouched flakes, and débitage. At some sites, such as Vértesszöllös, the stone used for artifacts consisted primarily

of small pebbles, so morphological variability was further restricted by the raw material. Assemblages without handaxes are termed *Clactonian* in northern Europe and *Tayacian* in the south, but their relationship to the biface-rich Acheulean is uncertain.

Handaxe industries are found throughout western Europe but tend to be less common in eastern Europe. Noteworthy Middle Pleistocene sites of the Early Paleolithic include Clacton, Swanscombe, and Hoxne (Britain); Terra Amata, Abbeville, and St. Acheul (France); and Torralba and Ambrona (Spain). Levallois prepared-core technology first appears at the end of the Acheulean, which gives way to the Mousterian (European Middle Paleolithic) between 200 and 150 Ka, although the latest Early Paleolithic industry, the Micoquian, continues into the Early Late Pleistocene (ca. 130–70 Ka).

See also Abbevillian; Acheulean; Africa; Africa, East; Africa, North; Africa, Southern; Ambrona; Arago; Archaeological Sites; Asia, Eastern and Southern; Asia, Western; Biface; Bodo; Buda Industry; Chilhac; China; Chopper-Chopping Tools; Clactonian; Cleaver; Core; Early Stone Age; Economy, Prehistoric; Europe; Fire; Flake; Florisbad; Handaxe; Hope Fountain; Hoxne; Hunter-Gatherers; Indonesia; Jabrud; Jabrudian; Kalambo Falls; Kanjera; Kapthurin; Karari; Laetoli; Lainyamok; Lazaret; Levallois; Lithic Use-Wear; Lokalalei; Man-Land Relationships; Melka Kontouré; Micoquian; Middle Paleolithic; Monte Peglia; Mousterian; Nihewan; Oldowan; Olduvai Gorge; Olorgesailie; Paleolithic; Pa-

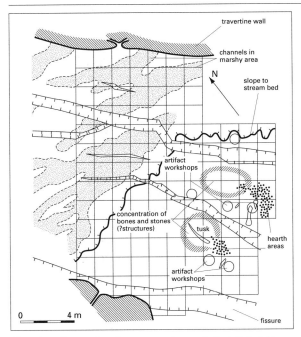

Plan view of bone and artifact concentrations at the Early Paleolithic Bilzingsleben site (eastern Germany). From R. Klein, The Human Career, *University of Chicago Press, 1989.*

leolithic Lifeways; Prepared-Core; Přezletice; Primate Societies; Raw Materials; Retouch; Ritual; Saldanha; Site Types; Soan; Soleihac; Spear; Speech (Origins of); Stone-Tool Making; Stranská Skála; Swanscombe; Tabūn; Tabunian; Takamori; Tata; Tayacian; Tighenif; Torre In Pietra; 'Ubeidiya; Vallonnet; Venosa sites; Xihoudu; Zhoukoudian. [N.T., K.S.]

Further Readings

Bar-Yosef, O. (1994) The Lower Palaeolithic of the Near East. J. World Prehist. 8:211–265.

Bordes, F. (1970) The Old Stone Age. New York: McGrawHill.

Gamble, C. (1986) The Palaeolithic Settlement of Europe. Cambridge: Cambridge University Press.

Huang, W., and Hou, Y. (1997) Archaeological evidence for the first human colonisation of East Asia. Indo-Pacific Association Bulletin 16(3):3–11.

Larick, R., and Ciochon, R.L. (1996) The African emergence and early Asian dispersals of the genus *Homo*. Am. Sci. 84:538–551.

Petraglia, M.D., and Korisettar, R., eds. (1998) Early Human Behavior in Global Context: The Rise and Diversity of the Lower Paleolithic Record. New York: Routledge.

Phillipson, D.W. (1993) African Archaeology, 2nd ed. Cambridge: Cambridge University Press.

Schick, K.D., and Dong, Z. (1993) Early Paleolithic of China and eastern Asia. Evol. Anthropol. 2:22–35.

Schick, K.D., and Toth, N. (1993) Making Silent Stones Speak: Human Evolution and the Dawn of Technology. New York: Simon & Schuster.

Svoboda, J. (1987) Lithic industries of the Arago, Vértesszöllös, and Bilzingsleben hominids: Comparison and evolutionary interpretation. Curr. Anthropol. 28:219–227.

Wu, R., and Olsen, J.W., eds. (1985) Paleoanthropology and Paleolithic Archeology in the People's Republic of China. New York: Academic.

Wymer, J. (1982) The Palaeolithic Age. New York: St. Martin's.

Early Stone Age

First stage in a tripartite system for the African Stone Age (originally Earlier, Middle, and Later), formalized by South African archaeologists A.J.H. Goodwin and C. Van Riet Lowe in 1929 for South Africa. The concept was later expanded to include Acheulean, Oldowan, and related early industries (Karari, Hope Fountain) from eastern, central, and northern Africa, and even from some areas of Asia, such as the Indian subcontinent. As originally defined, the Earlier Stone Age (ESA) referred to flake-and-core industries without prepared cores or Mousterian influences and included the Stellenbosch (= Acheulean), Victoria West, and Fauresmith industries of South Africa. Later, the three-stage scheme was modified to a five-stage scheme, with the transitional stages First Intermediate and Second Intermediate interposed between the Earlier and Middle, and the Middle and Later Stone Ages, respectively.

Development of separate nomenclature for the African Stone Age reflected recognition of substantial differences between Africa and Europe in technological and economic development. Initially, it was also thought that African development was retarded with respect to that of Europe; this is now known to be incorrect. Major differences between Africa and Europe during the Early Paleolithic/ESA include the more than 2 Myr of stone-tool manufacture in Africa, as opposed to less than 1.0 Myr in most of Europe (e.g., Vallonnet); the greater elaboration of pebble-tool industries in Africa, now known from Europe as well (Buda industry); and the wider diversity of African tool forms (e.g., cleavers), technologies, and industries.

Since the 1960s, new African archaeological data have made it difficult to sustain a single chronostratigraphic scheme for the entire continent. Recommendations include dropping the term *Early Stone Age,* substituting the (equally vague) term *Early (or Lower) Paleolithic,* using only specific industry terms (*Oldowan, Karari, Acheulean*), or instituting the Modes 1 and 2 of J.G.D. Clark's 1968 scheme for technological stages for simple pebble or flake industries (Oldowan) and biface industries (Acheulean), respectively.

The earliest stone-tool industries of Africa, consisting of split cobbles and simple flakes made largely of quartz, date between 2.6 and 2.1 Ma, in the Omo and Hadar (Gona sites) regions of Ethiopia, at Lokalalei in West Turkana (Kenya) and at Senga-5 in the Semliki Valley of Zaire. The oldest flake tools from Sterkfontein (South Africa) may also approach this age, and it has been proposed that basalt boulders from the Ndolanya Beds at Laetoli may represent Mode 1 cores or anvils. Except for a few possible handaxes from ca. 2–1.5 Ma contexts at Sterkfontein, the more formally shaped bifaces of the African Acheulean do not appear until 1.6–1.5 Ma. After their initial appearance, Acheulean tools continue in relatively unchanging form, along with industries consisting of simple Oldowan-type flakes, scrapers, backed knives, and pebble cores, well into the Middle Pleistocene. Late Acheulean handaxes do exhibit more refined flaking and flatter and more even contours. They are often associated with prepared core technology and occasionally, as at Baringo, with blades made on prismatic cores. The Acheulean is replaced by Middle Stone Age industries between 250 and 130 Ka.

Although different ESA industries have often been attributed to different cultures, different ethnic groups, or even different hominids, more recent arguments suggest that ESA industries represent a stable, possibly biologically mediated, level of simple technological responses to the environment. Interassemblage differences are attributed to differing activities, social groupings, raw material economies, depositional histories, or other site-formation factors.

One of the major controversies in ESA research (as with the Early Paleolithic of Europe) concerns the relationships between handaxe and nonhandaxe industries. The function of handaxes themselves and the underlying reasons for their symmetry are not clear. Use-wear analysis suggests that they were multiple-purpose cutting, chopping, piercing, or scraping implements, the "Swiss army knives" of their day. Other suggestions include use as projectiles, as cores, or as caches of raw materials. They are often associated with butchery of very large mammals, such as elephant, hippopotamus, rhinoceros, and giant buffalo, probably representing scavenging at death sites rather than hunting. In many regions (e.g., Olduvai), they are preferentially associated with stream-channel deposits, while flake-tool assemblages without handaxes are more often located on lakeshores. This situation is reversed in the Middle Awash Valley of Ethiopia, however, where in one area Acheulean butchery sites occur close to a former lakeshore.

See also Acheulean; Africa; Biface; Buda Industry; Cave of Hearths; Chesowanja; Early Paleolithic; Economy, Prehistoric; First Intermediate; Handaxe; Hope Fountain; Later Stone Age; Melka Kontouré; Middle Awash; Middle Stone Age; Natron-Eyasi Basin; Oldowan; Olduvai; Olorgesaile; Paleolithic; Second Intermediate; Senga-5; Sterkfontein; Stone-Tool Making; Swartkrans; Taphonomy; Turkana Basin; Vallonnet. [A.S.B.]

Further Readings

Clark, J.D. (1970) The Prehistory of Africa. New York: Praeger.

Clark, J.D. (1994) The Acheulean industrial complex in Africa and elsewhere. In Corrucini, R.S., and Ciochan, R.L., eds. Integrative Paths to the Past: Paleoanthropological Advances in Honor of F. Clark Howell. New York: Prentice Hall, pp. 451–469.

Goodwin, A.J.H., and Van Riet Lowe, C. (1979) The Stone Age cultures of South Africa. Ann. S. Afr. Mus. 27:1–289.

Phillipson, D.W. (1993) African Archaeology, 2nd ed. Cambridge: Cambridge University Press.

Potts, R. (1988) Early Hominid Activities at Olduvai. New York: Aldine de Gruyter.

Ecology

Adaptation and evolution through natural selection result from the interactions of living organisms with their surroundings, or *environment.* Ecology (from the Greek *oikos,* a house or household) is the science that studies such interactions. To an ecologist, the environment is all those living and nonliving things that impinge upon an organism or group of organisms and that may influence their growth, survival, and reproductive success.

Population ecology studies the interactions between the environment and members of a single species. It usually pays special attention to the dynamics of population growth and decline and the influence on these processes of such factors as food supply, predation, and disease. Community ecology concerns itself with multispecies interactions and especially with questions of coexistence and competition between species. The plant and animal communities of any given area, together with their inanimate surroundings, form an *ecosystem,* in which solar energy is captured by green plants (primary producers) and transferred along food chains to several levels of animal consumers (from herbivores to top carnivores). Ecosystems are dynamic and highly complex, and their study frequently involves mathematical modeling techniques.

An important concept in ecology is that of the *niche,* the functional position of an organism (or population) within an ecosystem. This is not so much the physical location of an organism as a description of its pattern of interactions with the rest of the system. With the proviso that all such ecosystems are local (which the species as a whole may not be), the ecological niche (or econiche) of an extinct organism can be reconstructed from fossil assemblages and a knowledge of present-day ecosystems. Such paleoecology can provide crucial insights on the causes of events in human evolution.

See also Adaptation(s); Diet; Man-Land Relationships; Paleobiogeography; Paleoenvironment; Primate Ecology. [J.F.O.]

Economy, Prehistoric

Economic behavior can be defined as the subset of general cultural practices that involves the acquisition and transformation of matter and energy from nature, the distribution of these products among people, and the use or consumption of these products. Economic practices of both prehistoric and present-day groups are multidimensional entities shaped by the interaction of the perception of the environment by the group, the ideas people have about their needs and how to satisfy them, the knowledge available to exploit the resources, the technology used to do so, and the social relationships that govern acquisition, production, and distribution. Some of these variables can be observed directly in the archaeological record; others can only be inferred by analogy with ethnographically observed behavior.

Reconstructing the nature of the environment in which a prehistoric group lived, including the climate and the distribution of organic and inorganic resources, is usually the first step in investigations of prehistoric economies. Information for this comes from such disciplines as botany, climatology, geology, and zoology. *Site-catchment analysis,* a particularly fine-tuned application, is directed to reconstructing what resources were available within a reasonable distance from sites under study (usually a two-hour walk or a 5-km

Storage pit under excavation at the Gontsy Late Paleolithic site in Russia. Courtesy of Olga Soffer.

radius around a site). This research strategy is most effective where local environments have changed little since the sites were occupied. Data on reconstructed paleoenvironments, including such variables as the availability, abundance, and predictability of key resources, have also been used to model human economic behavior. A variety of *optimal foraging* models delimit the most effective mix of resources that would have been harvested in a given region through different seasons and isolate suitable locations for doing so. Although such studies give clues about why particular locations may have been selected for occupation, they basically indicate what was *available* but not what was *used*. Evidence for the latter comes from the archaeological remains left behind at the sites. This information is used in both site-catchment analyses and predictive models for insights into actual vs. optimal economic decision making in the past.

Past subsistence practices—what food people ate, what materials they used, and how they obtained both—are reflected in the kinds of inventories and features and in their distribution at sites. Remains of plants and animals consumed provide information about prehistoric diets. Since morphological differences exist between domesticated plants and animals and their wild progenitors, organic remains indicate whether a particular group depended on wild products gathered from nature or grew their own food.

The study of animal bones by archaeozoologists (or zooarchaeologists) indicates not only what animals were hunted, but also at what age they were killed and often in what season the hunting took place. In general, more specialized and seasonally restricted use of a location by prehistoric hunter-gatherers implies more sophisticated planning and scheduling of economic activities. Furthermore, the kinds of animals hunted and the age-sex profiles of different species indicate what hunting methods were used and whether wild or domesticated taxa were harvested. The prevalence of herd animals at a particular site, for example, suggests hunting by mass drives; solitary species suggest stalking and individual kills.

The kinds of body parts found at a site—meat-bearing hindquarters or nutritionally impoverished skulls or foot bones—can be used to infer if the hunters were the first meat eaters who had access to the prey or if they exploited some parts of an animal killed by other carnivores. Under some circumstances, such data can help distinguish active hunting from scavenging. In other circumstances, such information can help determine if the hunters had lots of meat available to them and could be very selective, such as during the early fall season, for example, or if they hunted during the lean times and had to use every scrap of meat obtained.

Plant remains, which in general preserve poorly and are the most difficult to recover archaeologically, yield information about what species were harvested and about the season

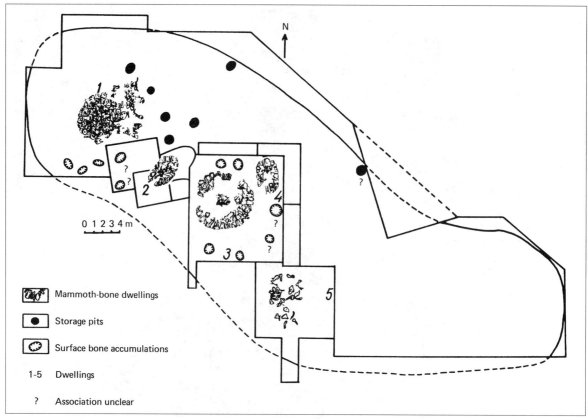

Distribution of storage pits and of surface bone piles at the Mezin Late Paleolithic site. Courtesy of Olga Soffer.

or seasons when this harvesting took place. Direct evidence for past diets is also obtained from coprolites (human feces) and from bone-chemistry analysis of human remains.

Tools and implements, too, help reveal economic practices. For instance, sickle blades with wear polish resulting from harvesting cereals imply plant collecting, as do grinding stones and pestles; bows and arrows indirectly attest to hunting; nets and fishhooks are evidence for fishing; and fire-cracked rocks in hearths point to cooking of food.

Other aspects of technology provide valuable clues about both the organization of production and social and economic relationships. High levels of standardization, for example, suggest that artifacts were produced by a small group of specialists and imply a more complex division of labor than that found in simple societies where all members are capable of making, and do make, everything they use. The presence of exotic materials and the use to which they were put often indicate exchange with distant groups and give clues to social networks.

Features found at sites similarly can yield information about past economies. First, the elaborateness of the structures (e.g., houses, storage facilities) reflects the degree of permanence of occupation. Ephemeral features in general suggest short-term occupations and imply group mobility; an increased investment of labor in dwellings and other facilities is associated with more sedentary lifeways. Such features as drying racks or smudge pits used in large-scale processing and preservation of food, as well as the presence and content of storage bins, pits, or rooms, indicate that the

economy in question involved logistical organization and delayed consumption rather than simple "feed as you go" foraging.

The distribution of inventories and features at sites is also important. Equal distribution of food and other remains among households at a site suggests an open and equal access to goods and resources. Finding most storage facilities associated with one or two households, on the other hand, suggests that the resources were controlled by a small group of individuals. Similar inferences can be drawn from the distribution of valuable nonlocal materials and from the comparison of the size and contents of the dwellings. Exotics consistently concentrated in large-size households suggest the existence of unequal access to resources, as do differences in size and elaborateness of dwellings for same-size social units.

Finally, settlement patterns within a region also can yield information. For example, finding early agricultural villages clustered exclusively in river valleys suggests the use of simple floodplain irrigation, while a more scattered pattern across the landscape suggests dry farming.

See also Archaeological Sites; Hunter-Gatherers; Man-Land Relationships; Paleolithic Lifeways, Site Types; Storage. [O.S.]

Further Readings

Binford, L.R. (1978) *Nunamiut Ethnoarchaeology.* New York: Academic.

Fagan, B. (1997) *In the Beginning,* 9th ed. Boston: Little, Brown.

Jochim, M.A. (1981) Strategies for Survival: Cultural Behavior in an Ecological Context. New York: Academic.

Ehringsdorf

Site in eastern Germany where fossil hominids were recovered from travertine deposits during commercial and controlled excavations between 1908 and 1925. The most significant specimens are an adult cranial vault, an adult mandible, a child's mandible, and postcranial elements. Found in association with artifacts of early Mousterian type, the fossils appear to represent early Neanderthals, although it is not clear whether they date from ca. 120 Ka or (more probably) from slightly more than 200 Ka.

See also Europe; Neanderthals. [C.B.S.]

Ekgmowechashalinae

Subfamily of omomyid tarsiiform primates consisting of the single genus *Ekgmowechashala*, a dentally highly modified, North American Early Miocene form. This genus, like *Washakius*, has incisors distinctly smaller than the canines and has the derived combination of upper-molar mesostyle and lower-molar mesostylid. It is likely to have been derived from the vicinity of *Washakius* and not from a form like *Rooneyia*. The extreme adaptive similarity of the teeth of *Ekgmowechashala* to fruit-eating relatives of raccoons suggests a habitual diet of soft fruits in the remnant warm forests of the Early Miocene of the Rocky Mountain states.

The 1980s transfer by M.C. McKenna of this genus to the probably dermopteran Eocene Plagiomenidae, with two genera—*Tarka* and *Tarkadectes*—referred to the (alleged plagiomenid) subfamily Ekgmowechashalinae, is highly unlikely. *Ekgmowechashala* has its hypoconulid well displaced buccally toward the hypoconid (like in *Washakius*). This condition is totally unlike that in plagiomenids and in the two fossil plagiomenid genera, mistakenly associated with *Ekgmowechashala*, that twin the hypoconulid and entoconid similarly to tupaiids, mixodectids, microbats, and living dermopterans. *Ekgmowechashala* has a well developed hypocone (as in *Washakius* and *Rooneyia*) and conules on the buccal half of the molars, a complex morphological condition entirely unlike *Tarka* (the only putative "ekgmowechashaline" with a known upper molar). The latter lacks a hypocone, has conules lingually placed on the molar, and has the characteristic stylar cusps seen in mixodectids, plagiomenids, and galeopithecids. The underlying assumption in associating *Ekgmowechashala* with plagiomenids is that the buccal cusps of the omomyid are stylar cusps rather than what they are: a small mesial accessory cuspule and the paracone and metacone. The occlusal mechanics of superimposed upper- and lower-molar outlines leave little doubt concerning the homology of the cusps on *Ekgmowechashala* on one hand, and undoubted plagiomenids and galeopithecids on the other.

See also Anaptomorphinae; Archonta; Dermoptera; Microchoerinae; Microsyopidae; Omomyidae; Omomyinae. [F.S.S.]

El Wad

Rockshelter on Mount Carmel in Israel excavated in the 1930s and 1970s. El Wad contains a sequence of occupations from Middle Paleolithic, Upper Paleolithic, and Epipaleolithic times. The Epipaleolithic Natufian occupation (Level B) dates to ca. 12–11 Ka and contains several adult and juvenile burials with *Dentalium* shell ornaments.

See also Asia, Western; Natufian. [J.J.S.]

Emiran

Name given by D. Garrod to a putative Middle-Upper Paleolithic transitional industry from Southwest Asia. Marked by the presence of Emireh points and *chamfrein* endscrapers (i.e., endscrapers sharpened by a lateral tranchet flake), the Emiran was initially recognized at Emireh, El Wad, Kebara, and other Levantine cave sites. Subsequent investigations, however, revealed these to be deposits mixed by spring activity. The term *Emiran* is no longer generally used, although Emireh points (triangular points with inversely retouched or thinned bases) and *chamfrein* endscrapers continue to be recognized as markers of the early Upper Paleolithic in the Levant.

See also Asia, Western; El Wad; Emireh Point; Kebara. [J.J.S., A.S.B.]

Further Readings

Garrod, D.A.F., and Bate, D.M. (1937) The Stone Age of Mount Carmel. Oxford: Clarendon Press.

Emireh Point

Pointed flake or blade with a base thinned by bifacial retouch. In the Levant, Emireh points have been found at Ksar 'Akil, El Wad, Kebara, and Boker Tachtit, where they are considered markers of the Middle–Upper Paleolithic transition.

See also Asia, Western; Boker Tachtit; Emiran. [J.J.S.]

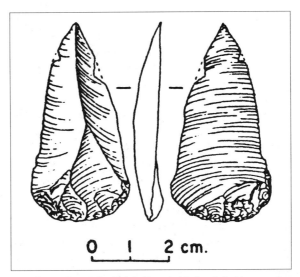

Emireh point from Boker Tachtit. From A. Marks, ed., Prehistory and Paleoenvironments in the Central Negev, *vol. 3, 1979, Southern Methodist University Press.*

Engis

Cave near Liège (Belgium) in which Belgian physician P.-C. Schmerling's systematic excavations in 1829–1830 demonstrated the great antiquity of Paleolithic humans. Fossil mammals, Mousterian stone tools, and fossil hominins were discovered at this site. One skull from Engis has deteriorated, and its morphology is unknown. The cranium of a hyper-robust male from Engis has been recognized as dating only to ca. 8 Ka. The third fossil, a partial cranium of a child, is a Neanderthal. Although unrecognized as such until the 1930s, this child was the first discovery of a Neanderthal fossil.

See also Europe; Homo sapiens; Neanderthals. [C.B.S., J.J.S.]

Eocatarrhini

A parvorder (between infraorder and superfamily) of catarrhines, including the extinct families Pliopithecidae and Propliopithecidae, as well as the "*Dendropithecus*-group"—thus, the "archaic" catarrhines. The taxon was originally defined by L. Ginsburg and P. Mein in 1980 with essentially the same contents, although they placed *Dendropithecus* and some others in the Hylobatidae.

This group is basically a paraphyletic assemblage of conservative taxa lacking the derived characters of the modern (or eucatarrhine) catarrhines (Cercopithecoidea and Hominoidea). Nonetheless, it is a useful way to refer to all of these early taxa, as opposed to the eucatarrhines.

See also Anthropoidea; Catarrhini; "Dendropithecus-Group"; Eucatarrhini; Pliopithecidae; Propliopithecidae. [E.D.]

Eocene

Epoch of the Early Cenozoic era, beginning ca. 54 Ma and ending ca. 34 Ma. The Eocene is typified in shallow marine strata of the Paris-London Basin, which interfinger with mammal-bearing beds laid down on adjacent coastal plains. This well-documented correlation between marine and nonmarine faunas in the type area supports a reliable worldwide chronostratigraphy. Confirmatory regional correlation and dating are provided by the integration of the paleomagnetic time scale with Eocene planktonic microfossil zonation and the mammalian sequences of North America and western Europe. Regional subdivisions of the continental Eocene have been defined in terms of mammalian history and/or evolution in North America, Europe, South America, and, increasingly, Asia. The African Eocene, except for the Fayum, is represented by isolated small faunas, and that of Australia is almost unknown.

The Eocene is of great interest for the study of primates, which were abundant and diverse in North America, Eurasia, and Africa. In the northern continents, the first euprimate (modern primate) families, the Adapidae and the Omomyidae, appeared in Early Eocene sites together with the earliest representatives of such major groups as perissodactyls, artiodactyls, sciuromorph (northern) rodents, carnivores, and whales. The earliest-known tarsioids and anthropoids (i.e., parapithecids and oligopithecids) come from rocks of Middle and Late Eocene age. The African Eocene

primates occur with African endemic forms such as hyraxes, proboscideans, elephant-shrews, and hystricomorph (southern continent) rodents, as well as with marsupials, palaeoryctids, creodonts, pangolins, and other ancient mammal groups that are also known from Europe. From the absence of more modern Eurasian groups, it can be assumed that connection between African and Holarctic faunas was limited or nonexistent after the Early Eocene.

Direct connection between North America and Europe via Greenland during the Early Eocene (Sparnacian or Wasatchian) is evidenced by the astonishingly strong similarity between the mammal faunas in the two areas. The connection was severed by the widening of the North Atlantic in Cuisian/Bridgerian times. Shortly after the Euroamerican faunal province came to an end, connection between Europe and Asia was made, or strengthened, by closure of the Turgai Strait in the Caucasus suture. The Indian subcontinent, together with the Anatolian and Irano-Afghan microplates, was drawn up against the Asian landmass during the Eocene, but the vertebrate faunas that these formerly African lands carried with them have not been discovered to date. South America, like Australia, remained, in the words of G.G. Simpson, in "splendid isolation" until the simultaneous arrival in South America of the primitive platyrrhines, such as *Branisella,* and cichlid fishes, boid snakes, and southern rodents (ancestral to guinea pigs and capybaras) from Africa. This remarkable transatlantic disperal may date to the Eocene and certainly occurred before the Late Oligocene.

The plant remains of the Eocene suggest a continuation of the warm, moist climate of the Paleocene, and there are indications that the beginning of the Eocene had the warmest global climate of the Cenozoic. This period of warming may be correlated with the great faunal turnover of Euroamerica at the beginning of the Eocene. The unusually warm climate extended as far as the Eocene circumpolar region, which coincided fairly well with the present-day Arctic. Ellesmere Island, with a paleolatitude of at least 76°N (78°N today) had a rich fauna of primates and plagiomenids (possible Dermoptera) during the Early and Middle Eocene, despite the winter darkness of such latitudes. To appreciate this climate, we should consider that plant assemblages of this age from southern Alaska indicate a mean annual temperature of ca. 22° C, similar to the southern reaches of Mexico today. At the end of the Eocene, however, paleofloras of temperate broad-leaved deciduous and coniferous forests began to develop in the higher latitudes, which has been interpreted as evidence for a high mean annual range (greater than 30° C) and a low mean annual temperature (less than 10° C). Even during this cool part of the Eocene, the North Pole would have been at least 25° C warmer than today, and, during the warmest phase of the Eocene, the polar regions may have been 30–35° C warmer than today.

With the sharp cooling that began at the end of the Eocene, the diverse primate fauna of Eurasia and North America was almost completely wiped out, with the last surviving species becoming extinct by the Late Oligocene. Only Africa and Madagascar had tropical primate faunas, and there the endemic stocks of primates that had developed by the Late Eocene, as documented in the Fayum beds of Egypt, continued to flourish. In the late Middle Eocene (Bartonian), Fayum-like primates, probably cercamoniine adapiforms or tarsioids, lived in Burma and China, while other characteristic Fayum mammals have been found from beds of Middle Eocene age in Turkey, India, and Romania. These finds suggest that exchange was widely possible between the landmasses bordering the Tethys, if not to Eurasia proper, in the mid- to later Eocene.

See also Africa, North; Americas; Asia, Eastern and Southern; Cenozoic; Fayum; Oligocene; Paleocene. [F.S.S., J.A.V.C.]

Further Readings

Prothero, D.R. 1995 The Eocene-Oligocene Transition: Paradise Lost. New York: Columbia University Press.

Prothero, D.R., and Berggren, W.A., eds. 1992 Eocene-Oligocene Climatic and Biotic Evolution. Princeton: Princeton University Press.

Savage, D.E., and Russell, D.E. (1983) Mammalian Paleofaunas of the World. Reading, Mass.: Addison-Wesley.

Szalay, F.S., and Delson, E. (1979) Evolutionary History of the Primates. New York: Academic.

Eoliths

From the Greek for *Dawn Stone,* a term used to denote crudely fractured stones that were originally thought to be of hominid manufacture. Such eoliths had been described, for example, from in and below the Crag deposits of East Anglia, England. Most of these collections are now thought to have been produced by natural forces, such as wave action, frost fracture, fire, pressure from moving ice sheets, or rock fall. [N.T., K.S.]

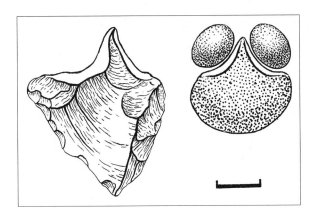

Left to right: eolith from river gravel at Piltdown; diagram to illustrate how such an eolith could have been produced by soil-creep under periglacial conditions. After K. P. Oakley, Man the Tool-Maker*, 1963, British Museum (Natural History). Scale = 2 cm.*

Eosimiidae

Extinct family of tarsioid primates known from the Middle Eocene of China. This family, described in 1994, is known from two species, *Eosimias sinensis* from fissures of Jiangsu Province and *E. centennicus* from the Heti Formation of the Yuanqu Basin of Shanxi Province. These tiny primates (ca. 100 g) represent an important addition to our knowledge of primate evolution. They have been strongly advocated to represent basal anthropoids, a hypothesis that does not appear to be supported by available evidence.

As yet, only lower teeth are known, but *E. centennicus* is represented by a nearly complete mandible, which allows the evaluation of many features vis-à-vis early anthropoids. The conformation of the symphysis is not as expected in a basal anthropoid, as it falls well within the range displayed by such omomyids as *Tetonius, Absarokius, Loveina,* or *Washakius*; it is particularly similar to the nearly vertical orientation of the symphysis of *Tarsius.* The vertical implantation of the incisors is also particularly similar to *Tarsius,* but omomyids such as *Loveina, Washakius,* or *Ourayia* also display vertical incisors. While *Eosimias* does not have the advanced guillotinelike incisor and canine complex shown by the carnivorous tarsiers, its vertical incisors and large canines display a condition structurally ancestral to the anterior dentition of tarsiids. The three eosimiid premolars are tarsiidlike, although not reduced in relative size as in tarsiers, which have hypertrophied molar teeth compared to their small premolars.

The lower molars in the two species of eosimiids display strong derived similarities to those of living *Tarsius,* far more so than to basal anthropoids. *Tarsius* is unique among euprimates in its strongly constructed shearing trigonid structure, probably a derived condition in euprimates. As in tarsiers, in *Eosimias* the trigonids are both hypertrophied and lack the distally progressive reduction of the paraconids. Both families display strong shearing crests both mesially and distally. This, like the other dental attributes of eosimiids, is decidedly unlike the inferred basal anthropoid condition but rather similar to tarsiids. The talonid construction is equally unlike that of basal anthropoids. In the latter, the hypoconulid tends to be close to the entoconid. In *Eosimias,* the hypoconulid is poorly expressed, and it is central on the distal crest of the talonid, as in most other tarsiiforms. The third lower molar talonids of *Eosimias* are narrow like those of *Tarsius eocaenus* described from the same Shanghuang fissures.

See also Anthropoidea; Euprimates; Haplorhini; Omomyidae; Strepsirhini; Tarsiidae; Tarsiiformes; Tarsioidea; Teeth. [F.S.S.]

Further Readings

Beard, K.C., Tao, Q., Dawson, M.R., Wang, B., and Li C. (1994) A diverse new primate fauna from Middle Eocene fissure-fillings in southeastern China. Nature 368:604–609.

Beard, K.C., Tong, Y., Dawson, M.R., Wang, J., and Huang, X. (1996) Earliest complete dentition of an anthropoid primate from the late Middle Eocene of Shanxi Province, China. Science 272:82–85.

Epigravettian

Upper Paleolithic industries of Mediterranean Europe characterized by backed microblades but poor or lacking in geometric microliths or microburins. In Italy, Epigravettian industries with leaf-shaped points begin shortly after 20 Ka, contemporary with the Solutrean and Magdalenian of southwestern Europe. The final phases, with short endscrapers, thumbnail scrapers, and some geometric microliths, at ca.12–10 Ka, are equivalent in some areas to the Romanellian. *Epigravettian* implies a continuity, expressed in the backed microblades, with the earlier Gravettian industries of western and central Europe.

See also Epipaleolithic; Gravettian; Late Paleolithic; Magdalenian; Romanellian; Solutrean; Stone-Tool Making; Upper Paleolithic. [A.S.B.]

Epipaleolithic

Term used in place of *Mesolithic* to describe final Late Pleistocene and Holocene assemblages that reflect a continuation of a Paleolithic way of life, based on hunting of large herbivores, from ca. 12 Ka to as late as 3 Ka, in northern Europe. Tool kits are highly variable but often include small tanged or backed points, scrapers and burins, a wide range of bone and antler tools including barbed harpoons, and some geometric microliths reflecting the development of composite tools. Specific industries may include the reindeer-hunting cultures of the North European plain (Hamburgian, Ahrensburgian); the Maglemosian of the North European plain; the Azilian, the Sauveterrian, and the Tardenoisian of France and Belgium; the Asturian of Spain; the Romanellian of Italy; the Creswellian of England; and comparable industries from Provence, Portugal, and other areas of Europe. Some authors limit the use of the term *Epipaleolithic* to industries of southern and southeastern Europe, as well as Africa, where greater continuity exists between Late Pleistocene and Early Holocene adaptations due to greater environmental continuity over the period involved.

Other users of *Epipaleolithic* reserve the designation *Mesolithic* for industries that reflect economic intensification in the direction of domestication, sedentism, or environmental modification. The Natufian culture of the Levant would thus be a clear example of Mesolithic; the Kebaran of the Levant and the later Ibero-Maurusian of North Africa, as well as much of the Later Stone Age of sub-Saharan Africa, would be Epipaleolithic. Economic intensification is characteristic of the Epipaleolithic but tends to be reflected in specialized procurement of single resources (reindeer, red deer) or of new kinds of resources that require advanced technologies (birds, fish, seals, and marine/lacustrine resources generally). Either of these economic strategies requires considerable scheduling of resource use, according to limited seasonal availability.

One major difference between Upper Paleolithic and Epipaleolithic cultures in Europe is the apparent disappearance of widespread imaging traditions based on animals. The few images associated with these sites are either abstract (Azilian) or represent schematic human figures (Asturian).

See also Azilian; Creswellian; Domestication; Economy, Prehistoric; Hamburgian; Hunter-Gatherers; Ibero-Maurusian; Kebaran; Late Paleolithic; Later Stone Age; Maglemosian; Man-Land Relationships; Mesolithic; Paleolithic Lifeways; Romanellian; Sauveterrian; Stone-Tool Making; Tardenoisian; Upper Paleolithic. [A.S.B.]

Further Readings
Bonsall, C., ed. (1989) The Mesolithic in Europe. Edinburgh: John Donald.
Champion, T., Gamble, C., Shennan, S., and Whittle, A. (1984) Prehistoric Europe. New York: Academic.
Koslowski, S.K., ed. (1973) The Mesolithic in Europe. Warsaw: Warsaw University Press.
Mellars, P., ed. (1978) The Early Postglacial Settlement of Northern Europe. London: Duckworth.
Phillips, P. (1975) Early Farmers of West Mediterranean Europe. London: Hutchinson.
Straus, L.G., ed. (1986) The End of the Paleolithic in the Old World. BAR International Series 284. Oxford: Archaeopress.
Straus, L.G., Eriksen, B.V., Erlandson, J., and Yesner, D.R., eds. (1996) Humans at the End of the Ice Age: The Archaeology of the Pleistocene-Holocene Transition. New York: Plenum.

ESR (Electron Spin Resonance) Dating

Dating of archaeological material and Quaternary strata according to the electron spin resonance (ESR) of solid materials. As one of the methods of trapped-charge dating, ESR spectrometry measures free electron charges at defects within mineral lattices that resonate at distinct frequency peaks (with distinct "g" values) representing different trap sites. The intensity (amplitude) of the peaks reflects the number of trapped electron charges that have accumulated in the sample through the effects of background radiation since the trap sites were formed, or since they were last zeroed. The original peak intensity is calculated from the equivalent radiation dose (DE) by the additive-dose method using controlled artificial radiation. The ratio of the additive-dose energy to the increased activity in the sample after dosing is a function of its age.

To be used for dating, the ESR signal sites must be sensitive to background radiation, so that the signal intensity is directly proportional to the natural dose rate, and must have lifetimes at least an order of magnitude greater than the age of the sample. The sites must also be robust (not subject to fading other than the thermal effect) and must not have been recrystallized or otherwise affected so that the number of traps is changed. Most, but not all, ESR-datable materials are carbonates or phosphates and are zeroed at the time of deposition because they were freshly crystallized. Materials that meet the above criteria are usually tooth enamel, speleothems (stalagmites and the like), mollusc shells, or corals. The lifetimes of ESR signals in these materials are close to or greater than 1.0 Myr, and all are radiation sensitive and relatively stable. Zeroing due to heating is also possible for flint or other siliceous artifacts.

Unsuitable materials include calcretes and spring-deposited travertines, which often display a significant initial signal, and bone tissue. The hydroxyapatite in bone is extremely susceptible to postmortem recrystallization, and bone usually takes up about 10 times as much ambient uranium as fossil teeth do.

Tooth enamel from archaeological sites is the most widely used subject for ESR dating, using the frequency peak at g = 2.0018, closely followed by analyses of speleothems using g = 2.0005. Dosimetry must be carefully determined and includes corrections for attenuation by the activity of β-particles, which may be emitted from radioisotopes in adjacent sediment or from within the fossil material itself. In tooth enamel, for instance, the signal is often modified significantly by ambient uranium ions that exchange with the phosphorus of dentine and enamel, and by evolution *in situ* of radioactive daughter isotopes of uranium. The ESR dating limit of enamel is more than 2 Ma, with a precision of ca. 10 percent of the age, and Miocene ESR ages have been reported. The minimum sample size is ca. 1 g of tooth enamel; therefore, only the teeth of larger animals (bovids, cervids, equids) are generally useful.

For analysis of tooth material, the enamel and dentine are reduced to a powder. Weighed portions of the enamel powder are exposed to gamma rays to determine the dose-response curve, while the uranium concentration is measured in both the enamel and the dentine. In cases in which the internal, U-generated radiation dose is large, the calculated age critically depends on the history of uranium uptake. The possible U-uptake models include early uptake (EU), in which the present U-content is assumed to have been established soon after deposition, and linear uptake (LU), which assumes a constant rate of uptake since deposition. The EU model leads to a calculation of the lowest possible age for a set of ESR data. Using U-series analyses of the enamel and dentine, it is possible to test which of these models best describes the U-uptake history of a tooth. Analyses of teeth from Israeli sites have suggested early U-uptake for most samples, while sites in other countries exhibit more continuous, quasi-linear uptake.

ESR dating has been used in assessing the age of numerous paleoanthropological sites, ranging in age from Acheulean levels in Morocco to the "archaic *Homo sapiens*" (or *Homo heidelbergensis*) site of Petralona (Greece), the "early modern human" sites at Qafzeh and Skhūl in Israel and Border Cave and Klasies River Mouth in South Africa, and Neanderthal sites such as Krapina. ESR studies of the australopith site at Sterkfontein (South Africa) indicate an age beyond the maximum limit of the technique, or more than 2 Ma.

See also Geochronometry; Trapped-Charge Dating. [H.P.S.]

Further Readings

Blackwell, B. (1995) Electron spin resonance dating. In N.W. Rutter and N.R. Catto (eds.): Dating Methods for Quaternary Deposits. St. Johns, Newfoundland: Geological Society of Canada, pp. 209–268.

Grun, R. (1993) Electron spin resonance dating in paleoanthropology. Evol. Anthropol. 2:172–181.

Grun, R., and Stringer, C.B. (1991) Electron spin resonance dating and the evolution of modern humans. Archaeometry 33:153–199.

Rhodes, E.J., Raynal, J.-P., Geraads, D., and Fatima-Zora, S. (1994) Premières dates RPE pour l'Acheuléen du Maroc atlantique (Grotte des Rhinocéros, Casablanca). C.R. Acad. Sci. (Paris), ser. 2, 319:1109–1115

Ethnoarchaeology

Collection and use of ethnographic data by archaeologists interested in behavior relating to material culture. The term was first used in the American Southwest, where archaeologists are fortunate in being able to draw on a rich ethnohistoric record, itself complementing robust and longstanding indigenous cultural traditions, some of which are thought to be traceable into the prehistoric past. More recently, this and comparable terms, such as *action archaeology, living archaecology, archaeoethnography,* and *archaeological ethnography,* have been applied to research among groups as diverse as hunter-gatherers in Australia, Alaska, and Africa; tribal agriculturalists in the Philippines and nontribal farmers in Central America; villagers and pastoral nomads in Africa, Europe, and western Asia; and potters in India, Peru, and elsewhere. Observations made among ethnographically documented groups considered analogous in specific ways to societies known archaeologically are used to support inferences based on analysis of prehistoric materials, as well as to suggest ways in which archaeological data may be collected and analyzed (e.g., how sites and regions might be more effectively sampled and how archaeologists' typologies might be reevaluated or refined in light of native systems of classification). Ethnoarchaeological research since the 1960s has illuminated a variety of subjects traditionally of interest to archaeologists. These include the manufacture, use, curation, and disposal of tools and ceramics; subsistence strategies, butchering, modification, and redistribution of animal parts; identification of activity areas and objects associated with them; internal organization of houses and villages and the relationship of differences among rooms to differences in activities, social relations, and economic status; interaction among ethnic groups and material markers of ethnicity and of boundaries among groups; and symbolic and ideological contexts for the creation and use of objects and structures.

Not all forms of human behavior observable today existed in the past, nor is it likely that all past adaptations have survived to the present. For example, the validity of applying studies of present-day hunter-gatherers to archaeological remains predating *Homo sapiens sapiens* has been questioned. This challenge has heightened some researchers' appreciation of the potential applications of research in primate and carnivore ethology to investigations of the behavior of the earlier hominins, particularly with respect to subsistence, settlement, and social organization. General ecological principles relating to responses to resource distributions, travel costs, predation threats, and other environmental variables have considerable potential for suggesting constraints within which *presapiens* groups may have operated and possible ranges of variation that may have characterized their adaptive strategies; such hypotheses can be tested in the archaeological record. A growing body of information about hunter-gatherers in diverse habitats is beginning not only to reveal points of difference but also to suggest some

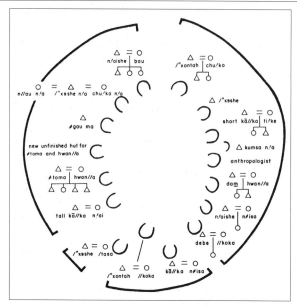

Plan of contemporary dry-season camp in Kalahari region of southern Africa. Each semicircular hut is labeled with the name of the occupants: a married couple (triangle male, circle female, = marriage symbol) and children, or single individual (note anthropologist's hut at center right). From Yellen, 1977.

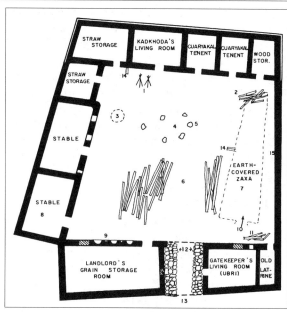

Floor plan of contemporary house in Hasanabad village (Iran). Key: (1) yogurt-churn; (2) wood; (3) grain storage pit; (4) rock salt for animals; (5) salt; (6) poplar poles; (7) sloping cover of zaxa; (8) wooden threshing machine storage area; (9) animal mangers and hitches; (10) entrance to covered zaxa; (11) wood; (12) stone platforms; (13) entryway; (14) wooden drain spout; (15) wall, 2.7 m high. Special terms: Kadkhoda = headman; zaxa = underground stable. From Archaeological Ethnography in Western Iran, *by P.J. Watson, © 1979 by the Wenner-Gren Foundation for Anthropological Research, New York.*

shared features that may have relevance to understanding pre-sapiens time ranges, as well as more recent periods.

Ethnoarchaeological research projects with agrarian groups and with pastoralists do not face quite the same challenge, since these adaptations were developed by members of our own subspecies, in the comparatively recent past. Even in such research, however, it is important to specify why one has selected a particular locality and how one is applying analogical models to archaeological remains. A research bias favoring contemporary hunter-gatherers, work designed in some cases to answer questions about our Paleolithic ancestors, is gradually being balanced by ethnoarchaeological work among farmers and herders. A related geographic bias toward the marginal areas occupied by most modern food-collecting peoples is increasingly complemented by research in more temperate zones in other parts of the world, some of it by archaeologists interested in Neolithic and later periods.

See also Archaeology; Culture; Primate Societies. [C.K.]

Further Readings

Binford, L.R. (1978) Nunamiut Ethnoarchaeology. New York: Academic.

David, N.C. (1998) Keyword Bibliography of Ethnoarchaeology and Related Topics. Version 3.1. http://www.ucalgary.ca/UofC/faculties/SS/ARKY/ethnarky.html

Hodder, I. (1982) Symbols in Action. New York: Cambridge University Press.

Kent, S., ed. (1987) Method and Theory for Activity Area Research. New York: Columbia University Press.

Kramer, C., ed. (1979) Ethnoarchaeology: Implications of Ethnography for Archaeology. New York: Columbia University Press.

Yellen, J. (1977) Archaeological Approaches to the Present. New York: Academic.

Ethology

Study of animal behavior from an evolutionary perspective (from the Greek *ethos,* meaning custom or habit). Its roots lie in C. Darwin's ideas on the evolution of instincts as developed in the 1930s by European zoologists K. Lorenz and N. Tinbergen. Ethology uses observation, experimentation, and the comparative method to investigate the proximate causes of behavioral acts, the relative contributions of inheritance and learning to these acts, and the adaptive significance and evolutionary history of different patterns of behavior within and across species.

See also Primate Societies; Sociobiology. [J.F.O.]

Eucatarrhini

A parvorder (between infraorder and superfamily) of catarrhines including the living superfamilies Cercopithecoidea and Hominoidea—thus, the modern catarrhines. The taxon was originally defined (Delson, 1977) to include all catarrhines except the Parapithecidae, then thought to be archaic members of the infraorder Catarrhini; the parapithecids were termed Paracatarrhini. Since then, the parapithecids have been shown to probably be the sister taxon of Catarrhini plus Platyrrhini, and the paracatarrhines have been elevated to infraorder rank and tentatively broadened to include the Oligopithecidae. Here, the sister taxon to Eucatarrhini is the Eocatarrhini, or archaic catarrhines, including the Propliopithecidae, Pliopithecidae, and *Dendropithecus* and its possible allies. This was the arrangement proposed by L. Ginsburg and

P. Mein in 1980, although they formally included Parapithecidae in Platyrrhini and *Dendropithecus* and some others in the Hylobatidae.

The eucatarrhines first appear in the fossil record in the latest Oligocene, when the proconsulid hominoid *Kamoyapithecus* is known. Other proconsulids range through the Early and apparently into the earliest Middle Miocene, when they are succeeded by the Hominidae. The Cercopithecoidea appear later, with *Prohylobates* and *Victoriapithecus* of the later Early and Middle Miocene. It is generally thought that the last common ancestor (LCA) of the eucatarrhines was an Oligocene descendant of a propliopithecid (or later eocatarrhine) stock. This LCA would have been broadly similar in many ways to *Proconsul;* in fact, some researchers have removed the proconsulids (as defined here) from the Hominoidea, considering them to lack the synapomorphies of the eucatarrhines.

See also Anthropoidea; Catarrhini; Cercopithecidae; Eocatarrhini; Hominoidea; Paracatarrhini. [E.D.]

Further Readings

Delson, E. (1977) Catarrhine phylogeny and classification: Principles, methods, and comments. J. Hum. Evol. 6:433–459.

Ginsburg, L., and Mein, P. (1980) *Crouzelia rhodanica,* nouvelle espèce de Primate catarhinien, et essai sur la position systématique des Pliopithecidae. Bull. Mus. Nat. Hist. Nat. (Paris) 2C:57–85.

Harrison, T. (1987). The phylogenetic relationships of the early catarrhine primates: A review of the current evidence. J. Hum. Evol. 16:41–80.

Euprimates

A major taxonomic division of primates, here ranked as a semiorder, that encompasses all primates except the archaic forms. The taxonomic unit was formally named in 1977 by R. Hoffstetter and independently in 1979 by F.S. Szalay and E. Delson, who developed the concept in detail as a suborder. Although there is much controversy surrounding the inclusion of archaic forms within the primate order, the euprimates are accepted by all workers as "true" primates, which is exactly what the term implies. Here, they are contrasted with the archaic semiorder Plesiadapiformes.

The following (presumably) derived features, which are the diagnostic characteristics of the euprimates in contrast to other groups, were present in the given combination for the first time in the last common ancestor of the semiorder Euprimates: (1) continuous postorbital rings; (2) advanced orbital convergence; (3) enlarged brain compared to archaic primates, suggested by the increased neural skull in proportion to the facial one, and an increased height of the occiput in early representatives compared to an archaic primate like *Plesiadapis;* (4) stapedial and promontory arteries inside the middle ear cavity, like the carotid in archaic primates (e.g., *Plesiadapis*), enclosed in a bony canal; (5) nails instead of claws (falculae) on all digits of the hand and foot except for the specially and secondarily modified toilet claws on the foot—it is possible that the modified toilet claw is a more an-

cient feature, an enhanced expression of a primitive therian grooming claw; (6) general elongation of the tarsal bones compared to the archaic forms; (7) a flattened and elongated ilium (the anterior and top portion of the hip bone) for the origin of the gluteus medius muscle that is greatly enlarged for leaping-related locomotion; (8) a deep and elongated groove for the knee cap (patella) on the distal end of the femur, also indicating a habitual leaping component in the locomotion; and (9) highly derived grasping adaptations in the hindfeet related to climbing and particularly leaping.

There are additional detailed and consistent characteristics in the dentition, hand, foot, and other areas of the postcranium that all support the hypothesis that the first euprimates were distinct from their archaic ancestors in the way they adapted to the arboreal environment, particularly in their grasp-leaping locomotion and correlated neural adaptations unique among other placental mammals. Euprimates is a holophyletic taxon within Primates.

See also Archonta; Plesiadapiformes; Primates. [F.S.S.]

Further Readings

Szalay, F.S., and Lucas, S.G. (1996) The postcranial morphology of Paleocene *Chriacus* and *Mixodectes* and the phylogenetic relationships of archontan mammals. Bull. New Mex. Mus. Nat. Hist. Sci. 7:1–47.

Szalay, F.S., Rosenberger, A.L., and Dagosto, M. (1987) Diagnosis and differentiation of the Primates. Yrbk. Phys. Anthropol. 30:75–105.

Europe

Continental area with the longest, most nearly continuous record of primate (including human) evolution. Europe does not have the most ancient primates (as does North America), nor a good series of *Homo erectus* fossils and very early primates (as in Asia), and its fossil record lacks the broad representation of almost all primate groups and most major events in catarrhine and human history characteristic of Africa. What does distinguish Europe is that it has a good representation of both early and later primates and many human types and the longest history of the study of paleoanthropology and geology. As a consequence, the definitions of Cenozoic and most other time-scale subdivisions (epochs and stages), as well as of many types of lithic industries, technologies, and artifacts, are based on European type sections, especially from the Mediterranean and Paris-London basins and from southwestern France.

Europe is the smallest mainland continent, with an area of 10 million km², of which only the southern two-thirds is potentially habitable by nonhuman primates. Western Europe was faunally connected to North America but not to Asia in the Early Cenozoic; Africa was isolated; a seaway divided central Asia from most of eastern Europe. Asia and Europe were in contact by the mid-Cenozoic, and faunal interchange with Africa via western Asia became possible early in the Miocene. Late in that epoch, intermittent contact was probably feasible across the Mediterranean Basin, both in the center (ca. 11–9 Ma) and in the far west (ca. 6–5.3 Ma). At this time, the mainly forested environments present since the Mesozoic were increasingly restricted northward, so that steppes dominated most of southern Europe from 8 to 5 Ma. The Mediterranean Basin became desiccated at the end of the Miocene as the result of tectonic contact with Africa in the west, preventing sufficient inflow of Atlantic water to keep the basin filled. After massive downcutting of river channels emptying into the basin (e.g., Rhone and Nile delta areas), a channel in the Rif area of Morocco refilled the Mediterranean with Atlantic water (and fossils), marking the beginning of the Pliocene ca. 5.2 Ma. Humid monsoon-type forest spread through southern Europe, but then global climatic cooling led to more open conditions in the later Pliocene and Early Pleistocene (ca. 3–1.0 Ma). A number of local mountain ranges that had risen mostly during the later Cenozoic were the centers of regional glaciation through the Pleistocene, as was the Scandinavian sector to the north. Latitudinal zonation of climatic belts typifies Europe today and probably did so through much of the Cenozoic.

Rise of Primates

Primates first appeared in the European fossil record in the Late Paleocene. *Plesiadapis* occurred in France at Cernay (and similar sites) and in Germany at the Walbeck fissure-fill, which also yielded the unique specimens of *Saxonella*. Plesiadapids continued into the Early Eocene in England, France, and Belgium (the important locality of Dormaal),

alongside *Phenacolemur* and the first euprimates: the notharctid *Cantius* and the anaptomorphine omomyid *Teilhardina*. More than a dozen genera included in the Adapiformes ranged through the Eocene of Europe, from Portugal to England to northern Germany. The greatest number of localities are in southern France, especially the group of fissure-fillings and stratified sites in the Quercy region. Microchoerine omomyids coexisted with adapiforms at many, if not all, of the localities in the Middle and Late Eocene. In general, they were small, while adapiforms ranged in size from tiny to that of a cat, filling the niches taken by both notharctids and omomyids in North America. Just after the beginning of the Oligocene (34–33 Ma), a major faunal turnover known as the *Grande Coupure,* (Great Cutoff) took place, and all primates disappeared from the European fossil record throughout the rest of the Oligocene and Early Miocene.

Only in the early Middle Miocene (ca. 17–16 Ma) do primates again appear in Europe, as a result of emigration from Africa. Pliopithecids were apparently the first to arrive, probably via the sub-Alpine route along the northern shore of the Mediterranean from western Asia. At this time, a major inland sea extended roughly east-west in the center of Europe and down to meet the Mediterranean in the Adriatic region.

Pliopithecus and allies were mainly restricted to the west and north of this seaway, from Spain through to Poland and Hungary (but also in Romania), between 16 and 11 Ma.

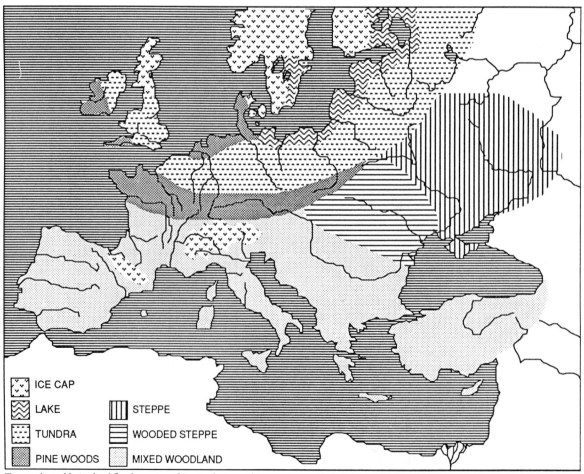

ICE CAP   LAKE   TUNDRA   PINE WOODS   STEPPE   WOODED STEPPE   MIXED WOODLAND

Topography and latitudinal floral zonation of Europe during a Pleistocene interstadial, slightly cooler than today.

Slightly younger is the first European hominid, *Griphopithecus*, known from a single tooth at Engelswies (Germany, ca. 15+ Ma) and a few others from Neudorf (Czech Republic, ca. 14 Ma); these appear to be closely similar to the large sample from Paşalar, Turkey. *Dryopithecus* arrived, or evolved locally, still later, perhaps by ca. 14 Ma, and sometimes occurred alongside the pliopithecids. At least three species are known from many localities: *D. fontani, D. laietanus,* and *D. ?brancoi,* and a fourth may occur in Spain; teeth from Udabno (Georgia, ca. 12 Ma) might represent *D. fontani* or a distinct species. Cranial and postcranial remains of *Dryopithecus* are known from the early Late Miocene of Can Llobateres (Spain, 9.6 Ma) and Rudábánya (Hungary, ca. 10

Ma), but opinions differ as to the affinities of this genus. It appears to have conservatively thin molar enamel and nearly gibbonlike nasopalatine morphology, the orbits are widely spaced, and its humerus and ulna display several features more like those of "modern" hominoids than is known for *Griphopithecus* or the African *Kenyapithecus*. Some authors have suggested that *Dryopithecus* may lie near the base of the orangutan (pongine) or African ape/human (hominine) clades, but it is probably more reasonably placed antecedent to that split, in the subfamily Dryopithecinae. Another member of that group may be the Italian "swamp ape" *Oreopithecus*, previously thought to be a cercopithecoid. More intensive studies have shown that, although it has distinctive

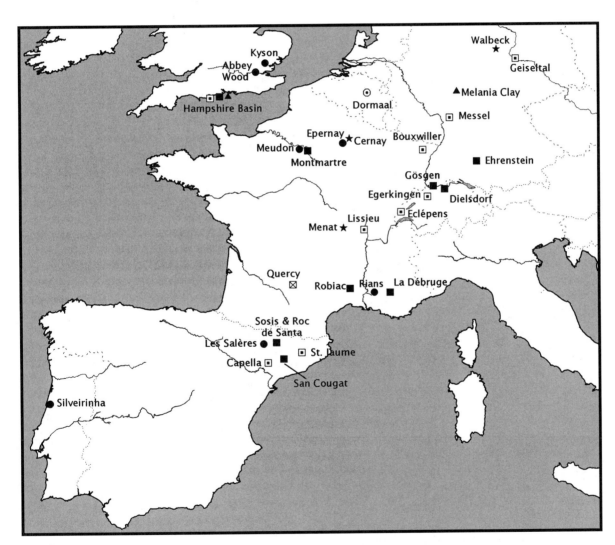

Selected European Late Paleocene to Early Oligocene fossil primate localities. Age and included taxa are indicated according to the key at left:

★ Middle-Late Paleocene – Plesiadapiformes

● Early Eocene – Plesiadapiformes, Adapidae

⊙ Early Eocene – Plesiadapiformes, Adapidae, Anaptomorphinae

▣ Middle Eocene – Adapidae, Microchoerinae

■ Late Eocene – Adapidae, Microchoerinae

⊠ Early-Late Eocene – Adapidae, Microchoerinae

▲ Earliest Oligocene – Adapidae

teeth, which converge in some ways on those of ancestral Old World monkeys, its postcranium and some cranial features ally it with later Hominidae. Most specimens are known from a series of sites in Tuscany dated to 8–7 Ma; a few teeth are also known from Sardinia. One last hominid genus may also belong to the Dryopithecinae or, more likely, to the Homininae. *Graecopithecus* is represented by a partial skull and numerous jaws (but no postcrania) from Greek localities dated ca. 9.5–8 Ma. It shares some canine reduction with Hominini, and its molars have very thick enamel, but otherwise it is rather gorillalike in facial morphology, conforming to the morphotype for hominines; no derived characters are shared with Ponginae.

Cercopithecoids appeared in Europe in the Late Miocene, when *Mesopithecus pentelicus,* a semiterrestrial colobine, was common in the southeastern part of the continent at Pikermi and Saloniki (Greece), Titov Veles (Yugoslavia), Kalimanci (Bulgaria), and Grebeniki (Ukraine), all ca. 9–8 Ma. The range of this species continued eastward at least into Afghanistan. One premolar tooth from Wissberg, in the Eppelsheim-area "*Deinotherium*-Sands" of Germany, may date to 11 Ma.

With the aridification of southern Europe, ca. 6–5 Ma, all primates disappeared except a few poorly dated colobines known from forested localities in Hungary. The return of humid forests saw the spread of macaques (presumably from North Africa—two teeth are known in eastern Spain in the latest Miocene) and two new colobines: a smaller and more arboreal species of *Mesopithecus* and the moderately large-bodied, terrestrial *Dolichopithecus ruscinensis.* Between 5 and 3 Ma, these species are often found together at localities between Spain and Ukraine and as far north as Germany (Wölfersheim) and southern England (Red Crag). Later Pliocene and Pleistocene cooling probably led to the extinction of the colobines, but macaques indistinguishable from the living *M. sylvanus* of Gibraltar and North Africa persisted into the earlier Late Pleistocene across all of Europe from England and Spain to the Caucasus. The large-bodied, terrestrial, baboonlike *Paradolichopithecus* was apparently a local macaque derivative that converged on the savannah baboon niche. It is known from only a few sites in the later Pliocene of Spain, France, and Romania, and also from Tadzhikistan (central Asia).

Earliest Human Colonization

The date and nature of the earliest human occupation of Europe are controversial. Europe was clearly occupied over a wide area between 500 and 300 Ka, an interval discussed in the following section. A smaller number of sites have been suggested to date before 500 Ka, but most of these have been criticized on one or more grounds: the artifactual nature of the material (Chilhac, Kärlich, Nevers [Bourbonnais sands], Přezletice, St. Eble, Stranská Skála, Vallonnet, Venta Micena), the basis of the dating (Isernia), or the association between the dated material and the artifacts (Chilhac III, Monte Peglia, Monte Poggiole, Solheihac). In the past, many claims of Late Pliocene and Early Pleistocene sites were based on the argument that simple tools—pebble cores and minimally modified flakes—necessarily indicated great antiquity.

Today, archaeologists recognize that such simple tools occur in assemblages of every prehistoric period and that hydrodynamic factors can, in some cases, mimic the appearance of human flintknapping. Accordingly, the acceptance of claims about early human sites in Europe (as in other regions) must depend heavily on biochronologic evidence and geochronometric determinations. In the early 1990s, such data only weakly supported any of the purported early occurrences.

Moreover, until the mid-1990s, indisputable human fossil remains were entirely lacking in Europe before ca. 500 Ka (or 600, if the oldest possible ages for the Mauer [Germany] mandible and Boxgrove [England] tibia are taken). In addition, unlike northern Africa and Asia, Europe lacked evidence for the presence of pre-"archaic *Homo sapiens*" populations, whether of *H. erectus* or another earlier species. In view of the clear documentation for much earlier human occupation in western (and eastern) Asia, as well as in northeast Africa ('Ain Hanech), the later occupation of Europe appeared to be due to an inability on the part of early humans to exploit temperate forested environments.

The discovery in 1991 of a human mandible at Dmanisi (Georgia) of probable *H. erectus* or *H. ergaster* affinities, in association with unspecialized (Mode 1) lithic artifacts lacking in bifaces, initiated a new period of inquiry into the timing of the earliest European occupations. The dating of this find is problematic, owing to its uncertain stratigraphic relationship to an underlying basalt dating to ca. 1.8 Ma, as well as to burrows containing fauna and sediments of reversed polarity that were excavated into the normally polarized sediment overlying the basalt. Thus, while the Dmanisi mandible is likely to be of Early Pleistocene age, its exact placement before 780 Ka is in some doubt. A date in the Matuyama Chron before the Jaramillo Subchron (ca. 1.4–1.1 Ma) seems most likely, given the associated fauna, the morphology of the fossil, and the dating of other finds from the region, such as 'Ubeidiya in Israel. Middle Pleistocene discoveries near the mountainous boundary between Europe and western Asia (e.g., Yarimburgaz in Turkey, Azych in Azerbaijan) confirm the early human occupation of this general region.

At the other end of the European region, in the Gran Dolina Cave of the Sierra de Atapuerca (Burgos, Spain), Level TD-6 has yielded a series of more than 70 human fossil remains, also associated with an assemblage of more than 200 lithic artifacts, among which bifaces are absent. This occurrence has been dated by paleomagnetism as below the Brunhes-Matuyama boundary, but almost certainly above the Jaramillo event (ca. 1 Ma). Of particular importance is the presence of an Early Pleistocene chronostratigraphic marker in the microfauna from the site (*Mimomys savini*), which serves to confirm the early date. Similar fauna and tools have been recovered from a lower horizon (TD-4), which may approach the Jaramillo. Preliminary analyses of the human remains have led some to suggest that derived characters suggestive of affinities with the Neanderthal lineage are already present in the Gran Dolina sample.

Two other discoveries of simple flake artifacts in southern Spain (Orce region)—at Fontenueva and Barranco del

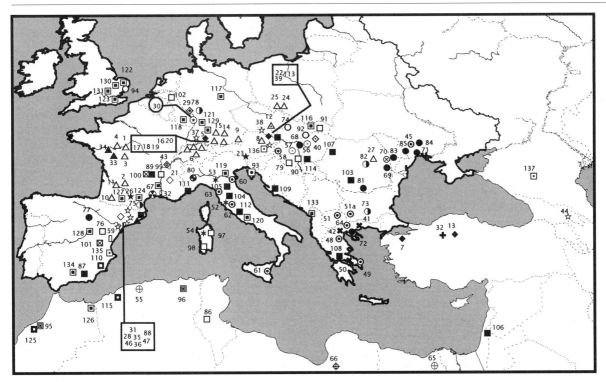

△ Middle Miocene: Pliopithecidae

▲ Late Miocene: Pliopithecidae

◆ Middle Miocene: Griphopithecus

★ Middle Miocene: Dryopithecus

☆ Late Miocene: Dryopithecus

✳ Late Miocene: Oreopithecus

✚ Late Miocene: Ankarapithecus

✖ Late Miocene: Graecopithecus

◇ Middle Miocene: Pliopithecidae & Dryopithecus

⬨ Middle Miocene: Pliopithecidae & Griphopithecus

◈ Late Miocene: Pliopithecidae & Dryopithecus

◈ Late Miocene: ?Pliopithecidae & Dryopithecus

◈ Late Miocene: Pliopithecidae & ?Dryopithecus

✪ Late Miocene: Dryopithecus & ?Mesopithecus

▯ Late Miocene: Macaca

▣ Pliocene: ?Macaca

▢ Pliocene: Macaca

◼ Early Pleistocene: Macaca

▣ Middle Pleistocene: Macaca

▪ Late Pleistocene: Macaca

◼ Pliocene: Paradolichopithecus

⊠ Pliocene: Macaca & Paradolichopithecus

▣ Pliocene: Theropithecus (& ?Macaca?)

▢ Early Pleistocene: Theropithecus

◼ Middle Pleistocene: Theropithecus

⊕ Late Miocene: Macaca: Macaca & Colobinae

⊕ ?Early Pliocene: Colobinae

◐ Pliocene: Macaca & Mesopithecus

⊙ Late Miocene: ?Mesopithecus (cf. ?Dolichopithecus)

◉ Late Miocene: Mesopithecus

○ Pliocene: Mesopithecus

● Pliocene: Dolichopithecus

◑ Pliocene: Mesopithecus & Dolichopithecus

◉ Pliocene: Macaca, Mesopithecus & Dolichopithecus

⊗ Pliocene: Paradolichopithecus, Mesopithecus & Dolichopithecus

Map of Europe (heavy outline) showing major Middle Miocene to Late Pleistocene fossil localities with primates. Symbols indicate age and included primates, while numbers represent site names (in approximate chronological order), as follows: 1, Pontlevoy-Thenay; 2, La Condoue; 3, Manthelan; 4, Pontigné; 5, Engelswies; 6, Elgg; 7, Pasalar*; 8, Göriach; 9, Trimmelkam; 10, Sansan; 11, Liet; 12, Neudorf; 13, Candir*; 14, Gallenbach; 15, Stätzling; 16, Ziemetshausen; 17, Stein Am Rhein; 18, Rümikon; 19, Kreuzlingen; 20, Diessen am Ammersee; 21, La Grive; 22, Klein Hadersdorf; 23, St. Stefan; 24, Opole; 25, Przeworno 2; 26, St. Gaudens; 27, Taut; 28, Castel de Barbera; 29, Eppelsheim; 30, Wissberg; 31, El Firal (Seu de Urgell); 32, Sinap Tepe*; 33, Doué la Fontaine; 34, Magné le Vicomte; 35, Can Ponsic; 36, Can Llobateres; 37, Swabian Jura sites; 38, Mariatal; 39, Götzendorf; 40, Rudabányá '20; 41, Nikiti-1; 42, Ravin de la Pluie, Xirochori-1; 43, Priay; 44, Udabno*; 45, Grebeniki-1; 46, La Tarumba I; 47, Terrassa; 48, Ravin des Zouaves, Vathylakkos, Dytiko; 49, Pikermi; 50, Pyrgos; 51, Titov Veles; 51a, Kalimanci, Kromidovo; 52, Monte Bamboli, Baccinello V2, Montemassi, Casteani, Ribollo; 53, Serrazano; 54, Fiume Santo; 55, Menacer (Marceau)*; 56, Hatvan; 57, Polgardi; 58, Baltavar; 59, Casablanca-M; 60, Brisighella (Monticino); 61, Gravitelli; 62, Baccinello V3; 63, Casino; 64, Maramena; 65, Wadi Natrun*; 66, Sahabi*; 67, Montpellier; 68, Pest(szent)lörinc; 69, Beresti; 70, Malusteni; 71, Kuchurgan valley sites; 72, Megalo Emvolon; 73, Dorkovo; 74, Ivanovce; 75, Serrat d'en Vacquer; 76, Orrios 7; 77, Layna; 78, Wölfersheim; 79, Csarnota 2&3; 80, Fornace RDB; 81, Ciuperceni 2; 82, Baraolt-Capeni; 83, Budey; 84, Kotlovina; 85, Novopetrovka; 86, Ain Brimba*; 87, Moreda-1a; 88, Cova Bonica; 89, Vialette; 90, Beremend; 91, Vcelare 2; 92, Hajnacka; 93, Sandalja; 94, Red Crag; 95, Ahl Al Oughlam*; 96, Ain Jourdel*; 97, Capo Figari; 98, Is Oreris; 99, St. Vallier; 100, Senèze; 101, Puebla de Valverde; 102, Tegelen; 103, Graunceanu; 104, Valdarno; 105, Mugello; 106, 'Ubeidiya*; 107, Betfia; 108, Tourkoubounja 2; 109, Razvodje; 110, Cueva Victoria; 111, Vallonet; 112, Monte Peglia; 113, Deutsch-Altenburg; 114, Somssichhegy 2; 115, Tighenif*; 116, Gombasek, Zlaty Kun; 117, Voigtstedt; 118, Hohensülzen; 119, Zoppega II; 120, Ranuccio; 121, Mosbach-2; 122, Cromer; 123, Swanscombe; 124, St. Estève; 125, Thomas Quarry III*; 126, Ain Mefta*; 127, Montsaunès; 128, Ambrona; 129, Heppenloch; 130, Hoxne; 131, Grays Thurrock; 132, Orgnac; 133, Gajtan; 134, Solana de Zamborino; 135, Cova Negra; 136, Kugelsteinhöhle; 137, Kudaro*. * indicates locality outside geographic area, but included for comparison. The site numbers enclosed in boxes correspond to unnumbered symbols.

Leon—have been similarly dated by paleomagnetic analysis to before the Brunhes-Matuyama boundary, possibly before the Jaramillo. A third Orce-region Early Pleistocene site, Venta Micena, has yielded some stone artifacts and a skull fragment described as hominid; this designation has been widely disputed.

Between the eastern and western extremities of Europe, the best evidence for human occupation pre-500 Ka derives from Italy. From the Po Valley to the southern region of Molise, a number of sites have suggested early occupation of this region. The evidence from the northern cave sites of Monte Peglia and Monte Poggiole is controversial, as the association between artifacts and dates is uncertain. In the south and center, however, three open-air sites are definitely indicative of pre-500 Ka occupation in association with fluvio-lacustrine systems. The best known of these is Isernia-La Pineta, a multiple-horizon site in alternating fine-grained sediments and fluvial gravels. The archaeological levels were dated older than 730 Ka, but some dated material may be reworked volcanic crystals. The artifacts are surely older than an overlying layer dated to 500 Ka, but they could be close to that age, which would still make them significant. Artifacts were made primarily on flint and by the predominant use of the bipolar technique; refitting suggests that at least some of the material is in primary context. Some flakes may have been utilized in butchery activities, possibly related to the large herbivore skeletons (rhinoceros, bison, and elephant) found at Isernia.

Another locality in southern Italy, Notarchirico, in the Venosa group, is a similar multi-horizon open-air site in fluvio-lacustrine sedimentary contexts with associated volcanic tuffs and a large herbivore fauna. In the case of Notarchirico, however, the tuff overlying the oldest horizons is in primary context and appears to date to ca. 650 Ka by TL (thermoluminescence) and tephrostratigraphy in relation to a regional volcanic sequence. The artifacts in these basal horizons include several bifaces, which are the oldest such tools in a securely dated context in Europe. A human femoral shaft is comparable to those of *H. erectus* and presumably to the poorly known "archaic *Homo sapiens*" postcranium.

Finally, in central Italy (south of Rome), similar deposits at Ceprano have yielded a well-preserved human calvaria and stone tools. An Early Acheulean horizon with bone tools is correlated to the ca. 450 Ka level at nearby Ranuccio, which has produced two human incisors. The Ceprano calvaria derives from a lower, otherwise sterile layer that is correlated to a local 700 Ka basalt. It has been termed "late *Homo erectus*" but seems better interpreted as "archaic *Homo sapiens*" (= *H. heidelbergensis*). Still lower in the sequence is a level with fauna and Mode 1 artifacts, from which the skull may have been ultimately derived. An age of 800 Ka has been suggested for the lowest horizon.

Thus, the oldest human occupation in Europe now appears to date to at least 1.1 Ma and to be characterized by human populations initially (in the east) of *H. erectus* type but later (by ca. 800 Ka) by populations with some derived "archaic *Homo sapiens*," if not Neanderthal, features. Associated simple flake industries almost always lack bifaces. This evidence is found across the southern third of the European landmass but is absent from more northerly areas. Before 500 Ka, bifaces also appear but are not numerous. It is possible that this early occupation was intermittent rather than continuous. The area of origin of the first Europeans is unknown. The distribution of sites in the Levant, the Caucasus, Italy, and Spain suggests that any one or more of four routes (trans-Bosphorus, trans-Caucasian, trans-Sicilian, or trans-Gibraltar) might have been possible, although in descending order of likelihood.

Why is there so little clear-cut evidence for an Early Pleistocene human presence in Europe? The scarcity of Early Pleistocene sites from Europe at first seems especially puzzling when compared to the record for Asia, but, in fact, the differences are not so striking. Fragmentary hominin remains are associated with both Developed Oldowan and Early Acheulean assemblages and a temperate Eurasian faunal assemblage at 'Ubeidiya at ca. 1.4 Ma, and human remains with Mode 1 tools from Dmanisi date only slightly younger. In eastern Asia, human fossils unaccompanied by artifacts in Java surely predate 1.0 Ma and may extend back toward 1.8 Ma, but the associations between fossils and dates are still in question; only Sangiran in Java has yielded more than one or two specimens older than ca. 750 Ka. In China, both the date and the identity of the putative 1.8 Ma Longgupo fragments (and scant artifacts) are questioned, and the two teeth from Yuanmou may well date to less than 600 Ka. The Lantian Gongwangling fragmentary cranium is clearly *H. erectus*, and, although it is surely older than 780 Ka, it may not be over 1.1 Ma as claimed. Similarly, archaeological residues without human remains from Nihewan are probably close to 1.0 Ma, but other claimed sites of similar antiquity in China (e.g., Xihoudu) are questionable. Given the rough comparability in temperate area between China and Europe, the number and quality of sites are extremely similar. Only tropical Java has produced more, and that is basically the bonanza of Sangiran. All of this evidence pales in comparison to Africa, but even there, the 1.3–0.6 Ma interval is low in human fossils although well stocked with Acheulean sites (as is western Asia after 1.0 Ma).

Thus, there are really two related questions: Why are all signs of human occupation so scarce? And why are bifaces rare in Europe before 300 Ka when they were so common in Africa? One possibility is that colonization was limited by climate. In this model, the Levant and adjacent parts of western Asia were colonized intermittently from Africa during periods of more open, savannah-like conditions, much like those to which hominins had adapted in the African tropics. Europe, on the other hand, was characterized from the Pliocene onward by relatively long, cloudy winters and a short growing season, adaptive constraints quite different from those of the subtropics. (Regions of China apparently colonized by humans by at least 1.0 Ma are south of 40° N latitude; almost all of Europe is north of this line, excepting only Sicily, southern Sardinia, southern Greece, and parts of Iberia). From the Late Pliocene to the early Middle Pleistocene, glacial cycles lasted ca. 40 Kyr, with slow cooling and warming phases. After ca. 900 Ka, the cycles spanned ca. 100 Kyr and were characterized by long cooling trends of higher amplitude, followed by rapid warming and short interglacial

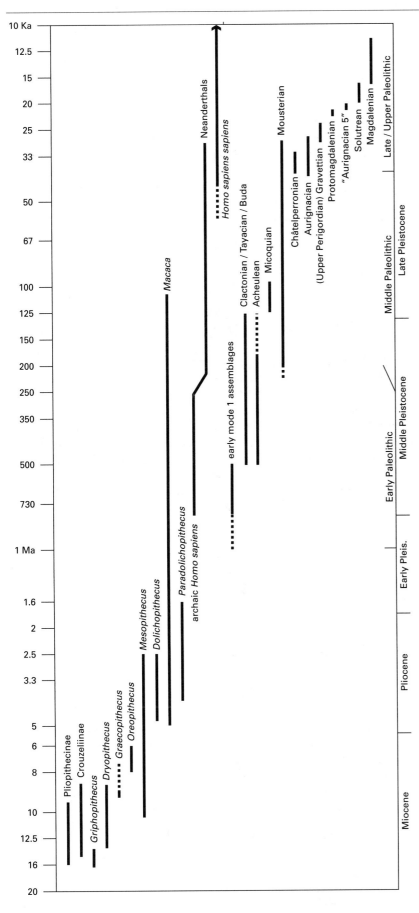

Time ranges of European primate (including human) taxa and archaeological industries. Note: time scale is logarithmic.

intervals. (Warm phases seem to have lasted only 10–20 Kyr from 2.5 Ma onward.)

There are no clear signs of a major shift in the African archaeological record accompanying the transition to longer and higher-magnitude glacial cycles after 0.9 Ma, as one would expect if climate were the sole limiting factor on hominin settlement. However, as noted, the African record is poor from 1.3–0.9 Ma. The greater number of Eurasian sites after this time is *a* signal, but it appears counterintuitive to have *more* humans when the climate is harsher, unless the humans themselves had changed in the interim. It is tempting to suggest that "archaic *Homo sapiens*" was the result of such a change, whether it originated in Africa or western Eurasia.

A related possibility is that colonization of Europe may have required both reliable hunting to survive the longer winters and effective control of fire. Early African *H. erectus* may have obtained animal protein primarily through scavenging, rather than hunting. Controlled fire has been documented in both eastern and southern Africa from ca. 1.6–1.3 Ma onward, but it is rare there, and apparently undocumented in the pre-0.5 Ma record of Europe, so it may not yet have been fully controlled. C. Gamble suggested in 1994 that the delay in colonizing Europe was due to the poor resource base during the winter, which required foragers to cover more ground in smaller groups; this, in turn, required an intensification of social life or, more specifically, of the mental construction of a social life among individuals who were not always present in a face-to-face relationship. Social memory and planning among primates is a major component of primate intelligence and may be indirectly reflected in increasing brain size.

It seems likely that humans did occupy Europe during the Early Pleistocene, but only intermittently and in small numbers, leaving behind only short-term use and expedient tool kits. Why didn't these tool kits contain bifaces? If bifaces served a raw-material-storage function in Africa and in western Asia, the population densities of Europe may have been too low to support this type of reoccupation and reuse strategy. Analogous situations occur in the Early Paleolithic of eastern Asia (east of Movius' line) and the earliest Paleoindian occupation of the Americas. In Asia, it has been suggested that Mode 1 stone tools were used to make more specialized tools from bamboo or that humans arrived there before the Acheulean was "invented" in Africa. In the Americas, putative pre-Clovis tool kits without finely worked fluted points are usually dismissed as poorly dated or of natural origin, but in all three areas it has been suggested that the earliest occupants either lost knapping skills on the trail or had not yet discovered sources of possibly different raw materials than they had been used to using. As always, more data are required to test these hypotheses, but into the late 1990s such data were available in Europe only after 500 Ka.

Archaic *Homo sapiens* and the Acheulean: The Later Middle Pleistocene

The evidence for a hominin presence in Europe is substantially better for the period 0.5–0.25 Ma, and few researchers dispute the validity or the antiquity of the numerous archaeological and paleontological sites assigned to this period.

Sites yielding substantial archaeological remains from this period include Arago, Barbas, Terra Amata, and the Somme River Gravels near Abbeville and St. Acheul in France; Bilzingsleben and Kärlich in Germany; Vértesszöllös in Hungary (perhaps younger than the others); Atapuerca, Torralba, and Ambrona in Spain; and Boxgrove, Clacton-on-Sea, Hoxne, and Swanscombe in southern England. Of these, all except Arago and Atapuerca are stream-channel or lakeshore–beach deposit sites, reflecting the relative predominance of such localities in the archaeological record of this period. The archaeological remains from these sites are broadly comparable to those found in Africa and western Asia during the same (and earlier) periods. In general, there are two kinds of lithic associations: Acheulean assemblages, which include large bifacially flaked core tools; and other assemblages lacking bifaces and composed primarily of pebble cores, retouched-flake tools, and pounding tools. The latter assemblages are known by many regional names (e.g., Tayacian, Evenosian, Buda industry, Clactonian) and differ from one another in few ways other than in the raw materials utilized and the relative frequencies of certain tool types, such as single-blow notched pieces (Clactonian) or crudely shaped points (Tayacian). All are broadly comparable to the Developed Oldowan industries from African Early and Middle Pleistocene sites. While it is difficult to unite these European industries with the broadly contemporaneous Acheulean, from which they differ technologically, there is little reason to suppose they represent the activities of distinct hominin populations. It seems far more reasonable to attribute the differences to situational variables, such as the local raw materials or the kinds of activities being performed, or to drift in the tool-making traditions of various hominin groups.

Some Middle Pleistocene sites, such as Torralba and Ambrona, feature residues of human activity in close association with large-mammal skeletal remains (elephant and horse, in the case of Torralba and Ambrona). Recent studies suggest that many such sites, traditionally seen as kill sites, may instead reflect hominin scavenging of natural death-sites, such as the edges of lakes or seasonal ponds. Circular patches of ash and carbonized bone at several sites, such as Terra Amata and Vértesszöllös, point to human control of fire, which would have been essential for survival through European winters. At least two sites, Terra Amata and Bilzingsleben, contain strong evidence for the manufacture of artificial shelters—in these cases, probably huts or windbreaks. Apart from typological similarities between lithic assemblages, which may reflect little more than the technological simplicity of those industries, there is little evidence of long-distance transport of raw materials or long-distance cultural connections among hominin groups living in Europe during this time. In this respect, the European record differs little from that seen in Africa and Asia during Middle Pleistocene times.

Sites with human fossil remains dating to this period are known throughout mid-latitude and southern Europe, with the exception of the Black Sea region. Some of the most notable Middle Pleistocene hominin fossil sites include Atapuerca (Spain); Arago and perhaps Montmaurin (France); Swanscombe and Boxgrove (England); Bilzingsleben, Stein-

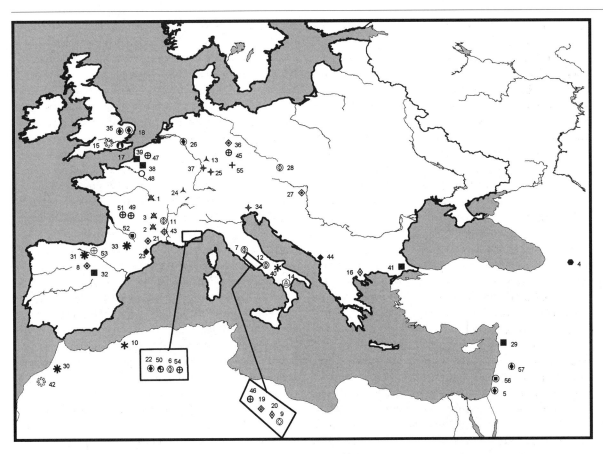

Map of Europe (heavy outline) showing major localities with hominin fossils and archaeological inventories older than Late Pleistocene (>130 Ka). Symbols indicate age, taxon and cultural allocation, while numbers represent site names (in approximate chronological order), as follows: 1, Bourbonnais; 2, Saint Eble; 3, Chilhac; 4, Dmanisi*; 5, 'Ubeidiya*; 6, Vallonet; 7, Monte Peglia; 8, Atapuerca TD6; 9, Ceprano; 10, Tighenif*; 11, Soleilhac; 12, Isernia; 13, Mauer; 14, Venosa sites; 15, Box Grove; 16, Petralona; 17, Swanscombe; 18, Clacton; 19, Ranuccio; 20, Pofi; 21, Arago; 22, Terra Amata; 23, St. Estève; 24, Vergranne; 25, Steinheim; 26, Kärlich; 27, Vértesszöllös; 28, Stranská Skala; 29, Latamne*; 30, Salé*; 31, Atapuerca Sima; 32, Torralba & Ambrona; 33, Montmaurin; 34, Visogliano; 35, Hoxne; 36, Bilzingsleben; 37, Reilingen; 38, Saint Acheul; 39, Abbeville; 40, Altamura; 41, Yarimburgaz; 42, Thomas Quarries*; 43, Orgnac; 44, Gajtan 1; 45, Ehringsdorf; 46, Castel di Guido, Monte delle Gioie, Ponte Mammolo and Rebibbia—Casal de Pazzi; 47, Biache; 48, Levallois; 49, La Chaise; 50, Lazaret; 51, Fontéchevade; 52, Pech de l'Azé; 53, Lezetxiki; 54, Grimaldi (Grotte du Prince); 55, Hunas; 56, Tabun*; 57, Jabrud*. * indicates locality outside geographic area, but included for comparison.

Legend:

⊠ ?Mode 1 ("geofacts"?)

⬣ Homo erectus & Mode 1

▲ Early "archaic Homo sapiens"

⊹ Late "archaic Homo sapiens"

✛ Early Neanderthal

◇ ?Early "archaic H. sapiens" & ?Mode 1

◆ Early "archaic H. sapiens" & Mode 1?

◆ Mode 1 tools

◈ Early "archaic H. sapiens" & Mode 1

◍ ?Mode 1 tools

■ Acheulean

❋ Early "archaic H. sapiens" & Acheulean

✳ Late "archaic H. sapiens" & Acheulean

✱ ?Early "archaic H. sapiens" & Acheulean

◍ ?Early "archaic H. sapiens" & Mode 1 & Acheulean

◐ Mode 1 & Acheulean

◌ Early "archaic H. sapiens" & Mode 1 & Acheulean

◮ Late "archaic H. sapiens" & Mode 1 & Acheulean

⊕ Early Neanderthal & Acheulean & Early Mousterian

○ Early Mousterian

⊕ ?Early Neanderthal & Early Mousterian

⊕ Early Neanderthal & Early Mousterian

⊕ ?Early Neanderthal & ?Early Mousterian

◙ Acheulean & Early Mousterian

⊕ Early "archaic H. sapiens" & Mode 1 & Acheulean
& ?Early Mousterian

heim, Mauer, and perhaps Reilingen (Germany); Vértesszöllös (Hungary); and Petralona (Greece). The taxonomy of these fossils is highly controversial: Although some specimens have been attributed to *H. erectus*, most authors refer to them as "archaic *Homo sapiens*" or, more recently, *H. heidelbergensis* (originally coined by Schoetensack in 1908 for the Mauer mandible). Many, if not all, specimens exhibit a mosaic pattern of primitive features undoubtedly reflecting their *H. erectus* ancestry mixed with derived characteristics resulting from a combination of genetic drift and natural selection for morphological adaptations, perhaps to colder climates. The range of estimated cranial capacities overlaps the mean of the later *H. erectus* sample from Asia but may average somewhat higher. Some fossils (e.g., Bilzingsleben) exhibit the typical angulated occipital region of *H. erectus*, while others (Petralona, Atapuerca, Steinheim, Swanscombe, Vértesszöllös) have a more rounded occipital region and a reduced and more inferiorly directed occipital torus. Similarly, the faces of Petralona, Atapuerca, Steinheim, and Arago are quite pneumatized and exhibit both midfacial prognathism and the divided superciliary arches of the later Neanderthals, while retaining some primitive features not found in the latter group. In the presence of characteristics shared with later Neanderthals, the Middle Pleistocene Europeans differed from their African contemporaries. There can be little doubt that the wide swings of the climatic pendulum during this period led to the isolation of many European populations and, consequently, to morphological divergence due to small groups breeding in comparative isolation. (This same hypothesis could also be applied to Africa and eastern Asia, where the periodic expansion of deserts and tropical rain forests would have been formidable isolating mechanisms.)

Hominin fossils dating to 0.25–0.13 Ma exhibit additional morphological characteristics suggesting close association with the distinctive Weichselian (last glacial) West Eurasian Neanderthals. Among the most important remains are those from Ehringsdorf (Germany); Pontnewydd (Britain); and Lazaret, Biache-St. Vaast, La Chaise, and Fontéchevade (France). Some scholars term this group *early Neanderthals,* emphasizing both their connections to, and their differences from, the later, or *classic,* Neanderthals. Others consider them late archaics (or *pre-Neanderthals*), little different from their predecessors, while another school hardly distinguishes them from the "classics." If a formal taxonomic distinction is drawn between *H. heidelbergensis* and *H. neanderthalensis*, it is the "early Neanderthals" that most often fall into limbo. On the other hand, under a model of the accretion of derived Neanderthal characteristics over time in the European human lineage, this group fits well with their beginnings of the occipital bun and suprainiac fossa, taurodontism, and other features, as discussed by D. Dean and colleagues in 1998.

Shifts in the accompanying lithic industries for this period include the development of prepared-core (Levallois) techniques and an increasing number of Acheulean bifaces exhibiting secondary thinning and careful shaping seemingly beyond the minimum amount necessary to produce a functioning cutting edge. A tendency for more controlled shaping of retouched-flake tools has also been noted, and assemblages with few handaxes and many such shaped flake tools are often termed *Premousterian* or *Early Mousterian,* blurring the traditional typological distinction between the European Early and Middle Paleolithic. Instead, there seems to have been a transition interval, with both Mousterian and Acheulean-like assemblages being manufactured between ca. 200 and 150 Ka, after which the Mousterian was dominant (although the Micoquian of the earlier Late Pleistocene represented a continuation of Early Paleolithic styles and forms). This pattern and timing is rather similar to that seen in Africa, where the Middle Stone Age (MSA) also began ca. 200 Ka and may have briefly overlapped the final Acheulean.

Additional evidence for the construction of simple shelters (Lazaret, Ariendorf) and somewhat more convincing evidence for technologically assisted hunting of large mammals (Lehringen, La Cotte de St. Brelade) date to the period 250–130 Ka. On the whole, however, the archaeological evidence for the final Middle Pleistocene differs little from that from 500–250 Ka. The difficulties of precisely dating a relatively patchy European archaeological and paleontological record make it difficult to adequately evaluate models proposing either long-term regional continuity or, alternatively, repeated cycles of colonization and extinction or population bottlenecking among Middle Pleistocene European hominins. Inasmuch as there is scarce evidence for hominin activities in boreal forests or tundra, however, it seems reasonable to suppose that Middle Pleistocene climatic fluctuations caused significant shifts in the distribution and demographic structure of hominin populations.

The Middle Paleolithic and the Classic Neanderthals

Traditionally, European prehistorians have distinguished a Middle Paleolithic (ca. 110–35 Ka) from the preceding Early Paleolithic on the basis of declining frequencies of large Acheulean core tools, increasing use of prepared-core techniques, increasing numbers of retouched-flake tools, more numerous cave occupations, and the evolution of distinctive Neanderthal populations. As noted above, however, there are essential continuities in all of these areas between the Middle Paleolithic and its Acheulean and Premousterian predecessors. Because of this, many scholars now recognize the Early/Middle Paleolithic distinction to be somewhat arbitrary, at least in Europe.

During the Eemian interglacial (ca. 130–115 Ka), Neanderthals appear to have spread widely across Europe and into Southwest Asia, with representative European sites including Saccopastore (Italy), Krapina (Croatia), and Gánovce (Czech Republic). Fewer sites of this age are known, in part because of the interglacial scouring of caves due to an increase in glacial meltwater and precipitation and in part because of the lack of sedimentation, whether of cold-fractured detritus in rockshelters or of wind-blown loess in open-air sites.

During much of the last or Weichselian glaciation (ca. 115–30 Ka), Neanderthals were the only hominids in Europe. They exhibit a number of derived morphological characteristics, including pronounced mid-facial prognathism and a heavily pneumatized face; robust, doubly arched

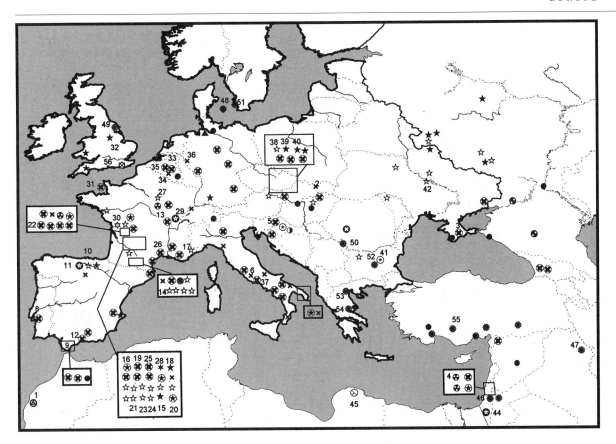

Map of Europe (heavy outline) showing major localities with hominid fossils and archaeological inventories younger than Middle Pleistocene (<130 Ka). Symbols indicate age, taxon and cultural allocation, while numbers represent site names (grouped in approximate chronological order—older than 90 Ka, 90–10 Ka, and younger than 10 Ka, mostly from west to east). All important sites shown as symbols, but only a selection is numbered and identified, as follows: 1, Jebel Irhoud*; 2, Gánovce; 3, Kiik-Koba; 4, Mount Carmel (Skhul, el-Wad)*; 5, Krapina; 6, Saccopastore; 7, Bañolas; 8, Figueira Brava; 9, Forbes Quarry; 10, Altamira; 11, Castillo; 12, Zafarraya; 13, Arcy sur Cure; 14, Aurignac; 15, Combe-Capelle; 16, Combe-Grenal; 17, Cosquer; 18, Cro-Magnon; 19, La Chapelle aux Saints; 20, La Ferrassie; 21, La Madeleine; 22, La Quina; 23, Lascaux; 24, Laugerie Haute; 25, Le Moustier; 26, L'Hortus; 27, Pincevent; 28, Roc de Combe & Le Piage; 29, Solutré; 30, St.-Césaire; 31, Cotte-de-St.- Brelade; 32, Mother Grundy's Parlour; 33, Engis; 34, La Naulette; 35, Spy; 36, Neandertal; 37, Monte Circeo; 38, Dolni Vestonice; 39, Mladec; 40, Predmosti; 41, Bacho Kiro; 42, Mezhirich; 43, Sungir*; 44, Boker Tachtit; 46, Jericho*; 47, Jarmo*; 48, Maglemose; 49, Star Carr; 50, Lepenski Vir*; 51, Vedbaek; 52, Karanovo; 53, Nea Nikomedia; 54, Sesklo; 55, Catal Hüyük*; 56, Piltdown. * indicates locality outside geographic area, but included for comparison. Note that (?) in symbol key indicates an industry usually present at these sites but possibly questionable at some. Numbers in boxes refer to neighboring symbols; not all boxed symbols are identified by number.

Legend:

- Acheulean & ?Early Mousterian
- Late Neanderthal & Mousterian (& sometimes Acheulean)
- Late Neanderthal & ?Mousterian
- Late Neanderthal
- Mousterian
- early? H. s. sapiens & Mousterian
- "Pre-Aurignacian" & early? H. s. sapiens & Mousterian & Upper Paleolithic
- Late Neanderthal & (?) Mousterian & Upper Paleolithic
- ?Late Neanderthal & Mousterian & (?) Upper Paleolithic
- Late Neanderthal & H. s. sapiens & Mousterian & Upper Paleolithic
- H. s. sapiens & Mousterian & Upper Paleolithic
- Mousterian & Upper Paleolithic
- Late Neanderthal & Chatelperronian
- Chatelperronian & Aurignacian
- Homo sapiens sapiens
- Upper Paleolithic
- H. s. sapiens & Upper Paleolithic
- H. s. sapiens "wraith" & Upper Paleolithic
- Post Paleolithic (Epipaleolithic, Mesolithic, Neolithic)
- Piltdown forgery

supraorbital torus; large nasal cavity with medial projections; a long, low cranial vault with lambdoidal flattening; occipital bunning and a suprainiac fossa; and a juxtamastoid crest larger than the mastoid process. Molar teeth have enlarged pulp cavities and partially divided roots (a condition known as taurodontism), and these teeth are placed forward of the ramus, creating a retromolar gap. Many Neanderthals also exhibit extreme linguo-labial paramasticatory wear on their anterior dentition, suggesting that these teeth were habitually used as a "third hand" in object manipulation. Postcranially, the hypertrophy of Neanderthal skeletons provides numerous indications of extreme strength, such as enlarged articular surfaces and relatively large cortical bone segments. As one would expect for hominins repeatedly stressed by cold conditions, Neanderthals have relatively shorter distal limbs than do contemporaneous populations from warmer climates, such as the early modern humans from Skhūl and Qafzeh in the Levant. Western or classic, Neanderthals were somewhat more derived than eastern European and Southwest Asian varieties, which seem to have changed little from the interglacial populations. This is presumably a result of greater adaptation to cold climate in the west, where the Neanderthals were closer to the harsh climates near the ice front.

There is intense argument about the phyletic position and taxonomy of the Neanderthals. Some authors consider them a distinctive temporal subspecies, *Homo sapiens neanderthalensis*, extending back to 130 Ka, 200+ Ka (the earliest Mousterian), or beyond (Atapuerca, Steinheim, even Petralona and Arago). This view is compatible with either the concept of Neanderthals as a long-separated lineage that was replaced by anatomically modern humans with little, if any, interbreeding, or the view that anatomically modern Europeans were descended, at least in part, from some Neanderthal population. An alternative taxonomy recognizes the species *Homo neanderthalensis* for some or all of the European lineage, perhaps separating this species at some point in time (and morphology) from an earlier *H. heidelbergensis*. Proponents of this view all see the Neanderthals as an evolutionary dead-end.

In either case, Neanderthal fossils extend from Gibraltar and Zafarraya in southern Spain to Belgium (Spy, Engis), across Germany (Neander Valley) and Italy (Monte Circeo), through the Czech Republic (Kulna), Hungary (Sübalyük) and Croatia (Vindija), and into Ukraine (Kiik-Koba) and western Asia. The largest series is found in France, with important specimens from La Chapelle-aux-Saints, La Quina, La Ferrassie, Le Moustier, and Saint-Césaire. Many of these specimens are poorly dated but appear to range between 100 and 40 Ka. The youngest-known Neanderthals include those from Saint-Césaire (36 ± 3 Ka), Arcy-sur-Cure (Grotte du Renne, 33.8 ± 0.7 Ka), Zafarraya (ca. 33–30 Ka), and Figueira Brava (Portugal, 31 ± 0.7 Ka). It is especially intriguing that the latest populations appear to have inhabited southern Iberia, perhaps seeking refuge from the advancing "moderns," even in warmer environments than usual. Northern sites of this period are poorly known, but one might predict finding additional late Neanderthals in northwestern Europe, another marginal region.

Neanderthals are associated most consistently with the Mousterian archaeological complex in Europe. In Southwest Asia, early anatomically modern humans (at Skhūl and Qafzeh) as well as Neanderthals are found with Mousterian assemblages; in Morocco, Mousterian tools are associated with the transitional archaic-modern Jebel Irhoud population. The essential characteristics of the Mousterian, described above, probably reflect increasing use of hafted stone tools in place of heavy core tools such as Acheulean bifaces. Variants of the Mousterian have been recognized on the basis of relative frequencies of Acheulean bifaces, blanks struck with the Levallois technique, and a wide range of morphologically distinct retouched tools. F. Bordes used this typology to identify six major Mousterian variants: Typical, Denticulate, Charentian (with Ferrassie and Quina subvariants), Mousterian of Acheulean Tradition (with MTA A and MTA B subvariants), Vasconian, and Asinipodian, the latter two being found mainly near the Mediterranean coast. Bordes argued that the differences between these industries reflected different Neanderthal cultures or ethnic groups. In contrast, L. Binford ascribed the same variation to functional variability (i.e., differing relative frequencies of tasks carried out at specific sites). Much Mousterian variability is now understood to reflect the influence of raw materials, mobility patterns, and tool function, use, and resharpening, as well as sequential changes in culture. There are broad typological and technological continuities across much of the European Mousterian. Nevertheless, some regional differences are apparent (e.g., the relatively higher frequencies of bifacial core tools in eastern Europe). The very end of the Middle Paleolithic witnesses the development of typologically distinct industries with restricted geographic distributions, such as Uluzzian (Italy), the Mousterian of Acheulean Tradition (central France), and the Altmuhlian (central-southeastern Europe). Some key Mousterian sites include Le Moustier, Combe Grenal, La Ferrassie, La Quina, L'Hortus, La Chapelle-aux-Saints, Pech de l'Azé, and Le Regourdou (all in France); Krapina (Croatia); Monte Circeo (Italy); and Gorham's Cave (England).

Occasional blade technologies appear especially after 100 Ka in the Lower-Middle Rhine region of Germany, northern France, and the Netherlands. Leaf-shaped points, which may have been hafted, are an even later phenomenon in the east, dating to 70 Ka or later. Changes in ranging pattern, food procurement, and lithic technology are also documented for central Italy after 55 Ka. Indeed, some authors have interpreted these and other technological developments (an increase in Upper Paleolithic tool forms) as indications of earlier contact between Neanderthals and anatomically modern humans; blades and points are a prominent feature of African Middle Paleolithic industries from the beginning, and of Southwest Asian industries, as well. (In the latter case, the points are rarely leaf shaped and almost never bifacially worked). Most authors, however, see these developments in Europe as purely local variants of Middle Paleolithic industries.

On the strength of the faunal evidence from archaeological sites, Middle Paleolithic Neanderthals appear to have practiced somewhat more predatory strategies or more effective scavenging than their predecessors. Numerous ashy concentrations from Mousterian sites attest to control over fire, although there are few signs of *warmth banking*, such as heating stones around hearths. Some Mousterian sites feature substantial (more than 1 m in diameter) pits that may have served as storage places, but this interpretation is controversial. Like their predecessors, some Mousterian sites (e.g., Molodova 1, Level 4) feature alignments of bones and stones that could represent simple shelters, but there are few clear signs of internal structure to Mousterian occupations. Most sites are probably palimpsests (multiple overlays) of numerous short-term occupations. Whether because of their biological or their cultural adaptations, Neanderthals may have been the first inhabitants of the cold steppe and periglacial regions of northeastern Europe.

As with the Early Paleolithic, there are few signs of long-distance transport of raw materials. Unlike Early Paleolithic sites, however, some Mousterian sites contain skeletons of adults and juveniles in anatomical articulation. The more complete skeletons have been interpreted as burials, although this is disputed by some scholars. Some perforated bones and teeth and lumps of mineral pigments (ocher and manganese), including those with signs of use (which are called *crayons*), as well as a putative bone flute from Divje Babe (Slovenia), may hint at more complex symbolic dimensions to Mousterian behavior, but most of this evidence involves singular finds from sites scattered widely in space and time.

Modern Humans and the Upper Paleolithic

The term *Upper Paleolithic* is used widely in Europe to refer to blade-and-burin industries that show the social, economic, and symbolic intensification typical of the Late Paleolithic as understood in this book. The latter term is used globally (like Middle Paleolithic), while the former is here restricted to Europe and southwestern Asia (analogous to Mousterian or MSA). In Europe, the appearance of anatomically modern humans coincides with a technological transition from Middle Paleolithic prepared-core technologies to Late Paleolithic prismatic-blade industries. Whether the Middle-Upper Paleolithic transition is meaningfully linked to the phyletic transformation or the extinction and replacement of Neanderthals is the subject of major debate.

The Middle-Upper Paleolithic transition occurred during a period of moderate climatic amelioration ca. 38–30 Ka, and it seems to have taken different forms and followed different time trajectories in different parts of Europe. The earliest Upper Paleolithic industry in France is the Châtelperronian, which is represented at such sites as Arcy-sur-Cure (Grotte du Renne), Saint-Césaire, Le Piage, Roc de Combe, and Le Moustier. The Châtelperronian features Levallois prepared-core, as well as prismatic-blade, techniques and numerous steeply backed blades. A number of worked-bone objects, including awls, and perforated and incised animal teeth have also been found in Châtelperronian contexts. Because of its backed-blade component, the Châtelperronian was once regarded as the earliest phase of a developmental sequence culminating in fully Upper Paleolithic Perigordian/Gravettian industries (and thus was often called Perigordian I). Now, most researchers regard the Châtelperron-

ian as an outgrowth of late Western Mousterian (most likely the MTA B) with an infusion of Late Paleolithic cultural elements. It is difficult to tell whether the seemingly Upper Paleolithic components of the Châtelperronian reflect indigenous innovations or influences from contemporaneous Aurignacian cultures. Châtelperronian occupations may be stratified between Aurignacian occupations at Le Piage and Roc de Combe.

Following discoveries of Neanderthal remains in Châtelperronian levels at Grotte du Renne and Saint-Césaire, many researchers associate the Châtelperronian with relict Neanderthal populations. A similar interpretation seems plausible for the transitional Uluzzian industry from Italy and Greece. From the British Isles to the North European Plain, to Germany, Poland, and the Carpathians, a number of such transitional industries (the Lincombian, Altmuhlian, Szeletian, and Jermanowican) feature large, bifacially thinned points. The hominin fossil associations for these industries are not yet clear. While Mousterian and transitional industries may continue in very limited areas (e.g., southern Spain) until ca. 30–28 Ka, after this date there are no known Mousterian sites or Neanderthal remains.

The arrival of the Aurignacian, the first fully Upper Paleolithic industry in most areas, represents an abrupt discontinuity with past industries. In no case can the Aurignacian be derived from a local predecessor. The earliest Aurignacian sites, predating 40 Ka, are in the Balkans (Bacho Kiro and Temnata, both in Bulgaria). By ca. 40–38 Ka, Aurignacian sites are known from the central Danube Basin (e.g., Istállöskö) and northeastern Spain (Arbreda, Castillo). The late survival of Neanderthals and Mousterian industries in southern Iberia suggests that the Spanish Aurignacian sites represent a diffusion from the east rather than a separate movement of anatomically modern humans across the straits of Gibraltar—in any case, Aurignacian-like industries are absent in North Africa at this time.

Indeed, the Aurignacian has no known antecedents outside Europe, particularly in the region from which anatomically modern humans might most reasonably have migrated: North Africa and Southwest Asia. The Aurignacian is found in the Levant, but only after ca. 36 Ka, where it appears to represent an intrusive cultural element into a sequence of local Upper Paleolithic industries derived from Mousterian (Ahmarian, transitional industry at Boker Tachtit). This Levantine Aurignacian has been compared to the Aurignacian of the Balkan region and may represent a migration from that area into western Asia. The Aurignacian as a whole may possibly be derived from Mousterian industries farther east, such as the Zagros Aurignacian or the Baradostian of Shanidar (Iraq) and Warwasi (Iran), but this is very debatable. It is more likely that the Aurignacian represents a European adaptation by a new population to the unique conditions and opportunities of that region, much as Clovis may have represented a new and dynamic response to the opportunities of North America. Such innovation may spread relatively rapidly, although it is now clear that the Aurignacian and the Upper Paleolithic in general took at least 6 Kyr to reach much of the European continent and more than

10 Kyr to entirely supplant Mousterian industries and associated Neanderthals.

Faunal assemblages from Aurignacian sites indicate a wide range of hunting strategies, with a greater emphasis on reindeer than seen in most Mousterian sites. Faunal assemblages associated with this and later Upper Paleolithic industries feature larger proportions of steppe and tundra species, such as mammoth, horse, ibex, and reindeer, reflecting the increasingly colder conditions. Much of the faunal evidence points to Upper Paleolithic groups intercepting large mammal herds at strategic points along migration routes, a strategy that implies considerably greater logistical planning and flexibility than is evident in the Mousterian. Aurignacian sites also include small, deep pit-hearths with heating stones, capable of high temperatures and long-term heat conservation. Mediterranean shells found far inland, ivory from outside the apparent range of mammoths, and exotic flint materials from many Aurignacian sites point to exchange networks that were more extensive than Middle Paleolithic ones. Aurignacian sites also contain some of the earliest Paleolithic images, in the form of musical instruments and carved bone and ivory figurines, as well as other carved, incised, notched, and perforated objects with multiple symbolic meanings. The earliest occurrences of parietal art from French sites such as Chauvet and Gargas may date to the later phases of the Aurignacian.

The identity of the early Aurignacian groups is one of the greatest mysteries of Upper Paleolithic archaeology. Early modern humans were first recovered at the classic site of Cro-Magnon in France, but their association with the early Aurignacian industry at the type site is uncertain, due to the nature of the 1869 excavations. Most purportedly early Aurignacian skeletal remains are either highly fragmentary (e.g., Vindija, Barma Grande) or in questionable stratigraphic associations (e.g., Combe Capelle, Engis 2, Grotte des Enfants [Grimaldi], Mladeč).

Aurignacian industries are followed by Perigordian or Gravettian ones, characterized by backed points, ca. 28–20 Ka. A variety of hafted projectile-point types suggests increased sophistication in hunting weaponry. Although Gravettian sites are linked by backed-tool technology and carved female figurines, such as the "venuses" of Willendorf (Austria), Lespugne and Laussel (France), and Dolni Věstonice (Czech Republic), the degree of regional variation across the vast area involved suggests the presence of ethnic signatures in the archaeological materials. The eastern European variant of the Gravettian, extending through Ukraine and Russia, is particularly rich in carved female and animal figurines and in elaborate burials (e.g., Sungir). At Dolni Věstonice figurines of clay and loess were apparently baked at temperatures of up to 800°C, possibly as part of a ritual sequence. Storage pits and piles of mammoth bones for food, fuel, and hut or windbreak construction reflect a greater degree of planning in daily life. Textile impressions on clay pellets from this site suggest the manufacture of twined baskets or other twined fabrics by Gravettians.

During the last glacial maximum (22–18 Ka), northern Europe—including England, Belgium, northern France, and Germany—was either abandoned or very sparsely populated. The same gap in occupation is evident in many central and eastern European sites, including those of Ukraine and Russia. In southern France and Spain during this time, on the other hand, Solutrean industries reflect greatly improved hunting specializations as well as the most refined stone-tool technology of the Paleolithic, with beautifully flaked foliate and shouldered points. Bone needles with eyes suggest refinements in dress and personal adornment, while elaborate bas-reliefs decorate the walls of some rockshelter living sites, such as at Roc de Combe and Cap Blanc (France).

In northern and western Europe and extending to Poland, Austria, and the Czech Republic, Magdalenian industries (18–11 Ka) with increasingly specialized economies, microlithic technology, and elaborate bone working complete the classic Upper Paleolithic sequence. This sequence is based on deeply stratified sites such as Abri Pataud, Laugerie Haute, Roc de Combe, La Madeleine, and La Ferrassie, all in southwestern France. New Magdalenian hunting implements include the barbed point, harpoon, atlatl, and an array of fishing implements and net weights; the evidence indicates extensive use of fish and birds and specialized reindeer hunting at suitable intercept locations. A number of free-standing structures known from open-air sites include simple huts and clusters of tent foundations (possibly windbreaks) such as at Plateau Parrain, Gönnersdorf, and Pincevent. Magdalenian sites also represent the high point of large-scale ritual and symbolic activity, documented not only in the elaboration of carved bone and antler objects in living sites, but also in deep painted-cave sites like Font-de-Gaume, Lascaux, and Altamira. Indeed, most of the painted, sculpted, carved, and engraved images that make up the rich record of Upper Paleolithic art date to this period. Microregional variations in tool types and art forms suggest ethnic differentiation on a new and more intensive scale. One interpretation is that the Magdalenian was a period of population growth and eventual resource stress, which resulted in increasing territoriality, intensification of symbolic behavior, and the greater use of small-scale resources. This conclusion is borne out by bioarchaeological studies that have shown greater indicators of stress (Harris lines, enamel hypoplasias) in Magdalenian skeletons than in those of the Solutrean or early Upper Paleolithic.

In southern and eastern Europe, a tendency to microlithic tool technologies is also evident but without the specific cultural markers of the Magdalenian. These industries are sometimes grouped as Evolved Gravettian or Epigravettian and contain endscrapers, burins, perforators, backed and truncated blades, bone awls, needles and points, and numerous microlithic tools at sites such as Grimaldi (Italy), Kostenki-Borshevo (Russia), and Molodova and Mezhirich (Ukraine). On the Russian Plain, elaborate dwellings of mammoth jaws and tusks alongside much simpler ones, as well as considerable differences in the quantities of exotic materials, some from hundreds of miles away, imply the existence of trade routes, social stratification, and interpersonal and intergroup complexity on an unprecedented scale for Paleolithic people, far beyond that seen in western Europe.

The Early Postglacial: Mesolithic and Neolithic

Deglaciation began ca. 18 Ka and accelerated rapidly after that point to ca. 8 Ka. During this period, sea levels rose rapidly and steppe-tundra zones retreated northward, replaced by successive waves of boreal and deciduous forest. The archaeological cultures of this period are called *Mesolithic,* and they differ from their predecessors primarily in featuring larger proportions of microliths that have been truncated and backed into geometric forms, such as crescents, triangles, trapezoids, and rectangles. The appearance of these microliths is generally thought to signal the greater use of the bow in hunting. Mesolithic subsistence was based to a greater extent on hunting of solitary and small herd-game, as well as on fishing and birding. On the newly deglaciated North European Plain, sites such as Hohen Viecheln suggest that the first human occupants of these regions (e.g., Ahrensburgian and Hamburgian groups) continued late-glacial hunting adaptations, focus on reindeer and elk. Later North European Mesolithic groups, such as the Maglemosian, increasingly focused their efforts on red deer, wild cattle, and marine mammals. Mesolithic cultures from the temperate forests of Europe, such as the Azilian, Tardenoisian, Sauveterrian, and Montadian, furnish evidence of scheduled exploitation of forest resources, including acorns, hazelnuts, wild cattle, boar, fallow deer, red deer, and ibex. The British waterlogged site of Star Carr has provided detailed information about Mesolithic economic activities, including evidence for domesticated dog. In general, the Mesolithic witnesses a decline in long-distance connections between different regions and an increasingly local and regional scale of social organization. Later Mesolithic sites are concentrated around more productive estuarine areas, where prolonged shellfish collection created enormous middens (piles of discarded shells). The cemetery of Vedbaek (Denmark) provides evidence for complex Mesolithic mortuary rituals. Both the quantity and the quality of representational art declines markedly at the Paleolithic-Mesolithic transition.

Neolithic farming economies featuring cereal cultivation and domesticated sheep, goat, cattle, and pigs first appear in southeastern Europe ca. 8 Ka and nearly simultaneously along the Spanish and French Mediterranean. In southeastern Europe between 8 and 6 Ka, sites such as Karanovo, Aichilleon, and Sesklo provide long sequences of Early Neolithic occupations whose architecture, ceramic designs, and mortuary practices clearly point to influences from earlier Neolithic cultures in Anatolia. The origins of the Southwest European Neolithic (called the *Cardial Neolithic* after distinctive *Cardium* shell impressions in its pottery) are less clear. The presence of Cardial Neolithic sites on the Moroccan coast could suggest dispersal of agriculture to Europe from North Africa. The period between 7.5 and 6.5 Ka witnessed the spread of agriculture into temperate Europe. The first phase seems to have involved a rapid dispersal, probably an actual physical migration of peoples along the Danube, where the Linearbandkeramik culture is associated with rich loessal soils. The spread of the Neolithic along the Atlantic coast is less well documented, but it appears to have been accompanied by *Megalithic* traditions involving large earthen barrows and stone chambered tombs. By 5.5 Ka, Neolithic farmsteads had been established in the northernmost reaches of the British Isles and Scandinavia. Trade patterns in the Neolithic were extremely complex, involving the dispersal of flint, stone axes, amber, shells, gold, copper, tin, and other materials through a variety of overlapping networks. These trade networks appear to have been a significant factor in the rise of Bronze Age chiefdoms and states.

See also Abbevillian; Abri Pataud; Acheulean; Adapidae; Adapiformes; Africa; Altamira; Ambrona; Anaptomorphinae; Arago; Archaeological Sites; Archaic Homo sapiens; Asia, Eastern and Southern; Asia, Western; Atapuerca; Aurignacian; Azilian; Bacho Kiro; Biache-St. Vaast; Bilzingsleben; Blade; Bordes, François; Burin; Catarrhini; Cenozoic; Ceprano; Cercopithecidae; Cercopithecinae; Chatelperronian; Chauvet Cave; Chilhac; China; Chopper-Chopping Tools; Clactonian; Colobinae; Cro-Magnon; Cyclostratigraphy; Dmanisi; Dolni Věstonice; Domestication; Dryopithecinae; Early Paleolithic; Economy, Prehistoric; Engis; Eocene; Fire; France; Gargas; Glaciation; Gravettian; Grimaldi; Griphopithecus; Hamburgian; Handaxe; Holocene; Hominidae; Hominoidea; Homo sapiens; Isernia; Istallöskö; Kostenki; Krapina; L'Escale; L'Hortus; La Chapelle-aux-Saints; La Cotte de St. Brelade; La Ferrassie; La Quina; Lagar Velho; Lantian; Lascaux; Laugerie Sites; Le Moustier; Lehringen; Levallois; Longgupo; Magdalenian; Maglemosian; Mauer; Mesolithic; Mezhirich; Microchoerinae; Middle Paleolithic; Miocene; Mladeč; Modjokerto; Molodova; Monte Peglia; Montmaurin; Mousterian; Neanderthals; Neolithic; Nihewan; Notharctidae; Omomyidae; Oreopithecus; Paleobiogeography; Paleocene; Paleolithic; Paleolithic Calendar; Paleolithic Image; Paleolithic Lifeways; Paromomyidae; Périgord; Perigordian; Petralona; Pincevent; Plate Tectonics; Pleistocene; Plesiadapidae; Plesiadapiformes; Pliocene; Pliopithecidae; Ponginae; Pontnewydd; Prepared-Core; Přezletice; Raw Materials; St. Acheul; Saint-Césaire; St. Eble; Sangiran Dome; Sauveterrian; Saxonellidae; Scraper; Sea-Level Change; Site Types; Soleihac; Solutrean; Star Carr; Steinheim; Stone-Tool Making; Stranská Skála; Swanscombe; Szeletian; Tardenoisian; Tarsiiformes; Tayacian; Terra Amata; Time Scale; Vallonnet; Venosa Sites; Vérteszöllös; Vindija; Yuanmou. [E.D., A.S.B., J.J.S.]

Further Readings

Adovasio, J.M., Soffer, O., and Klima, B. (1996) Upper Palaeolithic fibre technology: Interlaced woven finds from Pavlov I, Czech Republic, c. 26,000 years ago. Antiquity 70:526–534.

Andrews, P., Harrison, T., Delson, E., Martin, L.B., and Bernor, R.L. (1996) Systematics and biochronology of European and Southwest Asian Miocene catarrhines. In R.L. Bernor, V. Fahlbusch, and H.W. Mittmann (eds.): Evolution of Western Eurasian Late Neogene Mammal Faunas. New York: Columbia University Press, pp. 168–207.

Antunes, M.T., and Santinho Cunha, A. (1992) Neanderthalian remains from Figueira Brava Cave, Portugal. Géobios 25:681–692.

Bogucki, P. (1996) The spread of early farming in Europe. Am. Sci. 84:242–253.

Bonifay, E., and Vandermeersch, B., eds. (1991) Les Premiers Européens. Paris: Comité Travaux Historiques Scientifiques.

Cunliffe, B., ed. (1994) The Oxford Illustrated Prehistory of Europe. New York: Oxford University Press.

Dean, D., Hublin, J.-J., Holloway, R., and Ziegler, R. 1998. On the phylogenetic position of the pre-Neanderthal specimen from Reilingen, Germany. J. Hum. Evol. 34:485–508.

Dennell, R. (1983) European Economic Prehistory: A New Approach. London: Academic.

Dennell, R., and Roebroeks, W. (1996) The earliest colonization of Europe: The short chronology revisited. Antiquity 70:535–542.

d'Errico, F., Zilhão, J., Julien, M., Baffier, D., and Pelegrin, J. (1998). Neanderthal acculturation in Western Europe: a critical review of the evidence and its interpretation. Current Anthropology 39(supplement):S1-S44

Gamble, C. (1986) The Palaeolithic Settlement of Europe. Cambridge: Cambridge University Press.

Gamble, C. (1994) Timewalkers: The Prehistory of Global Colonization. Cambridge, Mass.: Harvard University Press.

Hublin, J.-J., Spoor, F., Braun, M., Zonneveld, F., and Condemi, S. (1996) A late Neanderthal associated with Upper Palaeolithic artefacts. Nature 381:224–226.

Larick, R., and Ciochon, R.L. (1996) The African emergence and early Asian dispersals of the genus Homo. Am. Sci. 84:538–551.

Mellars, P. (1996) The Neanderthal Legacy: An Archaeological Perspective from Western Europe. Princeton: Princeton University Press.

Roebroeks, W., and Kolfschoten, T. van, eds. (1995) The Earliest Occupation of Europe. University of Leiden Press.

Soffer, O. (1985) The Upper Paleolithic of the Central Russian Plain. New York: Academic.

Stringer, C.S., and Gamble, C. (1993) In Search of the Neanderthals: Solving the Puzzle of Human Origins. London: Thames and Hudson.

Turner, C., ed. (1996) The Early Middle Pleistocene in Europe. Rotterdam: Balkema.

White, R. (1986) Dark Caves, Bright Visions: Life in Ice Age Europe. New York: Norton.

Whittle, A. (1985) Neolithic Europe: A Survey. New York: Cambridge University Press.

Evolution

Hypothesis that all organisms are descended from a single ancestor by a process that Charles Darwin termed, aptly and simply, "descent with modification." More generally, evolution has been applied to change within any historical system, including the physical universe and its component parts, especially the solar system, the Earth itself, and its climate. Within biology, evolution or its equivalent (e.g., *évolution* in French, *Entwicklung* in German) has meant ontogenetic as well as phylogenetic (i.e., true evolutionary) development. As applied to hominids, evolution is taken in the usual biological (phylogenetic) sense insofar as anatomical and physiological features are concerned; behavioral evolution within hominids is generally termed *cultural evolution*. This entry considers only biological evolution.

The two fundamental aspects of biological evolution are both implicit in Darwin's concept of descent with modification. The first is the simple precept that life has had a history and that organisms alive today are interrelated by virtue of descent from a remote common ancestor. Evolutionary history is termed *phylogeny*. The second basic sense of evolution forms the focus of this entry: the processes, or patterns of causation, that underlie patterns of evolutionary change through time.

The Russian-born geneticist and naturalist Theodosius Dobzhansky once remarked that "nothing in biology makes sense except in the light of evolution." And, indeed, the intricate patterns of similarity and difference among all living organisms can be explained scientifically in no way other than by a notion of genealogical interrelatedness. Although the writings of Greek and Roman savants provide suggestive hints that they entertained notions of the interrelatedness of living beings, it was not until naturalists of the seventeenth and eighteenth centuries began a serious and systematic study of living plants and animals that early versions of modern evolutionary conceptions began to take shape. The great Swedish naturalist C. Linnaeus (Carl von Linné), whose *Systema Naturae* proved to be the forerunner of our modern system of classification, sensed variation around basic anatomical themes, although he later rescinded his doctrine that new species could arise from ancestral species. Most early naturalists were content to arrange living forms in order from the more simple to the more complex, deviating little from the ancient concept of the *Scale of Nature*. Similarly, the overall trend of the fossil record, in which more complex ("higher") forms of life appear in younger rocks lying above the older rocks containing simpler ("lower") forms of life, was interpreted as a form of simple progressivism, often seen as loosely equivalent to the order of Creation as given in Genesis. Alternatively, some paleontologists, like the Frenchman Baron G. Cuvier, noting the many instances of extinction and subsequent proliferation of newer, different faunas and floras, attributed the changing complexion of the fossil record to a series of multiple catastrophes and creation events.

Yet, despite the prevalent attempt to reconcile observations on the fossil record and living plants and animals with received biblical interpretation, early scientists such as Buffon, G. St. Hilaire, and Lamarck held definitely evolutionary views. Lamarck, in particular, is noteworthy in that he put forward a coherent theory on how life might have changed through time. Lamarck agreed with other biologists who postulated that features acquired during the lifetime of an organism may be passed on to descendants—the "inheritance of acquired characteristics" discredited by A. Weismann in the late nineteenth century. (It is not generally appreciated that Darwin also accepted the inheritance of acquired characteristics as a legitimate means of evolutionary change, emphasizing this process especially in later editions of his *On the Origin of Species*—notably the sixth, the one most often reproduced today—after his own theory of natural selection had been so strongly attacked).

It was Darwin who brought respectability to evolution as a legitimate scientific notion. Darwin's epochal *On the Origin of Species* was first published in 1859; the initial edition of 2,000 copies sold out on the first day, testimony indeed that evolution was an idea whose time had come. Although earlier authors had articulated the notion of natural selection, and although British naturalist A.R. Wallace had produced a manuscript that so nearly coincided with Darwin's own formulations that Darwin was shocked by the similarity of the very phrases both used, nonetheless it was Darwin's exposition, long awaited by his colleagues throughout the Western world, that transformed evolution from a daring, heretical, and even irrational notion into a hypothesis of undoubted respectability. Because of Darwin's efforts, evolution became *the* theory of life's history, a conjecture whose overall truth was so evident, supported as it was by facts and arguments from paleontology, embryology, comparative anatomy, and geographic distribution of plants and animals, that overnight most scientists and a large segment of the educated public embraced the notion that evolution has occurred. Yet, for all the evidence Darwin adduced in the *Origin*, his main argument that life has evolved sprang from his promulgation of the process of *natural selection,* a notion that still lies at the center of modern evolutionary theory. It is both ironic and instructive that, whereas the basic idea of evolution was accepted in most quarters immediately upon publication of the *Origin*, Darwin's notion of natural selection sustained withering criticism from the outset and continues to attract critics to the present day. Thus, it is something of an oversimplification to conclude that Darwin succeeded, when all others failed, in convincing the world that life had evolved because he, and he alone (save Wallace), had come up with a convincing mechanism to explain how life evolves.

But for all its critics, the simple, direct idea of natural selection remains an accurate description of a common dynamic process in nature, based on sound premises and their logical consequences. Selection has been modeled mathematically, mimicked in the laboratory, and analyzed in the wild to such an extent that there can be no doubt of its status as the main source of deterministic change in the evolutionary process.

Natural Selection

Both Darwin and Wallace experienced a sort of "Eureka!" when the concept of natural selection fell into place for each of them. Darwin said that he well remembered the spot in the road where he was riding in his carriage when all became clear. That was in 1838. Wallace saw much the same in a malaria-induced feverish dream on the Spice Island of Ternate in 1858. Both men had read a pamphlet by T. Malthus, published in 1798, a tract dealing with the perils of overpopulation in humans. From Malthus, they learned of the natural tendency for geometric increase of sexually reproducing organisms, unless breeding was checked by some factor, most obviously food supply. Both men realized that Malthus's analysis of the human condition applied equally well to any sexually reproducing species. Darwin, writing in the *Origin,* calculated that a single fertile pair of elephants would leave 15 million elephants within 500 years, assuming a generation time of one offspring every ten years, which he reckoned was a conservative estimate. The conclusion is obvious: Elephants have not overrun the Earth; hence, there must be some natural check on their potentially geometric increase. Of all the offspring born each generation, only some are destined to survive and reproduce. Presumably, those individuals best suited to the demands of life that are faced by all organisms of any given species will, on average, be the ones that manage to survive and to reproduce.

Nothing was known about the mechanics of heredity in the mid-nineteenth century. Yet, as Darwin soon discovered, every animal breeder realized two cardinal facts. In each generation, there is variation in a breeding population; not all organisms are alike. It was also known that, in general, organisms tend to resemble their parents; some factor of heredity ensures that particular traits of parents are inherited by at least some of their offspring. These two observations had immediate practical consequences in animal husbandry. Darwin begins his *Origin* with an account of variation under domestication, reflecting his apprenticeship at the hands of pigeon fanciers, who were selecting only those organisms that carried the traits they desired to see passed along and even enhanced. Pigeons lacking the desired traits were not allowed to breed. This artificial selection is an exact analogue of natural selection, the only difference lying in the actual agent of selection. In nature, instead of a Master Breeder, there is the competition engendered by a world of finite resources and harsh physical realities, such that only a limited few, those best suited to the exigencies of the day, will manage to reproduce. Their offspring will tend to inherit the characteristics of the parents that led to their success. Yet, the variation present in each generation has the effect that, should conditions change and a different spectrum of features prove advantageous, the mindless force of selection will shift gears and begin to favor organisms with a different set of characteristics. It will be they who will tend to out-survive and out-reproduce their conspecifics, and thus it will be their traits that will be passed on to the next generation—not exclusively, but preferentially. Natural selection is deterministic: Organisms that do better in coping with life's exigencies produce more offspring, hence, in today's understanding, leave more genes. But natural selection is also stochastic, or probabilistic: Only on the average will organisms best suited to the exigencies of life tend to survive and reproduce with greater frequency than those less well matched to their environmental conditions.

Adaptation

The theory Darwin developed offered an alternative, noncreationist explanation of the apparent design in nature: the often remarkably close fit exhibited by an organism's physical makeup, or morphology (*phenotype* in modern terms), and behavior, and the roles played by the organism in extracting energy, surviving, growing, and reproducing in its environment. For the will of a supernatural Creator, Darwin substituted the mindless mechanism of natural selection. Change in organic form through time reflects changing adaptations wrought by natural selection working on a groundmass of variation. Evolution, to Darwin, was essentially adaptation, and the theory of evolution remains strongly centered on the notion of adaptive origin, maintenance, and modification of organismic phenotypes—the morphologies, behaviors, and physiologies of organisms.

Darwin's ideas on why organisms tend to resemble their parents differed widely from modern concepts of genetics; nor was anything known of the ultimate source of phenotypic variation when Darwin was writing the *Origin*. Beginning ca. 1900 with the simultaneous rediscovery (by three different geneticists) of the nineteenth-century experiments of the Austrian monk G. Mendel, the science of genetics began to develop, quickly bringing a realization that factors of heredity (genes) were located on chromosomes within the nucleus of eukaryotic organisms. Many of the early discoveries of genetics seemed at odds with Darwinian formulations. For example, H. DeVries, a Dutch botanist and cytologist, thought that the conspicuous mutations of the evening primrose *Oenothera* implied that new species could arise by sudden disruptions of the hereditary material of a single organism and that natural selection was, consequently, an unnecessary construct. Later geneticists argued that mutations were mostly deleterious and large-scale in their effects (these being the easiest to detect in the laboratory), and thus the spectrum of finely intergradational variation required by Darwin, and observed in the wild in many populations of organisms, seemed not to be based on mutation. These and similar apparent incongruities were resolved in the 1920s and 1930s, particularly through the efforts of three mathematically inclined geneticists, R. Fisher and J.B.S. Haldane in England and S. Wright in the United States. The way had been paved for a full rapprochement between the traditional Darwinian visualization of the evolutionary process and the understanding of heredity as of the mid-1930s: an understanding that, while remaining in outline form in modern genetics, has been greatly augmented and partly supplanted by the revolution in molecular biology begun in the 1950s with the analysis of the structure of DNA (deoxyribonucleic acid) and the later understanding of the nature of the genetic code itself. Discovery of certain self-organizing aspects of DNA has altered our picture of genetic change to some degree; but it is remarkable that Darwin's basic formulation of natural selection still stands as the major force for maintenance and change of organismic adaptations. Despite great inroads of discovery into the contents of Darwin's "black box" of heredity, the essentials of the Darwinian position on adaptation through natural selection remain; his was a genuine discovery of a dynamic process in nature.

The Modern Synthesis

It was T. Dobzhansky who effected the fusion between the new genetics and the Darwinian view, in his book *Genetics and the Origin of Species* (1937). The systematist E. Mayr followed shortly thereafter, in 1942, with his *Systematics and the Origin of Species*. Both zoologists emphasized the essentially adaptive nature of geographic variation within species. Dobzhansky, in particular, was concerned to link patterns of variation in organismic phenotypes to the principles of genetics, but both men were also concerned to explain patterns of discontinuity in nature, the existence of species, and their mode origin. Their discussions of isolating mechanisms—features of the environment and of organisms themselves that initiate or act to strengthen a separation between two species—added a novel element to evolutionary theory. Both concluded that reproductive isolation is the factor underlying phenotypic gaps between species.

Soon thereafter, paleontologist G.G. Simpson attempted a reconciliation between the data of the fossil record and the emerging science of genetics (*Tempo and Mode in Evolution*, 1944). Arguing that gaps between species in the fossil record are, for the most part, the products of poor preservation, Simpson nonetheless took the gaps between large-scale biological entities, such as families and orders, as reflecting something real about the evolutionary process. In his concept of *quantum evolution,* Simpson explained gaps as reflecting the relatively sudden shift in adaptations of a population from one peak in the adaptive landscape to another, a shift relatively so rapid that most events were not likely to be preserved in the fossil record. Simpson was addressing large-scale features of the evolution of life; earlier, following Darwin's lead, Dobzhansky had written that, however reluctantly, it was necessary to put "a sign of equality" between *microevolution* and *macroevolution*. Microevolution—small scale, generation-by-generation change in gene content and frequency within natural populations—reflects the interface between the mechanics and the principles of population genetics, where the dynamics of natural selection (and the essentially chance effects of genetic drift) enter in. Macroevolution is generally understood to be large-scale changes in organismic form. The essential ingredient of the Modern Synthesis insofar as macroevolution is concerned was to return to the Darwinian position that macroevolution is nothing but microevolution summed up over geological lengths of time: What small change can be effected within a few generations turns to large-scale change over millions of years. This view essentially reduces the question of evolutionary mechanics to the manageably observable processes of generation-by-generation genetic change. The grand simplicity of this view is one of the strengths, as well as the potential major weakness, of both Darwin's original view and modern evolutionary theory.

Competing macroevolutionary theories, still very much focused on organismic phenotypes, came especially from the paleontologist O. Schindewolf and the geneticist R. Goldschmidt, both of whom formulated notions of sudden jumps ("saltations") to explain gaps between species, genera, orders, and so on. The founders of the Modern Synthesis were concerned to refute saltationist claims and to uphold the Darwinian notion of gradual adaptive modification as the dominant theme in the evolution of life.

Soon after Simpson's work was published, the Modern Synthesis was complete, and evolutionary biology entered a long period of essential agreement based on the original Darwinian formulation of adaptation through natural selection. There have, however, been important advances in the study of selection and adaptation, and there has been, as well, some extension of the important work of Dobzhansky and Mayr on the nature of species and the general problem of discontinuity among biological entities.

Modern Evolutionary Theory

By the 1960s, with the advent of biochemical methods to assay genetic variation, it became apparent that organisms are a good deal more genetically variable than had been expected. In particular, for many enzymes there seem to be a number of variations, so many that it has been assumed that many must be selectively neutral (i.e., the variants are equally viable, all performing the particular role of the enzyme equally well). Thus, the variation can accumulate without the mediation of natural selection, a model of evolutionary change that some have called *non-Darwinian*. The existence of variants that are equally functional in a given environment, however, is not, on the face of it, counter to a Darwinian worldview—only, perhaps, to an "ultra-selectionist" perspective that assumes that selection is constantly winnowing all but the very best from the environment, a hypermechanized view of biological nature hardly in accord with the experiences of most biologists.

Perhaps more important has been the strengthening of the very notion of natural selection within the mainstream of evolutionary theory. In response to the suggestion that natural selection may work on entire groups of organisms (*group selection*), biologist G. Williams presented a careful analysis of the nature of selection and adaptation in his influential book *Adaptation and Natural Selection* (1966). Pointing out that selection can act only on variations that exhibit a spectrum of success at any given moment, Williams attacked the notion that selection can be for the good of the species, hence casting doubt on the very idea of group selection, claiming that the evidence for such was slight and that the few bona fide examples seemed not to be important. Selection operates to maximize the reproductive success of individuals at any moment. Williams's formulation led directly to the *selfish gene* concept of R. Dawkins, who saw selection acting not so much on phenotypic properties of organisms, which would convey differential reproductive success to the organisms carrying the features, but rather on the underlying "immortal" genes themselves. This view represents a sort of *ultra-Darwinism*.

Such formulations of selection theory, when coupled with the analyses of W.D. Hamilton (who formulated the theory of kin selection), have led directly to the discipline of sociobiology. The tendency of organisms in social systems to behave cooperatively, and to varying degrees altruistically, is an apparent enigma, particularly from the standpoint of selection acting to benefit organisms, specifically by maximizing the spread of their genes over those of other, conspecific organisms. Hamilton's analyses showed that cooperative, altruistic behavior should be greatest among close relatives (i.e., organisms that share proportionately more genes than would be the case if two organisms were randomly sampled from the population at large). Thus, modern trends in selection theory were reconciled with observations of the social structure of a variety of organisms, and sociobiology has become an important empirical and theoretical aspect of modern evolutionary biology. The relationship of sociobiological principles to human sociocultural evolution is highly contentious and beyond the scope of this entry.

Another important theme in contemporary evolutionary theory stems from the move by Dobzhansky, Mayr, and others to incorporate the notion of *discontinuity* (between species), especially the idea that species are reproductive communities separate from other such communities and that new species arise from old by a process of speciation. The theory of *punctuated equilibria* represents an application of speciation theory to the fossil record and is based on the observation, known to Darwin and contemporary paleontologists, that most species exhibit little or no change throughout the vast bulk of their histories. Thus, adaptive change, rather than being continual, gradual, and progressive, is actually a rare event and considered, under punctuated equilibria, to occur generally during speciation—when new reproductive communities form from old ones. The fossil record seems to support the notion that species are discrete entities in time as well as space. Recognition that species may be spatiotemporally bounded, discrete entities has led to a revival of interest in theories of differential species originations and extinctions, thus contributing to patterns of stability and cumulative change of organismic phenotypic attributes through time. For example, trends (linear change through long periods of time, such as increase in brain size in hominin evolution over the past 2 Myr) are always considered to be the direct result of long-term directional natural selection under Darwinian and synthesis-based evolutionary theory. Yet, such trends may well reflect differential survival (and/or origination) of species whose component organisms differ with respect to the phenotypic feature undergoing directional change. Thus, natural selection may not be inexorably changing the frequency of the trait on a generation-by-generation basis, but rather only during speciation events, with the bulk of a species' subsequent history marked by little or no change at all. The accumulation of numerous speciation events may lead to the sort of long-term protracted macroevolutionary change we can identify as a trend. The recognition that species are real, spatiotemporally bounded entities increases the number of entities seen to play a role in the evolutionary process. Recent work in molecular biology indicates that the complex organization of the genome contains elements, such as transposons, that are capable of biasing the replication of genetic information and thus of influencing the course of evolution. Several lines of inquiry have been expanding the scope of evolutionary theory beyond the strict, traditional domain of explanation of the maintenance and modification of the phenotypic traits of organisms through time.

See also Adaptation(s); Adaptive Radiation; Darwin, Charles; Dobzhansky, Theodosius; Genetics; Genotype; Non-Darwinian Evolution; Phenotype; Phylogeny; Sociobiology; Speciation; Species; Wallace, Alfred Russel; Wright, Sewell. [N.E.]

Further Readings
Darwin, C. (1859) On the Origin of Species. . . . London: Murray.

Dawkins, R. (1976) The Selfish Gene. Oxford: Oxford University Press.

Dobzhansky, T. (1951) Genetics and the Origin of Species, 3rd ed. New York: Columbia University Press.

Eldredge, N. (1985a) Time Frames. New York: Simon & Schuster.

Eldredge, N. (1985b) Unfinished Synthesis. New York: Oxford University Press.

Futuyma, D.J. (1979) Evolutionary Biology. Sunderland, Mass.: Sinauer.

Mayr, E. (1942) Systematics and the Origin of Species. New York: Columbia University Press.

Simpson, G.G. (1944) Tempo and Mode in Evolution. New York: Columbia University Press.

Simpson, G.G. (1953) The Major Features of Evolution. New York: Columbia University Press.

Williams, G.C. (1966) Adaptation and Natural Selection: A Critique of Some Current Evolutionary Thought. Princeton: Princeton University Press.

Evolutionary Morphology

The study of the morphology of organisms in a comparative biological perspective and in accordance with the principles of modern Darwinian evolutionary theory, particularly as it relates to commitment to an understanding of functional and adaptive evolution. Its aim is to shed light on the evolutionary history of the morphology of organisms, a prerequisite for tested taxonomic properties against which phylogenies may be tested. Foundations for all areas of systematic studies depend on accurate descriptive morphology. But to create accurate descriptions for the taxa under study, a comparative framework is often essential. To be successful, endeavors in this field should be a blend of traditional comparative and descriptive morphology and the newest available concepts of functional and ecological morphology, all efforts handled within the framework of the theoretical principles of evolution and phylogeny.

Workers active in this field, one that cuts across all systematic specialties of organisms, have realized that in order to have a balanced perspective on any morphological characteristic, three distinct, yet completely interrelated, constraints that determine morphology must be taken into account. These are: (1) the morphogenetic constraints that manifest themselves through the biochemical programs of growth patterns and that also represent the constraints of physical organizations; (2) the functional-adaptive constraints that result from organism-environment interactions; and (3) the phylogenetic constraints (the history-related morphogenetic constraints) that exert a profound influence on all characters of organisms through the genotype itself, a fundamentally important initial condition for the construction of an organism. Mere consideration of these perspectives is not sufficient. Testing, in the form of nomological-deductive and historical-narrative explanations of the sundry hypotheses considered, is an essential part of the practice of evolutionary morphology, in contrast to what has been called *constructional*—or, in some cases, *functional*—*morphology*. All of these constraints are testable and completely compatible with an expanded neo-darwinian synthesis of population evolution by various genetic and epigenetic mechanisms and natural selection.

The foundations of evolutionary morphology are descriptive and comparative morphology, ideally undertaken within the context of some definite questions of mechanical function, ecological or behavioral adaptation, or phylogeny or of some hypothesis relating to principles of evolutionary change. "Pure" modern descriptions, or many descriptions

from the old comparative anatomical literature, lack this conceptual orientation and testing framework and, therefore, are usually of little use. Comparisons and new descriptions often yield not only new basic information, but also new insights into previously noted but unsolved problems. Clearly defined questions that encompass all of these goals, and attempts to solve them, are not possible in all descriptive studies. Yet, it is this problem-oriented framework that can make a description of scientific value. It follows from the foregoing that the success of a descriptive and comparative study is often more dependent on the sufficient complexity of characters chosen and questions posed than on the descriptive details that some structure may provide.

Functional anatomy within evolutionary morphology is concerned primarily with the understanding of the mechanical properties of morphology, and it interdigitates with physiological studies. Separating the concepts of form and function is difficult. Form is usually understood as the material shape (or molecular configuration) and structure of parts of organisms, whereas function (or physiology) can be defined as all of the chemical and physical properties of a specified form.

Ecological and behavioral morphology within evolutionary morphology concerns itself with the understanding of an organism's form-function in the natural environment and the selectional forces that may be responsible, among other factors, for the nature of its characters. For example, reasons for the existence of an enlarged hyoid bone in the throat of howler monkeys become clear only when territorial interactions, through intimidating howling, are observed in nature. Thus, the environmentally related aspect of a character, its relation to specific selectional forces, is referred to as its *biological role* or *biorole* or *adaptive function*, a concept distinct from physiological or mechanical function (although often conflated with that idea). Students of evolution should have some ideas of the bioroles of features before they can hope to successfully begin to understand the evolutionary history of these traits and, therefore, intelligently arrange the polarity of morphoclines (evolutionary transformation series). Parsimony-driven analysis using taxic outgroups is not a valid substitute for character analysis in phylogenetics.

A concept of fundamental importance in evolutionary morphology is that of *homology*. Because equivalent parts or areas of organisms are studied, it is paramount to understand clearly what those equivalencies are. Given organic evolution, organisms may possess attributes that remained relatively unchanged, or that at least can be identified as (modified) equivalents, from their common ancestor. We term these attributes *homologies* or *homologues*. A theoretical definition of a homologous feature in two or more organisms would specify that homologues are those features that are hypothesized to have been present in the last common ancestor of the specified organisms. It is critical that the concept of similarity is not included in this definition. The operational, or practical, testing of such hypotheses is a complex biological research undertaking that, in the final analysis, is based on the recognition and evaluation (heavily process-steeped and not merely phenetically clustered) of various kinds of similarities between the proposed homologues. Taxonomic-outgroup-generated homology, as practiced by taxic methods of character analysis, sidesteps the methodological directives of evolutionary morphology (or behavior, or molecular structure) to test homology hypotheses.

If a set of observed similarities is rejected as a homology, then this refuted homology hypothesis turns into a hypothesis of independent evolution of those features—in other words, *convergence* (= *analogy*). It is important to realize that homology is *not* an intrinsic property of an aspect of an animal. It is a specified relationship tied to (tested) evolutionary history of these traits that depends on corresponding aspects (parts, behaviors, biochemistry, etc.) of other species. It is for this reason that the conditions of homology must be clearly specified by students of morphology and students of behavior or molecules. Nails, but not claws (falculae), at the end of the digits of primates are *euprimate* homologies, the conditional statement telling us that it was the last common ancestor of euprimates in which this feature first appeared, a diagnostic apomorphy of that clade of mammals.

The essence of evolutionary morphology, then, is the methodological enforcement of an intimate interplay of accurate descriptive, comparative, and functional anatomy tied to rigorous testing, all within the conceptual discipline of systematic biology. A close feedback exists between these activities and the observation of bioroles in free living organisms.

See also Cladistics; Evolutionary Systematics (Darwinian Phylogenetics); Functional Morphology; Paleobiology. [F.S.S.]

Further Readings

Bock, W.J. (1977) Adaptation and the comparative method. In M. Hecht, P. Goody, and E. Hecht (eds.): Major Patterns in Vertebrate Evolution. New York: Plenum, pp. 57–82.

Evolutionary Systematics
(Darwinian Phylogenetics)

The study of the biological diversity of organisms, their phylogenetic (evolutionary) connections, their functional-adaptive biology, and all kinds of other relationships between them. It is sometimes considered distinct from *taxonomy*, which is the theoretical study of classification, its foundations, procedures, and rules. Taxonomy, however, is clearly dependent on the results of systematic studies, although some advocate that "natural groups" can be obtained independently of the complex biological investigations necessary for their tested reality, by merely following axiomatized rules when comparing lower-level taxa. A fundamental issue of distinction, with far-reaching consequences that cannot be discussed here, relates to the species concept for sexually reproducing organisms employed by some members of the cladistic school (that designates a lineage between splittings as the theoretical basis for the species) and the evolutionary school (that distinguishes between a lineage and a species in theory and the multidimensional species taxon of practical species-level taxonomy based on tested models of living

species). However, lines of distinction in phylogenetic analysis are sometimes difficult to draw between purely cladistic systematics and the Simpsonian, or evolutionary, school. In light of the expanded theoretical base provided the evolutionary school since the 1960s by W.J. Bock, Darwinian phylogenetic systematics is a better designation of the modern evolutionary school that considers functional-adaptive analysis a key component in character evaluation. The Simpson-Mayr school of systematics, while insisting on the consideration of sundry evolutionary mechanisms for systematic analysis, has not been specific and theoretically clear either about the importance of *tested* synapomorphies, as well as the fundamental significance of rigorous character analysis independent of taxic-outgroup analysis for obtaining taxonomic properties. The issues are much more complicated than convenient (human group–defining) labels imply, because both cladistics and Darwinian phylogenetics are interested in the unraveling of the one and only history of organisms, and practitioners of these approaches, unlike pheneticists, are committed to the understanding of phylogeny. The theoretical perspectives and methodological priorities on which they base their analyses, however, are different, and they also have distinct preferences about how to translate a phylogeny into a practical classification. Phylogenetic evaluation of lineages and taxa requires classification, an enterprise fundamentally controversial because it is, by definition, artificial at least in point of time—the stem of any taxon.

Phylogenists (both the cladists and the Darwinian evolutionists) believe that the core aim of systematics should be the understanding of phylogeny), and they base their phylogenetic hypotheses on the understanding of homologous characters. Yet, the word *phylogeny* means different things to cladistic and evolutionary systematists. Evolutionists insist on causal understanding of the taxonomic properties against which a specific phylogeny (meaning the history of organisms; their "descent with modification," as Darwin called it; or the paths of this history) may be tested. This view of "genealogy" includes both ancestor-descendant and sister-group relationships that result from a split lineage. Darwinian phylogenists concentrate their research efforts on processual (evolutionary—hence, the original designation for this school) understanding of traits, and on character analysis, in order to understand or explain the most probable path of transformation of homologous characters.

Before the analytical aspect of character analysis can really begin, systematists should ascertain the distribution of the characters studied (i.e., their pattern) in all taxa. But rather than rely only on simple rules for interpreting this pattern to make sense of character evolution (i.e., which characters were primitive [ancestral or plesiomorph] and which advanced [derived or apomorph]), evolutionary systematists use various biological research approaches to establish a degree of confidence in a proposed phylogeny of homologous characters. These research programs of Darwinian phylogenetics attempt to understand not only *what* characters are available, but also *how* these function, how they transformed, for what bioroles (which subsumes the *why* question) they evolved, and, whenever the fossil record permits, *when* they appear. All of these studies have important bearing on the interpretation and testing of the evolution of characters and the determination of the polarity (direction of transformation) of traits used in phylogenetics.

Functional-adaptive analysis-based systematics adheres to the notion that the evolutionary process results in either stasis or evolution and that the result of the evolutionary process is ultimately the modification of descendants relative to their ancestors. The path of descent (i.e., how species are related to one another given that the relationships can be of either the ancestor-descendant or sister-group kind), a consequence of evolution, results in the enormous variety of organisms that lived in the past and that are extant today. To understand this history, evolutionary systematists believe, the known samples of living and fossil organisms should be interpreted in the light of what we know of all available and relevant biological and evolutionary processes. The (process-based) pattern, as Darwinian phylogenists understand it, is only the evidence (data) retrieved from the study of the organisms themselves. The *establishment* and *interpretation* of this pattern, even the identification of what is or is not a species different from others, is "theory-drenched," or at least based on causal mechanism dependent assumptions. In other words, assumptions based on biological and evolutionary processes are utilized to make interpretations in all aspects of systematic activity. The demonstration of the pattern of phylogeny is the result of a tested, theory-steeped, analytical procedure, and is not something that can be creditably accomplished with the use of a simple assumption that evolution is a fact or that all transformations can be assumed to be parsimonious for the sake of consistency.

Evolutionary systematists believe that, because much evolutionary change is adaptive, the understanding of the functional-adaptive aspect of the characters of organisms helps in understanding the evolution of many different, but homologous, characters. Ancestral conditions often leave unmistakable influence in altered features, particularly if the features involved are complicated ones and the appropriate analyses are conducted.

It follows from the above that Darwinian phylogenists who lean more toward an evolutionary, process-steeped systematics, and who do not believe that a meaningful separation of systematics from evolutionary theory, particularly adaptive evolution, is desirable or possible, concentrate on the understanding of character transformation (evolution) of the organisms they study. Any information from biological and paleontological studies that bears on the extinct and extant samples may hold significant clues for the probability of one as opposed to another transformation. With the knowledge of as many character transformations (i.e., character phylogenies) as possible, using shared and derived features weighted in a biologically *a priori* manner (complex features being most valuable and simple, or "loss," characters least valuable), the systematist constructs a taxon phylogeny, using both sister-group and ancestor-descendant concepts for the taxa themselves.

The classifications constructed by evolutionists (phylogenists, some "evolutionary" cladists, etc.) attempt to reflect evolutionary history, both the history of branching and descent and the extent of divergence (from a measure of dissimilarity) as well as the relative extent of the adaptive radiation, as much as this is possible in a classification. It is clearly understood by Darwinian phylogenists that the aim of their endeavors is to understand phylogeny and not merely to construct a classification that single-mindedly reflects the latest (often entirely untested) branching hypothesis. This latter goal, while arguably impossible to achieve on a piece of paper, is shunned primarily because it simply attempts to duplicate in words a phylogenetic tree.

Only those taxonomic groups that include the last common ancestor of all included species (*monophyletic groups,* i.e., either *paraphyla* or *holophyla*) are constructed and named under the evolutionary paradigm. Whenever information permits and traditional channels of communications justify this, all of the descendants of a common ancestor are included in a group (*holophyletic groups*). Groups that represent the initial radiation of the close relatives of some very successful descendants (e.g., the primate family Omomyidae), but of which the exact affinities of its various subgroups to later descendants are not clear, are contained in monophyletic taxa that do not include all of the descendants (*paraphyletic groups*) of the last common ancestor. In fact, all ancestral species that evolved into other ones or split to give rise to other lineages are paraphyla (often dubbed *stems* to avoid the term *ancestor*). Paraphyletic groups (sometimes called *horizontal taxa*) can also be justified by their utility in allowing future readjustments of group relationships without the necessity for an entirely new classification that a cladistic system would dictate. Paraphyletic taxa are often well diagnosed by the derived attributes of their single common ancestor compared to its specifically designated (or hypothetical) ancestry and by the (subsequently) primitive characters that are shared by their varied descendants that diversified from one another. Paraphyla are real, not unnatural, and paraphyletic taxa are often a practical necessity as well. Their use in taxonomy, along with holophyletic taxa, allows extremely useful statements concerning stages of evolutionary change exemplified by radiations (many, if not most, genera are such taxa). They also permit both compatibility with traditional systems of classification and steady refinements to incorporate new understanding of both the extinct and the extant record, without attempting to treat fossils as some peculiar manifestations of life (*plesia*), as some cladistic classifications attempt to do.

See also Classification; Evolutionary Morphology; Phylogeny; Systematics. [F.S.S.]

Further Readings

Bock, W.J. (1977) Foundations and methods of evolutionary classification. In M. Hecht, P. Goody, and E. Hecht (eds.): Major Patterns in Vertebrate Evolution. New York: Plenum, pp. 851–896.

Bock, W.J. (1981) Functional-adaptive analysis in evolutionary classification. Am. Zool. 21:5–20.

Szalay, F.S., and Bock, W.J. (1991) Evolutionary theory and systematics: Relationships between process and pattern. Z. Zool. Syst. Evolut.-Forsch. 229:1–39.

Exotics

Archaeological materials, especially lithics, originating at distances of more than 30 km from the site where they are found. While rare exotic stones are present even in the oldest Paleolithic sites, such as Olduvai Gorge (Tanzania), their scarcity at Early and Middle Paleolithic sites and the lack of patterning in either the use of these materials or the directionality of the sources suggest that their presence at the sites resulted from the mobility of groups occupying the sites. The voluminous presence of different kinds of exotics (lithics, marine shells, amber) found at many Late Paleolithic sites, the special use made of these nonlocal materials, and the disparate but patterned sources of origin for these materials all suggest that these exotics were transported via exchange networks and that their distribution at the sites reflects past social relationships rather than mobility of the groups themselves.

See also Jewelry; Late Paleolithic. [O.S.]

Extinction

Final extinction of a species follows when environmental changes or mere accident overwhelms the last breeding population. Extinction is usually portrayed as the failure of a species in its one chance to leave a descendant at the end of its life, but this is hardly correct. Direct succession of one species by another, by evolutionary transformation of the final few members of a dying population, is probably very unusual. The same challenge to adapt or die is faced constantly by genetically isolated clusters of individuals on the fringes during the entire existence of species. Few, if any, of these myriad opportunites to adapt actually result in a new species. Seen in this light, speciation is not the alternative to extinction but an uncommon by-product of the extinction process.

Organisms are adapted by selection according to a host of physical and biological factors, ranging from soil chemistry and climate to parasites and population density, to which the name *environment* may be applied. Populations become extinct if their adaptations fail to cope with gradual or cyclic changes to any factor in their environment or, more rarely, through relatively sudden and widespread changes. In the latter instances, the consequence may be *catastrophic* or *mass extinctions,* in which numerous taxa become extinct simultaneously. The circumstances of mass extinction include plain annihilation (i.e., regional cataclysms such as a meteorite impact or megavolcanic explosion) or unprecedented extremes in normal variations of environmental factors.

Most species, however, become extinct in relatively stable environmental conditions, in which extinction affects relatively few species at a time (often a key species and its specialized associates). This is *background extinction,* which (without begging the question) is linked directly to reduced breeding populations. With fewer individuals, lethal or inhibiting variations can spread throughout a population faster than selection can compensate, and reduced numbers also

make a population more vulnerable to "final accidents," such as an epidemic disease or destruction of a vital resource.

A major distinction between catastrophic and background extinction, aside from a (perhaps illusory) perception that the events of greater scope also involve more precipitous rates of decline, is that catastrophic extinctions of numerous species tend to mark the end of higher categories as well. Analysis of background extinction generally involves a search for biological mechanisms of ecology and evolution, whereas the studies of catastrophic extinction tend to focus on geologic and even planetary factors.

Competition and Extinction

Since favorable as well as unfavorable variations are fixed more rapidly in smaller groups, crises that isolate parts of a population or reduce its numbers overall tend to stimulate evolution as well as background extinction. In other words, extinction is often accompanied by origination as part of the same process. *Competitive extinction* in past faunas is hard to document, but dramatic modern examples such as the replacement of the native red squirrel by the imported grey in eastern North America are not rare, and they indicate that relatively high levels of competitive extinction probably were associated with faunal interchange during periods of low sea level in the past. The special case in competitive extinction known as *evolutionary replacement*—competitive exclusion of an ancestral species by a daughter species—is even less common and seems to be mainly a projection of the Victorian worldview upon the face of nature.

The empty niche left by an extinct taxon may not be filled immediately, if ever. Interestingly, species of a group that vanishes in a mass extinction are more likely to leave unexploited niches behind them than when a single species vanishes, because of the lack of related forms that are preadapted for the opportunity. The fossil record shows, for instance, that the disappearance of the predaceous dinosaurs left a world without carnivores in the earliest Tertiary. It was believed that this niche was initially filled by phororacids, giant flightless birds of the Early Paleocene, but it now appears that at least some phororacids were vegetarians. Only after several million years did the first mammalian carnivores, adapted from insectivores, appear in the fossil record. In other circumstances in which a new species may appear to move into a niche abandoned by its direct ancestor, the decline of the ancestral species may, in fact, have been caused by subtle changes in the niche, and the new species will occupy a habitat that itself is new in some respect. While this looks like competitive replacement, it may be simple opportunism. Clear evidence for opportunistic rather than competitive replacement in the fossil record is documented by instances in which an extinct species (or group) is replaced by a taxon that is arguably less fit than its immediate precursor.

Living Fossils and Extinction Rates

Some species, in particular the various "living fossils," such as horseshoe crabs and lungfishes, have so much redundancy in their genetic code that inbreeding has relatively little effect, and thus relatively few individuals make up a viable population. This confers upon the species a degree of immunity from extinction. In such lineages, the genetic variability has gradually decreased through feedback from reiterated selection for a highly successful phenotype. The potential for adaption is suppressed for the sake of stabilizing a successful model that is able to survive almost any disaster. In the opposite strategy, some successful groups such as cichlid fishes are unusually labile, replacing one species with another at every minor opportunity.

Extinction rates are measured in macarthurs, or taxonomic units per million years. These units are not named after the famous general who made a philosophy of extinction ("Old soldiers never die—they just fade away"), but rather in honor of R.H. MacArthur, whose 1972 book *Geographical Ecology* introduced modern concepts of extinction dynamics. When averaged over large groups of species, such as the molluscs or mammals, or, using higher categories such as families, over all life forms, extinction rates have been cited as an indication of changes in global environment. Since a family or an order survives in the fossil record if a single one of its species survives, analysis at higher taxonomic levels is most sensitive to the catastrophic extinctions, with their geological implications.

Mass Extinctions

Major catastrophic extinctions, in which more than 20 percent of animal families (meaning more than 50 percent of species and nearly all individuals) disappear, have always been interesting subjects of speculation. The best known, at the end of the Cretaceous, is the extinction of the dinosaurs, actually a heterogenous group of large animals whose only common characteristic is the failure of its members to survive into the Cenozoic, together with diverse marine invertebrates such as ammonites, tetracorals, belemnites, and rudistids. Other groups, such as the planktonic foraminifera, survived this event by just one or two species. The evidence supports a massive bolide impact as the proximal cause, but it is also clear that this final blow came during a period of lowered sea level, greatly reduced diversity among many groups (the pterosaurs, for instance, had declined to just a few giant, highly specialized species), and high environmental stress.

Three other mass extinctions of this magnitude are recorded: at the end of the Ordovician, within the later Devonian, and near the end of the Triassic, but these pale in comparison with the great mass extinction at the end of the Permian in which more than 50 percent of families and perhaps as many as 96 percent of all marine-animal species were eliminated. A lesser, but very noticeable wave of extinctions, known as the *Grand Coupure* (Great Cutoff), in land-mammal faunas occurred early in the Oligocene. The beginning of the Cambrian, when shelled life-forms appeared in abundance in a number of unrelated phyla, may also have followed an extinction event. These catastrophic extinctions occurred, as in the end-Cretaceous, during periods of lowered sea level and worldwide environmental stress, and in some there is again evidence of massive bolide strikes. It may be that collisions with large meteorites are not rare on the geological scale, but only those that impact during periods of ecological disruption can synchronize a wave of extinctions among groups that are struggling to survive.

Evidence has been cited for periodicity in mass extinctions at ca. 29 Ma, which may coincide with the near approach of a normally indetectable dwarf companion of the sun aptly termed Nemesis. As with many other periodicities, however, the data have been criticized as being selected from a more random context.

Pleistocene Overkill

The extinction of many groups of large mammals at the end of the Pleistocene, 11.7 Ka, has engendered spirited debate among anthropologists. Many view this wave of extinctions as the result of human predation. Others, citing the need for scientific caution, have objected to drawing such conclusions from the available, mainly circumstantial, evidence. Behind scientific caution, however, many in the second camp have expressed a reluctance to convict preagricultural peoples of such wanton environmental vandalism, considering the fact that in existing cultures such as the Inuit and !Kung there is a functional equilibrium between large-prey species and hunting pressure.

In the most recent instances of preindustrial human colonization of large unspoiled territories, however, the case against unsophisticated humankind, armed with nothing more than the Neolithic hunting kit, appears to be irrefutable. In Madagascar, New Zealand, and Hawaii, subfossil remains and isolated survivors of formerly diverse and widespread biota give unequivocal testimony of far-reaching extermination beginning with the first few generations of human settlement. In some instances, these depredations are documented in oral histories, as in clear descriptions of the extinct flightless moa in Maori legend. The remains of specialized faunas, no longer with us, have also been found in prehistoric kitchen middens on New Caledonia, Hispaniola, Sardinia, and Taiwan.

Objectors have pointed to the large regions with hunter cultures, such as Australia, New Guinea, and forested regions of Southeast Asia and Africa, as areas where the Late Pleistocene extinction rates among large vertebrates have not been extraordinary, and where humans are said to live in harmony with nature. The last two are regions with a long period of human habitation, however, and the hunted fauna may be adapted to preindustrial human predation so that harmony is a result more of *could not* rather than *would not*. In the case of Australia, discoveries in Kow Swamp and elsewhere document a remarkable Pleistocene fauna of much greater variety than fauna in the present, dominated not by the lean and speedy kangaroo but by giant, slow-moving marsupials and a "komodo dragon" top predator that vanished in the past 20 Kyr.

P.S. Martin, a leading student of Pleistocene extinctions, has pointed out that the sudden decline from 79 to 22 large-mammal species that followed human immigration into North America was not only catastrophic in the definition given above, but was also unaccompanied by significant extinctions in parts of the ecology (perching birds, plants, small mammals, fish) that are less affected by human predation. Worldwide, the timing of large-mammal extinctions during the last glacial and postglacial, down to the colonization of outlying islands noted above, also can be shown to follow the expansion of human populations. Martin has noted that overkill may be associated with the abundance and innocence of prey species and the absence of real or cultural limits on human behavior in the first phase of colonization. The "harmony" seen in existing hunting cultures comes later, like the new sense of ecological management in industrial societies, as the remaining prey becomes more difficult to secure.

Perhaps the most dramatic evidence of Late Pleistocene overkill may be the sudden wave of extinction in the proboscidea, an extremely diverse and successful group with a panglobal distribution. At the beginning of the Weichsel (Wisconsinian) glacial, at about 125 Ka, diverse proboscidean species representing four distinct families—elephantids (mammoths and elephants), mammutids, mastodonts, and stegodonts—were the dominant large mammals of all continents but Australasia and Antarctica. By the time the Early Holocene expansion of humans was over, ca. 10 Ka, the proboscidean fauna of the "new lands" in North America, South America, and northern Eurasia was gone, and just two species of elephant that had co-evolved with the early human hunters survived in southern Asia and Africa. In many areas from which proboscideans suddenly vanished—Spain, Ukraine, Siberia, and North America—the archaeological record begins coincidentally, usually with evidence of human predation on these "walking meat lockers," as they have been called. Neolithic innovations in weapons, technology, and social structure may have launched an "elephant rush," which carried humankind across the Bering Strait in pursuit of a dwindling resource.

Modern Extinctions

Studies of global mass extinctions indicate that there may be a variety of causes. Dramatically sudden catastrophes appeal to the imagination, but, in most instances, detailed study of the fossils and strata suggests that mass extinctions represent secular increases in extinction rates over an appreciable, if geologically short, interval of several million years, in some instances punctuated by a bolide impact. To give a sense of scale to the word *short* in this context, the changes in land and marine biota in the earlier part of the Holocene, from 12 to 5 Ka, simply as the result of Neolithic predation and resource appropriation, would seem catastrophically rapid and extensive in the geological record. These 7,000 years of rapid worldwide change are recorded in ca. 7 cm of sea-floor sediments, or ca. 1.75 m of alluvial-terrace deposits, at average deposition rates. The rapidity and scope of the Early Holocene changes pale, however, against the effects of the geometric increases in human population and ecological disruption over the past 500 years, let alone the impact of industrialization and urbanization in the last 100 years. These effects have wrought a global transformation of envronment and biota that would be recorded as one of the greatest dislocations ever seen, in less than a centimeter of strata in the deep-sea record. Since change at this pace must soon end, one may wonder what new balance will be recorded in the meters of deep ocean sediment that will come to overlie this final single stratum.

See also Holocene; Pleistocene; Speciation. [J.A.V.C.]

Further Readings

Elliott D.K., ed. (1986) The Dynamics of Extinction. New York: Wiley.

Hallam, A. (1984) The causes of mass extinctions. Nature 308:686–687.

Martin, P.S., and Klein, R.G., eds. (1984) Quaternary Extinctions. Tucson: University of Arizona Press.

Unwin, D.K. (1986) Extinction—back to basics. Mod. Geol. 10:261–270.

Eyasi

Fossil hominin remains recovered in Tanzania between 1935 and 1938. Parts of at least two crania were found, and there has been dispute about their age and significance. They appear to represent late Middle or early Late Pleistocene nonmodern hominins, with a long, low skull and large brows but an occipital torus morphology with some modern characteristics. Discoveries from Ngaloba (Tanzania) and Eliye Springs (Kenya) may represent the same East African hominin population.

See also Africa, East; Archaic Homo sapiens; Natron-Eyasi Basin. [C.B.S.]

F

Family

Principal family-group category of the classificatory hierarchy, falling immediately below the superfamily and above the subfamily. The *International Code of Zoological Nomenclature* requires that all family names end in the suffix "-idae."

See also Classification; Nomenclature. [I.T.]

Fayum

Huge depression in the province of the same name in northern Egypt, yielding the world's largest and most diverse fauna of early anthropoids. These fossils come from upper Eocene and lowermost Oligocene strata of the Jebel Qatrani Formation, in the upper 500 m of a succession cut back into the Saharan plateau to the west and southwest of the Birket (lake) el-Qarun. The Jebel Qatrani Formation is made up of deltaic and estuarine beds that conformably overlie the Qasr el-Sahgha Formation, a near-shore shallow marine and lagoonal sequence of late Middle Eocene (Bartonian) age. The Qasr el-Sagha, in turn, overlies the open-marine early Middle Eocene (Lutetian) Mokattam beds. Whale bones from the Qasr el-Sagha, found in the 1870s by botanist Georg Schweinfurth, were the first vertebrate fossils reported from Africa. The Qasr el-Sagha has also yielded remains of various tethytheres (sirenians, embrithopods, and primitive proboscideans) and anthracotheres and scraps of creodont carnivores, but no primates. Other exposures of Bartonian and possibly younger lagoonal-deltaic beds farther west, at Dor el-Talha in Libya, have similar faunas. The antiquity of primates in Africa is established, however, by the recovery of a variety of strepsirhines and haplorhines (including anthropoids) in Paleocene to Middle Eocene sites west of Egypt as well as the occurrence of a parapithecid, *Biretia,* in beds at Nementcha, Algeria, that can be correlated by faunal arguments to a Bartonian age like that of the Qasr el-Sagha Formation.

The highly fossiliferous deposits of the Jebel Qatrani Formation were first collected by the British Museum (Nat-ural History) at the turn of the twentieth century, followed by major expeditions from the American Museum of Natural History in New York. Since 1960, work has gone forward under the direction of Elwyn Simons, first at Yale and later at Duke University. The formation has yielded thousands of specimens in a magnificent representation of African land mammals, including a wide diversity of tethytheres (sirenians, hyraxes, proboscideans, moeritheres, the unique rhinolike *Arsinoitherium*), anthracotheres, Southern Hemisphere rodents, bats, elephant shrews, and numerous and diverse primates. The fauna also contains descendants of Early Eocene or Middle Eocene immigrants from western Eurasia such as palaeoryctids, creodonts, didelphid marsupials, and a pangolin. The upper lip of the Fayum Escarpment is formed by the Widan al Faras Basalt, dated at 31 Ma, which rests on a regional unconformity truncating the Jebel Qatrani beds.

The environment of the Jebel Qatrani deposits was a shallow sea bordered by moist, tropical coastal forest growing on a sandy substrate. Fossil plants are extremely abundant and, together with the inferred habitats of the fossil mammals and lower vertebrates, indicate estuarine river-gallery forests, with large vine-draped trees and mangroves, in an area of seasonal rainfall drained by slow-moving tidal rivers. The Nile River system did not then exist, and local drainage was westward into a proto-Sirtean Gulf.

Fossil primates from the Fayum come from four distinct levels in the Jebel Qatrani Formation. Species turnover is nearly 100 percent between these levels, indicating significant elapsed time or environmental change, but there is less difference in genera between the two upper-level faunas than between these faunas and the two lower-level faunas. The lowest level, JQ-1, contains the important site L41 near the base of the Jebel Qatrani Formation. This is the earliest well-documented African primate fauna, the fragmentary Maghreb specimens notwithstanding. The taxa identified comprise diverse anthropoids, including three parapithecids, *Serapia, Arsinoea* and a species of *Qatrania*; an oligopithecid, *Catopithecus*; and *Proteopithecus*, a genus of uncer-

View of the Jebel Qatrani Formation (early Oligocene) in Fayum Province (Egypt). The line of cliffs in the background is capped by a basalt layer dated at ca. 31 ma. Courtesy of J.G. Fleagle.

tain affinities. From this level also comes *Plesiopithecus,* provisionally classed as a lorisiform with an enlarged procumbent incisor, and the cercamoniine (or protoadapine) adapiforms *Aframonius, Wadilemur* and *Anchomomys.* Hyraxes at this level are notably abundant and diverse. In JQ-2, typified at Locality E ca. 100 m above the base of the formation, occur remains of a possible omomyine, the parapithecid *Qatrania,* and the oligopithecid *Oligopithecus.* This level has been known classically as the Lower Fossil Wood Zone because of the abundance of large silicified tree trunks.

In the middle levels of the Jebel Qatrani Formation, Zone JQ-3, are found remains of the parapithecid *Apidium,* as well as *Propliopithecus,* a genus with dental characteristics that place it near the ancestry of all later catarrhines. More advanced species of *Apidium* and other parapithecids (*Qatrania* and *Parapithecus* or *Simonsius*) occur in the upper level, JQ-4, together with *Propliopithecus* and *Aegyptopithecus.* Also from the upper level are sparse remains of a possible lorisid and a very small primate, *Afrotarsius,* which displays many primitive characters of the protoanthropoid stock.

The age of the Jebel Qatrani beds is controversial, because of the poor correlation between its mammal faunas and those of Eurasia. From the late nineteenth century onward, researchers considered the invertebrates of the Bartonian Stage, such as those in the Qasr el-Sagha beds, to represent the uppermost Eocene, so the overlying Jebel Qatrani fossil beds entered the literature as Oligocene. Reassessment of the mi-

cropaleontology in the stage stratotypes, however, realigned the Bartonian to Late Middle Eocene, succeeded by the Priabonian Stage in the Late Eocene. This opens a time interval of ca. 3 Myr between the Bartonian-Priabonian boundary (37 Ma) and the Eocene-Oligocene boundary (34 Ma). The JQ-1 and JQ-2 levels are now generally assigned to Late Eocene age, but some question remains about the upper levels. Provisional paleomagnetic analysis is interpreted to place the Eocene-Oligocene boundary between the lower and upper levels, but the imprint of the global sea-level lowering at that time is not evident in the coastal-plain sequence represented here. The Early Oligocene age of JQ-3 and JQ-4 is supported, nevertheless, by the presence of Fayum-like faunas from lower Oligocene marine beds in Oman. Fayum-like fossils have also been found in shallow-marine lower Oligocene beds at Zallah, in eastern Libya. In both Oman and Libyan sites, the abraded and isolated condition and intertidal context of the mammal fossils allows the possibility that these remains were, possibly, reworked from upper Eocene sands.

The Fayum basin also contains an oasis where archaeological excavations have yielded the earliest evidence in Africa of the cultivation of southwest Asian cereal crops, ca. 7 Ka, along with a bone harpoon and backed microliths of southwest Asian types.

See also Africa, North; Afrotarsius; Anthropoidea; Catarrhini; Notharctidae; Oligocene; Oligopithecidae; Oman; Parapithecidae; Plesiopithecus; Propliopithecidae. [R.F.K., J.A.V.C.]

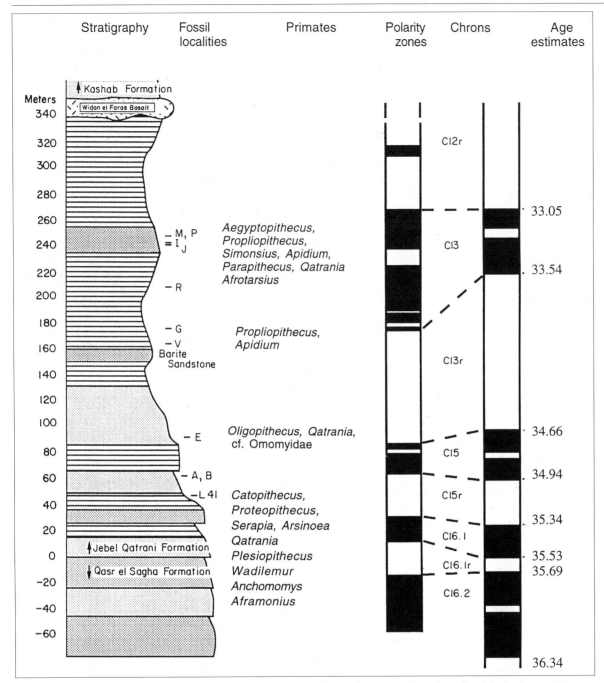

Section through the Jebel Qatrani Formation, Eocene-Oligocene of the Fayum, showing the various quarries (lettered) and the distribution of the primate taxa recovered. Courtesy of Richard F. Kay.

Further Readings

Fleagle, J.G., and Kay, R.F., eds. (1994) Anthropoid Origins. New York: Plenum.

Kappelman, J. (1992) The age of the Fayum primates as determined by paleomagnetic reversal stratigraphy. J. Hum. Evol. 22:495–503.

Krzyzaniak, L., and Kobusiewicz, M., eds. (1984) Origin and Early Development of Food-Producing Cultures in Northeastern Africa. Poznan:

Simons, E.L. (1992) Diversity in the Early Tertiary anthropoidean radiation in Africa. Proc. Nat. Acad. Sci. USA, 89:10743–10747.

Simons, E.L. (1997) Discovery of the smallest Fayum Egyptian primates (Anchomomyini; Adapidae). Proc. Nat. Acad. Sci. USA 94:180–184.

Van Couvering, J.A., and Harris, J.A. (1991) Late Eocene age of the Fayum mammal faunas. J. Hum. Evol. 21:241–260.

Fejej

Plio-Pleistocene sequence exposed in the Turkana Basin of southernmost Ethiopia. Abundant faunas spanning the Pliocene-Pleistocene boundary come from FJ-5, dated by its association with Hadar Orange Tuff to an age close to 1.7

Ma, and FJ-1, which comes from below Shungura Tuff H-1, close to 1.9 Ma. Artifacts are numerous at both levels. Early Pliocene faunas are found at two levels. The age of FJ-4, below two basalt flows with $^{40}Ar/^{39}Ar$ ages of 3.94 and 4.06 Ma in stratigraphic order, has been confirmed by paleomagnetic analyses that date the fauna between 4.00 and 4.18 Ma. Heavily worn dental remains from this level are among the oldest specimens attributed to *Australopithecus afarensis* (they might better be referred now to *A. anamensis*). FJ-3 is a *Nyanzachoerus kanamensis* fauna below basalts dated to 4.4 Ma. Oligocene sediments, with abundant fossil wood, also crop out below basalt dated to 34.2 Ma at Fejej Police Post.

See also Australopithecus afarensis; Australopithecus anamensis; Hadar; Turkana Basin. [J.A.V.C.]

Further Readings

Asfaw, B., Beyene, Y., Semaw, S., Suwa, G., White, T., and Wolde-Gabriel, G. (1991) Fejej: A new paleoanthropological research area in Ethiopia. J. Hum. Evol. 21:137–143.

Kappelman, J., Swisher C.C., III, Fleagle, J.G., Yirga, S., Bown, T.D., and Feseha, M. (1996) Age of *Australopithecus afarensis* from Fejej, Ethiopia. J. Hum. Evol. 30:139–146.

Fells Cave

Stratified Paleoindian archaeological site in the Straits of Magellan (Chile). Excavated by J. Bird in the 1930s, Fells Cave contained the bones of horse and guanaco, as well as distinctive Fells Cave fishtailed projectile points and groundstone disks. The site suggests that humans had reached the tip of South America between 11 and 10 Ka.

See also Americas; Paleoindian. [L.S.A.P., D.H.T.]

Fire

One of the most important technological innovations during the course of human evolution was the controlled use of fire, which played a critical role in the spread of hominid populations out of Africa and into colder climates. The benefits of fire production were enormous. Fire could be used to provide warmth; to produce light; to cook foods, increase digestibility, kill parasites, or detoxify; to keep away dangerous animals and pests; to drive game; to work wood and other materials; and to rejuvenate stands of plants. Many anthropologists have also stressed the strong socialization pressures on a group of hominins clustered around a fire. Finally, the control of fire was a prerequisite for two critical technological innovations: pottery and metallurgy.

The earliest evidence of hominin use of fire is controversial. One major problem is finding distinctive features in the archaeological record that can serve as certain evidence of deliberate fires. Even in the modern and recent ethnographic record, fireplaces used for warmth or cooking are not always elaborate affairs that would leave a lasting record over time. Human-made fires may be large or quite small; often they are casual affairs burned on the surface of the ground, perhaps used very briefly; or they may be made in shallow pits dug in the ground. The stone-lined hearth commonly associated with camp fires is by no means universal and may be a relatively recent phenomenon in prehistory. Proposed evidence for hominin use of fire includes charcoal, baked (hardened and usually discolored) sediment, thermally altered bones, stones and/or sediment, and a feature like a hearth structure (usually a concentrated area of ash and charcoal, sometimes bordered by rocks).

By the Middle Paleolithic, there is fairly widespread evidence for controlled use of fire by human groups, but prior to 150 Ka this evidence is controversial. The ash and charcoal produced by fires do not survive well in the early prehistoric record, particularly in tropical regions where organic materials are in general highly perishable. In the case of fires used for long or successive periods of time, especially with very hot fires, there may be localized baking and discoloration, particularly reddening, of the underlying earth. In the absence of deliberate hearth structures, though, it can be difficult to distinguish the results of natural brushfires from evidence of fire produced by human agency. Nevertheless, prehistoric investigators have found several intriguing signs of the possible control of fire in the Early Paleolithic.

The claims for the earliest evidence come from Africa. Localized areas of apparently baked sediment have been discovered at Koobi Fora and Chesowanja (Kenya), dating to ca. 1.5 Ma. Paleomagnetic studies of realignment of iron-oxide minerals suggest baking of these patches of sediment at consistently high temperatures, but these studies remain inconclusive and await further testing. Paleomagnetic evidence from the Acheulean site of Gadeb (Ethiopia) is also equivocal but could point toward baking of discolored stones in a fire. However, distinguishing these from baked areas that could be produced by natural brushfires in such deposits may prove difficult. Paleomagnetic analysis of some cone-shaped, baked patches of earth near sites in the Middle Awash Valley (Ethiopia) does indicate burning, but their shape may indicate natural burning of tree stumps. At Swartkrans (South Africa), a small percentage of the fossil animal bones from the Early Stone Age layer (Member 3), dated about 1.5 Ma, exhibited chemical and physical modification suggesting that they had been burnt. Cut-marked bone has also been found in this deposit.

During the Middle Pleistocene, several sites in Africa, Asia, and Europe appear to show signs of more habitual use of fire. Some of the best known are Zhoukoudian (China), Vértesszöllös (Hungary), Vallonnet Cave, Lazaret, and Terra Amata (France), and Kalambo Falls (Zambia), although some researchers are skeptical that all of these represent solid evidence of hominin-controlled fire. At Zhoukoudian, the evidence has been questioned. Many levels with putative ash deposits have been identified, not in localized hearths but in layers, some of them quite extensive and several meters deep. L.R. Binford has suggested that these layers may represent spontaneous combustion of deposits of organic material or guano left in the cave by owls or other raptors. The burned bones reported from the cave could then be coincidental casualties of smoldering fires engulfing bone brought in by hominins, carnivores, or other agencies and not represent refuse of cooked food. Chemical analysis of the sediment by Weiner et al. in 1996–1997 suggested that it did not, in fact, contain ash, although some of the bone was indeed burned. Other bones were manganese-stained rather than blackened by fire. The lack of structured hearths and the possible use of living space in a way unlike that in later periods of time are also problematic here, but unfortunately we do not know what the cultural remains associated with the early use of fire should look like.

There are other early occurrences in Asia with reported evidence for fire, including Xihoudu, Lantian, and Yuanmou (China). At Xihoudu, the evidence is in the form of discolored mammalian ribs, antlers, and cracked horse teeth. These black, grey, and grey-green specimens have been analyzed and interpreted as charred bone. At Lantian, a "wood ash" and bits of charcoal have been reported in a layer slightly above one yielding a fossil hominin cranium, and the site of Yuanmou has yielded apparent charcoal and burned bone. While such finds remain problematic in view of the questions being raised about the hominin role in early prehistoric fires, these instances are nevertheless of interest.

In Europe, two small hearths situated in an apparent hut structure have been reported at Lazaret (France). Likewise, the nearby site of Terra Amata in Nice has features apparently involving charcoal and burned bone in depressions partly lined with rocks that have been interpreted as hearth structures. At the site of Vértesszöllös (Hungary), fragments of burned bone have suggested the use of fire.

The evidence for relatively early hominin control of fire during the Early Paleolithic is suggestive, although not overwhelming as yet. A traditional view has been that the hominids' spread out of tropical Africa into the colder, temperate regions of the Old World was hindered until they gained mastery over the use and making of fire. As yet we do not have enough evidence to support or refute this hypothesis. It is likely, although, again, there is no definite evidence, that the earliest hominid populations to use fires first experimented with maintaining those produced by such natural phenomena as lightning strikes, spontaneous combustion, and volcanic events before they actually understood the logistics of *producing* fire.

Ethnographically, the most common form of making fire is the drill technique of twirling one piece of wood into another to produce enough friction to make the wood dust or kindling smolder. This is usually enhanced by blowing until the material flames up. More elaborate forms of fire making by friction include the bow-drill, pump-drill, saw, and plow techniques. Striking a flint against an iron-rich rock, such as a pyrite, can also produce a spark that can be used to light kindling. Such pyrites are known from the Late Paleolithic.

See also Asia, Eastern and Southern; Chesowanja; Kalambo Falls; Lantian; Lazaret; Paleomagnetism; Turkana Basin; Vallonnet; Xihoudu; Yuanmou; Zhoukoudian. [N.T., K.S.]

Further Readings

Barbetti, M. (1987) Traces of fire in the archaeological record, before one million years ago. J. Hum. Evol. 15:771–781.

Bellomo, R.V. (1994) Early Pleistocene fire technology in northern Kenya. In S.T. Childs (ed.): Society, Technology, and Culture in Africa. MASCA Research Papers in Science and Archaeology 11 (Supplement). Philadelphia: University of Pennsylvania Press, pp. 16–28.

Binford, L.R., and Ho, C.K. (1985) Taphonomy at a distance: Zhoukoudian, "the cave home of Beijing man"? Curr. Anthropol. 26:413–442.

Brain, C.K., and Sillen, A. (1988) Evidence from the Swartkrans cave for the earliest use of fire. Nature 336:464–466.

Clark, J.D., and Harris, J.W.K. (1985) Fire and its roles in early hominid lifeways. Afr. Archaeol. Rev. 3:3–27.

Gowlett, J.A.J. (1984) Ascent to Civilization: The Archaeology of Early Man. New York: Random House.

Harrison, H.S. (1967) Fire-making, fuel, and lighting. In C. Singer, E. Holmyard, and A.R. Hall (eds.): A History of Technology, Vol. 1. Oxford: Clarendon, pp. 216–237.

James, Steven R. (1989) Hominid use of fire in the Lower and Middle Pleistocene. Curr. Anthropol. 30:1–26.

Jia, L. (1980) Early Man in China. Beijing: Foreign Languages Press.

Oakley, K.P. (1956) Fire as a palaeolithic tool and weapon. Proc. Prehist. Soc. 21:36–48.

Perlès, C. (1981) Hearth and home in the Old Stone Age. Nat. Hist. 90:38–41.

Shipman, P., Foster, G., and Schoeninger, M. (1984) Burnt bones and teeth: An experimental study of color, morphology, crystal structure and shrinkage. J. Archaeol. Sci. 11:307–325.

Weiner, S., Xu, Q., Liu J., Goldberg, P., and Bar-Josef, O. (1998) Evidence for the use of fire at Zhoukoudian, China. Science 281:251–253. See also Wu, X. (1999) Letter to Science and reply by Weiner et al. Science 283:299.

First Intermediate

Term proposed at the Third Pan-African Congress in 1955 to refer to a group of African Paleolithic industries intermediate between the Acheulean or Early Stone Age, and the Middle Stone Age industries, such as Lupemban and Stillbay. The term includes the Sangoan, Fauresmith, and Acheuleo-Levalloisian industries with evolved bifaces, picks, and Levallois or other prepared-core technologies. Since the contemporaneity of these industries is no longer accepted, it has been recommended that the term be dropped.

See also Acheulean; Early Paleolithic; Early Stone Age; Levallois; Lupemban; Middle Paleolithic; Middle Stone Age; Sangoan; Second Intermediate; Stillbay. [A.S.B.]

Fission-Track Dating

Age measurements according to the accumulation of crystal defects, or *tracks,* caused by spontaneous fission of ^{238}U (uranium) nuclei in igneous minerals and glasses. This fission is relatively slow, but the technique is exquisitely sensitive because the measurements are made on single atoms. The damage caused by the massive particles resulting from each fission event appears as elongated, tear drop–shaped pits tapering toward the final resting place of the fission particle when a polished surface or flat crystal face is etched with an appropriate reagent, such as hydrofluoric or phosphoric acid. The tracks, which range in length from ca. 10 to 20 μm depending on the mineral and the etching procedure, are commonly counted in an acetate film peeled from the etched surface, in order to reduce the optical interference from flaws and reflections in the sample itself. The number of tracks per unit area, or *track density,* is determined under an optical microscope at 500 to 2500× magnification. The sample is then irradiated with a measured dose of neutrons in a research reactor, and the surface is reground, etched under the same conditions, and the track density is recounted. The increment in fission tracks, from induced fission of the much rarer isotope ^{235}U, allows calculation of its abundance in the sample and thus the quantity of ^{238}U according to the natural ratio of the two isotopes. Thus, the age can be determined from the ratio of the induced to the spontaneous tracks, in a calculation that also takes into account the unrelated (and trackless) decay of ^{238}U by alpha-particle emission. A standard of known uranium content is normally irradiated along with the sample to monitor the neutron flux in the reactor.

The most suitable minerals for fission-track analysis are high-U minerals such as zircon, sphene, and apatite. Low-U materials such as feldspar and obsidian have much lower track densities and require several days of laborious counting to record a sufficient number of tracks for an accurate age. Normally, only minerals found in volcanic deposits are used to date surface sites, since these crystals were formed, or heat-annealed, close at the time of deposition. In principle, it is also possible to date nonvolcanic materials that have been heated sufficiently to anneal any preexisting tracks. Archaeological materials, however, would seldom be sufficiently heated to assure complete annealing, except for glass and ceramic glazes, or obsidian artifacts that have been heated almost to the point of melting. When volcanic ash layers are sampled, primary volcanic ejecta must be distinguished from reworked volcanic sediment. Furthermore, some U-rich igneous materials—of which apatite and volcanic glass are the prime examples—tend to anneal over time through recrystallization and chemical attack. Sphene, and especially zircon, is more stable. Controlled heat-annealing and recounting in irradiated samples are used to calculate a correction for the susceptibility of spontaneous tracks to be lost over time.

Fission-track dating is applicable over an age range from a few hundred thousand years to billions of years before present. For any particular material, the practical lower dating limit is determined by the time allocated for counting an adequate number of tracks. Assuming that no more than 20 hours is allocated per sample to find at least 100 tracks in a

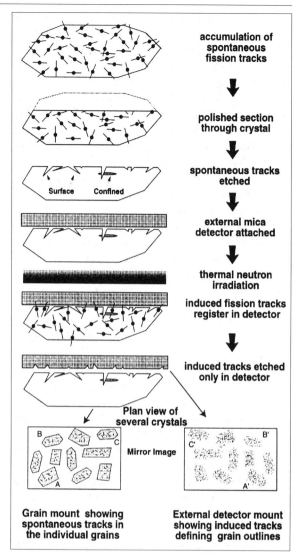

The use of an external detector allows a comparison between naturally accumulated fission tracks in a mineral grain, and the fission tracks induced by a measured dose of thermal neutrons. Since the natural decay rate of uranium is known, the age of the grain can be calculated by a comparison of the spontaneous fission tracks generated over time, and the concentration of parent uranium in the grain as represented by the induced tracks. The method has the advantage of providing fission-track age determinations for each individual mineral grain. Spontaneous tracks in a grain are exposed by chemical etching of a freshly cleaved or cut surface and counted. A uranium-free detector (plastic, or more often muscovite mica) is sealed against the surface and the sample is then irradiated. The detector is etched to reveal a mirror image of the grains showing induced tracks only. From K. Gallagher, R. Brown and C. Johnson, 1998, Fission track analysis and its applications to geological problems, Annual Reviews of Earth and Planetary Science, 26:519–572. By permission of Annual Reviews, Inc.

material with a total uranium content of 5 ppm, such as a typical obsidian, then the youngest age that can be measured is ca. 20 Ka. Archaeological and hominid-bearing deposits have been dated by fission-track analysis in East Africa (e.g., in studies of the KBS Tuff) and in Java, and the technique has been widely used by vertebrate paleontologists.

See also Geochronometry; Potassium-Argon Dating; Quaternary; Uranium-Series Dating. [H.P.S.]

Further Readings

Gleadow, A.J.W. (1980) Fission track age of the KBS Tuff and associated hominid remains in northern Kenya. Nature 284:225–230.

Naeser, C.W., and Naeser, N.D. (1988) Fission track dating of Quaternary events. In D.J. Easterbrook (ed.): Dating of Quaternary Sediments. Special Paper 227. Geol. Soc. Am. pp. 1–12.

Westgate, J.A. (1988) Isothermal plateau fission-track age of the Late Pleistocene Old Crow tephra, Alaska. Geophys. Res. Lett. 15:376–379.

Westgate, J.A., and Naeser, N.D. (1995) Tephrochronology and fission-track dating. In N.W. Rutter and N.R. Catto (eds.): Dating Methods for Quaternary Deposits. St. Johns, Newfoundland: Geological Society of Canada, pp. 15–28.

Flake

Characteristic spall removed from a stone core during artifact manufacture. A flake is characterized by a striking platform, or butt; a dorsal surface that may exhibit scars of previous flake removals from a core; and a ventral (release) surface with a bulb (semicone) of percussion, a bulbar scar *(éraillure),* ripples or waves curving away from the point of percussion, and fissures or hackle marks radiating out from the point of percussion (see illustration in STONE-TOOL MAKING). Flakes may represent by-products of tool manufacture, may be tools in their own right, or may serve as blanks for production of flake tools.

See also Core; Stone-Tool Making. [N.T., K.S.]

Flake-Blade

Flake nearly twice as long as wide, fitting the metrical definition of a blade, but manufactured on a flake core rather than a specialized blade core. Flake-blades are characteristic of certain tool industries, such as the late Mousterian, that are probable precursors to the early Upper Paleolithic of France (the Chatelperronian). Usually, Mousterian flake-blade industries do not have the standardization and carefully prepared blade cores of true blade industries of the Upper Paleolithic. Some Middle Stone Age industries from South Africa are also characterized by flake-blades.

See also Blade; Châtelperronian; Flake; Middle Stone Age; Mousterian; Prepared-Core; Stone-Tool Making; Upper Paleolithic. [N.T., K.S.]

Florisbad

Open-air site near Bloemfontein (South Africa), where in 1932 a partial hominin skull was discovered in sandy sediments around an ancient spring within, or intrusive into, Peat Level 1. Direct dates for the fossil indicate an antiquity of 260 ± 35 Ka. Associated artifacts consisted of nondiagnostic cores and flakes, together with a preserved wooden tool that resembles the handles of curved throwing sticks used by Australian Aboriginal hunters.

The human fossil consists of a frontal bone and facial fragments, which have recently been reconstructed. The broad

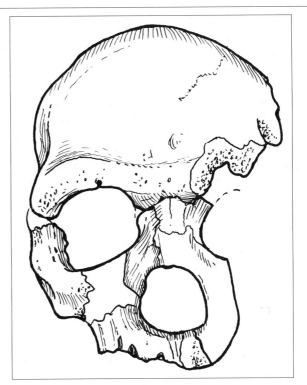

Facial view of the Florisbad partial cranium.

frontal bone is accompanied by a broad face and palate. The cranial bone is thick, the frontal moderately low, and supraorbital development is strong by modern standards. Less robust than the Kabwe fossil, Florisbad provides a morphological link between the archaic humans found with the Acheulean (e.g. Saldanha) and more modern-looking fossils from the later Middle Stone Age (MSA) (e.g., Klasies River Mouth).

An *in situ* MSA butchery floor in a younger horizon (at the top of Peat 2) is now dated to ca. 120 Ka. It contained conjoinable flakes and flake-blades on discoidal and Levallois-type cores, comparable to the Pietersburg industry.

See also Africa, Southern; Archaic Homo sapiens; Middle Stone Age. [J.J.S., A.S.B, C.B.S.]

Further Readings

Grün, R., Brink, J.S., Stringer, C.B., Franciscus, R.G., and Murray, A.S. (1996) Direct dating of Florisbad hominid. Nature 382:500–501.

Kuman, K., and Clarke, R.J. (1986) Florisbad: New investigations at a Middle Stone Age hominid site in South Africa. Geoarchaeology 1:103–125.

Flying-Primate Hypothesis

A short-lived view of the origin and relationships of bats and primates. The hypothesis, enunciated in 1986 by J.D. Pettigrew, proposed that members of the order Chiroptera (bats) were *diphyletic*—they evolved their flying adaptations twice independently, once in the ancestry of the more numerous microbats (Microchiroptera) and another time in the first fruitbat (Megachiroptera). This stillborn hypothesis was put forward because of similarities in the visual pathways of fruitbats and living primates that were subsequently considered *synapomorphies* (shared derived characters) because of Pettigrew's convictions that neural pathways are less subject to convergent evolution, and his (and his associates') argumentation using exclusively taxonomic-outgroup-driven cladistic analysis (even of wing characters) to justify the rejection of the taxonomic properties of the Chiroptera. Several rebuttal studies that followed showed that the bats are monophyletic and that a careful look particularly at the comparative biology of the neurological features that were offered as evidence for the flying-primate hypothesis revealed that they were probably convergent. There is no single line of evidence that unequivocally supports special relationships of primates with bats within the Archonta. The closest living relatives of the bats may be the relic colugos (two monotypic genera) of the order Dermoptera.

See also Archonta; Dermoptera; Primates. [F.S.S.]

Folsom

Projectile-point style dating to 10 Ka at Blackwater Draw and representing the middle range of the Paleoindian tradition. Folsom points are relatively small and lanceolate, made by pressure flaking, and thinned by a single channel flute detached from each face. First discovered at the Folsom site (New Mexico), they are best known from Lindenmeier (Colorado), where they occur with unfluted points, various scrapers, choppers, and bones of *Bison antiquus*.

See also Americas; Blackwater Draw; Paleoindian; Stone-Tool Making. [L.S.A.P., D.H.T.]

Fontéchevade

The two fragmentary fossil hominids from the late Middle Pleistocene levels of the Fontéchevade Cave in France have received an inordinate amount of attention because of the significance accorded them in the *presapiens* theory proposed by French paleoanthropologist M. Boule and developed by H.V. Vallois. Fontéchevade 1 is a small fragment of frontal bone from around the center of the browridge area, yet it lacks any development of a supraorbital torus. Vallois argued that it was an adult specimen and hence of fundamentally modern type, despite its antiquity, but other workers have suggested that it may derive from an immature skull or is intrusive from later levels. Fontéchevade 2 consists of a larger part of the cranial vault but does not preserve the browridge area. Nevertheless, Vallois postulated that the forehead and torus development would have been of modern type. Other workers studying the specimen have noted its Neanderthal-like shape. Statistical tests on cranial measurements also align the specimen with early and late Neanderthals rather than with modern humans, and few workers now support Vallois's interpretations.

See also Neanderthals; Presapiens; Vallois, Henri Victor. [C.B.S.]

Forensic Anthropology

Branch of anthropology that deals with the identification of, and the causes of, morbidity and mortality in individual remains. In many ways, the skeleton records the life history of an individual. It shows not only characteristics due to phylogenetic position and population affinity, but also variations due to trauma, diet, and disease. Forensic anthropologists commonly use this record to identify unknown skeletal remains, in conjunction with information gathered by the medical examiner, the police, the court system, and other forensic specialists.

The same strategy and skills help in the analysis of prehistoric skeletons. Anthropologists first of all carefully note the context in which bones are found, their stratigraphy and positioning, in order to address the manner and cause of death and the antiquity of the remains. Knowledge of skeletal anatomy helps determine whether the remains are human, represent more than one individual, are male or female, young or old, or show racial affinities. These identifications depend on fairly predictable life-history changes but are best stated cautiously. A useful rule of thumb: To reach the most likely identification, consider all possible observations together. An individual's age, sex, and race are not really separate questions. For example, the cranium of an adolescent male may look like that of a female because it is not yet fully developed. An individual's skeleton may look younger or older than his or her chronological age depending on the pattern of growth characteristic of the population or ethnic group.

In addition to generalized population parameters, such as sex, age, and race, indicators of more specific or individualistic life events may be seen in the skeleton. For example, a healed fracture of the forearm indicates that the individual broke an arm and was able to survive the episode. In the case of contemporary material, such traumas and other disease conditions (e.g., a pattern of arthritis or a dental abscess) may create a profile of specific insults that can be matched against medical or dental records. Toward this end, some forensic anthropologists also reconstruct facial parts from the skull itself, estimating the thickness of fat, muscle, and skin over various portions of the face.

The American Association of Forensic Anthropologists has been growing considerably as more and more physical anthropologists participate in this kind of investigative research. Involvement of anthropologists in the identification of war dead has greatly increased the precision of skeletal identification through the detailed study of large numbers of identified remains. New techniques using the microstructure of bone for aging, and multivariate discriminant functions for sexing, have resulted from initial forensic work on such remains.

See also Bone Biology; Ontogeny; Paleopathology; Race (Human); Sexual Dimorphism; Skeleton. [C.J.D.]

Further Readings

Krogman, W.M., and Iscan, M. (1986) The Human Skeleton in Forensic Medicine. Springfield, Ill.: Thomas.
Stewart, T.D. (1979) Essentials of Forensic Anthropology. Springfield, Ill.: Thomas.

Fort Ternan

Western Kenyan Middle Miocene stratified site, dated to 14 Ma by numerous potassium-argon (K/Ar) ages on included

Life-History Variation Used
to Identify Skeletal Remains

Women bear children; men do not.

Sex Determination from the Pelvis

	Female	**Male**
	Evidence of enlarged pelvic dimensions:	No evidence of enlarged pelvic dimensions:
Inlet	Elevated sacroiliac articulation Preauricular sulcus present	No elevation of articulation Sulcus not present
Cavity	Quadrangular pubis shape Pubis long relative to ischium	Triangular pubis shape Ischium as long as pubis
Outlet	Obtuse subpubic angle Wide greater sciatic notch	Acute subpubic angle Narrow greater sciatic notch

Men are generally larger and more muscular than women.

Sex Determination from the Skull and Long Bones

	Female	**Male**
	Evidence for small size with unremarkable muscle development:	Evidence for large size with pronounced muscle development:
Long bones	Small joints Muscle markings not pronounced	Large joints Muscle markings pronounced
Cranium	Small supraorbital tori Small mastoid process Minor nuchal crests	Pronounced supraorbital tori Large mastoid process Pronounced nuchal crests
Mandible	Pointed chin Obtuse gonial angle	Square chin Square gonial angle

Processes of growth and aging proceed through fairly predictable stages.

Age Determination

	Child	**Adolescent**	**Young adult**	**Older adult**
Teeth	1st permanent molars erupt	2nd permanent molars erupt	3rd permanent molars erupt	Cusps show wear
Limb bones	Secondary ossification centers appear	Arm/leg epiphyses fuse	Medial clavicle fuses	Joints show arthritis
Cranium	Metopic suture closes	— — —	Spheno-occipital suture closes	All vault sutures close
Pelvis	Pubis and ischium fuse	Ilium fuses to pubis/ischium	Secondary growth centers fuse	Pubic symphysis shows remodeling

tuffs and bracketing lavas. Discovered by Fred Wicker in 1959 during building-stone quarrying on his farm on the north slope of Timboroa (Tinderet) volcano, and excavated largely by L.S.B. and M.D. Leakey in the 1960s, the main site has yielded a large and diverse collection of fossil mammals that indicate a more open habitat than at the nearby 15-Ma site at Maboko Island. Elsewhere in Kenya, Alengerr and Kipsaramon in the Baringo sequence, and Nachola in the Samburu Hills, have similar fauna, including hominoid specimens, and are probably of the same general age. Fort Ternan is the type site of *Kenyapithecus wickeri* and also yields remains of a proconsul-like species.

See also Africa, East; Baringo Basin/Tugen Hills; Climate Change and Evolution; Kenyapithecus; Maboko. [J.A.V.C., A.H.]

Further Readings

Shipman, P., Walker, A., Van Couvering, J.A., Hooker, P.J., and Miller, J.A. (1981) The Fort Ternan hominoid site, Kenya: Geology, age, taphonomy, and paleoecology. J. Hum. Evol. 10:49–72.

Fossil

The primary source of knowledge about extinct life. In its original sense, *fossil* (from the Latin *fossa*, an excavation) meant anything curious that was dug up and thus included minerals and stones. With the development of paleontological sciences, the meaning became more restricted, to denote actual remains or other indications of past organisms. Any definition remains slightly vague, however, in terms of both the materials referred to and their context. Fossils normally carry with them some sense of antiquity. Therefore, bones or shells of animals buried quite recently, geologically speaking, or found in late archaeological situations, are sometimes designated as *subfossil* to indicate this distinction. Implications of some essential chemical or physical change are implied by the term *fossilized*, although the actual ways in which something can become preserved for geologically significant intervals of time are various. These depend in part upon the environment of burial, some circumstances being more favorable to the preservation of fossils than others.

A fossil can be an actual part of an organism, in which case it is usually some hard part, such as a piece of the skeleton of a vertebrate or wood from the trunk of a tree, that is suited to resist mechanical and chemical destruction. Most hominoid fossils are of this kind, being parts of the skeleton of the creatures concerned.

Another category comprises *trace fossils*. These are indications of the life or behavior of organisms that do not involve remains of the organisms themselves, such as the feeding burrows of invertebrate animals. There can be problems in relating a particular kind of trace fossil to the organism responsible for it. A hominid example of a trace fossil is the sets of footprints preserved in volcanic ash at Laetoli (Tanzania), believed to have been produced by *Australopithecus afarensis* 3.6 Ma.

See also Australopithecus afarensis; Laetoli; Taphonomy. [A.H.]

Further Readings

Rudwick, M.J.S. (1985) The Meaning of Fossils: Episodes in the History of Palaeontology, 2nd ed. Chicago: University of Chicago Press.

France

Country in western Europe with one of the longest and most complete records of human and primate evolution in that continent. During the Paleocene, *Plesiadapis* flourished in France, which has yielded the best cranial and postcranial samples of the genus in the world. Archaic primates, such as *Phenacolemur*, persisted into the Eocene alongside early euprimates, such as the adapids *Cantius*, *Donrussellia*, and *Adapis*, the microchoerine *Necrolemur*, and the anaptomorphine *Teilhardina* (in neighboring Belgium). The major faunal change *(Grande Coupure)* at the beginning of the Oligocene saw the end of European primates for nearly 20 Myr, but by the Middle Miocene France began to receive anthropoid emigrants from Africa. The pliopithecid *Pliopithecus* was first described from France, where it still has its greatest distribution: It arrived ca. 16 Ma, is known from ca. 20 localities (especially the type site, Sansan), and persisted until ca. 10 Ma. The dryopithecine (or potential hominine) hominid *Dryopithecus* was a slightly younger form, known especially from St. Gaudens (ca. 13–12 Ma). A variety of cercopithecid monkeys characterized the Pliocene and Early Pleistocene, such as the colobines *Dolichopithecus* and *Mesopithecus* (5–3 Ma) and the cercopithecines *Paradolichopithecus* (3.5–1.5 Ma) and *Macaca,* which arrived at the start of the Pliocene (5 Ma) and persisted into the later Middle Pleistocene (less than 250 Ka). Many of these primates were first described from French localities, some in the nineteenth century.

France has a long history of paleoanthropological studies, including such famous names as J. Boucher de Perthes, E. Lartet, M. Boule, H. Breuil, D. Peyrony, F. Bordes, C. Arambourg, H.V. Vallois, J. Piveteau, and A. Leroi-Gourhan. These workers led France to be recognized as the cradle of prehistoric research, with a wide variety of human fossils and archaeological assemblages claimed to span more than 1 Myr. Unlike many other Paleolithic areas with gaps in their prehistoric record, France shows an uninterrupted increase in the number of archaeological sites from the Middle Pleistocene to the Holocene.

The earliest evidence for human occupation comes from the southern part of the country. Numerous finds of rolled and weathered quartz pebbles and cobbles, possibly flaked by early humans, have been found together with bones of Villefranchian (Late Pliocene to Early Pleistocene) mammals (including *Elephas meridionalis,* which became extinct ca. 900 Ka), especially in the gravels of Chilhac in the Massif Central and at a number of localities along the Roussillon terraces near the Spanish border. Sites such as St. Eble in the Massif Central and others described in the Paris Basin probably do not represent human occupation but instead contain naturally flaked stones. One of France's oldest claimed sites, Vallonnet, is a small cave located on the Mediterranean coast near the town of Menton, west of Monaco. The 10 pieces in its lithic inventory of choppers and utilized flakes are recognized by some scholars as being true artifacts, but others think they are of natural origin. Paleomagnetic and paleoenvironmental data, and an association with remains of final Villefranchian fauna, suggest that Vallonnet may have been occupied ca. 1 Ma (or perhaps ca. 800 Ka) during a warm and dry interval. Soleihac, on the Massif Central, claimed as the earliest open-air site, is interpreted as a camp on a lakeshore beach at the side of an extinct volcanic crater. The archaeological inventory there consists of small retouched flakes and fragmented bones of Villefranchian mammals scattered over a 100–150 m² area. There is also a 6- × -1.5-m alignment of basalt blocks, which may represent the oldest evidence for a habitation structure in Europe. All of these occurrences are disputed on the basis of their dating and/or context.

Later in the Middle Pleistocene, the archaeological record becomes more prolific. Perhaps ca. 400 Ka, hominins occupied a beach area at Nice called Terra Amata over successive summers. No human fossils have been found there, but a large number of archaic *Homo sapiens* remains and archaic artifacts were recovered from the apparently contemporaneous Arago Cave near the eastern Pyrenees, close to where both *Dolichopithecus* and earlier artifacts are known. Generally similar hominid fossils are known from Montmaurin, and Acheulean archaeological assemblages of comparable age (400–200 Ka) include those from the type site of St. Acheul, the Abbeville gravels, and the Atelier Commont, on the Somme River. The Neanderthal lineage is especially well represented in France, beginning with the Biache skull of ca. 200 Ka, and the probably slightly younger Fontéchevade, Lazaret, and La Chaise fragments, all of which are early members of this group, mainly associated with an Early Mousterian industry. Other famous Neanderthal fossils from the Weichselian (ca. 110–30 Ka) include La Chapelle-aux-Saints, La Ferrassie, Le Moustier, La Quina, and Saint-Césaire, the youngest in France. These sites and many others have yielded a vast inventory of Mousterian artifacts, burials, and paleoenvironmental data.

The western European Upper Paleolithic was defined in France, with a sequence of Chatelperronian, Aurignacian, Gravettian (Perigordian), Solutrean, Magdalenian, and Azilian industries. These are often found superposed in caves, rockshelters and open-air encampments, associated with burials of anatomically modern humans (the Cro-Magnons, named after an early French discovery), mobile and parietal art, calendrical and numerical notation devices, and grave goods.

Because Paleolithic research has had the longest history in France and has been conducted by the largest number of scholars, it was perhaps inevitable that the chronocultural sequence developed for French materials, most notably those from southwestern France, was extended, with minor, if any, modifications over the entire Pleistocene Old World. Such an extension has subsequently proven to be erroneous on any but the grossest of scales as sequences from such places as central and eastern Europe, Siberia, Western Asia, Africa, Australia, and the New World show very different patterns of change through time.

See also Acheulean; Adapidae; Anaptomorphinae; Archaic Homo sapiens; Cercopithecinae; Colobinae; Dryopithecus; Early Paleolithic; Europe; Homo sapiens; Microchoerinae; Neanderthals; Paleolithic Image; Paromomyoidea; Plesiadapoidea; Pliopithecidae; Upper Paleolithic. [E.D., O.S.]

Further Readings

Gamble, C. (1986) The Palaeolithic Settlement of Europe. Cambridge: Cambridge University Press.

Frere, John (1740–1807)

British antiquarian. A former sheriff of Suffolk and Member of Parliament, Frere is remembered for his discovery of flint artifacts in apparent association with extinct mammalian fauna at Hoxne (Suffolk). Although he correctly recognized the great antiquity of these artifacts, his published account in *Archaeologia,* the organ of the Society of Antiquaries, in 1800 was refuted. It was not until 1859 that Frere's opinion was finally vindicated by the work of J. Prestwich (1812–1896), who demonstrated a concordance between the finds made by J. Boucher de Perthes (1788–1868) in the Somme River Valley and those found in similar river-valley systems in England, such as Hoxne. Frere is the great-great-great-grandfather of archaeologist M.D. Leakey.

See also Boucher de Perthes, Jacques; Hoxne; Paleolithic. [F.S.]

Functional Morphology

The study of the relationship between form and function. It seeks to explain what a structure is for, what it does, why it exists. The study of functional morphology focuses on those distinctive features of an animal's morphology that reflect structural adaptations to its environment and way of life. It attempts to determine the functional significance of a trait in terms of adaptation to the animal's conditions of existence—what does the trait allow or aid the animal in doing? A second goal is to understand how such a trait may have evolved, what selective advantage it may have conferred; did it originally arise for its present function or was it part of some other structure that served as a preadaptation for its present function? Function, however, is just one of several factors that influence form. Others include phylogenetic history, developmental constraints, and the constraints of architecture and materials. A complete explanation for why an animal looks the way it does would necessarily include all of these aspects.

The classic, or traditional, approach to studying the relationship between form and function is by use of the comparative method. As the name implies, it entails comparison of the morphologies of different animals. Usually two types of comparisons are made: (1) a comparison of the habits of animals with similar morphologies—if they share certain habits, the implication is that these habits are related to the function of the structure in question; (2) a comparison of the morphologies of animals with similar habits—a convergence of morphological features suggests that the features are related to the habits shared by the animals.

The comparative method can produce only a correlation between form and function. One must always keep in mind that similarities between animals could be due to common phylogenetic history or simply to accident. The probability that similarities in morphology are related to functional factors can be increased if the particular structural pattern is always associated with the particular habit or environmental feature (i.e., if one makes many comparisons, perhaps in very diverse taxa, and the same association comes up again and again). Two other ways that one can increase the confidence in an association between a particular form and function are (1) to look at a number of features in the species being compared to see if similarities can be found in other traits that might also be related to the shared habits, and (2) to determine whether closely related species with different habits lack the morphology in question.

Once an association between a form and a function has been made with the comparative method, a more direct analysis of why this association exists usually involves a series of more or less well-defined steps. It begins with a question that generally takes the form, How does this work? The second step is to make a morphological description of the system, including all of the elements affecting the mechanical functioning of the system. The third step is to construct a structural model of the system based on the anatomical description. The structural model represents an abstraction of the real system that includes only its essential aspects. The fourth step of the analysis is to construct a functional model of the system, which is essentially a dynamic version of the structural model. This often involves using the principles of mechanics (the study of forces and their effects) as applied to biological systems (i.e., biomechanics). To be useful, the functional model should make predictions about how the system operates. These predictions can then be compared to independent functional or experimental observations, thus making the functional model testable. The testing of the functional model is the fifth and final step in a functional morphological study. Most commonly, testing involves making additional functional observations using a variety of technical methodologies. These include results from electromyographic, cinematographic, or radiographic studies, as well as measurements of strain, stress, or pressure, to mention a few.

This view of how to do functional morphology is strictly mechanistic. It clearly is directed toward understanding how something works. However, as part of evolutionary morphology, functional morphology also seeks to identify structures as evolutionary adaptations and to contribute to understanding the process of adaptation (i.e., how the evolution of a trait is brought about by natural selection). To do this, one needs additional information. One perspective on identifying adaptations involves theories of optimization and efficiency. These concepts share in common a notion of a well-designed structure, one that approximates some engineering ideal. If the structure/function complex seems to approach these notions of efficiency and good design, it is taken as an indication that the observed configuration has been brought about by natural selection and contributes to the fitness of the species in question. The identification of adaptations also usually requires some knowledge about the evolutionary history of the species in question.

The goal of functional morphology is often to discover relationships between morphology and the behavior of an animal so that these associations can be applied to the interpretation of fossil material. Four criteria have been suggested for assessing whether a morphological trait observed in an extinct animal may have a particular adaptive (functional) meaning: (1) the trait must be found in some living species, since, without a living analogue, it is impossible to assess the adaptive significance of a trait; (2) in all extant species that possess the trait, it must be related to the same adaptive role; (3) there must be no indication that the trait appeared in the lineage before it came to have its present adaptive role; and (4) it must be shown that the morphological trait has some functional relationship to an adaptive role. In other words, simply showing that a correlation exists between a trait and a behavior does not prove the two are functionally related.

See also Adaptation(s); Biomechanics; Evolutionary Morphology; Locomotion; Musculature; Skeleton; Skull; Teeth. [S.G.L.]

Further Readings

Fleagle, J.G. (1979) Primate positional behavior and anatomy: Naturalistic and experimental approaches. In M.E. Morbeck, H. Preuschoft, and N. Gomberg (eds.): Environment, Behavior, and Morphology: Dynamic Interaction in Primates. New York: Gustav Fischer, pp. 313–326.

Homberger, M.G. (1988) Models and tests in functional morphology: The significance of description and integration. Am. Zool. 28:217–229.

Kay, R.F. (1984) On the use of anatomical features to infer foraging behavior in extinct primates. In P.S. Rodman and J.G. Cant (eds.): Adaptations for Foraging in Nonhuman Primates. New York: Columbia University Press, pp. 21–53.

G

Galagidae

The extant African galagos (or, less appropriately, bushbabies) are an ecologically, behaviorally, and morphologically diverse group that constitutes the family Galagidae. This is classified, together with the families Lorisidae and Cheirogaleidae, in the strepsirhine superfamily Lorisoidea. The extant galagos comprise at least 11 species that are restricted to sub-Saharan Africa, where they occupy habitats ranging from dense tropical forest to open-woodland savannah. The extant species are classified in three genera, two of which are, in turn, divided into subgenera. Several extinct strepsirhines are also included in this family.

Living galagos are small-to-moderate-size primates with mean adult body weights ranging from 70 g in the smallest species, *Galagoides demidoff*, to 1,150 g in the largest greater galago, *Otolemur crassicaudatus*. Males typically are solitary, while females usually live in small groups. Galagos feed primarily on exudates, fruits, and invertebrates. The smaller-bodied galagos favor invertebrate prey supplemented seasonally by exudates and fruit. Medium- and larger-bodied species feed year round on exudates and/or fruits and generally eat fewer invertebrates. Galagos have never been observed to eat leaves. All are nocturnal and use scent-marking behaviors and a variety of vocalizations as individual advertisements within a social context. During the day, they usually sleep in groups in semipermanent nests or inside hollow trees. Although galagos are predominantly arboreal, their habitats extend from the ground to the upper canopy. All species are active quadrupedal runners and agile bipedal leapers. Species of the genus *Galago* are extremely adept at leaping between vertical supports in a way that closely parallels the locomotor behavior of the Asian tarsiers.

All galagos have an adult dental formula of 2.1.3.3. The lower incisors and canines are procumbent and, together with the caniniform P_3, are arranged in a tooth comb, which is homologous to the condition seen in most extant lemuroids. The premolars and the molars are brachydont and bunodont, lacking primitive crests, cingula, or high pointed cusps. M^1 and M^2 both possess a hypocone. The pinna of the ear is prominent and mobile. The eyes are large, the ros-

trum typically reduced, and the petromastoid region inflated. The galagids are similar to lorisids and differ from cheirogaleids in having an ectotympanic outside of the auditory bulla.

The most distinct specializations of the living galagos are found in their postcranial anatomy and are associated with their active running and leaping mode of locomotion. All galagids possess long hindlimbs with greatly elongated calcanea and navicula. Members of the genus *Galago* have the longest hindlimbs relative to forelimbs of any living primates and can easily perform vertical leaps in excess of 2 m. The galago tail is long and hairy, usually exceeding the length of the head plus body. Unlike the tarsier, which uses a similar form of arboreal posture and locomotion, galagos do not use their tails for support while vertically perched. All digits have flat nails except the second pedal digit, which has a clawlike grooming nail. The grasping ability of both the hand and the foot are greatly enhanced by broad, flat, terminal digital pads.

Galago species are the most highly specialized members of the family and occupy the largest geographic and habitat range. Populations in each of the three species of the lesser galagos *G.* (*Galago*) inhabit dry woodland savannah, while species of the needle-nailed galago *G.* (*Euoticus*) are found in dense tropical forests. All galagos in this genus are characteristically vertical-clingers and leapers. They feed extensively on gums obtained by scraping the bark off trees with their tooth comb. All digits of the needle-nailed galago species, except for the second pedal, which retains the grooming nail, have nails with a raised central ridge that gives them a sharp, pointed, or needlelike, tip.

Galagoides species are the least morphologically specialized. They have long, pointed snouts and rely more extensively upon the primitive quadrupedal running, rather than leaping, mode of locomotion. Their diet consists mainly of fruits and animal prey. Both dwarf galagos (*G.* [*Galagoides*]) and squirrel-like galagos (*G.* [*Sciurocheirus*]) occupy heavily forested habitats ranging from dense undergrowth near the forest floor to more-open habitats in the upper canopy.

The greater galago genus *Otolemur* is the largest and most terrestrial of the galagos. Unlike *Galago*, with which it

Dwarf and Greater Galagos: Galagoides demidoff, *the smallest species (above) and* Otolemur crassicaudatus, *the largest.*

very similar to *G. senegalensis* but has specializations that preclude it from ancestry of the living species.

The relationships of the East African Early and Middle Miocene lorisoid species *Komba robustus, K. minor* and *K. winamensis, Progalago dorae, P. songhorensis,* and *Mioeuoticus bishopi* to living lineages of galagos are unclear. D.L. Gebo has suggested that all lorises and galagos evolved from a quadrupedal leaping ancestor. He characterized *K. minor* and *P. songhorensis,* based on their tarsal bones, as cheirogaleid-like primitive leapers, while *K. robustus* possessed specializations associated with a lorisidlike mode of slow-climbing and suspensory locomotion. M.L. McCrossin's 1992 study of the recently discovered *K. winamensis* from Maboko Island (Kenya) recognized *Progalago* and *Mioeuoticus* as lacking galago craniodental and postcranial specializations and as being more closely related to the lorises. While he identified galago specializations in *Komba,* he concluded that it probably diverged in the Early Miocene prior to the last common ancestor of the extant galagos. J.H. Schwartz, on the other hand, has suggested that *Progalago* fits better with the Galagidae; its relationships here are left indeterminate.

Family Galagidae
 Galago
  G. (*Galago*)
  G. (*Euoticus*)
 Galagoides
  G. (*Galagoides*)
  G. (*Sciurocheirus*)
 Otolemur
 † *Komba*
Family indeterminate
 † *Progalago*
†extinct

See also Africa, East; Cheirogaleidae; Diet; Lemuriformes; Locomotion; Lorisidae; Lorisoidea; Skull; Strepsirhini; Teeth. [T.R.O.]

Further Readings

Bearder, S.K. (1987) Lorises, bushbabies, and tarsiers: Diverse societies in solitary foragers. In B. Smuts, D. Cheney, R. Seyfarth, R. Wrangham, and T. Struhsaker (eds.): Primate Societies. Chicago: University of Chicago Press, pp. 11–24.

Gebo, D.L. Postcranial adaptation and evolution in Lorisidae. Primates 30:347–367.

Kingdon, J. (1971) East African Mammals, Vol. 1. New York: Academic.

McCrossin, M.L. (1992) New Species of Bushbaby from the Middle Miocene of Maboko Island, Kenya. Am. J. Phys. Anthropol. 89:215–233.

Nash, L.T., Bearder, S.K., and Olson, T.R. (1989) Synopsis of Galago species characteristics. Int. J. Primatol. 10:57–80.

Walker, A.C. (1987) Fossil Galaginae from Laetoli. In M.D. Leakey and J.M. Harris (eds.): Laetoli: A Pliocene Site in Northern Tanzania. Oxford: Clarendon, pp. 88–90.

is sympatric over most of its range, the greater galagos are not found in either dense forests or the open sub-Saharan woodlands that stretch between east and west Africa. *Otolemur* is not fully adapted to vertical clinging and leaping, but these galagos are active quadrupedal leapers and use a form of bipedal hopping when crossing open country. *Otolemur crassicaudatus* has been reported to travel up to 3 km across open acacia savannah in southern Africa.

Fossil Record

The galago fossil record spans most of the Neogene. Specimens indistinguishable from *Galago senegalensis* have been reported from 1.75 Ma beds at Olduvai Gorge (Tanzania) and 3–2 Ma deposits along the Omo River (Ethiopia), which have also yielded specimens attributed to the extant species *Galagoides demidoff.* Additional specimens reported from the Omo sites have been assigned by H.B. Wesselman (1984) to an extinct greater galago species: *Otolemur howelli.* The diversity of species identifiable in the Omo deposits demonstrates the existence of the three extant galago genera by the end of the Pliocene. A.C. Walker (1987) has attributed several 4–3 Ma specimens collected at Laetoli (Tanzania) and the Baringo Basin (Kenya) to *Galago sadimanensis,* which is

Facial views of (a) Large-eared greater galago, Otolemur crassicaudatus*; (b) Garnett's or small-eared greater galago,* Otolemur garnettii*; (c) Allen's galago,* Galagoides (Sciurocheirus) alleni*; (d) Elegant galago,* Galago (Euoticus) elegantulus*; (e) Matschie's galago,* Galago (Euoticus) matschiei*; (f) Senegal galago,* Galago (Galago) senegalensis*; (g) Somali galago,* Galago (Galago) gallarum*; (h) Mohol or South African lesser galago,* Galago (Galago) moholi*; (i) Zanzibar galago,* Galagoides (Galagoides) zanzibaricus*; (j) Thomas' galago,* Galagoides (Galagoides) thomasi*; (k) Demidoff's galago,* Galagoides (Galagoides) demidoff. *All drawn to the same scale. Figure prepared by D. Eden. Courtesy of Todd R. Olson.*

Wesselman, H.B. (1984) The Omo Micromammals. Contrib. Vert. Evol. 7:1–219.

Gánovce

Czech locality yielding hominid remains recovered from travertine deposits in 1926 and 1955. They include a natural endocranial cast with a capacity of ca. 1,320 ml, some cranial fragments, and natural molds of postcranial bones. The site also contained Mousterian (Taubachian) artifacts and is usually attributed to the last interglacial, ca. 130–100 Ka.

See also Europe; Mousterian; Neanderthals. [C.B.S.]

Gargas

A cave in the Hautes-Pyrénées, France, with incised animals attributed to the Gravettian, ca. 28–20 Ka. It is best known for the more than 200 red and black negative hand stencils with missing joints or bent fingers and for accumulations of incised ribbonlike *macaronis* interlacing the walls and the animals. Some of the handprints have been reused by overmarking, suggesting that the maker may have returned to renew the images. The macaronis were periodically extended or added to with branching bands. The meaning of the handprints and the macaronis have been the subject of much debate. A. Leroi-Gourhan (1967) suggested that the handprints, which are found in many Franco-Cantabrian caves, represent a system of signs. A. Marshack has suggested that the macaronis, also found in many Franco-Cantabrian caves as well as in homesites across much of Upper Paleolithic Europe, represent a water-related motif.

See also Gravettian; Late Paleolithic; Paleolithic Image. [A.M.]

Further Readings

Barrière, Cl. (1976) L'Art Parietal de la Grotte de Gargas/Palaeolithic Art in the Grotte de Gargas. 2 Vols. Mémoires de l'Institut d'Art Préhistorique de Toulouse no. III/BAR Supplementary Series 14(1). Oxford: British Archaeological Reports.

Leroi-Gourhan, A. (1967) Les Mains de Gargas: Essai pour une étude d'ensemble. Bulletin de la Société préhistorique française. 63(1):107–122.

Marshack, A. (1977) The meander as a system: The analysis and recognition of iconographic units in Upper Paleolithic compositions. In P. Ucko (ed.): Form in Indigenous Art: Schematization in the Art of Aboriginal Australia and Prehistoric Europe. London: Duckworth; New Jersey: Humanities Press, pp. 286–317.

Garrod, Dorothy Anne Elizabeth (1892–1968)

British archaeologist responsible for important excavations in Europe and the Levant. In 1925–1926 she directed work at the Devil's Tower (Neanderthal) site at Gibraltar; in 1928 she conducted research in southern Kurdistan. Shortly thereafter she excavated the Shukbah Cave, near Jerusalem, and between 1929 and 1934 she was director of excavations at the Mount Carmel sites in Israel (then Palestine), which led

to the discovery of skeletal and cultural remains of primary importance to the understanding of hominid evolution during the Middle Paleolithic. In 1939 she became the first woman to receive a professorship at Cambridge University, where she was professor of archaeology until 1952.

See also Keith, [Sir] Arthur; McCown, Theodore D.; Neanderthals; Skhūl; Tabūn. [F.S.]

Gene

Segment of DNA (deoxyribonucleic acid) responsible for the production of a specific functional macromolecule. Its direct product is called RNA (ribonucleic acid), which may itself perform a cellular function or simply bear the instructions for the production of a specific protein, which in turn performs the function. The production of RNA from a DNA molecule is *transcription;* the production of protein from an RNA molecule is *translation.* Use of the term *gene* is occasionally extended to refer to DNA stretches that are not themselves transcribed but that may have significant structural properties or affect the transcription of neighboring genes.

See also Allele; Genetics; Genome; Genotype; Molecular Anthropology. [J.M.]

Genetics

Defined by W. Bateson in 1906 as the study of "the physiology of heredity and variation." The laws of heredity and variation were unknown to C. Darwin, who nevertheless recognized them as the major unanswered questions in his own nineteenth-century theory of evolution. The field of genetics is thus essentially a twentieth-century endeavor, and we now acknowledge that evolution is, in its fundamentals, the genetic divergence of populations across time and space. The nature of those changes and how they result in what we recognize as evolution are studied by the numerous subdisciplines of genetics.

Genetics has traditionally been a sister discipline to physical anthropology, of great interest to students of human origins and prehistory. To an earlier scientific generation, genetics formed a basis for racial classifications of humanity, but modern interests focus upon the causes of individual differences within human populations, mechanisms of microevolutionary change, and the primary basis of relationships among the primates.

Classical Genetics

Austrian botanist G. Mendel derived the basic tenets of heredity in the mid-1860s. His work, however, was not appreciated until the turn of the twentieth century, apparently because contemporary studies of heredity conflated intergenerational transmission with organismal development, while Mendel's research involved only the former. It was only several decades later that biologists such as A. Weismann effected a rigorous separation between the processes of heredity and development, permitting Mendel's work to be seen in a new light. Mendel's Law of Segregation states that inheritance is packaged into units (later called *genes*) that ordinarily occur in pairs but separate from each other at some stage

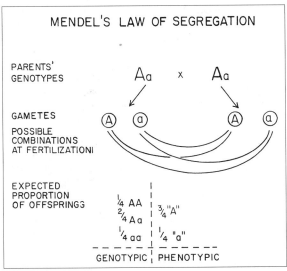

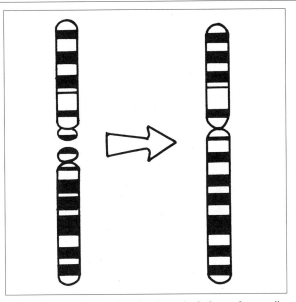

Human chromosome 2 was formed as the result of a fusion of two smaller chromosomes, easily identified among the chromosomes of the great apes and Old World monkeys. The pattern of bands observable are Giemsa, or G-bands. Courtesy of Jon Marks.

Mendel's Law of Segregation describes the behavior of a trait determined by a single gene. Here two heterozygotes (genotype Aa) produce two classes of gametes (A and a). Since, presumably, fertilization occurs at random, we expect three classes of genotypes (AA, Aa, and aa) approximately in the ratio of 1:2:1. Since the heterozygote has the same phenotype as the dominant homozygote, we expect two phenotypic classes in the ratio 3:1. Thus a couple, each heterozygous for Tay-Sachs disease (caused by a recessive allele), has a 25 percent chance of producing an offspring afflicted with the disease. Courtesy of Jon Marks.

of the reproductive cycle. The expression of a gene may depend upon the constitution of its partner: If they differ, one may conceal the effects of the other. A pair of genes that differ from each other are called *alleles;* the allele whose effect is masked is *recessive;* the expressed allele is *dominant.*

Mendel's Law of Independent Assortment states that the separation of any pair of alleles during the reproductive cycle is random with respect to the separation of any other pair (i.e., combinations of alleles do not travel together). We now know this to be true only for genes that are unlinked, or located on different chromosomes. Alleles that are on the same chromosome have a small probability of becoming unlinked in the next generation by a process known as crossing-over.

While Mendel's laws lay the foundation for our understanding of heredity, we now know their direct applicability to be rather limited. To observe Mendel's laws operating, it is necessary that the genetic constitution *(genotype)* be directly translated into an observable character *(phenotype)* that can be assessed in the organism and that a sufficient number of offspring from each mating be available for the investigator to establish the pattern of inheritance. The development of an organism is an extraordinarily complicated process; it follows that most characters directly attributable to single-gene variations manifest themselves as pathologies. It is no surprise, therefore, that much of our knowledge of classical genetics comes from the fruitfly, *Drosophila,* rather than from our own species. Indeed, simple Mendelian inheritance is usually demonstrable for humans only in the case of familial genetic diseases or in biochemical variants, such as the blood type.

Cytogenetics

Cytogenetics is the study of the cellular components of heredity, the chromosomes. Shortly after the rediscovery of

Mendel's laws, it became apparent that these microscopically observable structures were themselves the bearers of the genes, which were shown to be arranged linearly along the length of the chromosomes. Chromosomes were also seen to be the structures that actually do segregate during the reproductive cycle, physically following the letter of Mendel's law. The chromosomal basis of primary sex determination (females being XX and males XY) suggested that chromosomes might be the vehicles bearing the genetic instructions into the next generation. The general relations among chromosomes, genes, and inheritance were established largely through the research of T.H. Morgan and his colleagues on *Drosophila.*

Chromosome sizes and shapes are generally constant for each cell of the body and characteristic as well of the species from which they come. Rearrangements of the chromosomes may occur in some individuals, however. When such a rearrangement does not alter the amount of genetic material, but merely redistributes it, the rearrangement is *balanced* and is accompanied by few or no clinical manifestations. When the rearrangement does involve a change in the quantity of material, it is *unbalanced,* and many syndromes are known to be the result of such rearrangements. Cri-du-chat syndrome, for example, is due to a deletion in chromosome 5, and Down's syndrome is due to a duplication of at least part of chromosome 21.

Since balanced rearrangements usually have no effect upon the phenotype, we find that closely related species may frequently vary in the numbers, shapes, and sizes of their chromosomes, and variation in chromosome form may be useful as phylogenetic characters. The chromosomes of the great apes, for example, differ but little from those of humans. The most noteworthy difference is the fusion of two chromosome pairs in a human ancestor, creating the human state of 23 chromosome pairs per cell, as opposed to the 24 chromosome pairs in the cells of the great apes.

Quantitative Genetics

While the followers of Mendel's work developed a particulate theory of inheritance, a different school of thought followed F. Galton in studying the inheritance of *quantitative characters*. Quantitative characters are those that are continuously distributed, such as weight or height, rather than discretely distributed, such as albinism or sickle-cell anemia. Discrete traits could often be shown to follow Mendel's rules of particulate inheritance, but continuous traits could not. Indeed, these traits (e.g., skin color) often appeared to blend in offspring. Genetic studies of continuous traits were initiated by Galton and refined by K. Pearson and R. Fisher, in terms of the correlations between relatives for values of the trait under study. The modern science of statistics was born in the study of quantitative genetics.

A schism between the Mendelian and the Biometric approaches soon developed over the role of heredity in Darwinian evolution. If heredity were primarily Mendelian, then evolution must proceed by the substitution of a "tall" allele for a "short" allele, or a "black" allele for a "white" allele. This is a *saltational* view of evolution, in which populations jump across character states. If, on the other hand, evolution is gradual, as Darwin conceived it, then the discrete characters and the Mendelian rules that govern their inheritance are interesting but irrelevant, because those rules would not describe the changes in average values of phenotypic distributions that are the main foci of Darwinian evolution.

The rivalry between the two schools was effectively resolved by Fisher, who showed in 1918 that if several genes contribute additively to a single character, then the biometric data are accountable under Mendelian inheritance. For example, it has been proposed that the difference between the skin color of African and European Aboriginals is due to the cumulative effects of five to seven genes.

While the rivalry between classical and quantitative genetics no longer exists, the difference in emphasis remains. Classical genetics concerns itself with the material foundations of biological diversity and the hereditary mechanisms; quantitative genetics is more abstract and more statistically refined, and it studies only phenotypic products.

Population Genetics

The field of population genetics dates to shortly after the rediscovery of Mendel's laws, when G.H. Hardy and W. Weinberg independently showed that the operation of these laws could be mathematically extrapolated from a single individual to an entire population. Now colloquially called the Hardy-Weinberg Law, this extension of Mendelian laws describes the allocation of alleles into organisms (i.e., the relationship between allele frequencies and genotype frequencies) and shows that the relative frequencies of two alleles in a population will remain unaltered if the only forces operating upon them are those of Mendelian segregation and assortment.

By 1932, four mathematically oriented biologists (S.S. Chetverikov, R.A. Fisher, S. Wright, and J.B.S. Haldane) had published major works describing the perturbations that would occur to the genetic composition of populations under various circumstances. These circumstances represent deviations from the conditions of the Hardy-Weinberg equilibrium. The powerful mathematical model that combines these factors into a single theory is S. Wright's (1970) *shifting balance* or *adaptive landscape,* which emphasizes the interaction of deterministic forces (natural selection) and stochastic forces (genetic drift) in producing evolutionary novelties. The fundamental construct of population genetics is the *gene pool,* a summation of all possible gametes in a population. The gene pool is partitioned every generation into groups of pairwise combinations, or *genotypes.* The gene pool can change through time or can be divided geographically: This is the formal basis for the study of microevolution.

Three genetic processes operate at the cellular level in individuals to promote genetic diversity: *mutation* (constantly generating new alleles), *independent assortment* (transmitting new combinations of chromosomes into the next generation), and *crossing-over* (transmitting new combinations of alleles on the same chromosome into the next generation). This genetic diversity is distributed in populations and affected by four factors: *inbreeding* (making populations more homozygous); *natural selection* (making populations more adapted to local circumstances); *genetic drift* (making populations nonadaptively different); and *migration, or gene flow* (homogenizing different populations).

The major drawback of population genetics is that, while the perturbations in the gene pool can be modeled with a high degree of sophistication, relatively little is known about either the translation of genetic differences into anatomical characteristics or the generation of reproductive incompatibilities among different parts of a population.

Molecular Genetics

Molecular genetics studies the transmission, function, and variation of the hereditary material, DNA (deoxyribonucleic acid). The structure of DNA is the famous double helix, deduced by Watson and Crick in 1953. The inner part of the molecule contains the sequence of nucleotides (adenine, guanine, cytosine, thymine) that regulates the form and production of proteins and governs cellular processes. A gene is, therefore, an informational segment of DNA; the total DNA contribution of one parent is a *genome.* It is now known, however, that very little of the DNA actually is genic in nature. The vast bulk of genomic DNA lies between genes, is not expressed phenotypically, and is either functionless or has, at best, a very cryptic function.

The fundamentals of gene function were elucidated in the 1960s. The nucleotide sequence of genic DNA is informational when read in groups of three, or *codons.* In the nucleus, DNA is used as a template for the production of a molecule of messenger RNA (ribonucleic acid) (mRNA), whose structure conveys the information encoded by the DNA into the cytoplasm. After certain modifications to the mRNA molecule, the codons are translated into a precise sequence of amino acids, which constitutes a protein. This process of translation is mediated by a different class of RNA molecules, transfer RNAs (tRNA).

Variation is produced at the molecular level by several processes, most of which are only sketchily understood. First and foremost are random-point mutations, the substitution

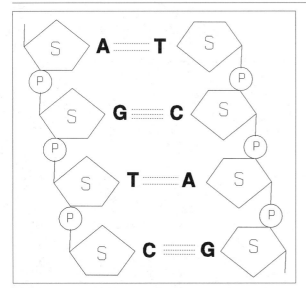

Molecular structure of the DNA molecule. S and P indicate the sugar and phosphate components, respectively, of the DNA "backbone." The sequence of bases in the center of the molecule encodes the genetic information. On opposite strands, Adenine (A) and Thymine (T) are joined by two bonds; Guanine (G) and Cytosine (C) are joined by three bonds. The two DNA strands are held together by weak bonds (dotted) joining the nucleotide pairs. Courtesy of Jon Marks.

The early breakthroughs in the study of molecular evolution in the 1960s produced expectations that molecular studies would solve all, or at least many, of the existing questions of evolutionary biology. Unfortunately, this has not turned out to be the case. While some questions have been resolved, others have remained unanswered, and still other questions have been generated by the study of the evolution of macromolecules.

Developmental Genetics

This subfield is concerned with the translation of the organism's genotypic instructions into its phenotypic characters. This is still largely unexplored terrain, with nearly all of the data coming from very few organisms: fruitfly, frog, sea urchin, nematode worm, and mouse.

The two most important late-twentieth-century research areas are *genetic regulation* (the processes by which genes are turned on and off) and *cell differentiation* (the processes by which the cells of a growing embryo become progressively more specialized). These are related by the fact that cell differentiation apparently results from the selective expression of genes.

Genetic regulation is poorly understood and involves molecular controls over the rate and efficiency of both transcription and translation. These controls are known to include the chemical modification of nucleotides, such as methylation; altered DNA conformations, such as the "left-handed" Z-DNA structure; folding of the DNA or mRNA molecule, changing its accessibility to transcription or translation; interactions of genes with other macromolecules, such as regulators or repressors; post-transcriptional changes in the mRNA, such as intron removal; post-translational modifications in proteins; and even the frequencies of certain codons in the gene, which may limit the rate of translation via the availability of certain tRNA molecules.

of one nucleotide for another (or insertion or deletion) at a specific site. Sickle-cell anemia is traceable to a single-point mutation in the beta-globin gene. Next, there are processes that produce duplications or deletions of DNA segments and often lead to tandemly repeated DNA sequences (families of genes lying adjacent to one another). These gene families are often coordinated in their regulation and evolution. Finally, there are processes in which a foreign piece of DNA is inserted or deleted. An example is the interpolation of the nearly one million *Alu* sequences, each about 300 nucleotides long, throughout the human genome.

gene

transcription

precursor mRNA

processing

mature mRNA

translation

protein

A gene composed of double-stranded DNA is transcribed in the cell nucleus, yielding a single-stranded mRNA molecule. The mRNA is processed by removing some stretches, "capping" one end, and adding a "tail" of adenines to the other end. The instruction in the processed or "mature" mRNA is then translated outside the nucleus to yield a specific protein. Courtesy of Jon Marks.

In the fruitfly, *Drosophila,* mutations that affect the most primary aspects of development are being carefully analyzed: determination of polarity in the embryo (dorsal/ventral; anterior/posterior, etc.) and laying down of the body segments. Some of these genes are expressed within hours of fertilization of the egg and contain a DNA sequence that codes for a protein region of about 60 amino acids, the *homeo domain,* which appears to have the property of binding to DNA. The corresponding DNA sequence, a 180-base-pair *homeobox,* has been found to be very similar in mammals—which is surprising, given the magnitude of biological difference between mammals and insects. There appear to be about 40 homeo-box-containing genes in humans, distributed in four chromosomal clusters. In humans, the expression of homeo-box-containing genes has been found in neural cells of the very early embryo and appear to have a role in spatially orienting its cells, as in the fruitfly.

See also Gene; Genome; Genotype; Molecular Anthropology. [J.M.]

Further Readings

Cavalli-Sforza, L., and Bodmer, W. (1970) The Genetics of Human Populations. San Francisco: Freeman.

Crow, J.F. (1986) Basic Concepts in Population, Quantitative, and Evolutionary Genetics. New York: Freeman.

Falconer, D.S. (1981) Introduction to Quantitative Genetics, 2nd ed. New York: Longman.

Lawrence, P.A. (1992) The Making of a Fly: The Genetics of Animal Design. Cambridge, Mass.: Blackwell.

Lewin, B. (1994) Genes V. New York: Oxford University Press.

Wright, S. (1970) Random drift and the shifting balance theory of evolution. In K. Kojima (ed.): Mathematical Topics in Population Genetics. New York: Springer-Verlag, pp. 1–31.

Genome

Totality of genetic material, or DNA (deoxyribonucleic acid), contained in a gamete, or reproductive cell. It was once thought that the genome simply consisted of protein-coding sequences, linked end to end. We now know that the human genome contains ca. three billion nucleotide pairs; this figure varies little among extant reptile, bird, and mammal species. Some lungfish are known, however, with 50 times more DNA per cell. Among amphibians alone, genomes are known to range from about one-third to 25 times the size of the human. There is, thus, no clear relationship between organismal evolution and genome size.

About 90 percent of the human genome consists of intergenic DNA (i.e., DNA that lies between genes). On the average, only about 10 percent of any gene is actually informational. Protein-coding sequences are now known to be interrupted by noncoding stretches, often quite lengthy, and are also flanked by noncoding sequences. Thus, only about 1 percent of the genome appears to be functional or informational and, hence, important in organismal evolution.

The genome is often arbitrarily divided into two components, *repetitive* and *unique-sequence,* which are of roughly

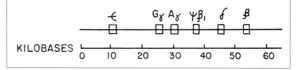

A minuscule segment of the human genome is the betaglobin gene cluster, located on chromosome 11. The actual protein-coding sequence of each gene is 438 nucleotides, but the five functional genes occupy nearly 70,000 nucleotides in the genome. Courtesy of Jon Marks.

equal proportion in humans. Repetitive DNA actually forms a continuum of sequences that vary both in length and in frequency of repetition. The most highly repetitive and simplest genomic DNA is called *satellite* DNA; this constitutes 4 percent of the human genome and is scattered across all of the chromosomes, generally localized in the region around the centromere. Unique-sequence DNA also forms a continuum of sequences, which, while often not literally unique, are at least not highly redundant. This DNA component contains the genes, as well as other elements as yet to be well characterized.

Genes are located in clusters that form as the result of tandem duplications of an ancestral primordial gene. A derivative copied gene is superfluous and, therefore, may accumulate mutations that either enable it to take on a new, related function or shut it down because of incapacitating mutations. In the latter case, it becomes a *pseudogene.* Sometimes, by processes not yet understood, the duplicate gene can be corrected against the original, so that the two (or more) appear to evolve in concert. Often, the new function is similar to the old but is specialized for a different developmental stage.

The human beta-globin cluster, for example, is responsible for producing part of the hemoglobin molecule, which transports oxygen in the bloodstream. It is located on chromosome 11 and spans ca. 70,000 nucleotides. It consists of an embryonic gene (ε), two fetal genes (Gγ and Aγ, which are corrected against each other), a pseudogene (ψβ1), and two different adult genes (δ and β), but all bear profound similarities to one another.

In a microevolutionary context, we may note that a single nucleotide change in the β gene is the cause of sickle-cell anemia, a genetic syndrome afflicting many human populations. In a macroevolutionary context, we find that the fetal-embryonic genes duplicated from the adult group ca. 200 Ma in an early eutherian mammal; the subsequent duplications occurred in a later mammal ca. 120 Ma, and the fetal genes duplicated in the catarrhine lineage ca. 40 Ma.

The alpha-globin gene cluster is located on human chromosome 16, and its genes code for the other hemoglobin subunit. The alphas and the betas diverged from each other ca. 400 Ma. The frog *Xenopus* still retains the close physical linkage between the alpha and the beta genes, while the jawless fishes retain but a single globin gene.

See also Gene; Genetics; Molecular Anthropology. [J.M.]

Further Readings

MacIntyre, R., ed. (1985) Molecular Evolutionary Genetics. New York: Plenum.

Genotype

Genetic constitution of an individual. As any human has two copies of each gene, parts of the genotype are often represented by a pair of letters. Different genotypes can have identical expressions, as occurs when one allele is dominant (A) to another (a) for a particular trait. Here the heterozygote (Aa) is phenotypically identical to one of the homozygotes (AA), despite the difference in genotype.

See also Allele; Genetics; Phenotype. [J.M.]

Genus

Rank in the hierarchy of classification that lies below the family group (including tribes and subtribes) and above the subgenus. The first component of the italicized and latinized species name (e.g., *Homo sapiens*) is the name of the genus (in this case, *Homo*). Genera are, in essence, monophyletic groupings of species, each species included within the genus bearing a different second (specific) name. No absolute rules determine how many related species should be included within a given genus, but, as with any inclusive taxon, monophyly is essential. Remarkably, given the fact that genera may contain widely differing numbers of species and, hence, of branching events, genera do tend to possess an individual Gestalt reality; it is rarer than one might expect that in the living biota one has to puzzle over the allocation of "intermediate" species to one genus or another.

Each genus must be defined by a *type species,* with which all other species placed in the genus must be compared. The valid name for a genus is the first half of the binomen first applied to its type species according to the provisions of the *International Code of Zoological Nomenclature.*

See also Classification; Nomenclature; Species; Subgenus; Systematics; Taxonomy. [I.T.]

Further Readings

Eldredge, N., and Cracraft, J. (1980) Phylogenetic Patterns and the Evolutionary Process. New York: Columbia University Press.
International Trust for Zoological Nomenclature. (1985) International Code of Zoological Nomenclature. Berkeley: University of California Press.

Geochronometry

The quantitative measurement of geologic time. *Geochronology* is the broader subject, which includes both quantitative age determinations and relative methods of dating, such as biochronology, to determine the order of events in Earth history. Most geochronometric methods are based on the fact that the decay of long-lived radioactive isotopes leaves a meaningful record in the rocks, either as daughter isotopes, physical damage, electrons trapped in energy wells, or deviation of the isotopic composition of a sample from that of similar material being formed at present. A second method of obtaining the age of a stratum, that of counting backward from the present on the basis of cyclic events in the geologic record, has taken on new vitality with the validation

beginning in the 1980s of Milankovitch's 1930–1940 calculations of an orbital imprint on past climates.

In addition, some progressive chemical changes in geological and fossil materials, such as racemization of organic molecules, fluorine uptake, and hydration, are used to estimate age in circumstances in which effects of external environmental influences (primarily temperature and groundwater chemistry) can be eliminated from analyses.

Placing an event in time must be distinguished from establishing the time interval over which a process has operated. In varved (annually or otherwise periodically layered) sedimentary sequences, ice layers, tree rings, coral growth, and other seasonally inflected records, it may be possible to state quite accurately the duration of a counted interval or the amount of time that separates two events in the counted interval, without being able to state the age of the interval itself with anything like comparable accuracy. For some purposes this is sufficient, but more commonly the age of the strata is desired as well.

Some iterative (i.e., successive but not predictable) features of the geological record are useful in geochronology, although they do not yield quantitative geochronometric measures of geologic time by themselves. Once a relatively complete and accurate model of an iterated sequence has been developed, the age calibration of a few points gives chronological meaning to the rest. This can provide dating in situations that cannot be gained in any other way, but they are not geochronometric methods since they depend on other dating techniques for their calibration.

Isotopic dating methods that provide reasonably precise ages for Tertiary and Quaternary strata are of greatest interest in paleoanthropology. Methods such as uranium-lead dating do not provide sufficiently precise ages for geologically young materials to be of much use. Other methods (e.g., ^{210}Pb dating and some uranium-disequilibrium methods) are applicable over too short a time period to be used in paleoanthropology but are of value in archaeology. The methods of greatest importance to hominid studies are potassium-argon (K/Ar) and its variants; fission-track dating; and uranium-disequilibrium dating. Radiocarbon dating is applicable to Late Pleistocene materials. In general, these methods cannot be applied to fossil materials themselves, so attribution of an age to a fossil requires thorough understanding of the stratigraphic relation between the dated materials and the fossils.

Some methods of interest in paleoanthropology and primate paleontology are tabulated in the accompanying table.

Each method records the time elapsed after an event that "starts the clock." For crystalline solid systems, the starting event is the moment at which some blocking temperature is reached, below which daughter products cannot escape or be erased (e.g., K/Ar, Ar/Ar, Rb/Sr, fission track). In other systems, it is the moment of crystallization itself (e.g., uranium-disequilibrium series, K/Ar in part, carbon-14 in part). In still other systems, the event may be the moment at which input stops, either by the death of the organism (e.g., carbon-14) or by burial (electron trapping in part). One principal task of a geochronologist is to determine how the

Method	Age-sensitive ratio (esp. isotopic)	Age range (yr)	Typical error percentages	Examples of datable material
Carbon-14	$^{14}C/^{12}C$	10^2-5×10^4	± 1-5%	Organic materials, carbonates
K/Ar	$^{40}Ar/^{40}K$	10^4-10^9	± 1-5%	Feldspar, biotite, amphibole, fine-grained lava, Mn-oxides from paleosol, glauconite
Ar/Ar	$^{40}Ar/^{39}Ar$	10^3-10^9	± 0.1-1%	Feldspar, biotite, amphibole, fine-grained lava, Mn-oxides from paleosol, glauconite
Trapped-charge: TL, OSL, ESR	Quantity of trapped electrons vs. annual dose	10^3-10^6	± 5-15% (TL, OSL) ±10-20%(ESR)	Quartz, calcite (bone, tooth enamel)
Fission-track (FT)	Track density vs. U concentration	10^3-10^9	± 1-5%	Zircon, sphene, apatite, glass, etc.
Rb/Sr	$^{87}Sr/^{87}Rb$	10^6-10^9	± 1-5%	Igneous rocks and minerals (normally requires analysis of more than one mineral in sample)
Th/U	$^{230}Th/^{234}U$	10^2-10^5	± 1-5%	Marine and non-marine carbonates including speleothems and travertines
Pa/U	$^{231}Pa/^{235}U$	10^3-10^5	± 1-5%	Marine and non-marine carbonates including speleothems and travertines
Pa/Th	$^{231}Pa/^{230}Th$	10^3-10^5	± 1-5%	Marine and non-marine carbonates including speleothems and travertines
Amino-Acid	D/L isomers	10^3-10^6	?	Ratite eggshell; other egg and mollusc shell

TL = Thermoluminescence; OSL = Optically stimulated luminescence; ESR = Electron spin resonance

Major geochronometric methods with age ranges, typical error estimates and types of material suitable for dating.

event that is being dated is related to the item of interest, and this requires all of the geological skill that can be brought to bear on the subject.

Even though determination of age-sensitive ratios in samples may be precise analytically, the ratios may yet be inaccurate because the relations between the materials measured and the event in question are not properly understood. For example, a measured K/Ar age on a mineral separate may yield an age of 10 ± 0.1 Ma and be a perfectly good determination in the analytical sense. If, however, this age is associated with fossils of Pleistocene age, it is patently inaccurate, probably from contamination of the sample by older grains. Unfortunately, inaccuracies are not always so obvious, and misplaced values, even for important events, may remain undetected for many years; the history of geochronometry is replete with painful case histories. The controversies over East African dating of the Rusinga *Proconsul,* the KBS Tuff, the Afar hominines, and the *Homo erectus* at Yuanmou (China) and Sangiran (Java) are vivid examples in the field of paleoanthropology.

Ages obtained on isolated samples and without independent backup should be regarded with great caution. Each method of dating has inherent weaknesses that can lead to inaccuracy. For all methods, however, the most difficult errors to detect are those hidden in small perturbations, and those for which independent information about the timing of the dated events is meager. It has become the hallmark of a good dating program to reduce random error and sample accidents by systematically overdoing everything. Internal redundancy is achieved by analyzing duplicate samples, by analyzing the same sample several times, and by collecting and analyzing samples from parallel traverses wherever possible. Nevertheless, the analysis or interpretation of a whole set of samples may be biased by some external influence, such as a regional thermal event or geological miscorrelation of the dated section, and such pervasive systematic errors are exposed only by comparison with the timing of similar or identical events from other geographic localities, by repeat analyses in different laboratories, or by the application of a different dating method.

See also Cyclostratigraphy; ESR (Electron Spin Resonance) Dating; Fission-Track Dating; OSL (Optically Stimulated Luminescence) Dating; Potassium-Argon Dating; Radiocarbon Dating; Radiometric Dating; Stratigraphy; Tephrochonology; Time Scale; TL (Thermoluminescence) Dating; Trapped-Charge Dating; Uranium-Series Dating. [F.H.B.]

Further Readings

Bishop, W.W., ed. (1978) Geological Background to Human Evolution. Edinburgh: Scottish Academic Press.
Rutter, N.W., and Catto, N.R., eds. (1995) Dating methods for Quaternary deposits. St. Johns, Newfoundland: Geological Society of Canada. Geotext 2.

Gesher Benot Ya'acov

Middle Pleistocene open-air site in the northern Jordan Valley (Israel) excavated in the 1930s by Stekelis and in the late 1980s to early 1990s by Goren-Inbar. The site is waterlogged, preserving fossil wood, bones, and stone tools. Two broken hominin femora were recently found among old collections from this site. Large basalt flakes struck from prepared cores at this site suggest possible cultural links with the Acheulean of North Africa. A basalt flow below the artifact horizon has been dated to 0.9 +0.15 Ma, which suggests a date in the late Early to early Middle Pleistocene for the site.

See also Acheulean; Asia, Western. [J.J.S.; A.S.B.]

Further Readings

Goren-Inbar, N. (1992) The Acheulian site of Gesher Benot Ya'aqov: An African or Asian entity. In T. Akazawa, K. Aoki, and T. Kimura (eds.): The Evolution and Dispersal of Modern Humans in Asia. Tokyo: Hokosen-Sha, pp. 67–82.

≠Gi

Middle and Later Stone Age open-air pan-margin site in northwestern Botswana. The Middle Stone Age horizons, dated to between 85 and 65 Ka, provide evidence of hunting of large animals such as giant buffalo (*Pelorovis*), giant zebra (*Equus capensis*), and warthog, not only in the form of faunal remains but also in the preponderance of finely trimmed small triangular stone points among the artifacts. On the basis of present-day analogies with modern hunting patterns in the area, ambush hunting at ≠ Gi is likely to have been a regular seasonal activity during the late fall to early winter, when water sources had dried up elsewhere. The Later Stone Age (LSA) horizons, beginning ca. 24 Ka, also provided evidence for ambush-hunting practices in the predominance of points over scrapers and in the teeth and horn cores of large animals, including kudu and white rhinoceros (*Ceratotherium simum*). Small pit hearths with associated lithic artifacts and faunal remains probably indicate the location of Later Stone Age hunting blinds, as these features are found below present-day blinds, indicating a long-term use-history for these features. Large pit traps were also constructed at the site. Bone points dating to at least the middle part of the LSA (ca. 8–7 Ka or possibly earlier) link the site in stylistic terms to the historic population of *ju* hunter-gatherers.

See also Africa; Africa, Southern; Later Stone Age; Middle Stone Age. [A.S.B.]

Further Readings

Brooks, A.S., and Yellen, J.E. (1987) The preservation of activity areas in the archaeological record: Ethnoarchaeological and archaeological work in the northwest Ngamiland, Botswana. In S. Kent (ed.): Method and Theory of Activity Area Research: An Ethnoarchaeological Approach. New York: Columbia University Press, pp. 63–106.

Gibraltar

The Rock of Gibraltar contains many caves, and two of these have produced Neanderthal remains. An adult (female?) skull was blasted from Forbes' Quarry in 1848, and a child's skull was excavated from the Devil's Tower rockshelter in 1926. Both show typical Neanderthal features, although the adult specimen is small and gracile and cannot be dated accurately. The child is remarkable for its large brain size (ca. 1,450 ml) for an individual of less than five years of age. Gorham's Cave has yielded Mousterian levels dated ca. 48 Ka and Gravettian dated ca. 28 Ka.

See also Europe; Neanderthals. [C.B.S.]

Gigantism

The development of radically larger body size is common in small mammal species isolated on islands, apparently because the inevitable impoverishment of the island fauna selects for more generalism in the surviving species. Cope's Rule, the tendency of successive species to become larger in

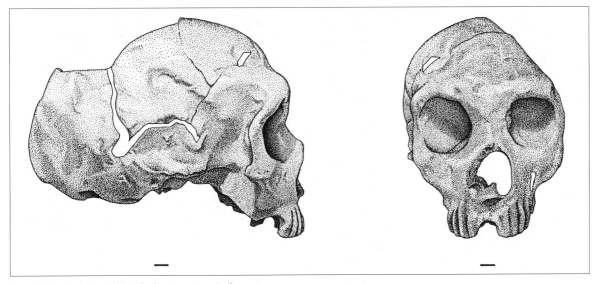

Lateral and facial views of the Gibraltar 1 cranium. Scales are 1 cm.

the course of evolution, generally, if not always, holds true. Many groups originate with a small body size relative to the adaptively optimal size. Also, in herbivores, increased body size in itself is advantageous in that reduced heat loss permits the use of less nutritive and more widely available food; in most cases, for example, only above ca. 15 kg can mammalian herbivores subsist entirely on grass and leaves. Individuals may also show phenotypic size increase in response to improved food supply, but abnormally large body size in an individual is usually pathological, especially when caused by hyperpituitarism.

See also Dwarfism; Rules. [D.P.D., R.L.B.]

Gigantopithecus

Extinct giant hominoid first recognized by G.H.R. von Koenigswald on the basis of a single M_3 purchased in a Hong Kong drugstore in 1935. Since then, more than 1,000 other specimens, mostly isolated teeth but including four massive mandibles, have been recovered from the Siwalik Hills and from the karst caves of southern China and Vietnam. The Chinese species, *Gigantopithecus blacki,* is thought to span the Early Pleistocene and most of the Middle Pleistocene. The earlier *Gigantopithecus giganteus* (= *G. bilaspurensis)* dates to ca. 9–6 Ma in the Siwalik sequences of Indo-Pakistan. This species is smaller than the Pleistocene Chinese form, and it thus appears that *Gigantopithecus* increased in size from Late Miocene to Late Pliocene time, if not throughout the Pleistocene. The youngest specimens may date to ca. 400 Ka in northern Vietnam, where *Gigantopithecus* occurs alongside *Homo* cf. *erectus,* an association also present somewhat earlier in China. Despite its occurrence in almost a dozen sites, no cranial or postcranial elements of *Gigantopithecus* have ever been recovered, probably as a result of porcupine bone-eating in caves.

There has been much discussion concerning the taxonomy and ecology of *Gigantopithecus.* A few workers have argued that this genus should be classified as a hominin ances-

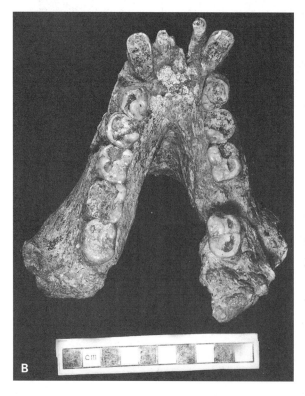

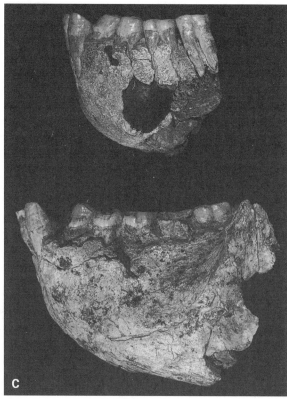

Mandibles of Gigantopithecus blacki *from Early Pleistocene of Liucheng, southern China: occlusal views of (a) subadult female (M_3 not yet erupted) and (b) adult male, left lateral view of adult female (above, M_3 lost) and (c) male. Scale bars in cm.*

tor because of its small incisors and stubby canines. In fact, however, the canines have a large diameter like those of apes, and their reduction in height is probably due to premolarization: They are worn flat on the tips from grinding use like premolars rather than puncturing like the usual catarrhine canines. Molars and premolars are large and rather flat, with very thick enamel, and the deep mandibles further reflect an adaptation to heavy chewing of harsh foodstuffs (in part, bamboo?). *Gigantopithecus* was probably derived from a *Sivapithecus* (or possibly *Lufengpithecus*) ancestry, and it is usually classified in the Ponginae. The best estimate is that *Gigantopithecus* increased in size as an adaptation to dietary pressure, much as did *Theropithecus*. The body size of *Gigantopithecus* is nearly impossible to estimate realistically, as there are no weight-bearing bones known, and the animal might well have been macrodont (i.e., with teeth and jaws especially large for body size).

See also Asia, Eastern and Southern; China; Dragon Bones (and Teeth); Hominidae; Hominini; Hominoidea; Koenigswald, Gustav Heinrich Ralph Von; Ponginae; Siwaliks. [G.G.P., E.D.]

Further Readings

Ciochon, R., Long, V.T., Larick, R., González, L., Grün, R., de Vos, J., Yonge, C., Taylor, L., Yoshida, H., and Reagan, M. (1996) Dated co-occurrence of *Homo erectus* and *Gigantopithecus* from Tham Khuyen Cave, Vietnam. Proc. Nat. Acad. Sci. USA 93:3016–3020.

Glaciation

Glaciation refers to the formation of glaciers, or *glacierization,* but the term is also used in a broader sense to include the activities of glaciers, such as their effect on the landscape and their action as an agent of transport and deposition of rock debris. Regions presently or formerly covered by glacial ice are termed *glaciated.*

Models of glacial buildup and decay are complicated and subtle in detail, but the basic process is a simple balance between supply (by snowfall) and withdrawal (by melting). In Antarctica, where melting rates are very low because of the year-round subfreezing temperatures, ice builds up even though the total annual precipitation compares to that of the Mojave Desert. In many low-latitude mountain ranges, the summer temperatures are quite warm, but glacierization occurs because the winter snowfall still exceeds the summer melt. The Antarctic conditions of constant dry cold also occur at high altitudes, and even near the equator, great mountains such as Kilimanjaro in Tanzania and Ruwenzori in central Africa, Carstensz in New Guinea, and the Andean peaks of Ecuador support glaciers that are derived primarily from nightly frosts.

Water is a substance that has the property of expanding slightly when it freezes. Pressure can reverse this process, causing ice to collapse back to water. For this reason, glaciers flow readily through internal deformation and by sliding on films of water where the ice presses against bedrock. Normally, the ends of glaciers are more or less stationary fronts,

where the rate of melting or calving equals the rate at which the flowing ice arrives. Under stable climate conditions, the ice front may remain in one narrow zone for many years, while rocks, sand, and clay brought by the ever-flowing ice keep piling up. The warmer the ice, of course, the more easily it liquefies under pressure; by the end of summer, the slow rise in the body temperature of ice at the lower end of a mountain glacier can cause the layers of ice at the base to abruptly liquefy and send a mass several miles long skating ponderously downhill in a *jokul-laup,* Icelandic for ice-run. It has also been calculated that ice caps, especially in volcanic areas, must eventually collapse from the slow absorption of terrestrial heat flow that normally radiates into the air.

By convention, the term *interglacial* in Pleistocene climatostratigraphy is reserved for periods when the great ice sheets melted completely from temperate lowlands, as at present, while the term *interstadial* refers to the periods when the ice sheets only contracted. In both instances, however, melting was due to relatively elevated global air temperatures and to concurrent changes in monsoonal storm tracks during the warm peaks of orbitally controlled climate cycles. The actual regressions of the ice front were delayed, however, until well into the warm-climate cycle because of the immense thermal inertia and high albedo (reflectivity) of the continental ice masses. In each instance the end was catastrophically rapid once it began and was synchronous with deposition of widespread sheets of ice-rafted debris on the floor of the North Atlantic and North Pacific oceans. These deposits are evidence that the glacial episodes ended abruptly in continent-scale *jokul-laups,* termed *Heinrich events,* that sent mountains of ice rumbling into the sea to spread icebergs far beyond normal latitudes.

Evidence of Glaciation

The former presence of glaciers can be reconstructed from the sediments, landforms, and fossils that remain after the ice has melted. The sedimentary evidence is in the form of *drift* (ice-deposited sediments) and in the secondary effects of glaciation on ocean waters and climate that can be seen in nonglacial strata. Drift includes *till* (stony clays) deposited directly from glacial melting, stratified till or *outwash* laid down under the influence of currents in lakes and estuaries, *diamictite* or deep-ocean tills composed of fine clays and scattered pebbles and boulders deposited from the melting of glacial ice at sea, and *loess* formed of wind-blown glacial dust.

Till is laid down in certain characteristic ways that are identified by the shape and extent of the resulting deposit. These include *moraines,* ridges of loose till built up from the material riding on the ice, or in it, which mark the melting zones along the margins and bottom of the glacier; *kames, eskers,* and *drumlins,* mounds or sinuous ridges of till deposited beneath the ice in meltwater channels or in fissures; *kettles,* depressions in the moraines left by the melting of solitary blocks of ice under the debris; and *erratics,* solitary rocks that were carried by glaciers (or by icebergs floating in the ocean) to resting places far outside their expected occurrence.

Outwash and diamictite build up in layers, and, in protected basins, the glacial clays may settle out in fine layers reflecting each summer's season of melting. The individual seasonal layers are termed *varves,* and varved deposits have been used to construct prehistoric time scales in the same way that tree rings have been used in the southwestern United States. Annual accumulation layers have also been detected in glacial ice itself, and cores taken in Greenland and Antarctica have been analyzed to show year-by-year variations in atmospheric carbon dioxide, carbon-14 production, and other conditions back to the Middle Pleistocene. Sedimentary varve chronology, on the other hand, has not been extended much past the end of the last glacial, but it has yielded important information about changes to vegetation and human occupation in northern lands.

Loess is deposited as blankets of yellow-brown, highly porous silt downwind from the continental ice sheets in the central United States, central Europe, and Ukraine, and, above all, on the North China plains, where total thickness locally exceeds 100 m. The fine, often limy dust, known as *rock flour,* is produced by the grinding of the boulder-studded glacial ice against bedrock. Rock flour is carried in suspension by glacial meltwater (causing the flat powder-blue color of glacial lakes) and settles out on mudflats, where it is exposed to the cold, dry winds that blow constantly off the glaciers. Late summer near the Pleistocene glaciers must have been a time of repeated, choking dust storms, and the loess plains of the United States and China have proven to be particularly subject to renewed wind erosion when droughts reduce the soil moisture.

The effects of glaciation on landscape, when adequately preserved, are unmistakable. On relatively low-relief terrain, the entire ice sheet passes over the land like giant sandpaper, removing soil and loose rock and grinding the bedrock down to gently rolling swells and hollows. Where the ice covers the entire landscape, its base can "flow" uphill over obstacles and out of depressions, grinding down the land with regard more to its variations in hardness than to slope or preexisting drainage. The result of this random excavation, and the irregular dumping of glacial debris, is that glaciated flatlands are very poorly drained. Stream patterns are incoherent, and the land is dotted with swamps, ponds, and gouged-out lakes. Some glacial lakes, such as the Great Lakes of the central United States, Lake Winnipeg, and Great Slave Lake, are among the largest in the world. Glacial excavation was also responsible for the beautiful lochs of Scotland, the Swiss lakes, and the Baltic Sea Basin.

Where mountains protrude above the surface of the moving ice, their sides are hollowed out into steep cliffs with knifelike junctures quite unlike those resulting from normal erosion; the Matterhorn, Jungfrau, and other toothlike peaks in the Alps owe their odd shape to this effect. Some ranges are sliced away until only isolated pegs, called *monadnocks* (after Mount Monadnock in New Hampshire) or *nunataks,* remain. Mountain valleys like Yosemite, through which glacial ice has passed, are scooped out to a distinctive U-shaped profile, unlike the V-shaped profile of nonglaciated valleys. In northern regions where such valleys were carved far below modern sea levels during the glacials, their drowned lower reaches are

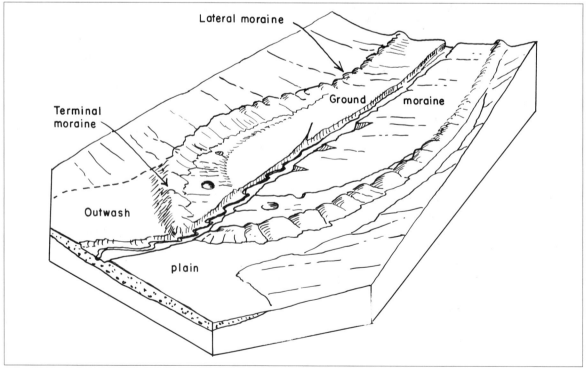

Moraines. Debris brought by flowing ice accumulates in terminal, lateral, and ground moraines and is redeposited as outwash terraces by meltwater. As the glacier retreats, successive outwash plains are developed upstream. After Flint (1971).

seen as the deep, winding inlets known as *fjords.* The most durable evidence of past ice ages, however, is flattened, glossy surfaces with deep, parallel grooves, called *striated pavements,* which are formed on hard bedrock by the weight and abrasive power of kilometers-thick, rock-studded ice sheets. Continental ice sheets are documented for Late Precambrian, Devonian, and the great Permo-Carboniferous episode by pavements that look as fresh as those of latest Pleistocene age on the gneiss outcrops in New York's Central Park. Tillites and striated pavements of Late Carboniferous and Early Permian age in South America, Antarctica, central and southern Africa, Australia, and India document the presence of a great ice sheet in Gondwanaland before the supercontinent began to fragment in the Triassic.

Glaciation also has an effect on sea level because of the vast amounts of water that move rapidly between the oceans and the ice caps. The coastal landscapes of today, with the shelf-break at the edge of the continental shelves at ca. 300-m depth, as well as the stair-step alternations of cliffs and terraces going inland, are the products of sudden drops in sea level and equally abrupt rises during Pleistocene glacial cycles. "Normal" landscapes of the Early Cenozoic and Mesozoic, when sea-level changes were much smaller, consisted of gently sloping coastal plains that extended for hundreds or even thousands of kilometers inland and of a comparably shallow offshore shelf.

The Ice Ages and Evolution

Fossil evidence of glaciation is partly negative—snakes have not yet repopulated the island of Ireland since it was last cov-ered by ice—and partly positive. For instance, the fossil remains of cold-adapted life-forms are found embedded in glacially influenced deposits (e.g., with glacial erratics, loess, or glacial outwash debris), while nonglacial beds interstratified with the glacial beds contain fossils of distinctly more warm-climate types. The fossil record also contains clear indications that a great many interisland and intercontinental migrations were synchronized with periods of glacially lowered sea level.

A circumstantial linkage between human evolution and major glacial episodes has been apparent for some time. It may be theorized, so far without much testable support, that the global climate changes involved in shifting from interglacial to glacial conditions had major effects on all continental environments and that this stimulated evolution in human populations. Be that as it may, the earliest known *Homo erectus* is coeval with Eburonian cold-climate maximum at the beginning of the Pleistocene, 1.8 Ma, and the transition to "early sapiens" (*H. heidelbergensis* of some authors) dates to the early part of the great Elster glacial climax ca. 500 Ka.

Human invasion of the Americas appears to have been controlled by glaciation as well. Between 127 and 12 Ka, most of Canada and the north-central United States was covered by a dome of ice several kilometers thick, centered on the west side of Hudson's Bay. The North American ice, termed the Laurentide ice sheet, extended as far south as the present sites of New York, Cincinnati, and Kansas City and fed icebergs into the sea along a front that stretched from Manhattan to Cape Breton Island. In central Alberta, the Laurentide ice met ice flowing down onto the plains from

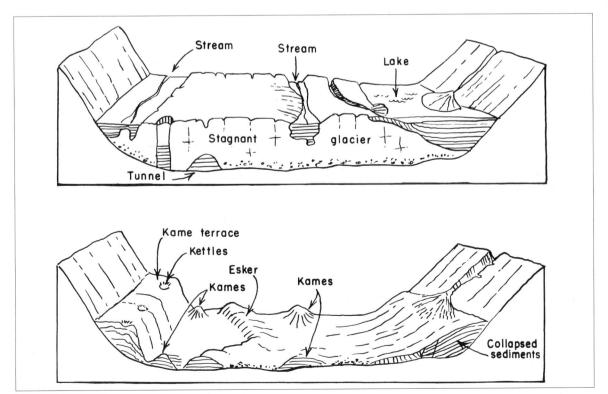

Kames and eskers. As stagnant ice (above) melts, bodies of sediment under the ice are exposed and those on the ice are left unsupported. After Flint (1971).

the Cordilleran (Rocky Mountains) ice cap, which occupied the interior from Colorado to the Yukon and emptied into the sea all along the coast of British Columbia and the Alaskan Panhandle. Although the lowlands of Beringia were open for most of this time, the way south was blocked by ice from sea to sea. This must have been a virtually impassable barrier until the breakdown of the ice sheet 11,400 years ago, because reliably documented human occupation in all parts of the New World (south of Alaska) appears to have begun just at this time.

During glacial episodes in Eurasia, the Scandinavian ice sheet buried all of Ireland and most of England and extended past the future sites of Berlin, Warsaw, and Moscow to join with ice flowing down from the mountains of the northern Urals and the Tamyr Peninsula. In addition, in all mountain regions, including those of the tropics and the southern high latitudes such as Tierra del Fuego, the Falklands, and New Zealand, the glacial fronts formerly extended as much as 2 km of elevation below their present melting limits. In Africa, this lowering of climatic zones brought the environment of the montane forest zone down onto the broad African Plateau, allowing biotic exchange in ecosystems that are restricted to high-altitude refugia (islands in the sky) during interglacials, such as today.

Continental glaciation and ice ages appear to be linked to the presence of an isolated polar continent, like Antarctica today. On such continents, uninterrupted circumpolar currents and airflow act to divert warmth from reaching the polar region, so that ice caps will expand even under the mildest global conditions. The refrigerating effect of the melting ice on the neighboring ocean will feed back, lowering world temperature and inducing ever greater volumes of ice and ever greater cooling of the ocean basins. At some point, the stabilizing effect of a warm ocean is lost, and the slight variations in insolation from orbital cycles will begin to cause increasingly violent oscillations between cold and warm periods—winter and summer, and glacial and interglacial—that we associate with modern climate. The present Antarctic ice sheet began to grow in the Oligocene, ca. 32 Ma, as continental drift widened the circumantarctic seaway, and reached modern dimensions ca. 3 Ma. The average temperature of sea water (save for the thin sun-warmed film above the thermocline) has dropped from ca. 20°C in the Eocene to ca. 4°C today, the coldest since the Permian. No change toward a warmer ocean and a nonglaciated world can be envisaged until the present arrangement of continents and ocean currents changes, which could be a long time. The Permo-Carboniferous Ice Age, when Gondwanaland lay across the South Pole, lasted ca. 80 Myr from start to finish, and at least 22 major glacial cycles—comparable to the four that have been logged so far for the Pleistocene—are represented in Dwyka-age tillite sequences in Antarctica.

Continuing basic changes in climate and ocean circulation during the Pleistocene are indicated by eastward progression of the accumulation centers in North America, as the names of the maximal advances—Nebraskan, Kansan,

Pleistocene glaciers of the northern hemisphere. Shaded areas are the regions usually covered by ice during a glacial maximum. Note that Beringia is normally ice-free even during a glacial advance but that the way south is blocked by the Cordilleran (and West Siberian) ice sheet(s). Actual shorelines (during glacial regression of sea level) not shown. After Flint (1971).

Illinoian, and Wisconsinian—would indicate. According to the area covered by ice sheets, and by temperature estimates from deep-sea proxy records, the Illinoian, or Elster, glacial maximum of ca. 450 Ka was the most severe of the Pleistocene, and the interglacial that followed was the mildest. The trend toward ever more extreme climate changes is continuing.

See also Climate Change and Evolution; Cyclostratigraphy; Holocene; Pleistocene; Sea-Level Change. [J.A.V.C.]

Further Readings

Bowen D.Q. (1978) Quaternary Geology. Oxford: Pergamon.

Denton G.H., and Hughes, T.J., eds. (1981) The Last Great Ice Sheets. New York: Wiley.

Prentice, M.L., and Denton, G.H. (1988) The deep-sea oxygen isotope record, the global ice sheet system, and hominid evolution. In F.E. Grine, (ed.): Evolutionary History of the "Robust" Australopithecines. New York: Aldine de Gruyter, pp. 383–403.

Prothero, D.R., and Berggren, W.A., eds. (1992) Eocene-Oligocene Climatic and Biotic Evolution. Princeton: Princeton University Press.

Gladysvale

South African karst-cave breccia in dolomitic limestone, ca. 13 km east of Sterkfontein and Swartkrans. The site was heavily mined for lime from 1902 until 1928 but was not known to be fossiliferous until it was investigated by R. Broom in 1936 and subsequently by C. Camp and F.

Peabody in 1948 and A. Keyser in 1988. The first hominine fossil was found in April 1992 by L. Berger, but only two teeth attributable to *Australopithecus africanus* have been recovered to date. These fossils were found in mine rubble, and it has not been possible to establish their provenance with reference to either of the two breccia units that have been identified *in situ*. The upper unit, termed *Pink Breccia*, has been tentatively dated to the Middle Pleistocene, and indeterminate hominid material has been recovered from this unit. The fauna from the Pink Breccia indicates a predominantly savannah environment. The lower unit, termed *Stony Breccia*, appears to have accumulated under wetter, more subtropical conditions than are found in the environment at present. Faunal correlations place Gladysvale between ca. 2.5 and 1.7 Ma.

See also Africa, Southern; Australopithecus africanus; Broom, Robert; Sterkfontein; Swartkrans. [F.E.G.]

Golden Spike

Informal term for a physical point in a stratigraphic section that defines a chronostratigraphic boundary. Pioneered by the Stratigraphic Committee of the London Geological Society, the "golden spike" has been useful in resolving intractable and unending problems arising from conceptual definitions. In the 1950s and 1960s, with improved correlation techniques, it became obvious that the boundaries of geological ages and epochs, as defined in geographically separate type sections, left significant gaps and overlaps, and it was concluded that "golden spikes" at the base of each type-section would be the most practical definition of the mutual top and bottom of succeeding units.

These same improvements in correlation also began to expose the inadequacy of local redefinitions of ages and stages that had long been used in regions at a distance from the typical region, not to mention in different disciplines, where the original definitions could not be well applied. These problems were particularly acute in the later Cenozoic, and especially in the Pleistocene, due to the differing criteria used by anthropologists, glaciologists, and vertebrate paleontologists, among others.

In resolving the conflict of definitions, the committee proposed the principle that "base defines boundary," which sets the rule that each successive unit extends up to, and no further than, the base of the next. The committee further proposed that each unit have as its sole definition a physical reference point at the base, located in an appropriate geological exposure. From this "golden spike" (in actual fact, often an iron bar) the recognition of the unit in other areas is a matter of correlation rather than redefinition. The location, or relocation, of a "golden spike" is a matter of international agreement. The principles of the committee have been fully adopted in modern stratigraphical codes, although often termed a GSSP (Global Stratigraphic Section and Point).

See also Biochronology; Cenozoic; Pleistocene. [J.A.V.C.]

Further Readings

Ager, D.V. (1984) The stratigraphic code and what it implies. In W.A. Berggren and J.A. Van Couvering (eds.): Catastrophes in Earth History. Princeton: Princeton University Press, pp. 91–99.

Salvador, A., ed. (1994) International Stratigraphic Guidelines, 2nd ed. Boulder: Geological Society of America.

Gönnersdorf

Magdalenian open-air site, dating to the Bølling period ca. 12 Ka, found on the right bank of the Rhine River near the city of Köln, Germany. The site contained remains of floors for three large oval tents delimited by postholes, as well as a smaller hut structure. The floor of the large tent was paved with ca. 400 schist plaquettes engraved with stylized depictions of animals and humans (mostly females). Other features included an inside cooking hearth filled with fire-cracked rocks and a nearby mammoth-scapula construction that served as a cooking tripod. A number of stone tools were made on exotic flint coming from distances of more than 100 km. Perforated shells used for decoration came from the Paris Basin and the Mediterranean coast. Faunal remains from the different dwellings suggest that some were occupied during the winter while others were used during the summer months.

See also Exotics; Jewelry; Late Paleolithic; Magdalenian; Upper Paleolithic. [O.S.]

Gorjanović-Kramberger, Dragutin Karl (1856–1936)

Croatian paleoanthropologist. Between 1899 and 1905, Gorjanovic-Kramberger carried out excavations at Krapina, a Paleolithic rockshelter ca. 40 km west of Zagreb (Yugoslavia). This work yielded some 800 fragments of fossil hominids, a large collection of faunal remains, and several thousand stone tools. Gorjanović-Kramberger concluded that these Mousterian remains represented a population of Neanderthals, which he considered to have been directly ancestral to anatomically modern *Homo sapiens*.

See also Krapina; Neanderthals. [F.S.]

Grade

Ill-defined term, derived from the archaic notion of the *Scala Naturae*, that loosely denotes a "level of organization." The epithet *monkey*, for example, applies to members of both the Ateloidea and the Cercopithecoidea, although together these do not represent a monophyletic grouping. In this case, the grade *monkey* denotes those living primates that are in some intuitive way more evolved than the strepsirhine primates but less evolved than the apes and humans; the only characteristics they share are medium body size, moderate brain size, and the general presence of a moderately long tail. This contrasts to the more rigorous concept of a *clade*, such as Catarrhini or Platyrrhini, some members of each of which are monkeys. Other grades among primates include *ape* and *prosimian*.

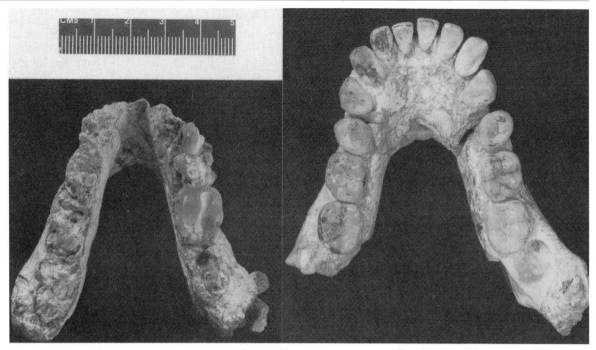

Occlusal view of two female mandibles of Graecopithecus freybergi, *lined up so that the second molars are alongside each other. On the left is an aged (and damaged) individual which is the holotype of the species. On the right is a subadult individual which has been made the type of* "Ouranopithecus macedoniensis" *but probably represents the same species. Courtesy of Peter Andrews.*

Within the human lineage, the notion of grades has been used to obscure the necessity for the precise delineation of species; as long as forms of more or less similar brain size or archaeological context could be grouped together as a grade, there was no need to inquire as to whether the grouping actually corresponded to an identifiable biological reality. Thus, while the notion of the grade may occasionally be useful in a vague, vernacular sort of way, it should never be employed when species or monophyletic taxa are under discussion.

See also Ape; Clade; Monkey; Monophyly; Prosimian; Scala Naturae. [I.T.]

Graecopithecus

A moderately well-known genus of hominoid primate from the European Miocene sometimes thought to be close to the origin of the great apes and humans. The type specimen of *Graecopithecus freybergi* was described in 1972 from Pyrgos, near Athens, on the basis of a damaged mandible with two teeth preserved. Since then, much more abundant remains have been found at three localities in northern Greece, and these have been assigned to a separate genus and species, *Ouranopithecus macedoniensis*, although there are no significant distinctions separating them. The northern sites, especially Ravin de la Pluie, are probably of later Vallesian age (early Late Miocene, ca. 9.5 Ma), while Pyrgos may be up to 1 Myr younger. One cranium and several maxillae and mandibles (but no postcrania) are known, and these preserve some characters that may link them with the hominine lineage, i.e. the African apes and humans. The form of the browridge and muzzle, suggesting development of klinorhynchy, and the morphology of the subnasal region, which is similar to that of the hominines, both suggest rela-

tionship with this clade. An alternative view sees *Graecopithecus* closely related to *Dryopithecus*, with both genera included in the Dryopithecinae.

See also Clade; Dryopithecinae; Dryopithecus; Europe; Hominidae; Homininae; Hominoidea; Skull. [P.A.]

Grande Coupure

Originally proposed in 1909 by H.G. Stehlin to denote a major event in mammalian history, the *Grande Coupure* denotes the wholesale replacement of archaic lineages in central and western Europe by modern ungulate and carnivore groups from North America, and by cricetids, murids, and other advanced rodents from Southeast Asia, during the Early Oligocene, ca. 33.5 Ma. Stehlin saw this change as a single event that coincided with the end of the Eocene and as the greatest revolution in mammalian faunas during the entire Tertiary. Although Stehlin's idea of perfect sychronicity has not survived, modern stratigraphers still recognize a massive turnover beginning in the basal Oligocene (Rupelian or Stampian). This time was, in fact, marked by an episode of unprecedented global cooling with a significant series of expansions of the Antarctic ice cap and consequent sea-level regressions, coinciding with very high extinction rates in marine invertebrates, including molluscs and microfauna, which has been termed the *End-Eocene Event* by marine paleontologists. The length of time involved in the mammalian turnover, however, is a subject of debate, since the immigrant taxa do not all appear in the European record at the same time. Revised concepts of the Oligocene in Eurasia have also contributed to uncertainty in this regard.

The African mammal fauna appears to have been revolutionized sometime in the Early Oligocene, in an episode

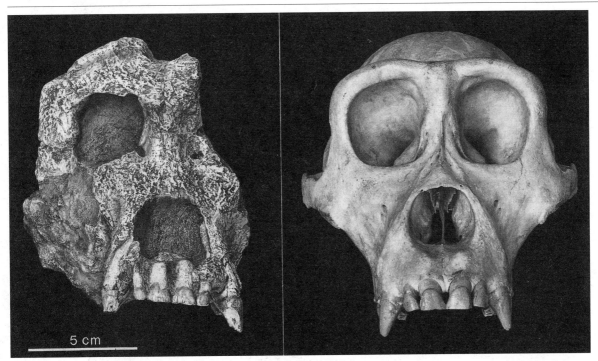

Facial view of male Graecopithecus freybergi *(cast, on the left) and female* Gorilla gorilla, *showing overall similarity in muzzle and browridge structure.*

of immigration that could perhaps be included as part of the *Grande Coupure*, although the evidence is found only in the comparison of the Eo-Oligocene "before" of the Eayum (Egypt) and the Early Miocene "after," in East Africa, for instance at Lothidok, Songhor, and Rusinga. The diversity and degree of evolution in the Early Miocene descendants of the immigrant lineages, however, make an Early-to-Middle Oligocene age for this momentous transition much more likely than a later time. Equids did not enter Africa at this time, and some of the rodent lineages that did invade were of indigenous European Eocene stock; but, with these exceptions, the post-Fayum immigrants into Africa were from groups that were also part of the *Grande Coupure* in Europe: rhinoceroses, chalicotheres, primitive hornless ruminants (tragulids, gelocids, moschids), suids, fissiped carnivores (mustelids, viverrids, arctocyonids, felids), ochotonids, and the Asian-origin rodents such as dendromurids and cricetids.

The introduction of this diversity of new mammals and their explosive adaptation (most notably in the ruminants, which rapidly gave rise to giraffids and bovids) had a predictably strong effect on the indigenous African groups. By the Early Miocene, ca. 20 Ma, some, such as the tenrecs, hyraxes, African hyaenodonts, and Southern Hemisphere rodents, were greatly reduced, while others, such as barytheres, embrithopods, African lorises and marsupials, and possibly the last mainland lemurs, had become extinct. On the other hand, the advanced proboscideans and, above all, the catarrhine primates adapted to the new conditions and entered the Miocene with a wide diversity of successful new lineages.

In South America, ancestral platyrrhines (not far removed from, but more primitive than, Fayum anthropoids) and Southern Hemisphere rodents first appear in Late Oligocene faunas, but may have entered much earlier, raising the possibility that intercontintal interchanges in the Early Oligocene were almost worldwide in scope. Further evidence for a South Atlantic crossing between Africa and South America at about this time comes from the disjunct fossil and living distribution of parrots, boid snakes, iguanas, cichlid fishes, and various insects on both continents.

See also Cenozoic; Fayum; Miocene; Oligocene; Sea-Level Change. [J.A.V.C.]

Further Readings

Prothero, D.R. (1995) The Eocene-Oligocene Transition: Paradise Lost. New York: Columbia University Press.

Prothero, D.R., and Berggren, W.A., eds. (1992) Eocene-Oligocene Climatic and Biotic Evolution. Princeton: Princeton University Press.

Savage, D.E., and Russell, D.S. (1983) Mammalian Paleofaunas of the World. Reading, Mass.: Addison-Wesley.

Van Couvering, J.A., Aubry, M.-P., Berggren, W.A., Bujak, J.P., Naeser, C.W., and Wieser, T. (1981) The Terminal Eocene Event and the Polish connection. Palaeogeog. Palaeoclimatol., Palaeoecol. 36:321–362.

Gravettian

Early Upper Paleolithic industrial complex of Europe, ca. 28–19 Ka, characterized by straight-backed points and burins. While the broadest use of this term sometimes includes the Upper Perigordian complex of southwestern France, the Gravettian is more often restricted to industries from eastern France, southern Germany, Austria, Czechoslovakia, southern Poland, Russia, Ukraine, Romania, Yugoslavia, Greece, Italy, and Mediterranean Spain. These in-

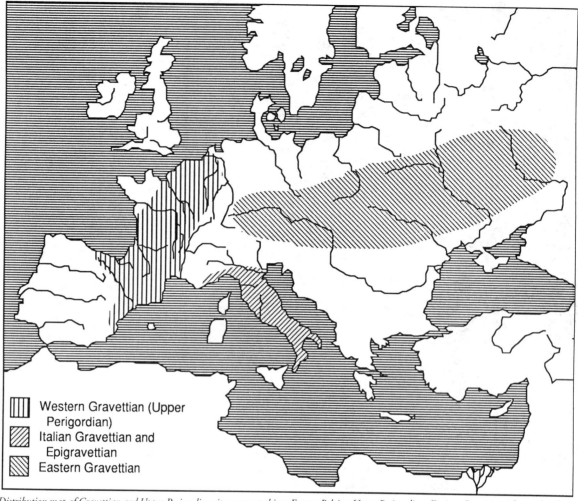

Distribution map of Gravettian and Upper Perigordian sites, separated into Franco-Belgian Upper Perigordian, Eastern Gravettian of central and eastern Europe, and Italian Gravettian and Epigravettian.

dustries are distinguished by regionally specific forms but lack the specific tool types that mark the various stages of the Upper Perigordian (with the exception of Font Robert tanged points and Noailles burins). Early Upper Paleolithic industries with backed *and* Font Robert points from Belgium and northern France are most often grouped with the Upper Perigordian. In eastern Europe, local variants of the Gravettian, such as the Pavlovian, the Molodovan, and the Streletskayan, each with distinctive point forms (e.g., Kostenki shouldered points, bifacial tanged points, triangular concave-based points with bifacial pressure flaking), are grouped as the Eastern Gravettian. Eastern Gravettian sites suggest greater economic specialization, technological skills, and social complexity than are known from other contemporaneous regions. Exploitation of large herd animals, especially mammoth, formed the basis for this adaptation, which included large-scale meat storage; use of bone for fuel in deep pit-hearths; construction of huts or tents using mammoth bone for support when wood was unavailable (Pavlov, Dolni Věstonice, Dömös, Kostenki I,1); baked-clay animal figurines fired to temperatures of ca. 800°C (Dolni Věstonice); elaborate burials with numerous ornaments and tools (Sungir); and large numbers of female, or "venus," figurines in bone, stone, and ivory (Kostenki I,1, Dolni Věstonice,

Willendorf, Pavlov, Předmosti). Long-distance trade is attested to by the appearance of shells at inland sites and by the presence of foreign stone. A mammoth tusk with elaborate incised patterns from Předmosti and other carved pieces in bone and ivory hint at symbolic and ritual complexity. Human remains associated with Gravettian sites in this region are essentially of modern type, although some (e.g., Předmosti) exhibit extremely robust brow- and nuchal-ridges, which have been used to suggest local retention of Neanderthal characteristics.

In the Mediterranean area, Gravettian industries are associated with fewer details of cultural elaboration, although female figurines are known from several sites (Savignano, Grimaldi). In Italy, Noailles burins are numerous and are associated with gravettes and backed bladelets as early as 27 Ka; other Gravettian assemblages contain Font Robert points and/or truncated pieces, all hallmarks of Perigordian V substages in southwestern France. The latest Gravettian levels, at ca. 20 Ka, contain geometric elements that presage the subsequent development of Epigravettian industries in this area. Engraved and painted slabs are rare or absent in the southern facies of the Gravettian, although an engraved ibex on bone and a slab fragment with part of the outline of a horse were recovered from Paglicci (Italy), in addition to a

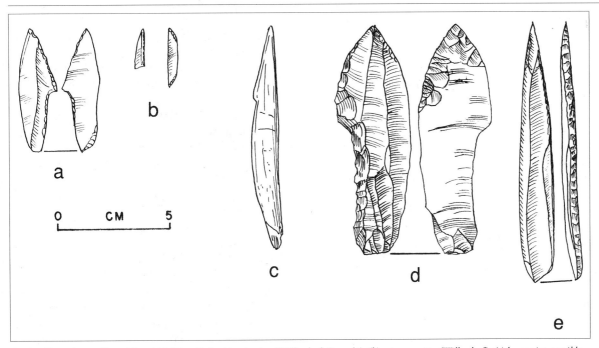

Eastern Gravettian artifacts: (a) and (d) Kostenki shouldered points (Willendorf, Kostenki); (b) microgravettes (Willendorf); (c) bone point, possibly barbed (Willendorf); (e) Gravette point (French Perigordian IV, but typical of all regions).

human burial with elaborate grave goods from an underlying Gravettian level at the same site.

The Gravettian occurs during a major cold phase of the last glaciation. Although brief warmer fluctuations are represented at some sites (e.g., Dolni Věstonice), glacial conditions appear to have prevented the occupation of the northern European plain during the entire interval.

See also Aurignacian; Bacho Kiro; Dolni Věstonice; Economy, Prehistoric; Epigravettian; Exotics; Jewelry; Kostenki; Lagar Velho; Late Paleolithic; Man-Land Relationships; Molodova; Paleolithic Image; Paleolithic Lifeways; Pavlov; Perigordian; Předmosti; Storage; Sungir; Upper Paleolithic. [A.S.B.]

Further Readings

Gamble, C. (1986) The Palaeolithic Settlement of Europe. Cambridge: Cambridge University Press.

Svoboda, J., Ložek, V., and Vlček, E. (1996) Hunters Between East and West: The Paleolithic of Moravia. New York: Plenum.

Valoch, K. (1968) Evolution of the Palaeolithic in central and eastern Europe. Curr. Anthropol. 9:351–368.

Engraved bone with ibex and chevrons (Italy), outline emphasized.

Gregory, William King (1876–1970)

American paleontologist. While a student at Columbia University (1899–1910), Gregory became assistant to H.F. Osborn (1857–1935) at the American Museum of Natural History in New York City. In 1921, 11 years after joining the museum full-time, Gregory founded the Department of Comparative Anatomy (later incorporated into the Department of Vertebrate Paleontology). Although his interests in vertebrate paleontology ranged from fish to reptiles and mammals, he had a particular interest in paleoprimatology. During his highly productive career, he published a number of influential works in this area, such as his 1920 monograph on *Notharctus.* He also published extensively on the evolution of the mammalian dentition, with particular reference to human origins. Gregory was the first American to endorse R.A. Dart's view that *Australopithecus* was a hominid. Among the several books he wrote was *Evolution Emerging* (1951), which summarizes his lifework. [F.S.]

Grimaldi

Complex of nine cave sites on the Italian Riviera near Menton. Of these caves, the most important are the Grotte du Cavillon, the Grotte du Prince, and the Grotte des Enfants, all of which were excavated in the late 1800s and early 1900s. These caves contain a similar succession of occupations, beginning with an alternating sequence of hyena den deposits and Mousterian occupations. These are overlain by Upper Paleolithic Aurignacian and Gravettian occupations.

Grotte des Enfants is notable for elaborate burials and for female "venus," figurines found in what were then termed the *Upper Aurignacian* levels. Three skeletons in two burials are reliably attributed to these levels, which have subsequently been redesignated as Gravettian. Their estimated age is thus not older than ca. 28 Ka. The earliest burial occurs in the lower part of Level E and contains one male and one female skeleton in flexed positions. Level F featured a burial of an adult male in an extended position with his head resting on a stone slab. These burials are accompanied by deposits of red ocher. The children after which the cave is named come from the upper levels of the site (Level N) and probably date to ca. 12 Ka. Many of the "venus" figurines from the Grimaldi caves are made of steatite, and they exhibit a wide range of forms.

Grimaldi played an important role in the development of theories about the origins of racial variation in modern humans. At a time when modern humans were seen as originating in Europe and migrating from there over the rest of the world, M. Boule and H.V. Vallois argued that the Grimaldi skeletons displayed Negroid affinities and represented the founding population of modern Africans. The skeletons have also played a part in twentieth-century Afrocentric theories about the African origins of modern Europeans. The attribution of the skeletons to the Gravettian levels, however, suggests that they are unlikely to have been among the first Europeans of modern aspect. In addition, a recent study has suggested that the "Negroid" features of the skeletons were much exaggerated by poor reconstruction.

See also Aurignacian; Europe; Gravettian; Homo sapiens; Modern Human Origins; Paleolithic Image; Perigordian; Upper Paleolithic. [J.J.S., A.S.B.]

Griphopithecus

Miocene hominoid primate known from Turkey and central Europe. Some of the earliest hominids outside Africa come from two sites in Turkey, Paşalar and Çandir, dated to ca. 15 and 14 Ma, respectively. Only a single mandible is known from the latter, but the former site has produced numerous upper and lower jaws and postcrania and a sample of more than 1,200 isolated teeth. Two species are probably present at Paşalar, *Griphopithecus alpani* (type from Çandir) and *Griphopithecus* sp.; they differ in minor but consistent features of the upper incisors and some other teeth. Four cheek teeth from Neudorf-Sandberg (Slovakia), dated 15–14 Ma, appear to represent another species of this genus, *G. darwini*. A single lower molar from the even older site of Engelswies in southern Germany (ca. 16–15 Ma, as yet incompletely published) may be referred to this European species, as may perhaps the partial humerus and ulna from Klein Hadersdorf (Austria) dated ca. 14 Ma and previously named *Austriacopithecus*. All of these taxa are grouped with the African hominids of similar age, *Kenyapithecus wickeri* from Fort Ternan, in the tribe Kenyapithecini of the subfamily Kenyapithecinae. They have thick-enameled teeth, robust jaws, and postcrania that are little different from Early Miocene specimens from Kenya. The naso-alveolar region retains the ancestral hominoid morphology, although it may be slightly advanced over the *Proconsul* condition and show similarities with *Dryopithecus*.

Griphopithecus was a medium-size hominoid predating the divergence of the great apes and humans. The thick enamel on its teeth and the microwear on the molars suggest a diet of small hard objects that is different from the diet suggested for *Proconsul* and also from later thick-enameled forms such as *Sivapithecus*.

See also Asia, Western; Dryopithecinae; Europe; Hominidae; Hominoidea; Kenyapithecus; Paşalar; Proconsulidae; Sivapithecus. [P.A.]

Guitarrero Cave

Paleoindian cave site in the Andean foothills of central Peru. Excavated by T. Lynch, the cave contained a series of lozenge-shaped or tanged projectile points dating between 11 and 10 Ka and also preserved a wide range of perishable artifacts-fragments of textiles, baskets, and wooden and bone tools previously unknown from this early period. The more recent deposits contained abundant plant remains, including cultivated beans.

See also Americas; Domestication; Paleoindian. [L.S.A.P., D.H.T.]

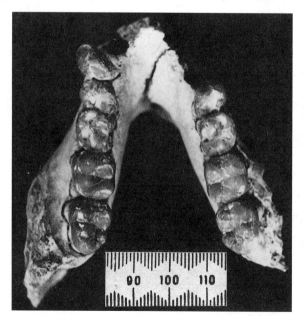

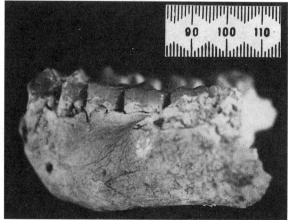

Mandible of Griphopithecus alpani *from middle Miocene deposits at Candir, Turkey. Left, occlusal view; right, buccal view. Courtesy of Peter Andrews.*

H

Hadar

Collecting area in exposures of Middle Pliocene age, between 3.4 and 2.3 Ma, in the west-central Afar region of Ethiopia. The name derives from a large wadi named Kada Hadar by the local Afar people. Approximately 100 km² of badland terrain underlain by the richly fossiliferous strata, defined as the Hadar Formation, have been explored and mapped since investigations of the site began in the early 1970s. The Hadar area has yielded a well-preserved and diverse mammalian fauna, including abundant remains of early hominins.

The Hadar Formation, 180–300 m thick, is subdivided into four stratigraphic members by volcanic marker beds, which give their names to the overlying member. The majority of the fossil vertebrates and all of the hominin fossils are derived from the three upper members: Sidi Hakoma, Denen Dora, and Kada Hadar. Neither the top nor the bottom of the formation is exposed, so its limits are not yet defined. Radiometric dating has established that the uppermost Hadar hominin-bearing levels date to ca. 2.3 Ma. Dating of the lower units was controversial throughout the 1980s but has since been resolved through the application of single-crystal laser-fusion ^{40}Ar/^{39}Ar dating to the marker tuffs as well as to newly sampled volcanic units, through correlation of some of the tephra bodies into the Turkana Basin, and through magnetostratigraphy.

Paleoenvironment

The Hadar Formation consists of interbedded, alternating sands and silty clay units deposited in the channel and extensive floodplain of a major meandering river, close to where it emptied into a lake. From time to time, the lake expanded, leaving layers of stratified lacustrine mud within the sequence. Microfauna and pollen suggest that the area lay at an elevation near 1,500 m, ca. 1,000 m higher than today. Paleoclimatic history can be inferred from the sedimentological and macrofaunal evidence, which indicates that from the time of the Basal and Sidi Hakoma members (ca. 3.4–3.25 Ma) through the time of the lower Kada Hadar Member (3.25–3.18 Ma), the regional environment was far more extensively vegetated and humid than today. At certain levels,

however, calcareous paleosols indicate a drier climate with patches of grasslands. From the middle of the Kada Hadar Member (ca. 3.18–3 Ma), grasslands became more extensive and rainfall became more seasonal. Despite the shifting environmental conditions of this 400 Kyr interval, the hominins from the lower part of the Hadar Formation display no appreciable anatomical changes. After 2.95 Ma, the rate of sedimentation slowed dramatically, and gravel-bearing streams entered the area from the Ethiopian Escarpment to the west, possibly due to tectonic movements, while aridity continued to increase.

Paleoanthropology

Hadar's paleontological significance was recognized in 1968 by the French geologist M. Taieb during areal geological mapping of the Afar Basin. Taieb invited D.C. Johanson, Y. Coppens, and J. Kalb to join in a survey of the area. Fieldwork began in 1973; by 1976, more than 6,000 vertebrate fossils had been recovered, including nearly 250 specimens of hominins. The first of these, in 1973, was a knee joint from Afar Locality (A.L.) 128/129. Numerous mandibles, maxillae, and teeth were added to the hominin inventory during the 1974 season, but the year is best remembered for the discovery of the partial skeleton of a female hominin ("Lucy") at A.L. 288, stratigraphically the highest and youngest hominin found during this first phase of exploration. In the two subsequent seasons, work was concentrated on the remarkable hillside at A.L. 333, where hundreds of skull and skeletal fragments representing at least 13 adult and subadult hominin individuals were recovered on the surface and *in situ*.

After a 14-year hiatus, field work resumed in 1990, as the Hadar Research Project (directed by Johanson, W.H. Kimbel, and R.C. Walter of the Institute of Human Origins). In the four seasons that followed, more than 50 hominin fossils were recovered, some of which are significantly younger than Lucy, and the geochronometry of the Hadar hominin-bearing sequence was improved dramatically. Included in the new hominin sample were the first fairly complete Hadar skull (A.L. 444–2), a partial upper limb skeleton

Outcrops of Pliocene sediments at Hadar, Ethiopia; view looking NW at the A.L. 333 hominin locality (located at black arrow). The resistant unit near the top of this ca. 40 m thick section is the DD-3 sand (see stratigraphic section): the level of in situ hominin remains is roughly 2 m below this unit near the center of the photo. Courtesy of IHO (Institute of Human Origins at Arizona State University).

with associated skull fragments (A.L. 438–1), a humerus (A.L. 137–50), and several mandibles and maxillae, especially an upper jaw closely associated with Oldowan lithic artifacts (A.L. 666–1) from sediments in the uppermost part of the stratigraphic sequence. Current dating permits the assignment of specific ages to many of the individual hominin finds. For example, the A.L. 444 skull dates to ca. 3 Ma; the "Lucy" skeleton, to ca. 3.18 Ma; the A.L. 333 hominin assemblage, to ca. 3.2 Ma, and the abundant material from the lower Sidi Hakoma member to levels as old as 3.4 Ma. All Hadar fossils are permanently housed in the National Museum of Ethiopia in Addis Ababa.

After comparative studies of the Hadar hominins from the 1973–1976 collections revealed detailed similarities to specimens described, but not named, from the Pliocene site of Laetoli in Tanzania, the material was formally united in the species *Australopithecus afarensis* Johanson, White and Coppens, 1978. This taxon is distinguished from other *Australopithecus* by its markedly primitive skull and dental anatomy, a diagnosis reinforced by new Hadar finds after 1990 such as the A.L. 444 skull. Although some workers considered the Hadar hominin material to be so widely variable that more than one species could be represented, the newer collections tended to corroborate the original interpretation that the Hadar fossils could be attributed to a single species with marked sexual dimorphism in body size (comparable to

that seen in the largest living hominoids, the orangutan and gorilla).

The Hadar hominin pelvis, knee joint, and foot indicate a fundamentally human adaptation to upright posture and a bipedal, striding gait. Analysis of the slightly older (3.5 Ma) hominin footprint trail at Laetoli has supported this general anatomical interpretation. The departure, however, of *A. afarensis* from the modern human condition in such features as relatively more robust upper limbs, relatively longer forearms, and more strongly curved hand and foot phalangeal bones, has led some workers to conclude that the Hadar hominins were also more adapted to arboreal activity than modern humans are.

Fossil evidence of a second hominin taxon, a maxilla with partial dentition, was discovered at Hadar in 1994 during a survey of upper Kada Hadar Member sediments in the Makaamitalu drainage of the Kada Hadar tributary. Found on the surface closely associated with Oldowan stone tools at A.L. 666, the maxilla derives from an artifact-bearing horizon less than 1 m below the BKT-3 tephra, dated by ^{40}Ar/^{39}Ar to 2.33 Ma. Derived features such as reduced subnasal prognathism; a relatively wide, deep palate; and details of cheek-tooth morphology unambiguously tie the A.L. 666 maxilla to early species of the *Homo* lineage, with closest affinities to *H. habilis* (as known in levels younger than 1.9 Ma at Olduvai Gorge [Tanzania] and Koobi Fora [Kenya]). *Australopithecus* has not been documented in these young Hadar deposits.

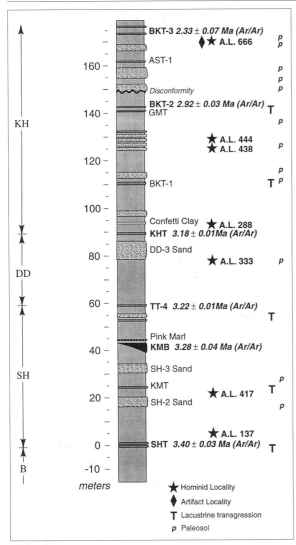

Generalized stratigraphic section of the Hadar Formation. At left the Basal (B), Sidi Hakoma (SH), Denen Dora (DD), and Kada Hadar (KH) members with a composite magnetostratigraphy indicating the position of the Kaena (K) and Mammoth (M) subchrons. Stars indicate important hominin specimens. Volcanic markers are Sidi Hakoma Tuff (SHT), Kada Mahay Tuff (KMT), Triple Tuff (TT-4), Kada Hadar Tuff (KHT), and Bouroukie Tuffs (BKT); KMB refers to the Kadada Moumou Basalt. Courtesy of IHO.

Stone tools have not been found below the upper part of the Kada Hadar Member. In the 1975–1976 season, Oldowan artifacts were discovered in exposures along the Gona, a tributary to the Kada Hadar from the west, in strata contiguous with the Hadar Formation. Excavations undertaken by S. Semaw and J.W.K. Harris in 1992 and 1993 uncovered Oldowan artifacts in primary contexts along the eastern bank of the Gona. These tools are certainly younger than 2.95 Ma, but geological studies to determine their precise age and stratigraphic relationship to the Makaamitalu drainage archaeological and paleontological occurrences are not yet completed. In 1994, similar tools were found at Makaamitalu in the Upper Kada Hadar Member.

See also Afar Basin; Africa; Africa, East; Australopithecus afarensis; Laetoli; Middle Awash; Oldowan; Sexual Dimorphism; Turkana Basin. [W.H.K., R.C.W.]

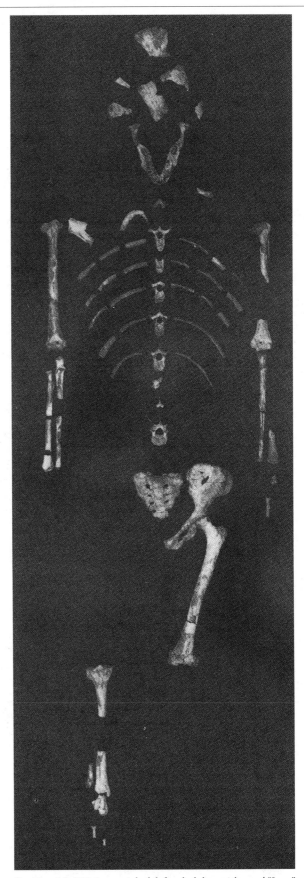

Specimen A.L. 288-1, a partial adult female skeleton nicknamed "Lucy." This is the most complete specimen known of Australopithecus afarensis. Courtesy of IHO and the Cleveland Museum of Natural History.

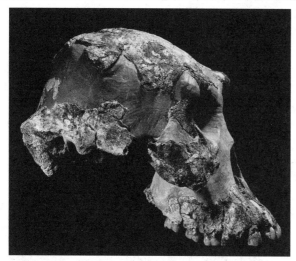

The 1992 cranium of Australopithecus afarensis *from A.L. 444, ca. 3.03 Ma (mandible not shown). Courtesy of IHO.*

Further Readings

Aronson, J.A., and Taieb, M. (1981) Geology and paleo-geography of the Hadar hominid site, Ethiopia. In G. Rapp and C.F. Vondra (eds.): Hominid Sites: Their Geological Settings. Boulder: Westview, pp. 165–195.

Bonnefille, R., Vincens, A., and Buchet, G. (1987) Palynology, stratigraphy, and paleoenvironment of a Pliocene hominid site (2.9–3.3 m.y.) at Hadar, Ethiopia. Palaeogeog., Palaeoclimatol., Palaeoecol. 60:249–281.

Harris, J.W.K. (1983) Cultural beginnings: Plio-Pleistocene archaeological occurrences from the Afar, Ethiopia. Afr. Archaeol. Rev. 1:3–31.

Johanson, D.C., Taieb, M., and Coppens, Y. (1982) Pliocene hominids from the Hadar Formation, Ethiopia (1973–1977): Stratigraphic, chronologic, and paleoenvironmental contexts, with notes on hominid morphology and systematics. Am. J. Phys. Anthropol. 57:373–402.

Kimbel, W.H., Johanson, D.C., and Rak, Y. (1994) The first skull and other new discoveries of *Australopithecus afarensis* at Hadar, Ethiopia. Nature 368:449–451.

Kimbel, W.H., Walter, R.C., Johanson, D.C., Reed, K.E., Aronson, J.L., Assefa, Z., Marean, C.M., Eck, G.G., Bobe, R., Hovers, E., Rak, Y., Vondra, C., Yemane, T., York, D., Chen, Y., Evensen, N., and Smith, P. (1996) Late Pliocene *Homo* and Oldowan tools from the Hadar Formation (Kada Hadar Member), Ethiopia. J. Hum. Evol. 31:549–561.

Tiercelin, J.-J. (1986) The Pliocene Hadar Formation, Afar depression of Ethiopia. In L.E. Frostic, R.W. Reneaut, I. Reid, and J.-J. Tiercelin (eds.): Sedimentation in the African Rifts. Oxford: Blackwell, pp. 221–240.

Walter, R.C. (1994) Age of Lucy and the first family: Single-crystal $^{40}Ar/^{39}Ar$ dating of the Denen Dora and lower Kada Hadar Members of the Hadar Formation, Ethiopia. Geology 22:6–10.

Walter, R.C., and Aronson, J.L. (1993) Age and source of the Sidi Hakoma Tuff, Hadar Formation, Ethiopia. J. Hum. Evol. 25:229–240.

Haeckel, Ernst Heinrich (1834–1919)

German zoologist and philosopher. Haeckel was an early proponent of the Darwinian evolutionary synthesis in Germany. His *Generelle Morphologie der Organismen* (1866) contains the first formal phylogenetic tree purporting to depict the course of human evolutionary history. In this regard, Haeckel predicted the existence of a phylogenetic link between humans and the apes, namely the "missing link," with a blend of ape and human traits. To this hypothetical construct, he gave the name *Pithecanthropus,* the term later employed by E. Dubois to describe the fossil hominid remains he discovered in Java. Besides being the originator of the famous dictum "ontogeny recapitulates phylogeny," Haeckel was also a leading exponent of monistic philosophy. Haeckel's entire academic career was spent at the University of Jena (Germany), where he was appointed full professor in 1865.

See also Dubois, Eugene. [F.S.]

Hahnöfersand

Isolated frontal bone that was recovered without any associated material from river deposits near Hamburg (Germany). The frontal is interesting because of its thickness and flatness, suggesting archaic affinities, although the browridge is of robust but modern type. Because of radiocarbon and amino-acid dates of ca. 36 Ka, the specimen has been claimed to represent a transitional or hybrid type between a Neanderthal and an early-modern population, but both morphological and chronological interpretations of this fossil remain problematic.

See also Europe; Homo sapiens. [C.B.S.]

Hamburgian

Late Paleolithic industry of northwestern Europe associated with late glacial Zone I and II pollen diagrams, ca. 10.5 Ka, defined by A. Rust on the basis of such open sites as Meiendorf, Stellmoor, and Ahrensburg, near Hamburg (Germany). At these sites, a Paleolithic way of life based on reindeer hunting, using tanged flint and barbed bone points, continued after it had disappeared from southern Europe. Piles of reindeer bones at these sites have been interpreted as supports for skin tents or remains of processing stations.

See also Economy, Prehistoric; Epipaleolithic; Harpoon; Holocene; Late Paleolithic; Man-Land Relationships. [A.S.B.]

Handaxe

Characteristic artifact of the Acheulean technological stage (also found in some Mousterian industries), normally a large bifacial implement of either pointed or ovate planform. Along with cleavers, this artifact type represents the first definite, deliberately stylized form of artifact in prehistory. These artifacts, made from large flakes, large cobbles, or nodules, are found in many parts of Africa, Europe, and the Middle East, as far east as India. Acheulean handaxes, along with cleavers, picks, and knives, are often also called *bifaces,* although the latter term is also commonly applied to bifacially worked tools from later times and other parts of the

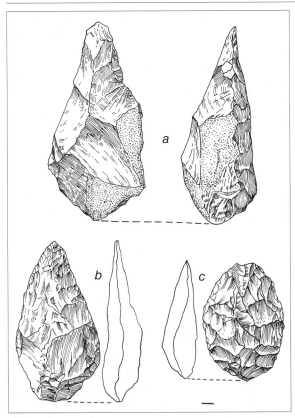

Handaxes: (a) crude pointed handaxe with relatively few, large flake scars; (b) refined pointed handaxe; (c) ovate handaxe. Scale is 1 cm.

world. Microwear analysis suggests that some Acheulean handaxes were used as butchery knives, but a range of other functions is possible as well.

See also Acheulean; Biface; Cleaver; Early Paleolithic; Mousterian; Stone-Tool Making. [N.T., K.S.]

Haplorhini

A suborder of the primate semiorder Euprimates, including the tarsiers and their relatives (hyporder Tarsiiformes, including Omomyidae, Tarsiidae, and Eosimiidae) and the "higher" primates (or hyporder Anthropoidea, including infraorders Platyrrhini and Catarrhini). The Haplorhini is a holophyletic taxon, named in 1918 by R.I. Pocock (and recognized by students before him without a formal naming of the taxon), and it is based on the special derived attributes shared between the Southeast Asian tarsiers and fossil relatives and the living and fossil anthropoid primates. The following osteological attributes, which allow the concept to be tested against the fossil evidence, were probably present in the last common ancestor of this suborder: (1) shortened facial skull; (2) olfactory process located above the interorbital septum; (3) reduced olfactory lobe and enlarged temporal lobe; (4) carotid artery entry of the skull medially, and promontory branch slightly larger than the stapedial one; (5) petromastoid and squamosal pneumatized (extreme reduction, or elimination, of this condition in *Tarsius* is derived); (6) crural (lower leg) and tarsal modifications that include conditions in known omomyids and fossil tarsioids more

similar to anthropoids (*Tarsius* is extremely derived) than to strepsirhines, both the living lemuriforms and the extinct adapiforms as well.

Among the first to notice shared advanced similarities for Haplorhini was A.A.W. Hubrecht. In 1897, after examining a series of embryos of *Tarsius*, he noted that features of the placenta and fetal membranes were not like those of other lemurs, the group with which the tarsiers were classified in Prosimii, but rather like those of anthropoid primates. Hubrecht knew of the Eocene tarsiiform fossils (the primates we group today in the Omomyidae) that were discovered earlier from North America, and he concluded that the tarsiiforms were an ancient and distinct lineage derived from the lemuriforms (strepsirhine primates). Hubrecht's studies on this important problem have been corroborated and further developed by W.P. Luckett. The development of the placenta and various fetal membranes, including body stalk, allantois, and yolk sac, consists of a complex series of steps, and the very complexity of construction of these features provides a character constellation of great systematic significance.

In addition to these studies on the placenta and fetal membranes, Pocock's initial observations on the special similarity of the external nose of tarsiers to that of anthropoids (in spite of some primitive primate retentions in *Tarsius*) have been elaborated upon and fully confirmed. Modern strepsirhine primates (living lemuroids and lorisoids) have an outer nose structure quite similar to what is considered the ancestral condition for both placental and marsupial mammals (a condition broadly understood as *strepsirhine,* a term that, when used taxonomically, is not restricted to a description of the nasal tissue or the shape of the nostrils). On the other hand, the ancestors of living tarsiers and anthropoids lost the naked rhinarium (wet and hairless nose skin), the cleft in the upper lip, and the philtrum (the median part of the rhinarium that is connected to the gum, after passing between the two halves of the upper lip) and greatly reduced the vibrissae ("whiskers"; also called sinus hairs because of the well-developed venous sinuses around their follicles) into short and stiff structures. Their nasal area is instead covered with hairy skin, although the nasal opening is similar to the crescent-shaped, primitive mammalian condition retained in some lemuriforms and in the platyrrhine anthropoid *Aotus.* Tarsiers, like anthropoids, have the derived mammalian condition of a relatively free upper lip that is continuous and untethered from one side to the other; moreover, this lip is mobile, unlike that of any living strepsirhine primate.

The third important area of special similarity between tarsiers and anthropoids living today is the construction of the retina at the back of the eyes. Like the previous two character complexes, this cannot be assessed in fossils. In strepsirhine primates, as in many other mammals, there is a layer of tissue behind the retina called the *tapetum lucidum* that somehow plays a role in light gathering and reflection. Tarsiers and anthropoids, however, not only lack this primitive mammalian condition, but also have a retina that contains, within an area called the *macula lutea* (yellow spot), a special area of great visual accuity, marked by a depression and called the *fovea centralis.* It is probable that the greatly enlarged eyes of tarsiers, like those of the nocturnal platyrrhine *Aotus*, have become relatively very large, even when compared to the enlarged eyes of other nocturnal mammals, because the common ancestor of anthropoids and tarsiers lost the tapetum lucidum, probably as an early adaptation to diurnality. All subsequent nocturnal haplorhines, however, had to compensate for the absence of this tapetum lucidum if they were to secondarily pursue a nocturnal way of life.

The fourth area of special similarity shared among the living haplorhines (and also indicated in the fossils where the appropriate anatomies are preserved) is the nature of the arterial circulation in the middle ear. The vessel that embryonically courses through the stapes is not functional in extant adult haplorhines. The emphasis in these living primates is on another branch of the carotid, the promontory artery, in the supply of blood to the brain. In lemuroids, the primitively large stapedial and vertebral arteries fulfill this role, while for this purpose, the lorisoids capture a newly recruited vessel, the ascending pharyngeal artery.

The fifth area of special similarity shared by living (and fossil) haplorhines is a character of exceptional importance (it can be examined in fossils) as it relates to the construction of the skull. The olfactory process of the brain passes below the interorbital septum in strepsirhine primates, but in all living haplorhines and in the known fossil omomyid skulls it passes above the persistent fetal septum formed by the orbitosphenoid bone. This fact is a strong indicator that the ancestral haplorhine species fundamentally reorganized the development of the skull due to some adaptive shift involving the visual and the olfactory, and maybe even the feeding, mechanisms. Any argument to the effect that shortening of the face will result in similar and independent developmental constraints is weakened by the fact that short-faced strepsirhines like the living lorisids did not develop along the haplorhine lines.

The taxonomic concepts Strepsirhini and Haplorhini, then, are not simply descriptive of nasal conditions in primates. The two terms are formal names, which are not affected by what we know or do not know of the nose or fetal membrane evolution of living or fossil primates. It is equally important to understand that the fossil groups included within the Haplorhini, the various subfamilies of the Omomyidae, are allocated to this suborder because they either share derived osteological features with living haplorhines or with the deduced common ancestor of the living species, or they possess traits that are part of well-understood transformational homologies. Omomyids are not considered haplorhine primates because we assume their nasal area (not only the nostrils) to have been of the haplorhine type. Similarly, linking of such fossil groups as the Adapidae with the Strepsirhini, or the Omomyidae with the Tarsiiformes within the Haplorhini, does not depend on the assumption of the presence of particular soft anatomical features in the fossils—there is no reliable access to such information in extinct species. On the contrary, the sharing of derived osteological attributes between the fossil forms and the respective living groups makes it probable that the former possessed the appropriate soft anatomical characters.

The evolution of the Haplorhini, particularly their pre-Eocene history, is poorly understood. We assume that the first lineage of haplorhines was, broadly, not unlike a small species of lemur that had already evolved an explosive, grasp-leaping mode of locomotion that allowed long and precise jumps from branch to branch in the canopy. In addition to such heritage, however, this first haplorhine had a commitment to a diurnal mode of life that was revolutionary for primates at that time. The known omomyids, with the suggested but unlikely exception of the Middle Eocene genus *Shoshonius* and its close relatives, were not particularly closely related to the tarsiids. But there is little doubt that the family Omomyidae was more recently related to the living Haplorhini than to the Strepsirhini, which includes not only the living tooth-combed primates (Lemuriformes) but also the Paleogene Adapiformes. The common ancestral root of the Haplorhini stems from as yet unknown animals that lived in the Late Cretaceous, or more likely Paleocene, forests of the Old World, possibly Africa or Southeast Asia. The dentally distinct Tarsiidae are known from the Middle to Late Eocene of Eastern China, along with another distinct lineage of tarsioids *(sensu stricto),* the Eosimiidae (based on *Eosimias,* tarsioid tarsiiform primates that are neither omomyids nor anthropoids). Together, these forms suggest that the early ties among the omomyids, tarsiids, and anthropoids go far back in the Paleogene. The exact relationships among the earliest representatives of these haplorhine groups cannot be readily discerned: They are not supported with convincing and tested transformational homologies (for ancestry) or synapomorphies (for sister-group relationships).

See also Adapiformes; Anthropoidea; Euprimates; Omomyidae; Primates; Shoshonius; Strepsirhini; Tarsiiformes. [F.S.S.]

Further Readings

Beard, K.C., Qi, T., Dawson, M.R., Wang, B., and Li, C. (1994) A diverse new primate fauna from Middle Eocene fissure-fillings in southeastern China. Nature 368:604–609.

Szalay, F.S., and Delson, E. (1979) Evolutionary History of the Primates. New York: Academic.

Szalay, F.S., Rosenberger, A.L., and Dagosto, M. (1987) Diagnosis and differentiation of the Primates. Yrbk. J. Phys. Anthropol. 30:75–105.

Harpoon

Barbed spear point that is a recurrent artifact form at many sites of the Late Paleolithic, particularly the Upper Paleolithic of western Europe and the Later Stone Age of Africa, as well as the Mesolithic of Europe. Harpoon heads are especially typical of the last, or Magdalenian, phase of the Upper Paleolithic (ca. 17–11 Ka), though there is evidence that may suggest early use of harpoon technology by Middle Stone Age times at the site of Katanda in Zaire. The Magdalenian harpoon head, barbed on one or both sides, is normally made from a piece of antler, although prehistoric harpoons elsewhere are also made from bone or ivory. Technically, a

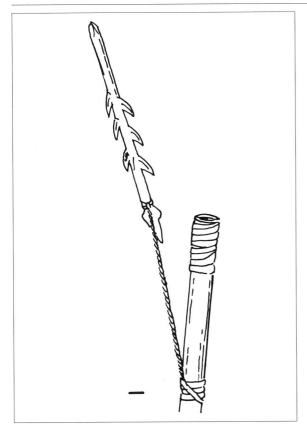

Magdalenian harpoon and possible mode of attachment to a spear shaft. Scale is 1 cm.

harpoon involves a head, or point, that is detachable upon penetration of the animal and usually tethered with a cord to the shaft or foreshaft of a spear, although the term is sometimes applied to elongate, barbed points even if they are not detachable. Ethnographic examples of harpoon use, such as among many Eskimo groups, suggest that prehistoric harpoons could have been used for hunting or spearfishing.

See also Katanda; Magdalenian; Raw Materials; Spear; Stone-Tool Making; Upper Paleolithic. [N.T., K.S.]

Haua Fteah

Large cave in Cyrenaica (Libya) excavated by C.B.M. McBurney in the 1950s. An extensive series of archaeological deposits was sampled, producing mainly tools of Levallois-Mousterian affinities. A distinctive blade-based industry, the Pre-Aurignacian, was excavated in levels within the Mousterian sequence dated by radiocarbon at more than 47 Ka. Later horizons produced the best evidence for the Dabban and eastern Oranian (Ibero-Maurusian), as well as Neolithic industries. Two posterior mandible fragments, from an adult and a subadult, were recovered in 1952 and 1955 from levels dated at ca. 47 Ka. They have low and broad ascending rami but lack the retromolar space characteristic of Neanderthals.

See also Africa; Archaic Homo sapiens; Dabban; Ibero-Maurusian; Late Paleolithic; Middle Paleolithic; Mousterian; Pre-Aurignacian. [C.B.S., A.S.B.]

Hayonim

Cave and terrace site in the Nahal Yitzhar, western Galilee, Israel, excavated since the 1960s. The main cave contains a deep Upper Pleistocene sequence (Levels B-E), including Natufian, Kebaran, Levantine Aurignacian, and Mousterian levels. The bottom of this sequence has not been reached. The terrace occupation is Geometric Kebaran and Natufian and features large, rectangular stone pavements. The Natufian cave occupation contains circular stone structures with flagstone floors, under which numerous primary and secondary burials have been found. Burials missing their crania suggest possible links to later Early Neolithic mortuary rituals. Early remains of domesticated dog also are known from the Natufian occupation. Studies of commensal microfauna (rodents and sparrows) and analysis of gazelle remains indicate a multiseasonal Natufian occupation at Hayonim, suggesting that the site could have been a permanent village occupied by several hundred individuals. The Levantine Aurignacian levels preserve numerous bone tools and traces of several distict hearths. These levels also contain an incised limestone slab, one of very few decorated objects from the Upper Paleolithic of the Levant. The Mousterian levels are complex and have been deformed by karst activity and subsidence. Only fragmentary human remains (teeth and phalanges) have thus far been recovered from the Middle Paleolithic levels.

See also Asia, Western; Kebaran; Levantine Aurignacian; Mousterian; Natufian. [J.J.S.]

Heliopithecus

Middle Miocene hominoid primate from Saudi Arabia, possibly a synonym of *Afropithecus.* Some fragmentary remains of a fossil hominoid from Ad Dabtiyah (Saudi Arabia), including a maxilla and some isolated teeth, have been described as *Heliopithecus leakeyi.* The morphology is similar to that of *Kenyapithecus* and *Afropithecus,* and it is likely that they are related. Provisional systematic placement of this taxon is with *Afropithecus* in the hominid tribe Afropithecini. The site is dated to ca. 16 Ma, at which time the Arabian Peninsula was directly connected to eastern Africa.

See also Afropithecus; Asia, Western; Kenyapithecus; Paleobiogeography. [P.A.]

Hemanthropus (Hemianthropus)

Purported hominin taxon based on a small number of "drugstore" fossil teeth purchased by Dutch paleoanthropologist G.H.R. von Koenigswald in Asia in the 1930s. Although he referred these teeth to what is here termed the *Hominini,* this assignment is far from certain for all the specimens. Since no specimens were recovered *in situ,* dating is impossible; the source is thought to be southern China but even that is uncertain. Some of the hypodigm may represent hominins (presumably *Homo erectus*), but at least part of it may be referable to some form of Miocene hominoid. Von Koenigswald originally named the specimens *Hemianthropus peii* but later changed this generic nomen to *Hemanthropus* because the former name had already been used.

See also Asia, Eastern and Southern; China; Dragon Bones (and Teeth); Homo erectus; Koenigswald, Gustav Heinrich Ralph von. [G.G.P.]

Hexian

Cave deposit in Hexian county, Anhui Province (China) with human remains of late Middle Pleistocene age. It had been dated ca. 200 Ka on the basis of hominid morphology and associated fauna, but work by R. Grün and colleagues in 1998 doubled that age, to 410 Ka. In 1980, this karst cave locality yielded a partial cranium of *Homo erectus*. The specimen has been classified as a "progressive" form, which apparently shows affinities to the hominids recovered from the upper deposits of Locality 1 at Zhoukoudian (China). The Hexian specimen (from Longtandong Cave) has an estimated cranial capacity of ca. 1,025 ml. The associated fauna is also interesting because it seems to represent a mixture of cold-adapted northern mammals and more tropical southern elements. Artifacts, including apparently intentionally flaked molar teeth of *Rhinoceros*, are associated with the fossil cranium.

See also Asia, Eastern and Southern; China; Homo erectus; Zhoukoudian. [G.G.P.]

Further Readings

Etler, D., and Li, T. (1994) New archaic human fossil discoveries in China and their bearing on hominid species definition during the Middle Pleistocene. In R.S. Corruccini and R.L. Ciochon (eds.): Integrative Paths to the Past: Paleoanthropological Advances in Honor of F. Clark Howell. Englewood Cliffs, N.J.: Prentice-Hall, pp. 639–675.

Grün, R., Huang, P.-H., Huang, W., McDermott, F., Thorne, A., Stringer, C. B., and Ge, Y. (1998) ESR and U-series analyses of teeth from the palaeoanthropological site of Hexian, Anhui Province, China. J. Hum. Evol. 34:555–564.

Huang, W., Fang, D., and Ye, Y. (1982) Preliminary study of the fossil skull and fauna from Hexian, Anhui. Vert. PalAsiatica 20:248–256.

Wu, R., and Dong, X. (1982) Preliminary study of *Homo erectus* remains from Hexian, Anhui. Acta Anthropol. Sinica 1:2–13.

Higher Primates

Anthropoid primates (monkeys, apes, humans, and their extinct relatives), as distinguished from the lower or prosimian members of the order. This term originally dates to a *scala naturae* view of evolution, which posited lower forms of life evolving into higher ones. It has come back into use as a way of referring to anthropoids as opposed to the paraphyletic group of lower primates. Anthropoids may be considered higher in terms of their greater relative brain size, social complexity, and other features, all of which link them to humans.

See also Anthropoidea; Brain; Lower Primates; Primate Societies; Primates; Prosimian; Scala Naturae. [E.D., I.T.]

Hoabinhian

Broadly and often nebulously defined archaeological techno-complex found throughout mainland Southeast Asia. Originally proposed by Colani in the 1930s on the basis of assemblages from Vietnam, the Hoabinhian seems to span the last 10 Kyr. This industry includes unifacially worked flakes, cores, polished flakes, and cord-marked pottery in what are presumably its later phases. There is a great deal of variation in Hoabinhian assemblages. It may well be that the Hoabinhian as it is recognized today does not constitute a single archaeological entity (i.e., culture, tradition, industry, or facies).

See also Asia, Eastern and Southern. [G.G.P.]

Hoanghonius

Middle Eocene primate from northern China. *Hoanghonius* is a poorly known and enigmatic genus that is linked by some authors to the dentally primitive early anthropoids *Oligopithecus* and *Catopithecus*. It is considered by others to be an adapiform. The detailed similarities of the lower molars, particularly the closely twinned entoconid and hypoconulid cusps of *Oligopithecus* and *Hoanghonius*, are somewhat canceled out by the less similar upper molars of the Asian genus and the African *Catopithecus*.

The issues of possible relationships are further complicated by the mid-1990s description by C. Beard and others from the Middle and Late Eocene of China, in addition to undoubted adapids, omomyids, and tarsiids, of the alleged anthropoid *Eosimias*. This small eosimiid primate (a tarsioid, in a strict sense) has special dental similarities with tarsiids but represents a distinct lineage. It shows no convincing uniquely shared special similarities to any undoubted anthropoid, a designation much more securely attached to the Late Eocene diminutive *Algeripithecus* from the Algerian Sahara.

See also Anthropoidea; Eosimiidae; Haplorhini; Oligopithecidae. [F.S.S.]

Holocene

The most recent interval in the geologic time scale. Synonyms for *Holocene* are *Postglacial* and *Recent*, in recognition of the fact that this chronostratigraphic unit is widely understood to be equivalent to the current interval of interglacial climate. Scientists do not formally agree on the status of the Holocene. Some workers treat it as the last epoch of the Cenozoic, but many others consider it to be a subdivision of the Pleistocene epoch because it is much briefer than the other epochs and because its climate is a continuation of Pleistocene conditions. *Holocene* means "entirely new," in reference to the fact that all of its fossils belong to living or artificially extinguished species, in contrast to the "mostly new" Pleistocene assemblages.

The name and faunal definition of *Holocene* are consistent with the criteria for Cenozoic epochs proposed by Charles Lyell in 1833, but the internal subdivision of the Holocene and even its traditional boundary have been identified with climatostratigraphic transitions. Under international guidelines, all global chronostratigraphic units must

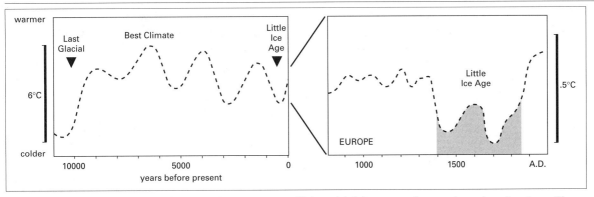

Climate change during the Holocene. Left: Following the Younger Dryas cold phase, global climate generally warmed, to a thermal maximum ("best climate") around 7–6 Ka. The last of several episodes of global cooling is termed the Little Ice Age. Right: About 1,000 BP, climate in the northern hemisphere was again optimal, and the Vikings expanded into Greenland and Newfoundland. The succeeding Little Ice Age bottomed in the 1700s, without continental glaciers forming, and climate has steadily warmed since then. From T. Van Andel, 1986, New Views on an Old Planet; *by permission of Cambridge University Press.*

be defined by physical reference points, or boundary-strato-types, in marine sequences. A boundary-stratotype for the base of the Holocene has not been adopted, but proposals are under study. The consensus would favor a level related to the beginning of the present regression of continental ice caps in the Northern Hemisphere. The retreat of the southern edge of the Scandinavian ice sheet from the Salpausselka moraine line in northern Europe is considered to be the characteristic example, and this is correlated to the paleo-botanical transition from the Younger Dryas cold-climate flora to the more modern Preboreal flora. That event was conventionally dated to 10 Ka, but subsequent dating in the 1990s indicates that it took place more than a thousand years earlier.

Thermal inertia in giant ice sheets causes them to persist until they catastrophically crash, rather than to melt gradually, under warming conditions. Heinrich events, catastrophic mass-melting episodes at the end of major glacial phases during the Pleistocene, spread conspicuous layers of ice-rafted debris across the floor of the North Atlantic. The wide swings in Quaternary climates also affected ocean circulation, slowing or accelerating the recycling of short-lived cosmogenic isotopes such as ^{14}C and ^{10}Be in the biosphere; this factor, called the *reservoir effect,* had significant effects on the apparent age of fossilized organic matter. The youngest Heinrich event, H_0, was synchronous not only with the Scandinavian regression of the Younger Dryas, but also with collapse of the Hudson ice dome in North America and the retreat of Siberian and Alaskan ice fronts. The H_0 layer has the same age as the end of the last significant cold-water phase in the Pacific (as measured in coastal sediments of California, Mexico, Japan, and New Zealand), the end of the last cold-climate regime in Greenland ice cores, and the end of glacial climate conditions in several European lakes. The Younger Dryas, the final cold-climate cycle in the Weichsel glacial age, is thus considered to have ended with a sharply defined, globally synchronous event. Differing adjustments for the reservoir effect on cosmogenic isotope abundances lead to ages for the Younger Dryas-Preboreal boundary, widely understood to be the

beginning of the Holocene, that vary between 11.2 and 11.4 Ka.

The climate cycles that preceded the Younger Dryas are the Bolling-Allerod interstadial, ending at ca. 13 Ka, and the Last Glacial Maximum, ending with Heinrich H_1 at 16.5 Ka. As in other interstadials, the continental ice sheets of the Hudson's Bay and Scandinavian centers contracted sharply but did not disintegrate at the beginning of the Bolling-Allerod; the last time that Holocene degrees of climate and glacial retreat were reached, with no sea-level ice sheets below the Arctic Circle, was during the Eemian interglacial that ended ca. 127 Ka.

The Holocene can be divided into three climatic stages with differing air-temperature and precipitation regimes. The earliest, from 11 Ka to 3 Ka, or 9000 to 1000 BCE, was the *anathermal* stage, cooler and mostly wetter than today. Between 1000 BCE and ca. 1400 CE was the *hypsithermal* (or altithermal) stage, also known as the *climatic optimum,*

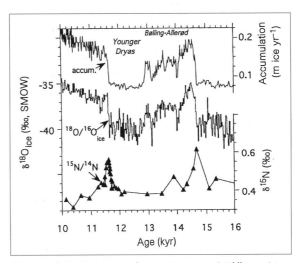

Ice accumulation (top curve) and oxygen isotope ratio (middle curve) in Greenland ice core GISP2 document the suddenness with which glacial ice sheets collapse in the early stages of an interglacial. The nitrogen isotope ratio (lower curve) also reflects such collapses, but less clearly. The end of the Younger Dryas is the internationally agreed criterion for the beginning of the Holocene. Reprinted by permission from J.P. Severinghaus et al., 1998, Nature, *v. 391. © Macmillan Magazines, Ltd.*

when climate was warmer and mostly drier than today. The *medithermal* stage, from 1400 to 1900 CE, reached a relatively cold, wet-climate minimum ca. 1650 CE known as the Little Ice Age. It is not widely appreciated, due to current concerns about ozone depletion and carbon dioxide loading, that a steady, worldwide increase in annual average temperatures following the Little Ice Age was stronger in the nineteenth than in the twentieth century, at least up to 1950.

See also Climate Change and Evolution; Glaciation; Pleistocene; Stratigraphy. [J.A.V.C.]

Further Readings

Kennett, J.P., and Ingram, B.L. (1995) A 20,000-year record of ocean circulation and climate change from the Santa Barbara Basin. Nature 377:510–513.

Denton, G.H., and Hughes, T.J., eds. (1981) The Last Great Ice Sheets. New York: Wiley.

Hominidae

As used in the present work, the family comprising the great apes and humans. It is linked with the Hylobatidae and the extinct Proconsulidae in the superfamily Hominoidea.

A word of explanation is needed before going on to describe the subfamilies and genera contained in the Hominidae. In the past—when it was thought that there was a broad distinction between apes and humans, with the apes in one family, the Pongidae, and humans in another, the Hominidae—Hominidae was generally used to contain humans and their immediate ancestors. With the recognition that some apes are more closely related to humans than they are to other apes, this convention starts to break down, for, if the concept of Pongidae can no longer be applied to the apes, the taxonomic level of difference between the apes must be reflected by a reduced level of taxonomic difference between humans and the apes most closely related to them.

One way of equating taxonomic levels would be to recognize all hominoid groups at the same family level. This would allow the retention of Hominidae for just humans, but it would also require Pongidae for the orangutan, Gorillidae for gorillas and chimpanzees (or Panidae also for the chimpanzees), and Hylobatidae for the gibbons. This is taxonomically valid, but it creates an imbalance with the other major catarrhine group, the Cercopithecoidea. In this superfamily, only one family is recognized, and the diverse species and genera, which are much more numerous than those of the hominoids, are divided between two subfamilies. It is more consistent and logical, therefore, to divide the hominoids at a similarly lower taxonomic level, and this is what is done here. The major divisions of the modern Hominidae are the two subfamilies Ponginae and Homininae. Among living forms, Ponginae includes just the orangutan (generic name *Pongo*), and the Homininae includes the African apes and humans *(Homo, Pan,* and *Gorilla)*. It would have been equally possible, in paralleling the discussion above, to have recognized more than these two subfamilies in order to emphasize the distinctiveness of humans, for instance, by restricting Homininae to humans and having Gorillinae (and possibly Paninae as well) for the African apes. This also lacks consistency with other catarrhine groups, and, for this reason, is not used here.

The hominids include the largest of all extant primates. Other primates in the past have matched or exceeded them in size (such as *Gigantopithecus*, a derivative of the *Sivapithecus* group in eastern Asia, and *Archaeoindris*, a subfossil lemur from Madagascar), but no living group comes close to them in body size. Probably linked with this in some way, the degree of sexual dimorphism (the differences in size and morphology between males and females of the same species) is generally high, certainly much higher than in the gibbons. Gorillas and orangutans show the greatest amount of sexual dimorphism, humans and chimpanzees the least, but a number of fossil genera appear to have been at least as sexually dimorphic as any of the living hominids. *Sivapithecus,* which is related to the orangutan, had levels of sexual dimorphism similar to that of the living ape, and the largest species were only slightly smaller in overall size. Indeed, *Gigantopithecus* has already been mentioned as being even larger and was probably a member of this clade; thus, increased body size and sexual dimorphism appear to be ancient characteristics of this part of the hominid lineage.

The African apes and humans, which form the other part of the hominid clade, are more variable in size. The gorilla is the largest hominid species and the chimpanzee the smallest,

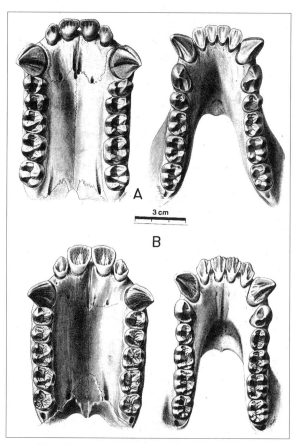

Upper (left) and lower male dentitions of A) gorilla and B) orangutan. From E. Selenka, Menschenaffen, Studien über Entwickelung und Schädelbau. Liefg. 2. Kapitel 2. Schädel des Gorilla und Schimpanse, *1899, Kreidel.*

and sexual dimorphism matches these size differences. The fossil genus *Graecopithecus* may belong to the African-ape-and-human clade, and the species *G. freybergi* (sometimes called *Ouranopithecus macedoniensis*) was nearly as large and as dimorphic as the gorilla. Some later taxa of australopiths belonging to the human lineage appear also to have been extremely variable. The fossil genera *Dryopithecus* and *Kenyapithecus* are grouped in the hominid clade, and the way these genera have been divided into species makes it appear that they were not variable at all. If, however, some of these species are combined, as the lack of morphological differences between them seems to indicate they should be, the new combinations in some cases may have as great a degree of sexual dimorphism as gorillas. Much needs to be done to resolve this problem.

Based on fossil evidence and the molecular clock, the time of origin of the hominids was ca. 17 Ma. The early fossil evidence is restricted to Africa, so the origin of the group was almost certainly African. The hominids subsequently diverged into two groups, of which one, Ponginae, left Africa and migrated early in its history to Asia, where it is now represented by the orangutan. The other group, Homininae, may have remained mainly in Africa until soon after 2 Ma (although the above-mentioned European fossils may belong here as well). An alternative view put forward in 1998 by C. B. Stewart and T. Disotell suggests that none of the Middle Miocene African hominoids were hominid but that the Eurasian colonizing lineage divided there (perhaps after *Dryopithecus*) into a pongine clade and the ancestors of Homininae (e.g., *Graecopithecus*). The latter group then re-entered Africa and differentiated into gorilla, chimpanzee and human lineages. The detailed history of the African apes is not known, although the recently named fossil *Samburu-pithecus* from Kenya may throw some light on their origin. The human lineage is well documented by fossils covering most of the last 4.5 Myr, and the earliest human fossils have all come from Africa.

See also Ape; Catarrhini; Dryopithecus; Graecopithecus; Homininae; Hominoidea; Hylobatidae; Kenyapithecus; Miocene; Ponginae; Samburupithecus; Sexual Dimorphism. [P.A.]

Further Readings

Andrews, P. (1992) Evolution and environment in the Hominoidea. Nature 360:641–646.

Ciochon, R.L., and Corruccini, R.S. (1983) New Interpretations of Ape and Human Ancestry. New York: Plenum.

Stewart, C.-B. and Disotell, T.R. (1998) Primate evolution in and out of Africa. Curr. Biol. 8:R582–R588.

Szalay, F.S., and Delson, E. (1979) Evolutionary History of the Primates. New York: Academic.

Wood, B.A., Martin, L., and Andrews, P., eds. (1986) Major Topics in Primate and Human Evolution. Cambridge: Cambridge University Press.

Homininae

Subdivision of Hominidae containing humans, chimpanzees, and gorillas. This subfamily name is not always used in this sense; more commonly, it signifies just humans and their ancestors, or even just *Homo* as opposed to the australopiths. This view was acceptable while humans and apes were still considered to make up the major subdivisions of the Hominoidea, but, if one accepts that the African apes are more closely related to humans than are the orangutan and gibbons, it becomes useful if not necessary to denote this grouping with a name. The name that has priority is Homininae.

The relationships of the species within Homininae are ambiguous. Some evidence indicates that humans and chimpanzees share a common ancestor after the divergence of gorillas, while other evidence indicates that gorillas and chimpanzees share a common ancestor after the divergence of humans. This is an important issue from the point of view of human evolution, for the correct interpretation of character change during the evolution of our species depends on knowing what the starting point was, and this, in turn, depends on correctly identifying our closest living relative.

The main evidence supporting relationship between chimpanzees and gorillas (i.e., for an African-ape clade to the exclusion of the human lineage) comes from their shared morphology. There are many characters, but most of these relate to two complexes of the skull and the limb bones. The sinus development of chimpanzees and gorillas is alike in the great extent of the maxillary and fronto-ethmoidal sinuses, and correlated with the latter are the great development of the supraorbital torus and the expansion of glabella. The elongation of the premaxilla and the narrowing of the incisive fossa may also be related, and the whole complex appears to be associated with klinorhynchy, the rotation of the face inferiorly with respect to the basicranium.

The same argument applies even more to the complex of characters related to knuckle-walking. This is an unusual form of locomotion by which the African apes use the knuckles of their hands to take their weight when walking. This both extends the lengths of their arms and enables them to hold objects in their bent fingers even when walking and running. This form of locomotion is not practiced by orangutans, even though they live in similar habitats, are of similar size, and have many similarities in posture and gait; and this makes the identical adaptations in the chimpanzees and gorillas all the more significant. They share numerous characters of the elbow, wrist, and hand that are concerned mainly with stabilizing the joints when they are fully extended by deepening fossae, enlarging guiding ridges, and shortening tendons. The complexity of these changes, which are completely shared by chimpanzees and gorillas, makes it unlikely that they could have been developed independently; rather, it suggests that they were already present in their common ancestor. Since humans share none of these characters, it would appear that the African apes shared a common ancestor after the divergence of humans.

In addition to the characters just described are other morphological features that support an African-ape clade. There is also evidence from the chromosomes and molecular data, but much of this is ambiguous. Some interpretations of the chromosomes, for instance, are taken to provide support for a relationship between humans and chimpanzees, and much of the evidence from molecular anthropology also supports this view.

Certain amino-acid substitutions are shared uniquely by humans and chimpanzees; since these are not present in any other hominoid, they are strong evidence for the human-chimpanzee relationship. There are many DNA substitutions similarly shared, which indicate that humans and chimpanzees had a common ancestor after the divergence of the gorilla and that chimpanzees are, therefore, our closest living relatives.

There is no immediate solution to this conflict in evidence over the relationships within the Homininae. It is unfortunate that for the time of divergence of African apes and humans, probably 7–5 Ma, the fossil evidence is almost nonexistent. Two groups of fossils can be assigned to this subfamily: the australopiths and other related fossils that are on or near the direct ancestry to humans, and the single fossil of *Samburupithecus* (from Kenya). In addition, some authorities believe that the Miocene taxa *Graecopithecus* and *Dryopithecus* belong to the Homininae. The evidence for this is, at best, equivocal and consists of claims of similarity in the supraorbital region, the naso-alveolar region, and the relatively high angulation of the face with respect to the cranial vault, or klinorhynchy. The latter cannot be observed directly, because the known skulls are too incomplete, but its presence is inferred on the basis of characters such as the presence of African-ape-like supraorbital tori.

The australopiths clearly belong in the Homininae. They were bipedal and had already developed many characters of the teeth and skull that are otherwise unique to humans. Their fossil record is good back to nearly 4.5 Ma, with direct evidence of bipedalism at ca. 4 Ma, and some fragmentary fossils are known back to 6–5 Ma. Before that, however, almost nothing is known except the single maxilla from Samburu Hills in the Kenyan Rift Valley, and the interpretation of this specimen is difficult. It comes from deposits closely dated to 9.5 Ma, and it is remarkably gorillalike in its morphology. Whether this resemblance to gorillas is derived or merely ancestral for the subfamily is hard to say, but in its molar proportions, premolar morphology, and cusp development on the molars it shares characters with the gorilla and with nothing else. In other words, these characters are otherwise unique to the gorilla, and their presence on *Samburupithecus* could indicate relationship. If this is so, it could indicate that the gorilla had diverged from chimpanzees and humans by this 9.5 Ma time period and that, therefore, the latter two species are related more closely to each other than either is to the gorilla, thus supporting the evidence from molecular anthropology.

Homininae
    Homo
    †*Australopithecus*
    †*Paranthropus*
    Pan
    Gorilla
    †*Samburupithecus*
    ?†*Graecopithecus*
    ??†*Dryopithecus*
†extinct

See also Ape; Australopithecus; Dryopithecus; Graecopithecus; Hominidae; Hominoidea; Locomotion; Molecular Anthropology; Molecular "vs." Morphological Approaches to Systematics; Samburupithecus; Skull. [P.A.]

Further Readings
Andrews, P. (1992) Evolution and environment in the Hominoidea. Nature 360:641–646.

Begun, D.R. (1994). Relations among the great apes and humans: New interpretations based on the fossil great ape *Dryopithecus*. Yrbk. Phys. Anthropol. 37:11–63.

Ishida, H., ed. (1984) Study of the Tertiary hominoids and their palaeoenvironments in East Africa. African Study Monographs, Supplementary Issue 2. Kyoto: Kyoto University.

Patterson, C., ed. (1987) Molecules and Morphology in Evolution: Conflict or Compromise. Cambridge: Cambridge University Press.

Wood, B.A., Martin, L., and Andrews, P., eds. (1986) Major Topics in Primate and Human Evolution. Cambridge: Cambridge University Press.

Hominini

Tribe containing taxa on the human lineage after its separation from any apes; corresponds to Hominidae of many previous authors. In this work, Hominidae and related taxa are used in a strictly cladistic sense, and if a term is required to denote the broadest concept of humans, it is *Hominini*. This tribe includes the genera *Ardipithecus*, *Australopithecus*, *Paranthropus* and *Homo*, each of which is discussed in detail.

In briefest outline, fossils and molecular studies indicate that the last common ancestor (LCA) of a hominin and an ape probably lived in Africa 8–5 Ma—paleontologists would often prefer an older date within this range, molecular anthropologists a younger. This common ancestor presumably was similar in many ways to a chimpanzee, in that hominins are derived compared to African apes in almost all studied features of morphology. Two functional complexes of some interest are less clearly understood, however. The modern chimpanzee and gorilla share locomotor adaptations to knuckle-walking, which most morphologists consider one or more detailed synapomorphies (shared derived characters). If that is the case, it is unlikely that the LCA had this adaptation, but others have suggested that knuckle-walking was indeed present in the LCA and lost in the (first?) hominins. Similarly, the morphocline and polarity of molar enamel thickness and formation speed is not clear among hominoids. For some years, it was thought that thick, fast-formed enamel characterized early hominids as compared to a thin, fast-formed enamel in hylobatids, proconsulids, and many other higher primates; thinner or more slowly formed enamel among hominids would thus be derived. But more recent studies have not confirmed this model for either modern taxa or fossils. For example, kenyapithecines include forms with thin enamel (*Otavipithecus*), thick enamel (*Griphopithecus* and *Afropithecus*), and in between (*Heliopithecus* and perhaps *Kenyapithecus*); the supposed early hominine *Graecopithecus* has very thick enamel nearly comparable to that found in *Paranthropus* species. *Ardipithecus ramidus* is distinguished from *Australopithecus* species by relatively thin enamel, although this is based upon observation rather than precise measurement. If the polarity of enamel thickness within Homininae runs from thick to thinner (or hyperthick in *Paranthropus*), then the LCA of humans and apes might have had relatively thick tooth enamel like *Homo* and *Australopithecus*; in this case, *Ardipithecus* is anomalous and might represent a convergence toward African apes, perhaps related to its forest habitat. But if the pattern were random, or if thin enamel were ancestral for modern hominines, the LCA might have had thin enamel like *Ardipithecus*.

Whatever the morphology of the African ape–hominin LCA, by ca. 4.5 Ma at the latest some of the hominin features or trends had become established, including reduction in the canine-premolar complex and anterior shifting of the foramen magnum. Soon after, species of *Australopithecus* document the development of bipedalism as the typical hominin locomotor pattern, with all of its attendant derived morphological modifications. Further dental and postcranial modifications and, eventually, increased brain size and complexity and tool use continued to characterize the successive lineages of the Hominini into the Pleistocene.

See also Ardipithecus ramidus; Australopithecus; Brain; Hominidae; Homininae; Homo; Locomotion; Molecular "vs." Morphological Approaches to Systematics; Paleolithic; Paranthropus; Teeth. [E.D.]

Further Readings

Begun, D.R. (1994) Relations among the great apes and humans: New interpretations based on the fossil great ape *Dryopithecus*. Yrbk. Phys. Anthropol. 37:11–63.
Conroy, G.C., Lichtman, J.W., and Martin, L.B. (1995) Brief communication: Some observations on enamel thickness and enamel prism pattern in the Miocene hominoid *Otavipithecus namibiensis*. Am. J. Phys. Anthropol. 98:595–600.

Hominoidea

Superfamily to which apes and humans belong. It can conveniently be divided for modern forms into the lesser apes, Hylobatidae, and the great apes and humans, Hominidae. Little is known about the evolution of the hylobatids, but the divisions within the hominids are better documented. Within this group, the orangutan was the first to branch off from the others, leaving a group comprising the African apes and humans, here called the Homininae. Thus, the nearest living relatives to humans are either or both of the African apes, but it is not clear yet whether chimpanzees and gorillas are more closely related to each other or whether one of them is more closely related to humans.

Hominoid Origins

By comparing all of the living species of hominoid, we can make inferences about the morphology of their common ancestor. These inferences are based on the likelihood that if all or most of the living species possess the same character or state, then that character or state was probably also present in their common ancestor. The alternative is to suppose that

the character evolved independently in each of the living hominoids, and, while this might have occurred in some instances, it is not likely. The majority of characters present in every animal are inherited from more or less remote ancestors, ranging from basic characters like a backbone (in all vertebrates), warm-bloodedness (in all mammals), nails instead of claws on the hands and feet (in all euprimates), or a reduced number of premolars in the jaw (in all catarrhines).

All of these characters are present in the hominoids, but they are not diagnostic of the group, since they are present in other animals as well. What we want is to identify those characters present only in (living) hominoids, and the following abbreviated description includes just such characters. These are the defining characters for the superfamily that were present in its common ancestor, by comparison to earlier catarrhines: The middle part of the skull is expanded, although overall size is no greater than in other catarrhines; the palate is deep and the sinuses are enlarged; the incisors are broader, the molars longer, and the differences between the premolars are reduced; the clavicle is elongated; the trapezius muscle inserts onto the clavicle; the humeral head is rounded, more medially oriented, and larger than the femoral head; the deltoid insertion is low on the humerus; the elbow joint is adapted for stability and for mobility in the articular surfaces for the ulna and radius; the wrist joint is adapted for mobility; the femur has asymmetrical condyles; the iliac blade of the pelvis is expanded; the talus neck and calcaneus are short and broad; the metacarpals have broad distal ends; numbers of vertebrae are lumbar 5, sacral 4–5, caudal 6 (tail is lost); a vermiform appendix is developed.

Having established the probable morphology of the ancestral hominoid on the basis of the comparative method, we can now look at the fossil record to see if any fossils fit this pattern. In the Early Miocene of East Africa is a group of fossil species with the generic name *Proconsul*. Several species are known from partial skulls and limb bones, and these show that *Proconsul* had acquired a number of the defining hominoid characters listed above. For instance, they have expanded skulls, reduced heteromorphy of the premolars, rounded and enlarged humeral heads, and the adaptations for stability of the joints (although not the ones for mobility). These lead to the conclusion that *Proconsul* was a hominoid, and we can now say a little about hominoid origins on the basis of what we know about these species.

Proconsul species lived in Africa in the Early Miocene. The earliest record is ca. 23 Ma, although fragmentary jaws of a similar form (*Kamoyapithecus*) are known back to ca. 26 Ma. The origin of the hominoids was, therefore, somewhat earlier than that. Such an age also makes sense in terms of the time of highest diversity of African hominoids, between 20 and 17 Ma, when there were more species present than anywhere today; this diversity would have taken at least several million years to develop, suggesting an origin perhaps 28–25 Ma. Moreover, this date closely corresponds to estimates of hominoid divergence based on the molecular clock.

The place of origin of the hominoids is difficult to determine based on the comparative method alone, because living hominoids are divided equally between Africa and Asia. The fossil evidence, however, is exclusively African for about the

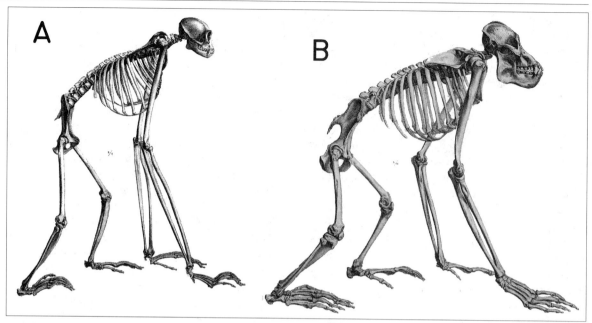

Male skeletons in right lateral view of (A) gibbon, and (B) orangutan. From H.M.D. de Blainville, Ostéographie. I: Primates, *1839, Baillière.*

first 10–12 Myr of hominoid history, with no reliable evidence for fossil hominoids in Europe or Asia until ca. 16–15 Ma.

Gibbon Divergence and Hominid Origins

The earliest branching point within the living hominoids is that dividing the gibbons from the rest of the apes and humans. The fossil species of *Proconsul* just discussed branched off earlier than the divergence of the gibbons, because the former lack several postcranial features shared by both gibbons and great apes, such as those related to adaptations for mobility in the forearm and wrist joint. Thus, *Proconsul* provides no information on gibbon origins. The gibbons themselves are a highly derived group, with many distinctive features; despite this, no fossil taxon has been found that shares any of these distinctive characters. The latter include characters of the forelimb related to the gibbons' brachiating mode of locomotion (characters not present in the great apes), the lack of sexual dimorphism in body size and in such aspects of their skull and jaws that are related to this (e.g., equal-size and large canine teeth), and their distinctive social structure and complex vocalizations. The branching event that gave rise to the gibbons also produced the great apes and humans—hominids, as defined here—and evidence for this split would also provide some indirect evidence for gibbon origins.

The ancestral morphotype for the hominid clade can be defined as follows: The skull has distinct mastoid processes, large medial pterygoids, lengthened premaxilla and increased alveolar prognathism, and reduced incisive foramen; the dentition has spatulate lateral incisors, robust canines, elongated premolars, and molars with thick enamel; the tooth rows are wide apart, the maxillary and mandibular bodies deep; the elbow joint has increased adaptations for stability in the trochlear region; the ulnar styloid process does not contact carpal bones; the hindlimb is reduced in length so that the intermembral index (the relationship of forelimbs to hindlimbs) is high; the deltoid muscle is greatly developed; and the pectoralis abdominis is missing.

Several fossil groups must be considered as potential hominids in relation to this list of characters. The earliest of these are the late Early Miocene (17 Ma) hominoids from Buluk and Kalodirr (Kenya) named *Afropithecus turkanensis.* Their hominid characters include a very deep mandibular body and symphysis, as well as molar teeth with thick enamel. The material is relatively complete, with parts of a skull, several jaws, and postcrania little different from *Proconsul,* but the descriptions published so far (1999) do not allow any further conclusions to be drawn. Another recently described fossil comes from the Ad Dabtiyah site (Saudi Arabia, which at this stage of the Miocene was connected with Africa and separate from Eurasia). This is about the same age as Buluk, and the fossil hominoid from there, *Heliopithecus leakeyi,* has at least one hominid character in its upper premolar elongation. It also has slightly thicker molar enamel than in the ancestral hominoid state, but it has not reached the full thickness seen in all other early hominids. These hominid taxa are placed in the tribe Afropithecini, and three other taxa of probably somewhat younger date may also belong to this group.

Otavipithecus from Namibia is known by a single partial mandible and is smaller than the other species, while a group of large specimens from Moroto (Uganda) recently named *Morotopithecus* are like *Afropithecus* but appear to have more modern postcrania. Specimens from Maboko and especially Nachola (both Kenya) previously termed *Kenyapithecus africanus* probably do not belong to that genus but are more like *Afropithecus* and its allies.

Kenyapithecus wickeri from Fort Ternan (Kenya) and species of *Griphopithecus* from sites in Turkey and central Europe date between 15 and 14 Ma. They have thick molar tooth enamel like *Afropithecus* (thicker than some other afropithecins) but more modern postcrania. On the other hand, they have less advanced postcrania than the European

Dryopithecus, whose enamel is thin. Given the uncertainty surrounding the determination of polarity for enamel thickness, it seems most reasonable to place *Griphopithecus* and *Kenyapithecus* together in the tribe Kenyapithecini, in turn linked with the Afropithecini in the subfamily Kenyapithecinae.

Placing greater weight on the postcranial evidence and some questionable cranial features, *Dryopithecus* is placed in its own subfamily, Dryopithecinae, probably near the origin of the two modern hominid subfamilies. *Dryopithecus* fossils from Rudábánya (Hungary) and Can Llobateres (Spain) show adaptations of the elbow joint and other limb elements very close to those of the living hominid species, and the naso-alveolar region, while not as developed as any of the living great apes, is more derived than the condition seen in *Proconsul* or the kenyapithecines. Some workers argue that *Dryopithecus* shares the klinorhynch condition with the African apes (see below), while others have suggested that it shares facial morphology with pongines. *Dryopithecus* species are known from Spain through Georgia ca. 13–8 Ma, and rare thin-enameled fossils from eastern Asia have also been referred to this genus. Two other more derived European genera, *Oreopithecus* and *Graecopithecus*, are here placed in different subfamilies but might instead be included in the Dryopithecinae.

The evidence from these fossils indicates that the divergence of the hylobatid and hominid clades occurred at least 17 Ma, probably in Africa. The initial changes leading to the hominid clade included enlargement of the premolars, deepening of the jaws, thickening of molar enamel, and stabilizing of the elbow joint. It is likely that in all of these characters the ancestral gibbons, which by definition must have been present alongside the hominids, would have retained the primitive condition. It is, in fact, possible that the early gibbon ancestors retained ancestral characters in most respects, making them difficult to identify in the fossil record, for they would have been little different from the ancestral hominoids. Generalized catarrhines that have been identified under a variety of names are known from Middle and Late Miocene sites as far apart as Kenya and China (e.g., *Micropithecus* from Africa and "cf. *Dionysopithecus*" from eastern Asia). Since these lack any definite hominoid characters, they are here included with *Dendropithecus* in a poorly defined grouping intermediate between pliopithecids and proconsulids. If further evidence revealed the presence of either hylobatid or hominid characters, they might eventually be included in one of these two clades.

Dates from the molecular clock are in general accord with the dates from the fossil evidence. DNA-DNA hybridization data give an age range of 22–18 Ma for gibbon divergence, based on assumed divergence dates for the orangutan of 16–13 Ma. A similar, if slightly younger date, is given by the clock from nuclear DNA-sequencing data, whereas sequencing of mtDNA indicates a younger divergence date still.

Orangutan Divergence

Probably the most solid evidence for any of the branching points within the Hominoidea is available for the orangutan lineage. The orangutan is highly derived, in both its morphology and its molecules. For these characters, the African apes and humans (the Homininae) share the same character

states as gibbons, and often with cercopithecoid monkeys as well, so that they are assumed to retain the ancestral condition for hominoids or catarrhines, respectively. In fact, within Hominoidea the hominines are characterized mostly by retention of ancestral characters, and this makes them a difficult clade to define. Among the defining characters of the pongine clade (based on modern *Pongo*) are these: The skull has an expanded and flattened zygomatic region, giving the face a concave aspect, no glabellar thickening, narrow distance between the eyes, no browridges, and a rotated premaxilla giving a smooth floor to the nasal cavity and an extremely reduced incisive canal with no incisive fossa; in the dentition, the upper lateral incisors are very small relative to the central, the molar enamel is of intermediate thickness, and the molars have a flattened dentine surface and deeply wrinkled enamel; and the articular surfaces of the limb bones are adapted for extreme mobility at the elbow, wrist, and hip joints. None of the fossils so far discussed (with the possible exception of *Dryopithecus*) share any of these pongine characters. They all retain the ancestral condition, where it is known, in these characters and, therefore, have no direct link with the pongine clade.

On the other hand, many of these characters are present in a widespread group of fossils generally placed in the Middle to Late Miocene Asian genus *Sivapithecus*, which is thus grouped with the orangutan clade. Included in *Sivapithecus* are a number of forms that used to be separated as distinct genera, including particularly *Ramapithecus*, which at one time was thought to be directly ancestral to humans. The Turkish fossils known as *Ankarapithecus* were previously included in *Sivapithecus* but they are distinct from the Indo-Pakistani material. Both share at least some of the facial characters detailed above for the pongine clade, and where they differ they retain the ancestral hominoid condition. They can thus be interpreted as within the pongine clade but as less advanced than the living orangutan. Their age range is from 12.5 to ca. 7 Ma, with the earliest good evidence for pongine affinities coming from Pakistan. Some researchers have assigned a number of other fossils to *Sivapithecus* (or to the pongine clade in general), such as those from Lufeng (China), Ravin de la Pluie (Greece), and Rudábánya (Hungary), but there appears to be little justification for this.

The conclusion from the fossils, therefore, is that the branching point of the pongine clade was at least 13–12 Ma and maybe more, if the Turkish *Griphopithecus* proves to be near the ancestry of this group. No specimen known from Africa can be included in this clade, but since the earliest hominoids are all African, it appears likely that the pongines originated from a sivapith-like form somewhere in Africa. The age range for the divergence of the orangutan is 16.4–12.7 Ma based on sequencing of nuclear DNA, while a younger date of 12.1–9.7 Ma is given by sequencing of mtDNA.

Hominines

The last group of hominoids, and the sister group to the pongines, is that containing the African apes and humans. This is a hard group to define because it has so few shared derived characters, particularly of features likely to be preserved as fossils. Chimpanzees, gorillas, and humans share

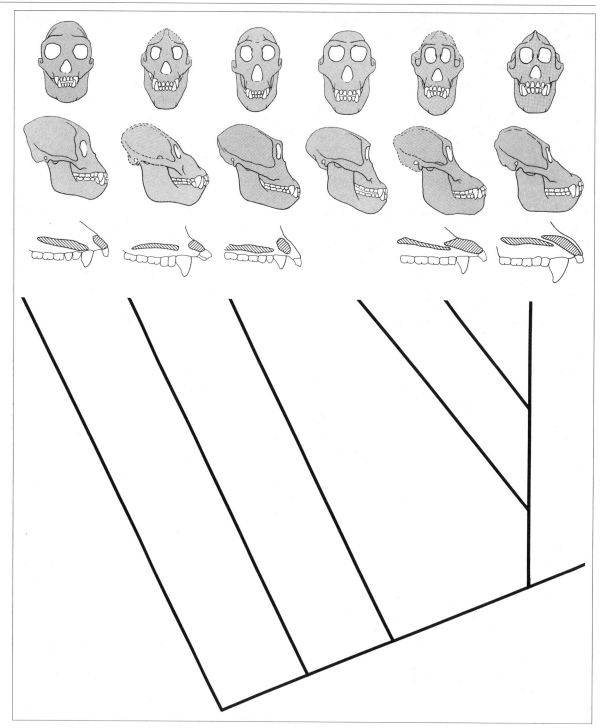

A cladogram of relationships of the Hominoidea, with illustrations of the frontal and right lateral views and nasopalatal sections of selected genera. From left to right: Proconsul, Afropithecus, Dryopithecus, Ankarapithecus *(nasopalatal details unclear),* Sivapithecus, Pongo, Graecopithecus, Gorilla, Pan, Australopithecus, *and* Homo. *Not to scale. Reconstructions of fossils modified by L. Meeker and E. Delson after various sources.* Afropithecus *based on sketch by A. Walker; its nasopalatal section is taken from the Moroto palate, now placed in* Morotopithecus, *while the* Afropithecus *face may show a pattern more like that of* Sivapithecus. *Nasopalatal sketches represent cross-section through midline of palate and nasal cavity, showing dental outlines, body of premaxilla (/////) and maxillary surface (\\\\\) on either side of incisive canal. In* Homo, *the "premaxilla" is fused with the maxilla. See text for discussion of the details of this region. Dashes indicate tentative reconstruction when remains unknown.*

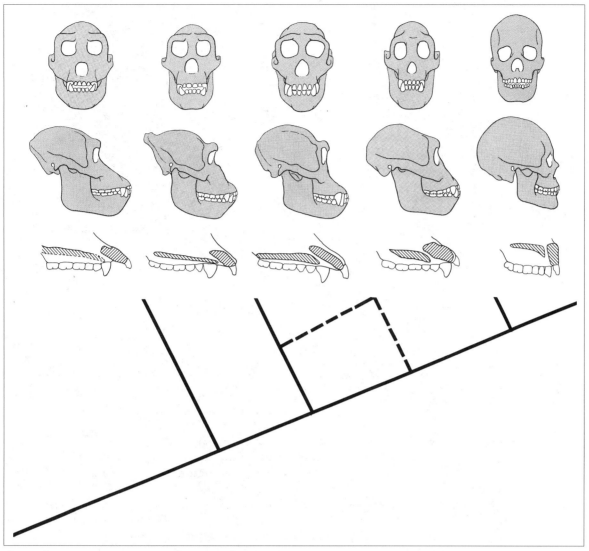

Continued.

the following list of characters, which are taken to define the node: The skull has a true frontal sinus developed; the browridges form a continuous bar across glabella, and a postorbital sulcus is developed; middle-ear depth is increased; two of the wrist bones (os centrale and scaphoid) are fused; the prostate is subdivided; apocrine glands are scarce and eccrine glands abundant; there is a large axillary organ; and the aorta type is distinctive. At the molecular level, several amino-acid residue substitutions are uniquely shared in this clade, as are large numbers of DNA substitutions. Weak as this evidence is, it is still much stronger than that linking any other hominoid species with humans. The evidence put forward suggesting that humans are specially related to either orangutans or chimpanzees is poor in both cases, and the same applies to the evidence, or lack of it, linking the three great apes together.

The situation is not made any easier by the lack of any early fossils that can be definitively assigned to this clade. A frontal sinus has been reported for some of the genera mentioned earlier, but it is not certain if these structures are homologous with the hominine frontal sinus. It has been observed in *Dryopithecus* and it may be present in *Graecopithe-*

cus, where it has been claimed to be associated with development of African-ape-like browridges, but the presence of the latter and the significance of the former are both uncertain. The latter genus apparently shares one hominine character in the presence of a narrow incisive canal due to the overriding of the premaxilla above the maxilla, giving this region an African-ape type of morphology in *Graecopithecus*, but this character is not present (or is at best incipient) in *Dryopithecus*. It is possible that either or both of these European forms may be early hominines, but a more conservative view places them both in a more primitive subfamily, Dryopithecinae.

One fossil that is of interest to the hominine branching event is *Samburupithecus* from Samburu Hills (Kenya), which raises the question of the relationships within the hominine clade. The Samburu fossil is dated at 9.5 Ma, and it has a morphology very close to that of gorillas. Only a single upper jaw is known, but the molar and premolar proportions and shape, and the cusp morphology of the molars, are all similar to the condition in gorillas. The polarity of these characters is hard to determine, but it is possible that they are gorilla synapomorphies.

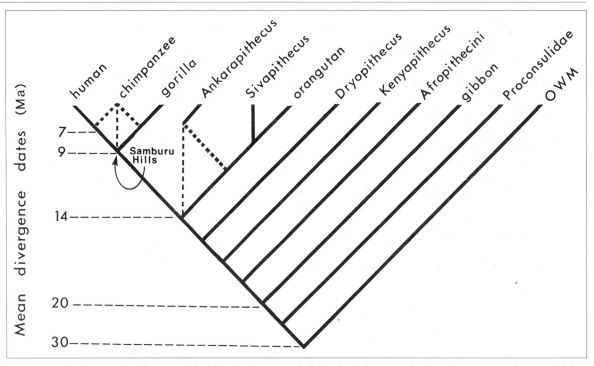

Relationships of the hominoids. Both recent and fossil hominoid taxa are included on this cladogram, and estimated ages are assigned to several of the major branching points based on the oldest record of the fossils contained within the respective clades. Where multiple possible relationships are indicated by interrupted lines, the heavier (diagonal) line is judged more likely than the lighter (vertical) alternative. DNA sequencing and hybridization studies suggest a date between 27 and 25 Ma for the hominoid-cercopithecoid divergence.

Evidence from comparative morphology supports the existence of an African-ape clade distinct from humans. Chimpanzees and gorillas share a major complex of characters relating to knuckle-walking, with about 10 characters of the elbow, wrist, and hand, depending upon how they are counted. They also share some characters of the chromosomes and DNA at the molecular level. In contrast to this is the abundant molecular evidence that indicates a closer link between humans and chimpanzees and that is supported by some morphological evidence: broad lower incisors, spatulate I^2, broad lower molars, vertical mandibular ramus, and the anterior edge of the incisive fossa posterior to P^3. These morphological characters shared between chimpanzees and humans are not very convincing, however, when set against the knuckle-walking complex of characters shared by chimpanzees and gorillas. As far as it goes, the single fossil from Samburu Hills supports the chimp-human relationship, if its gorilla affinities are correct, for it might imply the early separation of the gorilla clade from that linking humans and chimpanzees. Similarly, the European *Graecopithecus* (ca. 10–8 Ma) has been suggested as most similar to gorillas in certain characters, but these features may be hominine symplesiomorphies.

The scarcity of fossils makes it hard to say anything about the time and place of the origin of the hominine clade. Since humans and African apes have Africa as the only common geographical factor, that seems the likely place of origin, and this fits with *Samburupithecus*. On the other hand, if *Graecopithecus* and/or *Dryopithecus* are, in fact, hominines, the clade could have originated in Eurasia and then returned to Africa. Early human ancestors of the genus *Australopithe-*

cus are known only from Africa, but their fossil record starts long after the (human-chimpanzee) branching times indicated by the molecular clock. The latter are 10–6 Ma (DNA-DNA hybridization) and 8.1–6.3 Ma (DNA sequencing), and since these dates have been shown to be concordant with fossil evidence, where available, it seems reasonable to accept them where fossil evidence is lacking.

See also Africa; Africa, East; Afropithecus; Ape; Buluk; Catarrhini; Dryopithecinae; Dryopithecus; Hominidae; Homininae; Hominini; Kenyapithecinae; Kenyapithecus; Molecular Clock; Ponginae; Proconsulidae; Samburupithecus; Sivapithecus; Teeth. [P.A., E.D.]

Further Readings

Andrews, P. (1992) Evolution and environment in the Hominoidea. Nature 360:641–646.

Begun, D.R. (1994) Relations among the great apes and humans: New interpretations based on the fossil great ape *Dryopithecus*. Yrbk. Phys. Anthropol. 37:11–63.

Begun, D., Ward, C., and Rose, M., eds. (1997) Function, Phylogeny and Fossils: Miocene Hominoid Evolution and Adaptations. New York: Plenum.

Ciochon, R.L., and Corruccini, R.S. (1983) New Interpretations of Ape and Human Ancestry. New York: Plenum.

Patterson, C., ed. (1987) Molecules and Morphology in Evolution: Conflict or Compromise? Cambridge: Cambridge University Press.

Szalay, F.S., and Delson, E. (1979) Evolutionary History of the Primates. New York: Academic.

Wood, B.A., Martin, L., and Andrews, P., eds. (1986) Major Topics in Primate and Human Evolution. Cambridge: Cambridge University Press.

Homo

Genus to which modern humans belong, named in 1758 by the Swedish naturalist C. Linnaeus. In the eighteenth century, genera and species were regarded as fixed entities, and no possibility of change through evolution was entertained. As described by Linnaeus, *Homo* was made up only of living humans belonging to one species, *Homo sapiens.* Fossil representatives of the genus were not uncovered until the middle of the next century. The first Neanderthal to excite real debate was found in Germany in 1856 and named as a new species in 1864. Still more archaic humans were excavated in Java in 1890 and 1891. *Homo* is now considered to contain at least two and perhaps as many as four or five extinct species in addition to living people. The earliest members of the genus appeared in eastern Africa before 2 Ma. These forms were followed by *Homo erectus*, which seems also to have evolved in Africa and then spread into other parts of the Old World tropics. By the Middle Pleistocene, populations of this species had reached such areas as northern China, where they were able to adapt to harsh environmental circumstances. *H. erectus* was eventually supplanted by somewhat less archaic people, including the Neanderthals, but fully modern *H. sapiens* did not appear until after 100 Ka. Since that time, humans have developed elaborate technologies that allow exploitation of the humid forests, the arid deserts, and even the Arctic regions. Virtually no part of the planet is closed to human habitation. *H. sapiens* is the most dominant of mammalian species and is just becoming aware of its responsibilities to preserve the Earth's resources and maintain the many fragile ecosystems on which all life depends.

Definitions of the Genus

Modern descriptions of *Homo* emphasize features that set this genus apart from other extinct or living groups of the family Hominidae, including the large apes. One often-cited definition was provided by W.E. Le Gros Clark in 1964. Clark suggested that *Homo* can be distinguished primarily on the basis of brain size, along with morphology of the skull and teeth. Since he recognized only the two species *H. erectus* and *H. sapiens,* he stipulated a relatively large cranial capacity (900–ca. 2,000 ml). His description also notes that the temporal muscles never reach to the top of the braincase to produce a sagittal (midline) crest. Earlier representatives of *Homo* show strong supraorbital development, but the facial profile is straight rather than projecting. The dental arcade is rounded in form, the canine teeth are small, and the last molar is reduced in size. Clark makes little mention of the postcranial skeleton, suggesting only that the limbs are adapted to a fully upright posture and gait.

In the same year (1964), important new discoveries from Olduvai Gorge in East Africa were announced by L.S.B. Leakey and his colleagues. These fossils consisted of several small skulls as well as postcranial material. Leakey argued that the Olduvai finds should be included within

Homo as a new species called *Homo habilis.* This could be done only if Clark's description of the genus were revised. Accordingly, Leakey, together with P.V. Tobias and J. Napier, characterized *Homo* as having a brain variable in size but larger on average than the brain of *Australopithecus.* Other aspects of cranial and dental anatomy were treated in much the same manner as by Clark, although several points concerning tooth size and proportions were elaborated. The pelvis and hindlimb were again said to be adapted to upright posture and a bipedal gait, and the hand is described as capable of fine manipulation.

Homo habilis was greeted by substantial controversy, but many paleontologists now accept the species as valid. Modern definitions of *Homo* emphasize other characters or complexes in addition to brain size, which varies considerably within the genus. Along with changes in the proportions of the brain, which are reflected in the enlarged side walls and frontal portion of the cranium, F.C. Howell lists reduction of the area at the back of the braincase occupied by the nuchal (neck) muscles. The size of the facial skeleton is also decreased, and there are changes in the architecture of the nose and cheek. Howell comments further on tooth size and patterns of dental wear. Like earlier workers, he notes that *Homo* species are built to walk erect and use the hands skillfully. To this anatomical description, he adds one more important characteristic. *Homo* may be recognized as the (first) hominid dependent on culturally patterned behavior. Even *H. habilis* made stone tools, and these artifacts tell us about the lifeways of ancient humans.

The First Species of *Homo*

Since the first traces of *H. habilis* were recovered at Olduvai Gorge (Tanzania) in the 1960s, more material has been found elsewhere in eastern Africa, particularly in the Koobi Fora region east of Lake Turkana (Kenya). At Koobi Fora, the fossils are scattered through a lengthy sequence of ancient lake deposits. One of the best-preserved crania of early *Homo* comes from a layer dated quite securely to ca. 2 Ma. Most other specimens are not quite this old, but none of the East African finds is younger than ca. 1.5 Ma. During this time period, *Homo* may have ranged into southern Africa as well. Evidence from the Malawi Rift and caves at Swartkrans and Sterkfontein in the Transvaal suggests this, although the bones are broken and are, therefore, hard to interpret with certainty. Other early specimens of *Homo* come from the upper Chemeron level in the Baringo Basin (Kenya) and the uppermost horizon at Hadar (Ethiopia).

Tobias has continued to defend his claim that all of this material should be referred to one sexually dimorphic species. However, not all authorities accept this appraisal of *H. habilis.* For some time, it has been apparent that the smaller skulls differ from larger ones in important ways, as do other parts of the skeleton. An alternative is to place the fossils in separate species. One advocate of this view is B.A. Wood, who recognizes only the Olduvai finds along with certain individuals from Koobi Fora as *H. habilis.* As characterized in this restricted sense, *H. habilis* has an average brain size close to 600 ml, and the facial bones and teeth are relatively small. There is less size dimorphism, but the limbs as

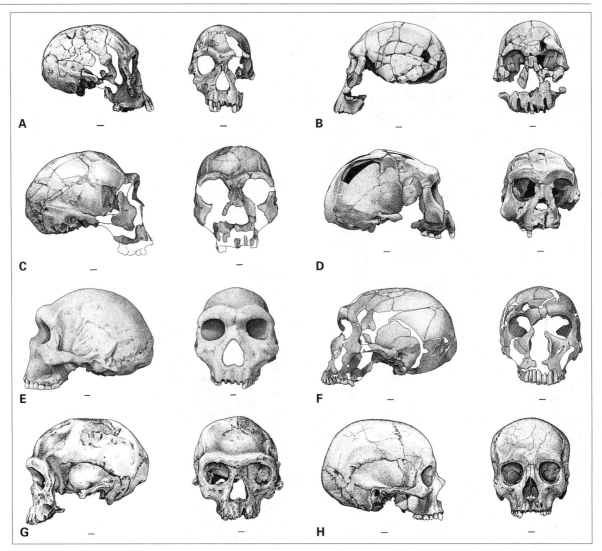

Lateral and frontal views of eight varieties (species, subspecies or populations, according to different authors) generally included in the genus Homo. *(A)* H. habilis; *(B)* H. rudolfensis; *(C)* H. ergaster *(=*H. erectus?*)*; *(D)* H. erectus; *(E)* H. heidelbergensis *(="archaic"* H. sapiens*);* *(F)* H. neanderthalensis *(=*H. sapiens neanderthalensis*);* *(G) archaic modern* H. sapiens; *(H) modern* H. sapiens.

judged from the small skeleton numbered OH 62 from Olduvai are generally primitive, showing resemblances to *Australopithecus*. Wood assigns the larger skulls and massive jaws from Koobi Fora to a separate taxon, called *Homo rudolfensis*. Postcranial bones that may belong to this species are more like those of later humans.

Other workers agree that two species are documented in the record, although they find that the hominids can be sorted slightly differently. For example, the cranial bones, lower jaw, and hand of one individual (OH 7) from Olduvai can be grouped with the larger specimens from Koobi Fora. Since OH 7 is the type for *H. habilis*, this name must be applied to an assemblage of fossils that is virtually the converse of *H. habilis* as treated above. Such a taxon, which includes much of the material referred by Wood to *H. rudolfensis*, would have a voluminous braincase and a flat, rather *Australopithecus*-like face—together, potentially, with more modern-looking postcranial bones. If this interpretation is accepted, then the second species represented at Olduvai and Koobi Fora is still unnamed (although *H. microcranous* has

been proposed by W. Ferguson based on Koobi Fora specimen ER 1813). The latter small-brained hominids have shorter faces, coupled with chimplike forelimbs and short legs.

However this question is resolved, it is clear that the earliest representatives of *Homo* are contemporaneous. Probably both species evolved before 2 Ma. One apparently survived for only a brief interval, but the second lived into the Early Pleistocene so as to overlap in time with *H. erectus*. The phylogenetic relationships of these hominids are obscure, but it can be argued on various grounds that the smaller species is unlikely to be ancestral to *H. erectus*. The large-brained group seems also to differ from later humans, especially in facial form, although its body proportions are rather modern. Evolutionary links as indicated in the accompanying figure must be considered tentative.

Homo erectus and Later Humans

H. erectus is known to have frequented the same East African localities as earlier *Homo*. This species is represented by sev-

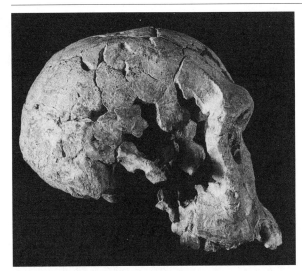

This skull numbered KNM-ER 1813 from Koobi Fora represents an early member of the genus Homo. *Some authorities refer it to* Homo habilis, *but others point to the relatively small brain, short face, and small teeth as evidence that* KNM-ER 1813 *may represent a still unnamed species contemporary with* Homo habilis. *See next figure. Photo by Philip Rightmire, courtesy of National Museum of Kenya.*

Asia. Just when *H. erectus* first reached the Southeast Asian tropics is uncertain, but a number of well-preserved fossils have been found at Trinil, Sangiran, and other sites in Java. *H. erectus* was present in China as well as Java during the Middle Pleistocene.

As with *H. habilis*, there is a difference of opinion concerning taxonomy. Some authorities prefer to emphasize the special features of the Asian fossils and claim that the name *H. erectus* should be retained only for specimens from Eastern Asia. In this view, the hominins from eastern Africa are better placed in a separate species called *Homo ergaster*. However, the anatomical distinctions among these populations are not very great, and it may still be argued that *H. erectus* is a widespread polytypic species having its origin in Africa.

All of these people differ from earlier *Homo* in important ways. Even the oldest *H. erectus* crania from East Africa have internal capacities of 800–900 ml, and one large braincase from Olduvai Gorge has a volume well in excess of 1,000 ml. Some of the younger specimens from Asia show a slight increase over this figure. The skull itself is long and low in outline. Individual bones tend to be thicker than is usual for *H. habilis*, and buttresses or crests are prominent. Brows over the orbits are especially thick and projecting. The rear of the cranium is strongly angled, and a transverse shelf of bone is present on the occiput. The face and jaws are large relative to the overall size of the braincase, but the cheek teeth especially are much reduced compared with those of *Australopithecus*. Postcranial parts recovered from the Turkana sites suggest that *H. erectus* had a relatively slender build and was about as tall as more recent humans.

eral incomplete crania, lower jaws, and other bones recovered at Olduvai Gorge. More material, including a nearly complete skeleton, has been collected near Lake Turkana. Some of the Turkana fossils date to ca. 1.8 Ma, while specimens from Olduvai are younger. During the Early Pleistocene, populations of *H. erectus* seem to have been distributed widely across Africa. Probably well before 1.0 Ma the species passed through the Levant into other parts of western

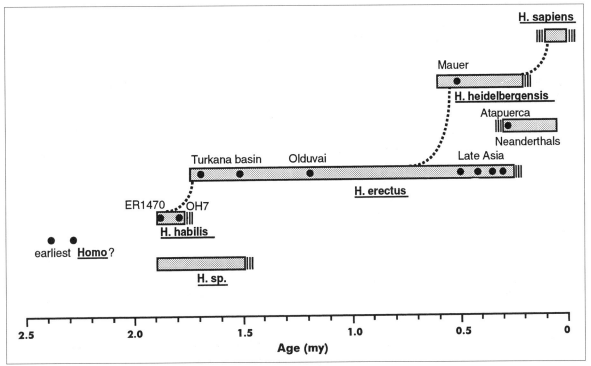

Durations and possible evolutionary relationships of Homo *species.* Homo habilis *is a relatively large-brained form, but it seems only marginally more acceptable than contemporary* Homo sp. *as the ancestor to* Homo erectus. *As documented from sites in Asia and Africa,* Homo erectus *survived into the middle Pleistocene. This long-lasting lineage evolved toward anatomically advanced humans, grouped here as* Homo heidelbergensis *(Europe and Africa) and* Homo sapiens. *The Neanderthals appear to have deep roots in western Europe, but their relationship to other middle Pleistocene populations is uncertain. Courtesy of Philip Rightmire.*

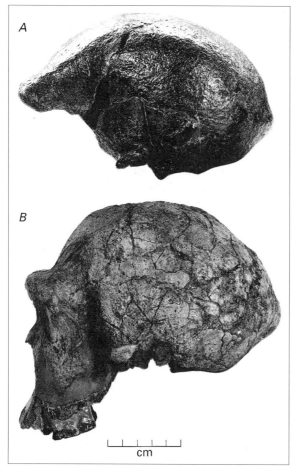

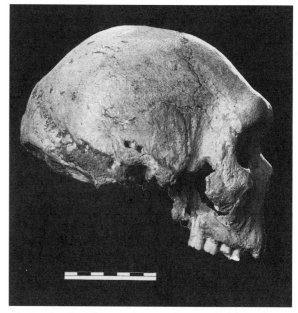

The exceptionally well preserved cranium from Petralona in Greece has thick brows and a low vault reminiscent of Homo erectus. Other characteristics of the face and braincase align this specimen with more advanced humans. It is often described as "archaic" Homo sapiens, but it can be argued that Petralona and certain other Middle Pleistocene hominids are better placed in a distinct species, called Homo heidelbergensis. See two figures back. Scale in cm. Courtesy of Philip Rightmire.

The cranium of Sangiran 2 from Java (A) compared to KNM-ER 3733 from Koobi Fora (B). These two specimens are similar in many respects and are usually grouped together as representatives of Homo erectus. Some authorities prefer to set KNM-ER 3733 and other East African remains apart from the Asian material, as Homo ergaster. Photos by Philip Rightmire; courtesy of Philip Rightmire (A) and National Museum of Kenya (B).

Sometime in the Middle Pleistocene, *H. erectus* was followed by more advanced humans. The skulls of these people are still archaic in general appearance but exhibit features that set them apart from *H. erectus*. One individual from Petralona Cave in northern Greece is very well preserved. This cranium is low in outline, with a strong brow. The rear of the braincase is not sharply curved, however, and several small but important details of cranial base anatomy are modern. Endocranial volume for Petralona is expanded well beyond the average for *H. erectus*. Another useful assemblage has been excavated at Arago Cave (France), and additional remains have been recovered at such sites as Lake Ndutu, Kabwe, and Saldanha in sub-Saharan Africa, and Dali in China. None of these fossils has been accurately dated, but the oldest may be 500 Kyr or more. They are usually described as "archaic *Homo sapiens*." This way of classifying them emphasizes broad similarities to later populations, including living humans. However, it can be argued that the crania and jaws are so different from modern ones that they must represent separate species. The Mauer (Germany) jaw, for example, along with Petralona and other European and African specimens, can be referred to *Homo heidelbergensis*, as in the figure.

Neanderthals make their appearance in Europe and southwestern Asia in the later Middle Pleistocene, although researchers vary somewhat in the definition of this group. Some important fossils from the Sierra de Atapuerca (Spain), dated to ca. 300 Ka, may be about the oldest recovered so far (1998). These populations possess a suite of distinctive anatomical characters, by which they can easily be recognized. Since many Neanderthal sites have been investigated, we know quite a lot about how these people lived. Their Mousterian flake tools are quite sophisticated, and their caves contain abundant indications that fire was used regularly for cooking and for warmth. Simple graves show that the dead were buried intentionally, perhaps for the first time in human history. The Neanderthals continued to inhabit parts of Europe until ca. 30 Ka. After this date, they disappear from the record. The populations that succeed them in Europe and Western Asia have fully modern skeletons and must have resembled people of today. Just where these anatomically modern groups originated, and whether such people may have existed for a considerable time in Africa or elsewhere as contemporaries of the Neanderthals, are important questions. Firm answers are not available, but it is clear that by 35 Ka modern *H. sapiens* occupied nearly all regions of the Old World.

Evidence for Early Cultural Activities
Stone artifacts have been recovered from a number of the sites yielding early *Homo*. These tools and waste materials provide clues concerning human behavior. One especially informative locality is Olduvai Gorge. Crude chopping tools and sharp flakes of the Oldowan industry are common at

several levels in Bed l, where they often occur with animal remains. This association of artifacts with bones traditionally has been taken as evidence that the hominins hunted animals, brought them to their living sites, and butchered the carcasses with the Oldowan implements. The situation at Olduvai and other Early Pleistocene sites is now known to be more complicated than this. Taphonomic studies have demonstrated that such assemblages may be formed by various agencies, not all related to hominid activities.

Continuing research on the Olduvai material does suggest that early humans used animal products. That cutmarks on some of the Bed I bones must have been produced by stone tools has been shown with the aid of scanning electron microscopy (SEM). This finding, however, does not prove that all of the animals were hunted. SEM analysis makes it clear that the Olduvai bones carry signs of rodent or carnivore tooth damage as well as definite evidence of cutting. It is likely that some of the game was killed by large cats or other carnivores. Probably, the Olduvai hominids were able to obtain such carcasses only after these had been fed upon by other animals. The people may well have hunted small antelopes and other prey, but they functioned as scavengers as well.

The supposition that hominids used the Olduvai sites as home bases can also be questioned. There is little indication that people actually lived at the spots where the animal bones accumulated, and such areas must have been attractive to a variety of dangerous predators. Perhaps these sites were treated simply as convenient caches of stone artifacts and raw materials, to which animal parts could be transported for rapid processing. If this is the case, then we do not know where the hominids were living or whether their social patterns resembled those of later hunter-gatherers. Certainly the first *Homo* species engaged in cultural activities, but these early people probably behaved quite differently from *H. sapiens*.

There is evidence that *H. erectus* possessed more sophisticated technological skills. Stone industries associated with these populations in Africa and Asia show more diversity. There is still little indication that *H. erectus* hunted large animals systematically, however. At many of the Middle Pleistocene sites where Acheulean tools and bones are concentrated, it is difficult to be sure whether the game was killed or scavenged by humans or by other carnivores. Some of the animal remains may represent natural deaths and may not document the activity of predators at all. Given these uncertainties, it can be argued that advanced hunting techniques were not developed until Late Pleistocene times.

Another question concerns the acquisition of language by early members of the *Homo* lineage. Evidence bearing on this issue is indirect and subject to several interpretations. Some anatomists have claimed that even ancient brains show enlargement of the regions associated with spoken communication. Others disagree, and, in fact, the number of well-preserved braincases from which detailed casts can be prepared is small. Anthropologists approach this question from the perspective offered by the archaeological record. Some suggest that even crude Oldowan artifacts imply a capacity for language. Alternatively, it may be argued that the Oldowan represents only opportunistic stone working, while Acheulean tools are more carefully formed and often display impressive symmetry. Perhaps *H. erectus* was the first hominid to use symbols and speak effectively. Critics point out that the link between technology and linguistic behavior has not been firmly established and note that simple tools could have been made by hominids lacking language. Just when *Homo* developed the linguistic skills that characterize modern humans is, therefore, not clear.

Continuing Questions

A traditional view is that the evolution of *Homo* was a process of gradual, progressive change. *H. habilis* is widely presumed to have evolved from an australopith ancestor. This ancient species of *Homo* resembles australopith in a number of features, although there are signs of increased encephalization and reduction in tooth size. Near the beginning of the Pleistocene, *H. habilis* was transformed into *H. erectus*. Trends begun early in the history of the genus were continued, to produce a larger brain and cheek teeth still more reduced in comparison with *Australopithecus*. Paleontologists favoring this view regard these species as successive segments of a single lineage. Middle Pleistocene populations of *H. erectus* are said, in turn, to show steady evolution toward the anatomy characteristic of *H. sapiens*, and all three taxa are linked in an unbroken progression of slowly changing forms.

This interpretation of the fossils can be challenged. Some paleontologists see indications that the evolution of *Homo* was more complicated, involving several lineages and substantial variations in the rate at which morphological change occurred. *H. habilis* and its companion species are still too poorly known to provide much information in this regard, but one of these lineages must have gone extinct. The older skulls of *H. erectus* from eastern Africa look much like the later ones from Java and China, and it can be argued that evolution slowed during the middle of the Pleistocene. The pace quickened again with the origin of more modern humans. Precisely when and where our own species emerged is not known, but this event may have taken place in a restricted geographic area. Some, perhaps many, archaic populations became extinct during this time. It is not obvious why the tempo of evolution varied during the Pleistocene or why some groups became extinct while others flourished. Gaining a better understanding of these processes is an important item on the agenda of modern paleoanthropology.

See also Acheulean; Africa; Asia, Eastern and Southern; Asia, Western; Baringo Basin/Tugen Hills; Clark, [Sir] Wilfred Edward Le Gros; Dali; Europe; Genus; Hadar; Homo erectus; Homo ergaster; Homo habilis; Homo rudolfensis; Homo sapiens; Kabwe; Mauer; Mousterian; Ndutu; Neanderthals; Oldowan; Olduvai Gorge; Petralona; Pleistocene; Saldanha; Speciation; Species; Speech (Origins of); Trinil; Turkana Basin. [G.P.R.]

Further Readings

Delson, E., ed. (1985) Ancestors: The Hard Evidence. New York: Liss.

Howell, F.C. (1978) Hominidae. In V.J. Maglio and H.B.S. Cooke (eds.): Evolution of African Mammals. Cambridge, Mass.: Harvard University Press, pp. 154–248.

Isaac, G. (1978) The food-sharing behavior of protohuman hominids. Sci. Am. 238:90–108.

Le Gros Clark, W.E. (1978) The Fossil Evidence for Human Evolution, 3rd ed. Chicago: University of Chicago Press.

Mellars, P., and Stringer, C., eds. (1989) The Human Revolution: Behavioural and Biological Perspectives on the Origins of Modern Humans. Edinburgh: Edinburgh University Press.

Potts, R. (1988) Early Hominid Activities at Olduvai. New York: Aldine de Gruyter.

Rightmire, G.P. (1990) The Evolution of *Homo erectus*: Comparative Anatomical Studies of an Extinct Human Species. Cambridge: Cambridge University Press.

Smith, F.H., and Spencer, F., eds. (1984) The Origins of Modern Humans: A World Survey of the Fossil Evidence. New York: Liss.

Tobias, P.V. (1991) Olduvai Gorge, Vol. 4: The Skulls, Endocasts, and Teeth of *Homo habilis*. Cambridge: Cambridge University Press.

Wood, B.A., and Collard M. (1999) The human genus. Science 284:65–71.

Wood, B.A. (1991) Koobi Fora Research Project, Vol. 4: Hominid Cranial Remains. Oxford: Clarendon.

Homo antecessor

Hominid species described in 1997 from fragmentary fossils discovered in the TD6 (Aurora) level of the Gran Dolina cave site, Atapuerca Hills, Spain. The sediments at this level lie about one meter below a magnetic polarity shift from reversed to normal that is believed to represent the Matuyama/Brunhes boundary. The fossils themselves thus probably date to slightly in excess of 780 Ka, making them the oldest known hominids from Europe (with the possible exception of the Ceprano calvaria from Italy).

The fossils themselves include a variety of postcranial and cranial fragments representing the remains of at least six individuals. The most complete of these specimens is a partial lower face of a juvenile, with several teeth preserved; in addition, there is a fragmentary right frontal, also juvenile, and a small piece of mandibular corpus with two molars. In naming the species *Homo antecessor,* Bermudez de Castro and colleagues pointed particularly to characters of the midface that distinguish this new taxon from known representatives of *Homo ergaster, Homo erectus,* and *Homo heidelbergensis,* and from the much younger hominids from the neighboring Atapuerca site of the Sima de los Huesos. They observed that in the paranasal region *Homo antecessor* shows closer resemblance to *Homo sapiens* than do any of the other *Homo* species just noted. However, they suggested at the same time that the configuration of the *Homo antecessor* midface is plausibly ancestral to that of the Sima de los Huesos form and of the Neanderthals, as well as to that of *Homo sapiens*. Accordingly, they proposed that *Homo antecessor* represents a lineage that subsequently bifurcated to give rise (ul-

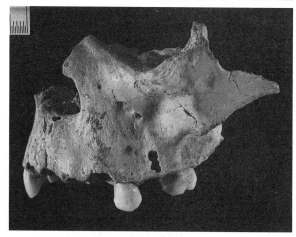

Oblique facial view of the juvenile holotype lower face of Homo antecessor. *The specimen presents nearly modern morphology in such areas as the prognathic mid-face, deep canine fossa, and sharp inferior nasal margin. Courtesy of J.-L. Arsuaga; photo by J. Trueba.*

timately) to *Homo sapiens* on the one hand, and to a *Homo heidelbergensis—Homo neanderthalensis* lineage the other.

Commentary on both the new species and this interpretation of its phylogenetic status has been mixed, centering on the fact that as juveniles the principal TD-6 fossils do not show the full adult morphology. However, the individuals involved are sufficiently well developed to show a distinctive conformation that does indeed seem to justify the creation of a new species; and while the phylogenetic position of *Homo antecessor* will doubtless be the center of much future debate, there is no question that these fossils, albeit in a very limited anatomical region, show much closer resemblances to *Homo sapiens* than do any others of comparable antiquity.

See also Atapuerca; Ceprano; Homo; Homo erectus; Homo heidelbergensis; Homo neanderthalensis; Homo sapiens. [I.T.]

Further Readings
Bermudez de Castro, J., Arsuaga, J., Carbonell, E., Rosas, A., Martinez, I., and Mosquera, M. (1997) A hominid from the Lower Pleistocene of Atapuerca, Spain: Possible ancestor to Neanderthals and modern humans. Science 276:1392–1395.

Kunzig, R. (1997) Atapuerca: The face of an ancestral child. Discover 18 (12):88–101.

Homo erectus

Extinct form of human known to have inhabited the Old World. This species probably originated in Africa, where it may have evolved nearly 2 Ma from earlier *Homo*. Following this African origin, populations of *Homo erectus* seem to have spread into Asia and probably into parts of Europe. Fossil remains of these people have been recovered from numerous localities. At many other sites, stone tools and animal bones suggest the presence of *H. erectus*, even though traces of the toolmakers themselves are absent. This evidence has been accumulating since the end of the nineteenth century. Some particularly important discoveries have been made more recently, and we now know a great deal about where and when

H. erectus lived, what these people looked like, and how they adapted to the Pleistocene environment.

First Discoveries in Asia

The first fossils were brought to light by E. Dubois, a young Dutch physician who traveled to Indonesia to search for the missing link. His first specimen turned up in 1890, and in 1891 a skull cap was excavated from the bank of the Solo River at Trinil in central Java. Several years later, after a remarkably complete and modern-looking femur had also been recovered at Trinil, Dubois named the Java hominid *Pithecanthropus erectus*, or upright ape-man. Apart from a few limb fragments, no further discoveries were made at this time. More substantial traces of these archaic humans did not appear until the 1920s, when fossils were found far to the north, near Beijing (China). This site at Zhoukoudian proved to be very rich, and well-preserved parts of many individuals were dug out of different levels in the cave. It is most fortunate that this material was described without delay by the German anatomist F. Weidenreich, as nearly all of it was lost during World War II. Since the war, continuing work at Zhoukoudian has produced a few new fossils, along with stone tools, animal bones, and evidence of fire. Accumulations of ash and charcoal have been interpreted as hearths by the excavators, who suggest that the cave was occupied by Middle Pleistocene hunters and foragers seeking shelter.

Since 1936, other sites in Indonesia have yielded additional relics. In the Sangiran area of Java, early discoveries were made by the Dutch paleontologist G.H.R. von Koenigswald, who followed Dubois in referring most of his material to *Pithecanthropus*. Von Koenigswald's collecting activities were interrupted during World War II, but Sangiran has become the most important of the Javanese localities. Remains representing more than 40 human individuals have been found in these ancient lake and stream deposits. Several more fossils, mostly incomplete crania, have been collected at other sites in central and eastern Java. Most workers now refer these assemblages to *H. erectus*, and the name *Pithecanthropus* has been dropped.

Geographic Distribution

For more than 50 years following Dubois's initial discoveries, virtually all of the fossils attributable to *H. erectus* were found in eastern Asia. It was not until 1954 and 1955 that three lower jaws and a single parietal bone from Ternifine (Algeria) made it clear that the species had lived in northwestern Africa as well. The site at Ternifine (now Tighenif) consists of sands and clays stratified in a small Pleistocene lake. Stone artifacts occurring with the fossils include bifaces and cleavers, and this industry is best described as Acheulean. Evidence of *H. erectus* has come also from the Atlantic coast of Morocco. Fragmentary lower jaws and other specimens are known from Sidi Abderrahman, near Casablanca, and from the Thomas Quarries located nearby. The only more complete cranium from northwestern Africa was picked up near Salé in 1971. This Salé braincase is small, and it is possible that the rear of the skull has been deformed. Nevertheless, the specimen resembles *H. erectus* in a number of respects.

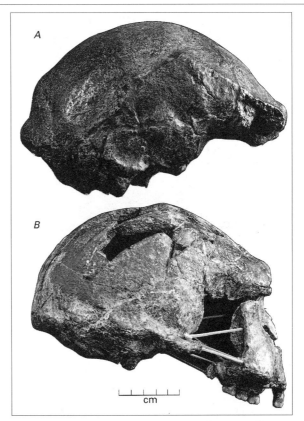

Two representatives of Homo erectus *from Java. The cranium of Ngandong 6 (A) is quite large but similar in its proportions to Sangiran 17 (B). It is probable that both individuals are male. Courtesy of Philip Rightmire.*

Many more fossils have been discovered in eastern Africa. Several of the most important and best-studied localities are Olduvai Gorge (Tanzania) and Koobi Fora and Nariokotome (northern Kenya). Olduvai has provided a great deal of information about the living habits, food preferences, and cultural activities of earlier hominids. *Australopithecus* and *H. habilis* are both documented in the lower levels of the gorge, while traces of *H. erectus* occur in Bed II, as well as in more recent deposits. A partial cranium (OH 9) of *H. erectus* was found in the upper part of Bed II by L.S.B. Leakey in 1960. More material, including several lower jaws, another broken braincase, and a hip bone together with part of the lower limb, shows that *H. erectus* lived at Olduvai for a substantial period of time. Stone tools associated with some of the fossil assemblages are of Acheulean manufacture.

Koobi Fora lies on the eastern shore of Lake Turkana. R. Leakey has directed fieldwork in this area since 1968. Vast quantities of animal bones have been collected, and a number of excavations carried out. As at Olduvai Gorge, it is clear that several forms of extinct human lived in the basin, and one of the species represented by the fossils is *H. erectus*. Some of the crania are well preserved and rival the best of the specimens from eastern Asia. A nearly complete skeleton has also been recovered. Unfortunately, the bones of this Koobi Fora individual are severely affected by disease, but a second skeleton, free of pathology, has been excavated at Nariokotome on the western side of Lake Turkana. Investigations of this adolescent boy from Nariokotome are yield-

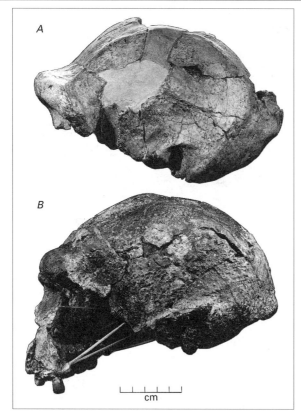

Hominid 9 from Olduvai Gorge (A), found in 1960, was one of the first discoveries to show that Homo erectus *lived in Africa as well as Asia. In size and overall appearance, it is close to Sangiran 17 from Java (B). Courtesy of Philip Rightmire.*

ing valuable details about the body size and proportions of earlier humans.

Hominids must also have been present in Europe at an early date. Signs of their occupation are preserved in caves and at open sites located in France, Italy, and Germany. Assemblages of chopping tools and faunal remains have been uncovered at the oldest localities, which are thought to be of Early Pleistocene age. The toolmakers probably resembled *H. erectus*, but establishing their identity has been difficult. Most of the ancient sites do not contain much human bone. In 1991, however, a mandible with teeth was found at Dmanisi (Georgia), and this jaw promises to shed new light on the first inhabitants of Europe and western Asia. The Dmanisi fossil shares numerous anatomical features with *H. erectus*.

Dating

Assemblages of *H. erectus* differ considerably in absolute age. The remains from the Turkana Basin are certainly among the oldest recovered so far. One of the most complete crania (KNM-ER 3733) from Koobi Fora was located in deposits ca. 1.8 Myr old, and the boy (KNM-WT 15000) from Nariokotome is dated to ca. 1.5 Ma. The Olduvai hominids are somewhat younger. The large braincase of OH 9 dates to ca. 1.4 Ma. Ages of another incomplete cranium and the hip and limb bones from Bed IV cannot be judged easily, as the rocks from this part of the Olduvai sequence cannot be dated radiometrically. Nearly all of these East African fossils are more ancient than any from Algeria or the Atlantic coast

of Morocco. The site at Tighenif may be of earliest Middle Pleistocene date, while the materials from Moroccan quarries are probably younger by several hundred thousand years. The latter may be close in age to the assemblage from Zhoukoudian. At Zhoukoudian, several methods have been used to gauge the antiquity of the many levels in the cave. Results suggest that the site was first occupied ca. 500 Ka and that *H. erectus* continued to make use of this shelter for perhaps 250 Kyr.

Dates for the Indonesian hominids are less certain. In some instances, the exact locations where fossils were found are no longer known, and these specimens may never be placed securely in a chronological framework. Other hominids, particularly those collected more recently at Sangiran, can be given provisional dates, subject to confirmation as more work is done. At Sangiran, *H. erectus* is present mainly in the Kabuh sediments. These levels were deposited during the Middle Pleistocene and probably during the Early Pleistocene as well. A few of the hominids may also have come from the uppermost Pucangan sediments, which underlie the Kabuh horizons. Such individuals may date to more than 1.0 Ma, and it is possible that they are nearly as ancient as *H. erectus* from East Africa. Nevertheless, it is likely that *H. erectus* appeared first in Africa and then spread into other regions of the Old World.

Anatomical Characters of *Homo erectus*

Many of the fossils from Southeast Asia and China are cranial bones, lower jaws, and teeth. A few limb bones have been recovered from the Javanese sites and from Zhoukoudian, but these fragments are not very informative. It is not surprising that descriptions of the species have emphasized the shape of the skull rather than the limbs. Discoveries in Africa are helping to fill out this picture. Postcranial parts and more skulls and teeth have turned up both at Olduvai Gorge and at the Turkana localities, and it is now possible to discuss the anatomy of *H. erectus* in some detail.

The cranium is distinctly different from that of other humans. It is low in profile and encloses a brain averaging a little less than 1,000 ml in volume. The side walls of the nose are thin and platelike, and there is a distinct nasal bridge. Construction of the nose may support the suggestion that *H. erectus* was adapting to life in a warm, arid climate. The browridges are prominent and thickened, even in smaller individuals that may be females. Just behind the face, the frontal bone is narrowed or constricted to an extent not seen in modern people. The forehead is flattened, but there may be a low ridge or keel of bone extending from the frontal onto the parietals in the midline. The parietal is relatively short. On its surface, the line marking the upper border of the temporal muscle curves downward toward the back, to produce a torus, or bulge, at the (mastoid) angle. Other crests in the mastoid region tend to be strongly developed. The skull is relatively broad at the base. The occipital bone, making up the rear of the braincase, is sharply curved. The division between its upper and lower parts is marked by a transverse torus, below which the neck muscles are attached. This area of muscle attachment is more extensive in *H. erectus* than in *H. sapiens*. Other features that distinguish *H.*

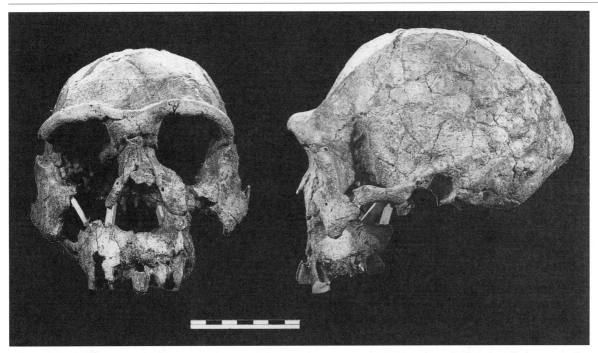

Facial and lateral views of KNM-ER 3733 from Koobi Fora. This very complete cranium is ca. 1.8 Myr in age. It displays essentially the same set of anatomical traits found in Asian Homo erectus *and is usually considered to be an early member of this taxon. However, some authorities place KNM-ER 3733 in* Homo ergaster *instead. Scale in cm. Photos by Philip Rightmire, courtesy of National Museum of Kenya.*

erectus are apparent on the underside of the cranium, particularly in the region of the joint for the lower jaw. The mandible itself is deep, very robust, and lacks any noticeable development of a chin eminence.

The part of the postcranial skeleton that has been most frequently preserved is the femur. Several of these thigh bones were recovered at Zhoukoudian and described by Weidenreich. More have been found in Africa, and it is now clear that the femoral neck is long, while the shaft is flattened from front to back and has a narrow (internal) medullary cavity. This robusticity is also seen in other parts of the skeleton, such as the adult pelvic bone found at Olduvai Gorge. Such a pattern may reflect a high level of biomechanical stress, and it suggests that *H. erectus* probably had a physically demanding lifestyle.

Limb bones also provide information about body size. One measure of size is stature, or height. A good estimate of stature cannot be obtained from the incomplete femora collected at Zhoukoudian, but dimensions of the skeleton from Nariokotome suggest that this individual was tall. Although he was not fully grown, the Nariokotome boy was ca. 160 cm in height. This individual, along with others from Olduvai and Koobi Fora, can be used to predict an average stature of 170 cm for early *H. erectus*, and this figure is close to that expected for modern adult males. Insofar as can be determined from the reconstructed pelvis of KNM-WT 15000, these hominids were also quite linear in body build. This finding, coupled with the form of the nose, indicates that African *H. erectus* may have inhabited open, arid environments.

Questions Concerning Taxonomy

It is generally assumed that the fossils found first in Asia and subsequently in Africa represent a single widespread species.

Since the mid-1980s, however, this view has been challenged. A key question concerns the material from the Turkana Basin, and it has been claimed that the early African crania lack certain special features that are present in the Asian populations. A midline keel on the vault, a parietal angular torus, characters of the cranial base, and overall thickening of the walls of the braincase are said to be absent at Koobi Fora but well expressed in the remains from Trinil, Sangiran, and Zhoukoudian. Facial and dental differences may also be apparent. These distinctions have prompted workers such as B.A. Wood to recognize two species. In their reading of the evidence, *H. erectus* as described originally by Dubois must be restricted to eastern Asia, while the Koobi Fora hominids are referred to a separate taxon called *Homo ergaster*. Into the late 1990s, the status of *H. ergaster* was uncertain. While there is variation among the various assemblages, a number of the fossils from Africa exhibit essentially the same set of traits as do those from Asia. The face of KNM-ER 3733 conforms in many respects to the anatomy of *H. erectus* as reconstructed from the Zhoukoudian specimens, and vault proportions are also like those of the Chinese and Indonesian crania. Few, if any, characters can be used to identify *H. ergaster*, and probably just one polytypic species was spread all across the Old World.

Role of *Homo erectus* in Human Evolution

Skulls identified as *H. erectus* are quite different from those of other humans. The low, heavily constructed braincase is not like that of earlier *Homo* or *Australopithecus*. The cranium and jaws can also be distinguished from those of *H. sapiens*. In other parts of the skeleton that have been studied closely, *H. erectus* again shows distinctive features. This complex of anatomical characters was well established in eastern

Africa at least 1.8 Ma. Populations of the species then seem to have flourished in Asia as well as Africa for well over 1.0 Myr. During at least part of this long span of time, *H. erectus* is the only form of human known to have inhabited the Old World. Therefore, it is likely that this species gave rise to more modern people sometime in the later Middle Pleistocene.

Just how this process took place is not clear. One line of reasoning holds that *H. erectus* changed gradually. Advocates of this view argue that the early African individuals have small brains coupled with relatively large jaws and teeth and thus appear more primitive than later finds. By contrast, the Middle Pleistocene skulls from Zhoukoudian exhibit some increase in brain volume and seem generally to be more appropriate ancestors for recent humans. Continuing evolution has carried not only the Zhoukoudian population but also other late *H. erectus* in the direction of *H. sapiens*. In this scenario, many archaic groups contributed to the genetic makeup of modern humans. Few if any bands of *H. erectus* became extinct, in the sense of leaving no descendants, and *H. sapiens* must have emerged in several different geographic areas.

If evolution proceeded in this fashion, then claims for regional continuity are plausible. Some anatomists and anthropologists, including Weidenreich, have suggested that there are discernible links between *H. erectus* assemblages and the humans who today occupy the same geographic areas. An example is provided by Zhoukoudian. Weidenreich and other scholars have argued that fossils from this cave exhibit morphological resemblances to living Chinese. These similarities are taken as evidence for biological continuity of populations extending from the Middle Pleistocene to the present. Comparable scenarios may be sketched for other regions. Some workers have claimed that *H. erectus* from Java is related, albeit distantly, to the recent indigenous populations of Australia. Fossils from Europe are said to fall into a progression beginning with archaic, *erectus*-like forms and ending with modern people, and the hominids from northwestern Africa have been interpreted in the same way.

The evidence for regional continuity, however, is often not convincing. In Asia, there are large gaps in the record. Few fossils seem actually to document the transition from *H. erectus* to *H. sapiens*. Even where the bones are more plentiful, their significance is questionable. It is difficult to identify anatomical characters that unequivocally link the Middle Pleistocene assemblages to later humans. Problems of this sort prompt some authorities to suggest a different evolutionary story. When all of the early and late *H. erectus* fossils are measured, there are, in fact, not many indications of steady change. It is true that brain size does increase in Asian populations like that at Zhoukoudian, but in other features the Middle Pleistocene specimens are not different from the Koobi Fora or Olduvai material. One can propose that little change took place during more than a million years. Perhaps *H. erectus* should be characterized as a stable species, within which trends are not readily apparent. If this is the case, then it is not surprising that evidence for regional continuity is hard to find. Populations within the species do, as expected, show a good deal of variation, but all are more similar to one

another than to later representatives of *H. sapiens*. Here we are left with little indication of the path actually followed when *H. erectus* evolved further. This transition to more modern people may have occurred relatively quickly, and it probably took place in a restricted geographic area. Confirming this hypothesis, or compiling solid evidence to support another view, is a major challenge to students of human evolution.

See also Acheulean; Fire; Homo; Homo ergaster; Nariokotome Site 3 (NK3); Olduvai Gorge; Pleistocene; Salé; Sangiran Dome; Sidi Abderrahman; Species; Thomas Quarries; Tighenif; Trinil; Turkana Basin; Weidenreich, Franz; Zhoukoudian. [G.P.R.]

Further Readings
Delson, E., ed. (1985) Ancestors: The Hard Evidence. New York: Liss.

Etler, D., and Li, T. (1994) New archaic human fossil discoveries in China and their bearing on hominid species definition during the Middle Pleistocene. In R.S. Corruccini and R.L. Ciochon (eds.): Integrative Paths to the Past: Paleoanthropological Advances in Honor of F. Clark Howell. Englewood Cliffs, N.J.: Prentice Hall, pp. 639–675.

Franzen, J.L., ed. (1994) 100 Years of *Pithecanthropus*. Frankfurt: Cour. Forsch. Inst. Senckenberg.

Rightmire, G.P. (1990) The Evolution of *Homo erectus*: Comparative Anatomical Studies of an Extinct Human Species. Cambridge: Cambridge University Press.

Walker, A., and Leakey, R., eds. (1993) The Nariokotome *Homo erectus* Skeleton. Cambridge, Mass.: Harvard University Press.

Wu, R., and Lin, S. (1983) Peking Man. Sci. Am. 248:86–94.

Homo ergaster

Extinct Pleistocene hominid from Africa. *Homo ergaster* is the earliest hominid species whose overall body size and shape and relative tooth size more closely resemble later *Homo* species than species belonging to either *Australopithecus* or *Paranthropus*.

Background

For much of the time since *Homo erectus* has been recognized as a hominid taxon (initially as *Pithecanthropus erectus*) it was widely accepted that it was an exclusively Asian species of archaic *Homo*. There was a broad consensus that the hypodigm of *H. erectus* consisted of two regional subsamples. The first comprised the remains recovered from exposures of the Kabuh and Pucangan Formations in and around the "Sangiran Dome" of Java, now Indonesia. The second comprised the *Sinanthropus pekinensis* remains recovered from the Locality 1 cave at Zhoukoudian and elsewhere in China. Subsequently, Weidenreich noted the similarities between the cranial remains of *Sinanthropus* and calvariae recovered from the Notopuro Beds at Ngandong in Indonesia, and these are now generally subsumed into the Asian hypodigm of *H. erectus*.

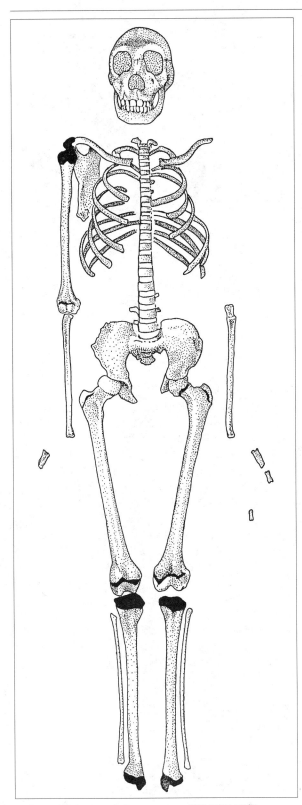

Skeleton of adolescent male Homo ergaster, *KNM WT-15000.*

was at least as old as, and probably older than, the oldest reliably dated remains from Indonesia (now thought to date 1.8–1.6 Ma).

Fossil Evidence

In the early 1970s, it became apparent that the remains of gracile hominids being recovered from what are now designated as the Okote and KBS Members of the Koobi Fora Formation at East Lake Turkana (Kenya) were drawn from more than one hominid species. Among this material was a well-preserved adult mandible, KNM-ER 992, which was discovered in 1971 and first reported in 1972. Initially, emphasis was placed on apparent similarities between KNM-ER 992 and *A. africanus*, but some observers were equally impressed by its resemblance to probable *H. erectus* mandibles from the Algerian site of Tighenif (formerly Ternifine) and from Olduvai. Further prospecting at East Lake Turkana—in 1975 and 1976, respectively—resulted in the discovery of two calvariae, KNM-ER 3733 and 3883. The latter was found in the same, Okote, Member as KNM-ER 992 (dating ca. 1.5 ma), but the former calvaria was recovered from the underlying KBS Member and is thus reliably dated at just less than 1.8 Ma.

The first description of KNM-ER 3733 stressed its similarity to *H. erectus*, but it became evident that, although KNM-ER 3733 and 3883 and *H. erectus* shared the same general cranial organization, when detailed comparisons were made the two East African calvariae were consistently less specialized, or derived, than *H. erectus*. In addition to the material already discussed, a further 14 specimens from East Lake Turkana are candidates for inclusion in the same species as KNM-ER 992 and 3733. One of these specimens, KNM-ER 730, is an associated skeleton; its importance was eclipsed in 1984, however, by the discovery at West Turkana of the associated skeleton KNM-WT 15000. This remarkably complete juvenile, probably male, skeleton provides copious information about the size and proportions of the skeleton as well as information about developmental history. Comparison of its cranial and mandibular anatomy with that of KNM-ER 992 and the two adult calvariae from East Lake Turkana (ER 3733 and 3883) leave little doubt that they all should be included within the same species. Remains attributed to *H. ergaster* span the time range between 1.9 and 1.5 Ma.

Taxonomy

The taxonomy of these early African *H. erectus* remains, as they are often called, was affected by a proposal made in 1975 by C.P. Groves and V. Mazák for a new hominid species, *Homo ergaster*. The mandible KNM-ER 992 was designated as the holotype, and the hypodigm included a fragmented skull and skeleton, KNM-ER 730; a juvenile mandible, KNM-ER 820; and an adult skull, KNM-ER 1805. Although subsequent research has thrown some doubt upon the wisdom of including the skull KNM-ER 1805 in the same species as KNM-ER 992, the species name *Homo ergaster* Groves and Mazák, 1975, is available if early *H. erectus*-like remains from East Africa are judged to merit specific distinction from *H. erectus*.

More recently researchers have suggested that there is evidence of *H. erectus* at sites in northern, eastern, and southern Africa. If these proposals are correct, then *H. erectus*, as represented by the Olduvai Gorge calvaria OH 9, was established in Africa by 1.1 Ma (now redated to 1.5 Ma), which, at the time, suggested that the African evidence for *H. erectus*

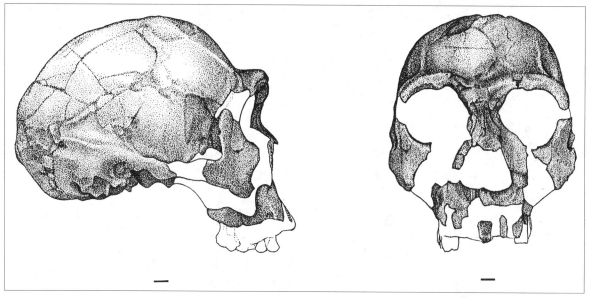

Side and front views of cranium KNM ER-3733, assigned to H. ergaster. *Scale is 1 cm.*

Morphological Characteristics and Relationships of *Homo ergaster*

Claims that *H. ergaster* can be distinguished from *H. erectus* rest on phenetic and cladistic evidence. The latter places relatively little stress on the possession of unique characters but does emphasize that *H. ergaster* possesses a unique combination of morphological features. The phenetic evidence suggests that both the shape and the size of the face and the morphology of the region around the temperomandibular joint differ when *H. ergaster* is compared with *H. erectus*. Likewise, the mandible and dentition of *H. ergaster* are generally more primitive than those of *H. erectus*. Whereas specimens attributed to the latter species rarely have an internally buttressed symphysis and mandibular premolars with a complex root system, mandibles attributed to *H. ergaster* usually, but not invariably, do. As suggested above, the distribution of cranial character states is not the same in *H. erectus* and *H. ergaster*. Members of the latter have a broader cranial vault, a shorter cranial base, a longer occipital, a wider nasal aperture, and a reduction in the width of the teeth.

Hypotheses about the relationships of *H. ergaster* have been generated using evidence from the cranium. These studies suggest that *H. ergaster* is less specialized, or derived, than *H. erectus* and that it is the sister group of *Homo sapiens*. This suggests that *H. ergaster* is a more plausible candidate for the ancestor of *H. sapiens* than *H. erectus* (*sensu stricto*). The epithet "early African" is usually used to preface *H. erectus* when this material is being referred to by those, probably in the majority, who do not accept *H. ergaster* as a separate species.

This was understandable and justifiable when the African material was generally believed to antedate the Asian hypodigm of *H. erectus* by at least 500 Kyr (see above). However, now that much earlier dates are being suggested for at least some of the *H. erectus* remains from Java, the African specimens may be approximately synchronic with *H. erectus* (*sensu stricto*). This would suggest that populations belonging to *H. ergaster* left Africa by at least 1.9–1.8 Ma and moved relatively quickly across the Old World.

See also Homo; Homo erectus. [B.A.W.]

Further Readings

Bräuer, G., and Mbua, E. (1992) *Homo erectus* features used in cladistics and their variability in Asian and African hominids. J. Hum. Evol. 22:79–108.

Groves, C.P., and Mazák, V. (1975) An approach to the taxonomy of the Hominidae: Gracile Villafranchian hominids of Africa. Cas. Pro. Min. Geol. 20:225–247.

Turner, A., and Chamberlain, A. (1989) Speciation, morphological change, and the status of African *Homo erectus*. J. Hum. Evol. 18:115–130.

Wood, B.A. (1984) The origin of *Homo erectus*. Cour. Forsch. Inst. Senckenberg. 69:99–111.

Wood, B.A. (1992) Early hominid species and speciation. J. Hum. Evol. 22:351–365.

Homo habilis

Extinct Late Pliocene species of hominid, presently included within the genus *Homo* and best known from sites in East Africa.

First Evidence

In 1964, L.S.B. Leakey, P.V. Tobias, and J.R. Napier proposed that a new species should be recognized and included within the genus *Homo*. They argued that several features of the hypodigm of the new taxon, *Homo habilis*, then known only from Olduvai Gorge (Tanzania), marked it out from the australopithecines. It was, however, significantly more primitive than *Homo erectus*, which hitherto had been the oldest and most primitive species of the genus *Homo*. Seven specimens, including the type, OH 7, were referred to *H. habilis* in the initial description; the authors made specific reference to a larger brain, narrower premolar and molar tooth crowns, and a modern humanlike foot skeleton as the main features that distinguished the Olduvai material from that attributed to *Australopithecus africanus*.

The proposal to recognize such a primitive new species of *Homo* did not go unchallenged. Some of their colleagues were unconvinced that the material was sufficiently distinct from *A. africanus* to merit the recognition of a new species, and others complained that the remains were indistinguishable from *H. erectus*. Subsequent discoveries at Olduvai, in particular the cranium OH 24 and the partial skeleton OH 62, have added crucially to our understanding of *H. habilis*, but the largest contribution to the hypodigm has come from Koobi Fora, now known as East Lake Turkana, in Kenya.

Koobi Fora Evidence:
The Case for Taxonomic Heterogeneity

During the 1970s, a steady stream of discoveries from Koobi Fora were either formally added to the hypodigm of *H. habilis* or implicitly added to it by being referred to as "early *Homo*." While many influential workers continued to support the integrity of that taxon, others were expressing doubts about the wisdom of assigning specimens that sampled such an apparently wide range of morphology to a single species. Some critics of the single-taxon solution suggested that the heteromorphy of *H. habilis* was due to the mixing of an earlier, more primitive, *Homo* species with remains belonging to a more recent, more advanced, *Homo* taxon. The discovery of OH 24 in the oldest levels of Bed I at Olduvai Gorge effectively refuted that scenario. Others suggested that the excessive morphological variation was due to the unwarranted amalgamation within *H. habilis* of two species, one "large brained" and the other "small brained." Crania such as KNM-ER 1470 and OH 7 were said to belong to the large-brained group, and KNM-ER 1805 and 1813 were linked with OH 24 in the small-brained taxon. Such has been the debate about the taxonomy of these remains that some specimens have been the subject of a remarkably wide range of interpretations. The skull OH 13 from Olduvai, for example, has been linked with taxa as widely different as *H. erectus* and *A. africanus*.

Although the hypodigm of *H. habilis* continues to be dominated by the evidence from Olduvai and Koobi Fora, material recovered from other sites has been likened to, or implicitly or explicitly assigned to, *H. habilis*. In East Africa, remains from Members G and H of the Shungura Formation in the Omo Valley have been attributed to *H. habilis*, but the suggestion that a cranial fragment from another site in the Omo region, at West Turkana, should be added to the hypodigm has been withdrawn. Two important specimens from southern African sites, the composite cranium SK 847 from the Lower Bank deposit of Member I at Swartkrans and Stw 53 from Member 5 at Sterkfontein, have both been linked with *H. habilis*.

Alternative Definitions of *Homo habilis*

Current interpretations of the material attributed to early *Homo*, or *H. habilis*, are polarized into two groups: those that accept a *single-taxon* solution and those that propose that the material should be subdivided into two species groups. Two schemes for subdividing the material have been proposed. One uses the criterion of size and stresses brain size in particu-

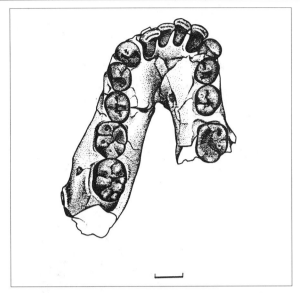

This mandible of hominid 7 from Olduvai Gorge was designated the holotype of Homo habilis *in 1964. Although the jaw itself is thick, the premolar and molar teeth are a little smaller than expected for* Australopithecus. *Two parietal bones found with the mandible suggest that OH 7 has a brain close to 700 ml. in volume. Scale is 1 cm.*

lar. In this version of the *two-species* solution, remains from Koobi Fora such as the relatively large-brained crania KNM-ER 1470, 1590, and 3732 and the mandible KNM-ER 1802 are linked with the Olduvai type specimen of *H. habilis*, OH 7. This hypodigm thus takes the species name *H. habilis* (*sensu stricto*). The same scheme recognizes a second, as yet unnamed, species group that includes the skull KNM-ER 1805 and cranium KNM-ER 1813 from Koobi Fora and the skull OH 13 and the cranium OH 24 from Olduvai. This scheme concentrates on the more complete specimens and effectively assembles species around the better-preserved specimens.

The second taxonomic scheme uses a different method to assess whether more than one taxon is justified. Workers using this scheme began by reviewing the nature and the degree of the variation among the fossils referred to early *Homo* from the Omo region (i.e., Koobi Fora and the Shungura Formation) and Olduvai against the background of information about intraspecific variation within species groups belonging to *Homo* and *Pan*. The results of this analysis suggested that, whereas the Olduvai part of the hypodigm of early *Homo* did not show excessive variation, the material from Koobi Fora and the Shungura Formation did. Because the Olduvai part of the hypodigm includes the type specimen, in this second scheme all of the Olduvai evidence has to be assigned to *H. habilis* (*sensu stricto*). Examination of the part of the early *Homo* hypodigm that comes from the Omo region, and mainly from Koobi Fora, suggests that it can be subdivided, using relatively consistent criteria, into two subsets. One, which includes specimens such as KNM-ER 1805 and 1813, resembles the Olduvai remains and is thus assigned to *H. habilis* (*sensu stricto*). The second, which includes the crania KNM-ER 1470 and 3732 and the mandible KNM-ER 1802, is referred to a separate species group, which takes the name *Homo rudolfensis*.

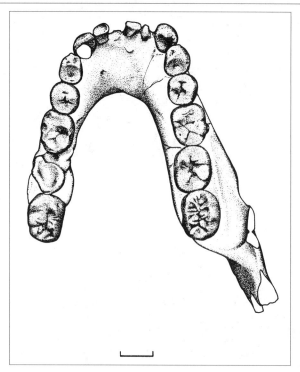

Homo habilis mandible OH 13 from Olduvai Gorge, Tanzania. Scale is 1 cm.

It is this second variant of the two-species scheme for early *Homo*, the one that recognizes the taxonomic homogeneity of the *H. habilis* remains from Olduvai, that is used as the basis for the description of the morphological characteristics of *H. habilis* (*sensu stricto*), henceforth referred to as *H. habilis*, that follows. Recently, W. Ferguson has made ER 1813 the holotype of *Homo microcranous*, a name that is unlikely to see further use—unless it is determined that ER 1470 and OH 7 are conspecific, an alternative that has been suggested by some researchers.

Morphological characteristics of *Homo habilis*
The cranium of *H. habilis* is larger and differently proportioned than that of *A. africanus*. The mean endocranial volume of *H. habilis* is 610 ml (range 510–687 ml) compared to a mean value of ca. 450 ml for *A. africanus*. The adult bones of

H. habilis are thin, like those of *A. africanus*, but unlike that taxon the suture pattern in *H. habilis* is complex with a tendency to form extra ossicles. The small but distinct frontal torus of *H. habilis* contrasts with the more flattened frontal morphology of *A. africanus*, and the shape of the parietal bones of *H. habilis*, with the coronal dimension exceeding the sagittal one, contrasts with the proportions of the parietal in *A. africanus*. A distinguishing feature of the facial skeleton of *H. habilis* compared with the australopith is the relative narrowness of the midface, combined with reduced subnasal prognathism and relatively short palate. The cranial base of *H. habilis* can be distinguished from that of *A. africanus* by the more coronal orientation of the temporal and a more anteriorly situated and, in undistorted specimens, more anteriorly inclined foramen magnum. The distinguishing features of the dentition are more marked in the mandibular than in the maxillary teeth. The crowns of *H. habilis* are generally narrower, with relatively smaller and less complex talonids and a generally simpler root structure, than their australopithecine counterparts.

What little is known of the postcranial skeleton of *H. habilis* suggests that it was little modified compared to that of australopiths such as *A. afarensis* and *A. africanus*. Information about limb proportions that can be obtained from OH 62 points to little sign of departure from the primitive ape condition of a relatively long forelimb and a relatively short hindlimb. The femora apparently retain the small heads and relatively long and narrow necks of the femora attributed to *A. africanus*. There are signs that the foot skeleton, in particular the midtarsal joints, may have been less flexible than in *A. africanus*, but the foot lacked the mechanisms that confer the rigidity during toe-off that is seen in early African *H. erectus* or *Homo ergaster* and in later species of *Homo*. Information about the hand of *H. habilis* suggests that, while it could have wielded stone artifacts, it shows little evidence of the dexterity that is so well developed in later *Homo* species.

Dating and Evolutionary Relationships of *Homo habilis*
The type and paratypes of *H. habilis* are among the most reliably dated components of the hypodigm, and they range in age from just over 1.8 to 1.6 Ma. Specimens attributed to *H. habilis* from Koobi Fora extend the age range of *H. habilis*

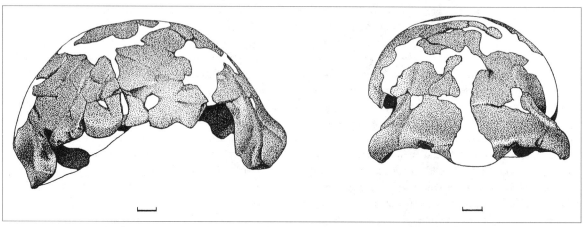

Fragmentary calotte of Homo habilis, *OH 16 from Olduvai Gorge, Tanzania. Scale is 1 cm.*

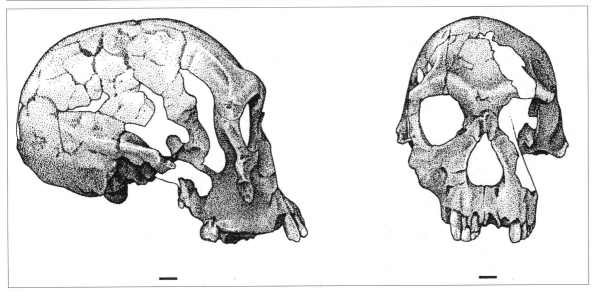

Female? cranium KNM ER-1813 from Koobi Fora, Kenya, often assigned to Homo habilis. *Scale is 1 cm.*

back to 1.9 Ma, but there is no unambiguous evidence for the species prior to 1.9 Ma or later than 1.6 Ma.

Whereas the first descriptions of *H. habilis* emphasized its "humanness" and stressed its distinctiveness with respect to *A. africanus*, more recent assessments acknowledge that, with respect to a grade classification, *H. habilis* shows much, if not more, in common with the australopith than with later *Homo*. This is reflected in functional measures such as relative tooth size and, to a lesser extent, encephalization. While it is true that the premolar and molar teeth of *H. habilis* are absolutely smaller than those of *A. africanus*, when the tooth crown areas of these teeth are corrected for body size, because of its small body mass of ca. 30 kg, *H. habilis* is no more or less megadont than *A. africanus*. When absolute brain size is related to body mass, *H. habilis* is more encephalized than *A. africanus*, but not to a degree that suggests a major grade shift in encephalization between *A. africanus* and *H. habilis*. However, there are sufficient derived features of the cranium, jaws, and teeth for *H. habilis* to be regarded as the sister taxon of all later, or temporally synchronic, species of *Homo*. The fact that the temporal range of *H. habilis* overlaps with that of early African *H. erectus* and *H. ergaster* does not exclude *H. habilis* from being ancestral to the latter two, but it certainly does not strengthen the case for *H. habilis* being ancestral to all other *Homo* species.

See also Australopithecus; Homo; Homo erectus; Homo ergaster; Homo rudolfensis; Leakey, Louis Seymour Bazett; Oldowan; Olduvai Gorge; Species; Turkana Basin. [B.A.W.]

Further Readings

Johanson, D.C., Masao, F.T., Eck, G.G., White, T.D., Walter, R.C., Kimbel, W.H., Asfaw, B., Manega, P., Ndessokia, P., and Suwa, G. (1987) New partial skeleton of *Homo habilis* from Olduvai Gorge, Tanzania. Nature 327:205–209.

Leakey, L.S.B., Tobias, P.V., and Napier, J.R. (1964) A new species of the genus *Homo* from Olduvai Gorge. Nature 4927:7–9.

Marzke, M.W., and Shackley, M.S. (1986) Hominid hand use in the Pliocene and Pleistocene: Evidence from experimental archaeology and comparative morphology. J. Hum. Evol. 15:439–460.

Rightmire, G.P. (1993) Variation among early *Homo* crania from Olduvai Gorge and the Koobi Fora region. Am. J. Phys. Anthropol. 90:1–33.

Wood, B. (1992) Origin and evolution of the genus *Homo*. Nature 355:783–790.

Wood B., and Collard, M. (1999) The human genus. Science 284:65–71.

Homo heidelbergensis

Species name created in 1908 by O. Schoetensack to receive the Mauer (Germany) jaw. In recent years this species name has increasingly been employed to accommodate a distinctive group of Middle Pleistocene human fossils from sites in Europe, Africa, and possibly Asia as well. These fossils include most of the earlier fossils (excluding Neanderthals and

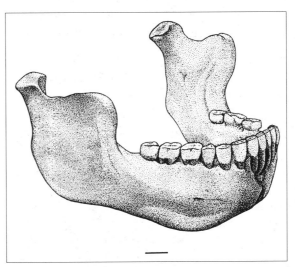

The Mauer mandible, type specimen of Homo heidelbergensis. *Scale is 1 cm.*

their relatives) that are otherwise dismissed as archaic variants of *Homo sapiens*. They include, in addition to the Mauer specimen, those from Arago (France), Petralona (Greece), Kabwe (Zambia), Bodo (Ethiopia), and possibly Dali (China). The species *Homo heidelbergensis* is potentially ancestral to all later hominids, including *Homo neanderthalensis*, on the one hand and *Homo sapiens*, on the other, although the vast cranial sinuses in at least some specimens may throw doubt on this.

See also Arago; Archaic Homo sapiens; Bodo; Homo; Homo sapiens; Kabwe; Petralona. [I.T.]

Homo neanderthalensis

Species named in 1864 by W. King to receive the original Neanderthal fossil from the Feldhofer Grotto (Germany). Since the mid-twentieth century, the Neanderthals, a distinctive group now known at many European and western Asian sites dating from the latest Middle Pleistocene to ca. 30 Ka, have been considered by most paleoanthropologists to represent a mere subspecific variant of *Homo sapiens*. However, as the magnitude of the Neanderthals' morphological difference from ourselves has come to be better appreciated, there has been an accelerating tendency to grant these extinct humans separate specific status, as *Homo neanderthalensis*.

See also Archaic Homo sapiens; Homo; Homo sapiens; Neanderthals. [I.T.]

Homo rudolfensis

Extinct Late Pliocene hominid species, presently included within the genus *Homo*, known from sites in East Africa and Malawi.

Taxonomic context

The species *Homo rudolfensis* is not recognized by all paleoanthropologists. Those who consider that "early *Homo*" shows no more variation than is to be expected within a single species are content to subsume all of this material into *Homo habilis* and see no need for an additional "early *Homo*" species. However, this "single-species" resolution of "early *Homo*" is being rejected by an increasing number of paleoanthropologists. They judge the variation within "early *Homo*" to be such that it is better reflected by a taxonomy that recognizes more than one species. For many years this second species was referred to as *Homo* sp. nov., but in 1986 the Russian anthropologist A. Alexeev gave it the species name *Pithecanthropus rudolfensis*. *Homo rudolfensis* (Alexeev, 1986) is increasingly being adopted as the formal designation for material that is included within "early *Homo*," but which can be distinguished from *H. habilis sensu stricto*. As yet, the diagnosis of *H. rudolfensis* rests on the cranial evidence, for there are no specimens of *H. rudolfensis* that preserve both the cranium and the postcranial skeleton. Suggestions that the Koobi Fora (Kenya) femora KNM-ER 1472 and 1481 should be assigned to *H. rudolfensis* are based on circumstantial evidence alone; until an associated skeleton of *H.*

rudolfensis is discovered, information about its postcranial anatomy must be regarded as conjectural.

Fossil Evidence

There is a natural tendency to regard well-preserved specimens as typical of the morphology of a species. Such fossils tend to provide the focus for species identification and species hypodigms become, in effect, clusters of specimens all of which depend for their taxonomic identity on sharing morphology with the focal specimen. As soon as it was discovered in 1972, it was perhaps inevitable that the cranium KNM-ER 1470 became pivotal for the debate about whether *H. habilis* (*sensu lato*) should be subdivided into more than one species. Thereafter, specimens were screened for their affinity with KNM-ER 1470, and two cranial specimens from what was then Koobi Fora (now called East Lake Turkana) were likened to it. One, KNM-ER 1590, included a substantial part of the cranial vault (calvaria) that resembled that of KNM-ER 1470 in size and morphology and provided the first direct evidence about the dentition of *H. rudolfensis*. The second specimen, the calvaria KNM-ER 3732, lacked any dental evidence, but it did preserve sufficient parts of the upper face to confirm that it shared features with KNM-ER 1470, such as the broad midface and the forwardly sloping malar region.

The case for recognizing more than one species among the early *Homo* remains from East Africa was strengthened by the results of a study of the degree and pattern of cranial, including mandibular and dental, variation within that material. The results suggested that, while "early *Homo*" material from Olduvai Gorge (Tanzania) did not show evidence of variability in excess of that expected within a single taxon, the part of the "early *Homo*" hypodigm from the Omo region, including that from East Lake Turkana, did show such evidence. This reinforced the claims of those who were emphasizing the apparently different organization of the face and palate, and, to a lesser extent, the cranial vault, between KNM-ER 1470-like crania and those attributed to *H. habilis sensu stricto*.

With such a taxonomic dichotomy in mind, it was possible to review less complete cranial specimens, as well as mandibles and teeth, from East Lake Turkana to see if they provided further evidence for a second early *Homo* taxon. The fragmented cranium, KNM-ER 3891, which includes a weathered palate and temporal fragment, shows evidence of a substantial and forwardly situated malar process and a stout zygomatic process, both of which are characteristic of *H. rudolfensis*. In the absence of a skull of *H. rudolfensis*, in which a mandible could be certainly associated with a cranium or calvaria, the likely morphology of the mandible and the mandibular dentition had to be inferred by extrapolating to the mandible the emphasis on heavy mastication that is suggested by the facial skeleton of *H. rudolfensis*. A particularly well-preserved mandible, KNM-ER 1802, which was found in 1973, a year after KNM-ER 1470, apparently provided such evidence. It lacked the detailed diagnostic feature of *Paranthropus boisei* yet shared with it an overall morphology that suggested a greater emphasis on chewing than is seen in the more gracile *H. habilis sensu stricto* mandibles from

Olduvai. The relatively large cross-sectional area of the corpus, the degree of talonid formation on the premolar and molar crowns, the complexity of the premolar root system, and the relative thickness and construction of the enamel of the postcanine teeth all pointed to an extension, both forward and backward, of that part of the tooth row that was functionally adapted to chewing. Other mandibular remains from East Lake Turkana, such as KNM-ER 819, 1482, 1483, and 1801, shared sufficient features in common with KNM-ER 1802 to be added, with varying degrees of confidence, to the *H. rudolfensis* hypodigm. More recently, an adult mandible found at Uraha (Malawi), estimated to date between 2.4 and 2.1 Ma, has been added to the hypodigm on the basis of its strong resemblance, in many points of detail, to KNM-ER 1802. In late 1996, a maxilla was described from the upper levels at Hadar (Ethiopia; dated ca. 2.3 Ma) that also may relate to this taxon. Some authors also include a temporal bone from the Chemeron Beds (Baringo Basin, Kenya) of similar age. The earliest evidence for *H. rudolfensis* therefore dates to ca. 2.5–2.3 Ma, and the most recent remains to be attributed to it are dated to 1.9 Ma, with just one possible member of the hypodigm, KNM-ER 819, dated to 1.6 Ma.

Morphological Characteristics and Relationships of *Homo rudolfensis*

The cranium of *H. rudolfensis* combines a large braincase—with a mean cranial capacity of 750 ml that substantially exceeds the upper limit of the range of *H. habilis* endocranial volume—a flat, wide, face and large tooth crowns. The midface is particularly wide, and the malar region is not vertical, or backwardly sloping, as it is in *H. habilis* but slopes forward. The robusticity of the mandible and the molarization of the premolars have already been commented upon; additional evidence for the accentuation of the chewing function is provided by the molar size order, which suggests that the M_3s are the largest molar tooth crowns.

The morphological characteristics of *H. rudolfensis* are such that, while in some aspects it resembles *H. habilis sensu stricto* and later *Homo* species, in others it resembles the "robust" australopith species included in the genus *Paranthropus*. Within that genus, the closest resemblances are with *Paranthropus robustus*, which is a species recognized only in southern Africa. It is the masticatory system, notably the face and dentition, that shows the closest links with *Paranthropus*. These similarities are the reason that some cladistic studies have concluded that it is only marginally more parsimonious to link *H. rudolfensis* with the genus *Homo* than with *Paranthropus*. Most hominid taxonomists are inclined to continue to accept a taxonomic solution that assumes that most of the phenetic resemblances between *H. rudolfensis* and *Paranthropus* are homoplasies. Only closer scrutiny of the details of these shared features will enable researchers to be clearer about whether the homoplasy hypothesis can be sustained. The alternative, that *H. habilis* (*sensu stricto*) and *H. rudolfensis* belong to different clades, would mean that they independently acquired the cranial features that have prompted their inclusion in *Homo*.

Despite its inclusion within the genus *Homo*, *H. rudolfensis* is scarcely less megadont than species of *Australopithecus*, and its relative brain size marginally exceeds that of the australopith. In the absence of firm evidence that *H. rudolfensis* is an obligatory biped, there is little evidence to support the claim of a major grade shift between *Australopithecus* and *Paranthropus* on the one hand, and *Homo* on the other. There is little doubt that the hypodigm of *H. rudolfensis* deserves recognition as a separate species, but its location within the genus *Homo* is still open to debate.

See also Africa; Africa, East; Australopithecus; Baringo Basin/ Tugen Hills; Brain; Hadar; Homo; Homo habilis; Paranthropus; Turkana Basin; Uraha. [B.A.W.]

Further Readings

Schrenk, F., Bromage, T.G., Betzler, C.G., Ring, U., and Juwayeyi, Y.M. (1993) Oldest *Homo* and Pliocene biogeography of the Malawi Rift. Nature 365:833–836.

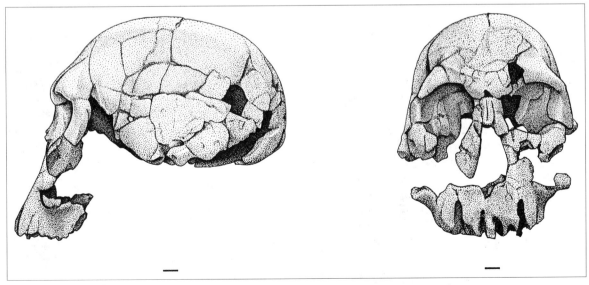

Lateral and facial views of KNM-ER 1470, holotype cranium of Homo rudolfensis *from Koobi Fora, Kenya. Scale is 1 cm.*

Wood, B.A. (1992) Origin and evolution of the genus *Homo*. Nature 355:783–790.

Wood, B.A. (1993) Early *Homo*: How many species? In W.H. Kimbel and L.B. Martin (eds.): Species, Species Concepts, and Primate Evolution. New York: Plenum, pp. 485–522.

Wood, B., and Collard, M. (1999) The human genus. Science 284:65–71.

Homo sapiens

Species to which modern humans belong. In the nineteenth century and the earlier years of the twentieth, it was common for workers who studied newly discovered fossil hominids to erect new species or even genus names for virtually every new find, even where the specimen was clearly closely related to previous finds. Thus, some years after the Neanderthal skeleton was discovered in 1856, it was made the type of a new species of the genus *Homo* called *Homo neanderthalensis*, and this practice was repeated by some workers for various other Neanderthal finds, such as those from Spy ("*Homo spyensis*"), Le Moustier ("*Homo transprimigenius mousteriensis*"), and La Chapelle-aux-Saints ("*Homo chapellensis*"). Similarly, the Broken Hill cranium was assigned to "*Homo rhodesiensis*" and later to "*Cyphanthropus rhodesiensis*," the Skhūl remains to "*Palaeanthropus palestinus*," and the Steinheim skull to "*Homo steinheimensis*."

During the period 1943–1964, however, a number of influential papers reexamined the basic concepts of hominid classification from the perspectives of more general paleontology and the developing field of population genetics. It was argued that, as living *Homo sapiens* represented a single polytypic species, so did fossil humans at any one time level in the past. Particularly important to these discussions was the status of the Zhoukoudian (China) remains (then commonly attributed to *Sinanthropus pekinensis*), and the Mount Carmel (Israel: Skhūl and Tabūn) remains (then commonly attributed to a single nonmodern population). The German anatomist F. Weidenreich, who described the Zhoukoudian fossils, actually regarded them as representing only a distinct race of early humans, despite his persistent use of a separate generic name for the material. This led several workers to suggest that the Zhoukoudian remains, in fact, represented merely a subspecies of an early human species, *Homo erectus*. T. McCown and A. Keith's interpretation of the Mount Carmel fossils as representing a highly variable single population led them to suggest that the taxonomic boundary between Neanderthals and modern *H. sapiens* had been broken down. The Mount Carmel "population" could be interpreted as a group close to the common ancestry of Neanderthals and modern humans, or a group in the process of evolving from a Neanderthal to a modern morphology, or even a hybrid population between two (closely related) forms.

Thus, reassessments of the fossil material suggested that no more than a single hominid species had existed at any one time in the Pleistocene and that *H. erectus* (including such geographical variants as "Java Man" and "Peking Man") and *H. sapiens* (including such variants as Neanderthals and modern humans) were polytypic species. This viewpoint was formalized by B. Campbell in the 1960s, when he proposed that *H. sapiens* Linnaeus 1758 should be subdivided into the following living or fossil subspecies: *sapiens* (modern humans), *neanderthalensis*, *steinheimensis*, *rhodesiensis*, and *soloensis* (for the Ngandong remains). This scheme was widely adopted after 1964, and a number of previous and new fossil discoveries have been incorporated into it under one or other subspecific categories. Subsequently, it has become common to differentiate the anatomically modern form of *H. sapiens* (*Homo sapiens sapiens*) from the other forms of the species by the additional epithets *modern* or *archaic Homo sapiens*. Thus, "archaic *Homo sapiens*" includes Middle or Late Pleistocene hominids that are distinct from, but supposedly closely related to, modern humans.

Modern *Homo sapiens*

Anatomically modern *H. sapiens* can be characterized by a number of anatomical features found in all living human populations. Many of these features are related to an overall gracility of the skeleton compared with archaic humans. Although living *H. sapiens* around the world display a remarkable variation in stature, physique, and weight (much of which can be attributed to environmental adaptations and nutritional factors), most modern humans are quite large bodied but have slenderly constructed bones and a less heavy musculature than was the case among archaic humans. This may well be an indication of the extent to which sophisticated behaviors found in all living humans have taken the selective weight off the skeleton (almost literally) through an emphasis on economy of effort rather than high activity and muscle power as the basic behavioral adaptation of the species.

Compared with archaic humans, modern *H. sapiens* have large brains (also found in Neanderthals), with an average volume exceeding 1,300 ml (but varying somewhat according to sex and body size). To house this large brain, there is a highly distinctive and derived cranial shape in modern humans. The vault is relatively short (front to back) and high, with a domed forehead and well-arched (rather than flattened) parietal. The base of the skull is narrow, as is the occipital bone. The occipital itself is rounded in profile, lacking the transverse torus and heavy neck musculature of many archaic forms, as well as the distinctive torus shape and suprainiac fossa found in Neanderthals. As in late Neanderthals, the skull walls of modern humans are relatively thin, and this lack of robusticity is also reflected in the small or nonexistent browridge and the gracile face and jaws with small teeth. The mandible itself is not thickened and has a bony chin on its outside, even in young individuals. The degree of flatness of the face and the shape of the nose vary in different populations, but in none of them is there the voluminous and projecting nasal region found in Neanderthals.

The whole skeleton of modern *H. sapiens* is slenderly built with thin-walls to the limb bones and only moderate muscularity. The scapula (shoulder blade) has less muscle attachment on the back edge; the pelvis is not robustly constructed, and it lacks the extended pubic ramus found in Neanderthals. There are also distinctive features of growth and development in modern humans compared with our closest

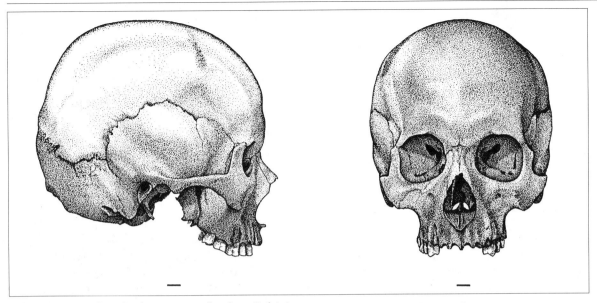

Side and front views of a modern human cranium from Egypt. Scale is 1 cm.

primate relatives, since humans have a long period of childhood growth and dependency, mature later, and complete growth much later than the apes. In addition, the life span of humans is such that there is often a long period of postreproductive survival, which is undocumented in the apes. The slow development of humans and the presence of postreproductive survival into old age may both be linked to the importance of intergenerational transmission of cultural information. Thus, old individuals may be provisioned, since they have a wealth of experience useful to younger, less expe-

rienced individuals. Similarly, the slow development of children allows them ample time to develop linguistic skills, which are of use in absorbing the complexities of the culture into which they have been born. Although this developmental pattern is found in all living human populations, there is little evidence (but much speculation) about when this distinctive pattern emerged.

Traditionally, it was believed that the human pattern of slow development was present in early hominids, such as the australopiths, *Homo habilis*, and *H. erectus*. However, new

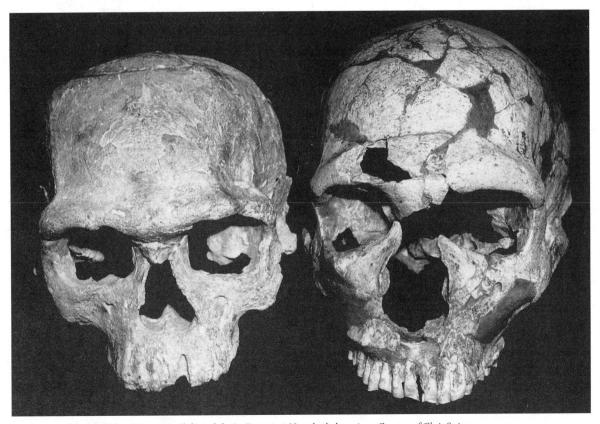

Comparison of the Jebel Irhoud 1 cranium (left) and the La Ferrassie 1 Neanderthal cranium. Courtesy of Chris Stringer.

techniques of determining more accurately the age at death of fossil remains of young individuals have suggested that the modern human growth pattern was not present in these early hominids. If this is so, the modern *H. sapiens* pattern may have originated quite recently, and its presence or absence in the Neanderthals is a topic of both speculation and research.

Origin of Modern *Homo sapiens*

Two extreme models have been proposed to account for the origin of modern people, with some workers adopting various intermediate positions. One extreme view (multiregional evolution) postulates that modern humans evolved locally in different parts of the world from already distinct archaic ancestors. This model of local continuity is sometimes termed the *Neanderthal-phase model,* since it envisages hominids of comparable evolutionary grade to the European Neanderthals giving rise to local descendant modern populations by parallel or polyphyletic evolution. Thus, in Europe, a direct unilinear evolutionary sequence might exist between the oldest European populations, represented by the Mauer (Germany) mandible, and modern Europeans via such intermediates as the Neanderthals and Cro-Magnons. Similarly, in China, the Lantian and Zhoukoudian *H. erectus* specimens could represent ancient ancestors for modern Asian peoples via such intermediates as the Maba, Jinniu shan, and Dali material. And in Indonesia, Javanese *H. erectus* fossils could represent populations that eventually gave rise to modern Australasian peoples via such intermediates as the Ngandong (Solo) and Kow Swamp fossils. In the *center-and-edge model,* the great variation found in recent and Pleistocene Australians is explained as a result of local evolution (from Indonesian *H. erectus*) combined with migration or gene flow from the Asian mainland (e.g., as represented by the Mungo fossils).

In the model of multiregional evolution, "racial" variation is very ancient, with "local" features traceable between ancient and modern populations over periods longer than 0.5 Myr. Variants of this model allow for significant gene flow to have occurred between the local lineages, so that speciation did not occur and so that the spread of the fundamentally similar anatomy of all modern peoples can be explained. In fact, some proponents of multiregional evolution have proposed that the taxon name *H. sapiens* should be extended to the whole human clade after the cladogenetic split from *H. habilis* (thus sinking *Homo ergaster* and *H. erectus,* as well as all later hominids, into *H. sapiens*).

In contrast to the local-continuity model, the *single-origin,* or *Noah's Ark, model* proposes that all modern humans derived from a single fairly recent common ancestral population. From this model, it follows that population movement or expansion, rather than local evolution, was the primary determinant of the spread of modern human characteristics during the last 50 Ka. As such, local racial features evolved *after* the anatomical features that are shared by all living *H. sapiens,* whereas, in the local continuity model, racial or local features were much more ancient. The geographical location of such a source population for all living humans is still uncertain, but most proponents of single-origin models favor Africa as the critical area, with a minority case also presented

for Southwest or Southeast Asia. The evidence for the earliest occurrence of anatomically modern fossils in these areas is discussed elsewhere (see ARCHAIC MODERNS), but there is support for the model that is independent of the fossil evidence from considerations of modern human skeletal variation and recently published genetic analyses. Different human populations show a fundamental similarity in anatomy, and it is difficult to believe that such a large number of characters in common could have evolved independently under very different environmental or cultural conditions in various parts of the world. Those features that distinguish modern humans from one another are relatively minor and could easily have been superimposed on a fundamentally modern anatomy inherited from a recent common ancestor. The genetic data that support a recent African origin for all modern *H. sapiens* come from many different kinds of analyses.

The most probable scenario has an African origin for modern morphological and genetic variation, probably during the African Middle Stone Age (MSA), which lasted from ca. 150 to 40 Ka. Ancestral populations probably resembled such specimens as Eliye Springs (Kenya) or Omo Kibish 2 (Ethiopia), while fossils approaching the modern condition in more respects occur at Guomde (Kenya), Ngaloba (Tanzania), Florisbad (South Africa), and Jebel Irhoud (Morocco). Specimens within the modern anatomical range can be recognized from such African sites as Klasies River Mouth, Border Cave, and Omo Kibish 1, all of which are likely to be older than 50 Ka, with actual or claimed MSA associations. The extent to which modern behavioral patterns were already present in MSA populations is still unclear, with some workers suggesting that there was a precocious appearance of "Upper Paleolithic" aspects in some MSA industries, while others argue that such changes do not occur until the end of the MSA. So it is also still uncertain whether there was a linkage or a decoupling between the morphological and behavioral changes that heralded the advent of modern *H. sapiens* in Africa.

Following an early Late Pleistocene establishment of modern features in Africa (and perhaps also Southwest Asia), the modern anatomical pattern probably first radiated by population expansion, migration, or gene flow from North Africa, through Southwest Asia, to eastern Asia and Australia. Modern humans may also have been present in Ukraine (Starosel'e) and eastern Europe (Krapina A and Bacho Kiro?) by 40 Ka and were probably widespread in Europe by 35 Ka, judging by the appearance of Aurignacian industries as far west as Spain and France by that time.

In all cases in which a hominid association with the Aurignacian is unequivocal, that hominid is always anatomically modern *H. sapiens,* and the European populations of these early-modern people are collectively known as *Cro-Magnons.* The term was formerly considered to be virtually synonymous with the term *Upper Paleolithic humans,* covering the period from ca. 35 to 10 Ka in Europe, but the discovery of a genuine Neanderthal associated with the early Upper Paleolithic Chatelperronian industry at Saint-Césaire (France) necessitates a revision of this usage. The term *Cro-Magnon* has come to cover a wide range of fossil material associated with different "cultures," such as the Aurignacian,

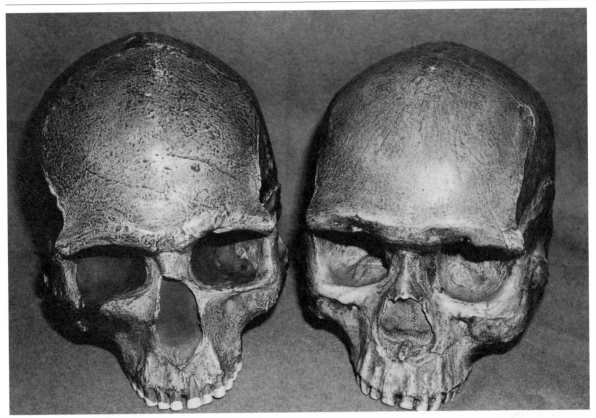

Two early modern human crania, each dated ca. 25 Ka: Předmostí 3 (left) from the Czech Republic, and Zhoukoudian Upper Cave 101 from China. Courtesy of Chris Stringer.

the Gravettian, the Solutrean, and the Magdalenian, and the extent to which it is legitimate to group this range of material is debatable.

While no one doubts that the Cro-Magnons do represent anatomically modern humans, they were undoubtedly distinct in a number of respects from modern Europeans. In some of these aspects, it is possible to see retained primitive characters, such as relatively large teeth and brows, but attempts to recognize these aspects as specifically retained from ancestral Neanderthals are generally unconvincing, and, in some respects, it is the Neanderthals who seem more derived in their characters. For example, the body proportions of the early Cro-Magnons were quite distinct from those of Neanderthals, since the lower portions of their arms and legs were elongated compared with the upper parts, whereas in the Neanderthals the lower portions were relatively shortened. In modern humans, this elongation is a pattern characteristic of warm-adapted populations, and this physique may be an early Cro-Magnon retention from African ancestors. Similar retentions may be observed in certain indices of facial shape (such as in possessing a shorter, flatter, and relatively broader face, with low orbits and short nose), and these features were present in Middle and early Late Pleistocene African specimens but not in Neanderthals.

Another feature that distinguished Neanderthals and early Cro-Magnons was the lower pelvic width/stature ratio of the latter, despite their overall similarity in estimated average body weight, probably comparable with that of modern Europeans. Cro-Magnon stature probably averaged more than 180 cm in males and ca. 167 cm in females, a signifi-

cant increase over typical European Neanderthals (males ca. 167 cm and females ca. 160 cm). This tall, slender physique of the Cro-Magnons certainly more closely resembled that of the Levantine Skhūl and Qafzeh specimens than that of the Neanderthals, since average stature in the European and Israeli early moderns was virtually identical. There is uncertainty about the ancestral African pattern, but the little evidence that exists (e.g., Broken Hill, KNM-ER 999) suggests that it was more similar to that found in Eurasian early-modern, rather than Neanderthal, skeletons.

However, certain early Cro-Magnon specimens from eastern Europe do not fit so neatly into this distinct Neanderthal/Cro-Magnon dichotomy. These include Předmostí 3, a specimen with some Neanderthal-like features in facial shape. This arguably indicates the possibility that some gene flow did occur between late Neanderthal and early-modern humans in Europe during a probable period of coexistence between about 40 and 30 Ka, and a possible hybrid fossil between the two groups has even been claimed from the site of Hahnöfersand (Germany). This specimen is dated at ca. 33 Ka by radiocarbon but can be interpreted in a variety of ways. If such hybridization did occur, it appears to have been on a limited scale, and even then there is no certainty that such hybrids gave rise to later Europeans.

Modern *Homo sapiens* Fossils from Outside Europe

Early-modern fossils have been discovered in Africa and Southwest Asia, but those so far discussed probably all date to more than 35 Ka. Unfortunately, there is a dearth of Late

Pleistocene human material from many of these areas, with the notable exception of the large North African collections from such sites as Afalou and Taforalt. What material there is suggests that, even at the end of the Pleistocene, there were still rather robust modern humans represented at such sites as Iwo Eleru (Nigeria), East Turkana (Kenya), and Springbok Flats and Boskop (South Africa). The Ishango skeletal material from eastern Zaire, recently redated to ca. 25 Ka, reflects a very robust but long-limbed population with some traits apparently linking them to modern Nilotic peoples. At the same time, there were other populations that already closely resembled the modern Khoisan (Bushman) peoples of southern Africa.

From the slender evidence available from central Asia, certain populations of the Late Pleistocene seem to have been physically and culturally related to those of the European Upper Paleolithic. Farther east, however, there is evidence of populations that may be related to modern aboriginal populations of eastern Asia and the Americas. Several partial skeletons from the Upper Cave at Zhoukoudian (China) may have represented a population close to the ancestry of Native Americans or Ainu (unfortunately, these specimens were lost at the same time as the main Zhoukoudian collection of *H. erectus* fossils). An isolated skull from Liujiang (China) and partial skeletons from Minatogawa (Japan) seem more similar in facial form to modern "Mongoloids" of Asia, suggesting that such "racial" differences were evolving by 20 Ka.

In Southeast Asia, there is possible evidence from the cave site of Niah (Borneo) that modern humans were present there by 40 ka, but this date needs further independent confirmation. Farther south, there is archaeological evidence that modern humans may have reached Australasia by 50 Ka, but the nature of the original colonists, and whether they represented a single population or multiple migrations from different source areas, is still unclear. The Mungo skeletons from southeastern Australia are dated at 34–24 Ka, and the most complete specimens (1 and 3) seem remarkably gracile by the standards of many early-modern humans from elsewhere in the world, or even in comparison with some populations today. The contrast is all the more marked because southeastern Australia was populated by much more robust peoples at the end of the Pleistocene, as represented by the Cohuna and Kow Swamp samples (now, unfortunately, reburied). Publications concerning this latter group have tended to emphasize the robusticity of some of the specimens, which is evident, but the sample also includes Mungo-like cranial and postcranial material.

One scenario postulates that two founder populations originally entered Australia, the first derived from Indonesian ancestors (such as Javanese *H. erectus* and the Ngandong material) and represented by the Kow Swamp, Cohuna, and Talgai specimens, while the other migrated into the region from the Asian mainland, as represented by the Mungo and Keilor fossils. These two groups coexisted through the later Pleistocene and eventually gave rise to modern Australian Aboriginal populations by hybridization. It is also possible to propose that there was only *one* founding population from either Indonesia or farther afield and that much variation was created within Australia as the huge unpopulated continent became colonized. This variation may also have been compounded by pathological factors and the practice of head binding, which was certainly responsible for some of the peculiarities in cranial shape among the Kow Swamp sample. What is probably the most archaic-looking specimen from Australia, however, might also be the most ancient, providing possible evidence of an Indonesian origin for at least some Pleistocene Australians. This skull (WLH 50) is still not published in detail, but if it can be accurately

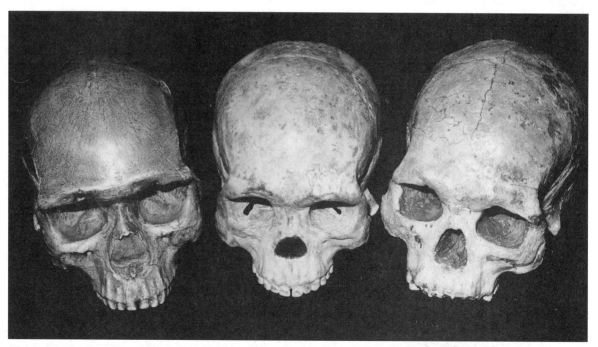

Three early modern human crania from eastern localities. From left: Zhoukoudian Upper Cave 101 and Liujiang (both China); Keilor, Australia. Courtesy of Chris Stringer.

dated it could throw further light on the mysterious origins of modern *H. sapiens* in Australia. It is very large and angular, with a broad base, its cranial proportions are modern and its great cranial thickness may be due to pathology, rather than a link with Indonesian *H. erectus*.

See also Archaic Homo sapiens; Archaic Moderns; Border Cave; Cro-Magnon; Florisbad; Ishango; Jebel Irhoud; Kabwe; Kibish; Klasies River Mouth; Kow Swamp; Lagar Velho; Lake Mungo; Modern Human Origins; Neanderthals; Ngandong (Solo); Niah; Zhoukoudian. [C.B.S.]

Further Readings

Howells, W.W. (1976) Explaining modern man: Evolutionists versus migrationists. J. Hum. Evol. 5:477–495.

Kimbel, W.H., and Martin, L.B. eds. (1993) Species, Species Concepts, and Primate Evolution. New York: Plenum.

Kimbel, W.H., and Rak, Y. (1993) The importance of species taxa in Paleoanthropology and an argument for the phylogenetic concept of the species category. In W.H. Kimbel and L.B. Martin (eds.): Species, Species Concepts, and Primate Evolution. New York: Plenum, pp. 461–485.

Smith, F.H., and Spencer, F. eds. (1984) The Origins of Modern Humans. New York: Liss.

Tattersall, I. (1986) Species recognition in human paleontology. J. Hum. Evol. 15:165–175.

Tattersall, I. (1992) Species concepts and species identification in human evolution. J. Hum. Evol. 22:341–349.

Turner, A. (1986) Species, speciation, and human evolution. Hum. Evol. 1:419–430.

Homology

Features of organisms that, by virtue of position, structure, or function, seem to be comparable are held to be homologous. In evolutionary theory, homologies are organismic attributes derived from a single ancestral condition. Thus, homologies may consist of very similar attributes (the eyes of all vertebrates) or very different ones (hair of mammals, feathers of birds, scales of reptiles). The term *homology* is usually contrasted with *analogy* (= *convergence*), in which attributes appear to be similar but have separate evolutionary origins (the wings of birds, bats, and pterosaurs are homologous as vertebrate forelimbs but analogous as wings; the wings of insects are only analogous with the wings of any vertebrate). By saying that certain features are homologous as structures of a given group, it is implied that the features so described are derived from the earlier structure in the ancestor of the broader group.

Evolution necessarily produces a complex nesting of adaptations (modified structures); these are homologies. In the reconstruction of evolutionary (phylogenetic) history, taxa (groups of species) are defined and recognized on the basis of features held in common, thus possibly derived from a single ancestral condition as homologies. Such restricted sets of homologous features are *synapomorphies*. Homology is a more general term (hair is a synapomorphy linking all

mammals; hair is homologous with the dermal structures—feathers and scales—of birds and reptiles, respectively).

See also Adaptation(s); Cladistics; Evolution; Phylogeny. [N.E.]

Further Readings

Eldredge, N., and Cracraft, J. (1980) Phylogenetic Patterns and the Evolutionary Process. New York: Columbia University Press.

Hooton, Earnest Albert (1887–1954)

American physical anthropologist. When Hooton left the University of Wisconsin in 1910 for Oxford as a Rhodes Scholar, he had every intention of continuing his studies in the classics. But at Oxford he came under the influence of the archaeologist R.R. Marett (1866–1943) and the anatomist A. Keith (1866–1955) of the Royal College of Surgeons, London. Hooton returned to America in 1913 to begin a career in physical anthropology at Harvard University (1914–1954), where he was an influential teacher and responsible for supervising doctoral students in physical anthropology, including the first generation of professionally trained physical anthropologists in the United States (such as H.L. Shapiro, W.W. Howells, and S.L. Washburn).

See also Howells, William White; Keith, [Sir] Arthur; Washburn, Sherwood L. [F.S.]

Hope Fountain

Early Paleolithic industry from southern and eastern Africa, named for a site near Bulawayo, Zimbabwe, and characterized by crudely worked flakes struck by direct percussion and exhibiting a variety of edge shapes, together with choppers, and bearing a superficial resemblance in technology and absence of handaxes to the Tayacian and Clactonian industries of Europe. Often interpreted by L.S.B. Leakey as evidence along with the Acheulean industry for two separate lineages of earlier Pleistocene hominids, Hope Fountain can also be interpreted as a functional or behavioral variant of a general Early Stone Age tradition that includes industries with and without handaxes. The industry occurs at the Hope Fountain site in Zimbabwe, in Olduvai Bed III (Tanzania) and at Olorgesailie (Kenya) and is probably early Middle Pleistocene in age, ca. 0.9–0.6 Ma.

See also Acheulean; Africa, East; Africa, Southern; Chopper-Chopping Tools; Clactonian; Early Paleolithic; Early Stone Age; Handaxe; Leakey, Louis Seymour Bazett; Olduvai Gorge; Olorgesailie; Stone-Tool Making; Tayacian. [A.S.B.]

Hopwood, Arthur Tindell (1897–1969)

British paleontologist. On graduating from the University of Manchester in 1924, Hopwood joined the Department of Geology of the British Museum (Natural History), where he remained until his retirement in 1957. In addition to establishing himself as an authority in the field of fossil molluscs, Hopwood also developed an interest in mammals, particularly fossil primates, and was a pioneer researcher with H.

Reck and L.S.B. Leakey at Olduvai Gorge (Tanzania) in the 1930s. He was responsible for describing *Proconsul africanus* from Koru, the first fossil hominoid found in Africa, during the mid-1920s. After his retirement from the museum, Hopwood became a professor at the Lycée Français, where he taught zoology.

See also Koru; Leakey, Louis Seymour Bazett; Reck, Hans. [F.S.]

Howells, William White (1908–)

American physical anthropologist. On completing his doctoral dissertation under the direction of E.A. Hooton at Harvard University, and following a short spell at the American Museum of Natural History in New York City, Howells received an academic appointment at the University of Wisconsin (1939–1954). In 1954, he returned to his alma mater, where he remained until his retirement in 1974. His interests are wide, ranging over the entire anthropological spectrum, as indicated by his highly popular book on the history and diversity of religion, *The Heathens,* published in 1948. In physical anthropology, he has researched problems ranging from craniometry to paleoanthropology, including the use of factor analysis in anthropometry, the role of Neanderthals in the evolution of *Homo sapiens,* and the application of discriminant-function equations to determine populational affiliation of human crania and range of variation within geographic populations. He is also an authority on the anthropology of Oceania.

He was awarded one of the first Charles R. Darwin Awards for Lifetime Achievement by the American Association of Physical Anthropologists in 1992. In the same year, the William White Howells Prize for a book in biological anthropology that combines technical excellence with broad public appeal was instituted by the Biological Anthropology Division of the American Anthropological Association.

See also Hooton, Earnest Albert; Neanderthals; Modern Human Origins; Quantitative Methods. [F.S.]

Further Readings

Howells, W.W. (1989) Skull shapes and the map: Craniometric analysis in the dispersion of modern *Homo.* Papers of the Peabody Museum of Archaeology and Ethnology, Harvard University 67:1–189.

Howells, W.W. (1997) Getting Here: The Story of Human Evolution, 2nd ed. Washington: Compass Press.

Howieson's Poort

Southern African Middle Stone Age industry, named for a site near Grahamstown, Cape Province (South Africa), and characterized by discoidal, Levallois, and blade technologies, backed and retouched blades, backed segments, and bifacial and unifacial leaf-shaped points. Ground and perforated ocher plaques are also associated with this industry. Originally grouped with transitional Second Intermediate industries, such as the Magosian, the industry has been shown to underlie classic Middle Stone Age levels at several sites, such as Klasies River Mouth. The Howieson's Poort is also some-

times associated with a shift to smaller prey animals along with evidence of a possible increase in rainfall. Other names for related industries in southern Africa include epi-Pietersburg, Umguzan, Tshangula (earlier variant), and South African Magosian. Its probable age is between 60 and 80 Ka.

See also Africa, Southern; Klasies River Mouth; Magosian; Middle Paleolithic; Middle Stone Age; Second Intermediate; Stone-Tool Making. [A.S.B.]

Hoxne

Open-air archaeological site in Suffolk (England), dated to the late Middle Pleistocene (Hoxnian interglacial), ca. 400–300 Ka, by stratigraphic and faunal correlation with the Middle Acheulean industry *in situ* in lake sediments. In 1797, Hoxne was the first site at which Paleolithic stone tools were recognized as such, by J. Frere.

See also Acheulean; Early Paleolithic; Europe; Frere, John. [A.S.B.]

Hrdlička, Ales (1869–1943)

American (b. Bohemia) physical anthropologist. On completing his medical training in New York City in the mid-1890s, Hrdlička became increasingly involved with anthropological expeditions from the American Museum of Natural History. These interests ultimately led to his appointment in 1903 as curator of the newly created Division of Physical Anthropology in the National Museum of Natural History (Smithsonian Institution), where he remained until his retirement in 1942. He is perhaps best remembered for his classic paper *The Neanderthal Phase of Man,* which was delivered in London as the Huxley Memorial Lecture of 1927. Prior to this paper, he had directed his research largely to understanding events leading to the emergence, dispersion, and differentiation of modern *Homo sapiens* in the Old World. After 1927, Hrdlička collected evidence in Beringia to support the hypothesis of the Asian origin of the American aborigines. Hrdlička also founded the *American Journal of Physical Anthropology* (1918) and the American Association of Physical Anthropologists (1928). [F.S.]

Human Paleontology

The part of paleoanthropology focusing on the study of human fossil remains, rather than Paleolithic archaeology or geological matters. Human paleontology had two independent origins, from human anatomy and vertebrate paleontology, which fused by the middle of the twentieth century. The earliest human fossils were recovered by naturalists and archaeologists and generally described by medical practitioners or paleontologists, who brought different backgrounds to their analyses. Eugene Dubois was one of the first paleoanthropologists, having actually set out to find early human remains. Marcellin Boule was the dean of human paleontologists in France early in the twentieth century, with H.V. Vallois and J. Piveteau as his successors. Raymond Dart in South Africa and W.E. LeGros Clark were major twentieth-century exemplars of the anatomist turned human paleontologist. The integration of these two viewpoints with those of archaeology and geochronology resulted in the discipline of paleoanthropology.

See also Boule, [Pierre] Marcellin; Le Gros Clark, [Sir] Wilfred Edward; Dart, Raymond Arthur; Dubois, Eugene; Paleoanthropology; Paleolithic; Piveteau, Jean; Vallois, Henri Victor. [E.D.]

Hunter-Gatherers

A very small number of people in the world today do not grow their food but obtain it by collecting plants, fishing, and hunting animals found in the area they occupy. The !Kung of the Kalahari Desert (Botswana), the Pygmies of the Ituri Forest (Zaire), and the Inuit (Eskimos) of northwestern Canada and Alaska are some of the better-known groups. This way of obtaining food, by harvesting what nature provides, is the oldest subsistence strategy known to us and has been practiced in one form or another for at least the last 2 Myr. In fact, it was the only way of obtaining food until the beginning of plant and animal domestication ca. 10 Ka. Hunter-gatherers have not done well in competition with food-producing societies since then. Their numbers have steadily dwindled, and they have been left in, or forced into occupying, the least productive regions of the world. While modern-day groups are found in marginal environments, such as deserts, tropical forests, or Arctic barrens, their predecessors in Paleolithic and Mesolithic times occupied the most productive habitats of both the Old and the New Worlds.

Studying hunter-gatherer adaptations known from the ethnographic record can help obtain insights into human adaptations in the past. At the outset, however, it has to be underscored that known groups are in no way living relics of ancestral lifeways. Contemporary hunter-gatherers, like their historically known equivalents, are as much a product of their histories as are other people. Furthermore, they are not a particular type of people predisposed for this way of life. At the same time, it is also true that, of all subsistence strategies practiced today, such as extensive and intensive agriculture, pastoralism, and industrialism, theirs is the closest to the way of life that prevailed throughout the Pleistocene and Early Holocene. Hunting-gathering, then, is the simplest and the most stable way of making a living that is still effective for some people in their particular habitats. Understanding the organization of this way of life provides us with a route for approaching the study of the past.

Subsistence Practices

Since hunter-gatherers use nature itself as a storehouse, their survival depends most directly on what, when, and where their habitats produce or are helped by them to produce (e.g., burning grasslands to stimulate new growth as practiced by Australian Aborigines). Needed resources, be they food, water, or other vital raw materials, are neither evenly nor predictably distributed across the landscape. Edible plants and game animals that these resources attract are found in scattered patches. In most parts of the world, seasonality is an important temporal variable that greatly affects the availability of food. In higher latitudes, for example, the shortness of the growing season restricts the availability of vegetal resources and of the animals that feed on them to the brief warm period. In lower latitudes, seasonal differences in rainfall affect the availability and distribution of food resources. Because of these and many other environmental differences, as well as nutritional requirements, the mix of foods harvested by hunter-gatherers can take many forms, depending on the nature, availability, and predictability of the resources in their habitat. While fishing and harvesting of shellfish may play major roles in food-procurement strategies of groups living along seacoasts and the shores of large lakes, groups occupying the continental interiors obtain the major portion of their nutrition from gathering wild plants and hunting animals. Since plants are more predictable in their location and less costly to obtain (one needs only to find them and exert just a little energy in capturing them), it is the plant resources that play the dominant role in hunter-gatherer diets worldwide. Since, in general, many more plants are found in tropical than in temperate-to-polar regions, and since the productivity of terrestrial environments decreases with increasing latitude, plants play a much greater role in diets of lower-latitude hunter-gatherers.

The structure of the resource base of a region (the abundance, availability, edibility, distribution, and predictability of food resources) profoundly affects both the size of the coresident group and the degree of mobility among hunter-gatherers. While adaptations based on harvesting food from nature in general require mobility and a small group size, these aspects of adaptation exhibit a good deal of variability. Although past hunter-gatherer studies stressed modal behavior, scholarship since the 1960s, focusing on the variability in hunter-gatherer adaptations, has emphasized the dichotomy between those groups who store food and those who do not, those who enjoy immediate returns on their labor and those whose returns are delayed, or those who invest more energy into traveling to obtain food and those who spend more time processing wild resources.

In reality, hunter-gatherer food-management strategies can probably be best understood when viewed as a contingency-dependent continuum. Strategies of simple foragers, occupying one end of this continuum, involve moving the entire coresidential group to the available resources. While the group is camped in one location, food search parties go out daily to harvest what is available within a reasonable distance from the camp. Such groups remain in an area until foods are depleted in the vicinity of their settlements and then move off to exploit other areas. Occasionally, when the productivity of local resources permits or requires it (abundant food or limited availability of water, for example), these small groups may be joined by other like-size ones for brief periods of time. In the course of their annual rounds, people employing this food-management strategy (in which food is not stored but is consumed immediately) occupy a number of short-term residential sites within a region. The regional archaeological record of such groups includes widely scattered, like-size, briefly occupied base camps together with a number of nearby special-purpose locations used in the course of resource procurement.

Logistically organized hunter-gatherers occupy the other end of the continuum. They use small, special-task groups to procure the food and bring it back to the group at large. In this strategy, most often encountered in regions with temporally or spatially clumped resources, such as herds of migratory animals or large seasonal runs of fish, food is harvested in quantities considerably beyond the daily requirements of the whole group. Much of this food is stored or cached for future consumption. Hunter-gatherers employing this strategy generally live in larger settlements that are moved less frequently than those of foragers. Among them, special food-procurement groups exploit larger territories and travel to greater distances from residential locations. These travels usually involve overnight stays away from the main residential locales. This organization of food procurement is clearly predicated on the availability of transport technology to bring the harvested resources back in bulk. The archaeological record of such groups includes at least two types of residential camps: large ones occupied by the whole group and small overnight camps occupied by food-procurement task groups. In addition, it may include special-purpose food-harvesting locations, as well as evidence for food storage in the settlements themselves or food caches scattered across the hunting territory.

Technology

All hunter-gatherers know much about the location of resources in their regions, as well as how and when best to exploit them, and their technology to do so is usually quite simple. They invest little energy in their tools and shelters yet are able to extract a sufficient return on their labor to support a significant proportion of nonproducers (e.g., the young and the old). Since the hunter-gatherer adaptation necessitates residential mobility, the number of tools and possessions is kept to a minimum. Multipurpose tools and implements are favored over special-purpose ones. Furthermore, since environmental conditions are far harsher in some regions, such as higher latitudes, and survival in these regions requires the use of more items of material culture (e.g., more clothing, more substantial shelters), it is not surprising that the elaboration of technology among hunter-gatherers shows a latitudinal gradation. Likewise, more mobile foragers possess simpler and fewer tools than do more permanently settled groups. These facts have numerous archaeological implications. First, other things being equal, we can anticipate finding more diversified inventories and more complex features among groups who occupied higher latitudes in the past than among groups who lived closer to the equator. Second, we can also anticipate richer and more elaborate archaeological records for groups living in larger numbers for greater lengths of time than for those smaller in size and more mobile.

Social Organization

Since the success of a hunting-gathering way of life depends on a close fit between the available resources and the number of people who can be supported, there are a few regularities

Artist's rendering of a base camp of modern foraging hunter-gatherers like the !Kung. After J. Jelinek, Strecha nad Hlavou, *Moravian Museum Brno, 1986.*

in group size and in social organization of hunter-gatherers. In general, coresident group size among present-day groups is small, averaging five to six nuclear families related to each other by ties of descent and marriage. Such a group of 25–30 people is called a *minimal band*. Membership in such bands is quite fluid, and families living in one band often move to join their relatives in another. When food supplies in their home territory are particularly low, the minimal band itself may temporarily break up into even smaller coresidential units, such as a single family. Conversely, when food supplies are abundant, a few minimal bands may camp together in an area. This fluidity and flexibility in group size and membership is more in evidence among simple foragers. Logistically organized groups that rely on stored resources exhibit more permanent group affiliation and residence, as well as larger coresidential units.

While, in general, food procurement in hunter-gatherer societies is a family or household undertaking, a number of important limiting mechanisms bring about a relatively equal distribution of goods and resources among the families. Perhaps the most important of these are strong reciprocal obligations among people that ensure that foods and other goods are shared. Obligations to share extend well beyond the household and eventually entail all other members of the coresidential unit. This emphasis on reciprocity, as well as ostracism when things are not shared, in effect makes the whole coresident group a minimal-subsistence unit. The prestige obtained by one's generosity, the threat of ostracism when this is not done, and the reality that frequent residential mobility itself imposes limits on acquisition of goods beyond one's immediate needs, result in both a paucity of material possessions and their rather equal distribution. Ethnographic research also suggests that hunter-gatherers are well aware that reciprocal obligations can lead to exploitation of the more productive individuals, and limit their productivity accordingly. Since residential mobility is a powerful factor limiting the amount of personal possessions owned by individuals, groups with reduced residential mobility exhibit a greater accumulation of possessions, invest more energy in their technologies and material culture, and have more strongly developed ideas about private property.

The relatively egalitarian economic and social relationships characteristic of simpler foraging societies have implications for the archaeological records of similar groups in the past. First, archaeological inventories left behind by prehistoric hunter-gatherers in general are sparse and simple. Furthermore, the nature and the quantity of the inventories differ little among households. Thus, remains of all past residential structures are similar in size and contain almost identical kinds and amounts of features and inventories. Similarly, we can anticipate few qualitative or quantitative differences in either features or inventories among like settlements on a regional level. All archaeological sites in a given region identified as the same type of occupations will be quite alike and differ from each other only by season of occupation.

Political Relationships

Political relationships among hunter-gatherers are more egalitarian relative to those found in societies who practice other subsistence strategies, and there are seldom any permanent leaders in band societies. While differences in status do exist, positions of higher status are generally earned and limited in scope, and there are as many positions of status as individuals within an appropriate age-sex category capable of filling them. This egalitarianism, however, is relative, and significant inequality between the young and the adults or between men and women have been amply documented in the literature. In general, however, positions of higher status are not institutionalized into offices, give their holders little special say in matters outside their particular area of competence, and do not bring significant economic advantages. Decision making among simpler hunter-gatherers is fairly evenly spread among the entire coresident group, and decisions are reached by consensus of those in appropriate age/sex categories rather than by the say of an individual who specializes in making decisions.

Research into group decision making indicates a strong positive relationship among fairly egalitarian sociopolitical relationships, residential mobility, and group size. Specifically, it appears that specialization in decision making by part-time or full-time leaders is tied to large groups of individuals interacting on a more permanent basis. While decisions by consensus, a hallmark of egalitarian sociopolitical relationships, are possible when groups are small and residential mobility is a viable option for individuals or families who do not agree, this form of decision making breaks down as the size of the group exceeds five to six households. The group then either disintegrates, as some families leave, or decision making becomes hierarchical. This can be situational and temporary, such as at temporary-aggregation locations, or more permanent. Thus, among logistically organized hunter-gatherers, as well as those who practice storage and delayed consumption, in which groups exceed the minimal band size of foragers (25–30 individuals), larger basal social units, such as extended or multifamily units or various kin-based descent groups (e.g., clans), become minimal social and subsistence units. This development of horizontal hierarchy is often accompanied by development of vertical hierarchy as well, in which a few permanent, often part-time, leaders specialize in making significant decisions. Thus, although hunter-gatherer societies are broadly characterized as egalitarian in political relationships, in reality these relationships grade from egalitarian to simple hierarchical ones, which, in some cases, carry not only social but also economic advantages as well.

Since differences in status are usually marked by specific items of material culture (e.g., pieces of personal adornment often made of hard-to-obtain or exotic materials), the existence of such differences in prehistory can often be inferred from the presence and distribution of such items at archaeological sites. Burials with differential grave goods offer one clue to past differences in status. A differential distribution of exotic jewelry or other nonutilitarian, costly-to-produce items among the households at a site offers another clue. In general, we can anticipate finding more evidence for sociopolitical differentiation among past groups who were logistically organized in their food-procurement pursuits or who practiced food storage than among foragers who employed group mobility in their subsistence strategies.

Origins of Hunter-Gatherer Adaptations

While we know that hominins harvested food from nature from the very beginning of their existence ca. 5 Ma, the origins of hunter-gatherer adaptations as we know them from ethnography are more difficult to pinpoint in time. Both the nature and the wealth of archaeological data from Late Paleolithic sites, dating in some parts of the Old World to before 50 Ka, indicate hunter-gatherer adaptations like those known from the ethnographic record, but how similar Neanderthal and earlier adaptations were to these lifeways is much debated. Some scholars have argued that the basic elements of foraging hunter-gatherer lifeways (i.e., division of labor between the sexes, food sharing, and seasonal mobility) can be traced all the way back to *Australopithecus*. Others insist that even inventories left behind by the Neanderthals differ significantly from those generated by present-day hunter-gatherer societies. Although these differences of opinion cannot be securely resolved yet, we can state with some degree of certainty that hunter-gatherer adaptations similar to those we know today have been around for at least the last 50 Kyr. Furthermore, it is quite likely that ethnographically known lifeways represent a mosaic of behavioral complexes that did not evolve in unison and were, in part, responses to historic factors. This suggests that, as we move back in time, we should anticipate finding a more patchy and incomplete record of human behavior that will be less analogous to present-day cases. Some parts of this record, especially those from more recent times (e.g., evidence for or against food sharing among the Neanderthals), will be easier to comprehend. Other parts, however, will be quite unlike what we know, and we shall have a difficult time interpreting them if we use only the organization of present-day hunter-gatherers as our baseline for reconstructing the past.

See also Aggregation-Dispersal; Economy, Prehistoric; Site Types. [O.S.]

Further Readings

Bettinger, R. (1991) Hunter-Gatherers. New York: Plenum.

Binford, L.R. (1980) Willow smoke and dog's tails: Hunter-gatherer settlement systems and archaeological site formation. Am. Antiquity 43:4–20.

Burch, E.S., Jr., and Ellanna, L.J., eds. (1994) Key Issues in Hunter-Gatherer Research. Oxford: Berg.

Kelly, R.L. (1983) Hunter-gatherer mobility strategies. J. Anthropol. Res. 39:277–306.

Lee, R.B., and DeVore, I., eds. (1968) Man the Hunter. Chicago: Aldine-Atherton.

Smith, E.A., and B. Winterhalder, eds. (1992) Evolutionary Ecology and Human Behavior. New York: Aldine de Gruyter.

Testart, A. (1982) The significance of food storage among hunter-gatherers: Residence patterns, population densities, and social inequalities. Curr. Anthropol. 23:523–537.

Woodburn, J. (1980) Hunters and gatherers today and reconstruction of the past. In E. Gellner (ed.): Soviet and Western Anthropology. New York: Columbia University Press, pp. 95–118.

Huxley, Thomas Henry (1825–1895)

British anatomist and physical anthropologist. Huxley was one of the first scientists to be converted to C. Darwin's views on evolution and became the foremost advocate of the Darwinian theory and its underlying materialist and mechanistic principles. Huxley's most influential and enduring book, *Evidences As to Man's Place in Nature,* published in 1863, contains the essential elements of his structural-functional argument for accepting Darwin's thesis of natural selection and the demonstration that, zoologically, the genus *Homo* is a primate. Huxley held that the presumed chasm between human beings and the apes had been greatly exaggerated by such anatomists as R. Owen (1804–1892), with whom Huxley had clashed earlier over this very issue. During the course of his influential career, Huxley held a number of prestigious positions, ranging from Hunterian Professor of the Royal College of Surgeons, London (1863–1869), to president of the Royal Society (1883–1885).

See also Darwin, Charles Robert; Evolution. [F.S.]

Hylobatidae

The gibbons, or lesser apes, are the smallest and, in many respects, the most primitive of the living apes. Both morphological and biochemical studies indicate that the gibbons are the earliest branch of living apes to evolve and are closest to the divergence of monkeys and apes. There is a single genus of living gibbons *(Hylobates),* with 10 species ranging in size from ca. 5 to 12 kg. All are from the rain forests of Southeast Asia, where they are abundant. In both numbers of species and numbers of individuals, they are the most successful of the living apes.

Like all catarrhines, gibbons have a dental formula of 2.1.2.3, and their molar teeth are simple with broad basins and small rounded cusps. There is no sexual dimorphism in the teeth of gibbons; both sexes have long, daggerlike canines. Gibbon skulls have short snouts, large orbits with projecting rims, and rounded, globular braincases that generally lack either sagittal or nuchal crests. The gibbon's most distinctive skeletal features are the long, slender limbs. They have relatively long hindlimbs, extremely long forelimbs, and long, curved fingers and toes. Like all apes, they have no tail. They are unusual among apes and resemble Old World monkeys in having ischial callosities (sitting pads).

In external appearance, gibbons are characterized by dense fur and coat colors ranging from black through gold and brown to silvery grey. While there is no size difference between male and female gibbons, in many species there are marked differences in pelage coloration.

All gibbons are totally arboreal. They are the most suspensory of all living primates and move primarily by brachiation and climbing, but they also run bipedally along branches. Gibbons are all primarily frugivorous, but various species supplement their diet to a greater or lesser degree with foliage or invertebrates. All gibbons (with one possible exception) live in monogamous social groups consisting of a single male, a single female, and their offspring. They advertise their territories with loud vocal duets and actively defend them from other families with fights and chases. In contrast with other apes, gibbons do not build nests for sleeping. Rather, when they sleep, they either sit hunched over on branches or recline at the end of tree limbs among the small twigs.

Authorities disagree over the exact number of gibbon species found on the islands of Southeast Asia; however, most believe that there are three main groups of lesser apes, often placed in separate subgenera.

The siamang [*H. (Symphalangus) syndactylus*] from Malaysia and Sumatra is the largest gibbon. It is a solid-black species with a large throat pouch and webbing between the third and fourth digits of its hands and feet. Siamangs are the most folivorous of the gibbons. Their social behavior is unusual in that the father transports the offspring and cares for it during the second year after birth.

The crested gibbon [*H. (Nomascus) concolor*] from China and Indochina is slightly smaller than the siamang. Males and females are strikingly different in pelage coloration. The ecology of this species is poorly known, but recent reports from China indicate that this gibbon may live in larger social groups than other species.

The remaining species of gibbons are more closely related to one another than to the siamang or the crested gibbon and thus are included in the subgenus *H. (Hylobates).* The hoolock gibbon (*H. hoolock*) is a large species from Burma, Bangladesh, and eastern India; it is sometimes placed in the subgenus *H. (Bunopithecus)* with an extinct Chinese form. Kloss's gibbon (*H. klossi*) is a gracile species from the Mentawai Islands off the western coast of Sumatra. Kloss's gibbon has an unusual diet of fruits and a large percentage of invertebrates, with no foliage.

The white-handed gibbon (*H. lar*) from Thailand, Malaysia, and Sumatra is the best-known species. Its diet consists predominantly of fruits, and it seems to specialize on fruit species that are found in small patches widely dispersed throughout the forest. As a result, white-handed gibbons travel over long distances each day in search of food.

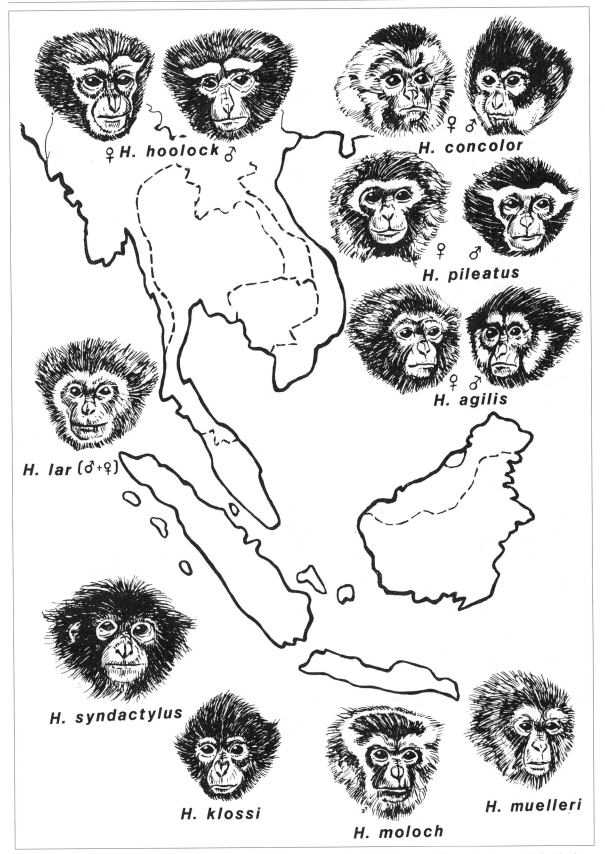

Map of the area of gibbon distribution in Southeast Asia, with portraits of males and females of the various gibbon species. Courtesy of John Fleagle.

The other hylobatids, the agile gibbon *(H. agilis)*, the pileated gibbon *(H. pileatus)*, the silvery gibbon *(H. moloch)*, and Mueller's gibbon *(H. muelleri)*, are similar to white-handed gibbons, and some authorities consider them geographical variants of the same species.

Over the years, paleontologists have identified many small catarrhines from the Miocene (23–5 Ma) as fossil gibbons. These include *Pliopithecus* from Europe, *Dendropithecus* and *Micropithecus* from Africa, and *Dionysopithecus* and *Laccopithecus* from China. All of these have (conservative) dental and cranial similarities to living gibbons. None, however, shows the unique skeletal adaptations that characterize the living hylobatids, and it is improbable that any is directly ancestral to modern gibbons. It seems more likely that small frugivorous catarrhines have evolved many times during the past and that the living hylobatids are the most recent radiation of small apes and the only one that has survived to the present day. Chinese and Southeast Asian Pleistocene fossils, mainly dental remains, probably represent *Hylobates* species close to living forms. The species diversity of gibbons today seems to be the result of the fluctuating land connections in the islands of Southeast Asia that resulted from sea-level changes during the Pleistocene.

Family Hylobatidae
    Hylobates
        H. (*Hylobates*)
        H. (*Symphalangus*)
        H. (*Nomascus*)
        ?*H.* (*Bunopithecus*)

See also Ape; Asia, Eastern and Southern; "Dendropithecus-Group"; Diet; Hominoidea; Ischial Callosities; Locomotion; Paleobiogeography; Pliopithecidae; Primate Societies; Sexual Dimorphism; Skeleton; Skull; Teeth. [J.G.F., F.J.W.]

Further Readings

Chivers, D.J. (1980) Malayan Forest Primates. New York: Plenum.

Preuschoft, H., Chivers, D., Brockelman, W., and Creel, N. (1985) The Lesser Apes: Evolutionary and Behavioral Biology. Edinburgh: Edinburgh University Press.

Hypodigm

The set of specimens upon which a systematist bases his or her concept of a species-level taxon. When a new species is named, or a previous one is revised through further study, it is possible for a taxonomist to examine the remains of only a small fraction of the total membership of that taxon, throughout its time and space range. Thus, it is important for other workers to know exactly which specimens were studied and used as the basis for the taxonomic concept. The *holotype* is the most pivotal member of the hypodigm, but the additional material allows for the understanding of at least part of the variability inherent in any taxon. Older concepts such as *paratypes* (secondary types that may reveal morphology not preserved in a holotype) or *topotypes* (secondary types from different localities) are now subsumed in the hypodigm.

See also Classification; Nomenclature; Systematics; Taxonomy. [E.D.]

Hyporder

Category in the classificatory hierarchy that falls between the suborder and the infraorder. This rank was devised in light of an awareness that a larger number of categories than traditionally recognized is necessary to accommodate the phylogenetic diversity of mammalian groups. In Primates, for example, the hyporders Tarsiiformes and Anthropoidea have been used within the suborder Haplorhini to reflect the phylogenetic distinctness of the tarsiers and their relatives from the "higher" primates (such as monkeys and apes, as well as their extinct relatives), which together form a monophyletic group, Anthropoidea.

See also Classification. [I.T.]

I

Ibero-Maurusian

North African Late Paleolithic or Epipaleolithic industry (also known as Oranian in the Eastern Sahara) dating to 20–9.5 Ka at numerous sites along the Atlantic and Mediterranean coast of North Africa (Taforalt, El Mouillah, Haua Fteah). It is associated climatically with cooler climates of the Mediterranean coast and, initially, with dessication of the Sahara. The "Ibero" in its name refers to a hypothetical cultural link, now discounted, with the Iberian (Spanish) Upper Paleolithic.

Ibero-Maurusian assemblages contain numerous pointed backed blades and bladelets that have been truncated by the microburin technique, and grinding and polishing stones. It is distinguished from the Capsian by the relative paucity or absence of geometric microliths, especially crescents, and from the partly contemporaneous eastern Oranian industry (e.g., Haua Fteah) by the scarcity of geometric microliths, burins, and large backed blades. Bone awls and other tools are also known from the Ibero-Maurusian. At El Mouillah, the type site, near Lake Marnia in the Oran district of Algeria, the Ibero-Maurusian occupation yielded numerous ostrich-eggshell fragments and pierced pebbles. Human remains of the *Mechtoid* type are associated with several Ibero-Maurusian sites in Morocco and Algeria, such as Taforalt. Among these Mechta-Afalou skeletons is the oldest-known example of trepanation.

See also Africa; Haua Fteah; Late Paleolithic. [A.S.B., J.J.S.]

Immunological Distance

The surface of a cell contains specific marker molecules (*antigens*) that identify the cell. Vertebrates, and mammals to an extreme degree, have evolved an immune system as a defense mechanism against infection by foreign cells. This sensitive system is stimulated by foreign antigens to produce highly specific molecules (*antibodies*), whose function is to destroy the foreign cell. In addition to cell-surface antigens, any substance that can elicit the production of antibodies is considered an antigen. Examples of the function of the immune system are the familiar blood-transfusion incompatibilities in which, for example, blood with type A anti-

gens is rejected by a patient with type O blood. An organism that has been exposed to a specific antigen can produce copious specific antibodies on subsequent exposure and is said to be *immunized* against the antigen; this is the basis for vaccinations.

The immune system possesses a property that makes it useful in primate systematics: *cross-reactivity*. A rabbit immunized against a specific human antigen (e.g., the protein albumin) will react also to the homologous antigen from a rhesus macaque. But its antibody production will not be as strong because the antigen is not quite identical. Since the antigenic difference between the human and the rhesus macaque is genetic in its basis, the amount of difference detectable in the immunological reaction is a rough estimate of a genetic *distance* between the two. Various methods, notably agar-gel diffusion and microcomplement fixation, were developed and refined in the 1960s for measuring such immunological distances among the primates.

See also Molecular Anthropology; Molecular Clock. [J.M.]

Further Readings

Goodman, M. (1963) Serological analysis of the systematics of recent hominoids. Hum. Biol. 33:377–436.

Sarich, V., and Wilson, A. (1967) Immunological time scale for hominid evolution. Science 138:1200–1202.

Incertae Sedis

Of uncertain taxonomic position. The term is placed after the name of a taxon at any level of the classificatory hierarchy to indicate that the affinities of that taxon are not precisely determined. The rank at which a taxon is placed as incertae sedis indicates the level at which the uncertainty exists. Thus, a large family well classified within itself, but of uncertain placement within an order, would be classified within that order, incertae sedis, and not allocated to any intermediate rank.

See also Classification; Systematics; Taxonomy. [I.T.]

Indonesia

Southeast Asian island nation yielding an important sample of *Homo erectus* and other hominin fossils. Occupying most of the longest archipelago in the world, Indonesia stretches along the equator for more than 5,800 km between Sumatra and central New Guinea and encompasses more than 14,000 islands. Many of the Indonesian islands occur around active or dormant volcanoes rising from the Sunda Shelf. The lowlands of the shelf, which are continuous with the Malayan Peninsula, were exposed several times during the Pleistocene by glacial-eustatic lowering of world sea level, and these periods of exposure provided periodic opportunities for interchange between the Indonesian islands and Southeast Asia.

Most of Indonesia is, or was until recently, heavily forested and relatively undeveloped apart from coastal strips, and only densely populated Java has yielded vertebrate fossil faunas of any significance. The principal collections have come from central and eastern Java, at Sangiran, Trinil, and

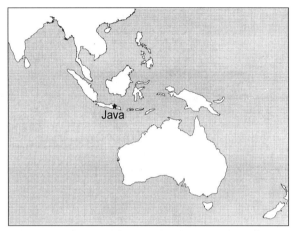

Location of Java in Indonesia and surroundings; star marks position of Solo River hominid sites on main map.

Ngandong (Solo). Paleoanthropologists generally agree that most of the early hominin specimens are attributable to *Homo erectus* at Trinil and Sangiran, an archaic form of *Homo sapiens* or a late form of *H. erectus* at Ngandong, and *H. sapiens sapiens* at Wadjak. Fossils of orangutan, as well as gibbon and cercopithecid monkeys, are also known.

Because Java is an island with a spinal chain of recently active volcanoes, there have been ample opportunities for radiometric dating of the hominin faunas of Java, but there is still little consensus about when this group first reached the island. One difficulty is that most of the Javanese hominin specimens were not recovered *in situ*, and placing them in a datable context has been problematical. While the consensus has favored a date for the earliest *Homo* later than 1.3 Ma, recent single-crystal argon-argon dating has placed the oldest finds at 1.89 Ma. The dating has important implications for the phylogeny and taxonomy of *H. erectus*, of which the holotype is the Trinil specimen. A more ancient age for the oldest Indonesian fossils could imply that Indonesian and possibly other East Asian forms of *H. erectus* represent a separate lineage from the African specimens that have gone by this name. The persistence of the Indonesian *H. erectus* lineage until relatively recent times, after modern *H. sapiens* had colonized Asia and Australia, is suggested by uranium-thorium dating of the Ngandong fauna at 50–25 Ka.

See also Asia, Eastern and Southern; Djetis; Dubois, Eugene; Homo erectus; Koenigswald, Gustav Heinrich Ralph von; Meganthropus; Ngandong; Sangiran Dome; Trinil. [G.G.P., E.D., A.S.B.]

Further Readings

Bemmelen, R.W. van (1949) The Geology of Indonesia, Vol. 1A: General Geology of Indonesia and Adjacent Archipelagos. The Hague: GP Office.

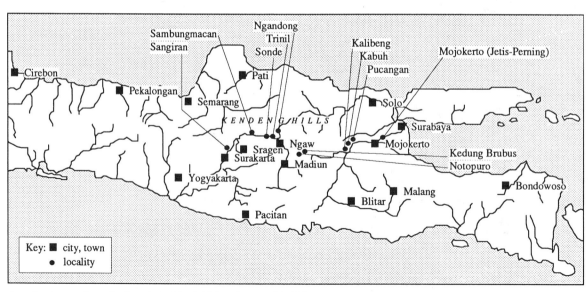

Central and eastern Java, showing principal hominid sites. Courtesy of G.G. Pope.

De Vos, J., and Sondaar, P. (1994) Dating hominid sites in Indonesia. Science 266:726–727.

Pope, G.G. (1985) Taxonomy, dating, and paleoenvironment: The paleoecology of the early Far Eastern hominids. Mod. Quatern. Res. Southeast Asia 9:65–81.

Sémah, F., Sémah, A., and Djubiantono, T. (1990) They Discovered Java. Jakarta: PT Adiwarna Citra.

Swisher, C.C., III, Curtis, G.H., Jacob, T., Getty, A.G., Suprijo, A., and Widiasmoro. (1994) Age of the earliest known hominids in Java, Indonesia. Science 263:1118–1121.

Swisher, C.C., III, Rink, W.J., Antón, S.C., Schwarcz, H.P., Curtis, G.H., Suprijo, A., and Widiasmoro. (1996) Latest *Homo erectus* of Java: Potential contemporaneity with *H. sapiens* in Southeast Asia. Science 274:1870–1874.

Theunissen, B., de Vos, J., Sondaar, P.Y., and Aziz, F. (1990) The establishment of a chronological framework for the hominid-bearing deposits of Java: A historical survey. In L.F. LaPorte (ed.): Establishment of a Geologic Framework for Paleoanthropology. Boulder: Geological Society of America, pp. 39–54.

Indriidae

Family of Lemuriformes that includes the extant genera *Indri*, *Avahi*, and *Propithecus*. All indriids occur exclusively on the island of Madagascar, and all are vertical clingers and leapers, with greatly elongated hindlimbs.

At a weight of ca. 6 kg, *Indri*, the babakoto, is among the two largest surviving lemurs and is particularly unusual in possessing only a vestigial tail. Although pelage coloration is variable, only one monotypic species, *Indri indri*, is recognized. Its habitat is the northern half of the eastern humid forest belt of Madagascar. Diurnal, the babakoto is pair bonding and subsists on a diet largely of leaves and fruit. Two recorded group home ranges were ca. 18 ha; there is little overlap between the ranges of different groups, which appear to space themselves by means of their loud, haunting vocalizations.

Avahi laniger, at ca. l kg the smallest indriid, is found throughout Madagascar's eastern rain-forest strip, as well as in areas of the northwest and the central west. Pair bonds are formed, although as many as five individuals have been seen in proximity, and small home ranges are aggressively defended. Diet is principally of leaves. Distinct eastern and northwestern subspecies are generally reckoned to exist, and the central-west form appears distinctive also.

Two indriids: Indri indri, *in midleap (left), and* Propithecus verreauxi verreauxi.

The most ubiquitous of the indriids is the sifaka, *Propithecus*. Three species are recognized: *Propithecus diadema* of the eastern rain forest (up to 7 kg body weight); the smaller (ca. 4 kg) *P. verreauxi* in the drier forests of the west and south of Madagascar; and the slightly smaller yet *P. tattersalli* in a highly restricted area of the far north. Each of the former two species contains local color variants recognized as separate subspecies. Some subspecies, at least, of *P. diadema* are probably pair bonding; others live in larger groups. *P. verreauxi* and *P. tattersalli* are generally seen in groups of from three to ten individuals, most commonly five. Most such groups contain more than one adult male, but it may be outsiders who mate with the resident females during the extremely brief breeding season. Home ranges are variable in size but, in the case of the smaller species, appear often to be ca. 8 ha or a little more. Diet is highly variable seasonally, fruit predominating at certain times of the year, leaves or seeds at others.

Family Indriidae
Indri
Propithecus
Avahi

See also Indrioidea; Lemuriformes; Teeth. [I.T.]

Further Readings

Harcourt, C., and J. Thornback (1990) Lemurs of Madagascar and the Comoros: The IUCN Red Data Book. Gland, Switzerland: IUCN.

Tattersall, I. (1982) The Primates of Madagascar. New York: Columbia University Press.

Tattersall, I. (1993) Madagascar's lemurs. Sci. Am. 268(1): 110–117.

Indrioidea

Superfamily of Lemuriformes that includes the families Indriidae, Daubentoniidae, Lepilemuridae, Archaeolemuridae, and Palaeopropithecidae. The last two of these consist of large-bodied genera (*Archaeolemur* and *Hadropithecus*, and *Palaeopropithecus* and *Archaeoindris*, respectively) that are recently extinct and known only as subfossils, but that can nevertheless be considered part of the modern Malagasy primate fauna. Lepilemuridae consists of the extant "sportive" lemur, *Lepilemur*, and the large-bodied subfossil form *Megaladapis*. Daubentoniidae contains only the highly specialized extant aye-aye, *Daubentonia*. Although it is considered here to be an indrioid, the aye-aye is extraordinarily autapomorphic, and its relationships are hard to determine definitively. Of the three living indriids two, *Indri* and *Propithecus*, are diurnal; the third, *Avahi*, is nocturnal. All indrioids are unique to the island of Madagascar, and, taking the extant and recently extinct forms together, the superfamily is by far the most diverse component of Lemuriformes. The lepilemurids traditionally were considered more closely related to the lemuroids than to the indrioids; however, characters of the dentition and of the postcranial skeleton suggest their inclusion in Indrioidea.

See also Archaeolemuridae; Daubentoniidae; Indriidae; Lemuriformes; Lemuroidea; Lepilemuridae; Palaeopropithecidae. [I.T.]

Further Readings

Mittermeier, R.A., Tattersall, I., Konstant, W.R., Meyers, D.M., and Mast, R.B. (1994) Lemurs of Madagascar (Tropical Field Guide No. 1). Washington, D.C.: Conservation International.

Schwartz, J.H., and Tattersall, I. (1985) Evolutionary relationships of living lemurs and lorises (Mammalia, Primates), and their potential affinities with European Eocene Adapidae. Anthropol. Pap. Am. Mus. Nat. Hist. 60: 1–100.

Tattersall, I. (1982) The Primates of Madagascar. New York: Columbia University Press.

Tattersall, I. (1993) Madagascar's lemurs. Sci. Am. 268(1):110–117.

Infraorder

Category in the classificatory hierarchy lying below the suborder and above the hyporder. Until the addition of the rank of hyporder, the infraorder was the rank intermediate between the superfamily and the suborder.

See also Classification. [I.T.]

Iron Age

Final step in the three-stage sequence of cultural development introduced in European archaeology during the early nineteenth century by C. Thomsen and J. Worsae. These Danish archaeologists arranged European prehistory into three successive developmental levels: Stone Age, Bronze Age, and Iron Age. These levels were seen as a unilineal developmental sequence from simple to complex cultures, as defined by the material employed to produce cutting tools, but the terms generally imply much more than technology.

The Iron Age is taken to mean a period of time ca. 3–2 Ka, when, in various parts of the world, the complicated technology of iron production and working was developed, highly centralized states emerged, warfare and imperial expansion were commonplace, and craft specialization and market economies developed. These cultural developments are not necessarily linked, and the use of the term in the context of unilineal schemes of cultural evolution is unwarranted. *Iron Age* remains as a term of reference for those parts of the world in which ironworking was developed, and it is best used to identify the early periods of development and use of the metal.

See also Bronze Age; Complex Societies; Europe. [B.B.]

Further Readings

Wells, P. (1984) Farms, Villages, and Cities: Commerce and Urban Origins in Late Prehistoric Europe. Ithaca, N.Y.: Cornell University Press.

Isaac, Glynn Llewellyn (1937–1985)

South African archaeologist. Isaac received his doctorate from Cambridge University in 1961 as a protegé of L.S.B. Leakey. He quickly established himself as a leader in African archaeology at the University of California, Berkeley, and in 1983 went to Harvard University. While his name is linked with the careful excavation of a number of East African archaeological sites, primarily Olorgesailie, Naivasha, and Peninj, he will probably be best remembered for his leading role in the East Turkana Research Project, of which he was coleader with R. Leakey from 1970 until his untimely death in 1985.

See also Africa, East; Leakey, Louis Seymour Bazeh; Olorgesailie; Peninj; Turkana Basin. [F.S.]

Ischial Callosities

Sitting pads found in all Old World monkeys and gibbons and sometimes in orangutans. They are cushions of fatty-fibrous tissue covered with a specialized skin, attached to an expanded ischial tuberosity. They enable monkeys and small apes to sit on branches during feeding and sleeping without either sliding off the branch or damaging other structures in the perineum. Whether they evolved independently in cercopithecids and hylobatids or were a feature of early eucatarrhines later lost in Hominidae is an intriguing problem in catarrhine systematics.

See also Catarrhini; Monkey. [J.G.F.]

Isernia

An open-air Early Paleolithic site in central Italy. Isernia–La Pineta features two major archaeological horizons in alternating fine-grained sediments and fluvial gravels, separated by a sterile level. The lower archaeological level contains sparse lithic and faunal remains. The upper level contains many stone tools and remains of large mammals packed together in clayey sediments. The faunal remains from Isernia include numerous specimens of *Bison schoetensacki* and lesser numbers of *Dicerorhinus hemitoechus* and *Elephas antiquus*. In one sector of the site, the archaeological levels were covered by a debris flow containing volcanic crystals dated to 730 ± 40 Ka. There has been considerable debate over whether volcanic crystals from such a derived deposit indicate the age of the site or come instead from older volcanics, although the crystals in question appear fresh. While the date of the debris flow is older than that obtained from *in situ* volcanic deposits in successively overlying strata (550 ± 50 and 470 ± 0 Ka, respectively), the oldest Isernia material could certainly be closer to the older of these latter two ages than is currently claimed (this younger date is also suggested by the microfauna); the age would still place this site among the oldest in Europe. To date, paleomagnetic data have been inconclusive.

The stone-tool industry consists of choppers and retouched flake tools struck from local flint and limestone river cobbles, predominantly by the bipolar technique to produce the maximum number of sharp flakes. The chop-pers are mostly made of limestone. The retouched tools are less common and consist mostly of denticulates, with lesser numbers of scrapers. Refitting of several groups of conjoinable artifacts suggests that at least some of the material is in primary context, although the preferential orientation of the fauna, together with considerable evidence of fluviatile abrasion, suggests considerable fluvial sorting and rearrangement. Use-wear studies suggest use of at least some flakes in butchery activities, perhaps in relation to carcasses of large herbivores such as rhinoceros, bison, and elephant. These concentrations have been interpreted by the excavators as evidence for specialized hunting, although others see Isernia as either a site where natural deaths of large mammals were scavenged by early humans or a coincidental juxtaposition of stone tools, faunal remains, and redeposited volcanic tuff.

See also Early Paleolithic; Europe; Lithic Use-Wear. [J.J.S., A.S.B.]

Ishango

Late Pleistocene open-air stratified site in eastern Zaire at the exit of the Semliki River from Lake Rutanzige (ex-Edward, ex-Amin). Excavated by J. de Heinzelin in the 1950s, the site shows a sequence of three strata of beach deposits with successive types (double-, single-barbed) of bone harpoons, small crude quartz tools, including microblade cores, and abundant fish and mammal remains. These strata of Ishangian cultural affinities are capped by levels of aceramic microlithic and ceramic Iron Age materials, also associated with fishing debris but not directly with beach deposits. Scattered human remains from the middle stage of the Ishangian culture have been attributed to very robust but entirely modern and long-limbed people comparable to the Nilotic peoples of this region today. Radiocarbon and amino-acid racemization determinations have suggested an age of ca. 25–20 Ka for the Ishangian bone-harpoon horizons and ca. 7 Ka for the microlithic horizon. A Late Pleistocene age for the Ishangian is also suggested by a recent study of the fauna, which includes giant forms of extant species. Analysis of the fish remains suggests considerable economic and technological sophistication, including the presumed use of nets and/or boats to take deep-lake species.

See also Africa; Economy, Prehistoric; Late Paleolithic; Later Stone Age; Mesolithic; Paleolithic Lifeways. [A.S.B.]

Further Readings

Brooks, A.S., and Smith C.C. (1987) Ishango revisited: New age determination and cultural interpretations. Afr. Archaeol. Rev. 5: 65–78

Istállöskö

Stratified Upper Paleolithic cave site in northeastern Hungary, ca. 15 km south of the Szeleta Cave. The two cultural layers found at the bottom of the deposit held faunal remains of large-size gregarious herbivores as well as numerous carnivores. Stone- and bone-tool assemblages containing diagnostic Mladeč-type bone points have been assigned to the eastern variant of the Aurignacian. Istállöskö also yielded one of the earliest-known musical instuments: a fragmentary bone flute. A fragment of an unerupted second molar found at Istállöskö belonged to an early anatomically modern *Homo sapiens.* Radiocarbon dating of bone found in the lower cultural layer gave dates between 44 and 40 Ka. A number of scholars have questioned the association of the dated bone with other cultural remains and have suggested that the much younger dates of ca. 30 Ka for the upper and 31.5 Ka for the lower layers are probably more correct.

See also Aurignacian; Europe; Late Paleolithic; Upper Paleolithic. [O.S.]

J

Jabrud

Archaeological site complex in the Anti-Lebanon Mountains of Syria near Nebek consisting of four rockshelters ranging in age from late Middle Pleistocene (Shelter IV) with a Tayacian industry to Neolithic (Shelter III). A long sequence in Shelter I contains a Pre-Aurignacian blade industry in the midst of Early and Middle Paleolithic levels; Shelter II materials were grouped as Aurignacian or Upper Paleolithic; and Shelter III preserves traces of the transition from Upper Paleolithic to Mesolithic.

See also Antelian; Early Paleolithic; Jabrudian; Late Paleolithic; Mesolithic; Middle Paleolithic; Natufian; Pre-Aurignacian; Tayacian; Upper Paleolithic. [A.S.B.]

Jabrudian

Early Paleolithic industry (probable age, later Middle Pleistocene). The Jabrudian, first defined by Rust at Jabrud Shelter I in Syria, is characterized by large numbers of side-scrapers, especially asymmetrical forms, and by few or no handaxes. The term has also been applied, probably erroneously, at Tabūn (Israel), where a Tayacian-like industry, also called Tabunian, is associated with Levallois technology and occurs both above and below the Pre-Aurignacian industry. All of these are better interpreted as variants of an early Paleolithic industrial complex.

See also Early Paleolithic; Levallois; Pre-Aurignacian; Stone-Tool Making; Tabūn; Tabunian; Tayacian. [A.S.B.]

Jarmo

Early Neolithic village site 11 km east of Chemchemal in Iraqi Kurdistan, occupied for several centuries ca. 9–8 Ka. Innovative multidisciplinary fieldwork at this 1.3-ha site, including three seasons of excavations during the period 1948–1954 directed by R.J. Braidwood, produced abundant artifactual, botanical, and osteological evidence of the transition from a hunting-gathering adaptation to food production, the development of ceramic technology, early village architecture, and long-distance trade in obsidian. Jarmo provided samples for radiocarbon dating during the developmental stages of this important archaeological tool; dates for Jarmo and Jericho were debated by their excavators.

See also Asia, Western; Domestication; Jericho; Neolithic. [C.K.]

Jebel Irhoud

Moroccan cave that has produced at least three hominin fossils, two adult skulls (Irhoud 1 and 2) and a child's mandible (Irhoud 3). These fossils were recovered during quarrying operations, but they were probably associated with an early Last Glacial fauna and a Mousterian industry found at this site. Electron spin resonance dates for levels above these fossils are 190–106 Ka. All three hominins show interesting combinations of archaic and modern characters. Irhoud I has an archaic vault shape, while its face is broad and flat with modern-looking cheek bones. Irhoud 2 has a modern frontal bone, while the parietal and occipital regions remain archaic in form. The child's mandible has large teeth but shows some chin development. Some consider the fossils to represent the local precursors of early-modern hominids from such sites as Dar-es-Soltane and Afalou.

See also Archaic Homo sapiens; Archaic Moderns. [C.B.S., J.J.S.]

Jerf 'Ajla

Rockshelter site near Palmyra, Syria, excavated in the 1950s and 1960s by American anthropologist C.S. Coon. The site contains a sequence of apparently early Middle Paleolithic industries with handaxes and thick scrapers in the lower levels and Levallois flakes and thick blade tools in upper layers. The antiquity of this site is uncertain, although sediment studies suggest deposition during cold, dry conditions.

See also Asia, Western; Coon, Carleton Stevens; Middle Paleolithic; Mousterian. [J.J.S.]

Jericho

Multilevel archaeological site at Tell es-Sultan, situated in the West Bank (Israel) between Jerusalem and the Jordan River. It was excavated for six seasons (1930–1936) by J. Garstang and for seven seasons (1952–1958) by K. Kenyon, who identified it with the biblical town, although not all researchers agree. The deposits are, in places, ca. 20 m thick and represent occupations ranging from aceramic (Pre-Pottery) Neolithic (PPN) through Chalcolithic, Bronze Age, and Iron Age periods. The PPNA and PPNB occupations (ca. 10–8 Ka) are estimated to have been ca. 2.4 ha in extent. These strata yielded complex structural remains (including retaining walls and a tower), evidence for long-distance trade in obsidian and other exotic raw materials, human skulls with faces of modeled plaster, and large plaster human figures.

See also Asia, Western; Jarmo; Neolithic. [C.K.]

Jewelry

Ostrich-eggshell beads from Africa are the earliest recognized examples of jewelry in the archaeological record. Early sites with beads include Level V at Mumba Shelter in Tanzania, a level with both Middle Stone Age points and large backed crescents dated to 60–40 Ka, a similar level at Enkapune ya Muto in Kenya dated to ca. 45 Ka, and an early Later Stone Age stratum in Border Cave (South Africa) dating to 45–33 Ka. Items of personal adornment, including diadems, beads, pins, pendants, bracelets, rings, and pectorals made of stone, bone, animal teeth, ivory, shell, and amber, are found in increasing numbers at Late Paleolithic sites in Eurasia after 40 Ka. The arrangement of beads and ornaments at early sites such as Sungir (Russia) suggests that jewelry was often sewn onto fur or hide clothing. The presence of jewelry in both burial and living contexts after 40 Ka is interpreted as indicating a newly emergent personal and social awareness. Stone beads from the Early Aurignacian of France reflect considerable time and effort invested in manufacture of these items. While items of jewelry found at the early Late Paleolithic sites are made predominantly of locally available materials, those found at sites dating after the glacial maximum (20–18 Ka) show greater percentages made of such exotic materials as fossil marine shells and amber.

See also Exotics; Late Paleolithic; Upper Paleolithic. [O.S.]

Further Readings

White, R. (1989) Production complexity and standardization of Early Aurignacian bead and pendant manufacture. In P. Mellars and C. Stringer (eds.): The Human Revolution: Behavioral and Biological Perspectives in the Origin of Modern Humans. Edinburgh: Edinburgh University Press, pp. 366–390.

Wymer, J. (1982) The Palaeolithic Age. New York: St. Martin's.

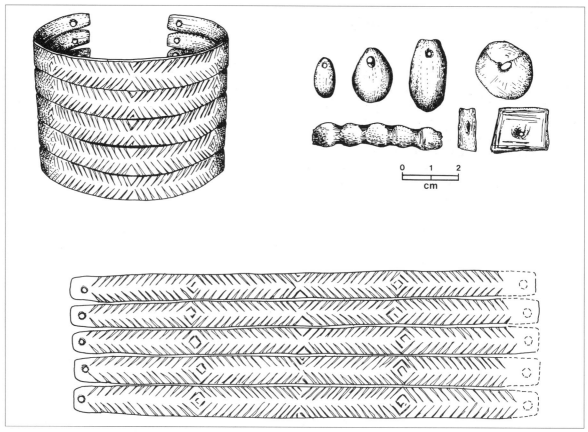

Ivory beads and bracelets from the Late Paleolithic site of Mezin (Russia). Courtesy of Olga Soffer.

Jia, Lanpo (Chia Lan-p'o or L. P. Chia) (1908–)

China's leading Paleolithic archaeologist. Jia was largely responsible, with Pei Wenzhong and Wu Rukang, for fostering the growth of paleoanthropology in China, particularly between 1949 and the late 1970s when foreign influence on Chinese science was minimal.

Largely self-educated (Jia graduated from the Huiwen Middle School in Beijing) and practically trained by his eminent contemporaries, including Pei Wenzhong, H. Breuil, and P. Teilhard de Chardin, Jia has been directly involved in the instruction of nearly all of China's living Paleolithic archaeologists. Jia's research in the field has been wide ranging, but he is best known for his interpretations of Early Paleolithic assemblages from Zhoukoudian Locality 1, the Nihewan Basin (Hebei Province) and Xihoudu (Shanxi Province); and the Middle Paleolithic materials from Xujiayao (Shanxi Province).

Jia is a senior research professor at the Institute of Vertebrate Palaeontology and Palaeoanthropology in Beijing. He is a member of the Chinese Academy of Sciences and the National Academy of Sciences of the United States, vice chair of the board of directors of the Chinese Archaeology Society, and a professor at Shanxi and Xiamen universities.

See also China; Wu, Rukang; Yang, Zhongjian; Zhoukoudian. [J.W.O.]

Further Readings

Jia, L.P. (1984) The Palaeoliths of China: Selected Works of Jia Lanpo. [In Chinese]. Beijing: Cultural Relics Press.

Jia, L.P. (1985) China's Earliest Palaeolithic Assemblages. In R.K. Wu and J.W. Olsen (eds.): Palaeoanthropology and Palaeolithic Archaeology in the People's Republic of China. Orlando: Academic, pp. 135–145.

Jian Shi

Hubei Province (China) cave deposit, dated to later Early or early Middle Pleistocene (ca. 1.0 Ma) by faunal correlation. This karst cave in Hubei Province (also known as Gao Ping) has yielded associated remains of hominins and *Gigantopithecus*. Three hominin molars recovered from the site were first attributed to *Australopithecus* cf. *africanus*, but most Chinese scientists now agree that two of them (belonging to one individual) are clearly aberrant and that all are best assigned to a species of *Homo*, probably *H. erectus*.

See also Asia, Eastern and Southern; China [G.G.P.]

Jinniushan

Middle Pleistocene hominin and Paleolithic locality in Yingkou County, Liaoning Province (China), dated to the late Middle Pleistocene, ca. 0.2 Ma by electron spine resonance (ESR) and uranium-series analyses, faunal correlation, and hominin morphology. Jinniushan (Golden Ox Mountain) is the site of a 1984 find of an unusually complete hominin specimen, which includes a cranium with a capacity originally estimated as 1,390 ml but now thought to be between 1,100 and 1,200 ml. The single individual is also represented by substantial postcranial material, including ribs, innominate (hip bone), leg fragments, and foot bones. The site of Jinniushan encompasses a number of fissure-infilling localities that have yielded artifacts and the fossils of at least 76 mammalian species. Evidence of fire in the form of burned animal bones and a hearth have also been reported. A uranium-series date of 0.3 Ma has been attributed to the fissure locality that yielded the hominin. Although the hominin has been referred informally to *Homo erectus*, it is now considered by all authorities to be an early member of *Homo sapiens*. While retaining many primitive characters, it shows few similarities to "archaic *Homo sapiens*" as this group is known from Europe and Africa. Furthermore, the hominin specimen may substantially postdate the mammalian remains, and an age of ca. 0.1 Ma may be possible. The taphonomic circumstances—very complete megafaunal skeletons and extensive cave microfauna—strongly suggest that the hominin locality was not an occupation site but instead a fissure faunal trap. Some Chinese workers dispute this interpretation.

See also Archaic Homo sapiens; Asia, Eastern and Southern; China; Homo erectus; Zhoukoudian. [G.G.P.]

Further Readings

Lu, Z. (1987) Cracking the evolutionary puzzle: Jinniushan Man. China Pictorial 1987(4):34–35.

Pope, G.G. (1992) The craniofacial evidence for the emergence of modern humans in China. Yrbk. Phys. Anthropol. 15(Suppl. 35):243–298.

K

Kabwe

Zambian site of the Broken Hill Mine, in which hominin fossils and Middle Paleolithic remains were exposed by mining operations and uncontrolled excavations between 1921 and 1925. The principal fossil discovery, the well-preserved cranium of an adult, appeared to derive from a deep narrow cave at the base of a dolomite hill, now removed by mining. Other finds, including a parietal, maxilla, humerus, sacrum, two ilia, three femora (of which two are fragmentary), and two tibiae, together with artifacts and fauna, were also collected from Kabwe, but their affinities and stratigraphic relationship to the original cranium are unclear, although fluorine, uranium, and nitrogen analysis suggests that the association may be valid.

The adult cranium exhibits a moderately large cranial capacity of ca. 1,280 ml; a moderately thick, long, and flattened vault; and a massive and pneumatized supraorbital torus. There is a centrally strong occipital torus like those of *Homo erectus* skulls, but the cranium is high with parallel-sided walls. It shows evidence of disease, such as dental caries and abscessing, and perhaps also a tumor in the temporal bone. Although the remainder of the Broken Hill hominin material (maxillary, cranial, femoral, humeral, and pelvic fragments) cannot be directly related to the cranium because of the uncontrolled manner in which the skull was excavated, a modern-looking tibia was closely associated. The postcranial bones, although robust, appear somewhat more modern than those of the Neanderthals, despite the presence of a strong *erectus*-like buttress on one of the pelvic bones. The faunal remains, 25 percent of which represent extinct species, include a short-necked giraffe (*Libytherium olduvaiensis*), a saber-tooth cat (*Machairodus*), an extinct buffalo (*Homoioceros baini*), and an extinct wildebeest (*Connochaetes laticornutus*). A late Middle Pleistocene antiquity for the cranium seems plausible, but the associations of the other material are less certain.

The artifacts from Kabwe were said to lack handaxes, picks, and cleavers, although bifacial tools typical of the Acheulean were recovered from an excavation ca. 170 m

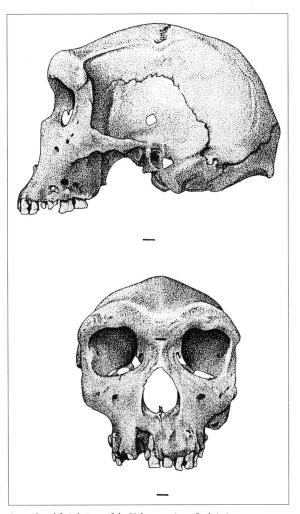

Lateral and facial views of the Kabwe cranium. Scale is 1 cm.

from the original site. This excavation, however, could not be related to the original cave fill sedimentologically or in terms of faunal remains. Although the Kabwe assemblage was placed in the Charaman, an early stage of the Middle Stone Age characterized by *ad hoc* scrapers, it could more likely relate to the Sangoan or even to a facies of the Early Stone Age without bifaces.

See also Archaic Homo sapiens; Homo sapiens; Woodward, [Sir] Arthur Smith. [C.B.S., J.J.S., A.S.B.]

Kafuan

Purported ancient split-pebble industry of sub-Saharan Africa defined by E.J. Wayland in 1934 on the basis of rolled material from the Kafu River in western Uganda. It was extended by C. van Riet Lowe to include materials from the Kagera Valley and the lower ferricrete horizon at Nsongezi, both in Uganda, as well as a supposed pluvial interval represented by the gravels incorporating these tools. Pluvials or periods of increased rainfall were once thought to be the tropical equivalents of, and synchronous with, glacials. The Kafuan has been shown to be invalid, due to the prevalence of natural fracturing in these water-laden deposits.

See also Early Paleolithic; Early Stone Age; Glaciation; Oldowan. [A.S.B.]

Kaitio Member

Plio-Pleistocene member of the Nachukui Formation, western Turkana Basin, Kenya. It consists of lake margin deposits above the KBS Tuff (1.9 Ma) and below the Lower Koobi Fora Tuff (1.6 Ma) in that area, equivalent to the KBS Member of the Koobi Fora Formation and to Members H and J of the Shungura Formation in southern Ethiopia.

See also Turkana Basin. [F.H.B.]

Kalambo Falls

Open-air stratified Pleistocene site in Zambia near the border with Tanzania close to the southeastern shore of Lake Tanganyika, with archaeological materials ranging in age, on comparative typological and faunal grounds, from probable Middle Pleistocene to Recent. The site, excavated by J.D. Clark between 1953 and 1966, yielded an unusually complete sequence of African Paleolithic industries, beginning with the Acheulean and continuing through industries with Sangoan (Chipeta), Lupemban, and Lupembo-Tshitolian (Polungu) affinities to a local microlithic Epipaleolithic culture (Kaposwa, ca. 4 Ka), followed by Iron Age horizons. At Kalambo Falls, the Sangoan and Lupemban horizons, which are among the very few stratified *in situ* occurrences of these industries, are both characterized by a wide range of small- and medium-size scrapers, as well as the core axes typical of these industries. Exceptional preservation of organic materials resulted in the recovery of roughly modified and fire-hardened wooden implements from the earliest Acheulean horizons. Radiocarbon dates on wood and charcoal of greater than 60 Ka for the Acheulean and 46–36 Ka for the Sangoan probably indicate ages for these industries that are beyond the range of this technique, rather than cultural conservatism.

See also Acheulean; Africa; Clark, J. Desmond; Early Stone Age; Iron Age; Later Stone Age; Lupemban; Middle Stone Age; Sangoan; Second Intermediate. [A.S.B.]

Kalochoro Member

Upper Pliocene member of the Nachukui Formation, western Turkana Basin, Kenya. It consists of fluvial and lacustrine beds above the Kalochoro Tuff (2.35 Ma) and below the KBS Tuff (1.9 Ma), equivalent to Members F, G, and lower H of the Shungura Formation in southern Ethiopia, and part of the upper Burgi Member of the Koobi Fora Formation of East Turkana.

See also Turkana Basin. [F.H.B.]

Kalodirr

Northern Kenya site, in Lower Miocene sandstones and tuffs of the Lothidok Formation, exposed in hills above the southwestern shore of Lake Turkana. There are numerous localities in three main exposures, in strata ranging between the 17.5 Ma Kalodirr Tuff up to a few meters above the 16.8 Ma Naserte Tuff. Localities at Moruorot (or Muruarot) Hill were first reported by C. Arambourg in 1943, and more extensive exposures in the same strata were later discovered on the Kalodirr and Kanukurinya streams to the northwest. The Kalodirr localities provide the type specimens of *Turkanapithecus kalakolensis*, *Afropithecus turkanensis*, and *Simiolus enjessei* in a context of fossil mammals closely similar to assemblages from paleo-lowland coastal sites in the Lower Miocene of Libya, Egypt, Israel, and Saudi Arabia, as well as from other Turkana Basin sites dated to this age range. Although Kalodirr also yields the northernmost example of *Proconsul africanus*, there is much less similarity to coeval paleo-highlands faunas from equatorial Kenya. In the upper Lothidok Formation, a middle Miocene fauna with *Kenyapithecus wickeri* and other primates has been recovered from Esha and Atirr localities in the Kalatum Member, dated between 13.8–12.2 Ma.

See also Africa, East; Afropithecus; Dendropithecus-Group; Kenyapithecus; Lothidok; Miocene; Proconsulidae; Turkana Basin. [J.A.V.C.]

Further readings

Boschetto, H.B., Brown, F.H., and McDougall, I., (1992) Stratigraphy of the Lothidok Range, northern Kenya, and K/Ar ages of its Miocene primates. J. Hum. Evol., 22:47–72.

Kanam

Western Kenya stratified sequence, with a lower unit of Late Miocene age, ca. 6 Ma, and an upper unit of Early Pliocene age, ca. 4.5 Ma, determined by potassium-argon (K/Ar) dating and faunal analysis.

Fossils at Kanam, on the shore of the Winam Gulf of Lake Victoria at the foot of Homa volcano, were discovered by the British geologist F. Oswald on his way out from investigations of Early Miocene fossils at Karungu in 1910. During L.S.B. Leakey's 1931–1932 expedition to eastern Africa, an assemblage of Mio-Pliocene mammals was collected here, together with a fragmentary hominin mandible of modern aspect that Leakey maintained had been found *in situ* with the rest. Leakey's team also discovered human cranial remains together with Middle Pleistocene mammals at the nearby Kanjera site. Together, these human fossils were used by Leakey to support an argument that the human line had an extremely ancient beginning and that such forms as *Australopithecus* and even *Homo erectus* were merely side branches.

Leakey's announcement of the new "*Homo kanamensis*" became the object of controversy because of its modern appearance and ancient date. Doubt was raised almost immediately by geologists who visited the site and reported that the context of the jaw could not be confirmed, but Leakey clung to this interpretation throughout his career. Work in the 1980s eventually documented the complexity of the slumped and faulted stratigraphy at Kanam, with the older faunal elements correlative to the Upper Miocene levels in the Lake Albert (Mobutu) Basin and the lower part of the Lothagam section, while the younger fauna matches best to Kanapoi in the southern Turkana Basin, Fejej Level 3, and Kuseralee in the Middle Awash. It is now widely concluded that the original Kanam mandible was probably washed in, like other Late Pleistocene mammal specimens picked up in the Kanam gullies, from Upper Pleistocene lake terrace beds overlying the Kanam sequence.

See also Africa, East; Fejej; Kanapoi; Kanjera; Leakey, Louis Seymour Bazett; Lothagam; Turkana Basin. [T.D.W.]

Further Readings

Pickford, M. (1987) The geology and palaeontology of the Kanam Erosion Gullies (Kenya). Mainzer Geowiss. Mitt. 16:209–226.

Reader, J. (1981) Missing Links. New York: Little, Brown.

Kanapoi

Lower Pliocene stratified sequence in Kenya ca. 100 km southwest of Lake Turkana, dated to between 4.16 and 4.05 Ma according to $^{39}Ar/^{40}Ar$ dating of associated basalts. The site, discovered in the 1960s by a Harvard University team headed by Bryan Patterson, consists of ca. 70 m of sediments yielding a Lower Pliocene mammalian fauna decidedly more evolved than that of Lothagam. Hominid remains from the site include an adult distal humerus collected by Patterson and a partial tibia and many jaws recovered by M.G. Leakey and colleagues. These fossils, in conjunction with other remains from the lowest part of the Koobi Fora sequence, have been recognized as a new taxon, *Australopithecus anamensis*, the oldest unquestioned hominin to date.

See also Australopithecus; Australopithecus anamensis; Lothagam; Patterson, Bryan; Turkana Basin. [T.D.W.]

Further Readings

Leakey, M.G., Feibel, C.S., McDougall, I., Ward, C., and Walker, A. (1995). New specimens and confirmation of an early age for *Australopithecus anamensis*. Nature 393:62–66.

Kanjera

Hominid and fossil mammal site, Early Pleistocene to Holocene in age, at the foot of Homa volcano on the south shore of Winam Gulf in western Kenya. This open site consists of a web of gullies cutting through fluvial, shallow lacustrine, and volcaniclastic sediments laid down, for the most part, prior to the formation of the modern Lake Victoria. Kanjera and adjacent Kanam were discovered by F. Oswald in 1911 on his return from mapping the Miocene beds at Karungu. Research on Kanam and Kanjera by L.S.B. Leakey held a controversial place in studies of human evolution and Quaternary stratigraphy from the 1930s to the 1950s. Fossilized hominin remains and early-to-middle Pleistocene fauna, handaxes, and simple cores were discovered in 1931–1932, leading Leakey to posit that hominins of modern appearance were of great antiquity. In addition, Leakey's Kanjeran Pluvial was based on the supposition that these beds represented a greatly enlarged Lake Victoria. Although several fragments of Kanjera Hominid 3 were believed to be *in situ*, stratigraphic provenance of the finds was never certain, and study of the entire sample collected through the 1980s shows that the hominin remains cannot be distinguished from anatomically modern humans. Based on recent excavations and geochemical study of the fossils since 1980, it now appears that the hominin sample comes largely from the sub-Recent terrace, ca. 3 m above the modern lake level, that rims the shoreline of Lake Victoria. Most of the faunal sample, however, comes from five fossiliferous beds, into which the terrace was cut, that span from ca. 1.8 (in isolated southern exposures) to 1.5 to 0.7 Ma in the main exposures. The type specimen of the extinct giant gelada *Theropithecus oswaldi* (a female cranium that Oswald deposited at the British Museum) is part of an unusual concentration of fossils of this species in an outcrop dated to ca. 1.3–1.0 Ma.

See also Africa, East; Cercopithecinae; Homo sapiens; Kanam; Leakey, Louis Seymour Bazett; Pluvials. [R.P.]

Further Readings

Behrensmeyer, A.K., Potts, R., Plummer, T., Tauxe, L., and Opdyke, N. (1995) The Pleistocene locality of Kanjera, Western Kenya: Stratigraphy, chronology, and palaeoenvironments. J. Hum. Evol. 29:247–274.

Kapthurin

Geological formation in the Tugen Hills west of Lake Baringo (Kenya) of Middle Pleistocene age. Fossilized bones and stone artifacts occur at a series of open sites in fluviolacustrine deposits dated ca. 780–240 Ka. The middle part of the Kapthurin Formation yielded two hominin mandibles and postcranial material (discovered 1966 and 1983), referred to "archaic *Homo sapiens*" (previously termed *Homo erectus*). The hominins are associated with Acheulean tools, including prepared cores, very early prismatic blade cores, and large blades at a higher stratigraphic level, but still before 240 Ka. Tools in the upper part of the formation may represent the youngest recorded Acheulean occurrences in East Africa.

See also Acheulean; Africa, East; Archaic Homo sapiens; Baringo Basin/Tugen Hills; Homo erectus; Prepared-Core. [R.P.]

Karain

A cave site in western Turkey preserving a deep sequence of Middle Paleolithic industries. The uppermost levels contain hearths and a regional variant of the Mousterian utilizing the Levallois technique. The lower levels feature thicker flakes struck without the use of the Levallois technique. These industries are separated by a calcite deposit dating to ca. 120 Ka.

See also Asia, Western; Levallois; Middle Paleolithic; Mousterian. [J.J.S.]

Karari

An escarpment east of Lake Turkana (Kenya) preserving stone-tool assemblages characterized by large core scrapers and assigned to the Karari industry, of Early Pleistocene age. Despite the unique presence of large scrapers, the Karari industry is otherwise similar to Oldowan and Developed Oldowan lithic assemblages of East Africa. Karari sites are concentrated within channel gravels and floodplain silts in the lower portion of the Okote Member of the Koobi Fora Formation, dated to ca. 1.6 Ma. Artifacts and fauna from these sites indicate transport and curation of stone by hominids and the use of lithic tools primarily of basalt in cutting meat, bone, and plant material. Acheulean sites are relatively rare on the escarpment.

See also Acheulean; Africa, East; Early Paleolithic; Isaac, Glynn Llywelyn; Oldowan; Scraper, Turkana Basin. [R.P.]

Kataboi Member

Lower Pliocene fluvial and lacustrine member of Nanchukui Formation, western Turkana Basin, Kenya. It occupies the interval between Moiti (3.9 Ma) and Tulu Bor (3.4 Ma) tuffs, equivalent to the Moiti and Lokochot Members of the Koobi Fora Formation (Kenya) and to the Basal Member and Member A of the Shungura Formation (southern Ethiopia).

See also Turkana Basin. [F.H.B.]

Katanda

Region on the Upper Semliki River ca. 6 km north of the source at Lake Rutanzige (formerly Lake Edward), which has yielded a series of open-air sites containing superimposed Early and Middle Stone Age horizons in fluvial and colluvial deposits dating to the Middle and early Late Pleistocene. Associated with the Middle Stone Age archaeological horizons at three of these sites is a series of worked bone artifacts including cylindrical points, a flat daggerlike implement, and

barbed bone points with finely grooved bases, presumably for hafting. Numerous fish bones at all three sites suggest that MSA peoples fished for large catfish; the fact that all the fishbones derived from large adults further indicates that this was a seasonally restricted activity which probably coincided with the spawning season. Dating results from five different techniques (TL, OSL, ESR, Uranium series, and amino acid racemization of mollusc shell) suggest that the age is greater than 70–60 Ka, possibly as old as 90 Ka. The Katanda materials thus constitute some of the earliest definitive evidence both for formal bone tools and for deliberate fishing activities.

See also Blombos; Bone Tools; Economy, Prehistoric; Klasies River Mouth; Middle Stone Age; Modern Human Origins. [A.S.B.]

Further Readings

Brooks, A.S., Helgren, D.M., Cramer, J.S., Franklin, A., Hornyak, W., Keating, J.M., Klein, R.G., Rink, W.J., Schwarcz, H., Smith, J.N.L., Stewart, K., Todd, N.E., Verniers, J., and Yellen, J.E. (1995) Dating and context of three Middle Stone Age sites with bone points in the Upper Semliki Valley, Zaire. Science 268:548–553.

Yellen, J.E., Brooks, A.S., Cornelissen, E., Mehlman, M.J., and Stewart, K. (1995) A Middle Stone Age worked bone industry from Katanda, Upper Semliki Valley, Zaire. Science 268:553–556.

KBS Member

Plio-Pleistocene stratigraphic unit in the Koobi Fora exposures on the northeast shore of Lake Turkana, Kenya. The term, from Kay Behrensmeyer Site, was initially used for locality FxJj1, with Oldowan tools. It was subsequently extended to the KBS Tuff, a volcanic-ash layer just below the site, and finally to all of the strata overlying the tuff up to the Okote Tuff. The KBS Tuff was one of the first to be dated at Koobi Fora, but the initially reported age of ca. 2.6 Ma was the basis for controversial proposals to extend the age of *Homo* beyond that of supposedly ancestral australopiths, even though the mammalian fauna of the KBS level was closely comparable with fossils in Shungura Bed H north of Lake Turkana, dated to ca. 1.8 Ma. After an acrimonious period of "dueling data" and repeated analyses, the age of the KBS Tuff was revised to 1.88 ± 0.02 Ma, approximately coeval with the oldest levels in Bed I, Olduvai Gorge, Tanzania, and the age of the overlying Okote Tuff was established at ca. 1.6 Ma.

The KBS Tuff is a widespread volcanic-ash layer 0.1 to 1 m thick over much of the northern half of the Koobi Fora region, and it is now identified with Tuff H-2 in the Shungura sequence and with the Kaitio Tuff of West Turkana as well. In many localities, it is a mixture of light grey and dark brown glass shards, giving it a distinctive salt-and-pepper appearance and making it a useful marker bed in the field. It commonly contains varicolored pumice clasts that are chemically identical to the glass shards and contain alkali feldspars used for age determination.

See also Africa, East; Oldowan; Tephrochronology; Turkana Basin. [F.H.B.]

Further Readings

Brown, F.H. (1994) Development of Pliocene and Pleistocene chronology of the Turkana Basin, East Africa, and its relation to other sites. In R.S. Corruccini and R.L. Ciochon (eds.): Integrative Paths to the Past. Englewood Cliffs, N.J.: Prentice Hall, pp. 285–312.

Kebara

Cave site located near Zikron Ya'acov on the southwestern escarpment of Mount Carmel in Israel. Kebara is a karst-solution cavity excavated since the 1930s that has produced Late Pleistocene fossil hominin specimens. Initial explorations by F. Turville-Petre revealed archaeological sediments, including a new Epipaleolithic industry, the Kebaran, which was named after the site. Excavations were later carried out in the 1950s–1960s by M. Stekelis and in the 1980s by a French-Israeli team.

The Late Paleolithic archaeological Levels of Kebara Cave are (from top to bottom): Natufian (Level B), Kebaran (Level C), Levantine Aurignacian (Level D), and Ahmarian (Level E). Both radiocarbon and thermoluminescence (TL) dating put the beginning of the Middle-Upper Paleolithic transition at Kebara at ca. 45 Ka. The underlying Levantine Mousterian sediments (Level F) date to 62–48 Ka on the basis of TL and electron spin resonance (ESR) techniques. The Mousterian sediments have been deformed by subsidence in the back of the cave.

Earlier excavations produced the remains of a child from Middle Paleolithic levels, but the more extensive recent work has already recovered the most complete trunk skeleton of a Neanderthal yet found. This presumed burial has no cranium, but it does include a massive mandible and a large-bodied skeleton of the entire upper part of the body of an adult male. The well-preserved scapulae and pelvis show the characteristic Neanderthal morphology. The preserved hyoid bone from this fossil has fueled debate about Neanderthal vocal capabilities.

Associated with these Neanderthal fossils are ashy patches (hearths?), numerous remains of gazelle (*Gazella gazella*), fallow deer (*Dama mesopotamica*), wild cattle (*Bos primigenius*), and wild boar (*Sus scrofa*). The Levantine Mousterian lithic industry is similar to that of Tabūn Cave Level B and Amud Level B, with predominatly unidirectional core preparation, numerous points and blades, and relatively few retouched tools. In the uppermost Mousterian levels at Kebara, however, there is a shift to more centripetal core preparation.

See also Ahmarian; Asia, Western; Emiran; Kebaran; Levantine Aurignacian; Natufian; Neanderthals; Speech (Origins of). [J.J.S., C.B.S.]

Further Readings

Bar-Yosef, O., Vandermeersch, B., Arensburg, B., Belfer-Cohen, A., Goldberg, P., Laville, H., Meignen, L., Rak, Y., Tchernov, E., Tillier, A.-M., and Weiner, S. (1992) Excavations in Kebara Cave, Mt. Carmel. Curr. Anthropol. 33:497–550.

Kebaran

Late Paleolithic industry (Neuville Stage VI) of the Levant, defined at Mugharet el-Kebarah on the Mount Carmel ridge in Israel and characterized by microblades and backed bladelets. Sometimes seen as transitional to the Mesolithic Natufian industry, the Kebaran coincides with the terminal Pleistocene, ca. 15–10 Ka. At Jabrud (Syria), variants of this industry, the Skiftian and the Nebekian, were recovered from Shelter III.

See also Asia, Western; Jabrud; Kebara; Late Paleolithic; Mesolithic; Stone-Tool Making. [A.S.B.]

Kedung Brubus

Eastern Java (Indonesia) fossil-collecting area of Middle Pleistocene age, ca. 0.5 Ma. One of E. Dubois's earliest discoveries in 1891 was a *Homo erectus* partial mandible at a site ca. 30 km from Ngawi in the Kendeng Hills. As with most other fossils from eastern Java, the exact provenance of the specimen is unknown. On the basis of mammalian fossils recovered from the exposure assumed to have yielded the mandible, a "Kabuh equivalent" age has been attributed to the specimen, which has been identified as that of a juvenile.

See also Asia, Eastern and Southern; Indonesia. [G.G.P.]

Keilor

A site near Melbourne, Australia, where a partial skeleton was found in 1940. Of gracile type, this individual is similar to those of Lake Mungo (Australia); the cranium was compared to Wadjak by F. Weidenreich, and to Liujiang by A. Thorne.

See also Australia; Lake Mungo. [A.T., J.T.L.]

Keith, [Sir] Arthur (1866–1955)

British anatomist and paleoanthropologist. For much of his career, Keith was conservator of the Museum of the Royal College of Surgeons, London (1907–1933). Prior to his appointment, he had been a demonstrator and lecturer in anatomy at the London Hospital Medical School (1895–1907). Although an earlier sojourn in Thailand (then Siam) in the period 1889–1892 had awakened his interest in the subject of human evolution, it was only after 1908 that he was able to devote himself exclusively to such matters. Largely as a result of his increasing commitment to the notion of the great antiquity of the modern human form, Keith withdrew from his earlier position that the Neanderthals had been the progenitors of modern *Homo sapiens*. Likewise, while accepting the Piltdown skull as a genuine fossil, he did not accept it as a precursor of the human lineage. In his general thinking on evolution, particularly in his later years, Keith emphasized the competition factor in human history and considered racial and national prejudice as inborn. In 1933, because of ill health, Keith gave up his post as conservator and became master of Buckston Browne Farm, the experimental research station of the College of Surgeons at Down in Kent, a post he held until his death.

See also Hooton, Earnest Albert; McCown, Theodore D.; Piltdown. [F.S.]

Kenniff Cave

Archaeological site in Carnarvon Range, Queensland, Australia. Excavated in 1962 by J. Mulvaney, this deposit was the first to demonstrate Pleistocene occupation of the continent. The earliest human presence at the shelter dates to 19 Ka.

See also Australia. [A.T.]

Kent's Cavern

British cave site near Torquay in southern England that contains both Upper Paleolithic and Early Paleolithic levels. The Upper Paleolithic remains from the Cave Earth levels date to 27–12 Ka. Brecciated deposits from the lower levels of the cave contain Acheulean handaxes. W. Pengelly's excavations at Kent's Cavern in the mid-1800s were among the first to reveal stone tools and bones of extinct mammals in sealed stratigraphic contexts. These discoveries were instrumental in establishing the presence of humans in Pleistocene times.

See also Acheulean; Early Paleolithic; Europe; Upper Paleolithic. [J.J.S.]

Kenyapithecinae

A subfamily of Hominidae including a variety of mostly African earlier Miocene fossil apes. For many years, the Miocene great apes, broadly speaking, were included in the subfamily Dryopithecinae, placed either in the Pongidae or the Hominidae, depending upon the viewpoint of the respective author. In 1992, P. Andrews reviewed the evolution and systematics of this group, distinguishing a number of subclades: Afropithecini, Kenyapithecini, and Dryopithecini. These three were interpreted as successively more derived (in a "modern ape" direction), especially based upon incomplete postcranial evidence. They shared hominid dental characters such as relatively enlarged upper premolars and (except for Dryopithecini) rather thick molar enamel, as well as an elbow-joint morphology indicative of greater stability than in earlier catarrhines. Continued reassessment of the relationships among these taxa has led to a modification proposed in this volume.

Dryopithecus is now seen to be probably more derived than the other genera in its postcranium, especially, and it is, therefore, placed in a distinct subfamily: Dryopithecinae may be near the common ancestry of the living Ponginae and Homininae, and several poorly known genera such as *Lufengpithecus* may be placed there tentatively. This isolation of *Dryopithecus* makes it necessary to provide a new name for the subfamily including Afropithecini and Kenyapithecini, and the term *Kenyapithecinae* is used here. All three of these taxa may be paraphyletic, or "horizontal," in nature, but they are diagnosable, and, with greater knowledge of the included

genera, their validity may become more certain. Each of these genera is discussed in the encyclopedia in a separate entry.

Kenyapithecinae
  Afropithecini
    † *Afropithecus*
    † *Heliopithecus*
    ?† *Otavipithecus*
    "† *Kenyapithecus*"
    ? *Morotopithecus*
  Kenyapithecini
    † *Kenyapithecus*
    † *Griphopithecus*
†extinct

See also Africa, East; Africa, Southern; Afropithecus; Asia, Western; Dryopithecinae; Dryopithecus; Griphopithecus; Heliopithecus; Hominidae; Homininae; Hominoidea; Kenyapithecus; Miocene; Morotopithecus; Otavipithecus; Proconsulidae. [E.D., P.A.]

Further Readings

Andrews, P. (1992) Evolution and environment in the Hominoidea. Nature 360:641–646.
Begun, D.R. (1994) Relations among the great apes and humans: New interpretations based on the fossil great ape *Dryopithecus*. Yrbk. Phys. Anthropol. 37:11–63.

Kenyapithecus

Middle Miocene Kenyan fossil hominoid. *Kenyapithecus* is definitively known only from Fort Ternan (14 Ma), but specimens from Maboko Island (15 Ma) and new collections from Nachola and Kipsaramon (ca. 15 Ma) in northern and central Kenya, respectively, have also been grouped in this genus by many authors. The genus was originally described by L.S.B. Leakey, who named the specimens from Fort Ternan *Kenyapithecus wickeri*. A previously described fossil from Maboko was later assigned by Leakey to this genus as a separate species, *K. africanus*. There is some doubt now as to the relationships of these species, for while *K. africanus* is very similar to the slightly earlier *Afropithecus* in its enlarged premolars, *K. wickeri* appears to be distinct. The Nachola specimens also appear to group with the afropithecins, and it is proposed that these specimens, together with those from Maboko, be placed in the tribe Afropithecini. A consequence of this is that *Kenyapithecus* proper from Fort Ternan should be distinguished by separate tribe identity, as Kenyapithecini.

Kenyapithecus was a small-to-medium-size hominoid primate, related to the great apes and postdating the divergence of the gibbons. It had robust jaws that, together with the thick enamel of its teeth, suggest a specialized diet. Its limb bones were more lightly built than those of *Dryopithecus*, but more modern than those of earlier African forms.

See also Africa, East; Ape; Baringo Basin/Tugen Hills; Dryopithecus; Fort Ternan; Griphopithecus; Hominidae; Hominoidea; Kenyapithecinae; Maboko; Miocene; Nachola; Teeth. [P.A.]

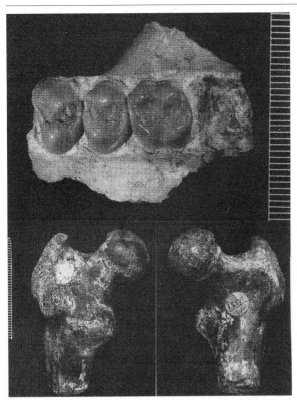

Occlusal view of upper jaw and anterior (right) and posterior views of a left femur of "Kenyapithecus" africanus from Middle Miocene deposits on Maboko Island (Kenya). Courtesy of P. Andrews.

Further Readings

Benefit, B.R., and McCrossin, M.L. (1995) Miocene hominoids and hominid origins. Ann. Rev. Anthropol. 24:237–256.

Martin, L., and Andrews, P. (1993) Species recognition in Middle Miocene hominoids. In W.H. Kimbel and L. Martin (eds.): Species, Species Concepts, and Primate Evolution. New York: Plenum, pp. 393–427.

Nakatsukasa, M., Yamanaka, A., Kunimatsu, Y., Shimizu, D., and Ishida, H. (1998) A newly discovered *Kenyapithecus* skeleton and its implications for the evolution of positional behavior in Miocene East African hominoids. J. Hum. Evol. 34:657–664.

Kenyon, Dame Kathleen (1906–1978)

British archaeologist. Trained in the field by G. Caton-Thompson and Sir M. Wheeler, she was highly regarded for her careful field methodology. She directed excavations in North Africa (Sabratha) and England during the 1930s and 1940s, but she is best known for her work at Jericho (1952–1958), where she uncovered a substantial Early Neolithic (ca. 10.3–8 Ka) settlement with tall encircling walls and towers, plastered human skulls, and evidence of long-distance obsidian trade, below later occupations. She also excavated in Jerusalem (1961–1967), helping establish the plans of the successive stages of the city. She maintained a long association (1935–1962) with the Institute of Archaeology, University of London, serving as secretary and later as lecturer in Palestinian archaeology; from 1962 to 1973, she was principal of St. Hugh's College, Oxford. She is the author of many books, among them *Digging Up Jericho* (1957), *Archaeology in the Holy Land* (1960), and *Excavations at Jericho*, vols. 1 (1960) and 2 (1964).

See also Asia, Western; Jericho; Neolithic. [N.B.]

Kibish

Three sites in the area of the Kibish tributary of the Omo River (Ethiopia) that produced hominin fossils in 1967. The most important specimens are an archaic and robustly built skull (Omo 2), lacking the face found on the surface, and a more fragmentary anatomically modern skull with associated partial skeleton (Omo 1). If both are correctly associated with Member 1 of the Kibish Formation, then they may date to ca. 130–100 Ka, but this date is still somewhat problematic. The morphological differences between Omo 1 and 2 are so great that they probably do not represent a single population. The archaeological associations for these fossils are indeterminate.

See also Archaic Moderns. [C.B.S., J.J.S.]

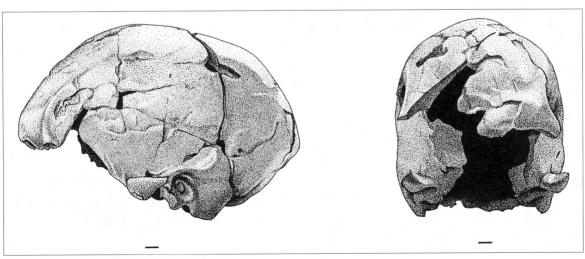

Lateral and frontal view of the Kibish 2 calotte. Scale is 1 cm.

Kirkbride, Diana

British archaeologist. In the 1960s, she discovered and excavated the Early Neolithic site of Beidha (ca. 10–8 Ka) in southern Jordan, exposing more than 2,000 m² and revealing four successive architectural stages, from small round structures to substantial, rectilinear multiroomed houses. In the 1970s, she excavated the Late Neolithic site of Umm Dabaghiyah (ca. 8 Ka) in northern Iraq, unearthing 12 levels, some of which revealed extensive wild onager hunting and hide processing activities, probably for trade with other localities.

See also Asia, Western; Beidha; Neolithic. [N.B.]

Klasies River Mouth

Coastal cave complex in South Africa that contains an early Late Pleistocene archaeological sequence and fossil hominin remains. Klasies is important because it appears to provide evidence for early-modern humans by 120 Ka and precursors of Late Paleolithic technology by 70 Ka, although the dating of this evidence remains controversial. The archaeological succession begins with a long sequence of flake-based Middle Paleolithic (African Middle Stone Age, MSA) levels, followed by levels of the Howieson's Poort blade-based industry. Flake-based MSA assemblages again overlie the Howieson's Poort in Rockshelter 1a. After a stratigraphic break, Later Stone Age deposits (chiefly a large shell midden) cap the Klasies sequence. Hominin specimens occur throughout the Klasies sequence, but assessments of their morphological affinities vary widely. Most are fragmentary and show clear variation, but some are indistinguishable in the form of the supraorbital torus and mandible from those of living humans. Shells from MSA levels provide early evidence for the exploitation of littoral resources. R. Klein's analysis (1976) of faunal remains from Klasies suggests a major increase in the effectiveness of hunting strategies with the appearance of Late Stone Age occupations. A second analysis of MSA faunal remains from Klasies, by L. Binford, suggests a prominent role for scavenging in hominid meat procurement.

See also Africa; Africa, Southern; Archaic Moderns; Howieson's Poort; Middle Paleolithic; Middle Stone Age; Modern Human Origins. [J.J.S., C.B.S.]

Further Readings

Binford, L.R. (1984) Faunal remains from Klasies River Mouth. New York. Academic Press.

Deacon, H.J., and Geleijnse, V.B. (1988) The stratigraphy and sedimentology of the Main Site sequence, Klasies River, South Africa. S. Afr. Archaeol. Bull. 43:5–14.

Klein, R.G. (1976) The mammalian fauna of the Klasies River mouth sites, southern Cape Province, South Africa. S. Afr. Archaeol. Bull. 31:75–98.

Singer, R., and Wymer, J. (1982) The Middle Stone Age at Klasies River Mouth in South Africa. Chicago: University of Chicago Press.

Koenigswald, Gustav Heinrich Ralph von (1902–1982)

Dutch (b. Germany) paleoanthropologist. From 1928 to 1930, von Koenigswald was an assistant curator at the Munich Geological Museum. After joining the Geological Survey of the Dutch East Indies, he discovered the remains of a number of fossil hominins in Java, including some of the Ngandong calvariae in 1933, the first Sangiran calvaria in 1937 (Pithecanthropus 11 = *Homo erectus*), and the *Meganthropus* mandibular fragments (also from Sangiran) in 1939. He also described four molars, attributed to *Gigantopithecus*, which he purchased between 1935 and 1939 in Hong Kong and Canton. When the Japanese occupied Java during World War II, von Koenigswald was imprisoned. After the war, he remained in Java until 1948, when he was appointed professor at the State University of Utrecht. He concluded his career as curator of paleoanthropology at the Senckenberg Museum, Frankfurt am Main.

See also Dragon Bones (and Teeth); Gigantopithecus; Homo erectus; Meganthropus; Ngandong (Solo); Sangiran Dome; Weidenreich, Franz. [F.S.]

Konso

Upper Pliocene to Lower Pleistocene group of sites (previously known as Konso-Gardula) in the southern extremity of the main Ethiopian rift valley, discovered in October 1991. Abundant fossil remains and artifacts occur throughout the sequence, spanning the time range between 1.9 and 1.3 Ma according to ^{40}Ar-^{39}Ar dating of interbedded tuffs; most material comes from levels dated ca. 1.9 and 1.4 Ma. Archaeological material from the lower horizon may include Oldowan assemblages, while artifacts from the upper level are assignable to early Acheulean, one of the oldest dated assemblages of this industry. Human remains from the upper horizon include a mandible attributed to early *Homo erectus* and a partial cranium and mandible (along with less complete remains) of a distinctive variety of *Australopithecus* (=*Paranthropus*) *boisei*.

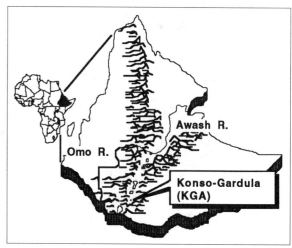

Map showing placement of the Konso paleoanthropological study area in the southern part of the main Ethiopian Rift. Courtesy of Tim D. White.

See also Acheulean; Afar Basin; Africa, East; Homo erectus; Paranthropus Boisei; Rift Valley. [G.S., T.D.W.]

Further Readings
Asfaw, B., Beyene, Y., Suwa, G., Walter, R.C., White, T.D., WoldeGabriel, G., and Yemane, T. (1992). The earliest Acheulean from Konso-Gardula. Nature 360:732–735.
Suwa, G., Asfaw, B., Beyene, Y., White, T.D., Katoh, S., Nagaoka, S., Nakaya, H., Uzawa, K., Renne, P., and WoldeGabriel, G. (1997) The first skull of Australopithecus boisei. Nature 389:489–492

Koonalda Cave

Huge limestone cave under the Nullabor Plain in southern Australia, entered by Aboriginal people as early as 25 Ka to mine for flint. Dating of burnt and discarded torches, bundles of saltbush twigs, indicates that artists were creating *macaroni* (meandering finger impressions) in soft cave walls more than 24 Ka.

See also Australia. [A.T.]

Koru

Locality in western Kenya exposing several levels of Early Miocene age, ca. 23–20 Ma according to potassium-argon (K/Ar) dating of pyroclastic biotite. Discovered in 1909 by a gold prospector, Koru was the first Miocene site found in Africa, only a year before fossils of the same age were discovered in the Namib diamond fields. Rich concentrations of fossil bone, mostly forest-adapted small to medium-size mammals, occur in red clays and silts sandwiched between hyperalkaline alnoitic (melilite-nephelinite) tuffs and flows of the Legetet Formation on Legetet Hill. Numerous specimens have also been found in red paleosols developed on underlying carbonatite volcanics of the Koru Formation. Early finds were natural exposures of Legetet Formation (Koru Red Beds, Maize Crib, Gordon's Farm), but others (Koru Lime sites) have developed as a result of quarrying in the carbonatites. The lowest level in this sequence, at Meswa Bridge near Muhoroni ca. 5 km from Legetet, is in sediments buried by a local carbonatite vent. Songhor, and the neighboring Chamtwara Beds, are probably correlative to the Legetet Formation. Koru is the type site of *Proconsul africanus, Xenopithecus koruensis,* and *Limnopithecus legetet* and also has yielded numerous important specimens of *Proconsul major, Micropithecus clarki,* and *Dendropithecus macinnesi.*

See also Africa, East; Leakey, Louis Seymour Bazett; Napak; Proconsulidae; Songhor. [J.A.V.C.]

Further Readings
Andrews, P.J. (1978) A revision of the Miocene hominoidea of East Africa. Br. Mus. (Nat. Hist.) Bull. Geol. ser. 30(2):85–224.
Harrison, T.E. (1981) New finds of small fossil apes from the Miocene locality at Koru in Kenya. J. Hum. Evol. 10(2):129–137.

Pickford, M.H., and Andrews, P.J. (1981) The Tinderet Miocene sequence in Kenya. J. Hum. Evol. 10:13–33.

Kostenki

Rich Late Paleolithic culture region on the River Don ca. 35 km south of the city of Voronezh (Russia). Some 25 single and multilayered open-air sites assigned to the related Gorodtsovskaya, Kostenki-Avdeevo, Kostenki-Borschevo, and Streletskaya industries are found in loesslike loam, humic beds, and colluvium (slope wash) along a 10-km stretch of the Don. They are situated at the river's edge, on two old river terraces, as well as at the edge of the interfleuve plateau up to 2 km away from the river.

The sites have produced rich and diverse inventories of stone and bone tools, portable figurative art including ivory "venus" figurines, animal figurines carved of bone and stone, and fragmentary remains of fired clay. Numerous complex features at the sites include pits and hearths. The alignment of these at some sites (e.g., Kostenki I-1, I-2, and IV) was traditionally interpreted as evidence for remains of rectangular longhouses measuring up to 35 m by 15 m. Subsequent research suggests that all of these features were not a part of a single dwelling but represent a number of occupational sequences at the sites. Other sites (Kostenki II, XI) contain remains of small round or oval mammoth-bone dwellings. Human burials have been found at Kostenki II, XIV, XV, and XVII. Occupation of the sites spans a period from ca. 36 to 11 Ka.

See also Europe; Gravettian; Late Paleolithic; Mezhirich; Rogachev, Aleksandr Nikolaevich; Russia; Sungir; Upper Paleolithic. [O.S.]

Further Readings
Klein, R.G. (1969) Man and Culture in the Late Pleistocene: A Case Study. San Francisco: Chandler.

Kota Tampan

Controversial localities in Perak district, northern Malaysia, proposed since the 1930s as one of Southeast Asia's earliest archaeological occurrences; the Tampanian industry. Reinvestigations of sites in the Kota Tampan area in the 1980s suggest that, while many are indeed Pleistocene workshops, none can be demonstrated to be older than ca. 31 Ka. No hominid fossils have been recovered from the Kota Tampan localities.

See also Pacitanian. [J.W.O.]

Further Readings
Majid, Z., and Tjia, H.D. (1988) Kota Tampan, Perak: The geological and archaeological evidence for a Late Pleistocene site. J. Malay. Br. Royal Asiatic Soc. 61:105, 123–134.

Kow Swamp

Site in northern Victoria, Australia, where an extensive burial area was excavated by A.G. Thorne in the period 1968–1972. Possibly reburied since, the remains of more than 50 individual humans are dated to 14.5–3 Ka. The Cohuna cranium, dated at ca. 14.5 Ka, was collected at the swamp much earlier, in 1925. Remains from these sites, and from Mossgiel, Coobool Creek, and the Willandra Lakes in New South Wales and Cossack in western Australia, show the morphology first described by German anatomist F. Weidenreich in 1945 as evidence of a link with the Pleistocene remains from Ngandong (Solo) in Java. Relative to other Pleistocene and contemporary populations, the Kow Swamp skeletal materials are distinguished by pronounced robusticity and thickening. The crania are of low dolichocephalic form, with flat foreheads, pronounced browridge development, and large prognathic faces. The contrast with the gracile remains, especially from Keilor, King Island, and the Willandra Lakes, has been interpreted as evidence that Australia's first migrants came from both Indonesia (robust) and East Asia (gracile) in a process that began at more than 60 Ka.

See also Australia; Lake Mungo; Modern Human Origins. [A.T., J.T.L.]

Krapina

Cave site in Croatia, excavated between 1899 and 1909 by D. Gorjanović-Kramberger, that produced a large number of fragmentary remains of adult and juvenile Neanderthals. Nine layers are numbered from the bottom up, with most of the human deriving from Layers 3 to 8. Biostratigraphic analysis has suggested that this site dates to the early part of the Würm Glaciation or the preceding interglacial. New electron spin resonance (ESR) and uranium-series dates combine to place at least Layers 1–6 (and perhaps 7–8 as well) ca. 130 Ka, thus early in the interglacial. The Mousterian lithic industry associated with these remains appears to be similar to the Quina variant of the French Mousterian, featuring large flakes that have been steeply and invasively retouched. The hominin fossil sample is characterized by a high incidence of taurodontism in the molar teeth (roots are undivided with expanded pulp cavities). The material includes several partial skulls, one of which has an associated facial skeleton, and many postcranial bones of robust morphology. Earlier researchers attributed the burning and fragmentation of the Krapina remains to cannibalism, or even to warfare with early anatomically modern humans, but it now seems more likely that this damage resulted from the disturbance of earlier burials by subsequent occupations. Defleshing and secondary burial may also have occurred at this site. Some authors continue to suggest that some cranial remains from Layer 8 may indicate more anatomically modern morphology.

See also Mousterian; Neanderthals. [J.J.S., C.B.S.]

Further Readings

Radovčić, J., Smith, F.H., Trinkaus, E., and Wolpoff, M. (1988) The Krapina Hominids: An Illustrated Catalog of the Skeletal Collection. Zagreb: Mladost.

Rink, W.J., Schwarcz, H.P., Smith, F.H., and Radovčić, J. (1995) ESR ages for Krapina hominids. Nature 378:24.

Kromdraai

South African stratified cave breccia site of Late Pliocene or Early Pleistocene age. Fossiliferous deposits in dolomitic limestone are located south of the Bloubank River ca. 3.6 km east-northeast of the site of Sterkfontein at 25°59′S and 27°47′E in Transvaal Province. The site consists of two elongate and narrow surface exposures of breccia ca. 9–10 m apart at their closest, known as Kromdraai A (the Faunal Site) and Kromdraai B (the Hominid Site). Kromdraai B consists of eastern (KBE) and western (KBW) breccia deposits, separated by a rib of dolomite bedrock. Five sedimentary units have been recognized in KBE, the third of which has yielded all of the hominin fossils thus far recovered from the Kromdraai localities. Three breccia units are recognizable at KBW, and it is uncertain how these relate to the KBE members, if at all.

The first hominin specimen from this site, in 1938, was described by South African paleontologist R. Broom as a

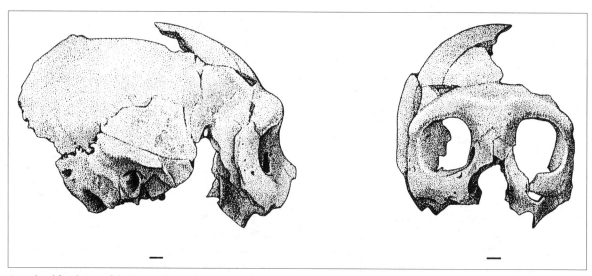

Lateral and facial views of the Krapina C partial cranium. Scale is 1 cm.

new genus and species, *Paranthropus robustus*. Excavations since then have yielded 13 additional specimens attributable to this "robust" australopith. At least one unquestionable lithic artifact, a chert flake, has been recovered from Kromdraai B. Interpretations of KBE paleoecology suggest that the breccias were accumulated at a time when rainfall was higher, and dense woodland more widespread, than in historical times. The faunal assemblages from Kromdraai A and B are not contemporaneous, and the age of the KBE hominin specimens is difficult to ascertain, since most of the time-diagnostic mammal species from KBE do not derive from Member 3. While there seems to be universal agreement that KBE Member 3 postdates Sterkfontein Member 4 and is, thus, younger than 2.5 Ma, its chronological relationship to the Swartkrans australopith-bearing breccias, which date between ca. 1.8 and 1.5 Ma, is not well established.

See also Breccia Cave Formation; Paranthropus; Sterkfontein; Swartkrans. [F.E.G.]

Further Readings
Grine, F.E. (1982) A new juvenile hominid (Mammalia; Primates) from Member 3, Kromdraai Formation, Transvaal, South Africa. Ann. Transvaal Mus. 33:165–239.

Vrba, E.S. (1981) The Kromdraai australopithecine site revisited in 1980: Recent investigations and results. Ann. Transvaal Mus. 33:17–60.

Ksar 'Akil

Lebanese rockshelter site near Beirut. Ksar 'Akil was excavated by J.F. Ewing in the 1930s and by J. Tixier in the early 1970s. This site contains a long (23-m) sequence of Late Pleistocene deposits, including the following industries: Epipaleolithic Kebaran (Levels I–VI), a complex (interstratified?) sequence of Upper Paleolithic Aurignacian and Ahmarian industries (Levels VI–XX), a Middle-Upper Paleolithic transitional industry (Levels XXI–XXV), and a Mousterian industry (Levels XXVI–XXXVII). The sequence of Middle and Upper Paleolithic industries at Ksar 'Akil has been used as a model for the Upper Paleolithic cultural succession in the Levant. Ksar 'Akil is especially important for the information it provides about the Middle-Upper Paleolithic transition in Southwest Asia and chronological change within the Upper Paleolithic. Radiocarbon dates from Ksar 'Akil suggest the Middle-Upper Paleolithic transition occurred at that site between 44 and 33 Ka. Hominin fossil remains from Ksar 'Akil were lost during World War II. These included a maxilla that was recovered from Level XXV and a reported burial of a juvenile ("Egbert") that was excavated from Level XVII.

See also Asia, Western; Late Paleolithic; Middle Paleolithic Mousterian; Upper Paleolithic. [J.J.S.]

Further Readings
Azoury, I. (1986) Ksar Akil, Lebanon: A Technological and Typological Analysis of the Transitional and Early Upper Paleolithic Levels of Ksar Akil and Abu Halka I, Levels XXV–XXXII. BAR International Series 289. Oxford: Archaeopress.

Bergman, C.C. (1987) Ksar Akil: A Technological and Typological Analysis of Later Paleolithic Levels of Ksar Akil II: Levels XIII–XVI. BAR International Series 329. Oxford: Archaeopress.

Ewing, J.F. (1963) A probable Neanderthaloid from Ksar Akil, Lebanon. Am. J. Phys. Anthropol. 21(2):101–104.

L

L'Escale

Cave in the Durance Valley of southeastern France (also known as St. Esteve Janson) with mid-Middle Pleistocene (Upper Biharian) fauna. The absence of *Equus stenonis* and *Elephas meridionalis* suggests a probable age of ca. 0.6–0.4 Ma. Although no archaeological industry was recovered, a thick ash layer was originally interpreted as the earliest evidence of anthropogenic fire in Europe but could well represent remains of naturally caused fires.

See also Europe; Fire. [A.S.B.]

L'Hortus

Middle Paleolithic cave site in southern France (north of Montpellier) excavated in the early 1960s. L'Hortus preserves early Late Pleistocene Neanderthal cranial and postcranial remains accounting for a minimum of 20 individuals (14 children and 35 adults). The lithic industry is a regional variant of the French Typical Mousterian. Spatially restricted concentrations of hearths, stone tools, and faunal remains at L'Hortus have been interpreted as signs of seasonal occupations.

See also Europe; Middle Paleolithic; Mousterian; Neanderthal; Ritual. [J.J.S.]

La Brea Tar Pits

Late Pleistocene and Holocene tar seeps at Rancho La Brea, Los Angeles, California. Incredibly abundant samples have been recovered, representing more than 565 species of plants, reptiles, birds, and mammals, from levels between 40 and 4 Ka. A single human skeleton, La Brea Woman, was recovered from one of the youngest layers.

See also Americas. [L.F.M.]

La Chaise

The La Chaise sites of Abri Bourgeois-Delaunay and Le Suard (Charente, France) have produced a number of hominid specimens associated with Mousterian and Late Acheulean assemblages. The skeletal material includes a calotte from Le Suard and both facial and parietal fragments of the same skull and a femoral diaphysis from Mousterian levels of Bourgeois-Delaunay. Both sets of fossils have Neanderthal affinities. Absolute dates for Bourgeois-Delaunay are: Level 7 = 114–71 Ka, Level 11 = 146–112 Ka. The hominid-bearing Level 51 of Le Suard dates between 151 and 126 Ka and is associated with an Acheulean industry.

See also Acheulean; Europe; Mousterian; Neanderthals. [J.J.S., C.B.S.]

La Chapelle-aux-Saints

Cave in France that in 1908 produced one of the most famous Neanderthal fossils, that of the Old Man of La Chapelle-aux-Saints. This fairly complete skeleton was studied by M. Boule in a series of monographs that greatly influenced paleoanthropological opinion about the Neanderthals for many years. The skeleton itself lay in a shallow depression in the marly basal sediments of the cave. The archaeological levels above the skeleton contain Mousterian artifacts and fauna indicating a cold climate, such as woolly rhinoceros, reindeer, ibex, bison, marmot, and cave hyaena. Dating of these levels places the site at ca. 60 Ka.

See also Boule [Pierre] Marcellin; Europe; Mousterian; Neanderthals. [C.B.S., J.J.S.]

Further Readings

Boule, M. (1911–1913). L'homme fossile de la Chapelle-aux-Saints. Annales de Paléontologie (1911)6:1–64; (1912)7:65–208; (1913)8:209–279.

La Cotte de St. Brelade

A late Middle to early Late Pleistocene rockshelter site on Jersey (British Channel Islands). Excavated since the early 1900s, the site preserves numerous archaeological levels dating to oxygen-isotope Stages 5 and 6 (ca. 200–75 Ka). Several levels contain dense concentrations of mammoth and

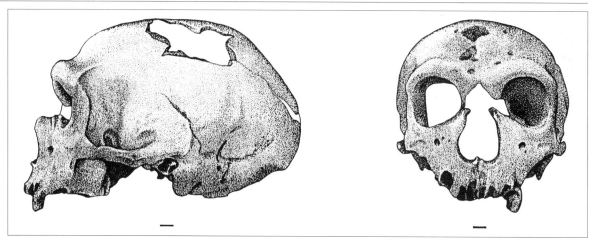

Lateral and facial views of the La Chapelle cranium. Scales are 1 cm.

rhinoceros bones together with stone tools. These concentrations have been interpreted as evidence of intercept hunting by driving herd groups over the steep cliffs. A partial set of Neanderthal teeth was also recovered from this site.

See also Europe; Middle Paleolithic; Mousterian; Paleolithic Lifeways. [J.J.S.]

Further Readings
Callow, P., and Coinford, J.M., eds. (1986). La Cotte de St. Brelade, 1961–1978: Excavations by C.B.M. McBurney. Norwich: Geo Books.

La Ferrassie
Rockshelter complex near Les Eyzies in the Périgord (France) excavated after 1902 through 1972. The lower levels of the site are Mousterian and have produced a sample of two adult and six immature Neanderthals. The specimens may derive from a cemetery complex. The adults are represented by partial skeletons and show clear evidence of sexual dimorphism. The adult male (La Ferrassie I) has a particularly well-preserved cranium with a capacity of more than 1,600 ml.

Recent dating suggests that the Neanderthal sample from La Ferrassie may date to ca. 70 Ka. One of F. Bordes' Charentian variants of the French Mousterian is named after La Ferrassie. The upper levels of this site date to less than 36 Ka and contain Châtelperronian, Aurignacian, and Perigordian levels. Historically, La Ferrassie has been treated as the model of the early Upper Paleolithic cultural succession in France, now much revised on the basis of more recent excavations, both at this site and in the Périgord region.

See also Abri Pataud; Aurignacian; Bordes, François; Châtelperronian; Europe; Late Paleolithic; Mousterian; Neanderthals; Perigordian; Peyrony, Denis; Sexual Dimorphism [C.B.S., J.J.S.]

Further Readings
Peyrony, D. (1934). La Ferrassie: Moustérien, Périgordien, Aurignacien. Préhistoire 3:1–92.

La Naulette
The Trou de la Naulette, a huge cave in Belgium, produced a human mandible and postcranial fragments in 1866. The

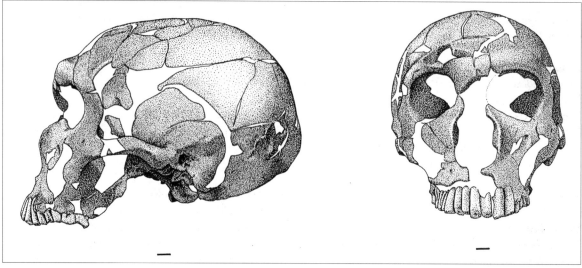

Lateral and facial views of the La Ferrassie I cranium. Scales are 1 cm.

specimen is of great historical importance: It was the first mandible of Neanderthal type ever discovered, and it was found in association with such cold-adapted mammals as reindeer and such extinct forms as mammoth and woolly rhinoceros.

See also Europe; Neanderthals. [C.B.S.]

La Quina

Rockshelter complex in the Charente (France). The upper shelter has produced a large sample of Neanderthal fossils. The most important of these include an adult partial skeleton (La Quina 5), an adult mandible (La Quina 9), and the skull of a child (La Quina 18). La Quina 5 has a long, relatively narrow cranial vault with a small endocranial volume but large brows, jaws, and teeth. It is not certain whether it represents a male or a female. Mandible 9 is one of the more modern-looking Neanderthal jaws, while the La Quina 18 child, ca. six years old at death, shows a number of Neanderthal characteristics but a brain size of only ca. 1,200 ml. Recent dating suggests an age of ca. 65 Ka for these fossils. La Quina gives its name to a French Mousterian variant characterized by large, steeply retouched side-scrapers. The lower shelter at La Quina contains a sequence of early Upper Paleolithic occupations.

See also Europe; Neanderthals; Mousterian; Upper Paleolithic. [J.J.S., C.B.S.]

La Venta

Area in western Colombia, including Middle Miocene Honda Formation fossil localities dated to 14–12 Ma. Recently, these faunal assemblages have been combined into the Laventan land-mammal age. Situated in a desertic depression of the Andean Mountain range near the Magdalena River, the La Venta badlands were once a subtropical-tropical forest floodplain and part of the greater Amazonian ecosystem. The area has yielded the richest series of fossil vertebrates and the most primates in northern South America. One of the significant features of La Venta primate fauna is that many of its forms are barely distinct from modern genera, suggesting an important degree of lineage stasis among New World monkeys. Primate genera known from the La Venta area include: ?*Aotus, Cebupithecia, Lagonimico* (slightly younger than the rest), *Laventiana, Micodon, Mohanamico, Nuciruptor, Patasola,* ?*Saimiri* (= *Neosaimiri*), and *Stirtonia.*

See also Americas; Atelinae; Callitrichinae; Cebinae; Patagonia; Pitheciinae. [A.L.R.]

Further Readings

Kay, R.F., Madden, R.H., Cifelli, R.L., and Flynn, J.J., eds. (1997) Vertebrate Paleontology in the Neotropics. Washington, D.C.: Smithsonian Institution Press.

Laetoli

Northern Tanzania site with Middle and Upper Pliocene strata, as well as Lower and Upper Pleistocene deposits, that

Pliocene hominid footprint excavated at the site of Laetoli in northern Tanzania. Photo by and courtesy of Tim D. White.

together span the period of 4.3–ca. 0.1 Ma according to potassium-argon (K/Ar) and faunal analysis. The local sequence now includes the Lower and Upper Laetolil Beds, the Ndolanya Beds, the Olpiro Beds, and the capping Ngaloba Beds.

Laetoli lies at the eastern edge of the Serengeti Plain on the Natron-Eyasi watershed in gullies at the head of the Side Gorge of Olduvai, ca. 50 km south of its juncture with the Main Gorge. Fossil beds were discovered here during a reconnaissance by L.S.B. Leakey in 1935, but the lone hominin tooth recovered at that time went unrecognized until 1979. Also during the 1930s, L. Kohl-Larsen worked the same beds on the opposite side of the watershed, in the headwaters of the Garusi River draining to Lake Eyasi. He found a fragmentary hominin maxilla with two premolars, together with an isolated molar and an isolated incisor. This material, known as the "Garusi hominid," remained enigmatic for many years, although it was named *Meganthropus* (later *Praeanthropus*) *africanus.*

During the 1970s, a team led by M.D. Leakey recovered abundant fossils from the Garusi gullies, including additional hominin remains from the Upper Laetolil Beds, which were dated to the Middle Pliocene (3.7–3.5 Ma). The homi-

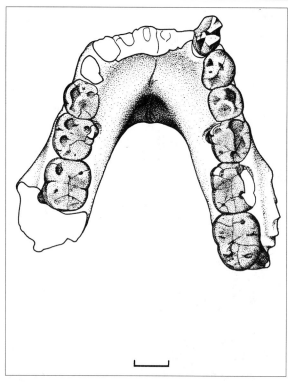

Occlusal view of the Laetoli LH4 mandible. Scale is 1 cm.

nin material included adult and juvenile mandibles, an adult maxilla, a partial juvenile skeleton, and some isolated teeth. One of these remains was subsequently made the type of *Australopithecus afarensis*, named after the region in Ethiopia where many more specimens of this taxon (including the famous "Lucy") have been found.

The Laetolil Beds formed as successive blankets of airborne volcanic debris, or ash falls, deposited on open, level ground in a dry and relatively treeless environment. In the late 1970s, abundant animal tracks in the ash were discovered, including (at Site G) the trail of three hominins. Excavation and analysis of these trails confirmed that these very early members of the Hominini were fully bipedal. No stone tools have been recovered from the Laetolil Beds.

The dominance of grasslands-adapted animals in the abundant Laetoli collection indicates that the ash falls did not have long-lasting effects on the ecology: They were either washed away from interfluves or readily vegetated between eruptions. The first scenario is clearly favored by the abundant trackways, which imply that the ash was still in an unconsolidated condition—possibly freshly erupted but clearly barren of plant life—when the terrain was able to support a diverse fauna. The uniquely preserved paleoecology at Laetoli is dramatically different from the usual water-laid sediment in which most fossils occur, including the slightly younger *A. afarensis* sites of Hadar in Ethiopia. On the other hand, the very diversity of mammal taxa preserved has suggested to P. Andrews, among other workers, that Laetoli was at least partly forested; there might have been gallery forests along watercourses or denser stands located away from the areas where sediments have been studied.

Later Pliocene faunal remains and possible stone artifacts are known from the Ndolanya Beds, dated to ca. 2.5 Ma. The Late Pleistocene Ngaloba Beds at Laetoli yield Middle Stone Age tools and the cranium of an "archaic *Homo sapiens*," LH 18, the Ngaloba cranium.

See also Africa, East; Archaic Homo sapiens; Australopithecus afarensis; Middle Awash; Middle Stone Age; Natron-Eyasi Basin; Ngaloba. [T.D.W.]

Further Readings

Andrews, P. (1989) Palaeoecology of Laetoli. J. Hum. Evol. 18:173–181.

Hay, R.L., and Leakey, M.D. (1982) The fossil footprints of Laetoli. Sci. Am. 246:50–57.

Leakey, M.D., and Harris, J.M. (1986) Laetoli: A Pliocene Site in Northern Tanzania. Oxford: Oxford University Press.

Lagar Velho

Open-air site in northern Portugal where the partial skeleton of a four year old child found in a 24,500 year old grave has been claimed to represent one of the last humans to show Neanderthal features. Portuguese archaeologists surveying this region of the Lapedo Valley (near Leiria, 90 miles north of Lisbon) in November 1998 found the first evidence of the burial by reaching into a rabbit hole at the base of a limestone cliff near a river, and drawing out some bones of the arm. Excavating nearby, they located a shallow grave containing bones covered with red ocher and a pierced shell. Most of the skeleton is present, including small pieces not yet fused to larger elements. The cranium had been crushed when the site was bulldozed for agricultural purposes, but the lower jaw was nearly intact; most of the postcranium is cracked but little distorted, and the cranium was being reconstructed in early 1999.

The bones are alleged to show an intriguing mixture of features typical of modern humans on the one hand and of Neanderthals on the other. There is a clear chin, and tooth proportions and morphology are like those of modern humans. Long bone shaft curvature and features of the radius and pubis are within the modern range, but the tibia is said to be as relatively short as those of Neanderthals of similar age and its proximal articular surface to be dorsally displaced. However, the tibial epiphyses are lacking, and the bone could be that of a robustly built anatomically modern youngster. The grave itself and the stone tools found nearby are identical to those of Gravettian sites known from Wales to Moravia at this time and always in association with anatomically modern humans. Previously, the most recent Neanderthal fossils were dated between 34–28 Ka.

The researchers who have worked on the new fossil interpret it as the result of interbreeding between Neanderthals and modern humans. Such a hybrid dating 4 Kyr after the previously known "last Neanderthal" suggested to them that this was not an isolated occurrence of interbreeding (a "love child"), but rather part of a long-term phenomenon. Other workers disagree, noting that the co-occurrence of features so clearly indicative of either modern human or

Neanderthal ancestry would only be found in at most a third-generation hybrid—after that time, the features would tend to grade to intermediate conditions. This interpretation would imply that Neanderthals persisted in Portugal far longer than previously thought. A third alternative is that this child is a fully modern human which either because of adaptation or genetic disorder had short legs (and arms) and a slightly distinctive symphysis. Further morphological and perhaps genetic analyses are awaited as the Encyclopedia goes to press.

See also Europe; Gravettian; Homo sapiens; Neanderthals; Skeleton. [E.D.]

Further Readings

Duarte, C., Mauricio, J., Pettit, P., Souto, P., Trinkaus, E., van der Plicht, H., and Zilhão, J. 1999. Proc. Natl. Acad. Sci. USA 96:7604–7609.

Tattersall, I. and Schwartz, J.H. 1999. Hominids and hybrids: The place of Neanderthals in human evolution. Proc. Natl. Acad. Sci. USA 96:7117–7119.

Lainyamok

Middle Pleistocene locality in southern Kenya, 8 km west of Lake Magadi. Surface bones and artifacts originally suggested that Lainyamok represented a hominin butchery area. Excavations showed that animal bones were gnawed by carnivores and were not associated with stone tools. A hominin maxilla and femoral shaft were found *in situ*.

See also Olorgesailie. [R.P.]

Lake Mungo

One of a series of dry lakebeds known as the Willandra Lakes, in western New South Wales, Australia; listed in the United Nations compilation of world heritage sites. The earliest dated human remains from Australia were excavated from the multilayered dune that marks Lake Mungo. The world's oldest cremation burial, Lake Mungo 1 (Willandra Lakes Human 1, WLH 1), dated to more than 35 Ka, involved a young, adult woman who was burnt on a funeral pyre. Her bones were smashed and refired, then buried in a small grave beneath the fireplace. Only 300 m away was the skeleton of Lake Mungo 3 (WLH 3), an adult male who was buried some 30 Kyr earlier than the Mungo woman, with a thick layer of powdered red ocher poured over his corpse at burial. Both of these skeletons are very delicate and gracile and have been linked to remains of similar age from southern China, such as Liujiang and Tzeyang. The extremely robust and archaic WLH 50, found close to Lake Garnpung, 20 km north of Lake Mungo, and dated by radiocarbon to more than 15 Ka and by electron spin resonance (ESR) to 50–30 Ka, is strongly reminiscent of the Ngandong (Solo) crania, but with an expanded braincase. A wealth of archaeological information has been recovered around the Willandra Lakes region.

See also Asia, Eastern and Southern; Asia, Western; Australia; Kow Swamp; Ngandong (Solo). [A.T., J.T.L.]

Land-Mammal Ages

Biochronological units based on regional First Appearance Datum events (FADs) and Last Appearance Datum events (LADs) of selected fossil mammal taxa or on other events in mammalian history. The datum events are historical (i.e., probabilistic) concepts whose existence is reconstructed from the observed spatial limits of fossil mammals in the field. The appeal to probability arises from the fact that mammalian fossils are too rare and scattered as regional stratigraphic markers, even where locally abundant to the eyes of vertebrate paleontologists, to support any other type of long-distance correlation.

The concept of regional land-mammal ages originated with the Wood Commission (1941), which aimed to use mammals in biostratigraphic correlation of the continental basins of western North America. Regional land-mammal-age sequences have been defined for South America, western and central Europe, the western part of the former Soviet Union, Siberia, the Indian subcontinent, and Australia. Locally based Late Cenozoic sequences for southern Africa and East Africa have been published, and a continentwide schema for the Afro-Arabian continent is under development; a preliminary version appears in the "Africa" entry.

In regions where fossiliferous formations are widely exposed and many collection sites are available, as in western North America, Australia, northern Spain, the Siwaliks, Tadjikistan, and the Gobi, the biochrons can be tested and refined according to superpositional stratigraphy, in which observed range limits control the application of land-mammal ages. In this environment, direct dating is a supplemental tool, and the history of taxa and communities is, in principle, deduced from stratigraphically ordered data.

In regions in which a stratigraphic context is lacking, such as the heavily covered terrain of Europe, or in the widely dispersed localities of South America, South Africa, and Siberia, the estimation of relative age between faunas is based almost entirely on determinations of evolutionary stage and evidence for extinction or immigration events, documented by the fossils themselves. Paleomagnetism and radiometric age determinations, where available, are vital controls.

Africa presents a special case, in that radiometric age determinations and tephrochronology in East Africa have superseded regional lithostratigraphy as well as evolutionary scenarios as the basic control over the age assignment of the spectacular Rift Valley collections and, by extension, the fossil faunas across the continent. This is at least in part because knowledge of the systematics, true age limits, and geographic range of the African fossil genera is still in a rudimentary state overall.

See also Africa; Biochronology; Cenozoic; Paleobiogeography; Paleomagnetism; Radiometric Dating; Stratigraphy; Tephrochronology; Time Scale (J.A.V.C.)

Further Readings

Kauffman, E.G. (1988) Concepts and methods of high-resolution event stratigraphy. Ann. Rev. Earth Planet. Sci. 16:605–654.

Lindsay, E.H., Fahlbusch, V., and Mein, P., eds. (1990) European Neogene Mammal Chronology. New York: Plenum.

Wood, H.E., II, Chaney, R.W., Clark, J., Colbert, E.H., Jepsen, G.L., Reeside, J.B., and Stock, C. (1941) Nomenclature and correlation of the North American continental Tertiary. Bull. Geol. Soc. Am. 52:1–48.

Woodburne, M.O. (1987) Cenozoic Mammals of North America. Berkeley: University of California Press.

Woodburne, M.O. (1996) Precision and resolution in mammalian chronostratigraphy: Principles, practises, examples. J. Vert. Paleo. 16:531–555.

Landscape Archaeology

An analytical and excavation method applied to archaeological materials distributed in a narrow stratigraphic interval of wide lateral exposure. Its goal is to establish spatial correlation between human activity traces, such as stone artifacts and cutmarked bones, and features of ancient habitats preserved in a single stratum such as a paleosol. The method has been developed in African Pleistocene studies as research on early human behavior expanded beyond the study of individual excavations of small spatial scope. It has been applied to examine human land use, transport of resources, habitat specificity of activities, and taphonomic issues. *Paleolandscape excavation*, as the method is sometimes called, widely samples an artifact-rich stratum in order to link separate excavations into a single geographic system and a restricted time interval. It maps the distribution of human activities relative to stone outcrop sources, ancient vegetation and topography, and the distribution of water sources, faunal remains, and other possible resources used by humans. This method incorporates many areas of field and laboratory study and especially relies on detailed investigation of the geologic context of archaeological remains. Paleosols and similarly confined strata that preserve original loci of human artifacts encompass a considerable span of time; thus, this method enables study of human activities and correlated environmental features typically spread over 10^2–10^4 years. The method has strong parallels in Late Pleistocene studies in Europe and Holocene archaeological studies in North America.

See also Archaeological Sites; Archaeology; Olorgesailie; Taphonomy. [R.P.]

Further Readings

Potts, R. (1994). Variables vs. models of early Pleistocene hominid land use. J. Hum. Evol. 27:7–24.

Lang Trang

Pleistocene-Holocene cave complex in western Thanh Hoa Province, northern Vietnam. Beginning in the late 1980s, exacavations conducted by Vietnamese and American scholars have yielded a rich Quaternary vertebrate assemblage, limited dentition of *Homo* cf. *erectus*, and both chipped- and ground-stone tools, the latter representing tens, if not hundreds, of thousands of years of occupation of the cave environs. Excavations of other cave localities in northern Vietnam have uncovered evidence of the direct association between *Homo erectus* and *Gigantopithecus*. One research focus of the Lang Trang Project is illuminating possible relationships between these two fossil primate species.

Located above the Ma River, the Lang Trang caves are solution cavities in massive karst limestone peaks that contain a weakly brecciated sequence of sediments likely representing the whole of the Quaternary period. Although no direct association has been established between occurrences of simply chipped stone tools, an early Middle Pleistocene *Stegodon-Ailuropoda* Fauna, and dentition of *Homo* cf. *erectus* in the lower part of the cave complex, electron spin resonance (ESR) dates thus far (1997) are in accord with a Middle Pleistocene antiquity.

The upper unit of Lang Trang IV contains a Holocene Hoabinhian burial and a later faunal complex suggesting that the fissure complex preserves the record of a complicated history of utilization spanning the period between the Middle Pleistocene and the early Holocene.

See also Asia, Eastern and Southern; Gigantopithecus; Hoabinhian; Homo erectus. [J.W.O.]

Further Readings

Ciochon, R.L., Olsen, J.W., and James, J. (1990) Other Origins. New York: Bantam.

Cuong, N.L. (1992) A reconsideration of the chronology of hominid fossils in Vietnam. In T. Akasawa, K. Aoki, and T. Kimura (eds.): The Evolution and Dispersal of Modern Humans in Asia. Tokyo: Hokusen-Sha, pp. 321–335.

Lantian

Fossil site group in Shaanxi Province, China, dated to the Middle Pleistocene or latest Early Pleistocene through paleomagnetic and faunal correlation. The "Lantian man" population of *Homo erectus* actually consists of two female specimens from two different localities: the Gongwangling cranium and the Chenjiawo mandible. The cranium occurs in paleomagnetically reversed sediments that have been assigned to the terminal part of the Matuyama [R] Chron (ca. 0.9–0.8 Ma). An alternative interpretation based on correlation of the surrounding paleosols to a local standard sequence places this specimen at 1.2–1.1 Ma. The Chenjiawo mandible reportedly came from a slightly higher level, in sediments of normal polarity, and thus has been assigned to the lower portion of the Brunhes [N] Chron (ca. 0.6 Ma). It has been suggested by An and Ho, however, that the strata in which the two specimens were found are, in fact, laterally correlative and that oxygen-isotope chronology and biostratigraphy in this interval indicate that the strata bracket the Jaramillo reversal at ca. 1.0 Ma. In either case, the Gongwangling cranium may represent the earliest known hominin fossil from mainland East Asia, depending on the resolution of controversy over the age of specimens from Longgupo and Yuanmou, also in China.

The poorly preserved cranium is low and robust, with thick bones and an estimated endocranial volume of 780 ml; it is considered to represent a female about 30 years old. There is a good deal of telescoping of bone fragments, especially of the occipital and parietal, which renders the vault size questionable. The mandible, also classified as female, probably belonged to an older individual; it exhibits agenesis of the third molars. A few stone tools, including an undoubted handaxe, and possible indications of fire have also been recovered from supposedly stratigraphically equivalent deposits in the same area.

See also Asia, Eastern and Southern; China; Homo erectus; Longgupo; Yuanmou; Zhoukoudian. [G.G.P.]

Further Readings

Aigner, J.S., and Laughlin, W.S. (1973) The dating of Lantian Man and his significance for analyzing trends in human evolution. Am. J. Phys. Anthropol. 39:97–110.

An, Z., and Ho, C.K. (1989) New magnetostratigraphic dates of Lantian *Homo erectus*. Quatern. Res. 32:213–221.

Larick, R., and Ciochon, R.L. (1996) The African emergence and early Asian dispersals of the genus *Homo*. Am. Sci. 84:538–551.

Muang, W., and Mou, Y. (1997) Archaeological evidence for the first human colonisation of east Asia. IPPA Bull. 16(3):3–12. Canberra: ANU.

Schick, K.D., and Dong, Z. (1993) Early Paleolithic of China and eastern Asia. Evol. Anthropol. 2:22–35.

Lartet, Edouard (1801–1871)

French paleontologist. Although Lartet was a lawyer by profession, his avocation was paleontology. He was encouraged by E. Geoffroy Saint-Hilaire (1772–1844) and subsequently by A. de Jussieu (1797–1853) of the Muséum d'Histoire Naturelle in Paris, and his explorations near his home (Gers) led to the discovery of the fossiliferous site of Sansan and the recovery of the first remains of the Miocene fossil apes *Pliopithecus* (1836) and *Dryopithecus* (1856).

Notwithstanding his admiration of G. Cuvier's (1769–1832) work, from the outset Lartet had been a supporter of the then minority view that human antiquity extended far back into the antediluvian period; he had eagerly endorsed J. Prestwich's (1812–1896) confirmation of the validity of J. Boucher de Perthes' (1788–1868) claims in 1859 for the antiquity of human artifacts in the Somme River terraces, with the results of his own excavations at Aurignac (Ariège) the same year. Furthermore, based largely on his own data, in 1860 he proposed the first Pleistocene chronology based on faunal remains. In addition, Lartet also pioneered, in collaboration with the English prehistorian H. Christy (1810–1865), the exploration of important cave sites (e.g., Les Eyzies, La Madeleine, and Le Moustier) in the Périgord and adjoining regions in the 1860s. The results of this work are summarized in their *Reliquiae aquitanicae* (1865–1875).

See also Boucher de Perthes, Jacques; Dryopithecus; Mortillet, Gabriel de; Pliopithecidae. [F.S.]

Further Readings

Grayson, D.K. (1983) The Establishment of Human Antiquity. New York: Academic.

Jones, R.T., ed. (1865–1875) H. Christy and E. Lartet: Reliquiae acquitanicae. London: Williams and Norgate.

Lascaux

Most important Ice Age painted cave in France, with ceilings and walls painted in an Early Magdalenian style, ca. 17–16 Ka. In addition to images of aurochs (wild cattle), bison, ibex, and deer, Lascaux has one imaginary animal (the unicorn), a bear, a rhinoceros, and a scene with a wounded bison and a supine, ithyphallic man. The cave is also rich in engravings and signs. Although only one reindeer image appears, numerous reindeer bones were excavated from the cave, indicating that the animals eaten were not necessarily those most represented in the art. Discovered in 1942, Lascaux was seen by thousands of visitors, but algae contamination appeared on the paintings, and the cave was closed to tourists. A copy of a major portion of the cave, Lascaux II, was built nearby and is open to the public.

See also Europe; Paleolithic Image; Upper Paleolithic [A.M.]

Late Paleolithic

As broadly defined here, a stage in human cultural development characterized by diversified blade- and microblade-tool (Modes 4 and 5) technologies, mainly occurring at the end of the Late Pleistocene ca. 50–10 Ka.

This stage was first recognized in southwestern France, where it was called the *Upper Paleolithic*. The similarity of cultural remains dating to this period from adjacent areas of Europe, and eventually all of the Mediterranean Basin, led to the adoption of this designation there as well. Archaeological inventories outside of Europe, however, are different enough to be distinguished as Late Paleolithic. In sub-Saharan Africa, Mode 4 technologies are rare, although they may appear during the Middle Stone Age, ca. 240–40 Ka. The Later Stone Age, first appearing between ca. 50 and 20 Ka in different regions, is mainly Mode 5 (except for some industries in Kenya and Ethiopia). Some scholars, especially those working in the North African Levant, call industries dated to 40–20 Ka Late Paleolithic and those after 20 Ka Epipaleolithic. Asian, Australian, and Pacific Island industries, as well as Paleoindian industries of the New World, are also Late Paleolithic in this broad conception of the term.

Important worldwide developments during this period included a deterioration of climatic conditions; the spread of anatomically modern humans (*Homo sapiens sapiens*) with new technologies; an explosion in the arts and other forms of symboling behavior in some parts of the occupied world; significant changes in subsistence practices and economic and social relationships; and the colonization of Australia, the Pacific Islands, and the Americas.

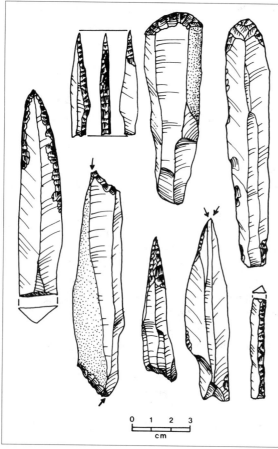

Late Paleolithic blade tools from Khotylevo II, Russia. Courtesy of Olga Soffer.

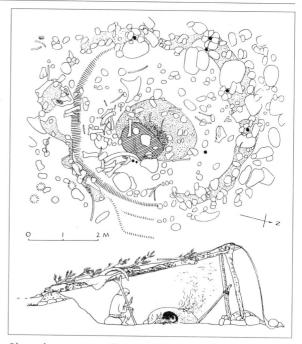

Plan and reconstruction of Late Paleolithic hut at Dolni Vestonice with a clay oven used to fire ceramic figurines. From J. Wymer, The Palaeolithic Age, *1982. Reprinted with permission of St. Martin's Press, Inc.*

Climates and Environments

Climatic conditions during the Late Paleolithic were significantly different from those of today. Late Pleistocene glaciers expanded to their greatest extent in both hemispheres, and mile-high sheets of ice covered all of northern Europe, Alaska, and Canada. This expansion of the ice, which peaked between 20 and 18 Ka, brought about much colder climates and a significant reduction in annual precipitation.

In higher latitudes, advancing ice sheets caused a profound change in the distribution of biotic communities and resulted in hyperzonality and a southward displacement of forest belts. In Europe, forests were found only around the Mediterranean; much of Eurasia was covered by a unique periglacial steppe. While cold and extremely continental in climate, this steppe was able to support large herds of such gregarious herbivores as bison, horse, mammoth, and reindeer.

Environmental data from Africa and southern Eurasia suggest that, at lower latitudes, this period saw increasing aridity, shrinkage of forests, and expansion of deserts onto former grasslands. A similar pattern of increasing aridity is documented in temperate Australia. Late Paleolithic climates and environments were generally considerably harsher than those of today.

Late Paleolithic People

Although Late Paleolithic industries succeeded those of the Middle Paleolithic at roughly the same time that Neanderthals were replaced by anatomically modern humans in much of Europe, the African and the Asian records are more complex and underscore that the relationship between the toolmakers and tool industries was not simple and straightforward. The discovery of both fully modern humans and Neanderthals with Middle Paleolithic tools in Western Asia and of Neanderthals with Upper Paleolithic ones in France indicates that both kinds of hominid used both kinds of industries. In Africa, the earliest Mode 4 (within the Middle Stone Age) tool kits and the earliest anatomically modern humans are even older.

Technology

Archaeological inventories at Late Paleolithic sites are extremely varied both in raw materials and in the tools fashioned from them. Advances in stone-tool making include a new way of preparing cores to produce long, thin, parallel-sided blades. Blades allowed a more economical use of nodules and permitted toolmakers to obtain far more working edge per unit of stone. The blades were then retouched into tools by a variety of techniques, among them finely controlled pressure flaking. We can see a decrease in the size of some tools made on blades during this period as well. The growing production of microblades after 20 Ka is probably related to the increasing role of hafting technologies and composite tools. These tools included stone-tipped spears, lances, spear throwers, and probably bows and arrows. These weapons permitted the killing of animals at far greater distances. A similar microlithization of tools is documented in Australia and on the Pacific Islands. Finally, techniques of grinding and polishing were used in Australia as early as 25 Ka ago to produce ground-stone tools, while in Eurasia and Africa they were employed to fashion stone and shell into beads and pendants. Late Paleolithic stone-tool makers were

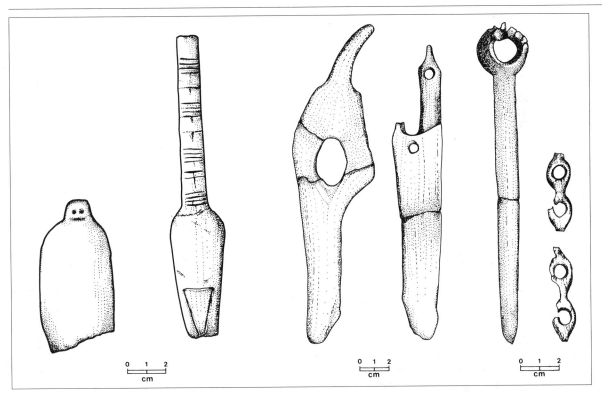

Worked and decorated ivory objects from the Mezhirich Late Paleolithic site. Courtesy of Olga Soffer.

much more selective than their predecessors in the raw materials they used, often preferring superior materials from some distance. High-quality chocolate-colored flint from the Holy Cross Mountains in central Poland, for example, has been found at sites up to 400 km away. Similar distances for superior exotics are widely documented in Australia and on the Pacific Islands, where they would have involved sea transport.

Late Paleolithic tool kits contain many more standardized tool types than those of the Middle Paleolithic. Two of these tools, end-scrapers and burins, are often found in great quantities. Overall, Late Paleolithic tool inventories also show increased variation from region to region and change more quickly through time. This patterned interregional and chronological variability, one reflecting less cultural evolution and more the nature of regional adaptations, is not universal, however: It is more prevalent in Europe and Africa than in parts of East Asia and Australia. For some areas around the Mediterranean, we can outline regional sequences of Late Paleolithic industries that replace each other through time in a manner similar to those in southwestern France. Archaeological records from other parts of Europe, as well as from much of Asia and Australia, although less studied, generally do not exhibit similar patterns of variability. Temporal patterning in these regions, however, may be affected by discontinuities in human settlement during the late glacial maximum.

In some regions of the Old World, Late Paleolithic industries overlie transitional ones that contain both Middle Paleolithic tools made on flakes and Late Paleolithic tools on blades. Such sequences, found, for example, in parts of central and eastern Europe, North Africa, and Siberia, suggest that Late Paleolithic industries may have evolved slowly from preceding Middle Paleolithic ones. In other regions, particularly in the northern latitudes of Eurasia, Late Paleolithic industries make a sudden appearance, indicating that their makers may have moved into these regions from elsewhere. This is clearly also the case in Australia, which was colonized only after ca. 50 Ka, as well as in the New World.

Among other Late Paleolithic technological innovations was the systematic use of a much wider spectrum of materials for tools, including antler, bone, ivory, and wood. Bone working, although present in the Middle Paleolithic, became especially elaborate; tools and implements ranging from spear throwers and shaft straighteners to harpoons, fishhooks, and eyed needles are repeatedly found at Late Paleolithic sites. Bone, especially in the higher latitudes of Eurasia, was burned as fuel in hearths and used as a construction material for dwellings. Another innovation was kiln-fired ceramics. Remains of fired-clay animal and female figurines have been found in North Africa, central and eastern Europe, Siberia, and Japan.

Significant new technology is also evident in features at Late Paleolithic sites. Carefully prepared hearths bordered with stones for heat retention and constructed with tangential air-flow channels for fire control have been found at sites in higher latitudes. Other hearths were surrounded by clay walls and served as kilns for ceramic production and possibly as baking ovens. Pits that measured up to 2 m in diameter and up to 1.5 m in depth were dug into permafrost and used first to store food and then to store bone and ivory for future use. In colder climates, large, elaborate dwellings measuring 20–30 m² were constructed from bones of large-size species like mammoths. Careful selection of skeletal parts for specific dwellings noted at sites with mammoth-bone dwellings on the central Russian Plain suggests that the construction of dwellings occurred on a planned sitewide basis. In Egypt, subterranean pit shafts into seams of flint cobbles suggest organized prehistoric mining activities.

Finally, the increase in both the size of residential sites (in some cases exceeding 10,000 m²) and the number of dwellings at sites indicates that people lived together on a permanent basis in greater numbers than during the preceding Middle Paleolithic period.

Cultural Explosion

The most distinctive feature of the Late Paleolithic is the appearance and proliferation of nonutilitarian symbolic behavior revealed in the production of art, decorative objects, jewelry, and musical instruments. Although a handful of Middle Paleolithic sites contain remains of coloring materials and one or two pieces etched with unpatterned lines, Late Paleolithic sites in many parts of Eurasia and Africa consistently feature decorative and decorated objects.

ART AND ENGRAVINGS

Art dating to this period comes in two forms, *parietal* and *mobiliary.* The first includes paintings and engravings on cave and rockshelter walls and is particularly well known in the Franco-Cantabrian region of western Europe, although examples have been found in Australia, Bulgaria, South Africa, Namibia, Zimbabwe, Tanzania, Ethiopia, and the Ural Mountains (Russia). Some sites in European Russia and Ukraine have also yielded painted mammoth bones, which, because of their weight, do not qualify as portable art objects but fit more closely the permanent mode represented by parietal cave art.

Late Paleolithic sites from the Czech Republic and Poland all the way to Siberia have yielded an abundance of mobiliary art carved out of stone, bone, and amber and modeled out of clay and subsequently fired in kilns. These human and animal figurines span a variety of styles, from the classic female "venus" figures to more abstract representations. The sites also contain great quantities and varieties of engraved and otherwise decorated objects, some of which were used for utilitarian tasks, like snow shovels, shaft straighteners, piercers, and awls. The function of other engraved pieces remains unclear, and scholars have interpreted them as early calendars, schematic maps, or other types of mnemonic devices. Engraving was done on bone, ivory, antler, and various types of stone. Engraved fragments of bone and ostrich eggshell are also known from Africa.

PERSONAL ADORNMENT

Jewelry and other items of personal adornment, such as beads and pendants, bracelets and rings, and pectorals and diadems, are also regularly found in Late Paleolithic sites and are especially numerous in higher latitudes. They were made from polished stone, ostrich eggshell, ivory, bone, antler, amber, marine shells, and drilled animal teeth. Their presence at the sites strongly suggests an emerged sense of personal and social identity, which may have been absent during the preceding period.

MUSICAL INSTRUMENTS

Finally, sites in northern Africa and Eurasia include whistles and flutes made of animal and bird long bones. Russian and Ukrainian scholars have also argued that some of the painted

Artist's rendering of dwelling 1, made from the bones of 95 mammoths, at the Mezhirich Late Paleolithic site. After J. Jelinek, Strecha nad Hlavou, Moravian Museum Brno, 1986.

mammoth bones found at Late Paleolithic sites on the Russian Plain were used as percussion instruments.

Burial

Planned disposal of the deceased in prepared graves began during the Middle Paleolithic, but the Late Paleolithic witnessed a dramatic increase in the amount of grave goods buried with the dead. Both single and multiple interments are known, and there is no clear pattern favoring either sex or any age category. The most spectacular of these burials, found in Sungir at the outskirts of the city of Vladimir in European Russia, contained a joint grave of two adolescents who were buried head to head with a wealth of grave goods, their clothing covered with ca. 3,000 sewn-on ivory beads each. The nearby grave of a mature male was equally rich and elaborate. At Předmosti, a Late Paleolithic site in the Czech Republic excavated at the beginning of the twentieth century, a mass grave covered by mammoth scapulae contained skeletal remains of more than 29 men, women, and children.

Subsistence Strategies

Like those who came before them, Late Paleolithic people made their living by hunting and gathering, but their food-procurement strategies were considerably more planned and effective. Organic remains at Late Paleolithic sites show that people had become finely tuned to local environmental conditions and organized their food procurement on a regional basis. This resulted in a good deal of regional differentiation in paleoeconomies and in the habitual use of such effective mass-harvesting techniques as drives, stampedes, and jump kills. The increasing presence in the inventories of such dangerous species as wild boars is witness that the invention of long-distance weapons, like bows and arrows and spear throwers, allowed hunters to go after animals more difficult to hunt. Remains of fur-bearing animals and aquatic and terrestrial birds suggest that trapping and snaring were practiced as well.

Groups living in lower latitudes harvested a wide variety of plant and animal resources. Coastal groups, such as those living around the Mediterranean and in southern Africa, harvested fish and shellfish, took birds, hunted medium-to-large-size bovids, and collected wild cereal grasses. Groups in Australia and on the Pacific Islands also fed on wild cereals, small mammals, lizards, fish, shellfish, birds, and bird eggs. Data from the Pacific Islands suggest that people may even have transported their favorite wild prey from island to island. The types of sites occupied in these regions indicate that people here were foragers who migrated to be near ripening resources.

Groups living in higher latitudes, especially on the huge Eurasian periglacial steppe, were confronted by far less predictable resources. These areas were characterized by a relative scarcity of vegetation but an abundance of animals. The latter, however, were available in huge numbers only during the short warm seasons and were sparse during the long, cold, winter months. Food management here meant mass-harvesting animals during the seasons of peak abundance and storing surplus food for use during the lean months. These storage economies, which involved both delayed con-

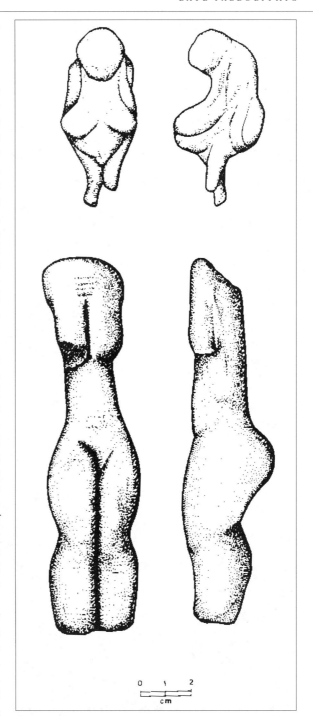

Carved Late Paleolithic ivory female figurines. Above: "venus" figurine from Khotylevo II, Russia; below: female figurine from Eliseevichi, Russia. Courtesy of Olga Soffer.

sumption and greater planning, organization, and cooperation on a permanent basis, indicate a more complex organization of subsistence pursuits than found among simple foragers.

A site-by-site comparison of organic assemblages recovered from many Middle and Late Paleolithic sites in all latitudes at first glance shows that Late Paleolithic sites contain concentrations of one or two species, while Middle Paleolithic ones show a greater range. A regional perspective, however, one that looks at all of the sites in a particular area, indicates not so much a narrowing of the resource base during the Late Paleolithic as an organizational change in subsistence behavior from "feed as you go" to planned food harvesting. Groups that lived in areas with diverse but predictable resources, which were generally found in lower latitudes, migrated to position themselves near the available resources and selectively harvested those that were most abundant in a given location. Groups in higher latitudes employed storage economies, harvesting and storing the most abundant animal species. Finally, the discovery of valued exotics at Late Paleolithic sites suggests that many groups during this period participated in long-distance exchange networks that linked them socially with groups living at considerable distances from them.

Sociopolitical Organization and Settlement Patterns

The elaboration and regionalization in Late Paleolithic technologies, the emergence of storage economies in parts of the Old World, the explosion in the production of art and jewelry, the use of exotic materials, the growing elaboration and differentiation in funerary inventories, and the increase both in the size of sites and in the permanence of their features—taken together, all of these indicate changes in sociopolitical relationships.

These changes, however, were not universal but regional and reflected local social and demographic realities. The more ephemeral nature of archaeological remains generated by groups in lower latitudes (few artifacts, insubstantial features) and the relative sparseness of such status goods as jewelry and art at these sites suggest that people probably lived in fairly egalitarian, small social units like those known ethnographically for band societies. Like their modern-day equivalents, these coresidential groups may have joined

other like-size groups at aggregation sites, where ceremonial behavior took place, including possibly the painting of cave and rockshelter walls.

Late Paleolithic groups in higher latitudes, especially those whose subsistence was based on storage economies, lived in larger groups and occupied residential locales for much longer periods of time. They did not undertake long-distance seasonal moves, nor did they break up into smaller social units during some seasons. Data on the distribution of stored resources and exotic and status goods, as well as on the differences in burial inventories, indicate that groups like those that occupied the central Russian Plain lived in larger and more complex, hierarchically organized social units, where positions of status and authority were restricted to just some members of the groups.

Colonization

Late Paleolithic people were able to adapt successfully to a wide variety of environments and to colonize Australia, the Pacific Islands, and the Americas. People from Southeast Asia may have arrived in Australia as early as ca. 50 Ka and soon afterward reached Melanesia (New Ireland). In doing so, they would have had to cross a large body of open water; they must have possessed seaworthy boats and considerable navigational skills. Those who peopled the Americas came from Siberia and crossed Beringia, a land bridge that connected Siberia with Alaska during the stadial periods of the last Ice Age but today lies submerged under the shallow Bering Straits. Although they may have come on foot, their technological skills and knowledge were sophisticated enough to permit them to survive in the cold and harsh tundra environments of Siberia and Alaska. There is much debate about the date of arrival of these first Americans, with some scholars arguing that it took place before 30 Ka and others dating the event sometime after 20 Ka.

See also Africa; Aggregation-Dispersal; Archaeological Sites; Australia; Economy, Prehistoric; Europe; Exotics; Hunter-Gatherers; Jewelry; Middle Paleolithic; Musical Instruments; Paleoindian; Paleolithic; Paleolithic Image; Předmosti; Ritual; Site Types; Storage; Upper Paleolithic. [O.S.]

Further Readings

Burenhult, G., ed. (1993) The First Humans. The Illustrated History of Humankind, Vol. 1. San Francisco: Harper.

Fagan, B.M. (1999) People of the Earth, 9th ed. Boston: Little, Brown.

Fagan, B.M. (1990) The Journey from Eden. London: Thames and Hudson.

Pfeiffer, J.E. (1982) The Creative Explosion. New York: Harper and Row.

Soffer, O. (1985) The Upper Paleolithic of the Central Russian Plain. Orlando, Fla.: Academic.

Parietal art from the Cosquer Cave, France: Ibex engraved on top of two black horses. Courtesy of Ministère de la Culture, Direction du Patrimoine; photo by A. Chêné, Centre Camille Jullian (CNRS).

Later Stone Age

Third stage in a tripartite system of nomenclature for the African Stone Age (Early, Middle, and Later), formalized in

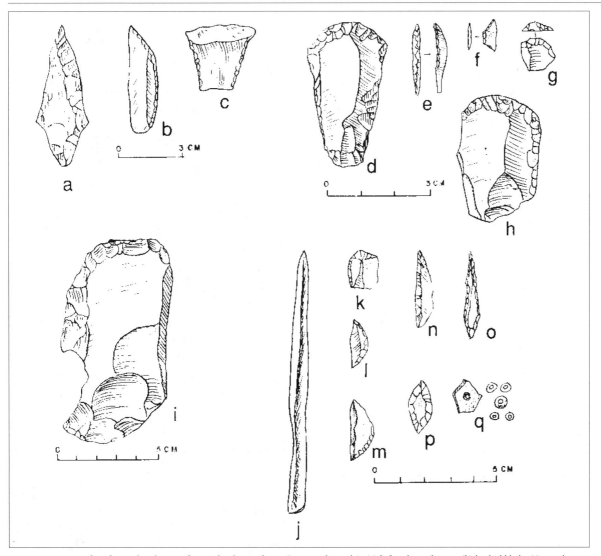

Later Stone Age artifacts from sub-Saharan Africa. Tshitolian industry (Zaire and Angola): (a) bifacial taned point; (b) backed blade; (c) tranchet. Smithfield industry (South Africa): (d) end-scraper (late phase); (e) backed blade; (f) lunate; (g) small convex scraper; (h) side- and end-scraper; (i–m) lunates; (n) straight-backed microlith; (o) awl; (p) double crescent; (q) ostrich-eggshell beads. After J.D. Clark, The Prehistory of Africa, *1970, Praeger.*

1929 by Goodwin and van Riet Lowe for South Africa and later expanded to microblade and other Epipaleolithic industries throughout Africa and on the Indian subcontinent. Original South African industries assigned to the Later Stone Age (LSA) included the microlithic Wilton industry and three phases of the Smithfield industry (A, B, and C), differentiated from the Wilton by its exclusively interior (noncoastal) distribution, abundance of scrapers, and relative lack of microlithic segments and backed bladelets.

Small tool size, bladelet technology, and hafting of arrows and other tools are among the most distinctive aspects of LSA industries across the continent; other features are widespread use of ostrich-eggshell and shell beads, bored stones that may have served as digging-stick weights, engraved and painted plaques, and an elaborate series of bone and wood tools, including hafts, points, linkshafts, net sinkers, fish gorgets, and barbed harpoons. Faunal remains indicate intensification of resource use through greater utilization of lacustrine and marine resources, as well as more consistent hunting of large plains game (giant buffalo, giant

zebra, giant haartebeest, large warthog) toward the end of the Late Pleistocene, possibly contributing to the extinction of several giant species at this time.

The earliest microblade technology is found in central Africa by ca. 20 Ka at sites in Zaire (Matupi), Uganda (Buvuma Island), Tanzania (Kisese), Kenya (Lukenya Hill), and Zambia (Kalemba). In eastern Zaire, where microlithic technology may date back to 40 Ka at Matupi Cave, sites in the Semliki Valley near Ishango indicate reliance on fishing technology in the form of bone harpoons by the final Late Pleistocene, ca. 20 Ka. Intensification of resource use is also reflected in faunal remains from Kalemba and other early sites of the Nachikufan industry. Microliths may be present as early as 25 Ka at Rose Cottage Cave in the Orange Free State (South Africa) but do not become widespread in this area until after 10 Ka. Southern African industries that follow the Middle Stone Age, dating to 30–10 Ka, are largely nonmicrolithic (Apollo-11, Border Cave) and are characterized by few formal tools, other than medium-to-large-size scrapers and an abundance of bone tools at some sites. In North Africa, Ibero-Maurusian industries are

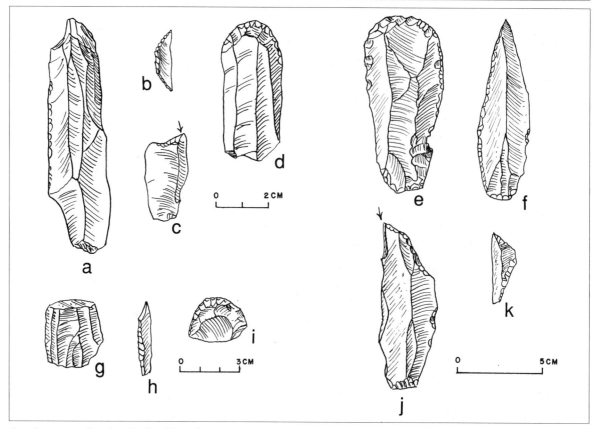

Later Stone Age artifacts from North and East Africa. From Gobedra (Ethiopia): (a) retouched blade; (b) lunate. Eburran industry (Kenya): (c) burin; (d) end-scraper. Ibero-Maurusian industry (Morocco): (e) alternate-ended microblade core; (f) backed bladelet; (g) short end-scraper. Capsian industry (Tunisia): (h) end-scraper; (i) backed blade; (j) burin; (k) microlith. After J.D. Clark, The Prehistory of Africa, 1970, Praeger; and D. W. Phillipson, African Archaeology, 1985, Cambridge University Press.

widespread by 14 Ka and may appear as early as 20–18 Ka. Later Stone Age technologies lasted into historic times in some areas, with the addition of small quantities of iron, indigenous pottery, and occasional herding of small stock. Interactions between hunters, fishers, and herders of the Later Stone Age and Iron Age agriculturalists and pastoralists were varied and complex and may have ranged from occasional contact through long-distance trade networks to intensive economic interactions and mutual dependency, as typified by ongoing pygmy-villager interactions in the Ituri Forest of Zaire.

Originally, the Later Stone Age was seen as parallel in age to the European Mesolithic but distinguished from it by continued dependence on large herd animals. As in the other stages of Goodwin and van Riet Lowe's scheme, the technological innovations of the Later Stone Age are now known to occur as early in Africa as anywhere in the world. As part of a general move to discard pan-African chronostratigraphic schemes, in view of the richness and diversity of Paleolithic adaptations throughout the continent, the term *Later Stone Age* is increasingly discarded in favor of J.G.D. Clark's use of Mode 5 to refer to industries with microlithic technology and composite tools.

In most areas, Mode 5 (LSA) industries directly succeed Mode 3 (Middle Stone Age, MSA) industries, with no intervening stage of widespread large-blade and burin technology comparable to the European Upper Paleolithic (Mode 4). Only in Kenya (the Eburran, previously the Kenya Capsian),

Ethiopia (Gobedra shelter), Somalia (Hargesian), and northeastern Africa generally (Dabban, Khormusan) are large-blade industries widespread between 40 and 10 Ka. Other aspects of the European Upper Paleolithic, however, such as images, body decoration, economic intensification, trade, and social complexity, have contemporary or earlier parallels throughout Africa in association with MSA and LSA industries.

See also Africa; Africa, Southern; Apollo-11; Border Cave; Capsian; Dabban; Early Stone Age; Economy, Prehistoric; Epipaleolithic; First Intermediate; Ibero-Maurusian; Late Paleolithic; Mesolithic; Middle Stone Age; Paleolithic; Paleolithic Image; Paleolithic Lifeways; Rose Cottage; Second Intermediate; Stone-Tool Making; Upper Paleolithic; Wilton. [A.S.B.]

Further Readings

Deacon, J. (1984) Later Stone Age people in southern Africa. In R.G. Klein (ed.): Southern African Prehistory and Paleoenvironments. Rotterdam: Balkema.

Goodwin, A.J.H., and van Riet Lowe, C. (1929) The Stone Age cultures of South Africa. Ann. S. Afr. Mus. 27:1–289.

Klein, R.G. (1994) Southern Africa before the Iron Age. In R.S. Corruccini and R.L. Ciochon (eds.): Integrative Paths to the Past. Englewood Cliffs, N.J.: Prentice-Hall, pp. 471–519.

Phillipson, D.W. (1993) African Archaeology, 2nd ed. Cambridge: Cambridge University Press.

Vermeersch, P. (1992) The Upper and Late Paleolithic of northern and eastern Africa. In F. Klees and R. Kuper (eds.): New Light on the Northeast African Past: Current Prehistoric Research. (Africa Praehistoria 5). Köln: Heinrich Barth-Institut, pp. 99–153.

Wadley, L. (1993) The Pleistocene Later Stone Age south of the Limpopo River. J. World Prehist. 7:243–296.

Laugerie Sites

Two adjacent rockshelters on the right bank of the Vézère River just upstream from Les Eyzies, Dordogne (France), with important Upper Paleolithic remains. Laugerie Haute is one of several deeply stratified rockshelters on which the classic succession of Upper Paleolithic industries in southwestern France is based. First excavated in 1868, the Laugerie Haute–sequence industries include Perigordian III (now VI), Protomagdalenian, Aurignacian V, Solutrean, and Early Magdalenian (to Stage III). The site is divided by a rock fall into eastern (Est) and western (Ouest) parts and dated by radiocarbon to 22–19.5 Ka. The nearby, younger shelter, Laugerie Basse, is a Middle-to-Late (Stages III–VI) Magdalenian site that also yielded the cranial remains of several individuals and a possible burial of an adult male.

See also Aurignacian; Europe; Magdalenian; Périgord; Perigordian; Peyrony, Denis; Protomagdalenian; Solutrean; Upper Paleolithic. [A.S.B.]

Lazaret

Cave on the Mediterranean coast near Nice (France) that contains late Middle Pleistocene (Rissian) deposits and Acheulean lithic assemblages. Hominid teeth and the parietal of a child were recovered. The latter specimen may represent an early Neanderthal and shows an extensive internal lesion that may have been caused by a meningeal tumor. In the upper parts of Lazaret, a number of large stones appear to have been arranged in an arc enclosing an area around several hearths in the back of the cave. The excavator, H. de Lumley, considers this arc to be the footings for a tentlike structure within the cave. Concentrations of small shells within this area could suggest the use of dried seaweed for bedding.

See also Acheulean; Early Paleolithic; Europe; Neanderthals [J.J.S., C.B.S.]

Le Chaffaud

French cave site in Vienne at which Upper Paleolithic art was first recognized. An engraving on reindeer bone of two deer was discovered at Le Chaffaud in the 1830s–1840s, but it was attributed to Celtic artists. In 1860, French paleontologist E. Lartet published the Chaffaud engraving together with similar objects from Massat, asserting their Pleistocene antiquity.

See also Europe; Paleolithic Image; Upper Paleolithic. [J.J.S.]

Le Gros Clark, (Sir) Wilfrid Edward (1895–1971)

British anatomist. During the 1920s and 1930s, Clark's work focused on primate evolution and the taxonomic status of treeshrews. After World War II, his main interest shifted to the early stages of hominid evolution. Having examined R. Broom's australopithecine collection in Pretoria in 1946, Clark returned to England, where he began a zealous campaign supporting the hominid affinities of these fossils, a viewpoint that initially met with considerable opposition. In 1951, with L.S.B. Leakey, he made an important study of the Miocene hominid fossils recovered between 1949 and 1951 by the British Miocene Expedition to East Africa. Two years later, he collaborated with J. Weiner and K. Oakley in the debunking of the celebrated Piltdown skull. From 1932 to 1962, Clark was professor of anatomy at Oxford University. Among his many papers and books, perhaps the most popular and enduring are *History of the Primates* and *The Antecedents of Man.*

See also Broom, Robert; Leakey, Louis Seymour Bazett; Oakley, Kenneth Page; Piltdown.

Le Moustier

French rockshelter site where the partial skeleton of a Neanderthal youth was excavated in dubious circumstances in 1909; much of the skeleton was destroyed by bombing in 1945. Stone tools from the Middle Paleolithic sequence of the cave gave the name Mousterian to the whole Eurasian cultural complex of the early Late Pleistocene, although it is not certain with which level the hominid itself was associated. Subsequent dating work suggests that Neanderthal occupation of the site was quite recent (less than 45 Ka). Early Upper Paleolithic horizons are also represented at the site.

See also Europe; Middle Paleolithic; Mousterian; Neanderthals; Upper Paleolithic. [C.B.S.]

Leakey, Louis Seymour Bazett (1903–1972)

Paleoanthropologist born in Kenya, the son of British missionary parents. Leakey spent his youth with the Kikuyu people of Kenya before going to Cambridge to study archaeology and anthropology (1922–1926). During his career, he held a variety of visiting academic appointments in British and American universities and was curator of the Coryndon Memorial Museum, Nairobi (1945–1951).

Primarily, however, Leakey was a fieldworker. After an initial introduction to field techniques at the Tendaguru dinosaur site in southern Tanzania in the early 1930s, he began his pioneering work on Rift Valley prehistory, summarized in his book *The Stone Age Races of Kenya,* published in 1935. It was in this same period that he began work on the Miocene faunas of western Kenya, where he uncovered new early hominoids at such sites as Rusinga, Songhor, and Fort Ternan. After his marriage to Mary Nicoll, Leakey focused his attention increasingly during the 1940s and 1950s on the search for hominid fossils at Olduvai Gorge (Tanzania). Finally, in 1959, there came to light a fossil hominid cranium, which he named *Zinjanthropus boisei* (now generally regarded as a species of *Paranthropus*). As a result of this discovery, the Leakeys embarked on an intensive study of the gorge that yielded a succession of fossil hominin remains, among them those of a second, more gracile form, promptly named *Homo habilis*. Leakey considered that *H. habilis* was a toolmaker that lived contemporaneously with the robust, noncultural *Zinjanthropus* and that the former species represented a hominin on the direct line to modern *Homo sapiens*. Summaries of his particular view and interpretation of human history can be found in several of his books, among them *Adam's Ancestors* and *Unveiling Man's Origins*.

See also Africa; Africa, East; Fort Ternan; Homo habilis; Leakey, Mary Douglas Nicoll; Olduvai Gorge; Paranthropus; Rusinga; Songhor. [F.S.]

Leakey, Mary Douglas Nicoll (1913–1996)

Kenyan (b. England) archaeologist who began working with L.S.B. Leakey, whom she married, in East Africa in the mid-1930s. Although she collaborated extensively with him on a variety of paleontological subjects, including fossil primates (she found the important 1947 cranium of *Proconsul* on Rusinga Island), she was by inclination and training an archaeologist. (In this regard, it is worth noting that she was the great-great-great granddaughter of J. Frere [1740–1807], the pioneer of British stone-age archaeology.) She was responsible for the systematic archaeological excavation of numerous sites at Olduvai Gorge (Tanzania) and in 1959 discovered there the cranium of *Zinjanthropus*. After the death of her husband in 1972, she reinitiated excavations at the Pliocene site of Laetoli (Tanzania) and continued to work at Olduvai until 1982. Besides her long-range work on the lithic industries of East Africa, she also conducted major studies of rock art in Zambia.

See also Africa; Africa, East; Laetoli; Leakey, Louis Seymour Bazett; Olduvai Gorge; Proconsulidae; Rusinga. [F.S.]

Further Readings

Leakey, M.D. (1971) Olduvai Gorge, vol. 3: Excavations in Beds I and II, 1960–1963. Cambridge: Cambridge University Press.

Leaky, M.D. (1983) Africa's Vanishing Art: Rock Paintings of Tanzania. New York:

Leakey, M.D. (1984) Disclosing the Past: An Autobiography. New York: Doubleday.

Leakey, M.D., and Roe, D. (1995) Olduvai Gorge, vol. 5: Excavations in Beds III, IV and the Masek Beds, 1968–1971. Cambridge University Press.

Lehringen

Late Middle Pleistocene open-air site in eastern Germany from which the remains of an elephant (*Elephas antiquus*), stone tools, and wooden objects have been recovered. Among the wooden objects is a 2.5-m-long sharpened wooden spear that was found wedged between the ribs of the elephant. To-

gether with the Clacton spear from England, Lehringen has been cited as evidence for hunting by Middle Pleistocene humans. It has been suggested that these spears may actually have been snow probes used to locate frozen carcasses.

See also Clacton; Europe; Paleolithic Lifeways. [J.J.S.]

Further Readings

Gamble, C. (1986) The Paleolithic Settlement of Europe. Cambridge: Cambridge University Press.

Lemuridae

Family of Lemuriformes that includes the extant genera *Lemur*, *Eulemur*, *Varecia*, and *Hapalemur*. It also includes the extinct *Pachylemur*, a close relative of *Varecia*. *Lepilemur*, often included in this family, is here classified in the indrioid family Lepilemuridae. Relationships within the family Lemuridae are debated: Some authors have called attention to a few behavioral similarities linking *Lemur* and *Hapalemur*, although the traditional *Lemur-Eulemur* link still appears more probable. The entire family is unique to the large island of Madagascar, off the southeastern African coast.

The genus *Lemur* contains the single species, *Lemur catta*, the ringtailed lemur of the south and southwest of the island. This is the only semiterrestrial lemurid, living in multimale groups of ca. 15 members and traveling mainly on the ground over home ranges of ca. 5–20 ha. Adult body weight is ca. 3 kg, and the diet is primarily fruit. Coloration is similar in both sexes. This contrasts with the five species of *Eulemur*, which are similar to *Lemur* in body size and proportions, but among which sexual dichromatism ranges from the subtle to the pronounced. Members of genus *Eulemur*, the "true lemurs," are, for the most part, arboreal quadrupeds.

E. mongoz, the mongoose lemur of northwestern Madagascar and the Comoro Islands, usually lives in monogamous pairs in small home ranges. Unlike the other species of its genus (which may, however, be active at night as well as during the day), the mongoose lemur is entirely nocturnal, at least seasonally. *E. macaco*, the black lemur of northwestern Madagascar, consists of two contiguous but subtly distinct subspecies, about neither of which a great deal has been published. Both appear, however, to live in multimale groups averaging 10 individuals. *E. coronatus*, in the north of the island, probably lives in groups of similar size and composition but may spend more time on the ground. *E. rubriventer*, of the eastern humid forests, is highly arboreal, pairforming, and principally frugivorous. The widely distributed species *E. fulvus* contains six subspecies, of which two have been well studied. *E. f. rufus*, found in southwestern Madagascar and part of the eastern rain forest, lives in multimale groups averaging 10 individuals; where studied in the west, its home ranges are only ca. 1.0 ha, overlap considerably, and are undefended. Leaves compose the bulk of the diet. The best-studied population of *E. f. fulvus*, native to northwest Madagascar and the central part of the eastern rain forest, is found on the island of Mayotte, the most southerly of the Comoro group. Its diet varies greatly between seasons but

Three lemurids: Eulemur fulvus *from Mayotte, grooming (above);* Hapalemur griseus griseus *(lower left);* Varecia variegata variegata *(lower right).*

overall consists primarily of fruit. These lemurs are seen in fluid, temporary "associations" of an average size of 10 individuals; they are opportunistic feeders but are primarily frugivorous at most times of year. Activity is evenly divided between the day and the night, with long rest periods at both times.

The ruffed lemur, *Varecia variegata*, is represented by a red-and-black and a black-and-white subspecies, only the first of which has ever been studied in the wild. With a body weight of ca. 4 kg, these primates are agile arboreal quadrupeds that live in the humid forests of eastern Madagascar. They are frugivorous and show some variability in social organization.

The bamboo (or gentle) lemurs, genus *Hapalemur*, occur primarily in eastern Madagascar, with isolates on the west coast and in the north. The smallest of the three species, *H. griseus*, contains three subspecies of which one, *H. g. griseus*, is found more or less throughout the eastern rain forest and is specialized for feeding on the young shoots of bamboo. Weighing ca. 2 kg, these lemurs are diurnal and crepuscular semierect arboreal quadrupeds and are found in groups averaging three individuals, although up to six have been observed together. *H. g. alaotrensis* is slightly larger bodied and lives only in the reed beds fringing Lake Alaotra in eastern Madagascar. In locomotion combining some of the characteristics of both quadrupeds and vertical clingers, these diurnal and crepuscular lemurs leap between vertical reed stems and are ready swimmers. Their diet is largely, if not entirely, composed of the leaves and shoots of *Phragmites* reeds and the buds and pith of papyrus; group sizes seem to vary seasonally. In the drier, seasonal forests of the west-central and northwestern coasts are found two isolates of the little-known and relatively small-bodied *H. g. occidentalis*, which apparently depends on the shoots of bamboo vines for much of its diet, although it has also been observed to eat fruit. A bamboo lemur presumed to be *H. griseus* has been observed on the Ankarana Massif in the north, and a distinct population exists at the southern extremity of the eastern rain forest but has not been adequately named.

The largest (ca. 2.4 kg) gentle lemur is *Hapalemur simus*, known only from two very limited areas of the eastern rain forest though apparently much more widespread formerly; subfossil remains are known from the center of Madagascar and are abundant in the far north. Probably diurnal, this lemur lives in small multimale groups and feeds largely on the pith of giant bamboo. The smallest and most recently discovered (1987) bamboo lemur species is *H. aureus*, also known only from a restricted area of the eastern rain forest. Weighing ca. 1.6 kg, the golden bamboo lemur lives in groups of two to six and feeds largely on the shoots of giant bamboo, which contain high concentrations of cyanide.

In common with all of the other Malagasy primates, members of Lemuridae are severely threatened by hunting and by the destruction of their forest habitat. All species are officially classified as endangered or threatened, and the populations of some, such as *H. simus*, have probably already fallen below the minimum necessary for long-term survival. A slightly larger close relative of the ruffed lemur is already known from subfossil evidence to have become extinct, probably since the arrival of humans on Madagascar.

Family Lemuridae
  Subfamily Lemurinae
    Varecia
    †*Pachylemur*
    Lemur
    Eulemur
  Subfamily Hapalemurinae
    Hapalemur
†extinct

See also Diet; Lemuriformes; Lemuroidea; Locomotion; Teeth [I.T.]

Further Readings

Harcourt, C., and Thornback, J. (1990) Lemurs of Madagascar and the Comoros. The IUCN Red Data Book. Gland, Switzerland: IUCN.

Mittermeier, R.A., Tattersall, I., Konstant, W.R., Meyers, D.M., and Mast, R.B. (1994) Lemurs of Madagascar (Tropical Field Guide No. 1). Washington, D.C.: Conservation International.

Tattersall, I. (1982) The Primates of Madagascar. New York: Columbia University Press.

Tattersall, I. (1993) Madagascar's lemurs. Sci. Am. 268(1):110–117.

Lemuriformes

Infraorder of primates that contains the living (and Neogene to subfossil) strepsirhines, or "lower" primates, of Madagascar, Africa, and Asia. These include the lemurs of Madagascar (families Lemuridae, Lepilemuridae, Cheirogaleidae, Indriidae, Daubentoniidae, Archaeolemuridae, and Palaeopropithecidae (the last two extinct), the bushbabies of Africa (family Galagidae), and the lorises and pottos of Africa and Asia (family Lorisidae). These families are classified into three superfamilies: Lemuroidea (Lemuridae), Indrioidea (Indriidae, Archaeolemuridae, Palaeopropithecidae, Lepilemuridae, and Daubentoniidae), and Lorisoidea (Lorisidae, Galagidae, and Cheirogaleidae).

The accompanying cladogram shows a recently proposed scheme of relationships among all living genera of Lemuriformes. In testimony of their common ancestry, all members of this group possess in common two striking attributes: a *dental comb* and a *toilet* (grooming) *claw*. The dental comb (tooth comb or tooth scraper) is formed by the procumbent front teeth of the lower jaw. Elongated and closely approximated to each other, these teeth lie horizontally forward and are used in grooming the fur, an important individual and social activity, and in feeding. The tooth comb is particularly elongate in species that use it for gouging resins from the bark of trees, but, although there has been much discussion about which function, grooming or dietary, is the primary one for which this specialized structure evolved, there has been no clear resolution of the question. In the indrioids (except for *Daubentonia*, in which a

Hypothesis of relationships among the extant lemurs and lorises, showing family groupings. After Schwartz and Tattersall, 1985.

single pair of continuously growing front teeth is found in each jaw), only two pairs of teeth, usually identified as the central and lateral incisors but alternatively interpreted as one pair of canines and one of incisors, are present in the tooth comb; in almost all other lemuriforms, six teeth are represented, two incisors and a canine bilaterally.

Like all other extant primates, the lemuriforms possess nails in place of claws, backing sensitive pads on the ends of all the digits. However, there is one exception: the second digit of the foot terminates in the toilet (grooming) claw. This structure is not found elsewhere among primates, although the callitrichines are secondarily clawed on all digits except the hallux, and, among the lemuriforms, *Daubentonia* shows very compressed and clawlike nails on the same digits. The replacement of claws by nails among primates reflects an increasing reliance on grasping (hence, potentially manipulative) hands and feet and the related enhancement of tactile sensitivity in these organs. Lemuriforms, however, use *whole-hand prehension* when manipulating objects, in contrast to the more precise forms of prehension characteristic of most "higher" primates.

The balance between the senses of vision and smell is less heavily tilted in favor of vision among lemuriforms than it is among the "higher" primates. Olfactory marking (thus, communication via smell) is of considerable importance to most lemuriforms, while color vision is less developed than in monkeys and apes in the diurnal forms and is understandably absent in most of the nocturnal ones. The visual fields of the left and right eyes of lemuriforms overlap sufficiently to provide a good field of stereoscopic vision, but, although the orbits are completely ringed by bone, they are not completely walled off in the rear as they are in other extant primates. Compared with body size, the brains of lemuriforms tend to be smaller than those of other primates, so that in the lemuriform skull the largest component tends to be the facial skeleton, which houses an elaborate olfactory apparatus, rather than the braincase. In nearly all lemuriforms, the middle-ear cavity is housed in a protruding and inflated *bulla* rather than within the structure of the skull base as in ourselves and our closer relatives, and the eardrum is located at the external surface of the skull rather than at the end of a

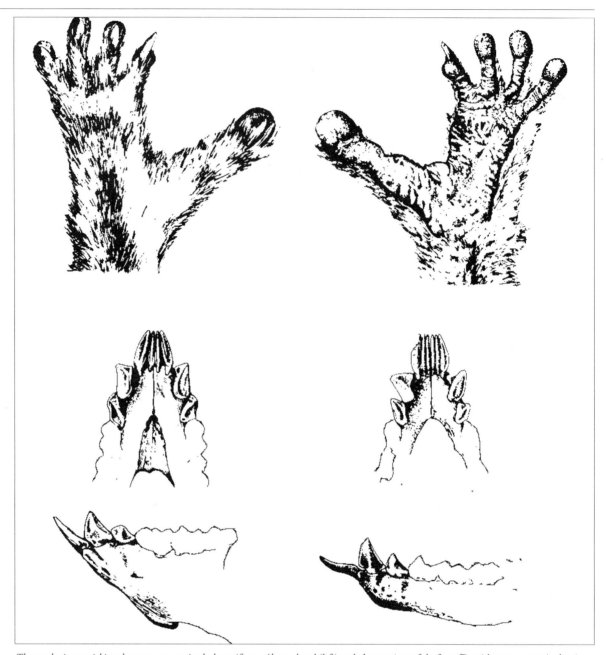

The two basic strepsirhine characters, as seen in the lemuriforms. Above: dorsal (left) and plantar views of the foot of Propithecus verreauxi, *showing the toilet claw. Middle and bottom: occlusal and lateral views of the dental scraper/combs of* Propithecus verreauxi *(left) and* Lemur fulvus.

bony tube. In the brain itself, lemuriforms tend to show less enlargement than do anthropoids of the *association areas*, the structures devoted to the integration of sensory inputs.

In body plan and in locomotion, the lemuriforms show great variety, although virtually all living forms are arboreal. Quadrupedalism takes many forms, from the deliberate slow-climbing of the lorisids—apparently related to manual predation—through the scrambling of the smaller cheirogaleids, to the agile bounding and leaping of the lemurids. Many lemuriforms, including the indriids, the galagids, and *Lepilemur*, prefer to hold their trunks erect and to leap between vertical supports, landing on, as well as pushing off with, their elongated hindlimbs. These forms also tend to use more suspensory behaviors when foraging in the trees. Most lemuriforms subsist primarily on leaves, fruits, and/or

flowers; insects form a large part of the diet of some of the smaller lorisoids, in particular, while other members of this group feed heavily on resins, at least seasonally.

Behaviorally, the lemuriforms have often been considered rather stereotyped. Recent studies, however, have shown that among the lemuriforms can be found almost the entire variety of types of social organization known among primates: male ranges overlapping those of more than one female; monogamous pairs with immature offspring; small groupings with a few adults of each sex, plus immature offspring; larger multimale-multifemale groupings with numerous immature offspring at various stages of development; even fluid and constantly reforming associations of individuals. Types of social organization are not grouped along systematic lines, however. Within-group social behaviors appear to be generally less complex among lemuriforms than are those exhibited among, say, Old World monkeys. This kind of thing is hard to pin down precisely, however, and a recent study has concluded that there is no quantum distinction between "lower" and "higher" primates in problem solving.

The primates of Madagascar are often referred to collectively as the lemurs and have generally been considered as descended from a single ancestor isolated on the island for many millions of years. This is not the case, however; the cheirogaleid lemurs are more closely related to the mainland lorisoids than to the other Malagasy forms. The term *lemur,* then, means simply Malagasy primate and has no strict systematic significance.

See also Archaeolemuridae; Callitrichinae; Cheirogaleidae; Daubentoniidae; Diet; Galagidae; Higher Primates; Indriidae; Indrioidea; Lemuridae; Lemuroidea; Lepilemuridae; Locomotion; Lorisidae; Lorisoidea; Lower Primates; Palaeopropithecidae; Primate Societies; Primates; Prosimian; Skeleton; Strepsirhini; Tarsiiformes; Teeth. [I.T.]

Further Readings

Doyle, G.A., and Martin, R.D., eds. (1979) The Study of Prosimian Behavior. New York: Academic.

Mittermeier, R.A., Tattersall, I., Konstant, W.R., Meyers, D.M., and Mast, R.B. (1994) Lemurs of Madagascar (Tropical Field Guide No. 1). Washington, D.C.: Conservation International.

Napier, J.R., and Napier, P.H. (1986) The Natural History of the Primates. Cambridge, Mass.: MIT Press.

Schwartz, J.H., and Tattersall, I. (1985) Evolutionary relationships of living lemurs and lorises (Mammalia, Primates) and their potential affinities with European Eocene Adapidae. Anthropol. Pap. Am. Mus. Nat. Hist. 60:1–100.

Tattersall, I. (1982) The Primates of Madagascar. New York: Columbia University Press.

Tattersall, I. (1993) Madagascar's lemurs. Sci. Am. 268(1):110–117.

Lemuroidea

Superfamily of Lemuriformes that contains the family Lemuridae. All of the lemuroids occur uniquely on the large island of Madagascar, ca. 450 km off the southeastern African coast. Lemuridae includes the four extant genera *Lemur, Eulemur, Varecia,* and *Hapalemur.* The genus *Lemur* contains the single species *L. catta;* the "true lemurs," genus *Eulemur,* embrace five species, of which one, *E. fulvus,* contains six subspecies and another, *E. macaco,* contains two. *Varecia variegata,* the ruffed lemur, also has two subspecies. *Hapalemur,* the bamboo lemur, includes the three species *H. griseus, H. aureus,* and *H. simus;* the former contains three distinct subspecies.

In other classifications, the Indriidae were sometimes included in the Lemuroidea, but they are here ranked as a separate superfamily with five families. *Lepilemur,* previously classified in the Lemuridae, is now seen as representing a distinct family of Indrioidea.

Lepilemur mustelinus *from eastern Madagascar.*

See also Indrioidea; Lemuridae; Lemuriformes; Lepilemuridae; Madagascar. [I.T.]

Lepilemuridae

Family of Indriiformes that contains the extant weasel or sportive lemurs, genus *Lepilemur,* and the extinct genus *Megaladapis.* The latter is a highly specialized form, but both genera share several distinctive features of the dentition, including the lack of upper permanent incisor teeth and certain characteristics of the lower molars.

Lepilemur is a genus of nocturnal lemurs widespread throughout the forested areas of Madagascar. Examination of such characters as pelage coloration, ear size, and certain cranial features reveals several distinctive populations of *Lepilemur,* along with some others that are less well defined. What is less certain, however, is at what taxonomic level all of these forms should be distinguished. They are karyotypically variable, but, since variability in chromosome number can be found even within the same forest, it is unclear to what extent karyotypic evidence is conclusive in species recognition. It seems a reasonably good bet, however, that when we know more about variation within the genus and about the precise distributions of the populations involved, we will conclude that several separate species exist among the more or less continuous *Lepilemur* populations in the forests that fringe Madagascar. Currently six or seven species tend to be recognized, according to taste. Although *Lepilemur* populations are found in a wide variety of forested environments, ranging from rain forest through seasonal gallery formations to

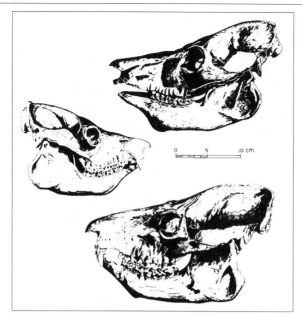

Crania in lateral view of the three species of Megaladapis: M. grandidieri *(above);* M. madagascariensis *(center); and* M. edwardsi *(below).*

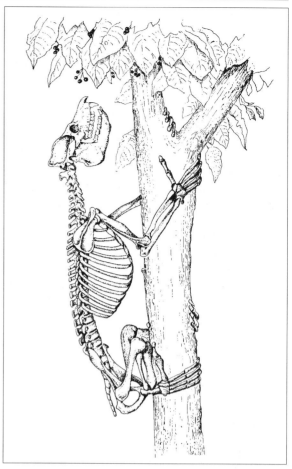

Skeletal reconstruction of Megaladapis edwardsi.

arid-adapted scrub forests, this lemur has been studied in detail in only one of these environments.

Lepilemur leucopus has been the subject of two studies in the arid south of Madagascar. Nocturnal in its activity but often observed awake during the day, the white-footed sportive lemur, as this form is cumbersomely known, is a specialized feeder on leaves. Small ranges (less than 0.4 ha) of males extensively overlap even smaller ranges of females, and male-female pairs of *range mates* may associate for part of the night's activity. Weighing ca. 0.5–1 kg, sportive lemurs are long-hindlimbed vertical clingers and leapers.

The large-bodied *Megaladapis* is perhaps the best known of the subfossil lemurs that became extinct subsequent to the arrival of human beings on Madagascar, ca. 1.5 Ka. Remains are known from marsh and cave deposits in central, northern, southern, and southwestern Madagascar. Some authorities recognize two species in this assemblage, others more. The largest-bodied of them, *M. edwardsi* (estimated at up to 80 kg), is found in sites of the south and southwest and is distinguished by its large dentition. This species attained the size of a St. Bernard dog, but the skull is disproportionately large, about 30 cm long. In sites of the same region occur also the subfossil remains of a smaller species, *M. madagascariensis*, with a skull ca. 20 percent shorter and a body weight estimated at 40 kg. Localities in the center of Madagascar have yielded bones of a closely related form often assigned to the species *M. grandidieri*. This form is distinguished by having a skull almost as long as that of *M. edwardsi* but molar teeth in the size range of *M. madagascariensis*. The morphology of all forms, including one from the Ankarana Massif in the north, is quite similar. As the illustration shows, the skull is greatly elongated in the braincase and the facial portion, even though brain size was relatively small. This elongation, together with an unusual upward flexion of the cranial base, is probably associated with cropping food with the front teeth. Also related

to this dietary adaptation is the lack of permanent upper incisor teeth, which were presumably replaced by a horny pad, as in some ruminants. With highly vascularized nasal bones overhanging the nasal aperture, it is even possible that in life *Megaladapis* possessed a small mobile snout. Unusually for a lemur, the ear cavity is entirely accommodated within the cranial base and communicates with the exterior via a bony tube.

Despite its great body size, *Megaladapis* was certainly arboreal, as attested by its extraordinarily long, curving extremities, among other features. In its locomotion, *Megaladapis* was probably a modified vertical clinger and leaper of limited agility. Its closest living locomotor analogue is said to be the koala of Australia, which progresses up tree trunks in series of hops and makes short leaps between vertical supports. Taken together, the characteristics of the skull and the postcranium of *Megaladapis* suggest the lifestyle of an arboreal browser, probably specialized for leaf eating like its living relative *Lepilemur*.

Family Lepilemuridae
    Subfamily Megaladapinae
        †*Megaladapis*
    Subfamily Lepilemurinae
        Lepilemur

†extinct

See also Indrioidea; Lemuriformes. [I.T.]

Further Readings

Mittermeier, R.A., Tattersall, I., Konstant, W.R., Meyers, D.M., and Mast, R.B. (1994) Lemurs of Madagascar (Tropical Field Guide No. 1). Washington, D.C.: Conservation International.

Tattersall, I. (1982) The Primates of Madagascar. New York: Columbia University Press.

Leroi-Gourhan, André (1911–1986)

French prehistorian. Leroi-Gourhan was a noted investigator who pioneered both the systematic study of Paleolithic cave art and sophisticated data-recovery and recording techniques in the excavation of Upper Paleolithic sites. His work at Arcy-sur-Cure and Pincevent elicited a great deal of paleoethnological information about human behavior during the Paleolithic. His wife, Arlette, was a leading practitioner of palynology in Europe and southwestern Asia.

See also Europe; Paleolithic Image; Paleolithic Lifeways; Pincevent; Site Types. [O.S.]

Les Trois Frères

Major Late Magdalenian engraved and painted cave, part of the Pyrenean Volp River (Ariège) group of cave sites that includes the shelter of Enlène and the cave of Tuc d'Audoubert through which the Volp flows. Les Trois Frères was discovered by three Bégouën brothers in 1914. It contains hundreds of engraved, and some painted, animal images (bison, horse, reindeer, lion, bear) as well as a unique, well-known painted and engraved dancing sorcerer in animal garb overlooking the main chamber of engravings. The associated cave of Tuc d'Audoubert contains a unique double clay sculpture of a bull and cow bison, with a tiny smaller bison (a calf?) on the floor nearby. The habitation site of Enlène contains more than 1,000 engraved stones. The three sites were utilized during the Middle Magdalenian and have carbon dates ranging from 14 to 13.5 Ka. Both Tuc d'Audoubert and Les Trois Frères contain the claviform motif, apparently a schematic "female," of this period and region.

See also Europe; Late Paleolithic; Magdalenian; Niaux; Paleolithic Image. [A.M.]

Further Readings

Bégouën, H., and Breuil, H. (1958) Les Cavernes du Volp: Trois-Frères-Tuc d'Audoubert. Paris: Arts et Métiers Graphiques.

Bégouën, R., and Clottes, J. (1984) Grottes des Trois Frères and Grotte du Tuc d'Audoubert. In L'Art des Cavernes: Atlas des Grottes Ornées Paléolithique Françaises. Paris: Ministère de la Culture, pp. 400–415.

Bégouën, R. et al. (1984–1985) Art mobilier sur support lithique d'Enlène (Montesquieu-Avantès, Ariège), Collection Bégouën du Musée de l'Homme. Ars Praehistorica 2/4:35–80.

Levallois

Prepared-core technology named after a suburb of Paris where flakes and cores of this type were first recovered and defined. Levallois technology is most characteristic of Middle Paleolithic industries but begins to appear before 200 Ka, in some cases in association with Early Paleolithic industries.

Levallois cores were carefully preshaped, or prepared, for the striking of flakes of a controlled shape and thickness. Centrally directed removals were generally used to create a square, ovoid, or other regularly shaped block of stone, which was more or less flat on the upper surface and markedly convex on the lower surface (planoconvex). The sides of the block were also convex (lateral convexities). A striking platform, at an acute angle to the upper, or flatter, surface was prepared at one end of the core by roughening or faceting. The Levallois flake was then removed from the upper surface by bringing the striking platform down sharply at an angle on an anvil. The large flake that often resulted was extremely thin for its size, conformed closely to the outline of the prepared core, and retained the pattern of centrally directed removals on its upper surface, as well as the facets of the striking platform.

Although not all of these features characterize every Levallois flake or core, the distinctive thinness of Levallois flakes, together with their regular shape, are suggestive of the use of the technology in a particular assemblage. Definitive determination of Levallois technology, however, can be made only by reconstructing the entire knapping process through refitting. Using the Levallois technology repeatedly on a block of stone required the knapper to maintain the convexities of the sides and lower surface, as well as the fundamental asymmetry of the way the block was struck. Levallois technology differs from discoidal technology in its focus on only the upper, flatter surface for the removal of flakes. In discoidal technology, on the other hand, each flake removal may serve as a striking platform for another removal simply by turning the core over, resulting in a symmetrical use of the core rather than an asymmetrical one. Removals from the upper surface of a Levallois core may be centrally directed or may be longitudinally organized from one or both ends, often resulting in bladelike blanks. The latter technique is more common in Western Asia and North Africa.

The industries made on Levallois flakes are often characterized by a lesser amount of secondary retouch than contemporaneous non-Levallois industries, as in the case of Ferrassie Mousterian (Levallois) vs. Quina Mousterian (non-Levallois) assemblages. Levallois points are pointed forms created entirely by preshaping on the core, with no secondary retouch.

Levallois technology produces large numbers of trimming flakes but relatively few Levallois flakes per core; it is used to flake both flint and coarser rocks, such as quartzite. It is particularly common in the Mousterian of Western Asia and North Africa. The Victoria West, a related technology that results in an elongated core, preshaped for striking repeated flakes from one end, is found in the final Early Stone Age of southern Africa.

Prepared-core technology like the Levallois is thought to have been an important development in human cultural evolution, both because the mental imagery needed to pre-shape a flake on the core required considerable cognitive ability and because it presaged the invention of blade technology.

See also Blade; Core; Early Paleolithic; Early Stone Age; Europe; Flake; Middle Paleolithic; Mousterian; Prepared-Core; Stone-Tool Making. [A.S.B.]

Further Readings

Bar-Yosef, O., and Dibble, H., eds. (1996) The Definition and Interpretation of Levallois Technology. Madison: Prehistory Press.

Boeda, E. (1996) Le Conception Levallois. Paris: CNRS.

Bordaz, J. (1970) Tools of the Old and New Stone Age. New York: Natural History Press.

Van Peer, P. (1992) The Levallois Reduction Strategy. Madison: Prehistory Press.

Levantine Aurignacian

An Upper Paleolithic industry from Western Asia dating to ca. 32–16 Ka (Ksar 'Akil 9–10, Hayonim D, El Wad E, Kebara E) and featuring distinctive nosed end-scrapers, burins, backed bladelets, and split-based bone points, and generally low numbers of blades. Because Aurignacian deposits occur in earlier periods in southeast Europe (e.g., Bacho Kiro and Temnata caves in Bulgaria), it seems likely that the Levantine Aurignacian was intrusive to the Levant, where it persisted alongside a different lithic tradition called the Ahmarian.

Further Readings

Bar-Yosef, O., and Belfer-Cohen, A. (1996) Another look at the Levantine Aurignacian. In A. Montet-White, A. Palma de Cesnola, and K. Valoch (eds.): The Upper Paleolithic. Colloquium XI: The Late Aurignacian. Colloquia of the XIII International Congress of Prehistory and Protohistory. Sci. Forli, Italy, 8–14 September 1996. Forli: A.B.A.C.O., pp. 139–150.

See also Ahmarian; Asia, Western; Aurignacian; El Wad; Hayonim; Kebara; Ksar 'Akil; Late Paleolithic; Upper Paleolithic. [J.J.S.]

Lithic Use-Wear

Modification of stone tools caused by their utilization. The adaptive role of stone tools is one of the most important questions in the study of human evolution, and, for more than a century, prehistorians have attempted the difficult task of trying to infer the function of Paleolithic artifacts. Early attempts tended to be based on simplistic morphological comparisons with ethnographic materials of known function or on common sense (i.e., asking the question, based on intuition, of what a likely activity was for a given artifact type). Contextual evidence, such as a Paleoindian Folsom point found between the ribs of an extinct form of bison, can also yield critical functional information, although dramatic evidence of this sort is relatively rare in the Stone Age record. Experimental archaeology is useful in showing the feasibility of whether a certain artifact form can, in fact, be used in a prescribed way, as well as the relative suitability of a particular tool for different tasks or of different tools for a given function.

At our present state of knowledge, however, the most reliable indications of stone-tool use are from use-wear studies—the examination of modification of stone-artifact surfaces that may indicate the activity for which they were used. These studies have their roots in the late nineteenth century, such as the observation that Neolithic flint sickle blades tended to have a bright, glossy appearance along their edge (corn/sickle/silica gloss) that could be replicated experimentally by cutting cereal grasses with hafted versions of similar artifacts.

The major pioneer in use-wear studies in the twentieth century was the Russian prehistorian S. Semenov, whose landmark *Prehistoric Technology* (1964) laid the foundation for most subsequent research. Semenov stressed the microscopic examination of prehistoric stone artifacts for traces of use-wear and proposed a number of types of modification still deemed important by researchers today: *edge damage* (breaking or chipping of an artifact edge); *polish* (modifica-

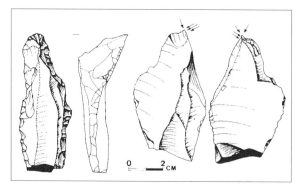

Levantine Aurignacian tools from eastern Sinai, Egypt. Left, steep end-scraper; right, busked burin (note burin-blow arrows). From I. Gilead, 1989, in O. Bar-Yosef and B. Vandermeersch, eds., Investigations in South Levantine Prehistory, *British Archaeological Reports, International Series, No. 497.*

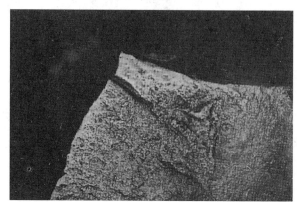

Close-up view (×100) of working edge of chert flake fragment from Koobi Fora, Kenya (ca. 1.5 Ma) showing polish caused by use on soft plant materials. Courtesy of L. Keeley.

tion of the surface of a stone artifact); and *striations* or scratches on an artifact.

Three major schools of use-wear study have developed since Semenov's publication, although none of them is incompatible with the others and some researchers have combined elements of all three. All of them use experimentation to discern patterns of wear from known functional activities and then apply these observations to prehistoric materials.

LOW-POWER OPTICAL MICROSCOPY

Using low-power magnification (normally less than 100×) and concentrating on edge damage, this approach is exemplified by the work of R. Tringham and colleagues and of G. Odell. It appears to be especially useful in separating major wear categories, such as damage produced by cutting relatively soft materials vs. scraping relatively harder materials.

HIGH-POWER OPTICAL MICROSCOPY

Using a higher powered, bright field magnification (usually 100–500×) and concentrating on polish as well as edge damage, this approach is exemplified by the work of L. Keeley, E. Moss, and P.C. Vaughan. It attempts to make fine distinctions among wear patterns produced by diverse functions (e.g., slicing, scraping, or sawing) and to specify the particular type of material to which a tool was applied (e.g., wood, soft plant, meat, bone, fresh hide, dry hide, antler). The principal criteria used in this technique are polish (a combination of brightness, luster, and texture), striations, pitting, and edge damage. At present this technique is restricted primarily to fine-grained siliceous materials, such as flint, chert, and chalcedony, of an unweathered and unabraded nature, in which optical polishes develop through tool use. Pieces must also be carefully cleaned to remove any adhering surface material.

SCANNING ELECTRON MICROSCOPY

Using much higher magnifications, researchers can examine topographic features of stone for surface modification or inclusions. This approach is exemplified by the research of P. Anderson.

An approach that incorporates both low-powered and high-powered optical microscopy appears to be the most reliable, as it maximizes the amount of information regarding damage or alteration incurred during stone-tool use. Expertise in microwear analysis is, to a large extent, a function of experience in analyzing experimental and prehistoric specimens. Since functional interpretations are subjective and criteria difficult to quantify, there are potential problems in assessing the reliability of an individual researcher's conclusions. To demonstrate proficiency, a set of blind tests using experimental, or ethnographic, materials of known function should be carried out to demonstrate the range of reliability of the particular technique and the practitioner. Studies by T.H. Loy suggest that organic residues on stone artifacts, especially blood residues, are diagnostic of the species that had been butchered with stone tools. Such residues may also be identifiable through DNA (deoxyribonucleic acid) analysis. Another approach uses microprobe analysis of the edge to detect adhering residues. Such organic-residue studies, once refined, should provide critical evidence of stone-tool function in the future and will greatly augment inferences made from use-wear analysis.

See also Paleoindian; Paleolithic Lifeways; Raw Materials; Stone-Tool Making. [N.T., K.S.]

Further Readings

Anderson, P. (1980) A testimony of prehistoric tasks: Diagnostic residues on stone tool working edges. World Archaeol. 12:181–194.

Coles, J. (1973) Archaeology by Experiment. London: Hutchinson.

Hayden, B., ed. (1979) Lithic Use-Wear Analysis. New York: Academic.

Keeley, L. (1980) Experimental Determination of Stone Tool Uses: A Microwear Analysis. Chicago: University of Chicago Press.

Loy, T.H. (1983) Prehistoric blood residues: Detection on tool surfaces and identification of species of origin. Science 220:1269–1270.

Moss, E. (1983) The Functional Analysis of Flint Implements Pincevent and Font d'Ambon: Two Case Studies from the French Final Paleolithic. Oxford: British Archaeological Reports.

Odell, G. (1979) A new improved system for the retrieval of functional information from microscopic observation of chipped stone tools. In B. Hayden (ed.): Lithic Use-Wear Analysis. New York: Academic, pp. 239–244.

Semenov, S. (1964) Prehistoric Technology. Bath: Adams and Dart.

Tringham, R., Cooper, G., Odell, G., and Voytek, B. (1974) Experimentation in the formation of edge damage: A new approach to lithic analysis. J. Field Archaeol. 1:171–196.

Vaughan, P.C. (1985) Use-Wear Analysis of Flaked Stone Tools. Tucson: University of Arizona Press.

Liucheng

Southern Chinese fossil locality of latest Pliocene-Early Pleistocene age, ca. 2 Ma based on faunal correlation. The Juyuandong Cave in Liucheng county, Guangxi Province has yielded three mandibles and more than 1,000 isolated teeth of *Gigantopithecus*, along with the remains of several other mammalian taxa. The cave is the unofficial type site for the *Gigantopithecus* Fauna, which is thought to present a more archaic aspect than the *Stegodon-Ailuropoda* Fauna of southern China. In fact, these two faunas are distinguished largely on the basis of the size of a few taxa.

See also Asia, Eastern and Southern; China; Gigantopithecus; Stegodon-Ailuropoda Fauna. [G.G.P.]

Further Readings

Pei, W.C. (1957) Discovery of *Gigantopithecus* mandibles and other materials in Liucheng of central Kwangsi in south China. Vert. Palasiatica 1:65–72.

Wu, X., and Poirier, F.E. (1995) Human Evolution in China: A Metric Description of the Fossils and a Review of the Sites. New York: Oxford University Press.

Llano Complex

Clovis-period (ca. 12–11 Ka) material culture centered on the High Plains of New Mexico, best known from the Blackwater Draw site. The assemblage is characterized by lanceolate, bifacially flaked projectile points, thinned by one or more fluting flakes. These points also exhibit basal and end grinding. Burins, scrapers, knives, and gravers accompany the stone (and occasional bone) points in the Llano assemblage. The name derives from the *Llano Estacado* (Texas and New Mexico), where the Clovis type site is located.

See also Americas; Blackwater Draw; Clovis; Paleoindian [L.S.A.P., D.H.T.]

Locherangan

Early Miocene fossil site in the western Turkana Basin (Kenya). Thin fluvial lenses in a 50-m section of lacustrine beds west of Kataboi have yielded a diversity of large mammals, including the primates *Afropithecus* and *Simiolus* and an indeterminate hominoid. Faunal correlation indicates an age of ca. 17.5 Ma.

See also Turkana Basin. [F.H.B.]

Locomotion

Animals are distinguished by their ability to move around in search of food, mates, and shelter. Primates, in particular, have evolved many types of locomotion in conjunction with their ability to exploit many habitats. Each of these methods is associated with anatomical specializations of the skeleton and musculature. The locomotor habits of most primates can be divided into five categories.

Primate Locomotor Modes

The most common type of primate locomotion is *arboreal quadrupedalism,* walking and running along branches. This is the most generalized type of locomotion among mammals and is probably the way in which the earliest primates moved. Most other locomotor specializations have evolved from this type of movement. The skeletal proportions of arboreal quadrupeds and many aspects of their musculature and limb joints indicate that the greatest mechanical difficulties presented by this type of locomotion are maintaining balance upon the irregular, unstable supports provided by tree branches. Thus, arboreal quadrupeds are characterized by grasping hands and feet. Their forelimbs and hindlimbs are similar in length and relatively short so that their center of gravity is close to the branch for stability, and many have a long tail for balance.

A few primates regularly walk and run across the ground, a type of locomotion that is called *terrestrial quadrupedalism.* Like arboreal quadrupeds, these species have forelimbs and hindlimbs that are similar in length. Because the ground is flat and stable, however, balance is less of a problem for them. Thus, they have shorter fingers and toes and longer limbs for higher speed. Many also have short tails.

The African apes use a special type of quadrupedal locomotion called *knuckle-walking,* in which they rest their hands on the knuckles of the third and fourth digits rather than on their palms or the tips of their fingers. This special hand posture enables them to walk quadrupedally on the ground using the long curved fingers they also need for climbing.

Many primates move by *leaping* to cross gaps between trees. In leaping, the propulsive forces come almost totally from the hindlimbs and back. Leaping primates have long hindlimbs, a relatively long, flexible back, and often a long tail. In many small primates, the ankle region is also elongated to aid in leaping. The concept of *vertical clinging and leaping* is sometimes used to describe those leapers (such as tarsiers, bushbabies, and sifakas) that hold themselves in a vertical posture between leaps. They have especially long hindlimbs and feet.

Larger primates often move by *suspensory locomotion,* such as swinging by their arms *(brachiation)* or climbing. In this type of locomotion, they usually hang below arboreal supports, and their limbs seem to function primarily in tension rather than compression. Suspensory locomotion enables a large species to spread its body mass over many slender supports and thus to forage in parts of a forest that it might not otherwise be able to reach. Suspensory primates are often characterized by long hindlimbs, very long forelimbs, and joints that permit a wide range of motion in many directions. They also have long hands and feet for grasping arboreal supports. They usually have a short, stiff backbone, and many have lost their tail.

Human Locomotion

The *bipedalism* that characterizes humans is one of the most unusual forms of locomotion that has evolved in the entire animal kingdom. The mechanical problems of balancing and moving our body atop two limbs have led to many of the distinctive anatomical specializations of our species. Our hindlimbs are long to provide a long stride. The human foot lacks the grasping abilities found in the feet of other primates and instead is a stiff propulsive lever with a long heel, short toes, and a hallux (great toe) aligned with the other digits.

During part of each stride in bipedal progression, our entire body weight is balanced over a single limb as the opposite limb swings forward for the next step. We have evolved many structural features to deal with this precarious situation. The human ilium (the largest bone in the pelvis) is short and broad to provide a large base for the attachment of the hip muscles that keep the trunk balanced over the lower limb. Humans are naturally knock-kneed, so that the lower part of our hindlimb is lined up close to the center of body mass. In addition, the curvature of our back helps keep the center of gravity lower for balance.

The first hints of human bipedalism appear in the fossil record more than 4 Ma, but many of the more subtle anatomical features we associate with this form of locomotion apparently came much later. There is considerable debate over the ecological factors that predisposed human ancestors to become bipeds. Early theorists linked the evolution

Representatives of various primate locomotion categories. Skeletons of similar forms are illustrated in the article "Skeleton." Courtesy of John G. Fleagle.

of bipedalism with the evolution of stone tools. This theory, however, seems to be contradicted by the paleontological record showing bipedal hominids well before the first stone artifacts. Some have argued that the selective advantage of bipedalism lay more generally in the freeing of the hands for transporting food or water from distant foraging sites to provision offspring or other family members. Others have linked the evolution of bipedalism with foraging in an open woodland environment in which food resources were widely scattered and required long-distance travel over flat terrain.

Although it is not possible to reconstruct the ecological conditions surrounding the origin of human bipedalism, the paleontological record clearly indicates that this locomotor adaptation was probably the first adaptive breakthrough that characterized the origin of hominins. The ability to walk on two legs preceded the later hallmarks of human evolution, such as the manufacture of tools and the enlargement of the brain.

See also Ape; Biomechanics; Functional Morphology; Hominidae; Hominini; Monkey; Primates; Skeleton. [J.G.F.]

Further Readings

Fleagle, J.G. (1998) Primate Adaptation and Evolution. Second edition. San Diego: Academic.

Gebo, D.L., ed. (1993) Postcranial Adaptation in Nonhuman Primates. DeKalb: Northern Illinois University Press.

Jenkins, F.A., Jr., ed. (1974) Primate Locomotion. New York: Academic.

Jungers, W.L., ed. (1985) Size and Scaling in Primate Biology. New York: Plenum.

Strasser, E., and Dagosto, M., eds. (1988) The Primate Postcranial Skeleton. London: Academic.

Lokalalei

Late Pliocene archaeological site in the Turkana Basin (Kenya) that has produced cores and unretouched flakes of Olduwan character, which are among the oldest known. The site, along the Lokalalei ephemeral stream west of Lake Turkana, is in the basal Kalochoro Member of the Nachukui Formation and dates to ca. 2.35 Ma.

See also Oldowan; Turkana Basin. [F.H.B.]

Lokalalei Member

Middle Pliocene member of the Nachukui Formation in the western Turkana Basin (Kenya). KNM-WT-17000, the best specimen of *Paranthropus aethiopicus*, derives from the basal part. It is bounded above by the Lokalalei (2.5 Ma) and below by Kalochoro (2.35 Ma) tuffs and is equivalent to the lower Burgi Member of the Koobi Fora Formation (Kenya) and Members D and E of the Shungura Formation (Ethiopia).

See also Turkana Basin. [F.H.B.]

Lomekwi Member

Middle Pliocene fluvial member of the Nachukui Formation, western Turkana Basin (Kenya), which has yielded several specimens of *Australopithecus*. It spans the interval between the Tulu Bor (3.4 Ma) and Lokalalei (2.5 Ma) tuffs, equivalent to the Tulu Bor Member of the Koobi Fora Formation (Kenya) and to Members B and C of the Shungura Formation (southern Ethiopia).

See also Turkana Basin. [F.H.B.]

Longgupo

Early Pleistocene cave locality in eastern Sichuan Province (China) containing a rich faunal assemblage and fossils of both *Gigantopithecus blacki* and a hominin provisionally classified as *Homo erectus*, along with stone artifacts.

Excavations conducted between 1985 and 1988 at Longgupo (Chinese for "Dragon Bone Hill") penetrated a thickness of ca. 17 m of fossiliferous deposits, apparently extending below the Plio-Pleistocene boundary (1.8 Ma). Biostratigraphic and palaeomagnetic correlations, as well as amino-acid racemization, have all been interpreted as evidence for a date in excess of 2 Ma for the hominin-bearing strata. These strata have yielded a hominin mandibular fragment with P_4-M_1 intact (Layer 8), a single isolated upper central incisor (Layer 7), and two stone artifacts: a flake tool from Layer 8 and a hammerstone from Layer 5. The Longgupo hominin fossils were identified as *Homo erectus* partly on the basis of their alleged antiquity and partly on the morphological similarities to African and Asian members of the *erectus*-level clade. At present, specialists are divided in their interpretation of these fossils, with some seeing closest similarities to African *Homo ergaster* teeth and others suggesting that the specimens are either pongine or indeterminate. Moreover, alternative (and younger) interpretations have been proposed for the age of the deposits.

See also Asia, Eastern and Southern; China; Chopper-Chopping Tools; Gigantopithecus; Homo erectus; Homo ergaster; Lantian; Yuanmou; Zhoukoudian. [J.W.O.]

Further Readings

Huang, W., Ciochon, R.L., Gu, Y., Larick, R. (1995) Early *Homo* and associated artifacts from Asia. Nature 378:275–278.

Huang, W., and Hou, Y. (1997) Archaeological evidence for the first human colonization of east Africa. IPPA Bull. 16(3):3–12. Canberra: ANU.

Huang, W.P., Fang, Q.R., et al. (1991) The Wushan *Homo erectus* Site. [In Chinese with English abstract]. Beijing: Haiyang.

Larick, R., and Ciochon, R.L. (1996) The African emergence and early Asian dispersals of the genus *Homo*. Am. Sci. 84:538–551.

Olsen, J.W., and Miller-Antonio, S. (1992) The Palaeolithic in Southern China. Asian Perspectives 31:129–160.

Lonyumun Member

Lower Pliocene lacustrine beds below the Moiti Tuff in the Turkana Basin (Kenya) dated between 4.2 and 3.9 Ma. It is recognized as the basal member of the Nachukui Formation west of Lake Turkana and of the Koobi Fora Formation to the northeast. Some of the oldest specimens of *Australopithecus* from the Turkana Basin come from its upper part in Koobi Fora Area 260.

See also Turkana Basin. [F.H.B.]

Lorisidae

Family of strepsirhine primates that includes the living lorises and pottos and their fossil relatives. The extant lorisids are distributed throughout sub-Saharan Africa (*Perodicticus*, the potto, *Arctocebus*, the angwantibo, and the recently described and very rare *Pseudopotto*) and Asia (*Loris*, the slender loris, in Sri Lanka and *Nycticebus*, the slow loris, in southern China and the large islands of the Southeast Asian archipelago). The galagos are sometimes included in Lorisidae but are here assigned to Galagidae.

All extant lorisids are nocturnal and essentially proteinivorous and are characterized by their extremely slow, cautious locomotion. To enhance the range of sizes of branches they can grasp with their hands, lorisids develop rudimentary second digits (one of the features that typifies the group), thereby permitting prehension between the first and third digits. There is also evidence that, to sustain the metabolic demands of maintaining muscular contraction while locomoting as slowly but as continuously as they do, lorisids have developed a collateral vascular supply to the limbs that aids in the elimination of accumulating lactic acid. As a group, extant lorisids have also been characterized by such features as the lack of a tail; expansion of the angular, or gonial, region of the mandible; marked frontation of the bony orbits, whose margins are elevated, or lipped; the presence in the auditory region of a stout but short lateral tubular extension of the ectotympanic; and dorsoventral compression of the distal femur. In their teeth, lorisids are distinguished by having lower premolars that are expanded lingually, but more striking is the configuration of the lower molars, which appear pinched into two components due to the centrally emplaced cristid obliqua, which isolates the protoconid and creates a deep hypoflexid notch.

Lorisids can also be described as differing from lemuroids and indrioids in aspects of the arterial circulation of the auditory region. Lorisids lack one of the branches within the auditory bulla of the internal carotid artery (the *stapedial*), thus retaining the promontory artery as the major internal artery, but they develop another artery, the *ascending pharyngeal* (anterior carotid), which branches off the internal carotid artery and courses medially around the bulla to anastomose, or network, with the promontory artery. These two features are indeed striking, but they are not unique to lorisids. Cheirogaleids (mouse and dwarf lemurs) and galagids (bushbabies) also develop an ascending pharyngeal artery, which is one of the major characteristics that points to the close relationship of these two groups with lorisids. The stapedial artery is lacking in some cheiro-

galeids, but it is more consistently absent in galagids, which, along with a suite of dental features, serves to join the latter group closely with the lorisids. Lorisids and galagids are also distinguished in their bony auditory region: The tympanic ring fuses in its entirety to the edge of the auditory bulla. Given the apparent relatedness of lorisids to galagids and, more broadly, to cheirogaleids, one might suggest that the last common ancestor of the extant lorisids had undergone secondary reduction of the calcaneus and navicular bones, which are otherwise typically more elongate in the other two groups of lorisoids.

Among the extant lorisids, close relationships are not between biogeographic neighbors. Rather, as G.G. Simpson and later J.H. Schwartz and I. Tattersall pointed out, it appears that the Asian *Loris* is most closely related to the African *Arctocebus*, while the Asian *Nycticebus* is most closely allied with the African *Perodicticus*. The former pair is united, for example, by the development of an anterior prolongation of the premaxilla (into a little snout) and such dental features as a large submolariform posterior upper premolar that bears a small hypocone, an anteriorly placed upper canine that is transversely rotated, buccal cingulids on the lower molars, and a large M³. *Nycticebus* and *Perodicticus* both possess a distinctive, "puffy" anterior maxillary region (created, in part, by the large root of the upper canine swelling out the bone of the maxilla), as well as relatively lower and broader upper and lower cheek-tooth cusps, which become so inflated (in fact, "puffy") in *Perodicticus* that shearing crests and tooth basins are virtually obliterated. *Perodicticus* and *Nycticebus* are also the two extant strepsirhines with the least procumbent and most robust (and, thus, least slender and elongate) tooth combs. These two primates are further distinguished among lorisoids in general by their possession of very stout and enlarged upper central incisors. In *Nycticebus,* emphasis on these teeth is evidenced in some individuals by the diminution of

The two African lorisids. Arctocebus calabarensis, *the angwantibo (left), and* Perodicticus potto, *the potto.*

the lateral incisors to very slender structures, and in others by the loss entirely of the lateral incisors.

Fossils whose affinities appear to lie with extant lorisids include *Mioeuoticus*, from the Miocene of East Africa, and *Nycticeboides*, from the Miocene of the Siwaliks of Indo-Pakistan. *Mioeuoticus* is broadly related to *Arctocebus* and *Loris*, whereas *Nycticeboides* appears to be closely related to *Nycticebus*. A third possible fossil lorisid is *Indraloris*, from the Miocene of Indo-Pakistan, which, although classified by some paleontologists as an adapid (or sivaladapid), shares with *Loris* specific and seemingly phylogenetically significant details of M_1 morphology, including a well-developed protostylid.

In 1996, Schwartz described a new lorisoid genus, *Pseudopotto*, which may have relationships to lorisids. This new taxon is based on two museum skeletons (one from Cameroon, the other less definitely located) that are less derived than any known lorisid in having a long tail and lacking a special feature of the distal ulna. *Pseudopotto* may represent the sister-taxon to the Lorisidae, but it has not yet been assigned to any family within Lorisoidea.

Family Lorisidae
   Loris
   † *Indraloris*
   † *Mioeuoticus*
   Arctocebus
   Perodicticus
   Nycticebus
   † *Nycticeboides*
Family unspecified
   Pseudopotto
†extinct

See also Adapidae; Cheirogaleidae; Galagidae; Locomotion; Lorisoidea; Skull; Strepsirhini; Teeth. [J.H.S.]

Further Readings

Martin, R.D., Doyle, G.A., and Walker, A.C., eds. (1974) Prosimian Biology. London: Duckworth.

Napier, J.R., and Napier, P. (1967) A Handbook of Living Primates. London: Academic.

Schwartz, J.H. (1986) Primate systematics and a classification of the order. In D.R. Swindler (ed.): Comparative Primate Biology, Vol. 1: Systematics, Evolution, and Anatomy. New York: Liss, pp. 1–41.

Schwartz, J.H. (1996) *Pseudopotto martini*: A new genus and species of extant lorisiform primate. Anthropol. Pap. Am. Mus. Nat. Hist. 78:1–14.

Schwartz, J.H., and Tattersall, I. (1986) Evolutionary relationships of living lemurs and lorises (Mammalia, Primates) and their potential affinities with European Eocene Adapidae. Anthropol. Pap. Am. Mus. Nat. Hist. 60:1–100.

Simpson, G.G. (1967) The Tertiary lorisiform primates of Africa. Bull. Mus. Comp. Zool. 136:39–62.

Szalay, F.S., and Delson, E. (1979) Evolutionary History of the Primates. New York: Academic.

Lorisoidea

Superfamily of strepsirhine primates including the Afro-Asian lorises (family Lorisidae) and galagos (family Galagidae), as well as the mouse and dwarf lemurs of Madagascar (family Cheirogaleidae). In this volume, Lorisoidea is included with the primates of Madagascar in the infraorder Lemuriformes rather than in its own infraorder, Lorisiformes, as has been more common practice over the past decades. On the other hand, Lorisoidea here contains not only Lorisidae and Galagidae (distinguished as full families), but also the cheirogaleids, which have traditionally been classified and thought of as closely related to the other, larger primates of Madagascar. Biogeographical proximity, however, does not guarantee phylogenetic relationship; thus, features of the hard- and soft-tissue anatomy of the auditory region and details of dental morphology present compelling reasons for associating the cheirogaleids with lorisids and galagids, despite the rejection of this view by A.D. Yoder and colleagues, mainly on the basis of molecular analyses. Within Lorisoidea, the lorisids and the galagids are the most closely related.

Fossils from Miocene deposits of East Africa and Indo-Pakistan are readily noted as having affinities with various lorisoids (*Komba* and *Progalago* with galagids and *Mioeuoticus*, *Nycticeboides*, and *Indraloris* with Lorisids), but J.H. Schwartz and I. Tattersall have recently suggested that certain Eocene taxa may also be related to lorisoids, either broadly (*Anchomomys*, *Periconodon*) or specifically (*Huerzeleris* with cheirogaleids and *Chasselasia* with galagids). Schwartz has even offered evidence that fossil "tarsioids" in general may be the sister group of Lorisoidea and that *Tarsius* is the primitive sister of this large clade. This hypothesis is not accepted elsewhere in the encyclopedia.

See also Adapidae; Adapiformes; Cheirogaleidae; Galagidae; Lemuriformes; Lorisidae; Molecular "vs." Morphological Approaches to Systematics; Notharctidae; Omomyidae; Strepsirhini; Tarsiidae; Tarsiiformes. [J.H.S.]

Further Readings

Schwartz, J.H. (1986) Primate systematics and a classification of the order. In D.R. Swindler (ed.): Comparative Primate Biology, Vol. 1: Systematics, Evolution, and Anatomy. New York: Liss, pp. 1–41.

Yoder, A.D., Cartmill, M., Ruvolo, M., Smith, K., and Vilgalys, R. (1996) Ancient single origin for Malagasy primates. Proc. Nat. Acad. Sci. USA 93:5122–5126.

Lothagam

Northern Kenyan stratified sequence of Late Miocene to Early Pleistocene age, with a Late Pleistocene capping layer, southwest of Lake Turkana. Discovered in the late 1960s by an expedition from Harvard University under the direction of B. Patterson, the Lothagam sequence has yielded a rich and diverse vertebrate assemblage from a succession of levels, most recently studied by M.G. Leakey and colleagues. The lowest fossiliferous unit, corresponding to what was previously termed Lothagam 1A-B and lower 1C, is now termed the Nawata Formation. Paleomagnetic stratigraphy, in view of an age of 8.3 Ma on basalt below the Nawata Formation, indicates that its base is just less than 8 Ma, and the top is 5.5 Ma, almost exactly coincident with the present age of the Miocene-Pliocene boundary (5.25 Ma). The Nawata is divided into two members, with the boundary (equivalent to the base of Lothagam 1C) at 6.25 Ma.

The West Turkana Nachukui Formation forms the upper part of the Lothagam sequence. The Apak Member, at the base, is a local unit dated between 5 and 4.7 Ma, underlying Lothagam basalt dated to ca. 3.7 Ma. The basalt is overlain by beds attributed to the Upper Pliocene Kalochoro and Lower Pleistocene Kaitio members, separated by the KBS Tuff (1.89 Ma). The Apak corresponds to the formerly designated upper Lothagam 1C. Nearly all Lothagam fossils have come from the Nawata and Apak units.

Several primates are known from Lothagam, including colobine and cercopithecine fragments from the Nawata Formation and an isolated lower molar of *Theropithecus,* from above the basalt, that is one of the oldest-known representatives of the genus. Patterson's team recovered an adult hominine mandible fragment with first molar from the basal Apak Member and two additional teeth were found later in the upper Nawata. The mandible displays several primitive features, and various workers have assigned it to *Ramapithecus, Australopithecus* sp., *A. africanus, A. afarensis,* and Hominoidea indet. Homininae indet. seems the most appropriate attribution pending recovery of more substantial material of this age.

The Lothagam area also exposes uppermost Pleistocene to Holocene horizons that have been excavated by L. Robbins. In these beds have been found bone harpoons, a crude nonmicrolithic industry on lava flakes, and human skeletal material of modern type, revealing various pathologies, including fractures.

See also Africa, East; Australopithecus; Homininae; Patterson, Bryan; Turkana Basin [E.D., A.S.B.]

Further Readings

Leakey, M.G., Feibel, C.S., Bernor, R.L., Harris, J.M., Cerling, T.E., Stewart, K.M., Storrs, G.W., Walker, A., Werdelin, L., and Winkler, A.J. (1996) Lothagam: A record of faunal change in the Late Miocene of East Africa. J. Vert. Paleontol. 16:556–570.

Lothidok Formation

Lower Miocene formation in the southwestern Turkana Basin between Lodwar and Kalokol, Kenya, with fossil-bearing beds in a complexly faulted section of conglomerates, sandstones, mudstones, and volcanics ca. 1,500 m thick. Specimens of *Turkanapithecus, Afropithecus, Simiolus,* and *Proconsul* come from basal levels, at Moruarot and Kalodirr, dated between 17.5 and 16.8 Ma by potassium-argon (K/Ar) ages on associated lavas. *Kenyapithecus* remains at Esha have been collected from upper levels dated to 13.2 Ma.

See also Africa, East; "Dendropithecus-Group"; Kalodirr; Kenyapithecinae; Proconsulidae; Turkana Basin. [F.H.B.]

Lothidok Site

Stratified Upper Oligocene site on the southwestern side of Lake Turkana (Kenya). This is the original site of Lothidok, or Losodok. Recent geological work has located it in the Eragaleit Formation, a sedimentary lens within thick lavas that underlie the Lothidok Formation proper. Dated between 27.5 and 24.3 Ma, this site yields the oldest-known member of Hominoidea, the proconsulid *Kamoyapithecus hamiltoni,* together with an early gomphothere, a hyrax, and an anthracothere.

See also Africa, East; Lothidok Formation; Proconsulidae; Turkana Basin. [J.A.V.C.]

Lower Primates

Prosimian primates, including the lemurs, lorises, galagos, tarsiers, their extinct relatives, and all early primates, as distinguished from the higher, or anthropoid, members of the order. This term originally dates to a *scala naturae* view of evolution, with *lower* evolving into *higher* forms of life. It subsequently has come back into use as a way of referring to this paraphyletic, or "wastebasket," group. Although tarsiers are often recognized as the closest living relatives of the anthropoids, and the extinct Plesiadapiformes are not closely related to any speciflc living primates, many authors prefer to refer to all members of this assemblage as if they were a natural group. The prosimians may be considered "lower" in terms of their lesser relative brain size and other features that separate them from the anthropoids.

See also Anthropoidea; Brain; Haplorhini; Higher Primates; Monophyly; Primate Societies; Primates; Prosimian; Scala Naturae; Strepsirhini; Tarsiiformes. [E.D., I.T.]

Lufeng

Upper Miocene lignite (brown coal) stratified sequence ca. 90 km northwest of Kunming, Yunnan Province, China. The Lufeng fauna is roughly equivalent to the Nagri or Dhok Pathan fauna of the Siwaliks of Indo-Pakistan, 9–7 Ma. The deposits have yielded several partial crania and numerous gnathic and dental remains of hominoids, but few postcranial specimens. The material had been grouped by some researchers according to size, with a larger species representing *Sivapithecus* and a smaller one *Ramapithecus.* Most workers, however, consider that, as with the Nagri hominoid material, the large and small forms represent a single sexually dimorphic species, here *Lufengpithecus lufengensis.* The affinities of this taxon are unclear, as it combines conservative broad interorbital spacing with somewhat pongine molars and autapomorphic, heavily buttressed anterior dentition and jaws; in this volume, *Lufengpithecus* is tentatively included in the Dryopithecinae. Other Lufeng primates include the crouzeliine pliopithecid *Laccopithecus* and the ?sivaladapine notharctid *Sinoadapis.*

See also Asia, Eastern and Southern; China; Dryopithecinae; Lufengpithecus; Notharctidae; Pliopithecidae; Sivapithecus; Siwaliks. [G.G.P.]

Lufengpithecus

A moderately well-known genus of hominoid primate from the Chinese Late Miocene whose precise systematic position remains unclear. *Lufengpithecus lufengensis* is surely known only from Lufeng, a site in southwestern China (Yunnan Province) that has produced the greatest abundance of fossil hominoid primates in the world. Well over 1,000 specimens are known, including several heavily crushed skulls, mandibles, and many isolated teeth but almost no postcranial elements. Originally described as two species attributed to *Sivapithecus* and *Ramapithecus,* all of the material is now generally assigned to a single species seen to be distinct from those genera. Claims have been made as to its relationship with the human lineage, and similarities have been suggested with the orangutan lineage, but its relationships remain unclear. It may tentatively be included in the Dryopithecinae as construed in this volume.

Lufengpithecus was a medium-size hominoid, probably with thin molar enamel and a conservative skull (with wide interorbital distance, no clear frontal sinus, weak browridges, and fairly simple incisive canal complex). The lower anterior dentition is somewhat pitheciin-like, with tall incisors and heavily buttressed canines, and the I^2 is quite small compared to I^1. The site of Lufeng consists of deposits derived from swamp forests dating to the Late Miocene (9–7 Ma). It is possible that at least some of the hominid fossils from the nearby Yuanmou Pliocene or late Miocene sites may also belong to this genus.

See also Asia, Eastern and Southern; Dryopithecinae; Hominidae; Hominoidea; Lufeng; Ponginae; Sivapithecus; Yuanmou [P.A.]

Lupemban

Central African Middle Paleolithic (Middle Stone Age) industry named for exposures on Lupemba Stream near Tshikapa in Kasai Occidental Province (Zaire). It was defined by H. Breuil on the basis of Levallois or discoidal prepared-core technology and backed or bifacially worked leaf-shaped points, many small enough to have been arrowheads. Core axes, particularly lanceolate forms, and discoidal cores are significantly smaller and thinner than in the Sangoan industry, also in central Africa. The Late, or Upper, Lupemban is further distinguished by occasional tanged points and by finer lanceolate and leaf-shaped points, similar to the younger Tshitolian. Although it is usually assumed to be a woodworking industry associated with areas that today are densely wooded, the Lupemban could also correspond to a Late Pleistocene period of major recession of the tropical-forest belt. This industry also occurs in a small-tool facies at Mwanganda's Village (Malawi) and at Peperkorrel (Namibia) in association with evidence of more open environments. The probable age is early Late Pleistocene, with some Zairian sites possibly falling within the range of radiocarbon dating.

See also Middle Stone Age; Sangoan; Stone-Tool Making; Tshitolian. [A.S.B.]

Lushius

Extinct primate from the Middle Eocene (ca. 47 Ma) of China whose systematic affinities are unclear. The only specimen is a maxillary fragment with three teeth. It was described in 1961 by M. Chow, who suggested that its affinities might lie with tarsiiforms. F.S. Szalay and E. Delson, however, thought that this cat-size primate possessed more of a primitive adapid *Gestalt* in its dental morphology. J.H. Schwartz argued, in turn, that a comparison with *Omomys* was the most compelling.

See also Adapidae; Asia, Eastern and Southern; China; Eocene; Omomyidae; Tarsiiformes. [J.H.S.]

M

Maboko

Middle Miocene site on the island of this name in the Winam Gulf of western Kenya. Fossil-bearing clays and silts beneath phonolite lava on the island, and on the nearby mainland at Majiwa Bluff and Kaloma, were first excavated by the British missionary W.E. Owen in the early 1930s. More than 1,000 primate specimens have been found, mostly by sieving the material in Owen's dumps and in recent excavations directed by B. Benefit and M. McCrossin. Twenty beds of sediment and tuff have been defined, with the majority of specimens coming from Beds 3 and 5 (counting up from the base of the section). Bed 8 is dated ca. 14.7 Ma and Bed 20 ca. 13.8 Ma, according to ^{39}Ar/^{40}Ar laser-fusion dates, in confirmation of previous faunally based estimates of 15 Ma for the primary fauna.

Correlative sites occur not far to the west at Ombo and Mariwa and on the opposite shoulder of the Nyanza Rift at Nyakach, near Sondu. The open-country aspect of the fauna is a radical change from the forest-adapted *Proconsul* communities from slightly older deposits in the Winam Gulf (e.g., Kulu Rusinga, ca. 16 Ma) and foreshadows the even more progressive aspect of the Fort Ternan local fauna (14 Ma). Maboko is the type site of the early kenyapithecine hominid "*Kenyapithecus*" *africanus* and the earliest well-documented cercopithecid, *Victoriapithecus macinnesi*. It has also yielded several *Dendropithecus*-like small catarrhines.

See also Africa; Africa, East; Cercopithecidae; "Dendropithecus-group"; Fort Ternan; Kenyapithecinae; Miocene; Rusinga; Victoriapithecinae. [J.A.V.C., E.D.]

Further Readings

Andrews, P.J., Meyer, G.E., Pilbeam, D.R., Van Couvering, J.A., and Van Couvering, J.A.H. (1981) The Miocene fossil beds of Maboko Island, Kenya: Geology, age, taphonomy, and paleontology. J. Hum. Evol. 10:35–48.

McCrossin, M.L., and Benefit, B.R. (1994) Maboko Island and the evolutionary history of Old World monkeys and apes. In R.S. Corruccini and R.L. Ciochon (eds.): Integrative Paths to the Past. Englewood Cliffs, N.J.: Prentice-Hall, pp. 95–122.

MacIntosh N.W.G. (1906–1977)

Australian anatomist and leader of the Sydney (Australia) school of biological anthropology in the 1960s and 1970s. MacIntosh excavated the Mossgiel and Nitchie skeletons, led detailed dating research at the Talgai cranium site, and conducted archaeological and art research in northern Australia. He was the author, with Stanley Larnach, of a series of monographs recording nonmetric features of eastern Australian and Tasmanian remains.

See also Australia; Talgai. [A.T.]

Madagascar

One of the world's largest islands, ca. 1,600 km long, and lying ca. 450 km off the southeastern coast of Africa. Madagascar has been approximately at this remove from the African continent for 120 Myr (i.e., since well before primates are known to have evolved); thus, the primate inhabitants of the island, known as the *lemurs,* as well as any later invaders, must have crossed a substantial water gap to get there. The fact that only such lower primates have successfully established themselves on Madagascar may say something about their ecological competitiveness, even though the relatives of these animals in Africa and Asia are supposed to have been crowded into nocturnal "refuge" niches by the later-appearing anthropoid primates.

As almost a microcontinent, Madagascar offers a wide spectrum of ecological zones, from semidesert to lush rain forest, and it is in this variety of settings that the most diverse surviving fauna of lower (strepsirhine, prosimian) primates has established itself, the ancestral forms having most probably, on present evidence, reached the island at some time during the Eocene. Ca. 30 species of lemur, many with diverse subspecies, are found on the island today; before the arrival of humans only ca. 1.5 Ka, at least a dozen more species existed, most of them much larger than the largest living lemur, which weighs ca. 6–7 kg. Surviving lemurs are grouped into five families: Lemuridae, Indriidae, Daubentoniidae, Lepilemuridae, and Cheirogaleidae; major extinct forms are grouped into Archaeolemuridae, Palaeopropithecidae, Lepilemuridae *(Megaladapis),* and Lemuridae *(Pachylemur).* No primate fossil record is known in Madagascar prior to ca. 10–5 Ka.

See also Archaeolemuridae; Cheirogaleidae; Daubentoniidae; Indriidae; Indrioidea; Lemuridae; Lemuriformes; Lemuroidea; Lepilemuridae; Lower Primates; Palaeopropithecidae; Prosimian; Strepsirhini. [I.T.]

Magdalenian

Late Upper Paleolithic European industry characterized by an extensive use of unretouched blades, as well as increasing production and use of microlithic blades, burins, scrapers, and borers. A distinctive feature of this industry, dated between 17 and 11.5 Ka, is fine bone-and-antler technology, including the production of first single- and then double-rowed barbed harpoons and of bone points, awls, needles, polishers, shaft straighteners, and spear throwers. Sites assigned to the Magdalenian have repeatedly yielded numerous remains of figurative engravings on antler, ivory, bone, and slate of both animals and somewhat abstracted female forms. Jewelry and other items of personal adornment are often found at Magdalenian sites and are included in elaborate burials, such as that found at Duruthy (France). Finally, the most spectacular Upper Paleolithic cave paintings, such as those at Altamira and Lascaux, also date to this period and are associated with this archaeological industry.

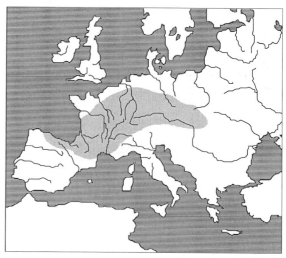

Distribution map of Magdalenian sites.

This Upper Paleolithic industry is named after discoveries made at the La Madeleine rockshelter at the outskirts of Les Eyzies in southwestern France. Its distribution, however, went far outside this classic Paleolithic region and includes both cave and open-air sites in northern France, Spain, Belgium, Switzerland, Germany, the Czech Republic, and southern Poland.

See also Altamira; Europe; Lascaux; Paleolithic Image; Upper Paleolithic. [O.S.]

Further Readings

Bordes, P. (1968) The Old Stone Age. London: Weidenfeld and Nicolson.

Gamble, C. (1986) The Paleolithic Settlement of Europe. Cambridge: Cambridge University Press.

Straus, L.G., Eriksen, B.V., Erlandson, J.M. and Yesner, D.R. (1996) Humans at the End of the Ice Age: The Archaeology of the Pleistocene-Holocene Transition, New York: Plenum.

Wymer, J. (1982) The Palaeolithic Age. New York: St. Martin's.

Maglemosian

Hunting and fishing Mesolithic culture of late pre-Boreal and Boreal times (ca. 9.5–7.7 Ka) on the North European Plain from the east Baltic to Britain. Most Maglemosian sites represent summer and fall lakeshore settlements, some with small individual or nuclear-family hut floors, in which both the hunting of forest species (aurochs, elk, red deer, roe deer) and the consumption of marine or lacustrine resources (fish, shellfish, seals) are reflected in the faunal remains, as well as in the artifacts. In addition to a stone industry with chipped-core axes and microliths, such as lunates and backed bladelets, Maglemosian sites have yielded wooden paddles, net weights, nets, floats, canoes, fishhooks, barbed and notched points and harpoons, and even nutshells due to the excellent organic preservation of wet sites.

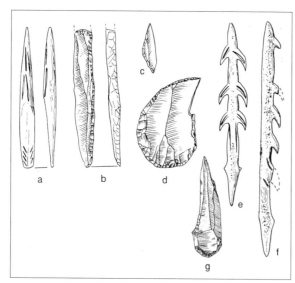

Representative artifacts of the French Magdalenian: (a) decorated bone point with beveled base (sagaie); (b) backed bladelet; (c) triangular microlith; (d) parrot-beaked burin; (e) bone harpoon with two rows of barbs; (f) antler harpoon with single row of barbs. The much earlier "Protomagdalenian" industry (represented by (g) end-scraper and double burin is placed by some authors at the end of the Upper Perigordian sequence but by others as an antecedent of the Magdalenian. Not to scale.

See also Bow and Arrow; Economy, Prehistoric; Epipaleolithic; Europe; Mesolithic; Star Carr; Stone-Tool Making. [A.S.B.]

Magosian

Purported African Paleolithic industry supposedly intermediate between the Middle and the Late Stone Age at Magosi rockshelter in northeastern Uganda, at Apis Rock (Nasera) in Tanzania, and by extension to other African industries combining bifacial points, Levallois and discoidal cores, and microliths or backed pieces. Later reinvestigation of the type site showed that the Magosian resulted from an admixture of an earlier classic Middle Stone Age horizon with bifacial points and Levallois technology, and a later microlithic horizon associated with a radiocarbon age of ca. 14 Ka. However, industries dating to the end of the Middle Stone Age (ca. 50–40 Ka) with no evidence of admixture, however, such as Level V from Mumba Hohle in Tanzania, also combine bifacial points with nonmicrolithic backed crescents and other geometric forms, as well as microblade cores. The earliest microblade cores in eastern and central Africa are dated to more than 40 Ka at Matupi Cave in the Ituri district of eastern Zaire.

See also Later Stone Age; Levallois; Middle Stone Age; Second Intermediate. [A.S.B.]

Mahgarita

A genus of Middle Eocene (Uintan, ca. 40 Ma) North American protoadapin adapid primate, known by excellent dental and good cranial material. This animal from the southern part of Texas is unusual for North America for a number of reasons. It is not a close relative of any of the Notharctinae (an endemic North American subfamily of the Adapidae), and its ties are with the slightly older (Geiseltalian) European genus *Europolemur* and the Middle Eocene Chinese *Adapoides*. The Texas primate and its European and Asian relatives (the Protoadapini) appear to be a clade distinct from the North American notharctines and adapins by the time of their appearance in the Early Eocene. The specific ties of these protoadapins to the rest of the Adapinae is unclear, particularly in light of the paucity of the relevant Asian fossil record beyond that of *Lushius* and *Adapoides*.

Mahgarita has a *Lepilemur*-size skull. Its mandibular symphysis is fused as in several other adapids (*Adapis*, *Leptadapis*, *Caenopithecus*), and it has robust canines. It is somewhat of a notorious genus in that its well-preserved ear region, known in considerable detail, has been a bone of contention concerning the origin of the anthropoids. The middle-ear cavity is closely similar to that seen in other adapids (both notharctines and adapines). While its ectotympanic is not preserved, it was probably ringlike (C-shaped) and not attached to the outside rim of the bulla. Entry of the inferior carotid artery was on the posterior and lateral surface of the bulla, unlike in tarsiiforms or anthropoids. The petromastoid, while well exposed, does not show the highly inflated, or pneumatized, condition seen in the earliest and all other living and fossil anthropoids. Contrary to some arguments, it shows no uniquely shared special similarities with anthropoids or putative anthropoid ancestors.

See also Adapidae; Adapiformes; Anthropoidea; Eocene. [F.S.S.]

Makapansgat

South African stratified cave breccias of Late Pliocene age, with the main fossil level between 3 and 2.6 Ma by faunal correlation. This extensive deposit, the largest of the South African early-hominin sites, is located ca. 16 km east-northeast of the town of Potgietersrust in northern Transvaal Province, at 24°12′S and 28°57′E.

Makapansgat is the remains of a system of karstic-solution chambers, of which ca. 1.5 ha are exposed. Fossil bones were recovered while the deposits were being excavated for lime between 1925 and 1935, but no hominins were recognized until 1947, when J.W. Kitching discovered material described the following year by R.A. Dart as a new species of *Australopithecus*, *A. prometheus*. Since then, reexcavation in the Limeworks rubble dumps has recovered several dozen specimens, all (including the original *prometheus*) attributable to the hypodigm of the earlier-named *Australopithecus africanus* from Taung. Five sedimentary breccia members have been recognized, although the basis for this lithostratigraphic division has been brought into question. All of the hominin specimens derive from Member 3 (the "Grey Breccia"), with a single exception from Member 4. Dart originally interpreted the nonhominid remains from Makapansgat as comprising food litter and osteodontokeratic (bone, tooth, and horn) artifacts of *Australopithecus*, but

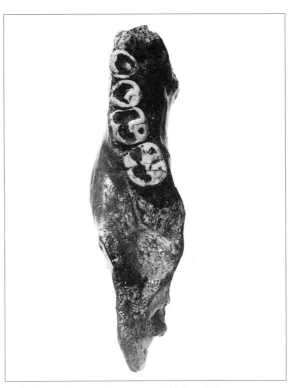

Occlusal view of a partial hominid mandible from Makapansgat. Photograph of cast.

these elements are now regarded as carnivore and/or scavenger assemblages, and no undisputed artifacts have been recovered from the *Australopithecus*-bearing breccias.

See also Africa, Southern; Australopithecus; Australopithecus africanus; Breccia Cave Formation; Dart, Raymond Arthur; Taung. [F.E.G.]

Further Readings

Dart, R.A. (1954) The minimal bone-breccia content of Makapansgat and the australopithecine predatory habit. Am. Anthropol. 60:923–931.

Delson, E. (1984) Cercopithecid biochronology of the African Plio-Pleistocene: Correlation among eastern and southern hominid-bearing localities. Cour. Forsch. Inst. Senckenberg 69:199–218.

Maguire, J.M. (1985) Recent geological, stratigraphic, and palaeontological studies at Makapansgat Limeworks. In P.V. Tobias (ed.): Hominid Evolution. New York: Liss, pp. 151–164.

Mal'ta

Late Paleolithic open-air site on the banks of the Belaya River, a tributary of the Angara River in Siberia (Russia). Archaeological inventories include bone and stone tools and portable art of bone and mammoth ivory, depicting birds and females in a manner distinct from that found in European sites. Features at Mal'ta include remains of 15 stone-slab and bone-curbed dwellings, some of which probably represent summer occupation, and others winter occupation. Other features include a child's burial, with ocher, jewelry, and grave goods, and a number of small cachepits. Mal'ta, like the nearby site Buret, dates to ca. 23–15 Ka. Stone-tool inventories from both sites are assigned to the Mal'ta-Buret industry.

See also Dyuktai. [O.S.]

Man-Land Relationships

Term referring to the interactions between human groups and their natural environment coined and developed by K.W. Butzer. As a concept, this perspective developed from ecology, which, in anthropology, gave rise to *human ecology,* a field that studies the relationship between people and their environment, both natural and social, in order to understand their adaptations at a particular point in time as well as changes in their lifeways through time. This paradigm is based on two assumptions: that humans, like all other living entities, are parts of particular ecosystems that differ from each other in important ways; and that adaptations are ultimately about obtaining the matter, energy, and information necessary for survival in the least costly way possible. The ecosystem consists of the sum total of all inert (e.g., climate, soils) and organic matter (living species of plants and animals), which are in a complex relationship with each affecting the other. For example, human groups in Arctic environments with long cold seasons when little food is available must contend with very different environmental

problems than those confronting groups in tropical forests where seasonal variation in temperatures are minimal and the supply of food is more equitably distributed throughout the year.

Given this, it follows that human adaptations, both past and present, can be productively viewed as specific cultural solutions to problems of survival posed by specific natural and social environments. To understand these adaptations, scholars have found it convenient to begin by separating out the two major components—man-land relationships (the natural environment and human utilization of that environment) and man-man relationships (social arrangements among individuals within a group and among different groups)—and considering each in turn.

In studying the man-land components of past adaptations in a specific region, prehistoric archaeologists most often begin by considering the overall characteristics of the natural environments, including such variables as climate (temperatures, precipitation, and their seasonal and long-term fluctuations); the nature, availability, distribution, and predictability of the biotic resources (what foods were available, which were eatable, how much was available, how costly and risky it was to obtain them); and the environmental limiting factors that created specific problems for groups in the area (e.g., the presence and severity or absence of seasonal fluctuations in food resources). Archaeological data obtained from the sites, including available technology, and season of death of prey animals are then used to understand how people who occupied the area perceived their natural environment and which strategies or combinations of strategies they chose to use to exploit the available resources (e.g., maximizing acquisition of energy, emphasizing acquisition of particular nutrients such as fats or carbohydrates, or minimizing risk).

See also Archaeology; Economy, Prehistoric; Hunter-Gatherers. [O.S.]

Further Readings

Butzer, K.W. (1982) Archaeology As Human Ecology. Cambridge: Cambridge University Press.

Campbell, B. (1984) Human Ecology. New York: Aldine.

Jochim, M.A. (1981) Strategies for Survival: Cultural Behavior in an Ecological Context. New York: Academic.

Martin, Rudolf (1862–1925)

German physical anthropologist. Martin's primary research interest was anthropometry, and he was responsible for producing a highly influential manual, *Lehrbuch der Anthropologie* (1914, 1928). This was subsequently updated by K. Saller (in three volumes) between 1956 and 1962. [F.S.]

Mauer

Sand and gravel pit at Mauer near Heidelberg (Germany) where a fossil human mandible was discovered accidentally in 1907. The associated fossil mammals suggest a Middle Pleistocene age somewhat later than the Cromerian interglacial but older than the Holsteinian (perhaps ca. 0.5 Ma).

The Mauer jaw is one of the oldest European fossil hominins yet discovered (approximately coeval with the Boxgrove site in England but younger than the lower level at Atapuerca, Spain, or perhaps Ceprano, Italy). Although it has been claimed that stone and bone artifacts have also been found at Mauer, in some cases there is doubt about their age and in other cases doubt about their identification as artifacts. The mandible has a thick body and a very broad ramus. There is no chin development, but the teeth are quite small, leading to the suggestion that this might even represent a female. Although there is no development of the retromolar space found in Neanderthal jaws, the mandible is long, indicating that the associated face was probably projecting. This specimen is the holotype of the species *Homo heidelbergensis*. This species is gaining currency among paleoanthropologists (to include the Arago and Petralona specimens as well as those noted above), although some workers still regard the Mauer jaw as representing a European form of *Homo erectus* or an archaic form of *Homo sapiens*.

See also Arago; Archaic Homo sapiens; Atapuerca; Boxgrove; Ceprano; Europe; Homo erectus; Homo heidelbergensis; Petralona. [C.B.S.]

Mayr, Ernst (1904–)

American (b. Germany) ornithologist and systematist. Mayr was a prominent figure in the movement responsible for the *new evolutionary synthesis* that emerged between 1937 and 1947. Following a stint at the University Museum, Berlin (1926–1931), and the American Museum of Natural History, New York (1932–1946), Mayr moved to Harvard University, where he spent the remainder of his career. Influenced by T. Dobzhansky's work, Mayr presented his own ideas in a 1940 paper, which led ultimately to the publication in 1942 of his influential book *Systematics and the Origin of Species*, followed by several major works of equally great influence. His recent contributions have been mostly historical and philosophical in nature.

See also Evolution. [F.S.]

McCown, Theodore D. (1908–1969)

American paleoanthropologist best remembered for his collaborative work with British anatomist and paleoanthropologist A. Keith in the mid-1930s on the preparation and description of the fossil hominids from Skhūl and Tabūn in Israel (then Palestine). Their 1939 report raised important questions about the biological affinity of Neanderthals to anatomically modern *Homo sapiens*. McCown later became professor of anthropology at the University of California, Berkeley.

See also Archaic Moderns; Asia, Western; Neanderthals; Skhūl; Tabūn. [F.S.]

Meadowcroft Shelter

Stratified archaeological site near Avella in southwestern Pennsylvania dating to ca. 20 Ka. J.M. Adovasio and colleagues have documented a sequence of more than 40 radio-carbon dates in perfect stratigraphic order. The oldest cultural date is considered to be 15.9 Ka; the oldest stone artifacts appear to date to 11.3–12.8 Ka. Evidence for human occupation (in lower stratum 11a) consists of occupation floors containing firepits, prismatic blades, biface-thinning flakes, flake knives, two bifaces, a wooden foreshaft, a piece of plaited basketry, and two human bone fragments.

The archaeology of Meadowcroft Shelter leaves many questions unanswered. The stone implements are few, small, and uninformative; they are surprisingly similar to much later artifacts. No diagnostic Early Archaic or Paleoindian artifacts occur. Pleistocene megafauna is likewise absent from stratum 11a, and this is surprising for deposits so old. The temperate character of the vegetation throughout the Meadowcroft stratigraphy (and particularly the presence of hardwood-forest macrofossils in stratum 11a) also seems anomalous, since, during a part of this time, the ice front was less than 75 km to the north. There is no stratigraphic unconformity to match the gaps in the radiocarbon dates in stratum 11a. These difficulties notwithstanding, Meadowcroft Shelter remains the only site providing solid support for human occupation of North America prior to 12 Ka.

See also Americas; Clovis; Folsom; Paleoindian. [D.H.T.]

Further Readings

Adovasio, J.M. (1993) The ones that will not go away: A biased view of pre-Clovis populations in the New World. In Olga Soffer and N.D. Praslov (eds.): From Kostenki to Clovis: Upper Paleolithic-Paleo-Indian Adaptations. New York: Plenum, pp. 199–218.

Adovisio, J.M., Donahue, J., Pedlar, D.R. and Stuckenrath, R. (1998) Two decades of debate on Meadowcroft Rockshelter. North American Archaeologist 19(4): 317–341.

Adovasio, J.M., Gunn, J.D., Donahue, J., and Stuckenrath, R. (1978) Meadowcroft Rockshelter, 1977: An overview. Am. Antiquity 43:632–651.

Dincauze, D.F. (1981) The Meadowcroft papers. Quart. Rev. Archaeol. 2:3–4.

Meganthropus

Hominoid genus recognized from two partial mandibles recovered by Dutch paleoanthropologist G.H.R. von Koenigswald in 1939 and 1941 in Java. The mandibles were described in 1945 by German anatomist F. Weidenreich from casts. Von Koenigswald thought that the 1939 fragment (Sangiran 5) and the 1941 fragment (Sangiran 6) represented a female and a male, respectively. Weidenreich disagreed and published Sangiran 5 under the nomen *Pithecanthropus dubius* because he doubted that the specimen was a hominid. He did, however, agree that Sangiran 6 was a hominid and published it under the generic name that von Koenigswald had suggested in a letter that accompanied the casts, *Meganthropus palaeojavanicus*.

Both specimens were described only from casts that von Koenigswald made and sent to Beijing prior to his internment in a Japanese concentration camp. Because of its large

Lateral view of the "Meganthropus" mandibular fragment discovered by G.H.R. von Koenigswald in 1941. Photograph of cast.

teeth and robust mandible, Weidenreich carefully considered the possibility that *Meganthropus* was pathological. In the end, he decided it was not, because the teeth, although extremely large, were proportionate to the large mandible. He also rejected the possibility of acromegaly because the mandible did not exhibit the exaggerated chin of modern acromegalics. Thus, the type of *Meganthropus* entered the literature as an Asian hominid that was less advanced than *Sinanthropus.* Subsequently, other fragmentary finds were also included in this taxon. Of particular interest are cranial and facial fragments (Sangiran 27 and Sangiran 31) collected in 1974 following the excavation of an irrigation ditch. These have also been claimed to document the presence of an Asian form of australopith, and have been referred to *Meganthropus.* Actually, the speculation that *Meganthropus* was an Asian australopith was introduced almost inadvertently as the result of South African paleontologist J.T. Robinson's initial arguments for the inclusion of australopiths in the Hominidae. He reasoned that the African australopiths were just as hominid in their morphology as *Meganthropus.* Subsequently, Robinson's arguments were augmented by speculations that australopiths were present in Asia. To date, however, no convincing body of evidence supports these hypotheses.

Relative to other specimens that have been included in *Homo erectus,* it is clear that previously known and recently reported *Meganthropus* specimens exhibit robust and extremely thick cranial bones. Nevertheless, nothing about the morphology of the specimens suggests a taxon other than *H. erectus.* The possibility that the specimens are aberrant should also be borne in mind since the taxon was actually named on the basis of a cast and newer cranial material has yet to be adequately described. It is also possible that the robusticity of *Meganthropus* reflects an insularized hominid population isolated on Java for hundreds of thousands of years. In any case, no consensus has been reached on the taxonomic and phylogenetic status of *Meganthropus.*

See also Indonesia; Koenigswald, Gustav Heinrich Ralph von. [G.G.P.]

Further Readings

Sartono, S. (1982) Sagittal cresting in *Meganthropus paleojavanicus* (V. Koenigswald). Mod. Quat. Res. Southeast Asia 7:201–210.

Sémah, F., Sémah, A., and Djubiantono, T. (1990) They Discovered Java. Bandung, Indonesia: Pusat Penelitian Arkeologi Najional.

Weidenreich, F. (1945) Giant early man from Java and south China. Anthropol. Pap. Am. Mus. Nat. Hist. 40:1–143.

Melka Kontouré

Central Ethiopian stratified sequence of Plio-Pleistocene age, dated ca. 1.7–0.1 Ma, by potassium-argon (K/Ar), paleomagnetic, and faunal correlations. Located ca. 50 km south of Addis Ababa, the composite Melka Kontouré stratigraphic column comprises 30 m of successive formations spanning the latest Pliocene and much of Pleistocene time. Stretching for ca. 5–6 km along both banks of the Awash River, the Melka Kontouré outcrops are mostly fluvial deposits, interspersed with volcanic layers that have permitted dating. The deposits contain abundant artifacts and faunal remains. More than 50 archaeological sites have been identified, and ca. 30 living floors have been excavated here by J. Chavaillon and coworkers.

The most important localities and their archaeological content are Garba (Oldowan through Middle Stone Age); Gomboré (Oldowan through Middle Acheulean); Simbirro (Middle Acheulean); and Karre (Oldowan). Hominin fossils have been recovered from both the Garba and the Gomboré localities.

From an Oldowan level at Garba IV comes a partial child's mandible attributed to early *Homo.* From another Oldowan level at Gombore 1B comes a partial hominin humerus. From a Middle Acheulean level at Gomboré II there is a parietal fragment attributed to *Homo erectus,* and from the Terminal Acheulean unit of Garba III comes a frontal bone of what may be a late *H. erectus.*

See also Acheulean; Africa, East; Homo erectus; Middle Stone Age; Oldowan [T.D.W.]

Further Reading

Chevaillon, J. (1976) Mission archéologique Francó-Ethiopienne de Melka-Kontouré. L'Ethiopie avant l'Histoire 1:1–11.

Mesolithic

Period or group of industries that falls between Paleolithic and Neolithic in time, technology, and economic development. In Lubbock's original (1865) division of the Stone Age into two epochs, the Paleolithic and the Neolithic were thought to have been separated by a hiatus, representing a time when mid-latitude Europe was abandoned after the retreat of the reindeer and their hunters to the extreme north. Subsequent excavations at Mas d'Azil (France) and other sites documented the existence of Early Holocene hunting-and-gathering cultures in mid-latitude regions. By the last quarter of the nineteenth century, several authors (e.g., A. Brown) had suggested independently the use of the term *Mesolithic* for these industries, although the first synthetic studies of European Mesolithic industries, compiled by J.G.D. Clark, were not published until the 1950s.

Definitions

The meaning of Mesolithic and the list of industries assigned to this interval are far from uniform. As with other subdivisions of the Stone Age, the term carries technological (microliths, composite tools), chronological (Early Holocene), and socioeconomic (broad-spectrum resource use, economic intensification, semisedentism) connotations. Some scholars reserve the designation *Mesolithic* for northern and western Europe, where societies adapted to forest-based subsistence, practicing hunting, gathering, and fishing, and using composite tools succeeded one another over perhaps 6 Kyr before the advent of domesticated stock and agriculture. In this view, societies that continued a *Paleolithic* way of life, characterized by nomadic hunting of large herbivores, or whose tool traditions continue relatively unchanged from Late Pleistocene to Holocene times, are referred to the *Epipaleolithic,* a term originally suggested by Obermaier as a synonym for Mesolithic. Such societies were found in the extreme north of Europe, where reindeer hunting continued to form the subsistence base, and in the Mediterranean Basin, where red deer and other forest species dominated both Late Pleistocene and Holocene assemblages and where Epigravettian industries continue with no abrupt shifts from the glacial maximum at ca. 20–18 Ka. into the Holocene. Epipaleolithic also refers to final Late Pleistocene and Holocene industries of North Africa.

In contrast to the use of Mesolithic to refer to specialized Holocene hunter-fishers of Europe, V.G. Childe and others reserved the Mesolithic (or *Protoneolithic*) designation for contemporaneous societies of southwestern Asia and northeast Africa that were experimenting with food production. The Mesolithic stage encompassed only those societies actually in transition between Paleolithic and Neolithic. In this view, it is the European Holocene industries that are relegated to the Epipaleolithic and whose adaptations are seen as a specialized dead end in human cultural evolution. To resolve these conflicting uses of the term, several authors (e.g., T.D. Price) have emphasized the chronological aspects of the Mesolithic and suggested that this phase incorporates all post-Late Pleistocene hunter-gatherers, whatever their location, dietary or technological specializations, or experimentation with domesticates (provided that most of the diet is still derived from wild resources). In such a definition, the Mesolithic industries of northwestern Europe constitute a large part of the universe under discussion, since domestication of food resources was not established in this area until relatively late, after 6 Ka. Paradoxically, the term *Mesolithic* is rarely used to refer to African Late Pleistocene and Holocene hunter-gatherers, although archaeological sites in southern Africa dominated by stone and bone tools and remains of wild animals are dated to the last 200 years.

In the New World, Holocene hunter-fisher-gatherers with a diversified subsistence base are referred to as *Archaic,* in an attempt to avoid the multiple connotations of the Old World terminology. American terminology is based primarily on stages of economic, rather than technological, development so that specialized hunter-fisher-gatherer societies that experimented with metals are still classed as Archaic, while early agricultural societies without pottery fall into the *Formative* period.

Broad-Spectrum Revolution

In 1965, K.V. Flannery introduced the concept of the *broad-spectrum revolution* to emphasize the shift in man-land relationships that took place in the final Late Pleistocene to Early Holocene. Even in such areas as the Levant, which experienced less of an environmental shift than mid-latitude Europe, Early Holocene adaptations were often different from their Late Pleistocene antecedents. Despite the argument over specific terminologies, there is now general agreement that the Mesolithic or its equivalent represented a level of more intensive exploitation of the natural environment. Small-scale resources like fish, shellfish, nuts, snails, birds, and tortoises were increasingly important in the diet of Holocene hunters, who developed new strategies and technologies for taking large nonmigratory forest and marine species. At Franchthi Cave in Greece, for example, tuna represent 50 percent of the faunal remains by the Late Mesolithic. Shellfish mounds from Hoabinhian sites in Southeast Asia, and abundant fish remains from other East and Southeast Asian

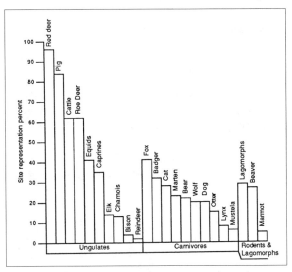

The presence of animals at 165 European Mesolithic sites expressed as percentages:

$$\frac{number\ of\ sites\ in\ which\ species\ occurs}{165\ sites}$$

After M. R. Jarman, in E. S. Higgs, ed., Papers in Economic Prehistory, *1972, Cambridge University Press.*

Early Holocene sites, demonstrate the worldwide extent of Mesolithic adaptations.

The scheduling of resource use was particularly important. Although the site of Star Carr in Yorkshire (England) was occupied by red-deer hunters in winter and early spring, Maglemosian lakeside sites of northern Europe reflect largely summer and fall occupations, when both nut harvesting and fishing opportunities were at a maximum. Seasonal movement from lowland winter camps to upland hunting settlements is documented for the Late Paleolithic and the Mesolithic of Greece. In the Archaic of the mid-Atlantic region of North America, occupation sites along rivers are concentrated in the spring and fall, when anadromous fish were running. North African Mesolithic populations exploited snails on a seasonal basis, and, in southern Africa, a possible seasonal round may have included coastal shellfish harvesting in one season and inland hunting and collecting in another, an adaptation that may also be reflected in the spatial separation and differing faunal inventories of Asturian and Late Azilian sites of Cantabria. In such widely separated areas as the Levant, Yorkshire, Kyushu (Japan), and Idaho, domesticated dogs appear in Early Holocene contexts, presumably as an aid to the tracking and killing of solitary forest prey.

The broadening of the subsistance base to include more species and a greater proportion of small-scale (low-trophic-level) resources did not occur suddenly, nor did it necessarily coincide with the major climatic shifts ca. 10 Ka. An increased use of marine resources, birds, and small game is evident in the later Upper Paleolithic (e.g., Magdalenian) of Europe, as well as in the Later Stone Age of Africa, which is well underway by 20 Ka. in central and eastern Africa.

Another feature of Mesolithic adaptations is the widespread practice of burning the land to maintain open areas and attract large game. In such diverse regions as the English moors, Australia, and the African savannah-woodland at the margins of the forest belt, previously forested areas did not regenerate following the last glacial maximum, due largely to human intervention.

Technologies

The most definitive and widespread, although not universal, characteristic of Mesolithic technology is the use of small, often geometric forms called *microliths*. Whether derived from small blade cores (microbladelet technology) or from regular-size blades that were divided into two or more, often triangular or trapezoidal pieces (geometric microliths, microburin technique), microliths formed the basis for a wide range of composite tools, including arrows, barbed fish spears, and sickles. Since the stone elements of composite tools could be easily replaced in a haft of worked bone, antler, or wood, composite tools may have represented a more efficient technology, as well as a way to create long detachable arrowheads, and curved stone cutting edges with multiple blades set in a sickle haft. The widespread use of very small (less than 2.5 cm) projectile points in the Mesolithic suggests that arrow points may have been designed to remain in the animal, possibly to dissolve a poison

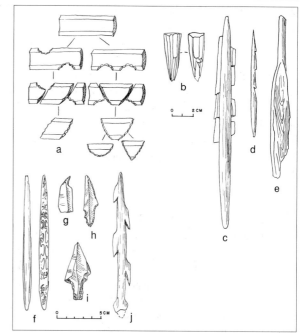

Mesolithic and Epipaleolithic technologies: (a) production of geometric microliths from segmented blades; (b) microblade core; (c) antler spear with hafted stone barbs; (d) barbed antler point (Star Carr); (e) antler mattock (Star Carr); (f) carved half-round bone wand (Ahrensburgian); (g) "zinken" or perforator; (h) tanged pont (Ahrensburgian); (i) tanged point (Lyngby culture); (j) biserial barbed antler point (Ahrensburgian).

into its bloodstream, rather than to kill the animal on contact. In Europe, the sequential forms of microliths, from tanged/shouldered points to triangles to trapezes, are often used to establish chronological and even cultural relationships (e.g., Azilian, Sauveterrian, Tardenoisian), although the regional distribution of these forms is extensive, and different forms coexist or overlap in time. *Lunates* (also called *segments* or *crescents*) are particularly common in Southwestern Asia (Natufian) and Africa (Capsian, Wilton).

Other innovations in stone technology are an increase in the use of ground stone (present in Africa from the Middle Stone Age on) for bowls, mortars, and pestles, in both the Old and the New World, reflecting an increased use of tubers and wild grains. In African Later Stone Age sites, bored stones, which may have served as digging-stick weights, also reflect an intensification of plant harvesting and possibly incipient cultivation. Chipped-stone axes were common in northern European Mesolithic contexts, and stone for axes was mined and transported over longer distances than before.

The development of Mesolithic bone-and-antler technology is equally distinctive. Bone, antler, and wood formed the hafts of such composite tools as sickles, as well as the points, barbed or smooth, of arrows, harpoons, fishhooks, and leisters. The detachable point, which may first appear in the Late Paleolithic of several areas, from Europe to central Africa, was as important an innovation in fishing as in hunting: It enabled the fisher to tire the prey and to land a greater proportion of the larger species. Other accoutrements of fishing, including the nets themselves recovered from sites in northern Germany and Scandinavia, demonstrate the use of various fishing strategies (nets, traps, weirs, harpoons, lines) by Mesolithic peoples. Dugout canoes and paddles indicate the widespread use of boats, whose presence is implied at an earlier date by the importation of obsidian from Melos to the Greek mainland during the final Late Pleistocene (18–12 Ka), as well as by the early peopling of Australia and Melanesia by ca. 50 Ka.

In a few places, entirely new materials were worked by Mesolithic peoples: cold-hammered metals, especially native copper, in Anatolia and parts of North America; basketry matting, first documented in the Late Paleolithic at Dolni Věstonice (Czech Republic) but becoming widespread in the North American Great Basin, northern Europe, and southern Africa; and ceramics in Japan, where pottery was in use as early as 12 Ka, as well as in the final Mesolithic (Ertebolle) of southern Scandinavia, 6.6–5.3 Ka, and of north Africa ca. 9000 Ka.

Settlement and Social Organization

The economic and technological developments of the Mesolithic also made possible a greater degree of sedentism, often based on fishing. At Eynan on Lake Huleh (Israel) and at Vlasac in the Iron Gates region of the Danube, stone foundations dating to 8 Ka or before attest to the permanence of dwellings. Elsewhere in Europe and western Asia, small lakeshore huts may have been seasonally reoccupied in alternation with rockshelters or forest camps. Within-settlement differentiation of activities and public vs. family areas is more marked than previously. Large Mesolithic cemeteries in southern Scandinavia and in the Sudan also argue for increased sedentism. Finally, the sizes of social territories, whose boundaries are reflected in trade networks, microlith styles, bone-point forms, and decorative motifs, are correspondingly reduced from Paleolithic times, from ca. 100,000 to 15,000–20,000 km² in northern Europe.

In certain areas (e.g., upland regions of western Asia, the Tehuacan Valley of Mexico, the Peruvian uplands, Greece, the Nile Valley, the Mississippi Valley, Southeast Asia), Mesolithic adaptations, especially semisedentism and scheduling of resource use within a defined territory, provided an economic, social, and technological milieu that favored experimentation with more intensive forms of procurement, leading ultimately to domestication of plants and animals.

See also Asia, Eastern and Southern; Asia, Western; Azilian; Bow and Arrow; Capsian; Çatal Hüyük; Creswellian; Culture; Diet; Domestication; Economy, Prehistoric; Epigravettian; Epipaleolithic; Ethnoarchaeology; Hamburgian; Haua Fteah; Hoabinhian; Holocene; Hunter-Gatherers; Ibero-Maurusian; Jarmo; Jewelry; Kebara; Kebaran; Late Paleolithic; Later Stone Age; Magdalenian; Maglemosian; Man-Land Relationships; Neolithic; Niah; Paleoindian; Paleolithic; Raw Materials; Romanellian; Sauveterrian; Sea-Level Change; Smithfield; Star Carr; Stone-Tool Making; Tardenoisian; Tshitolian; Upper Paleolithic; Wilton. [A.S.B.]

Further Readings

Childe, V.G. (1936) *Man Makes Himself.* London: Watts.

Childe, V.G. *What Happened in History:* Harmondsworth: Penguin.

Clark J.D., and Brandt, S., eds. (1984) *From Hunters to Farmers: The Causes and Consequences of Food Production in Africa.* Berkeley: University of California Press.

Clark, J.G.D. (1936) *The Mesolithic Settlement of Northern Europe.*

Clark, J.G.D. (1980) *Mesolithic Prelude: The Palaeolithic-Neolithic Transition in Old World Prehistory.* Edinburgh: Edinburgh University Press.

Deacon, H.J. and Deacon, J. (1999) *Human Beginnings in South Africa: Uncovering the Secrets of the Stone Age.* Walnut Creek CA: AltaMira Press.

Deacon, J. (1984) Later Stone Age people and their descendants in southern Africa. In R.G. Klein (ed.): *Southern African Prehistory and Paleoenvironments.* Rotterdam: Balkema.

Flannery, K.V. (1968) Archaeological systems theory and early Mesoamerica. In B.J. Meggars (ed.): *Anthropological Archaeology in the Americas.* Washington, D.C.: Anthropological Society of Washington.

Koslowski, S.K., ed. (1973) *The Mesolithic in Europe.* Warsaw: Warsaw University Press.

Lubbock, J. (Lord Avebury) (1865) *Pre-historic Times, As Illustrated by Ancient Remains and the Manners and Customs of Modern Savages.* London: Williams and Norgate.

Megaw, J.V.S., ed. (1977) *Hunters, Gatherers, and First Farmers beyond Europe.* Leicester: Leicester University Press.

Mellars, P., ed. (1978) *The Early Postglacial Settlement of Northern Europe.* London: Duckworth.

Obermeier, H. (1916) *El Hombré Fósil.* Madrid: Museo Nacional de Ciencias Naturales.

Price, T.D. (1983) *The European Mesolithic. Am. Antiquity* 48:761–774.

Straus, L.G., ed. (1986) *The End of the Paleolithic in the Old World.* BAR International Series 284.Oxford: Archaeopress.

Straus, L.G., Valentin, B.V., Erlandson, J.M., and Yesner, D.R. (eds.): (1996) *Humans of the End of the Ice Age: The Archaeology of the Pleistocene-Holocene Transition.* New York: Plenum.

Mezhirich

Major open-air Late Paleolithic site at the interfleuve of two minor tributaries of the Dnepr River in Ukraine, ca. 160 km south of Kiev. Excavations from 1966 on have revealed four round or oval surface dwellings, ranging in area from 12 to 24 m², that are made of mammoth bones. One of these had a semisubterranean entranceway to control the entry of cold air, as in historic Inuit dwellings. Other features include in-ground storage pits and hearths and surface bone piles. The clear selective patterning of specific bones evident in the construction of the dwellings suggests that they were built to conform to a particular village design plan. Radiocarbon dates assign the occupation of this cold-weather base camp at Mezhirich to ca. 15 Ka.

See also Europe; Kostenki; Late Paleolithic; Mal'ta; Sungir. [O.S.]

Micoquian

Final Early Paleolithic (Acheulean) industry found in western Europe during the Eemian and Early Weichselian, ca. 130–70 Ka. Named after the type site of La Micoque near Les Eyzies, Dordogne, in southwestern France, the industry is characterized by fine, thin lanceolate or foliate handaxes with concavoconvex outlines and by numerous side-scrapers and denticulates, including the convergent denticulate Tayac point. Levallois technology may be present to varying degrees.

See also Acheulean; Early Paleolithic; Europe; Handaxe; Levallois; Stone-Tool Making; Tayacian. [A.S.B.]

Microchoerinae

A subfamily of omomyid tarsiiform primates that occurs in Europe from the latest Early Eocene (Cuisian) to the latest Eocene. The following four recognized genera easily accommodate the modest known diversity of ca. 10–12 species: *Nannopithex, Necrolemur, Pseudoloris* (including *Pivetonia*), and *Microchoerus.*

The diagnostic characteristics of the last common ancestor of the subfamily, which delineate it from the other groups of omomyids, are not easily definable, yet there is no doubt about the monophyly of these primates. The dental formula, although debated in the literature, is different from other known omomyids in that there is one less pair of teeth in the lower dentition than in the upper one. The formula in the ancestral microchoerines, a species of *Nannopithex,* was probably two incisors, one canine, three premolars above and two below, and three molars. This peculiarity may have been the result of the probably early adaptive enlargement of the lower central incisors and the subsequent constraint this imposed on the evolution of the dentition. The molar teeth of the most primitive and oldest-known species of the genus *Nannopithex, N. zuccolae,* are reminiscent of the primitive North American anaptomorphines and omomyines. The greatly enlarged central incisors are similar to those seen in some anaptomorphines, and the known skulls of both *Nannopithex* (crushed) and *Necrolemur* show the same extreme inflation of the petromastoid portion of the petrosal bone as does the skull of the anaptomorphine *Tetonius.* The well-preserved crania of *Necrolemur* are one of the more important lines of evidence for cranial construction in the Omomyidae. The basicrania of these microchoerine skulls have been regarded by some, mistakenly, as showing special similarities to *Tarsius.* The microchoerine basicranium is, in fact, particularly unlike that of *Tarsius,* which is characterized by its extreme reduction of petromastoid pneumatization and derived circulation in contrast to microchoerines. On cranial grounds (including ear region), a strong case

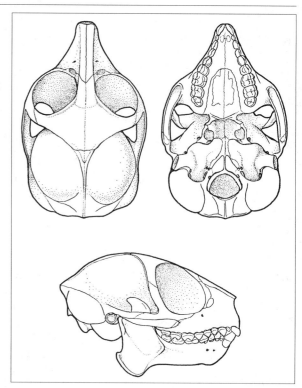

Skull of the European middle-late Eocene microchoerine omomyid Necrolemur antiquus. *Note the bulging area behind the auditory bulla, shared also with the anaptomorphine* Tetonius. *This advanced character does not occur in tarsiids or in known skulls of omomyines. Courtesy of Frederick S. Szalay, from Szalay and Delson, 1979.*

might be made for special affinity between anaptomorphines and microchoerines within the Omomyidae. One may speculate further that an early member of such an ancient omomyid clade was a good structural ancestor for the Anthropoidea. This is largely hypothetical, however.

Postcranial morphology is poorly known for the microchoerines. Information from the hindleg of *Necrolemur* suggests that tarsal elongation and distal fusion of the tibia and fibula, convergently tarsierlike in some adaptive respects, were more advanced than the homologous areas in the other omomyids. The ankle bone (astragalus) of *Necrolemur* shows many morphological differences from *Tarsius,* thus underlining the phylogenetic distinctness of the living tarsiers from this subfamily. The differences of microchoerines from the North American and Asian omomyids notwithstanding, the phylogenetic ties of the European subfamily to one of the major clades of the family is highly probable, and that would seem to make its independent family status unnecessary.

In spite of their relative morphological uniformity, the dental differences suggest divergent adaptive strategies for the two most derived genera, *Pseudoloris* and *Microchoerus.* The former was undoubtedly a predatory, or at least fully insectivorous, genus, whereas the latter displays the molar attributes associated with a diet including a greater proportion of plants than insects. The large incisors of the last common ancestor of the subfamily certainly suggest an initial adaptation to some form of exudativory in addition to feeding on animal (including insect) prey.

Subfamily Microchoerinae
　†*Nannopithex*
　†*Necrolemur*
　†*Pseudoloris* (incl. †*Pivetonia*)
　†*Microchoerus*
†extinct

See also Anaptomorphinae; Diet; Eocene; Europe; Haplorhini; Omomyidae; Omomyinae; Skeleton; Tarsiidae; Tarsiiformes. [F.S.S.]

Further Readings

Godinot, M., and Dagosto, M. (1983) The astragalus of *Necrolemur* (Primates, Microchoerinae). J. Paleontol. 57:1321–1324.

Godinot, M., Russell, D.E., and Louis, P. (1992) Oldest known *Nannopithex* (Primates, Omomyiformes) from the Early Eocene of France. Folia Primatol. 58:32–40.

Szalay, F.S., and Delson, E. (1979) Evolutionary History of the Primates. New York: Academic.

Microsyopidae

A family of Eocene mammals, known from North America and Europe, considered by some paleontologists to be archaic primates. In fact, they have been closely associated by some, mistakenly, with palaechthonin and micromomyin paromomyids. They range from tiny, mouse-size forms in the Early Eocene to almost cat-size ones in the Middle Eocene. Microsyopid cheek teeth are primatelike, but only convergently, and they have a pair of enlarged anterior incisors. This convergent nature of their dental morphology can, and should, be ascertained without recourse to any other characters. The twinned entoconid and hypoconulid, together with mesiodistally constricted trigonids, are reliable diagnostic traits of the lower molars. Known skulls show a relatively small brain, as in many archaic forms, and a related large sagittal crest in the larger species. Their basicranial morphology, particularly of the ear region, much valued by mammalian systematists, shows them to lack a petrosal bulla, which is present in all known primates identified by either dental or postcranial features. Their bulla was likely constructed of the entotympanic bone as in tupaiids and colugos. Microsyopid ear-region morphology also displays some derived similarities shared with the living colugos (flying lemurs) of the order Dermoptera. Remains of the hind foot, particularly the tarsus, which probably belonged to microsyopids, show unequivocally that these animals share the derived specializations of colugos to pedal hanging under branches. The remaining question is whether the closely twinned hypoconulid and entoconid of the lower molars and the dermopteranlike tarsal bones are homologously shared similarities with colugos or not. The living colugos are highly evolved gliders and have a membrane stretched not only between their limbs but between their digits as well.

Unlike other therian gliders, they are not capable quadrupeds. The structure of the tarsus, the best-known postcranial area for microsyopids so far, shows a complex of special similarities not only to colugos and Paleocene mixodectids but also to ptilocercine tupaiids and archaic primates (Plesiadapiformes).

Taxonomically, the microsyopids can be accommodated in two subfamilies: Microsyopinae and Unintasoricinae. The genera *Alveojunctus* from the Middle Eocene and the newly described *Picromomys* from the Early Eocene are uintasoricine microsyopids, not a new family of plesiadapiform primates as K.D. Rose and T.M. Bown contend in their concept of Picromomyidae. The mesiodistally compressed trigonids and twinned entoconid and hypoconulid of *Picromomys* strongly support its uintasoricine and microsyopid status.

The microsyopids, in spite of their enlarged incisor specialization, may be an early family of the order Dermoptera, but not the Primates. In fact, they may be relatives of the Eocene plagiomenids *Tarka* and *Tarkadectes*, which also sport an enlarged lower central incisor; these genera have been linked, incorrectly, to the omomyid *Ekgmowechashala*. In spite of studies of a somewhat distorted ear region of *Plagiomene*, the dental evidence still suggests that the Paleocene-Eocene Plagiomenidae are Dermoptera.

See also Archonta; Dermoptera; Ekgmowechashalinae; Eocene; Plesiadapiformes; Primates. [F.S.S.]

Further Readings

Rose, K.D., and Bown, T.M. (1996) A new plesiadapiform (Mammalia: Plesiadapiformes) from the Early Eocene of the Big Horn Basin, Wyoming. Ann. Carnegie Mus. 65:305–321.

Szalay, F.S. (1969) Mixodectidae, Microsyopidae, and the insectivore-primate transition. Bull. Am. Mus. Nat. Hist. 140:193–330.

Middle Awash

Upper Miocene to Upper Pleistocene stratified series in East-Central Ethiopia, dated by potassium-argon (K/Ar), tephrochronology, fission-track, and faunal analysis. This collecting area comprises sediments discontinuously exposed in a zone ca. 80 km long on both the eastern and western sides of the Awash River, between the town of Gewane and the collecting area of Hadar.

The Middle Awash region is part of the Afar Basin in the Ethiopian Rift and consists of an elongated fault-bounded block parallel to the rift wall that is traversed by the Awash River from south to north. The study region lies south (upstream) from the original discoveries of hominin fossils at Hadar and is divided into districts designated by abbreviations of local Afar names for the Awash tributaries (e.g., BOD = Bodo). The Middle Awash strata document a long and complex sedimentary and tectonic history over the last 6 Myr. Despite the dry and erosive environment, the sediments are exposed over less than 10 percent of this large area, and much of the potential for research is obscured by desert terrace and sand.

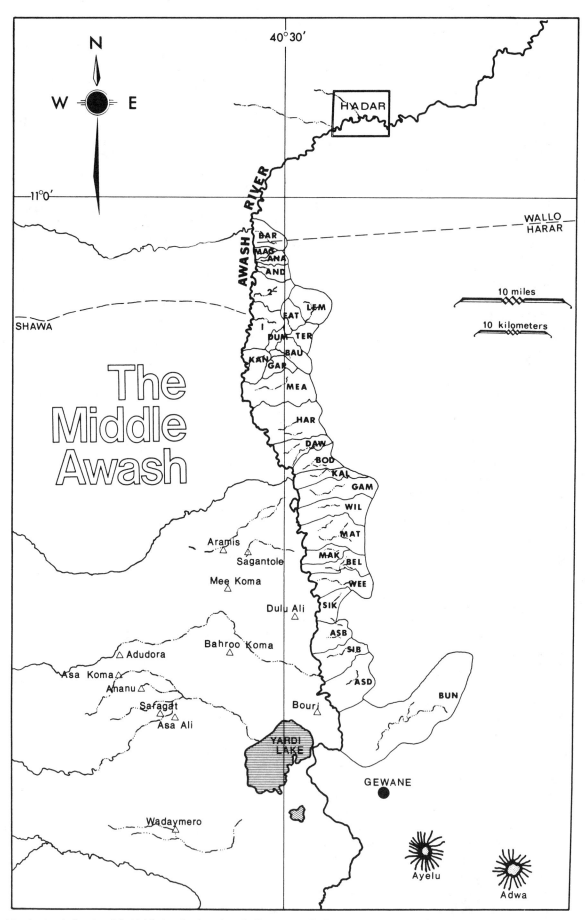

Map showing the location of the Middle Awash paleontological collection areas (for location map, see entry "Afar Basin"). Areas are given Afar names, usually indicating catchment areas of modern drainages that flow seasonally into the modern Awash River that bisects the study area. Major hominid-bearing areas include Bodo (BOD), Gamedah (GAM), Matabaietu (MAT), Belohdelie (BEL), and Maka (MAK) on the eastern side of the study area, and Bouri (BOU) and Aramis (ARA) on the west side. Intense tectonic activity has brought sediments of very different age into juxtaposition in the Middle Awash, and strata of such different ages are often found within some of the paleontological areas. Courtesy of Tim D. White.

Archaeologist J.D. Clark examines an Acheulean handaxe found eroding from Middle Pleistocene deposits in the Middle Awash Valley of Ethiopia's Afar Depression. The study area includes deposits on both sides of the modern Awash River. View is from the east side, toward the west where Pliocene deposits at Aramis are seen on the far left horizon. Photograph by and courtesy of Tim D. White.

The paleontological and archaeological potential of the Awash River Basin was recognized by the French geologist M. Taieb in the late 1960s. In 1976, the first paleoanthropological expedition to the region discovered a cranium of late *Homo erectus* (or early "archaic" *Homo sapiens*) from Middle Pleistocene levels at Bodo. In 1981, a second specimen was found at Bodo, together with archaeological material from there and at Hargufia. Pliocene hominins, consisting of a proximal femur from Maka and cranial fragments from Belohdelie, both predating the Hadar levels, were also found. Most recently, early hominin remains have been reported from the Aramis region that represent a new genus, *Ardipithecus*. At present, dozens of hominin specimens representing several species had been recovered from eight or more paleontological areas of the Middle Awash, along with thousands of other vertebrate fossil specimens.

Many Middle Awash volcanic strata have been radiometrically dated, with some tuff horizons correlated by chemical and petrological analysis with beds in the Gulf of Aden and Hadar and also with tuffs in the Turkana Basin of Kenya and the Lake Mobutu (Lake Albert) Basin in Uganda.

The westernmost Middle Awash study area, at the foot of the Ethiopian Escarpment, has important localities at Ananu and Adu Dora. Upper Miocene strata here are the oldest-known exposures in the study area, with faunal ages of 6–5 Ma based on similarity to Lothagam in northern Kenya and Sahabi in Libya. No primates are known from these western margin exposures. A *horst* (uplifted block) marks the center of the Middle

Awash study area, and Lower Pliocene sediments are exposed on and around the flanks of this central complex just west of the modern Awash River, with radiometric ages between 5 and 3 Ma. The vertebrate fossil assemblages from these sediments are similar to those from Kanapoi and Tabarin in Kenya, and primate fossils have been recovered from Middle Awash sites at Kuseralee, Amba, Urugus, Aramis, and Sagantole.

Most of the sedimentary deposits in the Middle Awash were laid down in and around relatively large, deep Middle Pliocene lakes between 4.5 and 3.7 Ma. The earliest Middle Awash hominin fossils come from this part of the section, in the Aramis drainage. Here, *Ardipithecus ramidus* is known by teeth, cranial parts, and most of a forelimb, as well as an undescribed partial skeleton, from a series of localities that directly overlie the Gàala Vitric Tuff Complex, dated at 4.4 Ma. Other hominin fossils, whose identification has been questioned given the several species that seem to overlap in this time range, were found in the Belohdelie drainage east of the Awash. The site is bracketed between 3.85-Ma Cindery Tuff above, and the VT-1 Tuff correlating with the 3.89 Ma Moiti Tuff of the Turkana Basin below. The big Middle Awash lakes disappeared at ca. 3.7 Ma, and the Maka unit, composed of sands and gravels from wadis and seasonal rivers on the east side of the basin, rests on the largely lacustrine sequence at Belohdelie. The Maka Beds, dated to ca. 3.4 Ma by the SHT Tuff and biochronology of the fauna, have yielded cranial and postcranial remains of hominins attributed to *Australopithecus afarensis*, together with a substantial assem-

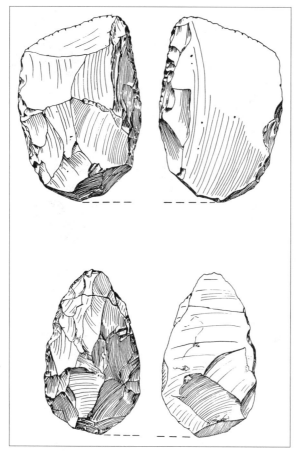

An Acheulean handaxe (below) and a cleaver made on basalt, from Bodo, Middle Pleistocene, Middle Awash study area.

Fragments of the Belohdelie cranium, the earliest cranial vault remains of a hominin. This Middle Awash specimen is dated between 3.9–3.8 Ma. Photograph by and courtesy of Tim D. White.

blage of fossil vertebrates. The material includes the most complete mandible of *A. afarensis*, very similar to the holotype from Laetoli in Tanzania, as well as a well-preserved adult male humerus. Maka thus joins Hadar and Laetoli as the third major locality yielding postcranial and cranial remains of this taxon, with an age equivalent to Laetoli and slightly older than Hadar.

With the demise of the deep Middle Awash lakes came more sporadic sedimentation in fluviatile systems and in small, ephemeral lakes. Strata from ca. 2.5 Ma are well represented in the east of the study area in the Wilti Dora, Gamedah, and Matabaietu drainages. In these beds, a series of highly fossiliferous sands and interbedded volcanic-ash horizons crop out intermittently over a lateral distance of ca. 20 km. Included in the abundant fossil vertebrate collections from these drainages are fragmentary hominid remains recovered in 1990. Oldowan tools are known from beds exposed farther to the north at Bodo, but these rocks appear to be younger, dated biochronologically to ca. 1.5 Ma. On the western side, sediments dated to 2.5 Ma. have yielded a new hominin species *Australopithecus garhi*, as well as cut-marked bones suggesting the manufacture and use of stone tools.

Spectacular Acheulean assemblages are known from the Middle Awash area. The earliest of these are on the western side of the Awash River, on the southern end of the study area, along a peninsula of high ground named Bouri. Here, human remains have been recovered with numerous mammalian fos-

sils and Early Acheulean handaxes. The fossils and artifacts are similar to those found farther inland in the Main Ethiopian Rift at Kesem-Kebena and Konso. Farther to the north and east of the river, in the drainages of Bodo, Dawaitoli, Hargufia, and Meadura, extensive Middle Pleistocene deposits crop out. Many fossil vertebrates, including the original Bodo cranium, have been recovered from these sites. Archaeological remains are abundant in the Bodo area, on the surface and in excavations, and include typical Acheulean materials and Developed Oldowan assemblages. Work in the Dawaitoli and Hargufia areas shows that these assemblages are related to the depositional environments: As the wadi fans became dominant, so did the Acheulean assemblages relative to the Developed Oldowan, indicating substrate preference and activity patterning by the hominid inhabitants. Volcanic strata in the Bodo region have been radiometrically dated to the Middle Pleistocene.

West of the Awash River, and north of Bouri, there are extensive deposits of Late Pleistocene age around Aduma. These Middle Stone Age occurrences, among the richest in Africa, are spatially extensive but stratigraphically constrained and are accompanied by a mammalian fauna. Similar assemblages are known in the Bodo area and north of Meadura. The presence of interbedded volcanic strata provides hope for future radiometric dating of these younger Pleistocene sites.

See also Acheulean; Afar Basin; Africa; Africa, East; Ardipithecus ramidus; Australopithecus afarensis; Australopithecus garhi; Bodo; Hadar. (T.D.W.)

Further Readings

Asfaw, B., White, T., Lovejoy, O., Latimer, B., Simpson, S., and Suwa, G. (1999) *Australopithecus garhi:* a new

A hominin mandible from Maka, Middle Awash, dated to ca. 3.4 Ma is on the left, compared to the mandible of "Lucy" (ca. 3.1 Ma) from the site of Hadar about 70 km to the north. The Maka mandible, assembled from 109 fragments recovered from Pliocene deposits on the east side of the Middle Awash study area, is the most complete lower jaw of Australopithecus afarensis. *Photograph by and courtesy of Tim D. White.*

species of early hominid from Ethiopia. Science 284:629–635.

Clark, J.D., Asfaw, B., Assefa, G., Harris, J.W.K., Kurashina, H., Walter, R.C., White, T.D., and Williams, M.A.J. (1984) Paleoanthropological discoveries in the Middle Awash Valley, Ethiopia. Nature 307:423–428.

Clark, J.D., de Heinzelin, J., Schick, K.D., Hart, W.K., White, T.D., WoldeGabriel, G., Walter, R.S., Walter, R.C., Suwa, G., Asfaw, B., Vrba, E., and H.-Selassie, Y. (1994) African *Homo erectus:* Old radiometric ages and young Oldowan assemblages in the Middle Awash Valley, Ethiopia. Science 264:1907–1910.

de Heinzelin, J., Clark, J.D., White, T., Hart, W., Renne, P., Wolde-Gabriel, G., Beyene, Y., and Vrba, E. (1999) Environment and behavior of 2.5 million-year-old Bouri hominids. Science 284:625–629.

Kalb, J.E., Oswald, E.B., Tebedge, S., Mebrate, A., Tola, E., and Peak, D. (1982) Geology and stratigraphy of Neogene deposits, Middle Awash Valley, Ethiopia. Nature 298:17–25.

Renne, P.R., WoldeGabriel, G., Hart, W.K., Heiken, G., and White, T.O. (1999) Chronostratigraphy of the Miocene-Pliocene Sagantole Formation, Middle Awash. Geol. Soc. Amer. Bull. 111:869–885.

White, T.D., Suwa, G., Hart, W.K., Walter, R.C., Wolde-Gabriel, G., de Heinzelin, J., Clark, J.D., Asfaw, B., and Vrba, E. (1993) New discoveries of *Australopithecus* at Maka in Ethiopia. Nature 366:261–265.

WoldeGabriel, G., White, T.D., Suwa, G., Renne, P., de Heinzelin, J., Hart, W.K., and Helken, G. (1994) Ecological and temporal placement of Early Pliocene hominids at Aramis, Ethiopia. Nature 371:330–333.

Middle Paleolithic

A cultural stage, defined largely on the basis of prepared-core technology and predominantly flake tools, that characterizes most of Europe, Asia, and Africa between ca. 200–150 Ka and 45–30 Ka. Synonyms for Middle Paleolithic in current use include Mode 3 (of J.G.D. Clark's five-mode framework for the Paleolithic) and Middle Stone Age (MSA; applied mainly to African and some South Asian industries).

The Middle Paleolithic differs from the Early Paleolithic by an increase in the proportion of prepared cores, especially Levallois cores, an increase in the size and complexity of retouched flake tools, and a decrease in the number of large core-tools, like Acheulean picks and handaxes. The Middle Paleolithic period also witnessed improvement in hunting technology and hunting abilities reflected both in the tools and in the faunal remains, the first sustained occupation of high altitudes and boreal-forest zones under cold climatic conditions, repeated occupations of rockshelters and caves, and an intensification of symbolic activities reflected in the first use of colored mineral pigments and the first burials.

The first mid-nineteenth-century formulations of European Paleolithic development divided the Paleolithic into two phases: an age of the caves, or Upper Paleolithic, and a precave age, or Lower Paleolithic. Originally included with the Upper Paleolithic as the first epoch of the caves, the Middle Paleolithic, or Cave Bear and Mammoth Age, was quickly recognized as a separate entity by E. Lartet, based on the material from the site of Le Moustier in the Dordogne (France). The Mousterian industries of Europe and Western Asia and the MSA industries of Africa and India are regional variants within a Middle Paleolithic framework that extended over most of the Old World. Middle Paleolithic industries are particularly widespread during the early part of the last glacial stage (ca. 110–40 Ka) but begin well before 200 Ka, as sites of this approximate age are known in East and Northeast Africa (e.g., Gademotta, Kukeleti, Bir Tarfawi), southern Africa (e.g., Twin Rivers, ?Florisbad), southwestern Asia (e.g., Tabūn), and a small region of northwestern Europe (e.g., Biache). While the Middle Paleolithic is generally replaced by Late Paleolithic industries at or before 30 Ka, it may have lasted until 20 Ka in some areas.

Regional Sequences

EUROPE

In Europe, most Middle Paleolithic industries are grouped in the Mousterian complex, although flake industries with leaf-shaped points (*Blattspitzen*) localized in southern Germany are often referred to a separate tradition, the Altmuhlian, and assemblages from most areas of western and central Europe, with small sharply pointed handaxes, are known as Micoquian. Middle Paleolithic industries characterized by blade technologies are particularly concentrated in northwestern Europe, including England, Belgium, northern France, and the Rhine Valley of Germany.

Important European Mousterian sites include Combe Grenal, Le Moustier, La Ferrassie, and La Quina in southwestern France, Cueva Morin in Spain, Grotta Guattari (Monte Circeo) in Italy, Asprochaliko in Greece, and Saltzgitter-Lebenstedt in Germany. Mousterian assemblages from Europe generally feature low-to-moderate percentages of Levallois débitage, and high but variable ratios of denticulates, notches, and side-scrapers. Mousterian assemblages from central and eastern Europe feature large numbers of

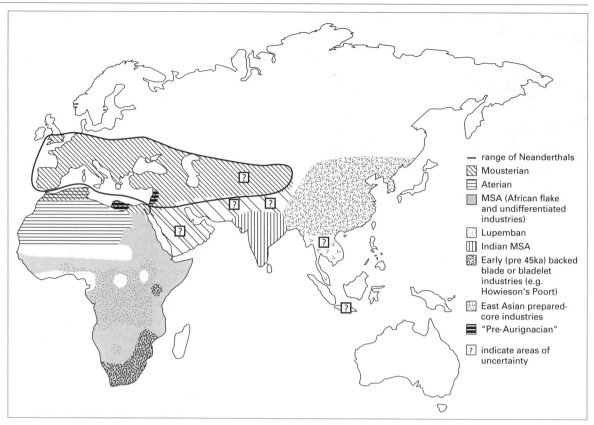

Map showing the distribution of major varieties of Middle Paleolithic industries.

thin, well-made handaxes and are sometimes distinguished as the Eastern Mousterian or the Micoquian. Examples of these assemblages are known from Kulna, Tata, and Konigsaue. Also in central and eastern Europe, a late Middle Paleolithic Altmuhlian industry featuring a wide range of thin, bifacial points is known from sites ranging in age from 60 Ka to less than 35 Ka (e.g., Kokkinopolis, Mauern F). Middle Paleolithic European sites predominantly date to the early last glacial period (oxygen isotope stages 5c to 3) ca. 100–35 Ka.

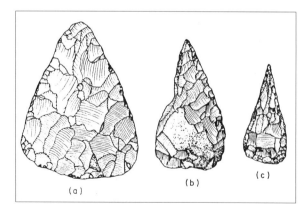

Middle Paleolithic handaxes from Europe (see also "Mousterian"): (a) Mousterian of Acheulean tradition; (b–c) Micoquian (Germany, France). From Champion, T., Gamble, C., Shennan, S., and Whittle, A., Prehistoric Europe, 1984, by permission of the publisher, Academic Press Limited London.

SOUTHWEST ASIA

This region is characterized by significant diversity in a small area. The Levant, in particular, differs from Europe in its very high frequencies of Levallois technology, early prevalence of blades, and frequency of trimmed and untrimmed points. In the Taurus and Zagros ranges of southwest Asia, Middle Paleolithic assemblages from Bisitun, Wawarsi, Shanidar, and Karain exhibit many continuities with the European Mousterian, generally featuring low Levallois indices and numerous scrapers. In the Caucasus, however, and in some parts of the Crimea, some assemblages feature abundant laminar Levallois débitage (e.g., Gouba, Nosovo, Erevan, and Starosel′e). In contrast to most European sites, after 150 Ka most Levantine industries, known as Levantine Mousterian, feature abundant Levallois débitage, with particularly high percentages of blades and pointed flakes, and a pattern of recurrent flaking from only one or both ends of the core, rather than a radial or centripetal flaking pattern around the entire periphery. Among the tool types common in the Levant there are also retouched points, many of which bear signs of hafting in trimmed and reduced butts or broken tips. Key Levantine Mousterian sites include Tabūn, Yabrud, Kebara, Amud, Skhūl, Qafzeh, Rosh Ein Mor, Nahal Aqev, Biqat Quneitra, Tor Faraj, and Tor Sabiha. The Mousterian levels at these sites have yielded not only evidence of modern humans (Qafzeh, Skhūl) along with the Neanderthals (Kebara, Tabūn), but also important evidence for symbolic behavior (Quneitra), burial with grave offerings (Qafzeh), and long-distance transport of shells (also at Qafzeh).

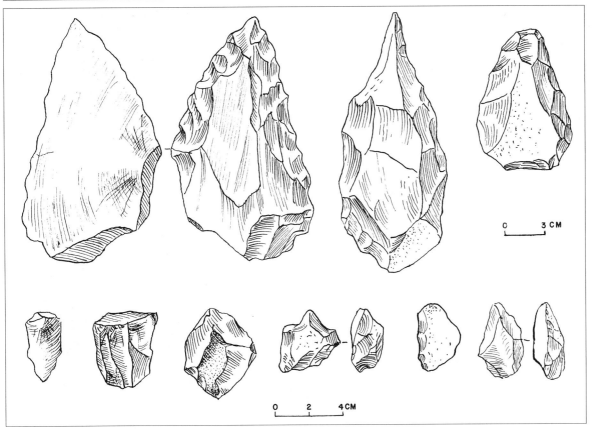

Middle Paleolithic lithic artifacts from China: large pointed flakes from Dingcun (top); small retouched flakes and cores, Xujiayao (bottom). After Qiu Z., in Wu R., and Olsen, J.W., eds., Paleoanthropology and Paleolithic Archaeology in the People's Republic of China, *1985, Academic Press.*

NORTH AFRICA

Along the Mediterranean coast and the Nile Valley, Middle Paleolithic industries, many dominated by side-scrapers as in Europe, have been referred to the Mousterian, and the high frequencies of Levallois technology in these industries suggests a close link with the Levant. The Levallois flaking pattern tends to be centripetal in the western part of the region, and uni- or bidirectional in the Nile Valley, producing a preponderance of blades in the latter case. West of the Nile, these Mousterian industries, associated with fossils such as Jebel Irhoud, may all predate ca. 100 Ka and are succeeded by a Middle Stone Age industry, the Aterian, that is characterized by tanged points, bifacial foliates, and scrapers and is limited to North Africa and the Sahara (e.g., Mugharet el-Aliya, Haua Fteah, El Guettar). In Libya, at the site of Haua Fteah, the Mousterian overlies an early blade industry, the Pre-Aurignacian, and underlies what may be an Aterian industry. In the Nile Valley, the Middle Paleolithic is variable both regionally and chronologically and incorporates four variants: the Mousterian and Aterian found elsewhere in North Africa, and the Khormusan and Nubian Middle Stone Age, which are restricted to the Nile Valley. All of these variants share with many other African Middle Paleolithic industries, and with the Levantine Mousterian, an emphasis on projectile points, whether untrimmed points made on special preshaped Nubian cores (Nubian Mousterian), tanged points (Aterian), bifacial foliates (Nubian Middle Stone Age), or bone points (Khormusan). The generalized Mousterian industries are probably at the base of the sequence during or before the last interglacial (ca. 130 Ka), while the Khormusan, which also contains burins and Upper Paleolithic tools, is late in the sequence.

EQUATORIAL AFRICA

Although the chronological relationships among Middle Paleolithic industries in this region remain imperfectly resolved, they are broadly divisible into three major industries. The earliest, the Sangoan, features large, heavy picks and is known mainly from inland localities, such as Kalambo Falls and Muguruk. Prepared cores are rare in the Sangoan, and it is possibly better described as a late survival of Acheulean technology (analogous perhaps to the Micoquian of eastern Europe). Sangoan industries have been dated to ca. 250 Ka at such sites as Eyasi (Tanzania). The Lupemban industry follows the Sangoan in many parts of western and central Africa. Lupemban assemblages feature thick, pointed lanceolates, some rather large backed microliths, and core-axes, the latter apparently used for woodworking. Along the East African coast and throughout much of the Eastern Rift, the same period sees the appearance of many industries (formerly grouped together under the rubric *Stillbay*) that feature both discoidal and prepared-core technology, as well as exceptionally well-made thinned bifacial points. Examples of the latter industries occur at Porc Épic, Pomongwe (the Tshangulan), Bambata Cave, Prospect Farm, and Mumba Rockshelter. The oldest of these industries are dated to ca. 240–200 Ka at Twin Rivers (Zambia) and Gademotta (Ethiopia).

SOUTHERN AFRICA

The early Middle Paleolithic (or MSA) of South Africa features a wide range of blank-production techniques, including some, such as the Pietersburg, with decidedly laminar Levallois-like blank-production methods. In most respects, however, most South Africa MSA industries exhibit the same basic range of flakes, blades, and points struck from discoidal and prepared cores as are also found in the rest of Africa, western Asia, and Europe. Only with the appearance of the enigmatic Howieson's Poort industry, probably ca. 80–60 Ka but possibly earlier, does this region exhibit a unique Middle Paleolithic industry. The Howieson's Poort, which is also known from Klasies River Mouth, Boomplaas, and Border Cave, features a prismatic blade industry, numerous backed geometric blade tools, and a substantial increase in the use of fine-grained lithic raw material. The Howieson's Poort anticipates many technological features seen in Late Paleolithic assemblages, but it is overlain by more primitive MSA industries at several sites.

SOUTHERN AND SOUTHEAST ASIA

On the Indian subcontinent, the Middle Paleolithic appears to be broadly comparable to other Middle Paleolithic assemblages, although a scarcity of detailed studies of assemblages from well-dated stratigraphic contexts limits generalizations about this region. Lithic assemblages of early Late Pleistocene age from insular Southeast Asia exhibit a wide range of variation within the broad outlines of pebble-core industries, some of which (e.g., Leang Burung in South Sulawesi) feature Levallois cores. The earliest human presence in Australia, Malakunanja II, is probably coeval with the late Middle Paleolithic of East and South Asia, although the lithic industries from this and other Late Pleistocene sites in Australia have more in common with Early Paleolithic pebble-core industries.

EASTERN ASIA

In China, the Middle Paleolithic is represented by several well-documented sites, but it has proved difficult to define regional industrial groupings comparable to those seen in Africa and western Eurasia. In general, there appear to be a large number of assemblages that continue Early Paleolithic pebble-core technology, with an occasional emphasis on bipolar core techniques (e.g., Xujiayao, Dali). Other assemblages, like those from Dingcun, feature rather large bifacial tools reminiscent of Acheulean picks. A singular series of rather well-made flake tools occurs at Zhoukoudian Locality 15. Ephemeral Middle Paleolithic occupations appear in southern Siberia. In Japan, Middle Paleolithic industries with scrapers, points, and borers on flakes from discoidal cores appear by 130 Ka.

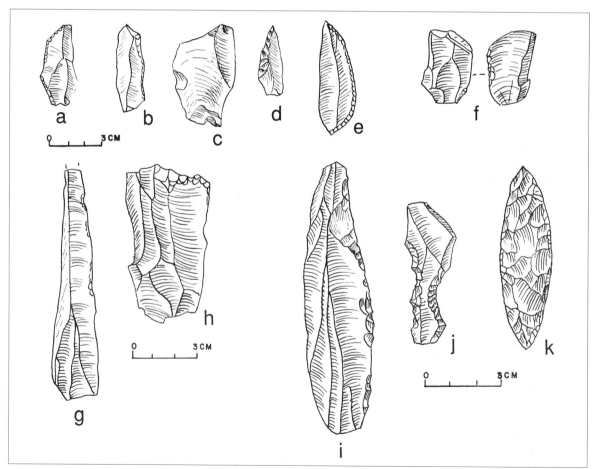

Blade tools of "Pre-Aurignacian," Howieson's Poort, and similar industries: (a-b) Lebanon: backed blades; (c,d,g,h) Libya: (c) burin, (d) retouched blade, (g) blade, (h) blade-core; (e-f; i-k) South Africa: (e) crescent, (f) burin, (i-j) scrapers, (k) bifacial point. (After C.B.M. McBurney, The Haua Fteah [Cyrenaica] and the Stone Age of the South-East Mediterranean, *1967, Cambridge University Press; and C.G. Sampson,* The Stone Age Archaeology of Southern Africa, *1974, Academic Press.)*

Hominid Fossil Associations

Both anatomically archaic and early-modern humans are associated with Middle Paleolithic assemblages. In Europe and western Asia, most fossils from Middle Paleolithic contexts are Neanderthals. In eastern Asia, a wide range of archaic-human forms occur (e.g., Dali, Maba). In Africa, hominins associated with Middle Paleolithic industries range from the archaic-looking (Kabwe) to more virtually modern forms (Omo 1, Border Cave?), with numerous specimens of intermediate morphology (Jebel Irhoud, Klasies River Mouth). Early-modern humans appear between 120 and 80 Ka in the Levantine Middle Paleolithic sites of Skhūl and Qafzeh. On the strength of present chronology, it seems likely that late-surviving populations of *Homo erectus* (e.g., Ngandong) were probably present in Southeast Asia in Middle Paleolithic times.

Behavior

SETTLEMENT

The distribution of Middle Paleolithic sites is similar to that of Early Paleolithic sites, concentrated in areas with permanent water and substantial and stable food sources. Nevertheless, savannah, steppe, and boreal-forest areas and montane zones witness an increasing human presence during Middle Paleolithic times. Indeed Middle Paleolithic people may have been the first to inhabit mid-latitude Europe during full glacial periods. This suggests that Middle Paleolithic groups had found strategies for coping with wide seasonal fluctuations in plant and animal resources. Yet, deserts, both tropical and polar, appear to have posed absolute limits to Middle Paleolithic settlement. There is no evidence for effective seagoing vessels from Africa or western Eurasia during Middle Paleolithic times, although some form of effective long-distance watercraft was clearly in use by the time Australia and New Guinea were colonized more than 50 Ka.

SITE STRUCTURE

Apart from those few sites containing probable burials (see below), most Middle Paleolithic sites provide little clear evidence of internal functional differentiation or of any arbitrary subdivision of space. Many cave sites are little more than juxtaposed concentrations of stone tools, bones, and ashes. A few sites, such as Molodova I, Cueva Morin, Grotte de Renne, Ariendorf, La Ferrassie, and Combe Grenal, along with Mumbwa (Zambia), feature alignments of large bones and/or rocks that some interpret as footings for huts, tents, or windbreaks. Such evidence is consistent with rather brief, perhaps single-season, occupations at most sites, although multiseasonal occupations may have occurred in some particularly favorable localities.

SUBSISTENCE

Although Middle Paleolithic sites have yielded few data concerning plant utilization, many sites contain rich faunal assemblages. Some, such as Combe Grenal, Grotta Guattari, Kebara Cave, and Klasies River Mouth, feature very diverse fauna, including most of the large and small mammals present in their respective regions. Tortoise remains are common at many sites, and there can be little doubt that rodents, birds,

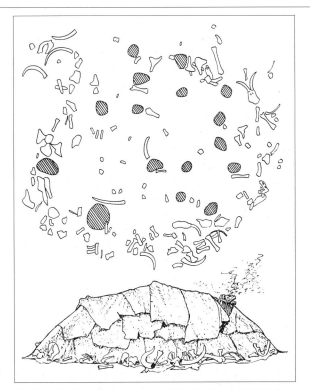

Site plan of a Mousterian structure, ca. 10 m. in diameter, at Molodova (Ukraine), showing hearth areas (shaded) and faunal remains. A hypothetical reconstruction of a skin, bone, and brush "hut" is shown below. From J. Wymer, The Palaeolithic Age, *1982. Reprinted with permission of St. Martin's Press, Inc.*

and invertebrates were collected by Middle Paleolithic humans. Coastal sites from Italy (Grotta Guattari), North Africa (Haua Fteah), and South Africa (Klasies River Mouth) indicate the collection of shellfish. Khor Musa (Egypt) provides evidence of fishing, as does Blombos (South Africa). The diversity of large mammals in many European Middle Paleolithic faunal assemblages suggests a more generalized hunting strategy than that seen in later Paleolithic times. Indeed, the relative frequency variation of large-mammal taxa among many Middle Paleolithic sites appears to be strongly influenced by local climatic conditions. R.G. Klein's 1970s study of large mammals from South African Middle Paleolithic faunal assemblages revealed a preponderance of attritional mortality profiles (frequencies of individuals in different age-classes mirroring natural mortality patterns), suggesting somewhat ineffective hunting strategies.

L. Binford's analysis of these same assemblages suggests that scavenging of carcasses at carnivore kills and other natural-death sites, such as areas around waterholes during a drought, probably also played a significant role in Middle Paleolithic subsistence. The rich faunal assemblage from the site of Quneitra on the Golan Heights between Israel and Syria may represent just such an occurrence. On the other hand, a 2.5-m-long wooden spear found embedded in an elephant carcass at the late Middle Pleistocene site of Lehringen (Germany) would seem to argue strongly for some technologically assisted hunting during Middle Paleolithic times, as does a stone point tip in a cervical vertebra of a *Pelorovis* at Klasies River Mouth.

TECHNOLOGY

Most of what is known about Middle Paleolithic technology concerns stone tools. Levallois prepared-core techniques occur in many Middle Paleolithic assemblages. This method of core preparation allows a considerable degree of control over the shape of the resulting flakes and an increased amount of cutting edge per unit mass of stone material. Middle Paleolithic assemblages, from Africa and the Levant in particular, show evidence of the application of the Levallois technique to the systematic production of blades and points. It seems likely that the increasing frequency of Levallois core preparation in Middle Paleolithic industries is linked to the use of hafted tools. Large core-tools, like handaxes and cleavers, continued to be made in some Middle Paleolithic industries, especially in Europe, although such tools are never very numerous. A wide range of scrapers, notches, and denticulates occur in Middle Paleolithic assemblages. The morphological differences between many of these tools, which were cataloged extensively by F. Bordes, now seem attributable to differences in the intensity of tool curation and the effects of repeated resharpening. Lithic use-wear studies suggest that most Middle Paleolithic tool types were used for a wide range of purposes, with woodworking figuring prominently in most assemblages. Basal modification and bifacial thinning of points and pointed flakes from many African Middle Paleolithic assemblages suggest their possible use as hafted spear points, and wear referable to the use of spears has been observed on Levallois points from the Levantine Mousterian. Most Middle Paleolithic assemblages are made of locally available materials, with only very small percentages of tool materials from sources farther than a few days' walk. This suggests that many of the technological differences between Middle Paleolithic assemblages may reflect local differences in raw-material availability. Bone, antler, ivory, or shell tools are rare in Middle Paleolithic assemblages, and such tools, like the flaked shells from Grotta dei Moscherini (Italy), simply reflect the shaping of these materials with the same techniques as applied to stone.

SYMBOLIC BEHAVIOR

The European Mousterian record has produced a number of claims regarding a cave-bear cult and such potentially symbolic activities as head-hunting and cannibalism. Most of the evidence for these activities is now regarded as naive interpretation of geological and taphonomic phenomena. For example, the occurrence of bear (*Ursus spelaeus* and *Ursus arctos*) remains together with Middle Paleolithic residues in caves such as Drachenloch and Le Regourdou probably is a result of the mixing of separate Mousterian occupations and cave-bear natural-death sites. Mineral pigments such as red ocher are found at many Middle Paleolithic sites, and it seems likely that this material was used for some symbolic purpose, perhaps body decoration. The earliest-known human burials occur in Middle Paleolithic times, primarily in Mousterian archaeological contexts, but in general burials are rare and do not follow a consistent pattern with respect to body position, orientation, and mortuary furnishings (grave goods). Except for those burials that occur in groups (e.g., La Ferrassie,

Skhūl, Qafzeh), most evidence presented in support of Middle Paleolithic symbolic behavior involves singular occurrences of artifacts or features in contexts thousands of years apart. Accordingly, there seems little basis to infer that the use of material culture as a medium for symbolic messages played a significant role in Middle Paleolithic culture.

Major Current Issues

THE ORIGIN OF THE MIDDLE PALEOLITHIC

The differences between later Early Paleolithic industries and early Middle Paleolithic industries are far from distinct in many regions. In Europe and the Levant, late Middle Pleistocene industries such as the Late Acheulean, Premousterian, and Levalloisian differ from the Mousterian industries that follow them in the same region primarily in terms of relative artifact frequencies. The distinction between Early Paleolithic and Middle Paleolithic is even less clear in eastern Asia. It is possible that the taxonomic distinction between Early and Middle Paleolithic in these regions masks a fundamental cultural and biobehavioral continuity.

BEHAVIORAL DIFFERENCES AMONG MIDDLE PALEOLITHIC HOMINIDS

Because at least some early fossils appear to be essentially modern in morphology, archaeologists are increasingly concerned about how the behavioral differences between these hominids and archaic humans like the Neanderthals may be reflected in the archaeological record. Thus far (1997), most comparisons of the archaeological record associated with Neanderthals and early-modern humans have focused on the Levantine Mousterian, in which examples of both hominid taxa occur in similar archaeological contexts. Few studies, however, have moved beyond superficial formal characterizations of the lithic and faunal record, in which one would expect to see continuities between hominid taxa sharing a recent common ancestor, to examine more subtle aspects of the record referable to specific behavioral processes (e.g., mobility patterns, technological strategies).

THE MIDDLE-UPPER PALEOLITHIC TRANSITION

Except in Australia and New Guinea, Middle Paleolithic industries are supplanted by Late Paleolithic industries featuring prismatic blade technology in most parts of the world ca. 54–35 Ka. Partly owing to the difficulties of dating sites from this time range with any great precision, this transformation of the Middle Paleolithic record has proven difficult to clarify. Many researchers have identified Middle-Upper Paleolithic transitional industries and have inferred biocultural continuity among the hominids from a specific region. Some of these, such as the Emiran of the Levant and the Magosian of East Africa, are demonstrably the result of geological mixing of separate Late and Middle Paleolithic assemblages. Many African sites, however, do demonstrate a gradual transition to Mode 5 technologies with microlithic forms appearing as early as 80–60 Ka. Other industries such as the Chatelperronian in western Europe and the Szeletian in central Europe, exhibit strong typological continuities with their Middle Paleolithic predecessors (the Mousterian of Acheulean tradition and the

Altmuhlian/Eastern Mousterian, respectively) but also feature prismatic blade techniques. Yet, these same industries differ typologically from their early Late Paleolithic successors and contemporaries in the same region (the Aurignacian in both cases). Thus, they may simply represent Middle Paleolithic assemblages infused with the rudiments of Late Paleolithic technology. Many regard the sites of Boker Tachtit (Israel) and Ksar 'Akil (Lebanon) as the best-documented cases of an indigenous Middle-Upper Paleolithic transition, although questions remain about the dating and industrial affinities of the final Middle Paleolithic assemblages at both sites.

See also Africa; Africa, East; Africa, North; Africa, Southern; Archaic Moderns; Asia, Eastern and Southern; Asia, Western; Bordes, François; Early Paleolithic; Europe; Homo; Homo neanderthalensis; Homo sapiens; Late Paleolithic; Levallois; Middle Stone Age; Modern Human Origins; Mousterian; Neanderthals; Paleolithic; Paleolithic Lifeways; Upper Paleolithic. [J.J.S.; A.S.B.]

Further Readings

Akazawa, T., Aoki, K., and Bar-Yosef, O. eds. (1998) Neanderthals and Modern Humans in Western Asia. New York: Plenum

Binford, L.R. (1984) Faunal Remains from Klasies River Mouth. New York: Academic Press.

Boeda, E. (1993) Le concept Levallois: Vaviabilité des Méthodes. (Centre de Recherches Archéologiques Monograph 9). Paris: CNRS.

Bordes, F. (1972) A Tale of Two Caves. New York: Harper & Row.

Chase, P.G., and Dibble, H.L. (1987) Middle Paleolithic Symbolism: A review of current evidence and interpretations. J. Anthropol. Archaeol. 6:263–296.

Clark, J.D. (1988) The Middle Stone Age of East Africa and the beginnings of regional identity. J. World Prehist. 2:235–303.

Clark, J.D. (1984) Cultures of the Middle Palaeolithic/Middle Stone Age. In J.D. Clark (ed.): The Cambridge History of Africa, Vol. 1. New York: Cambridge University Press, pp. 248–341.

Klein, R.G. (1978) Stone-age predation on large African bovids. J. Archaeol. Sci. 5:95–217.

Kuhn, S.L. (1995) Mousterian Lithic Technology: An Ecological Perspective. Princeton: Princeton University Press.

Mellars, P. (1996) The Neanderthal Legacy: An Archaeological Perspective from Western Europe. Princeton: Princeton University Press.

Qiu, Z. (1985) The Middle Palaeolithic of China. In Wu R. and J. Olsen (eds.): Palaeoanthropology and Palaeolithic Archaeology in the People's Republic of China. New York: Academic, pp. 147–186.

Stiner, M.C. (1994) Honor among Thieves: A Zooarchaeological Study of Neanderthal Ecology. Princeton: Princeton University Press.

Stringer, C.B., and Gamble, C. (1993) In Search of the Neanderthals. London: Thames and Hudson.

Middle-Range Theory

Archaeologists are increasingly aware of how little they know about how their sites were formed. In reality, the so-called facts of archaeology are contemporary observations made on the material remains of the past. Archaeological remains once functioned within an ongoing behavioral system; while these artifacts were being manufactured and used, they existed in their *systemic* contexts. But by the time the artifacts, features, and residues reach the hands of the archaeologist, they have ceased to participate in their behavior system, passing instead into *archaeological* contexts. To bridge the gap between these contemporary observations and past (unknown) behavior, archaeology requires external input from the behavioral world.

Geologists solved an analogous problem long ago. Employing the *doctrine of uniformitarianism*, they reasoned that the processes now operating to modify the Earth's surface are the same ones that operated long ago in the geological past. The study of modern glaciers has convinced geologists that moraines and striations are formed only through glacial action. Thus, when moraines and striated rocks are found in areas where no glaciers exist today, geologists can readily frame and test hypotheses explaining ancient glacial action. The observation of contemporary, ongoing processes provides the bridging arguments necessary to assign meaning to the geological objects of the past.

Using similar bridging arguments (or *middle-range theory*), archaeologists are learning to interpret the cultural remains of the past. Ethnoarchaeological and experimental studies bridge the gap between contemporary observation and relevant statements about ancient behavior. *Ethnoarchaeologists* work within a functioning behavior system, observing how artifacts, features, and residues are incorporated within a living system. By contrast, *experimental archaeologists* attempt to derive relevant processes by means of experimental replication. Much of this initial experimental work has concentrated on the manufacture and use of stone tools, although archaeologists are also exploring a wide range of problems, such as tool efficiency, processes of site destruction and preservation, and methods of ceramic manufacture.

Middle-range research links scientific ideas about the world to the world itself and attributes meaning to our empirical observations. Such research dictates the way that we perceive the past and is quite different from the research used to explain that past.

See also Archaeological Sites; Archaeology; Ethnoarchaeology; Lithic Use-Wear; Stone-Tool Making. [D.H.T.]

Further Readings

Binford, L.R. (1977) Gen. Intro. in Binford, L.R. (ed.). For Theory Building in Archaeology Essays on Faunal Remains, Aquatic Resources, Spatial Analysis and Systemic Modelling. New York: Academic Press.

Middle Stone Age

Second stage in a tripartite system for the African Stone Age, formalized by A.J.H. Goodwin and C. van Riet Lowe in 1929 for South Africa and later expanded to include pre-

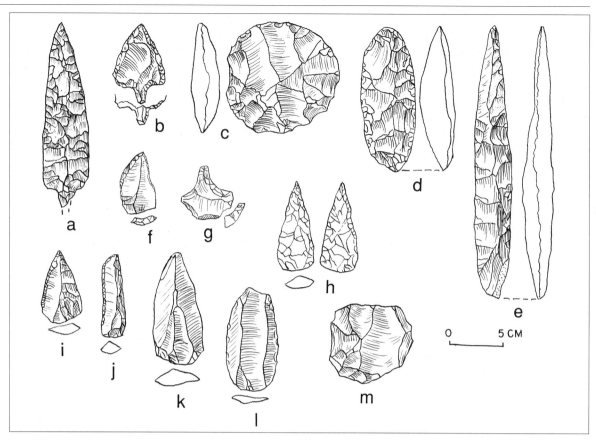

Middle Stone Age artifacts. Aterian industry (Algeria): (a-b) tanged points. Lupemban industry (Zaire): (c) disk; (d) end- and side-scraper; (e) bifacial lanceolate. Bambata industry (Zimbabwe): (f) backed flake with concave marginal retouch on working edge; (g) borer; (h) bifacial point. Pietersburg industry (South Africa): (i) unifacial point; (j) double side-scraper; (k) triangular flake from prepared core; (l) Levallois-type flake; (m) disk core. After J.D. Clark, The Prehistory of Africa, *1970, Praeger; and D. W. Phillipson,* African Archaeology, *1985, Cambridge University Press.*

pared-core (e.g., Stillbay, Bambata) and core-axe (Lupemban) industries from the entire continent, as well as from the Indian subcontinent. Originally included within the Later Stone Age as the Eastern Variant, the Middle Stone Age was separated from the Later, due to both stratigraphic evidence and the absence of microblade technology. Characteristic Middle Stone Age forms include discoidal and Levallois-type cores, convergent flakes with faceted striking platforms, flake blades and a variety of tools, such as side-scrapers and bifacial and unifacial points. Industries that combine prepared flake cores and microblade technologies were later placed in a separate transitional stage (the Second Intermediate), while handaxe industries with prepared flake-core technology, such as the Fauresmith, were referred to the transitional First Intermediate stage. These stages were dropped in the 1960s when stratigraphic studies showed that several "Intermediate" industries were either mixed (e.g., Magosian) or succeeded by non-microlithic MSA industries (e.g., Howieson's Poort).

Even within southern Africa, the term *Middle Stone Age* (MSA) includes a large number of regionally specific industries, such as the Pietersburg, Orangian, Stillbay, and Bambata industries, each with several phases of development, which differ in the forms and percentages of retouched points, knives, and scrapers and in the technology of blank manufacture. In the Cape Province of South Africa, a chronological variant, the Howieson's Poort, bears a superficial resemblance to Late Paleolithic industries in its preponderance of backed blades and geometric forms.

Middle Stone Age peoples were accomplished hunters, who regularly captured large antelope, zebra, and warthog at probable ambush locations, as well as a wide range of smaller game. Plant foods, reflected indirectly by large numbers of grindstones at some sites (e.g., Kalkbank, [South Africa] ≠Gi [Botswana]), shellfish, and ostrich eggs contributed to the MSA diet.

The technological sophistication of MSA industries, particularly in blade manufacture and possible hafting of projectile points, and the degree of regional and chronological specificity were widely interpreted as derivative Upper Paleolithic elements in a relatively backward context, at a time when the MSA was thought to coincide with the Upper Paleolithic of Europe. In the early 1970s, postassium-argon (K/Ar) dates for initial MSA occupations prior to the Late Pleistocene (more than 130 Ka) in Ethiopia and evidence from Tanzania (Laetoli) and southern Africa (where the earliest MSA now dates to ca. 200 Ka) suggested instead that MSA industries may represent technoeconomic and social advances lacking in the Middle Paleolithic of Eurasia but presaging later developments there. These advances, which include decorated stone slabs and incised ostrich eggshell from Apollo-11 Cave (Namibia), barbed bone points and seasonally limited fishing at the Katanda sites in Zaire, the transport of lithic raw materials over distances exceeding 250 km at sites such as Mumba Cave (Tanzania), and ostrich-eggshell beads at Enkapune ya Muto (Kenya) and Mumba Cave, may be contemporary with what are possibly the earliest examples of modern humans *(Homo sapiens sapiens)* at such South African sites as Border Cave, Cape Flats (Skildergat), and Klasies River Mouth, as well as with more archaic populations of *Homo sapiens,* as at Florisbad. Final dates for Middle Stone Age industries of southern Africa mostly predate 30 Ka.

Middle Stone Age core-axe industries of central Africa, such as the Lupemban and Kalinian, are poorly known from excavated contexts, with a few exceptions (e.g., Kalambo Falls, Zambia) but are thought to predate considerably a widespread recession of the tropical forest at ca. 20 Ka. In North Africa, the Aterian industry with its tanged bifacial points and scrapers is the local counterpart of the Middle Stone Age, between the last interglacial (ca. 100 Ka) and ca. 30–20 Ka. Since the term *Middle Stone Age* has been used as a general category for any industry with prepared cores lacking both handaxes and microliths, its use has been formally discontinued by the Pan African Congress of Prehistory and Quaternary Studies. Until the definition and the chronology of regional industries of the late Middle and early Late Pleistocene have been worked out, the congress has recommended the use of regionally specific industry names, combined with the Mode 3 designation of J.G.D. Clark, for flake industries with prepared cores to avoid implications of chronological, stratigraphic, and cultural uniformity across the African continent.

See also Africa; Africa, East; Africa, Southern; Amudian; Apollo-11; Aterian; Border Cave; Cave of Hearths; Early Stone Age; First Intermediate; Handaxe; Homo sapiens; Howieson's Poort; Kalambo Falls; Klasies River Mouth; Late Paleolithic; Later Stone Age; Levallois; Lupemban; Middle Paleolithic; Orangian; Paleolithic; Pietersburg; Pre-Aurignacian; Rose Cottage; Second Intermediate; Stillbay; Stone-Tool Making; Upper Paleolithic. [A.S.B.]

Further Readings

Clark, J.D. (1988) The Middle Stone Age of East Africa and the beginnings of regional identity. J. World Prehist. 2:235–303.

Deacon, H.J., and Deacon, J. (1998) Human Beginnings in South Africa: Uncovering the Secrets of the Stone Age. Walnut Creek, CA: AltaMira Press.

Klein, R.G. (1994) Southern Africa before the Iron Age. In R.S. Corrucini and R.L. Ciochan (eds.): Integrated Paths to the Past: Paleoanthropological Advances in Honor of F. Clark Howell. Englewood Cliffs, N.J.: Prentice-Hall, pp. 471–519.

Klein, R.G. (1978) Stone-age predation in large African bovids. J. Archaeol. Sci. 5:95–217.

Kleindienst, M.R. (1998) What is the Aterian: The view from Dakleh Oasis and the Western Desert, Egypt. In Proceedings of the First Dakleh Oasis Project Seminar. Oxford: Oxford University Press.

Phillipson, D.W. (1993) African Archaeology. 2nd ed. Cambridge: Cambridge University Press.

Volman, T.P. (1984) Early prehistory of southern Africa. In R.G. Klein (ed.): Southern African Prehistory and Paleoenvironments. Rotterdam: Balkema.

Wendorf, F., and Schild, R. (1992) The Middle Paleolithic of North Africa: A status report. In F. Klees and R. Kuper (eds.): New Light on the Northeast African Past: Current Prehistoric Research. (Africa Prehistoria 5). Köln: Heinrich-Barth-Institut, pp. 39–78.

Miocene

The Miocene epoch and series span the interval between 23.5 and 5.3 Ma in the later Cenozoic. *Miocene,* from the Greek meaning "moderately recent," was introduced in 1833 by Sir Charles Lyell for the marine strata representing the time when 40–60 percent of the molluscan species were extinct forms. Lyell later felt compelled to remind his readers in all six editions of *Elements of Geology* that, notwithstanding the inclusion of freshwater and volcanic rocks, ". . . the terms Eocene, Miocene and Pliocene were originally invented with reference purely to [marine] conchological data, and in that sense have always been and are still used by me" (6th edition, 1865, pp. 187–188). These data came, initially, from fossils found in Cenozoic basins in western Europe (the Lower Rhine Valley, the London-Paris Basin, the Bordeaux Basin, and the upper reaches of the Po Basin), and it is to these classical marine sequences that the modern definitions and subdivisions of this epoch have also been related.

The Miocene, like all chronostratigraphic units, is framed in a hierarchical series, and its limits are thus defined by its six subordinate stages, typified in the classical areas noted above. The Early Miocene is held by most modern stratigraphers to be time-equivalent to the Aquitanian and Burdigalian stages, founded on exposures in the vicinity of Bordeaux that Lyell cited in his analysis. The base of the Aquitanian thus defines the base of the Miocene, and a *golden spike* (physical reference point) in the Aquitanian stratotype at Moulin de Bernachon, near Saucats, has been employed as its definition. Micropaleontological correlations indicate that this level is equivalent to paleomagnetic Chron C6CN, as seen in deep-sea cores, and to marine deposits in California that are interbedded with radiometrically dated lavas. The dating from both lines of evidence agrees on an age of 23.7 Ma, but, since this may not relate precisely to the stratotype, the age of the boundary is rounded off to 23.5 Ma.

The Middle Miocene is equivalent to the Langhian and Serravallian stages, founded on exposures in the northern Appenine foothills that were among those most closely studied by Lyell. The underlying Bormidian stage in this area also includes strata noted by Lyell and has been proposed as an alternative definition for the Early Miocene. The base of the Langhian, a period of rising global sea level, is correlated to radiometrically dated magnetostratigraphy and microfossil zones (e.g., in the Vienna Basin, New Guinea, Japan, and California) at 16.5 Ma.

The Late Miocene is conventionally represented by the Tortonian and Messinian stages, also typified in the marine rocks of Italy. The base of the Tortonian, recently recorrelated to the worldwide time scale, is dated at 10.4 Ma, and the base of the Messinian, marking the beginning of a worldwide drop in sea level and the temporary desiccation of the Mediterranean Basin, is dated at 6.5 Ma.

Strata of Messinian age were not included in Lyell's discussion since they were mostly absent from the sections he studied due to Late Miocene erosion, and it has been argued that they could be considered as belonging to the Pliocene. Under modern stratigraphic principles, the top of the Miocene, however, is defined not by the highest-known Miocene but by the base of the known Pliocene. The Pliocene is clearly identified in Lyell's work as the deposits laid down in the post-Messinian transgression, and modern dating puts the beginning of this episode at 5.3 Ma.

Miocene Environments

The Miocene saw major changes in global climate, as conditions in the world ocean continued to shift toward the cold, unstable, thermally stratified "icehouse ocean" of today and away from the warm, stable, salinity-stratified "greenhouse ocean" of the Eocene and earlier. Thus, during the Early Miocene, the period between 19.5 and 16.5 Ma was warmer and had less seasonal variation than at any time since, as indicated by oxygen-isotope studies. In this interval, subtropical conditions extended well into higher latitudes, but even then, upwelling currents from the colder depths had already begun to generate onshore aridity in Namibia, North Africa, the Arabian and Iranian regions, and the western United States.

By the end of the Middle Miocene, ca. 12 Ma, the collapse of Tethys had closed the connection between the Mediterranean and the Indian Ocean at the head of the Persian Gulf, and free flow between the Indian Ocean and the Pacific had also been disrupted by closure in the Indo-Malaysian region. At the same time, new suture zones were added to those of the Eocene to form a continuous east-west mountain wall all across the Gondwana-Laurasia contact zone from the Alps and Carpathians through the Elburz, Tien Shan, and the Himalayas. This further impeded heat exchange between temperate and tropical weather regimes and contributed to the strength of the monsoon cycle in the Indo-Pakistan region. Conditions began to change noticeably to become more seasonal, with colder and colder winters at higher latitudes. By 11 Ma, as Miocene seas withdrew to their lowest point, great tracts of evergreen broadleaf forest in the temperate zones were replaced by communities that were better adapted to seasonal aridity and temperature change. The Canary Islands, where the requisite warm, stable conditions are perpetuated, are the last refuge of many members of the Miocene temperate woodland. After a slight warming trend and sea-level advance in the later Tortonian, ca. 8 Ma, the Miocene ended with a sharp drop in ocean levels and a new low in average global temperatures, which seems to be well correlated with a major expansion of the Antarctic ice sheet.

Miocene Faunas

The open-country habitats that developed in response to increased seasonality in the later Miocene have been termed *savannah, steppe,* and even *grasslands,* but they appear to have no real contemporary analogue, being a mosaic of closed-canopy forest, open woodlands, and grassy bush. In south-eastern South America and in Mongolia, open-country (e.g., semiarid and possibly seasonal) habitats with precociously developed *steppe faunas* appeared as early as the Middle Oligocene (30 Ma), probably in response to continental isolation during the great mid-Tertiary regression, combined with orographic effects of the Andean and Himalayan mountain zones. In most of the world's temperate and subtropical regions, however, open conditions did not develop until after global circulation changes in the Middle Miocene.

The tropical and subtropical forests were refuges for the more conservative animal groups, among which should be included the great apes and most monkeys and prosimians. The groups that colonized the open country, however, displayed conspicuous new adaptations. In dental morphology, many open-country herbivores (e.g., murid and cricetid rodents, rabbits, warthogs, antelopes, giraffes, rhinos, horses, hyraxes, and elephants) exhibited parallel trends toward ever-growing or continuously renewed teeth to cope with heavy wear, while others (bush pigs, bears, and hominoids), perhaps more omnivorous or more root oriented, adopted radically thickened enamel as an alternative way to deal with a more seasonal and abrasive diet. Seasonal food and water shortages in the open were met with various strategies not usually found in forest animals, including fossorial (subterranean) colonies, herding, synchronized reproduction, food caches, and (among carnivores) cooperative hunting, food transport, and den minding. The fossil record contains evidence that most of these trends began in the Middle Miocene, and the others may be inferred from the fact that many of the modern lineages that show this open-country behavior are first recognized at this time.

The carrying capacity of the open environment, with more sunlight reaching ground level and faster-growing and more diverse vegetation available, greatly exceeds that of the forest. Both abundance and seasonality are attested in the great mass-mortality fossil sites found in Middle and Late Miocene open-habitat localities (such as Valentine [Nebraska], Pikermi [Greece], Maragheh [Iran], and the Siwaliks [India-Pakistan]). *Mesopithecus* is fairly common at Pikermi, but rare at Maragheh, and many primates occur in Siwalik rocks. For the most part, however, Miocene primates appear to have favored the more closed and well-watered habitats even in savannah mosaic.

Miocene Biogeography

In the later Early Miocene, at ca. 18 Ma, sea-level decline exposed dry-land connections between Africa and Eurasia via key land bridges at the Bab el Mandab narrows between the Red Sea and the Gulf of Aden, and again in the shoaling contact between Mesopotamia and Iran in the Straits of Hormuz at the mouth of the Persian Gulf. The African fauna, specifically that of the coastal plains of East Africa and Arabia, found Eurasia much to its liking. Many of the endemic African lineages (tragulids, primitive antelopes and giraffids, proboscideans, creodonts, nimravine felids, and true chalicotheres, among others) appear at this time in Orleanian (Burdigalian) faunas of western Europe at the MN4b level, dated to ca. 17.5 Ma.

However, it is not until ca. 16 Ma (early Middle Miocene), by which time the proboscideans had already reached North America and sea levels had begun to rise, that the higher primates begin to spread out of Afro-Arabia. Plio-pithecids appear at this time in western and central Europe and in eastern Asia, and the kenyapithecine *Griphopithecus* in the Vienna Basin and Turkey. *Dryopithecus* spread westward, while pongines (*Sivapithecus* and *Ankarapithecus*) colonized a wide area from Turkey to Indo-Pakistan. Cercopithecids did not emerge from Africa until Late Miocene times, at ca. 11 Ma, concurrently with the expansion of more open habitats in temperate Eurasia and with the the first exposure of the Suez isthmus.

In North America, the last of the autochthonous lower primates became extinct before the Miocene. The earliest abundant South American platyrrhines are known principally from the Early Miocene of Patagonia and Chile and the Middle Miocene La Venta fauna of Colombia, but their last common ancestor with Old World primates was undoubtedly no younger than Middle Eocene.

See also Africa; Americas; Cenozoic; Climate Change and Evolution; Europe; Sea-Level Change. [J.A.V.C.]

Further Readings

Berggren, W.A., Kent, D.V., and Van Couvering, J.A. (1985) Neogene, part 2. In N.J. Snelling (ed.): The Chronology of the Geological Record (Geological Society Mem. 10). London: Blackwoods, pp. 211–260.

Berggren, W.A., Kent, D.V., Swisher, C.C., and Aubry, M.P. (1995) A revised Cenozoic geochronology and chronostratigraphy. In W.A. Berggren, D.V. Kent, and M.P. Aubry (eds.): Geochronology, Time Scales, and Global Stratigraphic Correlation (Special Publication 54). Tulsa: SEPM, pp. 129–212.

Russell, D.E., and Savage, D.E. (1983) Mammalian Paleofaunas of the World. Reading, Mass.: Addison-Wesley.

Mladeč

Cave (also known as Lautsch) in the Czech Republic in which skeletal remains of several adults and a child were recovered between 1881 and 1972 from deposits that had washed into the chimney of the cave. These deposits also contain Aurignacian stone and bone tools, forming the basis for the fossils' early Upper Paleolithic attribution (ca. 30–40 Ka). If this age and association are correct, the Mladeč sample may be among the earliest anatomically modern fossils from Europe. Several of the hominid crania are very robust and have even been regarded as Neanderthal-like. Unfortunately, much of the material was destroyed in a fire in 1945, but casts of the best crania have survived, as well as the most complete cranium (1), stored in Vienna.

See also Homo sapiens; Neanderthals; Upper Paleolithic. [C.B.S., J.J.S.]

Modern Human Origins: Introduction

The origin of modern humans is one of the most fiercely debated areas in paleoanthropology. The two major schools of thought are represented by the opposing notions of regional continuity in human evolution, and of a single unique origin, associated with a particular region of the world (see contrasting diagrams on the following pages). Both of these viewpoints were originally based on assessments of morphology, but in recent years both have appealed to genetic and archaeological evidence. Leading proponents of both morphological approaches summarize their positions below, followed by evaluations of the genetic and archaeological arguments by specialists in these fields. [I.T., E.D.]

Modern Human Origins: Multiregional Evolution

The *multiregional theory* has been developed to explain the emergence of modern humans and the sources of contemporary biological variation in humanity. The major process underlying the theory is known as *regional continuity*. The theory has several central elements, some of which it shares with rival theories.

First, it asserts that modern human variation can be traced back, through a single biological species, to a founding population that emerged in Africa, probably close to 2 Ma. This founding species, *Homo erectus*, expanded to occupy much of Africa and also spread into Asia and Europe.

Second, multiregional theory proposes that, since humans first began to colonize Asia and Europe, there has been continuous genetic linkage of all parts of the inhabited human range. While some local populations over the last 1–2 Myr may have become isolated for long periods or even extinguished in some cases, especially during glacial phases, these did not significantly alter the essential unity of the global human populations at all times.

Third, it suggests that regional variants—races or subspecies—of global *H. erectus* developed and that, in at least three major areas, these regional variants preserved their identity (at least as it can be observed skeletally) to varying degrees while being part of an evolution toward modernity. This phenomenon has been characterized as regional continuity.

Points two and three above can be combined to demonstrate that the multiregional model for human evolution, as for other evolving polytypic species, involves the combined influence of regional selection and unifying gene flow. In a living human population, from any part of the geographic range, there are selective forces producing or maintaining distinctive suites of skeletal and other features that contrast with the unifying traits seen in all populations. The multiregional model postulates that such forces have been operating at all times in our species, when it was restricted to Africa and when Europe, Asia, and Africa were all involved.

Fourth, the multiregional model rejects arguments for other human species later emerging anywhere in the human range, as well as for any globally replacing population arising from any one area. While there have been a number of major regional transformations, multiregionalism sees these as limited and stemming from various geographic zones, not just one. For some multiregionalists, *H. erectus* is merely a convenient term for the earlier part of an evolving chronospecies that resulted in *Homo sapiens*. Others regard *H. sapiens* as the only species involved, and thus as the only hominine species to have emerged from Africa.

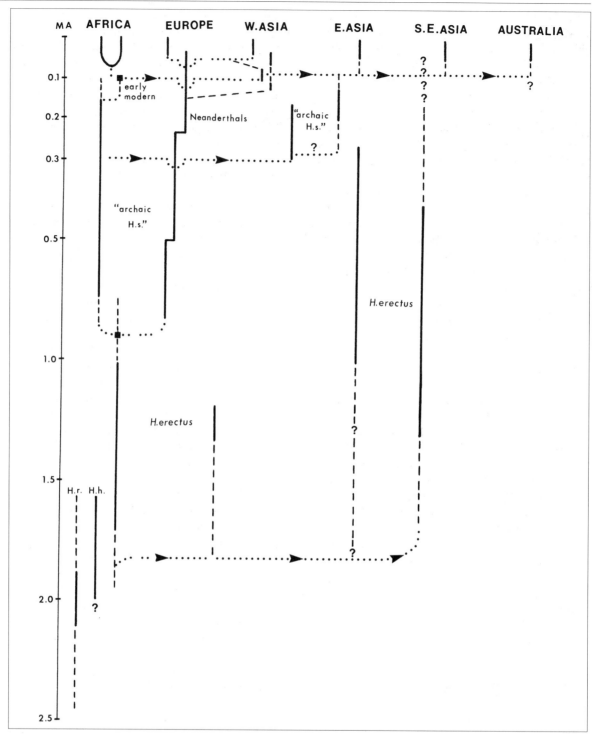

Diagrams contrasting the two main views of modern human origins: Left, single-origin (out of Africa); Right, multiregional. Both diagrams are based upon the same "data," namely the geographic distribution of human fossils as represented by solid vertical lines. Lateral "steps" in the Europe column indicate phases or species within a Neanderthal clade. Horizontal (or nearly horizontal) dotted lines represent interregional migration (semicircles in the European column indicate population movement from Africa to Asia bypassing Europe); thin horizontal lines with double arrowheads represent gene flow between regions. Dashed (semi-) vertical lines indicate postulated time extensions of known ranges. In the left diagram, taxonomic names are applied to various segments (H.h. = Homo habilis; H.r. = H. rudolfensis); on the right, all populations except the oldest Africans are included within Homo sapiens. By E. Delson and L. Meeker.

A number of genetic factors are important to the multiregional hypothesis. The principal one is that mitochondrial genetic (mtDNA) data indicate that only one of the two major theories of modern human origins can be correct. The fact that the human mitochondrial genome, while evidencing some minor variation, is essentially all of one type is important because it means that, in the absence of some evidence of another type, there is either complete replacement of earlier by later populations globally or there has been no replacement but merely continuous gene flow. As there has

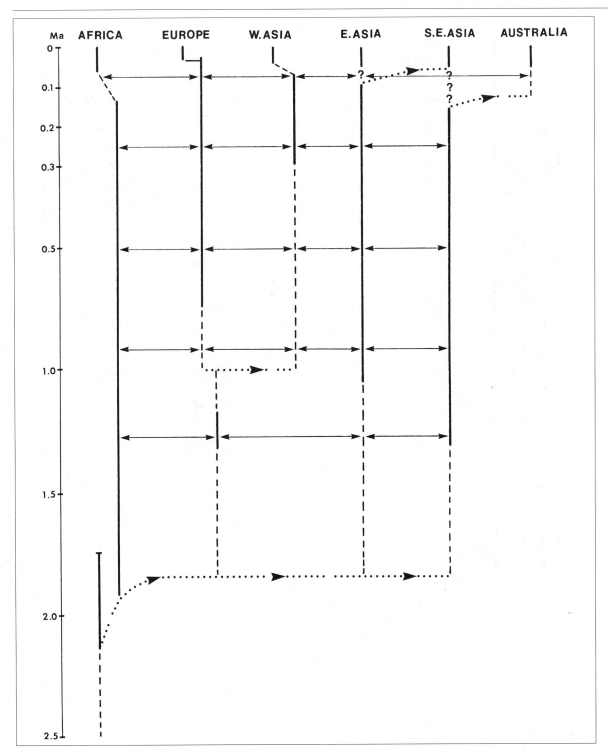

Continued.

been but one biological species involved, there can be no reason for nonincorporation of all mtDNA types in all modern populations from all areas.

Multiregionalists, using ethnographic evidence of modern human behavior, believe that it is most unlikely that a wave of replacement would extinguish indigenous mtDNA types. From this, multiregional theorists conclude that the root of contemporary variation lay in Africa, at a time that preceded the expansion of humans beyond that continent.

Any recent rooting of living mtDNA must be in error, based on a number of inappropriate assumptions about when the pongid-hominid diversion took place, as well as false demographic and geographic assumptions.

The essential skeletal rationale for the multiregional model was proposed by German anatomist F. Weidenreich in the 1930s, in his polycentric *trellis* concept of human evolution, with strong vertical lines representing regional lineages, linked together at all times by horizontal vines of

		Europe and Levant	Africa	East Asia	Australasia
Late Pleistocene	Late	Cro-Magnon Předmostí Mladeč	Afalou Lukenya	Shandingdong Ziyang Liujiang	Kow Swamp Wadjak Keilor
	Middle	Vindija Kebara La Ferrassie La Chapelle	Dar es Soltan	Maba	Lake Mungo 1, 3 Willandra Lakes 50
	Early	Qafzeh Krapina	Klasies	Dingcun Xujiayao	Ngandong
Middle Pleistocene	Late	Ehringsdorf Biache	Ngaloba Florisbad	Dali Jiniushan	Sambungmachan
	Middle	Zuttiyeh Petralona Arago Steinheim	Kabwe Ndutu	Zhoukoudian H Hexian Yunxian	?
	Early		Bodo Tighenif Olduvai 12	Zhoukoudian D, E, L Chenjiawo	Sangiran 2, 10 12, 17 Trinil
Early Pleistocene	Late		Olduvai 9	Gongwangling	Sangiran 4, 27, 31
	Middle		East Turkana 992		
	Early		West Turkana 15000 East Turkana 730, 3733, 3883		

Phylogenetic chart of Homo sapiens *evolution as interpreted under the multiregional hypothesis. This picture of a continuous, linked pattern of human evolution at well-dated sites around the world, leading to modern human groups in different geographic regions with distinct morphological features. Gene flow through interbreeding, as represented by the reticulating network of background lines, maintained these separate groups as part of a single species. After A.G. Thorne and M.H. Wolpoff,* Sci. Amer. *April 1992.*

genetic contact. Weidenreich clearly grasped the crucial notion that, throughout our evolution, certainly during *H. erectus* times, regional variation was matched by global unity. C.S. Coon accepted the vertical, or regional, variation in his writings but ignored the horizontal, or unifying, forces. Coon's idea that subspecies of *H. erectus* become subspecies of *H. sapiens* has been used to criticize multiregionalism by workers who are unaware that this theory builds on Weidenreich's work. After A. Thorne applied central and peripheral population theory to regional *H. erectus* varia-

tion, he and M. Wolpoff redefined Weidenreich's ideas for the Java-Australia skeletal sequence and later, with Wu Xinzhi, established them as the basis for a global concept of multiregionalism.

Weidenreich noted that there was a pattern that could be recognized in the Javan hominids available to him, from early materials such as Trinil to much later finds from Ngandong. There was a stability in many skeletal features over a long period, despite clear evidence of brain expansion and other modernizations. He also noticed that Aboriginal Australians shared many of these Javan traits, not just in isolation but as a repeated set of features. In other words, for Weidenreich the regional—subspecific or racial—features of the Javan erectines were almost the same as those that distinguish modern Australian Aborigines from their regional contemporaries.

Building on Weidenreich's work, multiregional theory sees a clear regional continuity in Southeast Asia-Australasia, based on the fact that the initial Javan population was at the geographic periphery of human Old World expansion and developed an easily recognized and relatively narrowly variable morphology. The Indonesian population, despite likely irregular gene exchange with nearby Asian populations and indirect exchange with more distant populations, shared in the modernizing changes that occurred within this evolving species. Some of the most important features that are present, in combination, in the Javan-Australian sequence are: a relatively robust cranium, retreating foreheads, a unique browridge form, large projecting faces, and large teeth. Cranial form tends to dolichocephaly and vault thickening.

For China, which also has an extensive set of recovered remains spanning a long period, there is a similar, but parallel, sequence visible in the hominid remains. The evolving regional features in this area include an early tendency to facial reduction and flattening, a high incidence of a unique shovel-shaped incisor form, and development of a thin-walled, brachycephalic braincase.

Europe displays the development of a long-term regional variant that can be seen in the Neanderthal skeletal form. It is clear that the arrival of new people in the Late Pleistocene results in the development of a new morphology, but, for multiregionalists, the process involves the incorporation of Neanderthal form not its replacement by exclusion. The Saint-Césaire individual from France and the Skhūl remains from Israel, for example, demonstrate the admixture of the two morphologies, and the central European sequence suggests a transition from one form to the other, again indicating incorporation.

Africa, despite being occupied for the longest period of time, presents the poorest record and, thus, the least-clear picture. As befits the original source area for a polytypic species, the early remains of *H. erectus* there are highly variable. Early evidence of more modern people is sparse, but the South African remains from Klasies River Mouth and Border Cave indicate that a gracile skeletal population had long-term stability there and that it was confined to that continent. This gracile morphology has commonly been mistaken for modern, rather than merely regional.

The eastern Mediterranean area has been the source of much debate about modern human origins because of the great variety of morphologies in the region. The gracility of some remains, particularly from Qafzeh, Israel, has led some to see a source in nearby Africa. However, these fossils lack distinctive African features. The presence of Neanderthal morphologies in the Levant and evidence for long-term links with East and South Asia suggest a complexity that is predictable in a region where three continents meet.

It is important for the multiregional model that the degree of stability of sets of regional features will vary from one area to another, even within any one area through time. Rates and extent of change will also vary in and between areas. With dynamic environmental change throughout the Pleistocene epoch, populations have been compressed geographically, have had altered demographic parameters, were isolated for varying periods by harsh environments or by sea-level rise, have had fluctuating genetic contact with other populations, and so on. Some regions will have experienced regular, continuous, low-level contact for very long periods, while others will have been subjected to relatively different histories. Change has taken place across the human range, but all areas have been influenced by all others rather than by a single one.

Cultural arguments are important to the multiregional model, which asserts that there is clear evidence of long-term tool-kit and behavioral regionality. East of Movius' line, which defines the eastern boundary of handaxe distribution, there is a chopper-chopping technology that is visible for more than 1.0 Myr and thought to be the source for Terminal Pleistocene stone industries in East and Southeast Asia, as well as Australia. There is no sign of the technological change that might be expected if major migrations or replacing populations had entered or left the East Asian area at some period in the later Pleistocene.

Language has been suggested as a mechanism for exclusion or extinction of populations, but there is confusion about what is meant by language and speech. Global brain expansion, including language areas of the brain, supports the notion of progressive language ability in evolving humans (and also demonstrates perhaps the most important single force of global gene flow in human populations). The hyoid and braincase apparatus of Neanderthals has suggested to some a speech barrier to gene exchange with more modern looking people, but this view ignores the multifaceted form that languages can take and the fact that gene exchange does not require mutual linguistic competence.

The considerable variability in living human populations is the product of a process traceable to founding regional groups in various parts of Africa, Asia, and Europe that were linked continuously for more than 1.0 Myr. While some contemporary variation may be attributable to recent adaptive or other processes, the underlying skeletal evidence indicates that some regional populations have maintained their individuality for hundreds of thousands of years. Gene flow and selection produce a complex pattern that, combined with similar influences in cultural development, suggests that our unity results from a process that has been going on since some of us first left Africa.

See also Archaic Homo sapiens; Archaic Moderns; Homo erectus; Homo sapiens. [A.T.]

Modern Human Origins: Out of Africa

The *Out of Africa model* of modern human origins is a special case of single-origin theories of human evolution that V. Sarich has called *Garden of Eden models* and W.W. Howells termed the *Noah's Ark hypothesis*. At the other extreme are polyphyletic models, such as C.S. Coon's, likened by Howells to a candelabra, in which the evolutionary lines are largely inde-

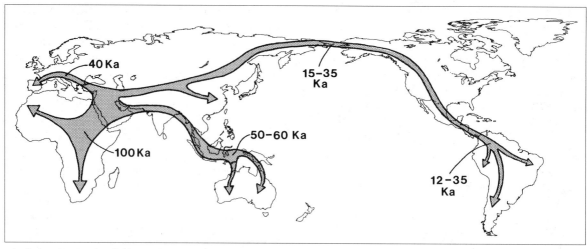

The deployment of modern humans over the past 100 Ka, from a source in Africa, based on paleontological and genetic evidence. After Stringer, C.B. and McKie, R., 1997, African Exodus: The Origins of Modern Humanity, *New York: Henry Holt.*

pendent of each other, and the multiregional models of F. Weidenreich, and M.H. Wolpoff, X. Wu, and A.G. Thorne, which combine multiple lineages and regular cross-cutting gene flow. In some ways, these extremes mirror the ancient philosophical debates between the models of monogenesis and polygenesis, but the present discussion utilizes many sources of data, such as the fossil and archaeological records and present-day morphology, genetics, and linguistic relationships.

Single Origin

The single-origin part of the model may depend on tracing back widespread modern features to a supposed single evolutionary source, or on finding an approximation to the supposed ancestral pattern in a particular region, which is then taken to be the place of origin. The latter approach has been used by C.G. Turner II in reconstructing the evolution of modern humans from dental morphological data. He concluded that present-day Southeast Asians were closest to the hypothetical ancestral dental pattern for modern humans and that, therefore, this region was the probable center of origin for modern humans. His approach also includes the recognition of a clear demarcation between archaic and modern humans in dental morphology in regions such as Europe, thus conflicting with supposed multiregional lineages. A single origin for modern humans has also been proposed by workers such as Howells and C.B. Stringer from comparisons of metrical variation in recent and fossil crania, where diversity in the archaic-fossil material is claimed to be both outside of, and greater than, the range of variation found in modern human samples.

A further implication of a single origin is that present-day regional differences between modern human populations could have developed only after that origin, and this provides a useful test of single-origin vs. multiple-origin models. In the latter, there should be clear morphological links between preceding archaic and succeeding early-modern specimens in each inhabited region. Several supporters of a single-origin model have argued that their research indicates only a recent development of regionality (see below).

Recent African Origin

The basis of models of recent African origin is usually the claim that anatomically modern fossils occur there at an earlier date than in other regions. Workers such as L.S.B. Leakey, D.R. Brothwell, and M.H. Day argued for an early presence of modern humans in Africa on the basis of sites such as Kanjera or Omo Kibish, but they did not make claims that Africa was necessarily unique in this respect. Such claims did not come until the 1970s, when new dating techniques began to move the chronology of the southern African Middle Stone Age back from its assumed Terminal Pleistocene position, coeval with the European Upper Paleolithic, to a time equivalent to that of the Mousterian/Middle Paleolithic. In 1975, J.D. Clark argued that the archaeological record of Africa indicated that this continent was, if anything, more advanced than that of other regions; in the same year, R.R. Protsch reported his new amino-acid and radiocarbon chronologies for southern African sites, indicating both the presence of modern humans more than 50 Ka and a Late Pleistocene persistence of archaic forms.

P.B. Beaumont and colleagues (1978), utilizing Stringer's research results on Northern Hemisphere hominids and their own work on southern African sites, proposed that the Sahara had acted as a major biogeographical barrier in later Pleistocene human evolution, with Neanderthals evolving to the north and modern humans to the south. Modern humans then spread with their African blade-based technologies, replacing the Neanderthals and other archaic humans. Workers such as G.P. Rightmire, G. Bräuer, and Stringer subsequently recognized a probable early *in situ* evolution of modern humans in Africa (based on material from sites such as Border Cave, Klasies River Mouth Caves, and Omo Kibish), but, while Rightmire initially remained cautious about global events, Bräuer developed his *Afro-sapiens hypothesis* of the spread of modern humans from Africa, accompanied by a degree of hybridization between dispersing modern humans and resident archaics such as the Neanderthals.

By 1985, Stringer was arguing for an African origin of modern humans by 70 Ka, a spread to the Levant (Skhūl and

Qafzeh) by 45 Ka, and a dispersal to Europe (ca. 35 Ka) and Australia (30 Ka). This Out of Africa scenario was heavily influenced by the presumed late Middle Palaeolithic age of the Skhūl-Qafzeh sample and the view that these specimens could represent the immediate ancestors of European early moderns, who dispersed into Europe with the development of Upper Paleolithic technologies, replacing the Neanderthals fairly rapidly in the Levant and Europe. At this stage, models of recent African origin were distinctly vague about events in eastern Asia, with Bräuer arguing that populations there could have hybridized with dispersing early moderns, while Rightmire and Stringer could see little evidence for post-*Homo erectus* continuity in the region.

The period 1986–1990 saw rapid changes in the way models of recent African origin were formulated. First, genetic data from nuclear and, particularly, mitochondrial DNA started to make a large impact on discussions of modern human origins. The mitochondrial Eve theory, based on analyses of maternally inherited mitochondrial DNA of living humans, argued for a sub-Saharan African origin of modern-human mtDNA ca. 200 Ka, followed by a dispersal of populations to the rest of the world. Furthermore, the lack of more ancient mtDNA lineages in non-African samples implied that these had been replaced by younger ones of African origin. The intense media interest generated by this work brought the debate on modern human origins to public attention, but it also led to a polarization and hardening of attitudes by scientists involved in the debate. While supporters of the models of recent African origin generally embraced the genetic conclusions enthusiastically, and often rather uncritically, opponents of such models now generally focused their critical attention on this research and often neglected the original palaeontological basis for African-origin models. Recent reanalyses have shown that the original mtDNA studies that formed the basis of the "Eve" theory were premature in their drawing of firm conclusions from these data, but, nevertheless, a growing body of both mtDNA and nuclear DNA research appears to support a recent African origin, albeit with more caution than before.

The second field to make a large impact on the debate about modern human origins was geochronology. Application of thermoluminescence (TL) and electron spin resonance (ESR) techniques began by essentially confirming the expected age of the Israeli Kebara Neanderthal skeleton, at ca. 60 Ka, but then proceeded to double the generally accepted ages for the Skhūl and Qafzeh early-modern-human samples from ca. 50–40 Ka to ca. 120–80 Ka. These methods have also been applied in Europe, establishing ages of 50–35 Ka for Neanderthals from sites such as Saint-Césaire and Guattari, and in Africa, where ESR dating has supported ages of 100–60 Ka for early-modern samples from Border Cave and Klasies River Mouth and 190–90 Ka for late-archaic specimens from Jebel Irhoud and Singa. The effect of these datings was to focus attention on the Levant as showing a presence of modern humans that could be as ancient as that of Africa and to emphasize the independence of the Neanderthal and early-modern lineages. The dating evidence for Singa and Jebel Irhoud also highlighted the importance

of North Africa as an additional and rather neglected source area for modern human origins.

The Evolution of Regionality

Because modern humans are skeletally rather similar and there is considerable morphological and metrical overlap between different populations, it is difficult to produce really effective discriminators between regional variants, which can then also be applied to fossil material. Nevertheless, this has been attempted, with followers of both multiregional and recent-African-origin models claiming support from their analyses. Howells has applied discriminant-function analyses, which can successfully classify modern crania, to Middle and later Pleistocene fossils. But while some early-modern crania can be classified appropriately, others cannot, and archaic and very early modern crania are too distinct to be classified successfully. Further general failures have been reported by workers such as Stringer, R.V.S. Wright, and Sarich, and these analyses seem to provide some of the strongest evidence against the ancient origin for present-day patterns of regionality expected from multiregional evolution. While multiregionalists have also cited continuity of morphological characters in support of their views, the only systematic multiregional comparisons of such characters have provided only limited support, or falsification, for such proposals. P.J. Habgood did identify some characters that were most consistently found in Australasian crania, but workers such as C.P. Groves, Stringer, and M.M. Lahr consider claimed regional-continuity characters to be generally either symplesiomorphies or homoplasies, without phylogenetic significance.

Status of Recent African Origin Models

Since the mid-1980s, models of recent African origin have moved from the margins to the center of the debate on modern human origins. Additional support has been added from fields such as archaeology and linguistics, but since the main paleoanthropological basis for the model was comparison of material in western Europe and Africa, new research on the Asian and Australasian fossil records has also had an impact. Interpretations of old and new Chinese discoveries have shown that at least one additional non-*erectus* archaic hominid, represented by specimens such as Dali, Jinniushan, and Yunxian, was present in the later Middle Pleistocene of China. While morphological contrasts between these specimens and classic *H. erectus* known from Zhoukoudian would appear to strengthen the case for recent African origins by negating claims for regional continuity, the generalized, or even advanced, morphological nature of some of these specimens also provides plausible alternative evolutionary sources for modern humans. It is too early to predict how much impact these fossils will ultimately have on the debate since general study access is not available for much of this important material and numerous chronological problems still prevent realistic reconstructions of local evolutionary scenarios.

For Australasia, the persistent morphological and chronological gap between the (presumed) late *H. erectus* material from Ngandong (Solo) and the Late Pleistocene and Holocene modern human material from sites such as Wajak (Java) and

Lake Mungo and Keilor (Australia), also prevents a clear picture from emerging. One large fossilized calvaria (presently undated) from Australia's Willandra Lakes region (WLH 50) is claimed to show morphological continuity with the Ngandong (Solo) specimens from Java. While there are some apparent structural similarities with these *H. erectus* partial crania, the metrics of the WLH 50 specimen indicate that it is more similar to early-modern specimens from other parts of the world. Until the identity of the earliest Australasian populations is fully understood, speculation about their nature is rather futile.

In Europe, the distinctive evolution of the Neanderthal lineage, with its roots in the Middle Pleistocene, has been increasingly supported by data from sites such as Atapuerca, Spain, while the fate of the Neanderthals seems to have been marginalization and extinction, with perhaps a degree of absorption into the gene pool of succeeding Upper Palaeolithic populations. However, there are still lingering doubts about the identity of the very earliest modern human populations in the region and their immediate place of origin (central Asia, the Levant, North Africa?). In the Levant, evidence for a long-term coexistence or alternation between early-modern and Neanderthal populations has provided an unexpected complexity to simple single-origin models, and the fates of both the earliest moderns and the last Neanderthals in the region are still unclear. In Africa, good evidence of the nature of the earliest manufacturers of the Middle Stone Age is still required, as well as clarification of when recognizably modern behavior had evolved—was it earlier than in other regions, and could it plausibly be linked with the African origin or spread of modern humans? Some other evidence also points to a greater complexity in the origin and dispersal of modern humans, notably the apparently close relationship between Australian and African populations in some phenetic, craniometric, and dental analyses. Howells's multivariate analyses have suggested this, and Turner's dental studies can also be interpreted in this way. Lahr's analyses have shown the relative distinctiveness of the Australian craniofacial morphology, and this is perhaps indicative of an early-modern-human dispersal to Australia, via tropical and subtropical regions, by Middle Palaeolithic founder populations retaining many of the original modern-human skeletal characteristics. In this latter case, cranial and dental similarities between Australia and Africa might be based on symplesiomorphies and would indicate a multiwaved dispersal of modern humans from Africa, rather than the single simple dispersal pattern originally envisaged by Out of Africa models.

See also Archaic Homo sapiens; Archaic Moderns; Atapuerca; Homo sapiens; Middle Stone Age; Neanderthals. [C.B.S.]

Modern Human Origins: The Genetic Perspective

In addition to the 3.2 billion nucleotides within a haploid human nuclear genome (which contain "the genetic instructions" as we commonly conceive them), a normal cell has a small bit of DNA (deoxyribonucleic acid) outside the nucleus as well. The mitochondria are organelles located in the cytoplasm, whose function is the generation of metabolic energy. A mitochondrion contains a genome of ca. 16,500 nucleotides, which code for many of the RNAs (ribonucleic acids) and proteins it uses.

Mitochondrial DNA (mtDNA) in humans has several properties that make it interesting for the study of human prehistory. It contains little noncoding DNA, unlike the nuclear genome. It accumulates mutations up to 10 times as rapidly as the nuclear genome, because mtDNA lacks the efficient DNA repair apparatus of the nucleus. Further, since it does not undergo meiosis and, therefore does not undergo crossing-over, mtDNA is transmitted intergenerationally as a single genetic unit.

Maternal Clonal Transmission

The most interesting difference between mtDNA and nuclear DNA, however, is its mode of transmission across generations. Nuclear DNA is passed on according to Mendelian rules, by virtue of the cycle of meiosis and fertilization, resulting in a child partaking of equal descent from each of its ancestors of a given generation.

By contrast, at fertilization the egg contributes mitochondria to the zygote; the contribution of the sperm is either minute or nil. As a result, a child is a mitochondrial clone of its mother and mitochondrially unrelated to its father. This generally unfamiliar pattern of inheritance is shown in the figure. While siblings are not genetically identical in the traditional sense (since Mendelian inheritance is quantitative), their mtDNAs are identical to one another and to that of their maternal ancestors.

This means that, although mtDNA is inherited faithfully, it does not track the same biological history as nuclear DNA. Imagine a peaceful village subjected to extensive one-way gene flow by a marauding army. Offspring will show the effects of that hybridization in their nuclear DNA but not in their mtDNA, which is exclusively that of their mothers.

The Mitochondrial Eve Hypothesis

Though the details of biological ancestry as told by mtDNA may be difficult to interpret, the coarse pattern may be easier to see. MtDNA is passed on maternally, yet accumulates mutations rapidly, and thus can be used as a genealogical marker, at least of maternal lineage. It is also easy to separate from the nuclear genome, and to analyze in the laboratory.

In 1987, R.L. Cann, M. Stoneking, and A.C. Wilson reported the results of a coarse survey of mtDNA diversity in the human species, with implications for its evolutionary history. They sampled the nucleotide differences from almost 150 different mtDNA variants worldwide and attempted to distinguish between two hypotheses derived from the paleontological record. On the one hand, F. Weidenreich in the 1940s had interpreted the fossil evidence as indicating strong local continuity between "archaic *Homo sapiens*" and anatomically modern *Homo sapiens* (later revised and expounded by C.S. Coon in the 1960s and by M. Wolpoff in the 1980s). This implied that Neanderthals were directly ancestral specifically to Europeans. Alternatively, in the 1950s F.C. Howell had elaborated a model of modern human origins that saw all modern humans as closely related to one another and descended from "archaic *Homo sapiens*"

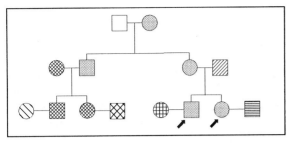

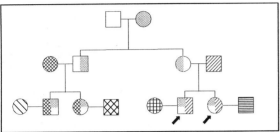

(Top) Clonal inheritance of mitochondrial DNA. The mtDNA of the brother and sister on the right-hand side in the third generation is identical to that of their maternal grandmother. (Bottom) Mendelian inheritance in the same family. The brother and sister carry only 25% of their maternal grandmother's genetic material. Courtesy of Jon Marks.

in one region of the world. This implied the emigration of a founding population and the general replacement of indigenous archaic-human populations by the descendants of the single non-European one (a view expanded and propounded by G. Bräuer and by C.B. Stringer in the 1980s and 1990s). In this *Out of Africa model,* Neanderthals were replaced by modern humans in Europe who evolved elsewhere and were not directly ancestral to them.

Cann, Stoneking, and Wilson linked the mtDNA variants into a tree of descent and observed that the deepest roots separated individuals of African ancestry from one another, while the differences among the mtDNAs from other continents lacked comparable depth. In other words, there appeared to be more mtDNA diversity within the sample of Africans than within the sample of Europeans or Asians. Since the node at the base of the tree represented the ancestor of all detectable mtDNA variants and was a woman (since men do not pass on their mtDNA), they somewhat whimsically named her "Eve." Further, they identified "Eve" as African because the base of the mtDNA tree appeared to be located within the highly diverse sample of Africans.

Finally, they attempted to determine when this mtDNA ancestor from Africa lived. Examining the mtDNA differences detectable in samples from the New World, Australia, and New Guinea, and knowing approximately when these areas were first settled by humans, they estimated that two mtDNA sequences will tend to diverge by ca. 2–4 percent every 1.0 Myr. Since the most divergent human mtDNA sequences differed by ca. 0.57 percent, Cann, Stoneking, and Wilson inferred that "Eve" lived ca. 200 Ka.

"Eve" and the Origin of Modern Humans

The coincidence of time and place between mitochondrial Eve and the earliest remains of anatomically modern humans suggested the possibility that they may actually have been the same.

A missing piece of the puzzle was supplied by comparative studies of mtDNA diversity in our closest relatives, the apes. S.D. Ferris and colleagues had found that, although the human, chimpanzee, and gorilla lineages were approximately as old as one another, chimps and gorillas appeared to have far more detectable mtDNA diversity than did humans. This, in turn, suggested a demographic event unique to human evolution, secondarily cutting back the mtDNA diversity in the species.

The most likely source of such a cutback in genetic diversity is a population bottleneck of the kind that frequently initiates speciation. In the *founder-effect speciation model* developed by E. Mayr, a small daughter population buds from an ancestral population but does not represent an adequate genetic sample of that population by virtue of its small size. If the daughter population thrives and expands, its genetic diversity will ultimately be traceable to the population bottleneck that marked its founding. The pattern of mtDNA diversity encountered in humans suggested such an event in human prehistory (see figure).

The Out-of-Africa hypothesis predicted that the majority of genetic diversity should be found among Africans and that all other human groups would, in essence, be a genetic subset of Africans. Alternatively, the *multiregional hypothesis* predicted that approximately equal amounts of genetic diversity should be found in Europe, Africa, and Asia. The "Eve" theory thus represented genetic evidence supporting one paleontological model (Out of Africa) and not supporting the alternative (the multiregional).

Critiques of the "Eve" Theory

The first wave of criticism centered on the fact that the African sample analyzed had actually been African-American, but subsequent studies of indigenous Africans have borne out the finding of greater diversity in Africa than in Europe or Asia (D.A. Merriwether et al.). Of course, the sampling of genetic diversity in human populations is only in its infancy, and it is conceivable that this finding is in error. Alternatively, it may represent the origin and spread of *Homo erectus* in Africa, long before *Homo sapiens.* For this, the date of a few hundred thousand years ago for the origin of the detectable variation is critical.

More damaging, however, was the recognition that the published phylogenetic tree was not the best tree derivable from the data. Again, however, the structure of the tree itself is of less importance than the relative amounts of genetic diversity on each continent.

Probably the weakest link in the mtEve theory is the relationship between the mtDNA ancestor and the origin of our species. Though both may date to ca. 200 Ka, this may be no more than a coincidence. If one traces back the origin of diversity in some genes (such as HLA), it appears to predate the split of humans and apes, while the diversity in other genes (such as β-globin) seems to be very recent. In the case of each genetic region, specific microevolutionary forces have shaped the gene pool; the origin of modern *Homo sapiens* is not necessarily the primary factor.

Nevertheless, if indeed Africans continue to show more genetic diversity than Europeans and Asians, and if humans really are depauperate in genetic variation relative to chimps

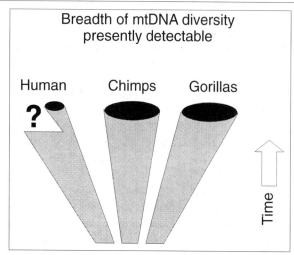

Although humans, chimpanzees, and gorillas have unique ancestries of about the same duration, humans have far less mtDNA diversity. This suggests a bottleneck in recent human prehistory. Courtesy of Jon Marks.

and gorillas, then it may be possible that these patterns are the result of a founder effect due to a speciation event marking the origin of our species in Africa, ca. 200 Ka. Regardless of the strength of these inferences, proponents of the multiregional model are presently concerned with explaining away the genetic data while proponents of the Out of Africa model invoke them. This represents a significant advance in the use of genetic data in anthropology: specifically to augment morphological or paleontological analyses rather than (as has occasionally been extravagantly claimed) to supersede them.

See also Homo erectus; Homo sapiens; Molecular Anthropology [J.M.]

Modern Human Origins: Archaeology and Behavior

The biological relationship of archaic to anatomically modern humans has been a major focus of research in paleoanthropology. Were the archaic forms in each region the direct antecedents of the modern ones? Or did modern humans develop in one area and spread from there? In the latter scenario, did they extinguish or absorb the populations they replaced? Where and when did the original population(s) of modern humans evolve, and by what routes did they expand? And, perhaps most intriguing, why did they evolve at all, and what about their adaptation allowed them to occupy most of the New and Old Worlds by 10 Ka?

While much of the debate has focused on fossil morphology, it is clear that these questions cannot be answered without reference to ancient behavior. The marked gracilization of modern humans must have been stimulated by behavioral changes that made the robust form and large teeth of archaic humans less important for survival. What were these behaviors? Did they appear in parallel in the various regions of the world, or does their distribution in time and space suggest a single origin and outward diffusion? Do modern and archaic humans, especially Neanderthals, share enough behavioral specializations to cast doubt on the existence of a species boundary between them? Morphology alone cannot account for the remarkable spread of

anatomically modern humans to eastern Siberia, Australia, and the New World, and the subsequent extinction of megafaunas in both of the latter, due at least in part to human activity. Since behavioral evidence is more prevalent in the buried record of later humans than the fossils themselves, it is this evidence that is more likely to yield information on migration routes and dates. To what extent were the earliest anatomically modern humans like ourselves, and what aspects of this behavioral repertoire were crucial to their success?

The Study of Behavior

The study of behavior rests on inferences drawn not only from the archaeological record, but also from the fossils themselves. These inferences are informed by analogies, stated or unstated, to living humans, living apes, and other species operating in similar environments. Where natural analogies do not exist, analogies may be created through experimentation. For example, bone points of various specific types may be hafted to spear shafts and propelled into animal carcasses to determine penetration and holding properties, or chimpanzees may be taught to make stone tools to see if they are capable of the complex mental imaging of the tool implied by advanced stone technologies such as Levallois.

Behavior may be inferred from fossils in several ways. Dental and facial morphology may suggest dietary patterns, as well as the extent to which food was processed before chewing. Dental anatomy can also reveal growth patterns relative to the modern human pattern of delayed growth, with its concomitant implications for learning and long-term child care. At the other end of the life span, the apparent ages of the oldest individuals can indicate the presence of the modern human pattern in which women survive their reproductive years by as much as a generation, a biological change that may have had selective value for survival of juvenile descendants. The shape of the cranium and endocranial cast may suggest changes in the relative importance of different areas of the brain. Basicranial morphology may indicate the capacity for an elaborate phonetic repertoire, which, in turn, has implications for language efficiency. Limb and trunk proportions are indicative of required levels of physical stress and movement, as well as of the need for physical rather than behavioral responses to climatic extremes.

Paleopathology, particularly the aggregation of wounds and traumas incurred by a fossil group, may suggest violent interpersonal behavior, especially if females bear a disproportionate number of traumatic injuries or if men suffer an unusual number of injuries to their defensive (usually left) arms. Traumatic injuries may also reflect a pattern of close encounters with large and dangerous animals. Nutritional insufficiencies due to either severe periods of illness or actual periods of starvation are reflected in pathological periods of growth arrest (Harris lines), enamel hypoplasias (growth defects on teeth), and porotic hyperostosis (spongy bone due to response of skull to anemia) and other indicators of anemias. Changes in these patterns may suggest changing hunting and food-gathering abilities, due either to improved technologies or to an increase in food supply whether through human colonization of a new area or to shifting patterns of resource exploitation.

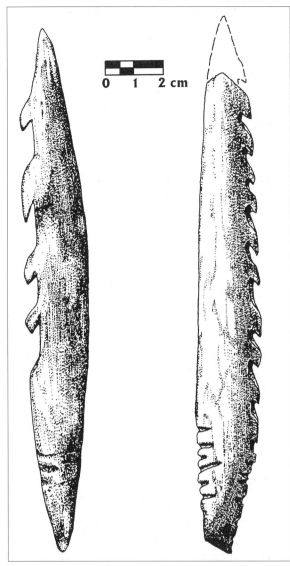

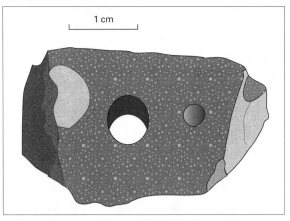

Drilled and ground ocher plaque from the MSA Howieson's Poort at Klasies River Mouth (South Africa). After Knight, C., Power, C., and Watts, I. (1995) "The human symbolic revolution: A Darwinian account" Cambr. Archaeol. J. 5:75–114.

Barbed bone points from Katanda 2 (left) and Katanda 16 (right), D.R. Congo (Zaire). Courtesy of J. Yellen.

Stable-isotope studies can also reveal dietary patterns and suggest changes in them, although the data can have differing behavioral implications. For example, does the 1991 suggestion by H. Bocherens and colleagues that Neanderthal bones contain very high values of the isotope ^{15}N, relative to modern humans, indicate that the Neanderthals were largely carnivorous, or that they usually died after a long period of starvation and reabsorption of their own energy stores, which mimics carnivory?

The archaeology of the fossils themselves—their disposition as a jumble of remains of multiple individuals or as a single articulated individual, in association with constructed pits, cairns, charcoal, ocher, or cultural objects interpreted as grave offerings—provides information on burial practices and, thus, on ritual and religious beliefs and practices. Additionally, cutmarks on the bones may point to cannibalism if they were done while the bone was fresh, or to secondary defleshing and burial if done when the bones were dry.

A somewhat different range of behaviors may be inferred from examining the archaeological record of stone tools, faunal remains, and archaeological sites. Stone tools tell us about cognitive abilities, especially planning ahead and conceptualizing, through their degree of standardization, through their technological and functional complexity, through raw-material-procurement patterns, and through patterns of curation and reuse. If regionally distinctive styles are present, stone tools may also tell us about the complexity of social patterning and ideology. Faunal remains provide information not only about hunting competence, but also about planning and conceptualization, about whether seasonality is indicated, about social organization and complexity, and about whether cooperative and logistical strategies were employed. Finally, archaeological sites themselves are perhaps the most interesting and neglected aspect of the archaeological record, since dense concentrations of materials on the buried landscape are usually the result of reuse and reoccupation. How do these nodes of prehistoric activity correspond to natural landscape features or to other such nodes? What does the resulting distribution and content inventory of the nodes suggest about prehistoric landscape use and reuse or about social organization?

What Is Modern Human Behavior?

Not so many years ago, it was thought that modern human behavioral capabilities and the human social pattern emerged very early, perhaps even in *Homo habilis* times, ca. 1.8 Ma. New ways of studying behavior, such as those mentioned above, have shown, however, that the earliest members of our genus were not competent hunters, did not have great planning depth in their activities as reflected, for example, in transport of stone from afar, and did not make standardized tools. Nor did they experience the long, drawn out juvenile and adolescent growth period of modern humans in which such skills are fully developed. The modern social pattern of long-term male-female monogamous pair bonding is not consistent with the extreme degree of sexual dimorphism present in these early humans. Indeed, the first members of the genus *Homo* may have been little more than toolmaking bipedal apes, who still may have slept in the trees.

Table 1. Behavioral attributes of modern humans as suggested by three recent authors

Hayden, 1993
Curation and foresight
Blades and bone tools
Ritual
Symbolism
Art
Language
Structured living spaces

Klein, 1995
Substantial growth in diversity and standardization of artifact types
Rapid increase in artifact diversity in space and change through time
First formal bone, ivory, shell artifacts
Earliest incontrovertible
Oldest organization of habitation space, hearths, structural ruins
Earliest evidence for ritual in art and graves
First occupation of Northeast Europe and North Asia
First evidence for modern hunter-gatherer population densities
First evidence for fishing and other intensive food procurement

Mellars, 1995
Improved blade technology
New forms of stone tools
Bone, antler, ivory technology
Personal ornaments
Art and decoration
Expanded distribution and trading networks

Table 2. Modern human technological, economic, social, and symbolic innovations

1. Technologies
Blades
Burins and bone technology
Complex hearths and use of fire
Hafted projectiles
Composite tools (e.g., harpoons)

2. Economic innovations
Competent hunting of targeted species
Seasonality and scheduling
Fishing and other small-scale resource use
Long-distance procurement of raw materials
Occupation of new environments

3. Social innovations
Encoding of regional human social groups in artifact styles
Long-distance trading networks

4. Symbolic innovations
Encoding of social groups and individual status in jewelry and personal ornament
Encoding of symbolic landscapes, histories, and rituals in rock art
Decoration of utilitarian objects
Notation

What is meant by *modern humans* when we talk about behavior rather than morphology? There are many trait lists in the current literature that seek to get at these distinctions (see Table 1). Like the early lists of traits that were thought to distinguish civilization from barbarism, however, none of these lists quite gets at the essence of what is meant by fully modern *human*. In Table 2, the lists are combined, reorganized, and expanded to reflect four domains of behavior, rather than trait lists as such, with the traits that provide evidence for modern competence in each domain grouped under that heading. In all of the four domains, the essence of the distinction between modern human behavior and its antecedents is the ability of modern humans to live within a cognitively structured world, rather than a naturally structured one. In such a world, there is a plan for the contingency that comes only once in three generations. You also know where you will be for dinner next Saturday, and maybe even what you will be eating. Such a world is composed of friends, of members of your society, and, most unusual for primates, of relatives you have met rarely or not at all. It may also be populated by past ancestors and their histories, whose persons and life stories may be commemo-

rated throughout your landscape, so that instead of trees, rocks, and water holes, you see history, myth, and validation of your right to be there. Modern humans relate to one another as members of groups and symbolize that membership in dress, behavior, speech, crafts, tools, and other physical expressions—in other words, a world of ethnic differences. When did this all start, and what is its relationship to biological modernity?

The Behavioral Evidence: Europe

The evidence for human behavior related to the origin of modern humans is usually sought in the period between 200 and 35 Ka (i.e., between the time when the first anatomically modern humans probably emerged and the time of the last Neanderthals). The archaeological remains attributed to this time range are usually put in a broad, basket category—the *Middle Paleolithic*. The use of this basket category to refer to archaeological remains in this time period may obscure major interregional differences and developments. The Middle Palaeolithic is a nineteenth-century European concept encompassing the flake tools of the Mousterian industries, which are distinguished by prepared cores and the relative paucity of both bifaces and blade tools. The worldwide emergence of prepared-core technology, which occurred well before 250 Ka, reflected a major change in cognitive planning and the conceptual organization of technology, as the shape of the flake was predetermined by prior shaping of the core. If we look at the Middle Paleolithic sites of different regions, characterized by different fossil hominid histories, do major behavioral differences emerge?

In Europe, the Middle Palaeolithic is not synonymous with Neanderthals. Some Mousterian industries date back to before the earliest Neanderthals of Biache, while the final Neanderthals are associated with an industry, the Chatelperronian, that used to be classed with the Upper Paleolithic because of the wealth of technologically more advanced and symbolic artifacts. Nor is the Middle Paleolithic synonymous with prepared-core technology, as some final Acheulean (Early Paleolithic) sites also exhibit prepared cores.

What can we tell about the behavior of the Neanderthals from their morphology? Neanderthal morphology is characterized by increased body mass, joint surfaces, and muscle markings and by shortened distal limb segments relative to the proximal. These imply a physical response to Ice Age scarcity and greater torsional strength of limbs, feet, arms, and hands. Neanderthals may have been the first hominids to successfully occupy Europe throughout a pleniglacial, beginning with a cold phase ca. 190 Ka. Other peculiarities of Neanderthals include a different body stance, as suggested by the Kebara pelvis; a high incidence of Harris lines and enamel hypoplasias, which suggest stress during growth; and little or no wear on the deciduous teeth, which could indicate a long nursing period and slow population growth or a more rapid individual transition from infancy to childhood than in ourselves. Neanderthals may also exhibit maximum sexual dimorphism for *Homo*. This might imply a different, more haremlike, social organization as in the very dimorphic gorillas or just greater selection for male effectiveness as providers. Females may also have been more stressed during growth, and, thus, smaller in stature, than modern humans.

The bones also tell us that some Neanderthals probably practiced cannibalism, while most populations buried their dead intact in simple graves. Healed injuries further attest to the rigors of Neanderthal life, possibly from close-range struggle with large prey. Some populations, such as those from Shanidar, bear more wounds than others. Many of the wounds appear to be from interpersonal violence, like the knife wound between the ribs of Shanidar 3. Healed wounds, on the other hand, also indicate that Neanderthals cared for the sick and injured, although few individuals appear to have survived into their 40s and none attained the age of 50. Other indicators of a difficult life are the high incidence of Harris lines and enamel hypoplasias, indicative of periods of illness and starvation during growth. Bone biochemistry of Neanderthals has suggested a very high degree of animal protein in their diets (or, alternatively, considerable starvation prior to death, during which the body cannibalizes itself, producing, as noted above, a chemical signal similar to that produced by carnivory).

The archaeology of the Middle Paleolithic of Europe also reflects the rigors of coping with the Ice Age. At least until 55 Ka, tools were relatively unspecialized and multipurpose and made from predominantly local raw materials, using both Levallois and nonprepared-core technologies. Curation and reuse of artifacts was limited. Blades and blade cores are rarely present, but do occur in a few sites, especially in the Middle Rhine

region of Germany. Thousands of sites in western Europe alone reflect repeated short-term visits to particular locations. Many fauna indicate competent hunting of prime-age animals at many sites, while others are characterized by a catastrophic age-at-death profile, suggestive of a mass ambush of an entire herd—at the Cotte de St. Brelade in Jersey, mammoths and woolly rhinos may have been driven over a cliff to their deaths. However, the relative absence or scarcity of hafted projectile points, at least in western Europe, suggests that the kill was usually made at close range with a wooden spear. Hafting seems to have been reserved for scrapers, which were used, according to microwear studies, to process the wooden tools, among other tasks. Fireplaces are small and rarely modified for forced-air or high-heat technologies, and heat treatment of stone materials is rare. Some sites in France have suggested seasonal late fall–early winter use for processing animal kills, particularly bovids. Specialized fishing sites and fishing technologies are unknown.

In social terms, European Mousterian sites are generally small or made up of multiple small-scale occupation horizons, suggestive of small-group size. Lack of substantial regional differentiation within Europe, together with the absence of evidence for trade over long distances, suggests that social organization above the face-to-face daily group was minimal. Although grave goods may, indeed, have been placed in some graves, and lumps of ocher or manganese, some faceted from use, are common, indisputable symbolic artifacts are rare in European Mousterian sites; one of the most convincing is a fossil nummulite with an incision from Tata in Hungary. The nature of Neanderthal language is difficult to resolve, given the present evidence; the major anatomical structures were there, including a modern hyoid bone in the neck. While the modern arrangement of tongue and vocal tract may not have been present, the rudimentary evidence for ritual, burial, and care of the sick suggests a certain linguistic sophistication. Yet, the evidence for a cognitively based world is limited; certainly, the absence of large-scale social networks and symbolic artifacts does not suggest a rich life of the mind. Symbols of ethnic identity and of large-scale social networks are essentially absent.

Late Mousterian and Chatelperronian European sites, from a time when the earliest modern humans were already present on that continent, are quite different from the classical Mousterian described above. They contain a substantial percentage of Upper Paleolithic, or blade, tools made on more specialized cores, as well as shells traded for long distances, bone tools, and perforated teeth for use as beads and amulets. Did they obtain these items from nearby modern human groups, or were they copying the behavior of such groups? M. Stiner has argued the latter, citing major changes in Neanderthal subsistence and ranging behavior that appear ca. 55 Ka, just before the first modern human fossils appear in Europe.

The end of the Middle Paleolithic in Europe, while less abrupt and more reflective of hybridization than the morphological transition from Neanderthals to modern humans, is nevertheless different enough from the succeeding cultures of anatomically modern Upper Paleolithic peoples for this changeover to have been characterized in the recent literature as "the human revolution," the "great leap forward," and "the big transition." However, studies of the Aurignacian, the earliest Upper Paleolithic culture, have suggested that this revolution, while marking a major transition from what had gone before, was not accomplished overnight. Aurignacian blades were crude, the technology for making beads and ornaments was rudimentary, and the earliest antler points were soon superseded by more sophisticated ones, hafted differently. Other inventions, the needle, the atlatl, and the fish weir, as well as the great mass of Ice Age art objects and cave paintings, came much later, although cave art discovered in the 1990s at the Chauvet Cave in France has been dated to the Aurignacian.

The Behavioral Evidence: The Levant

The Levant presents a very different picture during the Middle Paleolithic. In fact, the lumping of the Middle Paleolithic of this region with that of Europe under the term *Mousterian* masks many important distinctions. The lumping is largely due to the presence of prepared-core Levallois technology, which is actually much more prevalent in Levantine industries than in European ones and is quite different from that of Europe in many respects. In particular, Levantine Levallois technology tends to result in flakes being removed sequentially from opposite ends of the core surface, producing long, thin, and often bladelike blanks. European Levallois technology, on the other hand, is more likely to result in a centripetal flaking pattern in which blade forms are rare. Thus, some of the earliest Middle Paleolithic industries of the Levant, predating 200 Ka, are characterized by large blades on what appear to be prismatic blade cores, thought to indicate the advent of modern humans when they show up in Europe. Furthermore, the tools produced from the detached flakes or blades are different from European ones in the greater prevalence of retouched points in Levantine sites, particularly in what is now called Mousterian Type B. In addition, many of these points and the associated waste materials suggest clear evidence for having been hafted as projectiles, an important technology rare in much of Europe at this stage.

One of the major points made by archaeological critics of the Out of Africa hypothesis for modern human origins is that Neanderthals and modern humans living in the Levant cannot be distinguished archaeologically; therefore, they must represent different versions of the same evolving and intermingling population. Yet, the major differences between the Levantine Neanderthal sites and those of Europe, and the demonstrated abilities of European Neanderthals to assimilate aspects of modern human culture once contact is established, should suggest a very different interpretation—that Neanderthals and anatomically modern humans represented two very different human populations sharing elements of technology. Was one of these populations living in a more elaborate cognitive world? It is interesting that the best evidence for elaborate grave offerings in the entire Middle Paleolithic, worldwide, comes from Qafzeh in Israel, a site associated with remains of anatomically modern humans at 120–80 Ka. The most definitive symbolic artifacts in the Middle Paleolithic also come from this region, not only the pierced marine shells from one of the Qafzeh burials, but also an engraved stone from the site of Quneitra in the Golan

Heights, dated to ca. 54 Ka. Furthermore, there is evidence in the Israeli sites for long-distance movement of materials such as the shells mentioned above. Was this cognitive difference enough to maintain a population or species boundary between the two populations? Or were the boundaries more geographically maintained in a scenario in which moderns and Neanderthals occupied the Levant intermittently, but never simultaneously, a hypothesis that is untestable, given the error margins of modern dating techniques?

At the end of the Middle Paleolithic, the advent of Upper Paleolithic technologies in the Levant is both earlier and less abrupt than in Europe. A continuum of technological development from Levallois technology to blades can be traced through time at the site of Boker Tachtit in the Negev. The Aurignacian makes an appearance here, but later than in Europe and is, thus, probably intrusive from that region.

The Behavioral Evidence: Africa

If the Levant represents the overlap of two human populations from two different regions, then some of the reasons for its archaeological distinctiveness may lie in the homeland of the second population, in Africa. Some have argued that the Middle Paleolithic of Africa is just like the Middle Paleolithic elsewhere: a long period of flake tools and stagnation, followed by a rapid revolutionary change to blades, economic sophistication, long-distance transport, social complexity, and symbolic systems. This view ignores descriptions of the African Middle Paleolithic (or *Middle Stone Age*, MSA) published as recently as 1970. Before 1972, and the beginning of the revolution in dating this period, the Middle Stone Age of Africa was considered equivalent in time to the Upper Palaeolithic of Europe, so the discovery of associated anatomically modern skeletons at the South African sites of Border Cave, Klasies River Mouth, and Fishhoek came as no surprise. What was surprising was the relative lack of bone tools, art objects, and beads compared with Upper Paleolithic Europe. Other elements, however, such as the degree of regional differentiation, the ubiquitous presence of blades and blade cores along with flake industries, and the sophistication of projectile-point technology, were considered comparable to the European Upper Paleolithic. When new dates pushed the MSA back to 180 Ka, instantly the MSA became chronologically equivalent to the Mousterian instead of the Upper Paleolithic. Suddenly, attention focused on the anomalous modern-looking hominins associated with the MSA. The fact that many of the tools associated with those hominins recalled the Upper Paleolithic of Europe in both form and technology somehow faded into the background.

Elements of the kind of technological, economic, social, and cognitive developments traditionally associated with modern humans in Europe are present in Africa at what is now a much earlier date. Indeed, some of these behaviors appear before there is any evidence for anatomically modern humans, thus suggesting that the behavioral transition may have both preceded and stimulated the morphological one. Finally, the transition is not sudden or unidirectional as in Europe, suggesting that the revolutionary quality of the European transition may be an artifact of a cultural and biological discontinuity between indigenous and invading populations. In Africa, the transition is gradual, regionally diverse, and marked by many reversals.

What is the evidence for behavioral modernity in Africa? The following technological developments are the easiest to see in the archaeological record:

BLADES AND BLADE TOOLS

Blades made on prismatic blade cores antedate 240 Ka in the Kapthurin Formation (Baringo Basin, Kenya). Blades made on prismatic cores are also present at early MSA sites in Ethiopia, such as at the Gademotta sites, 235±5 Ka. Blade industries and finely made backed crescents are also characteristic of the MSA ca. 80 Ka in South Africa in the Howieson's Poort industry, as well as of the later MSA at Mumba in Tanzania.

BONE-WORKING AND BONE TOOLS

New evidence for hafted barbed bone points from three sites at Katanda in eastern Zaire suggests that this technology was present there by 80–60 Ka. Bone points have also been reported from Middle Stone Age levels at Blombos (South Africa). Scattered evidence for bone tools from several sites in South Africa has become more credible; previously, these were dismissed as probably intrusive.

HAFTED PROJECTILE POINTS

Projectile points with signs of hafting, including trimmed butts, consistently broken tips, standardized widths, and tangs or notches, are common in African MSA industries as far back as 180 Ka. Moreover, like projectile points of later periods, they show regional differentiation and, thus, possibly the beginnings of ethnic identity. Economic activities were also more sophisticated in the Middle Stone Age than previously thought.

ECONOMIC ACTIVITIES

Not only were large and dangerous prey animals such as the extinct giant buffalo, the giant zebra, and the warthog hunted seasonally from ambush at sites like ≠ Gi in Botswana, but many sites are characterized by fish remains, which are generally not present in Mousterian sites. This was true of the Katanda sites in Zaire, but also of several sites in the western desert of Egypt at Bir Tarfawi, as well as in Sudanese Nubia, and in the MSA levels of White Paintings shelter in the Kalahari and at Blombos. Fish remains also occur in Middle Stone Age sites of Ethiopia. The size of fish caught at Katanda implies that there it was a seasonal activity, conducted when the fish were spawning.

Mining and long-distance procurement of raw materials were also features of the MSA. In Egypt, flint mining began in the MSA; in Swaziland, mining for specular hematite occurred in the later MSA. At Mumba in Tanzania, between 1 and 3 percent of the MSA raw material was obsidian imported from the central highlands of Kenya, more than 300 km distant. All of these behaviors indicate greater planning depth and complexity than has previously been argued for the MSA.

SOCIAL COMPLEXITY

Social complexity and the existence of cognitive social maps were also more advanced in the MSA than in the Mousterian. Two examples can be cited from the data already mentioned—the transport of raw materials over distances equivalent to entire European countries and the differentiation of regional industries by projectile-point types.

SYMBOLISM

Symbolic artifacts and evidence of symbolic activities are still very limited for Africa. There is some suggestion that some of the rock art in many of the drier regions of Africa may predate 30 Ka, but the oldest reliably dated example so far is from Apollo-11 in Namibia in 27 Ka. However, pigments and grindstones used for processing pigments are widespread, from South Africa to Egypt, at 80 Ka and earlier. Klasies River Mouth (South Africa) and other sites contain ground ocher plaques with incisions or perforations. Incised fragments of ostrich eggshell are known from several southern African sites (Diepkloof, Elands Bay Cave, Apollo-11, and others) in levels dating as far back as 100 Ka, although the artifactual nature of the incisions is contested. Beads of ostrich eggshell appear in the MSA after 60–50 Ka at sites in Tanzania (Mumba), Kenya (Enkapune ya Muto), and South Africa (Border Cave, Bushman Rock Shelter, Cave of Hearths), but this is quite late in the Middle Stone Age. Equally late, but certainly predating 40 Ka, are bone fragments with notched edges, as at Klasies River Mouth, arguably of notational or mathematical significance. And burials do not seem to have taken place in the same context as in Eurasia; the only MSA cave burial described to date (Border Cave 3) is probably not MSA but intrusive. A late MSA burial from Taramsa (Egypt) suggests that this practice may have involved open-air localities rather than caves and rockshelters during the MSA. For the moment, given the limited state of exploration in Africa and the often poor preservation of organic remains, it is important not to take the absence of evidence as evidence of absence. Yet, the lack of proliferation of durable ostrich-eggshell beads and personal ornaments until very late in the period does suggest a continuing, rather than a sudden, behavioral transition from premodern to modern humans, which is only completed ca. 60–50 Ka. These objects, used widely by modern humans to symbolize group identity, status, and role, were clearly not important to early MSA people.

How does morphological evidence suggest differences between modern humans and Neanderthals and other archaics? The upper limbs of early-modern humans in Africa are less robust, suggestive of the development of projectile technology rather than close-range grappling with the prey. Smaller teeth and jaws, and emerging chins, may reflect less use of teeth as tools and more sophisticated manufacturing technologies. And the basicrania of early moderns suggest fully modern anatomical speech capabilities. Other evidence, comparable to the European studies of traumatic injury, nutrional deficiency, and gender differences in Neanderthals, requires larger fossil samples, especially of postcranial material, than are presently available for Africa.

This African MSA evidence has been criticized for its scarcity; there are, indeed, only a few bone tools, only a few beads, many sites characterized by discoidal and Levallois cores rather than blades, and only a few sites where long-distance procurement has been demonstrated. Yet, compared to the number of reasonably well-excavated sites from the MSA, the number that exhibit at least one of the behaviors discussed above is significant. Even in Upper Paleolithic Europe, many Aurignacian sites have few or no bone tools or ornaments, while others appear to have been regional manufacturing centers. The European bias of the archaeological record is quite overwhelming. Literally thousands of sites have been described for southwestern France alone, and more than 100 have been carefully excavated, while in East Africa, a region almost 100 times as large, the number of carefully excavated and dated MSA sites is less than 12.

Regional Discontinuity in Eastern and Southern Asia

The archaeological record of eastern and southern Asia between 200 and 35 Ka is very limited. In Southeast Asia, many sites dated to the end of this period (e.g., Kota Tampan) contain choppers and chopping tools that are indistinguishable from those in much older assemblages of the region. While the Siberian record of both fauna and artifacts suggests contacts and continuities with Russian and European sites to the west, the material from China, Korea, and Japan is more suggestive of regional isolation during this period. The earliest fossils assigned to anatomically modern humans in the region may be those from the sites of Liujiang in China, although the dates on fissure material of ca. 67 Ka may not relate directly to the fossils. Dates of 40 Ka for a modern child at Niah Cave in Indonesia are also controversial. More secure are the dates for fossils from the Upper Cave at Zhoukoudian in China (at ca. 25 Ka). Prepared cores appear in Chinese sites by ca. 250 Ka, but other evidence of behavioral advancement in the form of blades, burins, bone-working, projectile technology, long-distance movement of raw materials, regional styles, economic specialization, and symbolic expression are absent prior to 30 Ka. In brief, the evidence suggests a different trajectory of development in East Asia up to this point. If Upper Cave is the earliest evidence for modern humans, however, the associated archaeology of barbed-bone points, microliths, and perforated beads and pendants suggests an abrupt discontinuity with the past million or so years of cultural evolution in China and the possibility of an intrusive event, with cultural parallels in the African, rather than the early Upper Paleolithic European, record.

Out of Africa or Regional Continuity?

This overview of the behavioral evidence suggests that, during the Middle Paleolithic, different continental or subcontinental regions were characterized by different traditions. Evidence of behavioral modernity appears earlier in Africa than on the other continents, with the exception of the adjacent region of the Levant. Between 50 and 35 Ka in both Europe and eastern and southern Asia, there is a discontinuity with previous archaeological traditions. In Africa and the Levant, on the other hand, the evolutionary trajectory of culture is more gradual and more continuous, with little evidence of intrusion or discontinuity, at least in regions north of South Africa. This general pattern appears to support an Out of Africa (or Out of the Levant), rather than a regional, scenario.

Proponents of regional scenarios might counter that the earliest European industry associated with anatomically modern humans, the Aurignacian, is initially a purely European phenomenon, widespread on that continent, with no outside antecedents. This might well be taken as evidence of *in situ* evolution. The arguments turn more generally on issues of cultural, as opposed to genetic, transmission. When humans move into new environments, they may radically change their technology, settlement pattern, and subsistence strategy almost overnight, leaving very little evidence of their origins. This pattern is particularly characteristic of rapid or explosive geographic expansions of uncontested terrains not already occupied by other modern humans, as in the case of the initial occupations of the Arctic, Australia, and New Guinea, where the artifacts in question bear little resemblance to those of predecessors in genetically determined source areas. Perhaps the best-known example is the case of the Clovis tradition of North America, which bears little resemblance to the artifacts, hunting practices, or settlement patterns of the presumed Northeast Asian source area for the Clovis people.

If Africa is the cradle of behavioral as well as anatomical modernity, why did Out of Africa take so long to happen? Was it due to a final biological or cognitive transformation as R.G. Klein has argued? A final cultural transition to a cognitively structured world, as suggested by the patterning of symbolic evidence? Or was it due to changes in human relationships to the environment, as B. Hayden has proposed? To some extent, the absence of a dramatic cultural transformation in East and central Africa argues against a biological or cognitive transformation at or just before 40 Ka. The evidence from Africa and the Levant is also beginning to suggest that symbolic behaviors, indicative of cognitively structured environments, were more important to Middle Stone Age people than previously thought.

A possibility along the lines of Hayden's argument is that crowding of human populations in Africa and/or the Levant occurred as desirable environmental zones contracted with the onset of pleniglacial conditions and that this crowding led to the development of new strategies that eventually proved very useful in overcoming the Neanderthals. Chief among these may have been risk avoidance through social networks, which buffer the individual against environmental uncertainty in any one location. Distant networks are often maintained through exchange of goods, as well as through symbols of affiliation, and both of these features increase dramatically in the African record after 50 Ka, although less so in the Levantine record. Cultural elaboration, particularly of symbols representing ethnic identity, has been demonstrated to increase during periods of environmental stress.

Another possibility, suggested by the somewhat controversial Australian evidence for first occupation of that continent by 60 Ka, is that Out of Africa actually happened much earlier and was spread over a longer time period than we realize. In any case, the continuing development of new dating technologies will almost certainly demonstrate that the changes that led to modern humans and their spread throughout the world happened more gradually than current scenarios would suggest.

Although the focus of the Out of Africa scenario has been on the European evidence, the Australian and chronologically uncertain South Asian data may indicate a coastal colonization movement at an early date. The only artifacts that actually resemble MSA points from East Africa are found in the Indian Middle Stone Age, although dating is not at all clear. Early Australian lithic industries, however, bear little resemblance to those of other regions, and the early Australian rock art already contains characteristics of later artistic traditions on that continent, rather than any resemblance to rock-art traditions of East Africa or Asia.

In summary, the relatively limited data on behavioral change during the time when Neanderthals and other archaics were replaced by anatomically modern humans suggests that the change was early, continuous, and gradual in Africa but late (or later), discontinuous, and relatively abrupt elsewhere. To a limited extent, especially in view of problems of cultural vs. biological transmission, the behavioral evidence can be said to support the Out of Africa hypothesis.

See also Africa; Africa, East; Africa, North; Africa, Southern; Archaeology; Asia, Eastern and Southern; Asia, Western; Australia; Europe; Late Paleolithic; Middle Paleolithic; Middle Stone Age; Mousterian; Paleolithic Image; Paleolithic Lifeways; Paleopathology; Ritual; Stone-Tool Making; Upper Paleolithic. [A.S.B.]

Further Readings

Aiello, L. (1993) The fossil evidence for modern human origins in Africa: A revised view. Am. Anthropol. 95:73–96.

Barham, L.S. (1998) Possible early pigment use in South Central Africa. Curr. Anth. 39(5):703–710.

Beaumont P.B., de Villiers, H., and Vogel, J.C. (1978) A review and evaluation with particular reference to Border Cave. S. Afr. J. Sci. 74:409–419.

Binford, L. (1989) Isolating the transition to cultural adaptations: An organizational approach. In E. Trinkaus (ed.): The Emergence of Modern Humans: Biocultural Adaptations in the Later Pleistocene. Cambridge: Cambridge University Press, pp. 18–41.

Bräuer, G. (1984) The "Afro-European sapiens hypothesis" and hominid evolution in East Asia during the Late Middle and Upper Pleistocene. Cour. Forsch. Inst. Senckenberg 69:145–165.

Bräuer, G. (1989) The evolution of modern humans: A comparison of the African and non-African evidence. In P. Mellars and C.B. Stringer (eds.): The Human Revolution. Edinburgh: Edinburgh University Press, pp. 123–154.

Bräuer, G. (1992) Africa's place in the evolution of *Homo sapiens*. In G. Bräuer and F.H. Smith (eds.): Continuity or Replacement? Controversies in *Homo Sapiens* Evolution. Rotterdam: Balkema, pp. 83–98.

Brooks, A.S. (1996) Behavior and human evolution. In E. Meikle and N. Jablonski (eds.): Issues in Human Evolution, First Wattis Symposium. Calif. Acad. Sci. Memoir 21:135–166.

Brooks, A.S., Helgren, D.M., Cramer, J.S., Franklin, A., Hornyak, W., Keating, J.M., Klein, R.G., Rink, W.J., Schwarcz, H., Leith Smith, J.N., Stewart, K., Todd, N.E., Verniers, J., and Yellen, J.E. (1995) Dating and context of three Middle Stone Age sites with bone artifacts in the Upper Semliki Valley, Zaire. Science 268:548–553.

Cann, R.L., Stoneking, M., and Wilson, A.C. (1987) Mitochondrial DNA and human evolution. Nature 325:32–36.

Clark, J.D. (1975) Africa in prehistory: Peripheral or paramount? Man 10:175–198.

Clark, J.D. (1988) The Middle Stone Age of East Africa and the beginnings of regional identity. J. World Prehist. 2:235–305.

Coon, C.S. (1962) The Origin of Races. New York: Knopf.

Day, M.H., and Stringer, C.B. (1982) A reconsideration of the Omo Kibish remains and the *erectus-sapiens* transition. In H. de Lumley (ed.): L*'Homo erectus* et la place de l'Homme de Tautavel parmi les hominidés fossiles. Nice: C.N.R.S./Louis-Jean Scientific and Literary Publications, pp. 814–846.

Day, M.H., and Stringer, C.B. (1991) Les restes crâniens d'Omo-Kibish et leur classification à l'intérieur du genre *Homo*. L'Anthropologie 94:573–594.

Ferris, S.D., Brown, W.M., Davidson, W.S., and Wilson, A.C. (1981) Extensive polymorphism in the mitochondrial DNA of apes. Proc. Nat. Acad. Sci. USA 78:6319–6323.

Frayer, D.W. and Wolpoff, M.H. (1985). Sexual dimorphism. Annual Review of Anthropology 14:429–473.

Groves, C.P. (1989) A regional approach to the problem of the origin of modern humans in Australasia. In P. Mellars and C.B. Stringer (eds.): The Human Revolution. Edinburgh: Edinburgh University Press, pp. 274–285.

Grün, R., and Stringer, C.B. (1991) Electron spin resonance dating and the evolution of modern humans. Archaeometry 33:153–199.

Habgood, P.J. (1989) The origin of anatomically modern humans in Australasia. In P. Mellars and C.B. Stringer (eds): The Human Revolution. Edinburgh: Edinburgh University Press, pp. 245–273.

Hayden, B. (1993) The cultural capacities of Neanderthals: A review and re-evaluation. J. Hum. Evol. 24: 113–146.

Henshilwood, C. and Sealy, J.C. (1997) Bone artifacts from the Middle Stone Age at Blombos Cave, Southern Cape, South Africa. Curr. Anth. 38:890–895.

Howells, W.W. (1973) Cranial Variation in Man: A Study by Multivariate Analysis of Patterns of Differences among Recent Human Populations (Pap. Peabody Mus. Archaeol. Ethnol., Vol. 67). Cambridge, Mass.: Harvard University Press.

Howells, W.W. (1976) Explaining modern man: Evolutionists versus migrationists. J. Hum. Evol. 5:477–495.

Howells, W.W. (1989) Skull Shapes and the Map: Craniometric Analyses in the Dispersion of Modern *Homo*

(Pap. Peabody Mus. Archaeol. and Ethnol., Vol. 79). Cambridge, Mass.: Harvard University Press.

Klein, R.G. (1989) The Human Career. Chicago: University of Chicago Press.

Klein, R.G. (1992) The archaeology of modern human origins. Evol. Anthropol. 1:5–14.

Klein, R.G. (1995) Anatomy, behavior, and modern human origins. J. World Prehist. 9:167–198.

Knecht, H. (1993) Early Upper Paleolithic approaches to bone and antler projectile technology. In G.L. Petersen, H.M. Bricker, and P. Mellars (eds.): Hunting and Animal Exploitation in the Late Paleolithic and Mesolithic of Eurasia. Washington D.C.: American Anthropological Association, pp. 33–47.

Knight, C., Powers, C., and Watts, I. (1995) The human symbolic revolution: A Darwinian account. Cambridge Archaeol. J. 5(1):75–114.

Kuhn, S. (1995) Mousterian Lithic Technology: An Ecological Perspective. Princeton: Princeton University Press.

Lahr, M.M. (1994) The multiregional model of modern human origins: A reassessment of its morphological basis. J. Hum. Evol. 26:23–56.

Lahr, M.M. (1996) The Evolution of Human Diversity. Cambridge: Cambridge University Press.

McBrearty, S., Bishop, L.C. and Kingston, J.D. (1996) Variability in traces of Middle Pleistocene hominid behavior in the Kapthurin Formation, Baringo, Kenya. J. Hum. Evol. 30:563–579.

Mellars, P. (1996) The Neanderthal Legacy: An Archaeological Perspective from Western Europe. Princeton: Princeton Univ. Press.

Merrick, H.V., Brown, F.H., and Nash, W. (1994) Use and movement of obsidian in the Early and Middle Stone Ages of Kenya and northern Tanzania. In T. Childs (ed.): Society, Technology, and Culture in Africa (MASCA Research Papers in Science and Archaeology, Vol. 11 [Supplement]). Philadelphia: University of Pennsylvania Press.

Merriwether, D.A., Clark, A.G., Ballinger, S.W., Schurr, T.G., Soodyall, H., Jenkins, T., Sherry, S.T., and Wallace, D.C. (1991) The structure of human mitochondrial DNA variation. J. Mol. Evol. 33:543–555.

O'Connell, J., and Allen, J. (1998) When did humans first arrive in Greater Australia and why is it important to know? Evol. Anthropol. 6:132–146.

Ogilvie, M.D., Curran, B.K., and Trinkaus, E. (1989) Incidence and patterning of dental enamel hypoplasia among the Neanderthals. Am J. Phys. Anthropol. 79:25–41.

Pope, G.G. (1992) The craniofacial evidence for the origin of modern humans in China. Yrbk. Phys. Anthropol. 35:243–298.

Protsch, R.R. (1975) The absolute dating of Upper Pleistocene sub-Saharan fossil hominids and their place in human evolution. J. Hum. Evol. 4:297–322.

Rak, Y. (1990) On the difference between two pelvises of Mousterian context from the Qafzeh and Kebara caves, Israel. Am. J. Phys. Anthropol. 81:323–332.

Rak, Y. (1993) Morphological variation in Homo neanderthalensis and Homo sapiens in the Levant: A biogeographic model. In W.H. Kimbel and L.B. Martin (eds.): Species, Species Concepts, and Primate Evolution. New York: Plenum, pp. 523–536.

Rak, Y., and Ahrensburg, B. (1987) Kebara 2 Neanderthal pelvis: First look at a complete inlet. Am. J. Phys. Anthropol. 73:227–231.

Rightmire, G.P. (1984) Homo sapiens in sub-Saharan Africa. In F.H. Smith and F. Spencer (eds.): The Origins of Modern Humans. New York: Liss, pp. 295–325.

Smith, F.H., Falsetti, A.B., and Donnelly, S.M. (1989) Modern human origins. Yrbk. Phys. Anthropol. 32:35–68.

Stiner, M. (1994) Honor among Thieves: A Zooarchaeological Study of Neanderthal Ecology. Princeton: Princeton University Press.

Stoneking, M. (1993) DNA and recent human evolution. Evol. Anthropol. 2:60–73.

Stringer, C.B. (1985) Middle Pleistocene hominid variability and the origin of Late Pleistocene humans. In E. Delson (ed.): Ancestors: The Hard Evidence. New York: Liss, pp. 289–295.

Stringer, C.B. (1989) Documenting the origin of modern humans. In E. Trinkaus (ed.): The Emergence of Modern Humans. Cambridge: Cambridge University Press, pp. 67–96.

Stringer, C.B. (1992a) Reconstructing recent human evolution. Philos. Trans. Royal Soc. 337B(1280):217–224.

Stringer, C.B. (1992b) Replacement, continuity, and the origin of Homo sapiens. In G. Bräuer and F.H. Smith (eds.): Continuity or Replacement? Controversies in Homo sapiens Evolution. Rotterdam: Balkema, pp. 9–24.

Stringer, C.B. (1994) Out of Africa: A personal history. In M. Nitecki and D.V. Nitecki (eds.): Origins of Anatomically Modern Humans. New York: Plenum, pp. 149–172.

Stringer, C.B., and Andrews, P. (1988) Genetic and fossil evidence for the origin of modern humans. Science 239:1263–1268.

Stringer, C.B., and Bräuer, G. (1994) Methods, misreading, and bias. Am. Anthropol. 96:416–424.

Stringer, C.B., Hublin, J.-J., and Vandermeersch, B. (1984) The origin of anatomically modern humans in western Europe. In F.H. Smith and F. Spencer (eds.): The Origins of Modern Humans. New York: Liss, pp. 51–135.

Templeton, A.R. (1993) The "Eve" hypothesis: A genetic critique and reanalysis. Am. Anthropol. 95:51–72.

Trinkaus, E. (1983) The Shanidar Neanderthals. New York: Academic.

Trinkaus, E. (1986) The Neanderthals and modern human origins. Ann. Rev. Anthropol. 15:193–218.

Trinkaus, E. (1992) Morphological contrasts between the Near Eastern Qafzeh-Skhul and late archaic samples: Grounds for a behavioral difference. In T. Akazawa, K. Aoki, and T. Kimura (eds): The Evolution and Dispersal of Modern Humans in Asia. Tokyo: Hokusen-Sha, pp. 277–294.

Trinkaus, E., and Shipman, P. (1993) The Neanderthals. London: J. Cape.

Trinkaus, E., and Tompkins, R.L. (1990) The Neanderthal life cycle: The possibility, probability, and perceptibility of contrasts with recent humans. In C.J. de Rousseau (ed.): Primate Life History and Evolution. New York: Wiley Liss, pp. 153–180.

Turner, C.G., II (1987) Late Pleistocene and Holocene population history of East Asia based on dental variation. Am. J. Phys. Anthropol. 73:305–321.

Vandermeersch, B. (1981) Les hommes fossiles de Qafzeh (Israel). Paris: C.N.R.S.

Vigilant, L., Stoneking, M., Harpending, H., Hawkes, K., and Wilson, A.C. (1991) African populations and the evolution of human mtDNA. Science 253:1503–1507.

White, R. (1989) Production complexity and standardization in early Aurignacian bead and pendant manufacture: Evolutionary implications. In P. Mellars and C.B. Stringer (eds.): The Human Revolution. Edinburgh: Edinburgh University Press, pp. 366–390.

Wolpoff, M.H. (1989) Multiregional evolution: The fossil alternative to Eden. In P. Mellars and C.B. Stringer (eds.): The Human Revolution: Edinburgh: Edinburgh University Press, pp. 62–108.

Wolpoff, M.H., Wu, X., and Thorne, A.G. (1984) Modern *Homo sapiens* origins: A general theory of hominid evolution involving the fossil evidence from East Asia. In F.H. Smith and F. Spencer (eds.): The Origins of Modern Humans: A World Survey of the Fossil Evidence. New York: Liss, pp. 411–483.

Yellen, J.E., Brooks, A.S., Cornelissen, E., Mehlman, M.J., and Stewart, K. (1995) A Middle Stone Age worked bone industry from Katanda, Upper Semliki Valley, Zaire. Science 268:553–556.

Modes, Technological

Scheme or sequence of mainly Paleolithic technological stages devised by J.G.D. Clark in 1968 to avoid the use of local industrial terminology outside the area of its definition. For example, rather than discussing Oldowanlike or chopper-chopping tool assemblages in Europe, the less loaded term *Mode 1* could be applied to the Buda industry. Mode 1 implies simple flakes and cores; Mode 2, direct-percussion flaking of more formally shaped pieces; Mode 3, the wide use of prepared cores to yield flake variety; Mode 4, dominance of blades and burins; and Mode 5, microliths.

See also Paleolithic; Stone-Tool Making. [E.D.]

Modjokerto

Eastern Java (Indonesia) fossil-collecting area of Early or Middle Pleistocene age by dating and stratigraphic correlation. The Modjokerto infant hominid calvaria was supposedly excavated from a site north of Perning in East Java, and its provenance and taxonomic affinities have been a constant source of debate. German paleontologist G.H.R. von Koenigswald originally referred to the specimen as *Homo modjo-*

kertensis but subsequently referred it to *Pithecanthropus modjokertensis* and *Pithecanthropus robustus.*

Von Koenigswald's arguments as to its taxonomic affinities appear to have been strictly stratigraphic. An early whole-rock potassium-argon (K/Ar) date of 1.9 ± 0.4 Ma, often quoted for this fossil, probably has little or nothing to do with its actual age. And it now seems probable that the more recently published argon-argon (^{39}Ar/^{40}Ar) date of ca. 1.8 Ma, which appears on the surface to confirm the earlier date, was probably obtained on samples recovered at some distance from the actual site of collection. No fauna is associated with the specimen, and, as already implied, there is ongoing doubt as to whether the actual excavation site has been accurately identified. Although current estimates of the specimen's antiquity range from latest Early Pleistocene to Late Pleistocene, the absence of a reliable provenance for this specimen makes such estimates moot.

See also Asia, Eastern and Southern; Homo erectus; Indonesia; Koenigswald, Gustav Heinrich Ralph von; Potassium-Argon Dating. [G.G.P.]

Further Readings

Sartono, S., Sémah, F., Astadiredja, K.A.S., Sukedarmono, M., and Djubiantono, T. (1981) The age of *Homo mojokertensis*. Mod. Quatern. Res. Southeast Asia 6:91–101.

Swisher, C.C., Curtis, G.H., Jacob, T., Getty, A.G., Suprijo, A., and Widiasmoro (1994) Age of the earliest known hominids in Java. Science 263:1118–1121.

Molecular Anthropology

Systematic study of primate taxa using comparative genetic methods. Since evolutionary change involves change in the genes, a study of the genetic systems of primates should reveal the relationships of species. The subfield dates to G. Nuttall's pioneering work in 1902 on the immunological cross-reactions between the bloods of different species. Little progress was made in this area, however, until the studies of M. Goodman in the 1960s.

As immunological distances are a rough measure of protein (and, therefore, genetic) similarity, the first use of these data involved primate phylogeny and established that the African apes (chimpanzee and gorilla) are more closely related to humans than to orangutans. Another method that became available in the 1960s was the direct sequencing of the amino acids composing specific proteins, a more direct reflection of the genetic material. Protein-sequence data not only confirmed the immunological results, but also showed that humans, chimpanzees, and gorillas were genetically more similar to one another than had previously been imagined.

Concurrently, empirical data and theoretical advances pointed to the conclusion that most evolutionary changes in proteins are nonadaptive and not subject to the operation of natural selection. The spread of these *neutral* changes is governed by *genetic drift,* a statistical process. Consequently, any neutral mutation has a (low) probability of spreading through

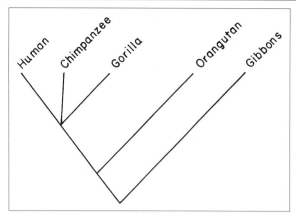

Molecular data show humans, chimpanzees, and gorillas to be approximately equally closely related to one another, but place the orangutan clearly apart from the African apes and humans. Courtesy of Jon Marks.

a population over time, and the spread of these mutations is simply a function of how often neutral mutations arise. Natural selection is here relegated to a primarily constraining role, limiting the rate at which a given protein can change but not affecting its evolution in a constructive, directional way.

Thus, although the vast majority of neutral mutations are lost shortly after arising, the laws of probability permit a few to spread through a population. They do so at a rate that fluctuates in the short run but approximates a constant rate in the long run. The amount of genetic difference between two species, therefore, could be taken as a measure of how long two species have been separated from each other.

Molecular Clock

The findings that molecular evolution proceeds at a roughly constant rate and that humans, chimpanzees, and gorillas are unexpectedly similar genetically can be reconciled in two ways, which represent the poles of a long-unresolved controversy.

Goodman and coworkers inferred that, since humans and the African apes are so similar genetically, the rate of molecular evolution in these species has been slowing down. Alternatively, A. Wilson, V. Sarich, and coworkers inferred that, since molecular evolution is constant, humans and the African apes must have diverged more recently than 4 Ma.

Sarich and Wilson argued that the prevailing opinion in 1967, that humans and African apes had diverged from each other by 15 Ma because the fossil *Ramapithecus* was a uniquely human ancestor, was flawed. Time has borne out their conclusion, but it also appears that the divergence dates calculated by Sarich and Wilson are somewhat underestimated and that there was, indeed, a slowdown in the rate of molecular evolution among the great apes and humans. These facts are being used to study the microevolutionary history of the human species, and of other primate species, using mitochondrial DNA (deoxyribonucleic acid) as genetic markers.

Recent technological advances have permitted trace amounts of DNA to be amplified into analyzable quantities, via the polymerase chain reaction (PCR). This opens the door to the study of DNA samples from prehistoric (unfossilized) bones, as well as from hair follicles, which can be collected noninvasively.

Cytogenetic Data

Techniques were developed in the 1970s for distinguishing the 23 chromosome pairs in the human karyotype, and, while these techniques have been most useful in clinical applications, they have generated evolutionary data as well.

Chimpanzees and gorillas share several chromosomal inversions, inherited from a recent common ancestor, as well as a unique distribution of C-bands. In humans, these bands, which distinguish areas where the DNA is more tightly condensed than elsewhere, appear only at the centromere of each chromosome; below the centromere of chromosomes 1, 9, and 16; and on the long arm of the Y chromosome. In the African apes, however, they appear at the tips of most chromosomes.

In general, the chromosomes of humans and the African apes appear highly similar when prepared by the common procedure of G-banding. The most significant difference seems to be a recent fusion of two chromosomes in the human lineage, reducing the number of chromosome pairs from 24 (retained in the great apes) to 23 and creating what we now recognize as chromosome 2 in the human karyotype.

Rates of chromosomal change vary widely across primate taxa. We find rapid rates of chromosomal evolution in the gibbons and the most arboreal cercopithecine monkeys, slow chromosomal evolution in the baboons, and a moderate rate in the great apes and humans.

DNA Studies

The development of molecular genetics in the late 1970s brought studies of molecular evolution away from phenotypes (even a protein or antibody reaction is, properly speaking, a phenotype) and down directly to the genotype. These studies examine direct aspects of the DNA nucleotide sequence itself or indirect measures of DNA divergence. As phylogenetic data, the results obtained from DNA studies support those obtained from protein analyses. For example, the specific relations among human, chimpanzee, and gorilla are as unclear in their DNA as in their proteins, yet these species all still cluster apart from the orangutan.

Mitochondria are organelles that exist in the cytoplasm of each bodily cell. Although subcellular structures, they contain their own genetic machinery and information encoded in a circular piece of DNA (which is ca. 16,500 nucleotides long in humans). While the evolutionary rules that govern change in mitochondrial DNA are still unclear, in primates their rate of change seems to be about tenfold higher than that of nuclear DNA. Moreover, mitochondria are inherited exclusively through the mother, in contrast to nuclear DNA. These facts have already been used to study the genetic splitting of the human races, using mitochondrial DNA as genetic markers. It has recently been proposed, based on the rate of change in this DNA, that the principal human groups diverged from one another ca. 200 Ka, a considerably more ancient date than usually thought.

Studies of DNA sequences across species have established that the neutral theory of molecular evolution is more applicable to DNA than to proteins. This is because the genome is now known to be very complex. Although a gene

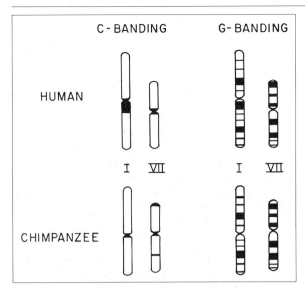

C - BANDING   G - BANDING

HUMAN

I   VII   I   VII

CHIMPANZEE

Despite some differences in C-banding (left) humans and chimpanzees share overwhelming similarities in their fine structure, as revealed by G-banding (right). Pictured are two chromosomes (1 and 7) from the human and their counterparts in the chimpanzee. Courtesy of Jon Marks.

codes for a protein, only a portion of the gene actually consists of coding instructions. These regions *(exons)* are interrupted by DNA segments *(introns)* that do not become translated into part of the protein molecule. Untranslated regions are also found at the beginning and the end of each gene. Further, most of the DNA in the genome consists of *intergenic* DNA (i.e., DNA that lies between genes). It is now clear that, between any two species, intergenic DNA is most different, intron DNA is slightly more similar, and exon DNA is least different. Further, differences in exon DNA fall into two categories: those that direct a different amino acid to become part of the protein *(replacement mutations)* and those that do not change the protein *(silent mutations)*. Silent mutations far outnumber replacement mutations in any gene compared across two species.

What this means is that the neutral theory proposed to explain protein evolution is really only a first approximation, since the mutations that actually are detectable in protein evolution represent the slowest-evolving part of the genome. These replacement mutations are affected by the constraints of natural selection to a greater degree than silent mutations, intron and untranslated mutations, or intergenic mutations.

Levels of Evolution

While evolutionary change is genetic change, and ultimately molecular change, it is impossible at present to associate any adaptive anatomical specialization of humans with any particular DNA change. We may analogize to what is known about phenotypic evolution in other organisms, such as the fruitfly, but we have never located a gene for bipedalism or cranial expansion, and it is likely that there are no genes "for" these traits in the sense that there is a gene "for" cytochrome C or beta-hemoglobin.

Thus, while it is certain that the processes of bone growth and remodeling are under genetic control, as are the

processes that govern the development of facultative responses to stresses on bone growth, such genes have not been located. Further, it is difficult to envision at this point how such genes work or what their primary product might be, much less how to isolate such a product.

Consequently, we are not able to explain at present how the primarily nonadaptive changes we find in the DNA account for the primarily adaptive morphological changes we find in the anatomy of the animal. This seems attributable less to any flaws in contemporary evolutionary theory than to our ignorance of how one gets phenotypic expressions out of genotypic information. It is, therefore, useful to conceive of evolution as a multilevel system: first, a level of the genome, where changes are clocklike over the long run and primarily unexpressed and nonadaptive; second, a level of the karyotype, where chromosomal rearrangements are primarily unexpressed and nonadaptive but may generate reproductive incompatibilities that facilitate the process of speciation; and third, a level of morphology, where changes usually track the environment, and individuals with certain anatomical characters outreproduce those with other similar anatomies, on the average.

See also DNA Hybridization; Genetics; Genome; Immunological Distance; Molecular Clock; Non-Darwinian Evolution. [J.M.]

Further Readings

Buettner-Janusch, J., and Hill, R.L. (1965) Molecules and monkeys. Science 147:836–842.

Devor, E.J., ed. (1992) Molecular Applications in Biological Anthropology. New York: Cambridge University Press.

Gillespie, J. (1986) Variability in evolutionary rates of DNA. Ann. Rev. Ecol. Syst. 17:637–665.

Goodman, M., Tashian, R., and Tashian, J., eds. (1976) Molecular Anthropology. New York: Plenum.

King, M.-C., and Wilson, A.C. (1975) Evolution at two levels in humans and chimpanzees. Science 188:107–116.

Marks, J. (1983) Hominoid cytogenetics and evolution. Yrbk. Phys. Anthropol. 25:125–153.

Marks, J. (1994) Blood will tell (won't it?): A century of molecular discourse in anthropological systematics. Am. J. Phys. Anthropol. 94:59–80.

Wilson, A.C., Cann, R.L., Carr, S.M., George, M., Gyllensten, U.B., Helm-Bychawski, K.M., Higuchi, R., Palumbi, S.R., Prager, F.M., Sage, R.D., and Stoneking, M. (1985) Mitochondrial DNA and two perspectives on evolutionary genetics. Bio. J. Linn. Soc. 26:375–400.

Weiss, M. (1987) Nucleic acid evidence bearing on hominoid relationships. Yrbk. Phys. Anthropol. 30:41–73.

Molecular Clock

Comparative studies of protein structure suggested the *molecular-clock hypothesis* to E. Zuckerkandl and L. Pauling in 1962: that proteins evolve at statistically constant rates and that a simple algorithm might, therefore, relate the amount of protein difference between two species and the time since divergence of those species from their last common ancestor. It presents a sharp contrast to anatomical evolution, in which rates of evolution are usually related to environmental exigencies and may fluctuate widely. The concept of a molecular clock was used by V. Sarich and A. Wilson in 1967 to modify earlier assumptions about the remoteness of common ancestry between humans and the African apes.

M. Kimura, a theoretical population geneticist, showed mathematically in the late 1960s that, if most genetic changes had no adaptive effect on the organism, the evolution of these *neutral* mutations would be essentially constant over the long run. While predictions of the neutral theory accord well with the empirical data of protein evolution, it is also possible that models based on natural selection can account for these data.

It is now clear that each protein has its own characteristic rate of change. The most fundamental proteins (e.g., histones, which package cellular DNA) evolve slowly, while globins (which transport oxygen) evolve more rapidly. Further, this rate may fluctuate in the short run, but it averages to a constant rate over the long run. DNA (deoxyribonucleic acid) evolution can be modeled along the same lines as protein evolution. The discovery that most of the genomic DNA is not transcribed or expressed makes it likely that most DNA evolution is more nearly neutral than protein evolution. This makes noncoding DNA a good candidate for the mathematical models of the neutral theory.

See also Immunological Distance; Molecular Anthropology; Non-Darwinian Evolution. [J.M.]

Further Readings

Avise, J.C. (1994) Molecular Markers, Natural History, and Evolution. New York: Chapman and Hall.

Gillespie, J.H. (1992) The Causes of Molecular Evolution. New York: Oxford University Press.

Kimura, M. (1983) The Neutral Theory of Molecular Evolution. New York: Cambridge University Press.

Li, W.-H., and Graur, D. (1991) Fundamentals of Molecular Evolution. Sunderland, Mass.: Sinauer.

Molecular "vs." Morphological Approaches to Systematics

Morphology has underlain almost all systematic hypotheses since the days of Linnaeus and Darwin. The development of techniques for determining genetic sequences and for analyzing them phylogenetically, as well as obtaining other measures of genetic similarity (e.g., DNA hybridization), combined with theoretical formulation of the *molecular-clock hypothesis,* have led to molecular systematic proposals. No small number of these have conflicted with prior views based on morphology. In part, these differences may relate to alternative approaches employed in analyzing and interpreting data, but they also may reflect aspects of mosaic evolution or erroneous acceptance of convergence or homoplasy as indicative of true relationship.

One of the more significant conclusions arising out of the early work on molecular evolution was M. Goodman's (1963) recognition that the African apes and humans formed a clade separate from the Asian apes. This he termed Hominidae, with Pongidae restricted to the orangutan and its relatives. By contrast, earlier authors had generally placed all of the great apes in Pongidae, with Hominidae restricted to *Homo* and, perhaps, *Australopithecus.* In 1963, Goodman lacked the data to indicate subdivisions within the hominid clade, and, since that time, a great deal of effort, both molecular and morphological, has gone into resolving the trichotomy among chimpanzees, gorillas, and humans. This issue makes an excellent case study of the relative merits of morphology vs. molecules.

NATURE OF MOLECULAR EVIDENCE

Earlier work on proteins and amino-acid sequences has given way since the mid-1980s to DNA (deoxyribonucleic acid) sequencing. This entails the identification of sequences of nucleotides in the genome of different species and comparing them for similarity. DNA sequences of nucleotides consist of unambiguous character states that are homologous if replicated unchanged from a common ancestor. Homology, however, cannot be independently demonstrated for nucleotide substitutions, and, in mitochondrial DNA (mtDNA), transitions (substitutions within either the purines or the pyrimidines) are so frequent that within 20 million years the genome becomes saturated with change, with some loci having multiple substitutions. The rate of change is much less in nuclear DNA, but transitions are still more abundant than transversions (substitutions between pyrimidines and purines), so homoplasy is still abundant. In addition to nucleotide substitutions, there are larger-scale deletions and insertions, where whole sections of DNA are removed from the DNA chain or inserted into it, and some types of DNA, such as those containing tandem duplicate repeats, are more likely to contain homoplasies than others. The pattern of change is analyzed stochastically to produce inferred relationships between taxa, and it is generally the case that different DNA sequences, and different parts of the same sequence, provide evidence for differing sets of relationships. When this occurs, the greater number of similarities in the most strongly supported cladogram are defined as homologies, and, by definition, those supporting other sets or relationships must, therefore, be homoplasies. Judgments about homology are, thus, dependent on the phylogeny accepted and do not provide independent support for the phylogeny.

NATURE OF MORPHOLOGICAL EVIDENCE

Even the simplest morphological features are much more complex than change in the DNA chain, and, accordingly, they are harder to interpret. Being complex, however, provides an independent means of identifying homology, in that two character states that are identical in every observable attribute are more likely to be homologous than to be the result of homoplasy. The ontogeny of the character state is one of these attributes that potentially is most useful, for the stages of development are unlikely to be the same where similar character states are independently derived. Two characters are homologous if they are similar in form, having the same embryonic development, and the character was present in the common ancestor of the two descendent species in which they are manifested. Lack of recognition of character attributes results in misinterpretation of the significance of the characters, which (given the complexity of most characters) is all too common. As for the molecular evidence, characters that appear to be homologous may provide evidence for different sets of relationships, with the post hoc recognition that those supporting the less parsimonious ones are, in fact, homoplasies. There is no difference in this respect between molecular and morphological evidence, although the latter has the advantage that an element of preanalysis judgment is possible based on the ontogenetic and structural attributes of the characters.

NUMBERS OF CHARACTERS

In molecular studies, single changes in protein or amino acid constitute characters, and, in DNA sequencing, point mutations resulting in nucleotide substitutions or insertion/deletions likewise count as single characters. Some of these characters are less liable to change and, therefore, less likely to arise in parallel, such as transversions mentioned above. Little information is available on correlative changes, however, and it may be questioned whether changes within one part of the genome are entirely independent characters. It may be safer to treat such changes, say within a 2kb section of DNA, as related changes within a single character complex, and character numbers should more realistically be based on the numbers of sections of the genome analyzed. Correlations are more readily determined for morphological data, and it is generally accepted that characters that are functionally correlated should not be treated as separate entities for purposes of phylogenetic reconstruction but should be seen as different aspects of the same (more heavily weighted) character. Some branching points in phylogenetic reconstructions are based on no more than single characters, but, in view of the widespread presence of homoplasy, this is a high-risk strategy.

Great Ape-Human Relationships

MOLECULAR EVIDENCE

An ever-increasing number of studies have been published on the molecular evidence for hominoid evolution. The great apes and humans form a test case for the application of molecular methods to phylogenetic reconstruction, and the addition of new data sets both adds to the numbers of character states available and increases the uncertainties arising from the data. The latter is the product partly of inadequate sample sizes, for even the most substantial analysis barely reaches the minimum projected DNA chain length necessary to resolve the African ape and human trichotomy. In addition to this, however, the question as to method of analysis also arises, for different methods applied to the same data set may produce different conclusions. For example, the maximum likelihood tree for the yh-globin sequence (2,000 base pairs) indicates relationship between chimpanzees and gorillas, whereas pairwise procedure on the same data supports

relationship between humans and chimpanzees, neither of them with any degree of significance.

Numerous analyses provide support for humans and chimpanzees sharing common ancestry, with gorillas and orangutans less closely related. One of the stongest lines of evidence supporting the chimpanzee/human grouping is the analysis of the β-globin by L. Bailey and others. This included the bonobo, which was grouped with the common chimpanzee more closely than with other hominoid species. This combination of the two species of chimpanzee was, in turn, grouped with humans, supported by seven transversions and four insertion/deletions. The chimpanzee clade shared only two transversions with the gorilla and no insertion/deletions (transitions are not included here for the reasons given above). If it is accepted that these data support a relationship between chimpanzees and humans, which seems reasonable, the post hoc recognition becomes necessary that the transversions shared by chimpanzees and gorillas (ca. 15 percent of total similarities) must be the result of homoplasy. If this homoplasy figure of 15 percent has any general significance, it should also be applied to the chimpanzee/human figure, so that the 11 shared features could be reduced by two. A binomial test of the human/chimpanzee pairing against the alternative chimpanzee/gorilla pairing showed a nonsignificant difference between them. DNA-DNA hybridization has also consistently supported the chimpanzee/human grouping, although some aspects of the method have been questioned. In nuclear DNA sequencing, the immunoglobin C_{e3} pseudogene, 28SrRNA, ITSI, X,Y pseudoboundary, a1, 3GT, immunoglobin Ca1, s-b intergenic region, and several other parts of the genome all have produced analyses supporting a human/chimpanzee clade, although other studies of these and short stretches of sex-specific and pseudoautosomal regions of the X and Y chromosomes have failed to resolve the trichotomy.

In a notable exception to the above studies, evidence from the involucrin gene favors relationship between chimpanzees and gorillas. In the original analysis, four repeat regions and seven nucleotide substitutions were found to be shared in gorillas and chimpanzees, compared with none shared between humans and chimpanzees. Analysis of the same data by parsimony reduced these numbers to one repeat region and four nucleotides, but still with none shared by humans and chimpanzees. This result has been criticized on the grounds that involucrin repeats are difficult to align and have a high likelihood of homoplasy, and that the repeats shared by gorillas and chimpanzees are not present in some gorilla individuals (i.e., are polymorphic for gorillas). It has been argued that this result, which is in striking contrast to the β-globin result, is the result of polymorphism in the common ancestor of African apes and humans, although a study of seven β-globin polymorphisms in humans showed that all seven arose in the human lineage after divergence from the apes. Polymorphisms have also been identified in chimpanzees and gorillas, and, although none so far (1999) have been found in orangutans, this could be because the distinction has not been made between the subspecies from Sumatra and Borneo.

MORPHOLOGICAL EVIDENCE

Many of the characters with similar states in the hominid clade are now recognized as either primitive retentions or the result of convergence. Some characters of forelimb related to knuckle-walking are common to chimpanzees and gorillas, and the degree of complexity of this adaptation supports a sister-group relationship between the African apes. The apparent absence of some of these characters from the bonobo may cast doubt on this conclusion. Some characters shared by chimpanzees and humans support relationship between them, but these are not such as to inspire confidence. Characters such as broader incisors and molars, more elongated alveolar process of the premaxilla, and vertical mandibular ramus are difficult to define precisely, have large ranges of variation, and have no justification in ontogeny. Density of hair is reduced in chimpanzees and humans, but it is continuing a trend of reduction that passes from hylobatids to orangutans to gorillas to chimpanzees to humans. C. Groves lists a number of characters, including the timing of epiphyseal fusion of the ankle vs. the elbow in chimpanzees and humans, and this has some ontogenetic justification; some of his other characters also appear valid, although no justification for homology is given. The conclusion from morphology, therefore, is that there is some support for both chimpanzee/human and chimpanzee/gorilla grouping, but no great weight can be put on any of the characters.

See also Cladistics; Hominidae; Homininae; Hominoidea; Homology; Molecular Anthropology; Molecular Clock; Numerical Cladistics. [P.A.]

Further Readings

Andrews, P. (1987) Aspects of hominoid phylogeny. In C. Patterson (ed.): Molecules and Morphology in Evolution: Conflict or Compromise? Cambridge: Cambridge University Press, pp. 23–53.

Begun, D.R. (1994) Relations among the great apes and humans: New interpretations based on the fossil great ape *Dryopithecus.* Yrbk. Phys. Anthropol. 37:11–63.

Cartmill, M., and Yoder, A., eds. (1994) Molecules and morphology in primate systematics. Am. J. Phys. Anthropol. 94:1–156.

Patterson, C., Williams, D.M., and Humphries, C.J. (1993) Congruence between molecular and morphological phylogenies. Ann. Rev. Ecol. Syst. 24:153–188.

Pilbeam, D.R. (1996) Genetic and morphological records of the Hominoidea and hominid origins: A synthesis. Mol. Phylogen. Evol. 5:155–168.

Yoder, A.D., Cartmill, M., Ruvolo, M., Smith, K., and Vilgalys, R. (1996) Ancient single origin for Malagasy primates. Proc. Nat. Acad. Sci. USA 93:5122–5126.

Molodova

Geographic region with three major stratified Paleolithic sites (Molodova I and V and Korman IV), located along the middle course of the Dnestr River in western Ukraine. The sites, which have received extensive attention from a multidisciplinary team of scholars, are found on the second terrace of the river; cultural remains are contained in both buried soils and colluvial deposits. Molodova I and V contain eight and 13 superimposed cultural layers, respectively. A sequence of radiocarbon dates indicates that they were occupied from at least 50 Ka to the close of the glacial Pleistocene, ca. 11 Ka. At both sites, a sequence of layers with Middle Paleolithic tools underlies those assigned to the Late Paleolithic. Extensive archaeological inventories of stone tools and faunal remains have been found in all layers. The Mousterian Layer IV at Molodova I contained bones of at least 13 mammoths arranged in a 10- by 7-m oval pattern that contained 15 hearths within it, as well as more than 44,000 pieces of lithics. This feature, dating to more than 44 Ka, has been interpreted as remains of the oldest mammoth-bone dwelling. A similar patterning of mammoth bone was also found in Level 11 of Molodova V. The consistency in stone- and bone-tool inventories from these sites has led East European researchers to assign the Late Paleolithic archaeological remains found here to a single, uniform, evolving Molodova industry, a local variant of the Eastern Gravettian technocomplex.

See also Europe; Gravettian; Late Paleolithic; Site Types. [O.S]

Further Readings

Klein, R.G. (1973) Ice-Age Hunters of the Ukraine. Chicago: University of Chicago Press.

Monkey

Grade or level of primate evolution characterized by moderate body and brain size, usually with a long tail, frugivorous or folivorous diet, above-branch quadrupedal locomotion, and multimale social organization. There are two main groups of monkeys in the modern primate fauna, the ateloids, or platyrrhines, of the Neotropics and the cercopithecids. At least one distinct group of fossil primates is also termed *monkey,* the Eocene-Oligocene parapithecids of North Africa. The most important evolutionary aspect of the concept *monkeys* is that it is not a phyletic term: Those animals called monkeys are not each other's closest relatives. Instead, it represents an informal grade of organization, such as those denoted by *ape, human,* or *prosimian.* Among the monkeys, the platyrrhines are the sister taxon of all of the Old World anthropoids or catarrhines. Similarly, the closest living relatives of the cercopithecids are the hominoids (apes plus humans), while the extinct parapithecids, once thought to be specially related to cercopithecids, are now thought to be the sister taxon of all other anthropoids. This confusing concept of monkey, having no real evolutionary meaning, arose before evolution was understood, as an outgrowth of the *scala naturae* thinking of the time. Nonetheless, we can use this concept to compare the two main types of living monkeys.

Platyrrhine Monkeys

The New World monkeys, or superfamily Ateloidea, include two families whose arrangement differs somewhat among

Brazilian Callithrix jacchus, *the common marmoset, clinging to a tree trunk which it has gouged for sap feeding. Photograph by W.G. Kinzey.*

authors. Here we recognize Cebidae and Atelidae. Ateloids are characterized by external noses with wide side-facing nostrils, three premolar teeth in both upper and lower jaws, mainly curved nails on fingers and toes, and generally long tails. By contrast, the cercopithecids have a narrower nasal septum with nostrils opening downward, only two premolar teeth, flattened nails, and tails varying in length from long to very short. Within the ateloids, the cebids are characterized by lightly built jaws and teeth, with the third molars reduced (in Cebinae) or lacking (in Callitrichinae); the thumb is often reduced as well, and the nails are clawlike in the callitrichines. Atelids have more robust jaws and zygomatic arches, deep mandibles, and large posterior teeth; one subfamily, the Atelinae, is characterized by a unique prehensile (grasping) tail—an independently evolved and less complex version of this organ is found in the cebines.

All platyrrhines inhabit rain forests or other densely wooded environments, none being at all terrestrial. Diets vary greatly among gums, insects, leaves, and fruits, both soft and hard skinned. In turn, the teeth of ateloids are varied and often distinguishable at the genus level. Social organization varies as well, with monogamy and a range of multimale patterns known. It is also interesting to note that ateloids are characterized by the early occurrence of extinct members of several modern lineages, either generic or subfamilial.

Catarrhine Monkeys

Two groups of Old World anthropoids may be called monkeys: the living Cercopithecidae and the extinct Parapithecidae. In addition to their features discussed by contrast to ateloids, cercopithecids retain ischial callosities, tough sitting pads that are probably an ancestral character of catarrhines. Their molars are uniformly bilophodont, with two parallel crests that interlock with those of opposing teeth.

The family Cercopithecidae comprises two living subfamilies, Cercopithecinae and Colobinae. The former have cheek pouches for the temporary storage of food and a mainly frugivorous-to-omnivorous diet, while the latter have a diet made up of large quantities of mainly young leaves and buds and are characterized by a complex stomach to process this hard-to-digest food. Colobine teeth are also taller and sharper than those of cercopithecines, for better shearing of leaves, and their thumbs are reduced and sometimes completely absent externally. Cercopithecines are quite variable in their environmental tolerance and locomotor adaptations, with terrestrial quadrupedalism having evolved independently several times, and at least twice more among the usually arboreal colobines. They range from desert margins in Arabia and North Africa through savannah, woodland, and rain forest to snowy regions of India and Japan. Most species have some form of multimale social organization, but unimale groups are common among the Cercopithecini. The baboons of sub-Saharan Africa (genus *Papio*) epitomize the terrestrial, omnivorous cercopithecine, with multimale troops involving intermale coalitions. One species ranges over most of the more open regions of the continent, while two species of forest baboons (mandrills and drills) inhabit small areas of western coastal forest. Their Asian equivalents are the macaques *(Macaca)*, of which numerous species divide up variable habitats more finely.

*Savannah baboons (*Papio hamadryas cynocephalus*) in Kenya. The male in the center is grooming a female. Note the size difference between the sexes and the open nature of the terrain. Courtesy of J.F. Oates.*

Nilgiri langur (Semnopithecus [Trachypithecus] johnii) *in South Indian rain forest, sitting on tree branch on its ischial callosities. Courtesy of J.F. Oates.*

Colobines are generally restricted to tropical forest habitats, but at least one living species and several extinct forms inhabited more open woodland or savannah. Unimale groups are common, but multimale troops and even monogamous units are known. The fossil record of the cercopithecids is well documented, with a variety of Asian species and several extinct European and African genera.

See also Ape; Atelidae; Ateloidea; Catarrhini; Cebidae; Cercopithecidae; Cladistics; Colobinae; Diet; Grade; Locomotion; Monophyly; Parapithecidae; Phylogeny; Platyrrhini; Primates; Prosimian; Scala Naturae; Teeth. [E.D.]

Further Readings

Fleagle, J.G. (1998) Primate Adaptation and Evolution, 2nd ed. San Diego: Academic.

Napier, J.R., and Napier, P.H. (1985) Natural History of the Primates. Cambridge, Mass.: MIT Press.

Szalay, F.S., and Delson, E. (1979) Evolutionary History of the Primates. New York: Academic.

Monophyly

A set of organisms, or taxon, is said to be *monophyletic* if it includes all (and only) those species descended from a common ancestral species. Noting that other, more liberal definitions have been adopted in the past, some biologists have used the term *holophyletic* for this strict conception of monophyly, but the definition given above has become pervasive in contemporary systematic biology. Thus, *holophyletic* is simply a synonym of *monophyletic*.

Taxa are *nonmonophyletic* if they fail to meet the definitional specifications of monophyly. Two types of nonmonophyly are sometimes distinguished. *Paraphyly* results when species are included in a taxon on the basis of shared possession of primitive *(symplesiomorphous)* characters; if a family of great apes (Pongidae) is recognized that excludes the genus *Homo* (placed in its own family, Hominidae), Pongidae is, in all probability, a paraphyletic taxon. *Polyphyly* generally refers to taxa thought to share derived states evolved independently. Thus, paraphyletic taxa tend to exclude species that should be included, while polyphyletic taxa include species that should be excluded. In practice, the two forms of nonmonophyly are often difficult to distinguish.

See also Cladistics; Hominidae; Homology; Phylogeny. [N.E.]

Monte Peglia

Bone breccia deposit containing numerous remains of early Biharian or latest Villafranchian fauna, found near the city of Orvieto in central Italy. A few heavily patinated limestone and quartzite implements with fresh fracture planes and no evidence for rolling or transport were also found in the breccia. The three considered as human-made include a chopper and two modified flakes; all bear extensive manganese concretions like those found on the nearby bones in the breccia. The remains are tentatively dated older than the Cromerian period (ca. 0.9 Ma), making this one of the earliest possible occurrences of artifacts in Europe.

See also Early Paleolithic; Přezletice; Stranská Skála; Vallonnet. [O.S.]

Monte Verde

Paleoindian site in south-central Chile that has been put forward as a candidate for pre-Clovis (i.e., pre-11.5 Ka) occupation of the New World. This open-air residential site has been extensively excavated by T.D. Dillehay and his colleagues, who have exposed four distinct zones of buried cultural remains. The foundations and fallen pole-frames of nearly a dozen residential huts have been excavated, with fragments of skin (perhaps mastodon) still clinging to the poles. Abundant plant remains survive in the deposits, which also contain numerous shaped-stone tools, including several grooved bola stones.

Dillehay argues that the upper layers of Monte Verde contain "well-preserved and clear, conclusive evidence" of human habitation dating to 14–12 Ka. Even more controversial are the deeper layers, where remains associated with possible cultural features and several fractured stones have been radiocarbon dated at 33 Ka. Although many archaeologists accept the later Monte Verde occupation as being of human origin, serious doubts remain about the earlier layers, which have not been excavated on large scale.

See also Americas; Paleoindian [D.H.T.]

Further Readings

Dillehay, T.D. (1989) Monte Verde: A Late Pleistocene Settlement in Chile, Vol. 1: Paleoenvironment and Site Context. Washington D.C.: Smithsonian Institution Press.

Dillehay, T.D., and Collins, M. (1988) Early cultural evidence from Monte Verde, in Chile. Nature 332:150–152.

Dillehay, T.D., and Meltzer, D.J. (1991) The First Americans: Search and Research. Boca Raton: CRC Press.

Montmaurin

French cave site, found in 1949, with several levels yielding human and other fossils and artifacts. The main, Niche, horizon, probably of mid Middle Pleistocene antiquity, produced a mandible that is thick and chinless with large teeth. Some workers regard it as Neanderthal-like in morphology, but it is distinct in a number of respects from anteneanderthal mandibles from such sites as Arago (France) and Atapuerca (Spain). Human remains from younger layers are more typically Neanderthal.

See also Arago; Archaic Homo sapiens; Atapuerca; Europe; Neanderthals. [C.B.S.]

Morant, Geoffrey Miles (1899–1964)

British biometrician. Morant was a disciple of K. Pearson's (1857–1936) Biometric School, as exemplified by his numerous studies and, in particular, the practical handbook on craniometry that he and L.D.H. Buxton (1889–1939) published in 1933. During the late 1920s, he conducted an influential biometrical study of European fossil hominid crania, the results of which were presented in a series of articles published in the *Annals of Eugenics* (1926–1931). With regard to his study of the European Neanderthals Morant, (1927), whose publication coincided with Ales Hrdlička's (1869–1943) Huxley Memorial Lecture in London, Morant (*contra* Hrdlicka) concluded that the Neanderthals were not only a relatively homogenous group, but also off the main line of human evolution. Another important publication of Morant's was *The Races of Europe: A Footnote to History* (1939), in which he attacked the utility of such things as the cephalic index and hair color in determining racial boundaries in Europe.

See also Hrdlička, Ales; Neanderthals. [F.S.]

Further Readings
Morant, G.M. (1927) Studies of Palaeolithic man, Part II: A biometrical study of Neanderthal skulls and their relationships to modern racial groups. Ann. Eugenics 2:318–381.

Morotopithecus

Ugandan Miocene hominoid primate which may be the earliest known member of Hominidae. In the 1960s, W.W. Bishop and colleagues collected craniofacial fragments at the site of Moroto 2 which were described in detail by D.R. Pilbeam. Originally these specimens, especially a nearly complete palate, were referred to *Proconsul major,* with which they compared well in size. A single thoracic vertebra was shown to have features in common with younger hominids but not seen in *Proconsul,* and later the dentition was shown to have thick molar enamel and relatively large and homomorphic premolars, although the incisive fossa opened directly onto the floor of the nose, as in *Proconsul, Hylobates,* and cercopithecids. Moroto was correlated faunally to ca. 17 Ma. P. Andrews and others recognized the Moroto specimens as early members of Hominidae, and when the genus *Afropithecus* was named for specimens from Kalodirr and Buluk (Kenya), the Moroto palate was generally included under that rubric, although Kalodirr postcrania appeared more like those of *Proconsul* and thus less "modern" than the Moroto vertebra.

In 1997, D. Gebo and colleagues described new specimens from Moroto. Basalt lava overlying the previously unfossiliferous site of Moroto 1 was dated closely to 20.6 Ma, and Moroto 2 was correlated to an equivalent horizon. A fragment of shoulder joint from Moroto 1 was argued to indicate relatively high mobility, as in living hominoids (and atelines), but not proconsulids. Partial femora from Moroto 2 also resemble those of living hominoids (and atelines), but not proconsulids or cercopithecids. Combining these features with the vertebral evidence indicating a shorter and stiffer backbone, Gebo and colleagues suggested that the Moroto primate was an arboreal climber and below-branch arm-hanger that practiced quadrupedalism and perhaps relatively slow-moving brachiation.

Gebo and colleagues gave the name *Morotopithecus bishopi* to the entire sample from Moroto 1 and 2, selecting the palate as holotype. *Morotopithecus* is surely a member of Hominidae and is here included in Kenyapithecinae (and tentatively in Afropithecini). Dentally, it is most similar to other members of that tribe, especially *Afropithecus,* from which it differs little: the amount of upper molar cingulum is intermediate between *Proconsul* and *Afropithecus.* However, the Kalodirr taxon appears to have a more angled and shut-down incisive canal than does *Morotopithecus.* Postcranially, the new genus was derived in the direction of living hominoids, compared to both *Proconsul* and *Afropithecus.* These features, and others discussed by Gebo and colleagues, leave uncertain the precise phylogenetic position of *Morotopithecus.* It is apparently older than *Afropithecus* but more derived postcranially (although perhaps less derived craniodentally). This may reflect the mosaic nature of earlier Miocene hominid evolution, with "modern" character states appearing independently in several taxa. *Morotopithecus* is older than most *Proconsul,* especially the better skeletal material, which leaves the latter genus as a "living fossil" in its own time (comparable to *Pliopithecus* and *Ankarapithecus*): such forms were less derived than close relatives which preceded them, underlining the nonlinear nature of catarrhine evolution and especially its fossil record.

See also Africa, Eastern; Afropithecus; Ankarapithecus; Diet; Hominidae; Hominoidea; Kalodirr; Kenyapithecinae; Pliopithecus; Ponginae; Proconsulidae; Skull; Teeth. [E.D.]

Further Readings
Gebo, D.L., MacLatchy, L., Kityo, R., Deino, A., Kingston, J., and Pilbeam, D. (1997) A hominoid genus from the Early Miocene of Uganda. Science 276:401–404.

Pilbeam, D.R. (1969) Tertiary Pongidae of East Africa: Evolutionary relationships and taxonomy. Yale Peabody Mus. Bull. 31:1–185.

Morphology

Quite simply, *shape,* and the study thereof. In the context of living organisms, the term is essentially synonymous with *anatomy,* which in fossil forms is effectively restricted to teeth and bones. The morphology of a human fossil, then, includes all of its attributes of form that can be detected by the eye, with or without the aid of a microscope.

See also Morphometrics; Skeleton; Skull; Teeth. [I.T.]

Morphometrics

Study of measurement of the shape of organisms. It is concerned with change in form, shape, and size in development and evolution and with the description and comparison of shapes. Statistical methods are used to summarize and compare shapes of samples of living and fossil organisms.

Traditional morphometrics is a term coined for the methods that depend on measurements taken between landmarks, or that represent distances like maximum widths or lengths. These methods have included, up to now, most data collected and analyzed using univariate and multivariate statistics.

New morphometrics, or geometric morphometrics, represents a departure from the use of distances in that the coordinates of points in two dimensions (2D) or three dimensions (3D) are the data recorded and used in the analysis. The distances of traditional morphometrics provide powerful summaries of shape and size, but they may also be defined from coordinates. However, they do not have the ability to archive the actual form of the organism in 2D and 3D. Landmarks and outlines recorded as series of x and y coordinates in 2D, together with surfaces as x, y, and z coordinates in 3D, allow us to reconstruct at least a cartoon of the organism and directly analyze the sets of points as they summarize shape and size. 2D and 3D digitizers connected to computers are becoming widely available as data-acquisition equipment, and laser scans, CAT scans, and magnetic resonance imaging (MRI) all may provide landmark, outline, and surface data automatically.

Landmark methods follow some of the pioneering early ideas of D.W. Thompson. Size may be estimated from all of the landmarks, and shapes compared by a number of procedures. Shape coordinates, for example, scale all distances between landmarks to a baseline between two of them (see figure), one landmark's x and y coordinates set to 0,0 and the other's to 1,0. They allow simple shape comparisons and direct use of multivariate statistics on the transformed data. Superimposition techniques, or Procrustes analyses, allow direct comparison of shapes by fitting one to another, or those from several organisms to an average form. These two methods are supported by computer-graphic software and provide information about affine shape differences (i.e., those that keep parallel lines parallel [square to rectangle or rectangle to parallelogram] and can be computed using linear transformations).

Thin plate spline analysis, based on the mathematics of the deformation of thin metal sheets, allows for analysis of shape comparisons that are more complicated, and duplicates some of the ad hoc procedures that Thompson had provided. Shape differences can be dissected into local and

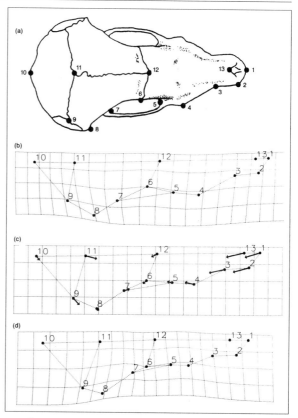

Visualization of the component of nonuniform shape change corresponding to the first canonical variate: (a) shows the locations of the landmarks on a dorsal view of the skull; (b) and (d) correspond to an extrapolation beyond the left and right ends of the first canonical vector axis (this exaggeration was necessary in order to make the differences visible); (c) shows the average positions of the landmarks with vectors pointing in the direction of positive changes along the axis. Plots produced using the TPSREGR program. Courtesy of L.F. Marcus.

global differences, and scores for sets of organisms compared to a reference—usually the average form—can be used for further multivariate statistical analysis (see figure).

Other landmark-based methods are Euclidean distance matrix analysis, which describes ratios of distances between landmarks for two organisms, and finite element scaling analysis, which subdivides the 2D or 3D landmark data into triangular or polyhedral elements, respectively, and records shape differences element by element.

Outlines recorded as closely spaced x,y coordinate pairs may be compared by Fourier techniques, which fit mathematical curves to the outline of each organism. The parameters of the curves for the separate organisms can be collected and analyzed using standard multivariate statistics.

Newer methods are being developed that combine outline and landmark data, and the methodology is being extended to surface data as well.

See also Morphology; Multivariate Analysis; Quantitative Methods. [L.F.M.]

Further Readings

Bookstein, F.L. (1991) Morphometric Tools for Landmark Data: Geometry and Biology. New York: Cambridge University Press.

Marcus, L.F., Bello, E., and Garcia-Valdecasas, A., eds.
(1993) Contributions to Morphometrics. Madrid:
Museo Nacional de Ciencias Naturales.

Marcus, L.F., Corti, M., Loy, A., Slice, D., and Naylor, G.,
eds. (1996) Advances in Morphometrics. New York:
Plenum.

Reyment, R.A. (1991) Multidimensional Paleobiology.
New York: Pergamon.

Rohlf, F.J., and Bookstein, F.L. (1988) Proceedings of the
Michigan Morphometrics Workshop. Ann Arbor: Museum of Zoology.

Rohlf, F.J., and Marcus, L.F. (1993) A revolution in morphometrics. Trends Evol. Ecol. 8:129–132.

Mortillet, Gabriel de (1821–1898)

French prehistorian. Following in the wake of Lubbock's
(1834–1913) definition of the *Paleolithic* and the *Neolithic* in
1865, De Mortillet pioneered a classificatory scheme for dealing with Pleistocene chronology in western Europe based on
stone-tool types. Specifically, he recognized five discrete stone-
tool types, recovered from French Paleolithic sites, representing industrial stages or *epoques* as "fossiles directeurs." This industrial sequence commenced with the Epoque de Chelles, or
Chellean (handaxes), which was followed by the *epoques* of Le
Moustier, Aurignac, Solutré, and La Madeleine. The Chellean
industry was essentially characterized by the handaxes found in
the gravel terraces of the Somme River Valley. These almond-
shaped artifacts had been made by striking flakes bifacially
from a flake or module so that the residual core formed the implement. J.J. Boucher de Perthes (1788–1868) called them
core-tools or "haches" (axes), whereas de Mortillet referred to
them as *coups de poing* (simple hand-hammers). By contrast,
the tools from Le Moustier (points, side-scrapers) were fashioned from flakes. De Mortillet believed that this *Mousterian*
industry represented a cultural bridge to the traditions of the
Upper Paleolithic: the Aurignacian, the Solutrean, and the
Magdalenian.

De Mortillet's chronological scheme, based entirely on
artifact similarities, superseded a prior one based on the association of these industries with a stratigraphic sequence of
successive large mammal faunas. Some years before (in the
early 1860s), E. Lartet (1801–1871) had attempted a similar
subdivision with "ages" based exclusively on the stratigraphic
succession of faunas with their associated artifacts: Epochs of
the Reindeer (*Rangifer tarandus*), Mammoth (*Elephas primigenius*), and Great Cave Bear (*Ursus spelaeus*) ages. Soon
thereafter, it was recognized that the cave bear and the mammoth were essentially contemporaneous, and this led F. Gar-
rigou (1835–1920) in 1863 to propose that the earliest period (i.e., Lower Pleistocene) had been dominated by ancient
elephants (*Elephas antiquus*) and that it had been followed by
the period of the mammoth and the cave bear, and then by
the age of the reindeer (Upper Pleistocene). De Mortillet's
Chellean was initially equated with the age of the ancient
elephant, whereas his Epoque du Moustier (Mousterian) was
associated with the period of the mammoth and the cave
bear. His Epoques d'Aurignac, Solutré, and La Madeleine
were all associated with the reindeer period. In later editions

of this work, however, the stratigraphic basis was dropped
and the Solutrean, with its flake and leaf-shaped points, was
placed before the Aurignacian, with its bone points, despite
stratigraphic evidence to the contrary.

As an advocate of Darwin's evolutionary theory, De
Mortillet was an eager supporter of the view that the genus
Homo had originated somewhere in the Tertiary period. This
Tertiary precursor, "Anthropithecus," he argued, stood
somewhere between the apes and man, and to characterize its
primitive tool industry he coined the term *Éolithique* (Dawn
Stone Age). De Mortillet was also responsible for founding,
in 1864, the journal *Materiaux pour l'Histoire Primitive de
l'Homme*, which he edited until 1870, at which time it was
taken over by E. Cartailhac (1845–1921). The journal was
later united with *Revue d'Anthropologie* and *Revue d'Ethnologie* to form *L'Anthropologie* in 1890.

See also Aurignacian; Boucher de Perthes, Jacques; Cartail-
hac, Emile; Lartet, Edouard; Le Moustier; Magdalenian;
Mousterian; Paleolithic; Pleistocene; Solutré; Solutrean.
[F.S.]

Further Readings

Daniel, G. (1976) A Hundred and Fifty Years of Archaeology. Cambridge, Mass.: Harvard University Press.

Hamy, E.T. (1870) Précis de Paléontologie Humaine. Paris:
Ballière.

Mortillet, G. de, and Mortillet, A. de (1900) Le Préhistorique. Paris: Reinwald.

Mousterian

Middle Paleolithic industries from Europe, western and central Asia, and North Africa named for the type site of Le
Moustier, Dordogne (France). Mousterian industries are
characterized by the use of both discoidal and Levallois
flaking techniques to produce flakes, blades, naturally
backed knives, and points. These are knapped, primarily by
direct percussion, into a wide range of forms, including side-
scrapers, retouched points, denticulates, and notches (see Figure). Some Mousterian industries also feature rather small,
symmetrical handaxes.

Geographical and Chronological Variation

Important Mousterian sites include La Cotte-de-St-Brelade
(Jersey); Le Moustier, La Quina, La Ferrassie, La Micoque,
Combe Grenal, and Pech de L'Azé (all in France); Cueva Morin
(Spain); Hohlenfels (Germany); Torre in Pietra and Saccopas-
tore (Italy); Erd and Tata (Hungary); Krapina and Vindija
(Croatia); Bacho Kiro (Bulgaria); Molodova (Ukraine); Karain
(Turkey); Teshik-Tash (Uzbekistan); Jabrud (Syria); Ksar 'Akil
(Lebanon); Shanidar (Iraq); Tabūn, Kebara, Qafzeh, and
Amud (Israel); and Djebel Irhoud, Haua Fteah, Khor Musa,
and Mughâret el-Aliya (North Africa). European Mousterian
industries may begin as early as the late Saale glacial (e.g., at
Biache-St. Vaast) ca. 200–150 Ka; in the Levant, the earliest
Mousterian (Tabūn D) may predate 250 Ka at Tabūn in Israel.
Most Mousterian sites, however, date to 130–36 Ka. Late Mid-
dle Pleistocene Acheulean assemblages featuring characteristi-

cally Mousterian industrial tools suggest that the distinction between the Mousterian and some of these Middle Pleistocene industries, especially the *Levalloisian* and the *Micoquian,* arbitrarily partitions a continuum of variability. The Mousterian *sensu stricto* does not occur in India, sub-Saharan Africa, or eastern or southeastern Asia, as the characteristic technologies and tool forms are not commonly found in these regions.

The use of the term *Mousterian* over so broad an area owes much to the influence of European and European-trained scholarship in Paleolithic archaeology and probably obscures significant technological variation. For example, Levallois technique is generally rather rare among European Mousterian assemblages, and, when it does appear, it is most often of the radial/centripetal variety (i.e., the core is prepared by flaking toward the center, followed by the striking of a single large flake). In southwestern Asia, the Levallois technique is very common, and usually takes the form of recurrent laminar preparation (i.e., the core is prepared by a series of parallel flake removals, after which a series of blades or points are detached). Similarly, while handaxes occur in many European Mousterian assemblages, especially in northern France, Belgium, and England, they are absent from some areas of France (Provence, Charente) and quite rare in southwestern Asian and North African Mousterian contexts. In Spain, a *Vasconian Mousterian* is distinguished by the addition of cleavers. Thinned bifacial points (*Blattspitzen*) occur in later Mousterian assemblages in central and eastern Europe (sometimes called Altmuhlian) and continue into the earliest Upper Paleolithic, or transitional, industries of eastern Europe (Szeletian, Jermanovician), where they form the basis for theories of Middle-to-Upper Paleolithic continuity. These tools do not occur in the Mousterian of western Europe or southwestern Asia. In southern Europe (Italy, Greece, the Balkans), Mousterian industries are often characterized by very small implements (*Micromousterian*).

Mousterian industries of southwestern Asia and North Africa are distinguished not only by the frequent use of Levallois technology but also by the prevalence of blades, whether made on Levallois cores or on prismatic blade cores. These occur both within the early stages of the Mousterian sequence and in a separate industrial stage (Pre-Aurignacian, Amudian, Mugharan) underlying the Mousterian at several sites (e.g., Tabūn, Jabrud, and Haua Fteah). Blades are also characteristic of the Teshik-Tash (Uzbekistan) assemblage. While the Mousterian, distinguished by the prevalence of Levallois technology and of characteristic points, scrapers, and denticulates, is common in the Nile Valley and eastern Sahara, it is rare in Northwest Africa, where a very generalized flake industry is often succeeded by a Middle Stone Age industry with bifacially worked tanged points called the *Aterian.*

One traditional notion about the Mousterian that has been overturned in recent years is the view that it represents a static, unchanging culture. Absolute dates based on thermoluminescence, electron spin resonance, and uranium-series dating indicate stage-wise changes in regional Mousterian industries from western Europe (e.g. the Ferrassie–Quina–Mousterian of Acheulean Tradition sequence at Combe Grenal) and southwestern Asia (e.g., the Tabūn D-C-B se-

quence). Furthermore, analyses of technological variation in several different areas, by S. Kuhn at Grotta Guattari and Sant'Agostino in central Italy and by Munday at sites in the central Negev in Israel, have shown significant changes in Mousterian technological organization in response to climatic fluctuations. Indeed, several purportedly Middle-Upper Paleolithic transitional industries, such as the Chatelperronian of Western Europe, the Uluzzian of Italy, and the Szeletian of East-Central Europe, exhibit far more technological and typological continuities with the Mousterian than they do with later Upper Paleolithic industries in the same region.

A second traditional notion about the Mousterian that requires care is the equation of *Mousterian* with *Neanderthal.* While it is true that the hominid remains found in most European and many western Asian Mousterian contexts are unambiguously Neanderthals, a few European Neanderthal fossils occur in post-Mousterian contexts, such as the Chatelperronian of Saint-Césaire and Grotte du Renne at Arcy-sur-Cure; this agrees with the view of some workers that the Chatelperronian is a product of Neanderthals who integrated some Aurignacian techniques into a Late Mousterian industry. At the other end of the time scale, there is uncertainty about the definition of both the earliest Neanderthals and the earliest Mousterian; sites such as Ehringsdorf (Germany) yield examples of both whose identity is sometimes questioned. Early-modern humans have been found together with Mousterian residues at Skhūl and Qafzeh (Israel), while Neanderthals are not found in the Mousterian of North Africa. (The modern human remains in Mousterian levels at Starosele in Ukraine are probably intrusive from a modern burial.) The Mousterian is, thus, the logical place to look for behavioral characteristics shared by Neanderthals and early-modern humans, although it is possible that many of these hominins' divergent behavioral characteristics are not reflected in gross patterns of lithic industrial variability.

The French Mousterian Debate

Partly because research on the Mousterian began in France, debate about the structure of the French Mousterian has tended to dominate discussion of this industry. Following the definition of the Mousterian by G. de Mortillet in 1887, the early part of the twentieth century witnessed unsuccessful efforts by H. Martin and others to recognize a simple cultural succession in the French Mousterian on the basis of diagnostic artifact types, an approach that had proven useful in constructing an Upper Paleolithic cultural sequence. In the 1950s, F. Bordes pioneered a different approach, defining distinct Mousterian variants on the basis of relative frequencies of Levallois technology, 63 flake-tool types, and 21 handaxe types (see Table, p. 456, and Figure, p. 457). Using graphs of the cumulative percentage of tool types in an assemblage, Bordes distinguished four major variants of the French Mousterian:

THE CHARENTIAN GROUP

Especially prevalent in the Charente district just to the north of the Dordogne, this variant is characterized by high numbers of scrapers and the absence or rarity of backed knives and handaxes. This, in turn, is subdivided into two variants:

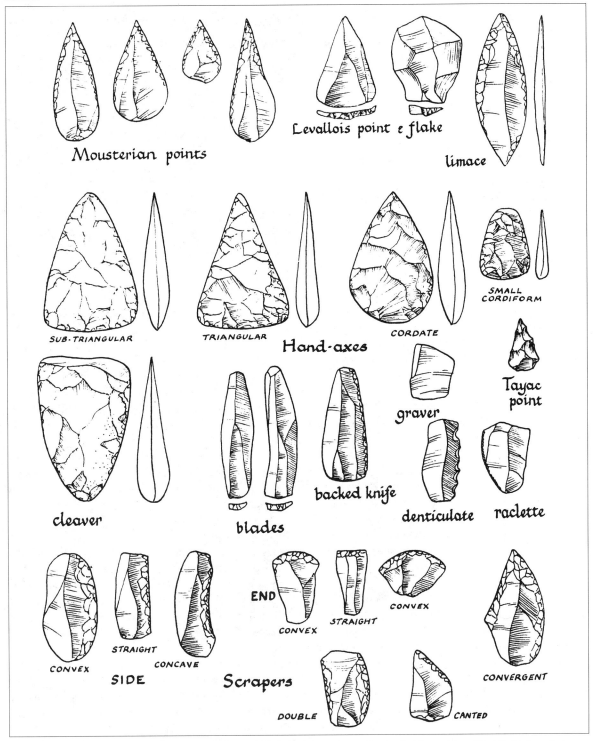

Characteristic French Mousterian stone tools. From J. Wymer, The Palaeolithic Age, *1982. Reprinted with permission of St. Martin's Press, Inc.*

the Quina type, with a low Levallois index and large numbers of Quina scrapers (thick, with stepped retouch) and transverse scrapers (scraping edge is opposite striking platform), and the Ferrassie type, with a high Levallois index and few Quina or transverse scrapers.

THE TYPICAL GROUP

This variant shows a medium but variable percentage of scrapers, variable proportions of Levallois débitage, and low percentage or absence of Quina scrapers, transverse scrapers, backed knives, and handaxes. Points are most common in this variant.

THE MOUSTERIAN OF ACHEULEAN TRADITION (MTA)

This variant is characterized by variable Levallois index, medium-to-low percentages of scrapers, few or no Quina scrapers, the presence of Upper Paleolithic types (burins, end-scrapers), numerous denticulates, and, most characteris-

Major assemblage variants in the Mousterian of Southwest France

Variant	Percentages of: Levallois types	Side scrapers	Upper Paleolithic types (Group III)	Denticulates Group IV	Quina retouch	Handaxes
Charentian		50–80		low		absent / rare
(a) Quina subtype	< 10				14–30	
(b) Ferrassie subtype	14–30				6–14	
Typical	very variable	> 50		moderate	0–3	absent / rare
Denticulate	very variable	4–20		60	0	low
Mousterian of Acheulean Tradition (MTA)	very variable				very low	
subtype A		25–45	seldom > 4	common		8–40
subtype B		4–40	strong	60		absent / rare

Table showing differences among major Mousterian variants.

tically, backed knives and/or handaxes. Two subdivisions of this type exist, one (MTA A) with triangular handaxes, the other (MTA B) with few, poorly made handaxes but numerous backed knives. MTA B is always later than MTA A.

THE DENTICULATE MOUSTERIAN
This variant shows a high percentage of denticulate and notched pieces, variable Levallois index, and all other types (scrapers, Quina scrapers, backed knives, handaxes) rare or absent.

With the exception of the Mousterian of Acheulean Tradition, which is also the only variant that changes consistently through time, much of the variability between the facies Bordes distinguished is due to two factors: changes in the percentage of scrapers from high to medium to low and changes in the Levallois index. Bordes attributed the variants to different ethnic groups whose technology changed little through time but who replaced one another in space with little admixture over a period of 50 Kyr, a hypothesis reflecting the notion—then shared broadly among French paleoanthropologists—that Neanderthals had a limited capacity to innovate. In contrast, L. Binford and S. Binford argued that the patterning of variability in Mousterian assemblages did not suggest stylistic or ethnic variables but rather the underlying patterning of different activities or combinations of activities. In this view, the different Mousterian variants represent special-purpose sites or base camps within a relatively unchanging pattern of activities. This functional argument has also been challenged, both by F. Bordes and D. de Sonneville-Bordes and by others, such as P. Mellars, on the grounds that regional differentiation and directional change through time do characterize some aspects of the Mousterian pattern, particularly with regard to the Mousterian of Acheulean Tradition. In addition, in the case of functional differentiation the correlation expected between the techno-typological variants of the stone-tool assemblages and faunal and/or locational differences had not been demonstrated. N. Rolland and H. Dibble, however, suggest that a significant amount of the technological and typological differences be-

tween French Mousterian variants may reflect differences in the intensity of lithic reduction arising from variation in settlement patterns and the availability of lithic raw material. Recent research by E. Boëda, L. Meignen, and others on cultural variation in the Mousterian has focused on reconstructing the *chaîne opératoire* (the sequence of technical operations from material acquisition through manufacture and use to discard) for Mousterian assemblages. To the extent that different Mousterian assemblages are characterized by different *chaîne opératoires*, the underlying causes of such differentiation—whether due to function, expediency, raw material, basic philosophical tradition, or other factors—are still much debated.

Behavioral Issues
Mousterian sites are associated with evidence for significant developments in economic, social, and cognitive behavior in comparison to the preceding industries of the Early Paleolithic. In addition, the Mousterian adaptation as a whole represents one of the first successful attempts to adapt to glacial and cold-steppe conditions in mid-latitude Europe.

SETTLEMENT PATTERNS
Wherever Mousterian industries are found, their appearance usually coincides with fluctuating, but generally cooling, climates. In Europe, this period (oxygen-isotope stages 5d–3, ca. 115–30 Ka) witnesses a gradual retreat of deciduous forests and their replacement throughout much of the continent, first by boreal forests and later by steppe-tundra. Although Neanderthals are often described as cold adapted, evidence of Mousterian occupation of actual tundra and periglacial zones is scarce. The first extensive human occupation of the plains and river valleys of Russia and the Ukraine, however, may date to this time. In southwestern Asia and North Africa, the distribution of the Mousterian coincides very closely with temperate woodlands, suggesting that extremely arid Saharo-Arabian deserts represented a formidable obstacle to settlement. It is assumed that most Mousterian settlements are of relatively short duration, although this needs to be verified by

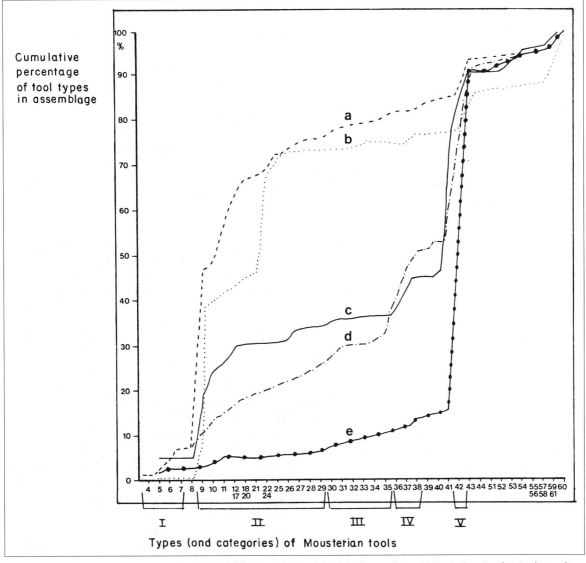

Cumulative graphs for Mousterian variants: (a) Ferrassie; (b) Quina; (c) Typical; (d) Acheulean tradition; (e) Denticulate. Based on Bordes type-list: I, points; II, side-scrapers; III, Upper Paleolithic tools; IV, backed knives; V, notched and denticulate pieces. After C. Gamble, The Palaeolithic Settlement of Europe, *1986, Cambridge University Press.*

further seasonality studies. In contrast to the Early Paleolithic, repeated occupation of caves and rockshelters is a common feature of the settlement pattern. The ephemeral nature of these occupations is further suggested by the widespread evidence of carnivore activity at Mousterian sites, presumably during the absence of the human occupants.

SUBSISTENCE

Little is known of Mousterian plant-food use, owing primarily to a lack of preservation. A few charred legume seeds were recovered from hearths at Kebara Cave in Israel, but these could equally well represent food or fuel for the fires. The large mammals whose bones occur regularly on Mousterian sites include cold temperate (Palearctic) species such as bison (*Bison*), wild cattle (*Bos primigenius*), horse (*Equus caballus*), onager (*Equus hemionius*), reindeer (*Rangifer tarandus*), red deer (*Cervus elaphus*), wild boar (*Sus scrofa*), ibex (*Capra* sp.), fallow deer (*Dama* sp.), and gazelle (*Gazella gazella*). The presence of carnivore remains (e.g., hyaena, wolf, cave lion)

or other evidence of carnivore disturbance at many Mousterian sites makes it difficult to reconstruct Mousterian predatory strategies unambiguously. Most Mousterian faunal assemblages feature a wide range of species, rather than a single focal species. Stable-isotope analysis of hominin and faunal remains from La Ferrassie in France suggests that Neanderthals secured regular access to meat and fat. The degree to which different Mousterian groups depended on hunting vs. scavenging to obtain meat and fat from these species is much debated, although the relative significance of these two subsistence strategies undoubtedly varied widely in time and space. Given the near-arctic environments of European Mousterian groups, it seems reasonable to suppose that animal fats were a major limiting resource in their subsistence strategies. This may explain the presence of large-mammal cranial remains (which are generally rich in fats) at many Mousterian sites. Evidence for exploitation of marine molluscs is also present at Mediterranean sites such as Haua Fteah and Gorham's Cave (Gibraltar).

The "witness section" in the lower shelter at Le Moustier (Périgord, France), type site of the Mousterian, with François Bordes. This sequence has been dated to 60–40 Ka.

SITE STRUCTURE

Mousterian cave occupations preserve concentrations of ash and burnt bone that are probably hearths. At a few sites (e.g., Grotte de Renne and Molodova I), excavators have identified concentrations of stone and bone that may be the footings for tents or windbreaks. In this respect, Mousterian sites do not differ significantly from Late Acheulean sites. At Combe Grenal, however, there is a very clear trace or cast of a posthole, while at several French sites (e.g., Baume-Bonne Cave in the southeast), a number of sharply delimited stone "pavements" or artificially constructed cobble floors, each measuring ca. 10 m², were recovered in excavation. The best evidence for the construction of living structures in Mousterian sites is provided by the excavation of pits up to 60 cm deep, dug into consolidated cave deposits (*eboulis*) at Combe Grenal, Le Moustier, and La Quina, possibly for the storage of food. The large oval arrangement of mammoth bones with interior hearths in Mousterian Layer IV at Molodova, usually interpreted as a hut foundation, may also have been a storage structure. Apart from these remains, there are few traces of installations or facilities that would suggest attempts to impose structure on living space, a frequent correlate of prolonged occupation.

TECHNOLOGY

Most Mousterian lithic assemblages are made on locally available raw materials, with only a small component produced on high-quality exotic flints. Studies by J.M. Geneste of raw-material economy among French Mousterian sites point to a consistent pattern of expedient use of local and/or low-quality raw materials paired with prolonged curation of symmetrical tools made of exotic materials. Very few recognizably modified bone tools occur in Mousterian contexts, although some pieces of bone and antler preserve wear traces from their use as flintknapping percussors. A few flaked-shell tools have been found in the Italian site of Grotta Guattari. The overall picture that emerges of Mousterian technol-ogy is one of simplicity. There are very few Mousterian tools that cannot be accurately replicated by a moderately skilled flintknapper in a few minutes. Exceptions to this generalization would probably include the East European bifacial points, some Mousterian handaxes, and the more symmetrical Levallois points. Lithic use-wear analysis of European and western Asian Mousterian stone tools indicates relatively weak form-function correlations. For example, many different kinds of tools formally described as scrapers, points, and knives all preserve the same type of microwear polish derived from woodworking. Some tools appear to have been hafted, and pointed tools from the Levantine Mousterian preserve wear from use as spear points.

SYMBOLIC BEHAVIOR

The question of Mousterian symbolic behavior has long been debated in Paleolithic archaeology, with much attention recently focused on Mousterian burials. While the clear majority of hominin fossils recovered from Mousterian contexts are isolated bones or fragmentary remains, the occurrence of skeletons in anatomical articulation in shallow pits at several sites (e.g., Amud, Kebara, Saint-Césaire, Shanidar, Skhūl, Regourdou, Qafzeh, La Ferrassie) suggests burial of the dead in at least some circumstances. Claims of grave goods in Mousterian burials are less readily substantiated, as the objects in question, usually stone tools and animal bones, differ but little from objects in the surrounding strata and may represent fortuitous associations. The ring of goat horns surrounding the burial of a child at Teshik-Tash and the masses of flower pollen associated with the burial of Shanidar 4 constitute very controversial evidence for burial practices. (The site of Regourdou, carefully excavated in the late 1950s, does suggest, however, that some of these objects were intentionally associated with the body.) Two of the strongest cases for Mousterian grave goods are burials of early-modern humans from the Levant, Qafzeh 9 (a boy holding a deer antler) and Skhūl 5 (a man clasping the mandible of a boar). A. Blanc's hypothesis of a Neanderthal "head cult," which was based on the discovery of an isolated cranium at Monte Circeo, is believed to be explicable by taphonomic factors, such as hyaena ravaging of a Neanderthal skeleton. A putative cave bear cult initially identified on the basis of concentrations of *Ursus spelaeus* remains in Mousterian levels at Drachenloch and other Alpine sites also appears likely to be a mistaken "cultural" reading of taphonomic phenomena.

On the more positive side, numerous occurrences of colored mineral pigments, including "crayons" of red and yellow ocher and manganese, occasional perforated animal teeth, shells, and rare fossilized molluscs from some Mousterian occupations hint at an aesthetic sensibility. A few pieces are considered to bear deliberate incisions of a symbolic nature, such as the fossil nummulite from Tata with a cross formed by the intersection of a natural crack and a deliberately incised line, and the incised plaque with a concentric design from Quneitra on the Golan Heights. In 1996, a possible bone flute was recovered in a Mousterian context in eastern Europe. In general, however, the evidence for a significant symbolic component in the Mousterian record is rather rare, and

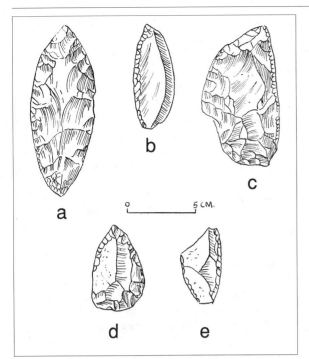

Mousterian tools from central and eastern Europe and North Africa: (a) leaf-shaped point (Germany); (b) side-scraper (Germany); (c) leaf-shaped point (Russia); (d) Mousterian point (Morocco); (e) double side-scraper (Morocco). In part after J.D. Clark, The Prehistory of Africa, *1970, Praeger.*

equivocal. This ambiguity need not imply that Mousterian humans did not use symbols in social contexts, but rather that these symbols were not encoded in durable media to the same degree as seen in Late Paleolithic times.

SOCIALITY

The presence of fragmentary, often burnt, human skeletal remains from Mousterian sites (e.g., Krapina) has led many to suppose that cannibalism played a part in Mousterian lifeways, as a subsistence option and/or as a mortuary ritual. Most researchers consider such damage to be explicable in terms of damage inflicted by carnivores or by subsequent human occupations on sites where human remains were exposed on the surface. At Krapina, where cannibalism has often been invoked to explain the condition of the remains, the practice of defleshing and secondary burial of the dead is a far more likely cause. The survival into late middle age of a Neanderthal with a useless right arm stemming from an early injury (Shanidar 1) carries implications about the cognitive and moral qualities of some Mousterian groups; although it is worth remembering that this same individual bears a probably fatal wound from having been stabbed in the back.

See also Acheulean; Africa, North; Amud Cave; Amudian; Archaic Moderns; Asia, Western; Aterian; Bacho Kiro; Biache-St. Vaast; Bordes, François; Chatelperronian; Cueva Morin; Culture; De Sonneville-Bordes, Denise; Drachenloch; Economy, Prehistoric; Europe; Flake; Flake-Blade; Hahnöfersand; Haua Fteah; Homo sapiens; Jabrud; Jebel Irhoud; Jewelry; Karain; Kebara; Ksar 'Akil; La Chapelle-aux-Saints; La Ferrassie; La Quina; Le Moustier; Levallois; Man-Land Relationships; Middle Paleolithic; Micoquian; Middle Stone Age; Modern Human Origins; Mortillet, Gabriel de; Mugharan; Musical Instruments; Neanderthals; Paleolithic Image; Paleolithic Lifeways; Pech de L'Azé; Pre-Aurignacian; Prepared-Core; Qafzeh; Quneitra; Regourdou; Ritual; Saccopastore; Saint-Césaire; Scraper; Shanidar; Site Types; Skhūl, Speech (Origins of); Stone-Tool Making; Szeletian; Tabūn; Tata; Teshik-Tash; Torre in Pietra; Uluzzian; Upper Paleolithic; Vindija. [J.J.S., A.S.B.]

Further Readings

Binford, L.R., and Binford S.R. (1966) A preliminary analysis of functional variability in the Mousterian of Levallois facies. Amer. Anthropol. 68(no.2 pt.2):238–295.

Blanc, A.C. (1961) Some evidence for the ideologies of early man. In S.L. Washburn (ed.): The Social Life of Early Man. Chicago: Aldine, pp. 119–136.

Boëda, F. (1993) Le Concept Levallois: Variabilité et Méthodes. (Centre de Recherches Archeologiques Monograph 9). Paris: C.N.R.S.

Bordes, F. (1972) A Tale of Two Caves. New York: Harper and Row.

Bordes, F., and de Sonneville Bordes, D. (1970) The significance of variability in Paleolithic assemblages. World Archaeol. 2:61–73.

Chase, P., and Dibble, H. (1987). Middle Paleolithic symbolism: A review of current evidence and interpretation. J. Anthropol. Archeol. 6:263–296.

Dibble, H., and Bar-Yosef, O., eds. (1996) Levallois Technology. Ann Arbor: Prehistory Press.

Dibble, H., and Rolland, N. (1992) On assemblage variability in the Middle Paleolithic of western Europe: History, perspectives, and a new sythesis. In H.L. Dibble and P.A. Mellars (eds.): The Middle Paleolithic: Adaptation Behavior and Variability. (Museum Monographs, No. 72). Philadelphia: University of Pennsylvania Press. pp. 1–28.

Gamble, C. (1986) The Palaeolithic Settlement of Europe. Cambridge: Cambridge University Press.

Goren-Inbar, N. (1990) Quneitra: A Mousterian site on the Golan Heights. Qedem (Monographs of the Hebrew University of Jerusalem 31). Jerusalem: Hebrew University of Jerusalem.

Kuhn, S. (1996) Mousterian Lithic Technology. Princeton: Princeton University Press.

Marks, A.E. and Chabai, V.P. (eds.) (1998) The Middle Paleolithic of Western Crimea Vol. 1: Liège:ERAUL 84 (Études et Recherches Archéologiques de l'Université de Liège).

Meignen, L., and Bar-Yosef O. (1988) Variabilité technologique au Prôche-Orient: L'example de Kebara. In M. Otte (ed.): L'Homme de Néandertal. Vol 4: La Technique. Liège: Études et Recherches Archéologiques de l'Université de Liège, pp. 81–94.

Mellars, P. (1996) The Neanderthal Legacy: An Archaeological Perspective from Western Europe. Princeton: Princeton University Press.

Rolland, N., and Dibble, H. (1990) A new synthesis of Middle Paleolithic variability. Am. Antiquity 55:480–499.

Stiner, M. (1994) Honor among Thieves: A Zooarchaeological Study of Neanderthal Ecology. Princeton: Princeton University Press.

Stringer, C.B., and Gamble, C. (1993) In Search of the Neanderthals. London: Thames and Hudson.

Movius, Hallem L., Jr. (1907–1986?)

American prehistorian. Movius directed excavations at several sites in Europe, of which the Abri Pataud in Les Eyzies, France, is the most important. In the 1940s, his synthesis of what was known about the prehistory of eastern and southern Asia gave rise to the term *Movius' line* to divide western areas with handaxe industries from those to the east that apparently were lacking in these symmetrical forms. In his later work, Movius was one of the first to advocate and carry out a multidisciplinary approach to the Paleolithic, which emphasized the contributions of the natural sciences, particularly in recognizing the complexity of rockshelter and cave deposits and devising appropriate excavation strategies. In addition, he was a pioneer in the statistical analysis of artifact types.

His excavations at Abri Pataud provided a much-needed revision to D. Peyrony's classic concept of parallel phyla in the early Upper Paleolithic by demonstrating that an important Middle Perigordian industry (previously termed Perigordian III, later changed to VI) was stratigraphically later than the "Upper Perigordian" industries of the region. This discovery and others suggested that the Aurignacian industries largely preceded the Perigordian ones and constituted the earliest true Upper Paleolithic of Europe. This, in turn, paved the way for a new concept of the remaining Lower Perigordian, or Chatelperronian, as a kind of final Middle Paleolithic, now thought to be the work of Neanderthals.

See also Abri Pataud; Aurignacian; Châtelperronian; Early Paleolithic; Movius' Line; Perigordian; Peyrony, Denis; Upper Paleolithic. [A.S.B.]

Further Readings

Bricker, H.M., ed. (1996) Le paléolithique Supérieur de l'abri Pataud (Dordogne): les Fouilles de H.L. Movius, Jr. (Documents d'Archéologie Française No. 50). Paris: Maison des Sciences de l'Homme.

Movius, H.L., Jr. (1944) Early man and Pleistocene stratigraphy in southern and eastern Asia. Pap. Peabody Mus. Archaeol. Ethnol. 19(3):1–113.

Peyrony, D. (1933) Les industries aurignaciennes dans le Bassin de la Vézère. Bull. Soc. Préhist Fr. 30:543–559.

Movius' Line

Imaginary line that seems to separate so-called handaxe from chopper–chopping tool assemblages in Asia. The term *Movius' line* came into use among archaeologists working in Asia after American prehistorian H.L. Movius, Jr., pointed out in the 1940s that the Paleolithic assemblages of East and Southeast Asia and India south of the Punjab differed from other Old World areas in the absence of handaxes and other Acheulean elements. Specifically, he suggested that the chop-per–chopping tool complex of eastern and southern Asia reflected its position as a largely isolated cultural backwater. Although Movius' line does seem to be "real" in that it demarcates eastern and southern Asia from other parts of Eurasia and Africa, many workers have suggested alternative explanations for the low frequency of bifacially worked tools in these areas, from the lack of suitable raw materials to a reliance on a largely nonlithic technology east of the line. The real significance of this differential distribution and frequency of artifact types is still the subject of much debate.

See also Acheulean; Asia, Eastern and Southern; China; Chopper-Chopping Tools; Indonesia; Movius, Hallam L., Jr. [G.G.P.]

Further Readings

Movius, H.L., Jr. (1944) Early man and Pleistocene stratigraphy in southern and eastern Asia. Pap. Peabody Mus. Archaeol. Ethnol. 19(3):1–113.

Pope, G.G. (1989) Bamboo and human evolution. Nat. Hist. 98(10):49–57.

Schick, K.D. (1994) The Movius line reconsidered: Perspectives on the earlier palaeolithic of eastern Asia. In R.S. Corrucini and R.L. Ciochon (eds.): Integrative Paths to the Past. Englewood Cliffs, N.J.: Prentice-Hall, pp. 569–596.

Mugharan

A term coined by A. Jelinek for the late Middle Pleistocene industry of southwestern Asia. The Mugharan (also known as the *Acheuleo-Yabrudian*) occurs mainly in caves, such as Tabūn (Level E) in Israel, Ras el-Kelb (Bezez C and Abri Zumoffen Levels 2–21), Jabrud Rockshelter 1a (Levels 11–18) in Syria, and Zuttiyeh in Israel. The main characteristics of Mugharan assemblages include thick, steeply retouched scrapers with plain platforms, handaxes with thin, symmetri-

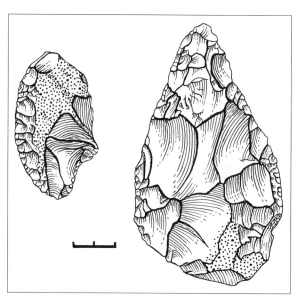

Mugharan tools from Mount Carmel: scraper (left) and small handaxe. After J. Coles and E. Higgs, The Archaeology of Early Man, *1975, Penguin. Scale = 2 cm.*

cal tips, and occasionally high frequencies of blades (in its Amudian facies). The hominin frontal bone from Zuttiyeh is associated with the Mugharan.

See also Amudian; Asia, Western; Jabrud; Mousterian; Tabūn; Zuttiyeh. [J.J.S.]

Mugharet/Mughara

Arabic for "cave/caves," a prefix often attached to the names of sites from southwestern Asia and Africa (e.g., Mugharet et-Tabūn = "cave of the oven"). [J.J.S.]

Multivariate Analysis

Statistical techniques for analyzing simultaneously many variables or characters measured on each individual unit under study. This is in contrast to *univariate* statistical analysis, which considers only one measured variable (*t*-test, analysis of variance, etc.) at a time. Some common methods are principal components, discriminant analysis, and factor analysis.

See also Morphometrics; Quantitative Methods. [L.M.]

Mulvaney, D.J. (1925–)

Historian and later Australia's leading prehistorian. Mulvaney carried out excavations in Arnhem Land, Willandra Lakes, and at Kenniff Cave in Queensland, where the first Pleistocene dates for indigenous occupation of Australia were demonstrated in 1962.

See also Australia. [A.T.]

Mumba

Rock shelter site near Lake Eyasi, Tanzania, which has yielded a deeply stratified series of occupations ranging from Middle Stone Age (Level VI) to Iron Age (Level I). Excavations were carried out in the 1930's by Kohl-Larsen, and in the 1970's by M.J. Mehlman. The oldest level, dated to ca. 130 Ka by uranium series, contained two hominid incisors of modern size and shape. Mumba cultural materials from Levels VI and V contain some of the oldest evidence for long-distance trade in raw materials, with obsidian derived from the central Kenya Highlands more than 300 km distant. Level V dated to 60–40 Ka at the top, also included some of the oldest ostrich eggshell beads and backed geometric forms of stone tools, possibly an east African equivalent of the Howieson's Poort industry in South Africa. A series of iron age burials were intrusive into the early Late Stone Age level (III) which is dated to ca. 25– 30 Ka.

See also Africa, East; Archaic moderns; Eyasi; Jewelry; Middle Paleolithic; Middle Stone Age.

Further Reading

Mehlman, M.J. (1991). Context for the emergence of modern man in eastern Africa: Some new Tanzanian evidence. In J.D. Clark, (ed.) Cultural Beginnings: Approaches to Understanding Early Hominid Lifeways in the African Savanna. Bonn: Forschungsinstitut fur

Vor- und Fruhgeschichte, Romisch-Germanishche Zentralmuseum Monograph 19:177–196.

Musculature

Mammals possess three types of muscle tissue: *smooth muscle* found in the walls of internal organs such as the intestines, *cardiac muscle* forming the walls of the heart, and *skeletal muscle*. All are distinguished by possessing the unique property of being able to shorten or contract. Smooth muscle and cardiac muscle are not under conscious control and are, therefore, sometimes called *involuntary muscle*. Since skeletal muscle is under conscious control, it is referred to as *voluntary muscle*. Skeletal muscles are what make movement possible in primates as in most other animals and are the focus of this entry. As the name implies, they are generally attached to bones, often via connective tissue bands or cords called *tendons*. One attachment site is called the muscle's *origin*; the other is its *insertion*. Usually, the origin is the more stable site, whereas the insertion is on the bone that moves. Muscles are actually composed of bundles of muscle cells, also known as *muscle fibers*. Muscle cells, in turn, contain a number of cylindrical elements known as *myofibrils,* which are composed of many serially repeating units known as *sarcomeres.* The sarcomere is the functional unit of the contractile system of the muscle and contains overlapping protein fila-

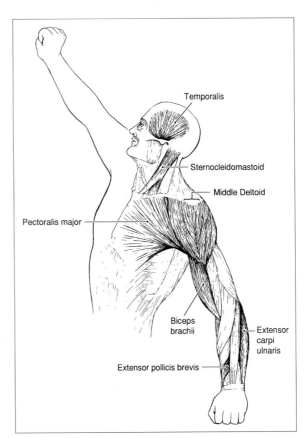

Examples of skeletal muscles from the human body. The temporalis and pectoralis major are examples of fan-shaped muscles. The sternocleidomastoid is a typical strap muscle, and the biceps brachii is a fusiform muscle. The middle portion of the deltoid is multipinnate in structure, the extensor carpi ulnaris is a bipinnate muscle, and the extensor pollicis is a unipinnate muscle. Courtesy of S.G. Larson, by L. Betti.

ments that slide past each other, reducing the length of the sarcomere when the muscle is activated. As the consecutive sarcomeres shorten, the entire muscle shortens, thereby bringing its attachment points on the skeleton closer together.

Muscle contraction, then, is due to the shortening of individual sarcomeres, and the arrangement of the sarcomeres has great significance for muscle performance. Two principles are helpful in guiding our understanding of the arrangement of sarcomeres: the forces of elements in parallel are additive and independent, while the forces of elements in series are nonadditive, and each element must exert the same amount of force to remain in equilibrium. Since myofibrils and muscle cells are arranged in parallel, their forces are additive. The amount of force a muscle can produce, therefore, is proportional to its cross-sectional area. However, consecutive sarcomeres of a myofibril are arranged in series, so lining up a lot of sarcomeres produces only as much force as one sarcomere.

These principles help us understand muscle architecture, the arrangement of muscle fibers within a muscle (see Figure). The fibers of some muscles are arranged in a simple parallel fashion. Included in this group are *strap muscles* that tend to be longer than they are thick, such as the sternocleidomastoid muscle in the neck or the sartorius muscle in the thigh. The number of parallel muscle fibers in a typical strap muscle is limited, and, therefore, such muscles generally cannot produce much force. However, since all muscles can shorten to approximately two-thirds of their length, a long strap muscle can produce a large amount of absolute shortening. Another parallel-fibered muscle, known as a *fusiform muscle,* packs more fibers into a thick muscle belly that tapers at the ends to attach to a cordlike tendon. An example is the biceps brachii muscle in the arm.

Pinnate muscles have fibers that insert onto tendons at an angle. The fibers are usually rather short, but there are many of them. Therefore, pinnate muscles are capable of producing high levels of force. However, since the fibers are generally short, they cannot shorten very much. Included in this group are unipinnate (e.g., the extensor pollicis brevis in the forearm), bipinnate (e.g., the extensor carpi ulnaris in the forearm), and multipinnate (e.g., the middle deltoid at the shoulder) muscles.

Fan-shaped muscles have very broad origins, and their fibers converge toward a much narrower insertion. Examples include the pectoralis major or temporalis muscles. Fan-shaped muscles very rarely act as a single unit; rather, different portions will contract at different times depending on the direction of force required. To understand how fan-shaped muscles work, it is necessary to understand how muscle recruitment is controlled. Motor neurons are the components of the nervous system that carry the signals for muscles to contract. Each motor neuron innervates a set of muscle cells within a muscle; the combination of a single motor neuron and all of the muscle fibers it innervates is called a *motor unit.*

A motor unit may include only a few muscle cells, several hundred muscle cells, or anything in between. This variation reflects the level of fine control by the nervous system. The nervous system recruits muscles by activating motor

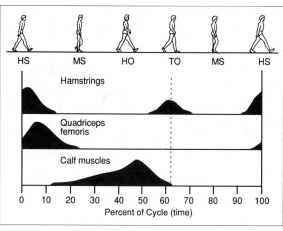

Pattern of recruitment of some human lower limb muscles during walking as revealed by electromyography. Activity in the quadriceps femoris during the initial period of right limb support phase prevents the knee from collapsing into flexion. As the knee passes behind the body's center of gravity during the second half of support phase, it is held extended by the weight of the body and the quadriceps femoris is no longer needed. The activity in the hamstrings at the beginning of support phase is also preventing a motion, namely, preventing the trunk from flexing forward at the hip during heel-strike. Similarly, the calf muscles prevent the ankle from collapsing into dorsiflexion in the second half of support phase. Courtesy of S.G. Larson, by L. Betti.

units; the more force is needed, the more units are activated. Although the fibers of a single unit can be scattered over an area of several centimeters within a muscle belly, they can be confined to particular regions. Thus, the nervous system can activate only those units within a region of a muscle, thereby permitting independent contraction of subparts of a muscle. This is especially important for fan-shaped muscles, in which the orientation of the muscle fibers changes quite radically across the breadth of the muscle, producing very different effects when each portion contracts.

Muscle fibers also differ in the particular forms of the contractile proteins that make up their individual sarcomere units. These differences alter their speed of contraction and resistance to fatigue. Three types of muscle fibers are generally recognized: slow twitch, resistant to fatigue (SR or Type I); fast twitch, resistant to fatigue (FR or Type IIA); and fast twitch, fatigable (FF or type IIB). These three types can also be classified on the basis of their method of energy metabolism: slow oxidative (SO), fast oxidative/glycolytic (FOG), and fast glycolytic (FG). As the name implies, slow-twitch fibers cannot contract quickly enough to produce rapid movements, but they are, however, able to produce sustained contractions. Fast-twitch fibers can contract very quickly, but most also fatigue relatively quickly. Muscles are usually composed of a combination of slow and fast fibers. Those that have a preponderance of one or the other are themselves classified as fast or slow. For example, the soleus muscle in the calf is composed primarily of slow-twitch fibers, whereas the rectus femoris in the thigh has a large percentage of fast-twitch fibers. Slow fibers are used for the maintenance of posture and are the first to be recruited during motion. During walking, for example, primarily slow-twitch fibers are used. However, when speed or direction is changed, when obstacles are to be avoided, or in behaviors requiring greater muscular effort such as leaping or running, both fast- and slow-twitch fibers are recruited.

When studying variation in skeletal muscle design, a distinction is generally made between the action of a muscle and its function. The *action* is what happens if the muscle were to contract in isolation (i.e., bring its two attachment sites together). The action of a muscle describes its full potential of possible contributions to motion, some of which may never be realized. The *function* of a muscle refers to its actual contribution to some motion or activity. The function may involve shortening, or maintaining constant length, or even resisting being lengthened. To discover the function of a muscle, it is necessary to know when a muscle is active as well as what it is capable of doing.

Determining when a muscle is active can be achieved through use of a technique known as *electromyography*. Since the signal for a muscle to contract involves a flow of ions, or charged particles, across the muscle cell membrane (an action potential), this change in electrical potential can be detected with a sensing device known as an electrode. A record of the changing electrical field during a muscle contraction is known as an electromyogram or electromyography (EMG). With this information about when a muscle is active, plus knowledge of its potential contributions to motion, one can then go about attempting to determine the muscle's function in some particular behavior.

The difference between a muscle's action and its function can be illustrated by the pattern of muscle use during human walking. The action of the quadriceps femoris in the thigh is to extend or straighten the knee, but during walking the quadriceps functions to prevent the knee from collapsing into flexion when the limb is supporting the weight of the body. In fact, most of the muscles used during human walking are functioning to regulate the rate at which a motion occurs or to prevent some undesired motion, rather than to cause a motion by shortening.

All mammals possess the same basic set of muscles, but, for each species, changes have been brought about by evolution so that their design and pattern of recruitment suit the functional demands of that animal's way of life. In general, human musculature is more similar to that of the living African apes (chimpanzees and gorillas) than to that of any other mammals. Indeed, as comparative anatomists have observed for more than 100 years, humans are more similar to the great apes than apes are to other primates. The unique aspects of human musculature are those associated with our bipedal gait and some features of the hand associated with human manipulative abilities. In most instances, these unique features of human musculature are extreme developments of variations found in chimpanzees and gorillas.

See also Biomechanics; Functional Morphology; Locomotion; Skeleton. [S.G.L., J.G.F.]

Further Readings

Winter, D.A. (1990) Biomechanics and Motor Control of Human Movement, 2nd ed. New York: Wiley, pp. 165–189 (Chap. 7: Muscle mechanics).

Mushabi

Open-air site complex in the Jebel Maghara, northern Sinai (Egypt), excavated in the 1970s. Mushabi contains a long sequence of Late Paleolithic (Geometric Kebaran and Mushabian) occupations dating to 14–12 Ka. Most sites contain one or more hearths and associated lithic scatters.

See also Africa, North; Asia, Western; Kebaran; Late Paleolithic; Mushabian. [J.J.S.]

Mushabian

Late Paleolithic industry of the Levant with North African affinities, characterized by numerous bladelets and the use of microburin technique for shaping tools and known primarily from sites in the Negev, Sinai, and southern Jordan between 14 and 11 Ka. Mushabian sites are generally small occupations near perennial water sources. The distribution of Mushabian sites through the southern Levant suggests that they represent a hunter-gatherer adaptation to steppe-desert conditions that was roughly contemporaneous with the Geometric Kebaran.

See also Africa, North; Asia, Western; Hunter-Gatherers; Kebaran; Late Paleolithic; Mushabi. [J.J.S.]

Musical Instruments

The oldest unequivocal musical instruments in archaeological context date to the Late Paleolithic period. Remains dating

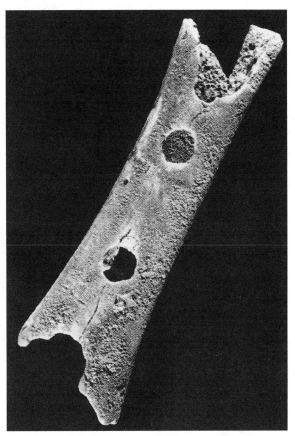

A Neanderthal flute? This fragment of cave bear femur with four perforations was recovered from Divje Babe Cave I in northwestern Slovenia, associated with Mousterian tools and ESR dated to between 82–43 Ka. Courtesy of Bonnie Blackwell.

from ca. 30 Ka and later of flutes and whistles made of perforated bird and bear bones and reindeer antler are found across Europe, from France (Isturitz) to Hungary (Istállöskö), the Czech Republic (Pekarna), and the Russian Plain region of Ukraine (Molodova V, Kostenki I). An ambiguous claim has also been made that the painted mammoth bones found at the Late Paleolithic sites of Mezin and Mezhirich (Ukraine) represent the earliest percussion instruments. Moreover, a perforated fragment of a bovid phalanx discovered in the pre-Aurignacian layer (possibly dating to before 130 Ka) in the Haua Fteah Cave (Mediterranean Libya) is claimed by some to be the remains of the earliest whistle on record.

In 1996, a fragment of cave-bear femur with four perforations was reported from Divje Babe Cave I in northwestern Slovenia, associated with Mousterian tools. This putative flute was dated by electron spin resonance (ESR) to 82–43 Ka by B. Blackwell and colleagues. Their conclusion was that it represents the first case of a Neanderthal musical instrument, but the matter is still questionable, as the holes may have been made by carnivore teeth.

See also Europe; Haua Fteah; Istállöskö; Kostenki; Mezhirich; Molodova; Mousterian; Neanderthals; Paleolithic Image; Pre-Aurignacian; Ritual. [O.S.]

Nachola

Locality at the base of the Aka Aiteputh Formation in the Samburu Hills, northern Kenya, on the eastern face of the rift escarpment north of Lake Baringo. Numerous teeth and jaw fragments of "*Kenyapithecus*" *africanus* but now assigned to *Sambinupithecus* *ishidai,* have been collected from this site, now dated to ca. 15.5 Ma.

See also Baringo Basin/Tugen Hills; Kenyapithecus; Samburupithecus. [P.A.]

Napak

Early Miocene hyperalkaline volcanic complex in eastern Uganda, with fossiliferous sediments beneath and within the main eruptive sequence of carbonatitic and nephelinitic flows and agglomerates, dated to ca. 20 Ma by potassium-argon (K/Ar) analysis of associated pyroclastic biotite. Collections made under the leadership of W.W. Bishop in the 1960s include the type of *Micropithecus clarki,* in association with *Proconsul major, P. africanus,* and *Limnopithecus legetet.* The abundant fauna, mainly of small forest-adapted mammals, compares with that of Koru and Songhor in western Kenya. From the somewhat younger Moroto volcanic complex to the north, a famous and nearly complete maxilla of a gorilla-size hominoid, originally placed in *P. major* and *Afropithecus,* but more recently named *Morotopithecus,* was pieced together over the years from fragments collected by expeditions under Bishop's direction.

See also Africa, East; Koru; Morotopithecus; Songhor. [J.A.V.C.]

Further Readings

Bishop, W.W., Miller, J.A., and Fitch, F.J. (1969) New potassium-argon age determinations relevant to the Miocene fossil mammal assemblages in East Africa. Am. J. Sci. 267:669–699.

Nariokotome Member

Upper Lower Pleistocene member of the Nachukui Formation, western Turkana Basin, Kenya. It spans the interval from Lower Nariokotome Tuff (1.3 Ma) to a level above Silbo Tuff (0.74 Ma), and it is temporally equivalent to all but the basal part of the Chari Member of the Koobi Fora Formation and to Member L of the Shungura Formation.

See also Nariokotome Site 3 (NK3); Turkana Basin [F.H.B.]

Nariokotome Site 3 (NK3)

Lower Pleistocene hominin site in western Turkana Basin, Kenya. Nariokotome is a major ephemeral stream west of Lake Turkana at about 4°10′N, on the south bank of which a nearly complete skeleton, KNM-WT-15000, was found in 1984. Only distal hand and foot elements are missing from the remains of a young male, ca. 160 cm tall at death, identified as *Homo erectus* (or *H. ergaster*). The site is in flood-deposited brown mudstone of the Natoo Member of the Nachukui Formation. The fossiliferous level overlies a correlative of the Lower Koobi Fora Tuff and underlies the Lokapetamoi Tuff, neither of which has been directly dated. The human remains are estimated to date 1.53 ± 0.05 Ma based on extrapolation from sedimentation rates between higher and lower dated levels, such as the Nariokotome Tuff (dated to 1.33 ± 0.05 Ma) and the KBS Tuff (1.89 ± 0.02 Ma).

See also Homo erectus; Homo ergaster; Turkana Basin. (F.H.B.)

Narmada

Valley in central India where more than 50 m of alluvial sediments have yielded an extensive Late or latest Middle Pleistocene mammalian fauna and numerous artifacts. In 1982, the cranium of a fossil hominin was recovered from gravel deposits at Hathnora east of Hoshangabad. Although this has been assigned to *Homo erectus,* it possesses a cranial

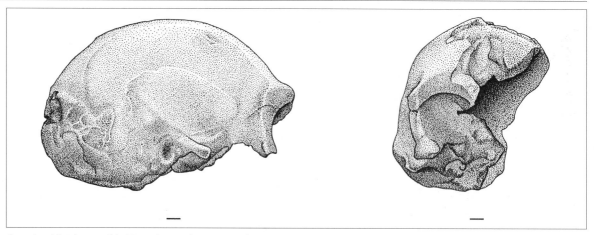

Lateral and facial views of the Narmada partial cranium. Scales are 1 cm.

capacity of 1,260 ml, and many workers think that it is best referred to an archaic form of *Homo sapiens*. A possible hominin clavicle from the same deposit was recovered in the early 1990s.

See also Archaic Homo sapiens; Asia, Eastern and Southern; Homo erectus. [G.G.P.]

Further Readings

Petraglia, M.D. (1998) The lower paleolithic of India and its bearing on the Asian record in M.D. Petraglia and R. Korisettar (eds.): Early Human Behavior in Global Context. New York: Routledge pp. 342–390.

Sankhyar, A.R. (1997) Fossil clavicle of a middle pleistocene hominid from the central Narmada Valley, India. J. Hum. Evol. 32:3–16.

Sonakia, A. (1985) Early *Homo* from the Narmada Valley, India. In E. Delson (ed.): Ancestors: The Hard Evidence. New York: Liss, pp. 334–338.

Sonakia, A. (1992) Human evolution in South Asia. In T. Akasawa, K. Aoki, and T. Kimura (eds.): The Evolution and Dispersal of Modern Humans in Asia. Tokyo: Hokusen-Sha, pp. 337–347.

Natoo Member

Lower Pleistocene member of the Nachukui Formation, western Turkana Basin, Kenya. Bounded by Lower Koobi Fora (1.6 Ma) and Lower Nariokotome (1.3 Ma) tuffs, it is approximately equivalent to Member K of the Shungura Formation and Okote Member of the Koobi Fora Formation. The skeleton KNM-WT-15000, ascribed to *Homo erectus*, comes from the base of this member.

See also Homo erectus; Nariokotome Site; Turkana Basin. [F.H.B.]

Natron-Eyasi Basin

The Tanzanian segment of the East African Rift is one of the primary sources of data bearing on human evolution. The major collecting areas are in the depression whose lowest points are occupied by Lake Natron, Lake Manyara, and Lake Eyasi, which lie to the north, east, and south, respectively, of the great intrarift volcanic massif centered on the Ngorongoro caldera in northern Tanzania. These modern lakes are only the present manifestation of topography in the unstable floor of the Tanzanian Rift, which has changed continuously since Miocene time. Thick sections of locally fossiliferous sediments that accumulated in one part or another of this restless zone have since been thrust up and exposed to erosion as the geological activity continues.

The Natron subbasin (named for the high sodium carbonate content of its waters) is the northernmost of the Tanzanian depocenters that have yielded fossil primates, including hominids and stone tools. The Natron catchment extends north into Kenya to the intrarift divide that separates it from the Magadi subbasin. In the Peninj area to the east of Lake Natron, there are ca. 80 m of exposed Lower Pleistocene sediments spanning the period ca. 1.5–1.0 Ma. The Peninj Beds, which are divided into lower (Humbu) and upper (Moinik) formations, contain fossil vertebrates and Acheulean artifacts that are similar to material at Bed II of Oldvai Gorge, which dates from the same time. A mandible of *Paranthropus boisei* was recovered from the lower beds in 1964 by a team led by G. Ll. Isaac and R. Leakey.

Olduvai Gorge, Tanzania's most famous fossil locality, is cut into the Serengeti Plain at the southwestern corner of the Natron subbasin. Discovered in 1911 and first worked by German scientists, Olduvai became the primary study area of L.S.B. and M.D. Leakey in 1931. Over the next 40 years, they recovered a wealth of archaeological and paleontological material, in a program that became increasingly interdisciplinary as they brought in geologists, geophysicists, sedimentologists, and vertebrate paleontologists to study and publish on the wealth of data available in the gorge. From the strata below the famous Bed I basalt (the anchor of the Olduvai paleomagnetic Subchron), which were laid down ca. 2 Ma, to the Upper Pleistocene deposits resting unconformably on the Ndutu Beds, the superimposed fossiliferous formations have yielded human remains that cover all of the stages in the evolution of genus *Homo*. Fossils of many other vertebrate and invertebrate fossils have also been recov-

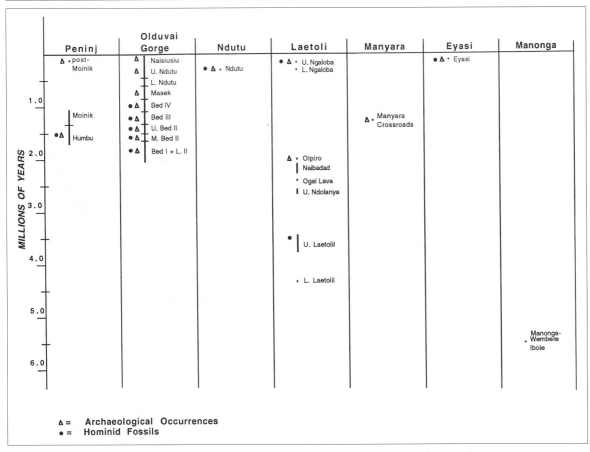

Temporal relationships between paleoanthropological areas of the Natron/Eyasi Basin, Tanzania. Courtesy of Tim D. White.

ered from these rich deposits that aid in the interpretation of the lifeways of the Olduvai hominids. From Bed I to middle Bed II, *Homo habilis* and *Paranthropus boisei* coexisted, and simple unretouched flake tools of the Oldowan industry are found. In middle Bed II, *Homo erectus* appears and is found along with Acheulean tools up through Bed IV. Middle Pleistocene Masek and Ndutu Beds and Upper Pleistocene Naisiusu Beds unconformably overlie Bed IV; the vertebrate faunas from these beds suggest a local climate with less extreme seasonal variation than today's. From Lake Ndutu, at the edge of the Serengeti Plain near the western end of the Olduvai Main Gorge, a cranium of "archaic *Homo sapiens*" was found in an archaeological horizon with Acheulean/Sangoan artifacts. A nearby rockshelter (Mumba) yielded a deep stratified sequence of Middle and Late Stone Age horizons. Late Pleistocene upfaulting exposed the beds of Olduvai to erosion from water draining to the east into the Olbalbal Depression at the foot of Ngorongoro.

Fossil beds older than Bed I are intermittently exposed in the Serengeti southwest of Olduvai, particularly at Laetoli, ca. 50 km from the principal Olduvai sites. Fossils were discovered here in gullies at the head of the northward-draining Olduvai Side Gorge by L.S.B. Leakey in 1935, but the first major discoveries were by a team organized by M.D. Leakey in the 1970s. The same beds are also exposed in the adjacent headwaters of the Garusi River, which drains south into the Eyasi Basin. At Laetoli, a discontinuous sequence of sedi-

ments spans the last 4 Myr. The earliest sediments, the Lower Laetolil Beds, have yielded no primates. The Upper Laetolil Beds, however, are very fossiliferous, particularly in their upper portion, which is dated to ca. 3.5 Ma. Here the remains of *Australopithecus afarensis* have been found along with footprint trails in volcanic ash. An abundant vertebrate fauna has been recovered from these beds along with the hominin fossils, but no stone tools are known. The overlying Ndolanya Beds have yielded faunas that can be dated to ca. 2.5 Ma, but no hominins (although it has been suggested that basalt boulders found there may represent Mode 1 cores or anvils). The Olpiro Beds, resting on the Ndolanya Beds, have Developed Oldowan stone tools and a limited vertebrate fauna. The Laetoli sequence is terminated by the Upper Pleistocene Ngaloba Beds, equivalent to part of the Ndutu Beds near Olduvai, which contain Middle Stone Age tools and have yielded the cranium of an "archaic *Homo sapiens*."

Lake Eyasi sits to the south of a steep fault escarpment where the Laetolil Beds in the Garusi drainage are dropped down below the rift floor. The modern lake is flanked to the north and east by deposits of Middle Pleistocene age that have yielded fossil vertebrate remains and Middle Stone Age tools. The first Eyasi fossil hominin was found by L. Kohl-Larsen's expedition in 1935, and, since then, other hominid fragments have been recovered from the surface of Pleistocene deposits east of the modern lake. In the Lake Manyara depression parallel to Eyasi depression in the eastern trough of the rift, L.S.B. Leakey reported limited artifactual material and fossil vertebrates dating to the Early Pleistocene, but, since his reconnaissance, little further work on the Manyara Crossroads area has been conducted.

Southwest of the Eyasi Basin, the Manonga Valley of north-central Tanzania contains fossiliferous sediments of Mio-Pliocene age from ca. 7 Ma to ca. 3 Ma. Discovered in the 1920s, the beds exposed in the Wembere-Manonga drainage system were deposited in a shallow, partly lacustrine basin. The area was visited by M.D. Leakey's Laetoli expedition in the late 1970s, and a team organized by T. Harrison that began work in the 1990s has recovered vertebrate remains from several different age levels. No primates have been recovered from these beds, but exploration has just begun.

The configuration of depositional basins in northern-central Tanzania is owed to the influence of the East African Rift system. Continuous and locally dramatic rearrangement of the sedimentation and erosion in this intensely active geological system have presented paleoanthropologists with unique opportunities to recover critical evidence of human evolution.

See also Africa; Africa, East; Eyasi; Laetoli; Ngaloba; Olduvai Gorge; Peninj. [T.D.W.]

Further Readings

Hay, R.L. (1976) Geology of the Olduvai Gorge. Los Angeles: University of California Press.

Kaiser, T., Bromage, T.G., and Schrenck, F. (1995) Hominid Corridor Research Project update: New Pliocene fossil localities at Lake Manyara and putative oldest Early Stone Age occurrences at Laetoli (Upper Ndolanya Beds), northern Tanzania. J. Hum. Evol. 28:117–120.

Harrison, T. (ed.) (1997) Neogene Paleontology of the Manonga Valley, Tanzania. New York: Plenum.

Leakey, M.D., and Harris, J.M. (1986) Laetoli: A Pliocene Site in Northern Tanzania. Oxford: Oxford University Press.

Mehlman, M.J. (1987) Provenience, age and associations of archaic *Homo sapiens* crania from Lake Eyasi, Tanzania. J. Archaeol. Sci. 14:133–162.

Mehlman, M.J. (1991) Context for the emergence of modern man in Eastern Africa: Some new Tanzanian evidence. In J.D. Clark (ed.) Cultural Beginnings: Approaches to Understanding Early Hominid Lifeways in the African Savannah. Monogr. 19. Forsch. Inst. Vor- und Frühgeschichte Bonn: Römisch-Germanische Zentral Museum pp. 177–196.

Taieb, M., and Fritz, B. (1987) Lac Natron. Paris: U.L.P.; C.N.R.S.

Natufian

An Epipaleolithic culture from the Late Pleistocene of Southwest Asia. The Natufian dates to ca. 12.5–10.3 Ka, contemporary with the initial Mesolithic adaptation in Europe, and is represented at numerous cave and open-air sites,

from the Levant, including the Israeli sites of Hayonim, El Wad, Kebara, 'Ain Mallaha/Eynan, Rosh Zin, and Hatoula. Natufian lithic assemblages are marked by the presence of distinctive lunate microliths, flaked-stone chisels and pecked-and-ground stone mortars. Bone artifacts include awls, spatulas, perforated animal teeth, polished bone beads, and *Dentalium* shell ornaments. Zoomorphic and anthropomorphic sculptures have also been recovered. Bone sickle handles and stone blades with distinctive *sickle polish* (wear resulting from cutting tropical grasses) suggest incipient cereal cultivation. Remains of early domesticated dog occur at several Natufian sites. The substantial, stone-lined hut foundations at several sites suggest prolonged occupations of the same sites, possibly multiseasonal sedentism. Other Natufian occurrences in the interior parts of the Levant, such as Abu Hureyra in Syria, suggest seasonal driving of gazelle.

The Natufian saw a simultaneous development of symbol systems that were drastically different from the rich animal art of the European Upper Paleolithic but, in some respects, reminiscent of European symboling traditions. These respects include the accumulation, in the Natufian, of incised sets of marks on nonutilitarian artifacts and the use of geometric motifs such as the multiple serpentine as decoration on utilitarian artifacts. The human face and head, in diverse forms, begin to assume particular symbolic importance. Both primary and secondary burials of adults and children, some with grave goods, occur at many Natufian sites. Some of these burials have had their crania removed, suggesting possible cultural continuity with local Neolithic cultures who practice this same mortuary ritual.

See also Asia, Western; Domestication; El Wad; Epipaleolithic; Hayonim; Kebara; Mesolithic; Neolithic. [J.J.S.; A.M.]

Further Readings

Bar-Yosef, O., and Valla, F.R., eds. (1991) The Natufian Culture in the Levant (International Monographs in Prehistory. Archaeological Series I). Ann Arbor: Prehistory Press.

Ndutu

Middle Pleistocene site west of Lake Ndutu in the Serengeti Plain (Tanzania). A partial hominin cranium, stone artifacts, and faunal remains were recovered from clays that underlie a volcanic tuff, ca. 0.4 Ma or younger, associated with the Masek Beds, or possibly the Lower Ndutu Beds, of Olduvai Gorge. The thickness of the cranial vault and the small cranial capacity (ca. 1,100 ml) resemble Middle Pleistocene specimens of *Homo erectus,* but the shape of the occipital and parietal regions suggests an association with later skulls attributed to "archaic *Homo sapiens.*" The artifacts consist of cores (especially spheroids), hammerstones, and flakes but few handaxes. This collection may represent a variant of the Acheulean or a Middle Pleistocene non-Acheulean assemblage.

See also Acheulean; Archaic Homo sapiens; Africa, East; Homo erectus; Natron-Eyasi basin; Olduvai Gorge. [R.P.]

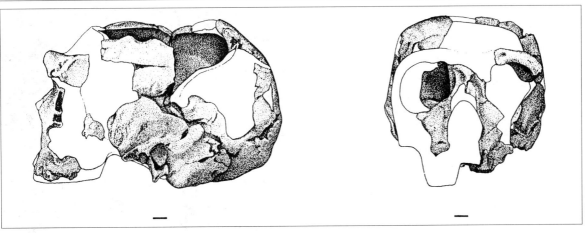

Lateral and facial views of the reconstructed Ndutu cranium. Scales are 1 cm.

Further Readings

Mturi, A. (1976) New hominid from Lake Ndutu, Tanzania. Nature 262:484–485.

Neanderthal

The 1856 discovery of a skull cap and partial skeleton in the Feldhofer Cave in the Neander Valley near Düsseldorf (Germany) was a momentous event. Although it was subsequently recognized that humans of this kind had already been found at Engis (Belgium) and Forbes Quarry (Gibraltar), the Neanderthal skeleton was the first to be described in any detail and recognized as a distinct human type. W. King in 1864 first named a new human species, *Homo neanderthalensis*, for the remains. Unfortunately, associated faunal or archaeological materials were not recovered, so the precise age of the specimen remains uncertain. The morphological features displayed by the skeleton, however, are consistent with those known in other last-glaciation Neanderthals, and the skull cap particularly resembles one found at Spy (Belgium) in 1886. The skull has a strongly developed and curved browridge, is flattened and elongated, and has a projecting occipital region. Brain size is ca. 1,400 ml, which is low for a Neanderthal individual sexed as male from the pelvis. The postcranial skeleton is robustly constructed with long bones that are thick walled and bowed (which led to erroneous suggestions that rickets was responsible). The Neanderthal humerus, however, does show a pathology of the elbow joint probably caused by a fracture.

See also Engis; Europe; Homo neanderthalensis; Neanderthals; Spy. [C.B.S.]

Neanderthals

Group of archaic humans known predominantly as Late Pleistocene European hominids of the early part of the Last glaciation (ca. 100–35 Ka). However, our lack of knowledge of their Middle Pleistocene antecedents and of their Asian representatives limits our perception of the Neanderthals, since they undoubtedly had a much wider distribution in time and space than this. The term *Neanderthal* is sometimes also used in a

wide sense to indicate fossils that are considered to represent their "grade equivalents" in various parts of the world, including eastern and southern Asia and Africa, although this unsatisfactory usage has declined as the special characters of the European specimens have been increasingly appreciated. As yet there is no evidence that true Neanderthals ever extended into Africa, but they were certainly present in western Asia from known occurrences in Israel, Iraq, and the former Soviet Union (including as far east as Uzbekistan, almost in Afghanistan). Their western limits reached as far as the Iberian Peninsula and the British Isles. To the north, they extended at least as far as northern Germany and Poland.

It is usually considered that the Neanderthals were cold adapted, as is indicated by their body proportions, and perhaps also by their facial shape, although they never extended into real Arctic habitats. They did, however, exist in a variety of temperate and boreal environments, including Mediterranean interglacial and northern glacial conditions. The first recognized Neanderthal discovery was made at the Feldhofer Cave in the Neander *Thal* (Valley; German spelling later

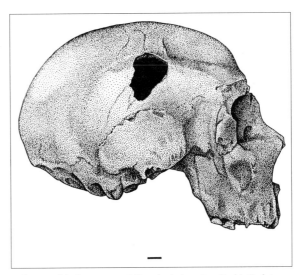

Side view of the Saccopastore 1 Neanderthal cranium (Italy). Scale is 1 cm.

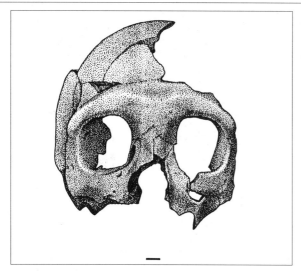

Facial view of the Krapina C partial cranium. Scale is 1 cm.

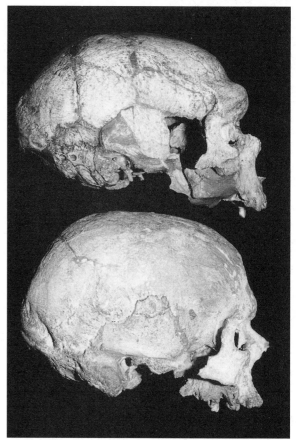

Comparison in side view of the La Chapelle Neanderthal cranium (above) with the early modern Cro-Magnon 1 cranium. Courtesy of Chris Stringer.

changed to *Tal*) (Germany) in 1856. Earlier unrecognized finds of Neanderthal type had been made at the Engis Cave (Belgium) between 1829 and 1830 and at a cave in Forbes' Quarry (Gibraltar) in 1848. Initial dispute about the significance of the unusual morphology of the Neander Valley partial skeleton was eventually settled by further fossil discoveries during the next 60 years that showed a comparable morphology, such as the Belgian finds from La Naulette and Spy and, in particular, the French finds from La Chapelle-aux-Saints, La Ferrassie, and La Quina. Important material of numerous but fragmentary Neanderthals from Krapina (Croatia). received less attention at the turn of the twentieth century, although it represented an equally informative and far larger source of data about the group. By this time, two different interpretations of the evolutionary significance of the Neanderthals were emerging. Some workers believed that the Neanderthals were the direct ancestors of living Europeans, while others believed that they represented a lineage of primitive hominids that had become extinct. As the sample increased and morphological variation was recognized in the fossils, further intermediate viewpoints were to develop between these extreme positions.

Neanderthal Characters

Many observations made on the relatively small sample of Neanderthals known by the early years of the twentieth century have been confirmed, while others have been shown to be misconceptions based on incomplete knowledge or preconceived ideas about the course of human evolution. Some Neanderthal features regarded as primitive are now known to be present in at least some modern populations; others appear to be rather specialized. Some supposedly aberrant features are, in fact, primitive for hominids and can be recognized in recent discoveries representing more archaic groups. Primitive features found in the Neanderthals include a long, low cranial vault, with a flattened top to the skull, and a short parietal arch. There is a primitive (for humans in general), well-developed supraorbital torus that is especially strong centrally, a large face with a broad nasal opening, a fairly large

dentition (especially incisors), and a mandible that, in most cases, lacks a bony chin. The cranial base is broad and, in some specimens at least, flattened rather than well flexed. The postcranial skeleton shares a whole suite of characters with those of earlier archaic humans, through an emphasis on strong musculature and thickened shafts to the bones.

Advanced (derived) characters that the Neanderthals appear to share with living humans include lateral reduction of the browridge, reduced development of the occipital torus, a relatively rounder occipital profile and longer occipital plane, a large brain, reduced facial prognathism, and unthickened ilium of the pelvis above the hip joint (acetabulum).

The Neanderthals also show their own special characters, present in most or all specimens but rarely found outside the group. These specialized features include the spherical shape of the cranial vault in rear view and the posterior position of the (usually very large) maximum breadth of the skull. On the occipital bone is a central depression at the upper limit of the neck musculature (a suprainiac fossa), and a prominent juxtamastoid crest along the lower margins of the bone. In the face are a number of special features associated with the phenomenon of midfacial projection, in which the enormous nose stands out from the swept-back and inflated cheek bones, and the teeth are similarly positioned far forward. This positioning of the teeth leads to the occurrence of a space behind the third molars (retromolar space). On the internal surface of the ascending ramus of the lower jaw,

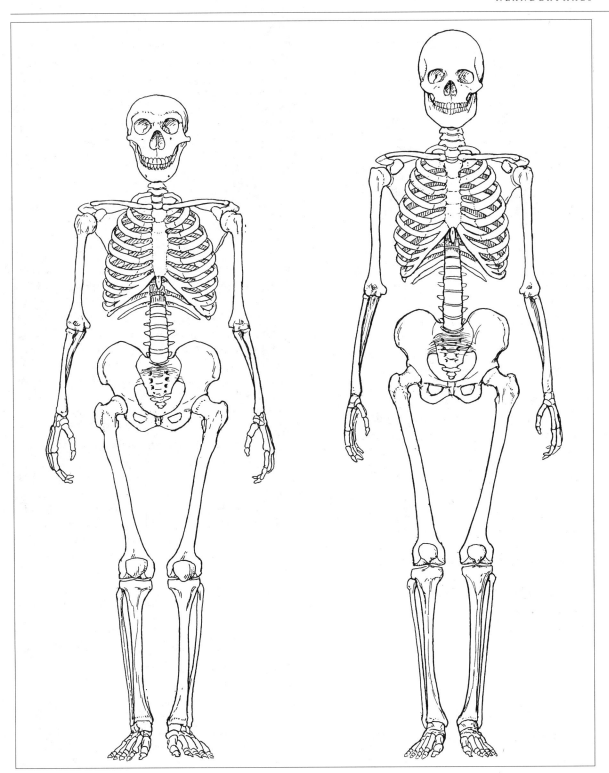

Comparison of a Neanderthal skeleton (left) with that of a modern human.

there is often an unusual shape (called *horizontal-oval,* or H-O) to the mandibular foramen or hole, which may be related to the strong musculature of the jaws in Neanderthals.

The rest of the skeleton shows other features that may be specialized in Neanderthals, although, because of limited information about these areas in earlier hominids, we cannot be sure. One aspect concerns the body proportions of Neanderthals, which may have been the result of cold-adaptation.

Another concerns the shoulder blade (scapula), which has on its back edge a well-developed groove for a muscle that runs to the upper arm. And at the front of the pelvis is a long and flattened pubic ramus in all Neanderthals (male and female) where this part has been preserved. This latter feature has been linked with the birth of large-headed infants in Neanderthal women (it has been suggested on this basis that gestation length in Neanderthals was as long as twelve months),

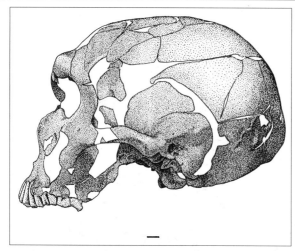

Side view of the La Ferrassie 1 Neanderthal cranium from France. Scale is 1 cm.

although this peculiarity has also—more convincingly—been related to locomotion. Neanderthals were certainly large-bodied by the standards of modern hunter-gatherers; by various means it is possible to estimate their body weight as ca. 65 kg (more than 140 lb) in males and perhaps 50 kg (110 lb) in females. This weight would have been for lean and heavily muscled bodies. Since many Neanderthals lived in relatively cold environments, it is not surprising, considering Bergmann's biological rule, that they were heavily built. Similarly, following Allen's rule, it would be expected that body extremities would be shortened if Neanderthals were cold adapted, and this also appears to be the case. As in present-day cold-adapted peoples, such as the Lapps and Eskimos, the forearms (radius and ulna) and shinbones (tibia and fibula) of European Neanderthals were proportionally shortened compared with the upper-arm and leg bones. This effect was less marked in the Neanderthals of Iraq and Israel. As well as being stockily built, the Neanderthals were fairly short in stature. Estimates from the long bones of their skeletons suggest that males averaged ca. 169 cm (5 feet, 6

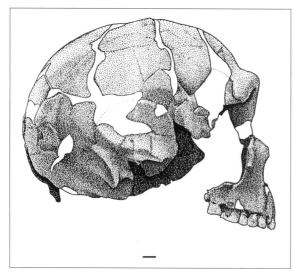

Side view of the Tabūn 1 Neanderthal cranium from Israel. Scale is 1 cm.

inches), while females averaged ca. 160 cm (5 feet, 3 inches). The Neanderthals were large brained, and their known average cranial capacity is larger than the modern average (more than 1,450 ml). In common with earlier humans, however, the brains of Neanderthals were low and broadest near the base, with small frontal lobes and large, bulging occipital lobes at the back. The significance for Neanderthal intellectual capabilities of the large size and unusual shape of their brains is still unclear.

Neanderthal Behavior

Behaviorally the Neanderthals certainly showed traits found in living humans, such as burial of the dead, care of disabled individuals (such as the Shanidar 1 man in Iraq), and at least a limited ability to communicate and to hunt large mammals. However, just as earlier workers may have overemphasized the potential differences between Neanderthals and living humans, so more recent workers may have overemphasized their possible similarities to us in behavior. Reassessments of Neanderthal behavior may well lead to indications of a significant inferiority in their cultural adaptations when compared with those of any modern hunter-gatherers. Thus, the Neanderthals may well turn out to have more in common with the behavior of primitive hominids than with people alive today. Their Mousterian stone-tool industries show a degree of specialization in the presence of tool kits for particular activities, yet many of the features of these "cultures" are invariant through long periods of time and large geographical areas, suggesting a lack of response to environmental parameters. Compared with the tool kits of anatomically modern hominids, such as the Upper Paleolithic peoples who produced the Aurignacian industry, Neanderthals made little use of bone, antler, or ivory and probably did not manufacture composite tools, such as hafted spears or harpoons.

Origin of the Neanderthals

The ancestors of the Neanderthals are thought to be the Middle Pleistocene hominids of Europe (and perhaps also of western Asia, although little is known of them). The extent and significance of supposed Neanderthal characters in such fossils, however, are matters of dispute. Early European fossils, such as those from Mauer and Bilzingsleben, are not complete enough to be conclusively classified but are primitive in the characters they do display. A number of Neanderthal features are present in such fossils as those from Arago (France), Petralona (Greece), Vértesszollöllös (Hungary), and Atapuerca (Spain), which are more usually classified as representing *Homo erectus,* "archaic *Homo sapiens,*" or anteneanderthals. Yet it is difficult to justify assigning any of these specimens to the Neanderthal group proper, and it is not until we reach the later Middle Pleistocene that Neanderthal-derived characters begin to predominate over more primitive ones.

The Swanscombe (England) "skull" displays a number of primitive features, such as its thickened, parallel-sided vault, but, in details of the occipital torus morphology, the presence of a suprainiac fossa, and the probable development of juxtamastoid crests shows clear Neanderthal affinities. Such affinities are even more obvious in the Biache St.

Vaast (France) partial cranium, since the spherical (in rear view), thin-walled vault and bulging occipital profile bear a particular resemblance to the form of the La Quina 5 Neanderthal (France). The Steinheim skull (Germany), which is probably also of later Middle Pleistocene age, is more enigmatic and perhaps more primitive, but its occipital region is reminiscent of that of Swanscombe and, hence, that of Neanderthals. The younger Fontéchevade specimens (France), like Swanscombe, were once directly linked in an evolutionary scheme with modern humans, via the "presapiens" lineage, but the more complete Fontéchevade 2, at least, is most plausibly regarded as an early Neanderthal.

Further probable early Neanderthals from the period between 200 and 100 Ka include the specimens from La Chaise (Abri Suard and Bourgeois-Delaunay) (all in France), Ehringsdorf (Germany), and Saccopastore (Italy). The last site produced an interesting association of two early Neanderthal crania with such fauna as elephant and hippopotamus, and these specimens differ from later specimens primarily in their smaller size and less developed midfacial projection and basicranial flattening. The Ehringsdorf site also produced Neanderthal-like cranial, mandibular, and postcranial bones from an interglacial environment, but it is unclear whether they date from the same last-interglacial period as the Saccopastore specimens (ca. 120 Ka) or derive from the previous interglacial (ca. 220 Ka). The La Chaise fossils, which include very Neanderthal-like mandibular and occipital specimens, mostly date from the period 150–100 Ka.

The large sample of early Neanderthals from the Croatian site of Krapina has been the subject of many interpretations since its discovery at the turn of the twentieth century. Some workers, noting the fragmentary condition and apparent variation displayed by the Krapina fossils, believed that they resulted from a battle between Neanderthal and early-modern populations that was followed by a cannibalistic feast. Other workers thought the specimens were related to the generalized Neanderthals from western Asia (the Zuttiyeh, Tabūn, and Skhūl fossils [all in Israel], at a time when these were regarded as representing a single early Late Pleistocene progressive population). Further study of the Krapina specimens, however, has confirmed that they do represent rather robust early Neanderthals, with large teeth and strong brows in some specimens. Where shoulder blades, pelves, and hand and limb bones are preserved, these seem to display the typical Neanderthal pattern described earlier. The large dental sample is especially important, since it derives from at least 15 individuals, many of whom were children, and the condition of taurodontism (unseparated roots in the molars with expanded pulp cavities) is especially developed. The real reasons for the fragmentary condition of the Krapina sample are uncertain, but ancient human interference seems to be at least partly responsible. Actual cannibalism by Neanderthals may have occurred, or skeletons may have been defleshed and broken up for ritual reburial.

Typical Neanderthals

The best-known Neanderthals are those from ca. 70–50 Ka in western Asia and 70–35 Ka in Europe. The western European specimens in this time range probably include the original Neander Valley partial skeleton (although its date cannot now be established accurately); the Spy Neanderthals from Belgium; the Devil's Tower and (perhaps) the Forbes' Quarry crania from Gibraltar; the Guattari Cave (Monte Circeo) skull and mandibles from Italy; and the La Quina, La Chapelle-aux-Saints, La Ferrassie, and Saint-Césaire partial skeletons from France. The latter specimens are particularly important, as the La Ferrassie assemblage is a group of late Neanderthal skeletons that may have made up a family cemetery of an adult male, an adult female, and young children, while the Saint-Césaire material is the youngest in age (associated with the early Upper Paleolithic Chatelperronnian industry) and establishes with a fair degree of certainty the contemporaneity of late Neanderthals and early-modern populations in Europe.

The eastern European material consists of less complete specimens but includes a lower jaw and other specimens from Subalyuk (Hungary), an upper jaw and other fragments from Kulna (Czechoslovakia), and the fragments from Vindija (Croatia). Some workers believe that the eastern European specimens show evolutionary trends that indicate a gradual progression toward a modern morphology, and the Vindija specimens certainly appear more gracile than the earlier Krapina hominids. No European specimens have yet been discovered, however, that display a clear transitional morphology between Neanderthals and early-modern humans.

The Asian Neanderthals differed in certain respects from their European counterparts. Variation in size, robusticity, and morphology is evident when comparing the Shanidar Neanderthals from Iraq with each other, or the male and female Neanderthals from the Israeli sites of Amud, Kebara, and Tabūn. Yet, these fossils and others from such sites as Kiik-Koba and Teshik-Tash (Uzbekistan) have major similarities in derived characteristics with European Neanderthals. The large Shanidar (Iraq) sample is especially important, probably spanning more than 15 Kyr and consisting of nine individuals of both sexes and various ages. The specimens include an adult man who had suffered extensive injuries sometime before he died (Shanidar 1) and one of the most massive but characteristic Neanderthal faces ever discovered (Shanidar 5). The Amud, Kebara, and Tabūn skeletons contrast markedly in lying at the extremes of size variation in Neanderthals. The Kebara man had the most massive jaw and skeleton, while the Amud man was the largest brained and tallest Neanderthal yet found. The Tabūn woman, however, was one of the smallest and most gracile of all Neanderthals. As with the eastern European specimens, some scientists perceive signs of evolution toward a modern morphology in the Neanderthals of Asia, but the dating of the specimens is not precise enough to construct valid evolutionary trends for the whole sample. Nevertheless, the Asian Neanderthals are less extreme than their European relatives when both are compared with modern humans. There may well have been as abrupt a transition between the Asian Neanderthals and the first modern humans as there was between the European Neanderthals and the first Cro-

Magnons. This is indicated by the non-Neanderthal morphology of the Qafzeh and Skhūl hominids, which, more than anything, argues against a direct evolutionary connection with Neanderthal ancestors.

Evolutionary Significance of the Neanderthals

The role of the Neanderthals in human evolution has been a subject of dispute for more than a century. In some respects, they seem to fill an intermediate position between earlier archaic hominids and modern humans. Yet, they also display unique characteristics that seem to have developed over hundreds of thousands of years in Europe. These special characteristics are rare or nonexistent in the succeeding anatomically modern peoples of Europe and western Asia, and the lack of morphological intermediates at the appropriate time between late Neanderthals and early moderns speaks against any direct evolutionary connection between the two groups. Additionally, it seems that in western Europe, and possibly elsewhere, Neanderthals and early-modern peoples may have coexisted for several thousand years. However, before it can be stated with confidence that the Neanderthals were not ancestors of any modern peoples, there are some tantalizing pieces of evidence that suggest otherwise. This evidence includes, as we have seen, the fossil material from eastern and central Europe, where some Neanderthal specimens are less extreme in their characteristics and some early-modern specimens appear particularly robust, and the evidence from Saint-Césaire that some Neanderthals were capable of producing Upper Paleolithic-style industries that were formerly thought to be exclusively the province of the European Cro-Magnons. Perhaps there was some cultural or genetic contact between these two very different peoples before the last Neanderthals disappeared, ca. 30 Ka.

See also Archaic Homo sapiens; Homo sapiens; Lagar Velho; Modern Human Origins. [C.B.S.]

Further Readings

Delson, E. (1985) Late Pleistocene human fossils and evolutionary relationships. In E. Delson (ed.): Ancestors: The Hard Evidence. New York: Liss, pp. 296–300.

Howell, F.C. (1984) Introduction. In F.H. Smith and F. Spencer (eds.): The Origins of Modern Humans. New York: Liss, pp. xiii–xxii.

Mellars, P. (1996) The Neanderthal Legacy: An Archaeological Perspective from Western Europe. Princeton: Princeton University Press.

Smith, F.H. (1984) Fossil hominids from the Upper Pleistocene of central Europe and the origin of modern Europeans. In F.H. Smith and F. Spencer (eds.): The Origins of Modern Humans. New York: Liss, pp. 137–209.

Spencer, F. (1984) The Neanderthals and their evolutionary significance: A brief historical survey. In F.H. Smith and F. Spencer (eds.): The Origins of Modern Humans. New York: Liss, pp. 1–49.

Stringer, C.B. (1982) Towards a solution to the Neanderthal problem. J. Hum. Evol. 11:431–438.

Stringer, C.B., and Gamble, C. (1993) In Search of the Neanderthals. London: Thames and Hudson.

Stringer, C.B., Hublin, J.-J., and Vandermeersch, B. (1984) The origin of anatomically modern humans in western Europe. In F.H. Smith and F. Spencer (eds.): The Origins of Modern Humans: A World Survey of the Fossil Evidence. New York: Liss, pp. 51–135.

Trinkaus, E. (1983) The Shanidar Neanderthals. New York: Academic.

Trinkaus, E. (1984) Western Asia. In F.H. Smith and F. Spencer (eds.): The Origins of Modern Humans: A World Survey of the Fossil Evidence. New York: Liss, pp. 251–293.

Trinkaus, E. (1986) The Neanderthals and modern human origins. Ann. Rev. Anthropol. 13:193–218.

Trinkaus, E., and Shipman P. (1993) The Neanderthals: Changing the Image of Mankind. London: Jonathan Cape.

Wolpoff, M.H. (1996). Human Evolution. New York: McGraw-Hill.

Nelson Bay Cave

Archaeological site on the southern face of the Robberg Peninsula on the Indian Ocean near the town of Plettenberg Bay, South Africa. Excavations by R. Inskeep in the 1960s and R.G. Klein in the early 1970s revealed abundant Later Stone Age (LSA) artifacts and associated faunal remains dating between 18 and 2 Ka, and Middle Stone Age (MSA) artifacts dating from ca. 120 to ca. 50 Ka. Extensive decalcification of the MSA deposits has removed any bone that may have been associated with the lithics. Lithics from the older LSA strata (18–12 Ka), coeval with the last glacial maximum of the Pleistocene, have been referred to the "Robberg Industry." The associated fauna is characteristic of coastal-plain grasslands. Changes in the fauna at ca. 12 Ka indicate encroachment of bush and a rising sea level with a concomitant increase in marine shells. Polished-bone tools are among the new elements in the artifacts at this level.

See also Africa, Southern; Die Kelders; Klasies River Mouth; Middle Stone Age; Later Stone Age. [F.E.G.]

Further Readings

Klein, R.G. (1972) The Late Quaternary mammalian fauna of Nelson Bay Cave (Cape Province, South Africa): Its implications for megafaunal extinctions and environmental and cultural change. Quatern. Res. 2:135–142.

Neogene

Biochronological term introduced by the Austrian paleontologist Moritz Hoernes (as *Neogen*) in 1856 to denote the younger faunas of the Cenozoic in the Austro-Hungarian sphere of influence in central Europe and the eastern Mediterranean. The fossils were dated to C. Lyell's newly minted Miocene and Pliocene, which at that time included levels that later went into Oligocene and Pleistocene. Hoernes, however, alluded specifically to the faunas and not the epochs in defining the term, and, in this sense, Neogene extends to the Recent. When Hoernes' coinage was revived by M. Gignoux in the early 1900s as a chronostratigraphic term, it applied only to the limited modern sense of Miocene and Pliocene, excluding Pleistocene, while the older epochs were grouped in Paleogene. Some researchers advocate Hoernes' original meaning, at least as regards including Pleistocene and Recent faunas, but the International Union of Geological Sciences has recommended the use of Neogene and Paleogene in Gignoux's sense to replace Tertiary in the standard chronostratigraphic scale. Thus, the Neogene extends from 23.5 to 1.8 Ma.

See also Anthropogene; Biochronology; Cenozoic; Miocene; Paleogene; Pleistocene; Pliocene; Quaternary; Tertiary; Time Scale. [J.A.V.C.]

Neolithic

Phase of human cultural development marked mainly by village settlement, domestication, and new implement types. In its earliest widespread usage among archaeologists, Neolithic (New Stone Age) referred to particular assemblages of chipped- and ground-stone tools known from prehistoric sites in the Old World. In stratified contexts, these tools reflected changes in technology of manufacture, tool morphology, and frequencies of types made in earlier periods. Increases in smaller tools, often made on snapped and retouched fragments of larger blades punched off prismatic cores; blades with edge sheen acquired in plant harvesting; and an increasing number and variety of pecked- and ground-stone objects (querns, mortars, pestles, knives, axes, adzes, hoes, net sinkers and other weights, and the like)—all combine to identify as Neolithic the assemblages at sites such as Jarmo in southwestern Asia, Lepenski Vir in Europe, and P'an-po (Ban Po) in China. By the beginning of the twentieth century, it was generally recognized that tools termed *Neolithic* had been used not by hunter-gatherers but by farmers and herders. Thus, while relating initially to stone-tool typology, the term *Neolithic* has taken on important derivative connotations.

During the first half of the twentieth century, archaeologists' efforts shifted from the necessary empirical description of cultural assemblages and, later, of their chronometric parameters to improving understanding of the internal workings of societies earlier thought of, somewhat simplistically, as ethnic groups. One example of the simplistic equation between cultural assemblage and ethnic group was Europe's Neolithic Linearbandkeramik folk (i.e., those who had made and used a particular ceramic assemblage with incised linear decorations). Among the archaeologists responsible for the important change in focus were J.G.D. Clark and V.G. Childe. In his influential work at the Holocene (Mesolithic) site of Star Carr in Yorkshire (England), Clark demonstrated that archaeologists could reconstruct many aspects of prehistoric economic organization, particularly in relation to subsistence and seasonality of settlement.

Childe, whose familiarity with several European languages gave him access to a large body of archaeological literature, suggested that there had been two crucial transformations in the course of the human career: a change from a food-collecting way of life to one based on plant cultivation and stock breeding, and the subsequent founding of cities and the development of complexly stratified societies. Childe referred to these as the Neolithic and Urban revolutions, respectively, and he formulated a hypothesis accounting for the change to reliance on produced rather than collected food on which later developments were based. This process, now referred to as *domestication,* was seen as intimately related to major climatic changes in southwestern Asia at the end of the Pleistocene after 13 Ka. Childe suggested that increasing desiccation caused aggregation of animals and people at oases and that this propinquity resulted in increasingly habituated and tamable domesticable animals. Childe's work also explicitly links technological change to shifts in environment, subsistence, and sociopolitical organization.

Immediately following World War II, Childe's hypothesis was examined in fieldwork designed and directed by R.J. Braidwood. In an ambitious multidisciplinary program, Braidwood coordinated experts in prehistoric archaeology, zoology, botany, geology, and ceramic technology. This fieldwork, carried out in northeastern Iraq, was designed, among other things, to document the process of domestication, with concomitant changes in settlement organization and technology, and to establish whether or not these transformations had occurred in tandem with significant Early Holocene climatic change in the hilly flanks of the Fertile Crescent (an arc-shaped area extending from the Levant to the mouths of the Tigris and Euphrates rivers). The team concluded that, while environmental change at the Late Pleistocene/Holocene boundary had occurred in this region, it had not been sufficiently drastic to have caused altering relationships among plants, animals, and people. More recently, however, H.E. Wright has used palynological evidence to show that the nature of Early Holocene climatic change varied locally within southwestern Asia, and that, in a number of areas, it involved increasing moisture rather than increasing aridity, as had been suggested by Childe. Wright now argues that climatic change at the end of the glacial Pleistocene was significant, affecting the geographic distribution of domesticable plants available to people. J. McCorriston and F. Hole have used botanical evidence to suggest that increasingly sedentary Early Holocene (ca. 10 Ka) cereal collectors in the southern Levant, faced with growing aridity brought on by longer hot dry summers, were forced to plant seeds to ensure adequate food supplies for the entire year; they believe that domestication in the southern Levant, as in other places in the world, stemmed from the chance convergence of several necessary preconditions, including the technology to process plants, the social organization to deal with delayed-return food sources, and the availability of annual plants that could be manipulated. Although it now appears that the precise nature of Late Pleistocene climatic change may differ from what was initially suggested by Childe, and while it was certainly far more complex and regionally varied, climatic change did, in some parts of the world (if not equally in all), affect distributions and associations of both plants and animals—transforming the stage upon which humans acted and from which they selected a few species for domestication.

Continuing disagreement about the precise timing and nature of the events of the Neolithic is due in large part to inadequate samples from representative sites and regions and

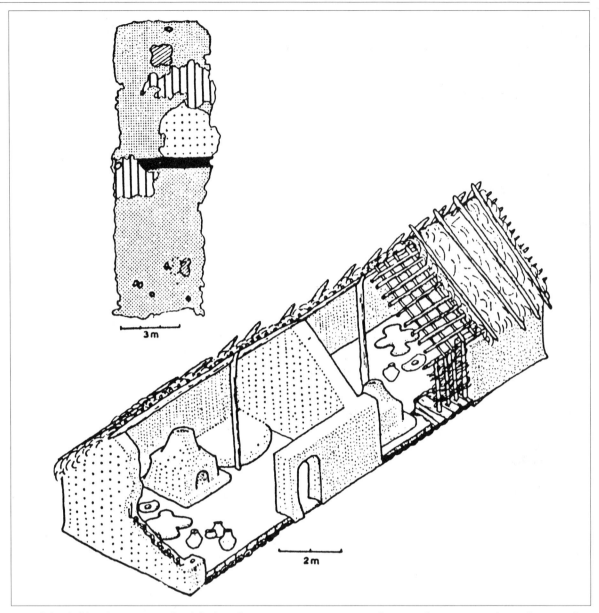

Ground plan (right) and reconstruction of Neolithic house from eastern Europe, ca. 5,500 BP After R. Tringham, Hunters, Fishers and Farmers of Eastern Europe, 6000–3000 BC, *1971, Hutchinson.*

to imprecision, despite ongoing improvements and refinements, in chronometric techniques. Nonetheless, research in a variety of geographic areas continues to demonstrate that Holocene changes in settlement patterns, food-procurement strategies, and technology were complex and highly varied and also that the rates at which changes occurred differed from one part of the world to another. In several world areas, people radically modified their relationships with plants and animals, and these altered relationships led, in turn, to other important cultural changes.

Even when wild ancestors of domesticates invaded new areas with ameliorating Holocene climate, not all societies took advantage of their presence. Some societies invented the complex of behaviors now identified as Neolithic; others failed to do so but were comparatively quick to imitate and modify such activities once exposed to them, using local species or importing foreign domesticates; yet

others continued to rely on the collection of wild plants and animals, as do a few groups even in the present day. Where domestication was autochthonous (indigenous), as in Mesoamerica and southwestern Asia, cultural complexes associated with plant and animal domestication were distinctive, and rates of change varied considerably. Of particular interest is the association of settled village life, and the radical alteration in land use that it implies, with an increasing reliance on domesticated species. In southwestern Asia, sedentary life appears to have predated domestication, while in Mesoamerica, where the domestication of maize and other vegetable species was a comparatively slower process, village life seems to have followed plant domestication by several millennia.

Neolithic, then, may be considered the complex of changes that, at the start of the Holocene and in many parts of the world, involved (1) radically altered relationships be-

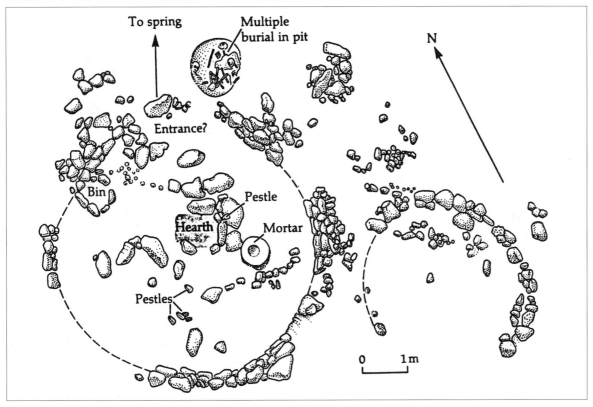

Plan of two structures from the lower level of Mallaha: a hearth is in the center of the larger structure, as are tools and a basin mortar. From Charles Redman, The Rise of Civilization: From Early Farmers to Urban Society in the Ancient Near East, *1978, W. H. Freeman.*

tween humans and the plants and animals on which they relied in many ways, (2) associated changes in land use (including settlement pattern), and (3) the technology by which humans adapted to their altered niches. The earliest manifestation of this complex of changes occurred in southwestern Asia, between 11 and 10 Ka. (and perhaps slightly earlier). Domestic plants and animals and changed technocomplexes appeared between 10 and 8 Ka. in Europe and possibly in Northeast Africa and by 8–7 Ka. in China (in the Yang-shao assemblage), where they were also associated with villages occupied for much if not all of the year. The idea of domestication and village life, along with some of the particular domesticated species, may have been introduced from southwestern Asia into Europe and East Asia, but tighter chronological controls must be established before routes, rates, and mechanisms of diffusion can be firmly identified.

See also Americas; Archaeological Sites; Asia, Eastern and Southern; Asia, Western; Broad-Spectrum Revolution; Childe, Vere Gordon; Complex Societies; Domestication; Late Paleolithic; Mesolithic; Paleolithic; Site Types. [C.K., N.B.]

Further Readings

Binford, L.R. (1968) Post-Pleistocene adaptations. In S.R. Binford and L.R. Binford (eds.): New Perspectives in Archeology. Chicago: Aldine, pp. 313–341.

Braidwood, R.S., and House, B. (1960) Prehistoric Investigations: Iraqi Kurdistan. (Studies: Ancient Oriental Civilization 31). Chicago: University of Chicago Press.

Childe, V.G. (1941) Man Makes Himself. London: Watts.

Clark, J.D., and Brandt, S.A., eds. (1984) From Hunters to Farmers: The Causes and Consequences of Food Production in Africa. Berkeley: University of California Press.

Flannery, K.V. (1969) Origins and ecological effects of early domestication in Iran and the Near East. In P.J. Ucko and G.W. Dimhlehy (eds.): The Domestication and Exploitation of Plants and Animals. London: Duckworth, pp. 73–100.

Flannery, K.V., ed. (1976) The Early Mesoamerican Village. New York: Academic.

Ford, R.I., ed. (1985) Prehistoric Food Production in North America. Ann Arbor: University of Michigan Press.

Megaw, J.V.S., ed. (1977) Hunters, Gatherers, and First Farmers beyond Europe. Leicester: Leicester University Press.

McCorriston, J., and Hole, F. (1991) The ecology of seasonal stress and the origins of agriculture in the Near East. Am. Anthropol. 93(1):46–69.

Reed, C.A., ed. (1977) Origins of Agriculture. The Hague: Mouton.

Young, T.C., Jr., Smith, P.E.L., and Mortensen, P., eds. (1983) The Hilly Flanks and Beyond: Essays on the Prehistory of Southwestern Asia Presented to Robert J. Braidwood. Chicago: University of Chicago Press (Oriental Institute).

Ngaloba

The hominid skull from Ngaloba (Laetoli Hominid 18) was discovered at Laetoli (Tanzania) in 1976. Middle Stone Age artifacts were reportedly associated with the discovery, which

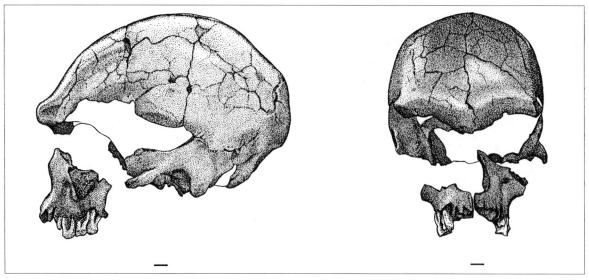

Lateral and facial views of the Ngaloba hominid cranium. Scales are 1 cm.

has an age of ca. 120 Ka by correlation with dated volcanics in the main part of Olduvai Gorge to the north. The skull comprises most of the cranial vault and the lower part of the face, which unfortunately cannot be directly fitted together because of damage. Brow-ridge development is archaic although not strong, and the frontal bone is long, low, and receding, while the occipital region is rounded. In this respect and in occipitomastoid crest development, the specimen is Neanderthal-like. Cranial capacity was originally quoted as only ca. 1,200 ml, but a higher figure (ca. 1,350 ml) has also been measured. The Ngaloba skull is generally regarded as an "archaic *Homo sapiens*" fossil, but some workers believe that it is relatively close to a modern human morphology.

See also Archaic Homo sapiens; Africa, East; Middle Stone Age. [C.B.S.]

Ngandong (Solo)

Middle Pleistocene deposits in eastern Java, usually dated at ca. 1.0–0.2 Ma by faunal correlation but possibly much younger (see below). Between 1931 and 1933, the calvaria, calottes, and tibiae of at least 12 fossil human individuals were excavated from the banks of the Solo River near Ngandong. The reconstructed cranial capacities range from 1,035 to 1,225 ml (n = 6). The phylogenetic and taxonomic status of these specimens has been debated ever since their discovery. Early workers thought that they might represent "neanderthaloid" forms. Few now accept this interpretation, but there is still much debate about whether to classify the Ngandong (also known as Solo) hominins, as an early form of "archaic *Homo sapiens*" or a late form of *Homo erectus*. The total morphological pattern includes characteristics of both: the relatively straight supraorbital torus and marked angulation at inion are reminiscent of *H. erectus*, while the cranial length, reduced postorbital constriction, and overall size suggest attribution to *H. sapiens*. Some have also suggested that the Ngandong specimens make a good morphological ancestor for Australian Aborigines.

The dating and taphonomic context of the Ngandong finds have also been a source of speculation. The hominids have generally been assigned a Late Pleistocene or latest Middle Pleistocene age. It has also been suggested, however, that the Ngandong vertebrate assemblage is a mixed time-transgressive assemblage, some components of which may have been transported and redeposited. Taphonomic considerations have also entered into longstanding contentions that some of the Ngandong crania bear evidence of cannibalism in the form of damaged or missing basicranial and facial regions. On the basis of current evidence, most workers attribute the preservation of the Ngandong crania to nonhominid taphonomic agencies. C.C. Swisher and colleagues have analyzed dental enamel from Ngandong faunal remains with extreme care using electron spin resonance (ESR) and uranium-series methods; they determined ages ranging between 50 and 25 Ka, far younger than previously estimated. If these dates hold up, they imply that *H. erectus* persisted in Java well after the time when modern *H. sapiens* arrived in Australasia. Other researchers have questioned whether this date actually relates to the human fossils, suggesting that the assemblage may be of mixed age or have been taphonomically disturbed.

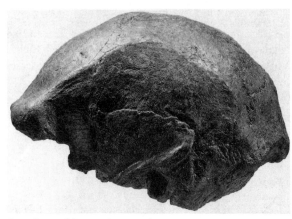

Lateral view of the Ngandong 12 calotte.

See also Archaic Homo sapiens; Asia, Eastern and Southern; Homo erectus; Indonesia; Ritual; Sangiran Dome; Taphonomy. [G.G.P.]

Further Readings

Santa Luca, A.P. (1980) The Ngandong Fossil Hominids: A Comparative Study of a Far Eastern Homo erectus Group (Yale University Publications in Anthropology No. 78). New Haven: Yale University Press.

Sémah, F., Sémah, A., and Djubiantono, T. (1990) They Discovered Java. Bandung: Puset Penelitian Artkeologi Nasional.

Swisher, C.C., III, Rink, W.J., Antón, S.C., Schwarcz, H.P., Curtis, G.H., Suprijo, A., and Widiasmoro. (1996) Latest Homo erectus of Java: Potential contemporaneity with H. sapiens in Southeast Asia. Science 274:1874–1878.

Thorne, A., and Wolpoff, M.H. (1981) Regional continuity in Australian Pleistocene hominid evolution. Am. J. Phys. Anthropol. 33:337–349.

Weidenreich, F. (1951) Morphology of Solo Man. Anthropol. Pap. Am. Mus. Nat. Hist. 43:201–290.

Niah Cave

Archaeological site in northern Borneo (Sarawak, Malaysia) with extensive late Pleistocene-Holocene (40–2 Ka) deposits. Most work has focused on the cave's largest opening, the West Mouth, where intensive excavation occurred in the 1950s and 1960s. Many human burials were recovered including a cranium known as the "Deep Skull," discovered in 1958 ca. 1.75 m below ground surface. Associated with this cranium were several postcranial bones (including a nearly complete femur), faunal remains, and a quartzite flake. If radiocarbon dates on associated charcoal accurately age this material at ca. 40 ka, then they represent the oldest anatomically modern remains yet discovered in Australasia. However, doubts have been raised about its context. The cranium is probably that of a young adult female and typologically is similar to people of Australo-Melanesian descent. Third molars are unerupted but all other age indicators are consistent with young adult status.

See also Archaic Moderns. [C.B.S., J.S.K.]

Further Readings:

Bellwood, P. (1997) Prehistory of the Indo-Malaysian Archipelago (revised edition). Honolulu: University of Hawai'i Press.

Niaux

An extremely deep cave in the Pyrenean foothills of the Ariège (France) discovered in 1906. The large central chamber, the *Salon Noir*, has black painted animals of different sizes and quality: bison, horse, male ibex, stags, lion. Some of the horses are in winter pelage, some of the bison are in summer molt, and the stags carry their autumn antlers. The nearby Late Magdalenian shelter of La Vache, facing Niaux, is rich in mobiliary art that also contains a diverse seasonal imagery. Analysis of the paints reveals the presence of two "recipes," suggesting two periods of painting, straddling 13.5–12.5 Ka.

Some of the Niaux animals have been killed with darts. Accumulations of signs and motifs occur outside the Salon Noir, strongly suggesting a variable use of the cave at different times and for different purposes. Many red-painted *claviforms,* a Middle Magdalenian motif purportedly representing the female figure, occur around the Salon Noir. A panel of sets of finger marks in the passageway below the Salon Noir, made by different paints, suggests different periods of ritual marking by persons visiting the Salon Noir.

See also Late Paleolithic; Magdalenian; Paleolithic Image. [A.M.]

Further Readings

Clottes, J. (1993) Les Cavernes de Niaux: Art Préhistorique en Ariège. Paris: Seuil.

Nihewan

Geological basin and formation in Hebei Province, ca. 150 km west of Beijing, China, containing Plio-Pleistocene through Holocene sediments, also known as Nihewan. Known since the 1920s as a rich paleontological locality, the Nihewan Basin has also yielded many archaeological sites ranging in age from the Lower and Middle Pleistocene Xiaochangliang, Donggutuo, Chenjiawan, and Maliang localities through Upper Pleistocene/Lower Holocene microlithic and Neolithic sites such as Hutouliang.

The Sanggan River and its tributaries have exposed long Quaternary depositional sequences throughout the basin yielding rich fossiliferous and archaeological occurrences in modern erosional cuttings and gullies. The Nihewan Formation itself includes stratified exposures in two main horizons: a lower level (Red Beds) dated ca. 2.5 Ma and an upper level (White Beds) dated ca. 700 Ka, both by faunal correlation. It has yielded associations of *Equus* and *Hipparion* and has long been considered the type site of the "Chinese Villafranchian" faunal assemblage. It is possible that *Hipparion*, which may have become extinct in the Early Pleistocene, derives from the Red Beds only, and that the *Equus* fossils came from the unconformably overlying White Beds.

Although H. Breuil suggested the Nihewan Basin's archaeological potential as early as the 1930s, it was not until a half-century later that subsequent investigations by Chinese and American researchers confirmed the rich Paleolithic record there. The oldest sites are all located on the eastern side of the basin. Paleomagnetic work has indicated that some of these sites, especially Xiaochangliang and Donggutuo, are stratified within a column of magnetically reversed sediments below a long sequence of normal strata. This appears to place them within the Matuyama Reversed Chron. Because the Jaramillo Normal Subchron may have been identified in the magnetically reversed sediments above the artifact-bearing layers, these sites may be somewhat older than 970 Kyr. Although no hominid fossils have yet (1997) been recovered in earlier Pleistocene contexts in the Nihewan Basin, these are the earliest well-documented Paleolithic occurrences yielding large artifact assemblages in eastern Asia.

Xiaochangliang has yielded numerous mammals in association with microdébitage, cores, and worked flakes and points. Some bones also exhibit distinct cutmarks. There is little doubt that this locality represents an early hominid activity site. Donggutuo, which has also been excavated, is located ca. 1 km from Xiaochangliang and appears to be a colluvial concentration of numerous flakes and very fragmentary faunal remains.

See also Asia, Eastern and Southern; China; Chopper-Chopping Tools; Xiaochangliang. [G.G.P., J.W.O.]

Further Readings

Pope, G.G., An, Z., Keates, S., and Bakken, D. (1990) New discoveries in the Nihewan Basin, Northern China. East Asian Tert.-Quatern. Newsl. 11:68–73.

Schick, K.D., and Dong, Z.A. (1993) Early Paleolithic of China and Eastern Asia. Evol. Anthropol. 2:22–35.

Schick, K.D., Toth, N., Wei Qi, Clark, J.D., and Etler, D. (1991) Archaeological perspectives in the Nihewan Basin, China. J. Hum. Evol. 21:13–26.

Teilhard de Chardin, P., and Piveteau, J. (1930) Les mammifères fossiles de Nihowan (Chine). Ann. Paléontol. 19:1–134.

Xu, Q., and You, Y. (1982) Four post-Nihewan Pleistocene mammalian faunas of North China: Correlation with deep-sea sediments. Acta Anthropol. Sin. 1:180–187.

Nomenclature

Zoological nomenclature is the process of naming the animal groups that one recognizes in nature. The rules by which names are applied are laid down in the *International Code of Zoological Nomenclature,* a publication issued and revised at intervals by the International Trust for Zoological Nomenclature. In its periodical, the *Bulletin of Zoological Nomenclature,* this independent international body also publishes comments and issues rulings by its commission, a committee composed of taxonomists from several countries, on the many problems of nomenclature that arise. The trust also maintains official lists of names and publications that the commission has accepted or rejected. The system of nomenclature laid down in the *Code* is often referred to as the *binominal* (not *binomial*) system. This is because the species, the basic unit of the system, is identified by two names, both of which are italicized and either of Latin derivation or latinized (given a Latin ending). Our species, for example, is *Homo sapiens.* The first name *(Homo)* is the name of the genus; the second *(sapiens)* is the specific name, and the combination of the two names is unique. Each species must be identified on the basis of a type specimen, or *holotype,* with which all other individuals allocated to the same species must be compared. The provisions of the *Code* apply only to taxa of the family-group or below and, among other things, prescribe endings for the names of families (-idae, as in Hominidae) and subfamilies (-inae, as in Homininae). The endings -oidea and -ini, respectively, are recommended for superfamilies and tribes.

See also Classification; Taxonomy. [I.T.]

Further Readings

International Trust for Zoological Nomenclature (1985) International Code of Zoological Nomenclature, 3rd ed. Berkeley: University of California Press.

Mayr, E. (1969) Principles of Systematic Zoology. New York: McGraw-Hill.

Non-Darwinian Evolution

Darwinian natural selection operates on physical or phenotypic variations of varying degrees of survival and reproductive value. Since, however, only a tiny portion of the genome is actually expressed in the phenotype, it follows that natural selection cannot be the major force guiding the evolution of the genome as a whole. It appears that most genetic change is adaptively neutral and simply indifferent to natural selection. Mathematically, the evolutionary rate of such genetic change is governed by rates of mutation.

See also Evolution; Genome; Molecular Anthropology. [J.M.]

Notharctidae

Family traditionally regarded as a group of Eocene, primarily North American, primates, related to the European adapids via the Holarctic genus *Pelycodus.*

As had happened with *Adapis* in the 1820s, *Notharctus* and *Pelycodus* (described in 1870 and 1875 by R. Leidy and E.D. Cope, respectively) were not recognized at first as being primates. By the turn of the twentieth century, these errors were corrected, and in 1902 H.F. Osborn suggested that the Early Eocene *Pelycodus* might be related to the Middle Eocene *Notharctus.* In his monographic study of *Notharctus,* W.K. Gregory argued that the European *Adapis* and its kin were also descended from *Pelycodus.* (Gregory also suggested that New World monkeys had evolved from *Notharctus,* but this scheme received no support from other systematists.)

Although specimens had been known since Osborn's study, it was not until 1958 that C.L. Gazin pointed out that the species known as *Notharctus gracilis* could be distinguished easily from *Notharctus;* this species he referred to J.L. Wortman's 1903 genus *Smilodectes,* which Gazin suggested had also evolved from *Pelycodus.* More recently, *Cantius* (very close to *Pelycodus*) and *Copelemur* (enigmatic, to say the least) have been added to the array of notharctids, as have various European taxa that had been lumped with *Adapis.* Breaking with tradition, J.H. Schwartz has argued that, if notharctids do, indeed, constitute a monophyletic group, they are probably the sister group of all proper strepsirhines, the whole being united by the possession of the lemurlike bulla.

The supposed family Sivaladapidae is usually said to include three or more later Miocene genera from the Indo-Pakistan Siwaliks and China: *Indraloris, Sivaladapis,* and *Sinoadapis* (from Lufeng). The first two forms have been known for decades, but only since the mid-1970s have fairly complete jaws of the latter two been recovered. Schwartz pointed out that *Sivaladapis* does not bear the distinctive dental features of an adapid. Rather, this primate (and also *Sinoadapis*), although resembling in some aspects of molar

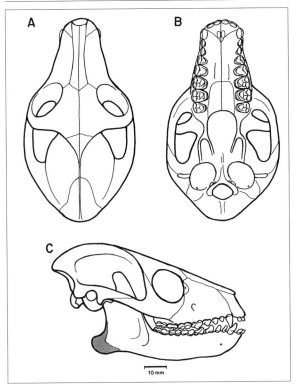

Three views of the skull of Northarctus tenebrosus. *Courtesy of Frederick S. Szalay, from Szalay and Delson, 1979.*

morphology the extant *Hapalemur*, shares with the North American notharctid *Smilodectes* such derived features as inwardly arcing cristids obliquae on M$_{1-2}$, thick buccal cingulids, and stout para- and hypocristids. Here these genera are united in a subfamily of notharctids. The other claimed Siwalik sivaladapid, *Indraloris*, is known from fewer specimens, but referred molars bear one of the unmistakable stamps of identity of the extant lorisid *Loris:* a well-developed protostylid, one of the dental features that distinguishes this genus from virtually all other primates. Other genera classified here as notharctids have also been suggested by Schwartz to have close phyletic ties to the Lorisoidea.

Family Notharctidae
    Subfamily Notharctinae
        †*Notharctus*
        †*Cercamonius*
    Subfamily Protoadapinae
      Tribe Protoadapini
        †*Protoadapis*
        †*Mahgarita*
        †*Pronycticebus*
        †*Microadapis*
        †*Europolemur*
        †*Barnesia*
        †*Adapoides*
        †*Buxella*
        †*Periconodon*
        †*Huerzeleris*
      Tribe Pelycodontini
        †*Pelycodus*

        †*Cantius*
        †*Laurasia*
        †*Agerinia*
        †*Donrussellia*
        †*Copelemur*
        †*Anchomomys*
    Subfamily Sivaladapinae
        †*Sivaladapis*
        †*Sinoadapis*
        †*Smilodectes*
†extinct

See also Adapidae; Adapiformes; Americas; Asia, Eastern and Southern; Europe; Lemuriformes; Locomotion; Lorisidae; Lorisoidea; Lufeng; Siwaliks; Teeth. [J.H.S.]

Further Readings

Gazin, C.L. (1958) A review of the Middle and Upper Eocene primates of North America. Smith. Misc. Coll. 136:1–112.

Schwartz, J.H. (1986) Primate systematics and a classification of the order. In D.R. Swindler (ed.): Comparative Primate Biology, Vol. 1: Systematics, Evolution, and Anatomy. New York: Liss, pp. 1–41.

Szalay, F.S., and Delson, E. (1979) Evolutionary History of the Primates. New York: Academic.

Numerical Cladistics

The goal of numerical cladistics is to obtain an optimal cladogram that, using coded character states, reconstructs the phylogenetic relationships among taxa. The data consist of a table or matrix of character codes, in which each taxon is coded for each character. Often, the characters are binary (presence or absence coded as 0 or 1) but multistate characters are also used. For all but the smallest data sets a computer program must be used to obtain the optimal solution. Different optimality criteria lead to different approaches or computer algorithms for their solution.

Parsimony Methods

Parsimony involves the minimum number of evolutionary changes and is the most popular optimality criterion. If there were no evolutionary reversals and no repeated evolution of the same character state (i.e., no homoplasy), then the length of the cladogram would be just the sum of the number of possible character-state changes over all characters. For example, with 20 binary characters, the tree length would be 20. This would be the most parsimonious solution. In real data, homoplasy is common, and true homology is not easy to evaluate.

A cladogram may be rooted or not. *Rooting* is done by including an outgroup in the analysis or by determining the ancestral state for each character. The latter is also called *polarizing*. Each character can be ordered or unordered, though this distinction is irrelevant for binary characters. Among unordered characters, any state can be reached from any other; in the case of ordered characters, a sequence is specified.

From a computational point of view, finding the most parsimonious cladogram is a time-consuming procedure, as the number of possible solutions grows exponentially with the number of taxa studied. In order to find the most parsimonious cladogram (i.e., the shortest tree), and know that you have it, the only rigorous solution for n taxa is to form all possible trees. The number of such rooted cladograms or trees is the product of the first n-2 odd integers greater than 1 (assuming only dichotomous branching and not allowing any of the taxa to occupy internal segments). For three taxa there are three possible cladograms, for four there are 3x5 = 15, and for 10 taxa there are 3x5x7x9x11x13x15x17 = 34,459,425 different possible trees. By 20 OTUs (operational taxonomic units) the number is truly astronomical—already near or beyond the capacity of the largest and fastest computers now available.

Algorithms, series of computational steps, that produce the least amount of homoplasy are either *exact* or *heuristic*. Current exact algorithms examine all possible solutions in a systematic way, or use a branch-and-bound strategy to find the shortest tree. This latter technique finds the length of a random tree and stops searching or prunes long sequences that produce longer solutions. Both of these approaches are too time consuming for all but the best-behaved data sets. Rules of thumb called *heuristic algorithms* search using what are called *hill-climbing techniques* but may only find local optima. *Branch swapping* attempts to exhaust the possibilities for reaching a true optimum. There may be many equally shortest trees, and suboptimal trees may be of interest. *Consensus trees* find the common parts of the solutions among equally short trees. *Bootstrap techniques* are sampling schemes that attempt to find confidence intervals for parts of the tree.

The length of a tree is the measure of its optimality. *Consistency indices* (ci) and *retention indices* (ri) indicate the amount of homoplasy for each character. ci is the minimum amount of possible change for a character divided by its actual change—which may range from greater than 0 to 1. ri ranges from 0 to 1 and depends as well on the maximum number of possible steps. Since the methods assume that characters evolve independently, overall indices may be computed as well by summing over the index for all characters.

Characters may be weighted in the analysis. In cladistics involving nucleotide-sequence data, for example, transitions (A to G, or C to T) are sometimes weighted less than transversions (other possible changes) since they are deemed less probable.

Character Compatibility Analysis

Compatibility analysis is another computational way to form cladograms. It looks for cliques of characters—the largest group of characters for a set of taxa—so that each character state arises only once. In other words, the method finds a set of characters for which there is no homoplasy over the taxa. Because characters showing homoplasy are discarded, the method has been criticized by users of parsimony methods. However, there are algorithms that, after finding the largest clique over all taxa, then find additional character compatibilities among those earlier discarded characters for smaller monophyletic groups or branches within the cladogram. There is some debate as to whether parsimony methods or compatibility-analysis methods are the algorithms that best reflect W. Hennig's original nonnumerical methodology.

Maximum-Likelihood Cladistics

J. Felsenstein has employed *maximum-likelihood methods* for estimating trees or cladograms. This method requires a probabilistic model for the evolutionary process and explicit assumptions about rates of evolution in the branches. It has been worked out only for the neutral or random walk model. Using standard statistical maximum-likelihood theory, one finds the tree-branching pattern and branch lengths that maximize the likelihood function. This function is computed over all possible trees to find the maximum-likelihood estimate. The computational task is very heavy. Maximum likelihood programs are available in the program package PHYLIP.

The strongest attraction of maximum-likelihood methods is that they take a statistical approach to estimating phylogenies. In addition, the method is quite general, as it can explicitly yield a parsimony solution and a maximum-clique solution as two extreme answers if appropriate statistical assumptions are made about rates of evolution. Some numerical taxonomic algorithms, if they are used to construct phylogenies, may also be viewed as maximum-likelihood methods when appropriate assumptions are made. However, maximum parsimony has been the most widely used procedure. Maximum-likelihood methods have been used most commonly by those who deal with allelic and molecular data.

Computer software for cladistic analysis is available from many sources. Among the most widely used software packages are PHYLIP, Hennig86, MacClade, and PAUP. The latter three are parsimony-based procedures, while PHYLIP includes all of the optimality criteria mentioned above. Hennig86 runs on an IBM PC or clones; MacClade and PAUP, on the Macintosh; and PHYLIP is platform independent.

See also Cladistics. [L.M.]

Further Readings

Felsenstein, J. (1988) Phylogenies and quantitative methods. Ann. Rev. Ecol. Syst. 19:445–71.

Maddison, W.P., and Maddison, D.R. (1992) MacClade: Analysis of Phylogeny and Character Evolution. Sunderland, Mass.: Sinauer.

Swofford, D.L., and Olsen, G.J. (1993) Phylogeny reconstruction. In W.D. Hillis and C. Moritz (eds.): Molecular Systematics. Sunderland, Mass.: Sinauer, pp. 411–525.

Numerical Taxonomy

Grouping of taxonomic units based on a numerical measure of (phenetic) similarity. Character states are coded as present or absent (coded 0 or 1), in rank orders, or as measurements on a continuous scale. Relationships are frequently presented in the form of a tree diagram, or *dendrogram.*

See also Cladistics; Numerical Cladistics; Phenetics; Quantitative Methods. [L.M.]

Oakley, Kenneth Page (1911–1981)

British geologist and paleontologist. On graduating from University College, London, in 1933, Oakley went to work as a geologist with the British Geological Survey. Two years later, he joined the Department of Palaeontology of the British Museum (Natural History), where he spent the rest of his career. As a result of his former connection with the Geological Survey, Oakley developed a consuming interest in vertebrate paleontology, especially paleoanthropology. He later acquired an international reputation for his work on analytical methods of dating bones, particularly the technique of fluorine dating. The application of this technique to bones in the Piltdown faunal assemblage contributed to the eventual exposure of the forgery, and it was also used to demonstrate that the Galley Hill and Bury St. Edmunds crania were not of Middle Pleistocene age as previously contended. Oakley produced a number of popular and technical books, including *Man the Toolmaker* (1949) and *Frameworks for Dating Fossil Man* (1964).

See also Geochronometry; Piltdown. [F.S.]

Obsidian Hydration

Obsidian—volcanic glass—has long been an important raw material for the manufacture of tools. Obsidian artifacts are found in archaeological sites on every continent except Australia and one day may rival ceramics as archaeology's most useful time marker.

Two geologists, I. Friedman and R. Smith, first began exploring this potential in 1948. Obsidian is a fairly dry rock, containing only ca. 0.2 percent water. But when a piece of obsidian is fractured, the fresh surface is exposed to the environment and absorbs water. The absorption, or *hydration*, process continues until the point of saturation, ca. 3.5 percent water. These zones, or rims, of hydration are denser than the unhydrated inside and have different optical properties. Whenever obsidian is broken, the hydration process begins anew. Friedman and Smith reasoned that the degree of hydration observed on an archaeological artifact could

measure how long it had been since that surface was created by the flintknapper. The principle behind obsidian-hydration dating is simple: The longer the artifact surface has been exposed, the thicker the hydration band will be. By making certain that the datable surfaces were only those exposed by deliberate flintknapping, obsidian hydration can be taken as a direct indicator of age.

Obsidian-hydration dating remains relatively simple, rapid, and cheap: Ten obsidian hydration dates may be run for the cost of a single radiocarbon determination. But obsidian dating is not without problems because the rate of hydration is not uniform throughout the world. Of the several variables that appear to influence the hydration rate, atmospheric temperature seemed to be paramount. Once a sufficient number of global samples were analyzed, Friedman and Smith constructed a world map describing the correlation between climate and hydration rates.

The geological source (and, hence, rate of hydration) remains another major factor in determining hydration rate. There are other lingering problems, such as artifact reuse, short-term temperature fluctuations, and variable amounts of available moisture. But as long as the restrictions are kept in mind, obsidian hydration provides a useful technique for dating archaeological sites.

See also Geochronometry. [D.H.T.]

Old Crow

Archaeological locality in the northern Yukon (Canada) that has yielded a series of bone tools thought to predate Clovis in antiquity. A bone apatite radiocarbon determination on a distinctive flesher provided an age of 27 Ka. But bone collagen from this artifact, recently redated by the accelerator-based radiocarbon method, provides a fairly modern age estimate (1.4 Ka). Significant questions linger regarding the age of this artifact and of the Old Crow bone assemblages in general.

See also Americas; Bone Tools; Paleoindian. [L.S.A.P., D.H.T.]

Oldowan

Oldest formally recognized set of stone-artifact assemblages of the Early Paleolithic. This lithic industry, or industrial complex, was defined on the basis of artifact assemblages from Bed I and lower Bed II at Olduvai Gorge (Tanzania), dating to ca. 1.9–1.6 Ma. It is characterized by pieces of stone (e.g., choppers, scrapers) modified by simple stone-on-stone chipping and the flakes detached by this process, thus a Mode 1 technology. As originally defined, the Oldowan is confined possibly to eastern Africa, although similar industries of simply modified stone cores and flakes dated to more than 1.0 Ma occur from northern to southern Africa. The term *Oldowan* has generally not been applied to stone assemblages outside of Africa. Assemblages of simple tools/cores and flakes, however, are found at archaeological sites from the Early and Middle Pleistocene in Asia and Europe. Some Oldowan-type artifacts, especially choppers, also occur in stone-tool assemblages up to the present. Because several hominin species occur at sites yielding Oldowan assemblages (or of similar age), there is some question as to who made these tools. Most paleoanthropologists consider that *Homo habilis,* which first appears in the fossil record at about the same time as the earliest Oldowan tools or slightly later, was probably the toolmaker.

Rocks modified by deliberate flaking, referred to as *tools* or *cores,* which characterize the Oldowan, are classified into several types: choppers, discoids, polyhedrons, scrapers, spheroids and subspheroids, burins, and protobifaces. Oldowan choppers are further divided into subtypes based on the relationship of the chipped edge to the original shape of the stone. Modification is often simple enough to identify the size and shape of the original stone as well. The Oldowan is also characterized by utilized material, such as battered hammerstones and anvils, and flakes with chipped edges thought to connote use; unmodified flakes, or débitage, which represent sharp-edged products detached from the large, chipped pieces; and manuports, or unmodified cobbles and other rocks that have been brought to a site by early humans. Based on spatially confined assemblages of these chipped rocks and related utilized and unutilized pieces, Oldowan archaeological sites are distinguished from natural occurrences of broken rocks by patterns of repeated flaking, and conchoidal fracture, evidenced by the tools/cores; and geologic contexts in which naturally transported and broken rocks do not occur.

Although defined on the basis of entire assemblages of artifacts, the usual predominance of choppers, in particular, and the absence of certain other types of chipped rock, such as bifaces, distinguish the Oldowan from related stone industries. At Olduvai, choppers represent from 28 to 79 percent of the tools/cores in Oldowan assemblages. Choppers made from rounded cobbles also typify the Pebble Culture assemblages of Morocco and Tunisia; however, choppers and other tool/core types of the Oldowan are made from varied shapes of raw material—angular lumps (e.g., quartzite) and irregular nodules (e.g., chert) in addition to water-worn cobbles. The KBS industry from Koobi Fora, ca. 1.9 Ma, is similar to the Oldowan in that it contains simply chipped pieces and flakes. Although some characteristic tool/core forms of

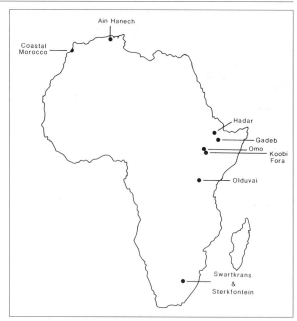

Map of some important Oldowan and Developed Oldowan sites in Africa.

the Oldowan, such as small scrapers, spheroids, and subspheroids, are rare in the KBS industry, the latter is considered to be part of the Oldowan. The younger Karari industry at Koobi Fora is also similar to the Oldowan, but the presence of large core scrapers distinguishes it from the Oldowan and other early stone industries. Bifaces are rare in the Karari artifact assemblages; their presence suggests an affinity with the Developed Oldowan.

Stone assemblages known from Ethiopia, Zaire, Kenya, and Malawi, as well as possibly South Africa, date to more than 2 Ma and may also be covered by the term *Oldowan.* Not all scholars would agree, however. Recently, H. Roche has suggested that these industries do not reflect the same conceptualization of the core and flakes to be removed from it that later Oldowan industries do, and she has proposed placing them in a *pre-Oldowan* category. Some of these earliest artifacts were apparently created by striking the core on an anvil and selecting useful flakes from the resultant shatter. Others reflect a more sophisticated flaking technology as at Lokalalei (Kenya).

The Developed Oldowan is an industry also defined at Olduvai. It is characterized by a poorer representation of choppers (less than 28 percent of all tools/cores) and a greater abundance of spheroids, subspheroids, and small scrapers. Bifaces also appear for the first time in the Olduvai sequence in the Developed Oldowan assemblages, which are prevalent from middle Bed II (ca. 1.6 Ma) through Beds III/IV (ca. 0.7 Ma). According to some researchers, bifaces, like handaxes and cleavers, indicate that the Developed Oldowan is part of the Acheulean industrial complex. M.D. Leakey maintained, however, that the Developed Oldowan is a tradition of tool manufacture continuous with the Oldowan and that both are characterized by the production of small (less than 10 cm) flakes, in contrast with the Acheulean.

All pieces modified by flaking in the Oldowan, as defined by Leakey, are referred to as *tools,* and the unmodified

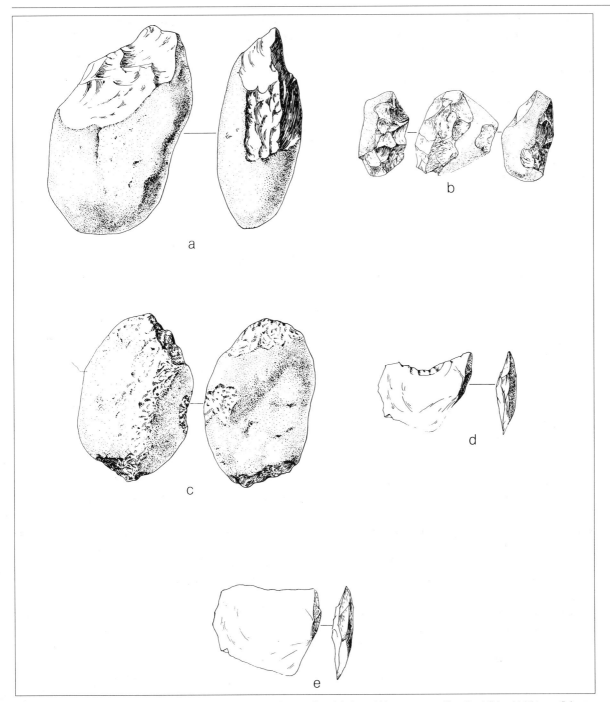

Typical artifacts from Oldowan assemblages at Olduvai Gorge: (a) chopper; (b) polyhedron; (c) hammerstone; (d) utilized flake; (e) débitage *flake.*

flakes are considered to be waste products. Nevertheless, other researchers have suggested that the flaked stones may represent mainly *cores* (i.e., by-products of manufacturing sharp flakes useful as implements). Indeed, studies of microscopic wear on the edges of siliceous stone tools from Koobi Fora (KBS and Karari industries) show that unretouched flakes were used for cutting plant and animal material. Oldowan assemblages at Olduvai are all associated with fossil animal bones, some of which bear cutmarks made by stone tools. Oldowan technology largely entailed making sharp-edged flakes and flaked pieces, many of which exhibit slight damage to the edges visible to the eye. Thus, Oldowan stone technology was devoted largely to production of cutting im-

plements. The presence of subspheroids, hammerstones, and anvils, though, also implies that implements were available for smashing or crushing functions. In fact, many of the major limb bones of animals on Oldowan sites show signs that the diaphyses were broken open, as people today do by pounding such bones in the middle to obtain marrow.

The Oldowan in East Africa persisted for at least 0.5 Myr with little evidence of change in artifact morphology or techniques of manufacture. This long stability in technology contrasts with heterogeneity in technology and artifact assemblages in time and space over the past 30 Kyr. Interpretations of "culture" implied by Oldowan toolmaking must incorporate ideas about conservatism and stability in behavior that are not evident over such long periods of time in the cultural behavior of modern humans.

See also Acheulean; Africa; Early Paleolithic; Homo habilis; Karari; Modes, Technological; Olduval Gorge; Paleolithic Lifeways; Stone-Tool Making. [R.P.]

Further Readings

Isaac, G.L. (1984) The archaeology of human origins. Adv. World Archaeol. 3:1–87.

Keeley, L., and Toth, N. (1981) Microwear polishes on early stone tools from Koobi Fora, Kenya. Nature 293:464–465.

Leakey, M.D. (1966) A review of the Oldowan culture from Olduvai Gorge, Tanzania. Nature 210:462–466.

Leakey, M.D., ed. (1971) Olduvai Gorge, Vol. 3. Cambridge: Cambridge University Press.

Potts, R., and Shipman, P. (1981) Cutmarks made by stone tools on bones from Olduvai Gorge, Tanzania. Nature 291:577–580.

Roche, H., Delagnes, A., Brugal, J.-P., Feibel, C., Kibunjia, M., Mourre, V. and Jexier, P.-J. (1999) Early hominid stone-tool production and technical skill. 2.34 Myr ago in West Turkana, Kenya. Nature 399:57–60.

Olduvai Gorge

Dry canyon in northern Tanzania exposing a sequence of Upper Pliocene to Upper Pleistocene strata, dated between 1.9 and ca. 0.01 Ma by radiometric, paleomagnetic, and faunal analyses. This famous site is a 25-km-long gash in the eastern edge of the Serengeti Plain where it drains to the Ol Balbal Depression at the foot of the Ngorongoro Caldera, with a 50-km tributary, the Side Gorge, extending far to the south.

Shaped in the form of the letter Y, Olduvai Gorge was first mentioned in 1911 by the German entomologist Kattwinkel, who noted the presence of fossils. Serious geological and paleontological research at Olduvai began in 1913 under German volcanologist and paleontologist H. Reck, who found that the most important geological, paleontological, and archaeological localities occur in the area where the Side Gorge joins the main canyon. Reck developed the basic stratigraphic nomenclature of Olduvai Gorge, which divides the ca. 100 m of section into Beds I, II, III and IV, from bottom to top. Reck's first expedition to Olduvai recovered a human skeleton numbered Olduvai Hominid One (OH 1) together with many extinct mammals from Bed II, but World War I brought this project to an end. Exploration resumed in 1931 when L.S.B. Leakey organized an expedition with Reck's guidance. Leakey recognized stone tools in the Olduvai sediments and initially accepted Reck's claims about the antiquity of the OH 1 skeleton, but he revised this interpretation after subsequent work showed that the skeleton was a relatively recent burial.

In 1935, Leakey led another expedition to Olduvai that recovered two human parietal fragments among large numbers of fossils and artifacts. This and subsequent expeditions were mostly devoted to surface survey of the gorge, but trial excavations had begun as early as 1931. Individual sites were identified according to the *korongo*, or gully, in which they were found.

Thus, FLK sites refer to "Frieda Leakey Korongo," named after Leakey's first wife. Work in this gully and others such as BK, SHK, DK, and HWK yielded many artifacts and fossils.

Large-scale excavations began in the 1950s in the Side Gorge. Thousands of artifacts and fossils were recovered, but hominin remains were elusive, and only isolated teeth were found. Finally, in 1959, M.D. Leakey discovered the cranium of a fossil hominin that was eroding from Bed I at FLK. This specimen featured enormous molars, molarized premolars, a small braincase, a flat face, and a large, anteriorly placed sagittal crest. In these and other regards, it resembled robust *Australopithecus* specimens from southern Africa. L.S.B. Leakey, however, was convinced that he had found Olduvai's toolmaker, a direct human ancestor. He first informally suggested the name "Titanohomo mirabilis" but later described the specimen formally under the binomen *Zinjanthropus boisei*. Today this specimen, OH 5, is often referred to as "Zinj," but, according to most scholars, the species *boisei* is better placed in the genus *Australopithecus* (or in this encyclopedia, *Paranthropus*).

The discovery of the Zinj cranium heralded the beginning of modern paleoanthropological research in eastern Africa, with interest centered on Olduvai until the late 1960s, when attention shifted to the Turkana Basin (Kenya-Ethiopia border) and the Afar (Ethiopia). Dating of volcanic rocks and tuffs interbedded with the fossil beds in the lowest levels exposed in Olduvai Gorge gave an age and a name to a geomagnetic-polarity interval that had previously been observed in volcanics of Germany and Czechoslovakia. With substantial financial support from the National Geographic Society, many new sites were opened. One of these, FLKNN in Bed I, yielded the remains (OH 7) of a second type of Early Pleistocene hominid, which Leakey and his colleagues P.V. Tobias and J. Napier named *Homo habilis* in 1964. With the recovery of *H. habilis*, Leakey changed his mind about "Zinjanthropus," relegating it to a side branch of human evolution. The original diagnosis of *H. habilis*, was based on fragmentary, partly immature material, and the species distinction was initially questioned by many anthropologists.

During the deposition of Bed I, the Olduvai region was characterized by a shallow, alkaline lake ca. 25 km across. Along the southeastern lakeshore, streams that arose from nearby volcanic highlands brought fresh water into the ancient Olduvai lake. The fossiliferous middle-to-upper Bed I sediments were laid down between 1.9 and 1.7 Ma in this lake and in the stream valleys that contributed to it. This deposition continued into the lower part of Bed II but was disrupted at ca. 1.6 Ma when faulting altered the topography of the basin, reducing the size of the lake. During Bed I and lower Bed II times, human occupation sites were clustered along the southeastern lake margin, as evidenced by an abundance of broken stones and bones, sometimes associated with the remains of humans themselves. These concentrations were at first thought to represent living floors, home bases, or campsites of early hominids, but interpretation of these sites became a controversial question for archaeologists in the 1980s.

The thick sequence Bed IV (sometimes subdivided as IVa and IVb or, more recently, into into four units) is suc-

View of the Olduvai Gorge with the Lemagrut volcano in the background. Photograph by and courtesy of Tim D. White.

ceeded by the Masek Beds, the Ndutu Beds (upper and lower), and the Naisiusu Beds. In some parts of the gorge, the red Bed III sediments cannot be easily separated from those of the overlying Bed IV. Bed III was initially interpolated to lie between 1.2 and 0.83 Ma, and Bed IV from 0.83 to 0.62 Ma, because the Brunhes/Matuyama paleomagnetic reversal, then dated at 0.73 Ma, was interpreted within Bed IV. The Masek Beds were thus placed between 0.62 and 0.4 Ma, the Lower Ndutu Beds between 400 and 75 Ka, the Upper Ndutu Beds between 75 and 40 Ka, and the Naisiusu Beds (above an unconformity) between 20 and 15 Ka. In the early 1990s reevaluation of the geochronometry at Olduvai Gorge has increased the age of the lowermost portion of Bed I, as well as Beds II, III, and IV. The upper part of Bed II is now dated to ca. 1.48 Ma, and the lower part of Bed III to ca. 1.33 Ma. Layers with a normal paleomagnetic polarity at the base of the Masek Beds are provisionally identified with the Jaramillo Subchron (1.07–0.99 Ma), although the Brunhes/Matuyama reversal (0.78 Ma), or even the Cobb Mountain Subchron (ca. 1.19 Ma) cannot be ruled out (see Table).

Remains of both *P. boisei* and *H. habilis* have been found in association with archaeological material in Olduvai Bed I. The tools themselves belong to the Oldowan industrial complex, dominated by crude cores, battered hammerstones, and many flakes. Although these artifacts were initially classified according to a detailed typology, it seems likely, based on the experimental work of American archaeologist N. Toth in the 1980s, that they are all related to the simple function of striking a core with a hammerstone to obtain sharp-edged flakes. The presence of foreign, imported stone clasts and crude tools made of fine-grained lavas, quartzite, and quartz in the clays and silts of Olduvai's lake-margin environments shows that humans carried stone there. Hammerstone-impact scars and cutmarks made by stone tools striking the bones of animals such as antelope have been recovered from Olduvai Bed I sites, leading some archaeologists to attribute the faunal remains to hunting behavior and central-place foraging. Some of the animal remains also show evidence of carnivore modification, leading other archaeologists to hypothesize that the animal remains were scavenged by the hominins from predator kills.

Human remains in Olduvai's upper Bed II, Bed III, and Bed IV have been attributed to *Homo erectus*. They include postcranial remains as well as the important OH 9 *H. erectus* cranial specimen, first called "Chellean Man" because of the abundant "Chellean" (now Acheulean) artifacts in the upper part of the Olduvai geological succession. The first appearance of large numbers of handaxes at Olduvai comes in the upper half of Bed II, perhaps ca. 1.6–1.5 Ma. Some sites feature high percentages of these bifacial tools, whereas other sites feature only core and flake tools similar to those found exclusively in Bed I. Human activity in Bed III and Bed IV times was largely confined to a main river system and tributary streams that flowed from the west into the basin. Therefore, much of the Acheulean and Developed Oldowan material was entombed in a disturbed archaeological context, unlike the well-preserved, more intact sites in Bed I.

By 1997, a total of 60 hominin specimens had been recovered from the Olduvai Gorge. Ca. 30 percent of these came from excavations, and the others were found on the

Age	P/M	Unit	m above base	Tuffs	Hominins	Archaeology
0.01*		(erosion)			OH 1 burial	LSA
		NAISIUSIU >10m thick				
		-------------------------- 110				
>0.03*		Upper				MSA
		NDUTU............... 99			OH 11, DK	MSA
		Lower				
~0.37+		-------------------------- 94				
	r	Norkilili Member			OH 23 FLK	Acheulean FLK
		MASEK 90			(in channel)	
[0.99]	N	Beds				
	N	Lower unit				
[1.07]	N	-------------------------- 80				Acheulean WK
	r	Bed IV 77		IVB		
	r	75		Tuff 4	OH 12? VEK	Acheulean HEB
~1.2	r	....			OH 28 WK	
	r					
	r	Bed III 70		Tuff 2		Dev.Oldowan? JK
1.33	r	-------------------------- 68		Tuff 1		
	r	Upper Bed II 66			OH 9 LLK	Acheulean,Dev.OldowanLLK
1.48	r			II-D		
~1.52	r	....		II-C		
	r	upper		up augitic ss		Acheulean EF-HR
	r	Middle Bed II		II-B	OH 13 MNK	Oldowan MNK
~1.65	r	....................lower...		lo augitic ss		
1.66	r	Lemuta Mb. 57		II-A		
~1.73	r	 55			OH 16 FLK-N	Oldowan FLK-N
[1.78]	N	Lower Bed II				
~1.8	N	-------------------------- 52				
1.75	N	51		I-F		
1.75	N	47		I-E		
1.76	N	Upper Bed I 38		I-D		
	N					
1.76	N	30		I-C		
	N				OH 62, OH 5	Oldowan FLK
	N				OH 7, 8 FLK	
1.80	N	21		I-B		Oldowan
	N	19			OH 24 DK-E	Oldowan DK-E
1.87	N	......Lava flow..........				
1.98	N	Lower Bed I 13		I-A		
[1.95]						
2.03	r	basal unit		Basal tuff		

Composite stratigraphic chart of Olduvai Gorge, compiled from several sources, especially Hay (1976, 1990), Tamrat et al. (1995) and Walter et al. (1991), with several dates from W. Kimbel (1997) in E.S. Vrba et al., eds. Paleoclimate and Evolution, with Emphasis on Human Origins, Yale University Press. The age column includes radiocarbon (*) and argon dates, as well as paleomagnetic correlations (in [ ]) derived from the paleomagnetism (P/M) column (N = normal, R = reversed polarity). Amino-acid racemization "dates" on bone between 60 and 30 Ka were reported for the upper unit of the Ndutu Beds, and ca. 20 Ka for the Naisiusiu, but such dates are now questioned (see AMINO ACID DATING). An argon date of 370 Ka has been obtained from nearby Kerimasi, probable source of the Masek Beds. An alternative interpretation of the normal polarity zone within the Masek Beds correlates this region to the lower Brunhes below the rarely observed Emperor reversed subchron dated ca. 0.49 Ma (which would thus be represented by the single reversed sample within the Norkilili member). This interpretation fits better with the Kerimasi date but depends on recognition of the questionable Emperor subchron and results in the extension of Beds III–IV to about the end of the Matuyama at 0.78 Ma. Geologic units column includes major formations (mostly "beds") and members, with approximate thickness as meters above base of idealized section; major tuffs are in separate column. Human fossils (OH = Olduvai hominid numbers) and archaeological residues (Old = Oldowan; Ach, Acheul = Acheulean) listed with abbreviated sites (FLK, EF-HR) in italics. Chart by E. Delson and J.A. Van Couvering.

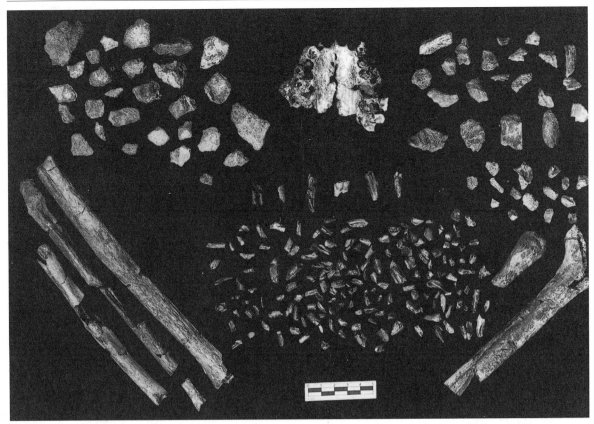

The OH 62 partial skeleton of Homo habilis *from Bed I, Olduvai Gorge. Arm bones to the left, leg bones to the right, cranial pieces and palate on the top, tooth fragments in the center. Photograph by and courtesy of Tim D. White.*

surface. In 1986, a very fragmented partial skeleton of a tiny adult individual (OH 62) was found in Bed I. This specimen, with a body size approximately the same as the much more ancient "Lucy" specimen from Hadar (Ethiopia), rekindled debate about the evolutionary and taxonomic status of *H. habilis.*

See also Acheulean; Africa; Africa, East; Homo erectus; Homo habilis; Leakey, Louis Seymour Bazett; Leakey, Mary Douglas; Natron-Eyasi Basin; Oldowan; Paleomagnetism; Paranthropus boisei. [T.D.W.]

Further Readings

Hay, R.L. (1976) Geology of the Olduvai Gorge. Los Angeles: University of California Press.

Hay, R.L. (1990) Olduvai Gorge: A case history in the interpretation of hominid paleoenvironments in East Africa. In L.F. LaPorte (ed.): Establishment of a Geologic Framework for Paleoanthropology. Boulder: Geological Society of America, pp. 23–37.

Leakey, M.D., ed. (1971) Olduvai Gorge, Vol. 3. London: Cambridge University Press.

Leakey, M.D. (1984) Disclosing the Past. New York: Doubleday.

Reader, J. (1981) Missing Links. Boston: Little, Brown.

Tamrat, E., Thouveny, N., Taieb, M., and Opdyke, N.D. (1995) Revised magnetostratigraphy of the Plio-Pleistocene sedimentary sequence of the Olduvai Formation (Tanzania). Palaeogeog., Palaeoclimatol., Palaeoecol. 114:273–283.

Toth, N. (1985) The Oldowan reassessed: A close look at early stone artifacts. J. Archeol. Sci. 12:101–120.

Toth, N. (1987) Behavioral references from early stone artifact assemblages: An experimental model. J. Hum. Evol. 16:763–787.

Walter, R.C., Manega, P.C., Hay, R.L., Drake, R.E., and Curtis, G.H. (1991) Laser-fusion ^{40}Ar/^{39}Ar dating of Bed 1, Olduvai Gorge, Tanzania. Nature 354:145–149.

Oligocene

Middle Cenozoic epoch, beginning at ca. 34 Ma following the Eocene and ending at 23.5 Ma with the onset of the Miocene. The Oligocene is divided into two global stages or ages, the Rupelian and the Chattian, which are typified in shallow marine sequences in the North German Plain. The internationally agreed GSSP (global stratotype section and point) that defines the base of the Oligocene has been designated at Massignano, near Ancona, Italy, at a level where deep-sea microfossils offer better control than in the German sections. The Massignano boundary coincides with the boundary between planktonic foraminiferal zones P17 and P18 and is within calcareous nannofossil zone CP16a and paleomagnetic-polarity reversal 13R1.

No formations of Oligocene age were included in Charles Lyell's review of European stratigraphy when he formulated the Eocene and the Miocene in 1833, and, in fact, he used the great difference between the fossils of these two epochs as a useful demonstration of a hitherto unappreciated vastness of geological time. Lyell was, therefore, unfriendly to the concept of an Oligocene epoch when August Beyrich proposed it in 1854, and held that the northern molluscan faunas of Germany could not be matched against the sub-tropical assemblages of France and Italy on which Eocene and Miocene were based. Correlating the Oligocene re-mained a problem until it was put to rest with the aid of planktonic microfossils. These showed that the Priabonian Stage of the Mediterranean Basin, which had been consid-ered to define the Lower Oligocene in that region and in the standard deep-sea zonation as well, was actually equivalent to the Lattorfian Stage of North Germany, which underlies the Rupelian. Because the original Oligocene begins with the Rupelian, the Priabonian had to be added to the concept of the Eocene, with the effect of shifting the Eocene/Oligocene boundary younger by ca. 4 Myr in most parts of the world. It also brought the marine boundary more into coincidence with the evidence from vertebrate paleontology in Europe and North America, which had been independently corre-lated to the German stages.

The most significant consequence to paleoanthropol-ogy arising from the realignment of the base of the Oligo-cene in the Tethys was to call into doubt the long-standing assignment of the Fayum primates to the Early and Middle Oligocene, an age assignment made originally on the basis that the Fayum Beds are apparently equivalent to the Pri-abonian. The matter is not yet resolved—preliminary paleo-magnetic evidence has been cited for basal Oligocene age of the upper Fayum levels—but all would agree that the Fayum primates must be considered to be significantly older than the platyrrhine *Branisella,* the earliest record of primates in South America dated from the Late Oligocene at ca. 26 Ma. The new alignment of the boundary also emphasizes that the spe-cialized and flourishing African forms were already strongly isolated from the contemporaneous, and declining, Late Eocene "prosimian" lineages in the northern continents.

The record of Old World Oligocene primates is almost unknown, if the upper Fayum levels are excluded. The Eurasian primate faunas only barely survived the climate changes at the end of the Eocene, with rare *Adapis* known in Germany and England. However, the presence of what may be derived adapiforms, *Sinoadapis, Sivaladapis,* and perhaps *Indraloris,* in the Miocene of eastern Asia suggests that isolated populations may have persisted in that region. Material that has been assigned to several Fayum genera as well as the unique adapiforms *Shizarodon* and *Omanodon* is reported (possibly reworked) from basal Oligocene marine deposits in Oman. At the end of the Oligocene, the earliest proconsulid, *Kamoya-pithecus,* occurs in strata dated to ca. 26 Ma in northern Kenya.

A few omomyid relicts must have lived on through the Oligocene in North America. *Rooneyia* comes from the Chambers Tuff of west Texas with an age of ca. 37.5 Ma, which must now be considered latest middle Eocene (and the adapiform *Mahgarita* is of equivalent age). *Macrotarsius* is found in a Late Eocene Chadronian horizon in Montana with an age between 36 and 34 Ma. Only the last North American

nonhuman primate, *Ekgmowechashala,* occurs in uppermost Oligocene, lower Arikareean beds in South Dakota dated to ca. 25 Ma, and in rocks of similar age from Oregon.

See also Cenozoic; Eocene; Fayum; Grande Coupure; Miocene; Oman. [J.A.V.C.]

Further Readings

Premoli Silva, I., and Jenkins, D.G. (1993) Decision on the Eocene-Oligocene boundary stratotype. Episodes 16:379–382.

Prothero, D.R. (1995) The Eocene-Oligocene Transition: Paradise Lost. New York: Columbia University Press.

Prothero, D.R., and Berggren, W.A., eds. (1992) Eocene-Oligocene Climatic and Biotic Evolution. Princeton: Princeton University Press.

Oligopithecidae

An extinct group of African (and East Asian?) archaic an-thropoid primates. Raised recently to the status of a family, oligopithecids are found principally in rocks of Late Eocene age in the Fayum Province (Egypt) in an area of badlands at the eastern edge of the Sahara Desert. Other fragmentary remains of oligopithecids come from Oman and possibly China and Thailand. Here, Oligopithecidae includes two moderately well known genera and species: *Oligopithecus savagei* and *Catopithecus browni,* as well as up to three less well understood species.

History of Study

The first recovered oligopithecid was *Oligopithecus savagei.* A single mandible was found in the Fayum at Quarry E in the Jebel Qatrani Formation by D. Savage in 1961 and de-scribed the same year by E.L. Simons, who immediately rec-ognized its anthropoid status. Because an Early Oligocene age was generally accepted for the Fayum fossil deposits at that time, he called it "Oligocene ape." A few teeth of *Oligopithecus* were recovered from Quarry E in the early 1980s.

These specimens were difficult to relate to modern pri-mates and remained of uncertain evolutionary relationship for 30 years following Simons's description of the single mandible. Simons's view was that, because of its dental for-mula (two rather than three lower premolars), *Oligopithecus* was an early catarrhine allied to *Aegyptopithecus* and *Proplio-pithecus* occuring at higher levels in the Fayum. Others were more impressed by the remarkably primitive structure of the molar teeth, especially the paraconids, high trigonids, and small hypoconulids, and thought that *Oligopithecus* might be the sister group to living catarrhines or even to living anthro-poids as a whole. A few workers even questioned whether *Oligopithecus* might belong with a poorly known European Eocene adapid group, the cercamoniines, and represent a linking form between anthropoids and the latter group.

In 1990, Simons described a closely related but older Fayum oligopithecid, *Catopithecus browni,* based on a com-plete skull. The skull has cleared up some of the debate about oligopithecids by showing that it was clearly at a monkey

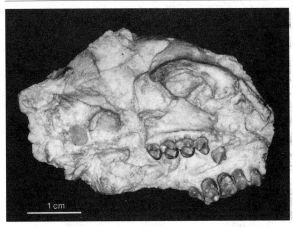

Right oblique infero-lateral view of crushed cranium of Catopithecus browni. *Scale bar 1 cm.*

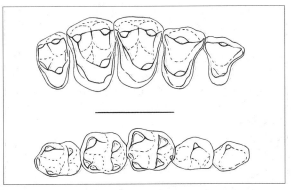

Occlusal view of upper right (above) and lower left P3-M3 of Catopithecus browni. *Scale bar = 5 mm. By C. Tarka, after Simons and Rasmussen, 1996, and photographs by E. Delson.*

Occlusal view of lower left C1-M2 of Oligopithecus savagei. *Compare with drawing above.*

grade of cranial organization, but scientists remain divided about its precise place in anthropoid phylogeny. Another possible oligopithecid, *Proteopithecus sylviae*, was at first referred to this family but is no longer believed to be so since it has three rather than two premolars, as first thought, and shares derived features with some more advanced anthropoids. Also in the 1990s, a French team described some fragmentary material of *Oligopithecus* from the Sultanate of Oman.

Three Asian species might also be related to the Oligopithecidae. *Hoanghonius stehlini* from the Middle Eocene of China was first reported in 1930, while its neighbor *Rencunius zhoui*, and *Wailekia orientale* from the Late Eocene of Krabi, Thailand, were only discovered in the mid-1990s. All have dental features reminiscent of *Oligopithecus*, but this may be superficial, and an alternative possibility is that they are related to cercamoniines or other adapiformes.

Age of the Oligopithecids

Most oligopithecid fossils come from the lower levels of the Jebel Qatrani Formation, which conformably overlies the marine and fluvial Qasr el Sagha Formation of Late Eocene age (ca. 37 Ma). *Catopithecus browni* occurs in Quarry L-41 from the lowest part of the formation and (based on preliminary paleomagnetic calibrations) may date between ca. 35.9 and 35.6 Ma. *Oligopithecus savagei* is younger and could be nearer 35.1–34 Ma (latest Eocene). A few teeth of oligopithecids from Oman may be slightly younger, perhaps earliest Oligocene. The Asian fossils are even older, *Hoanghonius* and *Rencunius* dating to perhaps 45 Ma, while *Wailekia* may date to 40–35 Ma.

Oligopithecid Adaptations

The anatomy of the oligopithecids is based principally on the skull and teeth, with little (as of 1999) published about the postcranial skeleton. The cranium of *Catopithecus* was similar in size and shape to that of *Saimiri*, the living squirrel monkey from South and Central America. Known specimens document the closure of the rear of the orbit and the fusion of the frontal bones in the midline, two important characteristics of anthropoids. On the other hand, two par-

tial mandibles suggest that the mandibular symphysis was not fused.

Oligopithecids have cheek teeth with well-developed shearing crests but not as extreme in this respect as primarily folivorous or insectivorous living primates. It appears likely that oligopithecids had a diet consisting primarily of fruit but with an important component of insects, like living *Saimiri*. One interesting and distinctive feature of the lower molars is the close appression of the hypoconulid and entoconid.

From the size of the teeth and skull elements, oligopithecids were much smaller than any living catarrhine and within the size range of living New World monkeys (platyrrhines). The two genera seem to have been between 600 and 1,000 g, about the size of *Saimiri*. A distal humerus and proximal portions of a femur from the same quarry as *Catopithecus* may belong to that oligopithecid. These show several prosimianlike features, including a large third trochanter on the femur and a long capitular tail on the humerus. These bones suggest that *Catopithecus* was an arboreal climbing quadruped somewhat like squirrel monkeys.

The brain size of *Catopithecus* cannot be estimated directly because the skull is crushed. However, the temporal lines, produced by the muscles of mastication, converge quite far toward the front of the skull, and there was a sagittal crest. This suggests substantial postorbital constriction and a relatively smaller brain than in living monkeys. The suggestion that *Catopithecus* had a small brain should not be surprising since the Early Oligocene propliopithecid *Aegyptopithecus* also had a small brain for an anthropoid.

The relatively small size of the eye sockets of *Catopithecus* suggest that the animals were daytime active (diurnal), as are the living anthropoids, but distinct from many prosimians with relatively large eyes (and eye sockets) and nocturnal habits. In sum, probably the closest living ecological parallels to the oligopithecid primates are found in small- to medium-size South American monkeys.

Phyletic Status of Oligopithecidae

As noted above, when Simons first described *Oligopithecus*, he identified it as a catarrhine on the basis of its having two premolars resembling those of *Propliopithecus*. However, the subsequent recovery of abundant new remains and the skull of the new genus *Catopithecus* further highlights the morphological paradox that had been recognized from the fragmentary remains. The cranial and dental material of *Catopithecus* shows that oligopithecids had reached the anthropoid, or monkey, grade of organization. They resemble living anthropoids and are dissimilar to Holarctic Eocene primates or modern Madagascar lemurs in having an anthropoid configuration in bony-ear structure (the ectotympanic bone for the tympanic membrane is fused to the lateral edge of the bony middle ear box; it was ringlike as in *Aegyptopithecus*, parapithecids, and living platyrrhines, not tubular as in all extant catarrhines), a bony partition between the eye socket and the space behind it that houses the jaw muscles (postorbital closure), closely packed cheek teeth, spatulate incisors, and projecting canines. This advanced combination of characteristics has led all authorities to accept their status as anthropoids.

At the same time, the molar dentition of oligopithecids was seen by many as similar to European adapids, particularly cercamoniines. These morphological similarities have thus led some to argue that anthropoids are derived from a cercamoniine adapid. However, the fact that oligopithecids have been linked (by Simons) with catarrhines (in the family Propliopithecidae) on the one hand, and to adapids on the other, has again called into question the role of parapithecids in early anthropoid phylogeny. In short, if primitive anthropoids resembled primitive parapithecids, then the primitive anthropoid dentition was quite unlike that of cercamoniines. This would mean that the resemblances between oligopithecids and cercamoniines must be homoplasies.

A more difficult and unresolved question concerns oligopithecid relationships within Anthropoidea. Opinion is divided as to whether oligopithecids are more closely related to the Old World (catarrhine) anthropoids or are an earlier offshoot of the anthropoid tree. As above, much of this controversy revolves around acknowledged conflicts in the distribution of anatomical resemblance. Many similarities between oligopithecids and some other anthropoids (e.g., the ringlike ectotympanic shared by oligopithecids, propliopithecids, platyrrhines, and parapithecids) are acknowledged primitive holdovers from the last common ancestor of all anthropoids and do not indicate a special relationship with any one group of anthropoids.

Oligopithecids have several apparent derived similarities with catarrhines. For example, they resemble early catarrhines like *Propliopithecus* in having a reduced premolar number, with the upper canine wearing against the lower third premolar. On the other hand, oligopithecids lack important derived cheek-tooth morphology shared by catarrhines and platyr-

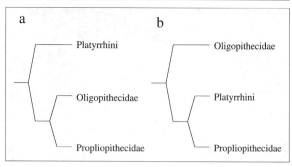

Conflicting views of the phylogenetic position of the oligopithecids. Courtesy of Richard F. Kay.

rhines (e.g., they still retain molar paraconids, and the P_4 and M_1 trigonids are still open; the upper premolars lack hypocones, and P^3 is still waisted). One or another of these sets of similarities must be homoplasies (evolutionary parallelisms), and the other set must be true homologies. The phylogenetic significance of this confusing set of apparent derived similarities can be cleared up only when we have more fossils documenting early anthropoid cladogenesis.

Oligopithecidae
   † *Oligopithecus*
   † *Catopithecus*
   ?† *Hoanghonius*
   ?† *Rencunius*
   ?† *Wailekia*
†extinct

See also Adapiformes; Anthropoidea; Fayum; Hoanghonius; Parapithecidae; Propliopithecidae; Skull. [R.F.K., E.D.]

Further Readings

Gebo, D.L., Simons, E.L., Rasmussen, D.T., and Dagosto, M. (1994) Eocene anthropoid postcrania from the Fayum, Egypt. In J.G. Fleagle and R.F. Kay (eds.): Anthropoid Origins. New York: Plenum, pp. 203–233.

Kay, R.F., and Williams, B.A. (1994) Dental evidence for anthropoid origins. In J.G. Fleagle and R.F. Kay (eds.): Anthropoid Origins. New York: Plenum, pp. 361–445.

Rasmussen, D.T., and Simons, E.L. (1988) New specimens of *Oligopithecus savagei*, Early Oligocene primate from the Fayum, Egypt. Folia Primatol. 51:182–208.

Rasmussen, D.T., and Simons, E.L. (1992) Paleobiology of the oligopithecines, the earliest known anthropoid primates. Int. J. Primatol. 13:477–508.

Simons, E.L. (1990) Discovery of the oldest known anthropoidean skull from the Paleogene of Egypt. Science 247:1567–1569.

Simons, E.L. and Rasmussen, D.T. (1996) Skull of *Catopitherus browni*, an early Tertiary catarrhine. Am. J. Phys. Anthropol. 100:261–292.

Simons, E.L., Rasmussen, D.T., Bown, T.M., and Chatrath, P. (1994) The Eocene origin of anthropoid primates. In J.G. Fleagle and R.F. Kay (eds.): Anthropoid Origins. New York: Plenum, pp. 179–202.

Szalay, F.S., and Delson, E. (1979) Evolutionary History of the Primates. New York: Academic.

Olorgesailie

Early to Late Pleistocene locality, dated 1.2–0.05 Ma, in the rift valley of southern Kenya known for concentrations of Acheulean handaxes and Middle Pleistocene fauna. The Olorgesailie Formation represents lake, lake-margin, and fluvial environments preserving a series of open sites. Dense accumulations of Acheulean handaxes occur in the middle part of the formation, ca. 780 Ka. Tools in several of these strata are associated with rich fossil accumulations of the extinct gelada *Theropithecus oswaldi*. The handaxe sites occur closest to the central axis of old stream channels, and nonhandaxe (scraper/flake) sites occur away from channels. According to excavations by Potts in the 1980s and 1990s, both kinds of site were deposited on the same ancient landscape and reflect spatial variants of behavior of the same toolmakers.

Olorgesailie documents a characteristic suite of Pleistocene large mammals, including the last-known occurrences of taxa such as *Elephas recki* and *Hipparion*, important in Early and Middle Pleistocene faunas. Once thought to encompass a brief time interval, Olorgesailie actually represents a long span calibrated by argon-argon (Ar/Ar) dating, including a revised upper Jaramillo paleomagnetic boundary (992 Ka) and the Brunhes/Matuyama boundary (780 Ka). Research has documented strong shifts in lake size and chemistry indicative of intensified paleoclimatic and tectonic activity during the Middle Pleistocene.

See also Acheulean; Africa, East; Early Paleolithic; Geochronometry; Isaac, Glynn Llewellyn; Landscape Archaeology; Paleomagnetism. [R.P.]

Further Readings

Isaac, G.L. (1977) Olorgesailie. Chicago: Univ. of Chicago Press.

Oman

At Dhofar, on the seacoast of Oman, Lower Oligocene (Rupelian) near-shore marine beds include two sandy layers with (mangrove?) root-marked horizons, indicating bayside or barrier-island accumulation. These deposits contain rare, abraded remains of mammals that have close affinities to the Late Eocene/?Early Oligocene Fayum fauna. The upper of the Dhofar fossil beds, at Taqah, yielded teeth of a propliopithecid referred to *Moeripithecus* (a Fayum taxon that has been synonymized with *Propliopithecus*), *Oligopithecus rogeri*, and two ?cercamoniine adapiforms, *Shizarodon* and *Omanodon*. Remains of a tarsiiform are also reported. The Dhofar fauna also includes hyraxes, a primitive proboscidean, an arsinoithere, rodents, insectivores, chiropterans, a marsupial, and a creodont. The rodents, in particular, have been said to be more primitive than the comparable forms in the Fayum Jebel Qatrani Formation.

See also Adapiformes; Africa, North; Anthropoidea; Fayum; Oligocene; Oligopithecidae; Propliopithecidae. [J.A.V.C.]

Further Readings

Roger, J., Sen, S., Thomas, H., Cavelier, C., and Al-Sulaimani, Z. (1993) Stratigraphic, palaeomagnetic, and palaeoenvironmental study of the Early Oligocene vertebrate locality of Taqah (Dhofar, Sultanate of Oman). Newsl. Stratig. 28:93–119.

Omomyidae

Family of mainly Eocene early tarsiiform primates from North America, Europe, and, more rarely, Africa and Asia. The family makes its unequivocal appearance in Europe and North America during the Early Eocene (Wasatchian and Sparnacian land-mammal ages) and survives into the late Middle Oligocene (Arikareean) in the genus *Ekgmowechashala*, sometimes wrongly considered to be a nonprimate plagiomenid. The Late Paleocene *Altanius* from Mongolia is probably an anaptomorphine omomyid, while the Late Paleocene *Altiatlasius* from Morocco, and perhaps the Middle Paleocene Chinese *Decoredon*, are possibly early omomyids, although their more specific ties are justifiably disputed.

The Late Paleocene to Early Eocene appearance of the Omomyidae is the first sign of the Haplorhini, roughly coinciding with the first (Early Eocene) record of the Adapiformes (a branch of the other major group of euprimates, the Strepsirhini). The other main subgroups of haplorhines do not appear until the Middle Eocene, with tarsiids and eosimiids (both within Tarsioidea sensu stricto) in China and the first possible anthropoids in North Africa. The spotty Paleocene through Middle Eocene record of omomyids suggests a possible Asian origin of not only the Euprimates, but also the Omomyidae, although African roots cannot be ruled out, particularly in light of *Altiatlasius*.

There is no serious doubt at present, based on convincing facts and reasoned arguments, that the omomyids are haplorhine primates. The known cranial features of the family can be distinguished from those of tarsiids, although the skull of the North American *Shoshonius* has a basicranial construction that recently prompted very weakly supported hypotheses of exclusive synapomorphy with tarsiids within the Haplorhini. The postcranial attributes are much less advanced in most omomyid genera than in *Tarsius*. The astonishing variety of dentitions known for such a relatively size-restricted group, particularly diversified during the Eocene, is a certain testimony that omomyids were an important component of the subtropical and tropical forest ecology of their day, at least in the Northern Hemisphere.

In briefly appraising the family, the following aspects of their paleobiology and phylogenetically significant traits are discussed in turn: morphology of the cranium and brain, dentition, postcranium, and taxonomic diversity.

Cranium and Brain

As expected, the number of known skulls of omomyids is limited, namely those of the Early Eocene North American *Tetonius*, and *Shoshonius*, the Late Eocene European *Necrolemur* (whose skull is exceedingly similar to that of *Microchoerus*, a somewhat younger descendant), and the late Middle Eocene North American *Rooneyia*. A crushed skull is known for *Nannopithex* from the Middle Eocene of Europe, and various facial fragments and palates of sundry genera reveal important confirmatory information concerning the interpretations from the more complete specimens.

Although the dentally very primitive omomyid *Teilhardina* from the earliest Eocene of Europe is unknown cranially, all other omomyids are known from either maxilla fragments or skulls that clearly indicate the presence of orbital rings, as in adapids. Omomyids had relatively large eyes and an orbital orientation that indicate highly stereoscopic vision. Perhaps as a causal consequence of the large stereoscopic orbits, they had relatively short and pinched snouts like those one observes today in lorisids and tarsiers. The problem of large eyes is not an easy one to contemplate. Relatively large eyes in a small primate do not necessarily mean a nocturnal way of life. The smaller a large-brained primate is, the relatively larger are its eyes compared to its cranium. In larger forms such as *Rooneyia*, the size of the eyes compared to the skull is only slightly larger than that of an ordinary diurnal platyrrhine primate. A genus such as the large-eyed *Necrolemur* probably represents a nocturnal radiation independent of tarsiids. It is also important to remember that tarsiers have enormously hypertrophied eyes probably because their retina seems to be constructed on the same plan as the diurnally adapted anthropoids.

A few natural casts of the inside of the neurocranium supply important information about the brain in omomyids. In spite of statements in the literature, members of this family had considerably larger brains (relatively) than other Eocene mammals of similar body size, and they also had relatively larger brains than the adapids. Although the Eocene adapids also had significantly larger brains than other mammals of their time, they were much less encephalized than the living lemuriforms, conflicting interpretations in the literature notwithstanding. In the small *Tetonius* and the larger *Necrolemur*, the olfactory bulb and the frontal lobe were relatively small compared to the enlarged occipital and temporal regions of the neocortex. The geologically younger *Rooneyia* further reduced the olfactory bulbs and enlarged the frontal lobe, attaining a relatively larger brain size compared to (an estimated) body size than other known omomyids.

Dentition

Dentition evidence is the most abundant available, and it allows important inferences about the relationships within the family, as well as a good approximation of the general food preference of the sundry known species. There is little doubt that the last good structural (but not necessarily actual) common ancestor of the known omomyids, like the European genus *Teilhardina* (not present in North America, other views notwithstanding), had two smallish incisors, a canine larger than either tooth preceding or following it, and the full primitive eutherian complement of four premolars and three molars. As in other groups of primates, however, subsequent omomyids showed widespread tooth reduction and modifications of the dental formula. Any generalization in the literature about *the* omomyid incisor morphology (or symphyseal structure) must be viewed with some skepticism because these areas are varied and still relatively poorly known. There is clear evidence, however, that when the lower incisors become enlarged, the central pair usually forms a spoonlike device, rather than anything sharply pointed like the anterior dentition of *Tarsius*. Some of the characteristic details of specific taxa are discussed under the subfamilies.

Postcranium

Although some have considered the omomyids too poorly known postcranially to allow their unequivocal association with other euprimates (hence, the concept of Plesitarsiiformes, now universally abandoned), they were, in fact, already well enough known in the 1940s to indicate their unequivocal euprimate (not archaic primate) ties, based on postcranial attributes. The characteristically modified pelvis with its flattened iliac blade expanded to accommodate the major muscles involved in jumping, the morphological details of the tibioastragalar joint and of the foot (all of these in *Hemiacodon* or *Shoshonius*), and the local abundance in mammal quarries where omomyids occur of diagnostically flattened terminal phalanges (almost certainly nail-bearing) are all ample testimony, from postcranials alone, that omomyids are more recently related to adapids than to archaic primates. There are also a number of postcranial traits of omomyids that corroborate their unity with haplorhines. While the tibioastragalar joint of euprimates is highly characteristic compared to other eutherian mammals, the relative rigidity and the less rotated tibial malleolus configuration of the upper ankle joint as known in omomyids and tarsiids differs slightly but consistently from the early strepsirhine condition. The variable anthropoid upper ankle joint is more similar to the primitive tarsiiform condition shown by omomyids (with an unfused distal tibia and fibula) than to that of strepsirhines, perhaps signaling special affinity rather than primitive euprimate retention. The astragalus of the omomyids retains such probably primitive euprimate features as a posterior astragalar shelf, usually more prominently present in most strepsirhines.

What we know of omomyid postcranial morphology suggests that, as in the first euprimates and the known strepsirhines, grasping was a fundamental modification of the extremities; the hypertrophy of pedal grasping ability suggests, along with the fast hip and knee joints, a mode of locomotion called *grasp leaping*. There is little doubt that the various species were fast and agile jumpers and branch runners that employed a firm and powerful grasp in probably most aspects of their postural and locomotor behavior. Some of these grasp leapers (e.g., *Necrolemur*) were undoubtedly fully capable to be habitual vertical clingers and leapers in the manner of tarsiers. As the postcranial diversity of omomyids is slowly becoming appreciated, it is obvious that, although they share common ancestral attributes, they were not any more stereotyped in their locomotor strategies than are the living lemuriforms. For most of the species, we lack even the more commonly found tarsal bones such as astragali and calcanea.

Diversity

The Omomyidae is probably a paraphyletic taxon, early in its history possibly including ancestors for both the Tarsioidea (Tarsiidae and Eosimiidae) and the Anthropoidea (Platyrrhini and Catarrhini). It is divided into four subfamilies: Anaptomorphinae, Omomyinae, Ekgmowechashalinae, and Microchoerinae. For purposes of balance with Tarsioidea, a monotypic superfamily Omomyoidea may also be recognized within Tarsiiformes. The size of omomyid species, estimated not from individual teeth (which are notoriously unreliable in predicting body size when it comes to specific taxa) but from the length of the tooth row, ranged from tiny forms such as the living pygmy marmosets to others comparable to medium-sized platyrrhines such as the pitheciines. There was probably no "typical" omomyid, and many of them were quite dissimilar to *Tarsius* in their way of life. Some of the species, however, as discussed under the respective subfamilies, were probably more representative of the primitive omomyid (the last common ancestor) than such late and modified forms as the highly frugivorous *Rooneyia* and *Ekgmowechashala*, or the small, possibly folivorous, *Macrotarsius* (present in both Asia and North America). Even the many described species are surely a mere tip of the iceberg when it comes to estimating the actual diversity, lineage, and taxonomic abundance of the Omomyidae.

Superfamily Omomyoidea (new)
    Family Omomyidae
        Subfamily Anaptomorphinae
        Subfamily Omomyinae
        Subfamily Ekgmowechashalinae
        Subfamily Microchoerinae
    Family Omomyidae?
        †*Decoredon*
        ?†*Kohatius*
        †*Altiatlasius*

†extinct

See also Adapidae; Adapiformes; Altiatlasius; Anaptomorphinae; Anthropoidea; Catarrhini; Decoredon; Ekgmowechashalinae; Eosimiidae; Euprimates; Haplorhini; Michrochoerinae; Omomyinae; Platyrrhini; Shoshonius; Strepsirhini; Tarsiidae; Tarsiiformes; Tarsioidea; Visual-Predation Hypothesis. [F.S.S.]

Further Readings

Dagosto, M. (1985) The distal tibia of primates with special reference to the Omomyidae. Int. J. Primatol. 6:45–75.

Szalay, F.S. (1976) Systematics of the Omomyidae (Tarsiiformes, Primates): Taxonomy, phylogeny, and adaptations. Bull. Am. Mus. Nat. Hist. 156:157–450.

Szalay, F.S., and Delson, E. (1979) Evolutionary History of the Primates. New York: Academic.

Szalay, F.S., Rosenberger, A.L., and Dagosto, M. (1987) Diagnosis and differentiation of the Primates. Yrbk. Phys. Anthropol. 30:75–105.

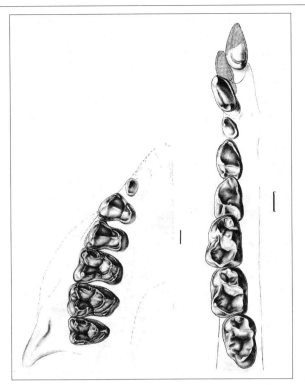

Upper and lower teeth in a reconstructed palate (left) and mandible (right) of the Middle Eocene omomyine omomyid Omomys carteri. *Note reconstruction of the anterior sockets of the palate. Scale is 1 mm. Courtesy of Frederick S. Szalay, from Szalay and Delson, 1979.*

Omomyinae

Subfamily of omomyid primates known primarily from the Eocene of North America, although two genera are now known from China. *Asiomomys* from the Middle Eocene of China (a form difficult to distinguish from *Stockia*, a California contemporary) is clearly a utahiin omomyine, while *Macrotarsius*, a mytoniinan omomyin first described from North America, is also resident in China at that time. The Asian genus *Hoanghonius*, previously considered as a possible omomyid, is possibly a representative of the Adapiformes or perhaps a stem anthropoid or a distinctive tarsiiform.

The omomyines are a diverse and adaptively complex clade, a long-lasting subfamily that ranges throughout the Early-Middle Eocene, a time span of ca. 16 Myr. These primates may be subdivided into the following tribes in order to express what we know of their phylogeny, diversification, and adaptations: Omomyini, Uintaniini, Utahiini, and Washakiini.

There are no credible explanations as yet why the omomyines dominated the Middle Eocene small-primate faunas of North America in contrast to the anaptomorphines. Postcranially, these two mainly North American subfamilies appear to have been similar to each other, and one of their few cranial differences is the smaller petromastoid of omomyines.

The tribe Omomyini consists of two subtribes, the Omomyina with the genera *Omomys* and *Chumashius*, and the Mytoniina containing *Ourayia* and *Macrotarsius*. All of the genera included in this taxon appear to share an interesting combination of a small hypocone (more a shelf in *Chumashius*) coupled with a lack of postprotocone fold on the upper molars. Although the first premolars have been lost from the omomyinans, they nevertheless appear to have retained relatively large canines and modest-size incisors, particularly in the Californian *Chumashius*. Both *Omomys* and *Chumashius* were in the size range of living marmosets and appear to have been highly insectivorous, judged from their somewhat shearing molars (for a primate) and sharp premolars. The subtribe Mytoniina contains the largest omomyids, and the included genera have somewhat molarized fourth premolars and molars suited primarily for a vegetarian diet. Whereas *Ourayia* may have been frugivorous, *Macrotarsius*, with its upper-molar mesostyles and lingual crests on the lower molars (both are extra cutting edges), was probably inclined toward a folivorous diet like the equally small living lemuroid *Lepilemur*.

The tribe Uintaniini contains the small genera *Steinius*, *Uintanius*, and *Jemezius*. *Uintanius* has transformed its third and fourth lower premolars into tall, trenchant blades, an adaptive theme that recurs independently not only among primates and marsupials, but also in other small mammals such as the extinct multituberculates. This group retains the more open lower molar trigonid construction of the Omomyinae. A premolar adaptation similar to that of *Uintanius* had evolved independently in the genus *Absarokius* (of the closely related subfamily Anaptomorphinae), but it is difficult to determine whether the selective agent responsible for these modifications and the biological roles performed in the two genera were similar. It is likely that in *Uintanius* the premolars were primarily a response for slicing insects, whereas the wider based premolars in *Absarokius* were serving some fruit- or seed-related masticatory activity. The poorly known genus *Steinius* retains all four premolars, has a relatively large canine, and appears to have a slightly hypertrophied central lower incisor, a recurrent theme in omomyid incisor adaptations. *Steinius* may be a primitive member of this tribe.

The tribe Utahiini contains three poorly known genera, *Utahia* and *Stockia* from North America, and the Asian *Asiomomys* that perhaps should not be separated on the genus level from *Stockia*. All three are characterized by the derived and extreme constriction of the trigonids on the lower molars and the concomitant enlargement of the talonid basins. Although upper molars are not known, this type of trigonid construction is closely correlated in platyrrhines and other primates with an enlarged hypocone. Whatever their dietary adaptation was, utahiinins clearly placed an evolutionary premium on a large lower-molar talonid and probably an upper-molar hypocone as well. These primates are the only ones known in addition to *Macrotarsius* that occur nearly synchronously in North America and Asia. Such biogeographic distributions greatly increase the probability for some common geographical center of origin for the tarsiiforms.

The tribe Washakiini is a varied group that can be characterized as having inherited from their last common ancestor a combination of a postprotocone fold and either an incipient hypocone or a strong postcingulum where the hypocone develops on the upper molars. This appears to be a decidedly herbivorous (at least more so than the Omomyini) radiation within the subfamily. The somewhat conservative (or perhaps differently derived) subtribe Hemiacodontina contains the most primitive but poorly known genus *Loveina* and the more advanced *Hemiacodon*, known not only from many jaws but also from various postcranial remains. Judged from uniquely derived dental attributes and a robust jaw, this genus had more of an herbivorous (?frugivorous) than insectivorous diet. The subtribe Washakiina includes the genera *Shoshonius*, *Washakius*, and *Dyseolemur*. All of these have an additional extra cutting edge on their lower molars, a metastylid, and some have another cutting edge on the upper molars, either a mesostyle or an additional conule, or both. Small as these animals were, they probably had a significant plant component in their diet. Small size, in spite of some of the primatological literature, is not always a good predictor of diet. Large groups within the immense rodent radiation are an ample testimony to the fact that small mammals can exploit high-energy resources such as a large variety of seeds without recourse to significant insectivory. It has been suggested that *Shoshonius* is actually a tarsiid, based on putative synapomorphies of its basicranium with *Tarsius*. While there are some suggestive similarities, *Shoshonius* is almost certainly part of the Omomyinae, which is, of course, paraphyletic as the Ekgmowechashalinae evolved from this group. *Shoshonius* is not a tarsiid.

The subtribe Rooneyina contains only the genus *Rooneyia* from the latest Middle Eocene of Texas. This genus is known from a single, albeit magnificent and justly famous, fossil skull. No lower teeth are known. The small canine of this genus makes it highly improbable that it gave rise to the younger *Ekgmowechashala*, as some previous literature suggested. The unique, low-crowned and bunodont cusps of the teeth of *Rooneyia* strongly suggest a primarily frugivorous diet.

Because there are so many genera in this subfamily, not all can be discussed in any detail; thus, temporal and geographic ranges are given here.

Subfamily Omomyinae
    Tribe Omomyini
        Subtribe Omomyina
            † *Omomys* (E.-M. Eoc.; NA.)
            † *Chumashius* (M. Eoc.; NA.)
        Subtribe Mytoniina
            † *Ourayia* (including † *Mytonius*; M. Eoc.; NA.)
            † *Macrotarsius* (M.-L. Eoc.; NA, As.)
    Tribe Uintaniini
        † *Steinius* (E. Eoc.; NA)
        † *Uintanius* (including † *Huerfanius*; E.-M. Eoc.; NA.)
        † *Jemezius* (M. Eoc.; NA)
    Tribe Utahiini
        † *Utahia* (E.-M. Eoc.; NA.)

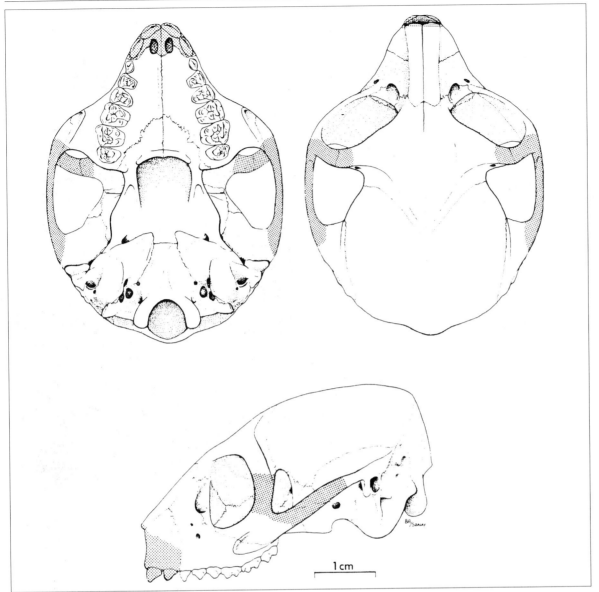

Slightly reconstructed skull of the Late Eocene omomyine omomyid Rooneyia viejaensis. *Courtesy of Frederick S. Szalay, from Szalay and Delson, 1979.*

†*Stockia* (M. Eoc.; NA.)
†*Asiomomys* (M. Eoc.; As.)
Tribe Washakiini
Subtribe Hemiacodontina (new)
†*Loveina* (E. Eoc.; NA.)
†*Hemiacodon* (M. Eoc.; NA.)
Subtribe Washakiina
†*Shoshonius* (E. Eoc.; NA.)
†*Washakius* (M. Eoc.; NA.)
†*Dyseolemur* (M. Eoc.; NA.)
Subtribe Rooneyina (new rank)
†*Rooneyia* (M. Eoc.; NA.)
†extinct; NA. North America; As. Asia

See also Anaptomorphinae; Ekgmowhechashalinae; Eocene; Hoanghonius; Microchoerinae; Omomyidae; Shoshonius. [F.S.S.]

Further Readings

Szalay, F.S., and Delson, E. (1979) Evolutionary History of the Primates. New York: Academic.

Ontogeny

Total life history of an individual organism, from roots meaning the "development of being." Ontogeny begins with conception and proceeds through embryonic development, when the formation of various structures and organ systems occurs, to fetal development, when these systems undergo further elaboration and growth. Following birth, the overall growth of these structures and the appearance of certain new features (such as teeth and secondary sexual characteristics) characterize the periods of infancy, childhood, and adolescence. The later stages of ontogeny are adulthood and, ultimately, death. Humans can be distinguished from other primates by their markedly prolonged life-history periods, from infant to adult.

Human growth and development form a complex process influenced by interacting genetic, hormonal, and environmental factors. Different tissues and body regions exhibit considerable variations in the timing and rate of their growth during ontogeny. These variations are of particular significance to evolutionary biologists, since phylogenetic transformations result from modifications of ontogenetic histories.

See also Allometry; Haeckel, Ernst Heinrich; Sexual Dimorphism. [B.T.S.]

Further Readings

Gould, S.J. (1977) Ontogeny and Phylogeny. Cambridge, Mass.: Harvard University Press.

Tanner, J.M. (1978) Foetus into Man: Physical Growth from Conception to Maturity. London: Open Books.

Orangian

South African Middle Stone Age industry closely related to the Pietersburg but largely restricted to the Orange Free State and differing from the Pietersburg in a greater emphasis on blades and the rare occurrence of true burins and trimmed points. These differences may also relate to the exclusive association of the Orangian with open sites and with the availability of abundant fine-grained isotropic raw material. The industry is best known from the open site of Orangia. The Orange Free State site of Rose Cottage may represent a rockshelter variant of this industry or a southwestern extension of the Pietersburg industry. The Orangian probably dates to more than 40 Ka, possibly as early as 130 Ka.

See also Border Cave; Florisbad; Howieson's Poort; Middle Stone Age; Pietersburg; Rose Cottage; Second Intermediate; Site Types; Stone-Tool Making. [A.S.B.]

Order

Principal major unit of classification within the Class. Human beings belong to the order Primates, together with the lemurs, lorises, tarsiers, Old and New World monkeys, and the lesser and great apes. Other mammalian orders include such familiar major groupings as the Carnivora, Rodentia, and Cetacea.

See also Classification; Primates. [I.T.]

Oreopithecus

European Miocene catarrhines, now classified in the subfamily Oreopithecinae, family Hominidae. There has been some controversy as to whether *Oreopithecus* is more closely related to the living hominoids or to the Old World monkeys. The latter, minority opinion is no longer followed here.

Oreopithecus bambolii was first reported in 1872 on the basis of a juvenile mandible. The original describer, P. Gervais, considered that it was most similar dentally to the gorilla but that it also had features in common with cercopithecids. Over the next 70 years, a variety of authors offered their opinions, mostly based on incomplete studies of poor replicas (casts). Some argued that *O. bambolii* was a hominoid,

Oreopithecus bambolii skeleton (cast) as originally recovered in 1958.

others that it was a cercopithecoid, still others that it was somehow intermediate between these major groups.

In 1915, G. Schwalbe placed *Oreopithecus* in its own family, which most authors continued to include in the Hominoidea. An additional dozen jaws and a few postcranial fragments were described from a cluster of five localities in the Tuscan region of North-Central Italy. The age of these fossils was also uncertain but generally estimated at ca. 12 Ma. In the 1990s more specimens have been recovered from a locality in Sardinia and from additional horizons in Tuscany; all are now dated close to 8–7 Ma.

In the late 1940s and through the 1950s, Swiss paleontologist J. Hürzeler reawakened scientific and popular interest in *Oreopithecus* through his restudy of known specimens and collection of new fossils. He argued that *Oreopithecus* was a close human relative, if not an ancestor (at that time, *Australopithecus* was poorly known and thought by many European scholars to be a distinctive ape). Hürzeler thought that *Oreopithecus* had a small canine and tooth proportions most similar to those *of Homo erectus*. He recognized that in some ways (e.g., a large central cusp on lower molars) *O. bambolii* was unique, but for him the majority of observed features were shared with human ancestors as he interpreted them. In 1958, with the aid of local Tuscan miners, Hürzeler recovered a partial skeleton of a young adult male. It was

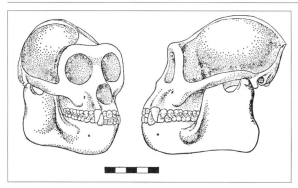

Reconstruction of the cranium of Oreopithecus bambolii *in oblique and lateral views. After Szalay and Berzi, 1973.*

badly flattened like most of the *Oreopithecus* fossils (which are found in a lignite, or soft brown coal, deposit laid down in a swampy forest). Hürzeler made a partial reconstruction of the skull, which indicated a large brain, supporting his view that *Oreopithecus* was a human forebear.

More recently, several researchers have studied parts of this skeleton, coming to quite different conclusions. The supposedly large brain has been shown to be based on the misinterpretation of large sagittal and nuchal crests as being the top of the skull and of crushed vertebrae as the rear; in fact, the brain is only about the size of that of monkeys of similar body weight. Male canines are quite large, and sexual dimorphism is high, as in most Miocene catarrhines. The gonial region of the mandible (where the corpus meets the ramus) is expanded, as in colobines and other leaf-eating mammals, and the molar teeth emphasize crests, for slicing leafy food items. The face is short and rather wide, admittedly as in humans, but also as in gibbons, colobines, and conservative catarrhines generally. Thus, almost all modern-day students think that *Oreopithecus* resembles humans only convergently, in a few characters, while they see closer phyletic links to either hominoids or cercopithecids.

A. Rosenberger and E. Delson have suggested that, in a number of dental features, *Oreopithecus* is intermediate in a homologous way between ancestral cercopithecids (e.g., victoriapithecines or the inferred common ancestor of all cercopithecids) and early catarrhines. For example, *O. bambolii* has elongate upper molars (while those of most hominoids are square or wide); reduced hypoconulids on dP_4-M_2; reduced cingulum on upper and lower molars, with remnants in the same places as seen (further reduced) in cercopithecids; molar cusps placed in transverse pairs (protoconid opposite metaconid, paracone opposite protocone, etc.), rather than offset as in hominoids, and with some development of transverse cresting; increased relief of molar teeth (tall cusps and deep clefts); and a partial approach to the mirror-image pattern of occluding uppers and lowers seen in Old World monkeys. It is clear that *Oreopithecus* is not bilophodont, as are modern cercopithecids, but neither was the earliest ancestor of monkeys. What Rosenberger and Delson were suggesting was that a common ancestor of cercopithecids and oreopithecids had already experienced selection for a number of shared trends before the two groups diverged in different directions.

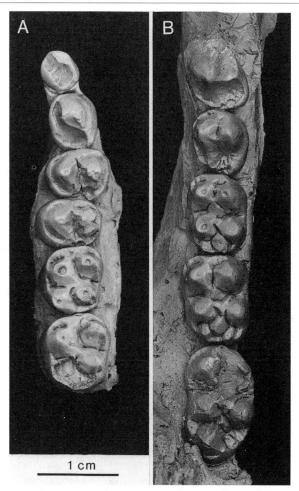

Occlusal views of Oreopithecus bambolii *from Baccinello, Italy: left P^2-M^2 of subadult female (left), left P_3-M_3 of male individual in other figures. Photographs of casts (for clarity of detail).*

T. Harrison has suggested that two or three African Miocene species are related to *Oreopithecus*. *Nyanzapithecus* species are poorly known, but their teeth look quite similar to those of *O. bambolii* in form and elongation. *Rangwapithecus* also presents some dental features similar to *Oreopithecus*, especially molar elongation and slight cresting. If these forms were truly close to the ancestry of *Oreopithecus*, it would imply a long independent history for the genus back to the Early Miocene and possibly support a link to cercopithecids. Other workers, such as F.S. Szalay, have considered that the foot of *Oreopithecus* is uniquely evolved, sharing no derived features with either hominids or cercopithecids.

But the majority of researchers today interpret *Oreopithecus* as a derived hominid, sharing most postcranial (and some cranial and dental) morphology with modern apes. Harrison has extended his research to review all known material of this genus, and, based mainly on his results, it appears that *Oreopithecus* shares 11 major, nearly independent complexes of the postcranium with the ancestral hominid morphotype. For example, the forelimb and hindlimb are adapted to different biological roles as evidenced by proportions; posture is relatively orthograde (upright); the joint complexes at shoulder, elbow, wrist, hip, and knee are similar in detail to those of hominids; and the hand and foot are adapted to powerful grasping. Moreover, there are a large number of synapomorphies shared with living hominids but not seen in Kenyapithecinae. Among these are detailed similarities of the vertebrae, ulna, pelvis, and various foot bones. In the dentition, the mesiobuccal surface of P_3 is short as in later hominids, rather than very long as in cercopithecids or intermediate as in early hominoids and eocatarrhines; the upper premolars are relatively large by comparison to the molars, intermediate between living hominids and other hominoids; and the upper molars are elongate as in cercopithecids and some modern hominids. In the skull, *Oreopithecus* lacks a subarcuate fossa on the temporal bone (a condition seen only in hominids, including *Dryopithecus*) and has nasopalatine and supraorbital torus constructions similar to those of gorillas (inferred as conservative for modern hominids).

Harrison thus joins such previous workers as W.L. Straus, Jr., and E. Sarmiento in considering that the above-noted dental features were evolved convergently by oreopithecids and cercopithecids, due to similar dietary adaptations. They argue that the detailed similarities in the shapes of the thorax (chest), and shoulder, elbow, and knee joints, must reflect a long period of shared ancestry between *Oreopithecus* and hominids (in our sense, not that of Hürzeler). It is difficult to argue that the shared postcranial features are all convergences due to similar locomotor adaptation, but, even if some of them are, it is more likely that the dental similarities to cercopithecids are also convergent.

Therefore, *Oreopithecus* is here included in the Hominoidea. But should it still be placed in its own family, or can it be ranked within the Hominidae, and, if so, where? The fossil hominid most similar to *Oreopithecus*, according to Harrison, is *Dryopithecus*, a slightly older and more widespread European form. The two taxa share a number of craniodental and postcranial features that link them to the modern hominids but place them as somewhat more conservative, perhaps near the common ancestry of Homininae and Ponginae. It is, in fact, possible that a species of *Dryopithecus* that became isolated in the Tusco-Sardinian geographical area might have been ancestral to *Oreopithecus*. One alternative might thus be to include the two genera in the same subfamily, which for reasons of priority would have to be termed Oreopithecinae. But, given the many unique features of *Oreopithecus*, it seems wiser at present to retain Oreopithecinae as a separate subfamily including only its type genus.

There is less argument about the paleobiology of *Oreopithecus*. The same features of the skeleton that indicate relationship to the hominids demonstrate that this animal had a longer forelimb than hindlimb; well-developed adaptations for raising the forelimb above the head, for a variety of movements at the elbow joint, and for flexibility of the wrist and mobility of the hindlimb; relatively erect posture during feeding and locomotion; and a flexible ankle with powerful grasping foot. Taken together, these functional interpretations allow reconstruction of *O. bambolii* as a powerful climber of vertical tree trunks and a suspensory arm swinger and arm hanger. There are similarities in this interpretation to both modern orangutans and chimpanzees, although not precisely to either ape.

The body weight of *Oreopithecus* was probably ca. 32 kg for a male, as estimated both by statistical analysis of weight-bearing joint surfaces (by W.L. Jungers) and by general comparisons of long-bone lengths (Szalay). This is nearly twice the weight estimated by several authors from anthropoid tooth size/body size ratios, implying that the dentition of *O. bambolii* was quite small for its probable body size. The dentition itself was apparently adapted to a folivorous diet, which fits well with the swampy forest habitat in which the species probably lived. Given seasonal variation in the availability of potential foods, perhaps aquatic plants or evergreen leaves were its staple diet.

See also Catarrhini; Cercopithecidae; Dryopithecinae; Dryopithecus; Europe; Hominidae; Hominoidea; Locomotion; Miocene; Skeleton; Teeth. [E.D.]

Further Readings

Azzaroli, A., Boccaletti, M., Delson, E., Moratti, G., and Torre, D. (1987) Chronological and paleogeographical background to the study of *Oreopithecus bambolii*. J. Hum. Evol. 15:533–540.

Clarke, R.J. (1997) First complete restoration of the *Oreopithecus* skull. Hum. Evol. 12:221–232.

Delson, E. (1987) An anthropoid enigma: Historical introduction to the study of *Oreopithecus bambolii*. J. Hum. Evol. 15:523–531.

Harrison, T. (1986) New fossil anthropoids from the Middle Miocene of East Africa and their bearing on the origin of the Oreopithecidae. Am. J. Phys. Anthropol. 71:265–284.

Harrison, T. (1987) A re-assessment of the phyletic position of *Oreopithecus bambolii* Gervais, 1872. J. Hum. Evol. 15:541–583.

Harrison, T., and Rook, L. (1997) Enigmatic anthropoid or misunderstood ape: The phylogenetic status of *Oreopithecus bambolii* reconsidered. In D. Begun, C. Ward, and M. Rose (eds.): Miocene Hominoid Fossils: Functional and Phylogenetic Implications, New York: Plenum, pp. 327–362.

Hürzeler, J. (1958) *Oreopithecus bambolii* Gervais: A preliminary report. Verh. naturforschenden Gesellschaft Basel 69:1–47.

Sarmiento, E. (1987) The phylogenetic position of *Oreopithecus* and its significance in the origin of the Hominoidea. Am. Mus. Novitates 2881:1–44.

Straus, W.L., Jr. (1963) The classification of *Oreopithecus*. In S.L. Washburn (ed.): Classification and Human Evolution. Chicago: Aldine, pp. 146–177.

Szalay, F.S., and Delson, E. (1979) Evolutionary History of the Primates. New York: Academic.

OSL (Optically Stimulated Luminescence) Dating

A method of trapped-charge dating closely related to thermoluminescence (TL) dating. In OSL, the length of time that a sample of sediment has been buried, while being exposed to natural background radiation, is determined from the intensity of characteristic light frequencies emitted by a sample when it is stimulated by light of a different wavelength. OSL signals are rapidly zeroed by the bleaching effect of sunlight, giving this method two advantages over thermoluminescence dating: Much less light exposure is needed to zero the OSL signal, and there is no residual signal after bleaching. In principle, any surficial sediment can be dated, including dune and beach sands, flood deposits, loess, and even shallow-water lacustrine and fluviatile sediments if they are laid down in clear water and exposed to sunlight for a few days before being covered. Wind-blown silt and sand washed into a cave during a flood may be deposited in an essentially zeroed condition as well.

Luminescence can be stimulated by monochromatic light from different sources, including optical laser light (typically a green argon laser), monochromatic light filtered from white light, or infrared from light-emitting diodes. Use of the latter, *called infrared stimulated luminescence* (IRSL), exploits emission from feldspar but not quartz, whereas optical or ultraviolet light can excite luminescence from both quartz and feldspar. Most modern thermoluminescence (TL) analysis systems can be adapted to OSL or IRSL by addition of a light source and suitable filters to prevent scattering of exciting light into the photomultiplier tube.

OSL, like TL, can date sediments ranging in age from a few Kyr to ca. 500 Kyr, with a precision of ca. ± 10 percent. Ambient dose rate measurements at the site are required.

See also ESR (Electron Spin Resonance) Dating; Geochronometry; Pleistocene; TL (Thermoluminescence) Dating; Trapped-Charge Dating. [H.P.S.]

Further Readings

Aitken, M.J. (1992) Optical dating. Quatern. Sci. Rev. 11:127–131.

Berger, G.W. (1995) Progress in luminescence dating methods for Quaternary sediments. In N.W. Rutter and N.R. Catto (eds.): Dating Methods for Quaternary Deposits, St. Johns, Newfoundland: Geol. Soc. Canada, Geotext 2, pp. 81–104.

Feathers, J.K. (1996) Luminescence dating and modern human origins. Evol. Anthropol. 5:25–36.

Godfrey-Smith, D., Huntley, D., and Chen, W.-H. (1988) Optical dating studies of quartz and feldspar sediment extracts. Quatern. Sci. Rev. 7:373–380.

Stokes, S. (1993) Optical dating of sediment samples from Bir Tarfawi and Bir Sahara East: An initial report. In F. Wendorf, A. Close, and R. Schild (eds.): Egypt during the Last Interglacial. New York: Plenum, pp. 229–233.

Otavipithecus

Genus of primate described in 1992 for the first Miocene hominoid fossils to be recovered from southern Africa. It represents a major extension of range for hominoids in Africa. The type specimen of *Otavipithecus namibiensis* is a gracile right mandibular corpus with all molars and a broken premolar. It was found in a block of breccia on the dump of the Berg Aukas mine in northern Namibia; small mammals in this and similar blocks suggest an age of ca. 13–12 Ma, while other blocks on the dump contain a younger, Mio-Pliocene small-mammal assemblage. Affinities have been suggested with kenyapithecines (*Afropithecus*) and with hominines, but it cannot be assigned with any confidence to either subfamily at this stage, although it is clearly a member of Hominidae.

See also Africa, Southern; Afropithecus; Dryopithecinae; Homininae; Hominoidea; Kenyapithecinae. [P.A.]

P

Pacitanian

Supposedly Early Paleolithic industry from Indonesia recognized by Dutch paleontologist G.H.R. von Koenigswald in the mid-1930s. The Pacitanian is represented by flake implements and so-called core choppers. The original designation refers to surface finds from terraces of the Baksoka Valley (Java). The Pacitanian has been shown on geomorphological grounds to date to less than 60 Ka. Furthermore, some now view it as a Javanese local variant of the broadly defined Hoabinhian of Southeast Asia. It now seems likely that a great many Pacitanian "artifacts" are, in fact, the result of natural nonhuman processes.

See also Asia, Eastern and Southern; Early Paleolithic; Hoabinhian. [G.G.P.]

Palaeopropithecidae

Extinct family of medium- to large-bodied lemuriform primates closely related to the indriids. Palaeopropithecidae contains four genera, together informally known as the *sloth lemurs*. Three genera are known from marsh and cave sites in the center, south, southwest, far north, and northwest of Madagascar: In ascending order of size, these are *Mesopropithecus* (body weight estimated at 10 kg), *Palaeopropithecus* (two or more species, 40–60 kg), and the huge *Archaeoindris* (160–200 kg). The fourth genus, *Babakotia* (ca. 15–20 kg), has only recently been described from the Ankarana Massif in the far north. Most sites probably date to ca. 3–1.0 Ka, though some may be several thousand years older. In any event, the subfossil forms they contain may be regarded as members of the modern fauna of Madagascar; they probably became extinct subsequent to the arrival of humans on the island, and their extinction seems to have been, at least in major part, a result of human activity. A skeleton of *Palaeopropithecus* discovered recently in the cave of Anjohibé in northwestern Madagascar, and skeletons of *Babakotia* and *Mesopropithecus* found more recently yet in the Ankarana, assume particular importance because their elements were associated. Most subfossil specimens known from Madagascar were excavated before World War II from marsh sites that were insufficiently drained and not systematically excavated. Positive association of different parts of the skeleton was, thus, rare; this led on occasion to profound disagreements over which postcranial elements should be matched with which skulls.

Adaptively, the three genera of palaeopropithecids form a series (from the relatively generalized *Mesopropithecus* to the extraordinarily specialized *Palaeopropithecus*) that tends toward greater and greater suspensory commitment. In the last of them, especially, the joints throughout the body are designed for flexibility—except in the long, curving extremities, which were built for powerful grasping. These adaptations for below-branch suspension are highly slothlike—hence, the group's informal name. The largest palaeopropithecid, *Archaeoindris*, was, however, clearly too large to have been a committed arborealist. Few postcranial bones are known (and none is definitely associated with any cranial remains), but it seems a fair bet that this lemur was highly terrestrial, probably with a niche similar to that filled in the New World by the extinct giant ground sloths.

The two smaller palaeopropithecid genera, despite their postcranial distinctiveness, are extremely indriidlike in cranial structure and dentition, and *Babakotia*, as its name suggests, bears a particular closeness to *Indri*. The two larger genera are more autapomorphic in cranial build. The skull of *Palaeopropithecus* is massively built and ca. 20 cm long. The face is elongated, and, while the overall proportions of the skull remind one of the long-faced *Indri*, the braincase is relatively smaller and bears nuchal and sometimes sagittal crests. The orbits are heavily ringed by bone, the nasal bones overhang the nasal aperture in a curious manner, and the gonial region of the mandible is vastly expanded. The middle-ear cavity is housed entirely within the base of the skull, without bulla formation, and an ossified tube leads to the outside. The dentition of *Palaeopropithecus* is fairly close in morphology to that of the much smaller indriids, especially to that of *Propithecus*. It also shows the reduction of the

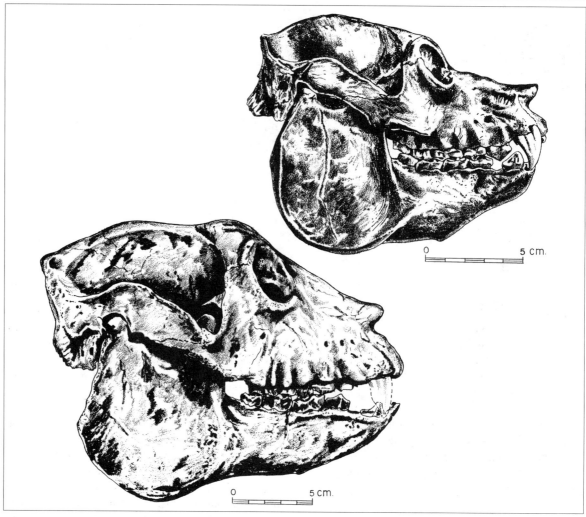

Crania in lateral view of Palaeopropithecus maximus *(above) and* Archaeoindris fontoynonti.

premolars to two in each quadrant, also characteristic of the indriids, but the tooth comb is reduced and stubby.

Archaeoindris is much less well known than its close relative *Palaeopropithecus*, only a single skull and a few other elements having been recovered in the center of the island. The skull is somewhat more than 25 cm long, massively built, and greatly deepened compared with that of *Palaeopropithecus*. This last feature gives it overall proportions vaguely reminiscent of *Propithecus*. Like *Palaeopropithecus*, *Archaeoindris* exhibits curious paired swellings of the nasal bones above the nasal aperture, lacks prominent auditory bullae, and has a bony tube connecting the eardrum with the exterior. Similarly, its cheek dentition closely recalls that of the indriines, though as in *Palaeopropithecus* it is a little more elongated, particularly in the lower jaw.

It was long unclear whether the palaeopropithecids or the archaeolemurids among the subfossil lemurs are the closest known relatives of the living indriids; our new postcranial knowledge of the palaeopropithecids indicates that a craniodentally conservative and postcranially generalized indrioid ancestor with three premolar teeth gave rise, on the one hand, to the three-premolared archaeolemurids and, on the other, to a two-premolared but still postcranially generalized lineage (with plenty of suspensory behaviors in its reper-

toire) that was ancestral to both the leaping (but still quite suspensory) indriids and the hanging palaeopropithecids.

Family Palaeopropithecidae
  † *Palaeopropithecus*
  † *Archaeoindris*
  † *Mesopropithecus*
  † *Babakotia*
†extinct

See also Archaeolemuridae; Lemuriformes. [I.T.]

Further Readings

Mittermeier, R.A., Tattersall, I., Konstant, W.R., Meyers, D.M., and Mast, R.B. (1994) Lemurs of Madagascar (Tropical Field Guide No. 1). Washington, D.C.: Conservation International.

Tattersall, I. (1982) The Primates of Madagascar. New York: Columbia University Press.

Paleoanthropology

As broadly defined here, the branch of anthropology including studies of primate and human evolution, prehistory, and the biological and geological backgrounds essential to the

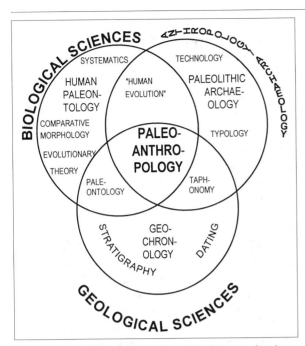

A "Venn diagram" showing the interrelationship of the many disciplines involved in paleoanthropological research.

study of these topics. This volume is essentially an encyclopedia of paleoanthropology (see "A Brief Introduction"), but that term is not as widely known as *human evolution and prehistory,* and some scholars still restrict its meaning to either its paleontological or its archaeological aspects. The unified nature of this concept owes much to the pioneering 1960s fieldwork of L.S.B. and M.D. Leakey at Olduvai Gorge (Tanzania), where a team of specialists was brought together to investigate fully all of the natural phenomena forming the background to the early fossil humans and their artifacts recovered there. F.C. Howell extended this approach at his excavations at Isimila (Tanzania), Torralba, and Ambrona (both in Spain), and especially at the Omo deposits (in Ethiopia), and his work more than anything else probably brought the term *paleoanthropology* into broader use to refer to this multidisciplinary approach rather than merely as a synonym for Paleolithic archaeology (or human paleontology).

See also Anthropology; Archaeology; Leakey, Louis Seymour Bazett; Leakey, Mary Douglas; Paleolithic; Paleontology; Prehistory; Primates. [E.D.]

Further Readings
Howell, F.C. (1965) Early Man. New York: Time-Life.

Paleobiogeography
Reconstruction of past biotic distribution patterns through integrations of the fossil record and geological history. The first step in analyzing the fossil record is *biostratigraphy,* to establish the lateral and vertical range of taxa in stratigraphic sequences and to identify the sharp changes in local diversity (i.e., coincident first or last occurrences among a number of taxa) that indicate major paleobiogeographic shifts. The sec-

ond step in analysis is to time-correlate the biostratigraphic data from different areas. *Time equivalence* is determined by various stratigraphic means—geological mapping, radiometric age determinations, tephrochronology, paleomagnetic and cyclostratigraphic correlation, and so on—and also by biochronological tests of compared faunas such as similarity coefficients and evaluations of relative evolutionary grade. A third constraint in paleobiogeographic models, mainly of interest in considerations of global distribution patterns and trophic variations, is the history of realignment of major land and sea provinces and the creation of topographic barriers as a result of plate tectonics.

Paleobiogeographical methods are somewhat controversial. The traditional approach is highly empirical and mostly inductive, taking the fossil record at face value to understand the biogeographic history of a given lineage, in terms of the biostratigraphic and biochronological ranges of its component taxa. From these data, the distribution of the lineage through time is inferred by assuming that the oldest fossils in a given area represent the ancestral taxa of related, younger taxa in the same general area.

Cladistic, or *vicariance,* paleobiogeography is based on the precept that scientific knowledge is basically conjectural and can never be confirmed but only falsified in a process of constant improvement. In this view, no direct ancestor of a taxon can be specified, but only the nearest level of phylogenetic (cladistic) relationship in a sequence of derived states. Under these assumptions, the primary goal of paleobiogeography is to analyze the geological record for evidence to explain the geographical relationships of the elements in the cladograms. It is assumed *a priori* that vicariance—the disjunct distribution of sister taxa (i.e., tapirs in Malaysia and South America, or struthioform ostriches, rheas, emus, and moas in the different Gondwana fragments)—implies that a common heritage was originally continuous across the area occupied by the descendant taxa, and that external forces have acted to break up the connection. In this view, dispersal in itself does not create vicariant taxa, nor do vicariant taxa separate from one another *in situ* and then disperse.

Both empirical and vicariance paleobiography depend on an independent geological framework for the past distribution of taxa including stratigraphy, biochronology, and time-correlation. While the traditional approach would merely integrate such a data set, the cladistic approach would use it to test a vicariance hypothesis. Dispersal hypotheses would be erected only when a vicariance hypothesis was rejected by relevant geological data. The failure to delineate species relationships precisely (in a cladistic fashion) risks erroneous reconstruction of the evolutionary pattern, which is, in turn, vital to paleobiological scenarios. Thus, the traditional empirical approach and the cladistic approach both require careful phylogenetic analysis to support paleobiogeographical reconstruction.

See also Cladistics; Paleontology. [R.L.B., D.P.D.]

Further Readings
Bernor, R.L. (1983) Geochronology and zoogeographic relationships of Miocene Hominoidea. In R.L. Ciochon

and R.S. Corruccini (eds.): New Interpretations of Ape
and Human Ancestry. New York: Plenum, pp. 21–64.

Nelson, G., and Platnick, N. (1981) Systematics and Biogeography: Cladistics and Vicariance. New York: Columbia University Press.

Paleobiology

An integrated part of both the biological and the geological sciences dealing with extinct life, especially the lifeways of extinct forms, in addition to the study of their evolutionary history. The number of different kinds of organisms that lived in the past is vastly greater than the number alive today. The numerous ways these organisms survived and the ecological communities they formed are the primary subject matter of paleobiology. The single most important activity of paleobiologists is the description of both the organisms and the sediments in which they are found, including the distributional and functional analysis of fossil animals and plants. Following descriptions and recognition of taxa, perhaps the most fundamental undertaking that involves the documentation of fossils and their spatial and temporal occurrence is the reconstruction of their evolutionary paths. Although this is an area of controversy, as well as an arena where opposing views of both theory and empirical interpretation meet head on, it is the aspect of paleobiology most visible in the scientific and popular literature. The evolutionary relationships of animals and plants can also be tied to their relationship with the environment in which they lived and evolved. This activity, commonly referred to as the reconstruction of the way of life of fossil species (literally, their paleobiology) makes up the second major area of this complex activity. Although the study of the relationships of fossil species and the understanding of their behavior and ecology are not quite separable from each other, and neither is completely independent from the developmental, historical, and functional-adaptive analysis of living species, these activities are usually pursued independently. In this brief overview, the various topics can be conveniently treated under systematic paleobiology and ecological paleobiology.

Systematic Paleobiology

Paleontology supplies us with the raw material for much of paleobiology: new organisms or better and more specimens of known ones and the description of the sediments in which they were buried. In addition to the systematic treatment of these forms the diversity described becomes the data base of a variety of paleobiological activities that are systematic in nature. The science of *systematics* deals not only with the delineation of species, but also with all relationships among them and, therefore, with the nature of evolutionary change between succeeding species. This inquiry leads to the evaluation of various hypotheses concerning the mode of life of past species, and information generated in this process of analysis becomes critical also in phylogeny reconstruction. Paleobiology, like all sciences, attempts to answer questions not only of "what" and "how," but also of "how did it come to be that way" ("why"), and, as a particular contribution of this science, the question of "when" as well.

The questions of why and when, applied to whole ecosystems of the past, involve studies in such disciplines as stratigraphy, paleontology, plate tectonics, and climatology, and virtually all other aspects of the earth sciences. When we question why a fossil species is constructed in a particular way and occurs in a time and place, we begin a complex series of analytical procedures that attempt to relate the lifestyle and subsequent adaptations, or at least known modifications, of that species to its hypothesized ancestral condition and various adaptations. The theoretical issues that relate to the biological roles of various parts of extinct species (as distinct from the function or mechanics of these components) or the evolutionary position of traits compared to other homologues are formidable. One has to make convincing connections between the morphology and mechanics (function) of fossil forms before the even more difficult association between form-function and postulated behavior can be established with any degree of probability. The major method to accomplish this for fossils is first to establish causal relationships between form and function in living forms and then, through a series of conceptual steps, use the comparative method to ask the appropriate questions. Usually, the well-established causal relationships in living taxa are used as analogies when applied to the fossils. There is considerable constructive disagreement over the specific conceptual methods, the logic and rules of applying such analogies, but ultimately it is some form of rigorous analogy argument that often supplies the best functional or behavioral explanation in paleobiology. This should not be confused with using fossils and morphology in living forms as simple analogies. Nevertheless, paleobiologists must always contend with the reality that, no matter how convincing the analogy applied to some fossil species is, biological roles often cannot be predicted with any degree of certainty from the form and function of parts of fossils. Similarly, morphologically based fossil species can never be matched with certainty with the tests embodied in the biological-species concept.

Clearly, however, there is a spectrum from near certainty to plain ignorance. The power of "predicting" paleobiological roles for taxa is increased if the focus is on the more recently acquired (derived) characters of a species. These characters, from a theoretical point of view, are more likely to reflect the mode of life of an organism than traits that this animal shares with many other distinct species inherited from a common ancestry. The analogy applied is even more powerful when one uses a feature that is independently derived (i.e., *convergent*) in two or more living species, and these features are causally explicable and exclusively correlated with the same biological roles. Such a feature in a fossil is likely to have performed the same bioroles.

Ecological Paleobiology

Reconstruction of fossil communities is an activity based equally on our understanding of living assemblages of organisms and the wealth and reliability of the fossil record of a locality or of a number of localities judged to be contemporaneous in the same area. Ancient environments are best explained when the animal and plant life and the geological evidence can be accounted for by the same hypothesis. Vertebrates, primates included, are often used in the understanding of sediments of various ages. While fishes and whales will certainly indicate extensive aquatic habitats, remains of primates with arboreal adaptations equally certainly suggest a forest environment. Thus, when all of the remains of animals and plants are carefully analyzed and special relationships between their adaptations and habitats can be shown with some degree of confidence, we arrive at a highly probable description of past ecosystems.

Macroevolution and Paleobiology

The way science solidifies its gains has a lot to do with the view that new and more complex theories, concepts, or even perceptions of the world are not accepted until the views they oppose have been shown to be inadequate explanations of evidence. This pragmatic and reductionist view of science maintains that, as long as existing hypotheses of science appear to account for observed patterns, the need for new theories must be demonstrated by showing that the older theories cannot, in fact, account for the known patterns of nature. This does not mean that nature can be explained at only one level of reality. One of the most contentious problems in paleobiology (and evolutionary theory) is whether the causal mechanisms acting on individual organisms and the subsequent processes that account for the evolution of species (that are really lineages through time) can also account for patterns of life we recognize (e.g., higher categories).

Some paleontologists have suggested that various patterns seen in the fossil record indicate evolutionary mechanisms other than those involved in the processes of phyletic evolution (*anagenesis*) and speciation (*full cladogenesis*).

Microevolutionary dynamics is an area firmly established in the admittedly incomplete but foundational outlines of a neo-Darwinian framework of the Modern Synthesis of the 1930s and 1940s. Proponents of punctuated macroevolution, however, argue for hierarchic theories of evolution with purported mechanisms above the Darwinian (organismic) level, such as species-selection theories, and punctuated trends that are not adaptive changes through time but merely expressions of shifts in variance of samples. While species selection is plausible (without the semantic approach of calling species "individuals," a taxonomically rooted and philosophically unhelpful confusion of taxa with organisms), evidence has not been marshaled that such proposed phenomena cannot be explained by neo-Darwinian mechanisms that, of course, would obviate hierarchic causality. It is widely held that the original definition of species selection is only an expression of natural selection acting on individuals viewed in a larger context. Species selection as a causal process of evolution is an interesting and proper model, but so far not a single substantiated example is known. The concept of *sorting* has been suggested as a macroevolutionary phenomenon, but, in reality, it simply means evolving through the constraints or facilitations of the inherited genotypes—a generality applicable to the becoming of all lineages. The proposition of punctuated trends would all but obviate the importance of adaptive evolution and natural selection in the realtime of evolutionary causality.

The most powerful candidate for such a "macro" mechanism or, more properly, phenomenon, which is not reducible to microevolutionary processes, originates from the well-documented and large varieties of extinction events that cut across taxonomic boundaries. From local to wholesale extinctions, without regard to the adaptations of various organisms, dying out creates a new spectrum of opportunities for the surviving lineages and, therefore, temporarily alters previously existing competitive relationships. But diversification (change and modification of all sorts of patterns), multiplication of lineages, and local to large-scale extinctions ultimately result in so-called megaevolutionary patterns that have their roots in either microevolutionary mechanisms or environmental factors that are either biotic or physical.

See also Cladistics; Ecology; Evolutionary Morphology; Evolutionary Systematics (Darwinian Phylogenetics); Functional Morphology; Paleontology; Plate Tectonics; Species; Stratigraphy; Systematics; Taxonomy. [F.S.S.]

Further Readings

Behrensmeyer, A.K., and Hill, A., eds. (1980) Fossils in the Making. Chicago: University of Chicago Press.
Boucot, A.J. (1990) Evolutionary Paleobiology of Behavior and Coevolution. New York: Elsevier.
Hoffman, A. (1989) Arguments on Evolution: A Paleontologist's Perspective. New York: Oxford University Press.
Szalay, F.S., ed. (1975) Contributions to Primatology, Vol. 5: Approaches to Primate Paleobiology. Basel: S. Karger.

Paleocene

The earliest epoch of the Cenozoic, spanning between 65 and 55 Ma. Paleocene strata are inconspicuous in Europe, and rocks of this age were not distinguished from the basal Eocene in C. Lyell's original schema, published in 1833. Shortly thereafter, studies of the highly fossiliferous Upper Cretaceous and Lower Cenozoic marine beds of the Gulf Coast in Florida and Alabama revealed the true extent of pre-Eocene strata at the base of the Cenozoic. After some debate, the American view, that a separate epoch was appropriate, was accepted by European authorities.

Paleocene-age rocks in North America, Europe, and Asia are the earliest to yield fossil primates, in a diversity that suggests that primates, like chiropterans, were already distinct from other placentals in the Late Cretaceous. Paleocene land-mammal ages in North America are, in ascending order, Puercan, Torrejonian, Tiffanian, and Clarkforkian. In Europe, the Danian and Selandian marine stages are roughly coeval with the continental Montian and more or less equivalent to the North American Paleocene up to the younger half of the Tiffanian. The Thanetian standard marine stage and the coeval mammalian faunas are equivalent to the rest of the North American Paleocene. Dating of the rocks and faunas is difficult, although the Paleocene spans 10 Myr.

Asian Paleocene sites are just beginning to yield primates or forms suspected to be primates (*Petrolemur, Decor-*

edon, Altanius). The earliest Cenozoic terrestrial faunas of Africa are from sites dated to the Thanetian-equivalent Tingitanian age, in Morocco, where the omomyid *Altiatlasius* has been described together with lipotyphlan ("insectivore") taxa, some of which are also known in the Thanetian of western Europe. The South American Paleocene is reasonably well known, but the earliest record of primates in this continent is in the Oligocene.

In Paleocene times, the geography of the world was quite different from the present, and the climate and vegetation were also strikingly different. Euroamerica was a continuous landmass across Greenland and northern Europe, and most of present-day Europe was separated from Asia by a major seaway, the Turgai Straits, where the Ural Mountains stand today. North America (more properly Euroamerica at that time) was intermittently connected to Asia at the Bering Straits. Africa, Indo-Pakistan, and the smaller continental masses that make up the cores of Italy (Apulia), Hungary (Pannonia), the Balkans (Rhodope), Turkey (Anatolia), Iran, Afghanistan, Burma, and Indochina were all separated from Eurasia by the Tethys Seaway, which stretched from the narrow Atlantic Ocean to the China Sea. The remnant of the Tethys is still closing, as Africa comes up behind the smaller plates that have already been sutured against the southern edge of Eurasia.

This was a world in which climate and vegetation distribution differed drastically from our own or that of the later Cenozoic. A change from the Cretaceous equable subtropical climates to a warm, but perhaps warm-temperate and less equable, climate appears to have occurred in the Paleocene. The Paleocene was probably characterized by broad-leaved evergreen forests almost as far north as 60°, and toward the equator south of these evergreen forests there were broad-leaved deciduous forests. It is likely that coniferous forests occupied the northernmost latitudes. Judged from paleobotanical evidence, the Paleocene was quite wet, in contrast to the Eocene to come. In the midlands of North America, a remnant of the Cretaceous seaway, the Cannonball Sea, that cut the continent into western and eastern halves during the end of the Age of Reptiles still persisted as far north as Montana. In North America, and presumably in the remaining northern land areas, there were extensive forests and woodlands with a subtropical and wet climate. This pleasant climate was warm, with no pronounced seasonality, as the palms, ferns, angiosperms, turtles, lizards, and crocodilians that occur together with the land mammals suggest.

In North America, the archaic Paleocene primate fauna was extensive. Judged from the still poorly known postcranial remains, they were capable tree dwellers much like some of the present-day squirrels and the more arboreal tree shrews (tupaiids).

The remarkable aspect of the Paleocene radiation of the archaic primates, as far as we can understand it from the relatively scanty remains from North America, Europe, and Asia, is that they display an extensive dental diversity. This clearly indicates that several major radiations were well established in the world during this time and that adaptive solutions in the ancestral species of these families played a key role in the further radiation of these groups, some of which

made it into the Eocene. The paromomyids represented a group most similar to the ancestral primates in their basic anatomy (although they are derived in many respects for specific ways of locomotion and ingesting food), and they display teeth that suggest they were feeding both on insects and on fruits and seeds. Some of these paromomyids are the smallest primates ever known, but they do not show the purely insectivorous adaptations of equally small insectivorans. The picrodontids were tiny, probably gum or pollen feeding forms, whereas the carpolestids and saxonellids may have specialized on fibrous vegetation. The widespread plesiadapids, while clearly arboreal, were primarily fruit, and perhaps to some degree leaf, eaters. The Paleocene holds the key to most of the many mysteries concerning the formative beginnings and initial divergent radiation of the several clades of the Primates that appear all of a sudden in the Eocene fossil record.

See also Carpolestidae; Eocene; Paromomyidae; Picrodontidae; Plesiadapidae; Plesiadapiformes; Saxonellidae. [F.S.S.]

Further Readings

Russell, D.E., and Zhai, R. (1987) The Paleogene of Asia: Mammals and stratigraphy. Mém. Mus. Nat. Hist. Nat. (Paris), ser. C, 52:1–487.

Savage, D.E., and Russell, D.E. (1983) Mammalian Paleofaunas of the World. Reading, Mass: Addison-Wesley.

Szalay, F.S., and Delson, E. (1979) Evolutionary History of the Primates. New York: Academic.

Paleodietary Analysis

The determination of the foods eaten by prehistoric peoples. Food is of special interest to prehistorians because it provides a fundamental link between human biology and behavior. While food is an obvious requirement for life, the specific choices made by prehistoric peoples from the universe of potentially edible foods are behavioral expressions. For this reason, paleodietary analysis is a key component of archaeological and paleoanthropological research.

The variety of expression made possible by human culture has increased the numbers of available foods and the ways these foods can be prepared and combined. This complexity of potential diets means that our investigations into prehistory must be limited to broad descriptive statements that we would never accept in characterizing our own diets. The aesthetic principles, subtlety of composition, and symbolism that make up what we know as *cuisine* are virtually invisible to archaeologists.

Paleodietary analysis is, thus, an art of knowing what kinds of questions *can* be asked. Prehistorians are mainly limited to "big picture" questions, such as whether a diet was nutritionally adequate, whether a particular plant or animal species was consumed, and the proportions of animal vs. plant, or marine vs. terrestrial foods in the diet. While such questions are limited in scope, answers to them are central to issues of subsistence and economy. In turn, paleodietary analysis is essential for understanding events as diverse as the origins of the human lineage and the transition from hunting and gathering to food production.

Reconstructing the diets of early hominids and prehistoric peoples includes three broad areas of scientific inquiry: (1) morphological and pathological analysis of human skeletons; (2) analysis of archaeological residues; and (3) chemical analyses of human and animal skeletons. Each category has its own advantages and limitations, which are, to some degree, complementary.

Anatomical Considerations

In contrast to specialized herbivores or carnivores, modern humans have a generalized dentition that reflects our omnivorous dietary pattern. This leaves us little in the way of signposts for those interested in specific foods consumed. On the other hand, certain early hominins, (e.g., *Paranthropus robustus*) had more specialized dental and cranial anatomy that was capable of generating and withstanding powerful forces during mastication. Such considerations clearly tell us that this species diet was different from that of contemporaneous hominins having less sturdy craniodental features (i.e., *Homo*) and that many of the food items consumed were likely to have been harder or tougher.

In addition to the gross anatomy that is readily observable to the naked eye, dietary inferences may also be obtained by measurements of the distribution of dental enamel thickness using CT (computed tomography) scanning. Studies of CT scans of early hominin teeth have concluded that, in contrast to *Homo*, *Australopithecus africanus* and *P. robustus* have thick enamel along the lingual and buccal walls, making it possible for these teeth to withstand substantial compressive forces from puncture crushing and grinding.

Analysis of microscopic scratches on tooth enamel can provide further insight. Studies of the dental microwear of a variety of primates have shown that patterns of scratches and pits on occlusal enamel surfaces are characteristic of certain diets. For example, leafy diets leave long, linear scratches due to abrasive particles such as opal phytoliths in the leaves and the grinding function of the dentition during mastication. On the other hand, small hard objects such as seeds or nuts leave characteristic pits. Studies of dental microwear have been used to suggest that robust australopiths had a diet that depended heavily upon hard objects, while little evidence was found for the consumption of leaves. Such data need to be interpreted with care since many foods (e.g., meat and soft fruits) may leave no characteristic enamel microwear at all.

Because anatomy can provide no direct evidence for the foods consumed, it is necessary to interpret such data in the context of other ecobotanical and archaeological evidence.

Archaeological Residues

Direct evidence of dietary constituents can be obtained from careful analysis of biological remains recovered from archaeological sites. Typical remains include the skeletons of hunted or scavenged animals, shells, and the durable parts of plants, such as husks. While such information is essential for identifying many of the foods that were eaten, it must be recognized that not all foods leave archaeological traces. Moreover, it is notoriously difficult to calculate the proportional importance of different classes of foods consumed from archaeological residues. For example, the archaeological record tends to skew the evidence of prehistoric diets toward meat eating because the bones of edible animals are more likely to survive than the remains of plant foods.

Coprolites (fossilized feces) are found at many archaeological sites and provide the most direct evidence available for the consumption of a particular food. Direct evidence of animal-protein intake can be found in coprolites from the identification of bone, hair, fish scales, fur, feather fragments, and shell parts. Evidence of the plant foods consumed is similarly found in the identification of seeds, nut fragments, and berry skins. As with other archaeological residues, such studies say little about the proportional importance of such items, since only undigested items are identifiable. Many foods leave no traces in coprolites at all.

The problem of proportional importance extends to inferences derived from tool technology. The stone blades used to butcher animals survive at archaeological sites, but wooden implements used to gather underground plant foods generally do not. Nevertheless, it is sometimes possible to make dietary inferences on the basis of unique tools or inferred tool function. A recent example is the demonstration that fine linear scratches on bone tools recovered from Swartkrans (ca. 2–1.5 Ma) in South Africa were likely to have been used to dig up underground corms of the edible lily *Hypoxis argentea*. An example from more recent periods is the demonstration that microscopic sheen on characteristic blades from Natufian sites in Israel is due to the harvesting of wild cereals. In addition to wear traces, artifacts may also bear chemical residues that suggest use in the procurement or preparation of foods. For example, grindstones from the Late Paleolithic of the Nile Valley have been shown to retain fatty-acid residues from Cyperaceae tubers, suggesting that these were ground for use as food. Additionally, projectile points and other stone tools may bear identifiable blood residues from particular species of prey animals, now identifiable in some cases by DNA (deoxyribonucleic acid) traces as well.

Chemical Analysis of Skeletons

Another dimension is provided by chemical techniques based on dietary signals that are registered in human and animal skeletons. These techniques include the measurement of stable-isotope ratios and trace elements. While the specific theoretical basis for each technique differs, all are based on the demonstration that a chemical signal exists in certain foods that ultimately resides in the skeletons of consumers. Because the techniques are quantitative in nature, they provide proportional information on the relative importance of classes of foods that is otherwise invisible from anatomical and archaeological data.

The use of chemical techniques depends upon two things: a sound understanding of the distribution of the variable in natural environments, and the demonstration that chemical changes in skeletons after interment (known as *diagenesis*) do not obscure or obliterate the signal. Because of diagenesis, chemical signals cannot be universally applied. As a general rule, controls need to be incorporated into chemical studies of archaeological and fossil skeletons to ensure that a meaningful biological signal is being retrieved. In spite of this constraint, chemical techniques have become an increasingly indispensable aspect of paleodietary analysis.

Perhaps the most widely applied such technique is the measurement of the stable carbon isotope ratio. Numerous studies have demonstrated that stable carbon isotope ratios ($^{13}C/^{12}C$, or $\delta^{13}C$) in an animal's tissues reflect those in its diet. For terrestrial animals, the most useful distinction relates to basic differences in photosynthetic mechanisms between two broad classes of plants: Plants using the C_3 (or Calvin-Benson) photosynthetic pathway discriminate markedly against ^{13}C, whereas plants using the C_4 (Hatch-Slack) pathway discriminate less against the heavier isotope. The C_4 group consists mainly of tropical and savannah grasses, whereas the C_3 group consists of temperate- and high-altitude grasses, all trees, and most shrubs. The two groups of plants are isotopically distinct, and these differences are passed along the foodchain to animals eating the plants, with some further fractionation.

In the savannah biomes of East and southern Africa, carbon isotopes clearly distinguish among grazers, mixed feeders, and browsers, and, in turn, among the predators eating these animals. Recent studies of carbon isotopes recovered from the dental enamel of *P. robustus* show that this species had a mixed signal indicating consumption of some grasses or grazing animals. In the Americas, the most significant distinction is between maize (corn), which is a C_4 plant, and virtually all other edible plants, which are C_3. As a result, it has been possible to monitor the development and spread of maize farming. Carbon isotopes clearly distinguish between marine foods and C_3 plant foods, so that it is also possible to monitor marine-protein input in environments such as Mediterranean biomes that are dominated by C_3 plants.

Nitrogen-isotope ratios ($^{15}N/^{14}N$, or ($\sigma^{15}N$) similarly distinguish between marine and terrestrial protein, since, in many environments, the collagen $\delta^{15}N$ of marine animals is more positive than terrestrial ones. Thus, it has been possible to use this index to infer marine-food consumption in many prehistoric populations. $\delta^{15}N$ also becomes more positive for each trophic level, so that it may be useful in determining whether an animal having an unknown diet is an herbivore, an omnivore, or a carnivore. For example, $\delta^{15}N$ has been used to argue that European Neanderthals were carnivorous.

The trace element strontium is particularly useful since it may also provide information on the proportional contribution of meat foods to the diet. The basis for using strontium is that, while 40–80 percent of dietary calcium is absorbed, only 20–40 percent of dietary strontium is absorbed. As a result, the strontium-calcium ratio (Sr/Ca) of an animal's skeleton is lower than that of the food it has consumed. The phenomenon is referred to as the *discrimination against strontium* or the *biopurification of calcium*. Because of this phenomenon, herbivores have lower Sr/Ca than the plants they consume, while carnivores have lower Sr/Ca than the herbivores they consume.

Biopurification does not result in uniform values within trophic levels since there is considerable variability in Sr/Ca at the base of foodwebs. Plant leaves tend to have lower Sr/Ca than do edible underground parts. This difference is transmitted to consumers, so that leaf-eating herbivores tend to have lower Sr/Ca than do root- and rhizome-eating ones. Thus, while there is considerable overlap in Sr/Ca between herbivores and carnivores, the reduction in Sr/Ca is always seen when prey-predator pairs are compared.

Sr/Ca analysis has been used to study the diet of the *P. robustus*. While this species was considered to be a vegetarian, surprisingly low Sr/Ca values for *P. robustus* were recorded, indicating the consumption of either leaves or high-trophic-level foods. Inasmuch as dental microwear studies for this species rule out leaf eating as a dietary specialization, it was concluded that *P. robustus* was likely to have been omnivorous.

Barium (Ba) is also an alkaline earth metal that is discriminated against in the digestive tracts of terrestrial mammals. Ca, Sr, and Ba are absorbed in the ratio of ca. 10:5:1, with the result that Ba/Ca is even more reduced in foodwebs than is Sr/Ca. A major difference between the geochemistry of Ba and Sr, however, is the depletion of Ba in the marine environment. Depletion occurs because seawater has abundant sulfite, which when combined with Ba to form barite (barium sulfate), precipitates out of the ocean. As a result, marine foods have very little Ba, and this makes it possible to use Ba to study the dependence of coastal populations on marine foods.

Zinc (Zn) is a transition metal that is *concentrated* at higher trophic levels, leading to the suggestion that skeletal Zn may be used to infer protein intake. The rationale is based on the recognition that Zn binds firmly to proteins; it also has been shown that there is a very high correlation between dietary protein and skeletal Zn in laboratory animals. While this avenue of inquiry is promising, insufficient data exist at present on the distribution of Zn in natural foodwebs to pursue archaeological applications. Moreover, Zn appears to bind firmly to the inorganic phase of bone and thus may be very susceptible to diagenetic loss.

As our understanding of the natural distributions of trace elements and stable isotopes develops, the paleodietary information available from such analyses is likely to expand in the coming years.

See also Diet; Economy, Prehistoric; Paleolithic Lifeways; Stable Isotopes (in Biological Systems); Teeth. [A.S.]

Further Readings

Hylander, W.L. (1988) Implications of *in vivo* experiments for interpreting the functional significance of "robust" australopithecine jaws. In F.E. Grine (ed.): Evolutionary History of the "Robust" Australopithecines. New York: Aldine de Gruyter, pp. 55–84.

Kay, R.F., and Grine, F.E. (1988) Tooth morphology, wear, and diet in *Australopithecus* and *Paranthropus* from southern Africa. In F.E. Grine (ed.): Evolutionary History of the "Robust" Australopithecines. New York: Aldine de Gruyter, pp. 427–448.

Price, T.D., ed. (1989) The Chemistry of Prehistoric Human Bone. Cambridge: Cambridge University Press.

Saunders, S.R., and Katzenberg, A., eds. (1992) Skeletal Biology of Past Peoples: Research Methods. New York: Wiley-Liss.

Sillen, A. (1993) Was *Australopithecus robustus* an omnivore? S. Afr. J. Sci. 89:71–72.

Thackeray, J.F., and Macho, G.A. (1992) Computed tomography and enamel thickness of maxillary molars of Plio-Pleistocene hominids from Sterkfontein, Swartkrans, and Kromdraai (South Africa): An exploratory study. Am. J. Phys. Anthropol. 89:133–143.

Unger-Hamilton, R. (1991) Natufian plant husbandry in the southern Levant and comparison with that of the Neolithic periods: The lithic perspective. In O. Bar Yosef and F.R. Valla (eds.): The Natufian Culture in the Levant. Ann Arbor: University of Michigan Press, pp. 483–520.

Paleoenvironment

In reconstructing human evolution, the primary evidence is in the form of fossil remains. These make it possible to define fossil species and, in comparing the species, to speculate on phylogenies that reflect the course that evolution may have taken. In addition, comparative anatomical work on fossils reveals broad behavioral aspects of these species, such as locomotion and feeding, as well as clues to more detailed refinements. Scientists, however, have increasingly come to realize that they cannot properly understand human evolution divorced from an understanding of the adaptive challenges of the environment that the form and behavior of the fossilized individual were shaped to meet.

Human evolution has proceeded through radical alterations in anatomy that are presumed to define a succession of biological species, with comparable changes in behavior. Evolutionary theory holds that morphological speciation comes about primarily in response to changes in the environment—factors external to the organism. This is why environmental data are fundamental to human evolution, but the issue is complicated by the fact that ancient environments may not have been analogous to modern ones and become more and more difficult to reconstruct as we go further into the geological past. Nevertheless, there is good evidence that world environments have varied considerably since hominins originated sometime between 10 and 5 Ma, and it seems clear enough that certain of the ever more extreme swings toward intervals of cold climate in the Pliocene and the Pleistocene were synchronous with human speciation events.

The study of paleoenvironments involves the analysis of a range of data from the stratigraphic record, some of them biotic, and others giving evidence of physical environment. In recent years, new techniques have dramatically expanded the scope and diversity of paleoenvironmental analyses, giving rise to the multidisciplinary approach that characterizes modern paleoanthropology. In addition, while many aspects of paleoenvironmental investigation are focused on hominid sites and regional context, a growing amount of information is being applied from paleoclimatic interpretations of cores and microfossils in deep-sea sediments and ice caps. The fluctuations of sea level, seen in stratigraphic studies of continental shelves, also tell of the timing and intensity of glacial climate phases.

Paleoenvironmental reconstructions depend heavily on assessments of contemporaneity, but most dating methods are too imprecise to discriminate the age of one event against another in the accelerated time frame of environmental change. The order of events must be obtained from stratigraphic analysis of sequences and their regional bed-by-bed correlation. To bring one regional study into relationship with another relies on independent means of correlation such as radiometric ages, isotope stratigraphy, or paleomagnetic stratigraphy. Geological studies also help in delineating contemporaneous landscapes, such as the location of lakes, volcanoes, and other features. Climatic interpretations of contemporaneous surface sediments, on the basis of chemistry (carbonate content), mineralogy (soil zeolites, clay minerals), soil structure (laterites, podsols, hardpan), isotopes (carbon and oxygen isotopic ratios, cosmically induced nuclides), and other features (wind-blown grains, current orientation, root casts, and bioturbation), are robust and widely used elements of environmental analysis.

The evidence of past vegetation is provided, for the most part, by *palynology*, the study of pollen and spores. Palynological material is best preserved in strata with neutral to acid pore water, such as swamp deposits and lake beds at higher latitudes and in areas with abundant vegetation. By and large, limy soils, and sedimentary basins in xeric regions, are too alkaline for reliable preservation of palynomorphs. This means that, in the Rift Valley setting, where most evidence for human evolution has been found, relatively little is known of the paleoflora.

The mammalian fauna associated with fossil hominids is generally well known and gives a good idea of the contemporaneous communities. Some fairly detailed inferences about environments can be made by assuming that extinct species had environmental requirements similar to the closest living phylogenetic and/or morphological counterparts. Care must be taken not to rely overmuch on simple analogy, however, because we are missing many modern counterparts to species whose fossils we find associated with those of the extinct forms of humankind, and whose role in human evolution might have been important as predator, prey, or habitat modifier. At certain periods, for example, more than one species of hominid coexisted, and, while we have no reason to believe that they interacted with one another any more intensely than with other members of the faunal community, it remains a possibility that the most effective competitor for a hominid might be another hominid.

Where sufficient diversity is recorded, the community structure can be analyzed to distinguish predator-prey ratios, social groupings, and adaptive guilds that are more reliable indicators of environment than inferences on a species-by-species basis. Age-structure in a sample is also significant; for instance, strong selection for certain age classes indicates seasonal breeding and mortality, as in grasslands biomes. Distinctive anatomical features, such as ever-growing cheek teeth in the case of grass feeders or digging specializations in fossorial mammals, are used to deduce the habits and habitats of extinct species.

It is always a temptation, when trying to understand human evolution and the faunas with which humans have been associated, to imagine that they were adapted to environments that were direct analogues of the present day. It is important, however, to realize that environments and ecology in the past could have been different in significant ways from anything we know of now; as one example, average temperature of the oceans below the thermocline was significantly higher in the Early Pliocene than today, and this would have affected tropical-storm systems in ways for which there are no modern comparisons.

See also Climate Change and Evolution; Cyclostratigraphy; Paleobiogeography; Pollen Analysis; Sea-Level Change; Stratigraphy. [J.A.V.C., A.H.]

Further Readings

Bown, T.M., and Kraus, M.J. (1993) Soils, time, and primate paleoenvironments. Evol. Anthropol. 2:11–21.

Butzer, K.W. (1971) Environment and Archeology. Chicago: Aldine.

Coppens, Y., Howell, F.C., Isaac, G.L., and Leakey, R.E.F., eds. (1976) Earliest Man and Environments in the Lake Rudolf Basin. Chicago: University of Chicago Press.

Vrba, E.S., Denton, G.H., Partridge, T.C., and Burckle, L.H., eds. (1995) Paleoclimate and Evolution, with Emphasis on Human Origins. New Haven: Yale University Press.

Paleogene

The older period of the Cenozoic era. Paleogene and Neogene are recommended by the International Union of Geological Sciences to replace the antiquated term *Tertiary*, but some workers compromise by making these subperiods of the Tertiary. The Paleogene contains the Paleocene, the Eocene, and the Oligocene epochs and covers the time from 65 to 23.5 Ma. The term also refers to the system of strata deposited during this time.

See also Cenozoic; Eocene; Neogene; Oligocene; Paleocene; Time Scale. [F.S.S.]

Paleoindian

First well-defined and widely recognized archaeological phase in the Americas, from the most ancient sites through those dating to 11 Ka.

Surely the most important, if least dramatic, event in the history of the Americas was the passage of that first human from Asia into the New World. Nobody knows exactly when this happened—perhaps 30 Ka or more—or even where. We do not know what these Paleoindians wore, spoke, looked like, or thought. We do not know why they left their Asian homeland or what conditions they encountered on their journey.

And, yet, there is no reasonable doubt that the first Americans did indeed travel from Asia during the Late Pleistocene. Biology, language, and archaeology all point to an Asian homeland; it is the timing and conditions surrounding their arrival that remain unknown.

But something is known about the environmental conditions that permitted this migration. The Pleistocene ice advanced and retreated according to a global pulse. As the glaciers grew, at times covering Canada to a depth of perhaps 3 km, sea levels simultaneously dropped, as much as 100 m. Depressed sea levels radically changed the Earth's appearance; the Bering and Chukchi seas retreated, leaving a land bridge more than 2,000 km wide at its maximum. This vast bridge was available to East Asians, some of whom crossed into a New World.

Clovis Culture

There is no question that Paleoindians were established in the New World prior to 12 Ka. The Clovis culture, named for an archaeological site in New Mexico, can be traced from northern Alaska to Guatemala, from the west to east coasts of the United States.

Clovis spear points, among America's most distinctive artifacts, measure up to 15 cm in length, (although some are as short as 4 cm); bases are concave; and a distinctive *fluting*, or channeling, extends from the base upward to half the length of the artifact. The Clovis (or Llano) complex documents the earliest well-dated association of human cultural (and skeletal) remains with extinct animals in North America. There are no established cultural antecedents for this culture anywhere in the New (or Old) World. Clovis sites are mainly mammoth kills, mostly dating to ca. 11.5–11 Ka. Archaeological remains usually include choppers, cutting tools, a variety of bone tools, and (very rarely) milling stones, as well as the characteristic Clovis fluted points. In many localities, the Folsom and Plano cultures succeed Clovis occupations.

At the end of the last glacial interval, the North American boreal forest was gradually replaced by deciduous forests; between 10 and 8 Ka, much forest was being replaced by grasslands. By this time, large portions of the Great Plains had thus become suited for occupation by large, gregarious herbivores. The bison began providing both material and spiritual focus for aboriginal lifeways on the Great Plains. These Paleoindians hunted a variety of big game, some now extinct: mammoth, caribou, musk-ox, and long-horned bison. Some think that changing climates and rapid shifts in vegetation so altered regional ecology that it no longer favored several of these species. Less water meant, among other things, fewer coarse grasses and reeds available for elephant herds. But many believe that humans, the world's most efficient predators, literally hunted these great beasts into extinction. A different pattern emerged in the eastern United States. Despite similarities in technology, the Paleoindian mode of life in this area differed from the pattern of big-game hunting found in the western plains. By 12 Ka, the floral and faunal resources available between the Ohio Valley and Ontario were sufficient to support scattered bands of hunters. The considerable homogeneity of tool forms in the Northeast suggested a single technological complex, adaptable to a wide variety of environments, from coastal plain to upland, from river valley to northern lakes. Animal bones

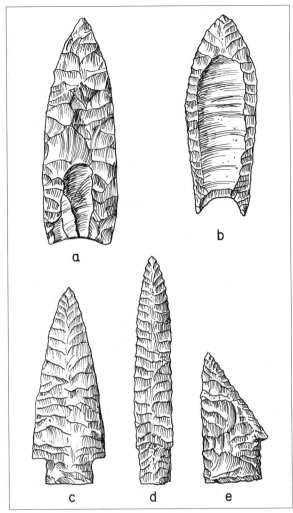

Some typical Paleoindian stone-tool types: (a) Clovis point; (b) Folsom point; (c) Scottsbluff point; (d) Eden point; (e) Cody knife. Not to scale.

found in association with these Paleoindian sites are usually woodland caribou.

There are many mastodon and mammoth finds in the eastern United States but no evidence that humans either slew or butchered these animals. Other foods, such as nuts, seeds, berries, fish, and fowl, were available and not beyond the procurement capabilities of these early populations. Eastern Paleoindians emphasized the exploitation of river-valley resources, thus beginning to adapt in the direction of later, more efficient gathering economies.

Hunting adaptations similar to Clovis can also be seen in early South American cultures. The diagnostic artifacts of this tradition are fish-tail projectile points from El Inga and other sites, which resemble Clovis points of North America. Established largely in Andean South America, this early hunting tradition seems to have begun in the Andean region, from where it spread eastward into the plains of Argentina and south to the tip of South America. Between 13 and 12 Ka, Paleoindians hunted mastodons at El Jobo in northern Venezuela. Their contemporaries in central Colombia and southern Chile seem to have concentrated on collecting plants and hunting smaller game. In southern Patagonia, people hunted horses and ground sloths ca. 11 Ka, but we

have no evidence that Paleoindians in central and northern Brazil ever hunted such big game.

The human fossil record for Paleoindians remains skimpy. Perhaps the earliest readily acceptable specimen is a complete cranium recovered from Cerro Sota Cave in Patagonia (Chile) by J. Bird in 1936. The skull is small, showing modest browridges and little facial projection, but, in all respects, the morphology of the Cerro Sota material is fully modern and consistent with the variability seen in native Americans from South America.

The oldest Paleoindian human remains in North America date from the Clovis period: Midland (Texas), Marmes Shelter (Washington State), Gordon Creek (Colorado), Anzick (Montana), and Buhl (Idaho). Although claims for a more extreme antiquity have been made, the evidence remains clouded. Aspartic-acid-racemization reactions suggested, for instance, that skeletons found near La Jolla, Del Mar, and Sunnyvale (California) ranged in age from 70 to 26 Kyr. But subsequent research, employing the accelerator-mass-spectrometry method of radiocarbon dating, now places these skeletons in the period between 6.3 and 3.6 Ka. Similar empirical problems exist for other reputedly pre-Holocene-age human fossils in the New World.

Pre-Clovis Cultures

Clovis is the earliest well-documented human population known in the Western Hemisphere. Decades of concerted research have provided no undisputed proof of a pre-Clovis human presence in North America. Perhaps the best evidence for a pre-12 Ka occupation comes from Meadowcroft Shelter in southwestern Pennsylvania. Accompanying a ladder of more than 40 radiocarbon dates is evidence of human occupation: firepits, stone tools, a piece of basketry, and two human bone fragments. The oldest cultural date at Meadowcroft is slightly more than 19 Ka. Yet, the evidence at Meadowcroft Shelter remains controversial; early stone tools are rare and identical to later artifacts; diagnostic Paleoindian artifacts are absent, as is Pleistocene megafauna. The temperate-vegetation evidence throughout the Meadowcroft sequence seems anomalous, since the ice front was less than 75 km to the north. In 1998, a new site, Cactus Hill (Virginia) yielded a pre-Clovis level similar to that at Meadowcroft and dated to 15–16 Ka.

Early radiocarbon dates are also available from South American sites. At Monte Verde, an open-air residential site in southern Chile, T. Dillehay and his colleagues have encountered four distinct zones of buried cultural remains. Nearly one dozen house foundations and fallen pole-frames of residential huts have been excavated, and fragments of skin (perhaps mastodon) still cling to the poles. Dillehay argues that the upper layers contain evidence of a human presence ca. 13 Ka. Even more controversial are the deep layers at Monte Verde that have produced two radiocarbon dates of 33 Ka associated with possible cultural features and several fractured stones.

Additional controversial sites throughout the Americas have yielded simple stone and bone assemblages from less definite cultural contexts. Unfortunately, the archaeology of each such site leaves many questions unanswered, and none of this evidence is universally accepted by New World archaeologists.

Despite such empirical difficulties, many specialists believe that humans reached North America long before Clovis, sometime prior to 40–30 Ka. Scholars favoring a pre-Clovis occupation of North America argue, among other things, that the great diversity in projectile points manufactured 12–10 Ka precludes the possibility of first migration from Asia only a couple of millennia before. The variety of ecological adaptations already evident by this date, ranging from interior Subarctic to coastal tropical, can be used to argue similarly. Moreover, there is no convincing demonstration that the precursor of Clovis technology came from Asia.

See also Americas; Blackwater Draw; Calico Hills; Clovis; Fells Cave; Folsom; Guitarrero Cave; Llano Complex; Meadowcroft Shelter; Old Crow; Plano; Sandia; Tlapacoya. [D.H.T.]

Further Readings

Adovasio, J.M., Donahue, J., Pedlar, D.R. and Stuckenrath, R. (1998) Two decades of debate on Meadowcroft Rockshelter. North American Archaeologist. 19(4):317–341.

Bonnichsen, R., and Turmire, K.L. (1991) Clovis: Origins and Adaptations. Corvallis: Center for the Study of the First Americans, Oregon State University.

Bryan, A.L., ed. (1986) New Evidence for the Pleistocene Peopling of the Americas. Orono: University of Maine Center for Study of Early Man.

Carlisle, R., ed. (1988) Americans before Columbus: Ice Age Origins. Pittsburgh: Department of Anthropology, University of Pittsburgh.

Dillehay, T.D., and Meltzer, D.J., eds. (1991) The First Americans: Search and Research. Boca Raton: CRS Press.

Dincauze, D. (1984) An archaeological evaluation of the case for pre-Clovis occupations. Adv. World Archaeol. 3:275–323.

Irving, W.N. (1985) Context and chronology of early man in the Americas. Ann. Rev. Anthropol. 14:529–555.

Soffer, O., and Praslov, N.D. eds. (1993) From Kostenki to Clovis: Upper Paleolithic-Paleo-Indian Adaptations. New York: Plenum.

Stanford, D.J., and Day, J.S., eds. (1992) Ice Age Hunters of the Rockies. Boulder: University of Colorado Press.

Paleolithic

Earliest division of the Stone Age, first defined by J. Lubbock in 1865 as the epoch of "the Drift [= Ice Age] when man shared the possession of Europe with the Mammoth, the Cave Bear, the Woollyhaired Rhinoceros, and other extinct animals." Today the term refers to Late Pliocene and Pleistocene archaeological sites worldwide that reflect the human coexistence with, and dependence on, extinct (and extant) large herbivores. Lubbock's definition succeeded those based on paleontology and biostratigraphy (e.g., those by E. Lartet and H. Christy) rather than on the characteristics of stone tools or human adaptations.

As the first stage of C.J. Thomsen's three-age system (Stone, Bronze, Iron), the Stone Age was initially divided by Lubbock into two epochs, Paleolithic and Neolithic, in accordance with a French division into "chipped stone" and "polished stone" ages. Since early definitions of the Paleolithic combined chronological (biostratigraphic), technological (chipped stone), and economic (big-game hunters) criteria, subsequent use of the term has been inconsistent, particularly at the chronological and geographic boundaries of the original definitions, which were based on Middle and Late Pleistocene European contexts. For example, African Paleolithic industries are often referred to a different system: Early, Middle, and Later Stone Age. These do not coincide in time with the Ice Age, and they include industries with ground-stone and occasionally metal objects, as well as evidence of economic intensification (e.g., fishing).

Boundaries and Divisions of the Paleolithic

Even the earliest chipped-stone industries, of which four are known between 2.6 and 2.1 Ma, are generally included in the study of Paleolithic archaeology. The inclusion within the Paleolithic of industries made by specialized hunter-fisher-gatherers of the Late Pleistocene and Early Holocene is more problematic, but where these industries appear prior to 20 Ka, as in Zambia and Zaire, their attribution to the Paleolithic is widely accepted. Thus, although the Paleolithic is intended to represent a stage of *cultural* evolution, it is often defined chronologically, particularly in Europe, and limited to industries occurring before the Late Pleistocene/Holocene boundary at ca. 10 Ka.

The Paleolithic is usually divided (especially in Europe) into three stages: Lower, Middle, and Upper, or, as in this volume worldwide, Early, Middle, and Late. The Early Paleolithic includes industries with handaxes and/or cleavers (Acheulean, Abbevillian, Micoquian), choppers and flakes (Oldowan, Buda), and unspecialized flakes (Clactonian, Tayacian, Hope Fountain). Prepared-core technologies (Levallois, Victoria West) develop only toward the end of this stage. In Africa the Early Paleolithic (or Early Stone Age) lasts more than 2 Myr, with only limited introductions of new tool forms (handaxes and cleavers at ca. 1.5 Ma) or economic strategies (a shift to rockshelter use, increased dependence on hunting of large herbivores by the later Middle Pleistocene, as at the Cave of Hearths). Control of fire may have been present from 1.5 Ma on or may have developed only later. In Europe and Asia, the earliest Paleolithic industries are dated to ca. 1.0 Ma or less (Vallonnet, Isernia, Atapuerca, Notarchirico, Nihewan, Xihoudu), although very scattered evidence of human fossils (Dmanisi, Modjokerto, Longgupo) and artifacts ('Ubeidiya) may indicate earlier intermittent human occupation of southern Eurasia. Handaxes appear by 650 Ka (Notarchirico) in Europe but are rare until ca. 400 Ka. They are generally absent from East and Southeast Asia but may occur in Middle Pleistocene contexts in South Korea (Chongok-Ni) and Japan (Takamori).

The Middle Paleolithic stage reflects increasing sophistication of stone-tool technology, economic patterns, and cognitive development. In both Europe and Africa, tools are frequently made on small, thin flakes of regular shape and are often preshaped on the core by Levallois or discoidal technology. European sites, usually rockshelters rather than

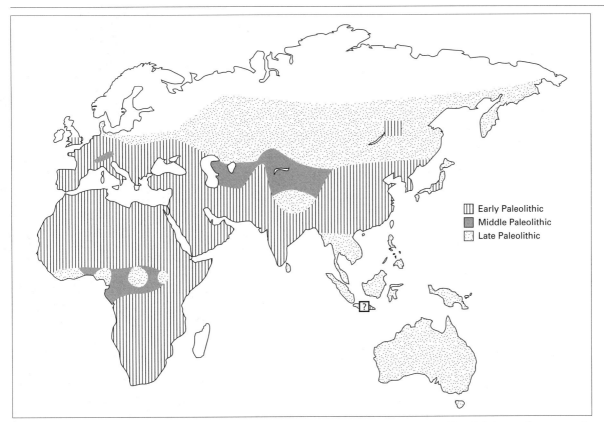

Map showing the approximate geographical extent of industries assigned to the Early, Middle, and Later stages of the Paleolithic period. Note especially the progressive extension of Paleolithic humans into less hospitable environments (e.g. northern Eurasia and the African rain forest).

stream channels, show evidence of considerable hunting skill and some degree of specialization on large herbivore prey species, as well as some of the earliest evidence for symbolic, aesthetic, and advanced cognitive behavior, in the form of "crayons" of coloring material, human burials with occasional grave goods, and rare examples of incised and perforated bones or teeth.

In Africa and Southwestern Asia, Middle Paleolithic industries are interspersed with horizons in which true blades are present. In addition, African Middle Paleolithic industries begin earlier than those in Europe (by 250–240 Ka, according to dates from Ethiopia, Kenya, and Tanzania), have more evidence of complex technologies (backing, hafting), and are occasionally associated with colored, notched, or incised objects of bone, stone, and ostrich eggshell. Unlike industries of the Early Paleolithic, those of the Middle Paleolithic exhibit a degree of regional specificity on a smaller-than-subcontinental scale, especially in southern Africa. Increasing interregional diversity suggests that Middle Paleolithic humans may have begun to be organized into discrete societies with different groups reflected in their styles of artifact manufacture or, alternatively, that patterns of economic exploitation were more tightly adapted to regionally specific resources.

Without question, the greatest shift in Paleolithic adaptations is that between the Middle and the Late Paleolithic (between 40 and 30 Ka) in Europe but possibly earlier elsewhere). In its strictest sense, the Upper Paleolithic is limited to Europe, and perhaps western Asia and northeastern

Africa, where the most characteristic innovations are the appearance of blade technology and the use of burins and other tools to work bone, antler, ivory, tooth, and shell. Faunal remains at particular sites are increasingly dominated by a single species (e.g., reindeer, horse, mammoth, red deer, ibex), indicating increased technological skill, scheduling of resource use, and possibly processing of meat for storage. Decorative beads and pendants were manufactured, and raw materials, such as stone, ivory, and shell, were traded over long distances, suggesting greater complexity of social organization. Finally, a profusion of carved, painted, modeled, or engraved images (whether on cave walls or on small pieces of bone, antler, ivory, or baked clay), together with rare but elaborate burials, as at Sungir, attest to an elaboration of symbolic behavior, possibly in response to the increased complexity and risk of economic strategies and/or to the greater requirements of expanded social interactions.

Although microlithic tools were made in many areas of Europe after 20 Ka, and economic specialization increases after this time with greater emphasis on small-scale resources, it is customary to place the limit of the Upper Paleolithic at the end of the last Ice Age, ca. 10 Ka, when large gregarious herbivores disappear from much of the area covered by Upper Paleolithic adaptations. In Africa, however, the transition from Middle to Late Paleolithic is much less abrupt and the coincidence of the final Paleolithic industries with the Pleistocene/Holocene boundary much less clear. Blade technologies are widespread in Africa during the Middle Paleolithic, and even microlithic technology appears in

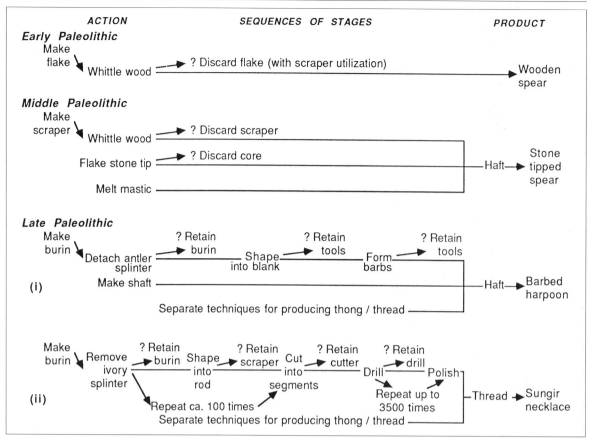

A comparison of the stages involved in representative tool making procedures in the Early, Middle, and Late Paleolithic. After R. Dennell, European Economic Prehistory, *Academic Press, 1983.*

some regions before 40 Ka. Economic and technological specializations such as seasonal fishing and boneworking are already present in the context of industries classed as Middle Paleolithic. Furthermore, in most of tropical Africa, large gregarious herbivores continue to be hunted through the final Pleistocene into the Holocene.

To avoid the Eurocentric Early, Middle, and Later (or Upper) Paleolithic divisions, and to separate the technological, economic, and social implications of the terms, J.G.D. Clark proposed five technological modes to describe the changes in Paleolithic industries: Mode 1, industries with simple flakes and cores/choppers (Oldowan, Clactonian); Mode 2, industries with some formally shaped tools and simple direct-percussion flaking techniques (Acheulean); Mode 3, industries with flakes struck from prepared cores (Mousterian, Bambata, Stillbay); Mode 4, blade and burin industries; and Mode 5, industries with microliths. In this scheme, the fact that Upper Paleolithic technology (Mode 4) is lacking over most of Africa would not obscure the fact that many of the same social, economic, and cognitive shifts, such as creation of images, long-distance trade, body ornamentation, diversification, and/or economic specialization, take place as early or earlier in Africa than the Middle/Upper Paleolithic boundary of Europe. The separation of technological from socioeconomic development also allows the discussion of Paleolithic stages to be extended to Australia, the Pacific, and the New World. These areas all appear to have been colonized from Asia between ca. 60 and 15 Ka by fully

modern (if somewhat robust) humans, who do not appear to have practiced a Mode 4 or 5 technology at the time of their arrival. Mode 4 idustries, called *Lithic* or *Paleoindian,* are widespread in North America by 12 Ka.

Aims of Paleolithic Archaeology

Paleolithic archaeology aims, first, to provide an inventory of the Paleolithic record so as to allow reconstruction of *culture history* through the definition and dating of regional industrial sequences and, second, to explain the variability in the archaeological record so as to shed light on Paleolithic lifeways (including particularly the technological, economic, social, ritual, and ideological aspects of Paleolithic societies at various times in the past) and their relationship to the formation of archaeological sites. Although both goals are inherent in most Paleolithic research, prehistorians trained in geology tend to emphasize sequences and culture-historical reconstruction, while those trained in anthropology (or ethnology) emphasize the reconstruction of past lifeways.

Recent syntheses have tended to combine the two approaches. The need to order assemblages from different sites in a chronological sequence has led to new approaches to age determination, particularly at sites beyond the range of radiocarbon (40 Ka), including microfaunal biostratigraphy, geochemical dating (e.g., thermoluminescence, electron spin resonance, oxygen-isotope ratios, uranium series, amino-acid racemization), and microstratigraphy. In addition to chronology, these techniques have yielded an improved understand-

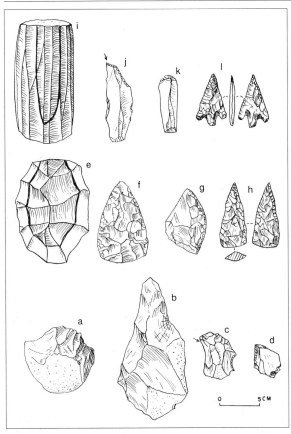

Representative artifacts of the Paleolithic. Early Paleolithic: (a) Oldowan chopper (Africa); (b) early Acheulean handaxe (Africa); (c) Clactonian flake tool (Europe); (d) flake tool (China). Middle Paleolithic: (e) Levallois core and flake removed from it (Europe); (f) Mousterian handaxe (France); (g) Quina convex scraper (Europe); (h) Pietersburg bifacial point (South Africa). Late Paleolithic: (i) prismatic blade core (Old World); (j) Capsian burin on blade (Tunisia); (k) Perigordian end-scraper (France); (l) Solutrean tanged point (Spain).

ing of paleoenvironments. Attention to formation processes and taphonomy has resulted in a consensus that most Paleolithic sites are palimpsests of repeated activities in a given location; that different sites within a group's annual range may have been used for different activities; and that the energy invested in objects, together with cultural rules of disposal and curation (retention for future use) are as important as technological capabilities, stylistic norms, and localized activities in determining the content of archaeological assemblages. The result is a shift to regionally based interpretive frameworks.

Human Evolution and Cultural Development

One of the major questions in Paleolithic research concerns the relationship between morphological and cultural change in the fossil and archaeological records, respectively. For example, is the *Homo habilis* to *Homo erectus* boundary correlated with the appearance of the Acheulean and other innovations, or the *neanderthalensis* to *sapiens* boundary with the shift from Middle to Upper Paleolithic? Recent evidence has suggested that morphological and cultural evolution are less clearly associated than previously supposed, particularly at the Middle to Upper Paleolithic boundary, where Neanderthals have been associated with Upper Paleolithic industries (Saint-Césaire, Vindija), and fully modern humans in

Africa with flake industries grouped with the Middle Paleolithic (Klasies River Mouth, Border Cave). In the Early Paleolithic, the correlation between human biology and culture is even less clear, with increasing speculation that some of the relatively similar, early stone-tool assemblages may have been produced by different hominin species, including *Australopithecus robustus*. Other ways in which morphological concerns impinge on Paleolithic studies concern the capacity for culture of *presapiens* hominids. Particularly in the early stages of the Paleolithic, the relatively unchanging simple technology and spatial distribution of tool types and sites suggest that, if entities comparable with human societies or cultures existed, they either did not recognize intergroup differences or did not symbolize them in the manufacture and use of implements. The extent to which Plio-Pleistocene hominins exhibited fully human behavior, such as food sharing, division of labor by sex, home bases, nuclear-family organization, provisioning of juveniles, hunting, or control of fire, has been much debated, as the earliest Paleolithic record provides little evidence for the existence of any of these behaviors. The record does show, however, that Early Pleistocene humans were unlike groups of chimpanzees in that they made, used, and discarded stone tools repeatedly at the *same* landscape points and also transported stone and carcass parts to these locations.

Another focus of this debate concerns the degree and interrelationship of language capabilities reflected in the Neanderthal skeleton and symbolic activities, including communication, reflected in the Middle Paleolithic archaeological record. In this case, some morphologists and archaeologists have advocated minimal symbolic and cognitive capabilities for Neanderthals, while certain of their colleagues have argued otherwise. The comparisons between the two kinds of data have led each side to reexamine its conceptions and pose new questions.

Regional Differences in Paleolithic Adaptations

Although study of the Paleolithic is still somewhat Eurocentric, investigators have realized that the continents and subcontinental regions of the Old World have profoundly different histories and patterns of human development. During the last million years of the Pleistocene, East Asian industries changed little from the Mode 1 forms recovered from the earliest sites, although there are a few bifacial forms (e.g., in Korea and Japan), and prepared cores appear in later Pleistocene contexts. Human morphological shifts, however, parallel those observed in Africa, although possibly at later time periods throughout. In sub-Saharan Africa, Mode 4 industries (e.g., Howieson's Poort) appear only intermittently within Mode 3 sequences (Middle Stone Age). A stage comparable with the European Upper Paleolithic in both technology and other aspects of economic and social intensification is lacking over much of the continent. On the other hand, fully modern humans appear earlier in sub-Saharan Africa than in Europe. Within Europe itself, the Mediterranean region has a different history of settlement and technological development, particularly at the end of the Paleolithic. Whether these regional differences were due to differing adaptations, ethnic groups, raw materials, or histories of human evolution and migration remains to be determined, but the shift in focus from a site-oriented perspective to a regional one is the most important step in a comprehensive understanding of the Paleolithic age.

See also Abbevillian; Acheulean; Africa; Americas; Asia, Eastern and Southern; Asia, Western; Australia; Biochronology; Buda Industry; Cave of Hearths; Clactonian; Early Paleolithic; Early Stone Age; Economy, Prehistoric; Epipaleolithic; Europe; Geochronometry; Glaciation; Handaxe; Hominidae; Homo; Homo erectus; Homo habilis; Homo sapiens; Hope Fountain; Howieson's Poort; Hunter-Gatherers; Late Paleolithic; Later Stone Age; Levallois; Mesolithic; Micoquian; Middle Paleolithic; Middle Stone Age; Mousterian; Neanderthals; Neolithic; Oldowan; Paleoenvironment; Paleolithic Image; Paleolithic Lifeways; Pleistocene; Prehistory; Prepared-Core; Raw Materials; Saint-Césaire; Site Types; Speech (Origins of); Stone-Tool Making; Storage; Stratigraphy; Taphonomy; Tayacian; Upper Paleolithic. [A.S.B.]

Further Readings

Clark, J.G.D. (1969) World Prehistory: A Brief Introduction. Cambridge: Cambridge University Press.

Gamble, C. (1986) The Palaeolithic Settlement of Europe. Cambridge: Cambridge University Press.

Klein, R.G., ed. (1984) Southern African Prehistory and Paleoenvironments. Boston: Balkema.

Klein, R.G. (1989) The Human Career. Chicago: University of Chicago Press.

Lubbock, J Chord Avebury. (1865) Prehistoric Tunes As Illustrated by Ancient Romans and the Manners and Customs of Modern Savages. London: Williams and Mangate.

Phillipson, D.W. (1993) African Archaeology, 2nd ed. Cambridge: Cambridge University Press.

Wu, R., and Olsen, J. (1985) Palaeoanthropology and Palaeolithic Archaeology in the People's Republic of China. New York: Academic.

Wymer, J. (1982) The Palaeolithic Age. New York: St. Martin's.

Paleolithic Calendar

The first book to describe the carved and engraved images and the bone and stone tools of the Reindeer Age in France (as the Upper Paleolithic, or Late Ice Age, was called at first) was published by E. Lartet and H. Christy in 1875. In that volume, the British anthropologist E.R. Jones described a number of bones incised with accumulated sets of tiny marks, which he considered to be "tallies," implying that they may have been hunting or gaming records. Jones documented the presence of comparable items made by hunters and farmers from many parts of the world in the historic period. Almost a century later, these Ice Age objects, which had begun to be found in both western and eastern Europe, were subjected to microscopic analysis to determine how they were made and accumulated. A. Marshack published several analyses that indicated that these "tallies" had often been accumulated over a considerable period of time, one set of marks being added sequentially to the next. The analyses indicated that the sets of marks were usually made by different engraving points and that they were often incised with different pressures, rhythms, and direction of marking, suggesting that they were, in fact, some form of record keeping or notation. Historic tallies made by hunters or by farmers of goods borrowed or lent did not show this form of continuous, sequential linear accumulation. The Upper Paleolithic notations sometimes had hundreds of marks, broken down into sets. An internal analysis of these sets indicated that they

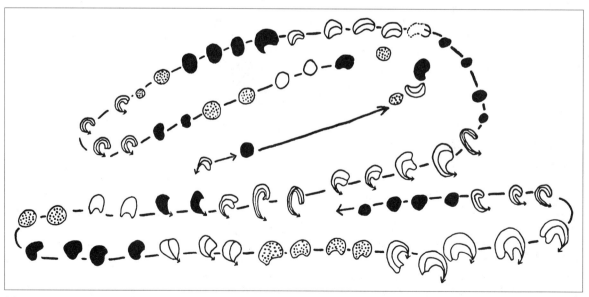

The serpentine notation engraved on a piece of bone from the early Upper Paleolithic (Aurignacian period, ca. 30,000 BP), rock shelter of Abri Blanchard, France. Sixty-nine marks were accumulated with twenty-six changes of point and style or pressure of marking. The notation images the waxing and waning of the moon and encompasses 2¼ lunar months, with the full moon periods at the left, the crescents and days of invisibility at the right. Courtesy of Alex Marshack.

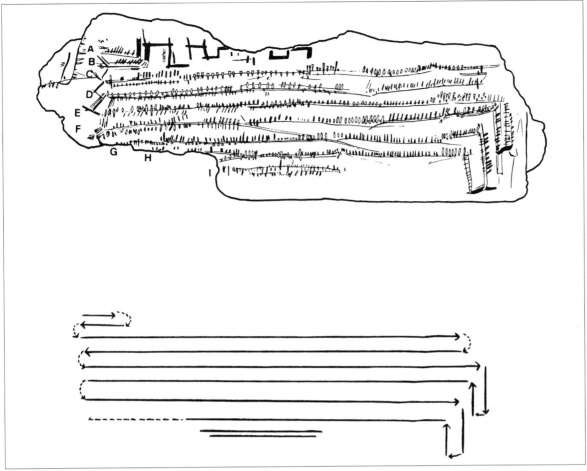

Notational engraving accumulated in a serpentine manner on a fragment of bone from the terminal Ice Age (late Magdalenian, ca. 11,000 B.P.) of Grotte du Tai, France. The entire plaque contains the notation for 3 ½ years. At far right the notation dips down because space ran out in marking lines D and E horizontallly. The serpentine model of accumulating the notation is indicated in the schematic model below. Courtesy of Alex Marshack.

were nonarithmetic, that they were not broken down into fives or tens. They provided no indication of an arithmetical counting system.

The sequences of sets, however, often closely tallied with observation of the phases of the moon, and the longer sets with an observation of passing lunar months. They therefore seemed to be records of the passage of time, marking off the phases of the moon and the passage of lunar months, or "moons," and the seasons. Since these analyses were published, it has become common among archaeologists to describe the hunting-and-gathering cultures and economies of the Ice Age as highly mobile and seasonally organized, with hunting groups often moving long distances to follow the migrating herds of reindeer, bison, horse, or mammoth, culling different species at different times for their antlers, meat, or skins.

The Upper Paleolithic notations, which were probably kept by tribal specialists, would have helped in planning and scheduling the complex sequence of social, cultural, and economic activity. Archaeologists have begun to acknowledge that there were probably seasonal periods for group dispersal and aggregation, with the latter periods involving barter and exchange and probably group rituals and ceremonies. True arithmetical and astronomical calendars, in which the year was established as an arithmetical sum, began to appear only with the political and religious temple organization that de-

veloped in the farming civilizations that arose some time after the Ice Age ended at ca. 10 Ka.

See also Late Paleolithic; Paleolithic Image; Paleolithic Lifeways; Upper Paleolithic. [A.M.]

Further Readings

Marshack, A. (1984) Hierarchical Evolution of the Human Capacity: The Paleolithic Evidence. Fifty-fourth James Arthur Lecture. New York: American Museum of Natural History.

Marshack, A. (1991a) The Roots of Civilization, rev. ed. Mt. Kisco, N.Y.: Moyer Bell.

Marshack, A. (1991b) The Tai plaque and calendrical notation in the Upper Paleolithic. Cambr. Archeol. J. 1(1):25–61.

Paleolithic Image

The first widespread body of imagery and symbol, or art, to appear in the archaeological record is from the Upper Paleolithic, or Later Stone Age, of Europe, popularly known as the last Ice Age, ca. 35–11 Ka. These images were made by the hunters of such extinct animals as the woolly mammoth, woolly rhinoceros, and large-antlered elk (*Megaloceros*), as well as reindeer, bison, horse, aurochs (wild cattle), ibex (wild goat), and deer. All of these species, along with lion, bear, wolf, fox, fish, seal, serpent, amphibians, migratory water birds, regional birds, insects, and plants, were depicted in the art of the European Ice Age. Images of comparable antiquity are documented for Africa, Asia, Australia, and some Pacific Islands. These images, painted, incised, or carved on antler, bone, ivory, and stone, began to be found in the habitation sites of the Ice Age hunter-gatherers of Europe more than a century ago, not long after C. Darwin published *On the Origin of Species* (1859) with its suggestion of a long evolutionary development for humans and other species. Darwin theorized that forms of humans must have lived on Earth long before the beginnings of written history and civilization. A few years after publication of the *Origin*, the validation of human-made stone tools, or handaxes, found in the soil with the bones of extinct animals began to document the ancient ancestry of modern humans.

Discovery of Ice Age Art

In 1865, the engraved outline of a woolly mammoth on a shaped piece of mammoth ivory was excavated at La Madeleine, a limestone rockshelter on the shore of the Vézère River in the Dordogne area of southwestern France. The engraving proved that humans capable of representational art had lived in Europe in a cold period when mammoth roamed the continent. In 1868, the skeletons of several Ice Age adults, including one woman, were found a few kilometers downstream on the Vézère, in a small cliffside burial cave called Cro-Magnon, within the farming village of Les Eyzies. The skeletons were of anatomically modern humans. It slowly became clear that the Cro-Magnons, as they came to be called, had displaced the Neanderthals, who had occupied Europe for the previous 100 Kyr. Found with the Cro-Magnon skeletons were beads of seashells that came from the Atlantic to the west and the Mediterranean to the southeast, indicating that these early humans not only made images but had walked or traded at great distances to secure symbolic materials. They were, then, modern humans in both their morphology and their ways of thinking, even though they were relatively ancient, prehistoric hunter-gatherers.

In the century that followed, hundreds of images were excavated from Ice Age habitation sites and burials across Europe, within those areas that lay south of the great ice sheets that blanketed northern Europe and the central region of the Alps. These habitation sites lay along the network of rivers that flowed to the Atlantic or to the Mediterranean and Black seas, within the area that today contains France, Spain, Italy, Germany, Austria, Czechoslovakia, and Ukraine. During the last Ice Age maximum cold phase, large portions of this area consisted of open steppe, some woodland along the rivers, and areas of permafrost tundra toward the north. Ice Age culture also dispersed into Siberia. The remains of homesites—including tents or huts constructed of poles, antler, and skins, with fireplaces, stone and bone tools, a burial, and a rich collection of carved and engraved images and costume pieces made of mammoth ivory—have been found at Mal'ta, on the Angara River in central Siberia, dated at ca. 16.5 Ka, near the end of the Ice Age.

The seemingly sudden explosion of art that developed across this vast area included many forms: a wide range of personal decoration, including necklaces, rings, bracelets, headbands, anklets, and pendants, as well as elaborately beaded clothes, along with a variety of nonutilitarian symbolic artifacts, such as carved ritual batons, wands, and strangely shaped objects. Bone tools began to be decorated with the images of animals, humans, signs, and motifs. There are occasional engraved and painted images of shamans in ritual costume. The library of imagery also includes imaginary or fantastic creatures. There are different types of human imagery: the best known are the human females from the early Upper Paleolithic or Gravettian period, ca. 28–23 Ka, the naked "venus" figurines carved in ivory and stone. Even earlier, in the Aurignacian period of France, ca. 30 Ka, one finds carved and engraved vulva images and occasional phalluses.

In the late Upper Paleolithic of western Europe, during the Magdalenian, a different style of representing the human female appears. It is usually the schematic, abstracted, headless image of a female body, known as the *buttocks image* because of a flat or concave front and an exaggerated, protruding rear. Musical instruments, including whistles, flutes, and percussion instruments, appear early. With these recognizable products, there begins to appear a number of prewriting, nonrepresentational symbol systems consisting of geometric signs and motifs and accumulations of sets of marks. Found in the homesites and the caves, these are among the major puzzles of the late Ice Age cultures. An internal analysis of the accumulated sets of marks, once thought to be hunting tallies, suggests that they may have been a form of notation or record keeping, perhaps marking the passage of months and seasons, an activity that would have been useful for scheduling both economic and ritual activity in the sharply delineated seasons of mid-latitude Europe. Within this huge and diverse body of symbolic materials are exquisite masterpieces of art, clearly made by trained specialists, although the majority of examples are artistically unexceptional, except for their early presence and extraordinary variety.

Sanctuary Caves: A Regional Development

In 1879, Altamira, a painted and engraved Ice Age cave, was discovered in the foothills of the Cantabrian Mountains of northwestern Spain. The depicted animals, including bison painted in red and black on the ceiling, were so startling that they were declared to be fake, until comparable images of bison, horse, ibex, and aurochs were discovered in 1895 in the small cave of La Mouthe in France, a short walk from the burial of Cro-Magnon and not far from the site of La Madeleine. Since then, almost 250 painted and engraved caves have been found among the limestone hills of southern France and northwestern Spain, the Franco-Cantabrian area. Rare examples of Ice Age cave art have been found elsewhere: underwater off the Mediterranean coast near Marseilles (Cosquer), on a tributary of the Rhône, the Ardèche (Chauvet) in eastern France, along the southern Mediterranean coast of Spain (La Pileta, Nerja), in the cave of Cucialat in Romania, and in the cave of Kapova in the Ural Mountains.

Top: three "venus" figurines made in the same style, from the early Upper Paleolithic of Europe (Gravettian, ca. 27–23 Ka) .Left: figure in mammoth ivory, from Kostenki (Ukraine); center: figure carved in limestone and covered with red ocher, from Willendorf (Austria); right: figure carved of mammoth ivory, from Lespugue (France). Bottom left: necklace of eighteen ibex heads and one bison head, carved from bone and incised, from Labastide (France), dating to the late Magdalenian. Bottom right: painting of a stag with full antlers, head up and mouth open, baying in the time of the autumn rut. A set of painted dots and a geometric sign accompany this work from Lascaux (France), dated ca. 16,500 BP Courtesy of Alex Marshack.

Upper Paleolithic cave engravings have been found in Italy and Sicily, and some Late Paleolithic engravings on rock walls have apparently been found in Siberia. Paintings on cave or rockshelter walls of later Pleistocene age are also known from Australia and southern and eastern Africa.

It was the powerful imagery in the Franco-Cantabrian sanctuary caves, and the dramatic stories of their discovery and validation, that for almost half a century turned the attention of archaeologists and the public away from the complexity and variety of the symbol systems that were being continuously found in Ice Age homesites across Europe. Most popular books on Ice Age art have focused on the caves, often providing highly imaginative descriptions of the rituals that were supposed to occur there. A few caves do provide evidence of group rites, but they are rare and never suggest large groups. On the clay wall of the cave of Montespan (France), the headless carving of a clay bear and the incised image of a horse were repeatedly stabbed with spears, perhaps in a ritual involving a few persons. In the cave of Tuc d'Audoubert (France), two carved clay bison were accompanied by a few heel prints of adolescents in the clay floor, suggesting a short hooflike ritual dance. In the Santander region of northwestern Spain, the cave of El Juyo has revealed a complex ritual altar that would have required the time and effort of a number of persons to construct, but it may have been a specialized sanctuary used by a few persons at special times. At Lascaux, the most important decorated cave in France, a scaffolding had been built to paint the high walls and ceiling, but whether the complex cave was a public sanctuary or a specialized place to be used at particular times is not known.

Many of the painted and engraved caves are too small or narrow for group rituals. A large proportion of the more complex compositions, signs, and images, even in the major caves, are in hard-to-reach, hidden, and narrow recesses where only one person at a time can enter. The evidence suggests that the caves were by and large used by few persons, sometimes by small specialized groups, often by individuals who did no more than add a single sign or motif to a larger composition or wall. At Gargas (France), among almost 150 negative hand prints in red and black paint, some with missing finger joints, an adult held an infant hand to the wall and blew paint over both hands. Such private usage does not indicate the overdramatized activity of supposed shamanistic performances as imagined by popular writers. Besides, there are engraved depictions on bone and stone of rituals being conducted outside of the caves.

Analysis of the homesite imagery and their modes of use suggests that different symbolic or ritual activities were conducted at living sites. These modes of homesite ritual activity were perhaps more common than the rituals performed in the caves. The evidence is found throughout Europe. At the living site of Dolni Věstonice (Czech Republic), in an area without sanctuary caves, a kiln was found in which clay "venus" figurines and animals had been ritually fired during homesite rituals. The presence of burials, often with stone and bone tools, symbolic artifacts, and elaborate costumes, also suggests a rich symbolic and ritual culture, within which the sanctuary caves were a specialized, regional development.

For almost a century, it was common to write about the animal and female images of the Ice Age and merely to note with some perplexity the rich and varied library of non-representational signs, symbols, and notations found, for instance, at Altamira, Lascaux, and the other Franco-Cantabrian caves. Many of these were at first interpreted as *hunting magic* and were even described as traps, snares, corrals, pitfalls, or weapons. Some of the structured images were thought to be huts or even dancing costumes. More recently, many of these nonrepresentational images have been interpreted by D. Lewis-Williams and others as visions of what the artist experienced while entering a trance or altered state of consciousness, perhaps in the course of a shamanistic ritual. While shamanism might have been practiced by Late Ice Age hunters of many regions, this explanation has been contested, and it certainly cannot account for the entire corpus of symbolic images, any more than could the *sympathetic magic* hypothesis of an earlier era.

Only slowly have researchers begun to realize that within the Late Ice Age, as in modern human cultures, there were dozens of symbol systems, each with its own iconography or set of images and its own modes of use. In the second half of the twentieth century, it has become apparent that the Ice Age images were more than just art, or the expression of primitive magic and the evidence of a simple, primitive philosophy. The images represented different, often complex concepts and mythologized referential systems. They were often the product of highly evolved specialized skills and technologies. Realization of this complexity, made possible by study of thousands of symbolic images and artifacts, as well as the discovery of dozens of major sanctuary caves, led to new, sophisticated methods for studying the categories of image and symbol and their manufacture and use. It became possible to begin internal and comparative analyses of widely dispersed images and traditions. Means of determining differences in paint mixtures and the dating of organic constituents in the paints made it possible to determine large spans of time between certain images, panels, and styles. These differed from the purely visual studies and tracings initiated by the Abbé H. Breuil, the foremost illustrator and interpreter of Ice Age art in the first half of the twentieth century. The new studies differ also from early efforts to explain the images and the supposed beginnings of art by reference to the images of historic primitive cultures or to changing anthropological theories about what images and symbols in a primitive culture should do and mean. A major step in the study of Ice Age art was initiated by French researchers who attempted to clarify the organization among the hundreds of images accumulated in the Franco-Cantabrian caves.

Mapping the Caves

Early in the second half of the twentieth century, the French archaeologists A. Laming-Emperaire and A. Leroi-Gourhan began to study the apparent relationships among the animal species depicted in the caves. They came to the conclusion that major species, such as the horse and bovids (bison and aurochs), were associated, or paired. To test this insight, Leroi-Gourhan began to catalog all of the images in a cave, charting the position of the animals, as well as the signs and motifs. These were visual studies, without internal analysis of any of the images or compositions. Leroi-Gourhan suggested that the apparent relationship between horse and bison in central areas of a cave represented an "opposition," a suggestion derived from the supposed polar thinking found among "primitive" peoples, as proposed by the structuralist theories that were then common in France among such anthropologists as C. Lévi-Strauss. According to this hypothesis, the horse, even if it was a mare, was "male," and a bison, even if it was a bull, was "female." Long, thin signs were considered male, while wide and round signs were female. This argument, which contained elements of Freudianism, has not been accepted by other archaeologists, particularly those working with the Ice Age images. For one thing, the oppositional associations that Leroi-Gourhan attributed to Ice Age art and thought do not occur in the homesite imagery, either in Leroi-Gourhan's Franco-Cantabrian area or in Ice Age homesites dispersed across Europe.

Leroi-Gourhan's visual and statistical studies did, however, provide the first systematic charts of where the major images and compositions in a cave were usually located. From these studies, he proposed an ideal model for a sanctuary cave, with opposed major animals in a central position and subsidiary animals and signs in the periphery. He also provided a catalog of the signs found in the caves, and he revised the chronology of developing styles for depicting animals within the Franco-Cantabrian region. He listed four major styles covering the 25 Kyr of animal art in his region, beginning with simple animal outlines and developing toward images of great realism, animation, and detail. Unfortunately, the scheme did not hold for the rest of Europe. The earliest animal images known, the Vogelherd carvings from the Early Aurignacian of Germany, ca. 32 Ka, are not in Leroi-Gourhan's Style I. They are instead highly sophisticated three-dimensional carvings of lion, horse, bison, and mammoth, with detailed rendering of the eyes, nose, mouth, ears, and hair. The Vogelherd lioness and horse have a grace and animation that would not be found in the Franco-Cantabrian area until thousands of years later, in the Magdalenian period.

Leroi-Gourhan's work nevertheless marked a major change in the systematic study of Ice Age art. His structural, topographic, cataloging, and stylistic studies made it possible for others, including many of his students, to begin the next stage of intensive, internal analytical inquiry.

Internal Analyses and Comparisons: New Questions and Methods of Study

It became evident through the work of the researchers who followed Leroi-Gourhan that the animal images in the homesites and the caves, particularly during the Magdalenian period of the Franco-Cantabrian area, 16–12 Ka, were more than mere images of species. A. Marshack stressed the fact that, as the Magdalenian tradition developed, the art increasingly depicted animals in terms of their dimorphic sexual and seasonal characteristics and behaviors: a horse in its summer coat (Lascaux) or winter coat (Niaux); a bison in summer molt (Lascaux, Altamira, Niaux) or its fall-winter coat (Lascaux); stags carrying mature antlers and baying during the autumn rut (Lascaux); hinds with fawns, cows with calves, juvenile ibex and deer with their springtime antler and horn buds; male salmon with the hook on the lower jaw that only the males acquire during the spawning season. The referential detail in these Magdalenian images of the Franco-Cantabrian area clearly did not represent an oppositional philosophy but were derived instead from the Ice Age hunters' observations of the diversity in animal behavior and appearance and the sequence of seasonal changes occurring in the Franco-Cantabrian ecology.

A radiocarbon date of ca. 32–30 Ka for the carbon in some of the paintings at Chauvet suggests that later Magdalenian traditions of dimorphic sexual and seasonal depiction may have begun as early as the Aurignacian. In Chauvet, there are images of male reindeer with a late, full growth of antler, horses in their summer pelage and with their serpentine pelage marker, and woolly rhinoceros lacking their winter hair but with mid-body skin fold visible in the summer. If these observations are validated, it would lend weight to the concept of very early *time-factored* symbol systems in the European Upper Paleolithic and lend support to the adaptive value of early notation. This tradition of depicting the seasonal and sexual characteristics of different species did not occur in other areas of Ice Age Europe where animals were always depicted as generalized species, without an indication of sexual, seasonal, behavioral, or age differences. The exception to this rule concerning animal depiction occurred in those neighboring areas into which the Magdalenian traditions temporarily intruded.

As a result of comparative studies of the Ice Age images throughout Europe, Marshack has suggested that the unique ecological and geographic conditions within the Franco-Cantabrian area may have contributed to the development of the referential mode of animal depiction. These conditions included wide areas of flatland steppe, cut by a tight network of rivers, that served as a human conceptual frame and a temporal-spatial organizational structure. These rivers ran through deeply cut, steep valleys in the interior region of limestone hills that provided abrupt altitudinal, microecological differences and gradations. These conditions supported a diversity of species during the Ice Age, including Subarctic, temperate, steppe, and alpine fauna; they produced sharp seasonal changes in the fauna and flora and fostered the arrival and departure of riverine, aerial, and steppic migratory species. It was the richness and diversity of this regional ecology, and the human cultural tapestry that was woven upon this frame, that was apparently the basis for the realistic referential animal art that developed in this area.

Other equally important symboling traditions developed during the Ice Age and were dispersed more broadly across Europe, reaching into Siberia. Female vulvas began to be carved and engraved on stones in rockshelters of the Dordogne region of France around Les Eyzies during the Aurignacian period, ca. 30 Ka. Abstracted vulvas of this type, carved in bone and stone, are found at Czech sites and on the Russian Plain, together with the more recognizable, full-

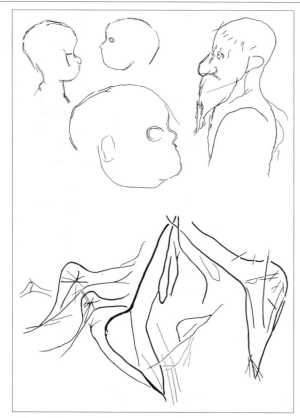

Top: incised heads of children, an infant, and an old man with a beard, all drawn on heavily overengraved limestone blocks found in the habitation site of La Marche (France), dating from the middle Magdalenian (ca. 16,500 BP.). Other stones here contain portraits of women, dancers, and animals and are overmarked as though used in rituals. The images were unscrambled from the heavy overengraving by L. Pales and T. De Saint Pereuse. Bottom: six abstracted and schematic female images, without heads, arms, or feet, incised on a limestone block found on the floor of the habitation site of La Roche (Lalinde, France), dated to the late Magdalenian. The large female in the center, apparently the first to be engraved, has two breasts; the figure at right has one breast; the other figurines are increasingly abstracted and schematized. Each of these "buttocks" images has been struck through by engraved lines as though they had been used in rituals. Courtesy of Alex Marshack.

figure "venus" statuettes. Vulva images were carved and painted on cave walls of the Franco-Cantabrian area during the Magdalenian period. Marshack has suggested that the early use of the vulva image in the homesite may have been a folk form of ritual activity, perhaps involving women concerned with the processes of menstruation, pregnancy, and birth, while the early masterpieces of carving known as the "venus" figurines may have been the product of skilled artisans making a more generalized, long-term image, with perhaps a wider range of meanings and uses. Female imagery in the Ice Age is complex. It includes slim, young females; buxom, mature, or older females; and pregnant and non-pregnant females. A Magdalenian image from Gönnersdorf (Germany) shows an infant being carried on a woman's back; abstracted images of the breasts and vulva symbolize the nurturant aspect of the female. Female images are sometimes associated with animals, plants, the phallus, the bison horn, and geometric signs, suggesting that it was often a generic symbol of the "feminine." Just as the Ice Age animal images represented more than a meal or hunting magic, the female

images apparently represented a recognition of periodicity and process in nature and were more than mere images of fertility magic or the erotic.

The prewriting, prearithmetic forms of notation that first appear in the Dordogne area of France, ca. 30 Ka, and the other sign and symbol systems throughout Ice Age Europe (and possibly elsewhere) document a range of nonrepresentational symboling modes, many of which may have been developed by a specialized elite, perhaps shamans. The simultaneous growth of folk images and ritual modes of using motifs, and the development over time of highly skilled artistic productions in carving, engraving, and painting, perhaps by persons trained and specialized in these skills, suggest that a cultural and symbolic complexity arose among these early hunter-gatherers of the European Late Ice Age that would not be reached again until the historic period.

The recognition of various types of symbol systems and modes of symbol use poses a set of questions about these early cultures different from those posed by previous efforts to find a single, unitary explanation for the "origins" of art and the seemingly "sudden" explosion of Ice Age art and creativity. The early attempts began with anthropological theories concerning primitive forms of thinking and involved concepts of *animism* and hunting and fertility *magic*. Leroi-Gourhan, when cataloging and classifying the Ice Age images, sought a simple, unitary explanation and, as a result, claimed that many of the images in the caves were male or female, within a closed conceptual system of oppositions. Subsequent analysis of how the images in the caves were made and used has indicated the presence of numerous symbol systems, each of which had its own iconography and mode of use or accumulation. Animal and female images could be used in a range of ways for different symbolic purposes. Many of the geometric signs and motifs found in the caves were periodically altered by additions that changed their original shape or form. Animal images were often used and reused, at times being killed by darts; at times being renewed by the addition of extra eyes, ears, muzzles, legs, tails, or backs; at times being used in association with a library of signs and symbols. Painted or engraved serpentine motifs were accumulated in the caves and on bone and stone in the homesites, at times so thickly as to give the appearance of macaroni. A study of these "macaroni" accumulations has suggested that they represented a system of periodic ritual marking, using a motif that may have been related to the symbolism of water.

A new generation of researchers have instituted systematic, methodological studies of the Ice Age images that go beyond what was possible with earlier visual studies of style and chronology and are not dependent on *a priori* anthropological theory. L. Pales and M.T. Saint-Pereuse performed a careful internal analysis of hundreds of intricately overengraved limestone tablets from the Magdalenian site of La Marche (France), unscrambling human portraits and animal images. Significantly, both the images and the stones were heavily overengraved as though by a ritual marking. B. and G. Delluc studied the carved and incised images on stone from the

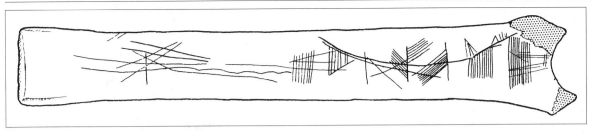

Engraved sets of marks, connected one to the other and accumulated sequentially on a fragmented piece of mammoth ivory. These markings were found with other forms of symbolic marking and accumulation in the later Late Paleolithic habitation huts of Mezhirich, on the Russian Plain. Such notational sequences and symbolic accumulations are found in habitation sites across Ice Age Europe, as well as in the Upper Paleolithic caves in western Europe. Courtesy of Alex Marshack.

Early Ice Age in the Dordogne area and found that the technique of working stone by slowly pecking out the outline of a preconceived image was far more sophisticated than the final, simple outline or bas-relief would indicate. G. Bosinski and G. Fischer studied more than 500 incised slates found on the floor of Gönnersdorf, a Magdalenian camp overlooking the Rhine in Germany, and found hundreds of accumulated female images in the buttocks style, a large number of which had been overmarked as though in ritual, while the stones themselves were heavily overengraved like the stones from La Marche. M. Lorblanchet employed microscopic and chemical means; J. Clottes has instituted studies of the paint mixes in different caves, panels, and images; often documenting great chronological differences among the images; and A. Marshack used ultraviolet, infrared, and fluorescence to study the paints in the caves and to determine the modes of use and reuse of animal images and signs. The Abbé Glory spent more than a decade tracing all of the incised lines in one intricately overengraved chamber at Lascaux, documenting in "the unknown Lascaux" a complexity of signs, symbols, "macaronis," and animal images that indicated that the famous paintings represented only a small part of the cave's original use and importance.

The complexity of the Ice Age symbol systems may be one measure of the complexity of the late Paleolithic cultures. Modern societies also use many types of image, symbol, and sign to mark the relevant categories and aspects of their cultures and to maintain the network of relations and activities that form the cultural tapestry. The first widespread and complex body of image and symbol found in the archaeological record indicates that these modes and capacities were present in the prehistoric Ice Age cultures, long before the beginnings of agriculture and civilization.

Precursors and Termination of Ice Age Art

The nearly 25,000-year development of image and symbol during the European Upper Paleolithic was a unique regional phenomenon that occurred under special geographic, climatic, and ecological conditions. When the climate warmed, the ice melted, and forests spread across Europe into what were once open grazing areas, the Late Ice Age cultures—and their art—disintegrated. New hunting-gathering ways of life appeared. The Franco-Cantabrian sanctuary caves were abandoned. Realistic animal art, the high point of Magdalenian creativity, virtually disappeared, although

some rock painting continued to be made in the hills of Spain and engraved rock art began to be made in the Subarctic, which had earlier been covered by the ice sheets. The Upper Paleolithic female images ceased being made. Representational art largely disappeared, although the mode of making and accumulating geometric signs and motifs, begun in the Late Ice Age, continued and developed; it became the dominant Mesolithic style.

The Ice Age cultural phenomenon raises a host of questions. Was the European development due to the arrival on the continent of anatomically modern and evolutionarily more advanced and competent forms of humanity? Opinions vary, but it may be significant that different types of anatomically modern humans in other parts of the world during this period did not develop the same symbolic and cultural complexity. In southwestern Asia, where modern humans also displaced the Neanderthals, no tradition of animal art, female imagery, or personal decoration arose during this period. There is, however, the rare evidence of engraving in the Mousterian period of southwestern Asia (e.g., Quneitra on the Golan Heights), as well as evidence for a crude beginning of painted animal art in South Africa and of geometric "macaroni" marking in caves of Australia, clearly made by different types of modern humans. Perhaps of greater significance is the (very) slowly accumulating evidence for forms of symboling in the earlier Mousterian period of the Neanderthals, suggesting that many of the traditions that later effloresced in the European Late Ice Age had their incipient beginnings in the earlier period.

It has long been known that the Neanderthals in Europe and Asia buried their dead, occasionally with symbolic grave goods, including flowers at Shanidar (Iraq) and tools, animal bones, and marked stones at La Ferrassie (France). These burials gave rise to the theory that the Neanderthals had arrived at an incipient religious awareness of death and an afterlife. It was widely believed, however, that the Neanderthals did not manufacture symbolic images or make personal decorations and that they therefore had no sense of "self" and lacked social complexity. It was even suggested that the Neanderthals had no capacity for full language and that such language began at the same time as Ice Age art. This assumed that other modern humans of this period, who did not develop comparable artistic traditions, may not yet have had language or social complexity. It is, therefore, significant that there is accumulating evidence for different forms of symbolic manufacture in the Mousterian period of the Neanderthals.

Carved-bone points for hunting large game also have been excavated from this period in Germany. Related to this capacity for working bone, at the Early Mousterian site of Tata (Hungary) a nonutilitarian oval plaque had been carefully carved and beveled from a section of mammoth tooth; it had then been colored with red ocher and was apparently handled or used, perhaps ritually, for a considerable period as evidenced by the hand polish along its edges.

These scattered early data became important when a Neanderthal skull was found in 1979 in a Chatelperronian level, ca. 34–32 Ka, at the French site of Saint-Césaire. Some years earlier, Leroi-Gourhan had excavated pendant beads from a Chatelperronian level at the site of Arcy-sur-Cure and had termed them the earliest-known examples of personal decoration made by anatomically modern man. The possibility now exists that the pendant beads were made and worn by Neanderthals.

The problem of the position of the Neanderthals in human evolution and of the Neanderthal capacity for symboling and even for human language is the focus of heated debate. If, as now seems possible, the Upper Paleolithic "revolution" in art and symbol represented a historical and cultural regional development, rather than a major evolutionary and genetically determined event, then the complex reasons for the "sudden" rise, the long development, and the sudden disappearance of Upper Paleolithic art and symbol must be explained by reference to a host of temporal, regional, historical, and social-cultural processes.

See also Aurignacian; Europe; Homo sapiens; Late Paleolithic; Magdalenian; Mousterian; Neanderthals; Paleolithic Calendar; Upper Paleolithic. [A.M.]

Further Readings

Chauvet, J.-M., Deschamps, E.B., and Hillaire, C. (1995) La Grotte Chauvet à Vallon-Pont-d'Arc. (Preface by J. Clottes). Paris: Seuil.

Clottes, J., and Courtin, J. (1994) La Grotte Cosquer: Peintures et Gravures de la Caverne Engloutie. Paris: Seuil.

Leroi-Gourhan, A. (1965) Treasures of Prehistoric Art. New York: Abrams.

Leroi-Gourhan, A. (1982) The Dawn of European Art: An Introduction to Paleolithic Cave Painting. Cambridge: Cambridge University Press.

Lewis-Williams, D. (1981) Believing and Seeing: Symbolic Meaning in Southern San Rock Paintings. New York: Academic Press.

Marshack, A. (1977) The meander as a system: The analysis and recognition of iconographic units in Upper Paleolithic compositions. In P. Ucko (ed.): Form in Indigenous Art: Schematization in the Art of Aboriginal and Prehistoric Europe. London: Duckworth, pp. 286–317.

Marshack, A. (1979) Upper Paleolithic symbol systems of the Russian Plain: Cognitive and comparative analysis of complex ritual marking. Curr. Anthropol. 20:271–311.

Marshack, A. (1991) The Roots of Civilization, rev. ed. Mt. Kisco, N.Y.: Moyer Bell.

Ucko, P., and Rosenfeld, A. (1967) Paleolithic Cave Art. London: Weidenfeld and Nicholson.

Paleolithic Lifeways

An important part of prehistoric investigation is the attempt to reconstruct the lifeways of early hominids. Some types of prehistoric behavior tend to leave evidence that is highly visible in the record, whereas others leave little or no direct evidence behind. Nonetheless, a primary goal of the prehistorian is ultimately to be able to make generalizations about hominid modes of life through time and space, including subsistence patterns, social organization, technology, and cultural norms and beliefs. Here, we first consider the methods employed to reconstruct Stone Age lifeways and then use these approaches to outline the major stages of Paleolithic adaptation through time.

Methods

Reconstructing Paleolithic lifestyles involves reconnaissance, survey, and meticulous excavation of Stone Age localities, followed by detailed identification and analysis of prehistoric remains. Such archaeological research aims to document patterns of technology, subsistence, and social behavior and to explain change or stasis in the prehistoric record. This reconstruction can be a subjective, imperfect science, since, as noted above, many aspects of hominid behavior leave few traces behind. Modern analogues, such as ethnographic, ethological, taphonomic, and geological studies as well as experimentation, can add valuable insights, but they must be used with caution. Researchers should be aware that concepts of ancient hominid lifeways have changed radically and often during the last two centuries. Theoretical perspectives and methodological innovations have brought about a new kind of rigor, sometimes referred to as the New Archaeology. This approach to the study of prehistory attempts to construct formalized, predictive explanatory models about the past, which are designed to be tested by the archaeological evidence.

DATING

Chronological placement of sites is critical in understanding changes in Paleolithic lifestyles through time. Relative dating techniques, such as stratigraphic superimposition, biostratigraphy, and artifact seriation, are often useful when one is trying to correlate one site or regional sequence with another. Chronometric techniques, such as radiocarbon, potassium-argon, and fission-track dating, have proved fairly reliable for dating suitable materials from Paleolithic sites.

ENVIRONMENTAL RECONSTRUCTION

Reconstruction of paleoenvironments helps prehistorians understand the geographic and ecological contexts in which fossil hominids are found. It can also augment our understanding of how early hominids adapted to new and varied environmental conditions through time.

Evidence for the flora of an area comes from fossil pollen, plant phytoliths, carbonized (burned) plant remains, leaf impressions in sediment, calcified root systems, and waterlogged or desiccated plant materials. Since many prehistoric species of plants have modern counterparts, it is often possible to predict reliably the types of climates and conditions that would have allowed such communities of flora to thrive, considering such variables as temperature, rainfall, sunlight, and soil chemistry.

Faunal remains, such as fossilized bones and teeth, mollusc shells, insect carapaces (rare in Paleolithic contexts), and footprints, can also yield valuable environmental clues, as many fossil taxa have similar modern descendants or near-relatives presumed to live under similar conditions. The faunal composition of a prehistoric assemblage may, therefore, yield clues to groundcover, rainfall, vegetation type, and proximity to water.

The sediments themselves may also contain environmental indicators. Isotopic and other geochemical studies may show how arid or wet an area was; soil formation may suggest how stable a landscape was and how much precipitation it received; and certain types of mineral alteration may indicate climatic conditions.

SUBSISTENCE AND PALEODIET

Reconstruction of the mode of procurement and range of foodstuffs for early hominid groups is based on both prehistoric evidence and patterns observed in modern animal species. Evidence of the types of foods that hominids consumed can come in a variety of forms. Plant foods, thought to be the staple for most hunter-gatherer groups, can be preserved as carbonized vegetable matter or pollen grains. In practice, however, it is often difficult to prove that pollen evidence necessarily represents the types of plants consumed by prehistoric human populations, since it could also represent the local and airborne background pollen in the vicinity of a Paleolithic site.

Other, sometimes subtle, forms of evidence are now being studied for indications of early human diet and subsistence. Among these are hominid tooth wear (macroscopic and microscopic polish and damage on teeth can indicate that materials had been chewed); microwear evidence on stone tools (microscopically detected damage and polish on stone-artifact edges can indicate the materials worked, such as cutting soft plants or slicing meat); trace-element analysis of prehistoric hominid remains (isotopic and trace-element proportions among common elements such as carbon, nitrogen, and strontium can indicate aspects of diet such as the proportion of grasses or the degree of carnivory); coprolite analysis (analysis of remains in fossilized hominid feces can reveal microscopic or trace-element evidence of materials consumed); paleopathology (certain osteological and dental features can indicate dietary deficiencies or abnormalities, such as dental hypoplasia); and artwork (pictorial representations in Upper Paleolithic artwork show some of the animals prominent in the minds of the hominids whether primary prey or not).

TECHNOLOGY

Paleolithic technologies permitted hominids to adapt to a wide range of environmental conditions. Reconstructions of prehistoric technological systems are based primarily on artifact representation and contextual associations, experimentation, use-wear studies, and ethnographic analogies.

Evidence for prehistoric technology is normally restricted to nonperishable materials: Such substances as wood, hide, and vegetable fiber are preserved only in exceptional conditions, such as dry caves or waterlogged, anaerobic sediments. Artifacts made out of stone, however, are durable and can be found in most situations. Bone preservation is variable, with alkaline sediments tending to be conducive to mineralization.

By far the most numerous types of technology found in the Paleolithic record are stone artifacts, including percussors, cores, débitage (flakes and fragments), and retouched pieces. Careful examination of such materials, combined with replicative experiments and refitting studies, can often be instructive in documenting which stages of stone reduction actually occurred at a prehistoric site. Use-wear studies on raw materials can also provide important information on the functional modes of artifacts. Bone tools tend to be rare until the Late Paleolithic, when a great diversity of artifact types can be seen for the first time. Other types of Paleolithic technology that may leave behind recognizable features are architectural structures (e.g., hut or tent foundations, postholes) and fire hearths.

SOCIAL ORGANIZATION

Getting a good grasp on early forms of hominid social organization is an important but difficult task for the Paleolithic archaeologist. Among the fundamental properties of social groups are the size of groups that operate together in some realm of life (e.g., regular mating relationships, foraging, territorial displays); the nature of relationships between males and females (their longevity, the investment of the male in the care and feeding of his young, matings of the female with plural males vs. monogamy or exogamy—preferred mating outside of the family group [i.e., the operation of an incest taboo]); and the type of group fissioning and fusing that might occur seasonally or for special activities. We need to know a number of these aspects of prehistoric social organization in order to understand the ancestry and evolution of modern human societies and to appreciate what might be basic biological or social norms in our lineage with a long period of development.

It is, however, extremely difficult to find any enduring evidence throughout most of the prehistoric record that will yield clues about social organization. We rely largely upon analogy with other primates and with hunter-gatherer groups to understand the full range of variation in the past. Group size was probably not large in the Paleolithic, as the subsistence demands of foraging human and nonhuman primates restrict the effective foraging group to a certain range, usually not much more than 25 to 100 individuals and fewer when resources are sparse or seasonally restricted. Most primates and human groups appear to have some sort of exogamous rule in operation or a prescription to marry or mate outside of the immediate or perceived family group. Many researchers believe that there may be an ancient biological basis for the human taboo against incest.

Male-female relationships are also difficult to define in prehistory. Nonhuman primates exhibit a range of mating and socialization patterns between males and females, from fairly long-term monogamous arrangements to more seasonally promiscuous behavior. In the latter cases, more dominant males tend to have better access to receptive females, but females in estrus tend to mate with multiple males. Thus, it is difficult to compare directly the complex marriage relationships among human groups with primate mating behavior per se. It has been suggested that the higher degree of sexual dimorphism evident in some early hominid taxa may be an indication of nonmonogamous mating behavior, with the larger male body size associated with competition among males.

Human groups, as a rule, have some form of marriage, with a network of social responsibilities connected to this bond, and it is thought that this tendency to form long-term male-female bonds has considerable prehistoric depth. This bonding is intrinsically connected to the development of the human family concept, with both parents, and often their relations, involved in duties and benefits regarding the offspring. It is difficult, however, to determine when this behavior pattern began. The first real evidence is perhaps among the Neanderthals, since at La Ferrassie (France) we find an adult male and female and several children buried in the same general area. Primate groups also appear to have a sense of territory that is under their proprietary interest. This tends to be defended by the group against incursions from other groups, even of the same species, although defensive behavior in such instances generally involves threat displays rather than physical violence. By analogy, it is thought that prehistoric human groups also tended to have a group-defended territory, but direct evidence is not yet available. It is only by relatively late in prehistory that we see definitive evidence for warfare or injuries inflicted by other humans.

RITUAL AND SYMBOLISM

The use of symbols—arbitrary sounds or images representing other objects or ideas—is a characteristic of all modern human groups. Symbols are conveyed in many forms, such as language, art, music, dance, and oral traditions. This symbolic behavior is sometimes called *nonutilitarian*, because it is often not directly related to immediate subsistence needs; nonetheless, it is an integral part of every modern human society and helps integrate individuals into the cultural beliefs and rules of their social group.

How far back such symbolic behavior can be traced is not clear. Language, music, dance, and oral traditions leave little direct evidence in the prehistoric record; other forms, such as art and rituals (e.g., burials), may have more prehistoric visibility. If one assumes that earlier (preanatomically modern) hominids possessed less sophisticated language abilities than modern humans, then the means of expressing and communicating ideas may have been different from those found in modern societies. The use of pigment for coloration, symmetry and finesse of stone artifacts, collection of unusual or exotic items, burial patterns and art styles have all been cited as evidence of such symbolic behavior.

See also Aggregation-Dispersal; Archaeological Sites; Bow and Arrow; Clothing; Diet; Economy, Prehistoric; Exotics; Fire; Geochronometry; Hunter-Gatherers; Lithic Use-Wear; Musical Instruments; Paleobiology; Paleolithic Image; Paleomagnetism; Primate Societies; Ritual; Site Types; Spear; Stone-Tool Making; Stratigraphy; Taphonomy.

Cultural-Historical Overview

HOMO HABILIS, HOMO RUDOLFENSIS AND *HOMO ERECTUS* (Ca. 2.5–1.0 MA)

The Oldowan industrial complex, associated with the first known flaked-stone tools, can be traced back to at least 2.5 Ma in East Africa and begins to be complemented by the large bifaces associated with the Acheulean complex ca. 1.5 Ma. Hominids contemporaneous with these industries are *Homo habilis* (and *Homo rudolfensis*) and early *Homo erectus*, as well as *Paranthropus boisei, P. aethiopicus,* and *P. robustus* (in South Africa). Most sites appear to be associated with tropical or subtropical grasslands and woodlands. Hominid toolmakers produced simple flaked- and battered-stone artifacts, including cores made on cobbles or blocks and a range of casually retouched flakes. Simple tools of organic materials, such as bone, horn, or wood, are also quite likely.

Little is known of territory size and land-use patterns, but the fact that both *Homo* and *Paranthropus* remains are sometimes found at the same localities suggests that at least two subsistence modes were in operation at this time. Most anthropologists assume that the larger-brained genus *Homo* was the principal toolmaker, but this cannot be demonstrated with certainty.

Oldowan hominids probably foraged for a variety of foodstuffs, of which vegetable foods like berries, fruits, legumes, seeds, roots, corms, and tubers contributed the bulk of the diet. Animal bones of taxa weighing an average of several hundred kg that are found at some Oldowan sites show indications of stone-tool cutmarks and probable hammerstone fracture. It is not clear how these bones were procured (scavenging or hunting), but an increasing number of researchers are favoring a scavenging hypothesis to explain the collecting of the larger animals' bones. Nonetheless, the recurrent association of such animal bones and flaked-stone artifacts in anomalous concentrations suggests that the processing of animal carcasses was a habitual, and perhaps frequent, behavioral pattern. It is possible that some control over fire had been developed, based on controversial evidence from Swartkrans (South Africa), Koobi Fora (Kenya), and other sites. There is no clear evidence for symbolic behavior during this time.

LATER *HOMO ERECTUS*/ARCHAIC *HOMO SAPIENS* (CA. 1.0–0.2 MA)

Of the numerous Middle Pleistocene Paleolithic sites throughout the Old World, few have the type of preservation that provides detailed information about hominid behavior. Many of these sites are geologically disturbed, found in high-energy fluvial regimes, suggesting that proximity to water was a major factor in site location.

Artist's impression of a late Homo erectus *occupation site.*

Hominids identified as classic *H. erectus* are known from the earlier part of this time period (e.g. the Sangiran, Zhoukoudian [China], Lantian [China], and Tighenif [Africa], materials). Between 500 and 200 Ka, however, many of the hominid fossils, such as those at Arago (France), Steinheim (Germany), Petralona (Greece), Saldanha (South Africa), Kabwe (Zambia), and Bodo (Ethiopia), appear to have more sapient features, including an expanded braincase, and are here designated as "archaic *Homo sapiens.*"

Many sites, especially in Africa, southwestern Asia, and western Europe, are characterized by the large bifacial forms, such as handaxes and cleavers, that are the hallmark of the Acheulean industry. These artifacts, especially in Africa, are sometimes found in astonishing numbers. Other artifact forms include a wide range of Mode 1 (Oldowan-like) cores and flakes, retouched flakes, and battered spheroids. The technological skill in producing bifaces and smaller flake tools seems generally to increase with time in many areas. Some Middle Pleistocene sites, especially in eastern Asia, are characterized by nonhandaxe industries (Mode 1). The reason for this technological dichotomy on either side of Movius' line is not well understood.

Although no direct evidence for clothing has been found during this time period, microwear polishes on stone tools from sites such as Clacton and Hoxne (both in Eng-

land) suggest that hide working was an important activity, perhaps with skins scraped so as to be worked into supple material for simple garments. Simple structural features, such as rock features and postholes, have been noted at several sites, including Terra Amata and Lazaret in France. These have been interpreted as huts or tents that were probably covered with branches and/or hides.

Evidence for fire comes from such sites as Zhoukoudian (China), Vértesszöllös (Hungary), Terra Amata (France), Kalambo Falls (Zambia), and Cave of Hearths (South Africa). It has been questioned, however, whether any of these instances show good evidence of hominid production or control of fire, although it seems that at sites such as Terra Amata possible hearth structures, ringed with stones, could indicate human control of combustible materials. As early hominins spread into more temperate zones, fire would have been a more important innovation, especially in the winter.

Numerous bones of a wide variety of animals are characteristic of many Middle Pleistocene archaeological sites, and at some occurrences, such as Torralba and Ambrona in Spain, the remains of large mammals are associated with stone tools. How much of these faunal materials are the result of hunting, scavenging, or incidental association is highly controversial.

No burials are known from this period, and claims for symbolic behavior have rested primarily on such evidence as

Artist's impression of a Neanderthal activity area.

pieces of red ocher found at some sites and the collection of unusual objects like rock crystals. The technological finesse involved in making large bifaces in the later Acheulean does suggest a strong sense of style, symmetry, and perhaps aesthetics. Although no representational art has been found in this period, a few sites, such as Bilzingsleben (Germany), have yielded bones with curious striations that do not appear to be utilitarian.

NEANDERTHAL AND CONTEMPORANEOUS HOMINID POPULATIONS (CA. 200–33 KA)

Beginning between 200 and 100 Ka, and lasting until ca. 40–30 Ka, new types of technologies emerged in many parts of the Old World. These are characterized by much less emphasis on the large bifacial tools of the Acheulean and more on recurrent types of flake tools (e.g., points, scrapers, denticulates) that were often made on flakes struck from prepared cores. Associated hominids in Europe are exclusively Neanderthals, while in the Levant, both Neanderthal and anatomically modern human populations appear to have been associated with these technologies. Before 100 Ka, later "archaic *Homo sapiens*" populations lacking the specialized Neanderthal morphology are known from East Asia and Africa. In Africa, however, at sites such as Klasies River Mouth Cave (and possibly Border Cave), it appears that anatomically modern or near-modern humans were associated with Middle Stone Age technologies at or before 100 Ka.

The diet of these Middle Paleolithic/Middle Stone Age people probably varied greatly geographically: In western Europe, for example, common faunal remains include such animals as reindeer, horse, bison, cave bear, rhinoceros, deer, and mammoth; in South Africa, such forms as Cape buffalo, *Pelorovis* (an extinct giant buffalo), and eland are numerous.

Although there is debate about the relative contribution of hunting and scavenging as a procurement mode for these animals, evidence from some sites suggests that these hominin populations were becoming more efficient and selective hunters.

The presence of Neanderthal burials in the prehistoric record, sometimes accompanied by what appear to be grave goods, suggests that communication skills and symbolic behavior may have been more complex than among earlier hominid groups and that a concept of an afterlife may have been a cultural norm. Interestingly, there is little evidence for artwork at this time, aside from a few engraved, bored, or artificially shaped pieces, as well as ocher from some localities.

HOMO SAPIENS SAPIENS (CA. 40–10 KA)

Although there are some hominid remains identified as a modern or near-modern form of human (*Homo sapiens sapiens*) between 50 and 100 Ka (e.g., at Klasies River Mouth and Qafzeh), it is during the Late Paleolithic that modern human morphology becomes widespread throughout the occupied Old World. The hunter-gatherers of the later part of the last glaciation often exhibited a much more sophisticated technological repertoire than earlier Paleolithic populations. Blades tend to supersede flakes as the primary blank form for a wide range of implements, including end-scrapers, backed blades, burins, and *percoirs*. Bone, antler, and ivory became more important during this time period and were worked into a wide range of implements, including points, needles, and harpoons. The evidence of needles strongly implies sewn or stitched clothing.

Architectural features are more common during this period as well. Besides the occupation of caves and rockshelters, open-air Upper Paleolithic sites have been found in western Europe with stone or posthole patterns that suggest

Artist's impression of an Upper Paleolithic campsite.

hut, tent, or teepee structures. In Ukraine, mammoth bones were widely used for building material, as well as probable site furniture and fuel.

Hunters tended to concentrate on certain types of game animals, such as reindeer in southwestern France and red deer in northern Spain. Fish and shellfish also appear to have been important foodstuffs for the first time in many areas. Many archaeologists suspect that the organizational skills of these later Upper Paleolithic hunter-gatherers were much more sophisticated than those of earlier hominins, an important development being the predetermined scheduling of subsistence activities to coincide with the seasonal abundance of different resources.

In the Americas, Paleoindian hunters were adept at bringing down mammoth and bison, as kill sites testify. In sub-Saharan Africa and much of the rest of the Old World, Late Paleolithic people hunted large game like Cape buffalo, antelope, and hartebeest. The shift toward microlithic industries in many places in the Late Pleistocene and Early Holocene suggests the development of efficient archery technology.

Symbolic behavior flourished during this time period; evidence includes such art forms as mobiliary carvings, engravings, and occasional fired-clay figurines, monochrome and polychrome paintings on cave walls, and bas-relief carvings on cave and rockshelter walls. A profusion of objects that appear to be elements of personal ornamentation also emerge at this time, and the use of ocher and other pigments continues. Burials appear to be more common than during Neanderthal times and are sometimes heavily endowed with grave goods, presumably for the afterlife.

The past 35 Kyr have seen little profound biological change in the human lineage, yet the pace of technological and subsistence innovation has increased at a tremendous rate with accumulated culture and perhaps better communications systems. The development of farming communities, pottery, metallurgy, and civilizations has occurred in the last 10 Kyr, to the point where human populations all over the world are changing their environments, sometimes to their own detriment, at an ever-accelerating pace.

See also Acheulean; Africa; Americas; Archaic Homo sapiens; Asia, Eastern and Southern; Australopithecus; Early Paleolithic; Europe; Homo; Homo erectus; Homo habilis; Homo rudolfensis; Homo sapiens; Late Paleolithic; Middle Paleolithic; Mousterian; Neanderthals; Oldowan; Upper Paleolithic. [N.T., K.S.]

Further Readings

Bordes, F. (1968) The Old Stone Age. New York: McGraw-Hill.

Campbell, B.G. and Log, J. (1989) Humankind Emerging, 8th ed. New York: Longman.

Coles, J.M., and Higgs, E.S. (1969) The Archaeology of Early Man. London: Faber and Faber.

Gamble, C.S. (1986) The Palaeolithic Settlement of Europe. Cambridge: Cambridge University Press.

Harris, J.W.K., and Yellen, J., eds. (1987) Papers dedicated to Desmond Clark. J. Hum. Evol. 13(8).

Klein, R.G. (1999) The Human Career, 2nd ed. Chicago: University of Chicago Press.

Lewin, R. (1999) Human Evolution: An Illustrated Introduction 4th ed. New York: Freeman.

Pfeiffer, J. (1985) The Emergence of Humankind, 4th ed. New York: W.H. Freeman.

Schick, K.D., and Toth, N. (1993) Making Silent Stones Speak. New York: Simon and Schuster.

Wymer, J. (1982) The Palaeolithic Age. New York: St. Martin's.

Paleomagnetism

Paleomagnetism is the geological record of the Earth's magnetic field. Most rocks contain iron-oxide minerals, which tend, with more or less scattering, to be aligned within the Earth's contemporaneous magnetic field when the rock is formed. The fossilized magnetic orientation in rock samples produces a field that, while almost indetectable, can be measured quite accurately with sensitive modern magnetometers in magnetically isolated conditions.

Two principal uses have been made of paleomagnetic data in the study of hominid paleontology. The first is chronological, based on the fact that frequent reversals in the polarity of the Earth's magnetic field during the Cenozoic have been accurately dated, which means that the identification of such a reversal in a fossiliferous sequence can afford a very reliable age determination. The second is geographical and is based on the fact that the Earth's magnetic field has remained relatively fixed with respect to the poles of rotation while large parts of the outer part of the Earth (the lithosphere) have moved. Observations of paleomagnetic directions in rocks of a given age permit reconstruction of the latitudinal, if not longitudinal, position of landmasses at the time and also the rotation of the landmasses during plate-tectonic movement. The presence of accreted microplates and foreign terranes within a continent can also be detected by their anomalous paleomagnetism.

The Earth's magnetic field has both horizontal and vertical components. If a magnetized needle is left free to rotate, the needle aligns itself in the magnetic field with the ends seeking the magnetic poles, thus revealing the horizontal component, or *declination*. If the needle is balanced on a point, it does not (in general) remain horizontal but fixes itself at a definite angle of inclination to the Earth's surface, revealing the vertical component, or *inclination*. This angle grows steeper near the poles and shallower near the equator, with the dependency given, to a first approximation by

$$\tan \text{inclination} = 2 \tan \text{latitude}.$$

In the Northern Hemisphere, the north-seeking, or "positive," end of a magnet also inclines downward, and the same for the south, or "negative," end in the Southern Hemisphere. The magnetic pole is where the inclination is vertical, or 90°, and the magnetic equator is where the inclination is horizontal, or zero.

If the declination and inclination of the field are mapped at a large number of points, the actual field is found to have a complex form. The magnetic equator is only approximately circular, and the magnetic poles are only approximately opposite each other. The magnetic field constantly changes its shape and orientation, but it can be reasonably estimated by imagining a stationary dipole magnet situated in the center of the Earth and aligned with the rotational axis. The calculated magnetic field produced by such a theoretical dipole is called the *geomagnetic field*. While the magnetic poles do not necessarily coincide with the rotational poles at any given time, it has been found that, when the positions of the actual magnetic poles are averaged over a long time period, the geomagnetic poles do coincide with the rotational poles. The long-term average of the Earth's magnetic field is called the *axial geocentric dipole field*, and the position of paleomagnetic poles from the rock record is computed with respect to this model field. During periods when the magnetic field was reversed, the end of a magnetized needle that we call "positive," or "north," would point to the South Pole and would be inclined upward rather than downward with respect to the magnetic pole in the Northern Hemisphere. It was this contradictory effect, found in the 1950s in certain Miocene lavas in Germany being examined for fossilized declination, that gave the first clue that the polarity of the Earth's magnetic field had been reversed in the geological past.

When igneous rocks cool from high temperatures in the earth's magnetic field, they acquire magnetization because their iron minerals tend to crystallize parallel to the field existing at that time. This is referred to as *thermoremanent magnetization* (TRM). Detrital fragments of the same minerals give a preferred magnetic orientation to sedimentary rocks when they settle in alignment with the Earth's field onto the depositional surface. This is *detrital remanent magnetization* (DRM). The crystallization of hematite in altered, secondarily reddened sediments also records contemporaneous magnetic orientation known as *chemical remanent magnetization* (CRM). Previously crystallized magnetic minerals may be overprinted with subsequent geomagnetic orientations through the influence of short, high-intensity fields (*isothermal remanent magnetization*, or IRM), such as those associated with lightning strikes, or by the influence of low-intensity magnetic fields over longer periods of time (*viscous remanent magnetization*, or VRM). If viscous effects for a sample are large, the sample is not suitable for paleomagnetic work. It is often possible, however, to "clean" the sample to remove the effects of both VRM or IRM by heating it in the absence of a magnetic field or by subjecting the sample to an alternating-frequency field. These procedures preferentially randomize the less stable, secondary magnetic phases and reveal the primary magnetization of a sample. The magnetization measured before any cleaning is the *natural remanent magnetization* (NRM).

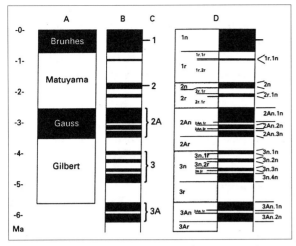

Geomagnetic polarity time scale for the last 5 Myr (Pliocene and Pleistocene). Black fill indicates intervals of normal polarity. Column A shows the named chrons (previously epochs) or major time intervals—chrons older than Gilbert are numbered rather than named. Column B increases the detail to show shorter intervals of opposite polarity within chrons, known as subchrons (previously events); those in the named chrons are also named (usually after the site where they were found), for example the Jaramillo normal subchron in the late Matuyama Chron, at about 1 Ma. An alternative system of numbering chrons and subchrons began with research on field reversals on the deep sea floor, where so-called magnetic anomalies were numbered outward from spreading ridges, as in column C. The modern system, in column D, incorporates the anomaly numbering system, so that chrons are numbered 1, 2, 2A, 3, 3A, 4, 5, etc., and the letters n or r appended to indicate normal or reversed polarity, respectively. In turn, subchrons are numbered following a decimal point in order from youngest to oldest. Thus, 2An.2r is the second reversed subchron and 2An.3n the third normal subchron, within the mainly normal chron 2A. From Kappelman (1993). © 1993 and reprinted by permission of Wiley-Liss, Inc., a subsidiary of John Wiley & Sons, Inc.

The timing of reversals of geomagnetic polarity is reasonably well known from the Jurassic to the present. It is especially well known for the last 10 Ma and can be used to refine the chronology at hominid fossil sites. The magnetic field is usually in one of the two opposed states, normal or reversed, but the intensity of the magnetic field may vary markedly, sometimes declining to such low levels as to be indeterminate. There is no practicably measurable difference, however, between the present declination and inclination of the normal field and those in the past. Consequently, the age of a rock sequence must be already approximately known before the polarity zonation can yield its chronological information. This preliminary age estimate may be based on radiometric dates or paleontological age. If a stratigraphic section is extremely thick, and there is reason to believe that the rate of sedimentation was more or less constant, a very rudimentary age estimate may be sufficient to find that part of the model polarity-reversal time scale that fits the pattern in relative thicknesses of the magnetic zones in the sequence. Because of the discontinuous nature of deposition in most continental settings, however, care must be taken to control for hiatuses through detailed geological analysis and by running parallel sampling traverses in widely spaced sections. Even so, short magnetozones may escape notice. In addition, certain rock types are more susceptible than others to remagnetization by viscous process and can lead to spurious local magnetozones that have no chronological significance because they arise from effects other than geomagnetic-field reversals.

The position of landmasses at various times in the past has been determined by paleomagnetic studies on the continents and by study of plate motions revealed by the geometry of linear magnetic anomalies on the ocean floor. Times of contact and separation between continents can be estimated, with obvious import for possible routes of primate dispersal. The paleolatitude, which emerges from remanent-inclination analysis, must be considered when making paleoclimatic reconstructions. Also, marked changes in oceanic circulation are clearly related to changing continental configurations as documented by sea-floor anomaly patterns. These circulatory changes are linked to other regional, and even global, climatic change.

Estimation of the times of reversal of the polarity of the Earth's magnetic field have been obtained in several ways. Initially, a Geomagnetic Polarity Time Scale (GPTS) was constructed for the past 4 Myr or so, and extended with less certainty back to ca. 12 Ma, by measuring radiometric ages of volcanic rocks in paleomagnetically analyzed sequences. The GPTS was refined and extended to earlier times by analogizing symmetrical magnetic intensity patterns, known as *marine magnetic anomalies*, in the sea-floor lavas paralleling midoceanic spreading centers. These anomalies are zones of positive and negative polarity in the remanent magnetism of the lavas, acquired as the lavas were emplaced along the spreading centers. The width of the anomalies presumably reflects the duration of a given geomagnetic polarity state if it is assumed that the rate of sea-floor spreading was constant, and, thus, when the dated GPTS was fitted to the youngest part of the pattern near the spreading centers, it was a simple matter to extrapolate the same time/distance ratio to more distant anomalies. To minimize the possibility that a given transect might be biased by local changes in the spreading rate, a global model anomaly pattern was developed by statistically "stacking" transects from different ocean basins. Interestingly, the transect in the South Atlantic from which the first approximation of an anomaly-based GPTS was developed proved to have one of the steadiest spreading rates of all.

The final refinement to the GPTS has been achieved by paleomagnetic analysis of oriented deep-sea cores, which sample the fine-laminated bathyal strata in which deposition was essentially continuous and sediment accumulation rates were notably constant. In these cores, which span the entire Cenozoic in numerous overlapping segments, the circumglobal biostratigraphy of planktonic marine microfossils is so detailed that each geomagnetic reversal has its own unique place in the evolutionary zonation of the microfossil groups. This helps control for missing or duplicated sections that distort the observed paleomagnetic profile, and greatly enhances the accurate correlation of any given paleomagnetic reversal to the model.

The deep-sea cores also preserve evidence of cyclic variations in the Earth's climate that are due to regular periodicities in axial tilt, equinoctal precession, and orbital shape. The timing of the cycles, as originally calculated by M.

Milankovich and recently refined by computers, is so precisely known, and the cycles are so closely spaced and regular, that the age of paleomagnetic reversals identified in this context can be established to a very high degree of accuracy, and with a level of precision approaching 10 Kyr. When this independent procedure for counting time was applied to magnetostratigraphy in Italian Pliocene and Pleistocene sections by researchers such as F.J. Hilgen the Paleomagnetic Laboratory of Utrecht University beginning in the 1980s, in a procedure that came to be known as *orbital tuning*, it confirmed earlier suspicions that the previously accepted radiometric dating of reversals in this period was on average ca. 6 percent too old. The corrected calibration has since been corroborated by new argon-argon (^{40}Ar/^{39}Ar) dating of the Olduvai Event at Olduvai Gorge (Tanzania) and by a similar redating of the Brunhes/Matuyama boundary.

See also Cyclostratigraphy; Geochronometry; Pleistocene. [F.H.B.]

Further Readings

Barendregt, R.W. (1995) Paleomagnetic dating methods. In N.W. Rutter and N.R. Catto (eds.): Dating Methods for Quaternary Deposits. St. Johns, Newfoundland: Geological Society Canada, pp. 29–50.

Hilgen, F.J. (1991) Astronomical calibration of Gauss to Matuyama sapropels in the Mediterranean and implications for the Geomagnetic Polarity Time Scale. Earth Planet. Sci. Lett. 104:226–244.

Kappelman, J. (1993) The attraction of paleomagnetism. Evol. Anthropol. 2:89–99.

McElhinny, M.W. (1973) Paleomagnetism and Plate Tectonics. Cambridge: Cambridge University Press.

Strangway, D.W. (1970) History of the Earth's Magnetic Field. New York: McGraw-Hill.

Paleontology

Study of ancient life by means of fossils. The field is conventionally divided into micropaleontology (concerned with fossil microorganisms), paleobotany (fossil plants, including spores and pollen), and paleozoology (fossil animals), which, in turn, includes invertebrate and vertebrate paleontology. Paleoanthropology lies at the interface of vertebrate paleontology, physical anthropology, and archaeology. Paleontology also embraces two parallel traditions: stratigraphic paleontology, which emphasizes the geological context of fossils and their applications in dating and correlating rocks, and paleobiology, which seeks to reconstruct the evolutionary history and life processes of the organisms represented by the fossils. Aspects of both traditions combine in the relatively new discipline of taphonomy, which studies the processes that lead to burial and fossilization of organic remains. Paleobiology has always owed much to neontology (the study of living organisms), especially to comparative anatomy and systematics. In certain cases, even the methods of biochemistry and molecular biology can be applied to fossil remains. The comparison of cladograms and phylogenies derived from paleontology and from biochemical and molecular-

genetic studies is also a currently active and fruitful field of research. Ultimately, the chief importance of paleontology to evolutionary biology is that it provides the only direct record of evolution and phylogeny and the only means of discovering and studying large-scale patterns and processes of evolution.

See also Archaeology; Evolution; Molecular Anthropology; Paleoanthropology; Paleobiology; Phylogeny; Stratigraphy; Systematics; Taphonomy. [D.P.D., R.L.B.]

Paleopathology

Study of disease in prehistory. In modern human populations, environmental insults to a healthy state are often related to a person's way of life. For example, children attending schools in large numbers are more likely to contract infectious diseases, while farmers are particularly subject to fungal infection from spores in the soil. Extrapolating from contemporary and historical patterns of health and disease, and working with archaeological information, paleopathologists can provide information about past lifeways and help measure adaptive success.

To achieve these goals, paleopathologists must place the occurrence and frequency of disease in biocultural context—that is, they must interpret information on skeletal diseases in light of the archaeological, ecological, and demographic data available. Abnormally low bone density, for example, can be a measure of nutritional stress. When observed in adolescent and young adult females, however, it signals some association with reproduction, especially if other individuals in the population show no loss of bone and if faunal and floral remains suggest a relatively complete diet.

Biocultural considerations are also important in the initial diagnosis of disease and abnormalities in skeletal material, which often involves an epidemiological perspective to rule out competing diagnoses. This approach considers the type of change observed in the skeleton, where in the body disease is found, what segment of the population shows the pathology (age/sex profile), and what kind of structure and environmental context characterize that population. Skeletal evidence for tuberculosis, for example, can be easily confused with a fungal infection: Both conditions tend to cause resorption of vertebral bodies. A soilborne fungal infection, however, might affect young adults who work close to the soil more than any other age segment, while tuberculosis would threaten all age groups under urban conditions but probably the immature and the elderly most of all.

In addition to specific disease conditions (possible syphilis, leprosy, and tuberculosis are frequently studied in prehistoric populations), other nonspecific indicators of health stress are apparent in the skeleton. Some of these signs of ill health are the product of disruptions to growth processes, such as Harris lines and enamel hypoplasias, found in long bones and teeth, respectively. Harris lines show up as bands of dense bone in radiographs, because cells at a growth plate stop proliferating and "run in place," causing denser bone to occur at that site than would be expected. When growth resumes, these lines of growth arrest become

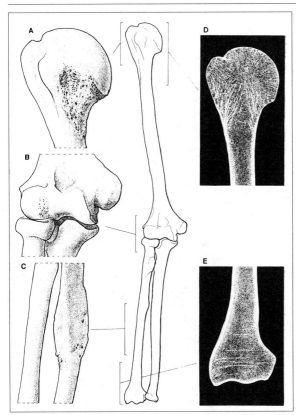

The field of paleopathology includes not only the study of obvious abnormalities, but also the analysis of normal variation that is related to the health status of a population. a) Infections are often distributed through the bloodstream, particularly affecting bone that is richly vascularized. In growing individuals metaphyses may be affected; in older persons muscle insertions may be common sites of infection. b) Osteoarthritis (OA) occurs commonly in older individuals, but is often localized to areas of joints that are stressed by habitual activities. "Atlatl elbow" refers to a pattern of OA observed in Amerindian groups that used throwing weapons. c) Fractures and other traumas can occur anywhere in the skeleton. Compression fractures on the front of the skull and midforearm breaks may signal interindividual conflict, while breaks near the wrist or ankle are more commonly the result of falls or accidents. d) All human populations show loss of bone with age. In radiographs bone loss can be seen as thin cortical bone or as spongy bone composed of sparse coarse trabeculae. When such loss occurs earlier in the life cycle than might normally be expected, it is considered to be evidence of poor health. e) Harris lines or lines of growth arrest, occur when growth halts and then resumes. When observed in radiographs, they have traditionally been interpreted as evidence of poor health, due perhaps to episodic stress such as might occur with seasonal patterns of food availability. There is some indication, however, that they may instead signal that individuals were healthy and could recover from such stressful episodes.

visible. Such punctuations in bone deposition can also be observed in histological sections of bone. Similar disruptions during tooth formation show up as areas of the tooth crown that are malformed and susceptible to cavities (hypoplasias). Episodes of Harris lines and enamel hypoplasias provide some information about when in the life cycle environmental stresses had the most impact in a prehistoric population but are most useful when analyzed in conjunction with other possible indicators of stress, including degree of asymmetry and sexual dimorphism, overall body size, and periostitis.

Of all the environmental contexts that can affect health, diet or availability of essential nutrients may be the most significant. Many of the above signs of ill health, in-

cluding the occurrence of specific infectious diseases, may be caused or exacerbated by nutrition in some way. The study of paleonutrition has, therefore, become an important focus within paleopathology. New techniques are available to quantify the biochemical composition of bones and evaluate the probable diet of an individual in prehistory. These focus on whether trace minerals, such as strontium, are present in high concentrations, as one would expect from a vegetarian diet of strontium-containing foods, and on whether carbon isotopes present in domesticated plants, such as maize, indicate dependence on such plants.

In several parts of the world, such as the mountains of Peru and the deserts of Egypt, environmental conditions as well as treatment of the dead have favored preservation of soft and hard tissues. The study of mummies can yield even more detailed information than is available from skeletal studies. A tuberculosis bacterium cyst was discovered in the lung of an Incan mummy, for example, offering proof of the existence of Precolumbian tuberculosis that can stand up under the scrutiny even of contemporary diagnosticians.

See also Archaeology; Bone Biology; Forensic Anthropology; Skeleton. [C.J.D.]

Further Readings

Brothwell, D.R. (1981) Digging Up Bones. Ithaca, N.Y.: Cornell University Press.

Buikstra, J.E., ed. (1990) A Life in Science: Papers in Honor of J. Lawrence Angel (Center for American Archeology Scientific Papers No. 6). Kampsville, Ill.: Center for American Archeology.

Cohen, M.N., and Armelagos, G.J., eds. (1984) Paleopathology at the Origins of Agriculture. New York: Academic.

Iscan, M.Y., and Kennedy, K.A.R., eds. (1989) Reconstruction of Life from the Skeleton. New York: Liss.

Ortner, D.J., and Putschar, W.G.J. (1981) Identification of Pathological Conditions in Human Skeletal Remains (Smithsonian Contributions to Anthropology No. 28). Washington, D.C.: Smithsonian Institution Press.

Powell, M.L., Bridges, P.S., and Mires, A.M., eds. (1991) What Mean These Bones? (Studies in Southeastern Bioarchaeology). Tuscaloosa: University of Alabama Press.

Steinbock, R.T. (1976) Paleopathological Diagnosis and Interpretation. Springfield, Ill.: Thomas.

Paracatarrhini

An infraorder of extinct, archaic anthropoid primates including the Parapithecidae and perhaps also the Oligopithecidae. This term was first defined by E. Delson in 1977 for the Parapithecidae, then thought to be archaic members of the infraorder Catarrhini. They were contrasted to the Eucatarrhini, for all later catarrhines. As the parapithecids are now more likely to be the sister taxon of both Catarrhini and Platyrrhini, Paracatarrhini has been elevated in rank to reflect this. The Parapithecidae combine a rather platyrrhine-like (or more conservative) postcranium and skull with derived dentition. The presence of a centrally placed conule on the upper premolars, and a tendency to emphasize various minor molar cusps, are defining autapomorphies of the family, while the presence of a midline distal hypoconulid on M_{1-3} suggests derived links with Catarrhini. The bulk of the evidence to date, however, supports a placement of the Eo-Oligocene parapithecids antecedent to the catarrhine-platyrrhine divergence.

The Oligopithecidae have not yet been shown to share any derived characters with the Parapithecidae. Nonetheless, it is suggested that these lesser-known forms may also predate the split between the modern anthropoid infraorders, and thus they can tentatively be included within the paracatarrhines.

See also Anthropoidea; Catarrhini; Oligopithecidae; Parapithecidae. [E.D.]

Further Readings

Harrison, T. (1987) The phylogenetic relationships of the early catarrhine primates: A review of the current evidence. J. Hum. Evol. 16:41–80.

Fleagle, J.G., and Kay, R. F. (1987) The phyletic position of the Parapithecidae. J. Hum. Evol. 16:483–532.

Fleagle, J.G., and Kay, R.F., eds. (1994) Anthropoid Origins. New York: Plenum, pp. 675–698.

Paranthropus

Genus name employed in reference to the clade that comprises the "robust" australopith fossils from the South African sites of Kromdraai, Swartkrans, and Drimolen (*Paranthropus robustus*), the geochronologically older sediments of the Shungura and Nachukui Formations of Ethiopia and Kenya (*P. aethiopicus*), and numerous later Plio-Pleistocene localities in Tanzania, Kenya, and Ethiopia (*P. boisei*).

The name *Paranthropus,* which means literally "beside man" or "next to man," was coined by R. Broom in 1938, when he described the first fossil hominid from the site of Kromdraai as belonging to the taxon *Paranthropus robustus.* Subsequently discovered australopith remains from the site of Swartkrans were also referred by Broom to *Paranthropus,* albeit to a separate species, *P. crassidens.* He regarded the Kromdraai and Swartkrans fossils as being so distinct from the *Australopithecus* specimens from Taung, Sterkfontein, and Makapansgat as to warrant their separation as a distinct subfamily, the Paranthropinae. Further work, principally by J.T. Robinson, served to substantiate the validity of recognizing the "robust" australopith fossils as representing a separate genus, *Paranthropus,* although he recognized the Kromdraai and Swartkrans fossils as composing a single species, *P. robustus,* and he did not consider that they were attributable to a separate subfamily. Robinson maintained that because *Paranthropus* and *Australopithecus* were on separate lines of evolution, and because they occupied different adaptive zones rather than different aspects of the same adaptive zone, their generic separation was fully justified. Robinson eventually came to view *Australopithecus* and *Homo* as constituting a single phyletic lineage and, therefore, proposed that

the genus name *Australopithecus* be recognized as a junior synonym of *Homo.* In 1959, a massively built australopith cranium was discovered by M.D. Leakey in Bed I of Olduvai Gorge, Tanzania. It was attributed by L.S.B. Leakey to a novel taxon, *Zinjanthropus boisei.* Robinson, who was quick to recognize its close affinities to *P. robustus,* proposed that *Zinjanthropus* was a junior synonym of *Paranthropus.* Thus, according to him, the Olduvai cranium was attributable to *P. boisei.*

Subsequent studies by several workers, including P.V. Tobias and M.H. Wolpoff, in which all australopiths were viewed as composing a single evolutionary grade of organization, questioned the generic distinctiveness of *Paranthropus.* These grade-oriented, phenetic studies influenced opinion such that, in the mid-1990s, most students of (and almost all textbooks on) hominid evolution regarded *Paranthropus* as a junior synonym of *Australopithecus.* Indeed, some individuals have even argued that all australopith fossils simply represent size and/or temporal variants within the range of variation of a single anagenetic species lineage.

Additional discoveries of "robust" australopith fossils, most notably those recovered by R.E.F. Leakey and his colleagues on the eastern shores of Lake Turkana, Kenya, have led to numerous studies by workers such as B.A. Wood, M.C. Dean, R.J. Clarke, and F.E. Grine that have highlighted their distinctiveness. Thus, despite the overwhelming scholastic influence that the "grade" paradigm has had upon anthropologists, a strong body of evidence has accumulated in which *Paranthropus* specimens have been shown to possess a host of derived morphological specializations that probably reflect significant functional differences between them and other early hominid taxa. Although there have been arguments to the contrary, this morphological evidence points overwhelmingly to the fact that the "robust" australopiths represent a monophyletic clade. Their characteristic craniodental traits are almost certainly related to trophic (i.e., dietary) parameters. *Paranthropus* specimens display so many craniodental features distinguishing them from representatives of other hominid taxa that there is good reason to believe that they constitute a unique and specialized evolutionary lineage.

Along these lines, both Robinson and Clarke have argued that, since the morphological differences between *Paranthropus* and *Australopithecus* are notably greater than those separating *Australopithecus* and *Homo, Paranthropus* had probably been separate from *Australopithecus* for a longer time than had *Homo.* As Clarke stated (1985, p. 172): ". . . if it is valid to place *Homo habilis* in a genus distinct from *Australopithecus,* it is far more justifiable to separate *Paranthropus* from *Australopithecus.*"

Robinson's view concerning early hominid phylogeny was adopted by T.R. Olson in his analysis of the Hadar and Laetoli fossils attributed by most workers to the species *A. afarensis.* Olson argued that the *Homo* and *Paranthropus* lineages were separate evolutionary entities and that they were already recognizable by the mid-Pliocene within the Hadar and Laetoli samples. Thus, according to him, the Hadar and Laetoli hypodigm of *Australopithecus afarensis* contains specimens belonging to different species, which made up the separate *Homo* and *Paranthropus* lineages. Accordingly, Olson has proposed that some of the Hadar fossils belong to the genus *Homo* (*H. aethiopicus*), while other of the Hadar and all of the Laetoli remains are attributable to the genus *Paranthropus* (*P. africanus*).

The question of the phylogenetic derivation of *Paranthropus* has been the focus of much of the work that has revolved around the interpretation of a nearly complete, albeit nearly edentulous cranium discovered in the 1980s by A.C. Walker in Pliocene sediments (ca. 2.5 Ma) of the Nachukui Formation on the western side of Lake Turkana. This specimen (with the catalog number KNM-WT 17000), which evinces a number of features that attest to its "robust" australopith affinities, has been interpreted by Walker and some of his colleagues as an early specimen of *Paranthropus* (= *Australopithecus*) *boisei*. They have argued that this fossil attests to the eastern African "robust" australopiths (= *A. boisei*) having evolved from *A. afarensis*, while the South African "robust" form (= *A. robustus*) evolved independently from *A. africanus*. Should this unlikely phylogenetic scheme prove true, it would mean that the "robust" australopiths would have to be divided into two genera: *Paranthropus* for the South African form and *Zinjanthropus* for the "robust" australopith fossils from eastern Africa.

Other workers, including W.H. Kimbel, D.C. Johanson, T.D. White, E. Delson, and F.E. Grine, interpret the cranium from the Nachukui Formation as representing a species distinct from *P. boisei*. According to this interpretation, this cranium and a number of penecontemporaneous fossils from the Nachukui (Kenya) and Shungura (Ethiopia) Formations might be referred to the species *Paranthropus aethiopicus*. The most parsimonious interpretation of the phylogenetic relationships among these various species is that *P. boisei* and *P. robustus* are more closely related to each other and to *P. aethiopicus* than any of them are related to any other hominid species. Should this arrangement be accepted, there can be little doubt about the validity of *Paranthropus* as a monophyletic taxon. While this is superficially similar to the arrangement proposed by Olson, it differs in that it does not necessarily recognize *Paranthropus* elements in the Hadar and Laetoli hominid samples. Rather, those fossils, which appear to represent a single species that does not possess any recognizable "paranthropine" synapomorphies, will likely have to be assigned a new taxonomic designation (i.e., they will not belong to the genera *Homo*, *Paranthropus*, or *Australopithecus*), for which the nomen *Praeanthropus africanus* is available.

Thus, although there is considerable difference of opinion regarding not only the generic distinctiveness of *Paranthropus*, but also the number of "robust" australopith species that are represented in the fossil record, there is almost universal agreement that these specimens display an extensive suite of unique cranial and dental features probably related to trophic specializations involving the generation and distribution of powerful masticatory forces. The cranial remains are reasonably interpreted as evidence for the existence of at least three species, and their shared features almost certainly attest to their common ancestry.

Characteristics of Paranthropus

The cranial and dental features that serve to distinguish the genus *Paranthropus* from other hominin genera include: a "dished" midface in which the pyriform aperture is set posterior to the level of the zygomatics; a depressed frontal trigone demarcated by strongly convergent superior temporal lines; a marked postorbital constriction; a nasion and a glabella that approximate each other in position; an internasal suture that tends to project above the frontomaxillary suture concomitant with superiorly expanded nasal bones; an infraorbital foramen that is situated in the lower half of the anterior surface of the zygomatic; a nasoalveolar clivus that passes smoothly into the nasal cavity; a hard palate that is very thick; a cranium that exhibits pneumatization and ectocranial superstructures (at least in presumptive males); a mastoid process that is laterally inflated relative to the supramastoid crest; a wide supraglenoid gutter; a thick zygomatic arch at the root of the frontal process; a petrous axis that is markedly angled to the sagittal plane, which results in a high petromedian angle; possibly a tendency for the occipital-marginal sinus to be enlarged relative to the transverse sinus; maxillary canine and incisor alveoli that tend to be aligned in the same coronal plane; incisors and canines that are relatively small compared to the sizes of molars and especially premolars; P_3 that tends to possess three roots; dP_3 "molarized" with anterior fovea centrally situated and walled by a complete mesial marginal ridge; very thick permanent molar enamel; a laterally inflated and relatively broad mandibular corpus with a large cross-sectional area at the level of M_1; a vertically oriented mandibular symphysis; and a wide extramolar sulcus of the mandible.

At least three species may be identified in the Plio-Pleistocene record of eastern (two species) and southern Africa (one species), although some workers, such as F.C. Howell and Grine, have maintained that the differences between the fossils from Swartkrans and Kromdraai attest to the presence of two *Paranthropus* species in South Africa. However, because the differences between the specimens from these two localities are subtle, and because the newly discovered fossils from Drimolen may warrant a reinterpretation of these differences, the "robust" australopith fossils from these three South African sites are considered to be attributable to a single taxon for present purposes. The three species recognized here are: *P. robustus*, *P. boisei*, and *P. aethiopicus*. Each is briefly discussed here and at greater length in separate entries.

P. aethiopicus

This species is represented by the nearly edentulous adult cranium, KNM-WT 17000, from the Lokalalei Member of the Nachukui Formation, a partial juvenile cranium from Submember E3 of the Shungura Formation, a partial mandible with teeth from the Lokalalei Member, a partial, edentulous mandible (cataloged as Omo 18-1967-18) from Submember C8 of the Shungura Formation, which is the holotype of this taxon, and a number of isolated teeth that

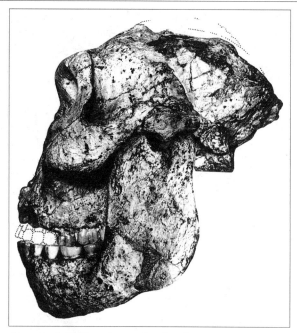

Composite skull of Paranthropus *from Swartkrans.*

range from Shungura Members C through G. The Omo 18-1967-18 mandible was described in 1967 by C. Arambourg and Y. Coppens, who attributed it in 1968 to the novel taxon *Paraustralopithecus aethiopicus.*

The adult cranium (KNM-WT 17000) displays a number of features that serve to differentiate it from specimens of *P. robustus* and *P. boisei,* and some of the isolated teeth—most notably the premolars—from the Shungura Formation lack several of the highly derived features of *P. boisei* homologues, according to work of G. Suwa, although penecontemporaneous deciduous premolars are virtually indistinguishable from those attributed to *P. boisei.* If the attribution of these various specimens to *P. aethiopicus* is correct, then this species may have a temporal range of between ca. 2.8 and 2.2 Ma. It shares with the other two species of *Paranthropus* almost all of the cranial derived features (synapomorphies) listed above as characterizing the genus, but few of the dental or mandibular features.

P. robustus

This is the type species of the genus *Paranthropus.* The holotype specimen, cataloged as TM 1517 in the Transvaal Museum, Pretoria, derives from the South African site of Kromdraai. It was described in 1938 by R. Broom. To date, only a handful of hominid fossils have been recovered from Kromdraai, and it is likely that all derive from Member 3 of the Kromdraai B East Formation. A decade after the recovery of the first Kromdraai specimen, Broom discovered fossils at the South African site of Swartkrans; these he assigned to another species, *P. crassidens.* Most workers consider the Kromdraai and Swartkrans fossils to represent a single species, *P. robustus,* with the vast bulk of the hypodigm of this taxon deriving from Swartkrans. Since 1992, specimens attributable to *P. robustus,* including a well-preserved cranium and mandible, have been recovered from the site of Drimolen,

also in South Africa. *P. robustus* fossils are known primarily from Member 1 of the Swartkrans Formation, although recent excavations by C.K. Brain have yielded specimens from Members 2 and 3.

The geochronological age of *P. robustus* is presently determined by associated faunal remains from Members 1, 2, and 3 of the Swartkrans Formation. There is no significant difference among the assemblages from these three units, and the age of the largest Member 1 assemblage has been estimated to be between ca 1.8 and 1.5 Ma. The geochronological age of the Kromdraai fossils is usually thought to be somewhat less than 1.5 Ma. The Drimolen *Paranthropus* fossils likely date from the same period of time.

Analyses of the faunal remains associated with *P. robustus* suggest that this species inhabited an environment that was somewhat more open than that associated with *Australopithecus africanus.* There are indications of riverine gallery forest habitats that appear to have been surrounded by large open grasslands.

P. boisei

The type of this species is a large, nearly complete cranium (cataloged as OH 5) that was discovered in 1959 in Bed I of Olduvai Gorge by M.D. Leakey. L.S.B. Leakey described it that same year as the new taxon *Zinjanthropus boisei.* The hypodigm of this species comprises fossils from Beds I and II of Olduvai Gorge and a mandible from the Humbu Formation at Peninj, near Lake Natron (Tanzania); a number of fine specimens from the Koobi Fora and Nachukui Formations (Kenya); a partial cranium from the Chemoigut Formation (Kenya); and a number of mandibles, isolated teeth, and a fragmentary cranium from the Shungura Formation (Ethiopia). A cranium attributable to *P. boisei* is known also from the site of Konso (Ethiopia).

The majority of the Koobi Fora fossils attributable to *P. boisei* derive from above the KBS Tuff, although several are known from below it (e.g., the mandibles KNM-ER 1469 and KNM-ER 1482 from the Upper Burgi Member). Undoubted *P. boisei* fossils are known from Members G, K, and L of the Shungura Formation, and from Bed II of Olduvai Gorge (i.e., specimen OH 3). Thus, undoubted *P. boisei* remains are known from ca. 2.3 to 1.4 Ma. Work by Wood and colleagues in 1994 suggests that *P. boisei* exhibited a degree of morphological stasis over this period.

The cheek teeth of *P. boisei* tend to be larger than those of *P. robustus;* dimensions for *P. boisei* premolars and molars are the largest recorded for any hominin taxon. Postcranial remains that are reasonably attributed to *P. boisei* suggest a species with some retained arboreal capabilities, especially in the configuration of its forearm skeleton. The proximal femur has a relatively small head and a relatively long, anteroposteriorly flattened neck. Craniodental remains and postcranial bones that have been attributed to *P. boisei* indicate a species with a considerable degree of size (presumed sexual) dimorphism. Reasonable body size estimates based upon attributed postcranial remains range from ca. 35 to 85 kg for the smallest and largest bones, respectively.

See also Australopithecus; Drimolen; Kromdraai; Olduvai Gorge; Paranthropus aethiopicus; Paranthropus boisei; Paranthropus robustus; Swartkrans; Synonym(y). [F.E.G.]

Further Readings

Clarke, R.J. (1985) *Australopithecus* and early *Homo* in southern Africa. In E. Delson (ed.): Ancestors: The Hard Evidence. New York: Liss, pp. 171–177.

Grine, F.E., ed. (1988) Evolutionary History of the "Robust" Australopithecines. New York: Aldine de Gruyter.

Olson, T.R. (1981) Basicranial morphology of the extant hominoids and Pliocene hominids: The new material from the Hadar Formation, Ethiopia, and its significance in early human evolution and taxonomy. In C.B. Stringer (ed.): Aspects of Human Evolution. London: Taylor and Francis, pp. 99–128.

Rak, Y. (1983) The Australopithecine Face. New York: Academic.

Robinson, J.T. (1954) The genera and species of the Australopithecinae. Am. J. Phys. Anthropol. 12:181–200.

Skelton, R.R., and McHenry, H.M. (1992) Evolutionary relationships among early hominids. J. Hum. Evol. 23:309–349.

Strait, D.S., Grine, F.E., and Moniz, M.A. (1997) A reappraisal of early hominid phylogeny. J. Hum. Evol. 32:17–82.

Suwa, G., White, T.D., and Howell, F.C. (1996) Mandibular postcanine dentition from the Shungura Formation, Ethiopia: Crown morphology, taxonomic allocation and Plio-Pleistocene hominid evolution. Am. J. Phys. Anthropol. 101:247–282.

Tobias, P.V. (1967) The cranium and maxillary dentition of *Australopithecus (Zinjanthropus) boisei*. Olduvai Gorge, Vol. 2. Cambridge: Cambridge University Press.

Walker, A.C., Leakey, R.E.F., Harris, J.M., and Brown, F.H. (1986) 2.5-My *Australopithecus boisei* from west of Lake Turkana, Kenya. Nature 322:517–522.

Wood, B.A., and Chamberlain, A.T. (1987) The nature and affinities of the "robust" australopithecines: A review. J. Hum. Evol. 16:625–641.

Wood, B.A., Wood, C., and Konigsberg, L. (1994) *Paranthropus boisei:* An example of evolutionary stasis? Am. J. Phys. Anthropol. 95:117–136.

Paranthropus aethiopicus

Taxonomic name used in reference to the earlier East African "robust" australopith fossils from the Shungura Formation (Ethiopia) and the Nachukui Formation (Kenya). These specimens span the time period ca. 2.8–2.2 Ma. The holotype specimen of this taxon is an edentulous mandible (cataloged as Omo 18-1967-18) from Submember C-8 of the Shungura Formation. It was described in 1967 by C. Arambourg and Y. Coppens, who attributed it in 1968 to the novel taxon *Paraustralopithecus aethiopicus*.

This species is represented by a nearly edentulous adult cranium (cataloged as KNM-WT 17000) from the Lokalalei Member of the Nachukui Formation, a partial juvenile cranium from Submember E-3 of the Shungura Formation, a partial mandible with teeth from the Lokalalei Member, and a number of isolated teeth that range from Shungura Members C through G. The adult cranium displays a number of derived features in common with *Paranthropus robustus* and *P. boisei*, which warrants its attribution to the same genus. On the other hand, KNM-WT 17000 differs from the crania of *P. robustus* and *P. boisei*, hence its attribution to a separate species. For the most part, the characters in which the *P. aethiopicus* cranium differs from those of *P. robustus* and *P. boisei* appear to evince more primitive states in the former. In addition, some of the isolated teeth—most notably the premolars—from the Shungura Formation lack several of the highly derived features of *P. boisei* homologues, although penecontemporaneous deciduous molars are virtually indistinguishable from those of *P. boisei*.

In their description and interpretation of KNM-WT 17000, A.C. Walker and colleagues suggested that, should this specimen be shown to be distinct from *P. boisei*, it might reasonably be accorded the taxonomic designation *P. aethiopicus*, the species name accorded the Omo 18-1967-18 mandible by Arambourg and Coppens. The Omo mandible and the 17000 cranium are of approximately the same geochronological age, but the KNM-WT 17000 cranium would have possessed a very large mandible, and its attribution to *P. aethiopicus*, which is based upon a much smaller jaw, holds by a rather tenuous thread of logic. Whether or not the name *P. aethiopicus* proves to be validly applied to the KNM-WT 17000 cranium, the name is at least available for this purpose, and there are very good reasons to attribute this specimen to a separate species from *P. boisei* and *P. robustus*. Alternatively, the name *Paranthropus walkeri* has been proposed by W. Ferguson with WT 17000 as holotype. *P. aethiopicus* will no doubt enjoy increased use in taxonomic discussion of early Hominini.

P. aethiopicus shares with *P. robustus* and *P. boisei* the following derived features (synapomorphies): a "dished" midface with the facial surface of the zygoma anterior to the level of the pyriform aperture; coincident glabella and nasion; an internasal suture that rises above the level of the frontomaxillary suture and is superiorly expanded; a nasoalveolar clivus that passes smoothly into the floor of the nose; marked ectocranial superstructures (at least in presumptive males); pneumatization of the temporal squama with strongly flared parietal mastoid angle; a broad anterior palate with lateral incisor roots set medial to the lateral margins of the pyriform aperture; maxillary incisor and canine alveoli aligned nearly in the same coronal plane; a very thick palate; a tympanic plate that is deep; a petrous axis that is strongly inclined to the sagittal plane, resulting in a high petromedian angle; dP_3 molarized with a centrally placed anterior fovea that is fully enclosed by a high mesial marginal ridge; and very thick (hyperthick) permanent molar tooth enamel.

It is similar to *P. boisei* and differs from *P. robustus* in possessing a heart-shaped foramen magnum, lacking anterior pillars, having no (or only a slight) Eustacian process of the tympanic bone; and in exhibiting parietal overlap of the

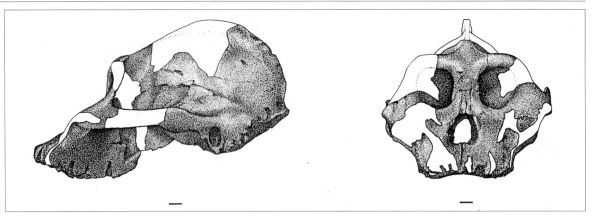

Lateral and facial views of the Paranthropus aethiopicus *(KNM-WT 17000) cranium from West Turkana, Kenya. Scales are 1 cm.*

occipital at asterion. On average, *P. aethiopicus* molar crowns approximate the sizes of *P. boisei* homologues, whereas *P. robustus* molars tend to be somewhat smaller. It is similar to *P. robustus*, and differs from *P. boisei* in possessing an inferior margin of the orbit that is rounded laterally, a maxillary trigon (zygomaticomaxillary step), and a tympanic that is vertically inclined with a distinct crest.

It differs from both *P. robustus* and *P. boisei*, and exhibits the presumably more primitive states (as evinced, for example, by *A. afarensis*) in the following features: strong alveolar prognathism; an anteriorly very shallow palate; a smaller cranial capacity (410 cc estimate for KNM-WT 17000 vs. a value of 530 cc for *P. robustus* and estimates of 500–550 cc for *P. boisei*); a cerebellum that flares laterally and protrudes posteriorly; the presence of an asterionic notch; a relatively flattened cranial base; a shallow mandibular fossa that lacks a distinct articular eminence; an external auditory meatus that is medially positioned relative to the lateral edge of the suprameatal roof of the temporal bone; the absence or very slight development of the vaginal process of the tympanic bone; and a foramen magnum that is positioned at the level of the bi-tympanic line as opposed to being situated well anterior to the line. Indirect evidence suggests that *P. aethiopicus* displayed considerable size (presumably sexual) dimorphism, to judge from the difference in the size of the Omo 18-1967-18 mandible and the mandible that would have been associated with the KNM-WT 17000 cranium (the latter approximates KNM-ER 729, a large *P. boisei* mandible, in size).

Postcranial remains from the Shungura Formation that may be attributable to *P. aethiopicus* include a large ulna from Member E that is notable for its considerable length and substantial dorsoventral curvature.

See also Australopithecus; Australopithecus afarensis; Australopithecus africanus; Paranthropus; Paranthropus boisei; Paranthropus robustus. [F.E.G.]

Further Readings
Grine, F.E., ed. (1988) Evolutionary History of the "Robust" Australopithecines. New York: Aldine de Gruyter.

Walker, A.C., Leakey, R.E.F., Harris, J.M., and Brown, F.H. (1986) 2.5-My *Australopithecus boisei* from west of Lake Turkana, Kenya. Nature 322:517–522.

Paranthropus boisei
Taxonomic name used in reference to the later East African "robust" australopith fossils from the Shungura Formation and Konso (Ethiopia); the Koobi Fora, Nachukui and Chemoigut Formations (Kenya); and Beds I and II of Olduvai Gorge and the Humbu Formation at Peninj (Tanzania). The type specimen (OH 5) was discovered by M.D. Leakey in Bed I of Olduvai Gorge in 1959. The earliest craniodental remains attributable to *P. boisei* are known from the Upper Burgi Member of the Koobi Fora Formation and from Member G of the Shungura Formation. The latest *P. boisei* specimen appears to derive from Konso. Thus, this species spans the temporal period from ca. 2.3–1.4 Ma.

Many of the morphological features that characterize the skull and dentition of *P. boisei* are shared with *P. robustus* and *P. aethiopicus*. For example, all three *Paranthropus* species possess a "dished" midface (in which the pyriform aperture is set posterior to the facial plates of the zygomatics); a depressed frontal trigone demarcated by strongly convergent superior temporal lines; nasion and glabella in near approximation; a nasoalveolar clivus that extends smoothly into the nasal cavity, a very thick palate; a high petromedian angle; incisors and canines that are relatively small in comparison to the sizes of the molars and especially the premolars; and very thick permanent molar enamel.

P. boisei differs from *P. robustus* primarily in that the former has sharply defined inferolateral orbital margins, greater maxillary depth with a concomitantly shelved palate, a "heart-shaped" foramen magnum, a strong postero-inferior slope to the tympanic bone, and a tendency to develop an inferiorly extended zygomatic "visor." In addition, *P. boisei* lacks the maxillary trigone, the discernible anterior pillars, and the prominent Eustachian process of the tympanic possessed by *P. robustus*. *P. boisei* cheek teeth tend to be larger than those of *P. robustus*. *P. boisei* differs from *P. aethiopicus* principally in that the former has sharply defined inferolateral orbital margins; less alveolar prognathism; an anteriorly deeper (shelved) palate; a deeper glenoid fossa with a well-

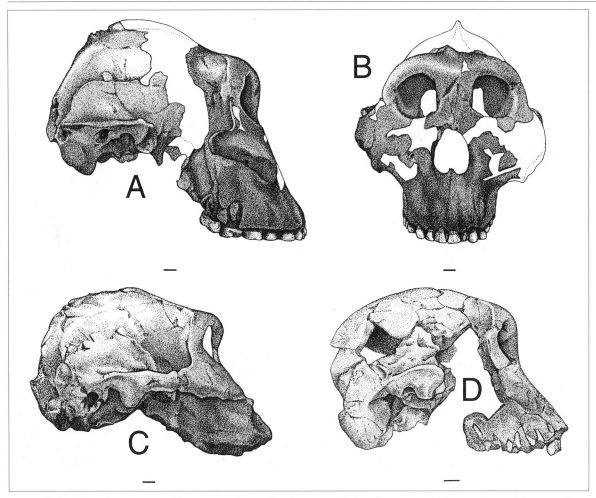

Crania of Paranthropus boisei*: OH 5, Olduvai Gorge, Tanzania (A, B); KNM-ER 406, Koobi Fora, Kenya (C); KNM-ER 732 (D) OH 5 and ER 406 are thought to be male, ER 732 to be female. Scales are 1 cm.*

developed articular eminence; a tympanic that extends to the lateral margin of the suprameatal roof; a more flexed cranial base; an anteriorly positioned foramen magnum; and a larger cranial capacity (500–550 cc vs. 410 cc).

Most of the morphological features that characterize the skull of *P. boisei* appear to be related to the generation and distribution of very powerful masticatory forces. In the absence of any contrary evidence, it seems reasonable to assume that these powerful forces were necessary to chew fibrous, tough, and/or hard objects. Such items would be consistent with a vegetarian diet that included fruits, seeds, and tubers.

Although crania, mandibles, and isolated teeth of *P. boisei* are by far the most abundant hominid fossils to be recovered from sediments that date to between about 2.3 and 1.4 Ma, there are comparatively few postcranial bones that can be attributed to *P. boisei* with reasonable certainty. Those postcrania that can be referred to *P. boisei* suggest a species that retained some arboreal capabilities, especially in the configuration of its forearm skeleton. The proximal femur has a relatively small head and a relatively long, anteroposteriorly flattened neck. The calcaneus and talus are generally humanlike, indicating a bipedally adapted foot, although the pedal elements also display some apelike features, as well as some unique traits. Body-size estimates for *P. boisei* range

from less than 30 kg to greater than 85 kg, and stature estimates have suggested values of ca. 148–168 cm. These estimates, although tenuous (because they are based on incomplete and referred long bones), indicate a species that exhibited considerable sexual dimorphism. This conclusion is supported by cranial and mandibular elements as well.

Recent studies have indicated that *P. boisei* probably exhibited a degree of morphological stasis in a variety of cranial and dental characters over the course of its ca. 1.0 Myr of existence. Reconstructions of the environment in which *P. boisei* fossils are found suggest that this species preferred fairly closed habitats that were in close proximity to water (e.g., gallery and marginal forests along rivers and lakes).

See also Africa, East; Australopithecus; Baringo Basin/Tugen Hills; Chesowanja; Konso; Natron-Eyasi Basin; Olduvai Gorge; Paranthropus; Paranthropus aethiopicus; Paranthropus robustus; Peninj; Turkana Basin. [F.E.G.]

Further Readings

Grine, F.E., ed. (1988) Evolutionary History of the "Robust" Australopithecines. New York: Aldine de Gruyter.

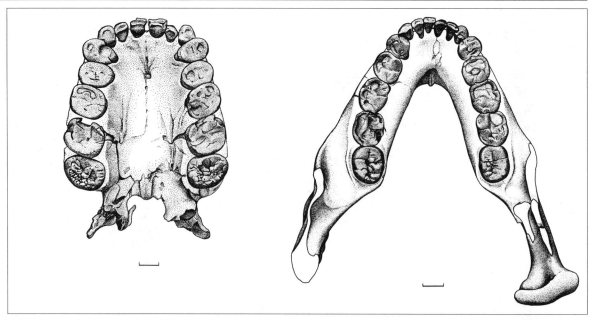

Left: Palate of P. boisei *OH 5, from Olduvai Gorge, Tanzania. Right: occlusal view of the* P. boisei *mandible from Peninj, Tanzania. Scale is 1 cm.*

Howell, F.C. (1978) Hominidae. In V.J. Maglio and H.B.S. Cooke (eds): Evolution of African Mammals. Cambridge, Mass.: Harvard University Press, pp. 154–248.

Rak, Y. (1983) The Australopithecine Face. New York: Academic.

Tobias, P.V. (1967) The cranium and maxillary dentition of *Australopithecus (Zinjanthropus) boisei:* Olduvai Gorge, Vol. 2. Cambridge: Cambridge University Press.

Wood, B.A. (1991) Koobi Fora Research Project, Vol. 4: Hominid Cranial Remains. Oxford: Oxford University Press.

Wood, B.A., and Chamberlain, A.T. (1987) The nature and affinities of the "robust" australopithecines: A review. J. Hum. Evol. 16:625–641.

Wood, B.A., Wood, C., and Konigsberg, L. (1994) *Paranthropus boisei:* An example of evolutonary stasis? Am. J. Phys. Anthropol. 95:117–136.

Paranthropus robustus

Taxonomic name used in reference to the "robust" australopith fossils from the South African sites of Kromdraai, Swartkrans, and Drimolen. The first of these specimens was discovered at Kromdraai in 1938. The fossil, which consists of the left half of a cranium, a right mandibular corpus, and several teeth, was obtained by R. Broom and described by him that same year. Broom noted that the face was flat, that the incisors and canines were small, and that the premolars and molars differed in their morphology and larger size from the Sterkfontein (South Africa) specimens of *Australopithecus.* He considered that the differences between the Kromdraai and the Sterkfontein fossils warranted their generic separation and made the Kromdraai specimen the type of a new taxon, *Paranthropus robustus.* A decade later, the first australopith fossil was recovered from the site of Swartkrans, several kilometers from Kromdraai along the Bloubank River. Broom observed that the mandibular corpus of the

Swartkrans specimen was similar in its robusticity to that from Kromdraai and that the teeth were morphologically similar to, but larger than, those from Kromdraai. He considered that the Swartkrans and the Kromdraai fossils were attributable to the same genus, *Paranthropus* but that the subtle differences between them warranted their specific separation. Broom thus named the Swartkrans specimen *P. crassidens.*

Several years later, on the basis of his study of larger samples of australopith fossils from Swartkrans and Kromdraai, J.T. Robinson argued that they could be accommodated in a single species, *Paranthropus robustus.* Robinson noted, however, that the Kromdraai and the Swartkrans fossils differed from each other in subtle dental features, and he suggested that these forms could be regarded as two subspecies (*P. robustus robustus* and *P. robustus crassidens*). Some workers (e.g., F.C. Howell and F.E. Grine) have more recently argued that the differences between the Swartkrans and the Kromdraai fossils may, indeed, warrant their specific separation. Fossils discovered at the site of Drimolen since 1992 are morphologically similar to those from Kromdraai and Swartkrans and most likely represent the same species. *P. robustus* fossils are known from Members 1 (both Lower Bank and Hanging Remnant deposits), 2, and 3 of the Swartkrans Formation. The faunal assemblages from these different stratigraphic units do not vary significantly, nor do the *Paranthropus* fossils appear to vary appreciably from Members 1 through 3. They probably date to between ca. 1.8 and 1.5 Ma on the basis of associated faunal remains. A preliminary attempt at thermoluminescence (TL) dating of quartz sand grains from these units suggested that the Member 3 fossils may be as young as 850 Ka. This would make them the youngest *Paranthropus* remains known in either southern or eastern Africa. However, the absence of significant differences in the faunal assemblages among these stratigraphic units indicates that they are temporally closer

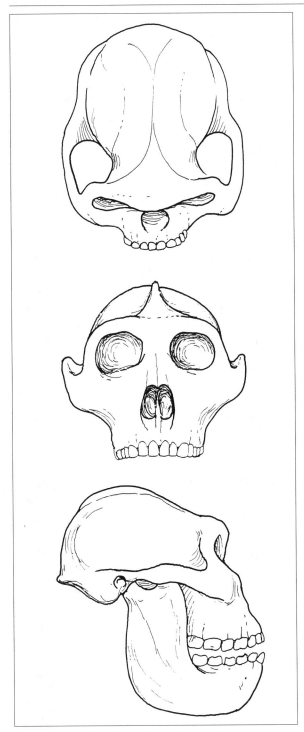

Dorsal, facial, and lateral views of Paranthropus robustus *cranium. Courtesy of Frederick E. Grine.*

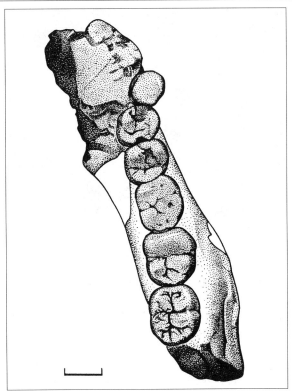

Occlusal view of the TM 1517 mandible of the Paranthropus robustus *holotype from Kromdraai, South Africa. Scale is 1 cm.*

to one another than implied by the TL date. The geochronological age of the Kromdraai hominid fossils is wholly unresolved; majority opinion would place them at somewhat less than 1.5 Ma. The Drimolen *Paranthropus* fossils also likely date from the same interval (i.e., ca. 1.8–1.5 Ma).

A substantial suite of features characterizes *P. robustus*. Many of these are shared with *P. aethiopicus* and *P. boisei*, but, in several traits, *P. robustus* differs from the other two species. Among the features that characterize *P. robustus* are a robustly constructed cranium with ectocranial superstructures;

substantial pneumatization of the cranium with marked lateral inflation of mastoid region; males with sagittal crest but lacking confluence of posteroinferior temporal and superior nuchal lines; temporal lines posteriorly divergent above lambda; a mastoid process not notably inflected and its tip medial to lateral margin of elongate and concave tympanic; marked angulation of the petrous axis to the sagittal plane resulting in a high petromedian angle; a tendency for the occipital-marginal sinus to be enlarged relative to the transverse sinus; a calvaria hafted to the facial skeleton at a low level, resulting in a low supraorbital height index; a low and slightly concave forehead with the frontal trigone delimited laterally by posteriorly convergent temporal crests; strong postorbital constriction; a strong and horizontally disposed supraorbital torus with a flattened "rib" of bone across the supraorbital margin and lacking twist between the medial and lateral components; a prominent glabella situated below the level of the supraorbital margin; nearly coincident nasion and glabella as a result of a low glabella and a tendency for the internasal suture to project higher than the nasofrontale; an orthoganthous bony face of moderate height; the piriform aperture set in the central facial hollow; the nasoalveolar clivus passing smoothly into the floor of the nasal cavity without strong demarcation; incisive canals open into the horizontal surface of the nasal floor without the presence of capacious incisive fossa; a tendency of the alveolar margins of the maxillary canine and incisor sockets to lie in the same coronal plane; a palate that is deep posteriorly and shallow anteriorly; relatively small incisors and canines compared with the large sizes of premolars and molars; a tendency of P_3

Lateral view of the SK 48 cranium of Paranthropus robustus *from Swartkrans, South Africa. Courtesy of Frederick E. Grine.*

to possess three roots; molarized dP$_3$ with the anterior fovea centrally situated and walled by a complete mesial marginal ridge; very thick permanent molar enamel; and a laterally inflated mandibular corpus.

Many of these traits appear to be related to the generation and distribution of powerful masticatory forces. Analyses of details of occlusal wear on the molar teeth indicate that the diets of *Australopithecus africanus* and *P. robustus* differed qualitatively and that the diet of *P. robustus* comprised hard objects. Studies of the carbon-isotope ratios of *P. robustus* tooth enamel indicate that this species had an overall reliance on C$_3$-based foods (trees, shrubs, forbs, and tubers), although C$_4$ grasses provided a substantial dietary contribution. Furthermore, strontium-calcium ratios determined from *P. robustus* cranial bones, if reliable, suggest that this species also may have consumed meat. Thus, the diet of *P. robustus* may have been fairly catholic, but its craniodental anatomy indicates a primary adaptation to the mastication of abrasive food items that required the application of powerful chewing forces.

Endocranial capacity estimates for *P. robustus* range between 450 and 550 ml, but only a single good specimen from Swartkrans is known (it has a volume of 530 ml). The paucity of good endocranial remains leaves this range of estimates open to question.

Because of the presence of *Homo* in the same sedimentary units at Swartkrans, it is difficult to correctly associate all of the hominid postcranial bones at that site. Nevertheless, there are several elements at Swartkrans that can be reasonably attributed to *P. robustus*, and there are a few from Kromdraai that also might belong to this species. In general, most of the postcranial remains of *P. robustus* appear to be morphologically similar to those of other *Australopithecus* and *Paranthropus* species for which homologous elements are known. Thus, the femur of *P. robustus* has a relatively small head and relatively long, anteroposteriorly flattened neck. The radius exhibited enhanced stability against medial displacement during pronation and supination, and aspects of its morphology appear to be related to enhanced capabilities of forearm-flexor, hand-extensor, and hand-flexor muscles. This is suggestive of arboreal capabilities. Foot bones, on the other hand, are indicative of bipedal locomotion. Hand

bones, especially pollical metacarpals, that may be attributable to *P. robustus* suggest an ability to have managed humanlike precision grasping, which may relate to the capacity to manipulate tools; in this regard, *P. robustus* differs from species of *Australopithecus*, such as *A. afarensis* and *A. africanus*. However, the humanlike nature of the foot and hand bones may be related to their derivation from individuals of early *Homo* rather than from *Paranthropus*.

Reasonable estimates of body size for *P. robustus* that are based upon postcranial elements rather than on postcanine tooth size range from ca. 42 to more than 65 kg. Although we still have little idea of how robust these "robust" australopiths actually were, it appears that they may not have been substantially larger than some species of *Australopithecus* (e.g., *A. afarensis* and *A. africanus*). Size dimorphism (i.e., presumed sexual dimorphism) in cranial, mandibular, dental, and postcranial remains of *P. robustus* appears to be rather less than the differences in size between elements attributed to both *P. aethiopicus* and *P. boisei*, and to species of *Australopithecus*, such as *A. afarensis* and *A. africanus*. However, it is unclear whether this apparent pattern reflects a specific reduction of body-size (sexual?) dimorphism in *P. robustus*, or whether it is a taphonomic artifact that reflects the preferred prey size of the predator responsible for the accumulation of *P. robustus* remains.

See also Australopithecus; Broom, Robert; Drimolen; Kromdraai; Paranthropus; Paranthropus aethiopicus; Paranthropus boisei; Robinson, John Talbot; Swartkrans. [F.E.G.]

Further Readings

Brain, C.K. (1993) Swartkrans: A Cave's Chronicle of Early Man (Transvaal Museum Monographs No. 8). Pretoria. Transvaal Museum.

Grine, F.E. (1981) Trophic differences between "gracile" and "robust" australopithecines: A scanning electron microscope analysis of occlusal events. S. Afr. J. Sci. 77:203–230.

Grine, F.E., and Susman, R.L. (1991) New *Paranthropus robustus* radius from Member 1, Swartkrans Formation: Comparative and functional morphology. Am. J. Phys. Anthropol. 84:229–248.

Howell, F.C. (1978) Hominidae. In V.J. Maglio and H.B.S. Cooke (eds.): Evolution of African Mammals. Cambridge, Mass.: Harvard University Press, pp. 154–248.

Lee-Thorpe, J.A., van der Merwe, N.J., and Brain, C.K. (1994) Diet of *Australopithecus robustus* at Swartkrans from stable carbon isotopic analysis. J. Hum. Evol. 27:361–372.

Rak, Y. (1983) The Australopithecine Face. New York: Academic.

Robinson, J.T. (1954) The genera and species of the Australopithecinae. Am. J. Phys. Anthropol. 12:181–200.

Sillen, A. (1992) Strontium-calcium ratios (Sr/Ca) of *Australopithecus robustus* and associated fauna from Swartkrans. J. Hum. Evol. 23:495–516.

Susman, R.L. (1988) Hand of *Paranthropus robustus* from Member 1, Swartkrans: Fossil evidence for tool behavior. Science 240:781–784.

Susman, R.L. (1994) Fossil evidence for early hominid tool use. Science 265:1570–1573.

Parapithecidae

Family of African Primates that includes the oldest and most primitive monkeys. As such, they are the key to understanding the origins of the anthropoid primates, the group that includes New and Old World monkeys, apes, and humans. Parapithecids are found principally in rocks of Late Eocene and Early Oligocene age in the Fayum Province (Egypt), in an area of badlands at the eastern edge of the Sahara Desert. Other fragmentary remains of parapithecids come from Algeria. As currently understood, Parapithecidae includes the following genera (with one species each unless otherwise indicated): *Apidium* (three species), *Arsinoea, Parapithecus, Serapia, Simonsius* (=? *Parapithecus*), *Qatrania* (two species), and possibly *Biretia, Algeripithecus,* and *Tabelia.*

History of Study

The first recovered parapithecid was *Apidium phiomense*, a name approximately translating into "little sacred bull of the Fayum." A single jaw of a young *A. phiomense* was found in the Fayum by the professional collector R. Markgraf early in 1907 and described by H. F. Osborn. Osborn suspected that it had primate affinities or that it was a hoofed mammal, hence the name. Later in the same year, Markgraf collected a more complete, adult lower jaw of a second kind of monkey for the Stuttgart Museum. This find was described by M. Schlosser in 1910 and 1911 as *Parapithecus* (meaning "next-to-an-ape") *fraasi*, and he erected the family name Parapithecidae for it. No other specimens of *Apidium* or *Parapithecus* were recognized or recovered until 1961. These two specimens were difficult to relate to modern primates and remained of uncertain evolutionary relationship throughout the 50 years that followed their description. Osborn could not decide whether *Apidium* might be an odd sort of pig or a primate, while others considered it a possible primitive hoofed mammal, a monkey, or an ancestor of the extinct Italian primate *Oreopithecus. Parapithecus* was never questioned as a primate, but its systematic position was widely debated partly because of damage to the specimen at the front of the jaw with possible loss of teeth and tooth sockets. This damage led to misunderstanding of the numbers and kinds of its teeth, information that would have been useful in judging its affinities. Opinions about its closest relatives thus ranged from tarsiers to monkeys, apes, or even humans.

No record has survived of the precise stratigraphic levels from which Markgraf recovered *A. phiomense* or *P. fraasi*. That both come from upper levels of the Jebel Qatrani Formation in the Fayum was clarified only by the collection of more specimens. Many new finds from the Fayum badlands (Jebel Qatrani Formation) have been made since 1961. It is now clear that parapithecids are anthropoids, although to which anthropoid group they belong is open to interpretation. E.L. Simons and his colleagues described seven new species of parapithecids, beginning with *Apidium moustafai* in 1962. In 1974, Simons named *Parapithecus grangeri*, which P.D. Gingerich in 1981 suggested be placed in a distinct genus he named *Simonsius;* there is still controversy over this distinction. Simons demonstrated that all of these species are closely related and assigned them to Parapithecidae. In 1983, another new kind of parapithecid primate, *Qatrania*, was described by Simons and R.F. Kay from an older level of the Jebel Qatrani Formation. In 1992, Simons described further new parapithecids, *Serapia* and *Arsinoea*, from the oldest part of the Jebel Qatrani Formation. From Algeria come fragmentary remains of other possible parapithecids (*Biretia*, described in 1988; and *Algeripithecus* and *Tabelia*, recovered in the 1990s). In 1994, Kay and B.A. Williams recognized two subfamilies, Parapithecinae for the more derived (Oligocene) genera and Qatraniinae for the conservative (Eocene) taxa.

Age of the Parapithecids

Most parapithecid fossils come from the Jebel Qatrani Formation, which conformably overlies the marine and fluvial Qasr el Sagha Formation of Late Eocene age (ca. 37 Ma). The top of the Jebel Qatrani Formation was eroded and then capped by volcanic flows dated at 31 Ma. Recent geochronologic studies of the Jebel Qatrani Formation allow us to place the Fayum parapithecids more precisely. The oldest genera, *Serapia* and *Arsinoea*, occur in the lowest part of the formation (Quarry L-41) and may date to ca. 36–35 Ma. *Qatrania* is the next younger and could be nearer 35–34 Ma. *A. moustafai* comes from a still higher stratigraphic level in the formation, at ca. 34 Ma. All of the other species are from the highest fossiliferous levels and date to 33.5–33 Ma. If this calibration based on paleomagnetic studies proves correct, Fayum parapithecids span the Eocene/Oligocene boundary at ca. 34 Ma. *Algeripithecus* and *Tabelia* are known from the site of Glib Zegdou, estimated to be of Middle Eocene age (ca. 42 Ma). *Biretia*, from Bir el Ater, seems to be of a similar age to the L-41 forms or *Qatrania* of the Fayum sequence, and some scientists believe that this poorly known animal may actually be the same as *Qatrania*.

Morphology of the Parapithecidae

Most of our knowledge of the anatomy of parapithecids comes from fossils of *Apidium* and *Simonsius*. Other taxa are known almost entirely from dental (and fragmentary mandibular) remains. Dentally, parapithecids are characterized by the presence of three upper and lower premolars (and, of course, three molars) and projecting canines. The cusps are generally low and rounded, but there are often extra accessory cusps, especially in *Apidium*. The upper premolars are distinct among primates in having an extra cusp between the two main cusps (i.e., a large ?paraconule between the buccal paracone and the lingual protocone). The lower molars present a moderate-size hypoconulid in the midline at the distal (back) end of the tooth, a feature that has long been used to associate the parapithecids with later catarrhines in which this cusp is important. The lower-molar trigonid and talonid are roughly even in height, another character typical of anthropoids. Dental features that vary among parapithecids are discussed below.

The skull of parapithecids is again known almost entirely from *Apidium* species, although there is one facial

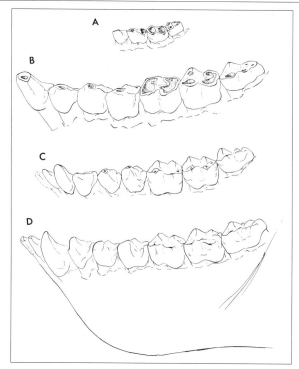

Lateral views of the lower teeth of four taxa of Fayum parapithecids: (a) Qatrania wingi; *(b)* Simonsius grangeri; *(c)* Parapithecus fraasi; *(d)* Apidium phiomense. *All drawings are to the same scale. Courtesy of Richard F. Kay.*

fragment of *Simonsius.* The orbits are fully closed off posteriorly (postorbital closure) and the frontal fused tightly in the midline, as in modern anthropoids. The braincase is apparently small for an anthropoid, suggesting a small brain. The external ear opening (auditory meatus) is ringlike, as in platyrrhines and the earliest catarrhines, without the tube that characterizes the more derived catarrhines. Known mandibles of most species indicate that the mandibular symphysis was fused before adulthood, as in later anthropoids; however, Late Eocene *Arsinoea* has an unfused symphysis. If *Arsinoea* proves to be a parapithecid (as of 1999, it is poorly known anatomically), this would provide evidence that the mandibular symphysis was fused independently in parapithecids and later anthropoids (catarrhines and platyrrhines). This would not be surprising since such more conservative anthropoids as oligopithecids also lack symphyseal fusion. Parapithecid teeth are also more derived than those of the Oligopithecidae.

Parapithecid Habitat and Adaptations

From all that can be learned concerning their anatomy and habitat, it is clear that parapithecids were monkeylike animals that resembled living squirrel monkeys from South and Central America in size, appearance, and probably habits. Parapithecid fossils come from continental sediments deposited by rivers, lakes, and streams in an area of low topographic relief. The Fayum region during the Oligocene, as evinced by sedimentological evidence, associated paleofloras, and vertebrate remains, had seasonal rainfall and was humid, subtropical to tropical, and densely forested (along the major streams at least). It is probable that there were savan-

nah woodlands in interstream areas. From the size of the teeth and skeletal elements, parapithecids were much smaller than any living African monkeys and closer in size to the smaller living New World monkeys. *Qatrania wingi,* the smallest, was as small as a marmoset, ca. 300 g. *Q. fleaglei, Serapia, Arsinoea, P. fraasi,* and *Apidium* were larger, between 700 and 1,300 g. *Simonsius* was the largest, probably weighing up to 1,800 g, the size of *Cebus,* the South American capuchin monkey.

Not all of the parapithecids are well known anatomically. What we know of their locomotion is based principally on study of bones of *Apidium.* To judge from the structure of its limbs and pelvis, *Apidium* was an agile, saltatory quadruped and highly arboreal. This animal had modifications in the lower leg bones that assisted in stabilizing the ankle joint during leaping. Indirect evidence suggests that *Simonsius* may have spent more time on the ground. This animal has high-crowned cheek teeth, a feature common in living ground-dwelling Old World monkeys. (Grit in food found on the ground subjects the cheek teeth to greater wear; higher molar crowns are selectively advantageous for resisting such wear.)

Most parapithecid species have low, rounded cheek-tooth cusps resembling the teeth of living, fruit-eating monkeys and apes. Cheek-tooth enamel of *Apidium* was relatively quite thick. Thick enamel suggests that *Apidium* species may have eaten hard nuts or seeds. *Simonsius* has cheek teeth with sharper cutting edges; these imply a greater leaf component in its diet, judged by analogy with the structure of cheek teeth among living leaf-eating mammals.

Apidium had projecting canines and small, vertically implanted lower incisors set in a lower jaw fused at the midline in front. Thus, this early group was already essentially anthropoidlike in using its incisors and canines for incision or separation of a bite of food. This differs from living strepsirhines, which have lower canines and incisors positioned in a comb for use mainly in fur grooming or bark scraping, not in incision. *Simonsius* is strikingly specialized by having lost its lower incisors. The projecting, robust, blunt lower canines of this animal touch one another in the symphyseal midline. Such a dental design would have served as a powerful puncturing device, although the functional details are unclear since the upper front teeth of *Simonsius* are still unknown. *Parapithecus* may have begun this specialization with the loss of permanent incisors and retention of just a single deciduous lower incisor as an adult. It is just as likely, however, that this species had two lower incisors in each jaw half, thereby resembling *Apidium.* The only known specimen of *P. fraasi* has symphyseal damage and may have lost one incisor from each side of the jaw post mortem. Incisor loss with canine enlargement has been reported recently in a Late Eocene Fayum ?strepsirhine called *Plesiopithecus;* otherwise, it is unknown in any other primate.

The relatively small size of the eye sockets of *Apidium* and *Simonsius* suggest they were daytime active (diurnal), as are almost all living anthropoids, but distinct from many prosimians with relatively large eyes (and eye sockets) and nocturnal habits. Probably the closest living ecological parallels to the parapithecid primates are found among South American monkeys.

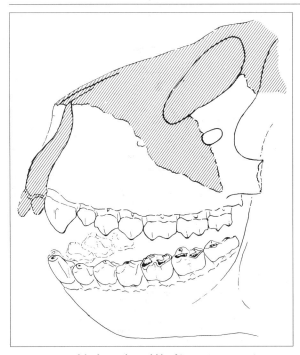

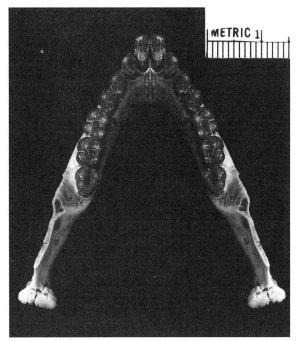

Reconstruction of the face and mandible of Simonsius grangeri *in lateral view. Anatomical features of note include postorbital closure and symphyseal fusion, indicating anthropoid status. Also, the orbits were small, indicating diurnal habits. Courtesy of Richard F. Kay.*

Occlusal view reconstruction of the mandible of Simonsius grangeri. *Right ramus of DPC 5527 with C-M3 printed together with its mirror image. Courtesy of Elwyn L. Simons.*

Anthropoid Status of Parapithecidae

Many cranial and skeletal parts are known for *Apidium* and some for *Simonsius*. These show that parapithecids had reached the anthropoid, or *monkey*, grade of organization. Parapithecids are more monkeylike than any primates of the Early and Middle Eocene. They resemble anthropoids (apes, humans, and Old and New World monkeys), and not Holarctic Eocene primates or modern Madagascar lemurs, in having reduced olfactory lobes of the brain, an anthropoid configuration in bony-ear structure (although the ectotympanic is not tubular, as in all extant catarrhines), a bony partition between the eye socket and the space behind it that houses the jaw muscles (postorbital closure), closely packed cheek teeth, spatulate incisors (except *Simonsius*), and projecting canines. This advanced combination of characteristics has led all authorities to accept their status as the oldest undoubted anthropoids.

A more difficult and unresolved question concerns parapithecid relationships within Anthropoidea. Opinion is divided as to whether parapithecids are more closely related to the Old World (catarrhine) or New World (platyrrhine) branch of anthropoids, or are a separate early branch.

Simons has often suggested that the parapithecids (especially *Simonsius*) were the ancestors or the sister group of living Old World monkeys, the Cercopithecidae, but on current evidence this would seem to be the least likely interpretation. Although there are a few similarities between the molars and the foot bones of cercopithecids and some parapithecids, the balance of evidence suggests that these similarities are caused by evolutionary parallelism (homoplasy). Otherwise, many unusual anatomical characteristics of living Old World monkeys and apes, but not of parapithecids,

must have evolved in parallel. Such a list would include independent loss of the front (second) premolars, shortening of the face, separate ossification of a tubelike extension of the bony ring (ectotympanic) that supports the eardrum, and features of the limb bones.

A few paleontologists suggest that parapithecids are in or near the ancestry of New World monkeys. This is not as farfetched as would seem from the present wide oceanic separation of Africa and South America. In the Late Eocene, the continents were closer together, and island chains may have intervened between them. Such a view gains support from the adaptive similarity between parapithecids and liv-

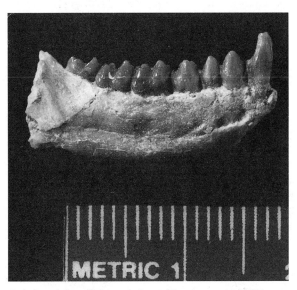

Right lateral view of holotype specimen of Serapia eocaena *(CGM 42286). Courtesy of Elwyn L. Simons.*

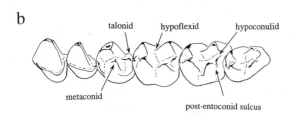

Dentition of early Parapithecidae from Fayum Quarry L-41: (a) Serapia eocaena, *left I2-M3; (b)* Arsinoea kallimos, *right P2-M3, slightly oblique. Note the large P₄ metaconid on* Arsinoea. *Courtesy of Richard F. Kay.*

ing small Neotropical monkeys. Parapithecids also show many anatomical resemblances to platyrrhines not seen in modern catarrhines (humans, apes, or Old World monkeys). For example, the tympanic bone of the ear is ringlike, resembling platyrrhines, rather than tubular as in catarrhines. What is important, however, is that most of these similarities seem to be holdovers from the last common ancestor of both of these groups and do not indicate an ancestor-descendant relationship. On the other hand, parapithecids have no special (derived) similarities with platyrrhines that would place them exclusively in the line of platyrrhine ancestry.

Another possible alternative is that parapithecids are the sister taxon to all later catarrhines. This view could be supported from dental evidence (and the cranial material is too scrappy to allow a definite conclusion). But the majority of known postcranial fossils are more conservative ("primitive") than not only all catarrhines, but than all platyrrhines as well. As with the parapithecid-cercopithecid hypothesis, this would require that several derived postcranial features shared by platyrrhines and catarrhines evolved twice, once in the parapithecid-derived catarrhines and again in platyrrhines. This is unparsimonious and thus tends to reject a special parapithecid-catarrhine relationship.

The likeliest hypothesis is that the parapithecids are an early side branch of anthropoid evolution. In other words, early Anthropoidea differentiated into two stocks, one leading to both platyrrhines and catarrhines and the other to parapithecids. This would explain the many persistently primitive features of skeleton, face, and dentition of parapithecids lost in the lineage leading to living Old and New World anthropoids. The conclusion that parapithecids are a group of primitive anthropoids in Africa 8 (or perhaps 15) Myr before the first record of platyrrhines lends support to the hypothesis of an African origin for that South American group.

Family Parapithecidae
    Subfamily Parapithecinae
        †*Parapithecus*
        †*Simonsius* (=? *Parapithecus*)
        †*Apidium*

    Subfamily Qatraniinae
        †*Qatrania*
        †*Serapia*
        †*Arsinoea*
    Subfamily indeterminate
        ?†*Biretia*
        ?†*Algeripithecus*
        ?†*Tabelia*
†extinct

See also Anthropoidea; Catarrhini; Diet; Fayum; Locomotion; Oligocene; Oligopithecidae; Platyrrhini; Propliopithecidae; Skeleton; Skull; Teeth. [R.F.K.]

Further Readings

Fleagle, J.G., and Kay, R.F. (1987) The phylogenetic position of the Parapithecidae. J. Hum. Evol. 16:483–531.

Fleagle, J.G., and Kay, R.F. (1994) Anthropoid origins: Past, present, and future. In J.G. Fleagle and R.F. Kay (eds.): Anthropoid Origins. New York: Plenum, pp. 675–698.

Fleagle, J.G., and Simons, E.L. (1995) Limb skeleton and locomotor adaptation of *Apidium phiomense*, an Oligocene anthropoid from Egypt. Am. J. Phys. Anthropol. 97:235–289.

Harrison, T. (1987) The phylogenetic relationships of the early catarrhine primates: A review of the current evidence. J. Hum. Evol. 16:41–80.

Kay, R.F., and Williams, B.A. (1994) Dental evidence for anthropoid origins. In J.G. Fleagle and R.F. Kay (eds.): Anthropoid Origins. New York: Plenum, pp. 361–445.

Simons, E.L. (1986) *Parapithecus grangeri* of the African Oligocene: An archaic catarrhine without lower incisors. J. Hum. Evol. 15:205–213.

Simons, E.L., and Kay, R.F. (1983) *Qatrania*, a new basal anthropoid primate from the Fayum Oligocene of Egypt. Nature 304:624–626.

Simons, E.L., Rasmussen, D.T., Bown, T.M., and Chatrath, P.S. (1994) The Eocene origin of anthropoid primates. In J.G. Fleagle and R.F. Kay (eds.): Anthropoid Origins. New York: Plenum, pp. 179–202.

Szalay, F.S., and Delson, E. (1979) Evolutionary History of the Primates. New York: Academic.

Paromomyidae

A family of archaic primates, currently in a serious state of flux. Under this family concept, in this encyclopedia, are united some of the most ancient and, in many ways at least, dentally similar archaic primates. There are as yet no satisfactory classifications of this very diverse but probably monophyletic group, certainly none that warrants the breaking up of the Paromomyidae into subfamilies: The grouping of genera into tribes yields taxa with diversity comparable to that seen in other primate tribes. Only a few of these tiny forms were in the size range of the common brown rat; the rest were usually smaller. Although some of the included species have such advanced characters as reduced dental formulae, new dental specializations, ear-region modifications, and probably other unknown unique features, the last common ancestor of the paromomyids was an archaic plesiadapiform. Paromomyids form the bulk of the superfamily Paromomyoidea, which also includes the rare Picrodontidae, but not the "picromomyids" that are uintasoricine microsyopids, and not primates.

Four or five tribes may be recognized within the Paromomyidae. They cannot be unequivocally related to one another within the family, largely because fossil evidence is mostly limited to the dentition. It is, furthermore, unwarranted to attempt linkage to other families within the Plesiadapiformes or outside of the Primates. While this is undoubtedly unsatisfactory at present (see conflicting classifications given as examples in the entry PLESIADAPIFORMES), the plethora of dental genera in this family awaits new evidence and understanding after which they may be united in two or more subfamilies or independent families. Unless otherwise indicated all genera are restricted to the western United States. The four tribes recognized here are the Purgatoriini, the Paromomyini, the Micromomyini, and the Navajoviini. Members of this assemblage have been (at various times in the past and today) referred to or linked with Microsyopidae, a family of contested affinities that some other paleontologists still believe to be part of the archaic primate assemblage Plesiadapiformes.

The diagnostic attributes of the tribe Purgatoriini are based on the genus *Purgatorius* from the Early Paleocene and doubtfully also from the Cretaceous. The dentition is relatively well known for *Purgatorius unio*, without question dentally the most primitive primate. In this animal, the trigonids of the lower teeth are still tall and prominent, in spite of the characteristically primate widening of the back part of the lower molars, the talonid. The Early Paleocene *Purgatorius*, along with the equally ancient *Pandemonium dis*, a plesiadapid from the famous Purgatory Hill locality, hint at the important dietary beginnings of the primates. Although the full eutherian dental formula appears to have been present in *Purgatorius* (three incisors, one canine, four premolars, and three molars in each quadrant of the jaws), the wide talonids suggest the evolution of extensive crushing function in addition to the ancient cutting ability of the trigonids. Insects and fruit likely made up the diet of the first arboreal archontans and primates.

The tribe Paromomyini is a much more varied assemblage of species, divided into the subtribes Palaechthonina and Paromomyina. Palaechthoninans are not far removed from *Purgatorius* in morphology, nor probably in lifestyle, but they have lost one of the incisors (probably the third pair) and slightly enlarged the central incisors to form a kind of spoon or scoop presumably useful for small animals that may have been exploiting the rich and widespread tropical and subtropical forests of the Paleocene. A crushed specimen of *Palaechthon* is the earliest indication of some of the proportions of the facial portion to the neural part of the skull in an early primate. As in the much bigger *Plesiadapis*, the smaller and older paromomyid also shows opossumlike proportions of its braincase to the rest of the cranium.

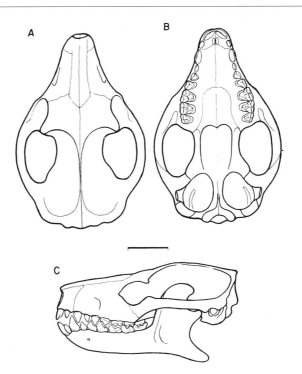

Reconstructed skull of the Middle Paleocene paromomyid Palaechthon nacimienti *from North America. Scale is 1 cm. Courtesy of Frederick S. Szalay, from Szalay and Delson, 1979.*

Paromomyinans represent a distinct radiation of the archaic primates, some of which managed to survive well into the late Middle Eocene of North America. They emphasized their central pairs of incisors to an extreme (although they never became ever-growing or rodentlike) and reduced the teeth between these and their last premolars. The square and relatively flat molars, with their trigonids reduced almost to the talonid level, strongly suggest a very considerable fruit component in their diet. They might have occupied a range of ecological niches not dissimilar to the burramyid and phalangerid phalangeriform marsupials of Australia and New Guinea. A recently described skull of *Ignacius* putatively displays an entotympanic bone in sutural contact with the middle-ear cavity in the roof of the tympanic cavity. Due to the crushing and plastic deformation of the *Ignacius* skull, this asserted departure from the petrosal bulla of primates could not be corroborated. The putative genus *Anasazia* was allocated to this group, but it is so far unrecognizable as to its validity or affinity.

The tribe Micromomyini also had enlarged lower incisors; the group contains the smallest-known primate, smaller than the living mouse-lemur. These astonishing early offshoots of the ancestral primate stock are now known from well-preserved postcranial elements; some of the species have enlarged their fourth lower premolar into a tall slicing device. The sharp and prominent antemolar dentition is emphasized to such a degree at the expense of the molars that it seems certain that micromomyinans, at least *Micromomys*, were thoroughly insectivorous like some of the small galagos. While these forms were possibly tiny gliders like the Australian marsupial possum *Acrobates*, their proposed close ties to the Dermoptera are doubtful.

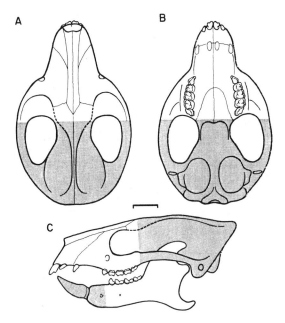

Reconstructed skull of the Early Eocene paromomyid Ignacius graybullianus *from North America. Scale is 1 cm. Courtesy of Frederick S. Szalay, from Szalay and Delson, 1979.*

The tribe Navajoviini includes small, dentally relatively nondescript primates that occur in the Late Paleocene and Early Eocene. Both the North American *Navajovius* and the European *Berruvius* and *Avenius* possess enlarged central incisors and molars that are assumed to have facilitated a primarily insectivorous diet. The exact affinities of the micromomyins and navajoviins are not known. Their closest ties are probably with the more primitive palaechthoninans or some other early group of primates, and not with microsyopids.

Family Paromomyidae
    (no consensus on subfamilies exists)
      Tribe Purgatoriini
          † *Purgatorius*
      Tribe Paromomyini
          Subtribe Paromomyina
              † *Paromomys*
              † *Ignacius*
              † *Dillerlemur*
              † *Pulverflumen*
              † *Simpsonlemur*
              † *Phenacolemur* (including † *Elwynella* and
                  † *Arcius*)
          Subtribe Palaechthonina
              † *Palaechthon*
              † *Plesiolestes*
              † *Palenochtha*
              † *Premnoides*
      Tribe Micromomyini
          † *Micromomys*
          † *Tinimomys*
          † *Chalicomomys*
          † *Myrmecomomys*

      Tribe Navajoviini
          † *Navajovius*
          † *Berruvius*
          † *Avenius*
† extinct

See also Archonta; Dermoptera; Microsyopidae; Picrodontidae; Plesiadapidae; Plesiadapiformes; Primates. [F.S.S.]

Further Readings
Gunnell, G.F. (1989) Evolutionary history of Microsyopoidea (Mammalia, ?Primates) and the relationships between Plesiadapiformes and Primates. University of Michigan Papers on Paleontology No. 27:1–154.
MacPhee, R.D.E., ed. (1993) Primates and Their Relatives in Phylogenetic Perspective. New York: Plenum.
Szalay, F.S., and Delson, E. (1979) Evolutionary History of the Primates. New York: Academic.
Van Valen, L.M. (1994) The origin of plesiadapid primates and the nature of *Purgatorius*. Evol. Monog. 15:1–79.

Paromomyoidea

A superfamily of the archaic primate semiorder Plesiadapiformes, of which the Plesiadapoidea is the other member. This group, along with the other archaic primates, has been in flux as to the suprageneric relationship of its individual members or whole collections of genera. Several tribes of this assemblage have been raised to family or higher categorical levels (e.g., Purgatoriidae, Palaechthoniidae, Micromomyiformes), and the Microsyopidae continue to be associated closely (if incorrectly) with the paromomyoids. Usually, two family-group taxa, the Paromomyidae and the Picrodontidae, are included in the superfamily Paromomyoidea. The diversity in the Paromomyidae based on dental criteria or various uncorroborated hypotheses regarding the phylogenetic ties of members of this taxon to forms outside of this group does not appear to warrant either association with other higher taxa or inflation beyond subfamily and tribal ranking.

Still, this is not the most satisfactory arrangement because various members of the group are only minimally known. This superfamily, in fact, represents only a convenient grouping of those archaic primates that are not admissible into the more clearly diagnosable Plesiadapoidea. Nevertheless, in spite of the suggestion by K.C. Beard to allocate various paromomyoids to two separate orders, this superfamily may turn out to represent a monophyletic group (of the paraphyletic variety), stemming from an early lineage from which only the Plesiadapoidea also arose. Thus, Plesiadapiformes probably gave rise to no other lineages, and, therefore, it may prove to be a holophyletic taxon.

See also Archonta; Dermoptera; Microsyopidae; Paromomyidae; Picrodontidae; Plesiadapiformes. [F. S. S.]

Parpalló

A cave shelter near Gandia (Valencia, Spain) excavated in the years 1929–1931. More than 5,000 incised limestone plaques document a single style of animal rendition and geometric-motif marking and accumulation that develops and increases in complexity from the Gravettian through the Solutrean and the final Magdalenian, ca. 28–14 Ka. Variants of this Mediterranean style extend into the Romanellian and Epipaleolithic cultures of Italy, the Azilian culture of France, and the Mesolithic cultures of Levantine Spain. Aspects of this style are also present at Parpalló on worked bone. Parpalló is the only site in western Europe within which one can follow the incremental development of a regional style of symboling across changing tool cultures and thousands of years of ritual-symbolic homesite marking. The engraving style includes both an overmarking and reuse of incised animal images and increasingly complex accumulations of motifs in the "macaroni" tradition (serpentines, zigzags, bands, ladders, etc.).

See also Azilian; Epipaleolithic; Gravettian; Paleolithic Image; Late Paleolithic; Magdalenian; Mesolithic; Solutrean. [A.M.]

Further Readings
Marshack, A. (1977) The meander as a system: The analysis and recognition of iconographic units in Upper Paleolithic compositions. In P. Ucko (ed.): Form in Indigenous Art: Schematization in the Art of Aboriginal Australia and Prehistoric Europe. London: Duckworth, pp. 286–317.

Pericot, L. (1942) La Cueva del Parpalló (Gandia). Consejo Sup. de Investigaciones Científicas, Inst. Diego Velázquez, Madrid.

Villaverde Bonilla, V. (1994) Arte Paleolítico de la Cova del Parpalló. 2 vols. Servei d'Investigació Prehistòrica, Diputació de València. Valencia.

Parvorder
Category in the classificatory hierarchy that falls between the infraorder and the superfamily. This rank was devised in light of an awareness that a larger number of categories than traditionally recognized was necessary to accommodate the phylogenetic diversity of mammalian groups. For example, in Primates the parvorders Eocatarrhini and Eucatarrhini have been used within the infraorder Catarrhini to reflect the phylogenetic distinctness of the Oligocene to Miocene archaic catarrhines (Eocatarrhini, a paraphyletic group in this case) from the cercopithecoids and hominoids, which together form the holophyletic group, Eucatarrhini.

See also Classification. [E.D.]

Paşalar
Middle Miocene site in western Anatolia, Turkey, dated to 15–13 Ma. The main fossiliferous deposit was accumulated extremely rapidly, so that the fossil assemblage forms a single-time accumulation, and the catchment area for both sediments and fossils is similarly limited, so that it is possible that the fossils preserved were derived from a limited number of animal populations. All sizes of mammal are preserved, including two proboscidean species, three rhino species, 19 shrews and rodents, 16 carnivore species, four suids, eight ruminants, and four other species. One kenyapithecine hominoid primate, *Griphopithecus alpani*, is fairly common, with a second much rarer (and unnamed) congeneric species also possibly present; together they constitute the second-most-abundant taxon preserved, with more than 50 individuals known from more than 1,000 specimens. Nonmammalian fossils are almost entirely absent from Paşalar, and the environment interpreted from the mammals is one of subtropical forest with marked seasonality of climate.

See also Asia, Western; Kenyapithecinae; Miocene; Taphonomy. [P.A.]

Further Readings
J. Hum. Evol. Special Issues: 19(4–5), 1990; 28(4), 1995.

Patagonia
Southern South America, including both Argentina and Chile. This region is famous for the rich Mesozoic and Cenozoic fossil sites first explored by the Argentine Ameghino brothers near the turn of the twentieth century. Its eastern portion is now a dry, steppelike grassland lashed by high winds coming off the South Atlantic, but warm, moist forests existed there during parts of the Tertiary. The fossil ateloid monkeys *Dolichocebus* and *Tremacebus* come from Colhuehuapian Early Miocene (ca. 21–19 Ma) sites (Gaiman and Sacanana, respectively), and a series of Santacrucian late Early Miocene (ca. 18–16 Ma) sites (Pinturas, Rio Gallegos, Monte Leon, Monte Observacion, Corriguen Aike) have yielded *Carlocebus, Homunculus*, and *Soriacebus*. A new site in Chile (on the Rio Las Leñas, dated ca. 20 Ma) recently provided *Chilecebus*. This fauna does not overlap with that from La Venta (Colombia) taxonomically, probably due to both temporal and ecological factors.

See also Cebinae; La Venta; Pitheciinae. [A.L.R.]

Further Readings
Flynn, J.J., and Swisher, C.C., III (1995) Cenozoic South American land mammal ages: Correlation to global geochronologies. SEPM Spec. Pub. 54:317–333.

Patterson, Bryan (1909–1979)
Anglo-American paleontologist and educator. Born in London and educated at Malvern College, Patterson immigrated to the United States in 1926 and joined the staff of the Field Museum of Natural History in Chicago. Beginning as a preparator, he rose to be Curator of Geology. In 1955, he moved to Harvard University as the Agassiz Professor of Vertebrate Paleontology, retiring in 1975 but remaining active in emeritus status until his death. Among his many honors, Patterson was elected to the U.S. National Academy of Sciences, and a museum in Guatemala was named after him. Pat (as he was known to friends and students) was probably one of the last paleontological scholars to rise to such eminence without benefit of graduate training.

His research spanned vertebrate history from the Late Paleozoic to the Late Pleistocene, throughout the Americas and in East Africa. He studied the dental remains of early mammals from the Early Cretaceous of Texas, resulting in a 1956 monograph that finally demonstrated the cusp homologies of tritubercular and tribosphenic molars, a problem since the time of Cope and Osborn. He also collected mammals, including primates, from the Paleocene and Early Eocene of the Debeque Formation in western Colorado and from the Middle Miocene of Loperot (in the "Turkana Grits") of Kenya. His most important paleoanthropological accomplishments came in the late 1960s, when he led several Harvard expeditions to the southwestern margin of Lake Turkana. There he located the Late Miocene and Pliocene sites of Ekora, Kanapoi, and Lothagam, each of which yielded important cercopithecine remains alongside early elephants and other mammals. At Kanapoi, the team recovered part of the distal humerus of a hominin, which Pat described in collaboration with W.W. Howells (and the brief assistance of E. Delson); this specimen is now part of the hypodigm of *Australopithecus anamensis*. From Lothagam, a partial ?hominin mandible, described in 1971, remains the oldest putative member of this taxon, although its taxonomic position is still uncertain.

See also Hominini; Howells, William White; Kanapoi; Lothagam; Picrodontidae; Teeth; Turkana Basin. [E.D.]

Paviland Cave

British Upper Paleolithic cave site in Wales excavated between 1822 and 1911. Initial exploration of Paviland Cave by D. Buckland in the 1820s revealed the fragmentary skeleton of an adult male lying on its back and covered with red ocher. The associated artifacts, stone tools and ivory objects, are said to have Aurignacian affinities, but the fossil itself dates to 18 Ka. Buckland, who was not prepared to acknowledge the antiquity of the human lineage, dubbed his fossil "the red lady of Paviland" and argued that she was a follower of the Roman army who had crawled into a cave to die. [J.J.S.]

Further Readings

Grayson, D. (1983) The Establishment of Human Antiquity. New York: Academic.

See also Aurignacian; Upper Paleolithic. [J.J.S.]

Pavlov

Complex of Late Paleolithic open-air sites (Pavlov I and II) at the foot of the Pavlov Hills, ca. 3 km southeast of Dolni Věstonice in Moravia (Czech Republic). These sites have yielded a huge inventory of stone and bone tools, portable art, and fragments of fired clay. Assemblages from the site were used to define the Pavlov industry, which researchers interpret as a regional variant of the Eastern Gravettian technocomplex. Features at Pavlov include remains of round, oval, and oblong surface and semisubterranean dwellings, as well as a burial of an adult male. The occupations are dated to ca. 25 Ka.

See also Dolni Věstonice; Předmosti. [O.S.]

Pech de l'Azé

Cave site near Carsac in the Dordogne (France). In 1909, the skull and mandible of a Neanderthal child were excavated from Mousterian levels now estimated to date to 90–60 Ka. According to a detailed report published years after the original find, the child may have been only ca. two years old at death, which has led to much discussion about its development and the presence or absence of Neanderthal characters. The face and cranial vault already show some Neanderthal features, and brain volume was probably large by the standards of modern two-year-olds (ca. 1,150 ml). The apparent random succession of Mousterian industries at this site and a nearby one (Combe Grenal) formed part of the basis for F. Bordes' interpretation of Mousterian industries as representing ethnic differences of long duration. Several manganese "crayons" were found in the Mousterian levels, bearing striae from use. The underlying Acheulean levels dating to 162–130 Ka contain an ox rib with what appears to be an engraved image.

See also Acheulean; Bordes, François; Europe; Mousterian; Neanderthals; Paleolithic Image. [C.B.S., J.J.S., A.S.B.]

Further Readings

Bordes, F. A Tale of Two Caves. New York: Harper and Row.

Pech Merle

A painted cave near the Lot River in the Quercy region of France. Discovered in 1922, it has ca. 60 animal figures and many signs. These are assigned, on the basis of their style, to three periods, ca. 22–10 Ka. The most famous single panel contains two spotted horses surrounded by negative handprints and additional spots. A butchered reindeer bone found under the horse panel was radiocarbon dated to ca. 18. Ka. Analysis of the paints in the horse panel reveals a use of different mixes for the different signs and sets of dots, suggesting a sequence of additions; the accumulation of hands around the two horses also suggests a sequence of ritual use. One wall in the cave contains rapidly sketched black outlines of mammoths and bison, some overmarked with red dots; a soft clay ceiling and one wall are finger-marked with images of "macaronis," females, mammoths, and a *Megaceros*.

See also Late Paleolithic; Paleolithic Image. [A.M.]

Further Readings

Lorblanchet, M. (1981) Les dessins noir du Pech Merle. In XXIᵉ Congrès Préhist. de France, Montauban/Cahors 1979, Vol 1., pp. 178–207.

Pedra Furada

Boqueirao da Pedra Furada, a large rockshelter in northeast Brazil, is a candidate for pre-Clovis (i.e, pre-11.5 Ka) occupation of the New World. N. Guidon and her colleagues claim an antiquity of 50 Kyr for the basal levels. The deposits are nearly 5 m deep, with abundant archaeological evidence for a later occupation of this site, including tools made of nonlocal chert. The lower levels contain extremely controversial "artifacts" made of local raw materials such as quartz and quartzite. An impressive sequence of 55 radiocarbon dates spans the last 42 Kyr. Proponents of the earliest occupational levels argue that the charcoal derives from human-built hearths; critics suggest natural brush fires as the most likely source. The claims for pre-Clovis occupation at Pedra Furada remain controversial, in part because the material remains and the site analysis are still unpublished.

See also Americas; Paleoindian. [D.H.T.]

Further Readings

Dillehay, T.D., and Meltzer, D.J. (1991) The First Americans: Search and Research. Boca Raton: CRC Press.

Guidon, N., and Arnaud, B. (1991) The chronology of the New World: Two faces of one reality. World Archaeol. 223:167–178.

Guidon, N., and Delibrias, G. (1986) Carbon-14 dates point to man in the Americas 32,000 years ago. Nature 371:769–231.

Guidon, N., Pessis, A.-M., Parenti, F., Fontugue, M., and Guérin, C. (1996) Pedra Furada, Brazil: Reply to Meltzer, Adovasio & Dillehay. Antiquity 70(268):408–421.

Meltzer, D.J., Adovasio, J.M., and Dillehay, T.D. (1994) On a Pleistocene human occupation at Pedra Furada, Brazil. Antiquity 68(261):695–714.

Peninj

Northern Tanzanian stratified sequence, with Lower Pleistocene Humbu and Moinik Formations dated by potassium-argon (K/Ar) and magnetostratigraphy. Located 80 km northeast of Olduvai Gorge, in upfaulted basin-filling sediments west of Lake Natron in northern Tanzania, this site was discovered in 1959. Archaeological studies by G.L. Isaac found Early Acheulean artifacts from two stratified localities, Bayasi and Mguludu, in the Humbu Formation. The Kamare locality at Peninj is a Late Acheulean surface assemblage derived from post-Moinik sediments. In 1964, a nearly complete mandible belonging to *Paranthropus boisei* was discovered in the Humbu Formation between key horizons dated 1.7 and 1.3 Ma. In the late 1970s, renewed explorations recovered many vertebrate and archaeological remains but no further hominins.

See also Acheulean; Africa, East; Isaac, Glynn Llewellyn; Natron-Eyasi Basin; Paranthropus boisei. [T.D.W.]

Further Readings

Mturi, A.A. (1987) The archeological sites of Lake Natron (Tanzania). Sci. Géol. Bull. 40:209–215.

Périgord

Medieval province of southwestern France centering on the Dordogne River and its tributaries (e.g., the Isle and the Vézère). This region of limestone plateaus, caves, and narrow, cliff-lined valleys is encompassed today in large part by the modern *département* of the Dordogne and is known for one of the greatest concentrations of Paleolithic paintings, engravings, and occupation sites of any area in the world, concentrated within 50 km of the village of Les Eyzies. The earliest systematic excavation of Paleolithic sites took place here, leading to the designation of many as type sites of Paleolithic industries, such as La Micoque, La Madeleine, La Gravette, and Le Moustier.

See also Abri Pataud; Aurignacian; Bordes, François; Cro-Magnon; Early Paleolithic; Gravettian; La Chaise; La Ferrassie; Laugerie Sites; Le Moustier; Magdalenian; Micoquian; Middle Paleolithic; Paleolithic Image; Pech de l'Azé; Perigordian; Peyrony, Denis; Regourdou; Solutrean; Tayacian; Upper Paleolithic. [A.S.B.]

Perigordian

Early Upper Paleolithic industrial complex of central and southwestern France (with brief extensions to northeastern Spain and the Paris Basin), 34–32 Ka and 28–21 Ka, named after the Périgord region at its geographical center. In 1933, D. Peyrony distinguished early Upper Paleolithic industries with stone points created by abrupt retouch or backing, then known as Lower and Upper Aurignacian, from the Aurignacian proper, or Middle Aurignacian, with its bone points, thick, carinate scrapers, and burins created by lamellar retouch. Like Peyrony's redefined Aurignacian, his Perigordian consisted of five stages and represented a *parallel phylum* to the Aurignacian, with the two phyla interpreted as the lithic signatures of two different ethnic groups who coexisted in the same area for ca. 15 Kyr.

On the basis of assemblages from the Dordogne sites of La Gravette, La Ferrassie, and Laugerie Haute, Peyrony defined his five stages as follows: Perigordian I, levels with large, relatively broad-backed points or knives known as Châtelperron points (La Ferrassie E); Perigordian II, with small semiabruptly retouched bladelets known as Dufour bladelets (La Ferrassie E'); Perigordian III, with truncated blades and small-backed Gravette points and bladelets (Laugerie Haute, base of sequence); Perigordian IV, with leaf-shaped points (*flèchettes*) and large Gravette points (La Gravette); and Perigordian V, in three successive facies represented at La Ferrassie Levels J, K, and L, respectively: Va, with tanged leaf-shaped Font-Robert points; Vb, with truncated blade segments; and Vc, with diminutive multiple-truncation (Noailles) burins and flat-faced (Raysse) burins.

This scheme has undergone several revisions. The original Perigordian II and its type fossil, the Dufour bladelet, have been relegated to the Aurignacian on the basis of such assemblages as Les Vachons (Charente). The Perigordian III, which was the only Perigordian originally recognized at Laugerie Haute, was found stratified *above* the Perigordian Vc at the Abri Pataud just across the Vézère River and was redesignated Perigordian VI. F. Bordes argued that the Protomagdalenian of Laugerie Haute should be relabeled Perigordian VII. Finally, the type fossils of the Perigordian Va, b, and c were found in differing combinations and stratigraphic order at Le Flageolet (Dordogne), which suggested that these

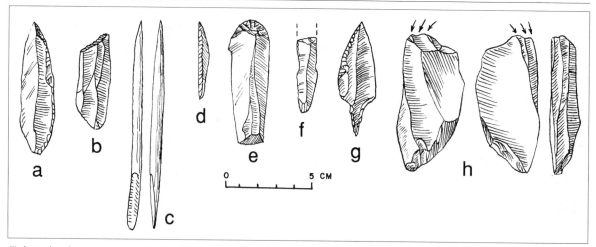

Tools attributed to various stages of the French Perigordian; note that Perigordian "I," or Châtelperronian, is now usually regarded as a distinct industry. (a) Châtelperron point (Perigordian I); (b) obliquely truncated blade (Perigordian I); (c) beveled-base bone point (Perigordian VI); (d) microgravette point (Perigordian VI); (e) end-scraper (Perigordian VI); (f) Noailles burin (Perigordian Vc); (g) Font Robert point (Perigordian Va); (h) Raysse burin [three views, Perigordian V c]. For a gravette point (Perigordian IV) see "Gravettian."

differences are not the signatures of different ethnic groups or stages of cultural evolution. As a result of these changes, which have largely eliminated the Middle Perigordian phases of Peyrony's scheme, the bulk of the Aurignacian now occupies a hiatus between the Lower Perigordian (or Châtelperronian) and the Upper (IV, V, and VI), with a minimal period of chronological overlap at each end. The *parallel phyla* concept has become hard to sustain. Although the technique of creating points through backing is widespread in Europe from 28 to 20 Ka, other specific hallmarks of Perigordian industries are lacking outside the core area, so that backed-point industries in eastern France and other countries are generally referred to as Gravettian. Châtelperronlike assemblages, however, are found in Spain (Cueva Morin), and industries comparable with the Perigordian V are found in Italy. Some authors have thus suggested that one or both of these industries, which have few or no Gravettes, be removed from the Perigordian technocomplex and designated separately as Châtelperronian and Noaillian. In any case, since the discovery of Neanderthal remains in association with Lower Perigordian (or Châtelperronian) industries at Saint-Césaire, the idea of ethnic or cultural continuity between a Lower and an Upper Perigordian has seemed increasingly untenable. Accordingly, the term usually refers today only to those industries formerly grouped as Upper Perigordian.

Perigordian industries (in the restricted sense just discussed) are associated with cold but fluctuating conditions. Faunal remains are dominated by reindeer, with horse and red deer increasing in warmer intervals and at the extreme south of the area. Trade networks are reflected in widespread use of nonlocal flint and in the occurrence of marine shells and ivory up to 400 km from probable sources. Bone tools, although not common, are carefully shaped and well polished, and several female (or "venus") figurines are associated with Perigordian industries at Pataud, Tursac, Laussel, Lespugue, and Brassempouy. Animal outlines were engraved on stone slabs and on utilitarian objects, and a few decorated caves and rockshelters have been attributed to Perigordian contexts: outlines of mutilated hands from Gargas, a carved

salmon bas-relief from Poisson, and simple engraved animal outlines at Pair-non-Pair. Living sites often contain complex arrangements of hearths, slabs, and postholes, suggesting elaborate structures or ordering of space.

See also Abri Pataud; Aurignacian; Bordes, François; Breuil, [Abbé] Henri [Edward Prosper]; Châtelperronian; Cueva Morin; Europe; Gargas; Gravettian; Homo sapiens; Jewelry; La Ferrassie; Late Paleolithic; Laugerie Sites; Paleolithic Image; Paleolithic Lifeways; Peyrony, Denis; Saint-Césaire; Stone-Tool Making; Upper Paleolithic. [A.S.B.]

Further Readings

Gamble, C. (1986) The Palaeolithic Settlement of Europe. Cambridge: Cambridge University Press.

Laville, H., Rigaud, J.-P., and Sackett, J. R. (1980) Rock Shelters of the Perigord. New York: Academic.

Peyrony, D. (1933) Les industries aurignaciennes dans le bassin de la Vézère. Bull. Soc. Préh. Fr. 30:543–559.

Wymer, J. (1982) The Palaeolithic Age. New York: St. Martin's.

Petralona

Cave site in northeastern Greece where, in 1960, a human skull encrusted in stalagmite was found in a deep level. It has been claimed that a whole skeleton was originally present, but this is unlikely. Because the original find spot was not studied carefully at the time of the discovery, many uncertainties about the associations and age of the skull remain to be resolved. Absolute dating by uranium series and thermoluminescence suggests that the skull may date as early as 200 Ka or as late as 350 Ka. Study of fossil mammals found elsewhere in the cave supports the more ancient age estimates, but claims for an antiquity of more than 700 Ka are unlikely. The skull itself shows an interesting combination of features found in *Homo erectus* and such later hominids as the Neanderthals. Brain volume was probably ca. 1,230 ml, and the skull is long, low, and extraordinarily broad across the base. Skull thickness is very great, particularly in the region of the occipital torus, yet the supraorbital torus and inflated cheek bones contain enormous sinuses (air spaces), larger even than those of Neanderthals. Browridge shape and nasal form are reminiscent of those of Neanderthals, but the upper and middle face are broader and flatter, as in other Middle Pleistocene fossils. The parietal region is expanded, as in other "archaic *Homo sapiens*" fossils, and it is with this group that the specimen is generally classified. Within Europe, the Petralona fossil can be grouped with those from Arago (France), Vértesszöllös (Hungary), and Bilzingsleben (Germany) as showing a number of retained *erectus*-like features, yet these specimens are now seen to probably lie near the origin of the Neanderthal lineage.

See also Arago; Archaic Homo sapiens; Bilzingsleben; Europe Homo erectus; Neanderthals; Vértesszöllös. [C.B.S.]

Petrolemur

Middle-to-Late Paleocene possible primate from southern China. This poorly sampled, enigmatic genus is known from a maxilla fragment and a juvenile mandibular fragment, each with five teeth. Although the samples are somewhat stratigraphically separated, the inferred occlusal relationships strongly suggest the congeneric nature of the two specimens. *Petrolemur*, although more likely referable to the Primates than to any other known order of mammals, is difficult to place within the generally recognized taxonomic framework for the Primates. It may represent a hitherto unknown group of archaic primates that flourished during the Paleogene of Asia.

See also Asia, Eastern and Southern; Paleocene; Primates. [F.S.S.]

Peyrony, Denis (1869–1954)

French schoolteacher and avocational prehistorian who excavated a number of major Middle and Upper Paleolithic sites in southwestern France, including La Ferrassie, Laugerie Haute, and Le Moustier. Like his predecessors H. Breuil and G. de Mortillet, Peyrony was concerned primarily with characterizing Paleolithic assemblages and placing them in relative chronologic sequence and did so by the use of an index fossil (the presence of a specific tool type considered diagnostic for a specific time period). Peyrony's delimitation of two contemporaneous Upper Paleolithic traditions, the Aurignacian and the Perigordian, challenged previously held assumptions that toolmaking traditions evolved unilineally.

See also Aurignacian; Breuil, [Abbé] Henri [Edward Prosper]; La Ferrassie; Laugerie Sites; Le Moustier; Mortillet, Gabriel de; Perigordian; Upper Paleolithic. [O.S.]

Phenetics

Study concerned with the similarity of organisms based on their phenotypic characteristics. In numerical taxonomy, this similarity is represented by a numerical index, and organisms are classified together based on overall similarity. This is in contrast to cladistics, which is concerned with relationship in terms of recency of common descent.

See also Cladistics; Numerical Taxonomy; Quantitative Methods. [L.M.]

Phenotype

Outward characteristics of an individual, usually the product of a complex interaction between the genetic constitution and the environment. Natural selection operates among phenotypes and, therefore, affects the genetic structure of a population only indirectly.

See also Genetics; Genotype. [J.M.]

Phylogeny

Evolutionary history of one or (more generally) a series of interrelated species: the course of ancestry and descent interlinking a series of species through time. A *phylum* in this context is simply an evolutionary lineage, not restricted to any particular rank in the Linnaean hierarchy. A series of species descended from a common ancestral species is said to be a *monophyletic taxon*, a *clade*, or simply a *lineage*.

Phylogeny As Evolutionary History

As C. Darwin pointed out in 1859, the process of "descent with modification"—his characterization of evolution—necessarily results in a pattern of nested resemblances interlinking all life-forms descended from a single common ancestor. When modifications occur within a lineage, they will be passed along to descendant organisms and ultimately to descendant species. These same novelties will be absent in collateral lineages. More closely related lineages will, therefore, tend to share a greater number of evolutionary novelties, reflecting a relatively more recent point of common ancestry. This observation has two interrelated consequences: (1) Darwin concluded that the notion of phylogenetic ancestry and descent explains why there is a nested pattern of resemblance linking all forms of life, a pattern previously recognized in early attempts to classify organisms. Put another way, the nested pattern of resemblance becomes the main prediction yielded by the conjecture that life has a single, unified phylogenetic history: If life has evolved, then there must be a single complexly internested pattern of resemblance linking all living creatures, past, present, and future. (2) Conversely, if there has been a phylogenetic history of life, that history can be reconstructed using standard procedures and principles of genealogical analysis developed both within and outside biological science. (For modern principles of phylogenetic [genealogical] reconstruction, *see* CLADISTICS.)

The daily experiences of systematists and paleontologists since before the appearance of Darwin's *On the Origin of Species* in 1859 have abundantly verified the notion that life has had a unified phylogenetic history. The oldest fossils yet discovered are ca. 3.5 billion years old (from sediments in Australia), only 0.5 billion years younger than the oldest-known rocks. The gross sequence of life-forms in the fossil record agrees with the spectrum of primitive-to-derived forms extant in the modern biota: The earliest fossils are of bacteria, which are small simple organisms lacking the complexities of cellular anatomy characteristic of all other forms of life (save viruses, which are obligate parasites). Single-celled eukaryotic (i.e., with complex nuclei encased in membranes, and intracellular organelles) organisms first appear in the fossil record ca. 1.3 billion years ago. All multicellular organisms—plants, animals, and fungi—were derived from single-celled eukaryotes. Multicelled organisms (animals) first appear in the Late Precambrian, ca. 700 Ma. The first great evolutionary radiation (*see* ADAPTIVE RADIATION) of animal life occurred at the base of the Cambrian period, ca. 570 Ma. Fungi and true vascular (land) plants appeared in the late Silurian, ca. 400 Ma.

The conventional classification of the major taxonomic entities does not accord with the actual phylogeny—genealogical affinities—of the taxa. Whereas it is conventional to recognize five kingdoms—Prokaryota, Protista, Fungi, Plantae, and Animalia—there is a basic dichotomy between Prokaryota and Eukaryota. Eukaryota is presumably a monophyletic group, marked by features of cellular anatomy that appear to be evolutionary novelties shared by all descendants of a common ancestor. Prokaryota, on the other hand, are all those organisms (bacteria) lacking the advanced features that define Eukaryota; thus, eukaryotes are predictably, and certainly, more closely related to some lineages of bacteria than to others. Recent work on bacterial anatomy and physiology has only confirmed the great heterogeneity of this group.

Likewise, the Protista are all eukaryotes lacking multicellularity; it has been known for more than a century that some forms of single-celled life are more plantlike, and others more animal-like. That classifications may be based on lines of genealogical descent is no guarantee that traditionally accepted taxa in classifications do, in fact, reflect the phylogenetic affinities of their constituent organisms.

Phylogenetic Patterns

There are some generalized patterns commonly exhibited by phylogenetic lineages through time. Typically, a lineage begins as a single species (perforce) producing a series of descendant species: Thus, the standing diversity (total number of species) at any one point in time typically increases within a clade. If there is a regular increase up to a point, followed by a regular, gradual decrease in species diversity up to the point of extinction, a graphic depiction of species diversity within a clade resembles a spindle; in general, such clade-diversity graphs are all called *spindle diagrams*. While the variation in spindle shapes is potentially limitless—so much so that simple classification and generalization of characteristic phylogenetic histories shared by a number of unrelated clades is both unrealistic and naive—there are at least four identifiable components to phylogenetic patterns.

ADAPTIVE RADIATIONS

These are typically rapid (in geologic time) expansions of species (and underlying phenotypic) diversity within a clade. Although clades may undergo a more gentle, progressive expansion in species diversity, adaptive radiations are common, often occurring at or near the beginning of a lineage. For example, the Devonian radiation within both the lungfishes and the coelacanth fishes produced by far the greatest

amount of species and morphological diversity within each of the groups; following the Devonian, diversity in both groups has remained very low consistently up to the present day.

Because adaptive radiations so often occur in the early phases of a lineage's phylogenetic history, it has long been postulated that adoption of a particular body plan (*Bauplan*) in an ancestral species confers the opportunity for radiation into a variety of ecological niches: The radiation is a consequence of the presence of a particular morphological complexion of the ancestor. But it seems more likely that lineages are especially well delineated if there is rapid diversification, for whatever reason, particularly early in their history; an early radiation establishes the lineage both in nature and, later, in the minds of systematists and paleontologists. Had the lungfish or the coelacanths not diversified, the probabilities are great that the lineages would not have persisted as they have, nor be recognized as major branches on the phylogenetic tree of vertebrate life.

Diversity reduction (in extreme form, including extinction, the ultimate fate of all species and higher taxa) is, of course, the converse of adaptive radiation and diversity expansion in general. The phenomena are related by the simple equation $D = S - E$, (i.e., species diversity is a reflection of speciation rate [S] less extinction rate [E]). Much of contemporary macroevolutionary theory is devoted to analysis of the controls of speciation and extinction rates within lineages.

STEADY-STATE

When neither speciation nor extinction rate exceeds the other for any great length of time, and when both rates are moderate, clade diversity remains roughly constant, the norm for a great number of clades through much of their phylogenetic histories. Such patterns are typically ended by periods of extinction that involve many other clades as well: Mass extinctions are cross-genealogical ecological events. During periods of steady-state, although new species continue to appear, generally little in the way of major anatomical change accrues within the lineage. This is arguably the case for the placental-mammal clade from the Oligocene on, with the possible exception of the hominoid subclade.

LIVING FOSSILS

Modern lungfish and coelacanths are considered living fossils. Although applied to a variety of not strictly comparable cases, this term most often means that living species bear a close anatomical resemblance to early members of the lineage and that the lineage is sufficiently old for there to have been a substantial amount of evolutionary change in other, closely related lineages. Both coelacanths and lungfish belong to the (clade) Class Osteichthyes (bony fishes); most numerous among bony fishes today are the teleosts, actinopterygian fish great in diversity and substantially changed from the primitive condition of actinopterygians of the Devonian. Although lungfish and coelacanths experienced adaptive radiations in their early history, for the vast bulk of their phylogenetic time species diversity was very low. Both speciation and extinction rates were low, which agrees with data on many lineages of living fossils suggesting that component organisms are generally broad-niched *ecological generalists*.

Ecological-niche theory has been a fruitful source of explanation for variation of characteristic rates of speciation and species extinction. Most species evolving in adaptive radiations seem, in contrast, to be *ecological specialists*, with concomitantly higher rates of both speciation and extinction.

TRENDS

Some lineages display a concerted, directional change in morphology of component organisms. For example, comparison of brain size in *Homo sapiens* with that of extant apes implies an increase in brain size in the phylogeny of our species. The fossil record of the past 4 Myr or so confirms that brain size in our lineage has, indeed, increased progressively. Yet, interpretation of such patterns in terms of the underlying evolutionary mechanisms (causal pathways) that produced them remains an item of serious debate in evolutionary biology.

Laboratory experiments, in which environmental conditions can be controlled and natural selection simulated, provide ample evidence that directional, generation-by-generation change in gene frequency and corresponding phenotypic expression can, indeed, proceed in a linear, directional manner, at least up to a point and for a limited number of generations, depending in part upon the nature of the available underlying variation. Darwin and virtually all later evolutionary biologists applied the model of generation-by-generation adaptive change under the control of natural selection to large-scale patterns of phylogenetic change, especially linear trends, which also involve modifications of adaptations, albeit on a scale considerably larger, in terms of amount of change and of time involved, than that encountered in laboratory circumstances.

Yet, the fossil record of most species, including those displaying phylogenetic trends between species within a lineage through time, indicates that the individual species involved tend not to undergo substantial change through time, especially in those very features shown to be involved in a long-term evolutionary trend. Except for examples involving size increase (or, more rarely, decrease) through time, the anatomical properties of component organisms remain remarkably stable in most species throughout the greater bulk of a species' history.

The solution to the apparent enigma of trends lies in the recognition that the actual *process* of phylogenesis involves speciation as well as the adaptive modification of phenotypic properties of organisms via natural selection. Phylogeny is a sequence of successive speciations and concomitant extinctions. Anatomical change in evolution, to the extent that it is deterministic, is under the control of natural selection. But the context for adaptive change seems, at least to some degree, to be in turn, under the control of the speciation process. According to the theory of punctuated equilibria, for example, most adaptive change occurs in conjunction with speciation (defined as the origin of a descendant from an ancestral reproductive community).

If species are real entities, with births (speciation), histories, and deaths (extinction), then the possibility arises that species themselves can be "sorted," in a manner analogous to, if not wholly comparable with, natural selection. Differential success of species, in which some species produce descendants at a faster rate or descendants that are less prone to extinction than others, will bias the distribution of species—hence, of phenotypes of constituent organisms within species—during the history of a lineage. The issue of species selection in macroevolution in general, and in the development of phylogenetic trends in particular, remains controversial. But patterns of phylogenetic history lie at the heart of testing rival theories of the evolutionary process.

See also Adaptive Radiation; Cladistics; Classification; Evolution; Speciation; Species; Taxonomy. [N.E.]

Further Readings

Eldredge, N., and Cracraft, J. (1980) Phylogenetic Patterns and the Evolutionary Process. New York: Columbia University Press.

Simpson, G.G. (1953) The Major Features of Evolution. New York: Columbia University Press.

Simpson, G.G. (1961) Principles of Animal Taxonomy. New York: Columbia University Press.

Wiley, E.O. (1981) Phylogenetics. New York: Wiley.

Physical Anthropology

Study of humans as biological organisms, in terms of both their evolutionary history and their anatomical and physiological function, and in contrast to *cultural anthropology*, the study of humans as social beings. In practice, physical anthropology also embraces the study of the origins, evolution, systematics, behavior, and ecology of our closest living relatives, the primates. The field thus consists of a patchwork of disciplines employing different methodologies, which are united by their ultimate focus on a single theme: humanity and its biological context. Major aspects of physical anthropology include the study of human evolution; human adaptation, variation, and genetics; human demography; forensic anthropology and paleopathology; and primate ecology, behavior, and evolution. These diverse areas of study are ultimately united in the broadest interpretation of the first: how modern humans, in all their diversity, came to be.

See also Anthropology; Forensic Anthropology; Paleoanthropology; Paleopathology; Primate Societies. [I.T.]

Phytolith Analysis

Archaeologists are now learning about both wild and domesticated plants by analyzing microscopic plant opal phytoliths (literally, "plant stones"). Phytoliths are formed when the silica ordinarily dissolved in groundwater is carried through plant roots and deposited in mineral form inside the plant. When dead plant material decays, the almost indestructible opal phytoliths are deposited in the ground. Phytoliths have been found in sediments older than 60 Myr. Distinctive

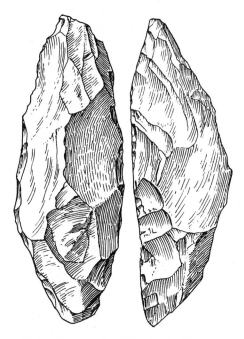

Sangoan pick from Sango Bay. From F. Bordes, The Old Stone Age, *1968, McGraw-Hill.*

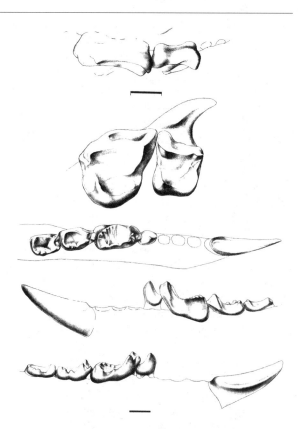

Upper and lower teeth of the Late Paleocene archaic primate Picrodus silberlingi. *Note the extreme flattening of the upper molars and the tremendously enlarged talonid and drastically reduced trigonid on the first lower molar. Scales are 1 mm. Courtesy of Frederick S. Szalay, from Szalay and Delson, 1979.*

phytoliths occur in members of the grass family, rushes, sedges, palms, conifers, and deciduous trees.

Phytolith analysis is superficially similar to pollen analysis, but there are differences. Some plants produce pollen but not phytoliths, and vice versa. Although pollen is produced in a single form, phytoliths vary considerably within a single species. Phytoliths are preserved under a wider range of soil conditions than pollen. These critical differences render the methods complementary.

Phytoliths have been recognized in archaeological sites for decades, but before 1970 deposits were only occasionally analyzed for phytoliths. Since then, interest in this unusual technique has exploded; today, the identification and analysis of phytoliths from archaeological sites hold great promise for reconstructing paleoenvironments and for tracking the process of plant domestication.

Although difficulties of taxonomy still plague phytolith analysis, considerable progress has been made. Phytoliths are being used to study rice, millet, barley, and wheat. Particularly important to American archaeology has been the identification of corn (*Zea mays*) phytoliths, which allowed the introduction date of maize to be pushed back by several millennia.

Further Readings

Piperno, D.R. (1988) Phytolith Analysis: An Archaeological and Geological Perspective. London: Academic Press.

See also Paleoenvironment; Pollen Analysis. [D.H.T.]

Pick

A heavy-duty tool often found in the Acheulean and Sangoan industries, usually produced by unifacially or bifacially working a large flake or cobble into a relatively thick, pointed form. Picks tend to be thicker and more crudely shaped than handaxes. One distinct form of pick, called a *trihedral*, has a triangular cross section.

See also Acheulean; Sangoan; Stone-Tool Making. [N.T., K.S.]

Picrodontidae

Tiny plesiadapiforms of the Paleocene of North America that are dentally among the most derived (i.e., most changed from a primate common ancestor) of all archaic primates. There are two known genera: *Picrodus* (including *Draconodus*) and *Zanycteris*. The latter is known by a crushed skull, but most of our knowledge of these primates is based on teeth and mandibles. The central incisors were enlarged, as in many archaic primates, and the antemolar dentition between the large incisors and the premolars was relatively unimportant compared to the large and highly modified molars. The first upper and lower molars are unusually enlarged compared to the more posterior ones, and they are modified in a most telling manner. The crowns of the teeth are expanded, and the enamel is heavily wrinkled on the molars. Emphasis is clearly on surface area, and the foods mashed were not particularly abrasive, judged from the low crowns of these molars. There are bats today that display molar characters convergently resembling the molars of picrodontids (with generally similar cheek teeth, these bats feed on nectar and pollen, a diet that is rich in energy and protein but very easy on the teeth). It is almost certain that picrodontids (without any implications of flying adaptations) were feeding on a diet of pollen, nectar, possibly tree exudates like gums, and maybe some nontoxic resins.

Picrodontids supply us with valuable evidence on just how widely plant foods were exploited by archaic primates and how exacting the adaptations of particular Paleocene archaic primates were to the resources of the tropical and subtropical forests of the world. They are included in the Paromomyoidea, along with the more common Paromomyidae, because of similarities in some molar features.

Family Picrodontidae
    † *Picrodus* (including † *Draconodus*)
    † *Zanycteris*
†exinct

See also Paromomyidae; Paromomyoidea; Plesiadapiformes; Primates. [F.S.S.]

Pietersburg

South African Middle Stone Age industry or group of successive industries (probably 130–40 Ka) with blade technology in addition to discoidal and Levallois cores, named after surface sites near Pietersburg, northern Transvaal, but best known from Cave of Hearths. Relatively few pieces have secondary retouch, but these include backed knives, side- and end-scrapers, and rare trimmed points. Regional variants or related industries include the Orangian (Orange Free State) and the Mossel Bay (Cape Province); as well as the Stillbay and other Middle Stone Age industries of southern Africa.

See also Apollo-11; Border Cave; Cave of Hearths; Florisbad; Howieson's Poort; Levallois; Middle Stone Age; Orangian; Rose Cottage; Stillbay; Stone-Tool Making. [A.S.B]

Pilgrim, Guy Ellock (1875–1943)

British geologist and paleontologist. Pilgrim spent his entire professional career (1902–1930) working for the Geological Survey of India (GSI), where he functioned as both a geologist and a paleontologist. During his tenure at the GSI, he conducted several important stratigraphical surveys in the Persian Gulf and northwestern India; of particular interest is his work on the Siwaliks in Indo-Pakistan. Prior to Pilgrim's investigations, the Siwalik Formation had been simply divided into a lower (unfossiliferous) and an upper (fossiliferous) section. Pilgrim demonstrated that there were, in fact, three distinct fossiliferous divisions in this upper section, each characterized by a distinct suite of vertebrate fossils. The result of this work was a steady stream of paleontological publications that include a series of major monographs on the fossil Giraffidae, Suidae, Carnivora, and Primates of India. Among the latter, Pilgrim identified two Miocene apes, *Dryopithecus punjabicus* and *Sivapithecus indicus*. In his evaluation of these fossils, he conjectured that the sivapithecines were ancestral to E. Dubois's *Pithecanthropus erectus* (now *Homo erectus*)—though, like many of his contemporaries, he did not consider *Pithecanthropus* to be on the main line of hominid evolution. On the other hand, he considered *Dryopithecus*

to be an Asiatic relative of the European dryopithecines and more closely allied to the hominoid apes. During the 1930s, G.E. Lewis of Yale University recovered similar material from the Siwaliks, which, along with Pilgrim's specimens, were later reevaluated by E. Simons in the early 1960s.

See also Dryopithecus; Dubois, Eugene; Hominidae; Lartet, Edouard; Piltdown; Ponginae; Sivapithecus; Siwaliks. [F.S.]

Further Readings

Pilgrim, G.E. (1915) New Siwalik primates and their bearing on the question of the evolution of man and the anthropoidea. Rec. Geol. Surv. India 45:1–74.
Pilgrim, G.E. (1927) A *Sivapithecus* palate and other primate fossils from India. Mem. Geol. Surv. India 14(n.s.):1–26.

Piltdown

Between 1912 and 1915, an unsuspecting scientific community was led to believe that the remains of an early fossil hominid had been sequentially recovered from a gravel bed located on the estate of Barkham Manor at Piltdown, a small village nestled in the Weald of Sussex (England). Essentially, these remains consisted of nine cranial fragments and a portion of a right mandibular corpus, plus a number of archaeological artifacts and a miscellaneous collection of mammalian fossils. Not until 40 years later were these remains declared to be a forgery, the elements of an elaborate scientific hoax. In the meantime, this bogus skull initially served to support an evolutionary scenario that rejected the phylogenetic significance of the Javan hominid *Pithecanthropus erectus* (now *Homo erectus*) and the European Neanderthals and, subsequently, the South African australopiths.

Both J.S. Weiner (1915–1982) and K.P. Oakley (1911–1981), who played an integral role in the exposure of the Piltdown forgery in 1953, strongly suspected that C. Dawson (1846–1916), a Sussex County solicitor and amateur geologist and collector for the Natural History Museum (the British Museum [Natural History], was the perpetrator of the fraud. According to the story Dawson recounted to the Geological Society of London on December 18, 1912, his interest had been aroused when (ca. 1910) he found a fragment of a human cranium tossed up by laborers excavating a gravel pit for road metal located on the estate of Barkham Manor. Subsequently, in 1911, he said, he picked up another and larger fragment of the same skull extracted from this gravel deposit. Impressed by the skull's general thickness, he took the fragments to his friend A.S. Woodward (1864–1944), keeper of palaeontology at the Natural History Museum. Woodward was excited by what he was shown; during the summer of 1912, he and Dawson worked feverishly at Piltdown, occasionally assisted by such trusted associates as P. Teilhard de Chardin (1881–1955), excavating and sifting through the earth previously removed from the gravel pit. Their labors yielded a further seven fragments of the skull, which, when fitted together, made up the greater part of the left side of a human braincase. They also found the right half of a seemingly apelike jaw with two molar

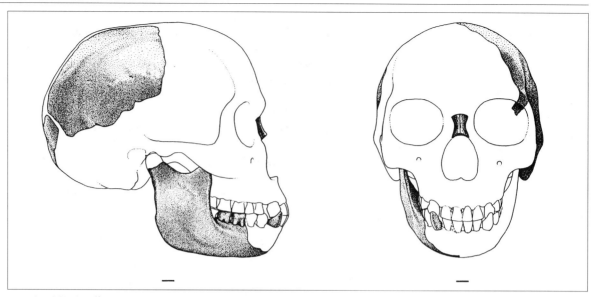

Lateral and facial views of the 1913 reconstruction of the Piltdown "skull." Scale is 1cm.

teeth, plus an assortment of fossil animal bones and "eoliths" (supposed primitive stone tools). Woodward was convinced that the skull cap and the jaw were associated and felt justified in creating a new genus and species to describe the remains: *Eoanthropus dawsoni* (Dawson's dawn man). It appeared to Woodward and his followers that *Eoanthropus* was a feasible alternative to *Pithecanthropus* of Java, then known only from scanty remains, as the ancestral form of modern humans.

In fact, the mammalian fossil fauna recovered from the site had been carefully selected and planted by the forger or forgers at the gravel pit to indicate that *Eoanthropus* had roamed the Sussex countryside during either the Late Pliocene or the Early Pleistocene.

From the time of the discovery's announcement, a number of scientists refused to accept the association of the cranium and the jaw as belonging to the same taxon, let alone the same individual. According to these critics, the jaw was that of a fossil anthropoid ape that had come by chance to be associated with human fossil remains in the deposit. In 1915, G.S. Miller (1869–1956), then curator of mammals at the National Museum of Natural History (Smithsonian Institution) in Washington, D.C., concluded from his study of the Piltdown casts that the jaw was actually that of a fossil chimpanzee. This and similar arguments, however, were dismissed by Woodward and his supporters as most improbable, given the fact that no fossil apes later than the Early Pliocene had been found in England or Europe.

Woodward's support of the monistic interpretation had been based on the apparent close association of the cranial and mandibular remains in the gravel, along with the evidence presented by the molar teeth, which were worn flat in a manner quite uncharacteristic of ape dentitions but commonly encountered among the most primitive extant human groups. In accordance with the notion that the Piltdown remains represented an early hominid, Woodward assigned to the reconstructed skull a relatively small cranial capacity of 1,070 cm³. Likewise, from his examination of the endocra-

nial cast of *Eoanthropus,* the neuroanatomist G.E. Smith (1871–1937) found evidence of primitive features, declaring it to be "the most primitive and most simian human brain so far recorded." But because the original skull used in the forgery had been broken in such a way as to preclude a definitive reconstruction, this permitted the anatomist-anthropologist A. Keith (1866–1955) of the Royal College of Surgeons to argue for an alternative assembly and to raise the cranial capacity upward to ca. 1,400 cm³—close to the approximate average of modern *Homo sapiens*—and thereby promote his particular views on the antiquity of the modern human cranial form and presapiens version of human evolution. And although Woodward's general reconstruction was subsequently "vindicated" by Teilhard de Chardin's fortuitous find of a canine tooth at the Piltdown gravel pit in 1913, this did not prevent Keith from continuing to advocate his reconstruction.

In 1917, the dualistic theory suffered a further setback when Woodward announced, shortly after the death of Dawson, the discovery of Piltdown II. These remains, consisting of two cranial fragments and a molar tooth and a fragment of a lower molar of a species of fossil rhinoceros, had reportedly been found by Dawson in 1915 at another site near Piltdown. However, despite considerable efforts by Woodward and later by others, the location of this second site was never discovered.

During the 1920s and 1930s, the remains of an even more primitive hominid—*Australopithecus*—were found in South Africa, though at that time they were not generally regarded as significant. However, these fossils, along with the spectacular discoveries at Zhoukoudian in China of a Middle Pleistocene hominin that was morphologically similar to the Javan *Pithecanthropus*, served to progressively undermine confidence in the monistic interpretation of the Piltdown skull and, more particularly, the prevailing paradigm of the preeminence of the brain in human evolution. Nearer to home, there were other findings that also served to cast a shadow of doubt over these enigmatic remains. In particular, the discovery of the Swanscombe skull in the mid-1930s led to comparisons with Piltdown and, ultimately, to the investigations by Oakley. In 1948, Oakley applied the newly developed fluorine-dating technique to a comparative study of the Swanscombe and Galley Hill remains, which reportedly had been found in similar geological circumstances. The Galley Hill remains had long been used by Keith and others to support the presapiens hypothesis. The results of the fluorine tests showed unequivocally that Galley Hill, unlike Swanscombe, was a comparatively recent specimen. Armed with these results, Oakley secured permission to extend his tests to the Piltdown skull. But, contrary to expectations, these initial tests were inconclusive.

It was not until 1953, when Weiner proposed his forgery hypothesis, that the remains were retested using a more sensitive fluorine methodology. The results of this new test revealed that the cranium and the jaw contained different amounts of fluorine and other elements—thereby providing for the first time evidence that the cranium and the jaw were not contemporaneous specimens. Based on the fluorine content, the cranium appeared to be considerably older than the jaw. In 1959, carbon-14 dating confirmed this conclusion. Furthermore, other chemical analyses conducted in 1953 revealed that both the human and the animal remains had been deliberately stained and that the human molar teeth had undergone artificial abrasion. Much later, using an immunological technique, it was shown that the Piltdown mandible and canine tooth had belonged to an orangutan (Lowenstein et al., 1982). The removal of the Piltdown enigma set the stage for a general acceptance of the South African australopiths as early hominids and the emergence of the modern interpretation of the hominid fossil record.

Since the discovery of the fraud, interest in the Piltdown affair has shifted to the possible identity of the forger or forgers. From a reconstruction of events and the apparent procedures adopted during the excavation of the site, there is little question that Dawson must have been intimately involved in the deception perpetrated at Barkham Manor. However, as Weiner (1955) first noted, while Dawson may have been an accomplished collector, there is every reason to doubt his ability to orchestrate such an elaborate scientific forgery; this has led to various scenarios in which Dawson has been portrayed either as an innocent dupe or as a scoundrel assisted by an expert second party. For example, R. Millar (1972) contested the case against Dawson, claiming that G. Elliot Smith was the primary culprit. Others, such as L.B. Halstead (1978), have contended that Dawson was duped by the Oxford geologist-paleontologist W.J. Sollas (1859–1930). Equally contentious is the case against the author A.C. Doyle (1849–1936) made by J.H. Winslow and A. Meyer (1983) and, more recently, by R. Milner and R. Anderson of *Natural History* magazine. Among the other individuals who have been implicated as Dawson's accomplice are Teilhard de Chardin (by S.J. Gould, 1980), the Sussex chemist S. Woodhead (P. Costello, 1985), Woodward (G.M. Drawhorn, 1994), and Keith (F. Spencer, 1990a, 1990b).

With the probable exception of the latter, which is grounded in a substantial body of circumstantial evidence,

all of these cases have rested exclusively on either suspicion or embroidered gossip and have not stood up to close scrutiny. More telling is the discovery at the Natural History Museum, London, of a trunk of fossils apparently belonging to M. Hinton, a former keeper of zoology there. These fossils were stained using a concoction of chemicals apparently identical to that used in coloring the Piltdown fossils and may represent "trial runs" for that effort. That Hinton was a close friend of Dawson's associate L. Abbott, that he held a bitter grudge against Woodward, and that he was one of the very few people with access to fossils of the kind found at Piltdown—all lead to the conclusion that Hinton possessed both the opportunity and the motive to carry out the fraud, in addition to the necessary access and expertise.

See also Clark, [Sir] Wilfrid Edward Le Gros; Keith, [Sir] Arthur; Oakley, Kenneth Page; Smith, [Sir] Grafton Elliot; Teilhard de Chardin, Pierre; Woodward, [Sir] Arthur Smith. [F.S.]

Further Readings

Costello, P. (1985) The Piltdown hoax reconsidered. Antiquity 59:167–171.

Drawhorn, G.M. (1994) Piltdown: Evidence for Smith Woodward's complicity (Abstract). Am. J. Phys. Anthropol. Suppl. 18:82.

Gould, S.J. (1980) The Piltdown controversy. Nat. Hist. 89(8):8–28.

Halstead, L.B. (1978) New light on the Piltdown hoax. Nature 276:11–13.

Lowenstein, J.M., et al. (1982) Piltdown jaw confirmed as orang. Nature 299:294.

Millar, R. (1972) The Piltdown Men. New York: Ballantine.

Spencer, F. (1990a) Piltdown: A scientific forgery. London: Oxford University Press.

Spencer, F. (1990b) The Piltdown Papers. London: Oxford University Press.

Weiner, J.S. (1955) The Piltdown Forgery. London: Oxford University Press.

Winslow, J., and Meyer, A. (1983) The perpetrator at Piltdown. Science 83(4):32–43.

Pincevent

This multilayered open-air site, located along the banks of the Seine River in the Paris Basin in France, was meticulously excavated and studied by A. Leroi-Gourhan and his colleagues in the 1960s and 1970s. Occupied during the warm weather months ca. 12 Ka, the site was a hunter's camp used to hunt reindeer. The four Upper Paleolithic layers indicate short-term residential occupation by a small group of hunters and their families who settled near a ford in the river to hunt migrating reindeer. Remains of living floors, some of which reach ca. 3,000 m² in size, show the presence of tents, curbed hearths, and work areas. Refitting of the bones from individual animals indicates how kills were shared among different hearth groups. The local availability of superior flint here resulted in abundant Late Magdalenian stone-tool inventories.

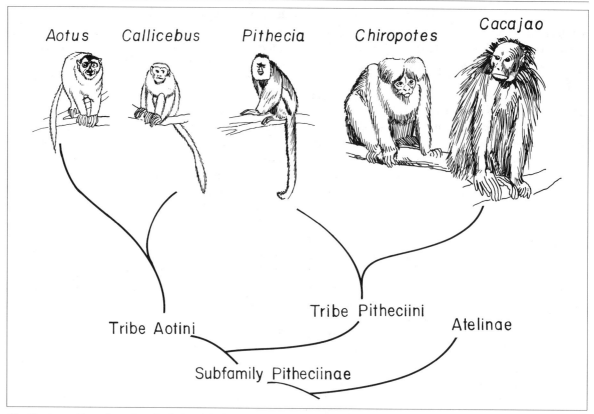

Classification and interrelationships of pitheciine ateloid monkeys. The tribe Aotini is now termed Homunculini. Courtesy of Alfred L. Rosenberger.

See also France; Leroi-Gourhan, André; Magdalenian; Upper Paleolithic. [O.S.]

Pitheciinae

Subfamily of platyrrhine atelid monkeys including the Pitheciini tribe of sakis (*Pithecia*) and uakaris (*Chiropotes, Cacajao*), a rather coherent group, as well as the nocturnal owl (*Aotus*) and the diurnal titi (*Callicebus*) monkeys, and their fossil allies. Older classifications tended to employ two or three subfamilies for the five genera, giving the impression that they were distantly related and adaptively heterogeneous. Thus, the realization that pitheciines are monophyletic as well as taxonomically diverse establishes them as a major factor in platyrrhine evolution that has no ecological counterpart of equivalent scale among the Old World primates. Owl and titi monkeys belong to the tribe Homunculini, named after the extinct *Homunculus*.

Pitheciines are hard-fruit and/or seed-predating frugivores. The more derived sakis and uakaris have unusually modified dentitions, with tall, narrow incisors; large, laterally splayed canines; flat-crowned, crenulate cheek teeth; and very robust jaws, enabling them to pry open and harvest seeds within well-protected shells. The homunculins exhibit various primitive aspects of this pattern. Hard-fruit- and seed-eating specializations allow uakaris to exploit vast "black water" areas of Amazonia that are inhospitable to many other primates. There the poor soils selected for a flora having a low diversity of tree species, many of which have evolved adaptations to resist predation by frugivores. This poses mechanical and possibly chemical or nutritional problems that "garden variety" frugivores are unable to solve.

Fossil pitheciines are known from several regions. From Patagonia, *Tremacebus* and *Homunculus* (of Santacrucian age, ca. 18–16 Ma) are classified as homunculins. The former, clearly allied with *Aotus*, was probably crepuscular and/or nocturnal. The latter may be either one of the most primitive members of the pitheciine subfamily or a relative of *Callicebus*. *Soriacebus*, also from the Santacrucian of Argentina, is a primitive member of the pitheciin clade, while the contemporary genus *Carlocebus* cannot as yet be placed properly within the subfamily. From La Venta (14–12 Ma) in Colombia, *Cebupithecia* is more closely related to the living saki-uakaris. *Mohanamico*, also from La Venta, was originally described as a probable pitheciine, but it is more likely a relative of the callitrichine *Callimico*. Another discovery at La Venta is a mandible and partial orbit indistinguishable on the generic level from modern *Aotus*; it is accepted here as *A. dindensis*, although it is occasionally confused with *Mohanamico*. In 1997, *Nuciruptor* was described as a basal pitheciine whose precise phyletic position is unclear. From a slightly older level than most of the primates (ca. 12.3 Ma) comes *Lagonimico conclucatus*, originally described as a tamarin relative but perhaps better interpreted as a generalized pitheciine. *Proteropithecia* (originally named *Protopithecia*) was described in 1998 as an early, conservative member of Pitheciini from Cañadon del Tordillo, Argentina, dated ca. 15.5 Ma. *Xenothrix* is a Late Pleistocene/Holocene pitheciine known from Caribbean cave deposits.

Subfamily Pitheciinae
    Tribe Pitheciini
        Pithecia

    Chiropotes
    Cacajao
    † *Cebupithecia*
    † *Soriacebus*
    † *Proteropithecia* (originally *Protopithecia*)
Tribe Homunculini
    (†)*Aotus*
    Callicebus
    † *Tremacebus*
    † *Homunculus*
incertae sedis
    † *Carlocebus*
    † *Lagonimico*
    † *Nuciruptor*
    † *Xenothrix*
†extinct

See also Americas; Atelidae; Ateloidea; Diet; La Venta; Patagonia; Platyrrhini; Teeth. [A.L.R.]

Further Readings

Kay, R.F. (1990) The phyletic relationships of extant and fossil Pitheciinae (Platyrrhini, Anthropoidea). J. Hum. Evol. 19:175–208.

Kay, R.F., Johnson, D. and Meldrum, D.J. (1998) A new pitheciin primate from the Middle Miocene of Argentina. Am. J. Primatol. 45:317–336.

Meldrum, D.J., and Kay, R.F. (1997) *Nuciruptor rubricae*, a new pitheciin seed predator from the Miocene of Colombia. Am. J. Phys. Anthropol. 102:407–427.

Rosenberger, A.L., Setoguchi, T., and Shigehara, N. (1990) The fossil record of callitrichine primates. J. Hum. Evol. 19:209–236.

Szalay, F.S., and Delson, E. (1979) Evolutionary History of the Primates. New York: Academic.

Piveteau, Jean (1899–1991)

French paleontologist, paleoanthropologist, and educator. Piveteau began his career under M. Boule at the Laboratoire de Paléontologie du Muséum National d'Histoire Naturelle, then worked for a time in the Paris École des Mines. He then moved to the Sorbonne, where he was named professor in 1942. In the early 1950s, he became the director of the Laboratoire de Paléontologie des Vertebrès et Paléontologie Humaine at the Université Paris VI. He was early elected to the Académie des Sciences, and in 1973 he served as its president. He trained many students over several generations in all areas of vertebrate paleontology. His early research (1920s) was on fossil reptiles, especially from Madagascar. In 1927, he wrote his first article on human evolution. Among his major works was the *Traité de Paléontologie*, which he edited in the 1950s and 1960s, covering the entire range of life history in 10 volumes. He wrote the final volume (1957), on primate and human evolution (from tupaiids to cave art). He also worked on Neanderthal fossils from Regourdou and La Chaise and wrote technical articles and general books on evolution, human evolution, the hand and its relationship to hominization, the history of science and the philosophy of his friend Pierre Teilhard de Chardin.

See also Boule [Pierre] Marcellin; La Chaise; Regourdou; Teilhard de Chardin, Pierre. [E.D.]

Plano

Terminal phase of the Paleoindian tradition. Plano-culture artifacts overlie the Clovis and Folsom levels at Blackwater Draw (New Mexico). Distributed for the most part on the High Plains of western America, the assemblage consists primarily of a series of long, unfluted lanceolate points with parallel-to-oblique pressure flaking; they are generally associated with the remains of extinct *Bison occidentalis* and *Bison bison*. The complex dates between 10 and 7 Ka and is well known from such sites as Agate Basin (Nebraska) and Hell Gap (Wyoming).

See also Americas; Blackwater Draw; Clovis; Folsom; Paleoindian. [L.S.A.P., D.H.T.]

Plate Tectonics

Plate-tectonic theory developed rapidly in the early 1960s, as evidence for the mechanism behind "continental drift" began to build from various sources in geophysics and deep-sea geology. The shape of the Atlantic Ocean had provoked speculation as soon as the first good maps appeared in the 1600s. Studies published by eminent geologists between 1880 and 1925, most notably those of H. Suess, A. Wegener, and A. duToit, described abundant data that were consistent with the separation of the supercontinent Pangaea into southern (Gondwana) and northern (Laurasia) parts by the formation of the equatorial Tethys Ocean, and the further breakup of the parts by the opening of the Indian and Atlantic oceans and the south polar straits. The term *Gondwana* refers to a site in central India where glacial tillites of the Ordovician ice age were discovered that had been generated under the same ice cap as tillites in South Africa, South America, and Australia—on the other side of the equator.

Early paleomagnetic studies in the 1950s by British geophysicist S. Runcorn and others, which showed that ancient magnetic-pole positions were incongruent between different continents but not within them, were also interpretable as evidence for continental separation and "drift." Others, however, argued that the present agreement between rotational and magnetic poles could be accidental and that "polar wandering" was relevant only to paleomagnetic data and not to the continents.

The problem came down to the fact that no faintly reasonable explanation could be found as to how entire continents could be induced to slide over, or plow through, the oceanic crust, and "drift" remained a subject of ill repute. The breakthrough came in the mid-1960s with clear evidence that the crust itself was moving, carrying continents with it, as A. Holmes and F.A. Vening-Meinesz had each supposed in the 1930s without being able to point to any evidence in support of their ideas.

Simultaneous and complementary studies of ocean-floor paleomagnetism and the newly defined Benioff zones of deep earthquakes, conducted by an unusually capable generation of young scientists at Cambridge University under E. Bullard, revealed that the Earth's crust is divided by the Benioff zones into seven major, and as many minor, plates, all moving independently and some carrying continents as passive freight. Movement in the plates, revealed by progressively older paleomagnetic domains in the sea floor, is almost entirely internal and bidirectional, away from *spreading centers*—linear volcanically active ridges in which new oceanic crust is continuously being formed—and toward marginal *subduction zones,* in which the cooled crust sinks down into the subcrust, where it is gradually reheated and recycled. Deep ocean trenches and subsiding foredeeps like the Persian Gulf are formed where subducting plates are driven beneath adjacent plates, creating the earthquakes and volcanoes of the Benioff zones. The great lateral-moving faults such as the San Andreas accommodate sideways motion between plates.

The basic source for the tremendous energy of plate tectonics, which creates mountain ranges, volcanoes, and oceans, is simply subcrustal heat and the force of gravity. The spreading centers are swollen upward with thermal expansion of the crust over zones of abnormally high heat flow, or *plumes*, in the subcrust. New crust is formed by the injection of basaltic magma along the crest of the spreading ridges, but the ocean crust is not so much pushed aside by the lava intrusions as it is pulled apart by gravity, allowing the lava to well up through rifts and partings. The crust slides off of the heated dome or ridge under its own weight, cooling and shrinking as it goes. The heat that drives this system appears to be a combination of the primordial heat-of-compaction, still dissipating from the core, and radioactive decay, mostly from the potassium-40 concentrated in the crustal rocks. Tidal and magnetohydrodynamic stresses, from solar-system gravitational and magnetic fields, respectively, may also contribute some internal heating. The friction volcanism associated with subduction zones—in particular the Ring of Fire surrounding the Pacific Basin—is reconversion of kinetic to thermal energy in the Benioff shear plane.

Continents play a major role in plate tectonics and appear to control the location of both spreading centers and subduction zones. It is generally agreed that new oceans begin under continents, in the form of rift valleys. The continental mass is a blanket of dry, thermally opaque material that blocks subcrustal heat flow. At some point, the trapped heat will lead to active updoming, with rifting along the stretched-apart crest. As the upper crust thins and heat flow increases in the zone of weakness, the rifts rip laterally to adjacent domes. Thus, the segments of the resulting rift valley can be seen to change course at each domal node, with a "failed" arm often extending from the external obtuse angle. (One example is the shallow Nyanza Rift Valley of western Kenya, which extends to Lake Victoria from the Mau-Aberdares apex.) Under the force of gravity, the process feeds on itself; the flanks of the dome slide away, and eventually the relatively hot basaltic core of the ridge is exposed, several thousand feet below sea level. This process has been much studied in the East African Rift system, where the Red Sea and Gulf of Aden segments have evolved into a true ocean separating Arabia from Africa during the past 35 Myr.

Subduction zones operate only where oceanic crust is being consumed. Continents, which consist mainly of granitic rocks with an average density of ca. 2.3, cannot be drawn down into the basaltic subcrust, which has a density of ca. 2.7 to 3. Because of their relative bouyancy, continents will stop plate motion when brought into the subduction trough. In such cases, subuction may continue, either by "flipping" to the opposing plate margin (if it is oceanic), which then begins to descend under the continent-bearing plate in the opposite direction, or, more commonly, by "jumping" back to a new subduction zone behind the jammed-up continent. (This has the effect of transferring the continent to the opposing plate.) The result is that a large percent of the total length of the world's subduction zones are located adjacent to, and are inclined beneath, continental margins; also, it is inevitable that the motion of continent-bearing plates (the plates of the Pacific Ocean Basin have always been wholly oceanic) will eventually bring continents together in subduction zones. The Alps, Carpathians, Taurides, Elburz, Tien Shan, and Himalayas all mark former subduction zones in which most of the Tethys Ocean has now disappeared. The continuing northward motion of the Afro-Arabian plate is now closing the Mediterranean remnant in a subduction zone extending from Sicily through southern Turkey and into the Persian Gulf.

As the Mesopotamian juncture began to close in the early to mid-Cenozoic, the previously isolated catarrhine fauna of Africa was exposed to periodic invasions of Eurasian mammals during low stands of sea level, notably just after the time of the Fayum fauna in the Early Oligocene, during the "Grand Coupure" intermigration event. Even as the juncture became permanent in the Early Miocene, however, plate motion opened a new barrier in the form of the deepening gulf of the Red Sea rift. Passage across the northern end, the present Suez isthmus, was not established until the Pliocene ca. 4 Ma., and mammalian migration between Africa and the outside world was possible only via the (presently submerged) Bab el Mandeb shallows at the south end of the Red Sea. The Early Miocene exchange brought dogs and hyaenas into Africa and allowed the emigration of apes, elephants, giraffes, and antelopes, among other indigenous African groups. More important in the long run, the redirection of ocean circulation that was caused by continental movement in the Cenozoic led to the thermal isolation of Antarctica. Refrigeration of the world ocean by contact with Antarctic glaciers since the Late Eocene, ca. 4 Ma., has profoundly affected climate, with ever-intensifying seasonality culminating in the Pleistocene ice ages. In this regard, as well as with respect to the paleobiogeography of Africa and Eurasia, plate tectonics has been a fundamental influence in human evolution (see maps in AFRICA entry).

Plate motion varies from place to place but (as a rule of thumb) is about as rapid as the growth of fingernails (i.e., ca. 3 cm/per year). From this it can be easily calculated that the two sides of the North Atlantic Ocean, ca. 8,000 km apart, have been moving away from each other at this rate for ca. 250 Myr (i.e., since the Late Triassic). Interestingly, calculations show that basaltic ocean floor generated in a Triassic spreading center will by today have cooled and contracted to the point that its density is the same as the underlying subcrust, and it will begin to sink by its own weight. This is undoubtedly the reason why there is no ocean floor anywhere that is older than Triassic. This has suggested a plate-tectonic megacycle, called the Wilson Cycle after the Canadian geologist J. Tuzo Wilson, in which worldwide continental dispersal (as heat builds up under the supercontinent of the previous cycle) is followed by coalescence into a new supercontinent (as rift-oceans cool and collapse). The Caribbean volcanic arc is the first sign that the overage North Atlantic Ocean has begun to "collapse" (i.e., to develop subduction zones along the coastlines).

See also Africa; Cenozoic; Climate Change and Evolution; Glaciation; Paleobiogeography; Paleomagnetism; Rift Valley; Sea-Level Change. [J.A.V.C.]

Further Readings

Condie, K.C. (1982) Plate Tectonics and Crustal Evolution, 2nd ed. London: Pergamon.

Schopf, T.J.M. (1980) Paleoceanography. Cambridge, Mass.: Harvard University Press.

West, R.M., ed. (1977) Paleontology and Plate Tectonics with Special Reference to the History of the Atlantic Ocean (Special Publications in Geology and Paleontology No. 2). Milwaukee: Milwaukee Public Museum.

Platyrrhini

Infraorder of New World anthropoid primates also known as the Ateloidea (previously Ceboidea). The scope of the platyrrhine adaptive radiation is remarkable. This has encouraged generations of primatologists to use the group as a natural laboratory of living analogues to examine morphological, behavioral, and ecological factors relevant to the evolution of hominids. For example, brachiation and antipronograde locomotor behaviors have counterparts among both the apes and the ateline New World monkeys. In fact, the anatomical similarities of upper-body shape shared by atelines and hominoids now support the theory that a type of arboreal climbing, rather than brachiation, preadapted protohominids to terrestrial bipedality. Similarly, the presence of hard-fruit masticatory adaptations in capuchin monkeys is serving as a dietary model for extinct hominoids with bunodont, thick-enameled cheek teeth. And the convergent evolution of fission-fusion social systems in spider monkeys and chimpanzees may shed light on the human condition, in which ordered social flexibility is a prevalent theme. Most recently, paleontologists have recognized that platyrrhines also share many similarities with the earliest members of the catarrhine radiation, the Fayum Oligocene primates, which may have behaved more like some of the modern New World monkeys than any of the apes or Old World monkeys to whom they are more closely related.

Their significance for broader questions notwithstanding, platyrrhines have been, until recently, less intensively studied for their own sake than have Old World forms. What they have to offer scientists is one of the order's most puzzling success stories. Where platyrrhines came from is hotly debated: from Africa, across a then narrow Atlantic Ocean; or from Central America, across an intercontinental gap now filled by Panama; or from North America, across the primordial island arc skirting the Carribean where the Antilles now stand? Why does platyrrhine phylogeny seem to have unfolded as a single but highly diversified radiation, unlike the prolific, multibranched catarrhine bush? Why do long-lived lineages seem to have dominated the macroevolutionary process? Why are there no terrestrial species?

Physically, the platyrrhines display an impressive array of body sizes, ranging from the 100-gm pygmy marmoset, *Cebuella pygmaea*, to the 10-kg woolly spider monkey, *Brachyteles arachnoides* (and a fossil relative perhaps twice as large). Their dietary spectrum includes exudativores, insectivores, moderate carnivores, and both soft-fruit and hard-fruit specialists, as well as folivores. Locomotor habits are equally diverse, including squirrellike runners, leapers, lethargic quadrupeds, climbers, and acrobatic arm swingers. These patterns tend to be phylogenetically distributed, and they indicate the ways in which the modern species have partitioned local habitats to allow for the coexistence of more than a dozen sympatric species in the lush communities around Amazonia. For example, the smaller callitrichines may be insectivorous and gumivorous scansorialists, while the larger, more agile atelines are more folivorous and frugivorous. The middle-size, leaping pitheciines may concentrate on harder fruits and seeds, secondarily upon insects or leaves, while the same-size, quadrupedal cebines dwell on concealed insects and forage for softer fruits when they are in season.

Because their fossil record is still poor, much of the interpretation and debate concerning the evolution of platyrrhines centers on the living species. The general pattern of their phylogenetic relationships, confirmed in outline by morphology and DNA (deoxyribonucleic acid) sequencing, indicates two major clades. These can be ranked at the levels of family (Cebidae, Atelidae). Within these are four subclades, ranked as subfamiles (Cebinae, Callitrichinae, Atelinae, Pitheciinae). All of the fossil forms, except perhaps for the earliest ones, *Branisella boliviana* and *Szalatavus attricuspis*, can be easily accommodated by this classification, although it has been commonplace to recognize many more higher taxa for both the living and the fossil forms. Nevertheless, opinions are not unanimous on these matters. Interpretation of the callitrichines (marmosets and tamarins) and the saki-uakaris (the pitheciines) are the keys to understanding platyrrhine history.

The callitrichines have convergently evolved features resembling primitive mammalian patterns, such as small body size, clawed digits, and unconvoluted brains, yet they are bona fide anthropoids. While the primitiveness or derivedness of these features has been a matter of debate for decades, the other important question—to which modern forms are marmosets most closely related?—had long been virtually ignored because it was thought to be imponderable without fossil evidence. The new neontological approaches, however, have indicated that the most likely answer to this question is that callitrichines are related to the cebines, *Cebus* and *Saimiri*. Also, they show that the evidence points

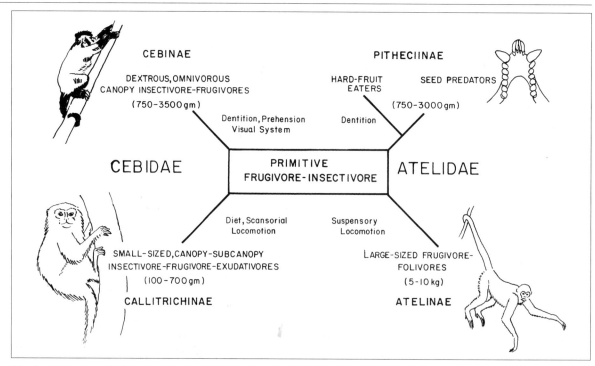

The platyrrhines as an adaptive array, with some of the major features of each of the four subfamilies indicated. Courtesy of Alfred L. Rosenberger.

emphatically to the interpretation that callitrichines are derived in many of their distinctive features. At least one extinct form, the nominal cebine *Laventiana*, supports this linkage as well.

The living pitheciine genera, in contrast to the famous callitrichines and atelines, have attracted little attention, perhaps because they are largely concentrated in the nearly impenetrable Amazon region about which we know little. Yet, current thinking is that these forms represent a segment of a larger adaptive radiation. We know as many as nine fossil genera belonging to this group. It is also noteworthy that

pitheciins have no adaptive counterpart among the Old World monkeys: They are a group of selective hard-fruit eaters. Thus, in a phylogenetic and paleontologic perspective, the pitheciins are more highly successful than one would infer from the living survivors. They have played an important, enduring role in the ecological community of platyrrhines since the Early Miocene.

See also Adaptive Radiation; Anthropoidea; Atelidae; Atelinae; Ateloidea; Callitrichinae; Catarrhini; Cebidae; Cebinae; Pitheciinae. [A.L.R.]

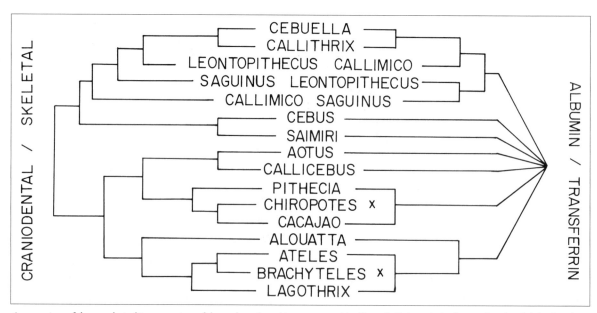

A comparison of the genealogical interpretations of the modern platyrrhine genera resulting from cladistic analysis of craniodental and skeletal evidence (left); and the serological evidence of combined studies of albumin and transferrin (right). Courtesy of Alfred L. Rosenberger.

Further Readings

Fleagle, J.G., Kay, R.F., and Anthony, M.R.L. (1997) Fossil New World monkeys. In R.F. Kay, R.H. Madden, R.L. Cifelli, and J.J. Flynn (eds.): Vertebrate Paleontology in the Neotropics. Washington, D.C.: Smithsonian Institution Press, pp. 473–495.

Hershkovitz, P. (1977) Living New World Monkeys (Platyrrhini), Vol. 1. Chicago: University of Chicago Press.

Rosenberger, A.L. (1986) Platyrrhines, catarrhines, and the anthropoid transition. In B.A. Wood, L. Martin, and P. Andrews (eds.): Major Topics in Primate and Human Evolution. Cambridge: Cambridge University Press.

Rosenberger A.L. (1992) Evolution of feeding niches in New World monkeys. Am. J. Phys. Anthropol. 88:525–562.

Pleistocene

Final epoch of the Cenozoic Era, beginning at 1.81 Ma. During the Pleistocene, the average temperature of the global ocean declined to the lowest values since the Permian, more than 200 million years ago, and the intensity and variability of global climate cycles reached a maximum, with repeated buildup and collapse of subpolar continental ice sheets in the Northern Hemisphere. The final part of the Cenozoic, in the interval since the melting of the most recent continental ice sheets at ca. 11.7 Ka, has often been regarded as a separate chronostratigraphic unit (the Holocene, or present, epoch), but, except for the level of human activity, it is not distinct from other nonglacial intervals of the Pleistocene.

The Pleistocene (from the Greek, "most recent") epoch was defined by Charles Lyell explicitly in terms of marine biostratigraphy. In the first edition of *Principles of Geology*, in 1833, he noted that the fossils in beds he assigned to "younger Pliocene" were markedly different from those of the older (standard) Pliocene. In a subsequent edition of 1839, Lyell renamed the younger beds as Pleistocene. At almost the same time, Louis Agassiz demonstrated that the "drift" of tillites and erratic boulders on the plains of northern Europe was due to vanished glaciers, and, in 1843, Edward Forbes recognized that the fossils of the Pleistocene reflected glacial conditions. Forbes coined the term *Ice Ages* for the epoch.

The Pleistocene epoch, like all chronostratigraphic units, is defined and subdivided on the basis of specific stratigraphic points in marine sequences. However, the overwhelming emphasis of Pleistocene studies has been on climatically induced changes to plant and animal associations, sediments, and geography, and this has led inevitably to the use of paleoclimatological interpretations rather than objective stratigraphic data in discussing Pleistocene history. Thus, the deposits attributed to a *glacial*, during times of ice

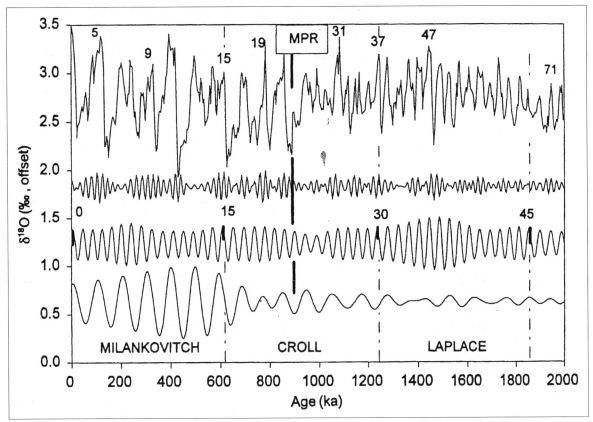

The oceanic oxygen isotope curve (top), a proxy for ice volume variation, reflects the influence of precession (21 Kyr), obliquity (41 Kyr) and eccentricity (100 Kyr) cycles on climate change over the past 2 Myr (lower three curves, extracted from the first through Fourier statistical analysis). The Pleistocene is divided into three climatostratigraphic chrons, each 15 obliquity cycles in duration. They document increasing instability of world climate, from the obliquity-dominated pattern of the Laplace Chron to the eccentricity-dominated pattern of the Milankovitch Chron. The Mid-Pleistocene Revolution (MPR) at 0.9 Ma marks a sharp increase in average ice volume and glacial coverage that is identified with the onset of the Elsterian or Illinoian glacial stage. (Note that the beginning of the Laplace Chron, because of the arbitrary definition at 15 cycles, is placed at 1.87 Ma, slightly older than the Vrica GSSP at 1.81 Ma.) From W. H. Berger et al., 1994, Geology, v. 22. By permission of the Geological Society of America.

advance and lowered average sea level and temperatures, or to an *interglacial*, during times of climate more or less like the present, have taken on the role of semiformal time-rock units in the Pleistocene. Even the resolution of the 1948 International Geological Congress in London, which specified that the base of the Pleistocene should be located at a physical point in marine strata at the base of the Calabrian Stage in southern Italy, stipulated that this definition was justified by evidence in these strata for a change from warm- to cold-climate conditions (i.e., the first appearance in the Mediterranean of "cold guests," molluscs that today live no farther south than the North Sea and the Baltics). It is now recognized that the migration of these northern visitors into the Mediterranean represent an intensification of cold-climate cycles that began in the Pliocene, rather than an idealized "first glaciation."

Different paleoclimatic proxies—the loess sequences in China, the paleofloral record of the Rhine delta, the paleoclimatic interpretations of dated fossils and sediments in North America and Europe, and the oxygen-isotope record of the deep-sea cores—all agree that a pronounced step in the progressive deterioration of world climate was seen at 2.5 Ma, during the Pretiglian cold phase in oxygen-isotope Stages 98 and 100. The earliest ice-rafted debris in deep-sea sediments of the North Atlantic and the North Pacific date from this level, indicating an expanded range for polar icebergs long after glaciers first began to calve at sea level in Greenland (7 Ma) and later in Norway (5.5 Ma).

The drastic reorganization of temperate mammal faunas at 2.5 Ma, known as the *E-L-E* (*Equus-Leptobos-Elephas*) *datum*, characterized the beginning of the classical (now middle) Villafranchian mammal age of Europe and the Tatrot Stage in the Siwaliks of Indo-Pakistan. It was assumed by vertebrate paleontologists and anthropologists to mark the beginning of the Pleistocene, and even today this definition has its advocates. It is worth noting, however, that, whereas this climate change was a shock to the animals and plants of the later Cenozoic, at its coldest the Pretiglian was still warmer than the present-day interglacial climates.

Early Pleistocene

The physical point that was eventually selected for the base of the Pleistocene, in deep-water marine strata exposed at Vrica, Calabria, is presently correlated to a level slightly below the top of Olduvai paleomagnetic Subchron, with an age of ca. 1.81 Ma. In the standard paleofloral sequences of the Rhine delta, this level is synchronous with the main (earlier) cold phase of the Eburonian Stage, and in deep-sea cores to the cold-water minimum of oxygen-isotope Stage 64. In continental sequences, this is also the level of the Olivola unit, at the beginning of the Late Villafranchian (Biharian) land-mammal age.

The Eburonian glacial-climate phase at the beginning of the Pleistocene (1.8 Ma) was more intense than the preceding Pretiglian cold phase (2.5 Ma) and was also significantly colder than the present interglacial, to judge from the presence of boreal molluscs in the Mediterranean and the first continental ice sheets in North America. The effects of

the Eburonian climates on Plio-Pleistocene mammalian faunas were, however, less conspicuous than those in the Pretiglian, because the latter represented the first exposure of Cenozoic biota to "winterizing" climate. Nevertheless, the basal Pleistocene Olivola mammal phase was marked by the evolution and rapid dispersal of the vole *Allophaiomys pliocaenicus* and the wolf *Canis etruscus*, as well as species-level replacements in most other lineages.

In Africa, faunas from sequences that span the upper part of the Olduvai Subchron exhibit a relatively high rate of replacement that has been attributed to environmental shifts. Human evolution at that time was marked by the divergence of *Homo erectus* from early *Homo*. The Waalian interglacial, following the Eburonian cold phase, appears to have offered the opportunity for *H. erectus* to migrate into southern Eurasia, where human remains and tools date to pre-Jaramillo levels in Georgia (Dmanisi), Israel ('Ubeidiya), China (Nihewan, perhaps Gongwangling and Longgupo), and Java.

Middle Pleistocene

At ca. 0.9 Ma, the Menapian cold-climate phase ushered in the ultimate "Ice Age" faunas and floras that continue to the present. The first major alpine glaciation, documented in the Günz terraces of southern Germany, dates from this cycle, and it is generally agreed that this is the beginning of the "classical" Pleistocene as Forbes and his contemporaries saw it. The Middle Pleistocene ends at the beginning of the next-to-last warm-climate cycle (Eemian) at ca. 127 Ka, following the Saale III advance in Europe, and Wisconsin I advance in North America. A precise definition for the Middle Pleistocene, the Ionian Global Standard Stage, has been proposed in deep-water marine strata of southern Italy. The base of the Ionian has been set just above the Jaramillo Subchron in strata deposited during oxygen-isotope Stage 25, the last warm-ocean peak before the Menapian at 0.92 Ma. Some have advocated that the Brunhes/Matuyama Chron boundary at 0.78 Ma should be the criterion for the base of the Middle Pleistocene, but this is inconsistent with the requirement that all chronostratigraphic units be defined by physical points in fossiliferous marine sediments.

The correlation of classical Middle Pleistocene subdivisions with the deep-sea record is tentative, due to the absence of effective dating methods for strata of this age. From the paleoanthropological point of view, the most important European horizon is the Holstein interglacial, generally correlated with the Hoxnian beds of England and the Steinheim beds of southern Germany, which have yielded skeletal remains of later "archaic *Homo sapiens*" and also archaeological material. Steinheim is also the type locality of the Steinheimian mammal fauna, which is characterized by many European species of large mammals (mammoths, mastodons, elephants, rhinos, hippos, lions, cave bears) that became extinct during the Late Pleistocene.

The marine deposits of the Holsteinian sensu stricto have been found to represent a warm maximum only ca. 15 Kyr long. This stage is correlated with some certainty to oxygen-isotope Stage 11 at ca. 400 Ka. This climatic optimum, the warmest of the Pleistocene, is followed by the Warthe glacial advance. A later warm interval, not recognized in the Alpine "classical" sequence, has been differentiated as the Wacken interglacial, equivalent to isotope Stage 9c; another possibility is that the Alpine Holsteinian may span Stages 11 and 9, with only a cool phase in between, thus deserving the old epithet "Great Interglacial." The true Saale glacial, which begins with the Drenthe glacial advance at ca. 250 Ka, is interrupted by distinct warm-climate peaks, the Treene and/or Ohe, equivalent to oxygen isotope Stages 7a and 7, dated to 230 Ka.

Late Pleistocene

The Late Pleistocene comprises the next-to-last interglacial, the last glacial, and (in the view of many stratigraphers) the present, or Holocene, interglacial. The chronology of this period is relatively well known from radiocarbon dating of pollen-bearing lake beds, uranium-thorium dating of emerged coral reefs, back-counting of varved (annually laminated) glacial lake beds, and cores drilled into the ice caps of Greenland and Antarctica. The Late Pleistocene begins with a very marked warm-climate interval, the Eem interglacial, which corresponds to the Tyrrhenian *Strombus*-bearing "Senegalian" faunas in high terraces of the Mediterranean and to the warm-ocean conditions of Peak 5e in the oxygen-isotope record, dated to ca. 127 Ka. Studies of carbon dioxide levels indicate that the Eemian interglacial climates, which lasted for ca. 10–12 Kyr, were warmer, at their maximum, than those of the present day. During the early part of the Weichsel "last glacial," between ca. 115 and 75 Ka, at least two major cold maxima in northern Europe alternate with three interstadials, the Amersfoort, the Brorup, and the Odderade. Studies of marine sediments of this age in the deep sea indicate that the main difference between the shorter, less extreme interstadial oscillations during a glacial advance and the longer, warmer interglacial conditions is that during the interstadials the temperature of the deep-ocean waters remains essentially unchanged, whereas they warm by 2–3°C during interglacials. Reforestation patterns, reflected in the pollen found in ancient lake beds, also distinguish between the climates of interstadials vs. interglacials.

The climate between ca. 75 and 12 Ka, following the Odderade interstadial, was predominantly cold and dry, with an environment that has been called *polar desert*. This interval, termed the Pleniglacial, was nevertheless interrupted by several ameliorations, or interstadials, during the middle (60–23 Ka) that have been recognized worldwide. The last of these, the Denekamp, between ca. 30 and 23 Ka, is particularly conspicuous and is known elsewhere by such terms as Würm 2/3, Farmdale, Plum Point, Stillfried B, Paudorf, Mologeshekskaia, and Gota-Alvi.

The end of polar-desert conditions and the waning of Weischel glaciation began ca. 16.5 Ka in a succession of warming events and readvances called the Late Glacial phase. This transitional period consists of the Bolling interstadial, the Older Dryas cool phase, the Allerod warm phase, and the Younger Dryas cool phase, as recognized in Denmark. The "final glacial" of the Younger Dryas dates from 13 to 12.2 Ka, with a pollen record indicating vegetation cover not un-

like the Holocene despite the presence of moraines in Norway, Sweden, and Finland (Salpausselka moraines), which demonstrate that the Weichsel ice sheet had not yet fully melted. The Laurentide ice sheets in Canada, as well as mountain glaciers around the world (Alps, Urals, western United States, Andes, Kenya), were also at glacial extent during this time. The Weichsel glacial age ended with a sharply defined, globally synchronous *Heinrich event* of massive iceberg-calving as the thermally overloaded ice sheets finally collapsed. Differing adjustments for the reservoir effect on cosmogenic carbon- and beryllium-isotope abundances lead to ages for the Younger Dryas/Preboreal boundary, widely understood to be the beginning of the Holocene, that vary between 11.2 and 11.4 Ka.

Considering the post-Weichsel as the final part of the Pleistocene, the world is now in the Flandrian interglacial. Following relatively cool and wet conditions until 1000 BCE, and the "thermal optimum" that lasted until ca. 1400 CE, the later Flandrian has been marked by a minor readvance of mountain glaciers, the "Little Ice Age," that peaked ca. 1650 CE. World climates returned to near-average Flandrian conditions by ca. 1900 CE.

In archaeological terms, the most conspicuous transition of the later Pleistocene in Europe is the one between the Middle and the Late Paleolithic. This appears to be contemporaneous with the transition between archaic and modern humans as far as the fossil record demonstrates and is interpreted to fall between 35 and 30 Ka in Europe. In Africa, these events seem to be significantly older, probably at ca. 50 Ka but in some interpretations as old as 90 Ka. Probably the most detailed succession of human artifacts, which at the same time contains various indicators of past climate, comes from the caves and rockshelters in the Périgord of southwestern France. This sequence is well dated by radiocarbon, while the changes in climate are interpreted from the changing shape and size of limestone fragments that make up the bulk of the cave sediments, as well as from pollen grains and animal bones found in the occupation levels.

Archaeologists first classified Pleistocene strata according to embedded stone artifacts, using the terms *Early, Middle*, and *Late Paleolithic*. Later, the Alpine stages came into wide use by archaeologists, who attempted to refine and subdivide this climate-based system for their own use. In the interval of the Riss and Würm, particularly, multiple subdivisions based on climatic oscillations resulted in frequent miscorrelations from one area to another because local conditions, usually conditions of preservation, prevented the record of climate change in any given region from being complete. One consequence, among others, is that the W 1/2 interstadial (i.e., the warm-climate interval between Würm-1 and Würm-2 advances) in French cave sites does not correlate to the W 1/2 interstadial in Austria and bears no relationship to the concept of the Würm Stage in the sequence of Alpine terraces.

Pleistocene in Africa

The earliest Pleistocene levels in Africa are reversed-polarity sediments laid down after the end of the Olduvai Subchron. At Olduvai Gorge (Tanzania) itself, this level occurs in the

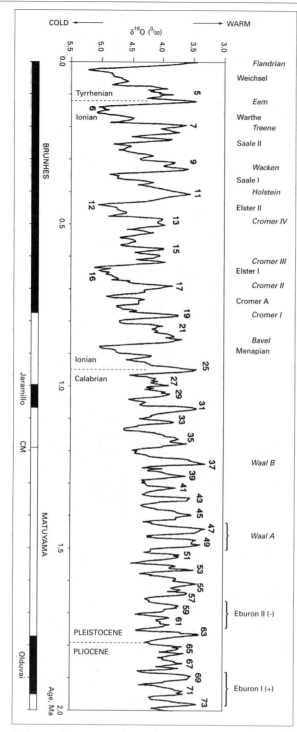

Pleistocene climatostratigraphy, correlating oxygen isotope ratios in benthic foraminifera from deep-sea core ODP Site 677 (from Shackleton, N.J. and Hall, M.A., 1989, in Becker, K., Sakai H., et al., Proceedings of the ODP, Scientific Results, vol. 111) and climatostratigraphic interpretation of the Plio-Pleistocene sequence in the Rhine-Scheldt delta of the Netherlands. The correlation of Waalian interglacials is approximate.

and Melka Kontouré). Fossil remains are rare in comparison, but, as far as the evidence allows, the base of the Pleistocene in Africa is closely coincident with the oldest fossil remains that can be attributed to *H. erectus* (placed by some in *Homo ergaster*), as distinct from coeval *Homo habilis* and *Homo rudolfensis*. A comparison of the mammal fossils suggests that Swartkrans (Member 1) and Sterkfontein (Member 5) in South Africa, and the 'Ubeidiya site in Israel, are close to this time, but confirmative dating is lacking.

No well-defined climate change has been identified with the beginning of the Pleistocene in Africa, but glacial deposits on Mt. Kenya, Kilimanjaro, and the Ruwenzoris show that mountain glaciers formerly extended thousands of meters lower in altitude than at present, demonstrating that Pleistocene climate swings also affected the tropics. The lakes of the Rift Valley show signs of cyclic "pluvial" rises and falls during the Pleistocene; in the American West, qualitatively similar changes in level of the great desert lakes coincided with periods of glacial advance, and it may be supposed that this is probably also the timing of the African pluvials, at least in a general way. In North Africa, coastal terraces with mammal fossils have been related to broad changes in sea level due to Pleistocene glacial oscillations. Fossiliferous beds in Morocco with late "archaic *Homo sapiens*" remains and tools at Thomas Quarries and Tighenif, and at Salé near Rabat, are dated to Holstein interglacial in this way.

See also Climate Change and Evolution; Cyclostratigraphy; Glaciation; Holocene; Pliocene; Quaternary. (J.A.V.C.)

Further Readings

Berggren, W.A., and Van Couvering, J.A. (1981) Quaternary. In Treatise on Invertebrate Paleontology, Part A, Introduction. Boulder: Geological Society of America, pp. A505–A543.

Bowen, D.Q. (1978) Quaternary Geology. Oxford: Pergamon.

Butzer, K.W., and Isaac, G.L., eds. (1975) After the Australopithecines. Hawthorne, N.Y.: Mouton.

Denton, G.H., and Hughes, T.J., eds. (1981) The Last Great Ice Sheets. New York: Wiley.

Sarnthein, M., Stremme, H.E., and Mangini, A. (1986) The Holstein Interglaciation: Time-stratigraphic position and correlation to stable-isotope stratigraphy of deep-sea sediments. Quatern. Res. 26:283–298.

Van Couvering, J.A., ed. (1996). The Pleistocene Boundary and the Beginning of the Quaternary. Cambridge: Cambridge University Press.

Plesiadapidae

An archaic primate family known from the Early Paleocene of North America and in the Late Paleocene to Early Eocene in both Europe and North America. Plesiadapids are the most successful early primates in terms of numbers of recognized paleospecies and the collected abundance of fossil individuals within these taxa. Species of the genus *Plesiadapis* are some of the most common Paleocene mammals, and

middle part of Bed II and correlates both radiometrically and paleomagnetically with the Okote Member at Koobi Fora (Kenya), Omo Shungura members J-K-L (southern Ethiopia), and lower Melka Kontouré (eastern Ethiopia). In all of these sequences, this level coincides with the earliest occurrence of Acheulean bifaces and cores, together with a brief continuation of Oldowan-style artifacts (at Olduvai they have been used as stratigraphic horizon markers (similar to the concept of *index fossils*) to date sedimentary rocks.

There are five recognized genera of Plesiadapidae. The oldest form is the newly described *Pandemonium*, from the Puercan Early Paleocene of North America; *Pronothodectes* occurs in the Torrejonian Early Paleocene of North America; *Plesiadapis* (including *Nannodectes*) and *Chiromyoides* are known from the Late Paleocene to Early Eocene of both North America and Europe; and the youngest genus, *Platychoerops*, is known from the European late Early Eocene.

Pandemonium is known from molar and a few premolar teeth, and in these features it is remarkably similar to the ancient paromomyid *Purgatorius*. The two somewhat younger and only slightly more advanced species of *Pronothodectes* display characters that are clearly antecedent to the three younger and more advanced genera. Although the central incisors are enlarged, a lateral pair is still retained, in addition to the canine and the second premolar. The premolars are upright and shortened, and the talonid on the third lower molars is characteristically expanded. The molars display the diagnostic ancestral features of the plesiadapids in having the upper-molar protocones somewhat more central on the lingual side of the tooth than in archaic primates, and correlated with this are the more vertical and less procumbent lower-molar trigonids.

The widespread genus *Plesiadapis* contains at least 15 paleospecies of varying degrees of justification for species-level distinction; many of these taxa are probably parts of the same lineage that do not deserve species ranking based on morphological distance models, but they are all retained in the same genus because morphologically they form a relatively undifferentiated group. In contrast to the probably ancestral *Pronothodectes*, members of *Plesiadapis* lose the lateral lower incisor but retain the upper one. The upper and lower incisors are highly characteristic not only of this genus but also of all of the other described ones. The robust and enlarged lower central incisors together form a broad-based shovel or scoop with a continuous marginal edge around them. This is most similar to what is seen in some marsupial phalangers, and it is emphatically not rodentlike. The enlarged central upper incisors have three distinct cusps on their outer edges and a more posterior (distal) one to stop the action of the lower incisors against it. These mittenlike upper incisors are as robust as the more simply constructed lower ones. It is not clear that the genus *Plesiadapis* is a strictly holophyletic group, as *Platychoerops* was derived from a species of *Plesiadapis*.

Chiromyoides is much more poorly known, even though five allegedly distinct species have been described, based on incisor structure. This genus is a super-robust version of the smaller species of *Plesiadapis*, and its rarity may be due in no small measure to an ecological role that may not have allowed great population densities. The mandible and muzzle are considerably shortened and deepened, and the enlarged incisors also suggest a greater loading of forces on the feeding mechanism. The lower incisors, as well as the anterior cusp of the upper central incisors, also have diagnostically sharp transverse cutting edges anteriorly. Assuming that *Chiromy-*

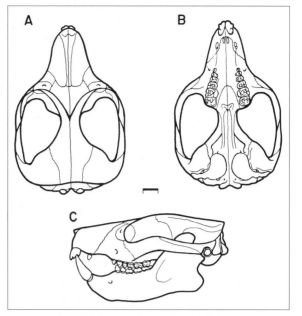

Reconstructed skull of the Late Paleocene plesiadapid Plesiadapis tricuspidens *from Europe. Scale is 1 cm. Courtesy of Frederick S. Szalay, from Szalay and Delson, 1979.*

oides was arboreal, a wood-gnawing and grub-hunting lifestyle such as seen in the lemuriform aye-aye and some marsupial possums (*Dactylopsila*), or hard-outer-shelled fruit feeding as in pitheciines may be the best living equivalents for this genus. Like *Chiromyoides*, *Platychoerops*, the youngest and largest plesiadapid, evolved from a stock of *Plesiadapis*. It had well-crenulated upper molars surrounded by broad cingula (ledges), suggesting a fully herbivorous diet like the many species of *Plesiadapis*.

Most of our knowledge of plesiadapid cranial and postcranial anatomy derives from a few well-preserved cranial specimens from Europe and rare postcranial remains from both sides of the Atlantic. All archaic mammals, including the archaic primates, had a relatively larger head-to-body size than modern lemurs possess. In spite of this large head, the brain was relatively small compared to the size of the skull or body, and the proportion of facial skull to neural skull in *Plesiadapis* was not dissimilar to that displayed by the living Virginia opossum. Yet, compared to similar-size contemporary nonprimates like the arctocyonids (ancient ungulate structural ancestors), known plesiadapids had relatively larger brains compared to their body size. The general shape of the skull was not unlike the broad and shallow skull of living marsupial phalangers such as the genera *Trichosurus* and *Phalanger*. The skull of *Plesiadapis* unequivocally shows one of the diagnostic primate characteristics, an encasing of the middle ear cavity by the petrosal, the same bone that houses the inner ear. Yet, unlike euprimates, this and other archaic primates have a reduced promontory artery and lack the postorbital bar; this latter feature is characteristic not only of the primitive euprimates, but it also evolved, convergently, in other groups of placental mammals.

Plesiadapid postcranial remains, like the cranium, display a tantalizing mixture of archaic mammalian features

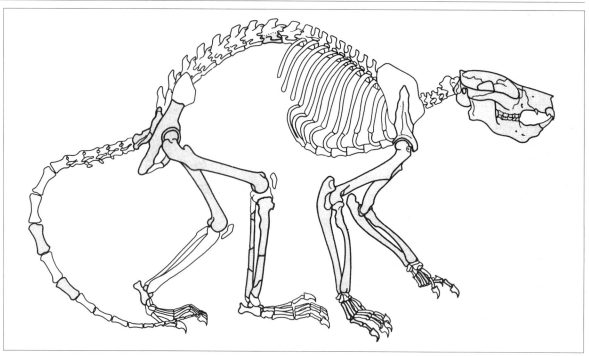

Reconstruction of the skeleton of Plesiadapis tricuspidens *from Cernay-les-Reims, France.*

intermixed with suggestive euprimate attributes and probably unique characters. Some important distinctions about the levels of homology are difficult to sort out because the archaic primates are relatively poorly known. The ability of the lower arm to rotate freely on the upper one, and the nature of the upper and lower ankle-joint articulations leave no doubt whatsoever that plesiadapids, or at least the nominal genus, were capable of performing activities found today in arboreal mammals. The very deep and laterally compressed terminal phalanges, which completely predict the shape of the claw in living mammals, indicate a claw structure like those found today in some of the most arboreal of clawed mammals, binturongs (viverrids), or the colugos and tree-roosting fruit bats. Although plesiadapids were probably arboreal, the structure of the knee, as seen from the groove for the patella (kneecap) on the femur, indicates that they were relatively slower moving than the rapidly jumping and grasp-leaping early representatives of euprimates (adapids and omomyids) or modern lemurids.

It thus appears that the Plesiadapidae were not only primarily herbivorous but also arboreal, although many of the species probably pursued survival strategies as mixed as any in the somewhat similar-size arboreal living mammals. We may think of these ancient primates as having occupied niches not entirely dissimilar to the arboreal phalangeroid marsupials, the phalangers and the various possums, and the living subtropical tree squirrels, species of the Sciuridae.

Family Plesiadapidae
   † *Pandemonium*
   † *Pronothodectes*
   † *Plesiadapis* (including *Nannodectes*)
   † *Chiromyoides*

   † *Platychoerops*
†extinct

See also Euprimates; Locomotion; Plesiadapiformes; Plesiadapoidea; Primates. [F.S.S.]

Further Readings

Gingerich, P.D. (1976) Cranial anatomy and evolution of Early Tertiary Plesiadapidae (Mammalia, Primates). University of Michigan Papers on Paleontology 15:1–141.

Szalay, F.S., and Delson, E. (1979) Evolutionary History of the Primates. New York: Academic.

Van Valen, L.M. (1994) The origin of plesiadapid primates and the nature of *Purgatorius*. Evol. Monog. 15:1–79.

Plesiadapiformes

Semiorder of primates that includes the earliest, archaic members of the order. The taxonomic concept was published by E.L. Simons in 1972 as an infraorder (but listed in his book as authored by Simons and I. Tattersall). It encompassed the archaic radiation of euprimatelike families, those probably monophyletically derived from an as yet unknown group that also gave rise to the Euprimates. The Plesiadapiformes, as used here, may eventually be shown to have given rise to the colugos (Dermoptera), and these, in turn, to their putative derivatives, the bats (Chiroptera).

The period since the mid-1980s has not only seen important discoveries of material, including new taxa, and significant studies dealing with these, but it has also resulted in some exceptionally confusing, and as yet still unconvincing (poorly or unacceptably tested), hypotheses about the relationships of these archaic relatives of modern primates. Nothing illustrates this confusion better than a comparison of three classifications (genera omitted): those of G. Gunnell (based primarily on dental evidence) and K.C. Beard (relying on characters of the postcranium and skull), compared with the classification that is utilized here.

Gunnell (1989)

Order Primates?
   Superfamily?
      Family Purgatoriidae
   Superfamily Plesiadapoidea
      Family Paromomyidae
         Subfamily Paromomyinae
         Subfamily Phenacolemurinae
      Family Plesiadapidae
      Family Carpolestidae
      Family Saxonellidae
      Family Picrodontidae
   Superfamily Microsyopidae
      Family Palaechthonidae
         Subfamily Palaechthoninae
         Subfamily Plesiolestinae
      Family Microsyopidae
         Subfamily Uintasoricinae
         Subfamily Navajoviinae
         Subfamily Micromomyinae
         Subfamily Microsyopinae

Beard (1993)

Mirorder Primatomorpha
   Order incertae sedis
      Family Purgatoriidae
      Family Palaechthonidae
      Family Microsyopidae
      Family Picrodontidae
   Order Dermoptera
      Suborder Micromomyiformes
      Infraorder Plesiadapoidea
         Family Plesiadapidae
         Family Carpolestidae
         Family Saxonellidae
      Infraorder Eudermoptera
         Family Galeopithecidae
         Family Paromomyidae

Classification Preferred Here

Order Primates
   Semiorder Plesiadapiformes
      Superfamily Plesiadapoidea
         Family Plesiadapidae
         Family Carpolestidae
         Family Saxonellidae
      Superfamily Paromomyoidea
         Family Paromomyidae
         Family Picrodontidae

The still poorly understood archaic primates, or plesiadapiforms, were quite distinct from the modern euprimates although their last common ancestor was probably fully arboreally adapted. In several ways, these ancestors might have been like some of their living archontan relatives, such as dermopterans or the possibly most primitive living tree-shrew, *Ptilocercus*. The facial and neural halves of the skull had proportions similar to what we see in a Virginia opossum today. Not only were they similar to opossums, at least superficially, in their degree of neural development, but they probably did not differ significantly from these in terms of locomotion. Despite the archaic proportion of their skulls, they could be distinguished from nonprimates by a complex of derived features. Among the most important of these characters are a special groove on the heel bone for a flexor tendon of the digits, some less clearly defined features of the molar teeth, and the developmental derivation of the auditory bulla (the chamber that houses the middle-ear ossicles) from the petrosal bone. This last character has received a challenge from the description of a new skull of a paromomyid, but the assertion that the bulla is entotympanic is based on equivocal evidence.

The Plesiadapiformes represent the first-known major radiation of the Primates, and they, along with the other archontans, composed the first wave of placental mammals that we know to have invaded the arboreal milieu and made use of the bounty offered by the flowering plants and the insects around them. Their classification into two superfamilies, the Plesiadapoidea and Paromomyoidea, recognizes the most corroborated monophyletic groupings (i.e., both holophyletic and paraphyletic taxa). The micromomyins probably represent a small group nested within the holophyletic Paromomyidae.

See also Archonta; Euprimates; Microsyopidae; Paromomyoidea; Plesiadapoidea; Primates. [F.S.S.]

Further Readings

Beard, K.C. (1993) Phylogenetic systematics of the Primatomorpha, with special reference to Dermoptera. In F.S. Szalay, M.J. Novacek, and M.C. McKenna (eds.): Mammal Phylogeny: Placentals. New York: Springer-Verlag, pp. 129–150.

Gunnell, G.F. (1989) Evolutionary history of Microsyopoidea (Mammalia, ?Primates) and the relationships between Plesiadapiformes and Primates. University of Michigan Papers of Paleontology No. 27:1–154.

Szalay, F.S., and Lucas, S.G. (1996) The postcranial morphology of Paleocene *Chriacus* and *Mixodectes* and the phylogenetic relationships of archontan mammals. Bull. New Mex. Mus. Nat. Hist. Sci. 7:1–47.

Plesiadapoidea

A superfamily of the archaic primate semiorder Plesiadapiformes. The three families that are united under this superfamily—Plesiadapidae, Carpolestidae, and Saxonellidae—almost certainly shared a common ancestor after the separation of this lineage from some stem lineage of paromomyoids. The Plesiadapoidea is monophyletic (its hypothetically acceptable last common ancestor is included in the group) and also probably holophyletic (it includes all known descendants of the common ancestor), and the relationships among the three included families, while not fully documented, appear to be resolved. The plesiadapids and the sax-onellids are probably more recently related to each other than either is to the Carpolestidae. The former families share a paraconule on P_3 in addition to the plesiadapoid condition of P_4; they also have both a parastyle and a metacone on these teeth. The plesiadapoid common ancestor, on the other hand, may be diagnosed as having had upper molars with more centrally placed and less mesially leaning proto-cones, correlated with less leaning trigonids, together with a distinct paraconule on the fourth upper premolar, in con-trast to its paromomyoid ancestry.

It has been suggested that the Plesiadapoidea, along with other taxa (of various authors) of the Plesiadapiformes, be transferred to the Dermoptera. There is, however, no sat-isfactory corroborating evidence that this taxon and the Der-moptera form a holophyletic clade when one examines ei-ther the cranial, dental, or postcranial evidence. Even if the Dermoptera do not prove to be the sister taxon of the Chi-roptera, the ties of the former, within a broader archontan grouping of Paleocene (and probably Cretaceous) arboreal placental mammals, are still considered controversial by many.

The plesiadapoid common ancestor was not far re-moved from the last common ancestor of all primates. It had, in each of the halves of the upper and lower jaws, two incisors, a canine, three premolars, and three molars. Its cheek-tooth morphology was probably not very different from the late Early Paleocene plesiadapid genus *Prono-thodectes,* or possibly very close to the morphology displayed by *Pandemonium.* The central incisors, as in all known plesi-adapoids, were characteristically enlarged, and the upper central incisors were three-pronged and somewhat mitten-like. This last characteristic, however, may have been a reten-tion from a paromomyid ancestry and, therefore, may not be an acceptable plesiadapoid diagnostic feature by itself. The petrosal construction of the auditory bulla in *Plesiadapis* has been questioned in light of the putative entotympanic bulla of the Early Eocene paromomyid *Ignacius.* Plesiadapoids persist into the Early Eocene in both North America and Europe.

See also Archonta; Carpolestidae; Dermoptera; Microsyopi-dae; Paromomyidae; Plesiadapidae; Plesiadapiformes; Pri-mates; Saxonellidae. [F.S.S.]

Plesiopithecus

A distinctive primate genus named from the Late Eocene (ca. 36 Ma) deposits of the Fayum, Egypt, and assigned to a new superfamily, Plesiopithecoidea, of which the species *P. teras* is the only known representative. A recently discovered and al-most complete skull shows that *P. teras* possesses a postorbital bar but lacks postorbital closure, even though its original de-scription emphasized the "archaic anthropoid" nature of its lower molars. The new material also suggests that this un-usual form retained four lower premolars. The latest (as of 1999) analysis proposes that, among known primates, *Ple-siopithecus* lies closest to the lorisoids, but its affinities will continue to be debated.

See also Fayum; Lorisoidea; Teeth. [I.T.]

Pliocene

Youngest epoch of the Cenozoic Era, occupying the interval between 5.3 and 1.8 Ma. The term, meaning "very recent time," was proposed by Charles Lyell in 1833 for the epoch in which nearly all of the fossils of marine molluscs and echinoderms were of extant species. Lyell initially included in the Pliocene all strata between the Miocene and the pres-ent, dividing it into an "older Pliocene" and a "younger Pliocene," but he subsequently renamed the "younger Pliocene" the Pleistocene. In standard marine sequences, the Pliocene consists of two stages typified in Italy, the Zanclean and the Piacenzian. Earlier literature refers to the Tabianian and Astian Stages, but these terms have been abandoned. A new, Upper Pliocene stage, the Gelasian, has been proposed to distinguish the youngest part of the epoch from the typi-cal Piacenzian.

In geological history, the boundaries of the Pliocene are synchronous with two striking events, the Messinian salinity crisis at its beginning and the first glacial episode of the Pleis-tocene at its end.

The Messinian Event

The *Messinian event,* also called "the death of an ocean," refers to a geologically brief period when the Mediterranean Basin was emptied by evaporation. The only strata that Lyell specifi-cally assigned to the "older Pliocene" in his original definition of the epoch, in Flanders and northern Italy, are separated from the Miocene beds by a major gap in deposition. In the North Sea Basin, as in most parts of the world, the depositional gap was the result of a transitory drop in global sea level at the end of the Miocene. In the Mediterranean Basin, however, the end-Miocene decline in sea level led to the final act in isolating the Mediterranean Sea from the world ocean, because compres-sion between Africa and Eurasia had already very nearly closed the shallow Miocene straits in Morocco and at the head of the Guadalquivir River Basin in southern Spain. Once the seaway had closed, the waters of the Mediterranean evaporated in ca. 0.2 Myr, leaving behind a sunken desert basin more than 2,000 km long and up to 5 km deep—perhaps the only time in the history of the Earth that a true ocean basin has been emptied of water. Deposits laid down during the period of increasing salinity and final evaporation are correlated with the Messinian Stage, the final stage of the Miocene. During the final million years of the Miocene, the three principal tributary rivers (Rhone, Po, and Nile) excavated canyons down to the floor of the Messinian desert that were twice as deep as the Grand Canyon. These canyons, now almost completely filled with Pliocene and Pleistocene strata, can be traced in the subsurface inland from the present river mouths for hundreds of kilome-ters, to Aswan in the case of the Nile and to the Italian lakes (the upper headwaters of the Italian canyon) in the case of the Po. It should be added that the Bosporus showed no such inci-sion, because at that time the Black Sea and the Caspian Sea drained via Armenia to the head of the Persian Gulf.

The base of the Pliocene in the Mediterranean repre-sents one of the most dramatic moments in geological history. The typical example is exposed in a sea cliff at Capo Rosello, near Realmonte in the Agrigento district of southern Sicily. The base of the cliff is formed by grey and black evaporite beds that were laid down in salt pans on the floor of the desiccated Mediterranean. These beds are directly overlain, in a knife-sharp contact, by chalk-white microfossil oozes that formed at the bottom of an ocean several kilometers in depth. The transition records the catastrophic flooding of the basin when ocean waters broke through the axis of the Gibraltar syncline. The flow from the Atlantic gouged out the present straits to a depth of more than 200 m, probably in a few weeks' time, while world sea level dropped by an estimated 10 m (30 feet). In Andalucia and Murcia provinces of southern Spain, African Late Miocene proboscidean faunas were succeeded by European Early Pliocene European mammals, reflecting the geographic shift of the water barrier between the continents. The living macaques of Gibraltar appear, however, to be Pleistocene migrants and not Pliocene refuges.

Hipparion Datum and the False Pliocene

In the later nineteenth century, German and Austrian geologists mistakenly correlated the Messinian evaporites of the Mediterranean Basin to similar-looking evaporite beds in central Europe (e.g., the famous salt mines of Kraków) that were, as we now know, of Middle Miocene age. At that time, however, most stratigraphers were forced to accept that the brackish water and continental beds of the widespread Pontian Steppe Formation that overlay the Polish salt were of Lower Pliocene age. The Pontian beds are characterized throughout central and eastern Europe by abundant remains of the three-toed equid *Hipparion*, an immigrant from North America. By the mid-1930s, using the *Hipparion datum* as a guide, American paleontologists had extended the central European concept of the Pliocene throughout Asia (including the Siwaliks) and back to the New World homeland of the hipparionines. It was not until the late 1960s that radiometric age analysis and marine micropaleontology combined to show that, whereas the advent of *Hipparion* in Eurasia dated to at least 10 Ma, the basal Pliocene of the Zanclean Stage in the Mediterranean was only half as old, at ca. 5.3 Ma. Continental faunas of the Pontian and its equivalents are now placed in the Late Miocene Vallesian and Turolian land-mammal ages.

Pliocene Climates and Fauna

The Pliocene was marked by increasingly wide swings in global climates, but without the intense short-term cyclicity of the Pleistocene. During the warm-climate intervals, the winter frost line retreated virtually to the Arctic Circle, and seasonal variation in rainfall was moderate, in contrast to cold winters and summer-dry seasonality during the progressively more intense cold-climate intervals. Significant expansion of ice caps during the cold-climate intervals is indicated by tillites and ice-rafted debris at high latitudes, as early as 3 Ma in Norway and Iceland, and evidence for worldwide lowering of sea level. The Early Pliocene warm-climate phase climaxed ca. 3.5 Ma, and modern instability of global climates shows its first signs at 3 Ma, when the 100,000-year

frequency of eccentricity-driven cycles start to appear in oxygen-isotope curves from deep-sea cores. This point also marks the beginning of the final decline in the long-term average of world temperatures that has continued to the present.

The Pretiglian glacial-climate maximum at 2.5 Ma, just above the Gilbert/Gauss paleomagnetic boundary, saw a permanent northward shift of Antarctic ice margins, a pulse of floating ice into the North Atlantic and North Pacific, and the earliest traces of mountain glaciation in western North America. Continental as well as marine climates were affected during the Pretiglian interval, with a clearly documented expansion of boreal paleofloral habitats at the expense of temperate woodlands in the higher latitudes, and a less well evidenced but widely suggested environmental crisis in tropical regions. The Pretiglian episode, which ends the typical Piacenzian marine deposits of Italy in a phase of lowered sea level and erosion, had a greater net impact on the fossil record of Pliocene shallow-marine and continental environments than the following, more intense, Eburonian glacial phase (1.8 Ma) at the end of the epoch. The intervening Gelasian warm-climate deposits were, however, deposited under pre-glacial—that is to say, typically Pliocene—rather than interglacial conditions, according to their content of tropical elements. This would suggest that the notable effects associated with the Pretiglian were due to a climate change that was more unprecedented than it was severe.

The continental Pliocene of Eurasia is characterized by the mammalian faunas of the Ruscinian and the Triversa, Montopoli, and Saint-Vallier faunal units that make up the earlier part of the Villafranchian. The Ruscinian and basal Villafranchian (Triversa) faunas reflected warm, equable habitats, with earliest Triversan dating to ca. 3 Ma. The transition to the Montopoli faunal assemblage at 2.5 Ma, coincident with the Pretiglian cold-climate interval, is classed as a major turnover. Many lineages became extinct, and new genera such as elephants (*Mammuthus*), horses (*Equus*), aurochs (*Leptobos*), and gazelles (*Gazella*) appeared, that were better adapted to the new conditions. The conspicuous, and obviously climate-related change at this level, which was known as the *Elephas-Equus-Bos horizon* by workers in the Siwaliks and later *Elephas-Leptobos-Equus datum* or simply *E-L-E*, throughout Eurasia, was long believed to be the continental equivalent of the Pliocene/Pleistocene boundary. So strongly was this held that the recommendation of the 1948 International Geological Congress in London, to formally define the base of the Pleistocene by the base of the marine Calabrian Stage in Italy, also included wording (at the insistence of L.S.B. Leakey) to equate this level in nonmarine sequences with the "base of the Villafranchian," meaning the Montopoli unit, which is now correlated to the Pretiglian climate shock at 2.5 Ma.

The transition from the Montopoli to the Saint-Vallier unit, at ca. 2.2 Ma, is marked by the extinction of *Hipparion* in Europe (but not in Africa, where it survived until ca. 1.6 Ma, or in eastern Asia) and the earliest forms of the characteristic Ice Age elephant, *Mammuthus meridionalis*. The cold climates of the Eburonian glacial age, at the beginning of the

Pleistocene, were coincident with a second major turnover, the Olivola faunal unit, in which wolves, lions, and several modern genera of voles and lemmings made their first appearances, and European and central Asian *Gazella* became extinct. The Middle Villafranchian Montopoli and Saint-Vallier units are essentially equivalent to the "Plio" part of the Plio-Pleistocene sequences of East Africa at Hadar, Laetoli, Olduvai Gorge, and Turkana Basin.

Hominid Evolution in the Pliocene

By the beginning of the Pliocene, the endemic Miocene hominids of temperate Eurasia were extinct. Intensified ocean cooling and expansion of the mid-latitude arid zone from India to Senegal had isolated the remaining tropical populations of hominids, with the orangutans and *Gigantopithecus* in Southeast Asia, and the australopiths and (presumably) chimp and gorilla ancestors in Africa. The hardier cercopithecids continued to adapt, however, to the deteriorating conditions in the northern part of their Miocene range.

In Africa, as in the higher latitudes, global climate change in the later Miocene at ca. 11 Ma led to increased seasonality, with the spread of grasslands and drought-resistant shrub and open forest. These trends intensified during the cold-climate cycles of the Pliocene. In Kenya, the earliest recognizable hominin remains, at Lothagam or Lukeino (ca. 6 Ma), and the oldest diagnosed australopiths, at Kanapoi and the lower levels at Koobi Fora (ca. 4.2 Ma), are found in open-country faunal associations, signaling that the postural and manipulative specializations of hominins were fundamentally associated with this widening habitat. The Pretiglian global cold event, at 2.5 Ma, coincided with a realignment of faunal province boundaries in Africa. Because the Pliocene fossil sites sample only small areas of southern and eastern Africa, the local effects of the regional biogeographic shifts are difficult to distinguish from evolutionary replacement, but it may be significant that this time of maximum seasonality coincided with the earliest-known examples of *Australopithecus africanus* and genus *Homo*.

See also Africa, East; Australopithecus; Cenozoic; Climate Change and Evolution; Cyclostratigraphy; Glaciation; Miocene; Pleistocene. [J.A.V.C.]

Further Readings

Azzaroli, A., Colalongo, M.L., Nakagawa, H., Pasini, G., Rio, D., Ruggieri, G., Sartoni, S., and Sprovieri, R. (1996) The Plio-Pleistocene boundary in Italy. In J.A. Van Couvering (ed.): The Pleistocene Boundary and the Beginning of the Quaternary. Cambridge: Cambridge University Press.

Shackleton, N.J., Hall, M.A., and Pate, D. (1995) Pliocene stable isotope stratigraphy of Site 846. In N.G. Pisias, et al. (eds.): Proceedings of the Ocean Drilling Program: Scientific Results, Vol. 138. College Station, Tex.: Ocean Drilling Program, pp. 337–356.

Vrba, E. S. (1982) Biostratigraphy and chronology, based particularly on Bovidae, of southern hominid-associated assemblages. In H. de Lumley and M.A. de Lumley (eds.): 1er Congrés International de Paléontologie humaine. Prétirage, Vol. 2. Nice: C.N.R.S., pp. 707–752.

Pliopithecidae

The pliopithecids are a group of catarrhines of small to medium size that were widespread through Eurasia during the Middle and Late Miocene. The family is first recorded in the earliest part of the Middle Miocene, and representatives are known into the Late Miocene from western Europe to China. There are no close relatives of the pliopithecids in Africa, and there is no evidence for relationship between them and the African small-bodied catarrhines of the Early Miocene such as *Dendropithecus*. They both constitute groups of primitive catarrhines, but the retention of simple ear regions and primitive humeri in the pliopithecids suggests that, in many respects, they retained more primitive characteristics than did the African small-bodied apes. It seems likely that they had independent origins in Africa during the Oligocene.

The pliopithecids made up one of the most diverse groups of fossil catarrhines during the Miocene. To date (1999), 13 species have been recognized, of which nine are restricted to western Europe and four to China. Three subfamilies are known, Crouzeliinae, Pliopithecinae, and a third as yet unnamed, with considerable overlap in such adaptations as body size and diet. All subfamilies include very small and moderately large species, and all contain folivorous as well as more frugivorous species. They are rarely found together, and even more rarely (in four of 74 localities where they are known) are they found with hominoid species such as *Dryopithecus*. There is probably some environmental aspect that separates them, but exactly what has not yet been discovered.

In addition to being diverse and relatively abundant in European Miocene sites, pliopithecids are also well represented by fossil material. Several partial pliopithecine skeletons are known from the fissure fillings of Neudorf Spalte in Slovakia, including an almost complete skull, and a partial face is known in China. Crouzeliinae is not so well represented, but there is an undescribed partial skull known from Hungary in addition to many good jaws and some postcranial specimens, and good cranial material has been described from China. The third group is known to date only by dentitions.

In the past, pliopithecids have been grouped with various other fossil primates. Originally, they were linked with the extant gibbons, but this was later recognized to be the result of superficial similarities in body size and long-bone gracility. In the 1980s, the gibbon relationship received some support from the discovery of a pliopithecid in China, namely *Laccopithecus robustus*. The pliopithecids have also traditionally been linked with *Propliopithecus* from Oligocene deposits in Egypt, but this has also been seen to be the result of shared primitive characters, and the Oligocene genus is better put into a separate more conservative family, Propliopithecidae. Both groups conform well to recent reconstructions of the ancestral catarrhine morphology, although both also have uniquely derived characters (e.g., in the elongated P$_4$ and the pliopithecine triangle on the lower molars of pliopithecids and the postcranial adaptations of the propliopithecids). Members of the two families also retain at least two characters in which they are more primitive than any other catarrhine (including *Dendropithecus*): an entepicondylar foramen on the distal humerus (also present in some platyrrhines and many strepsirhine primates) and a simple hingelike articulation of the carpometacarpal joint of the pollex. *Pliopithecus vindobonensis* is more derived than *Propliopithecus zeuxis* in having an external auditory meatus partly drawn out into a tube superiorly (though open inferiorly), as opposed to the simpler ringlike opening in the Fayum species, and the upper molars are relatively slightly longer as well.

All pliopithecids present a number of major features in addition to those shared with *Propliopithecus*. Among these are, in the cranium: a relatively short and broad face, of which the lower part is shallow; a narrow palate, in which the upper tooth rows converge anteriorly; a widely open incisive canal, only slightly angled posterosuperiorly, which allows a wide communication between the palate and the nasal fossa; subcircular, frontally directed orbits with a slightly protruding inferior rim and supraorbital torus (this circumorbital rim, superficially similar to that of gibbons, may represent either a specialization of the pliopithecids or a feature retained from the ancestral catarrhines); and a large neurocranium in relation to the facial skeleton, with well-marked temporal lines converging posteriorly, but not meeting to form a sagittal crest, even in males. Dentally, the pliopithecids are distinguished by several relatively derived features, such as: relatively slender and high-crowned lower incisors; mesiodistally short and high-crowned P$_3$, with a steeply inclined mesiobuccal honing face for occlusion with the upper canine; relatively long and narrow P$_4$ and lower molars, increasing in length toward the rear; and both M^2 and M^3 considerably larger than M^1.

The two better-known pliopithecid subfamilies are both represented at Sansan in France, where originally they were assigned to the same species: *Pliopithecus antiquus*. L. Ginsburg recognized their differences, however, and separated the crouzeliine at the genus level as *Crouzelia auscitanensis*. With the discovery of additional material, particularly from Rudabánya in Hungary, it was realized that two very different groups were represented, now recognized at the subfamily level. Crouzeliines differ from pliopithecines in having higher and more conical cusps on the upper molars with sharper occlusal ridges, a relatively larger trigon, and a diminutive distal basin with the hypocone isolated from the other cusps. The lower molars are more elongated with similarly higher cusps and sharper ridges. These are modifications generally associated with more folivorous diets, and unpublished studies of dental microwear show that crouzeliines have a pattern of fine parallel scratches similar to that of living folivorous primates. In contrast to these differences in the teeth, and in the dietary adaptations implied, the skulls of crouzeliines and pliopithecines are remarkably similar, all the more so when the best-known crania of the two groups are from Slovakia and China. This implies considerable uni-

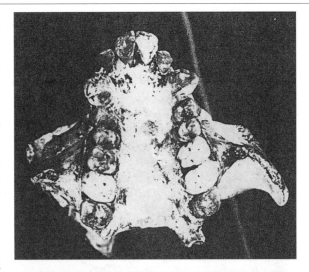

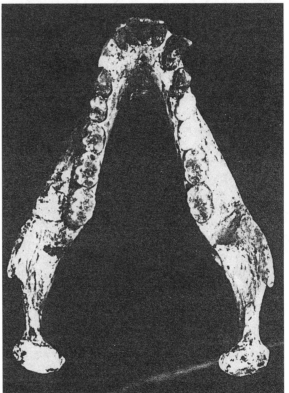

Upper (above) and lower jaws of Pliopithecus vindobonensis *from Middle Miocene deposits in the Czech Republic.*

formity in space and time, for the same morphology is apparently retained for a period of at least 4 Myr.

The subfamily Pliopithecinae contains five species, all assigned to the single genus *Pliopithecus*. Four are restricted to Europe, and one is known from China. *P. antiquus* from Sansan was the first noncercopithecid fossil catarrhine ever described, and it has a range extending into central Europe. The species is found in deposits dated from ca. 16 to 9 Ma, giving it a temporal range of ca. 7 Myr. Rather better known, but more restricted in time and space, is the species *P. vindobonensis* from Neudorf Spalte in Slovakia. This fauna dates to ca. 15–14 Ma, and the material consists of three partial skeletons and some isolated bones from additional individuals. The lower molars of *P. vindobonensis* lack the pliopithecine triangle and are more elongated, but in most other respects it is similar to the type species. It was originally assigned to a distinct subgenus, *Epipliopithecus*, but this has been seen to be unwarranted and the name has been dropped. The other major change in taxonomy of the pliopithecines has been the separation of the Göriach (Austria) specimens from the species *P. antiquus* on the basis of their larger size, broader P$_3$, and narrower lower molars. They are similar to the 16–15 Ma specimen from Elgg (Switzerland), *P. platydon*, and they are now assigned to this species. The recently described *P. zhanxiangi* from China is the largest of the pliopithecid primates, larger even than the largest of the crouzeliines, *Anapithecus hernyaki*.

The subfamily Crouzeliinae is taxonomically more diverse than the pliopithecines. Three genera are recognized, *Anapithecus* and *Plesiopliopithecus* from Europe and *Laccopithecus* from China. The Sansan species that provides the root for the subfamily name, *Crouzelia auscitanensis*, has been grouped with the prior-named *Plesiopliopithecus lockeri* from Trimmelkam in Austria, and both come from sites dated to ca. 14–13 Ma. A third species, *P. rhodanica* from La Grive-Saint-Alban, France, has recently been described. The best-represented crouzeliine from Europe is the younger species *Anapithecus hernyaki* from 10 Ma deposits at Rudabánya, Hungary. It is considerably larger than other species of crouzeliine, more than twice the size of *P. rhodanica*, the smallest species. It is approached in size only by the Chinese crouzeliine, *Laccopithecus robustus*, from Lufeng in Yunnan Province, which is the youngest pliopithecid, at ca. 9–7 Ma. Three recently described specimens from Terrassa, Spain, are intermediate in size between the small and the large crouzeliines, but they can be distinguished from all known species by a unique combination of characters of the premolars and molars. The P$_3$ is short, with a well-developed metaconid, while the P$_4$ is a long molariform tooth in which the talonid is almost twice as long as the trigonid and bears two distinct stylids. This is similar to *Anapithecus* and *Laccopithecus*, but the molar morphology is more similar to *Plesiopliopithecus*. It probably belongs to yet another genus of crouzeliine primate, as yet not named. Terrassa is the latest-known occurrence of pliopithecid in Europe, dated ca. 11–10 Ma.

Several controversial specimens require special mention. The first of these is an isolated upper canine from Eppelsheim in Germany (ca. 10 Ma). It was originally described as a cercopithecid monkey, but it is now recognized as a pliopithecid. This has significance for the identification of another specimen from Eppelsheim, the femur originally described as *Paidopithex rhenanus* and now generally identified as *Dryopithecus*. There is no evidence for this genus at Eppelsheim, however, and there is also no femur specimen with which it could be compared from that or any other site. It is at least as likely that the Eppelsheim femur belongs to a large pliopithecid as that it is a dryopithecine. Several isolated teeth from Salmendingen in Germany and Götzendorf in Austria have been attributed in the past to *Dryopithecus*, but, with the better understanding of crouzeliine morphology, it now seems possible that these belong to a species of crouzeliine; this issue is not yet finally resolved.

In the late 1990s, T. Harrison recognized that two species known mainly from the Chinese locality of Sihong (Jiangsu Province, dated ca. 17 Ma) are distinctive pliopithecids. *Dionysopithecus shuangouensis* was long seen as similar to the East African *Micropithecus*, but additional material documented closer similarities to the larger *Platodontopithecus jianghuaiensis*, once thought similar to *Proconsul*. *Dionysopithecus* also occurs slightly younger (16–15 Ma) in deposits in Thailand, but despite previous suggestions, not in Pakistan. These taxa both present a pliopithecine triangle on their lower molars. They are among the oldest pliopithecids anywhere and the oldest catarrhines in Asia.

Family Pliopithecidae
    Subfamily Pliopithecinae
        † *Pliopithecus*
    Subfamily Crouzeliinae
        † *Plesiopliopithecus* (including † *Crouzelia*)
        † *Anapithecus*
        † *Laccopithecus*
    Subfamily incertae sedis
        † *Dionysopithecus*
        † *Platodontopithecus*
†extinct

See also Asia, Eastern and Southern; Catarrhini; Dendropithecus-Group; Dryopithecinae; Dryopithecus; Europe; Miocene; Propliopithecidae; Skeleton; Teeth. [P.A., E.D.]

Further Readings

Andrews, P., Harrison, T., Delson, E., Martin, L., and Bernor, R. (1996) Systematics and biochronology of European and Southwest Asian Miocene catarrhines. In R.L. Bernor, V. Fahlbusch, and H.W. Mittmann (eds.): Evolution of Western Eurasian Late Neogene Mammal Faunas. New York: Columbia University Press, pp. 168–207.

Harrison, T., Delson, E., and Guan, J. (1991) A new species of *Pliopithecus* from the Middle Miocene of China and its implications for early catarrhine zoogeography. J. Hum. Evol. 21:329–361.

Wu, R., and Pan, Y. (1985) Preliminary observations on the cranium of *Laccopithecus robustus* from Lufeng, Yunnan, with reference to its phylogenetic relationship. Acta Anthropol. Sin. 4:7–12.

Zapfe, H. (1961) Die Primatenfunde aus der miozänen spaltenfüllung von Neudorf an der March (Devinska Nova Ves), Tschechoslowakei. Mem. Suisses Paléontol. 78:5–293.

Pluvials

Pluvials (literally, "rains") are Pleistocene paleoclimatic intervals in subtropical and tropical areas, marked by relatively cold, wet climate and a notable lowering in the elevation of ecozone boundaries. In the 1930s, East African archaeology was tied to four pluvials, the Kageran, the Kamasian, the Kanjeran, and the Gamblian, from oldest to youngest. These were assumed to reflect the four classic Ice

Ages in higher latitudes, as well as being the cause of four highstands of Lake Victoria that were made out in erosion surfaces around the lake. The *pluvial* concept fell into disrepute after World War II, with the somewhat premature debunking of the *four-glacials* concept, together with the failure of the simple model of pluvials under an avalanche of new data. Recent work indicates, nevertheless, that ancient lake levels in Africa can, in fact, be tied to global climate history.

See also Glaciation; Pleistocene. [J.A.V.C.]

Further Readings

McCall, G.J.H., Baker, B.H., and Walsh, J. (1967) Late Tertiary and Quaternary sediments of the Kenya Rift Valley. In W.W. Bishop and J.D. Clark (eds.): Background to Evolution in Africa. Chicago: Chicago University Press, pp. 191–220.

Pollen Analysis

Palynology, the analysis of ancient plant pollen and spores, is one of archaeology's more informative methods for examining prehistoric ecological adaptations. Most plants shed their pollen into the atmosphere, where it is rapidly dispersed by wind action. Pollen grains—microscopic single-celled organisms produced during plant reproduction—are present in most of the Earth's atmosphere, including, of course, archaeological sites. To conduct a pollen analysis, several sediment samples must first be removed, generally taken from the sidewall of an excavation unit. The individual pollen grains are isolated in the laboratory through the use of acid baths and centrifuging. Microscope slides containing the fossil pollen grains are then scanned at magnifications between 400× and 1,000×, and the grains are counted until a statistically significant number has been recorded. These figures are converted to percentages and integrated into a *pollen spectrum*. The pollen profiles are then correlated with the known absolute and relative dates for each stratum.

One of the most important applications of palynology is to reconstruct past environments. Fluctuating pollen percentages can indicate changes in prehistoric habitats. Once a regional sequence has been developed (often from noncultural deposits), archaeological samples can be statistically compared with the pollen rain from known extant plant communities. The ratio of arboreal to nontree pollen, for example, generally indicates the degree of forestation.

Recently, palynologists have employed the *pollen influx* method to estimate the actual number of pollen grains incorporated into a fixed volume of sediments over a particular time. Once the pollen influx is known, the number of years contained in a certain volume of sediment can be estimated. Total pollen influx can be estimated by adding a known number of *tracers* (such as *Lycopodium* spores) to each archaeological sample prior to pollen extraction. The ratio of the artificially introduced tracers to the fossil pollen grains permits the calculation of population estimates for each zone. The actual pollen influx for each stratigraphic zone can then be estimated from the average pollen content.

After several pollen diagrams from an area have been analyzed and integrated, a regional sequence can be constructed. At this point, pollen analysis can even function as a relative dating technique: An undated site can be placed in proper temporal sequence simply by matching pollen frequencies with the dated regional frequencies, just as in dendrochronology.

See also Dendrochronology; Geochronometry; Paleoenvironment; Phytolith Analysis. [D.H.T.]

Further Readings

West, R.G. (1971) Studying the Past by Pollen Analysis (Oxford Biology Reader). London: Oxford University Press.

Polytypic Variation

Because humans live in groups, the variation found among individuals can be analytically divided into two kinds: *polymorphic* and *polytypic*. The variation that exists *within* any group is polymorphic variation; the variation that exists *among* groups is polytypic variation. While polytypic variation is often more superficially obvious, approximately five times as much genetic variation is found within any human population as between populations.

See also Population; Race (Human). [J.M.]

Pondaung

Range of hills exposing upper Middle Eocene strata (40–38 Ma) near Mogaung, Burma, ca. 400 km north of Mandalay. The Pondaung beds have yielded fragmentary jaws and teeth of two primates, *Pondaungia* and *Amphipithecus*, each of which has been put forward as a possible early catarrhine. Recent reevaluation suggests that both were adapiforms. The Pondaung area was north of the Tethys Ocean in the Eocene, but it is possible that mammals known there might have dispersed westward toward Europe and North Africa in the Late Eocene; potential connecting taxa (not primates) are known in Nepal and Turkey.

See also Adapiformes; Anthropoidea; Catarrhini; Paleobiogeography. [E.D.]

Further Readings

Holroyd, P.A., and Ciochon, R.L. (1994) Relative ages of Eocene primate-bearing deposits of Asia. In J.G. Fleagle and R.F. Kay (eds.): Anthropoid Origins. New York: Plenum, pp. 123–142.

Ponginae

Subfamily of Hominidae containing the orangutan and a number of related fossil species. The orangutan is one of the three great apes, and formerly it was included with the chimpanzees and gorilla in a separate family, the Pongidae. Most authorities now believe, however, that the orangutan is more distantly related to humans than are chimpanzees and gorillas, and this is recognized by putting the former into its own subfamily and abandoning the concept of a great-ape clade. The family that combines all three great apes with humans is here called Hominidae.

Within Hominidae, the pongines are the most specialized group. In a great many characters, the African apes and humans retain the ancestral hominoid condition from which the orangutan has diverged, and this makes it easy to identify fossil orangutans, for they share at least some of the pongine specializations. It is less easy to identify hominine fossils because of the rarity of hominine specializations.

The main characters by which the pongines differ from other hominoids include the following: The skull has an expanded and flattened zygomatic region, and, together with a long upper face and great alveolar prognathism (projection of the lower face) this gives the face a distinctly concave shape when seen in side view. The lateral expansion of the lower face resulting from the large zygomatics contrasts with a much narrower upper face, which has relatively narrow orbits and a short distance between the orbits.

The browridges are not developed in the orangutan; this may be an ancestral hominoid character, since browridges are not present on any of the early fossil hominoids, such as *Proconsul*. However, there is some indication that strong browridges may be a hominid specialization: Prominent browridges are present on the African apes and fossil humans and perhaps on such early members of the hominid (hominine?) clade as *Graecopithecus*. If presence is a hominid character, the lack of browridges on the orangutan would have to be seen as a reversion to the ancestral condition and, therefore, as a derived character of the orangutan clade. On the other hand, it is not clear if the character state seen in *Graecopithecus* is really homologous with the condition in living hominines, and thus it is more likely that the orangutan simply retains the primitive condition in this respect.

The premaxilla in the orangutan is rotated upward relative to the maxilla, so that the alveolar end (where the incisors are emplaced) forms a nearly horizontal shelf projecting in front of the nose; this is responsible for the orang's alveolar prognathism and in part for the concave shape of the face, and it has also produced several changes in the morphology of the floor of the nose. The posterior end of the premaxilla is shifted posteriorly against the maxilla, and, because of the rotation, the two bones overlap; this results in the elimination of the incisive fossa, producing a smooth nasal floor, and in the great reduction in size of the incisive canals that carry blood vessels and nerves between the nose and the mouth. It has also resulted in the exaggeration of the airorhynch condition that was probably present to a lesser degree in Early Miocene hominoids such as *Afropithecus* and *Proconsul*. The African apes have reversed this trend in developing klinorhynchy, which is probably related to the great development of the browridges.

The dentition in orangutans is mainly noted for the thickened enamel on the molar teeth and the extreme degree of enamel wrinkling on the occlusal surfaces of the teeth. The enamel surfaces of the molar crowns are almost flat, as are the dentine surfaces beneath the enamel, and this seems to be related to the wrinkling of the crowns since these crenulations take the place of enamel/dentine ridges formed during tooth wear. Finally, the lateral incisors are small relative to the central incisors. These characters of the skull and dentition are unique to the orangutan. The African apes and humans are different from the orangutan but resemble the gibbons and monkeys and so must be said to retain the ancestral catarrhine condition. The discovery that a number of fossils also share the orangutan condition has led to a reassessment of the relationships of these fossils. Most of the specimens at present (1999) attributed to the genera *Sivapithecus* and *Ankarapithecus* can be shown to share some or most of these characters, particularly those of the nose and face, a finding made possible by the recovery of more complete fossil material from Turkey and Pakistan. The most complete specimen was described by D. Pilbeam in 1982 from Miocene deposits in Pakistan, and this adult individual of *Sivapithecus* has most of the face and jaws preserved. A less complete specimen from Turkey had been described a few years earlier, and, while some of these characters of the face and palate were indicated by this specimen, it required the more complete discovery from Pakistan to confirm the significance of these characters. These two specimens thus confirmed the existence of the orangutan lineage during this part of the Miocene. This gave a date of 10.5–7 Ma for the occurrence of this lineage, but more fragmentary fossils from earlier deposits in Pakistan pushed back the date of origin of the lineage to 13–12 Ma. The two more complete specimens were shown to have some aspects of the nasal and premaxillary morphology noted above to be characteristic of the orangutan. The 1996 publication by B. Alpagut and colleagues of a more complete skull from Turkey (see ANKARA-PITHECUS) has demonstrated that this species is less oranglike in the upper face than is *Sivapithecus*, thus implying that the genus *Ankarapithecus* should be revived for the several Turkish fossils.

In 1993, S. Moyà-Solà and M. Köhler described another fossil as having orangutan affinities. This is the partial skull from Can Llobateres, Spain, assigned to *Dryopithecus laietanus*. It lacks the pongine characters seen in *Sivapithecus*, but instead it has two others not present in that genus: a flat and forwardly projecting zygomatic bone, and multiple maxillo-zygomatic foramina. It seems most likely that these characters are ancestral retentions in *Dryopithecus* and the orangutan, but it is possible that the nasal and facial characters shared by *Sivapithecus* and the orangutan are ancestral retentions, or even conceivably that all of them are.

D. Pilbeam and colleagues presented new evidence from the postcrania in 1990 to show that the humerus of *Sivapithecus* is very similar to those of Early to Middle Miocene hominoids. It has long been thought that the features of the humerus present in the orangutan and the African apes are homologous and were, therefore, present in the last common ancestor of the great apes and humans, but, since some of these characters are absent from *Sivapithecus*, there is a problem if the fossil is on the orangutan lineage. One alternative is that *Sivapithecus* is not directly related to the orangutan and, therefore, the characters of the nose and face shared between them are not synapomorphies; another

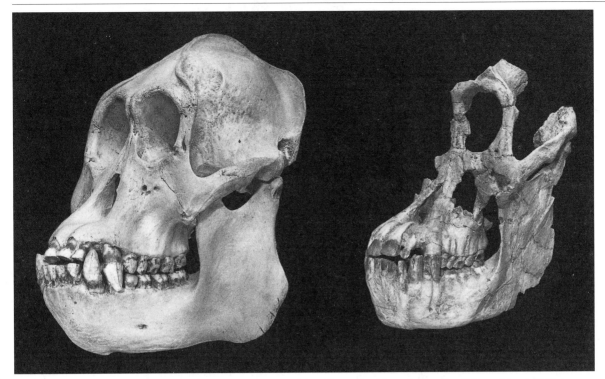

Oblique left lateral view of the cranium of modern Pongo pygmaeus *and Late Miocene* Sivapithecus indicus *from Pakistan. Photo by C. Tarka.*

possibility is that *Sivapithecus* is an orang relative that secondarily redeveloped features like the ancestral condition due to its locomotor adaptations. The resolution of this complicated matter must await further fossil evidence, but the most likely solution remains the link between *Sivapithecus* and the orangutan, so that the zygomatic characters seen in *Dryopithecus* and the orangutan are ancestral retentions, while the humeral characters shared between the great apes are homoplasies or lost in *Sivapithecus*.

Several other genera have been placed in the Ponginae with less certainty. *Gigantopithecus* from the Late Miocene of India and the Pleistocene of China and Vietnam is not known by facial or postcranial remains, but it has thick molar enamel and other features that suggest links to *Sivapithecus*. *Lufengpithecus* from the Late Miocene (9–7 Ma) of South China (Yunnan Province) was originally placed in *Sivapithecus*, but its distinctive facial and dental morphology (wide interorbital spacing combined with lightly built browridges; subnasal pattern unclear; tall and robust lower incisors and canines; small I^2; some molar surface wrinkling) led to its recognition as a separate genus. Most of its characteristics are either unique or conservative, so it is usually not included in Ponginae; here it is tentatively placed in Dryopithecinae, although the lack of known postcrania makes that assignment questionable. Other, probably comtemporaneous fossils from Hudielangzi and nearby sites in Yuanmou county, Yunnan Province have been termed *Ramapithecus* and *Homo*, but they appear to represent a pongine of uncertain generic affinity: A juvenile face has narrow interorbital spacing and ovoid orbits, both pongine characters. Many other specimens have been mentioned, but detailed descriptions have not yet been published. Fossil *Pongo* specimens are known from the Pleistocene of Indonesia, Indochina, and southern China, indicating a far wider range for this taxon than today, when it is restricted to portions of Sumatra and Borneo.

Subfamily Ponginae
    Pongo
    † *Sivapithecus* (including *Ramapithecus* and
           Sugrivapithecus, among others)
    † *Ankarapithecus*
    † *Gigantopithecus*
†extinct

See also Ankarapithecus; Ape; Asia, Eastern and Southern; Asia, Western; Catarrhini; Dryopithecinae; Dryopithecus; Gigantopithecus; Hominidae; Homininae; Hominoidea; Lufengpithecus; Miocene; Proconsulidae; Sivapithecus; Skull; Yuanmou. [P.A.]

Further Readings

Andrews, P., and Tekkaya, I. (1980) A revision of the Turkish Miocene hominoid *Sivapithecus meteai*. Palaeontol. 23:85–95.

Ciochon, R.L., and Corruccini, R.S. (1983) New Interpretations of Ape and Human Ancestry. New York: Plenum.

Moyà-Solà, S., and Köhler, M. (1993) Recent discoveries of *Dryopithecus* shed new light on evolution of great apes. Nature 365:543–545.

Patterson, C. (1987) Molecules and Morphology in Evolution: Conflict or Compromise. Cambridge: Cambridge University Press.

Pilbeam, D., Rose, M., Barry, J., and Shah, S. (1990) New *Sivapithecus* humeri from Pakistan and the relationship of *Sivapithecus* and *Pongo*. Nature 348:237–239.

Szalay, F.S., and Delson, E. (1979) Evolutionary History of the Primates. New York: Academic.

Ward, S.C., and Brown, B. (1986) The facial skeleton of *Sivapithecus indicus*. In D.R. Swindler and J. Erwin (eds.) Comparative Primate Biology, Vol. 1: Systematics, Evolution, and Anatomy. New York: Liss, pp. 413–452.

Pontnewydd

Cave in North Wales where fragmentary Neanderthal-like fossils and Acheulean tools occur in levels dating to 200 Ka. The lithic industry contains handaxes and flakes struck with the Levallois technique. The most significant feature of the Pontnewydd teeth is the presence of Neanderthal-like taurodontism in the molars, in which the tooth roots are undivided and the pulp cavity is enlarged.

See also Archaic Homo sapiens; Neanderthals. [J.J.S., C.B.S.]

Population

Interbreeding group of organisms (also called a *deme*). Collectively, the genotypes of the individuals in a population, or their gametes, constitute the gene pool of that population. Changes in the gene pool constitute microevolution. These changes may or may not affect the reproductive coherence of the population, thereby causing speciation and macroevolution.

See also Genetics; Race (Human). [J.M.]

Potassium-Argon Dating

A method of radiometric dating based on spontaneous decay of the unstable ^{40}K isotope. The decay of ^{40}K is relatively slow, with a half life of ca. 1.25 Myr, and the isotope occurs in only one out of 8,600 atoms of potassium. Most ^{40}K decay events proceed to ^{40}Ca by emission of a beta particle, and only 10.5 percent involve electron capture and gamma emission with decay into the ^{40}Ar isotope instead. Nevertheless, because of the abundance of potassium in granitic rock, it is calculated that the dual decay of this isotope is responsible for approximately one-third of the geothermal heat flow, nearly all of the background radioactive flux, and more than 99 percent of the argon in the atmosphere (ca. 1 percent of the total by weight). Radiogenic ^{40}Ca cannot be distinguished from the natural ^{40}Ca isotope of calcium, but *all* ^{40}Ar is radiogenic. This means that the amount of ^{40}Ar trapped within a mineral is a function of the age of the crystal and the amount of original ^{40}K (as a fixed percentage of total K, noted above). Applying the constant for the number of ^{40}K decay events per year ($\lambda = 5.543 \times 10^{-10}$ yr^{-1}) and a correction for any background, or atmospheric, ^{40}Ar that may have been incorporated at the beginning, year-ages can be calculated directly from the ratio of the parent and daughter isotopes.

Argon is a noble gas and does not combine or dissolve with other elements. Its atomic radius, however, is considerably larger than that of potassium, so that once the ^{40}Ar atom appears in place of its parent ^{40}K atom in the interlocked three-dimensional array of atoms that make up the *crystal*

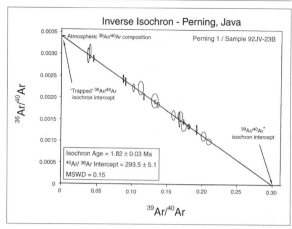

Isotope-correlation diagram ("isochron plot") of the ratios of ^{36}Ar and ^{39}Ar to ^{40}Ar obtained in incremental heating of neutron-irradiated hornblende crystals from Perning (Java). Dispersion about the isochron line is measured as MSWD (mean sum of weighted deviations). A low deviation, as in this example, represents the ideal in which all trials yield closely similar ages. MSWD over ca. 2.5 usually results from mineral or sample inhomogeneity. The isotope-correlation plot is more accurate than a simple weighted mean of the calculated ages because the atmospheric $^{36}Ar/^{40}Ar$ ratio in the sample is determined from the "y" intercept and not simply assumed. The ratio at the "x" intercept depends on the juvenile or radiogenic ^{40}Ar in the sample, and from these two points the isochron age, taking into account the neutron flux and other independent variables, can be calculated. From A. Deino, P.R. Renne and Carl C. Swisher, III, 1998, Evol. Anthropol. © 1998 and reprinted by permission of Wiley-Liss, Inc., a subsidiary of John Wiley & Sons, Inc.

lattice of a mineral, it is mechanically (not chemically) trapped for as long as the lattice is not degraded, or dilated by heat. This property of the K/Ar system has been ingeniously exploited in the step-heating analysis procedure, described below.

Sampling

Dating a stratum, such as a paleomagnetic boundary or a fossil bed, requires a potassium-bearing mineral whose isotopic age can be related to the age of the stratum. A second requirement is that changes, if any, to the argon or potassium content of the mineral after it crystallizes must be measureable. There are few such datable minerals that actually form within sediments at the time of deposition, as opposed to many (i.e., zeolites) that form postdepositionally. The potassium salt sylvinite is well suited on all accounts, but its occurrence is confined to certain rare types of playas. Glauconite (*green earth*), a hydrous iron-potassium silicate that forms abundantly on the seafloor under reducing conditions, has been used extensively by some laboratories, but doubts remain as to its reliability except under ideal conditions. By far the greatest number of K/Ar ages applied to Cenozoic stratigraphy, therefore, have been obtained on tuffs and lava flows interbedded with strata of interest, because eruptive rocks can be considered to crystallize at the geological moment that they are deposited in the sequence.

The K-bearing phases in igneous rocks are among the last to solidify. Most of the potassium in lavas and tuffs, therefore, is in the frozen matrix surrounding the larger, earlier-formed crystals. In the early days of Cenozoic dating, the analytical systems were still relatively insensitive, and it was often necessary to run dates on pulverized samples of the

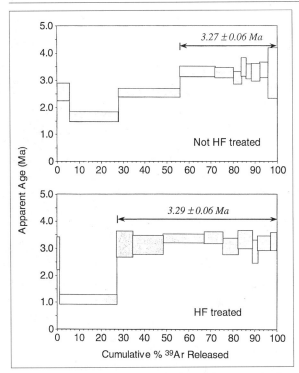

Step-heating ages in a whole-rock sample, the Kadada Moumou basalt, Hadar (Ethiopia). A spectrum of ages (shown on the vertical axis with 2 error envelopes) is obtained when different crystal phases release argon with increasing temperature, as monitored by incremental release of neutron-generated ³⁹Ar. Discordant younger ages are seen to come from low-temperature alteration products, while the age plateau at higher temperatures reflects older, more refractory unaltered phases, and represents the true or starting age of the sample. Dilute hydrofluoric acid treatment cleans the sample of weathering products and improves the signal from the original minerals. From A. Deino, P.R. Renne and Carl C. Swisher, III, 1998, Evol. Anthropol. ©1998 and reprinted by permission of Wiley-Liss, Inc., a subsidiary of John Wiley & Sons, Inc.

whole rock in order to get enough argon to measure accurately. This is still done in instances in which low-potassium rocks (e.g., olivine basalts) are dated, but it is difficult to control for weathering and argon loss in the relatively unstable matrix, even in the freshest-looking samples. Improved techniques and equipment have allowed researchers to concentrate on the more homogenous and less alteration-prone large crystals, or phenocrysts. The K-bearing igneous minerals that commonly occur as phenocrysts in eruptive rock are biotite mica, amphibole (hornblende), potassium feldspars (sanidine, anorthoclase, and the more potassic plagioclases), leucite, and nepheline.

⁴⁰K/⁴⁰Ar Total-Fusion Method

The application of argon radioisotope dating to Cenozoic rocks requires accurate measurement of extremely small amounts of radiogenic argon. The basic breakthrough came in the mid-1950s at the University of California, Berkeley, when techniques were developed for extraction and concentration of argon in an ultrahigh-vacuum environment that included a mass spectrometer. This remains the basic procedure in all Cenozoic argon-isotope dating today, since it is only the near-exclusion of atmospheric gases that makes it practical to process the tiny amounts of gas occluded in such young samples. In models of the original design, an external

microwave radiator is used to fuse the samples inside an evacuated chamber, and the expelled gas phase is passed through getters and condensers to further concentrate the argon. The amount of postcrystallization ⁴⁰Ar is the residual after subtracting initial atmospheric, or background, radiogenic argon. This correction is based on measurement of the natural isotope ³⁶Ar in the sample, and the fact that the ratio of ⁴⁰Ar/³⁶Ar in air and (usually) in magma is 295:1. The ⁴⁰K values are derived from wet chemical analysis of total potassium in separate splits of the samples. Multiple analyses, and careful attention to reagents and standards, bring the precision of K/Ar dates obtained in this way close to 0.7 percent (double standard deviation) under the best circumstances.

The basic accuracy of the ⁴⁰K/⁴⁰Ar total-fusion method (as opposed to its analytical precision) is vulnerable to several sources of error. One is the necessity of making argon and potassium determinations on separate splits of a sample of pulverized rock or separated crystals, the homogeneity of which can never be completely assured. Another source of error, at least in the early days, was the need to fuse relatively large samples (1 to 10 g) in order to obtain enough argon; under these circumstances, the potential for contamination by weathered (argon-deficient) or older (argon-amplified) material was very real, and often realized. A single fragment of Precambrian feldspar from a bit of wall rock caught up in a Pliocene eruption would contribute enough ⁴⁰Ar to seriously distort the age-signal from a thousand crystals of authigenic sanidine. A third potential source of error lies in compositional inhomogeneity of the phenocrysts themselves—in cases where the core portions of the mineral are isotopically older than the later phases—formed just before eruption. A fourth source of error is abnormalities in the isotopic ratios of ³⁶Ar and ⁴⁰K, which have been reported in some older rocks with complex thermal histories.

STEP-HEATING

Differences in lattice chemistry of minerals, including even small changes in the relative proportions within the same mineral, affect the temperature at which argon can escape. In minerals with zones of hydrothermally altered or weathered material in which argon leakage has reduced the apparent age, heating a sample in increments up to final fusion releases argon from the younger, lower-temperature phases before the older, less altered phases. Step-heating can, in theory, also separate the eruption age, recorded in the outermost zone of a phenocryst, from a significantly older core age and can isolate the geochronometric "noise" of older contaminant minerals. It cannot, however, distinguish mixed ages (i.e., as the result of partial thermal overprinting) in a compositionally uniform sample, since all argon would be released at the same temperature.

³⁹Ar/⁴⁰Ar Dating

This technique, now almost universally applied, irradiates samples with carefully metered neutron emissions at energies designed to convert a controlled percentage of the common ³⁹K isotope to ³⁹Ar, a relatively short-lived isotope that no longer exists in nature. In this way, the age of the sample can be calculated on a single extract of argon gas, in which ³⁶Ar gives the atmospheric correction, ³⁹Ar is a function of the potassium content, and ^{40}Ar is a function of the time since the crystal reached isotopic closure. Standard samples of known age and potassium content (usually sanidines from the Miocene Fish Creek Tuff of Nevada) are irradiated at the same time to control for variations in the neutron flux. The $^{39}Ar/^{40}Ar$ method can be combined with step-heating to obtain more precise dates of compositional phases. It offers greater accuracy than K/Ar step-heating, bcause the wet chemical assay of the latter technique gives only the potassium average of the whole sample.

Laser-probe fusion and customized mass spectrometers characterize the most advanced $^{39}Ar/^{40}Ar$ systems, capable of age measurements in suitable minerals as young as 0.1 Ma, even less. The microfocus of laser beams, projected through a transparent vacuum barrier, allows analysis of extremely small samples, often a single crystal. The interior volume of a laser line is orders of magnitude less than a radio frequency (RF) line, making higher vacuums attainable, while hand-picked small samples and crystals are less likely to be affected by contamination. Ultrasensitive mass spectrometers, created solely to measure the nuclides between mass 36 and 40, are required to analyze the microvolumes of gas liberated in this way. Extraordinarily well controlled and precise dating, at the younger limit of argon-isotope dating, is attained by step-heating. The temperature of the sample is gradually raised by incrementally tightening the beam of a defocused laser.

$^{39}Ar/^{40}Ar$ laser total-fusion dating can be highly efficient, since it is possible to automate the travel and firing of a laser across an array of dozens of tiny samples in a precisely machined carrier. Purification, mass spectroscopic analysis, computation, reporting, and purging can also be set to run automatically, even overnight, so that most of the time and effort in dating is loading the samples and checking equipment calibration.

See also Geochronometry; Radiometric Dating; Time Scale. [J.A.V.C.]

Further Readings

Chen, Y., Smith, P.E., Evensen, N.M., York, D., and Lajoie, K.R. (1996) The edge of time: Dating young volcanic ash layers with the ^{40}Ar-^{39}Ar laser probe. Science 274:1176–1178.

Dickin, A.P. (1995) Radiogenic Isotope Geology. Cambridge: Cambridge University Press.

McDougall, I. (1995) Potassium-argon dating in the Pleistocene. In N.W. Rutter and N.R. Catto (eds.): Dating Methods for Quaternary Deposits. St Johns, Newfoundland: Geological Society of Canada, pp. 1–14.

Preadaptation

Existing structure, item of behavior, or physiological process modified via natural selection to perform a new function. Preadaptations are often cited as intermediate stages in the development of complex adaptations (e.g., the evolution of flight in birds through stages of gliding and parachuting from heights).

See also Adaptation(s); Evolution. [N.E.]

Pre-Aurignacian

Pre-Late Paleolithic blade industry from the Levant, defined at Jabrud, Shelter I, in the Anti-Lebanon Mountains of Syria. Along with similar early blade industries from Ksar 'Akil (Lebanon) and possibly from Tabūn (Israel) and Haua Fteah (Libya), the industry is characterized by both Levallois and prismatic blade cores. At Jabrud, the industry also included burins and end-scrapers, including carinate forms that suggest Aurignacian affinities, in contrast to the Early Levantine Mugharan industry (previously known as the Amudian). The pre-Aurignacian is followed at most sites by an Early Paleolithic industry without handaxes, the Jabrudian, and then by several levels of Levalloiso-Mousterian, suggesting an age well in excess of 100 Ka. The appearance and subsequent disappearance of a blade industry contemporary with or preceding the Mousterian was once seen as evidence for a Southwestern Asian origin or at least early presence of modern *Homo sapiens*. New dates of 200 Ka or older for early blade industries at the base of the Mousterian sequence in Israel, however, suggest that blade technologies are not a particularly good indicator of modern humans or "the human revolution" since they predate the earliest modern skeletal remains in this region by ca. 100 Kyr.

See also Africa, North; Amud Cave; Amudian; Asia, Western; Aurignacian; Early Paleolithic; Haua Fteah; Jabrud; Jabrudian; Ksar 'Akil; Late Paleolithic; Levallois; Middle Paleolithic; Mousterian; Stone-Tool Making; Tabūn. [A.S.B.]

Předmostí

Late Paleolithic open-air site or complex of sites covering a few square kilometers, excavated at the beginning of the twentieth century near the city of Přerov in Moravia (Czech Republic). It remains unclear whether these finds came from a single or a multilayered site or whether they belonged to a single site or to multiple sites. Remains uncovered included more than 1,000 mammoths as well as a 4 by 2.5-m oval mass grave of articulated and disarticulated human remains belonging to 29 predominantly subadult individuals. Lithic and bone assemblages from Předmostí have been assigned to a number of Late Paleolithic industries, including the Aurignacian, the Szeletian, and the Pavlovian. The two radiocarbon dates for Předmostí indicate occupation at ca. 26 Ka.

See also Aurignacian; Dolní Věstonice; Europe; Pavlov; Szeletian. [O.S.]

Prehistory

Study of human cultures before writing. In Europe, a distinction is often made between *prehistory*, the study of the vestiges of past cultures in their geological context up to the origins of agriculture, and *archaeology*, the study of Neolithic and later societies in which historical and art-historical skills are used more than geological ones. Also in Europe, the study of cultures that lacked written records but existed on the fringes of literate societies is called *protohistory*. Only in the Western Hemisphere, where native American societies at the time of European contact often represented a direct continuum with the prehistoric past, is the study of prehistory integrally tied to anthropology, or ethnology.

Because prehistorians are almost entirely dependent on archaeological evidence to reconstruct the past, they must be able to extract the maximum amount of information from recovered objects and their geological, geographical, and environmental context. Increasingly, prehistorians must collaborate with physicists, chemists, botanists, zoologists, geologists, and geographers in order to reconstruct the ages of sites, the functions of objects, the sources of raw materials, the environmental setting of sites, and other pieces of the past. In addition to a familiarity with these disciplines, prehistorians must be able to draw on a knowledge of the ethnographic record.

See also Archaeology; Ethnoarchaeology; Geochronometry; Paleobiology; Paleoenvironment; Pollen Analysis; Raw Materials. [A.S.B.]

Further Readings

Daniel, G. (1964) The Idea of Prehistory. London: Pelican.
Daniel, G. (1967) The Origins and Growth of Archaeology. New York: Crowell.
Thomas, D.H. (1998) Archaeology. 3rd ed. Fort Worth: Harcourt Brace College Publishers.

Preneanderthal

Evolutionary scheme postulating that early and relatively unspecialized (generalized) Neanderthals could have been the common ancestors of both "classic" Neanderthals and modern humans. Such workers as S. Sergi, E. Breitinger, F.C. Howell, and W.E. Le Gros Clark were adherents of this scheme in the 1950s and 1960s. European specimens such as Steinheim (Germany), Swanscombe (England), and Ehringsdorf (Germany) were seen as representative of the preneanderthal group, and in Southwest Asia the Tabūn and Skhūl fossils from Mount Carmel (Israel) were believed to occupy a comparable position. The model has lost favor though, as opinions have become polarized about the phylogenetic position of the Neanderthals. Researchers now tend to see either late Neanderthals themselves or no members of the Neanderthal lineage at all as direct ancestors of modern humans. In addition, the dating and interpretation of the Mount Carmel fossils has considerably altered in recent years.

See also Modern Human Origins; Neanderthals; Skhūl; Steinheim; Swanscombe; Tabūn. [C.B.S.]

Prepared-Core

Technique of stone-tool manufacture in which the core is preformed to a shape suitable for the manufacture of a flake or flakes with a specific form. As stone technologies became more complex, the preparation of stone became more deliberate and refined: Cores were skillfully *prepared*, or flaked to a predetermined shape that would yield flakes or blades of a predictable size and shape.

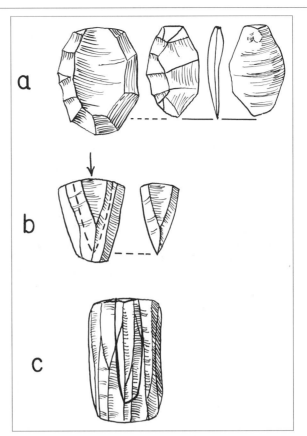

Three examples of prepared-core technique: (a) Levallois tortoise core (left) and the Levallois flake; (b) a Levallois point core (left) and the flake produced; (c) a blade core.

The earliest examples of prepared cores are the *Levallois* cores (and cruder, less standardized prepared cores often called *proto-Levallois*) of the Acheulean and Mousterian periods, in which a large flake was typically removed from one face of a bifacially worked (often disk-shaped) core form. Well-known examples of such early prepared cores include the Acheulean *Victoria West* industries of the Vaal River Valley in southern Africa with their circular and more pointed *hendebech* (hen's-beak) cores from which ovalshaped flakes were detached. From the Middle Pleistocene site of Kapthurin in the Baringo area of Kenya both Levallois cores and simple blade cores were recovered.

The classic Levallois, or *tortoise*, cores of the later Acheulean and Mousterian/Middle Stone Age of the Old World, producing symmetrical oval flakes, are characterized by radial preparation of a flattened dorsal surface and careful preparation (faceting) of the striking platform to achieve the ideal edge angle and contour to detach a relatively large, sharp flake. Such flakes ideally are thin and have a sharp, acute edge around most of their circumference, except for the platform, since, due to the core preparation, the flake intersects the flat, upper surface of the core. This contrasts with the contemporaneous *discoidal-core* technique, in which several flakes were struck from a bifacially worked, disk-shaped core, usually without elaborate platform preparation.

In northern Africa, at such sites as Tabelbala and Tachengit (Algeria), some Acheulean assemblages display an unusual prepared-core technique in which cleaverlike flakes were detached from large cores (*Tachengit technique*). And at some Acheulean sites in Africa, a large flake was detached from a boulder, and subsequently another large flake detached from the first flake, producing a flake blank with a bulb of percussion on *both* faces, the Kombewa, or *Janus*, flakes.

A sophisticated example of the prepared-core technique is evident in the production of Levallois points, in which intersecting scars on the core predetermined the shape of the final flake, a sharp point that may have been hafted to a spear. Such points are characteristic of the Middle Paleolithic. The blade cores of the Late Paleolithic and later periods are generally prepared to a cylindrical or prismatic shape for the production of a series of long, parallel-sided blades and also often involved careful preparation of striking platforms to maintain correct edge angles.

See also Acheulean; Blade; Cleaver; Core; Flake; Levallois; Middle Paleolithic; Middle Stone Age; Mousterian; Paleolithic; Stone-Tool Making. [N.T., K.S.]

Further Readings

Bordaz, J. (1970) Tools of the Old and New Stone Age. Garden City, N.Y.: Natural History Press.

Bordes, F. (1970) The Old Stone Age. New York: McGraw-Hill.

Clark, J.D. (1970) The Prehistory of Africa. London: Thames and Hudson.

Dibble, H.L., and Bar-Yosef, O. (1996) The Definition and Interpretation of Levallois Technology (Monographs in World Archaeology No. 23). Madison: Prehistory Press.

Isaac, G.L. (1982) The earliest archaeological traces. In J.D. Clark (ed.): The Cambridge History of Africa, Vol. 1: From the Earliest Times to c. 500 BC. Cambridge: Cambridge University Press, pp. 157–247.

Schick, K., and Toth, N. (1993) Making Silent Stones Speak: Hominid Evolution and the Dawn of Technology. New York: Simon and Schuster.

Presapiens

Term most clearly associated with the evolutionary scheme favored by the French paleoanthropologists M. Boule and H.V. Vallois. In their view, the European fossil hominin sequence recorded the separate evolution of the Neanderthal and the modern human lineages, with Swanscombe and, later, Fontéchevade representing ancient members of the presapiens lineage leading to modern humans. More recent research, by contrast, emphasizes the local, Neanderthal, affinities of these supposed presapiens fossils.

See also Archaic Homo sapiens; Boule, [Pierre] Marcellin; Fontéchevade; Neanderthals; Swanscombe; Vallois, Henri Victor. [C.B.S.]

Further Readings

Stringer, C.B. (1994) Out of Africa: A Personal History. In M. Nitecki and D.V. Nitecki (eds.): Origins of Anatomically Modern Humans. New York: Plenum, pp. 149–172.

Stringer, C.B., Hublin, J.-J., and Vandermeersch, B. (1984) The Origin of Anatomically Modern Humans in Western Europe. In F.H. Smith and F. Spencer (eds.): The Origins of Modern Humans. New York: Liss, pp. 51–135.

Přezletice

Open-air locality with four superimposed strata of Middle Pleistocene paleosols, lacustrine marls, and sands situated ca. 20 km northeast of Prague (the Czech Republic). At the time of deposition, this locality was on the shores of a lake close to the mouth of a small river. Numerous diverse animal remains from these strata are assigned to the Biharian complex. Archaeological inventories, including stone tools made of quartz and lydite, bone tools, worked bone, flecks of wood charcoal, and burned stone and bone fragments, were predominantly not *in situ*. The lithic assemblage, which includes both large and small tools and consists of some 335 pieces, has been assigned to the Preletician industry, a local variant of the proto-Acheulean. Faunal and floral remains indicate occupation during the Cromerian interglacial. A tooth fragment originally identified as human has been reassessed as nonprimate.

See also Acheulean; Early Paleolithic; Europe; Stranská Skála. [O.S.]

Primate Ecology

Study of interactions between primates and their environments. The natural environments of the great majority of living primates are the wooded regions of the tropics and subtropics in Central and South America, Africa (including Madagascar), and Asia. The largest number of primate species occurs in rain forests, vegetation that grows close to the equator in regions where annual rainfall is at least 1,500 mm and where no more than four consecutive months have less than 100 mm of rain. Tropical rain forests are dominated by tall broad-leaved trees, many of them evergreens, whose trunks and branches form a nearly continuous network above the ground. Tying many of the tree crowns together are woody stemmed lianas, the typical climbing plants of the rain forest. The diversity of species of plants and animals in the tropical rain forest is greater than in any other terrestrial environment, and in some West African areas as many as 15 primate species (including strepsirhines, cercopithecid monkeys, and great apes) may co-occur.

Away from the equator, where rainfall is lower and dry seasons more prolonged, tropical deciduous forests and savannah woodlands occur. These are also important primate habitats, but, in most cases, the number of species that live in them is much lower than in the rain forest. Here trees are generally smaller, are spaced farther apart, and frequently shed their foliage during dry periods. Continuous overhead pathways are rare, and primates, such as baboons (*Papio* sspp.), typically spend considerable periods of time on the ground. In savannah habitats, water is in relatively short supply, and its availability often affects the distribution of primates. In areas of low rainfall in the tropics, primates are usually absent, and, with the exception of humans and some macaques, few species of living primate have a significant part of their distribution within the temperate zone.

Since research on nonhuman primates is often undertaken either implicitly or explicitly to gain insights on human evolution and behavior, primate ecology has tended to concentrate on questions different from those pursued in the mainstream of ecological science. Although some primate ecologists have come from a biological background, many have been trained as anthropologists, psychologists, or anatomists, and this has led to a concentration on such topics as social and locomotor behavior. Primate ecology has also been influenced by the location of many study populations, remote from the temperate areas where the discipline of ecology (and many ecologists) has grown up. Not only has this tended to put primate ecology beyond the immediate view of the majority of ecologists, it has also limited the appeal of the subject to a relatively small number of people willing and able to work under unusual conditions. Remoteness from civilization and the nature of the animals have also limited the kinds of study techniques that can be used. Forest primates, in particular, are hard to capture without injury, and many field studies have, therefore, relied entirely on observational techniques. The most important piece of equipment in such field studies is a pair of binoculars.

The first scientific field studies of primates began in the late 1920s and early 1930s, sponsored by R.M. Yerkes, professor of psychobiology at Yale University. In 1931, one of Yerkes' research fellows, C.R. Carpenter, initiated studies on the population of howler monkeys (*Alouatta palliata*) on Barro Colorado Island in the Panama Canal, studies that have continued, with some interruptions, to the present day. A major surge in field studies began in the late 1950s, and in the next 25 years at least one population of most species came under scrutiny.

Although some progress has been made in understanding the dynamics of wild primate populations, the structure and functioning of primate communities, and foraging strategies (issues in the mainstream of ecology), most attention has focused on the ecological determinants of social organization. The evidence accumulated to date (1999) suggests that the distribution and abundance of food and the kinds and densities of predators are the environmental factors that have the most significant influence on the organization of primate societies.

Field studies have led to an awareness that nonhuman primates are of interest not only because of their close relationship to *Homo sapiens*, but also because they are a significant component of many of the ecosystems they inhabit. When not subjected to heavy pressure by human hunters, they are among the most numerous mammals in some tropical forests, particularly in Africa, where they can achieve a biomass (weight per unit area) approaching that of savannah ungulates. As medium-to-large-size consumers that are adept at arboreal life, have a broad range of more or less omnivorous diets, and are typically both long-lived and social (with low reproductive rates), primates occupy a special set of ecological niches and influence the functioning of rain-forest ecosystems in many ways.

Responding over millions of years to the pressures imposed by primates and other animals feeding upon them, some rain-forest trees and lianas have evolved flowers that may be pollinated by primates. Others have evolved fruits that attract primates; after digesting the pulp of these fruits, primates may unwittingly drop the seeds undamaged at opportune germination sites. Many plants have evolved mechanical and chemical defenses against animal depredations, and foraging primates must cope with this array of defenses as they search for food. Primate ecologists have only recently begun to unravel these complex systems of interaction between rain-forest primates and their food supply. Along with other fascinating problems presented by rain-forest ecosystems, these interactions may never be fully understood if present rates of forest destruction continue. The rapidity with which expanding human populations and consumer economies are destroying tropical forests and their primate populations is leading many primate ecologists to become increasingly involved in conservation efforts.

See also Diet; Ecology; Population; Primate Societies. [J.F.O.]

Further Readings

Bourlière, F. (1983) Primate communities: Their structure and role in tropical ecosystems. Int. J. Primatol. 6:1–26.

Chivers, D.J., Wood, B.A., and Bilsborough, A., eds. (1984) Food Acquisition and Processing in Primates. New York: Plenum.

Clutton-Brock, T.H., ed. (1977) Primate Ecology: Studies of Feeding and Ranging Behaviour in Lemurs, Monkeys, and Apes. London: Academic.

Milton, K. (1993) Diet and primate evolution. Sci. Am. 269:86–93.

Richard, A.F. (1985) Primates in Nature. New York: Freeman.

Terborgh, J. (1983) Five New World Primates: A Study in Comparative Ecology. Princeton: Princeton University Press.

Primate Societies

Primates, including humans, are social animals. When encountered in the wild, most primates are not alone. Instead, they are frequently in close proximity to other members of the same species. If one follows such a group for some time, it usually becomes apparent that it is not a transient phenomenon. Rather, it is a relatively stable, cooperative structure, whose members know each other well, have most of their nonaggressive social interactions with each other, and usually move in a synchronized fashion within the same limited geographical area (their home range). Members of one social group often behave aggressively toward members of another.

Although a primate social group typically contains individuals of both sexes and all ages, the actual size and composition of groups vary tremendously. Groups of monogamous primates, such as gibbons (*Hylobates*) and owl monkeys (*Aotus*), consist of a mated pair of adults together with a small

Some primates, such as this female black lemur (above), rarely leave the trees; others, such as this group of savannah baboons (below), range widely on the ground.

number of immature offspring. Many forest-living monkeys in Africa and Asia live in harem (or one-male) groups, which contain only a single fully adult male, several females (often three to eight but sometimes more), and the females' immature offspring; gorillas (*Gorilla gorilla*) also typically live in small harems. Groups of many species of baboon (*Papio*) and macaque (*Macaca*) are often large; groups of 30–40 are common, with several adult males and many females; occasionally, baboon groups number more than 100 individuals. Similar large multimale groups occur in some rain-forest primates, such as the squirrel monkeys (*Saimiri*) of Central and South America and the red colobus monkeys (*Procolobus badius*) of Africa.

While primate societies normally consist of one or another of these broad categories of social group, some do not. Chimpanzees (*Pan troglodytes*) and spider monkeys (*Ateles*) live in loosely coherent communities in which individuals may spend much time on their own or with just small subsets of their social network. Members of the community, however, do share a common home range and are familiar with each other. Gelada baboons (*Theropithecus gelada*) of the high-altitude grasslands of Ethiopia are organized into harem groups, but these groups share their range with many others, forming a band whose members often feed together. Individuals of the orangutan (*Pongo pygmaeus*) and of several species of small, nocturnal lorises and lemurs typically move and feed on their own yet belong to a local network of familiar individuals. Although galagos in such a network may forage on their own, they often share a sleeping nest with other individuals.

Not only do primate social groups vary greatly in size and structure, they also vary in the patterns of interaction that occur between individuals and in the patterns of migration in and out of groups. Social interactions, which involve communicative acts, are generally classed as *affiliative* (friendly or cooperative) or *agonistic* (competitive). Any one communicative act may involve a combination of visual signals, sounds, smells, or touch. Smell (olfactory communication) is used especially by lorises and lemurs, while loud long-range calls are particularly important in the signal repertoire of rain-forest monkeys and apes, which live in an environment whose vegetation interferes with long-range visual communication. Many affiliative interactions involve touch, of which grooming, in which one animal cleans the coat of another with its hands or mouth, is especially important.

In many primate societies, males leave the group in which they are born, while females stay in their natal group. Affiliative interactions, leading to the formation of close social bonds, are particularly common between animals that have grown up together. As a result, many primate groups have a social core of closely bonded female relatives. In these female-bonded primates, males will often compete with each other for the opportunity of mating with the females. In harem groups, this may lead to aggressive takeovers of whole groups by males migrating in from outside. These males may attack young infants. In a few non-female-bonded groups, especially those of chimpanzees and red colobus monkeys, females transfer out of their natal groups as they mature, and most social cooperation occurs between bonded males.

Grooming is an important component of the social behavior of these Mayotte lemurs (above); the dominant male of a group of Mauritian long-tailed macaques threatens an intruder (below).

In multimale groups (and especially in baboons and macaques), competition typically takes the form of dominance interactions, in which animals displace or give way to others (without overt aggression) on the basis of the outcome of previous interactions. Such dominance relationships, found in both males and females, have considerable stability and allow group members to be ranked in a linear hierarchy.

One of the major goals of those studying primate societies has been to explain these patterns of variation. Available evidence strongly suggests that much of the variation is the result of different phylogenetic inheritances (e.g., the size, structure, and functional features of a galago vs. those of a gorilla) interacting with a range of different environments. In any one environment, two of the most crucial sets of variables affecting social organization are the distribution and abundance of food and the risk of predation. Thus, a small-bodied forest-living nocturnal galago is not a conspicuous target for a predator, and by moving around with other galagos it may not be able to reduce significantly its risk of being preyed upon. On the other hand, insects (one of its main foods) are thinly scattered through its environment and searching for them in the company of other galagos would probably result in frequent competition over the same items. By contrast, day-active squirrel monkeys in the forests of Amazonia are obvious targets for visually hunting eagles, while one of their preferred foods (ripe figs) occurs in large aggregations when giant trees are in fruit. By moving about in large groups, squirrel monkeys may reduce their risk of predation without significantly lowering their feeding efficiency.

The distribution and clumping patterns of primate foods are thought to exert profound influences on social organization. Highly clumped foods, occurring in patches in which only one or a few primates can feed at one time, are likely to promote within-group *contest* competition and the establishment of the distinct dominance hierarchies exhibited by many baboon and macaque societies. Patches that are usually large relative to group size will produce a less direct *scramble* form of competition and more equable social relationships, as seen in some squirrel monkey and colobine societies.

Primate body size and mode of locomotion interact with food distribution to influence social organization, through their effect on the number of individuals that can efficiently move and feed as a unit. The food requirements of a single gorilla militate against large numbers of gorillas traveling together. However, the gorilla's staple food, the succulent stems and foliage of low-growing plants, occurs in denser patches than do the ripe tree fruits on which the closely related chimpanzee feeds. One tree crown can provide adequate food for far fewer chimpanzees (adult female weight 40 kg) than squirrel monkeys (adult female weight 0.6 kg), and this, combined with a chimpanzee's ability to cover long distances quite rapidly on the ground, probably explains the fission-fusion nature of chimpanzee society.

Finally, the number of adult males in a group seems to be closely related to the number of breeding females in a group and to the ability of a single male to monopolize them. Above a threshold determined not only by the total number of females but also by their dispersion and their reproductive synchrony, it can become uneconomic for a male to defend the females against all other males; then, a multimale group is likely to form. Once a multimale group exists, it may pay males to cooperate (especially with relatives) in warding off predators or competing primates (especially other males).

See also Ape; Diet; Locomotion; Monkey; Primate Ecology; Primates; Sexual Dimorphism; Sociobiology. [J.F.O.]

Further Readings

Cheney, D.L., and Seyfarth, R.M. (1990) How Monkeys See the World: Inside the Mind of Another Species. Chicago: University of Chicago Press.

Jolly, A. (1985) The Evolution of Primate Behavior, 2nd ed. New York: Macmillan.

Smuts, B.B., Cheney, D.L., Seyfarth, R.M., Wrangham, R.W., and Struhsaker, T.T., eds. (1987) Primate Societies. Chicago: University of Chicago Press.

Terborgh, J., and Janson, C.H. (1986) The socioecology of primate groups. Ann. Rev. Ecol. Syst. 17:111–135.

Van Schaik, C.P. (1989) The ecology of social relationships among female primates. In V. Standen and R. Foley (eds.): Comparative Socioecology: The Behavioural Ecology of Humans and Other Mammals. Oxford: Blackwell, pp. 195–218.

Primates

Order of mammals to which human beings and ca. 200 other living species belong. Classification of the group is not entirely settled; for example, all currently accepted classifications divide the living primates into two major groups (suborders), but zoologists differ as to whether *Tarsius,* the tarsier, should be classified with the lower primates (lemurs, lorises, bushbabies) in the suborder Prosimii or with the higher primates (New and Old World monkeys, apes, humans) in the suborder Haplorhini. In the classification adopted for this encyclopedia, the latter arrangement is provisionally preferred. As in the case of any other natural group, what essentially unites the primates is their common phylogenetic origin: All primates are descended from a single ancestor. Since evolution involves change, and Primates (spelled with a capital P and pronounced "pri-MAY-tees" only when used as a proper noun) has diversified considerably from that ancestor, we would not expect that this common origin would necessarily be reflected in the possession of a suite of diagnostic features by all members of the order. This turns out to be the case, at least in features that are observable in the fossil record, and it is probably for this reason that, following W.E. Le Gros Clark, recent students of Primates have generally characterized the order on the basis of several progressive evolutionary trends. Among these are the dominance of the visual over the olfactory sense, with the associated reduction of the olfactory apparatus and elaboration of stereoscopic vision; the improvement of grasping and manipulative capacities; and the tendency to enlarge the higher centers of the brain. Among those primates extant today, the lower primates more closely resemble forms that evolved early in the history of the order, while the higher primates belong to groups more lately evolved.

Trends, however, are of little use in providing a morphological definition of Primates with which the attributes of potential members of the order might be compared. Thus, R.D. Martin has recently reinvestigated this problem, finding that a number of universal or near-universal features do, indeed, demarcate living primates from all other placental mammals. Unfortunately near-universality is more generally the rule than universality, and such features cannot be

Representative living higher primates. Clockwise from upper left: tamarin (Saguinus; *Callitrichinae*); *spider monkey* (Ateles, *Atelinae*); *orangutan* (Pongo, *Ponginae*); *colobus* (Colobus, *Colobinae*); *chimpanzee* (Pan, *Homininae*); *human* (Homo, *Homininae*); *saki* (Pithecia, *Pitheciinae*); *macaque* (Macaca, *Cercopithecinae*). Not to scale; by D. McGranaghan. For lower primates, see illustrations in* STREPSIRHINI *and* TARSIIFORMES.

used in a rigid morphological definition, even (or especially) when such definition is based, as it must be, on an aggregation of animals already defined as Primates. Moreover, characteristics that do, indeed, definitively demarcate primates from other placentals, such as the possession of a brain that constitutes a significantly larger proportion of body weight at all stages of gestation, are impossible to apply to the fossil record, which is where the questions actually lie; for, follow-

ing the expulsion in the 1970s of the treeshrews from Primates, there has been no doubt about which members of the living fauna belong to Primates and which do not.

There is similarly no question about which typical Eocene (55–34 Ma) and later fossil forms are to be allocated to Primates, since by this epoch "primates of modern aspect" are present in the fossil record, and their aspect is modern enough to allay any doubts as to their phylogenetic affinities.

Skeletons of selected fossil primates. (a) Plesiadapis tricuspidens *(Plesiadapidae); (b)* Smilodectes gracilis *(Notharctidae); (c)* Propliopithecus
(= Aegyptopithecus*)* zeuxis *(Propliopithecidae); (d)* Proconsul heseloni *(Proconsulidae); (e)* Pliopithecus vindobonensis *(Pliopithecidae); (f)*
Mesopithecus pentelicus *(Cercopithecidae); (g)* Australopithecus afarensis *(Hominidae). Not to scale; by D. McGranaghan.*

The earliest primates, however, do pose a problem, and opinions have varied about whether the primates of the Paleocene epoch (ca. 65–55 Ma) should, indeed, be admitted to the order. This is because these forms are both adaptively different from, and have no direct evolutionary links with, any living representatives of the order; to express this, they are placed in their own primate semiorder, Plesiadapiformes. The plesiadapiforms are recognized as primates because of resemblances to later members of the order in their chewing teeth and locomotor anatomy; these serve quite convincingly to demonstrate the common origin of the two groups, which probably took place toward the end of the Cretaceous period, sometime more than 70–65 Ma. Found in both the Old and the New Worlds, the plesiadapiforms retained clawed hands and feet, possessed large, specialized front teeth, and were probably arboreal in habit. An alternative interpretation is that the plesiadapiforms are more closely related to the living dermopterans, or "flying lemurs," a group of Southeast Asian gliding mammals. This implies recognition of a supraordinal taxon Archonta, which would group treeshrews, dermopterans, and perhaps bats with primates (*see* ARCHONTA; CARPOLESTIDAE; EUPRIMATES; FLYING-PRIMATE HYPOTHESIS; PALEOCENE; PAROMOMYIDAE; PAROMOMYOIDEA; PICRODONTIDAE; PLESIADAPIDAE; PLESIADAPIFORMES; PLESIADAPOIDEA; SAXONELLIDAE).

Euprimates

No known plesiadapiform is a satisfactory candidate for the ancestry of the fossil "primates of modern aspect" or euprimates typical of the Eocene epoch. These later primates are grouped broadly into *lemurlike* forms, usually classified in the superfamily Adapoidea (*see* ADAPIDAE; ADAPIFORMES; EOCENE; NOTHARCTIDAE) and *tarsierlike* forms, generally classed as omomyids (*see* ANAPTOMORPHINAE; EOCENE; MICROCHOERINAE; OMOMYIDAE; OMOMYINAE), although this elementary division may ultimately prove to be oversimplified. Eocene primates from both the New World and the Old World already exhibit the trends noted above that mark modern primates as a whole. These arboreal creatures possessed grasping hands and feet in which sharp claws were replaced by flat nails backing sensitive pads; the face was reduced in response to a deemphasis of the sense of smell; the eyes were completely ringed by bone and faced forward, producing wide overlap of the visual fields (hence, stereoscopic vision) and suggesting a primary reliance on the sense of vision; and the brain was enlarged relative to body size when compared with other mammals of the time.

It is possible that the origins of some modern lower primates may be traced back to or through certain Eocene primate genera known in the fossil record. In any event, it is widely accepted that the antecedents of the living primates are to be sought somewhere within the Eocene primate radiation, even where the details of this ancestry remain unclear. In North America, the descendants of the Eocene primates gradually disappeared following the close of the epoch, while virtually all fossil lower primates from later epochs in Africa and Asia are quite closely related to the modern primates of those areas (*see* GALAGIDAE), except for *Afrotarsius* from the Fayum (Egypt) and possibly for a fragmentary strepsirhine recently found there. The bulk of living strepsirhine primates, known as the lemurs, survive in Madagascar. Since the recent (less than 1.5 Ka) arrival of humans in that island, many of the Malagasy primates have become extinct, notably the large-bodied climber-hanger *Palaeopropithecus,* the koalalike but huge *Megaladapis,* and the baboonlike *Archaeolemur* (*see* ARCHAEOLEMURIDAE; LEPILEMURIDAE; PALAEOPROPITHECIDAE). Extant Malagasy primates are grouped into five families (*see* CHEIROGALEIDAE; DAUBENTONIIDAE; INDRIIDAE; LEMURIDAE; LEPILEMURIDAE). Other living strepsirhines include the lorises of Asia and Africa (*see* LORISIDAE) and the bushbabies of Africa (*see* GALAGIDAE). All extant strepsirhines possess dental scrapers or tooth combs (*see* LEMURIFORMES; TEETH), and all retain the primitive mammalian external nose, with a moist, naked rhinarium and associated structures. Additionally, all are united by possessing a toilet (grooming) claw on the second digit of the foot (*see*

LEMURIFORMES; STREPSIRHINI). All strepsirhines possess grasping extremities, although their manual dexterity is generally inferior to that of the higher primates, in comparison with which their brains also tend to be relatively small.

Anthropoidea

The higher, or anthropoid, primates today are the dominant forms in all areas other than Madagascar. Their ultimate ancestry is obscure, but most researchers agree that it probably can be traced back toward the omomyid group of Eocene species. Of the living primates, tarsiers are commonly regarded as closest to anthropoids in details of nasal structure and placentation, the partial rear closure of the orbit, and the bony ear. In turn, some omomyids share dental, cranial, and postcranial structures with tarsiers, and some of the less extreme forms preserve incisor teeth that foreshadow the pattern characteristic of ancestral anthropoids (*see* EOSIMIIDAE; HAPLORHINI; TARSIIDAE; TARSIIFORMES).

Opinion varies more widely on the paleogeographic wanderings of early anthropoids, with two main views current: (1) a broadly protoanthropoid stock of omomyids was distributed in western North America and eastern Asia (where a later Paleocene species has recently been recognized), which diverged by the Early Eocene into two southward-expanding lineages: one entered South America to evolve into the platyrrhine New World monkeys, while the other spread across Eurasia into Africa as the ancestral catarrhines; or (2) a Eurasian protoanthropoid stock entered Africa by the Middle Eocene, where it divided into early catarrhines and a platyrrhine ancestor that rafted or island-hopped across the South Atlantic to reach the neotropics. A third alternative has been proposed in which a poorly known group of protoanthropoids (represented by new finds in Africa and/or Asia) was long distinct from both widespread Eocene taxa and gave rise to the modern lineages in an as yet unknown region. Each hypothesis has both morphological and paleogeographical problems to answer before one can be firmly accepted as more likely, but there is broad agreement on the monophyly of Anthropoidea if not on the date or place of divergence of the two infraordinal clades (*see* ANTHROPOIDEA; CATARRHINI; PALEOBIOGEOGRAPHY; PLATE TECTONICS; PLATYRRHINI).

The platyrrhines include two major divisions in most classifications, but not all researchers agree on the contents of these groups. Here, two families are accepted: the generally small-bodied Cebidae, with a lightly built masticatory system; and the mainly medium- to large-size Atelidae, with more robust jaws and teeth. Early members of both families are known by ca. 20 Ma, and most fossils can be closely linked to living genera. This pattern of *bathyphyly,* the long extension of evolutionary lineages, is a characteristic of the platyrrhines in strong opposition to the more bushy pattern of successive radiations seen in the catarrhines (*see* ATELIDAE; ATELINAE; ATELOIDEA; CALLITRICHINAE; CEBIDAE; CEBINAE; MONKEY; PITHECIINAE).

Living catarrhines are readily divided into the Cercopithecoidea (Old World monkeys) and the Hominoidea (lesser apes, great apes, and humans), but that distinction is not so easy to trace back into the past. Cercopithecoid monkeys are characterized by a bilophodont dentition and general skeletal adaptation to quadrupedal life on or near the ground, while hominoids share less derived teeth, a trend to larger brain and body size, and a complex of postcranial features emphasizing forelimb flexibility and suspension.

The earliest Old World anthropoid was once thought to be the later Eocene Burmese *Pondaungia,* but competition for this distinction has increased through the 1990s in the form of several equally poorly known taxa from North Africa and China. More definite are the latest Eocene and Early Oligocene (ca. 36–33 Ma) primates from the Fayum deposits of northern Egypt. *Catopithecus,* an oligopithecid from the latest Eocene horizon, has been shown to have at least a partially closed-off orbit, although it lacks symphyseal fusion and an anthropoid-like dentition. The family Parapithecidae includes species that share few features in common with living catarrhines but have a number of derived characters of their own. They may be considered either archaic members of this infraorder, little changed from its common ancestor, or more likely ancient anthropoids antedating the platyrrhine-catarrhine divergence. The Early Oligocene propliopithecids have reduced the number of their premolar teeth to the two seen in living catarrhines and have a more modern postcranial skeleton but still retain a conservative auditory region. It seems likely that they were similar to the common ancestor of the cercopithecoids and hominoids (*see* ANTHROPOIDEA; FAYUM; OLIGOCENE; OLIGOPITHECIDAE; PARAPITHECIDAE; PONDAUNG; PROPLIOPITHECIDAE).

Four main higher-primate groups existed in the Old World Miocene: the conservative pliopithecids of Europe and Asia, in many ways similar to the earlier propliopithecids; the African (and Asian) *Dendropithecus* and allies, which were slightly more derived postcranially; early cercopithecoids, known after ca. 19 Ma; and hominoids, first seen in the latest Oligocene, ca. 26 Ma. The third group apparently diverged from a dentally hominoid arboreal ancestor as a partially ground-dwelling lineage with a diet including more leaves and seeds than the mainly frugivorous hominoids. Although not common in the Early or Middle Miocene, Old World monkeys spread into Eurasia in the Late Miocene and possibly replaced most hominoids there as the climate deteriorated and forests shrank. The Colobinae retained conservative catarrhine facial proportions but adapted to a diet concentrating on leaves by increasing tooth relief and sharpness and developing a sacculated stomach for better digestion of cellulose. Most living species are arboreal, but two Pliocene lineages became highly terrestrial. Cercopithecines retained mainly conservative teeth and an eclectic diet but often developed elongated faces and, in a variety of lineages, a high degree of terrestriality (*see* CERCOPITHECIDAE; CERCOPITHECINAE; CERCOPITHECOIDEA; COLOBINAE; MIOCENE; PLIOCENE; PLIOPITHECIDAE; VICTORIAPITHECINAE).

Hominoidea

The last main group of Miocene catarrhines included the earliest members of the Hominoidea, especially the species of *Proconsul,* but perhaps also such other genera as *Kamoyapithecus* and *Rangwapithecus.* Known from 23 to 14 Ma, *Proconsul* was a quadrupedal frugivore that apparently shared a number of derived postcranial features with later apes. The classification of the Hominoidea varies widely among authors, but here three families are recognized: one for these early African forms; a second (Hylobatidae) for the gibbons and relatives, whose ancestry is not clear; and a third (Hominidae) for the great apes, humans, and extinct relatives. Middle and later Miocene African hominids are relatively rare, although several new forms have recently been discovered. *Afropithecus, Kenyapithecus,* and probably *Otavipithecus* are among the earliest members of this clade (known between 20? and 13? Ma), grouped here in the Kenyapithecinae.

Hominids (and pliopithecids) were able to enter Eurasia from Africa (probably via Arabia and western Asia) ca. 16 Ma, and at least four separate sublineages can be recognized until 8 Ma. *Griphopithecus,* known between 16 and 13 Ma in central Europe and Turkey, was a kenyapithecine. A more derived lineage apparently related to the living orangutan was represented in Turkey, Indo-Pakistan, and perhaps China mainly between 12 and 7 Ma. These species are commonly assigned to *Ankarapithecus* and *Sivapithecus,* although some members were previously separated as *Ramapithecus;* they share a number of facial synapomorphies with *Pongo,* but their limb bones are either more conservative or secondarily adapted to partly terrestrial life. *Gigantopithecus* was probably a very large member of this clade (Ponginae) known from a few 7 Ma specimens in Indo-Pakistan and many more from Pleistocene sites in China and Vietnam. Fossil hylobatids are also known from the latter time period onward, but it has not yet been possible to identify any older fossil as gibbonlike, because the living forms are characterized not only by generally conservative crania and dentition but also by a highly derived hominoid postcranium linked to their ricochetal brachiating adaptation.

The European genus *Dryopithecus* has been known the longest, but only recently have its crania been recovered. Along with relatively modern limb elements, these remains suggest a phyletic position more derived than the kenyapithecines but without the derived orangutan features of the Ponginae. *Dryopithecus* has been found across Europe at sites estimated to date between 13 and 10 Ma, and fragmentary fossils from China and India have also been tentatively referred here. The previously enigmatic *Oreopithecus* (from a few Italian localities dated ca. 8–7 Ma) is dentally specialized but postcranially most similar to *Dryopithecus.* These two could be sister taxa, but here each is placed in a separate subfamily. The final hominid clade, Homininae (African apes and humans), may be represented by *Graecopithecus,* known from northern and southern Greece ca. 10–8 Ma. Another member of this clade may be *Samburupithecus,* known by a single maxilla from Kenya (ca. 9.5 Ma).

The relationships among living hominids have not been unequivocally determined from comparative morphology, but, in combination with molecular studies (especially immunology and DNA hybridization and sequencing), one phylogeny has emerged as widely acceptable. Hylobatids are seen as strongly distinct from the hominids, implying a rather ancient divergence, although dates provided by *molecular clock* hypotheses are questionable. *Pongo,* the orangutan, is distinct from the African apes and humans; the subfamily

Ponginae is here recognized for the orang and its fossil relatives, as opposed to the Homininae. Views differ as to which was the first lineage to diverge among the hominines, with most molecular data placing chimpanzee closest to humans, but morphologists seeing little difference between chimpanzee and gorilla (*see* AFRICA; AFRICA, EAST; ASIA, EASTERN AND SOUTHERN; ASIA, WESTERN; BARINGO BASIN/TUGEN HILLS; DRYOPITHECINAE; EUROPE; HOMINIDAE; HOMININAE; HYLOBATIDAE; KENYAPITHECINAE; MOLECULAR ANTHROPOLOGY; MOLECULAR CLOCK; MOLECULAR "VS." MORPHOLOGICAL APPROACHES TO SYSTEMATICS; PONGINAE; PROCONSULIDAE; SAMBURUPITHECUS; SIWALIKS).

Hominini

Human evolution took place mainly in Africa in the Pliocene and the Early Pleistocene. Species of *Australopithecus,* the first-known bipedal hominine, range from ca. 4.2 to 2.2 Ma. Three species appear to more or less replace one another through this interval and may have eventually given rise to *Homo.* A collateral form may be represented by *Ardipithecus,* from deposits dated to 4.4 Ma in Ethiopia. Between 2.8 and 1.4 Ma, three species of the more "robust" *Paranthropus* are also known. Members of all of these species had large cheek teeth for their body size (means estimated at ca. 50–65 kg) and were omnivores that probably concentrated on vegetable foods. Their brains were large compared with those of great apes of similar body size, but, at 400–530 ml, they fell within the absolute size range of living-ape brains.

Significant brain-size increase is apparently evident for *Homo rudolfensis,* the earliest species placed in the same genus as living humans, and also probably the first stone-tool maker. Most fossils of this species are known from eastern Africa between 2 and 1.7 Ma, but a jaw from the Chiwondo Beds (Malawi) may date as early as 2.4 Ma, only slightly later than the oldest-known Oldowan tools, dated to ca. 2.7–2.5 Ma in Ethiopia. Another early species, *Homo habilis,* is known between 2 and 1.6 Ma in eastern and southern Africa. The earliest *Homo erectus* fossils (sometimes termed *H. ergaster*), at ca. 1.9 Ma, were apparently contemporaneous with both *H. rudolfensis* and *H. habilis,* but they differed in having a larger brain and body size, as well as cranial reorganization. By ca. 800 Ka in Europe and Africa, the fossil record yields specimens that are termed early (or archaic) *Homo sapiens* by some workers and *H. heidelbergensis* and/or *H. antecessor* by others. In turn, this group diversified into various regional sublineages or species (such as the Neanderthals in Europe and western Asia or the "Rhodesians" in sub-Saharan Africa). Eventually, anatomically modern humans evolved, probably in Africa, perhaps as long as ca. 120 Ka, developed a variety of Late Paleolithic tool kits, diverged into major geographic groups ("races"), and spread across the world displacing the other varieties by ca. 30 Ka (*see* ARDIPITHECUS RAMIDUS; AUSTRALOPITHECUS; BRAIN; HOMININI; HOMO; PALEOLITHIC; PARANTHROPUS). [E.D., I.T.]

Further Readings

Fleagle, J.G. (1999) Primate Adaptation and Evolution 2nd ed. San Diego: Academic.

Groves, C.P. (1989) A Theory of Human and Primate Evolution. Oxford: Clarendon.

Martin, R.D. (1990) Primate Origins and Evolution. Princeton: Princeton University Press.

Napier, J.R., and Napier, P.H. (1985) Natural History of the Primates. Cambridge, Mass.: MIT Press.

Shoshani, J., Groves, C.P., Simons, E.L., and Gunnell, G. (1996) Primate phylogeny: Morphological vs. molecular results. Mol. Phylogen. Evol. 5:102–154.

Szalay, F.S., and Delson, E. (1979) Evolutionary History of the Primates. New York: Academic.

Priority

Where different Linnaean names have been applied over the years to the same taxon, the valid name, the one that must be used to refer to that taxon, is the available name that has priority (i.e., that was published first). To be available, a name must have been published in accordance with the requirements of the *International Code of Zoological Nomenclature.* In the context of animal nomenclature, then, priority is seniority of available names as determined by publication date.

See also Classification; Nomenclature; Synonym(y). [I.T.]

Proconsulidae

Family of Early Miocene (and latest Oligocene) hominoids definitively known as yet only from East Africa. The earliest-known radiation of hominoid primates occurred at this time, with a number of closely related species and genera, of which *Proconsul* is the best known. This group produced the highest diversity of hominoids ever achieved at one place and time.

Four or five species are now assigned to the genus *Proconsul,* from such sites as Meswa Bridge, Rusinga Island, Songhor, and Koru (Kenya). The best known of these is *P. heseloni,* from Rusinga (18–17 Ma) and perhaps Fort Ternan (14 Ma), represented by two partial crania, six partial skeletons, and dozens of jaws. Estimates from postcranial elements suggest a body weight of ca. 11 kg (range 8–14 kg, probably reflecting sex dimorphism) for this species, but a somewhat higher value (average 17 kg, range 13–19 kg) has been obtained from dental elements; this has led to the suggestion that *P. heseloni* was somewhat megadont (i.e., had large teeth for its body size, which was comparable to that of a siamang). This form was long termed *P. africanus,* but that species from Koru and Songhor is now seen to differ from the Rusinga population in a number of dental proportions, which led to the latter being given a new name.

Proconsul nyanzae, also from Rusinga, is a larger species known from dentitions, a midface, and less complete skeletal remains. Estimates from postcrania suggest an average body weight of ca. 36 kg (range 26–46 kg), comparable to the size of the smallest chimpanzee varieties. On the other hand, dental estimates indicate lower values, between 22 and 35 kg, suggesting the microdont condition, opposite to that found in *P. heseloni.* Even larger and less well known is *P. major,* from Napak (Uganda), Songhor, and the Koru sites (apparently never found in association with either *P. nyanzae* or

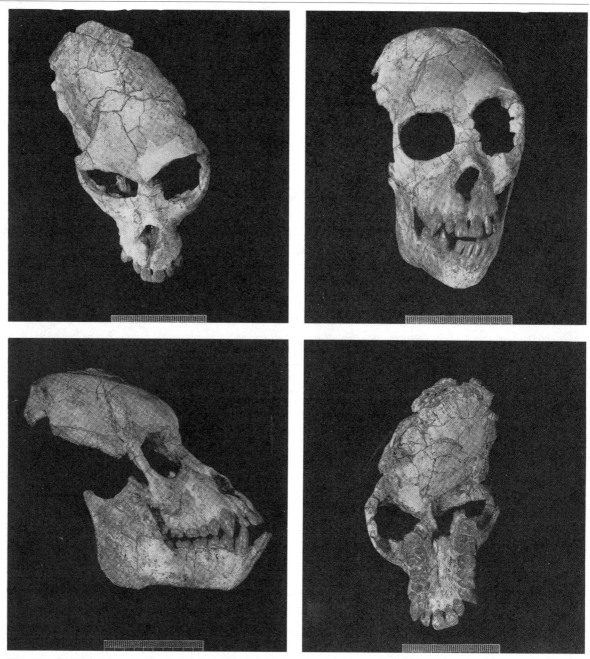

Four views of the Early Miocene Proconsul heseloni *skull found by M.D. Leakey in 1948 on Rusinga Island (Kenya). This is still one of the most complete specimens of a fossil (non-hominin) hominoid ever found. Courtesy of Peter Andrews.*

P. heseloni, but only with *P. africanus*). *P. major* postcrania yield weight estimates of 63–87 kg, in the range of male chimpanzees, orangutans, and gorillas but presumably representing both male and female fossils. Again, this species appears microdont, with dental estimates of body weight only in the 33–62-kg range. Another large form, as yet (1999) unnamed, is known from the earliest Miocene primate site, Meswa Bridge, where it is represented by teeth and a partial juvenile face.

Proconsul species are characterized by a mosaic of morphological features placing them clearly between the archaic catarrhines such as *Propliopithecus* and *Pliopithecus* on the one hand, and modern (or later Miocene) hominoids on the other. In fact, there is some argument as to whether they should be included in Hominoidea or placed with the "*Dendropithecus*-group" before the hominoid-cercopithecoid divergence. The former course is followed here because *Proconsul* specimens present such derived characters as expanded skulls, reduced heteromorphy of the premolars, rounded and enlarged humeral heads, and the hominoid adaptations for stability of the joints (although not the ones for mobility). Their upper molar teeth have large lingual cingulae and are relatively wide, the lowers have strong buccal cingulids, and all show thin to moderately thick enamel. The palate connects directly to the nasal floor, as in gibbons or monkeys, and the face is slightly airorhynch (relatively uptilted), but not as much as in pongines. The postcrania indicate a mainly branch-walking adaptation, and it has been argued that they had lost the external tail, another feature that would link *Proconsul* to hominoids. This genus is especially important because it appears to document an early stage in hominoid evolution, allowing tests of alternative hypotheses of adaptation and mosaic evolution near the origin of this group.

Proconsul was long thought to have been the oldest recognized hominoid, but the early 1990s redating of the Lothidok (Kenya) site to ca. 26 Ma revealed that its primate specimens were of latest Oligocene age. New fossils combined with those previously described document the presence of a species named *Kamoyapithecus hamiltoni*, which is generally similar to *Proconsul* but differs in dental details. It has rather wide molar crowns with large (but not crenulated) lingual and partial buccal cingulum; reduced distal cusps on M^3; M^2 slightly larger than M^3, both larger than M^1; ovoid P^4; probably thin enamel; and very robust canines (lowers also). The describers noted potential similarities to *Afropithecus* and distinctions from *Proconsul*, but it seems most likely to be a proconsulid rather than a hominid. Originally, this species was linked with *Xenopithecus koruensis*, a name proposed for a maxilla from Koru (Kenya) on the basis of minor differences in the upper molars from *Proconsul*. The larger species from Lothidok was later described as *Proconsul (Xenopithecus) hamiltoni*. The molars on these specimens shared the same bunodont, bilaterally expanded crowns with massive development of the lingual cingulum, but otherwise there is little reason to link them. *Xenopithecus koruensis* has been returned to synonymy with *Proconsul africanus*.

Also once described as subgenera of *Proconsul*, but now generally considered separate genera, are *Rangwapithecus*, with only one species, and the closely related *Nyanzapithecus*, with two. These are from the same sites as *Proconsul* and may best be placed in the family Proconsulidae however, it has been suggested that they might be related to *Oreopithecus*, now considered a hominid, in part because of their relatively elongate upper molars. *Limnopithecus*, often linked closely to *Dendropithecus* and its possible allies, may also be better placed in Proconsulidae, on the basis of its incisor and premolar morphology. If so, it would be the smallest proconsulid and one of the longest-lived, extending from Bukwa (Uganda, ca. 22 Ma) through the main Koru/Songhor/Napak/Rusinga sites possibly to Maboko Island (Kenya, ca. 15 Ma).

Proconsulid species ranged in body size from smaller than gibbons to the size of female gorillas. They thus span the size range of living apes. They were generalized arboreal primates, eating mainly fruit and living in tropical woodlands and forests with equable and nonseasonal climates. Some of the larger species may have been partly terrestrial, and some varied their diet with more leaves, but they lacked the extremes of adaptation seen in the living monkeys and apes. They survived in Africa until the Middle Miocene (15–14 Ma), giving way to apes that had thickened molar enamel and other dental specializations, the Hominidae.

Family Proconsulidae

† *Proconsul*

† *Kamoyapithecus*

?† *Rangwapithecus*

?† *Nyanzapithecus*

?† *Limnopithecus*

†extinct

See also Africa; Africa, East; Africa, Southern; Ape; "Dendropithecus-Group"; Diet; Fort Ternan; Hominidae; Hominoidea; Koru; Lothidok Site; Miocene; Napak; Oreopithecus; Ponginae; Primates; Rusinga; Skull; Songhor. [P.A., E.D.]

Further Readings

Andrews, P. (1978) A revision of the Miocene Hominoidea of East Africa. Bull. Brit. Mus. (Nat. Hist.) Geol. 30:85–224.

Andrews, P. (1985) Family group systematics and evolution among catarrhine primates. In E. Delson (ed.): Ancestors: The Hard Evidence. New York: Liss, pp. 14–22.

Harrison, T. (1986). New fossil anthropoids from the Middle Miocene of East Africa and their bearing on the origin of the Oreopithecidae. Am. J. Phys. Anthropol. 71:265–284.

Harrison, T. (1987a) The phylogenetic relationships of the early catarrhine primates: A review of the current evidence. J. Hum. Evol. 16:41–80.

Harrison, T. (1987b) A re-assessment of the phylogenetic relationships of *Oreopithecus bambolii* Gervais 1872. J. Hum. Evol. 15:541–583.

Leakey, M.G., Ungar, P.S., and Walker, A.C. (1995) A new genus of large primate from the Late Oligocene of Lothidok, Turkana District, Kenya. J. Hum. Evol. 28:519–531.

Rafferty, K.L., Walker, A.C., Ruff, C.B., Rose, M.D., and Andrews, P.J. (1995) Postcranial estimates of body weight in *Proconsul*, with a note on a distal tibia of *P. major* from Napak, Uganda. Am. J. Phys. Anthropol. 97:391–402.

Rose, M.D. (1994) Quadrupedalism in some Miocene catarrhines. J. Hum. Evol. 26:387–411.

Walker, A.C., and Teaford, M. (1989) The hunt for *Proconsul*. Sci. Am. 260(1):76–82.

Walker, A.C., Teaford, M.F., Martin, L., and Andrews, P. (1993) A new species of *Proconsul* from the early Miocene of Rusinga/Mfangano Islands, Kenya. J. Hum. Evol. 25:43–56.

Ward, C.V., Walker, A.C., and Teaford, M.F. (1991) *Proconsul* did not have a tail. J. Hum. Evol. 21:215–220.

Ward, C.V., Walker, A.C., Teaford, M.F., and Odhiambo, I. (1993) Partial skeleton of *Proconsul nyanzae* from Mfangano Island, Kenya. Am. J. Phys. Anthropol. 90:77–111.

Propliopithecidae

The earliest-known definitive catarrhine primates, mainly known from Oligocene deposits in the Fayum region of

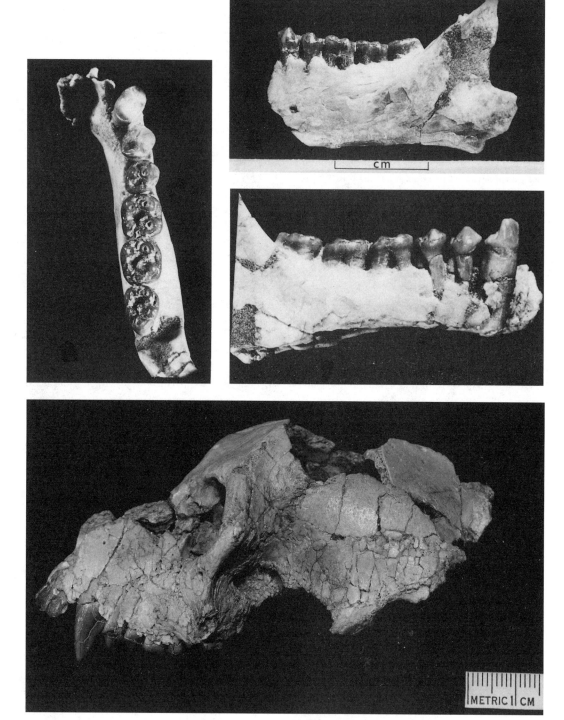

Above: Propliopithecus haeckeli, *left and right mandibular bodies and teeth. Below: lateral view of the first-discovered (and still most complete) cranium of* Propliopithecus (= Aegyptopithecus) zeuxis. *Subsequent finds have shown that the face in this specimen is abnormally long. Cranium courtesy of Elwyn L. Simons.*

Egypt. The first specimen was found early in the twentieth century by a professional collector, R. Markgraf, but more recent and much more extensive collections have been made by E.L. Simons, who has also recovered a great variety of other primates, mostly early anthropoids. The Fayum catarrhines have been given a number of names in the past, including *Propliopithecus haeckeli, P. ankelae, Aegyptopithecus zeuxis, Moeripithecus markgrafi,* and *Aeolopithecus chirobates,* but they should now be recognized as two to four closely re-

lated species of a single genus, *Propliopithecus,* grouped in a distinct catarrhine family.

These primates are known mainly from the Jebel Qatrani Formation in Egypt. The deposits making up this formation are exploited at a number of quarries, and *Propliopithecus* is known from Quarry V at 165 m above the base of the formation to Quarry M at 249 m above the base. Combining several radiometric dates on a basalt at the top of the formation with preliminary paleomagnetic calibration of the

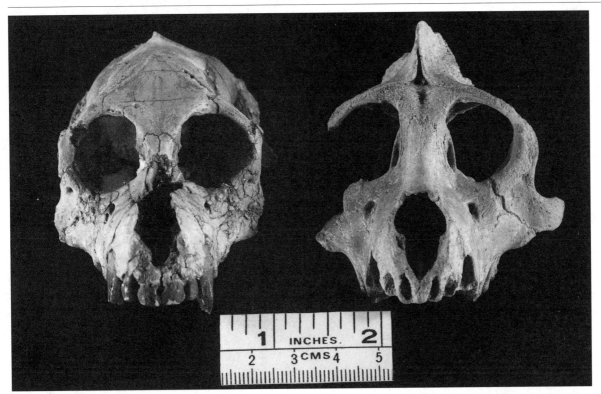

Faces of male Propliopithecus (= Aegyptopithecus) zeuxis: *left, young adult first-discovered individual, probably distorted; right, older adult.*
Courtesy of Elwyn L. Simons.

Fayum sequence, it is suggested that the propliopithecids date to 34–33 Ma, thus earliest Oligocene. Additional propliopithecid specimens have been reported from the Taqah locality in the Sultanate of Oman, on the central southeastern coast of the Arabian Peninsula; at the time, of course, this region was part of Africa. The relative age of the Taqah and Fayum deposits is somewhat controversial, but they are surely similar. The Taqah specimens were identified as *Moeripithecus markgrafi*, and certain characters were said to validate this as a distinct genus, but it seems best for now to consider *markgrafi* as a species of *Propliopithecus*, known also from an uncertain level in the Fayum. A single tooth from the Oligocene of Malembe in Angola may belong here as well.

The species of *Propliopithecus* range from smaller than most extant catarrhines to animals the size of gibbons. They have skulls with moderately projecting faces, wide interorbital spacing, tall canine teeth, and molars with broad crowns and low rounded cusps. Brain size is small, and there is a marked constriction between the face and the braincase (postorbital constriction). There is no development of the auditory tube of the external ear, a character present in all other catarrhine primates. The molars have well-developed cingula, apparently thin enamel on the surfaces of the crowns, and overall are very apelike, which has led many authorities to include the group with the apes. It is now thought that all of these features are those that characterize the ancestral catarrhine condition; they were present in the common ancestor of all catarrhines and, therefore, cannot be said to be diagnostic of any one group within the Catarrhini.

The postcranial morphology of *Propliopithecus* is more distinctive. The arm bones are relatively stoutly built. The distal articular surface of the humerus indicates a stable elbow joint, precluding full extension of the arm. This is also indicated by the morphology of the proximal ulna, which has a primitively long olecranon process. The fingers and toes are strongly developed and adapted for powerful grasping, and, overall, the postcranial morphology suggests quadrupedal climbing as the principal method of locomotion. In this it would have been like present-day howler monkeys of the tropical forest of South America. Some of these characters are probably primitive for the catarrhines, and this is particularly true of the retention of such characters as the entepicondylar foramen and the dorsal epitrochlear fossa on the humerus; but, taken all together, and in conjunction with the relative robusticity of the limb bones, this morphology is probably somewhat derived compared with the ancestral catarrhine morphotype.

The evidence from the postcranial skeleton is in contrast to the morphology of the skull and teeth just described. It is a good illustration of mosaic evolution, whereby some parts of the body evolve more rapidly and in a different way than do other parts. Just because *Propliopithecus* is the earliest-known catarrhine, and is primitive in some respects, it cannot be assumed that it is somehow primitive in all respects or that it is itself primitive. It shares some characters uniquely with other catarrhine primates (e.g., the loss of the second premolar), and this is sufficient to indicate its place as a member of the Catarrhini; but, in other respects, it lacks key catarrhine adaptations, as in the ear. It must, therefore, be recognized as a relatively primitive catarrhine, preceding the split between the two living superfamilies with which it shares no uniquely derived characters and, in fact, preceding the evolution of other somewhat less archaic extinct catarrhine groups.

The adaptation of the skull and teeth of *Propliopithecus* indicates that it lived on a diet of relatively soft food. It has neither the cutting edges to its teeth nor the strong musculature needed to cut up or crush tough or hard food, and it appears, therefore, that it must have had a diet consisting largely of fruit. Such a diet is consistent with the postcranial evidence that shows it to have been a slow and rather heavy-limbed climber in trees, which is where most fruit is found.

This is also consistent with the evidence available on the paleoenvironment in which *Propliopithecus* lived. Evidence from the sediments of the Jebel Qatrani Formation show them to have been laid down in low-lying lagoonal environments where the climate was probably hot and humid. The vegetation is known from the fossilized trunks of large tropical trees that are also commonly found in the deposits, and these show that the area surrounding the site was covered with tropical forests containing many large trees. These would probably have grown in a wet, hot climate without marked division into seasons. Still more information is available from looking at the other animals that are found in the same deposits as *Propliopithecus*. A large and varied mammalian fauna is present, and, although it is composed of animals very different from most living today, it is clear from the numbers of species, and from their adaptations, that the fauna as a whole indicates tropical forest.

Putting all of this together, we see the *Propliopithecus* species as small and monkeylike; they were adapted for climbing and lived in trees; they ate the fruit that grew on the trees; the trees were part of a lowland tropical forest growing close to the sea in a hot and humid climate, almost certainly not highly seasonal. This is a picture of a type of catarrhine primate that is the sister group to the living monkeys and apes and that is claimed by some authorities to be ancestral to all living monkeys and apes.

See also Anthropoidea; Ape; Catarrhini; Diet; Fayum; Haeckel, Ernst Heinrich; Locomotion; Monkey; Oligocene; Parapithecidae; Pliopithecidae. [E.D., P.A.]

Further Readings

Fleagle, J.G., and Kay, R.F. (1987) The phyletic position of the Parapithecidae. J. Hum. Evol. 16:483–532.

Harrison, T. (1987) The phylogenetic relationships of the early catarrhine primates: A review of the current evidence. J. Hum. Evol. 16:41–80.

Kay, R.F., Fleagle, J.G., and Simons, E.L. (1981) A revision of the Oligocene apes of the Fayum Province, Egypt. Am. J. Phys. Anthropol. 55:293–322.

Simons, E.L., and Rasmussen, D.T. (1991) The generic classification of Fayum Anthropoidea. Int. J. Primatol. 12:163–178.

Szalay, F.S., and Delson, E. (1979) Evolutionary History of the Primates. New York: Academic.

Thomas, H., Sen, S., Roger, J., and Al-Sulaimani, Z. (1991) The discovery of *Moeripithecus markgrafi* Schlosser (Propliopithecidae, Primates), in the Ashawq Formation (Early Oligocene of Dhofar Province, Sultanate of Oman). J. Hum. Evol. 20:33–49.

Prosimian

Member of the lower primates, including the lemurs, lorises, galagos, tarsiers, their extinct relatives, and all early primates. The Prosimii is a formal taxonomic grouping of primates, originally based upon the four modern groups mentioned but later extended to include the early fossils. The use of this term reflects the hypothesis that these animals are all part of a natural group and thus are each other's closest relatives, especially as contrasted with the Anthropoidea, or higher primates. Most current researchers do not accept that hypothesis, instead considering that the living tarsiers (and their extinct relatives) are the sister taxon of the anthropoids (forming the haplorhine group), while the living toothcombed prosimians (Lemuroidea and Lorisoidea) are a distinct clade, the Strepsirhini. The extinct, early Cenozoic Adapidae are probably also strepsirhines. Together, these two large groups compose the Euprimates, as opposed to the archaic Paleogene Plesiadapiformes. Thus, combining the plesiadapiforms, the strepsirhines, and the tarsiiforms in the single taxon Prosimii appears unnatural (paraphyletic) to many workers and is not followed here. Nonetheless, many authors desire to have a formal term that contrasts this assemblage to the anthropoids, and the concept of *prosimian* is, therefore, found in many textbooks and some research papers.

See also Adapidae; Anthropoidea; Euprimates; Haplorhini; Higher Primates; Lower Primates; Monophyly; Plesiadapiformes; Primates; Scala Naturae; Tarsiiformes. [E.D., I.T.]

Protomagdalenian

Upper Paleolithic industry dated ca. 22–21 Ka, defined by D. Peyrony on the basis of a level underlying the Solutrean at Laugerie Haute (France). Backed-bladelet technology and other aspects of the assemblage foreshadow the Magadalenian and represent a significant shift from the preceding backed-point technology of the Perigordian. The industry has also been referred to as Perigordian VII by D. de Sonneville-Bordes, due to the general use of backing technique and to the position of the industry in the sequence directly overlying the Perigordian VI (previously Perigordian III) at both Laugerie Haute and Abri Pataud.

See also Abri Pataud; De Sonneville-Bordes, Denise; Laugerie Sites; Magdalenian; Movius, Hallam L., Jr; Perigordian; Peyrony, Denis; Stone-Tool Making; Upper Paleolithic. [A.S.B.]

Further Readings

Bordes, F., and de Sonneville Bordes, D. (1966) Protomagdalénien ou Périgordien VII. L'Anthropol. 70:113–122.

Bricker, H.M., ed. (1995) Le Paléolithique supérieur de l'Abri Pataud (Dordogne): Les Fouilles de H.L. Movius, Jr. Documents d'Archaeologie Française 50. Paris: Editions de la Maison des Sciences de l'Homme, C.N.R.S.

Peyrony, D., and Peyrony, E. (1938) Laugerie Haute près des Eyzies (Dordogne) (Archives de l'Institut de Paléontologie Humaine, Mémoire 19). Paris: Masson.

Protosolutrean

The earliest Solutrean-related industry, dated ca. 20 Ka and found only at two sites in southwestern France: Laugerie Haute and Badegoule. It is characterized by unifacial points and the use of pressure flaking.

See also Laugerie Sites; Solutrean; Stone-Tool Making; Upper Paleolithic. [A.S.B.]

Psychozoa

A semitaxonomic term, of kingdom rank, employed by B. Rensch to reflect the great distinctions of humans from other animals. This concept has been used, rarely, by European authors, although it is, in essence, antievolutionary in denying the position of *Homo* as merely one member of one order of the Kingdom Animalia. [E.D., I.T.]

Q

Qafzeh

Cave site located in the Wadi el-Hadj, southeast of Nazareth in Israel overlooking the Esdraelon Plain. Qafzeh is important because it preserves remains of early-modern humans in a Middle Paleolithic archaeological context. Qafzeh Cave was first excavated in the 1930s by R. Neuville, the French consul in Jerusalem, and M. Stekelis, an Israeli prehistorian. A second series of excavations at Qafzeh was directed by B. Vandermeersch in the late 1960s and 1970s. The cave is a large karst solution cavity that has been filled by spring sediments, alluvium, and rock scree. The interior of the cave was the focus of the Neuville-Stekelis excavations, while Vandermeersch's work concentrated on the terrace and area around the entrance to the cave (the vestibule). Different numbering systems for the excavated layers have been used in different areas of the site.

Upper Paleolithic occupations from the interior of the cave (Levels D–E) contain an Ahmarian industry, as do the corresponding strata from the vestibule/terrace (Levels VII–IX). Human remains from Upper Paleolithic levels include two frontal bones. A stone mortar and pestle, probably for grinding ocher, were found in Level 9. Amino-acid-racemization analysis dates Level IX to 39 Ka.

The Middle Paleolithic occupations occur inside the cave in Levels F–L (Neuville) and Level 12–13 (Vandermeersch) and in Levels I–XXIV in the vestibule. Most of the hominid fossils occur in the vestibule in Levels XVII–XXIV. The antiquity of the hominid-bearing Middle Paleolithic levels of Qafzeh Cave has been established by thermoluminescence (92.5 Ka) and electron-spin resonance (100 Ka), indicating that the Qafzeh hominids are, together with the fossils from the nearby site of Skhūl, among the oldest hominids of modern morphology found in Eurasia.

Several of these fossils appear to be deliberate burials (Qafzeh 8, 9, 10, and 11). Qafzeh 11 is the skeleton of a child clasping the antler of a fallow deer (*Dama mesopotamica*) to its chest. Interestingly, the pit in which this body lies was dug into the soft bedrock at the bottom of the cave, an investment of effort that is unusual in comparison to other Middle Paleolithic burials. Qafzeh 9 (a young female) and Qafzeh 10 (a child) appear to have been part of a double burial. Many other fossils represent isolated cranial, dental, and postcranial fragments. Pieces of red ocher marked by incisions and abrasion, as well as stone tools worn from cutting red ocher, were recovered from these levels. Perforated shells of the cockleshell *Glycimeris* were also found. The nearest source would have been the shore of the Mediterranean, ca. 40 km to the west.

The robust but essentially modern morphology of the Mousterian-associated hominids from Qafzeh and the similar sample from Skhūl is considered by some researchers to represent the ancestral morphology that gave rise to the European Cro-Magnons. Other workers regard the Qafzeh hominids as part of a single polymorphic Levantine population that included the Skhūl modern humans and the Kebara, Tabūn, and Amud Neanderthals.

Faunal remains from the Middle Paleolithic levels of Qafzeh Cave indicate an early Last Glacial fauna and include desertic species of microfauna, such as *Gerbillus dasyurus*. Among the larger fauna, red deer (*Cervus elaphus*) is especially common.

The Middle Paleolithic assemblages associated with the Qafzeh hominids in Levels XVII–XXIV are similar to the Levantine Mousterian assemblages found in Tabūn Cave Level C and Skhūl Cave Level B (from which additional early-modern human fossils have been recovered). These assemblages feature predominantly centripetal modes of core preparation, numerous large, oval flakes, and variable numbers of points and scrapers. The affinities of the Levantine Mousterian assemblages from the *upper* parts of Qafzeh have been likened to those of both Tabūn B and Tabūn C. Because Tabūn B and Tabūn C assemblages have elsewhere been associated with Neanderthal fossils, some researchers have argued that this similarity of archaeological residues indicates cultural continuity between Levantine Neanderthals and early-modern humans from Skhūl and Qafzeh. Others maintain that this similarity is superficial, reflecting behavior patterns shared by a wide range of Upper Pleistocene

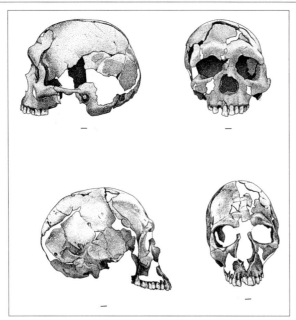

Side and front views of the two most complete early modern human crania from Jebel Qafzeh: Qafzeh 6 (above) and Qafzeh 9. Scale is 1 cm.

humans, and that it has no bearing on the Qafzeh hominids' biological relationship to the Levantine Neanderthals.

See also Ahmarian; Amud Cave; Archaic Moderns; Asia, Western; Kebara; Middle Paleolithic; Mousterian; Neanderthals; Skhūl; Tabūn. [J.J.S., C.B.S.]

Further Readings

Bar-Yosef, O., and Vandermeersch, B. (1993) Modern humans in the Levant. Sci. Am. 268(4):94–100.

Ronen, A., and Vandermeersch, B. (1972) The Upper Palaeolithic sequence in the cave of Qafzeh (Israel). Quaternaria 16:189–202.

Valladas, H., Reyss, J.L., Joron, J.L., Valladas, G., Bar-Yosef, O. and Vandermeersch, B. (1988) Thermoluminescence dating of Mousterian 'Proto Cro-Magnon' remains from Israel and the origin of modern man. Nature 331:614-615.

Vandermeersch, B. (1981) Les hommes fossiles de Qafzeh (Israel). Paris: Editions du C.N.R.S.

Quantitative Methods

In biology, these include numerical and mathematical descriptions or modeling of natural phenomena, as well as descriptive and inferential statistics. Relations between observed quantities can frequently be described in mathematical terms. Examples include the equation for geometric increase of a population through time or the change in size of an individual during growth, both as functions of time.

Mathematical Modeling

Mathematical modeling is used extensively in population ecology for modeling exchange of energy and resources in communities. In population genetics, the change in gene frequencies due to natural selection, mutation, migration, and the influence of population size can be incorporated into a mathematical model.

The model relating metabolic rate to body mass for warm-blooded vertebrates can be represented as a simple exponential equation. One starts with basic biological principles involving metabolic rate as a function of heat loss from body-surface area in relation to mass and deduces a model. The derived exponential equation describes the observed relation between calories consumed per unit time (metabolic rate) and body weight or mass and is descriptive and predictive for individual organisms and for mean tendencies of different taxa.

There are basically two types of mathematical models used in biology: *deterministic* and *stochastic.* In deterministic models, equations relating the variables in the model are used to compute results or draw graphs that tell exactly how much one variable changes as others change. For example, a simple equation can generate the shapes of most species of snails by choosing specific constants for each species in the equation for a logarithmic spiral.

The word *stochastic* is synonymous with probabilistic. In stochastic models, exact predictions cannot be made. Variables in the model have random components that lead to probability distributions for the variables of interest. Realistic models for population growth and population genetics for small populations are of this type. The population genetic phenomenon called *random drift* is based on a stochastic model that describes chance changes in frequency of genes from generation to generation as a consequence of the chance association of gametes in random mating populations. When the population is very small, all of the offspring may descend from just a few individuals who may not be typical.

For some deterministic models, linear algebra is a powerful tool. For example, the rate of increase in a population can be determined from the mortality rate and fecundity for each age group assumed to be constant from generation to generation. The methods of differential and integral calculus, including numerical integration, are required for other types of models. These methods frequently require the use of a computer for the extensive calculations involved.

Only the simplest stochastic models can be solved mathematically without the use of simulation or Monte Carlo techniques requiring repeated runs of the model on a high-speed computer. The phenomenon is simulated by specifying each parameter or feature and then randomly sampling possible values that may arise, using a random-number generator. Many repeated experiments are required to produce a distribution of results, in the form of a probability distribution. Some of the models used in evolutionary theory for speciation and proliferation of taxa are of this form.

Statistics

Statistics are among the most widely used of quantitative methods. Data are collected as measurements on a continuous scale (e.g., length, weight, angle, pH), meristic counts (number of teeth, digits, cusps), or frequencies of nominal variables (color, race, health, class, preference in a questionnaire).

Measurement data and counts may be summarized in terms of *descriptive statistics* that measure the average tendency (mean, median) or variation (standard deviation, coefficient of variation). Correlation coefficients are used to measure linear association of variables two at a time. Regression analysis is used to predict the value of one variable from others (what should the weight be of a male who is 49 years of age?). Frequencies are summarized by tabulations or converted to percentages and proportions. These descriptive statistics may be calculated for small samples (usually fewer than 30 observations), large samples, or even vast amounts of data (such as the results of a national census).

Most research studies that employ measurements or counts report such descriptive statistics in the form of tables or graphs. Numerical-taxonomy methods employ descriptive statistics to describe the numerical similarities or differences among taxa based on numerically coded characters. A computation rule, or algorithm, is used to find patterns of relationship among taxa based on the similarities or differences; these are then summarized in the form of a dendrogram, or treelike diagram.

Statistical inference is concerned with drawing conclusions about phenomena or populations based on experimental data or relatively small samples of observations drawn at random from populations of interest. We would like to make inferences about the larger body of data or the population sampled, using only the data at hand. One of the most common statistics used in inference is the *standard error*. We can compute a standard error for just about any statistic calculated from data taken at random from the population of interest. The standard error tells us how variable the statistic will be in repeated samples; thus, large samples have, on the average, smaller standard errors than small ones drawn from the same population. The standard error of the mean, for example, decreases inversely with the square root of sample size. Standard errors are frequently reported with a statistic and given with a plus or minus sign after the value of the statistic.

A *confidence interval* gives us the range of values that is likely to contain the true value of the parameter we are trying to estimate, along with the probability that intervals produced in the same way will contain the true value. Recording blood types for a random sample of people gives us an estimate of the blood-type frequencies for the population we have sampled. Confidence intervals for the frequencies will tell us how close we may be to the true values and the probabilities that the intervals will contain the true frequencies. The length of a confidence interval is frequently a simple function of sample size and frequently decreases roughly as the reciprocal of the square root of sample size (like the standard error of the mean). It takes a sample four times as large to halve the length of the interval. We may use general statistical results of this type in our design of statistical studies.

Descriptive statistics and confidence intervals are examples of estimates of unknown quantities. If we are interested in hypotheses about our experiments or about nature, we can formulate them as statistical hypotheses. For example, the statement that "the population that we have sampled is not evolving" may be translated into a statistical hypothesis

about the gene frequencies through time in a large random-mating population in which there is no effective selection, migration, or mutation. The statistical hypothesis would be "gene frequency is constant through time." We would test the hypothesis by observing gene frequencies through time and see if the differences we observe are due to chance or to evolution having occurred.

The statement that "the skull lengths are the same in two populations we are studying" is a hypothesis about a measurable quantity in populations of animals. A more specific statistical hypothesis might be "the mean skull length in population A is the same as the mean skull length in population B." This hypothesis is called the *hypothesis tested* or the *null hypothesis.* The alternative hypothesis is that "the mean skull lengths are different." A test of a statistical hypothesis is a mathematically rigorous way of evaluating our hypothesis based on data collected from samples drawn at random from the populations. We will reject the hypothesis tested if the observed difference is large enough. Large enough is larger than would have occurred by chance if the populations were, in fact, not different. We must choose this probability of rejecting the true hypothesis tested before we do the test. If we do this, we can deduce the properties of our test (i.e., its power of finding differences when they exist). Another name for the chance or probability of rejecting our true null hypothesis is *significance* level. One test for continuous variables, and appropriate for our data on mean skull lengths, would be Student's *t* test if certain assumptions about the distribution of the weights in the samples were valid and our samples had been drawn at random from the two populations.

The *analysis of variance* is used to test similarly formulated hypotheses about the equality of two or more means and is a powerful tool for analyzing sources of variation due to experimental manipulation in the laboratory or the effects of geography and time in natural populations.

Chi-square tests are used to test for independence of variables in count data and to compare frequencies or proportions in such data over various populations sampled. For example, if our null hypothesis is that the sex-ratio is the same over several populations, then a chi-square test would be appropriate. Chi-square and *t* tables are widely available for looking up values of the test statistic corresponding to our prechosen significance level.

Data collected about objects or phenomena usually consist of many observations on each object or experimental unit. Thus, on a single skull we might measure length, width, height, and any of a number of dimensions of interest. Collection-locality information might include, for each place, latitude and longitude, temperature, altitude, and a multitude of other features of that place at a given time. The majority of data collected are, therefore, multivariate in nature. Traditionally, however, the majority of statistical analyses look at variables one at a time and are known as *univariate statistical methods.* Analysis of variance and *t* tests are examples of univariate techniques.

Multivariate statistics, methods that look at many variables simultaneously, are being used more and more. The computations required are long and tedious but are made easier with the use of today's computers. Their interpretation, however, is more difficult. Still, the world is multivariate, and multivariate inferences are required and will become more common.

Some of the multivariate techniques commonly used are *multiple regression, principal-components analysis, factor analysis,* and *discriminant analysis.* Each method begins with many variables being observed for each individual or experiment. *Multiple regression* is concerned with predicting one or more variables from a whole suite of measured quantities. We may estimate brain volume as a function of a number of linear skull measures and also have a measure of how well our prediction does. Various stepwise procedures are available in computer programs for selecting an optimal subset of predictors in an orderly way. The presence of redundancy in the set of predictors, or *colinearity,* is reflected in high values of correlations among some of the predictor variables.

Principal-components analysis is a widely used data-reduction technique that depends on the presence of correlation among the measured variables. It is usually possible to find a relatively few indices or linear combinations of our original variables that summarize most of the information contained in all of our measured variables, so that a plot of two of the most informative linear combinations (called principal components) will give us a one-dimensional diagram or a very few two-dimensional diagrams that will show much of the structure of our multivariate data. We may be able to see trends associated with variables not in the analysis, or clusters of observations that help us understand our data, or we may be able to formulate hypotheses about groups not yet recognized as distinct. Analysis of residuals not explained by the principal components can be informative about unique variables or about cases not well expressed by the principal components.

Factor analysis, a multivariate method originally developed by psychologists, summarizes many measures in the form of a few common factors that explain all of the information shared by the variables. Thus, a large battery of intelligence tests administered to a number of subjects may be measuring general intelligence, mathematical ability, and language ability (the factors of the mind), although these factors cannot be measured directly. Factor analysis is widely used in the social sciences and is becoming more popular among biologists and geologists. Factor analysis may be used as a model-building and hypothesis-testing procedure, while principal-components analysis is exploratory, looking for not easily discerned pattern and structure in multivariate data.

Multivariate analysis of variance is a generalization of analysis of variance. It is concerned with any or all differences in a set of measured variables in an experimental or field condition. Do the skulls in populations A, B, and C differ in any measured dimension? If so, in which dimensions and how much do they differ? Can the observed differences be summarized by overall size changes in all variables or are the differences also in terms of shape differences? If the populations do differ, we can use an index based on a combina-tion of the characters to assign unknowns to the correct population and also to measure the probability of error of assignment. For example, we can assign a newly discovered fossil to one of a group of known populations or decide that it does not belong to any of them. This methodology, closely allied to multivariate analysis of variance, is *discriminant analysis.* Very similar techniques in engineering and operations research are called *pattern recognition.*

Plotting the results of our analysis of among-population differences, taking into consideration the variation and correlation within populations, is akin to principal-components analysis. We may have designated the groups or clusters beforehand, however, and want to see their relationships and differences. This method is called *canonical variates analysis.* Various descriptive measures of difference, called *distance statistics,* use all of the variables in the study and can be used to summarize relationships.

The exploratory multivariate techniques like principal components and multivariate distances are descriptive methods. Factor analysis may be used descriptively or inferentially. Models may be generated or specified and tested. Multivariate analysis of variance is an inferential technique. Cluster analysis and numerical taxonomy are descriptive multivariate methods.

Statistical Assumptions

All statistical tests require that we can properly make assumptions about our data so that we may use the test correctly and so that our chosen significance level will be what we say it is. The most important assumption is *random sampling.* Without random sampling, we can only present descriptive statistics for our data at hand and not make inferences about the sampled populations we are interested in. A sample is random if the probability of each observation being in the sample is known. In the most common form, *simple random sampling,* the probability is the same for all individuals entering the sample. More restrictive assumptions are required for tests like the *t* test, in which we must also know if variability is similar in the two populations sampled and that it follows the normal, well-known bell-shaped curve. There are statistical procedures that require fewer assumptions that are called *distribution-free* or *nonparametric* tests. These, however, are usually not associated with easily interpretable descriptive statistics.

See also Allometry; Morphometrics; Multivariate Analysis; Numerical Taxonomy. [L.F.M.]

Quaternary

The youngest period of the Cenozoic (from 1.8 Ma to the present), encompassing the Pleistocene epoch (or Pleistocene and Holocene epochs if these are considered to be separate). The term *Quaternary* originated in the earliest geological literature to apply to unconsolidated deposits, in contrast with *Tertiary* (lithified strata), *Secondary* (metamorphosed strata), and *Primary* (crystalline and igneous rocks). The latter two have long been abandoned, and formal action of the International Union of Geological Sciences in the

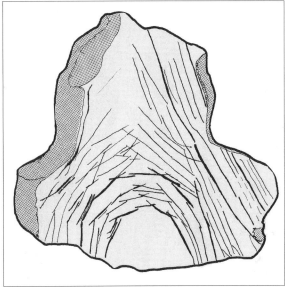

A flat cortex plate (7.2 cm) from the Mousterian site of Quneitra, the Golan Heights, with four nested semi-circles and surrounding vertical lines. Levantine Middle Paleolithic, ca. 54 Ka. Left, photograph; right, schematic rendition of the incised composition indicating the four central semi-circles—the faint markings surrounding the arcs are composed of straight, short, appended strokes that occasionally cross over each other. Courtesy of Alex Marshack.

1980s replaced the Tertiary, which had become a period of the Cenozoic, with Paleogene and Neogene. Proposals have been made to replace the Quaternary as well, with terms such as *Pleistogene* or *Anthropogene*. Others advocate extending the Neogene to the present, according to its original (1843) definition, and entirely erasing a separate period at the end of the Cenozoic.

See also Anthropogene; Cenozoic; Holocene; Neogene; Paleogene; Pleistocene; Tertiary. [J.A.V.C.]

Quneitra

Open-air Mousterian site on the Golan Heights (Israel-Syrian border) sealed under volcanic tuff until uncovered by excavations during the 1980s. Electron-spin-resonance (ESR) dating of tooth enamel suggested an age for the site of ca. 54 Ka, a period during which anatomically modern humans and Levantine Neanderthals inhabited the region and used a similar Mousterian technology. A plaquette of flint cortex (7.2 cm) found at Quneitra is incised with the earliest-known engraving to come from the Levant. The composi-

tion consists of a series of concentric semicircles surrounded by vertical lines. The intentional nature of the engraving was determined by microscopic analysis. The composition may have been made by anatomically modern humans as part of an incipient cultural shift that would lead to the Transitional Levantine Upper Paleolithic following the Mousterian. The engraving is ca. 20 Kyr earlier than the beginnings of Upper Paleolithic imagery in Europe.

See also Archaic Moderns; Asia, Western; Late Paleolithic; Middle Paleolithic; Mousterian; Paleolithic Image; Upper Paleolithic. [A.M.]

Further Readings

Goren-Inbar, N., ed. (1990) Quneitra: A Mousterian site on the Golan Heights (QEDEM, Vol. 31). Jerusalem: Institute of Archaeology, Hebrew University of Jerusalem.

Marshack, A. (1996) A Middle Paleolithic symbolic composition from the Golan Heights: The earliest known depictive image. Curr. Anthropol. 37:357–365.

R

Race (Human)

Arbitrarily defined and geographically localized division of humans. It is ideally equivalent to the zoological subspecies, but the social consequences of allocating humans to groups make it impossible to carry out microevolutionary systematics of humans as one would practice it for other species. For example, human race is transmitted in the United States by a mechanism of folk heredity: The offspring of an interracial marriage either adopts or is assigned the lower-status race of the two parents. And where the assignment to a race is politically significant, having one great-grandparent of a particular race often outweighs having seven of another.

The social nature of race is also evident from considering that Europeans were usually subdivided by an earlier generation into Nordic, Alpine, and Mediterranean races. Today, however, Europeans are rarely, if ever, subdivided, for the primary contrast being made is against peoples of sub-Saharan African descent. This reinforces our appreciation that human races are not basic biological units, but are, rather, constructs defined by the time, the culture, and the question being posed.

Races have traditionally been designated on the basis of phenotypic characters, such as hair or eyes. More recently, geneticists have tried unsuccessfully to designate races on the basis of the frequencies of blood-group alleles found within each presumptive race. Because the criteria used to define races are arbitrary, anthropologists have not agreed on how many races exist or what they are. For example, while many might agree that the aboriginal populations of Asia, Africa, and Europe constitute the equivalents of subspecies, there is no consensus about the aboriginals of North America and Polynesia or the Ainu of Japan. Thus, while J.F. Blumenbach (1835) and C.S. Coon (1962) both divided the human species into five races, Blumenbach separated the people of Asia and the Americas but grouped the peoples of sub-Saharan Africa together, while Coon divided the peoples of Africa into "Congoid" and "Capoid" and united the peoples of America and Asia into a single race.

Forensic anthropologists can use a battery of minor average differences to allocate an unknown skull into one of a few large racial groups with better-than-random success. This, however, does not validate those categories as the fundamental biological divisions of the human species—it only means that, *given* those categories, skulls can be reliably assigned to them.

A major difficulty with the concept of race is that the evolutionary model underlying it is unclear. What are often taken for representatives of "pure races" may be nothing more than people from populations best adapted to the most divergent conditions. There was probably never a time in which only a few homogeneous human populations existed in widely different parts of the world—the presumably original races. While populations do, indeed, differ biologically from one another, such differences are small and often represent localized physiological adaptations. This leaves us with a biological view of human populations that emphasizes both local adaptation and long-term genetic contact.

Human biological diversity is now recognized to be patterned in a way that defies its division into a small number of distinct groups. Individual characteristics, such as skin color, vary clinally (gradually across geography); different characters are usually distributed discordantly from one another; and there is invariably far more diversity within any defined human group than there is across the boundary separating it from another group. Populations at the end-points of a distribution will obviously differ significantly from each other, but that does not tell us that there is a small number of basic types of people or what they might be. As a result, populations are adopted as units of study and analysis, but their higher-order clusterings are acknowledged to be largely arbitrarily defined and not to designate fundamental biological categories.

The distribution of detectable genetic differences in the human species falls into two broad categories. The first constitutes *restricted polymorphisms,* possessed by a subset of the species—but a subset that does not correspond well to what we would identify as a race. For example, populations that have the Diego blood antigen are found only in East Asia and the New World. In those regions, however, the proportion of

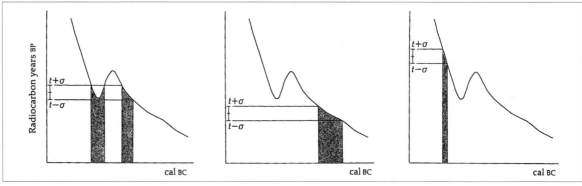

Calibration of ¹⁴C ages. Radiocarbon ages do not necessarily increase steadily with time because the amount of ¹⁴C in the environment is not constant, thanks to secular variation in the amount of CO₂ and CH₃ exposed to cosmic radiation in the upper atmosphere. In the figured example of a calibration curve, the difference between analyzed "radiocarbon years" (vertical axis) and counted calendar years (horizontal axis) in tree-ring sequences and ice cores is illustrated for the interval from 6–3 Ka. Some "wiggles" in the calibration curve are so severe, as in this segment, that the same radiocarbon age range can be one of two different calendar age ranges (left-hand figure). Note that the more precise a single radiocarbon age may be, the more likely it may fit to two different points in a wiggly calibration curve, but that locating the ambiguously dated sample in a stratigraphically ordered series of ages will resolve such conundrums. Note also that radiocarbon ages with the same error range can represent either a relatively precise (narrow) or imprecise (broad) range of calendar years depending on whether they fall on steeply or shallowly sloping parts of the correction curve (central and right hand figures, respectively). From S. Bowman, 1995, Radiocarbon Dating. *By permission of the Trustees of the British Museum.*

people with the antigen in a specific population varies from 0 to 40 percent (i.e., not only is the allele sometimes absent from populations in the region from which it is known, but those people who have it are also invariably a minority). The other pattern is that of *ubiquitous polymorphism,* in which diverse populations have all or most alleles—such as the ABO blood group. Neither pattern of diversity identifies races or permits the allocation of individuals to them.

Finally, the fact that races can and do freely interbreed makes their boundaries ambiguous and their historical existence ephemeral. Races thus seem to be principally constructs of culture imposed upon the biological variation in the human species. One of the fundamental roles of culture, indeed, is the assignment of symbolic meaning to subtle distinctions in nature. It has never been adequately demonstrated that human groups differ intrinsically in intelligence, or that any behavioral differences among them have a genetic basis.

See also Polytypic Variation; Population; Subspecies. [J.M.]

Further Readings

Marks, J. (1995) Human Biodiversity: Genes, Race, and History. New York: Aldine de Gruyter.

Montagu, A. (1964) Man's Most Dangerous Myth: The Fallacy of Race, 4th ed. Cleveland: World Publishing.

Radiocarbon Dating

Age determination based on measurements of the decay of the radioactive isotope carbon-14 (¹⁴C, or radiocarbon) to stable nitrogen-14 (¹⁴N) by emission of an electron charge (beta-particle) from the nucleus, leaving a proton in place of a neutron. The half-life of carbon-14 is 5,730 years; beyond about 10 half-lives (i.e., ca. 60 Kyr), the amount that remains is generally too small to measure with any accuracy. Carbon-14 is produced in the upper atmosphere by the reaction of cosmic rays with ¹⁴N, and it oxidizes there to CO_2.

The radioactive CO_2 enters the biosphere when the gas is taken up by plants and protists during organosynthesis and is recycled until it enters the fossil state. The present-day concentration of this nuclide in living organisms corresponds to a radioactivity of 13.6 disintegrations per minute per gram of carbon. The age (t, in years) of any ancient carbon sample can be calculated from measurement of its remaining ¹⁴C activity, A, according to the equation

$$t = [T\tfrac{1}{2}/0.6932]\ \ln(A/Ao)$$

where T½ is the half-life, 5,730 years, Ao is the ¹⁴C activity in atmospheric carbon dioxide at the time that the sample was formed, and ln is the natural logarithm (base e).

The value for A in the equation can be determined either by counting the beta-decay events directly or by establishing the concentration of remaining ¹⁴C atoms in the sample with an accelerator mass spectrometer (AMS). For measurement of β-activity, the carbon sample is converted into a liquid (usually benzene, C_6H_6), or to a gas (usually acetylene, C_2H_2), with a high carbon content. In liquid samples, the β-activity is measured by scintillometry, by adding a phosphor that emits a light flash when struck by a β-particle. In gas samples, the level of radioactivity is measured in a proportional counter similar to a Geiger counter. Both methods require very careful shielding to control natural background radioactivity.

Mass-spectrographic analysis of the ¹⁴C isotope is done on purified carbon (graphite) extracted from the sample and activated as positive ions to differentiate the ¹⁴C from the background ¹⁴N, which has the same mass. The main advantage of AMS is its ability to analyze samples as small as a few micrograms, whereas conventional β-counting requires the use of several grams to several milligrams (in the most modern, ultra-low-background systems) to provide a reliable date. The upper age limit of AMS dating is ca. 40 Ka, whereas β-counting can reach ages as old as 60 Ka.

Radiocarbon dating is principally applicable to samples of organically formed materials, including wood, charcoal, hair, coprolites, bones, and shells. Samples to be dated must meet stringent criteria of purity in order to exclude radiocarbon atoms introduced after the sample enters stratigraphic context, which would give an erroneously young age. For example, buried samples typically contain root hairs, fungal growths, or deposits from burrowing animals, which contribute younger carbon. A lesser risk is the introduction of "dead" carbon from rocks or groundwater, leading to erroneously old ages. Ideally, purified biochemicals such as cellulose (from wood) or collagen (from bone) should be analyzed. The carbonate of bone mineral is less useful because of the common effect of ion exchange with soil carbonate.

Inorganically deposited carbonates, such as travertine and speleothems, can be dated by radiocarbon, but a large correction must be made for dead carbon, because carbonate in springs and cave seepages has equilibrated with the carbonate in limestone or dolomite, which has essentially zero ^{14}C activity. Modern spring deposits can show less than 50 percent of modern atmospheric ^{14}C activity.

Correction Factors
Unadjusted dates, in which Ao is simply set equal to present-day ^{14}C activity, are said to be in *radiocarbon years*. There have been large variations in atmospheric Ao, however, over the time that carbon-14 dating is applicable, due primarily to the fact that the cosmic radiation flux in the upper atmosphere, and thus the production of radioactive carbon, varies inversely with the strength of the Earth's magnetic field. For the interval of 0 to 10 Ka, a correction curve has been built up through empirical calibration against counted tree rings, buttressed by dating of varved sequences in glaciers and lake beds. At many points in that interval, measured ^{14}C activity can be attributed to more than one age, because of "wiggles" in the curve of activity vs. time. In such instances, the age may be resolved by independent criteria, or it may be related to a stratigraphic set of ages that exhibits a characteristic variation curve. Calibration of the radiocarbon scale from 10 to 20 Ka is based on ^{14}C analyses of corals whose ages have been independently measured to ± 1 percent by mass-spectrometric ^{230}Th/^{234}U dating. The carbon-14 dates on marine shells and corals require further correcting for the lowered ^{14}C activity of carbon in sea water. This is the *reservoir effect*, a term for the prolonged sequestration of huge volumes of dissolved carbonate ion in the virtually abiotic water masses below the eutrophic zone. Finally, in the interval from 20 Ka to the lower limit of measurable activity, correction is based on the long-term variation in the magnetic-field strength recorded in paleomagnetic studies.

The small-sample capability of AMS opens the possibility for dating single amino acids or other uniquely biogenic molecules from samples of bone or wood, but the need for extreme purification of the sample greatly increases the cost. The most interesting applications of ^{14}C dating to human evolution are near the limit of the AMS dating range (40 Ka), where extreme care is necessary to obtain samples of adequate purity. Many ^{14}C dates from near this limiting time

are probably erroneously young due to contamination. A 40 Ka sample contains less than 1 percent of its original ^{14}C content, and contamination by only 1 percent of modern carbon will decrease its apparent age to ca. 35 Ka (about one half-life).

See also ESR (Electron Spin Resonance) Dating; Pleistocene; TL (Thermoluminescence) Dating; Trapped-Charge Dating; Upper Paleolithic; Uranium-Series Dating. [J.J.S.]

Further Readings
Aitken, M. (1990) Science-Based Dating in Archaeology. London: Longman.
Arnold, L.D. (1995) Conventional radiocarbon dating. In N.W. Rutter and N.R. Catto (eds.): Dating Methods for Quaternary Deposits. St. Johns, Newfoundland: Geology Society of Canada, pp. 107–116.
Cabrera Valdes, V., and Bischoff, J. (1989) Accelerator ^{14}C dates for early Upper Paleolithic (basal Aurignacian) at El Castillo Cave (Spain). J. Archaeol. Sci. 16:577–584.
Litherland, A.E., and Beukens, R.P. (1995) Radiocarbon dating by atom counting. In N.W. Rutter and N.R. Catto (eds.): Dating Methods for Quaternary Deposits. St. Johns, Newfoundland: Geology Society of Canada, pp. 117–124.
Taylor, R.E. (1987) Radiocarbon Dating: An Archaeological Perspective. Orlando: Academic.

Radiometric Dating
Measurement of the time elapsed since closure of a particular geochemical or biochemical system, as determined by analysis of the radioactive atoms and, in most cases, their daughter products contained within a sample. The time of closure may represent rapid cooling from high temperatures, as in volcanic rocks; cooling consequent on uplift of a portion of the Earth's crust, as in metamorphic rocks; incorporation in crystals or through precipitation by absorption on surfaces, as in deep-sea sediments; or cessation of carbon exchange consequent on death (the basis for radiocarbon dating). Stratigraphic judgment is often required to relate the dated material to the age of a particular fossil.

See also Geochronometry; Potassium-Argon Dating; Radiocarbon Dating; Uranium-Series Dating. [F.H.B.]

Raw Materials
Natural substances utilized in human technology. A wide variety of materials found in nature were used for technological ends in prehistoric times, in either modified or unmodified form. These include stone, wood, bone, horn, and hide. The role of such materials was governed by their availability, the functional requirements of the tools, and prevailing cultural norms regarding artifact manufacture.

Groups of Raw Materials
STONE
One of the most important materials for tool use and the one yielding the earliest archaeological evidence was stone

(evidence of percussive flaking of stone first appears in the archaeological record ca. 2.5 Ma). Rocks can be used or fashioned to serve in many activities, such as hammering, cutting, scraping, chopping, grinding, engraving, and perforating. Stone tools could have been used for animal butchery and the working of wood, hide, and, later, bone and antler.

During most of the Paleolithic, the predominant mode of working stone into tools was flaking (also called *chipping*), generally through direct or indirect percussion but also, by late in the period, through pressure. Not all stone sources are suitable for flaking, and the properties of a particular stone affect the manufacturing process. The flaking qualities, size, and shape of a given raw material influence the methods and techniques used to make an artifact as well as its resultant form. In most circumstances, the finer-grained the material (e.g., flint) and the more isotropic its structure (fracturing equally well in any direction with no preferential cleavage planes), the easier it is to control. Stone with superior flaking qualities often results in end products with a more standardized range of variation and an apparently higher degree of workmanship than those manufactured from coarser, non-isotropic stones.

The types of stone often used for tools include:

1. SEDIMENTARY ROCKS, such as
   a. *Cryptocrystalline* or *microcrystalline* silicas, including flints, cherts, jaspers, agates, chalcedonies
   b. *Opal*, an amorphous siliceous rock
   c. *Vein quartz*, a coarser-grained quartz, normally from geothermal veins in rocks
   d. *Silicified wood*, which often retains some of the preferential grain of the original wood
   e. *Silcretes*, or silicified sediments
   f. *Silicified limestones*
   g. *Quartz crystal*

2. METAMORPHIC ROCKS, such as
   a. *Quartzite*, in most cases metamorphosed sandstones
   b. *Indurated shale*, or shale subjected to high temperature and metamorphosed into a more homogeneous substance

3. IGNEOUS ROCKS, such as
   a. *Obsidian*, a superchilled volcanic lava (volcanic glass)
   b. *Volcanic lavas*, including basalts, trachytes, andesites, nephelinites, rhyolites, and phonolites
   c. *Ignimbrites*, rocks formed from hot ash-flows (welded tuffs)

The apparent sophistication in stone-artifact assemblages results from a combination of factors: the nature of the local or imported lithic materials, the functional requirements of the tools, the technological and functional norms of the social group, and the skill and motivation of the toolmaker. For example, at sites where raw-material sources are primarily small, poor-quality rocks, artifacts may be made in a casual way. This appears to be the case at Early Stone Age sites in the Omo Valley (Ethiopia), where small pebbles were apparently smashed into sharp fragments.

Even the typological distinction between the Developed Oldowan and the Early Acheulean at Olduvai Gorge (Tanzania) has been interpreted by some as being primarily a function of raw-material use. The poorly made bifaces of the Developed Oldowan are made predominantly of a quartz/quartzite from which it is relatively hard to produce large flakes; those of the Acheulean tend to be made of more easily worked lava from which the large flakes suitable for more finely worked Acheulean bifaces could be derived. In addition, experiments by P.R. Jones have shown that the superior flaking qualities and cutting efficiency of certain Olduvai raw materials, basalt and trachyandesite, may require less trimming and so yield a cruder, less sophisticated-looking end product than does the phonolite also common at Olduvai. Phonolite handaxes may appear more refined in terms of their relative thinness and number of flake scars, even when produced by the same experimental archaeologist, simply because the ones made in basalt and trachyandesite require less fashioning to produce functionally similar results.

The casual (*chopper-chopping tool*) industries of China and Southeast Asia, contemporaneous with Acheulean industries of much of the rest of the Old World but almost devoid of characteristic Acheulean handaxes and cleavers, may in part be a function of raw-material selection. H.L. Movius originally suggested that such Asian traditions were culturally separated from Acheulean groups to the west (Movius' line being drawn between the western and eastern traditions). However, G.G. Pope, among others, has suggested that the use of sharp strips of bamboo in many parts of Asia may have put less of a premium upon well-made stone cutting implements, so that these lithic assemblages seem cruder than their western counterparts.

WOOD

Next to stone, wood was almost certainly the most common raw material used in prehistory, but it is rarely preserved at earlier Paleolithic sites. The size, hardness, and ease of shaping would have had a profound effect on the types of artifacts that were made of wood. Normally, woods are easier to work in a relatively fresh rather than a seasoned condition. After the discovery of the controlled use of fire, charring and scraping would have been another efficient way of shaping wood into desired tools. The earliest definite evidence of a wooden artifact is an apparent wooden spear at the Early Paleolithic site of Clacton (England) ca. 300 Ka.

BONE, ANTLER, AND IVORY

Hard, durable parts of animal remains were made into a wide variety of forms, especially beginning in the Late Paleolithic. Antler is best worked when first soaked in water to soften it. Tools of these materials include percussors (soft hammers and punches), projectile points and harpoons, needles, and handles for hafted tools. Pieces of antler can be removed from a larger rack by the groove-and-splinter technique, in which a burin or a flake outlines a desired form on the outer surface of the antler, incising down to the spongy interior, at which point the piece can be pried or levered off. These materials can be worked with stone tools (scraped, sawed, incised, or ground). Worked bone and possibly ivory is known from the Middle Paleolithic of eastern Europe (Přezletice) and the Middle Stone Age of Africa (Katanda, Blombos, Khormusan sites, Kabwe), but worked bone, antler, and ivory become common in the archaeological record only during the past 40 Kyr.

Materials for Specific Activities

CONTAINERS

Humans are the only animals to make use of unmodified or modified materials as containers in which to carry other substances, such as foodstuffs, water, or material culture. It is likely that this extends well back in the prehistoric record. Materials used for containers might have included tree bark, large leaves, slabs of thin rock, hides (naturally dessicated or cured by human technology), eggshells, tortoise or turtle shells, skulls, horns, and wooden bowls. A pointed shaft of wood could also have functioned as a sort of spit for carrying small carcasses or larger pieces of meat. As material culture advanced, basketry and, ultimately, pottery were also common materials for containers. Examples of twined plant fibers, possibly baskets, mats, or textiles, are known from baked clay impressions at ca. 26 Ka in the Upper Paleolithic of central Europe (Dolni Věstonice).

WEAPONS AND HUNTING

For offensive or defensive weapons, the simplest could have been missiles of stone or wood and clubs of wood or bone. Simple spears could have been made of sharpened wood (with or without the use of fire) (e.g., the Clacton spear) or through mounting a projectile point of stone, bone, antler, horn, or ivory onto a wooden shaft. As technology became more complex, such weaponry as wooden or antler spear throwers and bows and arrows appeared by Late Paleolithic times. Lighter projected spears or arrows might have featured feather fletching to impart spin and stability to the shaft. There might have been slings of hide or vegetable material, and controlled fires and nets also could have been used in hunting, as well as snares, traps, and, after domestication, the dog.

PROCESSING PLANT FOODS

Interestingly, recent and modern hunter-gatherers do not normally use cutting tools in processing plant foods. Tools include stone or wooden hammers for cracking hard-shelled nuts and fruits or pounding vegetable remains, or wooden digging sticks for harvesting underground vegetation, such as roots, tubers, and rhizomes. A variety of containers help in the collection of these foodstufffs. It is likely that early tool-using hominids employed similar technologies. In the Middle Stone Age of Africa, grindstones were used widely to process tubers, seeds, and coloring materials. In Late Pleistocene and Holocene times (ca. 18–5 Ka), as more attention was probably paid to seed resources, the emergence of technologies for harvesting and processing these foods can be seen in the forms of stone sickle blades, bone and antler sickle hafts,

and grinding stones, such as those found in Late Paleolithic contexts in the eastern Sahara of Egypt. Groundstone axes and adzes become prevalent in many areas, particularly in regions of deforestation.

FISHING

Although shellfishing and freshwater fishing appear to be present in Africa from Middle Stone Age times, during the later Pleistocene and the Holocene fish and shellfish become more common as food worldwide. Materials for harvesting such resources could have included stone tools to remove shellfish from rocks, prying implements in a range of raw materials to open shellfish, and spears to catch fish. More sophisticated forms of fishing could have used vegetable and stone traps and weirs, net fishing with vegetable nets and stone weights, and line fishing with the use of hooks or gorges of such materials as bone, antler, and shell. The taking of deep-water species in the later Pleistocene to Holocene may imply the use of boats.

FIRE PRODUCTION

The principal combustible materials from which fire can be produced are wood, other types of vegetation (dried leaves, grasses, bark, fruits, seeds), bones, and dung. The artificial production of fire generally involves creating intense friction between harder pieces of combustible material (twigs or branches) through prolonged twirling or rolling and the subsequent ignition of dried tinder, in the form of vegetation or dung, to produce flames.

BINDING

By the Middle Paleolithic, there are indications that hafting of projectile points and perhaps other tools was becoming common. It is likely that either cordage was employed to tie or lash things together or an adhesive mastic was being used. Cordage could have been made of such materials as skin thongs, sinew, and rolled or braided vegetation. Adhesives or mastics could have been vegetable gums and resins or, in some areas, naturally occurring pitch.

STRUCTURES

Since the construction of simple structures in the form of sleeping nests is a common feature of the great apes, even early hominid populations probably exploited a range of materials for shelters. During the course of human evolution, these may have included wooded branches, poles, or large bones for the framework; stones for anchoring; and bark, branches, grass, leaves, mud, or hides for wall construction. Bedding materials may have included soft vegetation, hides, or feathers. Although claims have been made for Early Paleolithic structures (e.g. Terra Amata, France), the earliest clear evidence of artificial structures comes from the Middle Paleolithic site of Molodova, and evidence is not widespread until Late Paleolithic times.

CLOTHING

When clothing first became a necessity or a cultural norm, such materials as worked hides or beaten vegetation would most likely have been used. Probably by Late Pleistocene times true woven cloth made from plant fibers also emerged. Simple garments made from animal hides could have been produced in Early Paleolithic times, but there is no direct evidence (although microwear polishes on some Acheulean and Mousterian tools suggest hideworking was being being done). The oldest clothing portrayed in artwork, as well as the earliest bone needles, date to the Late Paleolithic, but the earliest preserved clothing dates to Holocene times.

See also Asia, Eastern and Southern; Clothing; Domestication; Europe; Fire; Oldowan; Stone-Tool Making. [N.T., K.S.]

Further Readings

Bordaz, J. (1970) Tools of the Old and New Stone Age. Garden City, N.Y.: Natural History Press.

Hodges, H. (1976) Artifacts: An Introduction to Early Materials and Technology. London: Baker.

Jones, P.R. (1979) Effects of raw materials on biface manufacture. Science 204:835–836.

Leakey, L.S.B. (1967) Working stone, bone, and wood. In C. Singer, E.J. Holmyard, and A.R. Hall (eds.): A History of Technology, Vol. 1. Oxford: Clarendon, pp. 128–143.

Leroi-Gourhan, A. (1969) Primitive societies. In A. Daumas (ed.): A History of Technology and Invention: Progress Through the Ages, Vol. 1. New York: Crown, pp. 18–58.

Merrick, H.V. (1976) Recent archaeological research in the Plio-Pleistocene deposits of the lower Omo Valley, southwestern Ethiopia. In G.L. Isaac and E.R. McCown (eds.): Human Origins: Louis Leakey and the East African Evidence. Menlo Park: Benjamin, pp. 461–482.

Movius, H.L. (1948) The Lower Palaeolithic cultures of southern and eastern Asia. Trans. Am. Philosoph. Soc. 38:329–426.

Pope, G.G., and Cronin, J.E. (1984) The Asian Hominidae. J. Hum. Evol. 13:377–396.

Schick, K.D., and Toth, N. (1993) Making Silent Stones Speak: Human Evolution and the Dawn of Technology. New York: Simon and Schuster.

Spier, R.F.G. (1970) From the Hand of Man: Primitive and Preindustrial Technologies. Boston: Houghton Mifflin.

Stiles, D. (1979) Early Acheulean and Developed Oldowan. Curr. Anthropol. 20:126–129.

Troeng, J. (1993) Worldwide Chronology of Fifty-three Prehistoric Innovations (Acta Archaeologica Lundensia, Series in 8o, No. 21). Stockholm: Almqvist and Wicksell.

Reck, Hans (1886–1937)

German volcanologist and paleontologist. In 1909, after receiving his doctorate in geology from Berlin University, Reck remained at the Geological and Paleontological Institute as an assistant to his mentor, W. von Branca. In the short inter-val between 1912 and the outbreak of World War I, Reck conducted three overlapping expeditions to Africa: to the dinosaur site Tendaguru (now Tanzania) in 1912–1913 under the auspices of the institute; to the German colonies in 1913, sent by the Prussian Academy of Sciences; and to Olduvai Gorge (Tanzania) in 1913 on behalf of the universities of Berlin and Munich. The primary aim of this latter expedition was to study volcanic formations in the Rift Valley, which provided Reck with an opportunity for the first rigorous search for Pleistocene human and animal remains in East Africa.

During his three months at Olduvai, Reck identified the four main beds, which he labeled I–IV. It was in Bed II that he reportedly found the remains of the "Oldoway" human skeleton, which he believed represented the first prehistoric human remains to be found in sub-Saharan Africa. It was later shown, however, that the skeleton was an intrusive burial of submodern age, with a radiocarbon date of only 15 Ka.

Although Reck retained an interest in African paleoanthropology, after World War I volcanologic studies constituted his major scientific activity. In 1931, however, he made a brief visit to Olduvai in the company of L.S.B. Leakey, who subsequently extended Reck's pioneering work at the gorge with spectacular results. In 1933, Reck wrote a popular book on Olduvai; in 1936, he published with L. Kohl-Larsen a survey of the animal and human remains found by the latter in the Lake Njarasa region.

See also Leakey, Louis Seymour Bazett; Olduvai Gorge. [F.S.]

Regourdou

Cave near Montignac, Dordogne, in southwestern France, yielding archaeological and human remains dated to ca. 80 Ka (Weichsel l) on faunal and sedimentological grounds. This site contained the skeleton of a young adult male Neanderthal at one end of a large stone-lined pit, divided by a wall of stone slabs. The other half of the pit contained the carefully arranged bones of a single brown bear (*Ursa arctos*). Associated faunal elements, flint tools of Quina Mousterian type, and stone structures suggest elaborate burial practices. The site, located close to the painted cave of Lascaux, was discovered by R. Constant and excavated by E. Bonifay in the years 1957–1961.

See also Europe; Middle Paleolithic; Mousterian; Neanderthals; Ritual. [A.S.B.]

Reilingen

Later Middle Pleistocene faunal assemblage from the town of Reilingen, near Heidelberg, Germany, including a partial cranium of *Homo*. The faunal elements were recovered from a gravel pit, mostly after quarrying, and, although there is some doubt about their association, several indicator species suggest that most of the specimens date to the Holstein interglacial. They may perhaps be correlated to ^{18}O Stages 11–9 (thus, ca. 400–350 Ka). Some elements, however, date as late as the Late Weichselian (ca. 40–20 Ka). The human fossil came from a deep level, and its preservation suggests that it was not mixed in from a higher (later) horizon, although, since it was not collected *in situ*, that conclusion is not certain. No artifacts were recovered from the gravels.

The *Homo* specimen includes both parietals and parts of the occipital and right temporal. The vault is large, with an estimated cranial capacity of ca. 1,430 cc. The occipital preserves a suprainiac fossa, a bilaterally developed occipital torus, and a strong convexity of its superior part, yielding an outline that may be incipiently bun-shaped. These features place the Reilingen cranium among the later Middle Pleistocene predecessors of the Neanderthals, such as Atapuerca, Steinheim, and Swanscombe.

See also Anteneanderthal; Atapuerca; Europe; Neanderthals; Steinheim; Swanscombe. [E.D.]

Further Readings

Dean, D., Hublin, J.-J., Holloway, R.L., and Ziegler, R. (1998) On the phylogenetic position of the pre-Neanderthal specimen from Reilingen, Germany. J. Hum. Evol. 34:485–508.

Retouch

Removal of flakes from a piece of stone. Sometimes the term *primary retouch* refers to the initial, roughing-out stages of stone reduction, while *secondary retouch* designates the more refined reduction of stone material, as in the case of bifacial thinning or the shaping of flake tools. Some archaeologists restrict the term to refer to the formation of flake tools.

See also Flake; Stone-Tool Making. [N.T., K.S.]

Rift Valley

Rift valleys form by failure and collapse of the cratonic continental crust on the crest of thermally expanded domal uplifts, and they widen as the crust slides away from the uplift. The East African Rift Valley system, one of the best-known examples, extends for a distance of 3,000 km. This elongated system is not a single curving valley but a series of connected rift segments, which follow a zig-zag course from one thermally uplifted dome to the next. The rift valleys are deepest, and the rift shoulders highest, in the crestal part of each dome. From north to south, the primary domes of the East African system are Palestine, Aqaba, Yemen, and Ethiopia. From the Ethiopia dome, the Eastern, or Gregory, Rift opens southward toward the Kenya and Eyasi domes, while to the west deep rifts transect domed-up highlands from Ruwenzori to the Zambesi. From the crest of each dome, a third, or *failed-arm,* rift normally propagates from the obtuse angle of the main rift junction; the most notable is the Winam (Kavirondo) Rift of western Kenya. The fact that each dome has its individual history explains why different parts of the East African Rift have different ages, from Cretaceous sediments in the Malawi segment and major Oligocene volcanism in the Ethiopian and Yemen domes to largely Pliocene volcanism and subsidence in the Eyasi region. Plate-tectonic studies indicate that all oceans (except the Pacific, which has no continents) originate by craton rifting, with the Atlantic Ocean, the Red Sea, and the Gulf of Oman as the most obvious examples. The Newark red beds of New Jersey and the valley of the Connecticut River, in which the first dinosaur in America was discovered, were deposited in a failed arm of the Atlantic Rift Valley, and the buried salt bodies of the Gulf Coast oilfields developed in a deep rift valley like the Dead Sea.

The East African Rift Valley of Ethiopia, Kenya, Uganda, and Tanzania has provided ideal conditions for the accumulation, preservation, and recovery of archaeological and paleontological remains. As Cenozoic rifting proceeded in eastern Africa, a series of elongate basins formed and disappeared. Lakes, ponds, and swamps in the rapidly subsiding basins trapped the sediments that rivers brought to them. Primates, including hominid species, left skeletal and cultural remains among the bones of thousands of other animals that lived and died in the basins, which became embedded in the sediments left by the ancient lakes and rivers. Because volcanic activity is closely associated with rifting, the fossil-bearing levels in many places were sandwiched between volcanic-ash horizons or lava flows, which can be used to obtain radiometric dates. The volcanism, in addition, is abnormally alkaline due to the great depths from which the magmas come, and this has fostered unusually complete preservation of faunas even in normally acidic environments, such as forests and highland swamps. In addition, the rift shoulders create rain shadow in the basins, also leading to the development of arid, alkaline burial environments that favor fossilization. Continuing tectonic activity then exposed many buried sections, making it possible to explore the abundantly fossiliferous layers in many places. The East African Rift Valley has, therefore, become a focus of the search for early hominids and traces of their activities.

See also Africa; Africa, East; Plate Tectonics; Stratigraphy. [J.A.V.C., T.D.W.]

Further Readings

Bishop, W.W., ed. (1978) Geological Background to Fossil Man. Edinburgh: Scottish Academic Press.

Ritual

Ritual acts can be defined as beliefs in action. Evidence for ritual behaviors is of special interest for the study of human evolution, because such behaviors imply the existence of a belief system shared by a group of people, and belief systems, or ideologies, play an integral role in human cultural systems today.

To ethnographers, rituals are institutionalized patterns of behavior that both express and reinforce group beliefs. Rituals involve the manipulation of symbols, often represented by special material objects, such as clothing, decoration, or artifacts. They take place at a set time and place and consist of behavioral acts that have become highly formalized and stereotyped. Religious rituals can take many forms and serve many ecological, ideological, psychological, and sociopolitical functions. Some rituals, such as baptismal or marriage ceremonies in our own culture, are individual oriented and mark a person's transition from one recognized social state into another. Other rituals, such as Thanksgiving or Christmas celebrations, are group oriented and express a relationship between a group of believers and the object or objects of their beliefs.

Evidence for prehistoric belief systems is notoriously difficult, if not impossible, to obtain directly. While a fairly direct relationship exists between a group's subsistence practices and the material remains that this behavior leaves behind at archaeological sites (e.g., remains of food prey, hunting and butchering tools), material evidence for past ideologies is far scarcer and more ambiguous. Evidence for rituals, which is archaeologically more accessible, can thus serve as an indirect indicator of the existence of belief systems in the past.

In general, the archaeological record of hominids before the advent of "archaic *Homo sapiens*" ca. 400 Ka contains few, if any, remains not associated with utilitarian behavior. With the appearance of this species, however, we begin to get increasing evidence for some sorts of ritual behavior.

Some scholars have argued that rituals or cults existed not only among "archaic *Homo sapiens*," but even among *Homo erectus* groups. Specifically, the discovery of highly fragmented and charred *H. erectus* remains belonging to a number of individuals and often bearing cutmarks and skinning marks at such sites as Zhoukoudian (China) has been used to argue for the existence of ritual cannibalism. Similar ideological explanations have been offered to account for more than 500 charred and splintered bones belonging to more than 50 Neanderthals of both sexes at the Krapina Cave (Croatia). A recent study has even suggested that, rather than ritual cannibalism, data from Krapina suggest the practice of defleshing the deceased and secondary reburial of their bones. Similarly ambiguous explanations have been offered to account for cutmarks and skinning marks and artificially made enlargements of areas around the foramen magnum found on the crania of various premodern *H. sapiens,* including the Bodo (Ethiopia), Petralona (Greece), and Monte Circeo (Italian Neanderthal) skulls.

The discovery of disjointed and apparently sorted skeletal remains of cave bears at such cave sites as Drachenloch (Switzerland) and Regourdou (France), in what appears to have been artificially made cairns or under large stone slabs, has been used to argue for the existence of bear cults among the Neanderthals. A reexamination of the evidence, however, suggests that most of these skeletal remains probably resulted from repeated deaths of bears in caves during hibernation and not from hominid ritual practices.

Our strongest evidence for the earliest ritual behavior comes from the way that "archaic *Homo sapiens*" disposed of their dead. Some intentional burials of Neanderthals are known from the Old World. Individuals of both sexes and of various ages were buried with grave goods in either artificially dug graves or under earth mounds. At Le Moustier in southwestern France, for example, an adolescent male was liberally sprinkled with red ocher, given grave goods, and buried in a flexed position ca. 40 Ka. The nearby cave site of La Ferrassie, dated to ca. 70–50 Ka, contained shallow pits and low mounds with burials of eight Neanderthals: an adult male, an adult female, four small children, one newborn infant, and one fetus. At the Teshik-Tash Cave (Uzbekistan), at least six pairs of mountain-goat horns may have been placed vertically around the grave of a Neanderthal youth who was buried perhaps 100 Ka. Finally, some researchers have argued that pollen remains of flowering plants found in the fill over a burial of an aged Neanderthal male at Shanidar (Iraq) indicate that flowers played a part in burial ceremonies ca. 60 Ka.

The existence of this way of disposing of the dead, one that entailed a much greater investment of labor than needed to be expended, implies ritual behavior and suggests that belief systems may have played a part in cultural practices of hominids who preceded anatomically modern humans. The advent of fully modern people, however, brought with it a veritable explosion in ritual and ideological behavior. The archaeological record of these Late Paleolithic people contains multiple evidence for this in the forms of burials, musical instruments, cave and portable art, and architectural elaboration in cave and open-air sites.

See also Bodo; Drachenloch; Homo sapiens; Krapina; La Ferrassie; Late Paleolithic; Le Moustier; Middle Paleolithic; Modern Human Origins; Musical Instruments; Neanderthals; Paleolithic Image; Petralona; Regourdou; Shanidar; Teshik-Tash; Zhoukoudian. [O.S.]

Further Readings

Gargett, R. (1989) The evidence for Neanderthal burial. Curr. Anthropol. 30:157–190.

Harrold, F.B. (1980) A comparative analysis of Eurasian Paleolithic burials. World Archaeol. 12:196–211.

Hayden, B. (1993) The cultural capacities of Neanderthals: A review and re-evaluation. J. Hum. Evol. 24:113–146.

Pfeiffer, J.E. (1982) The Creative Explosion. New York: Harper and Row.

Pfeiffer, J.E. (1985) The Emergence of Humankind, 4th ed. New York: Harper and Row.

Solecki, R. (1971) Shanidar: The First Flower People. New York: Knopf.

Robinson, John Talbot (1923–)

South African paleontologist. Between 1947 and 1951, Robinson was R. Broom's assistant at the Transvaal Museum, Pretoria, and as a consequence was intimately connected with the discovery and interpretation of the australopiths and other skeletal material recovered from the South African sites of Swartkrans, Makapansgat, and Sterkfontein. After Broom's death in 1951, Robinson remained in Pretoria and continued to work at the Swartkrans site. According to Robinson, the morphological dichotomy of the early fossil hominids from South Africa was correlated with behavioral and ecological differences, an idea that became known as the *dietary hypothesis.* The gracile (omnivorous) australopiths were considered to be in the ancestry of *Homo,* whereas the robust (herbivorous) forms were viewed as divergent and overspecialized hominids that eventually became extinct. In 1963, Robinson accepted a position at the University of Wisconsin. In 1972, he produced a major synthesis on the australopith postcranial skeleton, in which he deduced that these hominids were more arboreal than had hitherto been suspected. Around 1980, a debilitating stroke cut short his career.

See also Australopithecus; Broom, Robert; Makapansgat; Sterkfontein; Swartkrans. [F.S.]

Rogachev, Aleksandr Nikolaevich (1912–1984)

Russian archaeologist who for many years headed archaeological research at the Kostenki-Borschevo Late Paleolithic sites in Russia. His work there revealed that the classic French sequences for Paleolithic stone-tool industries, widely adopted by European archaeologists, were not suitable for analysis of Russian data. This led archaeologists to recognize local synchronic as well as diachronic Paleolithic industries (cultures).

See also Bordes, François; Kostenki; Peyrony, Denis. [O.S.]

Romanellian

Late Pleistocene Epipaleolithic industry, equivalent to the final stage of the Epigravettian and extending from southern Italy to the Mediterranean coast of France and the Rhône Valley between 12 and 10.5 Ka. Named after the type site of the Grotta Romanelli near Lecce (Puglia) in southern Italy, the industry is characterized by short, round end-scrapers, microgravette points, unifacial points, Azilian points with curved backs, microburins, and rare geometric microliths. Faunal remains suggest a greater diversity of resources than in the earlier phases of the Paleolithic, together with reliance on smaller species, such as rabbits and snails. At the Grotta Romanelli itself, the Romanellian is associated with a series of nine or more human burials.

See also Azilian; Economy, Prehistoric; Epigravettian; Epipaleolithic; Europe; Mesolithic; Stone-Tool Making; Upper Paleolithic. [A.S.B.]

Rose Cottage

Cave site near Ladybrand, Orange Free State (South Africa), with a long archaeological sequence ranging from Howieson's Poort at or near bedrock (age ca. 90 Ka), with a possible Middle Stone Age (MSA) level below, to a series of Wilton levels dated as late as AD 850. As at Klasies River Mouth, the Howieson's Poort level appears to be overlain by a flake-dominated Middle Stone Age industry (MSA 3 of T.P. Volman) lacking microliths, with possible affinities to the Orangian industry, which is otherwise limited to open-air occurrences. Most interesting is a pre-Wilton MSA level with utilized microblades and microblade cores, which may represent one of the earliest contexts for this technology in southern Africa, ca. 25 Ka or slightly younger based on a radiocarbon age of 25.6 Ka for the top of the underlying sand.

See also Howieson's Poort; Klasies River Mouth; Later Stone Age; Middle Stone Age; Orangian; Second Intermediate; Stone-Tool Making; Wilton. [A.S.B.]

Further Readings

Volman, T. (1984) Early prehistory of Southern Africa. In R.G. Klein (ed.): Southern Africa and Palaeoenvironments. Rotterdam: A.A. Balkema, pp. 169–220.

Rules

In ecology and evolutionary biology, there are several generalizations that are dignified by the title of "rules" but that are at best rules of thumb. Perhaps the best known of these are Bergmann's and Allen's rules. These state that members of a particular mammal group living in cold regions tend to be larger bodied (Bergmann's), and to have shorter limbs, ears, and other protruding body parts (Allen's), than those from warmer ones. The physiological basis for both of these generalizations lies in the relationship between body volume and surface area and in the necessity of shedding heat (by maximizing surface area relative to volume) in warmer climates and conserving it (by the reverse) in cooler ones. Other rules include Gloger's (melanins—skin and pelage pigments—tend to increase in warmer and more humid parts of a species' range) and Romer's (new adaptations often come about as responses to existing—not new—conditions). The main point to bear in mind about "rules" of this kind is that, despite their name, they do not represent laws that nature obeys but are simply observations about patterns that tend to recur in nature. [I.T.]

Rusinga

Island at the mouth of the Winam Gulf of Lake Victoria in western Kenya. Numerous Lower Miocene sites in the volcaniclastic Kiahera and Hiwegi beds of Rusinga and adjacent Mfwangano Island, closely dated to 17.8 Ma by $^{40}Ar/^{39}Ar$ analysis, and in the slightly younger, lacustrine Kulu Beds have yielded abundant and remarkably well-preserved fossils of vertebrates, invertebrates, and plants. The Rusinga fossil beds were discovered by British geologist E.J. Wayland in 1928, and the first hominoids by L.S.B. Leakey in 1931. At Karungu, in equivalent subvolcanic strata 50 km to the south on the far side of the Kisingiri volcanic complex, abundant fossils have been known since 1910, but no primates have been found.

A wide range of mammalian taxa from Rusinga and Mfwangano includes the most complete known specimens of Early Miocene primates, including the "First Family" group from Kaswanga Point, the famous 1948 *Proconsul* cranium from site 107, and the articulated postcranial elements from the Gumba Pot-hole site. The Rusinga primates were initially lumped with those of Songhor, Koru, and Napak, but refined dating indicates that Rusinga is ca. 2 Myr younger. The *Proconsul nyanzae* and *Proconsul heseloni* of Rusinga-Mfwangano are now held to be distinct from the earlier proconsulids. Of the Early Miocene catarrhine species, only *Dendropithecus macinnesi* and *Rangwapithecus vancouveringorum* (typified at Rusinga) and *Limnopithecus legetet* (typified at Koru) are common to both Rusinga and the earlier levels.

Rusinga and Mfwangano are unusual sites, in that they preserve forest-adapted mammals in desertlike alkaline floodplain sediments. Most fossils of forest-adapted mammals are known only from highly selective cave-floor accumulations because bones tend to decompose rapidly in acidic forest soils. The sediments of the Rusinga-Mfwangano Basin, which are also notable for preserving soft-bodied insects, fruit, and animal tissue, were strongly influenced by constant falls of hyperalkaline carbonatite-nepheline ash from the contemporaneous Kisingiri volcano. The chemistry, and thus the sedimentology, of material trapped in the downfaulted basin resembled that of a soda dry lake, although it actually lay in the midst of deep forest. Alkaline, carbonate-rich environments are highly conducive to fossilization. On the negative side, the volcanically induced "mock aridity" in the fossil beds here, and also at the Legetet and Napak volcanoes, led earlier workers to hypothesize that the Early Miocene hominoids were adapted to open country.

See also Africa, East; Koru; Napak; Proconsul; Rift Valley; Songhor. [J.A.V.C.]

Further Readings

Drake, R.E., Van Couvering, J.A., Pickford, M.H., Curtis, G.H., and Harris, J.A. (1988) New chronology for Early Miocene mammalian faunas at Kisingiri, western Kenya. J. Geol. Soc. London 145:479–491.

Harris, J.A., and Van Couvering, J.A. (1994) Mock aridity. Geology 23:593–596.

Russia

Largest nation in the modern world, with an area of ca. 17 million km², spanning 11 time zones and two continents: Europe and Asia. The European part is a broad expanse of relatively flat terrain terminating with the north-south-running Ural Mountains, which divide Europe from Asia. The larger Asian part, Siberia, is a geomorphic amphitheater where the interior plains are rimmed by mountains in the west, south, and east and open to the Arctic Ocean in the north.

Few fossil primates are known, although Cenozoic mammal localities are common. In the 1990s, however, fossils of a large colobine monkey similar to the European *Dolichopithecus* were recovered at Udunga near Lake Baikal. These are identical to material collected to the south, in Mongolia, and dated to ca. 2.5 Ma. These finds and the associated mammal fauna suggest a steppic migration route from Southwest Asia across Siberia during the Pliocene.

European Russia

The paleoanthropological record of European Russia is extensive but mostly confined to archaeological remains. Few Pleistocene human fossils have been recovered. The oldest, of Neanderthals, are confined to a molar found at the Middle Paleolithic site of Rozhok I near the Sea of Azov. Although small fragments of anatomically modern humans (*Homo sapiens sapiens*) have been found at a number of Late Paleolithic sites, complete skeletons have been recovered from burials at only a few sites, the best known being Sungir.

Data for human occupation of European Russia before the last interglacial (>130 Ka) are ambiguous and come from a few localities in the extreme south (e.g., Kudaro, Mikhailovskij Khutor) where artifacts claimed to be Mode 1 pebble tools as well as some surface finds of bifaces, stylistically dated to the Late Acheulean, have been reported. While territories to the southwest, south, and southeast of Russia (e.g., Crimea and the Dnestr region in Ukraine, the Caucasus) contain many stratified sites with Middle Paleolithic flake-tool inventories, such sites are rare within Russia and restricted to the southernmost parts of the country (e.g., Il'skaia, Rozhok, Sukhaia Mechetka). Higher latitudes contain evidence for a more ephemeral presence of hominids, which is restricted to lithic inventories dating to either the last interglacial or the very late Middle Pleistocene. These inventories, while containing such ubiquitous Middle Paleolithic tools as bifaces, points, side-scrapers, and denticulates, differ considerably from those identified at coeval sites in western Europe. This precludes identifying them using the classic Bordes type list or classifying them into Middle Paleolithic cultures or variants identified for territories farther west. A number of local classificatory schemes have been suggested for these materials by various Russian and Ukrainian scholars, none of which has found wide acceptance. No sites containing stratified Middle and Late Paleolithic inventories have been found to date in European Russia.

Late Paleolithic sites are far more numerous, dated to ca. 36–10 Ka and containing elaborate structures such as houses made of mammoth bones, storage pits, burials, jewelry, and portable art. Their distribution indicates expansion of human settlement to the north during warmer interstadial times ca. 25 Ka (e.g., Sungir at 56° N or Byzovaia at 64° N on the Pechora River, ca. 175 km south of the Arctic Circle) and a southward shift during colder and harsher stadial periods of the last glaciation. Cave art has been found at two sites in the Ural Mountains, Ignat'ev and Kapova.

Late Paleolithic inventories from European Russia do not fit the chrono-cultural sequence developed for western Europe. In their chronological sequence, local early Late Paleolithic industries—some with a strong presence of Middle Paleolithic elements and an absence of worked bone and jewelry (Streletskaia) and others blade-based and found with bone tools and items of personal adornment (Spitsyn)—change into what is termed the *Eastern Gravettian* and subsequent *Epigravettian* entities. While there is no consensus on just how many local cultures or technocomplexes can be identified at any point in time, some sites along the Don and the Seim rivers are recognized as belonging to the Kostenki-Avdeevo culture or cultural unity dating to ca. 22 Ka. As elsewhere in Europe, we can monitor a greater regionalization in human adaptations throughout the Late Paleolithic. Groups in the central part of the plain exploited large-size gregarious herbivores found in large numbers along the river valleys of that periglacial steppe, while those in the south focused more on exploiting steppe bison and, by the end of the Pleistocene, harvested wild cereals.

- ■ Acheulean
- ▼ Middle Paleolithic
- ▽ Middle Paleolithic & ?Neanderthal
- ● Late Paleolithic
- ◉ Late Paleolithic & modern humans
- ✚ "Eoliths"
- ★ Cercopithecidae

Eliseevichi ◉● Yudinovo
Suponevo
Mikhailovskij Khutor ●
Il'skaia ▼ ▽ Kostienki-Borshevo ◉ Sungir
Rozhok ▼ Sukhaia Mechetka
Kudaro ■ Byzovaia
Kapova ● ●Ignat'ev
Novoselovo ◉ Afontova Gora
Strashnaya ▼ ▽ ●●Kokorevo
Denisova Mal'ta-Buret'◉ ★ Udunga
Diring-Ur'akh ✚
Dyuktai
Ushki ◉
Filimoshki ✚

Above: The position of Russia (shaded) in Eurasia. Below: Selected Russian localities yielding human and monkey fossils and archaeological remains. The circles at sites indicate multiple symbols for these localities.

Siberia

As in European Russia, Pleistocene paleoanthropological materials have been found along the major river valleys and their tributaries, reflecting as much a pattern of research as past settlement systems. Similarly, the Siberian record also indicates the earliest evidence for hominid presence in the southern latitudes. Hominid skeletal remains here are even sparser, with some allegedly Neanderthal teeth found in the Middle Paleolithic layers of Denisova Cave; it seems unlikely that Neanderthals extended this far east, and the specimens may represent an Asian "archaic *Homo sapiens*." Burials containing remains of two children at Mal'ta and an adult at Ushki on Kamchatka, together with more fragmentary remains from the sites along the Enisei River (Afontova Gora, Novoselovo), belong to anatomically modern people and come from Late Paleolithic cultural layers.

A number of localities containing crude pebble tools are claimed to date to the Early or Middle Pleistocene (e.g.,

Ulalinka in the Altai and Filimoshki on the Amur River in the Maritime Far East) or even older (e.g., Diring-Ur'akh in Sokha or Yakutia). All of them come from gravel beds of uncertain stratigraphic integrity; their status as true artifacts is questioned by some scholars, and their dating is extremely controversial. Evidence for unequivocal occupation of Siberia comes from *in situ* materials recovered at Middle Paleolithic sites that are restricted to the extreme south. Mountainous (Gornyj) Altai contains a number of stratified cave and open-air sites with superimposed Middle and Late Paleolithic layers (e.g., Denisova, Okladnikov and Strashnaya caves). The same region also contains stratified Late Paleolithic sites whose lower layers date to the very early stage. These inventories, although sparse, show that the Middle-to-Late Paleolithic transition occurred in southern Siberia more than 42 Ka. The relatively recent discovery of unequivocal Middle Paleolithic materials in Siberia precludes their assignment to particular facies or cultures at present. What is clear, however, is that, although these inventories, like those in European Russia, show the use of both Levallois and non-Levallois core-reduction techniques for the production of flake tools, Siberian stone tools also do not fit the classificatory schemes and chrono-typological constructs developed for western Europe.

The same is true for Siberian Late Paleolithic materials found in much greater abundance. The presence of crude pebble tools together with many Middle Paleolithic elements (e.g., large side-scrapers, or *skreblos*) in most Late Paleolithic Siberian assemblages, which are found together with blade and microblade tools; worked bone, antler, and ivory, jewelry; and portable art depicting birds, animals, and humans, distinguishes this Late Paleolithic manifestation from that found in Europe and Africa. A number of regionally bounded Late Paleolithic cultures have been identified in Siberia (e.g., the Mal'ta-Buret' along the Angara River near Irkutsk, the Afontova, and the Kokorevo—one blade and the other flake based—along the Enisei River, the Dyuktai in northeastern Siberia), though some of them, like Dyuktai, are recognized by only some scholars. Siberian Late Paleolithic inventories do not show the patterned change through time identified for western Europe with one culture or technocomplex replacing another, and, at present, no uniform classificatory regional sequences exist to correlate them.

Chronometric dating and the distribution of these sites, which are more numerous in the southern parts of central and eastern Siberia than in the marshier western Siberia, indicate that these regions were permanently colonized by the makers of Late Paleolithic inventories shortly after the evolution of the periglacial steppe biomes there ca. 35–30 Ka. The Siberian Late Pleistocene climatic sequence—consisting of the Zyrianka glacial (70–50 Ka), the Kargin interglacial (50–25 Ka), and the Sartan glacial (25–10 Ka) periods—dates the initial spread of Late Paleolithic groups out of the more hospitable southern foothill and mountain regions into the more open northern latitudes during the Kargin period. Siberian Late Paleolithic sites, from the early phase onward, contain elaborate features such as burials, semisubterranean and surficial dwellings, and curbed hearths. As elsewhere, lithic inventories from many of these sites also show the use of superior exotic raw materials obtained from considerable distances.

In sum, the dating and distribution of Paleolithic sites and localities suggest that, although Russia, both in Europe and in Asia, may have been first colonized as early as the Middle Pleistocene, these hominids were few in number and only intermittently present. Permanent hominid occupation, on the other hand, occurred only in the Late Pleistocene, with earlier Middle Paleolithic groups restricted to more hospitable and geomorphically more diverse southern environments where foothills and mountains were found in close proximity to better-watered open landscapes. The makers of Late Paleolithic inventories were the first to successfully colonize all latitudes of Russia on a permanent basis, expanding their settlements to even the Arctic Circle by ca. 14–12 Ka. Finally, it is likely that Russia was populated from disparate areas, including central Asia, central and southeastern Europe, China, Mongolia, and Southwest Asia.

See also Asia, Eastern and Southern; Asia, Western; Afontova Gora; Colobinae; Denisova Cave; Dyuktai; Early Paleolithic; Europe; Homo sapiens; Kostenki; Late Paleolithic; Mal'ta; Mezhirich; Middle Paleolithic; Molodova; Neanderthals; Rogachev, Aleksandr Nikolaevich; Sungir. [O.S.]

Further Readings

Klein, R. G. (1973) Ice-Age Hunters of the Ukraine. Chicago: University of Chicago Press.

Kuzmin, Y.V., and Krivonogov, S.K. (1994) The Diring Paleolithic site, eastern Siberia: Review of geoarchaeological studies. Geoarchaeology 9:287–300.

Larichev, V., Khol'ushkin, Y., and Laricheva, I. (1987) Lower and Middle Paleolithic of Northern Asia: Achievements, Problems, and Perspectives. J. World Prehist. 1:415–464.

Larichev, V., Khol'ushkin, Y., and Laricheva, I. (1988) The Upper Paleolithic of Northern Asia: Achievements, Problems, and Perspectives. I: Western Siberia. J. World Prehist. 2:359–396.

Larichev, V., Khol'ushkin, Y., and Laricheva, I. (1990) The Upper Paleolithic of Northern Asia: Achievements, Problems, and Perspectives. II: Central and Eastern Siberia. J. World Prehist. 4:347–385.

Larichev, V., Khol'ushkin, Y., and Laricheva, I. (1992) The Upper Paleolithic of Northern Asia: Achievements, Problems, and Perspectives. III: Northeastern Siberia and the Russian Far East. J. World Prehist. 6:441–476.

Soffer, O. (1985) The Upper Paleolithic of the Central Russian Plain. Orlando: Academic.

Velichko, A.A., and Kurenkova, E.I. (1990) Environmental conditions and human occupation of northern Eurasia during the Late Valdai. In O. Soffer and C. Gamble (eds.): The World at 18,000 BP, Vol. 1. London: Unwin Hyman, pp. 255–265.

S

Saccopastore

Lowest and most recent terrace deposit of the Aniene River on the outskirts of Rome (Italy), where two early Neanderthal skulls were found in 1929 and 1935. The terrace deposit that yielded the skulls also contained fossil vertebrates, including hippopotamus and elephant (*Palaeoloxodon*), terrestrial molluscs, and pollen suggesting a mixed oak forest. These paleoenvironmental data suggested that Saccopastore should be attributed to the last interglacial (ca. 120 Ka). A few stone tools of Mousterian or Pontinian type, including a retouched point and a side-scraper, were also recovered. The skulls probably represent a male and a female, and it is interesting to note that the supposed female specimen shows the more marked Neanderthal characteristics, although both have relatively small cranial capacities.

See also Mousterian; Neanderthals. [C.B.S.]

Sagaie

Bone or antler points characteristic of the Upper Paleolithic (ca. 35–12 Ka), especially the Magdalenian period (ca.

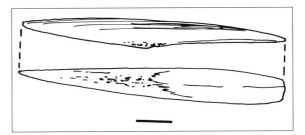

Sagaie. Scale is 1 cm.

17–12 Ka). These sturdy projectile points are normally pointed at one or both ends and are round or oval in cross-section. Some have beveled or incised bases. Very early examples of bone points are also known from the Mousterian of eastern Europe (ca. 45 Ka) and from the Middle Stone Age of Africa (ca. 90–60 Ka).

See also Magdalenian; Middle Stone Age; Mousterian; Spear; Upper Paleolithic. [N.T., K.S.]

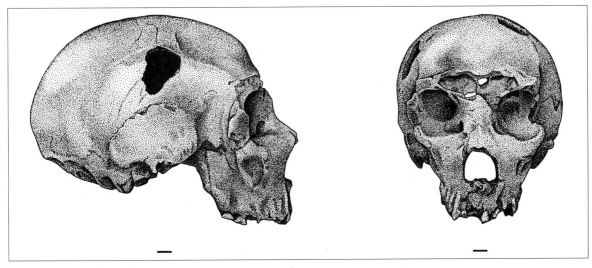

Lateral and facial views of the Saccopastore 1 Neanderthal cranium. Scales are 1 cm.

Sahabi

Collecting area in Mio-Pliocene estuarine strata of north-eastern Libya, ca. 90 km south of Ajdabiyan. Fossil bone in the Wadi es-Sahabi was discovered by Italian geologists in the 1930s, and expeditions directed by N.T. Boaz between 1975 and 1981 recovered an abundant fauna, including remains of the cercopithecoids *Macaca* and *Libypithecus,* as well as marine mammals. The main fossil beds rest on Upper Miocene evaporites that formed in the early stages of desiccation of the Mediterranean Basin, ca. 0.5 Myr before Pliocene inundation at 5.3 Ma. They are close in age to end-Miocene deposits at Wadi Natrun, Langebaanweg, and Lothagam.

See also Africa, North; Lothagam; Miocene; Pliocene; Sea-Level Change. [D.P.D., R.L.B.]

St. Acheul

Type locality of the Early Paleolithic Acheulean industry. St. Acheul is one of several localities (together with Abbeville and Moulin Quignon) along the Somme Valley near Amiens in northwest France where J. Boucher de Perthes first identified Paleolithic implements exposed by quarrying operations in the middle 1800s. These claims were not generally believed at the time they were made, although they were increasingly accepted after 1860 as discoveries of stone tools and fossils were made in sealed stratigraphic contexts.

Investigations in the late 1800s and early 1900s by V. Commont revealed a long sequence of terrace deposits containing deposits of Acheulean artifacts and vertebrate fossils of Middle Pleistocene age (ca. 400–250 Ka). In the early twentieth century, H. Breuil used collections from the Somme terraces around St. Acheul to formulate a developmental sequence for changes in the design of Acheulean handaxes, from crude Chellean protobifaces, to Abbevillian picks, to more symmetrical Acheulean handaxes.

One of the most important Acheulean sites in this region is the Atelier Commont (Commont's Workshop). This open-air site contains a rich assemblage of well-made handaxes and numerous retouched tools made on flakes. Some flakes from the Atelier Commont were struck using the Levallois technique.

See also Abbevillian; Acheulean; Boucher de Perthes, Jacques; Early Paleolithic; Europe; Handaxe; Levallois. [J.J.S., N.T., K.S.]

Further Readings

Grayson, D. (1983) The Establishment of Human Antiquity. New York: Academic.

Saint-Césaire

Rockshelter in Charente-Maritime (France), excavated by F. Lévêque, that in 1979 produced Neanderthal fossils from early Upper Paleolithic Châtelperronian levels dated to 36 Ka by thermoluminescence. These levels contain the typical range of Châtelperronian artifacts, such as backed blades, bone points, and perforated teeth. The more complete skeleton, which is clearly a Neanderthal, appears to be a secondary burial in a shallow pit less than a meter across in the higher of two Châtelperronian levels at the site. The main cranial parts consist of the right side of the front of a skull with the face and

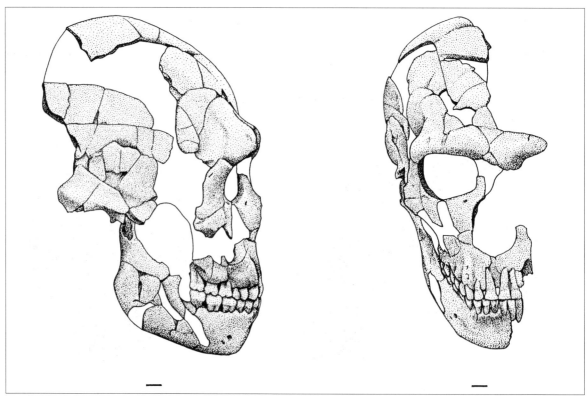

Lateral and facial views of the partial Neanderthal cranium from Saint-Césaire. Scales are 1 cm.

right half of the mandible. The form of the frontal bone, brows, face, and jaws is Neanderthal, although the nose and teeth are relatively small. The postcranial skeleton is fragmentary but Neanderthal-like in its robusticity. A second, more fragmentary Neanderthal is also present in the same levels. Until the discovery of the Saint-Césaire Neanderthal, the nature of the population responsible for the manufacture of the early Upper Paleolithic Châtelperronian industry was an enigma. Traditionally, prehistorians had viewed the Châtelperronian (also known as Perigordian I) as the earliest Upper Paleolithic industry, deriving it from the French Mousterian of Acheulean Tradition. On the basis of the Saint-Césaire and Grotte de Renne (Arcy sur Cure) Neanderthal discoveries, many researchers now associate the Châtelperronian with relict Neanderthal populations that lived roughly contemporaneously with the (presumed) early-modern human groups who produced the Early Aurignacian industry.

See also Aurignacian; Châtelperronian; Homo sapiens; Modern Human Origins: Out of Africa; Neanderthals; Perigordian; Upper Paleolithic. [J.J.S., C.B.S.]

Further Readings

Lévêque, F., Backer, A.M., and Guilbaud, M. (1993) Context of a Late Neanderthal (Monographs in World Archeology No. 16). Madison, Wis: Prehistory Press.

St. Eble

Locality in central France claimed to yield stone tools dated to more than 2 Ma. Fossil mammals from Le Coupet in the Auvergne/Velay district of the French Massif Central are dated to ca. 2.1–1.9 Ma by their relationship to over- and underlying potassium-argon-dated volcanic materials from the Mont Coupet and other volcanoes, as well as by biochronological correlation (mid-Villafranchian mammal age). The St. Eble roadside exposure presents a sequence of residual gravels, 3–4 m of slope deposits, and (on top) a volcanic breccia that has been correlated to the 2.1 Ma dated layer. Numerous quartz fragments and flakes have been isolated from the gravels and especially the slope deposits, most of which are not determinable as human artifacts. But several pieces have been claimed by E. Bonifay and colleagues to represent extremely early tools. These have not been published in detail, and most specialists question their artifactual

nature, preferring to see them as the most artifactlike of a large series of naturally flaked quartz cobbles.

See also Early Paleolithic; Eoliths; Europe; France; Stone-Tool Making [E.D.]

Further Readings

Bonifay, E. (1989) Les premières industries du Sud-Est de la France et du massif central. In E. Bonifay and B. Vandermeersch (eds.): Les Premiers Européens. Paris: Comité Travaux Historiques Scientifiques.
Delson, E. (1989) Oldest Eurasian stone tools. Nature 340:96.

St. Gaudens

Surface site in the Aquitaine Basin in southern France. The meager fauna is generally attributed to the Middle Miocene (13–12 Ma), but this is uncertain due to the limited diversity of the sample and inadequate stratigraphic control. The site is best known for remains of *Dryopithecus fontani*.

See also Dryopithecus; Europe; Miocene. [R.L.B., D.P.D.]

Saldanha

Middle Pleistocene open-site (also known as Elandsfontein) near Hopefield (South Africa) that has produced a hominid cranial vault, extensive faunal remains, and archaeological remains of probable Acheulean type. A partial human cranium lacking the face and base was discovered in an erosional basin in 1953. A mandible and skull fragment that may be associated were found a considerable distance away. The antiquity of the cranium is unknown, owing to its provenance on the surface, but comparisons with other erosional basins nearby suggest either Acheulean or (less likely) Middle Stone Age cultural associations and a probable age of 700–400 Ka, based on biostratigraphy. The Saldanha skull resembles the Kabwe (Broken Hill) cranium in its general shape, although it is somewhat less robust, with a smaller supraorbital torus and an endocranial capacity of ca. 1,225 ml. It may represent a female individual of the same kind of population. Some workers believe that this specimen may represent part of an evolving southern African lineage of hominids that gave rise to modern humans through such evolutionary intermediates as the Florisbad specimen.

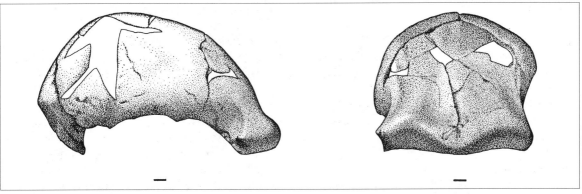

Lateral and facial views of the Saldanha (Elandsfontein) partial calotte. Scales are 1 cm.

See also Acheulean; Africa, Southern; Archaic Homo sapiens; Florisbad; Kabwe; Middle Stone Age. [C.B.S., J.J.S.]

Salé

Open-air site near Rabat (Morocco) in which a partial hominid skull was exposed by quarrying activities in 1971. These dunes are associated with the Middle Pleistocene Tensiftian transgression, tentatively dated to 400 Ka. The Salé fossil may thus be similar in age to the nearby sites at the Thomas Quarries and Sidi Abderrahman. A small faunal assemblage was recovered in the same deposits, but no stone tools were found. The skull is small, with a cranial capacity of only ca. 900 ml, but the vault is long, low, and relatively thick walled. Muscle markings are slight, suggesting derivation from a female individual. While most of these characters suggest assignment of the Salé skull to *Homo erectus*, there are also some more advanced characters that are found in *Homo sapiens* specimens. These include the basicranial proportions, an expanded parietal region, and a rounded occipital region with minimal development of an occipital torus. The occipital, however, is quite abnormal in its proportions, suggesting the presence of pathology. Because of its mosaic characteristics, the Salé skull's classification is not generally agreed upon. Some workers regard it as an evolved *H. erectus* specimen, while others believe it represents an "archaic *Homo sapiens*."

See also Africa, North; Archaic Homo sapiens; Homo erectus; Sidi Abderrahman; Thomas Quarries. [C.B.S., J.J.S.]

Sambungmachan

Fossil-collecting locality in central Java: Indonesia, dated to ?1.0–?0.2 Ma, based on lithostratigraphic correlation. A relatively complete hominid cranium was discovered in 1973 on the banks of the nearby Solo River.

Although the provenance of the cranium is known, there is no substantial agreement about its age. Estimates range from early Middle Pleistocene (ca. 500 Ka) to Late Pleistocene (50–35 Ka). The specimen seems advanced in its relatively large cranial capacity (1,035 ml), but there is disagreement as to whether it should be classified with the Ngandong hominids or with the presumably earlier *Homo erectus* specimens from Trinil and Sangiran.

See also Homo erectus; Indonesia; Koenigswald, Gustav Heinrich Ralph Von; Ngandong (Solo); Sangiran Dome; Trinil. [G.G.P.]

Further Readings

Sartono, S. (1979) The stratigraphy of the Sambungmachan site, central Java. Mod. Quatern. Res. Southeast Asia 5:83–88.

Sémah, F., Sémah, A., and Djubiantono, T. (1990) They Discovered Java. Jakarta: Pusat Penelitian Arkeologi Nasional.

Samburupithecus

Genus of Late Miocene East African Hominidae which may represent an early member of the African ape and human clade (Homininae). A single maxilla was recovered in the early 1980s from an Upper Miocene site in the Namurungule Formation, Samburu Hills, north of Lake Baringo in the Kenya Rift Valley. The fauna has been estimated to date ca. 9 Ma, and incompletely published K-Ar dates bracket the fossiliferous horizon closely at 9.5 Ma. In 1997, H. Ishida and M. Pickford named this specimen *Samburupithecus kiptalami* and interpreted it as a potential human ancestor the size of a gorilla.

The maxilla contains only the left P^3–M^3; the canine crown is broken but the size and shape of its root indicate that the individual was probably female. The premolars are large compared to the molars. The molar crowns are low and flat, probably with thick enamel and a high-relief dentin-enamel junction; M^3 is larger than either M^1 or M^2; cingulum is present around the protocone, but there is little around the hypocone and none buccally. The palate is moderately deeply arched—less so than in living African apes, but more than in proconsulids or kenyapithecines. The thick enamel and reduced cingulum are also characters that suggest a phylogenetic position intermediate between the groups mentioned: modern apes generally lack a cingulum entirely on their upper molars.

Pickford and Ishida provide a detailed comparison between *Samburupithecus* and a wide range of Miocene to living hominoids. They found that the Samburu taxon shared with Eurasian dryopithecines, pongines, and *Graecopithecus* the derived character states of enlarged upper premolars with a mesiobuccal flange of enamel on P^3 and deeply arched palate. However, they noted differences between the Eurasian genera and *Samburupithecus* in the position of the zygomatic root, the retention of some lingual cingulum, the high-relief dentin-enamel junction and large M^3. Contrary to the interpretations in this encyclopedia, they suggested that all Eurasian hominids were members of the orang clade (Ponginae) and inferred that *Samburupithecus* may have developed palatal arching in parallel with those taxa. Instead, they suggested that *Samburupithecus* was dentally most similar to early hominins and might represent a potential ancestor for that clade. An alternative preferred here is that *Samburupithecus* of Kenya and the contemporaneous *Graecopithecus* of Europe might represent early members of the Homininae with no further precision yet determined: a comparison of these two taxa would be of great interest.

See also Africa, East; Ape; Graecopithecus; Hominidae; Homininae; Miocene. [E.D., P.A.]

Further Readings

Ishida, H., and Pickford, M. (1997) A new Late Miocene hominoid from Keyna: *Samburupithecus kiptalami* gen. et sp. nov. C. r. séances Acad. Sci. Paris, Sci. Terre 325:IIa, 823–829.

Pickford, M., and Ishida, H. (1998) Interpretation of *Samburupithecus*, an Upper Miocene hominoid from Kenya. C. r. séances Acad. Sci. Paris, Sci. Terre 326:299–306.

Sawada, Y., Pickford, M., Itaya, T., Makinouchi, T., Tateishi, M., Kabeto, K., Ishida, S., and Ishida, H.

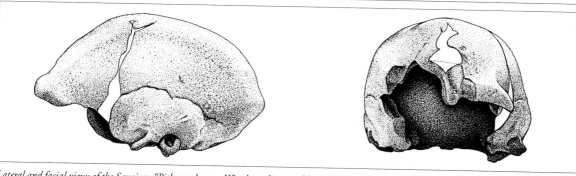

Lateral and facial views of the Sangiran "Pithecanthropus II" calotte discovered by G.H.R. von Koenigswald in 1937.

(1998) K-Ar ages of Miocene Hominoidea (*Kenyapithecus* and *Samburupithecus*) from Samburu Hills, northern Kenya. C. r. séances Acad. Sci. Paris, Sci. Terre 326:445–451.

Sandia

Paleoindian projectile points, considered by some to be the earliest form in North America, first found at Sandia Cave and subsequently at the Lucy site (both in New Mexico). Sandia points are lanceolate with contracting or square concave bases, partial to full fluting, and a distinctive unilateral shoulder. Dating is based strictly on geological contexts, the Sandia type apparently underlying and coincident with Clovis points (ca. 12–10 Ka). Questions have been raised about the authenticity of the Sandia artifacts; the matter remains unsettled.

See also Americas; Clovis; Paleoindian. [L.S.A.P., D.H.T.]

Sangiran Dome

Stratified sequence in central Java, spanning the interval between 2.3 and 0.2 Ma, according to stratigraphic, radiometric, and paleomagnetic evidence. The Sangiran Dome, an anticlinal fold in Neogene and Quaternary sediments ca. 10 km north of Surakarta, has yielded numerous early hominid fossils, most of which are assigned to *Homo erectus*. Dutch geologists in the nineteenth century recognized four formations in the exposed portion of the dome, an area ca. 6 km long and 3 km wide. The oldest beds, assigned to the Kalibeng Formation, are Pliocene marine clays, sandstones, limestones, and volcanic tuffs. Unconformably overlying the Kalibeng are more than 85 m of the Pucangan (Putjangan) Formation, composed of black clays, sands, and volcanic avalanches (lahars). Conformably overlying the Pucangan Formation are the fluvial sediments of the Kabuh Formation, beginning in a widely recognized marker bed, the Grenzbank, consisting of well-consolidated calcareous sands, gravels, and silts in a distinctive hard unit ca. 2 m thick. Many, if not most, of the hominids and other vertebrate fossils derive from just below or just above the Grenzbank. Above the Grenzbank, the upper 70 m of the Kabuh Formation is made up of gravels, silts, sands, and clays, with volcanic tuffs intercalated throughout the sequence. The Kabuh is overlain unconformably by more than

50 m of gravel, silts, sands, lahars, and tuffs assigned to the Notopuro Formation.

Because of the fossil human discoveries in the Sangiran area, many attempts have been made to date the sequence. Unfortunately, magnetostratigraphic interpretations have been contradictory and equivocal, as have potassium-argon (K/Ar) and fission-track analyses of tektites (presumed on mineralogical evidence to have been reworked from a single layer) in the middle and upper parts of the Kabuh. Recent radiometric and biostratigraphic studies cited by F. Sémah indicate that the age of the earliest hominids from Sangiran was overestimated, and that the oldest specimens may date to no more than 1.3 Ma. On the other hand, a recent series of argon-argon ($^{40}Ar/^{39}Ar$) determinations on volcanic clays from the lower part of the Pucangan Formation yielded ages of ca. 1.65 Ma, and a date of ca. 1.5 Ma has been attributed to volcanic crystals associated with the original *H. erectus* from the Solo River. No firm consensus has yet emerged.

See also Asia, Eastern and Southern; Homo erectus; Indonesia; Trinil. [G.G.P.]

Further Readings

Itihara, M., Sudijono, Kadar, D., Shabasaki, T., Kumai, H., Yoshikawa, S., Aziz, F., Soeraldi, T., Wikarno, Kadar, A.P., Hasibuan, F., and Kagemori, Y. (1985) Geology and stratigraphy of the Sangiran area. Indonesia Geologic Research and Development Centre Special Publication 4:11–45.

Pope, G.G. (1985) Taxonomy, dating, and paleoenvironment: The paleoecology of the early Far Eastern hominids. Mod. Quatern. Res. Southeast Asia 9:65–81.

Sémah, F. (1996) Plio-Pleistocene of Indonesia. In J.A. Van Couvering (ed.): The Pleistocene Boundary and the Beginning of the Quaternary. Cambridge: Cambridge University Press.

Sémah, F., Sémah, A., and Djubiantono, T. (1990) They Discovered Java. Jakarta: Pusat Penelitian Arkeologi; Nasional.

Swisher, C.C., Curtis, G.H., Jacob, T., Getty, A.G., Suprijo, A., and Widiasmoro. (1994) Age of the earliest known hominids in Java, Indonesia. Science 263:1118–1121.

Sangoan

Earliest stage, on stratigraphic grounds, of the Middle and Later Stone Age core-axe industries of central Africa. The Sangoan was named by British geologist E.J. Wayland for surface material found in the 1920s at Sango Bay (Uganda), on the west side of Lake Victoria, as well as from an *in situ* gravel deposit at Nsongezi, just to the north of the lake. The Sangoan is characterized by bifaces, particularly almond-shaped and cordiform types; prepared cores, polyhedrons, rostrocarinates, core-axes, and scrapers; and Sangoan picks. Extending throughout central Africa, from the Limpopo and Orange rivers north to the Sahel and east into Tanzania and Uganda, the industry is also associated at many sites, such as Kalambo Falls, with a small-tool component of scrapers, especially concave, notched, and denticulate forms, and other tools. The presence of concave scrapers, picks, and core-axes, together with the woodland or forest environment suggested at many sites, implies a connection with a woodland adaptation, possibly involving woodworking tools. At sites on the northeast side of Lake Victoria, however, such as Simbi, and at Kamoa (Zaire), the Sangoan is associated with a sand indicative of drier, more open conditions. Its probable age is later Middle Pleistocene, although sites of probable early Late Pleistocene age may be known from Zaire and Rwanda. Excavations in the Sangoan level at Eyasi (Tanzania), presumed to be the level that yielded a cranium of "archaic *Homo sapiens*" in the late 1930s, have been dated at ca. 250 Ka.

See also Early Stone Age; Eyasi; First Intermediate; Kalambo Falls; Middle Stone Age; Stone-Tool Making. [A.S.B.]

Further Readings

McBrearty, S. (1991) Recent research in Western Kenya and its implications for the status of the Sangoan Industry. In J.D. Clark, (ed.): Cultural Beginnings: Approaches to Understanding Early Hominid Lifeways in the African Savanna. Römisch-Germanisches Zentral Museum Forschungsinstitut für Vor- und Frühgeschichte (Monographie, Band 19). Bonn: Rudolph Mabel, pp. 159–176.

Mehlman, M.J. (1991) Context for the emergence of modern man in eastern Africa: Some new Tanzanian evidence. In Clark, op. cit., pp 159–176.

Sauveterrian

Second stage in the classic Mesolithic/Epipaleolithic sequence of inland France, ca. 9.5–7.5 Ka, characterized by diminutive tools, especially biconvex points on microblades, retouched on both sides. The type site is the Abri Martinet at Sauveterre-la-Lémance (Lot-et-Garonne) in the southern Périgord. Microblade industries from other areas, including eastern Europe, although dissimilar in other ways, are sometimes referred to this industry.

See also Azilian; Epipaleolithic; Mesolithic; Périgord; Stone-Tool Making; Tardenoisian. [A.S.B.]

Saxonellidae

A rare family of primates from the Late Paleocene of Europe and North America, based on the single genus *Saxonella*. Although this taxon is unique among archaic primates with its enlarged lower third premolar, there can be no doubt that it is derived from an ancestor that would be recognized as a plesiadapid on the basis of molar-tooth conformation. Like several plesiadapiforms (e.g., *Phenacolemur*), the very long enlarged incisor is the only lower tooth anterior to the characteristically enlarged third premolar. The somewhat trenchant (bladelike) specialization of this tooth, which occurs independently in both multituberculate and marsupial mammals, as well as in carpolestid primates, is called *plagiaulacoidy*. The trenchant edge of such a lower tooth usually works against a flatter upper one, although in such marsupials as kangaroos and some phalangers its upper occlusal counterpart is equally bladelike, with a serrated edge. *Saxonella* shared with other plesiadapoids the mittenlike enlarged upper incisors that must have provided an excellent grip on whatever the animal held in its mouth. A tiny distal end of a humerus from the same Walbeck (Germany) fissure in which the teeth occur, and associated by size, strongly suggests that this animal was fully arboreal.

An interesting aspect of saxonellid distribution is the fact that so far no picrodontids or carpolestids are known in Europe in spite of the fact that the equally small saxonellids and the larger plesiadapids occur on both sides of the then incipient North Atlantic.

See also Carpolestidae; Paromomyoidea; Plesiadapidae; Plesiadapiformes; Primates. [F.S.S.]

Scala Naturae

Preevolutionary doctrine claiming that the diversity of the organic world was divinely arranged as a qualitative continuum, ranging from lower to higher and more perfect forms of life. Gradistic classification, which groups taxa according to their hierarchical position within a series of ranks meant to reflect levels of adaptive progress, is a derivative of this principle. T.H. Huxley applied such concepts during the nineteenth century in one of the earliest successful attempts to place human origins in an evolutionary perspective.

See also Anthropoidea; Cladistics; Classification; Grade; Huxley, Thomas Henry. [A.L.R.]

Schlosser, Max (1854–1932)

German paleontologist. In 1887, Schlosser published the first major review of the fossil primates. Although this study was based, in large part, on his researches at Yale University, the primary focus was an assessment of the European fossil primate record. He is best remembered, however, for his work during the opening decades of the twentieth century on the fossil mammals of the Fayum Oligocene of Egypt; in particular, his provision of the first descriptions of the early catarrhines *Parapithecus* and *Propliopithecus*. He considered the latter to be an ancestral gibbon. Curiously, Schlosser has not been the subject of a major scientific biography.

See also Fayum; Oligocene; Pliopithecidae. [F.S.]

Further Readings

Schlosser, M. (1887) Die Affen, Lemuren, Chiropteren . . . des europaischen Tertiärs. Beitr. Paläontol. Österreich-Ungarns Orients 6:1–162.

Schlosser, M. (1911) Beitrag zur kenntnis der Oligozänen Landsäugetiere aus dem Fayum: Ägypten. Beitr. Paläontol. Österreich-Ungarns Orients 24:51–167.

Schwalbe, Gustav (1844–1917)

German anatomist and paleoanthropologist. Between 1899 and 1905, while a professor of anatomy at the University of Strasbourg, Schwalbe undertook a detailed study of the fossil hominid record and concluded that the European Neanderthals were sufficiently different from modern *Homo sapiens* to warrant the rank of a distinct species (*Homo primigenius*). He also proposed two possible arrangements for the then known fossil hominids: the pithecanthropines (i.e., E. Dubois's *Pithecanthropus erectus = H. erectus*), the Neanderthals, and the anatomically modern fossils of *H. sapiens*. In the first arrangement, now known as the Unilineal (or Neanderthal) hypothesis, the Neanderthals are portrayed as an intermediary line between the pithecanthropines and modern humans, while the second depicts the Neanderthals and the pithecanthropines as specialized offshoots from the human lineage. This latter proposal formed the basis of the *presapiens* theory that attracted considerable support during the first half of the twentieth century.

See also Dubois, Eugene; Neanderthals; Presapiens. [F.S.]

Scladina (Sclayn)

Cave site in south-central Belgium, with a more or less continuous sedimentary record running from early in the last interglacial through most of the last glacial. Level 5, toward the bottom of the sequence, encloses an abundant Middle Paleolithic stone-tool assemblage dated to 150–110 Ka. Above this, in Level 4A, fragmentary Neanderthal remains dated to ca. 75–70 Ka were found in 1993. These included most of the right half of the mandible of a child aged 10–11 years, a maxillary fragment and a first molar attributed to the same individual, and an isolated adult molar. There appears to have been no significant archaeological context for these human remains, but Level 1A higher in the sequence produced numerous artifacts of typical Mousterian aspect dated to 40–37 Ka.

See also Middle Paleolithic; Mousterian; Neanderthals. [I.T.]

Further Readings

Otte, M. (dir.) (1992, 1999) Recherches aux gróttes de Sclayn Vols. I, II. Liège: ERAUL (Etudes et Recherches Archéologiques de l'Université de Liège) 27, 79.

Scraper

Term used traditionally in prehistoric archaeology to describe pieces of stone, usually flakes or blades, with retouch along one or more sides or ends. This retouch is generally semiabrupt in nature, steepening the tool edge or making it less acute than a natural flake edge, thus rendering it more suitable

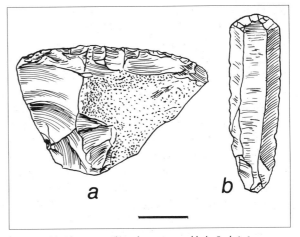

Scrapers: (a) side-scraper; (b) end-scraper on a blade. Scale is 1 cm.

for scraping rather than cutting activities. Found throughout the Paleolithic, side-scrapers (*racloirs*) are quite common in the Middle Paleolithic or Mousterian period (ca. 200–40 Ka), while end-scrapers (*grattoirs*) are typical of the Upper Paleolithic. Many of these scraper forms could have been used for such activities as hide scraping or woodworking, while more acute-edged versions could also have served as knives.

See also Flake; Middle Paleolithic; Mousterian; Retouch; Stone-Tool Making; Upper Paleolithic. [N.T., K.S.]

Sea Harvest

Coastal site consisting of a cluster of fossiliferous pockets with human remains on the northern shore of Saldanha Bay (South Africa). The pockets are depressions in sandstone underlying a lithified Middle Stone Age shell midden. The midden is provisionally dated between 74 and 60 Ka, and the age of the Sea Harvest accumulations is probably between 128 and 74 Ka. The material contains no lithic artifacts or other evidence of human culture, and the Sea Harvest bones appear most likely to have been accumulated by hyaenas. The human specimens consist of a distal manual phalanx and a maxillary premolar. The finger bone is comparatively large in relation to modern human phalanges. Its narrow shaft contrasts with the condition in European Neanderthals of this age range, and in this regard it is more like modern humans. The tooth is comparatively large with regard to the mean in modern humans, but it falls within the observed range for the premolars of modern Africans.

See also Africa, Southern; Border Cave; Homo sapiens. [F.E.G.]

Further Readings

Grine, F.E., and Klein, R.G. (1993) Late Pleistocene human remains from the Sea Harvest site, Saldanha Bay, South Africa. S. Afr. J. Sci. 89:145–152.

Sea-Level Change

Geological-scale variations in the location of the ocean strandline on the margins of the continents, due to the interaction of *eustasy* (global sea level) and the geodynamics of the continental shelf, are fundamental to understanding the role of paleobiogeography in hominoid evolution. The most significant secular variations in eustasy are in response to the Milankovitch band of astronomical cycles, which affect sea level over periods of 0.01 to 1.0 Myr. Compared to these inherently gradual rises and falls (but see below), the rate of local elevation change on the continental shelf itself, caused by tectonic and hydrologic processes, can be much more rapid. Historical and legendary accounts of catastrophic flooding on coastal plains are, therefore, related to regional changes in elevation rather than to changes in world sea level. A major exception to these generalities, however, is orbitally forced sudden rises in sea level during the Pleistocene, called *Heinrich events*. These rapid inundations resulted from the runaway collapse of continental ice sheets, when slow, global warming finally overcame the thermal inertia of the massive carapaces of ice.

ELEVATION CHANGES ON COASTAL PLAINS

Continental shelves are the aprons of sediment that pile up on the seafloor around the continents. On passive, nonsubducting margins of ocean basins, such as the east coast of North America or the Mediterranean and Indian Ocean coasts of Africa, the outer parts of the shelf are marked by continuous slow subsidence. The primary cause is the subsidence of underlying ocean crust, steadily cooling and shrinking at an average rate of ca. 1.0 cm per year. A secondary cause is compaction and dewatering of buried sediment. The continents themselves, on the other hand, are steadily (if less evenly) rising, from the combined effects of erosional unloading from the upper surface and accretion of new granitic material at the base. The Mesopotamian flood myths, including the biblical version, are based on the experience of life in a tectonically subsiding region. In many areas of the world, on the other hand, it is common to find the rising continent reflected in abandoned shorelines and terraces at successively higher elevations inland from the hinge line, with the oldest ones at the top. In volcanically active regions, such as the Bay of Naples, variations in geothermal activity can cause the land surface to inflate and subside by several meters in 100 years; the partially sunken Temple of Serapis illustrated by Charles Lyell in his famous textbook of geology in 1843 is now more or less at the same elevation above sea level as when the Romans built it.

Changing load can also affect local elevation, because the Earth's crust slowly adjusts to redistributed weight by the process known as *isostasy*. In areas such as Scandinavia and Hudson's Bay, the entire region is slowly rising, or rebounding, in response to the melting away of the Pleistocene ice sheets ca. 12 Ka. Other factors, such as changes in the local gravitational field due to slow shifts of mass in the Earth's deep interior, also have minor effects.

CHANGES IN MEAN SEA LEVEL

Close monitoring of mean sea level by agencies concerned with maintaining accurate elevation data has shown that the mean sea level has varied by only a centimeter or so since technically competent observations began, early in the 1800s, and there is no evidence that earlier Holocene sea levels were much different. This has not always been the case, however. The thick sequences of marine beds found in coastal basins of Europe (such as the North German Plain, the London-Paris Basin, the Gironde, Rhône, and Po valleys, and the lower Danube Basin), represent a history of deposition for more than 100 Myr. The sciences of stratigraphy and paleontology began as a study of these deposits, and it was long ago found that these sequences consist of distinct packets of strata, separated by major unconformities representing lengthy periods of erosion. The different packets appeared (on the basis of marine fossils) to be synchronous over wide regions. In the nineteenth century, European stratigraphers began to formally recognize the regional extent of these stratigraphic bodies as *stages* and *series* (and the time-equivalent *ages* and *epochs*), which are now fundamental units in global chronostratigraphy and the geological time scale.

Almost from the beginning, stratigraphers such as C. Depéret, H.E. Suess, and A. Grabau saw the regional extent of stages as evidence for worldwide cycles of *transgression*, or rising sea level with consequent deposition, alternating with *regression* and erosion on the coastal plains. However, the effort to modernize the geological sciences during the early and middle twentieth century brought with it an atmosphere of rigorous skepticism. In the absence of any techniques capable of accurately determining the true synchronicity of stages on a regional basis, most geologists took the conservative view that global transgressive and regressive events were more convenient than proven, and that the erosional unconformities might just as reasonably be ascribed to regional geological uplift and erosion. The idea that changes in the level of the world ocean could be responsible was ridiculed, not for lack of plausibility but for lack of proof.

In the 1960s, improved stratigraphic techniques began to support the concept of global sea-level change, just as the hitherto inexplicable concept of *continental drift* also began to emerge from disrepute. Newly refined global time scales, in which potassium-argon (K/Ar) analyses and paleomagnetic reversals were tied directly to the worldwide record of planktonic (free-floating) marine microfossils, revealed that transgressions and regressions in different areas were, in fact, closely synchronous. Work in California and New Zealand, where marine deposits show particularly clear evidence for climate change, also indicated that regressions were associated with cold climate and transgressions with warm climate. Evidence mounted rapidly, and, in the mid-1970s, a group of stratigraphers and geophysicists at Exxon Production Research (Houston), using data accumulated during the corporation's worldwide search for oil, produced a record of global transgressions and regressions over the past 300 Myr. The *Vail Curve,* named after group leader Peter Vail, showed beyond reasonable doubt that many of the major erosional unconformities found in continental-shelf sequences around the world must have been caused by real changes in mean sea level. The rise and fall leads to a predictable sequence of deposits on the outer shelf, including beds that tend to be hydrocarbon source rocks when deeply buried and other beds that tend to be impermeable reservoir

CENOZOIC TIME SCALE

Cenozoic sea-level changes (Vail Curve). The long-term curve shows an average of high sea-level stands and probably reflects changes in the volume of the ocean basins. The short-term curve shows variations down to 1 Myr long, probably due to glacio-eustatic changes, but omits very short-term changes (Milankovitch cycles). Sharp declines of 50 m or more led to net regression on subsiding continental shelves and were the most opportune times for interregional migration of mammal faunas. Courtesy of B. U. Haq.

of water in the ocean, but changes in the shape of the ocean basins affect sea level as well.

GLACIO-EUSTATIC CHANGE

The amount of water presently held in the world's ice caps, even during an interglacial, is enormous, amounting to ca. 30 million km^3. Ca. 80 percent of the world's ice is piled up on the Antarctic continent, where it reaches up to five miles in thickness, and virtually all the rest is on Greenland. It is calculated that if all of the ice in these masses were to melt, world mean sea level would rise by 70 m (220 feet). As far as we know (see below), this has not happened since the Eocene 50 Myr ago. However, estimates of glacial ice volume during the last Ice Age suggest that an additional 40–45 million km^3 were withdrawn from the seas when the Pleistocene glaciations were at a maximum. This would have lowered sea level by as much as 110–130 m (340–400 feet). The actual exposure of continental shelves during eustatic drawdown is due more to the rate of drawdown than to its magnitude, as is discussed below.

Geological evidence shows that an ice cap has been present on Antarctica at least since the Eocene, that it expanded greatly to reach sea level in the Oligocene, and that it began to attain close to its present size in the Miocene. In the Pliocene, glacial ice caps also began to build up during cold-climate cycles in Greenland, Baffin Island, Iceland, Scandinavia, and the northern Rockies, as well as in the southern Andes, Tierra del Fuego, and the Falklands. Finally, in the Pleistocene the cold-climate cycles produced huge, albeit unstable, continental ice caps on the Hudson's Bay, North Sea–Baltic, and Siberian lowlands, while every mountain range in the world (including tropical heights such as Mount Carstensz in New Guinea, the East African volcanoes, and the highlands of Ecuador) also developed glacial carapaces. Each major climate cycle in the Pliocene and the Pleistocene resulted in growth or reduction of the global ice volume and is faithfully reflected on the Vail Curve.

Glacio-eustatic sea-level swings of the frequency and magnitude indicated in the Vail Curve will always be the occasion of the first (or last) exposure of a land bridge between two moving continental blocks. Continental shelves continuously subside, with the highest subsistence rates farthest from the continent. When sea level also declines, the strandline moves down the shelf to the point at which the rate of sea-level lowering and the rate of subsidence are equal. The faster sea level recedes, the farther the strandline will move outward on the continental slope. Thus, the most likely time for intercontinental migration via exposed continental shelves would be coincident with the midpoint (not the nadir) of a major eustatic downswing, when rates of sea-level lowering are the most accelerated. At maximum rates of eustatic decline, shorelines recede all the way to the shelf edge.

As soon as the rate of eustatic lowering slows, the strandline will begin to climb back toward the continent. During rising sea level, the strandline moves very rapidly upslope because of the continuing subsidence on the shelf. The rapid transgression means that the basal sediments of a new stage cycle, resting on eroded strata that were exposed during the

seals. The analysis of strata in light of sea-level change, termed *sequence stratigraphy*, is now a major area of research in the oil industry.

Mechanisms of Sea-Level Change

Global mean sea level can be changed by more than one mechanism, according to present understanding. The most rapid major changes are caused by variations in the volume seaward excursion of the strandline, are virtually synchronous from the outermost to the innermost parts. Because water depth generally increases faster during a transgression than sediments can build up, the lower strata in each transgressive package are usually deposited in relatively deep water.

Many worldwide swings in sea level are indicated in the Early Cenozoic, and even in the Mesozoic, and it has been questioned whether these can be due to ice-volume changes. No other mechanism is known that could affect sea level so rapidly and profoundly, but it is possible that, in a nearly ice-free world, the shelf would be much shallower and flatter, and quantitatively small changes in sea level, due to relatively minor shifts in freshwater abstraction from the oceans, could cause the shoreline to migrate out to the shelf edge and back just as in the later Cenozoic.

TECTONO-EUSTATIC CHANGES

Changes in the average global rate of seafloor spreading, or plate tectonics, affect ocean-basin volume on a grander but slower scale. This is because the great submarine ridges that mark the spreading centers, such as the Mid-Atlantic Ridge, owe their elevation (up to 3 km above average seafloor depths) to the fact that their crustal rocks are newly formed and thus relatively hot and expanded. As the oceanic crust moves away from the spreading center, it gradually cools and shrinks, with a consequent decline in elevation. Thus, a significant increase in spreading rates would create relatively wider ridges of hot, expanded rock, and a slowdown of spreading rates would have the opposite effect of reducing the size of the midocean ridges. Such spreading-rate changes would, therefore, change the capacity of the ocean basins and the displacement of the ocean water. Calculations based on known spreading rates indicate that this effect could act to change sea level by several hundred meters, but only over a period of 50 Myr or more. Time-scale studies suggest that, in fact, the rate of seafloor spreading may have slowed down since the Middle Cretacous when seas were at least 300 m higher than today.

The linear extent of spreading centers can also change, with a similar effect on ocean-basin capacity. Spreading ocean basins are at a minimum when the continents are coalesced into one, as in the Ordovician and Permian Pangaeas, and these were times of maximum eustatic lowering. On the other hand, in the Middle Cretaceous the number of separate continents was greater than today, and eustatic levels were also at their highest.

Mountain-building is an effect of plate-tectonic motion and should change in intensity as spreading rates change. Higher rates of mountain uplift result in higher rates of erosion and an increase in the net volume of continental shelves and deep turbidites displacing water in the oceans. Ocean-volume changes created in this way are, however, relatively small compared to glacio-eustatic or tectono-eustatic changes.

THERMO-EUSTATIC CHANGES

Warm water is more expanded than cold water. It has been found that the average temperature of the oceans changed by 1–2° Celsius in response to the climate variations of the Pleistocene. While lagging somewhat behind the immediate effects of ice buildup and melting, the thermal contraction and expansion of the ocean emphasizes glacio-eustatic changes in mean sea level.

Sea-Level Change and Hominoid Evolution

Hominoids originated within the isolated primate fauna of Afro-Arabia, separated by ocean barriers from the rest of the world until the Early Miocene, ca. 17 Ma. Comparison of the Vail Curve and the fossil record suggests, however, that some major glacio-eustatic drawdowns may have been the occasion for transient interchange with South America or Eurasia in earlier periods.

The Late Paleocene and Eocene faunas of northern Africa contain evidence of Paleocene interchange with Eurasia in the presence of marsupials, palaeoryctids, pangolins, "prosimians," creodonts, and anomalurid rodents that diverge from the closest Eurasian relatives during the Eocene. In the Middle Oligocene (ca. 32 Ma), Cenozoic strandlines reached their lowest point. Redating of earliest anthropoids in South America to the later Oligocene makes it possible to theorize that the ancestral platyrrhines may have been able to cross the Atlantic from Africa during this great regression. African sciurognath rodents, cichlid fishes, boas, and various insects also dispersed into South America at about this same time, and coral-capped prominences along the submerged scarp of the Romanche fault that offsets the Mid-Atlantic Ridge suggest a possible island-hopping route.

The Middle Oligocene regression may also have been one of several that opened Africa to the immigration of a host of new mammal groups, following the time of the Fayum fauna. These are groups that appear in Europe no earlier than the Early Oligocene "Grande Coupure" and have Eocene fossil records in North America or Southeast Asia. Their descendants are found widely diversified in East Africa by the beginning of the Miocene, ca. 20 Ma, suggesting that the ancestors of African hedgehogs, rats, gerbils, squirrels, mole-rats, otters, weasels, cats, rhinos, pigs, hippos, tragulids, giraffes, and antelopes entered Africa no later than the Middle Oligocene. This mass immigration revolutionized the biological environment of the indigenous African mammal fauna, such that groups like the endemic sciurognath rodents, hyraxes, creodonts, and anthracotheres were greatly reduced in diversity by the Early Miocene, and marsupials, embrithopods, and adapiforms were extinct, while other groups such as anthropoids and proboscideans evolved important new lineages.

The immigration of catarrhines to Eurasia in the Early Miocene may also have been triggered by falling sea level. Kenyapithecines, first known from ca. 16 Ma in Turkey and central Europe, appear to have been among the first Afro-Arabian mammals to enter Europe via the eastern, Zagros land bridge, together with giraffids, bovids, tragulids, proboscideans, and the African endemic felids, chalicotheres, and rhinos. This bridge began to develop where the Mesopotamian shoulder of Afro-Arabia encountered Iran and Anatolia and was probably exposed for the first time by the major sea-level drop during the later Burdigalian (later Orleanian, MN-4b) at ca. 17 Ma. Pliopithecids first appear in China and Thailand by 18–16 Ma, presumably via an eastern branch of this route; rare Pakistani specimens of primates allocated to the *Dendropithecus*-group suggest that many lineages were exiting Africa at this time. Dryopithecines and pongines became common in Europe and southern Asia, respectively, ca. 14 Ma, coincident with the sharp drop in sea level recorded for the later Middle Miocene (Serravallian). This is equivalent to the mid-Astaracian of Europe and the upper Chinji levels of the Siwaliks of Indo-Pakistan. Fossils of oreopithecines are known only from later Miocene levels in Sardinia and Tuscany, but ancestors of these primates may also have found their way to the isolated Appenine landmass at this time. The coincidence of Weichselian glaciation and human colonization of the New World across Beringia, ca. 12 Ka, is well known.

Pleistocene Sea Levels and Archaeology

Ancient beach lines above the level of the modern Mediterranean have long been related to the interglacial melting of the ice sheets, and they are used extensively to define subdivisions of the Pleistocene in classical archaeology. The standard subdivisions, as defined by Déperet in the early 1900s, are (from oldest to youngest) the Sicilian (ca. 90–100 m above sea level [asl]); the Milazzian (50–60 m asl); the Tyrrhenian (30 m asl); and the Monastirian (20 m asl).

Present usage differs considerably from the classical model and also includes regressional (i.e., cold-climate, glacial) stages during which sea level dropped by 100 m or more from the interglacial levels. The Milazzian and Monastirian are no longer used because of evidence that they are based on local elevation changes rather than eustatic changes, and the Tyrrhenian high-sea-level phase has been divided into three substages. The relationship of some of the older beach levels to interglacial melting is also complicated by the fact that they include levels dominated by cold-water molluscan fossils.

The most widely accepted interpretation of Mediterranean sea-level stages, published by K.W. Butzer in 1964, is as follows:

ITALY	elev. asl	MOROCCO	elev. asl	CLIMATE	approx. age (*)
Versilian	+2	Mellahian	+2	Warm	5 Ka
Pontinian	−100	Soltanian		Cold	20 Ka
Tyrrhen.-III	+2	Ouljian	+5	Warm	80–60 Ka
		Pre-Soltanian		Cold	110–90 Ka
Tyrrhen.-II	+2–10	Pre-Ouljian	+5–10	V. Warm	127 Ka
Nomentanan	−200.	Tensiftian		Cold	0.2 Ma
		Kebibatan		Warm	?0.23 Ma
Tyrrhenian-I	+25–30	Anfatian	+25–35	Warm	0.3 Ma
Flaminian	—	Amirian		Cold	0.45 Ma
Sicilian-II	+50–60	Maarifian	+55–60	Warm	—
Cassian	—	Saletian		Cold	0.9 Ma
Sicilian-I	+100–110	Messaoudian	+90–100	Warm	—
Emilian	—	Regregian		Warm	ca. 1.1 Ma
Calabrian	—	Upp.			
		Moghrebian		Cold	ca. 1.8 Ma

(*) Ages modified by later workers

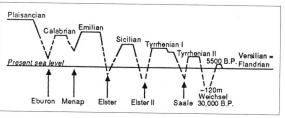

Mediterranean terrace levels, in order of age. The successively older terraces (identified by fossil shells on their surfaces) indicate a general decline of sea level through the Pleistocene as ice caps steadily increased in size. The gaps between terrace levels represent periods of erosion that correspond to the major glacial intervals.

The Pontinian regression is named for the Po Valley, where it is widely evidenced in boreholes, characteristically associated with cold-water molluscs presently living in the Baltic; some archaeologists use the term *Gravettian* for cultures of this age. A sea-level decline of the indicated magnitude was inadequate to expose a land bridge to Africa at Gibraltar or between Sicily and Tunisia, or to connect Crete or Cyprus to the mainland. However, Corsica and Sardinia were joined at this time in a single large island, and England and France were connected via the Dover lowlands, in which the Thames and the Seine rivers came together to drain into the North Sea. As noted, this was also the probable occasion for the immigration of humans into the New World, since the previous opportunity (Pre-Soltanian regression) seems to be much too old.

Tyrrhenian-II beaches are the most widespread of the Mediterranean levels and are characterized by molluscs, notably *Strombus*, which today range no farther north than Senegal. From U/Th ratios in corals embedded in Tyrrhenian beachrock, and by the magnitude of the warming event, this level is confidently attributed to the climax of the last interglacial maximum (Eemian), seen in oxygen-isotope curves as Level 5e, at 127 Ka.

There is some evidence that the long interval of mixed but mostly cold-climate conditions, which produced the erosional landscape of the Nomentanan, included a regression of as much as 200 m below sea level. The equivalent levels in North Africa, the Tensiftian, have yielded hominid remains at Rabat dated between 0.2 and 0.3 Ma. The Tyrrhenian-I warm-climate interval is represented in beach deposits with subtropical molluscs and extensive red soils, which may correlate to post-Mindel soils in the Alps and the Holsteinian of the Rhine delta. Flaminian regression is, therefore, regarded as correlative to the Elsterian (Mindel) glacial episode(s) (ca. 0.45–0.6 Ma), and the equivalent Amirian deposits in Morocco contain "archaic *Homo sapiens*" or "advanced *Homo erectus*" dated to about this age at Thomas Quarries and Salé.

Major changes in the mammal and the marine fauna, with many extinctions and intercontinental migrations, mark both the Cassian (i.e., end-Villafranchian) and the Calabrian (mid-Villafranchian) cold-climate intervals. Although most of the studied deposits of this age occur above sea level, this is probably due to local tectonism; the faunal revolutions suggest glacio-eustatic regression with the uncovering of land bridges, together with severe environmental

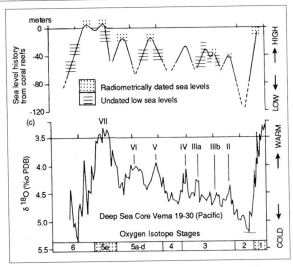

Sea-level variations (above) in the later Pleistocene, interpreted from coral reef lines on the tectonically rising coast of the Huon Peninsula, New Zealand. These are coincident with fluctuations in ice volume (below), recorded as variation in oxygen isotope proportions in deep-sea cores. After Aharon, P. and Chappell, J., 1986, Palaeogeog., Palaeoclimatol., Palaeoecol. 56.

stress. The Cassian regression is generally correlated to the Menapian (Günz) glacial episode in Europe, and the Calabrian to the Eburonian (upper Donau) cold-climate sediments.

Coral Reefs and Sea Levels

Charles Darwin was the first to observe that coral reefs, as ever-growing communities, would maintain themselves at sea level despite changes in elevation. The abandoned reef structures are conspicuous and geologically durable formations, and they are the best-dated markers we have of sea-level fluctuations over the later Pleistocene time. On the one hand, corals preserve the oxygen- and carbon-isotope ratios of the seas in which they lived and can be directly related to the history of global temperature and atmospheric changes. On the other hand, they are very suitable for radiometric dating by the uranium-thorium method, which is reliable to ca. 150 Kyr.

Rising seacoasts in geologically active areas, particularly in Barbados and the Huon Peninsula of New Guinea, have been analyzed because they preserve both high-stand and low-stand reefs. Supporting data have come from the Ryukyu Islands, Indonesia, and Haiti and from drilling records on islands in Micronesia. By measuring the rate at which the reef-bearing coastlines are being uplifted and the age of reef corals at each level, the relative motion of the mean sea level can be determined, rather than just the high and low elevations. These coral-reef studies produce sea-level curves that closely match those obtained from oxygen-isotope records, which reflect the variations in the amount of fresh water trapped in ice.

See also Africa, North; Cenozoic; Cyclostratigraphy; Europe; Glaciation; Plate Tectonics; Pleistocene; Radiometric Dating; Time Scale. [J.A.V.C.]

Further Readings

Butzer, K.W. (1975) Pleistocene littoral-sedimentary cycles of the Mediterranean Basin: A Mallorquin view. In Butzer, K.W., and Isaac, G.L., eds. After the Australopithecines. Hague: Mouton Publishers, pp. 25–71.

Denton, G.H., and Hughes, T.J., eds. (1981) The Last Great Ice Sheets. New York: Wiley.

Haq, B.U., Hardenbol, J., and Vail, P.R. (1987) Chronology of fluctuating sea levels since the Triassic. Science 235:1156–1167.

Wilgus, C., et al., eds. (1987) Sea Level Change: An Integrated Approach (Special Publication No. 42). Tulsa: Soc. Econ. Paleontol. Mineral.

Second Intermediate

Term proposed at the third Pan-African Congress in 1955 to refer to industries transitional between Middle Stone Age flake industries (e.g., Stillbay) and Later Stone Age industries with backed microliths. The term is no longer in use, since more careful stratigraphic work, especially at the type site of the most characteristic industry, the Magosian, has cast doubt upon its existence as a cultural evolutionary stage. Recent research at several sites in central, eastern, and southern Africa (e.g., Mumba-Hohle, Nasera, Rose Cottage Cave), however, has suggested that microlithic technology and Middle Stone Age points made on triangular flakes do coexist in several well-stratified and carefully excavated assemblages. The transition from Middle to Later Stone Age may be less abrupt and spread over a much longer time period than previously supposed.

See also First Intermediate; Later Stone Age; Magosian; Middle Stone Age; Stillbay. [A.S.B.]

Semiorder

Category in the classificatory hierarchy that falls between the order and the suborder. This rank was introduced to express the fundamental distinction within Primates between the modern Euprimates and the archaic Plesiadapiformes.

See also Classification; Euprimates; Plesiadapiformes. [I.T.]

Senga-5

Late Pliocene or Early Pleistocene open-air site in the Lusso (Kaiso) Beds of the Semliki Valley (Albertine Rift Valley) in eastern Zaire. The site, excavated by J.W.K. Harris in 1985–1988, has yielded numerous small quartz (and a few quartzite) flakes, simple pebble cores, and abundant remains of savannah mammals, tortoises, and fish in association with fossil wood and coprolites (fossilized feces). Sediments and molluscan fauna suggest deposition on or near an ancient beach. The suggested age of the fauna, based on correlations with the Omo sequence in the Eastern (Gregory) Rift Valley, is 2.3–1.9 Ma. The artifacts may be coeval with the fauna or intrusive from a more recent Pleistocene horizon.

See also Africa; Early Paleolithic; Early Stone Age; Oldowan; Olduvai Gorge; Paleolithic Lifeways; Stone-Tool Making. [A.S.B.]

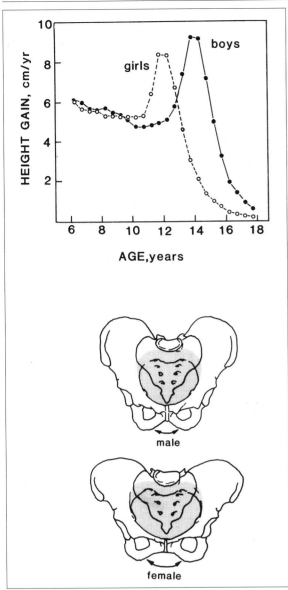

Above: sexual dimorphism in growth patterns of humans. Note the earlier and smaller spurt in growth of height gain per year versus age (weight gain per year exhibits a similar pattern) in the females. (After Tanner, 1962.) Below: anterosuperior views of human male and female pelves, illustrating the greater subpubic angle (arrows) and larger and differently shaped bony pelvic inlet (shaded area) in females. After J. Basmajian, Primary Anatomy, *Williams & Wilkins, 1982; courtesy of Brian T. Shea and J. Basmajian.*

Sexual Dimorphism

Intersexual differences in physical form. Many primates, like the majority of mammals, exhibit sexual differences in morphology, physiology, and behavior. Some aspects of sexual dimorphism result directly from differences in the male and female sex hormones. Examples include the external genitalia and secondary sexual characteristics established at puberty (in humans: female breasts, male beard, and shape differences in the bony pelvis related to enlargement of the birth canal). Other shape differences between the sexes in primates are related to the generally larger overall body size of males and thus result from allometry, or differential growth. The relatively smaller brains, relatively larger faces

(see Figure), and differing limb proportions of males compared with females in many primates are examples of such allometric components of sexual dimorphism. Although the differences in form between the sexes are usually described and analyzed at the adult stage, it is important to understand that these differences are merely the end points of sexually differentiated patterns of growth. Analysis of the ontogenetic bases of different patterns of sexual dimorphism can lead to insights into the ecological and social correlates of dimorphism.

Primate Dimorphism

The distribution of patterns of sexual dimorphism varies in interesting ways among the primates. In terms of overall body size, the haplorhines (tarsiers, monkeys, apes, and humans) are generally dimorphic, while the strepsirhines (lemurs and lorises) are not. Some of the strepsirhines, however, are sexually dichromatic (having different coat colors). Among the haplorhines, most species exhibit a moderate degree of dimorphism in overall size, with adult females being 75–90 percent of male weight. The most dimorphic primate species is the mandrill (*Mandrillus sphinx*), where males averaging 35 Kg weigh nearly three times as much as 13 Kg females. Other dimorphic primates include the gorillas and the orangutans among the apes, as well as the patas monkeys, the proboscis monkeys, and the open-country baboons; here females are roughly half the size of adult males. The lesser apes (gibbons and siamangs) and various New World monkeys (marmosets, tamarins, titi monkeys) are among the higher primates that exhibit little or no dimorphism in size. In a few primates, notably some marmosets and the spider monkeys, females may be larger than males in overall size. Canine teeth also exhibit sexual dimorphism in most higher primates, largely paralleling in degree the overall differences in weight, although there are a number of exceptions to this generalization.

The primates reveal other interesting examples of sexual dimorphism. For instance, orangutan males sport prominent cheek pads and enlarged laryngeal air sacs, giving them a characteristic facial appearance. Male mandrills have brightly colored faces and external genitalia, while male hamadryas baboons differ from females in the enlarged cape of hair about their shoulders. Cases in which males exhibit exaggerated versions of features also present in females include the prominent fleshy nose of the proboscis monkey and the specialized hyoid apparatus used by the howler monkey to communicate with conspecifics.

Sexual Dimorphism in Humans

Modern humans, with the majority of higher primates, exhibit a moderate degree of sexual dimorphism in body weight, although we are clearly an aberrant species in combining this size dimorphism with an almost total lack of canine-tooth dimorphism. Within our wide-ranging species, we also see varying degrees of dimorphism. It is difficult to trace patterns of sexual dimorphism reliably in the fragmentary fossil record, but the available evidence suggests marked differences in overall size between the sexes in the apes of the

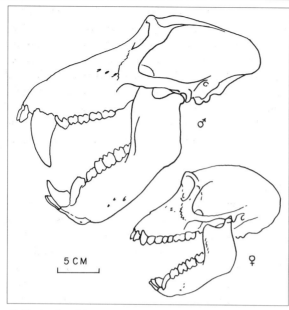

Skulls of male and female mandrill monkeys, illustrating the marked differences in size and shape between the sexes. Note particularly the extreme dimorphism in the canine teeth and the bony snout. After A.H. Schultz, The Life of Primates. *Universe Books, 1969; courtesy of Brian T. Shea.*

Miocene (23.5–5 Ma), as well as in the earliest hominins from which the lineage leading to modern *Homo* emerged. In the earliest australopiths, females may have been only three-quarters to one-half (or less) the size of males, depending on the part of the body examined and the potential error of the estimates derived. Canine size and dimorphism were reduced early in hominin evolution, a change of undoubted behavioral significance, as C. Darwin noted long ago.

Factors Influencing Sexual Dimorphism

A number of factors appear to be responsible for the variation in sexual dimorphism observed among primates. One important component is Darwin's notion of sexual selection, which is based on (1) competition among members of the sex that is more plentiful or in which some individuals are disproportionately successful at mating, and (2) choice of the more successful individuals in this competition by members of the opposite sex. Primatologists have generally viewed males as competing for access to, or choice by, females. Larger male body size, canine size, and such ornamental features as the cheek pads of male orangutans or the silvery pelage of fully mature male gorillas are believed to have evolved either for direct use in competitive interactions or as signals to females of the size and fitness of the male. A number of the bases of this argument, particularly the degree of male-male competition and variance in male reproductive success, are being examined in laboratory and field studies. It gains some support, however, from the empirical observation that sexual dimorphism among primates is generally strongest in polygynous, unimale, multifemale groups, such as hamadryas baboons and gorillas, and absent or weakest in monogamous, one-male, one-female groups, such as the lesser apes. This general relationship is also not without ex-

ception; for example, strongly dimorphic DeBrazza's monkeys (*Cercopithecus neglectus*) and patas monkeys (*Erythrocebus patas*) apparently do not exhibit strongly polygynous mating systems.

The need for males to protect females and their offspring from predators is another possible determinant of the degree of sexual dimorphism. The large canine and body size of males is seen as advantageous in defense and interspecific encounters, and the fact that terrestrial primates are often strongly dimorphic is cited as evidence of this purported relationship.

Another important influence on sexual dimorphism is the overall size of the species. For reasons not well understood, the degree of dimorphism tends to increase with body size, so that the most dimorphic taxa in a given group are also generally the largest bodied. Examples include the gorilla among the apes and the baboons among the Old World monkeys, although a few cases do not follow this general prediction.

Primatologists have begun to investigate the role of sex differences in niche utilization, feeding behavior, and other bioenergetic factors as influences on size dimorphism. The focus here is often on the possible advantages of smaller size in females, such as early reproduction, reduced energy requirements (particularly during pregnancy and lactation), and reduced feeding competition with males. Among humans, there appears to be a relationship between the degree of weight dimorphism and protein availability.

Future research will likely clarify these and other factors, but, clearly, sexual dimorphism in primates is a complex phenomenon manifested in various ways and influenced by multiple causes.

See also Allometry; Ontogeny; Primate Ecology; Primate Societies. [B.T.S.]

Further Readings

Campbell, B.G., ed. (1972) Sexual Selection and the Descent of Man, 1871–1971. Chicago: Aldine.

Clutton-Brock, T.H., Harvey, P.H., and Rudder, B. (1977) Sexual dimorphism, socionomic sex ratio, and body weight in primates. Nature 269:797–800.

Fedigan, L.M. (1982) Primate Paradigms: Sex Roles and Social Bonds. Montreal: Eden.

Frayer, D.W., and Wolpoff, M.H. (1985) Sexual dimorphism. Ann. Rev. Anthropol. 14:429–473.

Leigh, S.R. (1995) Socioecology and the ontogeny of sexual size dimorphism in anthropoid primates. Am. J. Phys. Anthropol. 97:339–356.

Plavcan, J.M., and van Schaik, C. (1992) Intrasexual competition and canine dimorphism in anthropoid primates. Am. J. Phys. Anthropol. 87:461–478.

Ralls, K. (1977) Sexual dimorphism in mammals: Avian models and unanswered questions. Am. Nat. 111:917–938.

Shanidar

Cave in the Kurdish hills of northern Iraq where the remains of nine Neanderthal adults and children were recovered from 1957 to 1961 in excavations directed by R. Solecki.

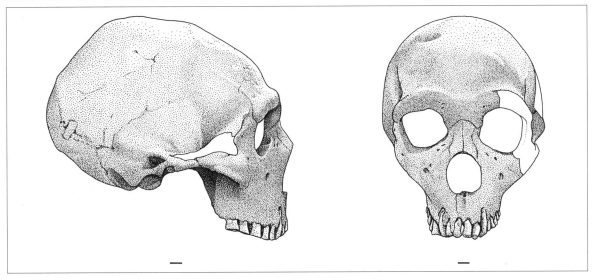

Lateral and facial views of the Shanidar 1 Neanderthal cranium. Scales are 1 cm.

The uppermost strata (Level B) contains an Epipaleolithic Zarzian occupation. Level C, which dates to 35–28.5 Ka, features an Upper Paleolithic Baradostian industry, which some researchers compare to the European and the Levantine Aurignacian, due to the prevalence of lamellar retouch producing carinate morphologies on chunky blanks in the Baradostian. Burins, however, especially truncation burins, are far more common in the Baradostian than in most Aurignacian assemblages. Neanderthal remains occur in Level D, which radiocarbon assays date to more than 46 Ka. The most important of these remains are a partial adult skeleton showing clear signs of disabling injury and disease, as well as a serious, possibly fatal knife wound in the back (Shanidar 1), an adult partial skeleton supposedly buried with flowers (Shanidar 4), and a very large and robust partial skull (Shanidar 5). Ibex (*Capra ibex*) is the most common large mammal represented in the Mousterian strata. The lithic industry of Level D, attributed to the Zagros Mousterian, is made on primarily local flints and contains numerous small, heavily retouched scrapers and low numbers of Levallois tools.

See also Asia, Western; Aurignacian; Baradostian; Epipaleolithic; Levantine Aurignacian; Mousterian; Neanderthals; Ritual; Upper Paleolithic. [C.B.S., J.J.S.]

Further Readings
Solecki, R. (1954) Shanidar Cave: A Paleolithic site in northern Iraq. In Annual Report of the Smithsonian Institution. Washington, D.C.: GPO, pp. 389–425.
Solecki, R.S. (1971) Shanidar: The First Flower People. New York: Simon and Schuster.
Trinkaus, E. (1983) The Shanidar Neanderthals. New York: Academic.

Shoshonius
North American Early Eocene (ca. 50 Ma) omomyine omomyid. The recent recovery of four skulls of *Shoshonius*

resulted in claims concerning the special affinities of this genus with the Tarsiidae. The hypothesis was based on putative synapomorphies (shared derived characters) of the basicranium of the omomyine and *Tarsius*. There are a number of suggestive similarities that certainly qualify as hypotheses of synapomorphies, to be tested by a careful functional-adaptive analysis, but the whole basicranium must be examined as an interrelated and causally interconnected unit of these animals, rather than atomized similarities of various degrees within the basicranium. The presence of (1) an inflated hypotympanic sinus and an intrabullar septum that divides the enlarged anterior chamber of the middle ear, (2) a basioccipital flange that overlaps the petrosal bulla itself, (3) ventrolateral entry of the carotid artery into the bulla, and (4) lateral pterygoid wings in contact with the anterolateral bulla wall certainly would seem to be significant similarities with *Tarsius*. An enlargement of the middle ear employing the expansion of the anterior chamber (hypotympanic sinus) will certainly expand that structure anteriorly, resulting in contact with the pterygoids, so the latter is likely the result of the enlarged anterior hypotympanic sinus. While the point of entry of the carotids is similar, the actual passage of the carotid (promontory) artery could not be more different in tarsiers and *Shoshonius*. In the latter, as in *Rooneyia* in which it is associated with a septum (and probably in other omomyines that we do not know cranially), the promontory artery crosses the promontorium, unlike in tarsiids. In tarsiers, the entry of the carotid into the bulla and into the cranial cavity is associated with an anterior septum only (of the hypotympanic sinus), and its vertical ascent bypasses the promontorium completely, more so than in anthropoids. The posterior septum derived from the posterior end of the promontory at its entrance into the bulla in *Shoshonius* is shared with *Rooneyia* and *Necrolemur* but not with tarsiers.

Shoshonius is almost certainly the sister taxon of *Washakius*; not only do they share extremely similar general molar patterns, but both have the undoubtedly derived metastylids and the extreme distolingual hypocones. Furthermore,

Shoshonius lacks the postorbital closure characteristic of tarsiers in spite of the fact that it appears to have relatively enlarged eyes. The special sister-group ties of this genus with tarsiers is not corroborated, although the possibility exists that the Omomyinae as a group may be more recently related to tarsiids than to other omomyids.

See also Anaptomorphinae; Microchoerinae; Omomyidae; Omomyinae; Tarsiidae; Tarsiiformes. [F.S.S.]

Sidi Abderrahman

A large quarry system along the Atlantic coast near Casablanca (Morocco) containing undated Upper Pleistocene coastal sediments (beach and dune deposits, and cave deposits in consolidated dunes) that have yielded Early Paleolithic artifacts at a number of sites, as well as some hominin fossils. At one site, Littorina Cave or Cunette, an Acheulean artifact associated with fauna including a partial mandible attributed to *Homo erectus* has come from these deposits. This human fossil may represent the same hominin population as that known from the nearby Thomas Quarries and Salé, although the specimen has also been assigned to the same group as the earlier Tighenif specimens from Algeria. Other site names applied to specific quarries in the Sidi Abderrahman group that have yielded artifacts and/or fossils include STIC Quarry and Thomas Quarries I, II, and III.

See also Acheulean; Africa, North; Archaic Homo sapiens; Early Paleolithic; Homo erectus; Pleistocene; Salé; Thomas Quarries; Tighenif. [N.T., K.S., C.B.S.].

Simpson, George Gaylord (1902–1984)

American paleontologist who held major appointments at the American Museum of Natural History (1927–1959), Columbia University (1945–1959), and Harvard University (1959–1970). While making numerous contributions to vertebrate paleontology (especially of the mammals), Simpson also made original and important contributions to the evolutionary synthesis that began to emerge during the decade following the publication of T. Dobzhansky's milestone work, *Genetics and the Origin of Species*, in 1937. Simpson's book *Tempo and Mode in Evolution* (1944), supplemented by *The Major Features of Evolution* (1953), embodies a perspective that was an integral feature of the modern evolutionary synthesis.

See also Dobzhansky, Theodosius; Evolution. [F.S.]

Site Types

Variety and distinctions of residential and special-purpose occupation localities seen in the archaeological record of hunting-and-gathering peoples. Ethnographic research among hunter-gatherers indicates that group size and subsistence activity are important aspects of settlement and are closely related to environmental conditions. Work on land-use patterns and group size of coresident units among these groups has revealed a number of cross-cultural regularities of significance to prehistoric archaeology. First, all ethnographically known hunter-gatherers are mobile in their subsistence pursuits. This mobility can occur both on the level of a few individuals and on the level of the group. A given group thus uses a number of site types over a season, a year, or a lifetime.

Reasons for Variability

The organization of subsistence pursuits among hunter-gatherers varies greatly in the extent to which the whole group is moved to the food resources. On the one hand, foragers constantly move the whole group to position it optimally in relation to the available resources. Logistically organized groups, those in which specialized procurement parties harvest specific resources and bring them back to the larger social group, constitute the other extreme of this scale. In this second case, the social group as a whole moves far less frequently. The existence of these different strategies of positioning groups vis-à-vis resources implies that we can anticipate finding very different occupation and settlement records for areas occupied by groups of hunter-gatherers in the past.

Another significant feature found among many hunter-gatherers is a pattern of group aggregation and dispersal, in which a large number of people living together during one season break up into smaller coresiding units during other seasons. This feature suggests that we can anticipate finding different sizes of residential settlements or camps for a given group of hunter-gatherers.

While sites used by hunter-gatherers vary along parameters that include the organization of subsistence behavior; the season, nature, and duration of occupation; and group composition and size, two broad classes of site types can be distinguished for these groups: *residential camps* and *special-purpose camps*.

Residential Camps

These are sites where a group of people spend some time and sleep overnight. The nature of overnight stays, however, differs between foraging and logistically organized hunter-gatherers. The former exploit their regions using group-mobility strategies, and it is the whole group that occupies residential sites, or *base camps*. Logistically organized groups send out food-procurement parties that exploit resources within a particular region. These task groups may occupy overnight camps away from the residential camp of the whole group.

Base camps, occupied by large and diverse social units comprising individuals of all ages and of both sexes for lengths of time exceeding a week or more, are locales in which the widest variety of activities takes place. These include the construction of shelters, tool and clothing manufacture and repair, food preparation and consumption, and other routines generally involving whole coresidential groups. Furthermore, because all ages and both sexes reside at these sites, age- and gender-specific behavior takes place here as well.

Since base camps are occupied by large social groups for relatively lengthy periods of time, archaeological correlates of base camps in a given region are found in large sites with thick cultural layers. Living floors at these sites have the widest array of features, such as dwellings, hearths, work areas, and storage facilities. Tool and implement assemblages contain a wide variety of items associated with diverse activities and may include a small number of nonutilitarian objects, such as jewelry and pieces of portable art.

Organic remains resulting from subsistence activities at these sites show both greater abundance and greater diversity than at other site types. Finally, since residence at base camps is not year-round but restricted to one or two seasons, remains of food debris at these sites can be used both to estimate the time of the year that they were inhabited and to offer clues about the size of the coresidential units.

Overnight stops are most often occupied by small groups of same-sex individuals in the course of their forays to procure food or resources for a larger coresidential unit. Thus, a group of hunters may stay overnight while hunting, or a trading party on an exchange expedition to a distant group may have to make temporary overnight camps during their trip. We can expect that people at such camps will cook and eat some food, and possibly repair or resharpen some tools, but also that the extent and the variety of these activities will be far more limited than those found at base camps.

Archaeological signatures at these types of sites include small size, thin cultural layers, and total absence or ephemeral presence of such features as shelters and hearths. Inventories of tools and implements are small and fairly uniform in composition. The amount and nature of organic remains reflect both the briefness of stays and the size of the group.

Special-Purpose Camps

These sites, variously termed *camps* or *locations* in the ethnographic and archaeological literature, are occupied for specific and finite purposes and include lithic workshops; hunting, ambush, and collecting camps; lookout spots for monitoring the movements of game animals; processing stations; ritual or ceremonial locales; and aggregation sites.

LITHIC WORKSHOPS

These are usually found near the outcrops of good-quality lithic materials and are the locations to which small groups of toolmakers come to obtain the necessary raw materials for making tools. Activities performed here include the quarrying of the rock itself and the shaping of the nodules into cores or, in some cases, into flakes and blades.

Since good quarry sites are repeatedly used over long periods of time, archaeological profiles generally do not show the same discrete spatial limits that other types of occupations exhibit. The scatter of lithic debris around quarries will be thick, extend over a large area, and be a product of numerous visits. These areas lack any residential features and have assemblages poor in cores but rich in unretouched cortical and waste flakes.

Occasionally, however, toolmakers may use discrete spots at distances from a few to a few hundred meters from the quarried outcrop for reducing the nodules into appropri-

ate preforms. These sites, like their equivalents near the quarry, lack such features as hearths or dwelling structures and have tool assemblages clearly related to the initial stages of lithic production. There are few or no food remains and no evidence for exploitation of any resources other than lithic. Since the task force visiting this location consists of only a handful of people, and since they spend a relatively short period of time obtaining the raw materials, the area with the lithic scatter is small and without any appreciable depth.

HUNTING, COLLECTING, AND AMBUSH CAMPS

These camps are occupied for short periods of time by a small group of people engaged in specific food-procurement tasks. They include locations for harvesting vegetable resources, spots for fishing and shellfish collecting, and kill sites where prey is dispatched. These camps range from spots where a single animal is killed or a few tubers dug up to mass kill sites where whole herds of animals are harvested by a large group of hunters.

Although varying from a few square meters to large areas, all of these sites generally exhibit short-term occupation by groups smaller than those found at the base camps in the region. They lack such features as dwellings, storage pits, and sizable hearths with thick ash deposits. They may, however, contains such features as drive lanes built to facilitate the taking of game. Tool inventories at these sites may be limited in number, homogeneous in kind, and associated with activities related to initial procurement and processing of specific food resources. Some resharpening of tools used in these activities may also take place here. Fewer organic remains may be found at these sites than at base camps, or they may represent just the one or two species being harvested.

Kill and ambush sites, especially those where mass harvesting took place, may contain sizable amounts of skeletal remains. The composition of these remains, however, is quite different from that found at base camps, containing a high percentage of parts with low nutritional value, such as skulls, vertebrae, and lower-limb extremities.

LOOKOUT SPOTS

Groups of hunters among both foragers and logistically organized hunter-gatherers may pause briefly during the hunt at specific spots to survey their prey, rest, snack, and resharpen their hunting implements. If such natural blinds as large rocks or thick bushes are present in the area, they will use them to conceal themselves from their prey. If natural barriers are absent, the hunters may build artificial blinds out of boulders or branches. These activities generate yet another type of special-purpose site in the archaeological record, one with some sort of a natural or human-made blind, a thin cultural layer with sparse remains of food debris, and possibly some lithic debris produced by tool resharpening. Repeated reuse of a blind, however, may produce a denser archaeological record.

PROCESSING CAMPS

Hunting or collecting task groups usually reduce their catches or harvests to easily transported parts of high food

Daily life at the Pincevent Magdalenian base camp in the Paris basin. After J. Jelinek, Strecha nad Hlavou, *Moravian Museum Brno, 1986.*

value. This processing is done adjacent to the kill, ambush, or harvest site and generates remains that differ from those at the kill, fishing, or collection spot itself. While such processing camps are more common for logistically organized groups, similar sites can occasionally be generated by foragers as well. This will occur when unusually large numbers of animals are killed in one spot or an especially large species is taken. On such occasions, one of the hunters may go back to the base camp to summon the rest of the group to help process the meat and bring it back to camp.

In the ethnographic present, these processing locations are adjacent to the kill or harvest ones, but the limited size of most archaeological excavations may uncover only shell middens or areas of primary or secondary butchering rather than the kill site itself. Remains found at these locales usually do not contain the tools used to take down the prey (arrows, spears, harpoons) but only implements used to cut, skin, butcher, and perhaps fillet it. Thus, the range of tools is much narrower than at base camps and similar in homogeneity, although not in tool types, to those at kill sites. The composition of the organic remains closely parallels that of kill or harvesting sites, as only one or two species are repre-

sented. Since the processing of meat or fish may also involve drying or smoking it, such features as shallow hearths or smoke pits and various forms of drying racks may also be found at these locations. Overall, however, whatever features or inventories are discovered, they are all clearly related to a finite set of activities associated with processing of particular resources.

RITUAL OR CEREMONIAL SITES

Both foragers and logistically organized hunter-gatherers often have special locations for ritual or cermonial purposes. These may include caves or rockshelters with sacred paintings, in- or above-ground cemeteries, and sacred sections of the regional landscape. While many rituals and ceremonies are conducted at the base camps themselves, when locations away from residential sites are used for these purposes the sacred activities generate material remains that differ significantly from those found at other types of sites.

Archaeological profiles of sites used for ritual or ceremonial purposes differ widely, depending on the types of ceremonies performed there and on the size of the group engaged in these activities. The most easily identifiable are cemeteries with in-ground interments. Other special-purpose ceremonial sites contain both material features and inventories that have numerous nonutilitarian components. Such locations have a minimum of remains clearly identified with subsistence- and maintenance-related activities, such as the manufacture or repair of tools or clothing. Although some evidence for food preparation and consumption can be expected at these sites, both the materials and the methods used in these activities may differ significantly from those found at residential base camps in the same region.

AGGREGATION SITES

Some hunter-gatherers, especially foragers who live in small coresidential groups and who use extensive seasonal mobility in their subsistence pursuits, join other like-sized groups during particular seasons at large residential base camps. Activities during these short periods of large gatherings include the expected subsistence-related component of food procurement and preparation, tool manufacture and repair, and shelter construction and use. In addition, large gatherings of this kind serve as special-purpose locales for finding mates, exchanging information and goods, and performing sacred rituals and ceremonies. Archaeological identification of aggregation sites is a difficult task, because they exhibit many similarities to base camps in the same region. Aggregation sites will, however, be generally much larger in size and contain more dwelling remains and hearths, but, due to the brevity of their occupation, they have relatively thin cultural layers unless they are subjected to repeated reoccupation. Inventories at these sites may include tool groups much like those at base camps but also have significantly more objects such as jewelry, engravings, portable art, exotics, or musical instruments, which are not related to everyday subsistence and maintenance activities but to the sphere of social and ritual interaction.

See also Archaeological Sites; Exotics; Hunter-Gatherers; Jewelry; Middle Stone Age; Musical Instruments; Paleolithic; Ritual. [O.S.]

Further Readings

Binford, L.R. (1980) Willow smoke and dog's tails: Hunter-gatherer settlement systems and archaeological site formation. Am. Antiquity 43:4–20.

Brooks, A.S., and Yellen, J.E. (1987) The preservation of activity areas in the archaeological record: Ethnoarchaeological and archaeoological work in northwest Ngamiland, Botswana. In S. Kent (ed.): Method and Theory of Activity Area Research. New York: Columbia University Press, pp. 63–106.

Butzer, K.W. (1982) Archaeology As Human Ecology. Cambridge: Cambridge University Press.

Jochim, M.A. (1981) Strategies for Survival: Cultural Behavior in an Ecological Context. New York: Academic.

Kelly, R.L. (1983) Hunter-gatherer mobility strategies. J. Anthropol. Res. 39:277–306.

Price, T.D. (1978) Mesolithic settlement systems in the Netherlands. In P.A. Mellars (ed.): The Early Postglacial Settlement of Northern Europe. London: Duckworth, pp. 81–113.

Soffer, O. (1985) The Upper Paleolithic of the Central Russian Plain. Orlando: Academic.

Sivapithecus

A Middle-to-Late Miocene Asian fossil ape, probably related closely to the orangutan. *Sivapithecus* was one of the earliest fossil apes to be discovered, fragments now thought to belong to it having been reported in India as far back as 1837. The name *Palaeopithecus* was first applied to Siwalik Miocene ape fossils, but it turned out that this name had previously been given to some Mesozoic trackways and was thus unavailable. *Sivapithecus indicus* was named in 1910 by G. Pilgrim for an upper tooth, and the species *sivalensis*, originally placed in *Palaeopithecus*, was transferred to the new genus. Many other genera were named for a variety of Siwalik Miocene ape fossils until 1965, when E. L. Simons and D. Pilbeam reviewed all of them and recognized only *Sivapithecus* (then as a subgenus of *Dryopithecus*) and *Ramapithecus*. Further study has led to the synonymy of *Ramapithecus* with *Sivapithecus* and the general recognition of four (now three) species. Two of these appear to be time-successive in the Indo-Pakistan Siwaliks between ca. 12.5 and 8.5 Ma, but, as the original type specimens are so fragmentary, there has been some controversy about which names to use. *S. indicus* is generally considered to date to ca. 9.5–8.5 Ma and to be represented by the best material, including a partial cranium and numerous postcrania from Pakistan. The older specimens (12.5–10.3 Ma) are usually termed *S. sivalensis*. A third, larger species, *S. parvada*, was named in 1987 for material from a single locality in Pakistan: Sethi Nagri (Loc. Y311), dated to 10 Ma. Teeth and jaw fragments from Xiaolongtan (Yunnan Province, China, perhaps ca. 13 Ma) may also represent a species of *Sivapithecus*, but they are too fragmentary to preserve the diagnostic features. Finally, specimens from the Yassiören locality in the Sinap Beds of Turkey (9.8 Ma) were originally termed *Ankarapithecus meteai* but, generally have been included as a fourth species of *Sivapithecus*. A recent find published by B. Alpagut and colleagues in 1996 suggests that they differ sufficiently in the upper face to merit retaining a separate genus.

The cranial remains of *Sivapithecus* from Pakistan reveal numerous derived similarities with *Pongo*. These include an expanded and flattened zygomatic region, giving the face a concave aspect; no glabellar thickening; narrow distance between the eyes; no browridges; and a rotated premaxilla, giving a smooth floor to the nasal cavity and an extremely reduced incisive canal with no incisive fossa. The upper lateral incisors are very small relative to the central, and the molar enamel is of intermediate thickness. The proximal humerus is less modern than expected for a member of the derived great-ape group, but it seems more likely that this reflects the adaptations of *Sivapithecus* itself, rather than contradicting the close relationship with orangutans implied by the craniodental remains.

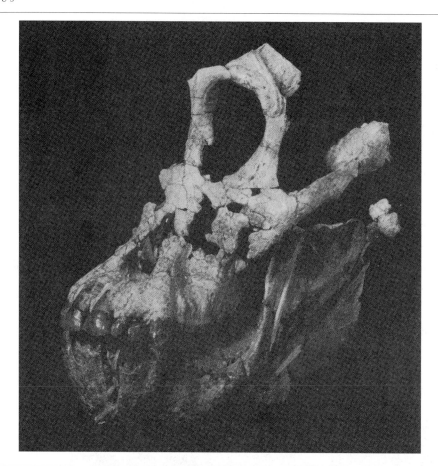

The face and lower jaw (in left oblique fronto-lateral view) of Sivapithecus indicus *from Late Miocene deposits in the Pakistan Siwaliks. It shows many characteristics of the face found also in* Pongo, *the orangutan. The lower panel compares the left lateral view of the face in a chimpanzee* (Pan), Sivapithecus, *and an orangutan. Courtesy of David Pilbeam.*

See also Ankarapithecus; Ape; Asia, Eastern and Southern; Asia, Western; Hominidae; Ponginae; Siwaliks. [E.D.]

Further Readings

Ward, S. (1997) The taxonomy and phyletic relationships of *Sivapithecus* revisited. In Begun, D., Ward, C., and Rose, M., eds. Miocene Hominoid Fossils: Functional and Phylogenetic Implications. New York: Plenum, pp. 269–290.

Siwaliks

Neogene strata in the Siwalik Range of northern India and Pakistan are exposed in a huge arc at the foot of the Himalayas extending from the Indus River to the Brahmapu-

tra, a distance of more than 2,500 km. In this vast fossiliferous region, the strata assigned to the Siwalik Group range in time from more than 18 Ma to less than 1.0 Ma, providing one of the most complete successions of mammalian fossil faunas in the world. Fossils, including large hominoids attributed to *Sivapithecus* and *Gigantopithecus,* have been collected from the Siwaliks intermittently since the early 1800s. Since 1973, the Geological Survey of Pakistan has worked with Yale and then Harvard universities in the Siwalik Group exposures on the Potwar Plateau south of Rawalpindi, enormously expanding the faunal sample and clarifying many geological and paleoenvironmental questions. Modern understanding of the Siwaliks and its fossil fauna depends largely on this work.

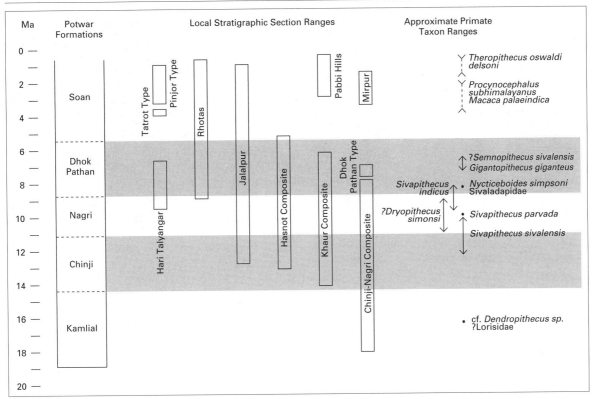

Stratigraphy of Siwalik deposits in India and Pakistan. Left column shows temporal range of formations (rock units, often used as time or faunal units) in the Potwar region of Pakistan, where the most detailed collecting has been done. Narrow columns indicate range of local sequences, mainly in Pakistan (Tatrot and Pinjor type sections and Hari Talyangar in India). Temporal range of Siwalik primates indicated at right: solid lines are well-dated ranges, dashed lines approximate and single dots isolated occurrences. Modified after Barry, 1995.

Siwalik Stratigraphy

The Siwalik Group is divided, in stratigraphic order, into the Kamlial, Chinji, Nagri, Dhok Pathan, and Soan formations. All of these units have been formally designated as lithostratigraphic bodies with type sections in the Potwar Plateau, but, in their original form, defined by British paleontologist G. Pilgrim in the 1930s, they were essentially fossil-mammal zones. Over the years, problems arising from conflicting usage of these names for faunal units, time units, and rock units was not helped by the difficulty, prior to the recent paleomagnetic work, of accurately dating the succession.

Outside the Potwar region, other correlative and older sediments are often broadly included in "the Siwaliks," but some are, in fact, quite distinct geologically. Parts of the Manchar and the Murree formations yield equivalent (or slightly older) faunas to the Kamlial, while Dera Bugti (Baluchistan) and correlates in the nearby Zinda Pir Dome are significantly older, extending the local faunal succession back to ca. 22 Ma. The Soan Formation is correlative with the Tatrot and Pinjor formations, originally defined in the Siwalik Hills of north India (see Figure). Due to the general lack of datable volcanics (other than rare ash layers suitable for fission-track analyses), geochronometry is based on paleomagnetic correlation of longer sequences, calibrated by faunal comparisons. Continuing changes in the calibration of geomagnetic polarity transitions result in small changes in the precise dates attributed to specific horizons, so that even the recent chart presented here was modified slightly, mainly

by increasing the ages of Middle–Late Miocene levels by as much as 0.5 Myr.

In the Potwar Plateau, the Siwalik Group measures several km in thickness and ranges from the Early Miocene, in excess of 18 Ma, to the Pleistocene at 1.0 Ma or less. The lithologic boundaries of the formations are time-transgressive, as must be expected. The sediments represent floodplain deposition in the subduction trough below the Himalayas suture zone, where the leading edge of the Indo-Pakistan plate is descending beneath the Eurasian plate. Erosion in this highly active uplift region produced sediment in vast volumes, which was spread out and buried in the subduction basin by streams large and small. The process shifted southward to the Indus, Ganges, and Brahmaputra floodplains in the Middle Pleistocene, when the Siwaliks zone became caught up in the suture folding. Siwaliks fossils are preserved in a variety of fluviatile sedimentary situations, but particularly in abandoned floodplain channels.

The environment appears to have been characterized by subtropical climate in a low-relief terrain of braided and meandering stream channels, with a variety of vegetation types, including swamp, gallery forest, floodplain forest, woodland, and grassland.

Siwalik Primates

Hundreds of specimens of large fossil hominoids have been collected from the Potwar area of Pakistan. Other significant collections come from India near Ramnagar, in the Kashmir district, and from the Hari Talyangar region north of Delhi (where the fauna is dated mainly between 9.5 and 8.5 Ma

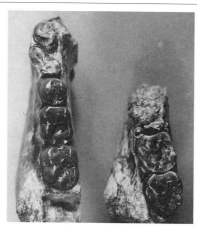
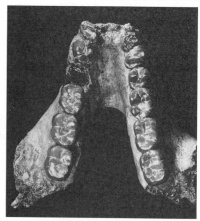

Occlusal views of selected Siwalik hominoids. Sivapithecus indicus *females, left to right: right maxilla with P3-M2 (ex-"Ramapithecus punjabicus"), left maxilla with C1-M3, left juvenile mandible with P4-M2 (ex-"Sugrivapithecus"), left mandible with M2-3 (ex-"Ramapithecus"); mandible of* Gigantopithecus giganteus.

but continues up to 6.5 Ma). Smaller catarrhines and strepsirhines are also known. The large hominoids belong principally to the genus *Sivapithecus,* including specimens formerly assigned to *Ramapithecus.* Many new specimens, including a well-preserved face and a large number of postcranial elements of *Sivapithecus,* are now known. These seem to indicate clearly that this genus is not on the human lineage as once thought but is more closely allied to the ancestry of the modern orangutan. Three species are recognized: *S. sivalensis* dated 12.5–10.3 Ma; *S. indicus* (represented by most material, especially at the U-sandstone horizon that is dated ca. 9 Ma on the latest time scale) between 9.5 and 8.5 Ma in Pakistan and India; and the large *S. parvada,* known only at Loc. Y311 (Sethi Nagri), dated ca. 10 Ma. Small, apparently thin-enameled hominoids are known from levels ca. 11.5–10.5 Ma and at Hari Talyanger; these have been called *S. simonsi* by R.F. Kay but are probably better referred to as *?Dryopithecus.* Specimens attributed to *Gigantopithecus* are rare, with an undated isolated tooth named *G. giganteus* usually synonymized with the ca. 7–6.5 Ma mandible of *G. bilaspurensis* from the upper levels near Hari Talyangar.

A small catarrhine previously referred to *?Dionysopithecus,* but now considered a possible member of the *Dendropithecus*-group and not a pliopithecid, is known mainly from levels dated ca. 16.1 Ma. Similar teeth have been reported at Hari Talyangar. The lorisid *Nycticeboides* derives from levels near the U-sandstone. Small archaic strepsirhines usually included in the Sivaladapidae also occur at this level in Pakistan and at Hari Talyangar, and they extend down into the Kamlial. Cercopithecid primates occur later in the sequence, with the small colobine *?Semnopithecus sivalensis* between ca. 7.5 and 6.5 Ma, and the cercopithecines *Macaca palaeindica* and *Procynocephalus subhimalayanus* probably between 3.5 and 2 Ma. A single specimen of *Theropithecus oswaldi delsoni* is known from Mirzapur, India, perhaps dating to 1.5–0.9 Ma.

As discussed mainly by J. Barry and colleagues, there are several intervals of major faunal turnover in rodent, artiodactyl, and primate taxa through the Miocene portion of the Siwalik sequence. As yet, the Pliocene segment is not well enough known to analyze. The greatest turnovers occur ca. 13 Ma and 8.5–8 Ma, which do not correspond closely to known global events. Small catarrhines are present before the first of these turnovers, while *Sivapithecus* first appears soon after it. The last occurrences of *Sivapithecus,* *?Dryopithecus,* *Nycticeboides,* and Sivaladapidae probably correspond to the second turnover, after which cercopithecids first appear (the oldest-known members of this family east of Afghanistan). In India, however, *Gigantopithecus* is found to at least 6.5 Ma, and in China it continues well into the Pleistocene. This faunal change in the Siwaliks is probably related to climate. For example, studies of soil carbonates reveal that there was a shift between 8 and 5 Ma from environments dominated by C_3 plants to those in which C_4 plants were more common— this may equate to forests being replaced by grasslands. Faunal elements that appeared during and after this time seem to be adapted to more open-country regimes. Prior to the 8 Ma turnover, a smaller turnover may have occurred ca. 10–9.5 Ma with the arrival of equids, but the environmental change, if any, had no major effect on the hominoids.

The great interest of the Siwalik region, and of the Potwar sequence in particular, lies in the information it provides about mammalian faunal change in one region over a long time period. The fact that hominoids are part of this fauna only adds to its value. In conjunction with work elsewhere, periods of successive isolation and connection with other parts of the world can be demonstrated and their effects on the fauna closely documented. The Siwaliks also present the best opportunity available for investigating the possible interactions of climatic events and mammalian evolution through the Neogene.

See also Adapiformes; Asia, Eastern and Southern; Cercopithecinae; Colobinae; Dryopithecus; Gigantopithecus; Hominidae; Hominoidea; Lorisidae; Miocene; Neogene; Paleodietary Analysis; Ponginae; Plate Tectonics; Sivapithecus; Stable Isotopes (in Biological Systems). [J.A.V.C., E.D., A.H.]

Further Readings

Badgley, C., and Behrensmeyer, A.K., eds. (1995) Long records of continental ecosystems. Palaeogeog., Palaeoclimatol., Palaeoecol., Vol. 115.

Barry, J.C. (1986) A review of the chronology of Siwalik hominoids. In J.G. Else and P.C. Lee (eds.): Primate Evolution. Cambridge: Cambridge University Press, pp. 93–105.

Barry, J.C. (1987) The history and chronology of Siwalik cercopithecids. J. Hum. Evol. 2:47–58.

Barry, J.C. (1995) Faunal turnover and diversity in the terrestrial Neogene of Pakistan. In E.S. Vrba, G.H. Denton, T.C. Partridge, and L.H. Burckle (eds.): Paleoclimate and Evolution, with Emphasis on Human Origins. New Haven: Yale University Press, pp. 114–134.

Skeleton

The human skeleton, like that of most primates, is relatively generalized by mammalian standards. Most primates have a primitive limb structure with one bone in the upper (or proximal) part of the limb (humerus and femur), a pair in the lower (distal) part (radius/ulna and tibia/fibula), and five digits on their hands and feet. Primates have retained many bones from our vertebrate ancestors that other mammals have lost, such as the clavicle, a bone that has been lost in the evolutionary history of most ungulates and many carnivores. Likewise, many mammals have reduced the number of digits on their hands and feet and reduced or coalesced the bones of their forearm and leg. In the number of separate skeletal elements and the configuration of their limbs, primates are more similar to the primitive mammalian skeletal morphology than are many other living mammals.

In general, the skeleton of a mammal has the skull (composed of cranium and mandible), in front, followed by the *postcranial skeleton*, which serves several functions, such as providing support and protection for the organs of the trunk. However, its primary functions and those that seem to account best for the major differences in skeletal shape, are those in respect to locomotion. In this capacity, the postcranial skeleton provides both a structural support and a series of attachments and levers to aid in movement. In humans, of course, the skull is placed *above* the postcranium, because of our upright posture. The primate skull is treated in detail in a separate entry.

Primate postcranial skeletons can be divided into three parts: axial skeleton (backbone and ribs), forelimb, and hindlimb.

Axial Skeleton

The backbone is made up of individual bones called vertebrae and is divided into four regions. The cervical, or neck, region contains seven vertebrae in humans, as in almost all mammals. The first two vertebrae, the atlas and the axis, are specialized in shape and serve as a support and pivot for the skull. The other cervical vertebrae are concerned with movements of the neck.

The second region of the backbone is the thorax. Humans have 12 thoracic vertebrae, while other primates have between nine and 13, each of which is attached to a rib. Most of the rotational movements of the trunk involve movements between thoracic vertebrae. The ribs are connected anteriorly with the sternum to enclose the thoracic cage, within which lie the heart and lungs. On the outside, the thorax is covered by the muscles of the upper limb. Primates exhibit considerable variability in the shape of the thorax. In quadrupedal species, the thorax tends to be relatively deep dorsoventrally and narrow from side to side. In suspensory apes and in humans, the thorax is broad, so that the scapula lies on the back.

The thoracic vertebrae are followed by the lumbar vertebrae. Humans have five lumbar vertebrae, but in other primates the number ranges between four and seven. Those species with long flexible backbones for leaping or running tend to have more lumbar vertebrae, while climbing and suspensory species have fewer vertebrae and, hence, a short, stiff backbone.

No ribs are attached to the lumbar vertebrae, but the latter have very large transverse processes for the attachment of the large muscles that extend the back. Most of the flexion and extension of the back takes place in the lumbar region. In most primates, the thoracic and lumbar vertebrae form a gentle curve with a dorsal convexity *(kyphosis)*. The human backbone is unusual in that the thoracic region has a dorsal convexity while the lumbar region has a ventral convexity *(lordosis)*. This extra curvature is related to our bipedal posture.

The next region of the backbone is the sacrum, a single bone composed of several fused vertebrae. The pelvis, or hip bone, is attached to the sacrum on either side, while the tail joins it distally. Humans have five sacral vertebrae; other primates have between three and seven. Primates with a tail generally have fewer sacral vertebrae, while tailless species have more. The last region of the spine is the caudal region, or tail. In humans and apes, this consists of three or four tiny bones all fused together, called the coccyx. In other primates, the caudal region forms a long tail made up of as many as 30 vertebrae.

The Forelimb

The primate upper limb is divided into four regions, most of which contain several bones. The most proximal part, nearest the trunk, is the shoulder girdle composed of two bones: the clavicle anteriorly and the scapula posteriorly. The small S-shaped clavicle is attached to the sternum anteriorly and to the scapula posteriorly. It provides the only bony connection between the upper limb and the trunk.

The flat, triangular scapula is attached to the sternum via the clavicle and is attached to the thoracic wall only by several broad muscles. The scapula varies considerably in shape among living primates. In suspensory species, this bone tends to be relatively long and narrow, with the glenoid cavity facing cranially. In quadrupedal species, it tends to be broad, with a laterally (or ventrally) facing glenoid. The human scapula is most similar to that of an orangutan.

The scapula articulates with the single bone of the upper arm, the humerus, by a very mobile ball-and-socket joint between the glenoid cavity of the scapula and the head of the humerus. Most of the large propulsive muscles of the upper limb originate on the chest wall or the scapula and insert on

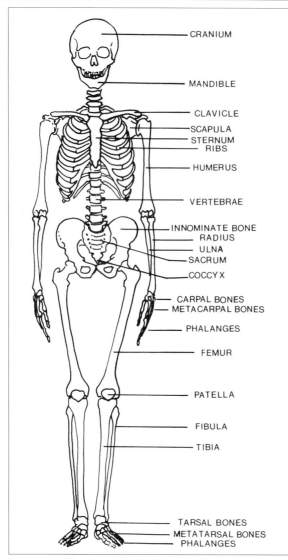

CRANIUM

MANDIBLE

CLAVICLE
SCAPULA
STERNUM
RIBS
HUMERUS

VERTEBRAE

INNOMINATE BONE
RADIUS
ULNA
SACRUM
COCCYX

CARPAL BONES
METACARPAL BONES

PHALANGES

FEMUR

PATELLA

FIBULA

TIBIA

TARSAL BONES
METATARSAL BONES
PHALANGES

Anterior view of a human skeleton, showing the principal bones of which it is composed.

the humerus; the muscles responsible for flexing and extending the elbow originate on the humerus (or just above on the scapula) and insert on the forearm bones. The human humerus is very similar to that of extant great apes in having a head that faces medially rather than posteriorly and in the distinctive distal articulation with a rounded capitulum and a spool-shaped trochlea.

Two forearm bones articulate with the humerus: the radius on the lateral, or thumb, side and the ulna on the medial side. The elbow joint is a complex region with the articulation of three bones. The articulation between the ulna and the humerus is a hinge joint, functioning in a simple lever system. Humans resemble apes and other suspensory primates in having a very small olecranon process on the proximal end of the ulna. In quadrupedal primates and most other mammals, the olecranon process is long and provides a powerful lever for extension of the elbow during quadrupedal walking and running.

The radius forms a more complex joint, since this rodlike bone rotates about the ulna. This movement of the radius and ulna is called *pronation* when the hand faces down and *supination* when the hand faces up. The muscles responsible for movements at the wrist and for flexion and extension of the fingers originate on the distal end of the humerus and on the two forearm bones. Distally, the radius and the ulna articulate with the bones of the wrist. The radius forms the larger joint, and in some primates (lorises, humans, and apes) the ulna does not even contact the wrist bones.

Primate hands are divided into three regions: wrist, metacarpals, and phalanges. The wrist, or carpus, is a complicated region. In most primates, it consists of nine separate bones aligned in two rows. In humans and in African apes, two of these have fused so that there are only eight bones. The proximal row articulates with the radius, and the distal row articulates with the metacarpals of the hand. Between the two rows of bones is a composite joint, the midcarpal joint, with considerable mobility in flexion, extension, and rotation.

The five rodlike metacarpals form the skeleton of the palm and articulate distally with the phalanges, or finger bones, of each digit. The joints at the base of most of the metacarpals are formed by two flat surfaces offering little mobility; however, the joint at the base of the first digit—the pollex, or thumb—is more elaborate in many species and shows special modifications associated with the requirements of manipulation and grasping. The joints between the metacarpal and the proximal phalanx of each finger allow mainly flexion and extension with a small amount of side-to-side movement (*abduction* and *adduction*) for spreading the fingers apart. There are three phalanges (proximal, middle, and distal) for each finger except the thumb, which has only two (proximal and distal). The joints between the phalanges are pure flexion and extension joints.

While all primate hands have approximately the same numbers of bones, the relative proportions of their hand elements can vary greatly in conjunction with particular locomotor needs. In arboreal species, the digits, and especially the phalanges, are relatively longer than in terrestrial species. Many arboreal primates have greatly reduced or even lost the pollex (thumb), while lorises have reduced the index finger for enhanced grasping abilities between the pollex and the more lateral digits. In suspensory primates, the digits are especially long. Species that rely on manipulative abilities for grasping insects, seeds, or other items tend to have a pollex and an index finger that are more similar in length. Humans show a large number of detailed modifications of hand structure in association with the hand's almost exclusive use as an organ of manipulation rather than as part of the locomotor system.

The Hindlimb

The primate hindlimb can be divided into four major regions: the pelvic girdle, the thigh, the leg, and the foot. These regions are comparable with the shoulder girdle, arm, forearm, and hand of the forelimb. The primate pelvic girdle is made up of three separate bones on each side (the ilium, the ischium, and the pubis) that fuse to form a single rigid structure called the innominate bone. In contrast with the pectoral girdle, which is mobile and loosely connected to the

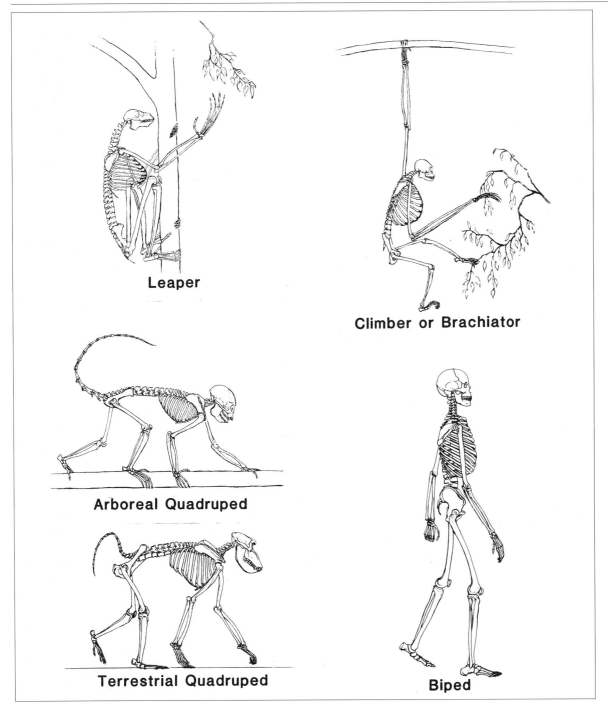

Leaper

Climber or Brachiator

Arboreal Quadruped

Terrestrial Quadruped

Biped

Lateral views of the skeletons of primates representing various locomotor types, showing differences in skeletal proportions. Courtesy of John G. Fleagle.

trunk, the pelvic girdle is firmly attached to the backbone through a nearly immobile joint between the sacrum and the paired ilia. The primate pelvis, like that of all mammals, serves many roles. Forming the bottom of the abdominopelvic cavity, the internal part supports and protects the pelvic viscera, including the female reproductive organs, the bladder, and the lower part of the digestive tract. The bony pelvis also forms the birth canal through which the newborn must pass. In conjunction with this requirement, most female primates (including women) have a bony pelvis relatively wider than in males of the same species. Finally, the pelvis plays a major role in locomotion. It is the bony link be-

tween the trunk and the hindlimb bones, and it is the origin for many large hindlimb muscles that move the lower limb.

The ilium is the largest of the three bones forming the bony pelvis. A long, relatively flat bone in most primates, it lies alongside the vertebral column and is completely covered with large hip muscles, primarily those responsible for flexing, abducting, and rotating the hip joint. The rodlike ischium lies posterior to the ilium, and most of the muscles responsible for extending the hip joint and flexing the knee arise from its most posterior surface, the ischial tuberosity.

This tuberosity also forms our sitting bone. The pubis lies anterior to the other two bones and gives rise to many of the muscles that adduct the hip joint. The ischium and the pubis join together inferiorly to form the ischiopubic ramus and completely surround the obturator foramen. The relative sizes and shapes of these three bones vary considerably among primate species in conjunction with different locomotor habits. The human pelvis is unique among all mammals in having a very short, broad ilium and a short, dorsally oriented ischium, associated with our bipedal locomotion.

The part of the bony pelvis that articulates with the head of the femur is called the acetabulum, and it lies at the junction of the three bones. The hip joint is a ball-and-socket joint that allows mobility in many directions.

The single bone of the thigh is the femur. The prominent features of this long bone are a round head that articulates with the pelvis, the greater tuberosity where many hip extensors and abductors insert, the shaft, and the distal condyles, which articulate with the tibia to form the knee joint. Most of the surface of the femur is covered by the quadriceps muscles responsible for extension of the knee. Attached to the tendon of this set of muscles is the third bone of the knee, the small patella. The human femur is unique among primates in having a large rounded head and a short femoral neck. The lateral condyle is larger than the medial one, and the shaft of the femur is angled medially so that the knee joint lies medial to the hip joint. This adaptation places our center of gravity closer to the midline and aids in balance during bipedal walking.

Two bones make up the lower leg, the tibia medially and the fibula laterally. The tibia is larger and participates in the knee joint; distally, it forms the main articulation with the ankle. The fibula is a slender splintlike bone that articulates with the tibia both above and below and also forms the lateral side of the ankle joint. Arising from the surfaces of the tibia and the fibula (and also from the distal-most part of the femur) are the large muscles responsible for movements at the ankle and those that flex and extend the toes during grasping or walking and running.

Like the hand, the primate foot is made up of three parts: tarsus, metatarsus, and phalanges. The most proximal two tarsal bones are those that form the ankle: the talus (or astragalus) above and the calcaneus below. The head of the talus articulates with the navicular bone. The navicular articulates with three small cuneiform bones, which, in turn, articulate with the first three metatarsals. The body of the talus sits roughly on the center of the calcaneus, the largest of the tarsal bones. The tuberosity of the calcaneus extends well posterior to the rest of the ankle and forms the heel process. The achilles tendon from the calf muscle attaches here, and this process acts as a lever for the entire foot. Anteriorly, the calcaneus articulates with the cuboid, which, in turn, articulates with the metatarsals of digits IV and V.

In nonhuman primates, the digits of the foot resemble those of the hand. Each of the lateral four digits has a long metatarsal followed by three phalanges. The shorter first digit, the hallux, is opposable like the thumb, or pollex, and has a mobile joint at its base for grasping. Primate feet show considerable differences from species to species in the relative proportion of different pedal elements, associated with different locomotor abilities. Arboreal species tend to have longer, more curved phalanges and usually a more opposable hallux, whereas terrestrial species have shorter digits.

Human feet are unique in their lack of an opposable hallux. Rather, all five digits are aligned side by side. In addition, we have relatively short phalanges, and the tarsals form a set of bony arches that make the human foot a more effective lever during bipedal locomotion.

Skeletal Proportions

Primates vary considerably in their overall body proportions, in association with differences in their locomotor habits. Leaping primates are generally characterized by relatively longer hindlimbs than forelimbs and a long flexible trunk, especially in the lumbar region. Arboreal quadrupeds usually

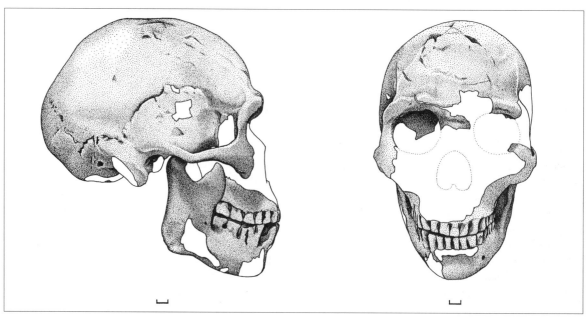

Lateral and facial views of the Skhūl 5 skull. Scales are 1 cm.

have a relatively long trunk and a long tail and forelimbs and hindlimbs that are more similar in length but short relative to trunk length or body size, as adaptations for balance. Terrestrial quadrupeds also have forelimbs and hindlimbs that are similar in length, but their limbs tend to be longer relative to body size, since balance is not a problem on the ground. Suspensory primates usually have relatively long limbs and long hands and feet to permit them to suspend their body from a wide range of supports. They usually have a short, relatively rigid trunk.

See also Bone Biology; Forensic Anthropology; Locomotion; Musculature; Skull; Tail. [J.G.F.]

Further Readings

Bass, W.M. (1971) Human Osteology. Columbia: Missouri Archaeological Society.

LeGros Clark, W.E. (1959) The Antecedents of Man. Edinburgh: Edinburgh University Press.

Shipman, P., Walker, A., and Bichell, D. (1985) The Human Skeleton. Cambridge, Mass.: Harvard University Press.

Skhūl

Rockshelter in the Wadi el-Mughara on the western escarpment of Mount Carmel (Israel). Between 1929 and 1934, excavations at Skhūl by T.D. McCown (supervised by D. Garrod) recovered a number of adult and child partial skeletons of early modern humans together with a Levantine Mousterian industry. These excavations removed virtually all of the sediments from this site. All of the human fossils occur in Level B, a highly brecciated layer with generally poor faunal preservation. The lithic industry from Skhūl Level B is broadly comparable to that at nearby Tabūn Level C and the lower levels from Qafzeh, where remains of early modern humans were also found. Initial radiocarbon and amino-acid racemization dates placed the hominid-bearing strata ca. 45–30 Ka, but more recent thermoluminescence and electron spin resonance dates place Level B between 120 and 80 Ka. Ten individual hominids (seven adults and three children) are probably represented in Level B, and the material includes three reasonably complete adult skulls and some well-preserved long bones from the adults and children. Many of the skeletons appear to have been intentionally buried; one adult (Skhūl 5) is clasping the jaw of a wild boar to his chest, and one infant (Skhūl 1) is buried in a highly flexed position. The Skhūl fossils were interpreted by their describers (McCown and A. Keith), together with the remains from the nearby site of Tabūn Cave, as a single population in the process of evolution into an early-modern type. The Skhūl material is now generally regarded as a robust early-modern population of western Asia that still retains some archaic features from nonmodern ancestors. Some workers consider the Skhūl specimens, together with those from Qafzeh, to represent the ancestors of the European Cro-Magnon populations; others continue to view them as part of the same population as the Levantine Neanderthals from Tabūn, Amud, and Kebara.

See also Amud; Archaic Moderns; Asia, Western; Cro-Magnon; Garrod, Dorothy Anne Elizabeth; Kebara; Keith, [Sir] Arthur; McCown, Theodore D.; Neanderthals; Qafzeh; Tabūn. [C.B.S., J.J.S.]

Further Readings

Akazawa, T., Aoki, K. and Bar-Yosef, O. eds. (1998) Neandertals and Modern Humans in Western Asia. New York: Plenum.

McCown, T.D. (1937) Excavations of Mughâret es-Skhūl. In D. Garrod and D.M.A. Bate (eds.): The Stone Age of Mount Carmel, Vol. 1: Excavations in the Wady el-Mughara. Oxford: Clarendon.

Skull

The primate skull (like that of all mammals) is composed of two elements: the cranium (including many fused bones) and the mandible or lower jaw. In turn, the cranium may be divided into two major components based on developmental and functional criteria: the neurocranium and the splanchnocranium, or viscerocranium. The neurocranium houses the brain and is made up of two parts distinguishable by the type of bone formation underlying each. The membranous neurocranium, so called because the bones develop via intramembranous ossification, forms the calvarium and comprises the frontal bone, parietal bones, the squamous (or flat) portions of the temporal bones, and the squamous portion of the occipital bone. The chondrocranium, or basicranium, develops from cartilage and comprises the ethmoid and sphenoid bones, as well as the petrous and mastoid regions of the temporal bones and part of the occipital bone. The basicranium serves as the floor of the neurocranium (and is, therefore, pierced by many nerves and blood vessels), and it also acts as a structural interface between the splanchnocranium and the neurocranium.

The splanchnocranium constitutes the rest of the skull, primarily the jaws and facial bones. The terms *splanchnocranium* and *viscerocranium* reflect the derivation of these bones from the embryonic visceral, or branchial, arches, which in primitive vertebrates line the wall of the digestive tract and support the gills. These bones develop via both membranous and endochondral ossification and, in the adult human state, are represented by the paired maxillae; inferior nasal conchae; nasal, lacrimal, zygomatic, and palatine bones; plus the single vomer and mandible. Since primate skulls are often described or measured, a system of landmarks, or defined points, has been developed to facilitate the process. Some of the most important landmarks are shown in the accompanying figure.

The primary functions of the skull are to gather and break down food for nourishment and to support and protect the brain and the soft tissues associated with the special senses of hearing, sight, and smell.

Primate Diversity in Skull Form and Function

The rich diversity of skull form evidenced by our order is best illustrated by consideration of the functional specializations of the soft tissues associated with the various skeletal regions. For example, the skull of modern humans is dominated by

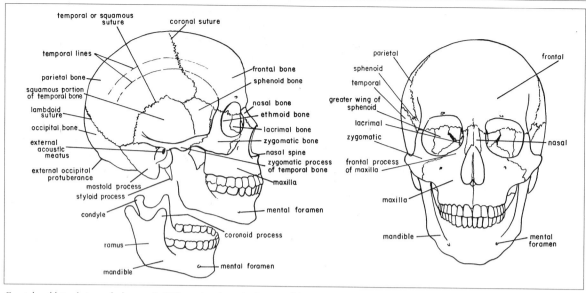

Frontal and lateral views of a human skull illustrating the major bones and features. Courtesy of Brian T. Shea.

the dramatically enlarged neurocranium, which houses our most salient morphological specialization, ca. 1,500 ml of grey matter. Because our enormous cranial vaults are combined with relatively small faces, teeth, and chewing muscles, human skulls lack the marked bony ridges or protuberances, such as the sagittal crest or supraorbital torus, often seen in other primates. In other cases, relatively large braincases and small facial skulls are related to the small overall body size of a species, as in the South American squirrel monkey (*Saimiri*) or the African talapoin monkey (*Miopithecus*), both of which may be dwarfed forms derived from larger ancestors. The basis for such shape changes is the differential, or *allometric*, growth of the facial skeleton relative to the neural skeleton, so that shifts in body size during ontogeny or among adults of closely related species result in a disproportionate change in facial size relative to overall skull size.

The orbits house the eyes and associated soft tissues and are particularly well developed in nocturnal species, such as the South American owl monkey (*Aotus*). Orbital hypertro-

phy reaches an extreme in the tarsier (*Tarsius*), where the weight of a single eyeball may exceed that of the brain, and the huge orbital cones envelop the facial skeleton. In general, however, the eyes exhibit a growth pattern similar to the brain, and thus the orbits usually decrease in relative size during ontogeny and among larger adults of a series varying in body size (compare the skulls of the two small species on the left in the accompanying figure with those of the large species on the right). The degree of development of the bony midface, or snout, is influenced by numerous factors. The strepsirhine primates generally rely more on olfactory stimuli in their social and feeding behavior than do the haplorhines; they also exhibit relatively larger faces that protrude in front of the neurocranium rather than being more recessed under the skull vault. The nasal fossae in these primates are filled with bony turbinals that are covered by olfactory and respiratory epithelium. Certain extant haplorhines, such as howler monkeys, baboons, and gorillas, also have secondarily enlarged faces, due primarily to the effects of large

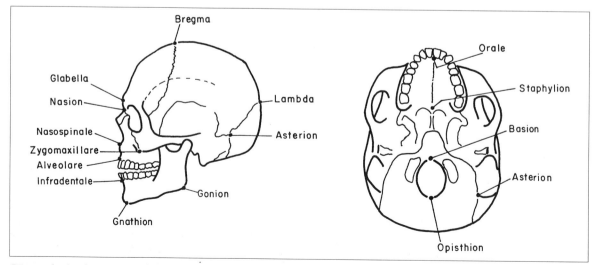

Diagram showing the major cranial "landmarks" used in skull descriptions and between which standard measurements are taken. Courtesy of Brian T. Shea.

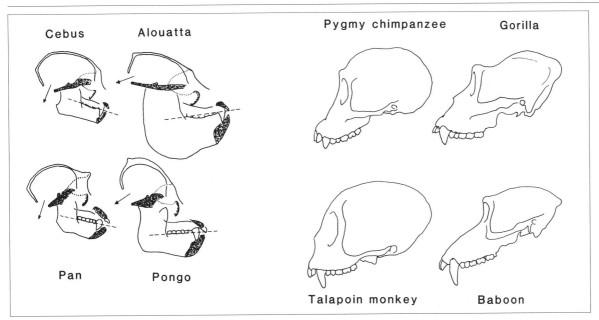

Left: differences in the positioning of the face relative to the skull base and cranial vault in howler monkeys (Alouatta) *and orangutans* (Pongo) *by comparison to unflexed relatives (capuchin monkey and chimpanzee, respectively). The upward or dorsal deflection of the face (airorhynchy) may be related to enlargement of structures associated with vocalization. Right: a comparison of skull shape in two pairs of closely related species differing markedly in overall body size. Above: female pygmy chimpanzee or bonobo* (Pan paniscus, *ca. 33 kg) and male gorilla* (G. gorilla, *ca. 170 kg); below: male talapoin monkey* (Miopithecus talapoin, *ca. 1.2 kg) and male savannah baboon* (Papio hamadryas anubis, *ca. 25 kg). Note the relatively enlarged faces and small braincases in the larger forms, resulting from differential growth in these regions as size increases. Courtesy of Brian T. Shea.*

body size and the positively allometric increase in the splanchnocranium and the canine teeth (see Figure).

Structures related to the production of sound may also affect skull form. In the howler monkey (*Alouatta*), the face is flexed upward, or dorsally, on an elongated and flattened skullbase, allowing for the suspension of an enlarged hyoid bone as part of a resonating chamber used to boom signals to conspecifics. The orangutan (*Pongo*) also exhibits a dorsally deflected splanchnocranium, perhaps related to the enlarged laryngeal sac, which functions as a resonating structure, especially in males. In *Homo*, a secondary flexion or bending of the skull appears to be related to a restructuring of the pharyngeal and laryngeal region, yielding an enlarged supralaryngeal tract vital to the production of the complex and subtle sounds that make up human speech.

The dentition affects the size and the shape of the splanchnocranium and also indirectly of the neurocranium, via related soft tissues, such as the chewing muscles, and bony support structures, such as the mandible and portions of the facial region. Larger teeth basically require a larger, more heavily buttressed maxillary and mandibular framework. An interesting example is seen in the intriguing and bizarre aye-aye (*Daubentonia*) from Madagascar. Here a deep and strongly flexed, beaklike face is related to the procumbent and continuously growing incisors that aye-ayes use to pry under tree bark for grubs and insects.

The chewing muscles, along with the teeth, the bony jaws, and other stress-bearing regions of the skull, compose a functional unit that affects skull form in an important and reasonably predictable fashion. The mechanical task of this unit is primarily to break down ingested food by repetitive opening and closing of the jaws. The masticatory muscles, primarily the

masseter, temporalis, and medial and lateral pterygoids, perform this function. The degree of force produced at the bite point can be roughly determined by taking a ratio of the *lever* (or power) *arm* of muscular effort, which is the distance from the jaw joint to the average line of action of the muscle, to the *load* (or resistance) *arm*, which is the distance from the jaw joint to the bite point. If one assumes a constant force input (i.e., muscles of the same size and power), a higher lever/load ratio reflects a mechanical situation capable of producing greater forces. Increased mechanical efficiency is often produced by moving forward the insertion of the masseter muscle and thus increasing the length of the lever arm, or by decreasing the length of the load arm, accomplished by shortening of the lower face or by tucking the palate underneath the upper face.

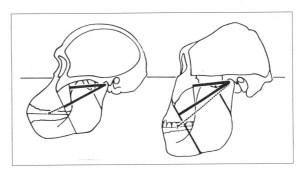

Illustration of cranial biomechanics using the early hominins Australopithecus africanus *(left) and* Paranthropus boisei. *The heavy solid lines represent the in-lever or power arms for the temporalis (shorter) and masseter chewing muscles, while the dashed lines represent the out-lever or resistance arms to the molar teeth. Note the higher ratio of in-lever to out-lever arms in* P. boisei, *providing increased mechanical efficiency and greater force production during chewing with the back teeth. After E.L. DuBrul, 1977,* Am. J. Phys. Anthropol., *47; courtesy of Brian T. Shea.*

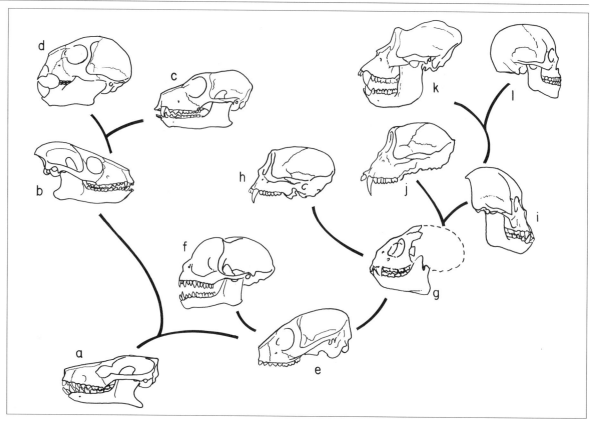

An array of skulls of extant and extinct primates, depicting the general evolutionary directions taken by some of the major taxonomic groups as well as some striking specializations. The diagrammatic linkages among these skulls reflect phylogenetic ties, but they do not represent the actual anatomical transformations among the species shown here. Several skulls are generalized, primitive designs indicative of ancestral patterns of important groups, as identified in parentheses: (a) Plesiolestes *(all primates); (b)* Notharctus *(euprimates); (c)* Lemur *(lemurs and lorises); (d)* Daubentonia*; *(e)* Rooneyia *(tarsiiforms and haplorhines); (g)* Apidium *(anthropoids); (h)* Cebus*; *(i)* Proconsul *(hominoids); (j)* Macaca*; *(k)* Gorilla*; *(l)* Homo sapiens. *Courtesy of Brian T. Shea. Not to scale.*

Within the hominins, the "robust" australopiths (*Paranthropus robustus, P. aethiopicus,* and *P. boisei*) in particular exhibit aspects of this configuration. These basic principles of cranial biomechanics also help us make sense of the differences in skull form between the two subfamilies of Old World monkeys: The folivorous, or leaf-eating, colobines with their short faces and deep jaws have higher ratios of lever/load arms compared with the frugivorous, or fruit-eating, cercopithecines with their long and prognathic faces.

Current Research and Prospects

A number of relatively new approaches and techniques in the study of primate and mammalian skull form have yielded promising results, and much additional research will be completed in these areas in the future. Experimental approaches to masticatory biomechanics have involved cineradiographic filming of jaw and tooth movement, electromyographic determination of muscle activity, measurement of *in vivo* bone strain in various portions of the face, and investigation of the histochemical properties of the chewing muscles. The integration of such information with results of studies of comparative anatomy and biomechanical modeling has resulted in significant advances in our understanding of skull function.

Another important area of work involves the genetic and developmental factors controlling skull growth and

form, since it is changes in these controls that result in evolutionary transformations of the skull. Studies in quantitative genetics, developmental abnormalities, and experimental approaches to intrinsic (e.g., developing tissue interactions) and extrinsic (e.g., hormonal) growth controls have provided new insights here. Finally, advances in evolutionary theory and the discovery of new fossil skulls of extinct primates also combine to provide important new information. Primatologists synthesize data from these and other fields in their continuing attempt to understand the form, function, and phylogeny of the skull of humans and nonhuman primates.

Evolution of Primate Skull Form

Our knowledge of cranial anatomy in the earliest primates is based largely on fossil remains of Paleocene forms such as *Palaechthon nacimienti* from North America and *Plesiadapis tricuspidens* from western Europe. These examples illustrate that the first primates were more similar to their mammalian contemporaries than to their later primate descendants or to any primates alive today. The skulls of these Paleocene primates generally resemble those of living treeshrews, with a long snout projecting in front of the relatively small braincase. Such a skull is designed to accommodate a large masticatory apparatus, with a long dental arcade and well-developed chewing muscles anchored to the skull vault, the zygomatic arches, and the lower jaw. The long face also reflects an acute sense of smell, whereas the eye sockets are relatively small, less frontated, and without the supportive postorbital bar characteristic of later primates. This combination of features has been used by some to argue that the earliest primates were nocturnal animals.

The fossil evidence indicates that plesiadapiforms had an ossified auditory bulla, a bony shell-like casing that envelops the chamber of the middle ear and its ossicles from below. According to some authors, this bullar capsule is formed by the petrosal bone, a derived homology that unites all of the primates as a monophyletic group. Other mammals have analogously evolved ossified bullae by incorporating different cranial elements into a middle-ear covering, such as the ectotympanic bone, whose primary function is to provide a collar for the tympanic membrane. Some mammals lack an ossified bulla entirely but encase the ear region with membrane or cartilage. The evolution of a bony auditory bulla may be related to the development of a hearing mechanism sensitive to low-frequency sounds.

The second major radiation of primates occurred during the Eocene epoch and produced a new type of cranial organization. Eocene adapiforms, such as *Notharctus*, and omomyids, as exemplified by *Rooneyia*, are characterized by a reduced snout, relatively larger brains, more frontally directed orbits, and a postorbital bar developed from processes of the frontal and zygomatic bones. The postorbital bar stabilizes the zygomatic arches by solidly fusing them to the braincase, providing a lateral truss that resists the twisting generated during unilateral mastication in a face that is shorter and with more frontated orbits than found in Paleocene primates.

The early omomyids were perhaps the first primates to adopt a diurnal activity pattern. Their skulls reflect this change from a dominance of the olfactory/tactile sense and corresponding enlargement of the portions of the brain associated with the sense of smell, the primitive primate pattern that characterized the plesiadapiforms and that persists among many extant strepsirhines. One of the important skeletal features reflecting this change in omomyids is the loss of the deep posterior recess of the nasal cavity that forms part of the separation of the eye sockets in most mammals. In the modern haplorhines, this space is occupied by the medial walls of the orbits, which have become frontated and closely spaced, enhancing the capacity for steroscopic vision. An orbital septum, or bony plate enclosing the posterolateral portion of the orbital space, is an important novel development in this group.

Anthropoids mark another adaptive transition in the evolution of the primate skull that is documented by such Oligocene forms as *Apidium*. In addition to a larger braincase, their faces are proportionately shorter and more vertical, the mandibular symphysis and frontal bones are rigidly fused early in life, and a greatly modified zygomatic bone extends laterally around the orbital fossa to form a postorbital partition that, in its detailed construction, is unique among the mammals. One explanation of this suite of features is that they signify a more active, forceful use of the incisor teeth in harvesting foods, powered by masseter and temporalis muscles of larger size and strength. With a fused man-

dibular symphysis, large loads can be carried by the solidly rooted, large, spatulate incisors that are typical of anthropoids, and power generated by muscles on either side of the head can be added together to increase the force of molar biting. Possibly to balance these forces and protect orbital contents from injury, the zygomatic bones have expanded in size and become firmly joined to the skull. The effect of this is to produce the postorbital plate, or septum, and reinforce the junction between the facial skull and the neurocranium. This basic anthropoid groundplan of skull form served as a foundation for marked diversification during Oligocene, Miocene, and Plio-Pleistocene times, yielding a broad array of extinct and extant monkeys, apes, and hominins.

Recent fossil discoveries of Miocene hominoid skulls, combined with a new perspective on the phylogenetic significance of certain cranial features, have rekindled debates over the origins of the African-ape clade. Previous schemes have characterized great-ape crania as either *klinorhynch* or *airorhynch*, depending on whether the facial skeleton is directed more ventrally or dorsally relative to the cranial base. While it has always been appreciated that the Asian orangutan has a particularly airorhynch skull relative to the other large-bodied hominoids, recent studies have raised the possibility that this feature is probably a shared primitive character of most known Early and Middle Miocene hominoid crania. In this view, a more klinorhynch skull represents a shared derived feature uniting humans, African apes, and certain Miocene forms perhaps specially related to this African clade (*Dryopithecus* and *Graecopithecus*, also known as *Ouranopithecus*, have been suggested as such possibilities). Moreover, certain other cranial features that have played a key role in phylogenetic and evolutionary debates, such as supraorbital-torus form, paranasal-sinus development, and nasoalveolar-clivus morphology, may covary with facial position and size to some extent, thus providing additional information of phylogenetic significance.

Another late-twentieth-century development has been the attempt to identify cranial features that link chimpanzees and hominins to the exclusion of gorillas, thus corroborating recent biomolecular phylogenies. However, much additional comparative data, an increased understanding of trait polar-

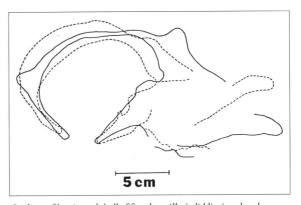

Outlines of hemisected skull of female gorilla (solid line) and male orangutan (dashed line) to show differences in positioning of the face, base and braincase. After Shea, 1985; courtesy of Brian T. Shea.

ity and homoplasy, and new fossil evidence from particularly the African-ape lineages are required before this suggestion can be accepted on the basis of cranial anatomy.

Evolution of the Human Skull

The evolution of skull form in our own lineage has been the subject of intense interest and debate since the discovery of the Taung child, formally named *Australopithecus africanus*, by R.A. Dart in the 1920s. This skull exhibited a counterintuitive mosaic of features, considering that common preconceptions, fueled by the fraudulent Piltdown skull, predicted that early hominins would have large, humanlike brains combined with primitive, apelike faces and teeth. The Taung skull was followed by even more impressive fossil remains from South Africa, and, from the late 1950s onward, the sediments of East Africa have yielded an unprecedented series of well-preserved skulls of humans and our close relatives. Combined with additional material from Asian and European sites, these African fossils permit us to sketch a fairly detailed, if ever-changing, scenario of human evolution over the past several million years based on craniodental remains.

Although specific phylogenetic connections are difficult to determine, particularly in the period 3.5–1.5 Ma, we can discern three primary groups of hominins, which are placed in the closely related but divergent genera *Australopithecus*, *Paranthropus*, and *Homo*. The australopiths (hominins other than *Homo*) are characterized, particularly in later and larger forms, by massive chewing teeth, well-developed sagittal crests, and large, heavily buttressed faces adapted to generating great chewing forces and withstanding the resultant bony stresses. Relative brain size exhibits no apparent increase through time within this group, although the australopiths are more highly encephalized than the great apes. Authorities have interpreted the most salient aspects of skull form in the australopiths as evidence of an increasing specialization on some type of hard-food items, such as roots and nuts, perhaps a dietary adaptation related to exploitation of drier and more open-country environments. It has never been clearly demonstrated that these specialized herbivorous hominins used any of the primitive stone tools found in eastern and southern Africa in the Plio-Pleistocene, and they disappear from the fossil record by ca. 1.4 Ma.

Another lineage of early hominins, in all likelihood derived from a primitive early australopith like *Australopithecus afarensis*, exhibited quite different skull morphology and general adaptations. In this group, the chewing teeth and associated masticatory apparatus became smaller and more gracile, while the brain literally exploded in an evolutionary sense, undergoing a three- to fourfold increase in overall size in a 3 Myr period. Skulls of the genus *Homo* combine a large and rounded cranial vault devoid of sagittal cresting with a smaller and flatter (orthognathic) face. The evidence of skull form and the archaeological record clearly suggest that, by ca. 2.5–2 Ma, our own genus had embarked on what would be a most successful evolutionary pathway, one characterized by behavioral flexibility and an adaptation to the natural environment based on culture.

Some interesting elaborations on this basic *Homo* pattern are seen in the well-known Neanderthal crania: The faces are enlarged and protruded in the nasal region and dominated by a heavy supraorbital torus, or browridge. Some have interpreted this morphology as evidence of cold adaptation in glacially isolated hominins, while others have suggested a link to use of an enlarged anterior dentition as part of a cultural tool kit.

In any case, a plentiful fossil record has revealed some haunting reflections that clearly inform us of the evolutionary pathways that culminated in our own species, *Homo sapiens*. Only time will tell whether this aberrant and highly encephalized species will avoid the fate of our closest cousins.

See also Adapiformes; Allometry; Anthropoidea; Australopithecus; Bone Biology; Dwarfism; Functional Morphology; Gigantism; Hominidae; Homininae; Hominoidea; Homo; Morphology; Omomyidae; Ontogeny; Paranthropus; Plesiadapidae; Ponginae; Primates; Sexual Dimorphism; Skeleton; Teeth. [B.T.S., A.L.R.]

Further Readings

Anderson, J.E. (1983) Grant's Atlas of Anatomy, 8th ed. Baltimore: Williams and Wilkins.

Begun, D.R. (1994) Relations among the great apes and humans: New interpretations based on the fossil great ape *Dryopithecus*. Yrbk. Phys. Anthropol. 37:11–63.

Biegert, J. (1963) The evaluation of characteristics of the skull, hands, and feet for taxonomy. In S.L. Washburn (ed.): Classification and Human Evolution (Publications in Anthropology No. 37). New York: Viking Fund, pp. 116–145.

De Beer, G.R. (1985) The Development of the Vertebrate Skull. Chicago: University of Chicago Press.

Enlow, D.H. (1982) Handbook of Facial Growth, 2nd ed. Philadelphia: Saunders.

Hanken, J., and Hall, B.K., eds. (1993) The Skull. Chicago: University of Chicago Press.

Moss, M.L., and Young, R.W. (1960) A functional approach to craniology. Am. J. Phys. Anthropol. 18:281–292.

Rak, Y. (1983) The Australopithecine Face. New York: Academic.

Shea, B.T. (1985) On aspects of skull form in African apes and orangutans, with implications for hominoid evolution. Am. J. Phys. Anthropol. 68:329–342.

Shea, B.T. (1988) Phylogeny and skull form in the hominoid primates. In J.H. Schwartz (ed.): Orang-utan Biology. Oxford: Oxford University Press, pp. 233–246.

Szalay, F.S., and Delson, E. (1979) Evolutionary History of the Primates. New York: Academic.

Weidenreich, F. (1941) The brain and its role in the phylogenetic transformation of the human skull. Trans. Am. Philosoph. Soc. 31:321–442.

Zingeser, M.R., ed. (1973) Craniofacial biology of primates. Symp. 4th Intl. Congr. Primatol., Vol. 3. Basel: Karger.

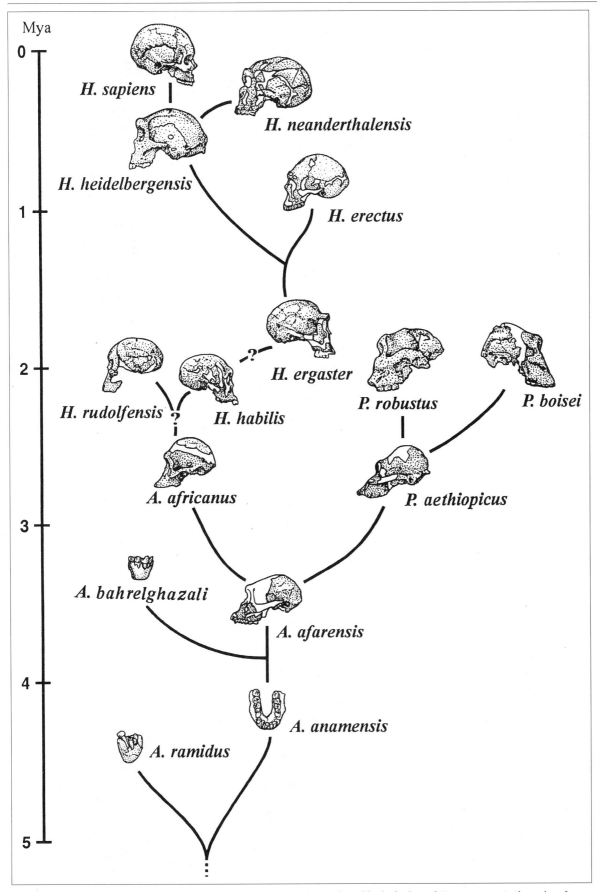

Evolution of hominin skulls. Two or three broadly defined phylogenetic trends are indicated by the fossil record. From a pattern similar to that of Australopithecus afarensis *increasingly large masticatory muscles and chewing teeth produced the strongly buttressed, deep faces of the robust lineage, which became extinct. A general decrease in tooth size, musculature, and face size, coupled with a dramatic increase in the size of the braincase, marked the* Australopithecus africanus–Homo sapiens *lineage, although the intervening details of phylogenetic and morphologic evolution are unresolved.*

Smith, [Sir] Grafton Elliot (1871–1937)

British (b. Australia) neuroanatomist and anthropologist. On receiving his doctorate of medicine in 1896 from the Medical School of the University of Sydney, Smith moved to England to continue his studies at Cambridge University. In 1900, he received the chair of anatomy at the Government School of Medicine in Cairo, where he remained until 1909, when he accepted the anatomy chair at Manchester University. Between 1919 and 1937, he served as the first director of the newly established Institute of Anatomy and Embryology at University College, London. Smith's interests were wide ranging. His most enduring contributions were in the area of comparative neuroanatomy, particularly as it pertains to primate evolution. Emerging from these studies was the notion that primate evolution involved an increasing elaboration of those areas concerned with sight, hearing, and touch and a corresponding decrease in the olfactory centers. Smith also brought his neuroanatomical expertise to bear on human paleontology and conducted a number of endocranial studies, including that of the celebrated Piltdown (England) skull. Although his endorsement and interpretation of the Piltdown remains identify him as an early supporter of the presapiens thesis, in later years Smith softened his antagonistic views on the evolutionary significance of the Neanderthals. Smith was also a vigorous advocate of an extreme form of diffusionism that claimed Egypt as the cradle of civilization.

See also Neanderthals; Piltdown; Presapiens. [F.S.]

Smithfield

Later Stone Age Late Holocene industry of the southern African interior, once called "Smithfield B,"named after nineteenth-century surface collections from near Smithfield, Orange Free State (South Africa). Late Pleistocene to early Holocene industries formerly termed "Smithfield A" are now included within the Oakhurst industrial complex. Former "Smithfield C" industries are now called "Interior Wilton" or "Post-Wilton". The industry is characterized by an abundance of end, side, and hollow scrapers; rarity or absence of backed microliths; and frequent association with ceramics and iron trade items. Faunal remains suggest a continuing dependence on hunting and gathering, although occasional herding of small stock may have been practiced. Its relationship to the Wilton industry remains unclear, as both are found in the interior up to historic times, although the Smithfield is much less widespread and also overlies the Wilton at several sites.

See also Hunter-Gatherers; Later Stone Age; Man-Land Relationships; Stone-Tool Making; Wilton. [A.S.B.]

Further Readings

Deacon, H.J. and Deacon, J. (1999) Human Beginnings in South Africa: Uncovering the Secrets of the Stone Age. Walnut Creek CA: AltaMira Press.

Soan

Paleolithic artifacts of uncertain age and affinity from the Indus and Soan river valleys in Pakistan and the Narmada Valley of India. Proposed in 1936 by H. de Terra and T.T. Paterson as a Middle Pleistocene tradition, the Soan Culture was distinguished from the Indian Acheulean (or Madrasian) by the absence of large bifaces and the dominance of chopper-chopping tools. Earlier Soan assemblages reportedly contained bipolar flakes and massive choppers, mostly unifacially flaked. The late Soan industry included choppers, scrapers, and flakes struck from prepared cores; indeed, some earlier workers argued that the morphology of later Soan artifacts converged on those produced by Levallois technology. Localities with artifacts in clear stratigraphic association are rare, so that the age, actual affinities, and typological range of this supposedly distinct archaeological entity remain highly uncertain. Soan assemblages, however, do seem to be distinct from Acheulean-like industries also present in India. The actual temporal range of these artifacts can only be estimated as broadly representative of the Middle Pleistocene. Soan-related artifacts reported from Pliocene contexts in Pakistan (ca. 2 Ma) are not universally accepted. Furthermore, some of the artifacts attributed to the Soan are undoubtedly the result of natural geological agencies.

See also Acheulean; Asia, Eastern and Southern; Chopper-Chopping Tools; Levallois. [G.G.P., J.W.O.]

Further Readings

Misra, V.N. (1987) Middle Pleistocene adaptations in India. In O. Soffer (ed.): The Pleistocene Old World: Regional Perspectives. New York: Plenum, pp. 99–119.

Dennell, R.W., Rendell, H., and Hailwood, E. (1988a) Early toolmaking in Asia: Two-million-year-old artifacts in Pakistan. Antiquity 62:98–106.

Dennell, R.W., Rendell, H., and Hailwood, E. (1988b) Late Pliocene artefacts from northern Pakistan. Curr. Anthropol. 29:495–498.

Sociobiology

Although the term *sociobiology* had been used before, it became widespread only after 1975, when E.O. Wilson's *Sociobiology: The New Synthesis* was published. Wilson's book, in which he defined sociobiology as "the systematic study of all social behavior," has stimulated intense debate and a great deal of research.

An outgrowth of ethology, sociobiology has been heavily influenced by population genetics and evolutionary ecology. It has yet to become the preferred term to describe all studies of social behavior. Rather, it is most frequently used to describe studies on the genetics and evolution of social behavior and societies. A society, according to Wilson, is "a group of individuals belonging to the same species and organized in a cooperative manner." Although Wilson introduced this definition in his 1971 book *The Insect Societies,* the definition applies equally well to other organisms, including primates, where the most common unit of society is generally referred to as a social *group,* or *troop.*

A key concept in sociobiology is that social behavior does have a significant genetic component and that the societies resulting from social behaviors are, therefore, able to evolve under selection. As Wilson has argued, a simple behavioral difference between two animals, which may have a genetic basis, can result in a significant difference in their patterns of interaction with other individuals. An example would be variation in tolerance of the close proximity of other particular classes of individual, such as adult males. Multiplied through a series of the interindividual interactions that build social relationships, such small differences can create very different social structures. If the original difference has some genetic basis and leads to a difference in individual reproductive success, then societal structure becomes subject to natural selection.

In addition to the concept that societies and their structure are adaptive in an evolutionary sense, another important tenet of sociobiology is that kin selection will operate to reinforce sociality. The theory underlying kin selection (a theory first clearly expounded by the population geneticist W.D. Hamilton) is that the apparently self-sacrificing altruistic acts that are often observed in social animals may not be self-serving in an evolutionary sense. If these acts are directed toward close kin sharing many genes with the altruist, they will tend to increase the representation of the altruist's genes in the next generation (and, therefore, its "inclusive fitness"). Efforts to promote the survival of one's own offspring are an obvious example of such kin selection, but the same principle can apply to brothers, sisters, and other relatives. Although the significance of such selection in the evolution of insect societies (in many of which all females inherit identical sets of genes from their fathers) is well established, its significance in vertebrate societies is less clear. It has yet to be adequately demonstrated, for instance, that kin selection (other than assistance to immediate offspring) has played a major role in the evolution of most primate societies.

An extension of kin-selection theory is group selection, a theory associated particularly with the writings of V.C. Wynne-Edwards. This theory (more properly called *intergroup selection*) holds that many apparently altruistic behaviors in social animals have evolved because they have tended to increase the long-term reproductive success of one distinct group in relation to another. This requires that social groups be both relatively isolated from one another genetically and potentially subject to extinction. It has been pointed out that extensive between-group migration, such as occurs in many primate societies, would tend to nullify the effects of such selection, especially in the presence of individuals with any genetically based tendencies to antisocial "selfish" acts. While much social behavior seems readily explicable in an evolutionary sense in terms of the reproductive advantages it brings to individuals, intergroup selection cannot yet be totally dismissed as a potentially significant factor in social evolution.

From an early stage, Wilson included human societies within the purview of sociobiology. This has brought sociobiologists into conflict with social scientists studying *Homo sapiens;* social scientists do not traditionally view human society from a Darwinian perspective, but rather emphasize the roles of learning and culture as determinants of human behavior. While the large brain of modern humans provides tremendous learning abilities (making *nurture* a particularly significant determining factor in human behavior), there is considerable evidence that this learning is built upon a genetic substrate (our *nature*) similar to that found in many other primate and nonprimate animals. For instance, large-scale studies of monozygotic and dizygotic human twins, separated early in life and reared apart, show strong heritability for many psychological (i.e., behavioral) traits.

See also Anthropology; Evolution; Genetics; Primate Societies. [J.F.O.]

Further Readings

Barash, D.P. (1982) Sociobiology and Behavior, 2nd ed. New York: Elsevier.

Betzig, L., Borgerhoff Mulder, M., and Turke, P. (1988) Human Reproductive Behaviour: A Darwinian Perspective. Cambridge: Cambridge University Press.

Bouchard, T.J., Jr., Lykken, D.T., McGue, M., Segal, N.L., and Tellegen, A. (1990) Sources of human psychological differences: The Minnesota study of twins reared apart. Science 250:223–228.

Gray, J.P. (1985) Primate Sociobiology. New Haven: HRAF.

Wilson, E.O. (1971) The Insect Societies. Cambridge, Mass.: Harvard University Press.

Wilson, E.O. (1975) Sociobiology: The New Synthesis. Cambridge, Mass.: Harvard University Press.

Wilson, E.O. (1978) On Human Nature. Cambridge, Mass.: Harvard University Press.

Soleilhac

Possible early open-air site in the commune of Blanzac, Haute Loire (central France), located on what was a small island in a shallow lake. Soleilhac is dated to ca. 1.0 Ma on the basis of its normal magnetic polarity (between reversed levels) and biostratigraphy. The faunal remains, which also suggest a late Early Pleistocene age (1.0–0.8 Ma), include several species of deer (cervids), which may have been butchered by hominins, and an elephant, which probably was not. A lithic assemblage of 400 choppers, flakes, fragments, and a protobiface occur in association with an elongated concentration of basalt blocs and animal bones. This concentration measures 25 × 2–4 m and is said by the experts to possibly represent the footings for a wind-break or hut.

See also Early Paleolithic; Europe. [A.S.B., J.J.S.]

Solutré

Open-air archaeological site in the Ardèche region of eastern France, dated to the Late Pleistocene by faunal and archaeological correlation, and by radiocarbon ages of greater than 30.4 to ca. 17 Ka. It was chosen in 1869 as the type site of the Solutrean industry. Located at the base of a cliff and reexcavated during the 1960s by J. Combier, Solutré contains archaeological industries identified as Mousterian, Lower Perigordian (Châtelperronian), Aurignacian, Upper Perigordian (Gravettian), Solutrean, and Magdalenian. Although considerably affected by cryoturbation and slumping, the

Upper Paleolithic levels also contain faunal remains of horse, reindeer, and bovids, whose spatial associations (e.g., partial articulation and sorting of skeletal parts) suggest repeated use as an ambush site or butchering station.

See also Archaeological Sites; Aurignacian; Economy, Prehistoric; Laugerie Sites; Man-Land Relationships; Magdalenian; Mousterian; Perigordian; Site Types; Solutrean; Upper Paleolithic. [A.S.B.]

Solutrean

Later Upper Paleolithic industrial complex of France and Spain, ca. 21–18 Ka (17 Ka in Cantabrian Spain), named after the open-air site of Solutré (Saône-et-Loire) in eastern France. The Solutrean is characterized by several forms of thin, leaf-shaped points, shaped by distinctive flat, highly invasive unifacial and bifacial retouch. Superficial resemblances between these points and leaf-shaped Mousterian points, the abundance of flakes, and the relative paucity of Solutrean bone working led to a placement of the Solutrean stage *between* the Mousterian and the Aurignacian by G. de Mortillet in 1881. In 1912, H. Breuil published a correct sequence for the French Upper Paleolithic, with a three-stage Solutrean phase (Lower, Middle, and Upper; or I, II, and III)

between the Aurignacian and the Magdalenian. A fourth stage, Protosolutrean, was added subsequently to distinguish the basal Solutrean at Laugerie Haute, with its generalized use of flat retouch without specialized point types, from the later stages.

Breuil's three stages were themselves distinguished by different forms of pressure-flaked stone points based on the Laugerie Haute sequence: from the unifacial point (Solutrean I, or Lower), to the classic laurel-leaf point (Solutrean II, or Middle), to the narrower willow-leaf and shouldered points (Solutrean III, or Upper), sometimes used to divide the Solutrean III into two successive stages, Upper and Final, respectively. Antler hafts or sleeves are also present at some sites, suggesting improvements in hunting technology. Although worked bone is rarer in the Solutrean than in the preceding early Upper Paleolithic industries, eyed needles are characteristic of the final stages.

In Spain, where the point types corresponding to Protosolutrean and Solutrean I are absent, the *earliest* Solutrean industries at 21.7–19 Ka are characterized by bifacially worked leaf-shaped points, while the final stages exhibit shouldered points, hollow-base laurel-leaf points, and bifacial barbed and tanged arrowheads. Important sites include Parpalló in Valencia and La Riera in Cantabria. Backed bladelets and burins are

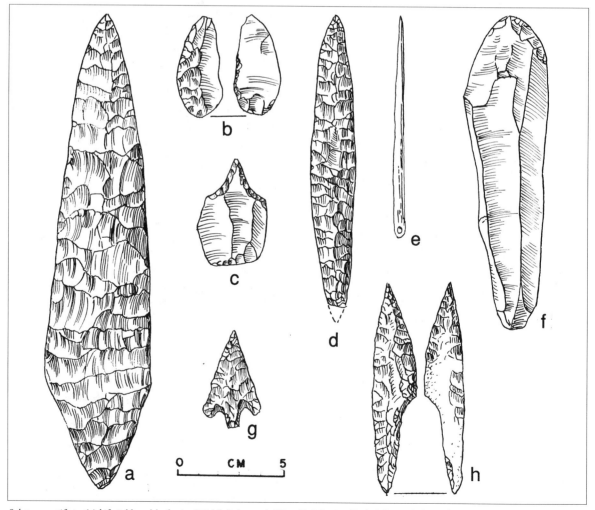

Solutrean artifacts: (a) bifacial laurel-leaf point (Middle Solutrean); (b) unifacial point (Early Solutrean); (c) perforator; (d) willow-leaf point (Later Solutrean); (e) eyed bone needle; (f) end-scraper; (g) tanged and notched point (Spanish Solutrean); (h) shouldered point (Final Solutrean).

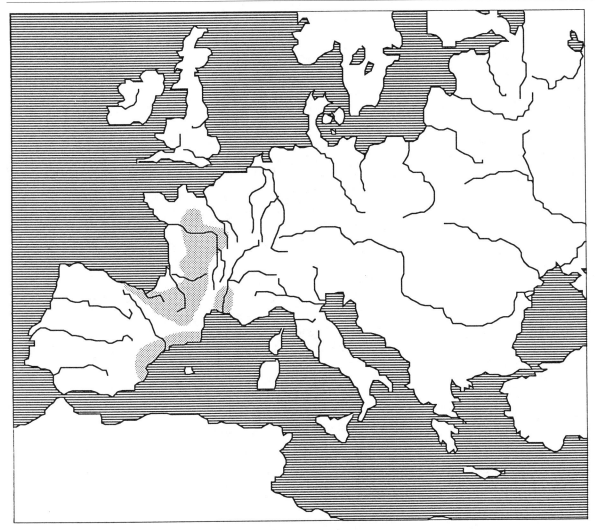

Distribution map of Solutrean sites.

also more common in the later Spanish industries than in southwestern France during the Final Solutrean. Another variant of the Solutrean, with shouldered points throughout together with laurel-leaf points in the Middle Solutrean, is recognized in Languedoc (Grotte de la Salpetriere, Gard). The Solutrean is absent in northern France and in Provence.

The Solutrean is the dominant industrial type of western Europe during the last glacial maximum (ca. 18 Ka), when northwestern and central Europe were apparently abandoned. The density of sites and the increasing elaboration of engraved, sculpted, and painted blocks and cave and rockshelter walls, as well as the possibly ceremonial nature of the largest and thinnest stone points, may reflect social intensification due either to crowding or to more scheduling of resource use within defined territories. The faunal remains from French sites are dominated by reindeer, with some later assemblages reflecting local increases in exploitation of ibex and horse. In Spanish Solutrean sites, ibex, red deer, and horse are the most common mammalian species, and resource intensification is reflected in large numbers of mollusc shells. Human remains from several sites are morphologically similar to those from Combe Capelle. Solutrean images are distinctive in the widespread use of large bas-reliefs of animals (Roc-de-Sers, Char-

ente, and Fourneau-du-Diable, Dordogne) and of painted and engraved plaques (Laugerie Haute, Parpalló).

See also Aurignacian; Bow and Arrow; Breuil, [Abbé] Henri [Edward Prosper]; Economy, Prehistoric; Homo sapiens; Hunter-Gatherers; Jewelry; Late Paleolithic; Laugerie Sites; Magdalenian; Mortillet, Gabriel de; Mousterian; Paleolithic Image; Paleolithic Lifeways; Parapalló; Perigordian; Protomagdalenian; Protosolutrean; Solutré; Stone-Tool Making; Upper Paleolithic. [A.S.B]

Further Readings

Gamble, C. (1986) The Palaeolithic Settlement of Europe. Cambridge: Cambridge University Press.

Smith, P.E.L. (1964) The Solutrean culture. Sci. Am. 211(2):86–94.

Wymer, J. (1982) The Palaeolithic Age. New York: St. Martin's.

Songhor

Paleontological site in western Kenya, in stratified sequence of Early Miocene age, ca. 20 Ma by potassium-argon (K/Ar) dating of interbedded biotite tuffs. First collected by L.S.B.

Leakey in 1952, Songhor is a small exposure, ca. 200 m wide and 15 m thick, of extremely fossiliferous red and brown clayey silts interlayered with, and overlying, micaceous alnoitic tuffs that abut the granite of Songhor Hill. Songhor Beds have been traced eastward into the Upper Mtetei Valley, where they correlate to the Chamtwara Beds, equivalent to the upper part of the Koru sequence in the basal strata of the nearby Tinderet volcanic complex. Songhor is notable for its diversity of fossil primates, including strepsirhines. Among catarrhines, it is the type locality for *Proconsul major, Rangwapithecus gordoni, Limnopithecus evansi,* and *Kalepithecus songhorensis.* Other species include *Proconsul africanus, Nyanzapithecus vancouveringorum, Micropithecus clarki,* and *Dendropithecus macinnesi.*

See also Africa, East; "Dendropithecus-Group"; Koru; Leakey, Louis Seymour Bazett; Napak; Proconsulidae; Rusinga. [J.A.V.C.]

Further Readings

Andrews, P.J. (1978) A revision of the Miocene hominoidea of East Africa. Br. Mus. (Nat. Hist.) Bull. Geol. ser. 30:85–224.

Harrison, T. (1981) New finds of small fossil apes from the Miocene locality at Koru in Kenya. J. Hum. Evol. 10:129–137.

Harrison, T. (1988) A taxonomic revision of the small catarrhine primates from the Early Miocene of East Africa. Folia Primatol. 50:59–108.

Pickford, M.H., and Andrews, P.J. (1981) The Tinderet Miocene sequence in Kenya. J. Hum. Evol. 10:13–33.

Spear

The earliest hunting or defensive weapons probably consisted of hand-held clubs or simple thrown missiles. The invention of a throwing or thrusting spear would have been a major innovation during the course of human evolution, emphasizing penetration and bloodletting rather than merely trauma from a blunt object.

Since the first spears were probably made from wood or horn, it is rare that very early forms of such artifacts would be preserved in the prehistoric record except under unusual conditions. The earliest examples of spears had been thought to come from the Middle Pleistocene site (ca. 300 Ka) of Clacton-on-Sea (England), which produced just the tip of a yew spear; and the early Late Pleistocene site (ca. 120 Ka) of Lehringen (Germany), which yielded a charred, scraped wooden point associated with an elephant carcass. Some of the pointed bone and antler pieces at the ca. 200 Myr old site of Bilzingsleben (Germany) may also be spear tips. In 1997, H. Thieme reported the find of three well-preserved wooden spears from Schöningen (eastern Germany), in interglacial deposits estimated to date to ca. 400 Ka. The spears average 2 m in length, with the thickest part of the shaft near the sharpened point, as in modern javelins. In addition to these apparently throwable spears, a stabbing spear may also be present at the site.

During the Middle Paleolithic over much of the Old World, a range of unifacially and sometimes bifacially flaked

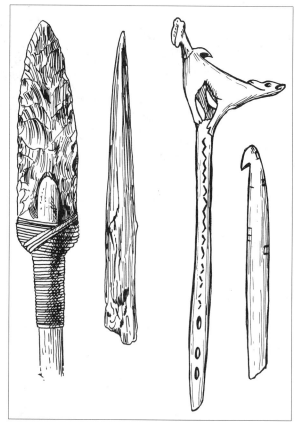

Left to right: reconstruction of possible hafting of Paleoindian Clovis point as a spear (point ca. 10 cm long); broken tip of late Early Paleolithic fire-hardened wooden spear from Clacton (England) (ca. 40 cm); two bone spear throwers, one engraved, from French Upper Paleolithic sites (shorter one ca. 18 cm long).

pointed stone-artifact forms occur that are usually assumed to be projectile points for spears, as are some specialized prepared-flake types (i.e., Levallois points). Such points are presumed to have been mounted on long, probably wooden, shafts. The base of such points may show modification to produce a morphology that would facilitate hafting (e.g., thinning, making a tang, or notching, and, in rare instances, possible evidence of mastic or natural adhesive). In North Africa, Aterian Middle Stone Age assemblages include tanged pointed forms that strongly suggest hafting to a shaft. In Europe, the first bone artifacts that appear to be probable spear points are found at the Middle Paleolithic site of Salzgitter-Lebenstedt (Germany). In Africa, the barbed bone points found in Middle Stone Age context at Katanda (Zaire) would also represent a form of hafted spear tip. Such hafted stone or bone projectiles could have involved the use of sinew, vegetable fiber, gum or resin mastic, or bitumen to help secure the point to a shaft. A Neanderthal male from the cave of Shanidar (Iraq) had a slightly healed cut on a rib that has been interpreted as a possible spear wound.

The Late Paleolithic industries of the Old World, as well as Paleoindian sites of the Americas, have a range of artifact forms that have been interpreted as spear points, including such lithic examples as Châtelperron points, Gravette points, Solutrean laurel- and willow-leaf points, and New World Clovis points. Bone points are common from the Au rignacian onward, and the Magdalenian harpoons were almost certainly part of a composite spear. Barbed antler artifacts interpreted as spear throwers (the Aztec word *atlatl* is sometimes used) are known from the Magdalenian; these tools can increase the velocity of a propelled spear, in turn increasing maximum distance of a throw as well as deeper penetration into an animal. Such artifact types as the Solutrean *pointe à cran* and the Paleoindian Folsom and Cumberland points may have been atlatl dart points.

Spear technology appears to be represented in Upper Paleolithic cave art—e.g., at Niaux, Font-de-Gaume, and most notably Lascaux (France). At each of these sites, animals (and, in a few cases, humans) appear to be shown with spears embedded in the bodies; at Lascaux, in the same scene as a wounded bison is an object that some prehistorians have interpreted as a bird-effigy spear thrower.

With the advent of archery during the last 10 Kyr, the spear became a secondary hunting weapon in many places, although it is still important in many modern hunter-gatherer technologies, including those of Australian and Tasmanian Aborigines, Pacific Islanders, Arctic Eskimos, the !Kung San, and Native Americans. The use of the spear or lance in military combat became obsolete only at the turn of the twentieth century.

See also Clactonian; Middle Paleolithic; Paleoindian; Paleolithic Image; Paleolithic Lifeways; Stone-Tool Making; Upper Paleolithic. [N.T., K.S.]

Further Readings

Thieme, H. (1997) Lower Paleolithic hunting spears from Germany. Nature 385:808–810.

Speciation

Formation of descendant from ancestral species. The process of species formation depends upon conceptions of what species are. Thus, if species are arbitrarily delineated segments of an evolving lineage of interbreeding organisms, new species are seen to arise by a process of phyletic evolution of the phenotypic properties of organisms within the lineage. Such phyletic transformation would include primarily the transformation of adaptations through natural selection and the random changes engendered by genetic drift.

However, if the conception of species followed is some version of the *biological species concept,* the process of speciation is seen to involve primarily the origin of a descendant reproductive community from an ancestral species. Anatomical differences between ancestor and descendant species, involving aspects of organismic phenotypes not involved directly in reproduction, are seen as ancillary and consequential rather than as direct causes of speciation. The prime question is always: How did a single reproductive community become divided into two (or more) reproductive communities?

Isolating Mechanisms

The geneticist T. Dobzhansky in 1937 coined the term *isolating mechanisms* for those causative agents that might play a role in either initiating or maintaining genetic isolation between two reproductive communities. Dobzhansky believed that natural selection was involved in the development of reproductive isolation, as the formation of hybrids between two incompletely separated protospecies would diminish the capacity of either species to adapt closely to the exigencies of their niches (or *adaptive peaks*). By the 1950s, Dobzhansky's classification of isolating mechanisms had taken on the form still accepted today. Dobzhansky saw a fundamental dichotomy in isolating mechanisms. Organisms that are prevented from interbreeding by *geographic isolation*—i.e., organisms living in separate places (*allopatry*)—never meet and thus cannot mate. He reserved the term *reproductive isolation* for instances in which organisms live in the same area *(sympatry)* but cannot or do not interbreed for a host of biological reasons, including lack of mutual attraction, mechanical inability, ecological isolation, and various degrees of incompatibility, in which hybrids are not viable. The last case is the strongest: Reproductive isolation is held to be complete when, if organisms attempt to mate, they cannot produce viable or fertile offspring. Dobzhansky referred to these factors as *mechanisms* because of his conviction that reproductive isolation is adaptively advantageous to species. The preferred view now is that geographic and biologic factors impeding reproduction among closely related organisms are a consequence of the ecological, distributional, and evolutionary histories of their species and populations. The question, though, remains: How is reproductive isolation typically developed?

In the 1930s and 1940s, Dobzhansky, and especially the biologist E. Mayr, favored the view that remains paramount in theories of speciation today: In most instances, reproductive isolation begins in geographic isolation. New species arise from old only when the ancestral species becomes fragmented, with gaps in spatial distribution preventing the free exchange of genes between populations that once experienced some gene flow. This is the essence of geographic, or allopatric, speciation.

Once geographic barriers have isolated portions of a species from one another, if sufficient evolutionary modification occurs in one or more populations such that reproduction is hindered or impossible should the populations once again come in contact, *speciation* is said to have occurred. Note that, while many species are fragmented into fairly isolated populations, speciation is by no means an inevitable consequence. The usual fate is local extinction of isolated populations or their merger back with other populations of the species, long before speciation can occur. Moreover, isolation of a population in itself does not guarantee the sort of evolutionary diversification required to lead to reproductive isolation when, and if, sympatry is reestablished.

There are several varieties, or modes, of allopatric speciation. Perhaps the simplest case involves climatic or other physical-environmental change, disrupting a formerly continuous distribution. When the Isthmus of Panama emerged ca. 3 Ma, communication between elements of the marine fauna of the Caribbean and the Pacific was cut off. Another situation involves relatively small populations near the periphery of a species' range; already adapted to the environmental extremes tolerated by members of a species, the organisms of the small, isolated populations may undergo fairly rapid adaptive change. Speciation in such circumstances may take place as rapidly as a few hundred, or thousand, years. The *founder principle* is an extreme situation of allopatric speciation, in which a single breeding pair, or a gravid female, successfully colonizes an outlying region, founds a new population, and perhaps leads to the evolution of a new species.

Sympatric speciation, in which reproductive isolation is developed without a period of geographic isolation, has been repeatedly invoked, especially for instances of parasites adapted to particular host species. Most such examples are readily interpreted as microallopatric—i.e., there is, indeed, physical separation between diverging populations. Nonetheless, theoretical models continue to emerge that suggest that speciation may be sympatric in some taxa.

Rates of Speciation

Rates of speciation tend to vary systematically between lineages—i.e., some lineages display greater characteristic rates of appearance of new species than others, often including their closest relatives. Moreover, rate of speciation tends to be positively correlated with rate of extinction. It has been suggested that ecological parameters may govern both speciation and extinction. In particular, ecological generalists (*eurytopes,* referring to organisms' abilities to tolerate a spectrum of environmental conditions or to draw upon a range of resources) appear more resistant to extinction, but less likely to give rise to new species, than ecological specialists (*stenotopes,* more narrowly adapted organisms).

See also Dobzhansky, Theodosius; Evolution; Mayr, Ernst; Species. [N.E.]

Further Readings

Bush, G.L. (1975) Modes of animal speciation. Ann. Rev. Ecol. Syst. 6:339–364.

Eldredge, N. (1985) Time Frames. New York: Simon and Schuster.

Mayr, E. (1963) Animal Species and Evolution. Cambridge, Mass.: Harvard University Press.

Species

Latin word meaning "kind," denoting its original sense in biological usage: Species are different kinds of organisms. Early attempts to classify organisms, first formalized by Linnaeus into the system still in use today, recognized species as the lowest-ranked category of a series of hierarchically arrayed collections of organisms. Each species is included in a genus, in turn included in a family, and so on. Human beings are members of the genus *Homo,* species *sapiens.* The latinized name for any species is always accompanied by its generic designation; thus, our species name is *Homo sapiens.* Species names are always italicized.

The notion of different kinds of organisms has long been associated with the recognition that "like begets like"—i.e. that species are associations of organisms that choose reproductive mates among themselves and do not, or cannot, mate successfully with organisms from other associations.

Thus, two ideas are bound up in most considerations of the nature of species: the notion of species as reproductive communities and the idea that organisms within a species resemble each other (as a rule) more closely than they resemble organisms within other species. Some concepts of species emphasize anatomical similarity as the major attribute of species, while others, including the *biological species concept* (currently the dominant view in biology), see species primarily as communities of reproductively interacting organisms.

Biologists have long debated the "reality" of species—i.e., are species actual entities or are they simply arbitrarily designated clusters of similar organisms? Pre-Darwinian thought saw species as immutable, fixed entities, as collections of organisms that had been "breeding true" since their initial creation some thousands of years before. William Whewell summarized this attitude succinctly as late as 1837, when he wrote: "Species have a real existence in nature, and a transition from one to another does not exist."

It is clear that C. Darwin and many biologists subsequent to the publication of his *On the Origin of Species* in 1859 saw the notion of evolution as antithetical to the concept of species as articulated by Whewell. Species fixity was discarded and, along with it, the pre-Darwinian conviction that species are "real" entities in nature. However real and discrete species may seem at any moment, most evolutionary biologists since Darwin have seen species as evolving lineages of sexually reproducing organisms; through time, the properties of the organisms are modified by evolution, and species are thought thereby to evolve by imperceptibly gradual degrees into descendants by direct transformation.

A number of biologists have remarked that Darwin did not discuss the origin of species in his epochal book of the same title. (Having effectively discarded the concept of species, Darwin was concerned instead to establish the notion that life has had a complex history and that such history could be understood through a theory of the origin, maintenance, and modification of adaptations through natural selection.) With the advent in the 1930s of the Modern Synthesis (by which the maturing science of genetics was integrated with Darwinian principles), evolutionists began to confront species as "real" entities. T. Dobzhansky and, subsequently, E. Mayr developed the *biological species concept,* which remains the basis of all modern evolutionary definitions. Mayr's short version of the definition is: "Species are groups of actually or potentially interbreeding natural populations, which are reproductively isolated from other such groups." A more recent definition accepts the core of the *biological species concept,* while generalizing it and stressing that new species arise from old and also referring to the close similarities usually found among organisms within species: "A species is a diagnosable cluster of organisms within which there is a parental pattern of ancestry and descent, beyond which there is not, and which exhibits a pattern of phylogenetic ancestry and descent among units of like kind" (based on Eldredge and Cracraft, 1980). Other species definitions are also current, if disputed; among these are Paterson's *recognition concept* of species as "that most inclusive population of individual biparental organisms which share a common fertilization system," and J. Cracraft's *phylogenetic species concept*, which takes a morphological perspective and regards species as minimum diagnosable units.

In 1942, Mayr wrote that, to justify a theory of the origin of species—i.e., any of the available models of speciation—one must suppose that species actually exist. Yet, the *biological species concept* is widely acknowledged, even by its proponents, to pertain to but a single instant in time; through time, the old Darwinian view is maintained, and species are considered to become transformed gradually into descendant species. More recently, work in paleontology, notably the theory of *punctuated equilibria*, coinciding with analyses by Ghiselin and Hull, has supported the notion that species are, indeed, "real" entities in the fullest sense. Species are lineages of reproducing organisms that may—or, as is perhaps more common, may not—become substantially modified through time; they have births (speciation), histories, and deaths (extinction). And, from time to time, they may give rise to offspring (descendant species). The implications of this view for evolutionary theory are great. If species are real entities in this sense, the history of life cannot be reduced simply to a Darwinian story of origin and modifications of organic adaptations. And we must consider the differential survival and reproductive success of species as well as organisms when we consider the dynamics of the evolutionary process.

Many specialized concepts of species continue to appear in the literature. For example, *chronospecies* are arbitrarily delineated segments of evolving lineages, while *morphospecies* are recognized solely by the perceived similarity among organisms. Most of these extraneous concepts, which are not in wide use, are ably summarized by A.J. Cain (1960). Arguments persist about whether asexual organisms form true species; the definition of Eldredge and Cracraft was intended to encompass asexual organisms, but it appears that the *biological species concept* is best suited to sexually reproducing organisms.

See also Classification; Darwin, Charles Robert; Dobzhansky, Theodosius; Evolution; Mayr, Ernst; Phylogeny; Speciation; Subspecies; Systematics; Taxonomy. [N.E.]

Further Readings

Cain, A.J. (1960) Animal Species and Their Evolution. New York: Harper.

Eldredge, N. (1985) Unfinished Synthesis. New York: Oxford University Press.

Eldredge, N., and Cracraft, J. (1980) Phylogenetic Patterns and the Evolutionary Process. New York: Columbia University Press.

Kimbel, W.H., and Martin, L.B. (1993) Species, Species Concepts, and Primate Evolution. New York: Plenum.

Mayr, E. (1942) Systematics and the Origin of Species. New York: Columbia University Press.

Mayr, E. (1963) Animal Species and Evolution. Cambridge, Mass.: Harvard University Press.

Speech (Origins of)

One of the most distinctive features of humankind is our unparalleled capability for communication. This is due, in large part, to our ability for speech. While many definitions of speech have been offered by those in diverse fields, here the term will refer to that unique form of rapid, verbal-vocal communication universally used by living humans.

Many components of human anatomy and physiology must interact to produce speech, but two basic human systems must be present: (1) a brain and associated nervous system sufficiently sophisticated to absorb, integrate, and direct the transmission of information; and (2) a peripheral anatomical system, what we generally term the *vocal tract,* which is capable of producing rapid, articulated sounds. The task in the study of human evolution is to determine when in our history a sufficiently developed brain and vocal tract first appeared that were capable of producing human speech.

Speech and the Brain

A traditional means of exploring when speech may have evolved uses endocasts—artificial or natural casts formed over time within braincases—as a vehicle to examine brain evolution and thus to gain insight into the development of speech. Workers who have used this approach, often referred to as *paleoneurology,* have been particularly interested in charting the development of specific areas of the brain that often relate to speech production or general language capabilities. Of special concern has been the region of the inferior frontal gyrus of the dominant cerebral hemisphere known as Broca's motor speech area. This region was first suggested as being intimately related to speech production in 1861, by the French anatomist and anthropologist P. Broca. He came to this conclusion after noting a significant loss of tissue in the area of the frontal lobe upon the autopsy of an individual who lacked the ability to utter more than a few meaningless sounds. Paleoanthropologists who followed Broca have often spent considerable time trying to assess the appearance of Broca's area in fossil endocasts and thus gain some insight into the speech abilities of these early hominids. For example, the presence of endocast markings that may represent this region have been cited by some to suggest the possibility of nascent speech abilities in early members of *Homo,* such as the East African hominid KNM-ER 1470, dated at more than 1.8 Ma.

While data from paleoneurology have provided valuable information, there have been limitations to their use in charting the evolution of speech. For example, precisely locating speech centers in the brain appears to be more complicated than originally thought by Broca. Further, considerable debate exists among endocast experts themselves as to what markings are present and what they may mean. Finally, paleoneurology cannot tell us much about the inner workings of the brain and, as a result, can provide only limited evidence as to the origins of hominid speech.

Evolution of the Vocal Tract

Another approach has emerged within the last few decades to address the question of when speech evolved. Rather than focus on the brain, this approach has concentrated upon reconstructing the anatomy of our ancestors' vocal tracts: the larynx (voice-box), pharynx, tongue, and associated struc-

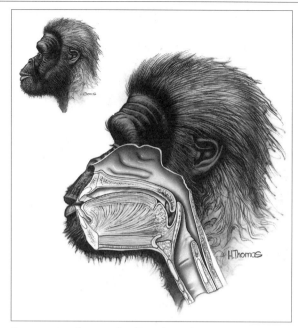

Reconstruction of an australopith's vocal tract during normal breathing through the nose (based on the Sts 5 cranium of Australopithecus africanus*). The larynx, or voice box, is positioned high in the throat, as in most mammals and in contrast to the considerably lower position found in adult humans. Due to this high position, during vocalization this australopith would have only a limited region above the larynx available to modify sounds generated at the vocal folds ("cords") as compared to ourselves. Courtesy of Jeffrey T. Laitman.*

tures. The ability to do this has been based upon data from both comparative anatomy and the fossil record. For example, studies on living mammals have shown that the position of the larynx in the neck is of prime importance in determining the way an animal can vocalize, as well as how it breathes and swallows. In almost all mammals, the larynx is positioned very high in the neck. This high position severely limits the space (part of the pharynx) above the larynx responsible for the major modification of sounds produced inside the larynx at the vocal folds (vocal cords). As a result, the vocal repertoire of most mammals is very limited. Interestingly, human newborns and infants, until approximately one and a half to two years of age, also have a larynx positioned high in the neck. Baby humans accordingly show a limited repertoire in the variety of sounds they produce.

After the first years of life, however, humans undergo a dramatic change in the anatomy of their vocal tract, with the larynx descending to a much lower position in the neck than that found in any other mammal. This lowered position significantly enlarges the portion of the pharynx above the larynx responsible for modifying sounds. In essence, the low position of the larynx provides us with the anatomy necessary to make the varied sounds of human speech. How to reconstruct the soft-tissue structures of our ancestors' vocal tract has, until recently, been a problem for those investigating the evolution of speech. Such structures as the larynx, comprising cartilages and membranes, are not preserved in the fossil record. Fortunately, one portion of the vocal-tract region that is preserved is its *roof,* as represented by the bottom of the skull, or *basicranium.* Studies of this region in living mammals have shown that the shape of the basicranium is related to the po-

sition of the larynx in the neck. Knowledge of basicranial anatomy can thus tell us quite a bit about the location, and thus the function, of an animal's vocal tract.

Discerning the relationships between the basicranium and vocal-tract structures in living mammals has enabled researchers to analyze the shape of fossil hominid basicrania and reconstruct the position of the larynx and related structures. Studies have shown, for example, that the australopiths exhibit basicrania similar in many important aspects to those of the living apes. In view of these basicranial similarities, it is likely that the vocal tracts of the australopiths were also similar to those of the extant apes, with a larynx positioned high in the neck. This suggests that the australopiths were restricted in the types of sounds they could make, probably being incapable of producing a number of the universal vowel sounds found in human speech patterns. While it is still not fully clear when change toward the human condition began, preliminary studies have shown that the basicrania and, by extension, the vocal tracts of some members of *Homo erectus* were already moving in the human direction. It was, however, not until the arrival of early *Homo sapiens,* ca. 400–300 Ka, that we find skulls with basicrania that indicate the presence of a vocal tract similar to our own. It was among these hominids that largely modern vocal tracts appeared, and our ancestors began to produce fully articulate speech.

One group of hominids who appeared after 300 Ka, however, may have had a vocal tract that differed from those of living people. These were the Neanderthals. Based upon evidence from the basicranium, nasal cavity, and paranasal sinuses, it appears that Neanderthals, particularly the late surviving western European group known as the Classic Neanderthals, may have had subtle, yet important, differences in their vocal-tract configuration and function when compared with that of people today. For example, their larynx was likely positioned slightly higher in the neck, thus anatomically restricting the area available to modify laryngeal sounds as compared to ourselves. While Neanderthals may thus have had some limitations on their vocal capabilities, their brain size and morphology suggest that they had the neural components for a highly complex form of language. As with many aspects of reconstructed Neanderthal behavior, the anatomy and function of their vocal apparatus and speech remain the subjects of differing opinions and ongoing debate.

See also Australopithecus; Brain; Broca, Pierre Paul; Homo erectus; Homo habilis; Homo sapiens; Neanderthals. [J.T.L.]

Further Readings

Budil, I. (1994) Functional reconstruction of the supralaryngeal vocal tract of fossil humans. J. Hum. Evol. 9(1):35–52.

De Grolier, E., ed. (1983) Glossogenetics: The Origin and Evolution of Language. Paris: Harwood Academic.

Laitman, J.T. (1984) The anatomy of human speech. Nat. Hist. 93:20–27.

Laitman, J.T., Reidenberg, J.S., and Gannon, P.J. (1992) Fossil skulls and hominid vocal tracts: New approaches to charting the evolution of human speech. In J. Wind

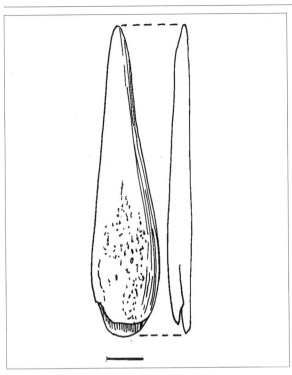

Split-base bone point. Scale is 1 cm.

et al. (eds.): Language Origins: A Multidisciplinary Approach. Dordrecht: Kluwer, pp. 385–397.

Lieberman, D.E. and McCarthy, R.C. (1999) The ontogeny of cranial base angulation in humans and chimpanzees and its implications for reconstructing pharyngeal dimensions. J. Hum. Evol. 36: 487-517.

Lieberman, P., Laitman, J.T., Reidenberg, J.S., and Gannon, P.J. (1992) The anatomy, physiology, acoustics and perception of speech: Essential elements in analysis of the evolution of human speech. J. Hum. Evol. 23:447–467.

Milo, R.G., and Quiatt, D. (1993) Glottogenesis and anatomically modern *Homo sapiens*: The evidence for and implications of a late origin of vocal language. Curr. Anthropol. 34:569–598.

Split-Base Bone Point

Diagnostic artifact form of the Early Aurignacian period of the Upper Paleolithic of Europe and western Asia, ca. 40–32

Ka. These points, actually made of split antler, indicate a gradual shift away from stone for spear projectile points. They are a precursor of the rich bone and antler technologies of later Upper Paleolithic times.

See also Aurignacian; Paleolithic; Spear; Upper Paleolithic. [N.T., K.S.]

Spy

Cave in Belgium, important as a site that, in the nineteenth century, produced confirmatory evidence for the existence of Neanderthals during the European Paleolithic. Two partial Neanderthal skulls and a partial skeleton were recovered in association with artifacts and extinct fauna in 1886. The two skulls show differences that may be attributable to sexual dimorphism.

See also Europe; Neanderthals; Paleolithic; Sexual Dimorphism. [C.B.S.]

Stable Isotopes (in Biological Systems)

Isotopes of an element are atoms whose nuclei contain the same number of protons but a different number of neutrons. All elements have at least two isotopes, while one element (tin) has as many as ten. A good analogy is that isotopes are to elements as alleles are to genes: They are the allowed variants that may exist in nature.

Isotopes are either unstable—i.e., radioactive—to some degree or stable. Atoms with unequal numbers of protons and neutrons tend toward instability, and the more unequal the number, the more unstable the atoms. This is true both of isotopes of a given element and, to some degree, of elements in general: Elements with many "excess" neutrons may always be radioactive. Carbon, for example, is an element with three important isotopes, ^{14}C, ^{13}C, and ^{12}C. (Isotopes are indicated by a number prefixed to the chemical symbol that is the total of nuclear particles.) ^{14}C, with six protons and eight neutrons, is unstable; it decays, by conversion of a neutron to a proton, to ^{14}N, an atom with a more stable configuration of seven neutrons and seven protons. In ^{13}C, the disparity of six protons and seven neutrons is insufficient to make this atom decay spontaneously. Therefore, like ^{12}C (which has six protons and six neutrons), it is stable.

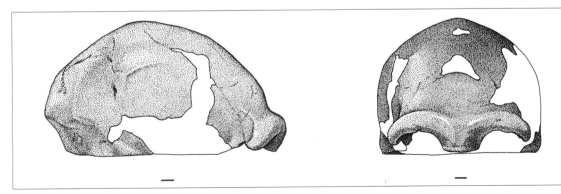

Lateral and frontal views of the Spy 1 calotte. Scales are 1 cm.

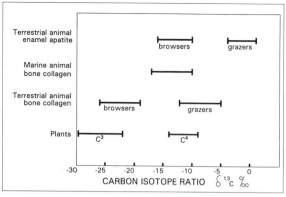

Diagram of modification of the carbon isotope ratio from plants to consumer tissues. The ^{13}C ratio is more negative (relatively less ^{13}C) in C_3 plants (trees and temperate grasses) than in those following the C_4 photosynthetic pathway (tropical grasses). The bone collagen (and to a greater degree the tooth enamel) of browsers which feed on C_3 plants is less negative than the source plants because of reduced isotopic fractionation, and the same is true for consumers of C_4 plants. Nonetheless, the difference between the two plant types is reflected in animal hard tissues and can be detected in fossils to allow inference of food types.

Measurement of stable-isotope ratios (in the example of carbon, ^{13}C to ^{12}C) in a variety of biological tissues can provide valuable biological, behavioral, and paleoenvironmental information. To understand what kind of information is available, it is useful to divide stable-isotope ratios into two general categories, light and heavy, according to their *atomic weight* (total number of protons and neutrons). The phrase *light stable isotopes* is used for isotopes of elements below atomic weight 50 (e.g., hydrogen [H], carbon [C], nitrogen [N], oxygen [O], and sulfur [S]), whereas *heavy stable isotopes* means isotopes of elements of atomic weight 50 and above (e.g., strontium [Sr] and lead [Pb]).

Stable-isotope ratios are measured in a *mass spectrometer*, operating on the principle that a beam of ions in a vacuum can be split by a magnetic field into a number of different trajectories determined by the mass and also the charge of the ions. All else being equal, heavier ions have higher momentum and are, thus, less deflected than lighter ones. Isotopes of an element will all carry the same ionic charge, allowing their slightly different mass to be accurately distinguished by magnetic deflection.

Mass-spectrometer design varies, depending upon which isotopes the instrument is designed to measure. Light-isotope mass spectrometers are designed to handle samples in the form of gases, usually $^2H/^1H$ (in H_2), $^{13}C/^{12}C$ (in CO_2), $^{18}O/^{16}O$ (in CO_2), $^{15}N/^{14}N$ (in N_2), and $^{34}S/^{32}S$ (in SO_2). Instruments for measuring heavy-element-isotope ratios are designed to handle solid samples, using thermal ionization of the sample on a filament.

Light Stable Isotopes

Owing to their mass differences, the physical behavior of isotopes of the same element differs. Although these differences are very small when compared with differences in behavior between elements, they nevertheless contribute to measurable variation in the isotopic composition of substances. For any given element, the chemical bonds involving relatively

light isotopes are weaker than those involving heavier ones. It takes slightly less energy to dissociate bonds involving light isotopes; as a result, they react more readily than heavy ones. In turn, light isotopes tend to accumulate in the reaction products of biochemical pathways; heavy isotopes tend to remain behind in unreacted molecules. The lighter isotopes of carbon, nitrogen, and oxygen are considerably more abundant than the corresponding heavier isotopes. For example, 98.9 percent of all carbon is ^{12}C, and only 1.1 percent is ^{13}C. As a result, reporting these ratios can be awkward. To make such reporting less cumbersome, geochemists express differences in light-isotope ratios in terms of parts per thousand, or *per mil* (the terminology is directly analogous to percent, which is parts per hundred). The per mil notation is expressed as ‰, to be distinguished from % (percent).

Relative measurements against a standard provide a more accurate determination of isotope ratios than absolute measurements. Therefore, the measurement of light isotopes is generally expressed as the difference from a standard, using the delta notation:

$$\delta \text{ in } ‰ = \frac{\left(R_{sample} - R_{standard}\right)}{R_{standard}} \times 1000$$

where R represents the isotope ratio (e.g., $^{13}C/^{12}C$). Examples of such notation are $\delta^{13}C$, $\delta^{15}N$, and $\delta^{18}O$.

$\delta^{13}C$

In just 15 years since the first application to the archaeological record, stable-isotopic measurements of carbon have become the best understood and widely applied chemical technique for dietary analysis of prehistoric skeletons. Since ^{12}C is a slightly lighter atom than ^{13}C, it reacts faster in most biochemical reactions, notably photosynthesis—i.e., plants use relatively more ^{12}C than ^{13}C when they fix atmospheric carbon dioxide; consequently, plants have considerably lower $\delta^{13}C$ than does atmospheric carbon dioxide. The process of alteration of the isotope ratio is called *fractionation*.

In photosynthesis, most plants fix atmospheric carbon dioxide initially into a phosphyoglycerate three-carbon molecule using the enzyme ribulose biphosphate carboxylase (the Calvin, or C_3 photosynthetic pathway). Certain plants, however, use the enzyme phosphoenol pyruvate carboxylase to fix atmospheric CO_2 into a four-carbon molecule (dicarboxylic acid) (the Hatch-Slack, or C_4 pathway). Plants that use the C_3 pathway strongly fractionate carbon isotopes, with the result that they are relatively depleted in ^{13}C; $\delta^{13}C$ for these plants range between −23 and −30 ‰. Plants using the C_4 pathway less strongly fractionate carbon isotopes; as a result, the $\delta^{13}C$ values for these plants generally range between −9 and −15 ‰.

Thus, the two groups of plants have differing $\delta^{13}C$, and the ranges do not overlap. Tropical and savannah grasses follow the C_4 pathway, while trees, most shrubs, and temperate grasses follow the C_3 pathway. A paleoenvironmental application is the measurement of $\delta^{13}C$ in pedogenic carbonate and organic matter from paleosols. For example, measurements of $\delta^{13}C$ in paleosols from the Miocene site of Fort Ternan (Kenya) have been used to show that the paleosols were likely to have been formed under wooded or forested conditions (rather than a grassland).

Because less significant fractionation occurs in animals during the incorporation of dietary carbon into tissues, the differences in the carbon-isotopes ratios of plants at the base of a food web are maintained. The most important of these tissues (from the archaeological point of view) is bone collagen, since the $\delta^{13}C$ values of the collagen reflect those of the dietary source of the carbon. For large animals, there is a further +5 ‰ fractionation between bone collagen and the dietary carbon source. Thus, diets consisting wholly of C_3 vegetation result in collagen values of ca. -26 to -19 ‰. Diets consisting wholly of C_4 vegetation result in collagen values in the region of -13 to -4 ‰. In tropical African ecosystems, it is, therefore, possible to distinguish clearly between the collagen of grazers and that of browsers.

Carbon-isotope relationships are very useful in New World archaeology because maize is a C_4 plant, while virtually all other edible New World plants are C_3. Thus, it has been possible to monitor the spread of maize agriculture in the Americas by measuring the $\delta^{13}C$ of human skeletons. Carbon isotopes also distinguish between marine and terrestrial foods in areas where the terrestrial plants are C_3 (such as Mediterranean biomes), since marine animals have relatively positive $\delta^{13}C$, in the region of -10 to -17 ‰. Because marine-animal $\delta^{13}C$ values overlap with those of C_4 plants, however, carbon isotopes cannot distinguish between marine foods and C_4 plants in human diets.

Carbon-isotope studies using collagen are limited by the longevity of the collagen itself, which rarely extends beyond the Holocene. Recent studies have shown, however, that dietary information can be recovered using the $\delta^{13}C$ of carbonate ions (CO_3), which are structurally incorporated into the inorganic phase of bones and teeth. While the carbon in collagen may be principally derived from dietary protein, that of carbonate is derived from dietary carbohydrates and lipids, via serum bicarbonate. One consequence of this is that the signal is derived from a mix of all dietary components, rather than from just protein. Another consequence is that carbonate ions in apatite are isotopically heavier than collagen carbon: The diet-apatite fractionation is as high as +12 to +13 ‰ for free-ranging herbivores, as opposed to +5 for collagen. Using $\delta^{13}C$ of enamel apatite carbonate, it has been possible to differentiate between grazing and browsing animals from the South African site of Swartkrans (ca. 2–1.5 Ma). Specimens of *Paranthropus robustus* from this site were found to have intermediate $\delta^{13}C$ (in the region of -8.0 ‰). Since virtually all edible plant foods in the region are C_3, the result suggested the consumption of grazing animals.

$\delta^{15}N$

Nitrogen-isotope ratios ($^{15}N/^{14}N$, or $\delta^{15}N$) similarly provide information that is useful in dietary reconstruction. Initial study of the $\delta^{15}N$ focused on the observation that plants that obtain nitrogen directly from the atmosphere (such as legumes) have lower $\delta^{15}N$ than other plants that rely on soil nitrites and nitrates to obtain N; consequently, $\delta^{15}N$ were first suggested as a means of identifying legumes in human diets. Subsequently, it was shown that the $\delta^{15}N$ also differentiate between marine and terrestrial protein—the collagen $\delta^{15}N$ of marine animals tend to be more positive than those of terrestrial ones—and are consistently fractionated by ca. 3–5 ‰ for each trophic level. Where skeletal proteins survive, the index is thus useful in determining the contribution of marine protein to diets and also whether an animal (or unidentified skeletal part) having unknown diet is a herbivore, an omnivore, or a carnivore. For example, relatively negative $\delta^{15}N$ have been used at European Paleolithic sites to suggest that European cave bears were likely to have been herbivores, while relatively positive $\delta^{15}N$ have been used to argue that "archaic *Homo sapiens*" (Neanderthals) were largely carnivorous.

One complication is that physiological adaptations to water stress in animals lead to more positive $\delta^{15}N$. As a result, bones from terrestrial animals from areas receiving less than 400 mm of rain per year may not be distinguished from the bones of marine animals.

$\delta^{18}O$

Oxygen-isotope ratios ($^{18}O/^{16}O$, or $\delta^{18}O$) have special importance for paleoclimatological research. Because fractionation is due to energy differences between isotopes, and since the energy of atoms increases with temperature, fractionation is temperature dependent. With increasing temperature, the energy difference between isotopes is lessened; as a result, less fractionation occurs. For this reason, the oxygen isotope exchange reaction between water and other molecules is temperature dependent. For example, the reaction between calcium carbonate and water:

$$CaCO_3^{16} + H_2O^{18} = CaCO_3^{18} + H_2O^{16}$$

can be used to infer the temperature at which fossil carbonates precipitated. The paleotemperature equation that allows the conversion of isotope values in $CaCO_3$ to water temperature is given in the form:

$$t°C = A - B\,(\delta^{18}O_{sample} - \delta^{18}O_{water}) + C\,(\delta^{18}O_{sample} - \delta^{18}O_{water})^2$$

in which A, B, and C are constants. The most extensive application of isotope thermometry has been in the construction of temperature curves from deep-sea sediment cores. Recent studies have also suggested that the phosphate $\delta^{18}O$ values obtained from calcified tissues are correlated to the $\delta^{18}O$ of an animal's drinking water. Thus, $\delta^{18}O$ measurements of fossil enamel apatite may have paleoenvironmental applications.

Heavy Stable Isotopes

In heavy elements, the mass difference between the stable isotopes is relatively small. As a result, there is no measurable fractionation in heavy-isotope ratios due to biochemical reactions. Therefore, such indices are direct measurements of the source of the element. For example, the $^{87}Sr/^{86}Sr$ incorporated into skeletons will reflect that of the ultimate source of the Sr—i.e., the parent rock of the soils from which food was obtained. Because modern marine $^{87}Sr/^{86}Sr$ (0.70923) differs from most crustal Sr, it is possible to use the $^{87}Sr/^{86}Sr$ as a tracer for marine foods. Moreover, $^{87}Sr/^{86}Sr$ ratios have also been used to study residential mobility patterns in prehistoric Southwest North America. Other heavy-isotope ratios that may be used as source tracers are as $^{208}Pb/^{204}Pb$, $^{206}Pb/^{204}Pb$, and $^{143}Nd/^{144}Nd$, although the use of such indices to trace migrations in archaeological peoples or fossil hominids requires further development.

See also Bone Biology; Diet; Paleodietary Analysis; Pleistocene. [A.S.]

Further Readings

Ambrose, S.H. (1992) Isotopic analysis of paleodiets: Methodological and interpretive considerations. In M.K. Sanford (ed.): Investigations of Ancient Human Tissues: Chemical Analysis in Anthropology. Gordon and Breach.

Bocherens, H., Fizet, M., Mariotti, A. Lange-Badré, B., Vandermeersch, B., Borel, J.P., and Bellon, G. (1991) Isotopic biogeochemistry (^{13}C, ^{15}N) of fossil vertebrate collagen: Application to the study of a past food web including Neanderthal man. J. Hum. Evol. 20:481–492.

Cerling, T.E., Harris, J.M., MacFadden, B.J., Leakey, M.G., Quade, J., Eisenmann, V., and Ehleringer, J.R. (1997) Global vegetation change through the Miocene/Pliocene boundary. Nature 389:153–158.

Cerling, T.E., Quade, J., Ambrose, S.H., and Sikes, N.E. (1991) Fossil soils, grasses, and carbon isotopes from Fort Ternan, Kenya: Grassland or woodland? J. Hum. Evol. 21:295–306.

DeNiro, M. (1987) Stable isotopy and archaeology. Am. Sci. 75:182–191.

Hoefs, J. (1987) Stable Isotope Geochemistry, 3rd ed. Berlin: Springer-Verlag.

Tieszen, L.L. (1991) Natural variations in the carbon isotope values of plants: Implications for archaeology, ecology, and paleoecology. J. Archaeol. Sci. 18:227–249.

Van der Merwe, N.J. (1982) Carbon isotopes, photosynthesis, and archaeology. Am. Sci. 70:506–606.

Star Carr

Mesolithic Maglemosian open-air site in Yorkshire (England) excavated in the 1950s by J.G.D. Clark and dated to ca. 9.5 Ka by radiocarbon, contemporary with the youngest Creswellian sites. A wet site with excellent organic preservation, Star Carr yielded remains of a brush pile or platform, in or at the edge of a former lake, possibly representing a dump rather than a prehistoric campsite, in association with barbed antler spearheads, bone awls, and scrapers, and a large series of antler frontlets, variously interpreted as ritual objects, hunting disguises, or a raw-material cache. A wooden paddle and a roll of birch bark suggested the presence and/or construction of boats. The stone industry included flint axes and geometric microliths, such as angular backed bladelets approaching trapezes, probably relating to arrow manufacture. The associated fauna is dominated by red-deer remains, possibly representing repeated winter hunting episodes, and it also includes the earliest European evidence for the domesticated dog. In contrast to other Maglemosian sites, fish remains were not recovered. The excavation and interpretation of the site reflect the economic approach to prehistory pioneered by its excavator.

See also Bow and Arrow; Creswellian; Domestication; Economy, Prehistoric; Maglemosian; Mesolithic; Raw Materials; Ritual; Site Types; Stone-Tool Making. [A.S.B.]

Further Reading

Clark, J.G.D. (1971) Excavations at Star Carr: an Early Mesolithic Site at Seamer near Scarborough, Yorkshire. Cambridge: Cambridge University Press.

Stegodon-Ailuropoda Fauna

Late Early to early Middle Pleistocene Southeast Asian paleontological assemblages usually characterized by the extinct proboscidean *Stegodon* and the giant panda *Ailuropoda*, together with the Malaysian tapir *Tapirus*, the orangutan *Pongo*, and other warm, humid-climate mammals. This regional (sub) tropical fauna, mainly found in south China and Indonesia, was distinct from that of temperate northern China, which had numerous cold-adapted forms. The *Stegodon-Ailuropoda* fauna has been distinguished from a presumably earlier *Gigantopithecus* fauna, found only on the mainland, and a Middle-to-Late Pleistocene "Sino-Malayan" fauna, also found in Java. The *Gigantopithecus* fauna contains certain taxa with smaller body size than related taxa in the *Stegodon-Ailuropoda* fauna, but the distinction may be merely ecological, rather than indicative of temporal difference.

See also Asia, Eastern and Southern; China; Gigantopithecus; Indonesia; Liucheng. [G.G.P.]

Steinheim

Middle Pleistocene quarry site near Stuttgart (Germany) which yielded a human fossil in 1933. The specimen is a nearly complete cranium but is distorted. Cranial capacity is small (less than 1,200 ml), and the cranial walls are thin, but the supraorbital torus is strongly developed. The occipital is evenly curved, and, in its present state of preservation, the position of maximum breadth of the skull is fairly high. The damaged face is small, relatively broad, and flat, with a large nasal opening and delicate cheek bones with an apparent canine fossa. Early researchers recognized broad similarities between the Steinheim and the Swanscombe (England) fossils, although they were placed on separate lineages in M. Boule and H.V. Vallois's presapiens scheme. Many now regard the Steinheim skull as an early member of the Neanderthal lineage, citing its nasal form, occipital-torus morphology, and suprainiac fossa. The specimen is of mid–Middle Pleistocene antiquity, perhaps comparable with that of Swanscombe or slightly younger; both are often dated to the north-

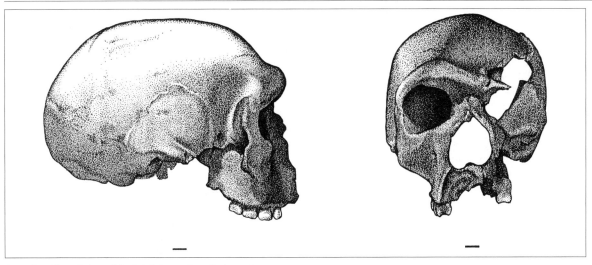

Lateral and frontal views of the Steinheim cranium. Scales are 1 cm.

ern European Holsteinian interglacial (ca. 350 Ka). No artifacts are directly associated with this fossil, although both Acheulean and flake industries are known from deposits of roughly the same antiquity.

See also Acheulean; Archaic Homo sapiens; Boule, [Pierre] Marcellin; Europe; Neanderthals; Presapiens; Swanscombe; Vallois, Henri Victor. [C.B.S., J.J.S.]

Sterkfontein

South African karst-cave breccia deposit in dolomitic limestone located south of the Bloubank River ca. 9.6 km north-northwest of the town of Krugersdorp. The site was initially quarried for lime in the 1890s, and fossil bones from these deposits were sent to the Natural History Museum in London in 1895. The first hominin specimen was recovered by R. Broom in 1936.

The site comprises six sedimentary (breccia) members. Field operations by Broom (1936–1939), Broom and J.T. Robinson (1947–1949), Robinson and C.K. Brain (1956–1958), P.V. Tobias and A.R. Hughes (1966–1991), and Tobias and R.J. Clarke (1991–) have resulted in the recovery of more than 500 numbered hominin specimens, all but one of which derive from Members 4 and 5. Several associated foot bones were reported from Member 2 in 1995. In late 1998, Clarke reported the location of most of the remainder of the skeleton of the same individual. The incompletely cleaned skull is similar to those from Member 4. The vast majority of hominin fossils come from Member 4, and these are attributed to *Australopithecus africanus.* The bulk of the hominin specimens that derive from Member 5 have been attributed to *Homo habilis.* It has also been reported that *Paranthropus robustus* remains are present in Member 5, but this claim has yet to be substantiated adequately.

The faunal remains from Member 4 suggest a date of ca. 2.8–2.5 Ma and the presence of comparatively wetter and more bush-covered conditions than during the accumulation of Member 5. Preliminary electron spin resonance (ESR) dates obtained from bovid tooth enamel from Member 4 suggest an age of ca. 2.4 Ma, which is consistent with the younger part of the faunal estimate. The Member 4 fauna has suggested to some that a considerable time period elapsed during the accumulation of this sedimentary unit. A forest component of the environment during the accumulation of Member 4 is attested to also by the presence of *Dichapetalum*

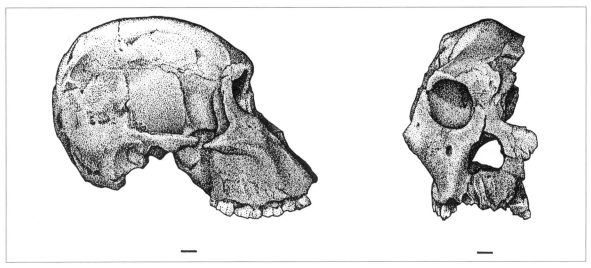

Side and front views of the Sts 71 cranium from Sterkfontein. Scales are 1 cm.

lianas. The faunal age of Member 5 is somewhat less secure, with an estimated date between 2 and 1.5 Ma. The hominin foot bones from Member 2 have been argued to be earlier than 3 Ma, and likely ca. 3.5 Ma, but this rests upon unsubstantiated geological inference, and as yet unpublished magnetostratigraphy; a date later than 3 Ma is more likely.

No artifactual material is known from Members 1 through 4. Paleolithic artifacts were first discovered in 1956 by Brain in Member 5 of what was initially referred to as the Extension Site. Subsequent work has yielded Early Stone Age artifacts attributable to the Oldowan and Early Acheulean traditions.

See also Acheulean; Africa; Africa, Southern; Australopithecus; Australopithecus africanus; Breccia Cave Formation; Broom, Robert; Early Stone Age; Homo habilis; Oldowan; Robinson, John Talbot. [F. E. G.]

Further Readings

Clarke, R.J. (1985) *Australopithecus* and early *Homo* in southern Africa. In E. Delson (ed.): Ancestors: The Hard Evidence. New York: Liss, pp. 171–177.

Clarke, R.J. (1998) First ever discovery of a well-preserved skull and associated skeleton of *Australopithecus*. S.AF.J.Sci.94: 460–463.

Clarke, R.J., and Tobias, P.V. (1995) Sterkfontein Member 2 foot bones of the oldest South African hominid. Science 269:521–524.

Kuman, K. (1994) The archaeology of Sterkfontein—past and present. J. Hum. Evol. 27:471–495.

Partridge, T.C. (1978) Re-appraisal of lithostratigraphy of Sterkfontein hominid site. Nature 275:282–287.

Schwarcz, H.P., Grun, R., and Tobias, P.V. (1994) ESR dating studies of the australopithecine site of Sterkfontein, South Africa. J. Hum. Evol. 26:175–181.

Stillbay

African Middle Stone Age flake industry, originally included as the eastern variant (as opposed to the variant localized around Cape Town itself) of the South African Later Stone Age. Named for surface collections at Still Bay on the southeastern Cape Peninsula (South Africa), the Stillbay industry is characterized by faceted striking platforms, discoidal and Levallois technology, and bifacial or unifacial leaf-shaped or triangular points, often thinned at the base for hafting. Although the exact definition or integrity of the industry is ambiguous, due to the lack of context for the type collections, the term was extended to other Middle Stone Age industries, such as the Bambata, and (by L.S.B. Leakey) to cover industries with faceted striking platforms in East Africa. One of the best *in situ* occurrences of a Stillbay-like industry is at Skildergat, near Cape Town, where the Fish Hoek cranium may be associated with this industry or represent an intrusion from an overlying Howieson's Poort horizon. In 1997, a new series of excavations in the Stillbay levels of Blombos Cave yielded bone points, incised ocher plaques, incised bone, and remains of large marine fish along with Stillbay points.

See also Africa; Africa, Southern; Apollo-11; Bambata; Blombos; Cave of Hearths; Florisbad; Howieson's Poort; Leakey, Louis Seymour Bazett; Levallois; Middle Paleolithic; Middle Stone Age; Modern Human Origins; Orangian; Pietersburg; Rose Cottage; Stone-Tool Making. [A.S.B.]

Further Readings

Henshilwood, C. and Sealey, J.C. (1997) Bone artifacts from the Middle Stone Age at Blombos Cave, Southern Cape, South Africa. Curr. Anth. 38:890–895.

Stone-Tool Making

The emergence of a flaked-stone technology during the course of hominid evolution marks a radical behavioral departure from the rest of the animal world and constitutes the first definitive evidence in the prehistoric record of a simple cultural tradition (i.e., one based upon learning). Although other animals (such as the Egyptian vulture, the California sea otter, and C. Darwin's Galapagos finch) may use simple unmodified tools, or even manufacture and use simple tools (as in the termiting and nut-cracking behavior of wild chimpanzees), a fundamental aspect of human adaptation is a strong reliance upon technology for survival and adaptation. Archaeological evidence shows a geometric increase in the sophistication and complexity of hominid stone technology over time since its earliest beginnings at 3–2 Ma.

Stone is the principal material found in nature that is both very hard and able to produce superb working edges when fractured. A wide range of tasks can be executed with even a simple stone technology, including animal butchery (hide slitting, disarticulation, meat cutting, bone breaking), woodworking (chopping, scraping, sawing), hide scraping, plant cutting, and bone and antler working. Although other perishable materials, such as wood, bone, horn, and shell, were probably used early in the evolution of hominid technology, tools made of stone are relatively indestructible and so provide the longest and most detailed record of prehistoric tool manufacture. Stone tools supplemented biology as a means of adapting to the environment during the course of human evolution, and the study of their manufacture and potential uses reveals important information about the evolution of human culture.

Antiquity of Stone Tools

Archaeological evidence indicates that a flaked-stone technology is one of a suite of biological and behavioral changes in early hominid ancestors involving a selection for greater intelligence and possibly marking the emergence of the genus *Homo* between 3 and 2 Ma in Africa. Before the advent of a flaked-stone technology, hominids could have possessed a relatively rich technology that would have left little or no visibility in the prehistoric record. Missiles, clubs, nut-cracking hammers and anvils, stick probes, and simple bark or shell containers may have been used by early *Australopithecus*.

The oldest-known archaeological sites bearing definite flaked-stone artifacts (Oldowan or Omo industry) include those found in Member F from the Omo Valley (Ethiopia), dated to ca. 2.4 Ma, the archaeological sites from the Gona region of Hadar (Ethiopia), at 2.5-2.6 Ma, the sites at Lokalalei (Kenya) at 2.34 Ma and possibly Senga-5 (Zaire), perhaps between 2.3 and 2 Ma. Other sites believed to be at least 1.5 Myrdd include those in Member E at Omo; Koobi Fora (Kenya) in and above the KBS Tuff; Olduvai Gorge (Tanzania) Beds I and II; and Peninj, west of Lake Natron (Tanzania). The stone artifacts from the South African caves of Swartkrans and Sterkfontein (Member 5) may be in this time range as well.

Raw Materials for Stone Tools

The typical types of rock from which flaked-stone artifacts are produced are relatively fine grained and hard and tend to fracture easily in any direction (i.e., they are *isotropic*). Commonly used rock types are flint or chert, quartzite, quartz, and various volcanic rocks, including obsidian (volcanic glass). Some materials, such as many flints or cherts, can be more easily worked after heat treatment (a controlled heating that alters crystal structure), a practice that may have begun in Late Paleolithic times.

The different types of raw materials vary widely in their overall geographic distributions and in the size, shape, quantity, and quality of material found at any one location. They may be found in *primary* geological context (at their site of origin or formation), such as a lava flow, quartz vein, quartzite layer, or flint nodule seam, or they may be in *secondary* (redeposited) context, such as cobbles in river gravels or rocks forming the pavement of desert surfaces.

Both the cultural rules regarding artifact design and the intended use of a tool influence what types of tools are found in the prehistoric record. Cultural norms and functional requirements for tools aside, the size, shape, quality, and flaking characteristics of the stone material also can strongly affect what sort of artifact may be made. More sophisticated, delicately flaked artifacts can generally be made in fine-grained materials like high-quality cherts and flints than are usually made in coarser-grained rocks. The relative abundance or scarcity of stone suitable for flaking affects the quantities and sizes of artifacts left behind at archaeological sites, so that artifacts made in rock available locally often tend to be larger and to be found in greater numbers than artifacts made from stone transported over greater distances.

In general, there is increasing selectivity in use of stone materials over time in the Paleolithic. Later Stone Age peoples tended to concentrate more on finer-grained, higher-quality rock sources, often quite localized in distribution and transported some distance to the archaeological site, than did hominids in the earlier phases of the Paleolithic, who appear to have exploited available rock sources in a more opportunistic fashion.

Principles of Stone Fracture

The type of fracture or mechanical failure of rocks observed in stone-tool manufacture is often called *conchoidal fracture*, named after the shell- or conchlike ripples or swirls generally evident in the artifacts manufactured in finer-grained materials. In stone-tool manufacture, a force is applied to the stone sufficient to break it in a controlled fashion. The stone usually fractures in alignment with its crystalline structure; thus, noncrystalline or finer-grained materials, especially isotropic materials with no preferential cleavage planes (such as obsidian or flint), tend to produce a smoother, more predictable fracture.

The stone is deliberately fractured (or *flaked*) either through a sharp, percussive blow (*direct* or *indirect percussion flaking*) or through the application of a compressive force (*pressure flaking*). The parent piece of rock is the *core,* and the spalls so removed are *flakes.*

The key to producing fracture in stone by flaking is to find core edges with acute angles (less than 90°). Thus, in manufacturing tools from rounded pieces of rock, such as stream cobbles, those with pronounced overhangs or with flattened edges tend to be easier to flake than more spherical pieces. When a hammer strikes the core obliquely and with sufficient force near one of these edges, a flake is detached, producing an associated scar (*flake scar*) on the core.

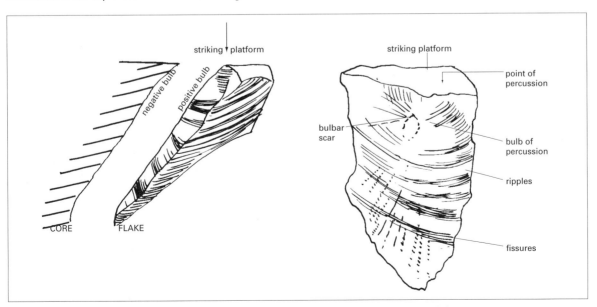

Left: the relationship between the core and the flake; right: major features of the ventral (release) surface of the flake.

Characteristics of flakes include, on the ventral, or *release,* surface (the face detached from the inside of the core), a striking platform (*butt*) at the top of the flake, a bulb of percussion (*semicone*), a bulbar scar (*éraillure*), ripples or waves, and fissures (*hackle marks*); and on the dorsal, or outer, surface of the flake (representing the surface of the core), a cortex (weathered surface of the core) and/or scars of previous flakes removed from the core. Cores and retouched pieces exhibit the negative features of flake release, particularly a negative (concave) bulb of percussion and the conchoidal ripples or waves of percussion.

Although some natural processes (e.g., high-energy fluviatile or glacial forces) can produce percussion flaking on pieces of stone, they do not exhibit the controlled, patterned removal of flakes characteristic of even the earliest stone industries. Early hominids clearly had a sound intuitive sense of geometry when flaking rock and expertly exploited acute angles on cores.

Procedures and Techniques of Stone-Tool Manufacture

Numerous techniques of working stone are known ethnographically and experimentally. They include:

HARD-HAMMER TECHNIQUE

Striking a core with a stone hammer to induce flaking. This is one of the most common techniques of flaking, used from the Early Paleolithic onward. The flakes tend to have large striking platforms and prominent bulbs of percussion. Cores characteristically have deep flake scars and prominent ridges between flakes.

ANVIL (BLOCK-ON-BLOCK) TECHNIQUE

Striking a core against a stationary anvil to produce flakes. This percussion technique is sometimes used in flaking very large cores. The features on flakes and cores are similar to hard-hammer percussion.

SOFT-HAMMER TECHNIQUE

Flaking a core with a hammer that is softer than the core itself, such as a softer stone or wood, antler, or bone. This technique usually produces flakes with relatively small platforms, diffuse bulbs of percussion, and flatter release surfaces. There is often a prominent "lipping" at the intersection of the platform and the release (ventral) surface. Cores tend to have relatively shallow flake scars and subtle ridges between flake scars. This technique is particularly effective in the thinning of bifaces (e.g., handaxes or projectile points). Often, striking platforms are faceted with numerous flake scars, which is an indication of preparing the core by steepening and regularizing the edge with a hammer or an abrader.

BIPOLAR TECHNIQUE

Setting a core on an anvil and hitting the core from above with a hammerstone. This technique was often used for very small or intractable, hard-to-flake raw materials. Flakes tend to have thin or punctiform (very small circular to oval) platforms and very flat release surfaces with small bulbs of percussion. Cores tend to be barrel shaped in platform and thin, with flakes removed from both ends.

PUNCH TECHNIQUE (INDIRECT PERCUSSION)

Often used for blade production. This technique consists of setting a punch (or indirect percussor) on the core and detaching blades by hitting the punch with a hammer. Blades tend to have small striking platforms and diffuse bulbs of percussion and are slightly curved in side view.

PRESSURE TECHNIQUE

Flakes can also be detached from a core or a retouched piece through compressive force or through exertion of pressure on the stone with a pointed tool (such as a piece of antler or bone). This technique, first observed in the prehistoric record during the Late Paleolithic, allows a stone worker to carry out controlled and meticulous flaking and was often used to finish finely made projectile points that had been shaped initially through percussion flaking. Flakes tend to be quite small and thin, often breaking when pressed off the core, with a small platform and diffuse bulbs of percussion, although it is also possible to produce more prominent, deep scars on a piece by pressure flaking. Pressure-flaked artifacts tend to exhibit shallow, regular flake scars. In Mesoamerica, a pressure technique may have also been used for the removal of obsidian blades from prismatic cores.

GRINDING AND POLISHING

Smoothing and shaping a rock (sometimes previously flaked into a rough shape) by grinding it against another rock. Such forms as axes and adzes were manufactured by this technique. Sometimes, abrasive sand and water were used in the grinding process. This technique is often associated with Neolithic farming communities in southwestern Asia, Europe, and North Africa, but it can be found also among some hunter-gatherer communities, as in parts of Australia.

Prehistoric Information from Stone Technology

The study of stone technology does not entail simply observing the techniques or procedures of artifact manufacture; ideally, it considers a complex series of prehistoric actions that surround the creation of a set of tools at an archaeological site. It is useful to view stone technology as a *system,* that encompasses the procurement of raw materials, the manufacture of tools from those materials, the transport of tools and raw materials, tool use, the resharpening and reshaping of the tools, artifact discard or loss, and the final incorporation of the stone tools within the archaeological record. Within each major component of this system, there are some basic questions that can yield important information about prehistoric behavior.

ACQUISITION OF RAW MATERIALS

What is the range of raw-material types exploited by prehistoric peoples? Are the sources *primary* (e.g., rock outcrop) or *secondary* (e.g., river gravel, surface erosion)? Is there evidence for selectivity in the acquisition of raw materials? Are certain materials used for some artifact forms and not others?

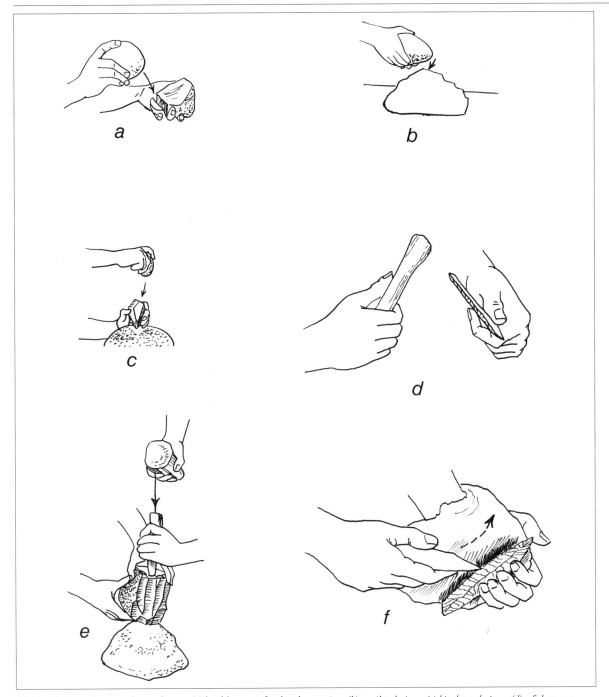

Major techniques of stone-tool manufacture: (a) hard-hammer, free-hand percussion; (b) anvil technique; (c) bipolar technique; (d) soft-hammer percussion; (e) indirect percussion or punch technique; (f) pressure flaking.

TRANSPORT OF RAW MATERIALS

Can distances from rock sources to prehistoric sites be measured? Transport of materials can occur at any stage of lithic reduction; for example, after a handaxe is roughed out at a quarry site, it may be transported and the final shaping of the artifact carried out at another locality. Transport of stone artifacts in a finished form is a major clue to the degree of *curation* (keeping things for future use) of artifacts by hominid groups.

MANUFACTURE OF STONE ARTIFACTS

What techniques and strategies were employed by prehistoric peoples in stone-artifact manufacture? A flowchart can be devised to explain the reduction of an unmodified piece of stone into deliberate end products and waste products. Can various stages of stone-artifact manufacture be recognized from unfinished tools at an archaeological site, or by the types of débitage (flakes and fragments) being removed from cores and retouched pieces? Can tools of manufacture (e.g., percussors, anvils, pressure flakers) be recognized at prehistoric sites? Can we talk about stylistic norms or "mental templates" of artifact design among the toolmakers? Are there other clues regarding the strength, skill, cognition, foresight, or preferential handedness of the toolmakers?

Is there contextual evidence to suggest how stone tools were used at a prehistoric site (e.g., cutmarks and points of percussion on bone; tool marks on wood, bone, or antler objects; organic residues on stone artifacts; or characteristic edge damage and microwear polishes on stone artifacts)? What was the adaptive significance of specific artifact forms?

REJUVENATION OR REUSE OF STONE ARTIFACTS

Is there evidence of resharpening, reuse, repairing, or rehafting of tools?

PATTERNS OF DISPOSAL

Is there evidence to suggest *why* stone artifacts ended up at a specific place? Were they discarded, lost, cached for future use, left as grave goods?

POSTBEHAVIORAL EFFECTS

How altered is the spatial distribution of these artifact forms from the original patterning on the landscape at the time of hominid occupation or site abandonment? Has there been any geological sorting of materials (e.g., fluvial winnowing of lighter materials)? Is there evidence of admixture of archaeological materials from different levels? Does the physical or chemical alteration of stone artifacts give clues to their mode of burial and diagenetic changes?

Major Stages of Stone Technology in Prehistory

Prehistorians often divide the Stone Age of the Old World (Africa, Europe, and parts of Asia) into technological stages:

PALEOLITHIC (OLD STONE AGE)

The Paleolithic is generally divided into three main stages according to the technological practices and major artifact types present:

1. Early Paleolithic (in sub-Saharan Africa called the Early Stone Age). This stage is often divided into:
   a. Oldowan, or Mode 1, technology, characterized by simple core forms (e.g., choppers, polyhedrons, discoids) associated débitage, and often casually retouched flakes (scrapers and awls). Hard-hammer percussion, bipolar technique, and anvil technique were employed. This stage has sometimes been called Pre-Chellean in Europe.
   b. Acheulean, or Mode 2, technology, characterized by large bifacial forms, especially handaxes or cleavers, a range of simpler core forms, and retouched flakes. Hard-hammer percussion, anvil technique, and, in later Acheulean industries, soft-hammer percussion were employed. These technologies were formerly referred to as Chellean in Europe, and the cruder bifacial forms sometimes assigned to the Abbevillian.
2. Middle Paleolithic, or Mode 3, technology (in sub-Saharan Africa referred to as the Middle Stone Age and in Europe mainly the Mousterian), usually characterized by a range of well-made side-scraper forms and unifacial

points and use of prepared-core techniques of toolmaking, especially the Levallois method. Hard-hammer and soft-hammer percussion were typically employed. The presence of apparent projectile points, as well as tanged artifacts of the Aterian (a North African variant of the Mousterian), suggests that hafting with cordage or mastic was practiced during this stage.
3. Late Paleolithic, or Mode 4, technology (termed the Upper Paleolithic in much of Europe and often in northern Africa and western Asia; rare in sub-Saharan Africa, but found in both Middle and Later Stone Age assemblages), characterized by blade industries, often associated with such artifact forms as end scrapers, burins, and awls. Bifacially worked points may be present, as well as a range of bone- and antler-tool forms. Hard, soft, and indirect percussion were typically employed, as well as some pressure flaking. Spear throwers are known from this period, and some small projectile points also suggest the possible use of bows and arrows.

MESOLITHIC

This is designated as Mode 5 technology (in sub-Saharan Africa, this technological stage is found among the microlithic technologies of the Later Stone Age). It is characterized by microlithic tools, particularly such geometric forms as triangles, trapezoids, and crescents, which were used to form composite tools. These technologies are often associated with the use of bows and arrows. In some areas, such as temperate Europe, flaked-stone axes were used, sometimes attached to antler sleeves, which, in turn, would be hafted to a wooden handle. Hard, soft, and indirect percussion were typically employed, as well as the *groove-and-snap* method of producing blanks for geometric microliths, and pressure flaking.

NEOLITHIC

This stage, designated as Mode 6 technology, is characterized by ground-stone tools, such as axes and adzes, and is usually associated with pottery. A wide range of flaked-stone tools was still employed, often with an associated blade technology. Hard, soft, and indirect percussion were used, as well as pressure flaking and grinding and polishing. Grinding stones for cereal processing, known from some Mesolithic sites, become more plentiful in early farming communities.

This system of classification of the major developmental stages of stone-tool making works reasonably well in western Europe but not necessarily elsewhere. For example, the later stone industries of the Americas constitute sophisticated traditions often centering on the manufacture of bifacial points, as well as unifacial scrapers, which do not fit well into this classification scheme.

Thus, in many geographical regions independent terminologies have been developed to subdivide industrial or economic stages of indigenous prehistoric inhabitants. In Southeast Asia and Australia, there are prehistoric technologies with ground-stone axes that would not normally be termed Neolithic, since these peoples in other regards are very different economically and technologically from the early farmers of western Asia, Europe, and Africa. It is also important to note that these technological stages did not develop at precisely the same rate in different geographic areas. For example, blade technologies appeared earlier in Southwest Asia than in western Europe.

Stone Tools As Cultural Markers

Stone artifacts can often serve as important cultural markers for certain chronological periods, technological stages, or regional styles during the Stone Age. Some tools, such as certain types of projectile points, may be restricted in time and space and, therefore, indicative of particular cultural systems, while others, such as side-scrapers, may represent forms found widely in different temporal and geographical contexts.

Role of Tools in Human Evolution

Some scientists, such as the anthropologist S.L. Washburn and the sociobiologist E.O. Wilson, have emphasized the interplay between learned behavior, such as technology, and genetic evolution, forming a feedback system that accelerated both biological evolution and cultural innovation (through a *biocultural feedback system* or *gene-culture co-evolution*).

From ca. 2.5 Ma to relatively recent times, stone tools provided a technological means to a wide range of functional and adaptive ends for our human ancestors. It is certain that tools have played an extremely important role in human evolution; particularly within the past 3–2 Myr, tools have constituted a vital part of our cultural adaptation to the environment, an adaptation based upon intelligent technological innovations designed to meet the requirements of the situations and environments faced by our ancestors. Prehistoric evidence of stone-tool making serves as the most continuous, lasting record of this human adaptation.

See also Acheulean; Bipolar Technique; Core; Early Paleolithic; Flake; Late Paleolithic; Lithic Use-Wear; Mesolithic; Middle Paleolithic; Modes, Technological; Prepared-Core; Raw Materials; Retouch; Sociobiology; Takamori; Upper Paleolithic. [N.T., K.S.]

Further Readings

Bordaz, J. (1970) Tools of the Old and New Stone Age. Garden City, N.Y.: Natural History Press.

Bordes, F. (1970) The Old Stone Age. New York: McGraw-Hill.

Hodges, H. (1976) Artifacts: An Introduction to Early Materials and Technology. London: Baker.

Leakey, L.S.B. (1967) Working stone, bone, and wood. In C. Singer, E.J. Holmyard, and A.R. Hall (eds.): A History of Technology, Vol. 1. Oxford: Clarendon, pp. 128–143.

Oakley, K.P. (1976) Man the Toolmaker. Chicago: University of Chicago Press.

Schick, K., and Toth, N. (1993) Making Silent Stones Speak. New York: Simon and Schuster.

Spier, R.F.G. (1970) From the Hand of Man: Primitive and Preindustrial Technologies. Boston: Houghton Mifflin.

Swanson, E., ed. (1976) Lithic Technology. The Hague: Mouton.

Storage

Food is preserved for consumption at a later time most commonly by salting, pickling, drying, or freezing. Ethnographic data on hunter-gatherers indicate two disparate subsistence behaviors. Groups found in lower latitudes generally consume immediately what can be harvested from nature. Groups in higher latitudes, where the availability and abundance of foods are more seasonally restricted, are prone to storing foods in large quantity during periods of their peak abundance and using these stores during the resource-lean months. These differences in subsistence behavior have significant impact on the settlement systems, coresident group sizes, and economic and sociopolitical relationships of ethnographically known hunter-gatherers. Because of this, evidence for food storage is of special interest to prehistoric archaeologists.

Unequivocal evidence for storage economies is first documented during the Late Paleolithic. Numerous in-ground storage pits measuring 1–2 m in diameter and up to 1 m in depth are repeatedly found in Late Paleolithic sites on the East European Plain (e.g., Dobranichevka, Eliseevichi, Mezhirich, Mezin, Radomyshl', Suponevo, Yudinovo) dating to ca. 20–12 Ka. Their contents indicate that Late Pleistocene groups first stored meat supplies during the late summer or early fall and reused the pits after consuming the stored resources to store the bones themselves for use as fuel and raw materials for the manufacture of tools, implements, and jewelry.

See also Economy, Prehistoric; Late Paleolithic; Mezhirich; Site Types. [O.S.]

Further Readings

Soffer, O. (1985) The Upper Paleolithic of the Central Russian Plain. Orlando: Academic.

Testart, A. (1982) The significance of food storage among hunter-gatherers: Residence patterns, population densities, and social inequalities. Curr. Anthropol. 23:523–537.

Stranská Skála

Jurassic limestone hill on the outskirts of Brno (Czech Republic), with three localities yielding Middle Pleistocene paleoanthropological materials. Paleosols inside two small caves, as well as the downslope scree outside the caves, contained remains of both large mammals and microfauna assigned to the Biharian mammal age. The cave deposits also contained ca. 40 artifacts, predominantly of hornstone and limestone, consisting of simple flakes, cores, choppers, and hammerstones. These materials are considered Cromerian in age and probably reflect occupation during the "Günz-Mindel" interglacial (perhaps ca. 600–400 Ka). Excavations both upslope and downslope from the cave and talus have revealed Late Paleolithic occupations.

See also Acheulean; Europe; Přezletice. [O.S.]

Stratigraphy

Stratigraphy is the study of the origin, physical characteristics, and spatial relationships of stratified rocks, primarily to understand the history of events documented in the strata. Layers of sediment are the principal object of study, but layered volcanic rocks, and even metamorphosed strata, can also be interpreted according to the three great principles of stratigraphy. The *principle of superposition* states that in an undisturbed sequence each stratum is younger than the one beneath; the *principle of original horizontality* states that strata are horizontal or nearly so when they are deposited; and the *principle of original lateral continuity* states that all parts of a stratum, however disrupted by later activity, were once joined in a single connected layer.

Rock strata may be classified by any of their properties or by inferred attributes, such as the time or environment of origin. In general, the units based on one set of properties do not coincide with units based on another, and a different set of units is thus needed for each classification. The three most common criteria by which strata are classified are lithology, fossil content, and age, and these give rise to the three main branches of stratigraphy: *lithostratigraphy, biostratigraphy*, and *chronostratigraphy*, respectively. Magnetostratigraphy, isotope stratigraphy, and cyclostratigraphy are also coming into wide use. Lithostratigraphic and biostratigraphic units are always limited because they depend on features that have finite vertical and lateral extent. Magnetostratigraphy, isotope stratigraphy, and cyclostratigraphy are based on global phenomena that, in theory, affect all sedimentary environments (and, in the case of magnetostratigraphy, igneous environments as well), but observing them is highly dependent on favorable circumstances. Only chronostratigraphic units are recognizable globally under all circumstances, because they are based on specified intervals of deposition rather than on specified processes of deposition.

Each of the stratigraphic categories has its own particular terminology, and the names of units in general do not overlap from one classification to another.

The thickness of lithostratigraphic units is not related explicitly to the passage of time, but in all other classifications there are exact geochronological equivalents. None of the stratigraphic-time units are inherently measurable in terms of years. On the one hand, magnetostratigraphy, isotope stratigraphy, and cyclostratigraphy are related to age-calibrated models, while, on the other hand, chronostratigraphic and biochronological time units are scaled to the rock record. In the stratigraphies that relate to year-calibrated ideal models, the distinction between the stratigraphic unit and time tends to be blurred by the fact that the identification of these units conveys an immediate age value to the rocks. The distinction between magnetozone and chron, for instance, is very seldom considered, and most writers use *chron* as if it were being observed directly in the strata; thus, *lower Matuyama Chron* is commonly used where the modifier *early* would be more appropriate. As for isotope stages and orbitally induced cycles, no attempt has been made to erect geochronological equivalents, because the lithologic expressions of these stratigraphies and the chronometric models are always treated as one.

In chronostratigraphy, however, the difference between rocks and time is essential. This relationship is made clear by a two-aspect terminology, so that Tertiary, for instance, is both a System of rocks and a Period of time. In order to express this, stratigraphers conscientiously use the modifiers *lower* and *upper* to refer to strata, and *early* and *late* to refer to age. The word *middle* is used for both position and time, although some stratigraphers prefer *medial* for time units. With this in mind, it is logically impossible to speak of a Lower Pleistocene age or an Early Pleistocene formation. These positional modifiers are capitalized, as a matter of taste, when they mean an exact and complete subdivision of a rock or time unit; lowercase is employed where the meaning is intentionally vague or where the terms are simply comparative.

The rock record is far from complete. It is broken by myriad gaps of varying length, which are expressed as buried surfaces. There are two primary genetic types of gap: *diastems*, which are due to the inherent transitions or pauses in a continuing depositional process—e.g., the intervals between floods on a floodplain—and *discontinuities*, which are due to changes or interruptions in the depositional process itself. These range from *condensed sections*, where deposition was markedly slowed, to *disconformities*, where deposition was completely interrupted. Disconformities are usually marked by indications of exposure such as weathering, chemical alteration, or signs of organic habitation (burrowing, root casts), as well as a difference between the strata. Erosion during exposure leads to the extreme discontinuity called an *unconformity*, in which previously buried strata are eroded. In some circumstances, diastems involving contemporaneous facies can mimic erosional unconformities—e.g., in delta systems where migrating gravel-filled distributary channels carve their way laterally through fine-laminated overbank deposits.

Lateral relationships between strata are of great importance, particularly in the reconstruction of ancient landscapes. Sands may be deposited along the shoreline of a lake at the same time that finer sediments are being deposited farther offshore and gravels are being laid down in stream channels. As a result, rock types change as the strata within a defined unit are traced laterally; these features are called *facies*. In treating facies, it is imperative to maintain accurate time correlation because the objective of studying facies is to document the lateral variations in lithology and paleontology (as lithofacies and biofacies, respectively) in order to understand the environmental conditions under which the strata were formed. The term *facies* has also been used to mean the rocks of a particular sedimentary environment, without regard to coeval lateral relationships, but such a unit is properly termed a *lithotope*. The equivalent paleontological term for an environmentally governed set of fossils is a *biotope*.

Depositional environments are not fixed in geographic position but change position as time passes. Thus, the shoreline of a lake advances and retreats as its water budget changes or as subsidence in the lake basin waxes or wanes. As the position of the shoreline changes, so, too, do the kinds of sediments being deposited at a particular spot. The fact that the sediments of coeval adjacent facies will also be deposited adjacent to one another in vertical succession is known as *Walther's Law.*

Factors that control the distribution of stratigraphic facies are manifold. In regard to lithofacies, some of the more important are the amount of sediment supplied to an area of deposition, the climate in the immediate region and also in the source area of the sediments, tectonic movements, changes in base level (for whatever reason), changes in the kind or degree of biological activity, and chemical changes in water bodies associated with the site of deposition. In regard to biofacies, external factors include geology, topography, water supply, water depth, latitude, and seasonality, but the internal dynamics of the biosphere also play a major role. Climatic changes and geological movements are completely or largely insensitive to changes in the other factors but may induce large changes in them, so climate and tectonics may be viewed as more basic controlling factors than the others.

STANDARDS IN STRATIGRAPHIC PRACTICE

Stratigraphy is strictly governed by international guidelines, based on earlier national stratigraphic codes of the United States, the United Kingdom, and the former USSR. The guidelines spell out standards for defining and using units, with a modern emphasis on unambiguous physical definitions—i.e., type sections and boundary-stratotypes—rather than interpretations of paleoclimate, biological evolution, or geological events. Another distinction of the modern guidelines is the accommodation of new stratigraphies that are based on instrumental or mathematical analysis of layered sequences.

LITHOSTRATIGRAPHY

Every stratigraphic unit is based on the lithified crust of the Earth, but lithostratigraphic units are the only ones based on rocks alone. Because such units are the basis of geological mapping, their only requirement is that they are clearly and reliably recognizable across a reasonable distance. The least lithostratigraphic unit is a *bed*, which is simply the smallest unit that can be depicted on geological maps, and, in fact, the term is very often applied to units that are made up of smaller, unmappable beds (i.e., laminae or strata). The basic unit of lithostratigraphy is the *formation*, which is any well characterized set of beds with consistent mappable characteristics and clear stratigraphic boundaries. The division of formations into *members*—or the combination of formations into *groups*—is a matter of convenience, and the same strata may be included in different formations where regional points of view overlap. Formations may consist of several lithic phases, or *facies* (for instance, alternating conglomerates and shales), and it is common for formations to grade laterally or vertically with others through facies changes. Two terms for regionally mappable units, from the old USSR code, are *horizon*, a lithological level that can be recognized throughout a wide region by some distinctive fossil or mineral property, and *suite*, a composite unit like a group but organized laterally, rather than vertically, by the inclusion of coeval facies, in order to have a regional scope (e.g., the lake beds, river gravels, and peats of an interior montane valley).

A formation is defined in terms of a designated type section where the rocks can be best described, measured, and revisited. The type sections of subsurface formations and beds, or formations that are badly exposed at the surface, can be designated in boreholes or mines. The names of formations consist of a unique title, usually taken from a local cultural or geographic feature, and a descriptive appellation that may be generic (i.e., Formation, Member) or specific (i.e., Shale, Grit, Trachyte). The combinations are always capitalized: Jebel Qatrani Formation, Kabarnet Trachyte, Lubur Grits. Members and beds can have titles like formations, or they can have completely descriptive names (Lower Member, White Tuff, Upper Gravels). There are many exceptions to standard nomenclature, especially in the older literature—e.g., the Old Red Sandstone, the Millstone Grit, or the Kupferschiefer—and custom still allows much variation. The Olduvai Beds, for instance, are a formation, and its members are both numbered (Bed I, Bed II) and named (Lemuta Member).

BIOSTRATIGRAPHY

Biostratigraphy classifies rock strata according to their included fossils, without reference to the evolutionary relationships or absolute age of the remains. The use of fossils to distinguish bodies of rock predates Darwin by a century or more and is still widely applied. The most commonly used criterion for the boundary of a biozone is the presence or absence of designated fossils, but other criteria, such as the morphology or evolutionary stage of the fossils, or the frequency or relative abundance of the fossils, are also employed. Being defined on the basis of organisms, biozones tend to be recognized over much greater lateral extent than formations and through greater thicknesses of strata. Certain marine planktonic microfossils, in particular, result from dispersal so rapid and extensive that their biozone boundaries have virtually the same geologic age around the globe.

Modern biostratigraphers recognize that the observations of fossils in the rock do not provide an accurate record of true biological history, because of incomplete preservation, incomplete sampling, and the human nature of paleontologists. For this reason, the limit of occurrence of a fossil in rock is known as a *datum level*, emphasizing that the stratigraphic observations are necessarily different from the inferred historical events—evolution, immigration, extinction—that they only approximately record. Some paleontologists use the acronyms FAD (First Appearance Datum) and LAD (Last Appearance Datum) to distinguish the bottom and top of a fossil taxon's observed stratigraphic range. In biochronology, *datum event* is used to refer to the historical equivalent of a datum level.

Among the several kinds of biozones, an *assemblage-zone* (or faunal-zone in vertebrate paleontology) is a body of strata defined by the joint occurrence of a group of specified fossils. *Range-zones*, which are bodies of strata defined by the fossils of one or two specified taxa, fall into several variants. A *total-range-zone* is the strata between the FAD and the LAD of a designated taxon; a *partial-range-zone* is the strata between the FADs of two designated taxa (or, rarely, the interval between the LADs of two designated taxa); and a *con-*

current-range-zone is the strata in which two designated taxa overlap. An *acme-zone* is a body of strata defined by the relatively high abundance of a designated taxon. All biostratigraphic units are identified by the name or names of their characterizing fossil taxa and the type of zone (e.g., the *Globorotalia margaritae* partial-range zone of tropical planktonic foraminifera in the lowermost Pliocene).

CHRONOSTRATIGRAPHY

Rocks that form during a specified interval of time are classified in time-stratigraphic (= chronostratigraphic) units. The objective of chronostratigraphy is to put all strata of the same age into the same chronostratigraphic unit. The boundaries of time-stratigraphic units are isochronous planes, independent of rock types or thickness. They are also independent of absolute-age measurement, and their application depends strictly on the first principle of stratigraphy: that the age of any stratum relative to another is established by their superpositional relationship. Chronostratigraphy is, therefore, capable of classifying strata in terms of their age relative to another stratum with great precision, no matter how old the rocks are. The extension of chronostratigraphic boundaries accurately from region to region, known as *time-stratigraphic correlation*, is one of the great and never-finished tasks of stratigraphers. For many years, regional correlations depended almost entirely on comparisons of biostratigraphic data, but radiometric dating, magnetostratigraphy, isotope stratigraphy, and cyclostratigraphy have brought new levels of accuracy to this procedure.

Chronostratigraphic units are hierarchal, and, in principle, the greater are defined in terms of the lesser, such that the boundaries of a system are defined by the boundaries of its oldest and youngest included series, and so on. *Stages* are the smallest units that are, in theory, capable of being correlated globally, and, therefore, stage boundaries (at least potentially) define all others in the hierarchy. One difficulty is that there have been many stages defined around the world, and it has been necessary to rule that the sequence of marine stages of western Europe are to be considered as the global standard stages (see "Time Chart" in the Introduction to this volume).

A stage is characterized in a *stage-stratotype*, which establishes its basic character and scope, but, because stratotype sections are designated in different places, there are usually stratigraphic overlaps and gaps between one stratotype and the next. To address this fact of life, the international guidelines recommend that "base defines boundary," so that the base of each unit is simultaneously the top of the one beneath, regardless of the upper limits of its stratotype. This makes the base all important, and the guidelines, therefore, recommend that every stage (and, thus, every unit in the hierarchy) eventually must be defined at its base by a *boundary-stratotype*, or unique physical reference point, to which the boundary is correlated around the world. This point, sometimes referred to as a *golden spike*, is a single stratigraphic plane in an accessible, appropriate, and easily correlatable section of beds—preferably, but not necessarily, located in the stage-stratotype section. Once defined, the boundary-stratotype may not be moved without formal action, even if new fossil finds or other evidence indicate that the reasons cited for its placement were in error. A number of boundary-stratotypes have been approved by the International Union of Geological Sciences for the status of GSSP, or Global-Boundary Stratotype Section and Point.

MAGNETOSTRATIGRAPHY

Paleomagnetic polarity is a feature that should be characteristic of all strata deposited during particular time intervals, because the magnetic field of the Earth is a global phenomenon. The isochronous boundaries between normal and reversed magnetozones are thus, in theory, ideal correlation tools. The practice, however, is more difficult, because many strata do not preserve paleomagnetic orientation. Furthermore, in those that do, paleomagnetic polarity reversals are indistinguishable from one another. This means that the identity of a particular reversal must be narrowed down in some way before a tenable correlation can be proposed. The usual method is to apply an external time scale, through correlation to a dated level or by direct dating of the magnetostratigraphic section. Another method is to match the studied section to the model of the calibrated paleomagnetic time scale, according to the thickness pattern of reversals or to the variations in geomagnetic intensity.

Another feature of magnetostratigraphic correlations that must be kept constantly in mind is that the isochroneity of the reversal boundaries is actually somewhat fuzzy because transitions—the interval in which the Earth has essentially no magnetic field—require at least 5 Kyr. Furthermore, the imprinting of a new polarity regime on strata can be delayed by thousands of years in certain environments. Bioturbation disorders the acquired polarity of seafloor sediments, and the fixation of detrital geomagnetic orientation in open-ocean marine deposits normally does not take place until the material is buried to ca. 40 cm. The time required for this depth of burial varies and is, of course, much longer in slowly deposited sediments. The age of a microfossil specimen is, therefore, synchronous not with the remanent magnetization in the horizon in which it occurs, but with that of a horizon ca. 40 cm below. Thus, the apparent microfossil "date" of a paleomagnetic horizon is always somewhat younger in deep-sea sediments than in the more rapidly deposited shallow marine equivalents.

ISOTOPE STRATIGRAPHY AND CYCLOSTRATIGRAPHY

These classifications, which reflect astronomically forced climate change, are not depicted as bounded units but as data curves in which the peaks are numbered starting from the present. The astronomical cycles are assumed *a priori* to have had globally synchronous effects, if not everywhere expressed in the same way or with the same intensity. All of the medium-high-frequency (10 to 100 Kyr) variations in oxygen and carbon isotope ratios in the later Cenozoic have now been related to astronomical cycles, and it is probable that this will prove to be the case in older strata as well. The correlation of isotope and insolation-cycle curves between one region and another is analogous to the correlation of tree rings or magnetostratigraphy, in that external evidence of age is combined with pattern recognition.

See also Biochronology; Climate Change and Evolution; Cyclostratigraphy; Geochronometry; Golden Spike; Paleobiogeography; Paleomagnetism. [F.H.B., J.A.V.C.]

Further Readings
Ager, D.V. (1981) The Nature of the Stratigraphical Record. New York: Halsted/Wiley.

Dunbar, C.O., and Rodgers, J. (1957) Principles of Stratigraphy. New York: Wiley.

Eicher, D.L. (1976) Geologic Time. Englewood Cliffs, N.J.: Prentice-Hall.

Salvador, A., ed. (1994) International Stratigraphic Guide, 2nd ed. Boulder: Geological Society of America.

Stratophenetics

Term coined by P.D. Gingerich in 1976 for a technique of reconstructing phylogeny. The technique follows three steps: (1) Stratigraphic organization of all fossil samples. This includes determining the number of biological species represented in each sample; arranging in chronological sequence all samples within a given stratigraphic column; and correlating separate columns to yield a composite column with all species in proper temporal order. (2) Phenetic linking of similar species populations in adjacent stratigraphic intervals to form a branching pattern of lineages. Lineages showing significant change through time are then divided arbitrarily into paleontological chronospecies. (3) Testing of the resulting phyletic hypothesis, by collection of additional fossils and judging whether the density and continuity of the fossil record is sufficient to render the hypothesis significantly more plausible than alternative hypotheses. This judgment involves considerations of paleogeography and functional interpretations of morphology as well as of morphology itself.

This stratophenetic method was originally applied by Gingerich to the Paleocene Plesiadapidae of western North America. The best subsequent examples of stratophenetic analyses have likewise been provided by Gingerich and his coworkers in studies of other Paleocene and Eocene mammal groups from the same region. The results of these studies have also been interpreted by their authors as strong evidence for the dominance of phyletic gradualism as opposed to punctuated equilibrium in mammalian evolution. Gingerich regarded the stratophenetic method as a codification of the traditional method of phyletic inference rather than as a novel approach. He introduced the term *stratophenetics* principally to distinguish this method from cladistics, which he regarded (1976) as "a narrower comparative method . . . sometimes based purely on morphology with little regard for time." Therefore, the most salient feature of the stratophenetic approach was conceived to be its reliance on stratigraphic superposition to indicate the temporal ordering of fossil forms and to provide a time dimension that cladistic analysis explicitly ignored. Gingerich acknowledged that his method required a relatively dense and continuous fossil record to provide accurate results. On the other hand, he emphasized that it made use of all evidence in the fossil record—temporal, geographic, and morphological—in contrast to cladistics, which used only morphology. Gingerich argued that cladistic analysis could best be used in evaluating competing hypotheses considered equally likely on stratophenetic grounds.

The stratophenetic method has been criticized on a number of grounds. Due to the nature of the samples—teeth—most stratophenetic analyses have been based on single characters, usually measures of tooth size. Character-state polarity has received little attention in this frankly phenetic approach; definition of chronospecies has often been based on scant morphological evidence and small sample sizes; linkage of species into lineages has been thought to be too subjective; and evolutionary change within restricted sedimentary basins has been too hastily inferred in preference to considering immigration of species as an alternative. Just as cladists condemn evolutionary systematics in general for inextricably commingling data on cladistic relationships with data on morphological distance, they condemn stratophenetics for intertwining systematics and biostratigraphy, potentially in a circular fashion. The interpretations of stratophenetic analyses as supporting phyletic gradualism rather than punctuated equilibrium have also been contested.

As usual in such epistemological disputes, some truth is to be found on all sides. The power of cladistic analysis is now well recognized, even by most evolutionary systematists, and it seems fair to say that the problem of character-state polarity must be taken into account in any systematic study, whatever the philosophy of the investigator. On the other hand, however, stratigraphic superposition, when used with due caution, is as valid and valuable as any of the other clues to character-state polarity, all of which are admitted to hold pitfalls for the unwary. It remains undeniable, furthermore, that paleontology alone gives access to the actual record of evolution. Numerical taxonomists as well as cladists have justly emphasized the necessity of examining multiple characters. In like fashion, the proponents of stratophenetics have once again underlined the need to focus all available lines of evidence on systematic problems. This insistence on the relevance of nonmorphological, and especially stratigraphic, data to phyletic reconstruction may be the chief contribution of the stratophenetic viewpoint, transcending differences of opinion on how best to avoid circularity in research design.

See also Cladistics; Evolutionary Systematics (Darwinian Phylogenetics); Phylogeny. [D.P.D., R.L.B.]

Further Readings
Gingerich, P.D. (1976) Cranial Anatomy and Evolution of Early Tertiary Plesiadapidae (Mammalia, Primates) (Papers on Paleontology No. 15). Ann Arbor: Museum of Paleontology, University of Michigan.

Gingerich, P.D. (1979) Stratophenetic approach to phylogeny reconstruction in vertebrate paleontology. In J.

Cracraft and N. Eldredge (eds.): Phylogenetic Analysis and Paleontology. New York: Columbia University Press, pp. 41–77.

Gingerich, P.D. (1984) Primate evolution: Evidence from the fossil record, comparative morphology, and molecular biology. Yrbk. Phys. Anthropol. 27:57–72.

Strepsirhini

Subgroup within the order Primates, typically recognized as a suborder. Loosely referred to as the "lower" primates, Strepsirhini includes the living lemurs of Madagascar, the lorises of sub-Saharan Africa and Southeast Asia, and the bushbabies, also of sub-Saharan Africa, as well as fossil and subfossil taxa thought to be either ancestral to, or extinct sisters of, the living forms. Here, the suborder Strepsirhini is subdivided into the infraorders Adapiformes and Lemuriformes. Adapiformes comprises three families of Eocene taxa, subsumed under the superfamily Adapoidea; one of these families, Adapidae, has traditionally been viewed as the group from which modern strepsirhines evolved. The infraorder Lemuriformes includes the extant lemurs and indriids of Madagascar and various subfossil relatives (distributed within the superfamilies Lemuroidea and Indrioidea) as well as the mouse and dwarf lemurs of Madagascar (family Cheirogaleidae), the lorises (family Lorisidae), and the bushbabies (family Galagidae), which together constitute the superfamily Lorisoidea.

History of Classification of Strepsirhini

Lemurs and lorises—the lower primates—were first grouped together in 1811 by the German systematist C. Illiger as Prosimii. Illiger kept a third lower primate, the tarsier, in its own group, Macrotarsi (a name that refers to the elongated tarsal bones of *Tarsius*), but in 1883 the British comparative anatomist W.H. Flower pulled together lemurs, lorises, and the tarsier as a single group of primates, distinguished from St. George Mivart's suborder of "higher" primates, Anthropoidea, proposed in 1864. Flower called his suborder of lower primates Lemuroidea, but Illiger's Prosimii eventually became the accepted taxonomic referent for this group.

In 1918, the British comparative anatomist R.I. Pocock argued that *Tarsius* had closer evolutionary ties to anthropoid primates than to lemurs and lorises because of similarities between the former taxa in the configuration of the lateral margin of the nostril. *Haplorhinism* is a condition among mammals in which the nostril is rounded aborally and is not discontinuous, or slit, as is the case in *strepsirhinism*. Anthropoid primates as a group are typically haplorhine, and, according to Pocock, so is *Tarsius*: He united these in the suborder Haplorhini. Lemurs and lorises had nostrils that bore slits laterally: Strepsirhini, created by the French comparative anatomist E. Geoffroy in 1812, was resuscitated as a suborder to receive these primates.

However, the hypotheses of Strepsirhini and Haplorhini as groups to replace the suborders Prosimii and Anthropoidea did not receive much support until the 1950s, when W.C.O. Hill published the first volumes of his monumental and influential treatise *Primates, Comparative Anatomy, and Taxonomy*. Volume 1 was entitled *Strepsirhini*, while Volume 2, which dealt with *Tarsius*, began the series of volumes included under the heading *Haplorhini*. This work emphasized the features that are today typically associated with Haplorhini: Haplorhine primates were further distinguished from strepsirhines by having a fused rather than divided upper lip and by lacking a moist, naked rhinarium that otherwise would proceed from the nasal region, through the split upper lip, to the membrane of the oral cavity. During the 1970s, studies on placental and fetal membranes, the bony and soft-tissue anatomy of the ear region, and the structure of the retina supposedly demonstrated the dissociation of *Tarsius* from the lemurs and lorises and the reality of the groups Strepsirhini and Haplorhini.

In 1980, however, the German primate anatomist H.O. Hofer pointed out that *Tarsius* and even some marmosets (New World anthropoid primates) are "strepsirhine"—i.e., the nostrils are not consistently aborally rounded—so that Pocock's original case for disbanding Prosimii and Anthropoidea was unfounded. In addition, Hofer demonstrated that, while *Tarsius* does, indeed, have a completely fused upper lip, this condition does not characterize all extant anthropoids. Rather, various New World monkeys possessed a vertical furrow in the midline of the upper lip, a feature that P. Hershkovitz also illustrated in his magnum opus on these primates. It is only among the extant catarrhine primates that one finds a completely fused upper lip, which would certainly lead to uniting these primates as a group, but not to arguing for the monophyly of Haplorhini. Thus, one of Hill's major criteria for linking *Tarsius* with Anthropoidea was unfounded. As F.S. Szalay had also done, Hofer questioned the homology of the fused and "dry" internarial region of the upper lip of *Tarsius* and anthropoids, since this condition is found in other mammals, such as horses and ungulates.

Defining Strepsirhini

Inasmuch as strepsirhinism is a condition common to many mammals—not just to lemurs and lorises but also to rodents, lagomorphs, carnivores, insectivores, bats, elephants, and treeshrews—the possession of such a configuration of the external nares (and even the upper lip) by any of these groups does not distinguish it from the others. Thus, being strepsirhine, while descriptively accurate, does not set apart a strepsirhine primate from any other strepsirhine mammal. But, as J.H. Schwartz and I. Tattersall have pointed out, one morphological feature does distinguish extant lemuroids, indrioids, and lorisoids as a group: They all possess a compressed, spikelike grooming claw on the second pedal digit. More recently, C.K. Beard and colleagues suggested in 1988 that extant strepsirhines are further distinguished among primates in having a unique configuration among their wrist bones. Specifically, in lemuriforms, Beard and colleagues described the os centrale as extending medially over the dorsal surface of the capitate to make contact with the hamate. To these distinctive characteristics we might add a third: the development of the anterior lower teeth (either six or four, depending on the specific taxon) into somewhat elongate and

Strepsirhine primates (clockwise from lower right): ruffed lemur, Varecia variegata *(representing the family Lemuridae); smallest of living primates, the mouse lemur,* Microcebus murinus *(family Cheirogaleidae); slow-climbing African potto,* Perodicticus potto *(family Lorisidae); and small, long-legged African bushbaby,* Galago senegalensis *(family Galagidae). All are characterized by the development of a grooming claw on the second digit of the foot (most visible in the illustration in the large animals).* Varecia, Propithecus, *and* Microcebus *occur only on the island of Madagascar. Of the five,* Microcebus, Perodicticus, *and* Galago *are nocturnal. The figures are drawn roughly to scale. Drawing by J. Anderton; courtesy of Jeffrey H. Schwartz.*

slender teeth whose crowns are tilted procumbently; this set of specialized teeth is usually referred to as a *tooth comb*. With the exception of *Daubentonia* (the aye-aye), all extant primates that possess a grooming claw also develop a tooth comb and an os centrale-hamate contact. If, indeed, these three features do unite as an evolutionary group lemuroids, indrioids, and lorisoids, and if the aye-aye is related to a specific group of lemurs, then we must conclude that this primate "lost" the tooth comb.

On the basis of extant taxa, a group of primates we might call Strepsirhini can be defined on the basis of its universal possession of a grooming claw and os centrale-hamate contact, and, secondarily, on the development of a tooth comb. Associating fossil taxa with extant strepsirhine primates is, however, problematic if we wish to state that any is a member of the larger group to which specific

lemurs and lorises belong. Beard and colleagues suggest that the pisiform attributed to *Adapis* links this taxon (and, by extension, Adapidae) with extant strepsirhines by virtue of its having a deeply excavated contact for the ulna styloid process—but not all extant strepsirhines have ulnocarpal contact. Beard and colleagues also suggest that Notharctidae can be united with a hypothesized adapid–extant strepsirhine group on the basis of features of the ankle: a laterally sloping talofibular facet, a lateral position of the groove for the flexor hallucis longus muscle, and, on the navicular bone, confluence of the naviculocuboid and mesocuneiform articular facets. Some of these features, however, are found in anthropoid primates and/or do not characterize all extant strepsirhines. And the only Eocene primate for which a grooming claw is known (from the Grübe Messel of Germany) is itself known only from damaged postcranial remains. Thus, we can suggest that this was a strepsirhine primate, but, without associated teeth or skull or taxonomically identifiable bones, the broader identity of which Eocene group or groups may have had a grooming claw remains unknown. Of the Eocene taxa, only among Adapidae is there a hint that the short crowns of the lower incisors are inclined forward into a miniature tooth comb, analogous to the diminished tooth combs of various subfossil lemurs.

But lest we think that, at least for the extant taxa, we can remain secure in an unquestionable security of the subordinal divisions Strepsirhini and Haplorhini, we must not forget about *Tarsius*. It possesses a grooming claw on its second pedal digit, which is more similar to the upright, conical grooming claw of lorisoids than lemurs. Even though it lacks a typical tooth comb, the tarsier's pair of lower anterior teeth are surprisingly similar in details of morphology—lateral flare, margocristid, central keel—to the lateral teeth of extant lemuriform tooth combs. And *Tarsius* can be compared quite favorably in dental and postcranial morphology with extant lorisoids, especially galagids and cheirogaleids.

Strepsirhini is, thus, well established as the larger taxon to which the modern tooth-combed prosimians belong. It may or may not be ultimately accepted that it embraces the living *Tarsius;* if it does, the name should be replaced by Illiger's Prosimii. The question as to which fossil taxa should be allocated to Strepsirhini seems set for indefinite debate.

See also Adapidae; Adapiformes; Anthropoidea; Cheirogaleidae; Galagidae; Haplorhini; Lemuriformes; Lemuroidea; Lorisidae; Lorisoidea; Lower Primates; Madagascar; Primates; Prosimian; Skull; Teeth. [J.H.S.]

Further Readings

Beard, K.C., Dagosto, M., Gebo, D.L., and Godinot, M. (1988) Interrelationships among primate higher taxa. Nature 331:712–714.

Hill, W.C.O. (1953) Primates: Comparative Anatomy, and Taxonomy, Vol. 1: Strepsirhini. Edinburgh: Edinburgh University Press.

Hill, W.C.O. (1955) Primates: Comparative Anatomy, and Taxonomy, Vol. 2: Haplorhini: *Tarsius.* Edinburgh: Edinburgh University Press.

Schwartz, J.H. (1984) What is a tarsier? In N. Eldredge and S.M. Stanley (eds.): Living Fossils. New York: Springer-Verlag, pp. 38–49.

Schwartz, J.H. (1986) Primate systematics and a classification of the order. In D.R. Swindler (ed.): Comparative Primate Biology, Vol. 1: Systematics, Evolution, and Anatomy. New York: Liss, pp. 1–41.

Schwartz, J.H. (1992) Issues in prosimian phylogeny and systematics. In S. Matano, R.H. Tuttle, H. Ishida, and M. Goodman (eds.): Topics in Primatology, Vol. 3: Evolutionary Biology, Reproductive Endocrinology, and Virology. Tokyo: University of Tokyo Press, pp. 23–36.

Schwartz, J.H., and Tattersall, I. (1985) Evolutionary relationships of living lemurs and lorises (Mammalia, Primates) and their potential affinities with European Eocene Adapidae. Anthropol. Pap. Am. Mus. Nat. Hist. 60:1–100.

Subfamily

Category of the classificatory hierarchy that falls immediately below the family. *The International Code of Zoological Nomenclature* requires that subfamily names end in the suffix "-inae." Informal use results in the ending "-ine," as in hominine for a member of Homininae. Thus, the informal term "australopithecine" implies the recognition of the formal subfamily Australopithecinae; as we do not recognize such a taxon, the informal "australopith" is used in this work.

See also Classification; Family; Nomenclature. [I.T.]

Subgenus

Category of the classificatory hierarchy that lies between the genus and the species and that is used to group species within genera. The subgenus name is formed by placing another latinized and italicized name in parentheses between the genus and the specific name as, for example, in *Hapalemur* (*Prolemur*) *simus.* The use of subgeneric designations is relatively rare in primate systematics.

See also Classification; Genus; Nomenclature; Species. [I.T.]

Suborder

Rank of the classificatory hierarchy lying immediately below the order and above the infraorder.

See also Classification; Infraorder; Order. [I.T.]

Subspecies

Units of classification within the species. Many species are *polytypic,* containing a number of recognizable variants in different geographical areas, and it is frequently useful to recognize these by formal names. A subspecies is named by adding a third latinized, italicized term at the end of the binomen denoting the species concerned, producing a *trinomen.* In this way, we arrive at subspecies names, such as *Eulemur fulvus rufus,* which designates a geographically discrete and readily recognizable variant of the species *Lemur fulvus,* a widely distributed inhabitant of Madagascar. In the human family, *Homo erectus pekinensis* is a subspecies name widely used to designate the "Peking Man" variant of *Homo erectus,* although it should be noted that, in general, subspecies of the same species in the living biota do not differ anatomically enough to be readily recognizable on the basis of the parts that are preserved in the fossil record.

While living subspecies are distinct and recognizable to the eye, however, they do not have a discrete identity in the way that species do. Conspecific subspecies owe their distinguishing characteristics to accidents of geographical separation and remain genetically compatible. When given the opportunity to interbreed, as when contact is reestablished, they will merge with one another. Thus, while any subspecies is a potential new species, speciation requires a genetic event that subspecies, by definition, have not undergone.

See also Classification; Nomenclature; Polytypic Variation; Speciation; Species; Systematics. [I.T.]

Subtribe

Category of the classificatory hierarchy that may be used between the genus and the tribe. No suffix is designated in the *International Code of Zoological Nomenclature*, but "-ina" is often used to terminate subtribe names. Informally, "-inan" may be employed, as in macacinan.

See also Classification; Genus; Tribe. [I.T.]

Sungir

Late Paleolithic open-air site at the outskirts of the city of Vladimir (Russia), dated to ca. 24 Ka. Archaeological remains include three burials with extremely rich grave goods. The skeletons of a 55–65-year-old male, a 7–9-year-old girl, and a 9–13-year-old boy were each covered with ca. 3,000 cut and drilled ivory beads (originally sewn onto their clothing) and with numerous pendants and necklaces of shell and animal teeth. Inventories found with the two juveniles, who were buried head to head in a joint grave, included numerous bone implements and ivory spears, including two that measured more than 2 m in length. Lithic inventories from Sungir are assigned to the Streletskaya industry.

See also Europe; Kostenki; Late Paleolithic; Mezhirich. [O.S.]

Superfamily

Highest of the family-group categories of the classificatory hierarchy, falling immediately below the hyporder (or below the infraorder in earlier classification schemes) and above the family. The *International Code of Zoological Nomenclature* recommends that all superfamily names end in the suffix "-oidea." Informal usage results in the ending "-oids," as in hominoids, for members of Hominoidea.

See also Classification; Family; Hyporder; Infraorder; Nomenclature. [I.T.]

Swanscombe

Open-air site in a gravel pit on a terrace of the Thames River in England from which Early Paleolithic archaeological assemblages and a hominid fossil have been recovered, together with artifacts and the remains of Middle Pleistocene mammals. Swanscombe contains a sequence of gravels and loams of late Middle Pleistocene age, probably dating to ca. 350–250 Ka. The Lower Loam horizon at the site contains Clactonian assemblages, and biostratigraphic analysis places these levels in the Hoxnian (Holstein, Mindel-Riss) interglacial. The Middle and Upper gravels, in which the hominid cranial remains were found, feature Acheulean assemblages in both Late Hoxnian interglacial and Early Wolstonian (Saale, Riss) glacial strata.

In 1935, an occipital bone was discovered in the upper Middle Gravels, followed by the left parietal of the same individual a year later, and the right parietal in 1955. The bones are thick by modern standards, but the occipital torus

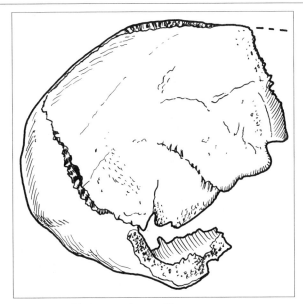

Lateral view of the Swanscombe partial braincase.

is only slightly developed, as are the muscle insertions, leading to the suggestion that the skull belonged to a female. The brain size of the Swanscombe woman was probably ca. 1,325 ml, and the overall cranial shape is rather modern, without the characteristic occipital angulation and torus development found in more archaic hominids or the bulging occipital plane found in many Neanderthals. Parietal curvature is rather flattened, however, with a short midsagittal length, while the occipital bone is broad, as in many archaic hominids. Three features, in particular, point to Neanderthal affinities. These are the gracile and double-arched occipital torus, the presence above the torus of a central depression (the suprainiac fossa), and the suggestion at the occipital margins that there was a developed juxtamastoid eminence. It seems likely that the Swanscombe woman was a member of an early Neanderthal population that lived in Europe in the Middle Pleistocene. Related fossils may include those from Pontnewydd (Wales), Biache (France), and Steinheim (Germany). The dating of the Swanscombe site and the Swanscombe hominid remain problematic. The whole stratigraphic sequence appears to postdate the local Anglian glaciation, indicating a post-oxygen-isotope Stage 12 age (c. 400 Ka or less), but it is unclear whether one or more interglacial cycles are represented in the Clactonian-to-Acheulean sequence of industries at the site.

See also Acheulean; Archaic Homo sapiens; Biache-St. Vaast; Clactonian; Europe; Glaciation; Neanderthals; Pontnewydd; Presapiens; Steinheim. [C.B.S., J.J.S.]

Swartkrans

South African karst-cave breccia deposit in dolomitic limestone located north of the Bloubank River, ca. 2 km northwest of the site of Sterkfontein. Fossil bones were recovered from the site during lime-mining operations in the 1930s, and the first hominid specimen was discovered by R. Broom and J.T. Robinson in 1948. This specimen was described in

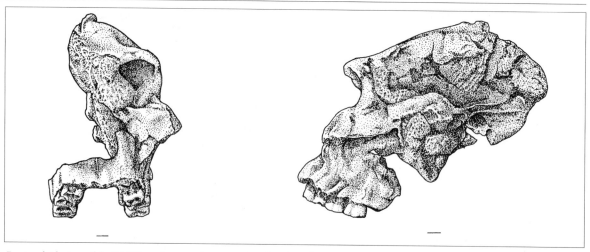

Front and side views of the SK 46 Paranthropus robustus *cranium from Swartkrans. Scales are 1 cm.*

1949 by Broom, who attributed it to a novel species of the "robust australopithecine" genus *Paranthropus,* namely *P. crassidens.* Although a few workers have resuscitated this species, most paleoanthropologists consider that the material is not specifically distinct from the Kromdraai *P. robustus.* Work by Broom and Robinson (1948–1949), Robinson (1951–1953), and, most recently, the extensive and meticulous excavations by C.K. Brain (1965–1986) have resulted in the recovery of the remains of more than 100 individuals of *P. robustus.* In 1949, Robinson discovered a fossil mandible of a more "advanced" early human, which Broom and he named *Telanthropus capensis.* Subsequent work by Broom, Robinson, and Brain has produced the remains of six individuals of what is now termed *Homo* sp. (probably cf. *Homo habilis* in Member 1 and cf. *Homo erectus* in Member 2). The *Homo* fossils derive from the same stratigraphic units as the *Paranthropus* remains. Thus, Swartkrans provided the first conclusive evidence for the contemporaneity of *Homo* and *Paranthropus,* since confirmed in the Koobi Fora and Shungura formations of the Lake Turkana sequence of East Africa.

Two sedimentary members were recognized and formally named by K. Butzer in 1976. At that time, the known *Paranthropus* fossils came only from the earlier Member 1 breccia, while *Homo* remains were known from both Members 1 and 2. The further work by Brain has resulted in the recognition of seven distinct units arrayed in five successive members: the Member 1 "Hanging Remnant," originally excavated as the "Pink Breccia" by Broom and Robinson (the source of most of the *Paranthropus* fossils); the Member 1 "Lower Bank" deposits, which have been recognized as the outer-cave equivalent of the Hanging Remnant; the calcified Member 2 breccia, originally sampled by Broom and Robinson and the source of the type mandible of "*Telanthropus capensis*" (cataloged as SK 15); together with the decalcified Member 2 deposits, from which both *Paranthropus* and *Homo* fossils have been recovered by Brain; Member 3, which contains several *Paranthropus* teeth together with burnt bone; Member 4, which yields Middle Stone Age artifacts; and Member 5, which is dominated by the bones of the extinct springbok, *Antidorcas bondi.*

While the Member 1 Hanging Remnant breccia has provided very few lithic artifacts, these are strikingly abundant in the Member 1 Lower Bank deposits, and these lightly calcified sediments have also yielded bone tools, characterized by smooth, tapering points. Ca. 60 of these bone tools were recovered from Members 1, 2, and 3 by Brain, who demonstrated that they were most probably used as digging implements to extract edible bulbs and tubers from the ground in the vicinity of the cave. The lithic artifacts from Members 1, 2, and 3 do not differ significantly from one another, and they may be assigned to a core/chopper/flake (Mode 1, or Oldowan) tradition, although there are hints that a biface technology might also be associated in Members 2 and 3. Several bones, predominantly from Member 3, also display the clear indications of having been cut by stone tools.

In 1984, Brain uncovered the first of 270 burnt bone pieces from Member 3, including two bone tools made of horncores and a hominid phalanx, which had been heated to various degrees. His experimental work with A. Sillen has demonstrated clearly that some of these bones were subjected to the prolonged, very high temperatures that are reached in campfires. The nonhominid vertebrate remains from Members 1, 2, and 3 suggest a relatively consistent fauna throughout the depositional history of these units. These bones suggest that the paleoenvironment remained relatively constant as well, with indications of high-veld grassland together with riverine woodland savannah conditions, and a Bloubank River that would have been considerably more substantial than at present.

The fauna from Members 1, 2, and 3 is of similar taxonomic composition, suggesting a date of between ca. 1.8 and 1.5 Ma for these units. Moreover, there are no appreciable differences among the numerous *Paranthropus robustus* fossils from these three strata. Bones of *Antidorcas bondi* from Member 5 have yielded radiocarbon (^{14}C) dates of ca. 11 Ka.

See also: Africa; Africa, Southern; Breccia Cave Formation; Broom, Robert; Fire; Homo erectus; Homo habilis; Oldowan; Paranthropus; Paranthropus robustus; Robinson, John Talbot. [F.E.G.]

Further Readings

Brain, C.K. (1981) The Hunters or the Hunted? An Intro-
    duction to African Cave Taphonomy. Chicago: Uni-
    versity of Chicago Press.

Brain, C.K. (1993) Swartkrans: A Cave's Chronicle of Early
    Man (Transvaal Museum Monograph No. 8). Pretoria:
    Transvaal Museum.

Brain, C.K., and Sillen, A. (1988) Evidence from the
    Swartkrans Cave for the earliest use of fire. Nature
    336:464–466.

Synonym(y)

Synonyms are different Linnaean names applied to the same taxon. The valid name for any animal taxon, the one that must be used for it, is the oldest name applied to it that conforms to the requirements of the *International Code of Zoological Nomenclature*. The valid name is the *senior* synonym; all others subsequently applied to the same taxon are known as *junior* synonyms and are not used in reference to the animal in question. When two forms formerly thought to have been distinct are discovered to be, in fact, the same, they are placed in synonymy, and the senior synonym becomes the valid name for the inclusive taxon. Thus *Pithecanthropus* Dubois, 1894 is a synonym of *Homo* Linnaeus, 1758.

See also Classification; Nomenclature; Priority; Taxon; Taxonomy. [I.T.]

Systematics

Study of the diversity of life and of the relationships among taxa, living and fossil, at the various levels of the taxonomic hierarchy. The late American paleontologist G.G. Simpson pointed out that systematics is at once the most elementary and the most inclusive component of zoology: The most elementary because any discussion of living things is dependent on some degree of systematization having been carried out, and the most inclusive because information gained from virtually every branch of biology can eventually contribute to the solution of systematic problems.

The primary goal of zoological systematists is to order the diversity of animal life into sets based on the relationships between the myriad kinds of animal. Early systematists arranged organisms into groups on the basis of the common similarities they saw among them, and the system of classification of living things introduced by the Swedish systematist C. Linnaeus in the mid-eighteenth century reflected his perception that a hierarchy exists in nature, a hierarchy reflected in the way that organisms seem naturally to fall into ever more inclusive sets. Human beings, for example, group naturally with the other higher primates at one level, with Primates as a whole at another, with all mammals at a yet higher level, and so on. Hence, the various ranks of Linnaeus's classificatory scheme—species, genera, families, orders—become ever more inclusive as one ascends the hierarchy of his classificatory system: Genera belong to families, families to orders, orders to phyla.

Following the advent of evolutionary thought in the mid-nineteenth century, the basis for this natural nesting of groups of organisms became apparent: The hierarchy of similarities among organisms results from varying propinquity of descent. Closely related organisms share many similarities because they inherited them from a recent common ancestor; more distantly related forms share fewer similarities because more evolutionary change has taken place in their respective lineages since a remoter common ancestry.

All modern systematists agree on the evolutionary basis for the order seen in nature. There is much disagreement, however, on how best to proceed in uncovering and classifying this order. Over the years, many schools of thought have emerged on how best to reconstruct the relationships among the various components of the living world and on how to classify them. Some systematists favor quantitative methods, others qualitative; some group organisms on the basis of general similarity, while others insist that only certain kinds of resemblance are of value in reconstructing evolutionary relationships.

Despite the misleading similarity in the names involved, the most important division between opposing schools of systematic thought is that between the *evolutionary systematists* and the *phylogenetic* (cladistic) *systematists* (or cladists). Both seek to order organisms into natural groups on the basis of shared *homologous* similarities, those inherited from a common ancestor. The phylogenetic systematists, however, insist that only *derived* homologous states, those representing unique *evolutionary novelties* acquired and passed along by the common ancestor, may be used in recognizing natural groups. In other words, in reconstructing evolutionary histories they reject the use of *primitive* similarities inherited from a remote common ancestor that also gave rise to descendants not belonging to the monophyletic group immediately under consideration. Phylogenetic schemes and classifications put forth by evolutionary systematists, on the other hand, tend to depend on overall resemblance between organisms rather than on inferred strict branching sequences in phylogeny. Since new characters tend to accumulate more rapidly in some lineages than in others, application of the two approaches can, on occasion, produce strikingly different phylogenies and classifications. Purely phenetic phylogenies produced by numerical taxonomists and others can be different yet, and differ among themselves.

See also Cladistics; Classification; Evolution; Evolutionary Systematics (Darwinian Phylogenetics); Monophyly; Numerical Taxonomy; Phenetics; Phylogeny; Simpson, George Gaylord; Stratophenetics; Taxonomy. [I.T.]

Further Readings

Eldredge, N., and Cracraft, J. (1980) Phylogenetic Patterns
    and the Evolutionary Process. New York: Columbia
    University Press.

Mayr, E. (1969) Principles of Systematic Zoology. New
    York: McGraw-Hill.

Simpson, G.G. (1961) Principles of Animal Taxonomy.
    New York: Columbia University Press.

Szeletian

Early Upper Paleolithic industry, dating to ca. 30 Ka, found in central Europe and named after the Szeleta Cave in the Bükk Mountains in northeastern Hungary, where it was first identified. It contains diagnostic bifacially worked leaf points and occasional split-base bone points together with Mousterian tool forms. Some scholars see the Mousterian component reflecting local evolution of the Upper Paleolithic, from the Middle Paleolithic; others interpret the evidence as indicating acculturation of Middle Paleolithic toolmakers to the advent of people making Upper Paleolithic (Aurignacian) tools; and still others suggest that the combination of tool types resulted from mixing of the different levels during excavation. Finally, it may also be that the Szeletian bifacial implements were just parts of specialized tool kits made and used by Aurignacian toolmakers.

Further Readings

Allsworth-Jones, P. (1986) The Szeletian and the Transition from Middle to Upper Palaeolithic in Central Europe. Oxford: Claredon Press.

See also Aurignacian; Châtelperronian; Europe; Istállöskö; Mousterian; Solutrean. [O.S.]

T

Tabūn

Deep cave at the entrance to the Wadi el-Mughara (Valley of the Caves) on the western escarpment of Mount Carmel (Israel). Tabūn Cave was first excavated between 1929 and 1934 by a team led by D. Garrod, later excavated by A. Jelinek between 1967 and 1973, and since the 1980s has been excavated by A. Ronen. Tabūn's extraordinarily deep (more than 20 m) series of occupations furnishes a model for the Early and Middle Paleolithic cultural succession in the Levant. Tabūn has yielded hominid fossils from Middle Paleolithic deposits.

The upper levels of the cave, Garrod's Levels B–D, comprise sandy silt and rocks deposited through a "chimney" in the roof of the cave and contain Levantine Mousterian lithic assemblages that Levantine prehistorians use as a model of the cultural succession in the Levant. Tabūn B, which comprises terra rosa sediments and much roof fall, features cores with primarily unidirectional-convergent preparation and high percentages of Levallois points and blades. Tabūn C, which comprises ashy sediments and roof fall, features cores with centripetal preparation, large numbers of broad, oval Levallois flakes, and many retouched tools. Tabūn D, a more sandy stratum, contains cores with unidirectional and bi-directional preparation, numerous elongated Levallois points, and blades. The lowest levels of the cave, Garrod's Levels E–G, comprise sandy sediments and contain Acheuleo-Jabrudian or Mugharan (Level E), Acheulean (Level F), and a poorly known Tabunian/Tayacian (Level G).

Most prehistorians traditionally assigned the Levantine Mousterian from Tabūn to 90–40 Ka. New thermoluminescence (TL) and electron-spin-resonance (ESR) dates, however, suggest a much greater antiquity, with the Levantine Mousterian spanning the period 180–50 Ka (ESR) or 270–50 Ka (TL).

The hominid fossils from Tabūn include a female Neanderthal skeleton (Tabūn 1) and a mandible, probably of a male (Tabūn 2), from Level C; a femoral diaphysis from Level E; and numerous isolated teeth, mainly from Level B. Tabūn 1 is the reasonably complete skeleton of an adult female with a relatively small skull (capacity ca. 1,300 ml) and body. Brow development is strong, and, although the occipi-

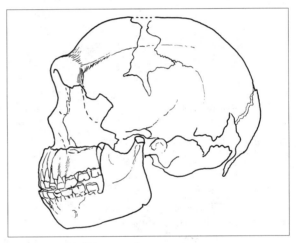

Lateral view of the Tabūn 1 cranium.

tal region is rather rounded, the specimen is clearly of Neanderthal type. The skeleton was the first one in which the unusual pubic-bone morphology characteristic of Neanderthals was recognized. The stratigraphic position of this fossil has been a major problem in Levantine prehistory. Garrod recorded the provenance of this fossil as the top of Level C, although she noted that the possibility of it being intrusive from Level B could not be ruled out. Jelinek has argued that Tabūn 1 could come from Level D. The separate mandible of Tabūn 2 is large, but it displays a slight chin and only small retromolar spaces. Its phyletic status and classification are less clear than those of Tabūn 1.

See also Acheulean; Amud Cave; Asia, Western; Garrod, Dorothy Anne Elizabeth; Kebara; Levallois; Mousterian; Mugharan; Neanderthals; Qafzeh; Skhūl; Tabunian; Tayacian. [J.J.S., C.B.S.]

Further Readings

Bar-Yosef, O. (1995) The Lower and Middle Palaeolithic in the Mediterranean Levant: Chronology and cultural entities. In H. Ullrich (ed.): Man and Environment in the Palaeolithic. E.R.A.U.L. 62:247–263.

Garrod, D.A., and D.M.A. Bate, eds. (1937) The Stone Age of Mount Carmel, Vol. 1: Excavations in the Wadi el-Mughara. Oxford: Clarendon.

Grün, R. (1993) Electron spin resonance dating in paleoanthropology. Evol. Anthropol. 2:172–181.

Jelinek, A. (1982) The Tabūn Cave and Paleolithic man in the Levant. Science 216:1369–1375.

Mercier, N., and Valladas, H. (1994) Thermoluminescence dates for the Palaeolithic Levant. In O. Bar-Yosef and R.S. Kra (eds.): Late Quaternary Chronology and Paleoclimates of the Eastern Mediterranean. Cambridge: American School of Prehistoric Research, pp. 13–20.

Tabunian

Name formerly given to an Early Paleolithic industry without handaxes found in Level G of Tabūn Cave, Mount Carmel (Israel). This industry has been compared to the French Tayacian, but the small samples of artifacts from Tabūn Level G, and the technological simplicity of the tools thus far recovered (essentially limited to pebble-cores, flakes, and a few simple retouched tools), preclude any precise assessment of its typological affinities. This term is no longer generally used by Southwest Asian prehistorians. Instead, most use the name Tayacian or Tayacian/Tabunian.

See also Asia, Western; Early Paleolithic; Tayacian. [J.J.S]

Tail

Humans and apes lack an external tail, but most other primates have them, and there is no doubt that protohominoid ancestors possessed a tail prior to ca. 25 Ma. There is debate as to whether a tail was still present in *Proconsul* species of the East African Early Miocene (23–15 Ma); at least one skeletal fragment has been interpreted as documenting the loss, but some authors question the identification.

The lowest part of the human vertebral column, the coccyx, is the bony remnant of the tail of our ancestors, and the muscles that support our pelvic organs from below are modified versions of the same muscles that move the tail in other primates. Most primates that are arboreal quadrupeds or leapers have a long tail. This appendage appears to serve primarily as an organ for maintaining balance during walking, running, and leaping in trees. In several of the larger New World monkeys, the tail is prehensile and is used as a "fifth limb" to grasp branches and food. In many of these species, this fifth limb lacks fur on the ventral surface. Rather, the skin has dermatoglyphics similar to the fingerprints found on the grasping surfaces of the hands and feet.

More terrestrial species often have relatively shorter tails, and several macaque species have lost the external projection altogether, which results in their being termed *apes* (e.g., *Macaca sylvanus*, the Barbary ape, and *M. nigra*, the Celebes black ape). Loss of the tail in suspensory primates, including the ape and human lineage, seems to be the result of two factors: Suspensory species do not need this organ for balance, and because they frequently adopt upright postures,

they can further benefit from rearrangement of the tail structures to support the pelvis from below.

See also Atelinae; Cebinae; Cercopithecinae; Locomotion; Proconsulidae; Skeleton. [J.G.F.]

Takamori

Area of Early Paleolithic open air sites in Miyagi Prefecture, in Northern Honshu, Japan which were discovered and excavated in the late 1980's and 1990's. Stratified within and below several meters of volcanic soils, the oldest levels of Takamori and nearby Kamitakamori are dated to ca. 500 Ka by several techniques including thermoluminescence (TL), optically stimulated luminescence (OSL), tephrochronology and a unique method of phytological seriation based on ratios of cold-adapted to warm-adapted species of bamboo. The dates appear internally consistant with other ages in the Japanese Paleolithic sequence. Particularly interesting at Kamitakamori are four storage pits dug into one of the oldest levels (16) containing carefully laid-out arrangements of small bifaces, rare in the Far East. The bifaces appear to have served as adzes, rather than points or axes, and are made on a range of exotic materials in several colors–red, blue, and grey, possibly representing early evidence of symbolic behavior, as well as complex procurement strategies for raw materials.

See also Acheulean; Asia, Eastern and Southern; Biface; Early Paleolithic; Movius' Line; Stone Tool Making. [A.S.B.]

Talgai

Australia's first human fossil, found after the floods of 1886 on the Darling Downs, Queensland. Now thought to date to at least 12 Ka, the cranium is that of an adolescent and is notable for its thickened vault bone, receding forehead, and large, protruding face with large teeth. These features characterize the "robust," or Java-like, Pleistocene morph that is found across Australia and believed to be the major genetic basis for modern Australians.

See also Australia. [A.T.]

Taphonomy

Taphonomy, the study of the processes affecting organic remains prior to fossilization, began as an ancillary field to paleoecology. The Russian geologist I.A. Efremov originated the term in 1940 to identify what he called the "transition of animal remains from the biosphere into the lithosphere." The word derives from the Greek *taphos*, ("burial") and *nomos* ("law").

Taphonomy considers two basic facts of paleontology. The first fact is that fossils (with rare exceptions such as insects in amber or animals smothered by volcanic ash or sandstorms) normally do not preserve the organism as it was precisely at the moment of death. Ancillary to this is the fact that fossil assemblages, likewise, are not (usually) the instantaneously preserved living communities. Animal fossils are just the remains of decomposed individuals, commonly the hardest parts, that become buried in sediments. In the case of vertebrates, we face the problem of discovering the meaning of piles of broken bones, in biological terms. To answer this question, and to reconstruct the paleoecology of these creatures with any confidence, we must assess the degree to which fossil assemblages constitute representative samples of the communities of animals from which they were derived.

Taphonomy encompasses a number of other concerns, some of which were already being debated when the word was invented. German scientists in the 1920s had coined a few relevant terms, such as *biostratonomy* (the study of the embedding of fossils in sediments) and *aktuo-* or *aktualpaläontologie* (the investigations of modern remains of animals in the contemporary environment). The goal of aktuopaläontologie, in particular, was to discover and understand the environments and events for which fossils are the only remaining evidence. This is really no more than a branch of actualism, or C. Lyell's uniformitarianism: the idea that the present is the key to the past.

Most of this early work concerned animals in the marine environment, but, in the early 1960s, E.C. Olson reintroduced the word *taphonomy* in his consideration of Late Permian terrestrial vertebrates of the United States and the (former) USSR. He stressed its importance and the need to keep it distinct from paleoecology, although the two subjects were closely related.

The science of taphonomy has developed along fairly independent lines around the world and has focused on slightly different subjects, depending mostly on the paleontological interests of the investigator. Much research in taphonomy has been carried out with a particular problem in mind, often of a paleoecological nature, beginning as a reaction to some other concern. The intention has often been to rectify preservational bias in an assemblage so as to reveal matters of paleoecological interest or to allow the assumptions and limitations of paleoecological conjecture to be more clearly stated.

Taphonomy is sometimes described as the study and evaluation of *information loss*. Others, however, see it as *information gain*, because the state of fossil material may provide unique data about the agents that cause preservational bias. Often, the agent of modification or collection can be of as much paleoecological interest as the fossil remains themselves.

This positive approach has led to investigations that are less disparate and more united in their aims. Such work has generated much basic information that has permitted the formulation of more general rules and principles that find wider application. Consequently, the relevance of taphonomy to matters other than paleoecology is also becoming realized. In a more recent and broader formulation, as the study of ways in which preservation affects the fossil record, it has important implications for biostratigraphy and evolutionary questions.

Subject Matter of Taphonomy

Efremov's simple description of taphonomy as the transition of animals from the biosphere to the lithosphere, although accurate, is operationally difficult because there are so many ways in which animals can become fossils.

A more direct, and perhaps more objective, approach to the practice of taphonomy is to enumerate and then explain the differences between fossil collections and living communities of animals. Most questions about sites and assemblages can then be framed and possibly answered in terms of these differences. For vertebrates, the most relevant organisms for hominid sites, they include the following: the animals are dead; there are usually no soft parts preserved; the skeletons are often disarticulated; bones are often concentrated together; bones are mostly damaged; parts of the skeleton occur in proportions different from their occurrence in life; remains are buried in sediment or other rock; bones are sometimes preferentially oriented within the rock; bones are altered chemically.

The list only partly illustrates the scope of taphonomy. For one thing, these distinctions all apply to individual animals. The question of how whole communities are represented in the fossil record also involves the association of different species and their numbers or relative proportions, or the numbers of individuals of different age or sex groups within each species.

There are two complementary lines of approach for tackling these issues. One, which could be referred to as *paleotaphonomy*, examines the content and context of fossil or archaeological sites in greater detail than has been usual. Another, *neotaphonomy*, is close to the idea of aktuopaläontologie and concentrates on the modern environment to find analogies to fossil situations. This can be in the form of observations of modern situations where bones naturally accumulate, such as a hyena den, and preferably in an environment where the modern animals are reasonably well known, permitting the relation between the modern bone assemblage and the community from which it is derived to be more easily understood. Alternatively, the work may be more experimental in nature, perhaps in laboratory situations, to study the effect of a limited and controlled range of specific processes on bones or standard forms. For example, experiments have been performed with flume tanks, or artificial stream tables, to investigate the effects of moving water on different skeletal elements and different kinds of bones.

The resolution of taphonomical studies extends from highly detailed work on specific fossil sites, from microstratigraphy or the analysis of microscopic scratches on bone, to matters on a much larger scale. Some environments, for example, are much more likely to preserve bone than are others. Fossils may have been more likely to be preserved at particular times in the past than during others. Such factors as these directly pertain to large-scale issues of paleobiogeography and evolution.

Taphonomy and the Hominid Record

Taphonomic factors clearly affect the nature of the hominid fossil record. On a global scale, taphonomical considerations largely constrain the availability of sites where hominids may be preserved. East Africa is famous for fossil sites in the Rift Valley, where a combination of richly productive habitats surrounding highly alkaline and rapidly subsiding sedimentary basins that were periodically flooded with lavas produced conditions highly favorable to the accumulation and preservation of bone. This rather unusual set of circumstances has had an undue impact on interpretations of the distribution of hominids on a world scale. In the rest of Africa and Eurasia, the right geological and paleoenvironmental conditions—basically, those in which the factors promoting the accumulation of fossiliferous strata were present and in which, at the same time, hominids were numerous—were much more limited. From this point of view, the abundance and diversity of fossil hominids in the East African fossil record obviously reflects local taphonomical rather than regional paleobiological factors.

Taphonomical factors have their effects on the distribution of hominids in time as well, and this, in turn, affects not only paleoecological inference but also how we see evolution as having taken place. If so many circumstances conspire to influence the preservation of a fossil, how can we know how accurately the first and last occurrences of the fossils of a particular species in the stratigraphic record actually represent the time of its local appearance and disappearance, let alone its true time of biological appearance and its final extinction worldwide? Taphonomy helps answer questions of time resolution in the fossil record that are essential for understanding the mode of evolution, such as discriminating between punctuated or gradualistic models. Taphonomy is also vital to questions of the influence of external forcing factors on evolution. It may provide insight into the question of whether events of speciation and climate that appear contemporaneous in the fossil record are truly synchronous.

On a finer scale, the contribution of taphonomy to paleoanthropology is to expose the factors that control and modify bone assemblages, to distinguish natural effects from the effects of human behavior. Paleoanthropologists and archaeologists have a vital interest in the accumulations of bone that may represent the food debris of hominids, as evidence of technology, domestication, social structure, and foraging strategies. Since the late 1960s, a good deal of taphonomical work, mainly in Africa, has specifically aimed at understanding hominid sites and behavior. Fundamental anthropological problems addressed by taphonomy include the identification of sites as having been produced by hominids; the recognition of bone tools; the determination of whether early hominids were hunters or scavengers; the analysis of butchery practices; the identification of human-inflicted vs. natural violence on human remains; the description of the meat component of the diet; and the distinctions between domesticated vs. hunted items. At the same time, taphonomy is valuable for critically examining the often wildly exaggerated claims of human activity in newly discovered bone assemblages.

These issues are often interrelated. The first of them, the identification of sites as having been produced by hominids, is fundamental. It applies particularly, but not exclusively, to early hominid localities: How is hominid involvement in a site to be recognized? This question has arisen a number of times since the beginning of the nineteenth century. A classic recent example relates to South African cave sites where australopiths have been found. Were the bones associated with the early hominids collected by them, or were they, along with the hominids, the food remains of carnivores? The

recognition of the australopith remains as predator garbage involved some of the earliest serious taphonomical work on hominids, carried out by C.K. Brain, among others.

Normally, for an occurrence to be regarded as a site, bones must be present in some quantity. The problem of the objective differences between a fossil collection and a living community initially relates to the concentration of remains: What processes result in bones becoming accumulated together? Not only hominids but also other carnivores, such as hyenas and leopards, collect bones, and a good deal of taphonomical work has studied such animals, distinguishing their collections from others. Flowing water also concentrates bones, prompting research on the effect of moving water on different parts of the skeleton. In practice, the question of bone-collecting agency leads to a close study of some of the other objective differences, notably damage to bones and the differential representation of skeletal parts. These factors, such as carnivores and moving water, leave their imprint on bone collections, but how do their effects differ from those of hominids?

Two of the notable features of the South African cave collections were the markedly different proportions in which parts of the animal skeletons were represented and the fact that the remains were broken in consistently repeated ways. R.A. Dart suggested, plausibly at the time (the 1940s), that the bones were the deliberately selected and modified tools and weapons of the hominids. Taphonomical work has since shown that the different proportions can be explained by such factors as the relative robusticity of different bones, their specific gravity, and the time of epiphysis fusion. The anomaly does not require human intervention. These factors also explain the characteristic patterns of damage, and, nowadays, with increasing knowledge of bone breakage by nonhuman agencies, researchers are generally much more critical of claims concerning bone tools.

A more recent example of this issue concerns the peopling of the New World. The earliest putative evidence for the arrival of humans in North America takes the form of bones claimed to show the effects of human working, some of them alleged to be artifacts. Taphonomical work on bone damage assists in discriminating between human agencies and other factors potentially responsible for creating these bone objects. In neither of these cases, the South African cave sites and the North American occurrences, have damaged bones been found with stone tools. Association of bones with artifacts has traditionally been axiomatic in affirming hominid involvement at a site, but even this criterion has come into question, some regarding certain associations as fortuitous. This objection has resulted in increased subtlety in taphonomical analysis, which has, for example, established microscopic distinctions between scratch marks produced by humans using stone tools and marks made by teeth of other carnivores. In turn, this endeavor has led to attempts to discriminate between scavenging and hunting behavior on the part of early hominids.

Inferences concerning the butchery practices of early humans here come into play, and the matter is a more explicit object of inquiry in other contexts. Part of the process of butchery is the dismemberment of carcasses. It is interesting to discover the ways in which skeletons fall apart under natural conditions and to compare this information with sequences of disarticulation deduced from archaeological sites. It appears that, like damage to bones, it is the nature of the skeleton that fundamentally controls sequences of dismemberment rather than the idiosyncrasies of any external agent. Consequently, human butchery practices are sometimes less distinctive than has been supposed.

Evidence of breakage and damage to human bones has been called upon to answer questions regarding human violence to other humans. Apparently unusual fractures on human specimens have frequently been attributed to violent or cannibalistic behavior. Rarely were they considered in the context of other possible causes. Taphonomy has demonstrated the need for caution in such assertions, refining the analysis of human remains in this respect.

Other anthropological issues rely upon the ability to answer questions regarding the numbers, or at least the relative proportions, of different species in an assemblage or paleocommunity. These questions are particularly difficult to answer because they require far more information about relative taxonomic and skeletal preservation if our reconstructions are to be treated with any confidence. Among these problems is the perennial one of estimating the relative amount of different meat food items at an archaeological site and what this means in terms of diet. Many of the obvious questions, such as how much meat of each particular species is consumed and how often, are hard to answer. Taphonomical work is helpful primarily by being critical of rash suggestions but also by providing positive information about the time interval represented by the accumulation of bones at particular sites.

Inferences about animal domestication and hunting also sometimes depend upon an estimation of the relative proportions of different age groups in a bone assemblage, and here again taphonomical factors are important. It is essential to be able to assess the relative survivorship of skeletons from animals of different individual age.

Taphonomy Today

These examples show, in brief, the relevance of taphonomy to important paleoanthropological issues. Most of our information about past hominids comes from fossil sites, and the essence of taphonomy is to understand the true nature of our data. Taphonomy began by assimilating procedures and information that many scientists were already considering. Is it simply, as someone once insisted, just a matter of doing paleoecology properly? Partly, but not entirely: By drawing together relevant information from a variety of fields, taphonomy focuses attention on an area that is not otherwise adequately examined. In the past, interpretation of bone assemblages associated with hominids was anthropocentric, with little concern for the many other natural processes involved in the formation of such accumulations. Today, a large number of studies with an explicitly taphonomical orientation have produced a formidable body of information regarding the nature and dynamics of such processes. Workers are coming to see this information as

being applicable to much broader problems that rely on the interpretation of the fossil and archaeological records, involving not just paleoecology but global paleobiogeography and the mode and tempo of evolution. Present-day taphonomical work is decreasingly a reaction to narrow problems at particular sites, although this remains valuable, and is increasingly designed to formulate rules, almost the laws Efremov hoped for, that are of much more general applicability.

See also Ethnoarchaeology; Fossil; Paleobiogeography; Sterkfontein. [A.H.]

Further Readings

Andrews, P. (1990) Owls, Caves and Fossils. Chicago: University of Chicago Press.

Behrensmeyer, A.K., and Hill, A. (1980) Fossils in the Making. Chicago: University of Chicago Press.

Behrensmeyer, A.K., and Kidwell, S.M. (1985) Taphonomy's contribution to paleobiology. Paleobiology 11:105–119.

Brain, C.K. (1981) The Hunters or the Hunted? An Introduction to African Cave Taphonomy. Chicago: University of Chicago Press.

Hill, A. (1978) Taphonomical background to fossil man. In W.W. Bishop (ed.): Geological Background to Fossil Man. London: Geol. Soc. London, pp. 87–101.

Lyman, R.L. (1994) Vertebrate Taphonomy. Cambridge: Cambridge University Press.

Shipman, P. (1981) The Life History of a Fossil. Cambridge, Mass.: Harvard University Press.

Tardenoisian

Third stage in the classic Mesolithic/Epipaleolithic sequence of inland France, ca. 8–6 Ka or possibly later, named after the type site of Fère-en-Tardenois. It is distinguished from earlier industries by the presence of geometric microliths, microburin technique, scalene triangles, trapezoids, and points with concave bases. The term is sometimes used to describe industries with geometric microliths from other regions, such as eastern Europe, as well as to distinguish northern French sites (Tardenoisian) from southern ones (Sauveterrian).

See also Azilian; Bow and Arrow; Epipaleolithic; Europe; Mesolithic; Sauveterrian; Stone-Tool Making. [A.S.B.]

Tarsiidae

Family of tarsiiform haplorhine primates represented today only by the living tarsier. No other modern primate presents as many radical anatomical specializations as the tarsiers, a group of four to six living species assigned to the genus *Tarsius*. And no other primate, except for humans and australopiths, has stimulated as much controversy. The tarsier's remarkable morphology enables an unusual, nocturnal predatory lifestyle, making the genus sufficiently divergent overall to warrant a taxonomic placement in its own family. Such a claim is reserved here for only one other living primate, the Malagasy aye-aye (*Daubentonia*), although many would obviously also rank *Homo* and its fossil allies in a unique family.

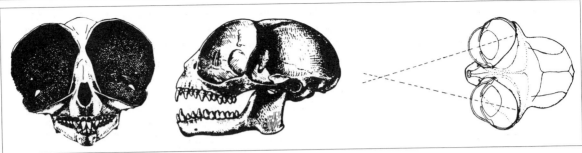

Frontal, lateral, and dorsal views of the tarsier skull with the eyeballs and optical axes shown in the latter. Courtesy of Alfred L. Rosenberger.

Tarsiers occur in the Philippines and on some islands of the Malay Archipelago, including Borneo, Sumatra, Sulawesi, and other minor islands in the chain. How long they have been isolated there, cut off from continental Asia, is unknown. Their peculiarities may or may not have an Early Cenozoic origin. Perhaps they evolved fairly recently and rapidly, partly in response to their relict distribution. Fossil tarsiids are still poorly known, by scrappy dental material from the Miocene of Thailand, the Eocene of China, and perhaps the Oligocene of Egypt.

Once it became clear that these phantomlike, long-legged mammals were not related to jerboas (Rodentia) or opossums (Marsupialia), as some early naturalists believed, tarsiers became the focus of a lively systematic debate, which continues. The discussion involves objective issues, such as the tarsier's correct genealogical position within the order Primates, as well as the subjective concerns and disagreements over the philosophies of classification and the methods of paleobiological reconstruction. The scope and the intensity of this dispute are a reflection of the problem: Morphologically aberrant taxa are difficult to comprehend evolutionarily, and at stake is the very basic picture of primate evolution during the Cenozoic. The two predominant views regarding classification are that tarsiids should be placed either with the lemur-loris *prosimian* group or, alternatively, with the anthropoids. Advocates of the latter view assign tarsiers and anthropoids to a larger taxonomic group, the *haplorhines,* and place the lemurs and lorises in the *strepsirhines.* This position presumes that tarsiers are the closest living relatives of the anthropoids, a point that is almost unanimously accepted by specialists. History, however, shows a preference for their classification in Prosimii, and many still adhere to this, both to preserve consistency and because they think that classifications need not mirror phylogeny so exactly. Some would argue further that tarsiers represent a prosimian grade of evolutionary progress equivalent to that of lemurs and lorises. Another relatively recent view, now essentially discarded, is that tarsiers are the only surviving descendants of the Paleocene group Plesiadapiformes. That view has been expressed in classifications that contrast "plesitarsiforms" and "simiolemuriforms" as phylogenetic sister groups.

Tarsiers are specialized, nocturnal, saltatory predators, a complex adaptation involving a number of anatomical systems. But none are so specialized as the visual system. Relative to body size, tarsiers have the largest eyes of any living mammal. Greatly enlarged eye sockets dominate the mor-

phology of the skull. A bony flangelike rim makes up the upper and lateral perimeter of the orbit as if to collar the huge eyes, each eyeball alone exceeding the mass of the brain. The eyes' receptor cells are all of the rod type, sensitive to low levels of light; color-sensitive cones are absent. As in owls and some deep-sea fishes, eye-socket shape is somewhat tubular, and each is set directly forward to provide a high degree of binocularity. Even given the large size of the eye socket, a tarsier's eye is larger still. More than half of it protrudes beyond the bone underneath the lid, so that the animal's face gives an unusually soft, rounded appearance. Because the eyes are too large to be moved efficiently by their extrinsic muscles, the whole skull is delicately balanced on the spine to facilitate accurate head-scanning maneuvers, including the capacity to swivel the head around, owl-like.

Why are tarsier eyes so much larger than those of other nocturnal primates? In part because, as haplorhines, tarsiers lack a tapetum lucidum. This is an accessory cell layer common in nocturnal strepsirhines and other mammals. Lying adjacent to the retina, it provides indirect stimulation of the photoreceptor cells by reflecting light back toward them, thus making the most of twilight and moonlight. The absence of a tapetum in tarsiers is compensated by an increase in eyeball size, and, like the presence of a central foveal spot on its retina, this also serves as a phylogenetic marker indicating close affinities with anthropoids, which have a similar derived pattern.

In addition to having very large external ears for collecting sound, tarsiers have an unusually enlarged middle ear. Unlike most other primates, their auditory bulla is partitioned into two discrete cavities. The eardrum opens into the external ear via a long bony tube, which also acts as a sound filter of some sort. These evolutionary novelties are still imperfectly understood, but observing the animals in the wild leaves no doubt that tarsiers use hearing first and vision second in locating and capturing prey.

The vertical-clinging-and-leaping locomotor style of tarsiers involves many muscular and osseous specializations of the postcranial skeleton. Most of these are strikingly developed in the hindlimb, whose bones are much elongated. The forelimb/hindlimb ratio, for example, yields an intermembral index of only 56, the hindlimb being nearly twice the length of the forelimb. The anatomy of the lower leg is also unique among living primates. The fibula is reduced to a sliver of bone up near the knee, while its lower two-thirds is completely fused to the tibia. A tight hinge joint for the upper an-

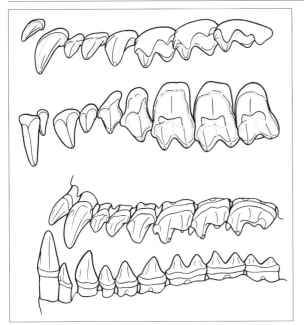

Lateral view of the right lower and upper toothrows of Tarsius syrichta, *top. Below, oblique views of the right toothrows of the same specimen. Courtesy of Alfred L. Rosenberger.*

kle results, so that rotation of the talus upon the tibiofibula is stablilized in the flexion-extension plane. Distal fusion also strengthens the bone against bending and twisting, which may be considerable at the beginning of a leap. Tarsier hands and feet are very large, giving the animal energetically efficient, passive purchase in a vertical-clinging position while waiting silently for food to arrive. The proximal part of the tail is also built to bend against a vertical trunk and to serve as a third base of support behind the pelvis. Perhaps most impressive is the exceptionally elongated leverage system of the foot, especially the calcaneum and navicular bones of the tarsus, which inspired the animal's taxonomic name.

The origins of tarsiids are still unclear. The family Omomyidae includes a number of forms that show important resemblances to the modern tarsiers. They were widely distributed in North America and Eurasia during the Eocene and survived until the Early Miocene. Many of the omomyids were probably diurnal, a feature of their haplorhine heritage. Among them are species known informally as necrolemurs, a reference to a morphological pattern exemplified in the genus *Necrolemur*. They are likely to have been nocturnal leapers, but less derived than tarsiers. Their European allies have been classified as either microchoerine omomyids or tarsiids. *Afrotarsius,* from the Egyptian Oligocene, may also turn out to be a member of the tarsiid group, and the recently discovered *Eosimias* from the Middle Eocene of China appears to be an even better candidate for placement near the ancestry of one of the most unusual members of the Primate order.

See also Afrotarsius; Anthropoidea; Eosimiidae; Haplorhini; Locomotion; Lower Primates; Microchoerinae; Omomyidae; Primates; Strepsirhini; Tarsiiformes; Tarsioidea; Teeth. [A.L.R.]

Further Readings

Beard, K.C., Qi, T., Dawson, M.R., Wang, B., and Li, C. (1994) A diverse new primate fauna from Middle Eocene fissure-fillings in southeastern China. Nature 368:604–609.

Cartmill, M., and Kay, R.F. (1978) Craniodental morphology, tarsier affinities, and primate suborders. In D.J. Chivers and K.A. Joysey (eds.): Recent Advances in Primatology, Vol. 3: Evolution. London: Academic, pp. 205–214.

Gingerich, P.D. (1978) Phylogeny reconstruction and the phylogenetic position of *Tarsius.* In D.J. Chivers and K.A. Joysey (eds.): Recent Advances in Primatology, Vol. 3: Evolution. London: Academic, pp. 249–255.

Niemitz, C. (1984) Biology of the Tarsiers. Stuttgart: Gustav Fischer.

Rosenberger, A.L. (1985) In favor of the necrolemur-tarsier hypothesis. Folia Primatol. 45:179–194.

Tarsiiformes

A subdivision of haplorhine primates (here ranked as a hyporder of the suborder Haplorhini), the sister taxon of the Anthropoidea. It includes the modern tarsiers and their putative close relatives in the fossil record. The three (possibly four or even six) living species of *Tarsius* and some poorly known Eocene and Miocene Asian species referred to *Tarsius* constitute the family Tarsiidae. Tarsiids, however, are merely the barely surviving representatives of a remarkably varied and widespread radiation of tarsiiform haplorhine primates that may have evolved sometime in the Late Cretaceous or Paleocene from a lemurlike strepsirhine primate, an unknown early representative of the Adapiformes (in a broad sense). The Oligocene African *Afrotarsius* is probably a tarsioid or a primitive anthropoid, but it is as yet so poorly known that more detailed allocation is unwise. The Middle Eocene Chinese *Eosimias* (and related undescribed Chinese fossil taxa) placed in the family Eosimiidae are not only tarsiiforms, but tarsioids more closely related to tarsiids than to omomyids or anthropoids. The family Omomyidae is a major radiation from an ancestry more primitive than the early tarsioids.

The number of claimed special derived similarities of the small Eocene *Eosimias* to early anthropoids does not stand up to broader comparative scrutiny. From symphyseal to dental attributes, most of the traits considered anthropoid occur, in fact, in various omomyids, characters that probably represent either primitive tarsiiform traits or convergent features. The diagnostic traits of *Eosimias*, such as the conformation of the trigonid structure on the molars, strongly signal a derived affinity with the tarsiids; hence, the designation of the Eosimiidae as tarsioid rather than anthropoid is far more appropriate.

The fossil animals treated under the Omomyidae and its various subfamilies share a number of significant similarities with the living tarsiers. The North American genus *Shoshonius* (and possibly the whole tribe Washakiini) has a middle-ear-chamber morphology that certainly hints that special ties with tarsiids may exist. However, the character complex underlying this hypothesis has not been critically examined, and the skull

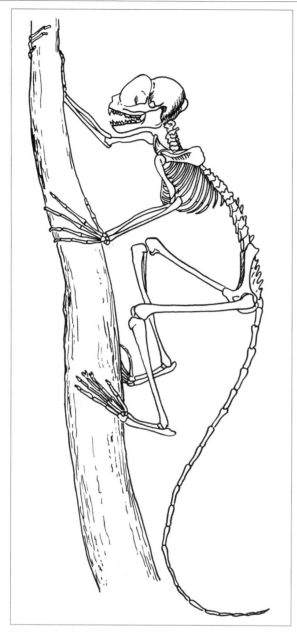

Skeleton of Tarsius, *in typical vertical clinging position.*

pared to the stapedial artery, which passed through the stapes (the stirrup bone). This last character complex suggests an early increase of fresh blood supply to the brain, which, in turn, implies an increase in visual acuity or brain enlargement, or both. The olfactory lobe was relatively reduced compared to contemporary (Eocene) strepsirhines, and the temporal lobe was relatively enlarged. These last features, although of soft anatomy, can be deduced from endocranial casts. Added to the cranial characters listed, there are a number of subtle, but important and telling, modifications in the postcranium of the known omomyids that suggest representative ancestral conditions for the living haplorhines.

In spite of the strong cranial and postcranial special similarities between omomyids and tarsiids, some authors have considered a number of superficially similar dental, cranial, and postcranial (particularly from the hindleg) features shared between *Tarsius* and galagos as synapomorphies. However, these supposed shared and derived features are entirely uninterpreted (i.e., untested) in the appropriate functional context and thus of little phylogenetic significance. It may also be noted that the shared grooming claws of tarsiers and strepsirhines are almost certainly primitive euprimate traits, while their loss in anthropoids is a derived condition.

There is a strong temptation for primatologists to consider living tarsiers as typical of the once greatly diversified, widespread, and undoubtedly locally abundant fossil tarsiiforms of the Eocene and the Oligocene. In fact, the only species we know that may have been very tarsierlike are the Chinese Eocene forms recently discovered by K.C. Beard and colleagues near Shanghuang. They have been dated to ca. 45 Ma and allocated to *Tarsius* based on cheek-tooth morphology. The study of tarsier morphology, fossils, and behavior reveals that these relict living species have a long, independent, complex, and unique history and that their characteristics reflect a series of lineage-specific adaptations that probably did not occur at the same time. The clade Tarsiidae, which we know now to be probably at least as ancient as the Eocene, may have separated from other haplorhines anywhere between 65 and 50 Ma.

The rat-size living tarsiers are carnivorous, taking every conceivable prey they can handle, from snakes to birds. Yet, it is certain, judging from their dental and gnathic (jaw) adaptations, that the fossil omomyid tarsiiforms had a wide range of dietary preferences. In addition to the insectivory and carnivory emphasized in some species, many were primarily either frugivorous or sap feeders, while some specialized on tough seeds, and others were, in spite of their relatively small size, probably partly leaf eaters. Such diverse feeding strategies probably demanded social and locomotor strategies quite distinct from what we observe in the tarsiers. The tarsioid eosimiids also display functional dental adaptations best interpreted as insectivorous-carnivorous.

The enormously enlarged eyes of living tarsiers necessitated a large number of correlated changes that render them unique among tarsiiforms. Yet, the need for such large eyes in the nocturnal tarsiers is intimately tied to the loss, early in haplorhine history, of the primitive mammalian tapetum lucidum behind the retina. Nocturnality may not have been the rule among Paleogene tarsiiforms. On the other hand,

morphology (e.g., orbital features) and the dentition of this group do not corroborate their status as tarsiids. The basicranial, dental, and postcranial shared and derived features of the omomyids, tarsiids, and eosimiids suggest that the taxonomic concept Haplorhini is a valid one. The following shared and derived features of the osteology of the living haplorhines are present in representative omomyids, and it is likely that these were some of the diagnostic haplorhine features in contrast to the strepsirhine ancestor of the earliest haplorhines.

The ancestral haplorhine had a shortened skull, and the olfactory process of its brain was above the midline septum of the facial skull. This interorbital septum was formed from the orbitosphenoid bone, which separated the eyes. The carotid artery, which at least partly nourishes the brain in most primates, entered the skull on the medial side of the middle-ear cavity (encased by the auditory bulla), and one of its branches inside the bulla, the promontory artery, was enlarged com-

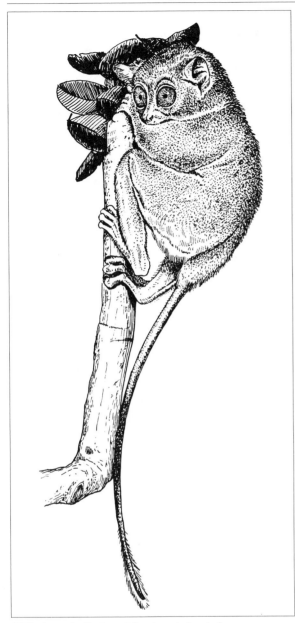

Philippine tarsier, Tarsius syrichta, *in typical vertical posture.*

The jumping ability of living tarsiers is phenomenal: They are capable of up to 1,500 leaps per night, averaging ca. 1,000. Yet, what we can deduce from the rather poorly known postcranial remains of Paleogene tarsiiforms suggests that the early and more primitive members of the group were not as committed to vertical clinging and bipedal grasp leaping as are living tarsiers. Most omomyids were probably rather like the other early euprimates: fast moving, primarily quadrupedal grasp leapers that displayed a range of landing strategies after leaping. Living galagos appear to be adapted either for landing on their hindlegs like tarsiers or habitually making contact with their forelimbs after a jump.

What caused the disappearance of such a widespread and successful radiation as the nonanthropoid haplorhine primates? This is one of the most important big questions concerning primate evolution. It may have been that, in addition to the effects of Cenozoic climatic deterioration, the primates that possessed the best biological adaptations to diurnal living were the very forms that had flourished from among the early tarsiiforms, whom they replaced. These completely diurnal and probably frugivorous early anthropoid primates came to dominate the forests, capable of competing even with the fruit-eating birds, and it is perhaps no accident that the only tarsiiforms that escaped this competition were species of the genus *Tarsius,* whose ancestor had turned nocturnal to survive.

See also Anthropoidea; Euprimates; Haplorhini; Omomyidae; Strepsirhini; Tarsiidae; Tarsioidea. [F.S.S.]

Further Readings

Beard, K.C., Qi, T., Dawson, M.R., Wang, B., and Li, C. (1994) A diverse new primate fauna from Middle Eocene fissure-fillings in southeastern China. Nature 368:604–609.

Hill, W.C.O. (1955) Primates: Comparative Anatomy and Taxonomy, Vol. 7: Haplorhini: Tarsioidea. Edinburgh: Edinburgh University Press.

Szalay, F.S., and Delson, E. (1979) Evolutionary History of the Primates. New York: Academic.

Tarsioidea

A superfamily of the Tarsiiformes, the sister taxon of Omomyoidea. The tarsioids consist of the living species of tarsiids (*Tarsius*) found in the Philippines and Indonesia, a relict distribution for this family, and the fossil Eosimiidae known so far from the Middle Eocene of China. Tarsiidae has been reported from the Miocene of Thailand, the Oligocene of Egypt (*Afrotarsius,* possibly not a tarsiid), and, more recently, as far back as the Middle Eocene of China, occurring together with Omomyidae and Eosimiidae.

While the living Tarsiidae can be clearly diagnosed by an impressive list of complex and, therefore, excellent characters, the phylogenetic and, hence, taxonomic status of the Tarsioidea is as yet restricted to jaw and lower-tooth attributes. The lower jaw, in spite of a lengthy discussion in the literature, does not provide evidence for anthropoid ties for the Eosimiidae, as these attributes are also similar to those found in sev-

the early tarsiiforms, like tarsiers, were probably different in some important ways from contemporary lemurlike strepsirhines. In spite of their probable prosimian (i.e., primitive euprimate) similarities to their nonhaplorhine relatives (such as grooming claws, a soft woolly pelage, and large or expandable membranous external ears), the omomyid tarsiiforms, many of them probably diurnal (active during the day), had not only shortened muzzles, but also probably an upper lip that was not cleft and that therefore allowed a greater range of facial expressions than we see in strepsirhines today. As suggested by the reduced olfactory bulb, and an admittedly assumed haplorhine nose and lip condition, the stage was set among the earliest tarsiiforms, the tarsiids, eosimiids, and omomyids (in a broad sense), for the evolution of primarily visual displays and communication in which an active face was increasingly favored by selection during the critical social interaction of these animals.

eral omomyoids. These broad similarities make such traits either ancient euprimate or haplorhine attributes. The lower molars of *Eosimias*, however, show strong derived similarities to those of living *Tarsius*. The trigonids are hypertrophied and lack the distally progressive reduction of the paraconids, as in tarsiers, but unlike in omomyoids or anthropoids. Significantly, the talonid construction is unlike that of basal anthropoids (oligopithecids), in which the hypoconulid tends to be close to the entoconid. In *Eosimias*, the hypoconulid is not only poorly defined, it is also central on the distal crest of the talonid. The three premolars behind the canines are tarsiid-like, but they are less reduced than in tarsiers, which have hypertrophied molar teeth compared to their small premolars.

The Tarsioidea is one of the more poorly known groups in the fossil record, but this is dramatically changing as new discoveries, such as the eosimiids, are brought to light. Tarsioid ties with the omomyoids and the anthropoids are increasingly secure, substantiating the concept of Haplorhini, although the fossil record undoubtedly stores many new exciting discoveries yet to come.

See also Afrotarsius; Anthropoidea; Eosimiidae; Euprimates; Haplorhini; Oligopithecidae; Omomyidae; Strepsirhini; Tarsiidae; Tarsiiformes. [F.S.S.]

Further Readings

Hill, W.C.O. (1955) Primates: Comparative Anatomy and Taxonomy. Vol. 7: Haplorhini: Tarsioidea. Edinburgh: Edinburgh University Press.

Szalay, F.S., and Delson, E. (1979) Evolutionary History of the Primates. New York: Academic.

Tata

Mousterian site in Hungary of probable Early Weichselian age (?110–70 Ka), excavated by L. Vértes, among others. The industry is distinguished by the use of Levallois technology, small size, numerous side-scrapers, and bifacial retouch on small points and handaxes. Finely ground pigments were recovered from Tata in an Early Mousterian context, together with a carved mammoth tooth and other incised bone objects. These represent some of the earliest carved and incised objects known.

See also Clactonian; Europe; Levallois; Middle Paleolithic; Mousterian; Paleolithic Image; Stone-Tool Making. [A.S.B.]

Taung

South African karst-cave breccia deposit in a limestone tufa, located ca. 10 km southwest of the town of Taung and ca. 130 km north of Kimberley. It is the type locality of *Australopithecus africanus*. The hominin skull was discovered at the Buxton Limeworks there in November 1924, having been blasted from a breccia-filled solution chamber in the Thabaseek limestone tufa, the oldest of five tufa carapaces that fan out from the Precambrian dolomites of the Gaap (or Kaap) Escarpment at Buxton. The cave from which the skull was reported to have been taken was obliterated by mining operations that continued to cut into the tufa for a number of years after the discovery of the hominin specimen.

The hominin skull was described in 1925 by R.A. Dart, who attributed it to the species *A. africanus*. The cave from which it reportedly came, known as the *Australopithecus* Cave, was only one of several fossiliferous cave deposits (e.g., Hrdlička's Cave, Spier's Cave) that were exposed in the immediate vicinity during the course of mining the tufa bodies in the Buxton Quarry. No artifactual material was recovered from the *Australopithecus* Cave.

The geochronological age of the Taung hominin site is a matter of dispute. Much of the so-called Taung Fauna probably derives from breccia deposits other than the *Australopitecus* Cave itself; thus, many of the earlier faunal-age estimates may not pertain directly to the hominin specimen. An ill-founded attempt at geomorphological dating in the early 1970s suggested a date of later than 870 Ka for the

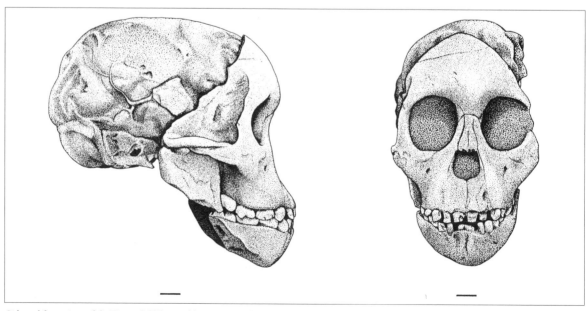

Side and front views of the Taung child face and brain cast. Scales are 1 cm.

hominin, which prompted speculation that the skull may be that of a "robust" australopith. Preliminary thermoluminescence analyses of calcite from the outer Thabaseek tufa have suggested a date in the vicinity of 1.0 Ma, but these may not date the tufa itself. Analyses of the cercopithecid fauna that derives from the *Australopithecus* Cave indicate a date of ca. 2.5–2 Ma, and the hominin specimen itself is morphologically more similar to those from Sterkfontein and Makapansgat than to the younger "robust" australopith fossils from Kromdraai and Swartkrans. Recent excavations and analyses of the Taung fauna suggest that most of the specimens, which derive from the Hrdlička deposits, have their greatest affiliation with elements from Sterkfontein Member 4. The hominin skull, however, probably derived from a cave system associated with the Dart deposits, which contain a fauna comprising seven extinct species. This fauna suggests that the hominin specimen may date to a period between the times represented by Makapansgat Members 3 and 4 (ca. 3 Ma) and Sterkfontein Member 4 (ca. 2.8–2.5 Ma).

See also Africa; Africa, Southern; Australopithecus; Australopithecus africanus; Breccia Cave Formation; Dart, Raymond Arthur; Kromdraai; Makapansgat; Sterkfontein; Swartkrans. [F. E. G.]

Further Readings

Berger, L.R. and Clarke, R.J. (1995) Eagle involvment in accumulation of the Taung Child fauna. J. Hum. Evol. 29:275–279.

Delson, E. (1984) Cercopithecid biochronology of the African Plio-Pleistocene: Correlation among eastern and southern hominin-bearing localities. Cour. Forsch. Inst. Senckenberg 69:199–218.

McKee, J.K. (1993) Faunal dating of the Taung hominin fossil deposit. J. Hum. Evol. 25:363–376.

McKee, J.K. (1994) Catalogue of fossil sites at the Buxton Limeworks, Taung. Palaeont. Afr. 31:73–81.

McKee, J.K., Thackeray, J.F., and Berger, L.R. (1995) Faunal assemblage seriation of southern African Pliocene and Pleistocene fossil deposits. Am. J. Phys. Anthropol. 96:235–250.

Peabody, F.E. (1954) Travertines and cave deposits of the Kaap Escarpment of South Africa, and the type locality of *Australopithecus africanus*. Bull. Geol. Soc. Am. 63:671–706.

Vogel, J.C. (1985) Further attempts at dating the Taung tufas. In P.V. Tobias (ed.): Hominid Evolution: Past, Present and Future. New York: Liss, pp. 189–194.

Taxon

Named unit at any level (rank) of the classificatory hierarchy (plural: taxa). The kingdom Animalia, order Primates, family Hominidae, and species *Homo sapiens* all are taxa. Informally, taxa above the level of the species are known as higher taxa.

See also Classification; Nomenclature; Systematics; Taxonomy. [I.T.]

Taxonomy

Theory and practice of classifying organisms. This has two separate aspects, in both of which theory and practice are intertwined: first, the process of classifying organisms, which can be done on the basis of various criteria, the most important of which is phylogeny; and second, the naming of the units recognized in the classification, which is governed by rules laid down in the *International Code of Zoological Nomenclature*. Thus, while the naming of taxonomic units is an objective process that must follow established procedures, the recognition of these units and their incorporation into the classificatory hierarchy is less clear-cut, the bases of any classification depending on the intentions of the classifier.

See also Classification; Phylogeny; Systematics. [I.T.]

Tayacian

Early Paleolithic flake industry found in Europe and possibly in western Asia during the later Middle Pleistocene (ca. 0.45–0.15 Ma; Late Elster to Saale glacial stages). Lacking or poor in handaxes and Levallois technology, the industry is characterized by large numbers of small, often crude flakes, denticulates, core-choppers, crude scrapers, and points, especially the *pointe de Tayac*. The type site, as defined by H. Breuil, is La Micoque, near Les Eyzies (Dordogne) in southwestern France, where some Tayacian levels are also referred to as pre-Mousterian. Other important sites with a similar industry include Arago, Ehringsdorf, Tabūn, and Jabrud.

See also Arago; Breuil, [Abbé] Henri [Edward Prosper]; Clactonian; Early Paleolithic; Ehringsdorf; Europe; Jabrud; Jabrudian; Tabūn; Tabunian. [A.S.B.]

Technology

System by which raw materials, including food items, are extracted and transformed for human use, or, more specifically, the set of behaviors or procedures carried out on a raw material, leading to its transformation. Succeeding stages of the Paleolithic (and later cultures) may be characterized in terms of the increasingly sophisticated technology used in the production of stone tools.

See also Mesolithic; Modes, Technological; Neolithic; Paleolithic; Stone-Tool Making. [A.S.B.]

Teeth

Organs that assist in the acquisition and mechanical breakdown of food and in several nondigestive functions, such as defense and display. Teeth have long been a subject of interest to comparative anatomists. First, because of their complexity and evolutionarily conservative character, teeth are important for determining evolutionary relationships among primates. Second, dental structure, when understood in functional and adaptive terms, is important for assessing dietary preferences and social structure of living primates. Moreover, because teeth are composed in large part of inorganic calcium salts, they are commonly preserved in the fossil record, so it has been possible using dental anatomy to trace evolu-

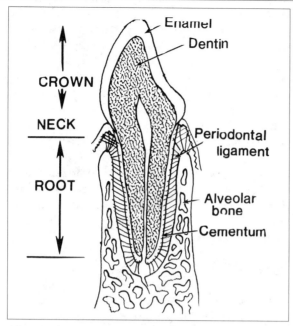

Schematic cross-section of a mammalian tooth. Courtesy of Richard F. Kay.

tionary changes in many primate groups and to reconstruct phylogenetic and adaptive patterns of extinct primates.

The mammalian tooth has a *crown*, a *neck*, and a *root*. In cross section, the tooth is composed of a column of *dentin* containing a *pulp cavity* with nerves and vessels. Covering the dentin of the root is a thin layer of *cementum*. The root is suspended in its bony crypt, or *alveolus*, by the *periodontal ligament*, which takes its origin from the alveolar surface and inserts into the cementum. On the crown, the dentin is covered by a hard, crystalline layer of *enamel*.

To fully appreciate the dental anatomy of primates, it is useful to consider that of their reptilian and mammalian forebears. Several major advances distinguish mammalian dentitions from those of reptiles.

The most obvious of these is *heterodonty*. The reptilian ancestors of mammals had simple conical teeth from the front to the back of the jaw. In contrast, mammals exhibit regionally differentiated tooth groups that serve special functions. From front to back on each side of the upper and lower jaw in the primitive mammalian dentition is a series of simple nibbling teeth, *incisors*, followed by a projecting and pointed *canine* used for grasping and stabbing purposes. Behind the canines is a series of increasingly complicated postcanine (or cheek) teeth, the *premolars* and the *molars*, used for separating a bite of food and chewing it to speed the digestive processes after swallowing. All of the lower teeth are embedded in the *mandible*; the upper incisors are in the *premaxilla*, the other upper teeth in the *maxilla*.

To simplify reference, the major tooth types are referred to by their initial letters: M, molars; P, premolars; C, canine; I, incisors. In a front-to-back sequence within tooth types, the teeth are referred to by numbers (e.g., M1, first molar; P2, second premolar). Upper and lower teeth are usually distinguished by super- and subscripts, respectively (e.g., M^2, second upper molar; I_1, first lower incisor); more rarely, uppercase letters are used for upper teeth, lowercase for lowers: m1 and M1.

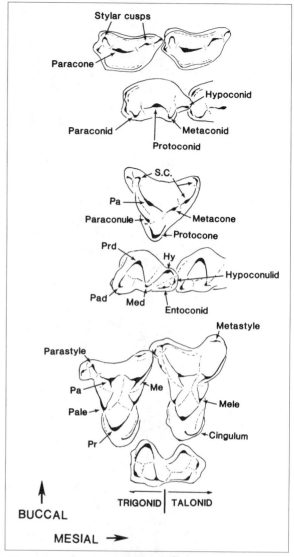

Three stages in the evolution of the tribosphenic molar. Top: Kuehneotherium *from the later Triassic; middle:* Aegialodon, *early Cretaceous (upper tooth reconstructed); bottom:* Kennalestes, *Cretaceous (Santonian). For each taxon upper-left teeth are at the top and lower-right teeth at the bottom. Tooth cusps are identified in full as they first appear and in abbreviated form thereafter. (Abbreviations: end, entoconid; hy, hypoconid; hyd, hypoconulid; me, metacone; med, metaconid; mele, metaconule; mes, metastyle; pa, paracone; pad, paraconid; pale, paraconule; pas, parastyle; pr, protocone; prd, protoconid; s.c., stylar cusps.) After Crompton and Kielan-Jaworoska, 1978; courtesy of Richard F. Kay.*

Note that numbering is based on supposed homology, not position; thus, the premolars of humans are known as P_3 and P_4, even though there are only two of them, since the anterior premolars present in remote ancestors have been lost.

Accompanying the development of heterodonty in the mammalian dentition was a change in the way teeth were replaced. Typically in reptiles, the tooth at each position (*locus*) in the jaw is replaced a number of times, and the total number of teeth increases with the continued growth of the animal throughout life. In mammals, the tooth at each locus is replaced only once, or not at all, and the total number of tooth loci is strictly limited. Thus, mammals have a set of "baby," or deciduous, teeth and a complement of adult, or permanent, teeth that erupt into position sequentially. Another way of looking at this picture is to consider the deciduous teeth and the permanent molars as the primary dentition, while the permanent incisors, canines, and premolars are the secondary, or replacement, dentition. These ideas make it clear that the deciduous postcanine teeth are premolars (dP), not milk *molars* as they are sometimes wrongly termed—they are replaced by the permanent premolars. In fact, this is the basic definition of the difference between molars and premolars.

The structure of mammalian cheek teeth has departed far from that of reptiles. The earliest mammals, such as *Kuehneotherium*, had upper and lower cheek teeth with a single cone (cusp), in front of and behind which were single small cusps. As in reptiles, the upper and lower teeth alternated in the jaws so that each lower tooth fit between, and internal to, two upper teeth. This primitive arrangement became modified by the increasing size of the accessory cusps, their rotation with respect to the principal cusp to form reversed triangles, and the addition of sharp crests between the cusps. The triangles of the upper teeth had the principal cusp located internally, whereas the principal cusp of the lower molar was external to the accessory cusps. As the molar teeth came together during mastication, the lower triangular teeth fit into the embrasures between the reversed upper triangular teeth. In this way, food interposed between the teeth was not only punctured between the cusps, but the crests joining the cusps moved across one another, producing a shearing action to cut the food. A further modification was the addition of a small heel onto the back of the lower cheek teeth that served initially as a "stop" to prevent food particles from being driven onto the gums. As this surface expanded, it served as a platform for crushing food against the upper principal cusp. The modifications just described served as the basis for the *tribosphenic molar* of therian mammals. This molar pattern underlies, and was ancestral to, that of the first primates.

Basic Characters of Eutherian Dental Structure

As judged from the study of Cretaceous eutherian mammals (placentals and marsupials) and living dentally primitive eutherians, the adult ancestors of primates had three incisors, one canine, four premolars, and three molars on each side of the mouth in upper and lower jaws. This configuration may be expressed as a *dental formula* of 3.1.4.3/3.1.4.3. The incisors and canines had a deciduous precursor; the first premolar (the one closest to the canine) apparently did not, but the second through fourth premolars had deciduous precursors. Permanent molars lacked deciduous counterparts. Thus, the primitive eutherian deciduous dental formula was 3.1.3/3.1.3.

The eutherian ancestor of primates had small, cylindrical to slightly spatulate incisors with blunt tips. The canines were larger than the incisors, slightly curved, and projected above the plane of the incisors and the premolars. The upper canine was the first tooth behind the premaxilla/maxilla suture. The premolars changed in shape from front to back. The first was a simple cone, compressed laterally. The second and third premolars showed an increased complexity by the addition of cusps and crests. The fourth of the series may have been a complex molarlike tooth.

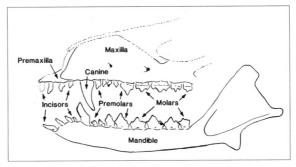

Reconstruction of the jaws and teeth of Kennalestes, *an early Cretaceous mammal, with the tooth fields identified. After Crompton, 1986; courtesy of Richard F. Kay.*

The three upper molars of the generalized eutherian ancestors of primates had three principal cusps arranged in a triangle, the *trigone*. The *protocone* was the sole lingual cusp. (According to anatomical convention, the side of each tooth closest to the front of the tooth arcade is its *mesial* side; the side farthest from the front of the jaw is its *distal* side. The tongue side of a tooth is the *lingual* side, and that closest the cheek is the *buccal* [or *labial*, if near the lips] side.) There were two buccal cusps, the *paracone* mesially and the *metacone* distally. A pair of sharp, curved crests led buccally away from the protocone defining a small central trigone basin. Between the protocone and the paracone was a *paraconule*, while between the protocone and the metacone was a *metaconule*. Protoconule and metaconule also each had a pair of crests running buccally from them to either side of the buccal cusps.

Buccal to the paracone and the metacone was a wide region called the *stylar shelf*. The strong development of the stylar shelf may be accounted for by the large size of the crests running mesiobuccally from the paracone and distobuccally from the metacone. The ends of those crests were supported by small cusps called the *parastyle* and the *metastyle*, respectively. The cusps of the upper and lower teeth served as puncturing devices in the initial stages of mastication. The crests were important during the precise cutting up of food before swallowing.

Lastly, mention should be made of the molar *cingulum*, a raised rim at the edges of the crowns. Upper molars of early mammals had a well-developed cingulum on the buccal margins of the stylar shelf and on the mesial and distal margins as well. The triangular shape of the upper molars of early mammals leaves a space, or *embrasure*, lingually between the protocones of adjacent molars into which the principal lingual cusp of the lower molars, the protoconid, fits (see below). The role of the cingulum was apparently to deflect away from the gums any food particles driven upward by the movement of the protoconid into this space. Incidental contact occurred, and wear was produced between the protoconid and the distolingual cingulum of the upper molars. Repeatedly in mammalian evolution, a small cusp raised fortuitously along this cingulum has been selectively enlarged as a *hypocone*.

Mesially, the lower molars of the generalized eutherian ancestors of primates had a triangular arrangement of cusps called the *trigonid*. The trigonid had a single cusp buccally,

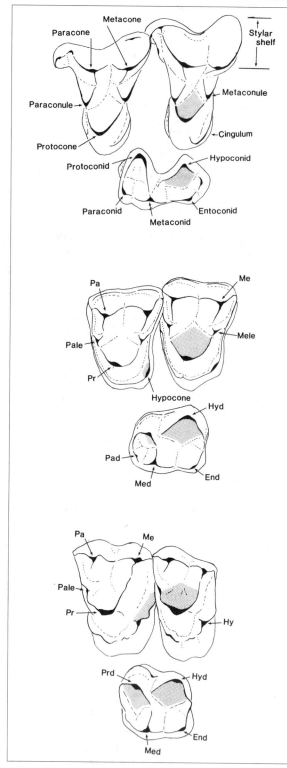

Upper and lower molars. Top: Kennalestes, *a Cretaceous mammal;* middle: Omomys carteri, *a middle Eocene primate; and bottom:* Saimiri sciureus, *a living monkey. Various features mentioned in the text are indicated. Crushing surfaces on the protocone and hypocone (if present) are indicated by stippling.* Kennalestes *after Crompton and Kielan-Jaworowska, 1970; courtesy of Richard F. Kay.*

the *protoconid*, with two lingual cusps, the *paraconid* mesially and the *metaconid* distally. Trigonid cusps were tall and pointed. A pair of sharp curved crests led lingually away from the protoconid toward the paraconid and the metaconid.

Behind the trigonid of each lower molar was a heel-like projection, the *talonid*. The talonid was primitively lowered well below the level of, and much narrower than, the trigonid. Centrally, the talonid was hollowed out as a basin enclosed by a raised rim of three cusps with their connecting crests. A buccally situated cusp, the *hypoconid*, supported short crests running mesially to the base of the trigonid and distally to the back of the tooth. Lingually was an *entoconid* with crests running up to the metaconid and toward a distal cusp, the *hypoconulid*. The triangle formed by the talonid cusps was reversed from that of the trigone of the upper molar, and the trigonid cusps were fitted into the embrasures between the upper cheek teeth. In the case of the first lower molar (M_1), the space was between the upper fourth premolar and first molar (P^4 and M^1); M_2 fit between M^1 and M^2; and so forth. The talonid basin was fitted under and around the protocone when the teeth were fully occluded.

Chewing Behavior in Mammals

The mechanism by which the teeth are used to bring food into the mouth, called *ingestion*, is accomplished with the incisor teeth assisted by the canines and premolars when more force is required to separate a bite of food. Once the food is in the mouth, *mastication* is the process by which it is broken up by the premolars and molars and mixed with lubricating and digestive juices before swallowing. The complex structure of the molars is best understood by reference to the masticatory process in living primitive mammals, such as the American opossum. In the beginning stages of mastication, large particles of food are punctured and crushed between the projecting and pointed cusps of the molars. After the food is sufficiently softened and divided, the masticatory process becomes more regular. The lower jaw is shifted to the side where chewing is to occur. The teeth are brought into position so that the lower and upper outer crests are vertically aligned and in contact. Guided by the structural fit between the molars, the lower teeth are moved upward and lingually in the *power stroke*. This movement is terminated when the talonid basin and the protocone contact in *centric occlusion*. Then the lower teeth are dropped out of occlusion as the jaws are opened in preparation for another masticatory cycle. In the masticatory process of structurally primitive mammals, chewing occurs on only one side of the jaw at a time, with only incidental contact occurring between the teeth on the opposite side of the jaw.

Precise fitting together of the cusps and the crests occurs during the power stroke only after the food is first thoroughly punctured and crushed. After puncture/crushing, the principal action is one of shearing, with the crests of the teeth being moved past one another. Several distinctive features of the molar crests of primitive mammals, such as *Kennalestes* of the Cretaceous, may be understood with reference to movements in the power stroke. In these forms, the protoconid and its associated concavely curved crests moved up-

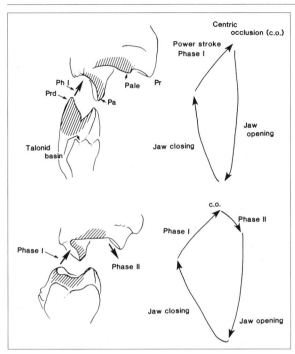

Jaw movements during chewing. Top: Cretaceous mammal Kennalestes; *bottom: living primate* Saimiri. *Each tooth pair is arranged to show how a lower molar protoconid and its crest (viewed from the back) moves, first, across the crest leading from the upper-molar paracone and, second, across the crest leading from the paraconule (viewed from the front). This movement is Phase I of the power stroke and terminates when the protocone fits into the talonid basin. In* Kennalestes, *or in living primitive mammals like the American opossum, the jaws are opened from the point of centric occlusion. In* Saimiri *and other primates a second phase (Phase II) begins at centric occlusion. In Phase II the protocone is dragged across the talonid basin before the jaws are opened. The path of the chewing cycle in* Kennalestes *and* Saimiri *viewed from back to front is illustrated on the right.* Kennalestes *after Crompton and Kielan-Jaworowska, 1970; courtesy of Richard F. Kay.*

ward and lingually into an embrasure between triangular upper molars. At first, protoconid crests engaged reciprocally curved upper molar crests running mesially from the paracone and distally from the metacone; any food trapped between them was sheared. Later, as the protoconid crests moved farther upward and lingually, they engaged a second set of concavely curved crests running from the paraconule and the metaconule. Thus, each lower-molar crest moved in sequence past a pair of upper-molar crests. This sequence of shearing events is called *en echelon* shearing. Emphasis was placed in early mammals on *en echelon* shearing crests associated with the triangular-shaped embrasures between the upper teeth and the mesial and distal sides of the protoconid. Other *en echelon* shearing blades were also utilized by the hypoconid as it moved upward and lingually into the trigone basin, but these were not as important.

At the apex of the upward and lingual movement of the lower teeth, the talonid basin closed against the protocone in centric occlusion. In primitive mammals, the jaws were then moved apart in preparation for the next chewing cycle. Thus, the interaction of the teeth to break down the food occurred up to and including centric occlusion with the emphasis on *en echelon* embrasure shearing. This part of the chewing cycle is called Phase I. Such crushing as was to be found oc-

curred between the protocone and the talonid basin as centric occlusion was reached. There was little or no grinding of the flat surfaces of the talonid across the protocone after centric occlusion. Later, in the evolution, these postcentric grinding movements (called Phase II) become more important.

Dentition of the Earliest Primates of Modern Aspect

The appearance of the teeth of the first euprimates, as exemplified by *Notharctus* from the Middle Eocene, is in marked contrast with the condition of primitive eutherians. The incisors of primitive euprimates were reduced to two on each side above and below and became more spatulate. Canines remained large and projecting. There were originally four premolars, but the number was soon reduced to three. Changes in molar structure were conditioned by the appearance and gradually expanded importance of Phase II of the power stroke of mastication. In early primates, such as *Omomys*, more of a premium was placed on the crushing surfaces of the talonid basin and the protocone. Following centric occlusion, rather than breaking off occlusal contact, as was done in early mammals, the expanded crushing surface of the talonid was dragged across the protocone in a grinding action. As Phase II crushing was enhanced, the importance of *en echelon* embrasure shearing declined. One cusp importantly associated with embrasure shearing, the paraconid, was greatly reduced or lost. The stylar shelf was reduced in size and importance as the embrasure-shearing crests leading mesially and distally from the paracone and the metacone, respectively, became smaller. Also, the second series of shearing crests associated with the paraconule and the metaconule was deemphasized for similar reasons. There was an increased importance of crests associated with the talonid basin and its crests and the protocone and its crests.

General Tendencies in Primate Evolution

The dentitions of living primates have departed widely from the primitive primate condition. The following summarizes a few of the specializations of the living forms.

INCISORS AND CANINES

Incisors of primates have become adapted for a variety of tasks, such as ingestion and grooming. Primitively, the paired incisors on each side of the jaw acted in concert with spatulate upper incisors for grasping and manipulating food items to position them for being cut away powerfully by the canines and the cheek teeth. Many kinds of early primates reduced the number of incisors and modified them into stabbing, gouging, or piercing teeth. Such structures apparently were useful for extramasticatory activities, ranging from killing or subduing prey to tearing bark from food trees to promote the flow of nutritious gum. Living strepsirhine primates have modified their lower incisors and canines to form a comb for grooming fur. Some strepsirhine species have further modified the tooth comb for the purposes of prying up bark or scraping gum. The incisors of anthropoids are more spatulate and are used for powerfully separating a bite of food for mastication. Some New World monkeys have evolved gum-scraping caniniform incisors.

CANINES

Whereas the lower canine became part of the tooth comb in lemurs, primitive projecting canines are retained in most living anthropoids, where they have many uses, including the powerful prying open of tough food. In many anthropoids, the canines of males are much larger than those of females. Canine sexual dimorphism is best accounted for by sexual selection and the role of males in protecting the social unit from predation.

PREMOLARS

Repeatedly in primate evolution, the premolars have been reduced in number and the premolar battery broadened and shortened. Only occasionally, among some Eocene forms, are four premolars found. More commonly, the number has been reduced to three or even two, as among the Old World monkeys and apes. A striking development among lemurs is the enlargement of the lower mesial premolar, P_2, into a caninelike tooth in association with the incorporation of the lower canine into the tooth comb. Among anthropoids, the front premolar, P_2 or P_3, is modified at the front for shearing against the upper canine. In some Old World monkeys, this development has reached an extreme in which the mesial surface of this lower premolar is elongate and its enamel migrates onto the root, forming a *hone* for sharpening the upper canine.

MOLARS

Many of the changes in occlusal patterns have been importantly mediated by selection for specialized diets. Since so many of the dietary specializations of primates (e.g., for leaf eating and fruit eating) have occurred in parallel in a number of independent lineages, there are a number of recurring themes in primate molar evolution. For example, there has been the tendency for a reduction in the height of the trigonid and a reduction of the crests running from the protocone, with an accompanying loss of the paraconid. Accompanying the lower-molar changes are a reduction of the importance of the stylar cusps and crests and loss of the paraconule and the metaconule and their crests. These changes are a reflection of a move away from the system of *en echelon* embrasure shearing, in which the protoconid and its crests are moved into the embrasures between the upper teeth. An increase in the importance of Phase II crushing and grinding may have been the driving force behind these changes. As the talonid basin (and its principal cusp, the hypoconid) and the protocone expanded, and with the appearance of the hypocone and expanded trigonid crushing/grinding surfaces, there was little space available for embrasure shearing. The emphasis has shifted to shearing crests that surround the crushing surfaces, such as those associated with the protocone and the hypocone. Thus, there has not always been a move away from shearing as such. Rather, there was a shift from embrasure shearing to shearing between crests on the edges of the talonid basin and the protocone.

Trends in Relation to Social and Dietary Selection

Teeth have become adapted for many specialized tasks in primates. Some of these are best understood as nondietary adaptations, while others have to do primarily with the diet.

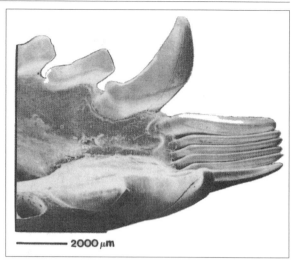

The lower teeth of a prosimian showing a tooth comb consisting on each side of the mandible of two incisors and a canine. Courtesy of Kenneth D. Rose.

Most nondietary specializations are restricted to the incisors and the canines. A good example is the strepsirhine tooth comb, with which the animal grooms its fur. Especially among anthropoid primates, there is a strong correlation between social structure and sexual dimorphism in the canines. Males and females of monogamous or polyandrous anthropoids tend to have similar-size canines, whereas the canines of polygnous species tend to be quite dimorphic. In extreme cases, the canines of males can be more than twice as large as those of females. Another factor influencing canine dimorphism is terrestriality. Primates that spend more time foraging on the ground tend to be more dimorphic than their arboreal close relatives.

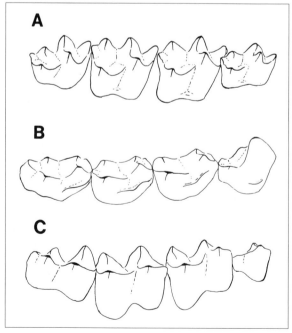

The lower cheek teeth of living primates with different diets: (a) insectivorous Galago senegalensis; (b) frugivorous Cheirogaleus medius; (c) folivorous Propithecus verreauxi. Note that the insectivorous and folivorous taxa have sharper cusps and longer cutting crests than do the frugivorous species. Courtesy of Richard F. Kay.

Primates eat many kinds of plants and animal foods, but each species tends to specialize on just a few. A part of this dietary specialization is modification in the structure of the teeth. Many primates are insect eaters, and this was the diet of the most primitive primates of the Paleocene and the Eocene. The front teeth of living insectivorous primates have structural designs that are often more a reflection of nonfeeding adaptations than strictly of dietary habits. For example, insect-eating strepsirhines have tooth combs that are essentially the same as their more frugivorous close rela-

tives. In contrast, the cheek teeth of all insect-eating primates are quite distinctive and stereotyped. The molars of insect eaters have sharply pointed cusps and well-developed, trenchant shearing crests. These structures assist in puncturing the tough chitinous exoskeletons of insects and in cutting up the insects to enhance the digestion of the chitin.

Primates have become adapted to a variety of plant diets. These adaptations can be fully appreciated only when the complex interplay of biomechanics and structural/ historical factors is understood. For example, adaptations of the front

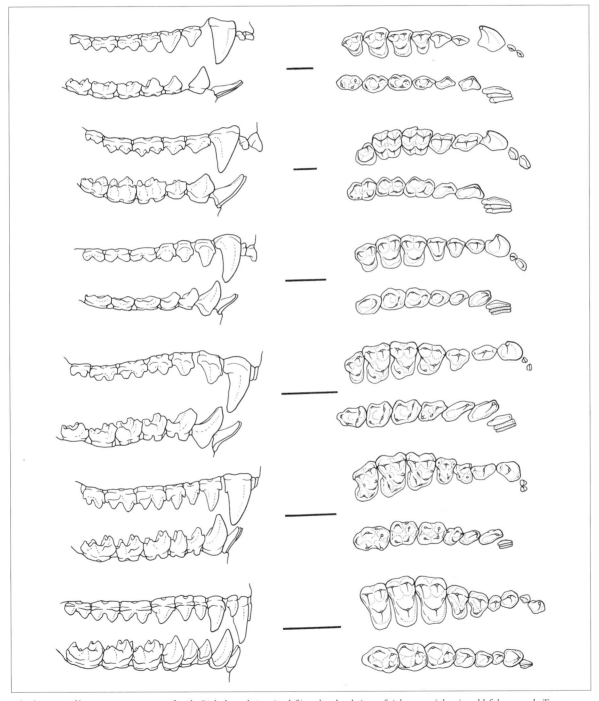

The dentition of living primates, one per family. Right lateral view (on left) and occlusal views of right upper (above) and left lower teeth. Top to bottom: Lemur, Propithecus, Cheirogaleus, Galago, Loris, Tarsius. *Scale bars = 5 mm. By L. Meeker, after specimens and W. Maier, Konstruktionsmorphologische Untersuchungen am Gebiss der rezenten Prosimiae (Primates),* Abh. Senckenb. naturforsch. Ges. *538, 1–158, 1980.*

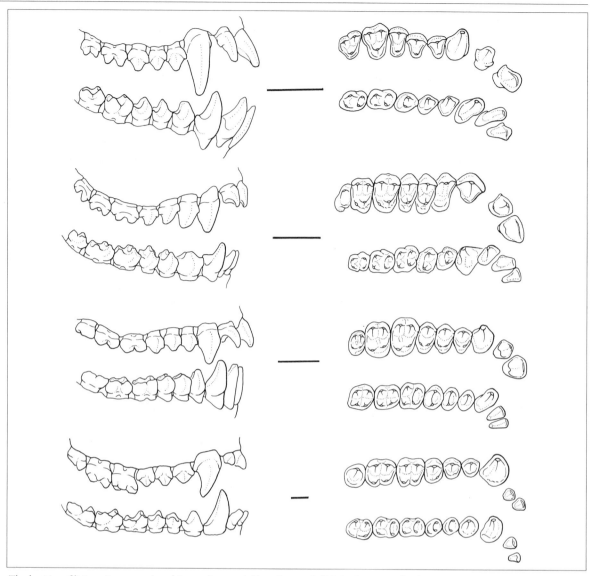

The dentition of living primates, continued (see previous page). Top to bottom: Callithyix, Saimiri, Callicebus, Alouatta; *scale bars 5mm. By L. Meeker.*

teeth for gum eating differ greatly in living strepsirhines and anthropoids, because the former began the adaptive process with a fully developed tooth comb, whereas the latter started with spatulate incisors and projecting lower canines. Gum-eating strepsirhines (species such as *Galago senegalensis*) have relatively elongate tooth combs to improve their ability to gouge bark and scrape gum. The same sort of adaptation has been achieved in some small gum-eating marmosets (e.g., *Callithrix jacchus*) by lateral compression, strengthening, and enlargement of typically anthropoid spatulate incisors. Anthropoids have evolved several other specializations of the front teeth for eating plant foods. Those that eat primarily fruits have enlarged incisors for husking and scraping, whereas those that eat mostly leaves requiring little incisal preparation have comparatively small incisors. The canines of seed-eating anthropoids are enlarged and tusklike.

There have been a number of adaptive changes in the cheek teeth of fruit- and leaf-eating primates. Primates that eat fruit or gum have flattened, rounded tooth cusps with an emphasis on crushing and grinding surfaces, but little shear-ing. In species adapted for eating seeds, the molars resemble those of fruit eaters, but the enamel is much thicker or has an interwoven crystalline structure to resist the greater forces engendered when seeds are broken. Species that specialize in eating leaves or other plant parts containing structural carbo-hydrates resemble insectivorous species in having strongly developed, trenchant cutting edges on the molars but tend to differ in that they often do not have sharply pointed cusps for puncturing.

See also Adaptation(s); Anthropoidea; Diet; Euprimates; Functional Morphology; Primate Societies; Primates; Skull; Strepsirhini. [R.F.K.]

Further Readings

Crompton, A.W., and Kielan-Jaworowska, Z. (1970) Molar structure and occlusion in Cretaceous therian mam-mals. In P.M. Butler and K.A. Joysey (eds.): Develop-ment, Function, and Evolution of Teeth. London: Academic, pp. 249–288.

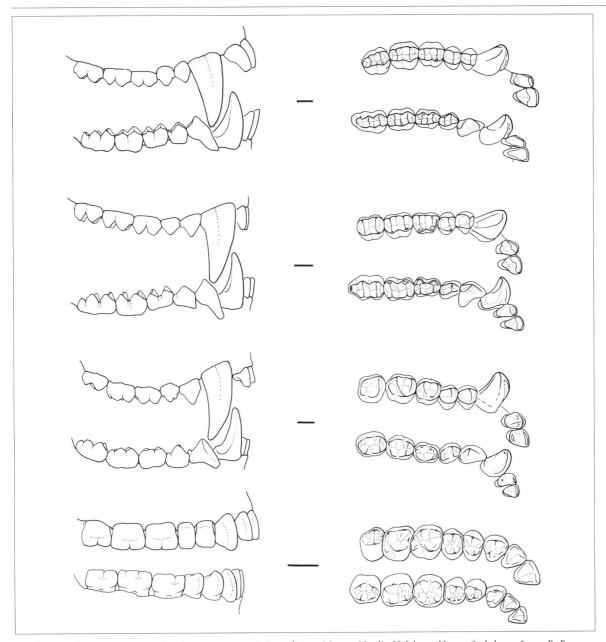

The dentition of living primates, continued (see previous pages). Top to bottom: Macaca, Nasalis, Hylobates, Homo. *Scale bars = 5 mm. By B. Akerbergs;* Homo *by L. Meeker, after specimens and W. Maier and G. Schneck, Konstruktionsmorphologische Untersuchungen am Gebiss der hominoiden Primaten, Zeitschrift für Morphologie und Anthropologie 72, 127–169, 1981.*

Hiiemae, K.M., and Kay, R.F. (1972) Trends in the evolution of primate mastication. Nature 240:486–487.

Kay, R.F. (1975) The functional adaptations of primate molar teeth. Am. J. Phys. Anthropol. 43:195–216.

Kay, R.F., and Covert, H.H. (1984) Anatomy and behavior of extinct primates. In D. Chivers, B.A. Wood, and A. Bilsborough (eds.): Food Acquisition and Processing in Primates. New York: Plenum, pp. 467–508.

Kay, R.F., and Hylander, W. (1978) The dental structure of mammalian folivores with special reference to Primates and Phalangeroidea (Marsupialia). In G.G. Montgomery (ed.): The Biology of Arboreal Folivores. Washington, D.C.: Smithsonian Institution Press, pp. 173–191.

Lucas, P.W., and Teaford, M. (1994) Functional morphology of colobine teeth. In G. Davies and J.F. Oates (eds.): Colobine Monkeys: Their Ecology, Behaviour, and Evolution. Cambridge: Cambridge University Press, pp. 11–43.

Teilhard de Chardin, Pierre (1881–1955)

French paleontologist, priest, and religious philosopher. Just as Teilhard's philosophical texts are a curious blending of science and religion, so was his career. As a young student of theology at Ore Place, Hastings in Sussex, England (1908–1912, 1913), Teilhard assisted in the diggings at Piltdown (England) in 1912 and is credited with discovering the canine tooth in 1913 that appeared to vindicate British paleontologist A.S. Woodward's reconstruction. Later, during the late 1920s and early 1930s, he was involved in the early excavations of *Sinanthropus pekinensis* at Zhoukoudian, near Beijing. While in

China, Teilhard also made some important contributions to paleoprimatology, as well as the fundamental observation of the strong separation between southern and northern Pleistocene faunas on the plains of China. These are not attributable to geographical barriers (such as mountain ranges), unlike such differences throughout the rest of Eurasia. Also while in China, he completed the manuscript for *Le Phenomène humain,* a meditative outgrowth of his scientific researches. In 1946, Teilhard, frustrated in his desire to publish his philosophical works and to teach at the Collège de France, moved to the United States. He spent the last five years of his life living in New York City, where he was associated with the Wenner-Gren Foundation for Anthropological Research.

See also China; Piltdown; Zhoukoudian. [F.S.]

Tephrochronology

Geochronologic correlation method based on comparison of tephra layers. *Tephra* is a general term for airborne fragments from explosive eruptions. The deposits called *volcanic ash* or *tuff* are layers of tephra, some of which spread out for a thousand meters or more downwind from the source. Their simultaneous deposition in different basins and environments, their datability, and their individual physical and chemical "fingerprint" make tephra sheets appealing to stratigraphers.

In general, tephra layers consist of a mixture of volcanic glass and minerals. The mineral proportion decreases with distance from the eruptive source because the mineral grains tend to fall out more rapidly than the glass shards. Each tephra cloud has a unique chemistry, however, because the parent magmas originate under a variety of conditions and sources, ascend at different rates, assimilate different amounts of wall rocks, and undergo different amounts of crystallization and fluid loss up to the point at which their vapor pressure exceeds the pressure of confining rock and they explode. Thus, the kinds, proportions, and composition of minerals in a tephra layer all reflect not only the unique history of the parent magma, but also that unique moment in the mineralogical evolution of the magma that is captured in the eruption.

Glass tephra represent the liquid magma, frozen and shattered by the sudden pressure drop. Compositional gradients in the liquid magma can give rise to a detectable range in composition of the glass erupted from the chamber, but, despite this variability, the glass tephra are often chosen to establish the individual character of a particular tephra layer because they are clearly of primary origin (i.e., not detrital), are readily separated from the minerals, and are usually the most abundant phase especially in distal parts of the tephra body. Major elements in the glass may be determined by electron probe microanalysis, wet chemistry, or X-ray fluorescence spectrometry; minor and trace elements are commonly determined by X-ray fluorescence spectrometry or neutron activation analysis. The abundance ratios of a few selected pairs of elements are usually sufficient to distinguish any glass. Weathering and secondary mineralization change the gross composition of the glass phase, but a number of elements are relatively immobile and can help identify glass that has been partly altered.

Once the elemental signature, or fingerprint, of the glass tephra has been established, it can be identified wherever this layer is sampled, with mineralogy as a reliable cross-check. When several tephra layers occur in sequence, recognition of the sequence is the ultimate in secure correlation. Mapping out tephra layers and establishing sequences is the branch of physical geology called *tephrostratigraphy*. In addition, if a tephra layer has been isotopically dated, or calibrated in the paleomagnetic time scale, then this dates all sections into which the tephra layer (or the sequence to which it belongs) is correlated. This application of tephrostratigraphy is called *tephrochronology*.

As an example, the tephrochronology used in studies of the Turkana Basin in Ethiopia and Kenya is summarized here using only the dated units. Note that the isotopically determined ages also fall in stratigraphic order. See also the more complete figure and table in AFRICA, EAST.

Omo (Ethiopia) Shungura Formation	West Turkana (Kenya) Nachukui Formation	East Turkana (Kenya) Koobi Fora Formation	Age (Ma)
	Silbo Tuff	Silbo Tuff	0.74
	Gele Tuff		1.25
	Nariokotome Tuff		1.33
Tuff L	Chari Tuff	Chari Tuff	1.39
Tuff J-4	Morutot Tuff	Morutot Tuff	1.64
Tuff H-4	Malbe Tuff	Malbe Tuff	1.87
Tuff H-2	KBS Tuff	KBS Tuff	1.89
Tuff G			2.32
Tuff F	Kalochoro Tuff		2.36
Tuff D	Lokalalei Tuff	Lokalalei Tuff	2.52
		Burgi Tuff	2.64
Tuff B-10			2.95
		Ninikaa Tuff	3.08
		Toroto Tuff	3.32
Tuff B	Tulu Bor Tuff	Tulu Bor Tuff	3.38*
	Topernawi Tuff	Topernawi Tuff	3.72
	Moiti Tuff	Moiti Tuff	3.89*

*Dates are from correlatives in the Ethiopian Rift Valley.

See also Geochronometry; KBS Member; Stratigraphy; Turkana Basin. (F.H.B.)

Further Readings

Westgate, J.A., and Naeser, N.D. (1995) Tephrochronology and fission-track dating. In N.W. Rutter and N.R. Catto (eds.): Dating Methods for Quaternary Deposits, St. Johns, Newfoundland: Geological Society of Canada, pp. 15–28.

Terra Amata

An open-air site located on a sandy terrace 26 m above the Mediterranean in southern France, near Nice. Terra Amata was discovered in 1965 and excavated under the direction of H. de Lumley. The upper levels of the site feature concentrations of stone tools, bones, and ashy sediments distributed in a roughly oval area measuring ca. 6 × 13 m. Ashy patches within this concentration are interpreted as hearths. Postholes and stone footings found near the edge of this concentration suggest a wooden superstructure, perhaps a hut or a windbreak. The lithic industry from Terra Amata features numerous picks, handaxes, cleavers, and flaked tools made from local beach cobbles. Faunal remains include *Elephas antiquus*, *Cervus elaphus*, *Sus scrofa*, and *Bos primigenius*, as well as burnt mussel shells. A hominid cranial fragment (*Homo* sp.) was also discovered. Thermoluminescence dates for burnt flints from Terra Amata suggest that the site formed between 350 and 250 Ka. Terra Amata was initially interpreted by de Lumley as the site of numerous repeated seasonal occupations. The stratigraphic integrity of these separate occupations was challenged by P. Villa, who found that artifacts from different levels at Terra Amata conjoined to each other.

See also Acheulean; Early Paleolithic; Europe; Paleolithic Lifeways; Site Types. [J.J.S.]

Further Readings

De Lumley, H. (1969) A Paleolithic camp at Nice. Sci. Am. 220(5):42–50.

Villa, P. (1983) Terra Amata and the Middle Pleistocene archaeological record of southern France (Publications in Anthropology, Vol. 13). Berkeley: University of California Press.

Tertiary

First, and principal, period of the Cenozoic, including Paleocene, Eocene, Oligocene, Miocene, and Pliocene epochs, in order of their age. G. Arduino, a seventeenth-century Italian natural philosopher, was the first to classify rocks according to their condition and to attribute this condition to their age. In a study of the northern Apennines of Italy, he divided the exposures into *Primary* (igneous), *Secondary* (metamorphic), *Tertiary* (consolidated strata), and *Quaternary* (unconsolidated strata). The first two terms had been largely abandoned by the 1830s, but Tertiary continued in use for the deposits lying above the chalk in the Paris and London basins. Lyell's 1833 characterization of the epochs within the Tertiary formalized its status in chronostratigraphy, but modern international opinion is moving in favor of replacing Tertiary with two approximately equal periods, the Paleogene and the Neogene.

See also Cenozoic; Neogene; Paleogene; Quaternary; Time Scale. [J.A.V.C.]

Teshik-Tash

Cave in Uzbekistan, where in 1938–1939 the partial skeleton of a ca. 9-year-old Neanderthal boy was found. The child was allegedly buried within an arrangement of goat skulls. The cranium and mandible are particularly well preserved and show clear Neanderthal features in the face, mandible, and cranial vault. The brain size of the child was already large (ca. 1,500 ml). Although it is often attributed to the last glaciation, the antiquity of the specimen is uncertain, but it is especially significant in indicating the eastern extent of Neanderthals during the late Pleistocene.

See also Asia, Eastern and Southern; Mousterian; Neanderthals. [C.B.S.]

Thomas Quarries

Three quarries near Casablanca (Morocco) which have produced Middle Pleistocene faunal material, Acheulean tools, and hominid specimens. The Thomas 1 quarry yielded a mandible in 1969; the Thomas 3 quarry, cranial fragments in 1972. The sites are of approximately the same age, close to that of the nearby finds from Salé and Sidi Abderrahman, ca. 400–300 Ka.

The Thomas 1 mandible is similar to those from Tighenif (formerly Ternifine) in Algeria, especially mandible 3, but is robust with large teeth, although the third molar is reduced in size. The Thomas 3 cranial fragments have not yet been studied in detail, but they include frontal, facial, and dental parts of a small individual, probably comparable with the Salé specimen in size. The associated teeth, like those of Salé, are large and heavily worn, yet the associated face is delicately built. A 1992 study using CT (computed tomography) scans has permitted the reconstruction of a nearly complete skull from the combined Salé and Thomas 3 remains, suggesting membership in "archaic *Homo sapiens*."

See also Africa, North; Archaic Homo sapiens; Homo erectus; Salé; Sidi Abderrahman; Tighenif. [C.B.S.]

Further Readings

Kalvin, A.D., Dean, D., Hublin, J., and Braun, M. (1992) Visualization in anthropology: Reconstruction of human fossils from multiple pieces. In A.E. Kaufman and G.M. Nielson (eds.): Proceedings of IEEE Visualization '92. Los Alamitos: IEEE Press, pp. 404–410.

Tighenif

Open-air site of early Middle Pleistocene age (ca. 800–600 Ka) in Algeria, previously known as Ternifine or Palikao. It is

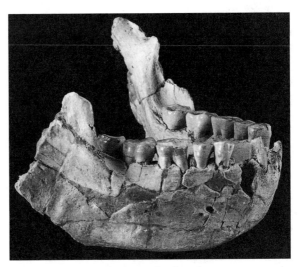

Homo cf. erectus *mandible from Tighenif.*

known for three mandibles and a parietal fragment attributed to *Homo cf. erectus* and for assemblages of Acheulean handaxes and flaked pebbles, associated with abundant faunal remains. The artifact and fossil horizons are now submerged under lake waters.

See also Acheulean; Africa, North; Homo erectus; Thomas Quarries. [R.P.]

Time Scale

The concept of a geological time scale, consisting of time values assigned to stratigraphic boundaries, is the basic formality of prehistory. The establishment of a realistic, if crudely calibrated, time scale was the great triumph of nineteenth-century Victorian geology, giving explanatory power to Earth history and underpinning the Darwinian revolution in biology. In modern geology, refinement of the time scale continues to be a major objective. Decay rates in radiometric isotopes are the most widely used calibration tool, but the geological record contains evidence of other natural processes that also proceed at predictable rates (e.g., radiation-dose accumulation, biomolecular differentiation, deep-sea sedimentation, astronomical cycles) and can be used to improve the time scale.

The antiquity of geological strata has been an issue since 1788–1835 when J. Hutton, J. Playfair, and C. Lyell first raised the argument that Earth history must be measured in millions of years in order to account for all of the geological strata built up by processes that could be observed at work in the modern landscape. This humbling view of humanity's place in the cosmos met with great opposition and remains a central issue among religious conservatives. Over the years, corroborative evidence for the antiquity of the Earth has mounted from other slow processes, such as biological diversification, radiometric decay, geomagnetic-polarity reversals, orbital cycles, and seafloor spreading, and each has been met with ingenious alternative explanations in "creation science" that have as their only rigorous test that they are in agreement with a scripturally based time scale, commencing with an act of universal creation ca. 8 Ka.

Within the scientific community, the nineteenth century saw two fundamentally different models of Earth history, the *uniformitarian* and the *thermodynamic*, with strongly different approaches to a geological time scale. The uniformitarian school, in what may be seen as an overreaction to the short-lived school of "catastrophists" who intended to accommodate the brief scriptural scenario, envisaged a steady-state world of ever-repeating cycles, and cycles within cycles, "without a vestige of a beginning, nor any prospect of an end." The timing of the cycles, the youngest of which Lyell recognized as the epochs of the Tertiary, could not be measured except by very rough estimates of depositional rates. A time scale without years, published in 1893 by H.S. Williams, calibrated the Phanerozoic (the eon of conspicuously fossil-bearing strata) with a reasonable degree of accuracy in terms of the *chrone*, a unit equivalent to the duration of the Eocene. In the same paper, Williams also introduced the term *geochronology*.

On the other hand, physicists exploring the laws of thermodynamics showed that energy in any system was available only because of its initial irregular distribution. By evening-out, or entropy, every system would eventually reach an average "heat death." W. Thompson (Lord Kelvin), working from flawed assumptions, calculated that the sun and its planets were following a path of entropy only 100 Ma in duration, with the solid Earth dating from not more than 20 Ma. Although most geologists came to see the application of first principles of physics as a more realistic way to look at Earth history, attempts to fit all of Earth history into this too-brief time frame were not very satisfactory.

The reconciliation of these two views followed the discovery of radioactivity by H. Becquerel. In itself, radioactive decay (primarily of potassium-40) accounted for most of the heat in the crust that Thompson had taken as evidence of a recently molten state of the Earth. In the 1930s, analysis of the decay processes of radium and uranium led further, to the first attempts at *radiometric* dating. When viewed as a process begun ca. 4.5 billion years ago, the progressive cooling of the solid Earth provides all of the time needed for the lengthy evolution of atmosphere and continents and, eventually, for the development of the metazoan fossil record under conditions that were essentially no different than today, at rates that accord with both the uniformitarian and the thermodynamic postulates.

The Cenozoic Time Scale

A chronologically calibrated time scale for the Cenozoic began to take shape in the 1950s, with instrumentation sensitive enough to make radiometric age determinations of the Neogene, including strata old enough (i.e., Miocene and Pliocene) on the one hand, and young enough (i.e., up into the Late Pleistocene) on the other, to be of interest to paleoanthropologists and archaeologists. The first dates used the *carbon-14* and *potassium-argon* (K/Ar) systems, followed by the development of *uranium-thorium* (U/Th) dating in the carbon-14 range and *fission-track* dating in the K/Ar range. In the 1970s, improvements to mass spectrometers and extraction lines made it possible to determine K/Ar ages on volcanics as young as Early Pleistocene, and the introduction of mass spectrometers doubled the range of the carbon-14 method. *Laser-fusion extraction* led to a further improvement in the quality of argon-isotope ages in the 1980s so that the upper limit of the K/Ar and fission-track methods, and the lower limit of carbon-14 and U/Th, leave only the Middle Pleistocene, between practical limits of 300 and 50 Ka, out of reach to accurate radiometric dating at the end of the twentieth century. *Trapped-charge* dating, such as *electron-spin resonance* (ESR) and *thermoluminescence* (TL), has the range but not the reliability to fill the gap as yet, and argon dates of the eruption of Mt. Vesuvius in AD 79 indicate that this system will continue to improve its precision as well as close the dating gap.

Cyclostratigraphy is a new development of enormous potential for the Cenozoic time scale. Based on the precisely calculated changes in solar radiation reaching the Earth's atmosphere that result from orbital cycles, the timing of the rhythmic variations in stable-isotope ratios from deep-sea cores has made it possible to "tune" the age of magnetostratigraphic reversals in these cores to a much higher level of accuracy and precision than has been possible heretofore with radiometric dating. The feedback into the radiometrically calibrated time scale has already been felt in Pliocene and Pleistocene studies, and the extension of *orbital tuning* into the Miocene is under way.

At the present time, most chronostratigraphic boundaries are dated in their stratotypes or other primary reference sections, by reference to the GPTS (Geomagnetic Polarity Time Scale), and according to fossil evidence, with cyclostratigraphy fast becoming a third dating tool. Radiometric dating is not normally obtainable in the type sections, and the accuracy of boundary ages depends first on the accuracy of correlation from other localities where reversals and fossils are dated, and second on the accuracy of the dating itself. Most of the best dates are from continental and shallow marine deposits, in which volcanics are better preserved and more abundant. The chronostratigraphic boundaries, as bedding planes in stratotype sections, seldom coincide exactly with magnetostratigraphic and biostratigraphic boundaries, and often the boundary age must be interpolated between such calibration points. Cyclostratigraphy promises to improve the quality and number of calibration points significantly.

The weakest link in the correlation chain that brings geochronology to the global time scale is the quality of the stratigraphy where the stage and epoch boundaries are defined. Virtually all stages, and thus all higher categories in the chronostratigraphic hierarchy, are typified in unconformity-bounded highstand tongues, in which substantial parts of the section are usually condensed or missing and in which calibrated paleontological and magnetostratigraphic data are difficult to apply.

Molecular time scales, which are biological in nature and are therefore independent of stratigraphy, have also been put forward. These time scales assume invariant and irreversible rates of differentiation in complex molecules, such as DNA, hemoglobin, and immune-system enzymes. Under these assumptions, the amount of difference between any two living species, in terms of their mutual difference from a third species, is a function of the time since they became genetically distinct. Quantification of this difference in years has proven difficult, with estimates of the human–great ape split ranging from 8 to 3 Ma. The basic tenet of invariant rates has also been questioned on theoretical grounds.

See also Biochronology; Cenozoic; Cyclostratigraphy; ESR (Electron Spin Resonance) Dating; Fission-Track Dating; Paleomagnetism; Potassium-Argon Dating; Radiometric Dating; Stratigraphy; TL (Thermoluminescence) Dating; Trapped-Charge Dating. [F.H.B., J.A.V.C.]

Further Readings

Berggren, W.A., Kent, D.V., Aubry, M.P., and Hardenbol, J. eds. (1995) Geochronology, Time Scales, and Global Stratigraphic Correlation (Special Publication No. 54). Tulsa: Soc. Sed. Geol.

Odin, G.S., ed. (1985) Numerical dating in stratigraphy, Part 1. New York: Wiley.

Renne, P.R., Deino, A.L., Walter, R.C., Turrin, B.D., Swisher, C.C.I., Becker, T.A., Curtis, G.H., Sharp, W.D., and Jaouni, A.R. (1994) Intercalibration of astronomical and radioisotopic time. Geology 22:783–786.

Tindale, N.B. (1900–1993)

Australian anthropologist and prehistorian. With J.B. Birdsell, he made the most extensive surveys of the Australian Aboriginal population, producing detailed maps of traditional tribal boundaries. He also excavated historically important sites on the Murray River in South Australia, at Devon Downs and Tartanga.

See also Australia; Birdsell, Joseph B. [A.T.]

TL (Thermoluminescence) Dating

Dating method for archaeological and geological deposits based on the emission of light from heated samples; one of the methods of *trapped-charge dating*. Thermoluminescence depends on the fact that raising the temperature of some materials releases energy, stored as trapped electron charges, in measurable amounts of visible light. A few milligrams of finely granulated sample are placed beneath a high-sensitivity light detector on an electrically heated platform in a vacuum chamber. The sample is heated at a constant rate (usually 5°C/sec), and a *glow curve* is constructed from measurements of the amount of light emitted at each increment. Energy from specific electron-charge traps is liberated at characteristic temperatures, with the longest-lived traps giving peaks at the highest temperatures. Thus, in mixtures of different minerals, such as in a pottery sample, the emitted light exhibits high-intensity peaks in particular wavelengths (seen as colors) in certain temperature ranges on the glow curve.

TL-datable materials from archaeological sites include quartz, feldspar, and flint (microcrystalline quartz) that have been zeroed by heating in cooking fires or in ceramic firing, and freshly formed calcite from stalagmites and tufa deposits. The age of ceramics can be determined with a precision of ca. 5–10 percent. Artifacts (e.g., points or knives) made of quartz or flint can be dated from the last time of heating; heated ("burned") flints can be recognized by the development of characteristic microfractures. The TL signal in quartz is stable up to at least 500 Ka and can be used to date Paleolithic sites where fire was used.

Burial age of Quaternary sediments can be approximately dated by TL, because the trapped-charge content in quartz and feldspar grains is gradually reduced during exposure to sunlight to values near (but not equal to) zero. The most datable sediments are those made up of grains that have been thoroughly exposed prior to burial, such as loess, dune sand, or beach sand. The apparent age is corrected by artificially bleaching a split of the sediment and subtracting for the residual TL activity.

Two sites at which burned flint was dated by TL are the cave of Qafzeh in Israel, where burials of anatomically mod-

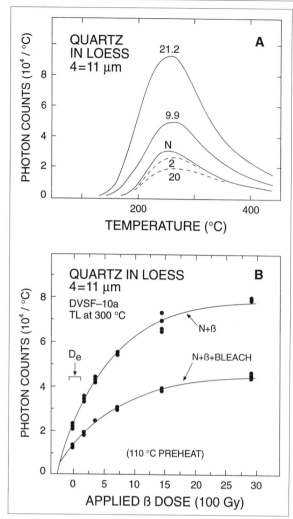

Top: glow-curve for a sedimentary sample zeroed by solar bleaching. Each curve shows the light intensity emitted (as photon counts) as temperature is increased at 5°C/sec. N is glow-curve for the natural sample; solid curves are for samples with added doses of 990 and 2200 Gy (gray); dashed curves are for samples which were bleached and then irradiated. The height of the glow curves at 300°C was used to construct additive dose curve.

Bottom: additive-dose curve for determination of equivalent dose (DE). N+β shows the height of the glow curve at 300°C and for added dose (multiple points represent repeat measurements). N+β+BLEACH shows 300°C points for samples that were bleached before β-dosing.

ern humans were shown to date from 92 ± 5 Ka, and Le Moustier in the Dordogne region of France, where layers containing Mousterian artifacts gave mean ages ranging from 56 ± 5 (at the base) to 40 ± 3 Ka just below the Châtelperronian, which gave a date of 43 ± 4 Ka. The ages increase downward and indicate a resolution of a few thousand years.

See also ESR (Electron Spin Resonance) Dating; Geochronometry; OSL (Optically Stimulated Luminescence) Dating; Pleistocene; Trapped-Charge Dating. [H.P.S.]

Further Readings

Aitken, M., and Valladas, H. (1992) Luminescence dating and the origin of modern man. In M.J. Aitken, C.B. Stringer, and P.A. Mellars (eds.): The Origin of Mod-

ern Humans and the Impact of Chronometric Dating. Princeton: Princeton University Press. pp. 27–39.

Berger, G.W. (1988) Dating Quaternary events by luminescence. In D. Easterbrook (ed.): Dating Quaternary Sediments (Special Paper No. 227). Boulder: Geological Society of America, pp. 13–25.

Berger, G.W. (1995) Progress in luminescence dating methods for Quaternary sediments. In N.W. Rutter and N.R. Catto (eds.): Dating Methods for Quaternary Deposits. St. Johns, Newfoundland: Geological Society of Canada, pp. 81–104.

Feathers, J.K. (1996) Luminescence dating and modern human origins. Evol. Anthropol. 5:25–36.

Hütt, G.I., and Raukas, A. (1995) Thermoluminescence dating of sediments. In N.W. Rutter and N.R. Catto (eds.): Dating Methods for Quaternary Deposits. St. Johns, Newfoundland: Geological Society of Canada, pp. 73–80.

Tlapacoya

Archaeological site in the Basin of Mexico, generally thought to be important in establishing a firm association between artifacts and bones of extinct animals. Although evidence for human use of the site is scanty, radiocarbon dates of 20 Ka derive from a hearthlike depression and a fallen tree immediately beneath which a bifacial blade was found. Andesite implements and a chalcedony scraper uncovered at this site have also been attributed to this early period.

See also Americas; Paleoindian. [L.S.A.P., D.H.T.]

Torre in Pietra

Open-air archaeological site located 24 km northwest of Rome (Italy), with two archaeological levels, first excavated by A.C. Blanc in the 1950s. The older level contains Acheulean artifacts in a disturbed horizon with associated fauna suggesting attribution to the penultimate (Saale or Riss) glacial stage (*Equus caballus, Elephas antiquus, Bos primigenius, Rhinoceros mercki,* and, more rarely, *Cervus elaphus* and *Megaceros*). Although this level also yielded one of the first potassium-argon (K/Ar) ages for the European Paleolithic, the samples are almost certainly in derived context, so that the date of 430 Ka should not be taken to characterize the level. The upper level contains a more temperate fauna, including fallow deer (*Dama dama*), suggestive of last-interglacial conditions. Due to the absence of bifaces and the presence of prepared striking platforms and other characteristics of Levallois technology, as well as a wide range of retouched flake tools, this later industry is referable to an early phase of the local Mousterian (Pontinian).

See also Acheulean; Europe; Middle Paleolithic; Levallois; Mousterian. [A.S.B.]

Transformation Series

Set of states of the same character in different members of a higher taxon of organisms that is believed to represent a morphocline from primitive to derived.

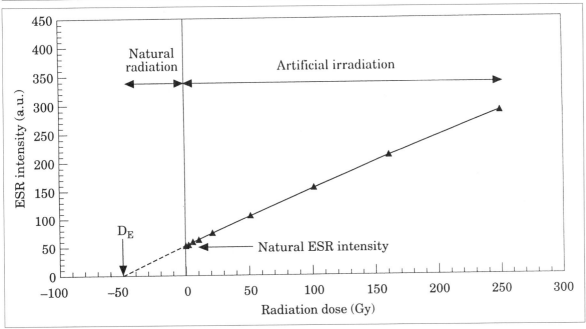

Typical response curve for trapped charge dosimetry. To arrive at the time value for the trapped charges accumulated in the sample, aliquots (portions) of the sample are successively dosed with increasing amounts of additional gamma rays (triangle symbols). The intensity of light given off (vertical axis) at the release temperature after each dose (horizontal axis) defines a curve (here a nearly straight line) that can be extrapolated back to zero intensity, or DE, , when the sample began to accumulate charges. The horizontal distance from DE to the vertical line of zero additional (artificial) dose represents the ancient dose generated by natural radiation. From R. Grün, 1996, J. Hum. Evol., 30. By permission of Academic Press, Ltd.

See also Cladistics; Cline; Evolutionary Morphology; Evolutionary Systematics (Darwinian Phylogenetics). [I.T.]

Trapped-Charge Dating

Different methods for determining the age of archaeological and geological material are based on the phenomenon of electron-charge trapping, among them thermoluminescence dating (TL), optically stimulated luminescence dating (OSL), and electron spin resonance dating (ESR). These methods all exploit the fact that, when crystal lattices are bombarded by background high-energy radiation, some of the energy is trapped in the form of electrons and holes (i.e., positive charges left after the ejection of electrons from an atom) at lattice defects in crystals. The age of crystallization, or the age of the last zeroing event, can be determined by measuring the trapped-charge levels that have accumulated since that time. Some trapped-charge sites are more unstable than others and are readily zeroed by exposure to moderate levels of transient heat and sunlight. Depending on the site, the lifetimes of trapped charges range from a few minutes up to millions of years, and they decrease with increasing background temperature.

Trapped charge dating consists of (1) measurement of the amount of trapped charge, expressed in terms of the equivalent radiation dose (DE) needed to duplicate the observed TL, OSL, or ESR signal; and (2) measurement of the ambient dose rate, d, at the site where the sample was stored. The equivalent dose is determined by the additive-dose method, in which several aliquots (portions) of the sample are given successively larger artifical doses of radiation, producing a curve of increasing signal intensity with dose. DE is the dose equivalent to that which would have raised the sig-

nal intensity from zero to its observed natural value (see Figure). The ambient dose rate, d, is the sum of external (d_{ex}) and internal (d_{in}) components, where the external dose rate is the sum of the background radioactivity from uranium (U), potassium (K), and thorium (Th) in the sample environment plus cosmic-ray dose, plus corrections for water content as a moderator and for radon leakage. The internal dose rate is determined from the U, K, and Th content of the sample itself. The age is then given by the ratio DE/d.

See also ESR (Electron Spin Resonance) Dating; OSL (Optically Stimulated Luminescence) Dating; TL (Thermoluminescence) Dating. [H.P.S.]

Further Readings

Aitken, M.J. (1985) Thermoluminescence Dating. London: Academic.

Treeshrews

The treeshrews comprise an order (Scandentia) of small mammals that is widespread throughout the forested areas of both insular and mainland Southeast Asia. The best-known treeshrew genus is *Tupaia*, the common treeshrew, which is represented by numerous species; but even this is poorly studied, and very little is known about the other five treeshrew genera in their native habitats.

The treeshrews are of particular interest to primatologists because, for many years, these mammals were considered to be the "most primitive" of the primates. Various authors pointed particularly to certain aspects of their brain and basicranial anatomy, as well as to their possession of a postorbital bar (a bony strut defining the lateral edge of the orbit that is also characteristic of all living primates), to justify the inclusion of the treeshrews in Primates; today, however, it is clear that this relationship cannot be substantiated. In some ways, *Tupaia* probably does resemble the earliest primates (e.g., in being a clawed, moderately small-bodied, opportunistic frugivore that lives in solitary-ranging pairs), but in general these are primitive eutherian mammal traits and not characteristically primate ones. Scandentia possibly forms part of a major group, Archonta, to which bats, colugos, primates, and maybe elephant shrews also belong, but this remains to be firmly demonstrated.

See also Archonta; Primates. [I.T.]

Further Readings

Luckett, W.P., ed. (1980) Comparative Biology and Relationships of Tree Shrews. New York: Plenum.

Tattersall, I. (1984) The tree-shrew, *Tupaia:* A "living model" of the ancestral primate? In N. Eldredge and S. Stanley (eds.): Living Fossils. New York: Springer-Verlag.

Tribe

Category of the classificatory hierarchy that lies below the subfamily and above the genus. Subtribes may, however, be interposed between the tribe and the genus. The *International Code of Zoological Nomenclature* recommends that the suffix "-ini" be used to terminate tribe names. Informal usage results in the "-in" ending, as in hominin.

See also Classification; Genus; Nomenclature; Subfamily; Subtribe. [I.T.]

Trinil

Fossil-collecting area in central Java dated to the Middle Pleistocene by lithostratigraphic correlation and associated mammalian fauna. Trinil is the name of a village on the Solo River in east-central Java, close to where E. Dubois unearthed the first evidence of *Homo erectus* in 1891. The evidence consisted of a molar, skull cap, and femur that Dubois christened *Pithecanthropus erectus*. Dubois's original find was initially the subject of much controversy. Not only did his contemporaries question the specimens' status as a hominid ancestor, but they also criticized his association of the femur with the skull cap. Decades later, Dubois modified his own

position and considered that the specimen represented some form of giant "gibbonoid" primate that was, nonetheless, ancestral to modern humans.

Today, paleoanthropologists are nearly unanimous in recognizing these specimens as the same species as the human remains at Sangiran. They were excavated from a gravel bed that has been correlated with the lower portion of the Kabuh Formation, whose Trinil Fauna is usually considered to span the Middle Pleistocene. However, controversy about the absolute and relative age of the locality and the fauna continues. Some workers think that the Trinil Fauna actually predates the reputedly Early Pleistocene Djetis Fauna. Others argue that they are the same age (i.e., early Middle Pleistocene). The only thing that virtually all workers agree on is that both the fauna and the hominid(s) were transported prior to deposition. Subsequent excavations, some on a massive scale, have failed to unearth more hominid finds from Trinil.

See also Asia, Eastern and Southern; Dubois, Eugene; Djetis; Indonesia; Pleistocene; Sangiran Dome. [G.G.P.]

Further Readings

Sémah, F., Sémah, A., and Djubiantono, T. (1990) They Discovered Java. Jakarta: Pusat Penelitian Arkeologi Nasional.

Theunissen, B. (1989) Eugène Dubois and the Ape-Man from Java. Dordrecht: Kluwer.

Theunissen, B., de Vos, J., Sondaar, P.Y., and Aziz, F. (1990) The establishment of a chronological framework for the hominid-bearing deposits of Java: A historical survey. In L.F. LaPorte (ed.): Establishment of a Geologic Framework for Paleoanthropology. Boulder: Geological Society of America, pp. 39–54.

Tshitolian

Central African Later Stone Age industry named after Bene Tshitolo, a Luba group occupying the plateau north of Bibange in Kasai Occidentale Province (Congo/Zaire). The Tshitolian is characterized by blade and discoidal-core technology; arrowheads with tangs, shanks, or wings; microlithic elements, especially *tranchet* arrowheads, trapezes, and segments, together with a continuation and refinement of such Lupemban forms as lanceolate and bifacial foliate points, biconvex core-axes, core and flake scrapers, and choppers. The

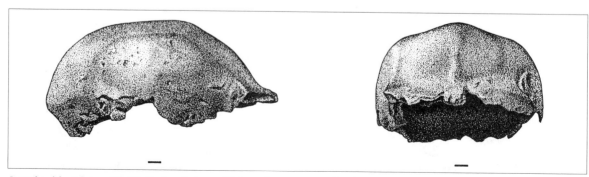

Lateral and frontal view of the Trinil calotte (holotype of Pithecanthropus erectus*) found by Eugene Dubois in 1891. Scales are 1 cm.*

industry is often associated with evidence of intensive grain and tuber exploitation or possibly cultivation in the form of pottery, bored stones, and grindstones. Radiocarbon ages range from ca. 13 to 2 Ka, and the distribution is restricted to forest and forest-savannah mosaics in and around the eastern Congo Basin, with possible extensions into the savannah areas of Rwanda and Burundi.

See also Africa; Later Stone Age; Lupemban; Mesolithic; Neolithic; Stone-Tool Making. [A.S.B.]

Tsodilo Sites

Tsodilo is a small area of rocky hills in northwestern Botswana just west of the Okavango drainage system. The Tsodilo hills contain both Early Iron Age pastoralist sites on their summits, and numerous small to medium rockshelters below containing cultural materials dating from the Middle Stone Age (MSA) to the Iron Age. Specularite was also mined here, beginning at least as early as the early Iron Age. Particularly interesting in the MSA horizons are a series of very small points from Rhino Shelter, many made on exotic raw materials, and evidence of fishing in the form of catfish remains from White Paintings Shelter before 40 Ka. In the Later Stone Age (LSA) horizons of White Paintings Shelter, bone harpoons occur with LSA stone artifacts and fish remains, possibly dating to as early as ca. 35 Ka. The hilltop sites of Divuyu and !Noma contain important evidence for early Iron Age movements of people from the north into southern Africa, at ca. AD 400–500. The exposed rock faces of the Tsodilo hills are decorated with more than 4,000 rock paintings, including scenes of both wild and domestic animals.

See also Africa; Africa, Southern; Iron Age; Later Stone Age; Middle Paleolithic; Middle Stone Age; Modern Human Origins. [A.S.B.]

Turkana Basin

The segment of the East African Rift in northern Kenya and southern Ethiopia occupied by Lake Turkana and its tributaries. From the headwaters of the Omo River in Ethiopia to where the smaller Kerio and Turkwel streams enter from the Kenya highlands, the distance from northeast to southwest is ca. 700 km. The lake level is presently several tens of meters below its pluvial outlet to the White Nile in southern Sudan, but the water is still relatively fresh and supports a wide variety of aquatic life, including Nile perch and crocodiles. Many important Plio-Pleistocene hominins have been recovered from sediments deposited in this basin, as well as a unique assemblage of Miocene hominoids and cercopithecoids.

The Cretaceous Lubur Series, which crops out in sheer cliffs in the rift shoulder northwest of the lake, yields a small but moderately diverse dinosaur fauna. Beginning with Late Eocene volcanism in the Ethiopian Rift segment to the north, by the Middle Miocene the length of the Turkana Basin had filled with immensely thick sequences of lavas and agglomerates, interbedded with locally fossiliferous sedimentary layers. The richest fossil sites, however, are in the

Upper Miocene to Pleistocene formations of stream and lake sediments, interbedded with numerous tuff layers and local lava flows, which were subsequently laid down in the Lake Turkana floodplain and the lower reaches of its tributaries.

The Eragaleit Beds in the Lothidok Range, bordering the lake on the southwest side, are the oldest investigated Cenozoic sediments in the region. These beds consist of coarse-grained sandstones bracketed by flows of the Kalokol Basalts with potassium-argon (K/Ar) ages of 27 and 24.5 Ma. In the current time scale, these beds are of Late Oligocene age. A sparse collection, long known in the literature as the Losodok Peak or Lothidok fauna, includes the oldest-known hominoid, the proconsulid *Kamoyapithecus hamiltoni* (formerly considered a species of *Xenopithecus*).

The Kalokol Basalts are overlain by the Lower Miocene Lothidok Formation, a thick body of fluvial beds, volcanic mudflow deposits and lavas in which the sites of Moruarot and Kalodirr have produced fossils of *Turkanapithecus, Afropithecus, Simiolus,* and *Proconsul,* dated between 16.8 and 17.5 Ma. The associated fauna is characterized by mammals that seem indicative of open, seasonal environments that have also been inferred at North African and Saudi Arabian coastal-plain sites of similar age but not in the coeval highland faunas of western Kenya. The clear implication is that the floor of the Turkana Basin at that time had a coastal-plain ecology, and, in fact, a whale has been recorded from the Early Miocene Loperot site to the south of Lake Turkana.

To the north of the Lothidok area, the small site of Locherangan west of Kataboi village has yielded Early Miocene fossils of *Afropithecus, Simiolus,* and an indeterminate catarrhine from a sequence of fluvial and lacustrine deposits. Early Miocene sites to the south of the lake include Napedet and Loperot (ca. 18 Ma), the latter producing fragmentary *Victoriapithecus* jaws. East of Lake Turkana, the Buluk site, dated to 17.5 Ma, has yielded fossils of *Afropithecus* that compare closely with those from the Early Miocene sites west of the lake. At the southern tip of the lake, local exposures of the Mwiti Beds, dated to 17.2 Ma, have Early Miocene faunas at Kajong and Lokalalei.

Faunas between 14 and ca. 8 Ma are rare. In the upper part of the Lothidok Formation, dated to ca. 13.2 Ma, fossils have been recovered from the Esha site, including specimens attributed to *Kenyapithecus.* Exposures at Nachola, an isolated area in the lower part of the Samburu Escarpment in the extreme southeastern part of the basin, have also yielded a mammalian fauna that includes numerous specimens attributed to *Kenyapithecus,* including a partial skeleton, dated just older than 15 Ma. A younger level at Baragoi, dated ca. 9.5 Ma, has produced the unique maxilla of *Samburupithecus,* perhaps the oldest African hominine.

The sites of Ekora, Kanapoi, and Lothagam, southwest of the lake, preserve a record of the Late Miocene and Early Pliocene in the basin. Kanapoi has yielded one of the oldest-known hominins, *Australopithecus anamensis,* from levels dated to ca. 4.2 Ma. Lothagam has several faunal levels, ranging from Late Miocene (ca. 8 Ma) into the earliest Pleistocene (more than 1.5 Ma). In contrast to earlier and later rocks, the lower part of the Lothagam deposits are brick red from sands

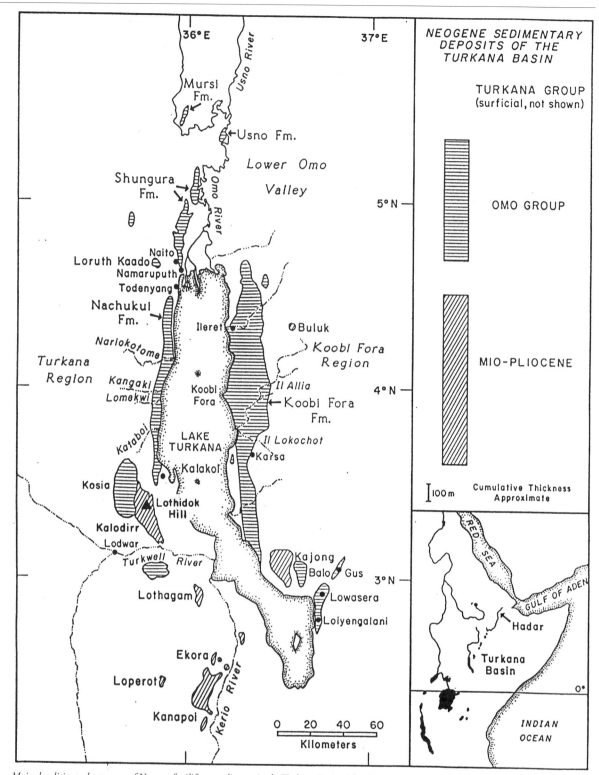

Major localities and exposures of Neogene fossiliferous sediments in the Turkana Basin. After F.H. Brown and C.S. Feibel, 1991, in J.M. Harris (ed.) Koobi Fora Research Project, Volume 3. *Oxford, Clarendon Press. Courtesy of F.H. Brown and Oxford University Press.*

and silts derived from weathering of a volcanic source terrane that lay to the south. The upper part of the sequence is dominated by detritus from a metamorphic basement source west of the rift valley. A mandible and two isolated teeth of an early ?hominin are known in layers dated ca. 6–4.7 Ma.

Each of the Miocene sites has its own character, source region, and stratigraphic style, but in the Plio-Pleistocene the

sites show a more uniform stratigraphic character, arguing for the establishment of basinwide depositional influences. At ca. 4 Ma, fissure eruptions of fine-grained basalt covered the northern half, at least, of the Turkana Basin as far south as Central Island. These basalts punctuate the change in sedimentary style from Miocene to Plio-Pleistocene and quite likely mark the inception of the Turkana Basin in its modern outline. De-

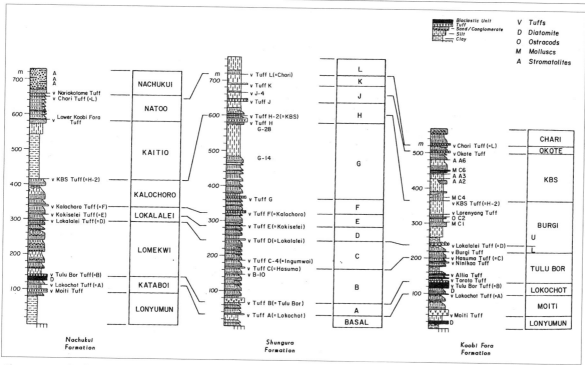

Chronostratigraphic framework for the Omo Group deposits of the Turkana Basin. Major marker tuffs ranging in age from the Moiti Tuff at 3.89 Ma to the Chari Tuff at 1.39 Ma correlate the exposed sequences in West Turkana (Nachukui Formation), Omo (Shungura Formation), and Koobi Fora areas. Courtesy of Craig C. Feibel.

posits of the Omo Group (4.2–0.6 Ma), with widespread formations that are recognized at Usno, Shungura, Fejej, Koobi Fora, and in the West Turkana sites, overlie these basalts in most places but are intruded by them in a few localities.

The next 4 Myr saw alternation of lacustrine and fluviatile conditions within the central Turkana Basin. Stratigraphic relations between these geographically separated exposures have been established through correlation of volcanic ash layers. In the Lower Omo Valley, the Mursi Formation underlies a fissure basalt dated near 4.2 Ma and probably overlaps in time with the highest part of the Lothagam and Kanapoi sequence. The Mursi Beds appear to represent the northern extension of an immense pre-Turkana lake, called Lonyumun Lake, which occupied essentially the entire basin. Few mammalian fossils have been recovered from Lonyumun Lake strata, but the deposits are rich in diatoms, ostracodes, molluscs, and fish remains. Ca. 3.9 Ma, the basin was captured by a major fluvial system that drained to the Indian Ocean. Remains of *Australopithecus* come from the lower levels of this fluvial system, which persisted until ca. 3.45 Ma, when the rift structure was reemphasized and a major new lake was impounded. Evidently, this lake did not reach as far northward as previously because fluvial, not lacustrine, conditions characterized the Shungura Formation in the Omo Valley. Lacustrine beds of this age southeast of the present lake contain mammalian fossils, mainly in lake-margin environments preserved in the Nachukui Formation. This lake phase came to an end ca. 3.36 Ma ago, and fluvial conditions are recorded in all exposed parts of the basin for the next 1.1 Myr with only minor lacustrine interruptions.

Many hominid fossils from the Shungura Formation come from this extended fluvial interlude (3.35–2.2 Ma), as do

many important specimens from the Nachukui Formation. These include NME Omo 18–1967–18, the type specimen of "*Paraustralopithecus*" (now *Paranthropus*) *aethiopicus*, and its probable conspecific KNM-WT-17000, which was initially described as *Australopithecus boisei*. Few hominid fossils are known from the Koobi Fora Formation in this time interval; this is partly because the last half of this interval is not represented at Koobi Fora due to a slight regional uplift east of the lake. Early stone artifacts are recorded from this interval in both the Shungura and the Nachukui formations, dating to ca. 2.35 Ma. The basin was once again inundated by a lake at ca. 2.1 Ma, which withdrew at ca. 1.9 Ma from the northern and eastern parts but persisted until ca. 1.7 Ma on the west side of the lake.

Between ca. 1.9 and 1.3 Ma, fluvial and lacustrine conditions alternated far more frequently than in the earlier history of the basin. Stromatolite layers and beds rich in molluscs, both deposited in shallow waters, provide important marker horizons for this interval. Hominids are very well represented from this interval at Koobi Fora and include specimens KNM-ER-406, -407, and -732 (all attributed to *Paranthropus boisei*); -1470, -1805, and -1813 (all considered as *Homo* sp.); and -3733 and -3883 (*Homo* aff. *H. erectus*). In the Nachukui Formation, remains of both a robust australopith and an exceptionally complete skeleton of an early variety of *Homo* (initially described as *H. erectus*) have been recovered from this interval. All of the well-documented archaeological sites from Koobi Fora occur in strata of this age, as well as a number of archaeological sites in the Nachukui Formation.

After 1.3 Ma, the record of deposition within the basin becomes increasingly sparse. The highest levels of the Shungura Formation probably date to ca. 1.0 Ma, but sedimentation continues until ca. 600 Ka in the Nachukui Formation. At Koobi Fora, the youngest strata of the Omo Group date to ca. 500 Ka, although these are well exposed only in the Ileret area. No hominid fossils have been recovered from this important interval.

Sometime between 700 Ka and the present, strata of the Omo Group were deformed and faulted, uplifting those parts of the old basin floor that are presently exposed around the lake. Displacement on individual faults may amount to several hundred meters, and nearly a kilometer of cumulative vertical displacement can be documented for the Shungura Formation across a series of faults. There is little evidence for deposition in areas around the lake from 700 to ca. 100 Ka, but the Kibish Formation, best exposed in the northern part of the Lower Omo Valley, represents a final phase. Several highstands of lake level are represented, the oldest dating to ca. 100 Ka and the youngest to ca. 10 Ka. Three calvaria of "archaic *Homo sapiens*" have been collected from the lower part of the Kibish Formation. At Koobi Fora, a cranium (KNM-ER-3884) was collected at the unconformity between the Koobi Fora Formation and the Galana Boi Formation, a deposit that is ca. 10 Ka at the base. Many Neolithic sites are known from the Galana Boi Formation, and Iron Age sites also exist at Koobi Fora.

Lake Turkana dropped to near its present level not more than 3.5 Ka, resulting in erosion and exposure of the younger deposits and local exhumation and further erosion of earlier strata.

See also Afar Basin; Africa; Africa, East; Lothagam; Rift Valley; Tephrochronology. [F.H.B.]

Further Readings

Boschetto, H.B., Brown, F.H., and McDougall, I. (1992) Stratigraphy of the Lothidok Range, northern Kenya, and K/Ar ages of its Miocene primates. J. Hum. Evol. 22:44–71.

Brown, F.H. (1994) Development of Pliocene and Pleistocene chronology of the Turkana Basin, East Africa, and its relation to other sites. In R.S. Corruccini and R.L. Ciochon, (eds.): Integrative Paths to the Past. Englewood Cliffs, N.J.: Prentice-Hall, pp. 285–312.

Brown, F.H. (1995) The potential of the Turkana Basin for paleoclimatic reconstruction in East Africa. In E.S. Vrba, G.H. Denton, T.C. Partridge, and L.H. Burckle (eds.): Paleoclimate and Evolution, with Emphasis on Human Origins. New Haven: Yale University Press, pp. 319–330.

Feibel, C.S., Brown, F.H., and McDougall I. (1989) Stratigraphic context of fossil hominids from the Omo Group deposits, northern Turkana Basin, Kenya and Ethiopia. Am. J. Phys. Anthropol. 75:595–622.

U

'Ubeidiya

Open-air Early Pleistocene site located in the northern Jordan Valley (Israel), south of the city of Tiberias. Early Acheulean and Developed Oldowan stone tools, a rich Late Villafranchian (Early Pleistocene) faunal assemblage, and hominid fossils have been recovered from this site. 'Ubeidiya was excavated between 1960 and 1974 by M. Stekelis, E. Tchernov, and O. Bar-Yosef, and later (1988–1994) by a French-Israeli-American team. The 'Ubeidiya Formation consists of four major beds (Li, Fi, Lu, Fu) representing two lacustrine-fluvial cycles that formed around a delta where a seasonal stream (Wadi Yavneel) flowed into the lake that covered the floor of the Jor-

dan Valley. The most significant stratigraphic feature of the site is an anticline (upward bending of strata) that tilts the 'Ubeidiya Formation sediments ca. 70° to the horizontal plane.

All of the 'Ubeidiya Formation sediments have reversed polarity and belong to the Matuyama Chron. The vertebrate fossils include *Pelorovis oldowayensis*, *Equus oldowayensis*, *Hippopotamus gorgops*, *Praemegaceros verticornis*, *Ursus etruscus*, *Kolpochoerus oldowayensis*, *Crocuta crocuta*, *Canis arnensis*, and *Macaca sylvanus*. Several hominid teeth and a cranial fragment, attributed to *Homo* sp. by P.V. Tobias, were recovered during the early 1960s, mostly from the surface. Biostratigraphic analysis of the fauna from the 'Ubeidiya Forma-

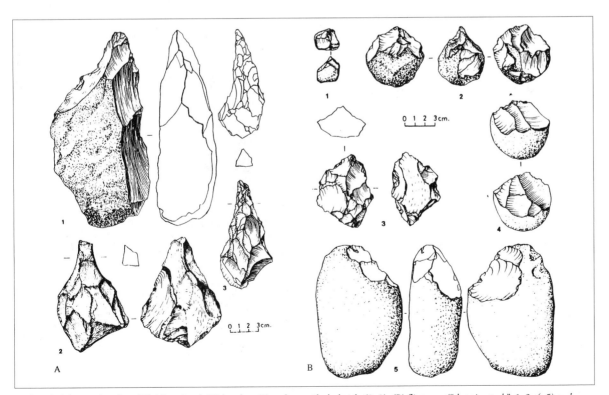

Early Paleolithic artifacts from 'Ubeidiya, Israel: (A) handaxe (1) and two trihedral picks (2, 3); (B) flint cores ("chopping tools"; 1, 2, 4, 5) and alternately retouched thick flake (3). From A. Horowitz, The Quaternary of Israel, *1979, Academic Press.*

tion establishes its rough equivalence with Tamanian (Russia), 'Ain Hanech (Morocco), and Olduvai Upper Bed II (Tanzania), suggesting an age of 1.4 Ma for the entire formation. If this date is correct, 'Ubeidiya is one of the oldest archaeological sites in Eurasia.

The archaeological features of the site include dense concentrations of stone tools in perilimnic deposits that early excavators described as *living floors*. These are now recognized to have resulted from wave action and flowing water. Many of the fossils and stone tools at 'Ubeidiya have either been redeposited or subjected to wave action, but smaller patches of fossils and stone artifacts in primary contexts are also known. The lithic assemblages vary widely in composition, but most are comparable to the Developed Oldowan B and the Early Acheulean of Olduvai Gorge, featuring numerous spheroids (mostly made of limestone), trihedral picks, and many awls, notches, and denticulates.

See also Acheulean; 'Ain Hanech; Asia, Western; Early Paleolithic; Oldowan; Olduvai Gorge. [J.J.S.]

Further Readings

Bar-Yosef, O., and Goren-Inbar, N. (1993) The Lithic Assemblages of 'Ubeidiya, a Lower Palaeolithic Site in the Jordan Valley (Monographs of the Institute of Archaeology, Qedem 34). Jerusalem: Hebrew University.

Tchernov, E. (1987) The age of the 'Ubeidiya Formation, an Early Pleistocene hominid site in the Jordan Valley, Israel. Israel J. Earth Sci. 36:3–30.

Uluzzian

An early Upper Paleolithic industry, dating to more than ca. 33 Ka, defined on inventories recovered from cave sites located mostly around the Uluzzo Bay, near Lecce in southern Italy. These inventories are dominated by Middle Paleolithic elements produced by bipolar percussion, including numerous side-scrapers, denticulates, and notched pieces. Distinctly Upper Paleolithic implements include the diagnostic small, curved, backed points, as well as bone points and perforated shells. Uluzzian layers in Cavallo Cave, where this industry was defined, have yielded two human teeth, one of which is considered anatomically modern while the second one apparently belonged to a more archaic hominin. Like the Châtelperronian in France and the Szeletian in central Europe, this industry is seen as a transitional one between the Middle and the Upper Paleolithic, possibly indicative of cultural interaction between Mousterian and Aurignacian peoples.

See also Aurignacian; Châtelperronian; Europe; Middle Paleolithic; Mousterian; Szeletian; Upper Paleolithic. [O.S.]

Upper Paleolithic

Stage of European and eastern Mediterranean Paleolithic development characterized by the development of blade and burin technology, proficient hunting of large game (possibly to extinction in some cases), and sophisticated working of organic materials (bone, antler, horn, ivory, tooth, shell), as well as a proliferation of jewelry and of carved/painted/ incised images on stone, organic materials, and cave and rockshelter walls.

Geographical and Chronological Extent

Since later Pleistocene archaeological developments in northwestern and sub-Saharan Africa, India, China, Southeast Asia, Australia, and the New World are substantially different from those in Europe, southwestern Asia, and northeastern Africa, the term *Upper Paleolithic* is often reserved for the blade and burin technologies of the latter regions. In this volume, the term *Late Paleolithic* is employed for later Late Pleistocene industries worldwide in a broader sense than simply the Upper Paleolithic, mainly of Europe. Also referred to as *Mode 4* (after J.G.D. Clark) or *Leptolithic*, Upper Paleolithic industries replaced flake and prepared-core industries, such as the Mousterian, ca. 40–35 Ka and were themselves replaced by microlithic technologies ca. 20–10 Ka. Thus, the Upper Paleolithic occurred during the maximum cold phases of the last glacial.

In most of Africa outside the northeast, a sustained blade and burin technological state is absent from cultural sequences, although blade technology itself appears sporadically within prepared-core and flake sequences (Mode 3, Middle Stone Age) at a much earlier date than in Europe. Painted images, decorative objects, bone working, and sophisticated hunting appear in Africa at an age comparable with, or even earlier than, that of the early Upper Paleolithic, but also in a Mode 3 (flake technology) context. A widespread shift to Mode 5 (microlithic) technology, accompanied by the more intensive exploitation of small-scale resources, begins in Africa by 20 Ka, well before the comparable shift to Mode 5 technologies in most European regions. Culture histories in southern and eastern Asia, the

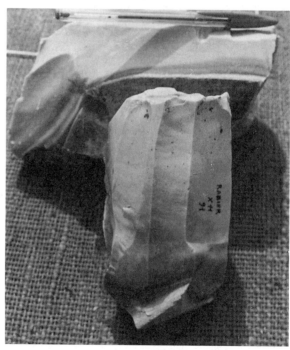

Very large Upper Paleolithic prismatic blade cores from Gravettian of Rabier (France). For illustrations of Upper Paleolithic tool types, see entries on specific industries.

Pacific, and the New World appear equally divergent from the European pattern. It is, thus, inappropriate to extend the European-based Upper Paleolithic designation beyond the limits of Europe and adjacent regions, exclusive of northwestern Africa. The significant exception is Siberia, where true Upper Paleolithic technologies (although in combination with flake tools), economic adaptations, and symbolic behavior were widespread after 20 Ka.

Divisions of the Upper Paleolithic

The classic division of the Upper Paleolithic into Aurignacian, Perigordian (Gravettian), Solutrean, and Magdalenian industries is based on the earliest explorations of sites of this age in southwestern France. The first definition of the Upper Paleolithic, by E. Lartet and H. Christy in 1875, was paleontological: their Cave Bear, Mammoth, and Reindeer Ages were based on the dominant animals in the faunal remains from many western European Upper Paleolithic sites. Prior to the Reindeer Ages, the Aurignacian of Aurignac, Le Moustier, and Abri Lartet was recognized as a transitional industry succeeding the Mousterian at the end of the Cave Bear and Mammoth Ages, followed by the Solutrean and the Magdalenian of Solutré, La Madeleine, and the Laugerie sites during the Reindeer Age.

Subsequent chronologies based on tool typologies rather than stratigraphy were developed by G. de Mortillet from 1867 to 1910. In these schemes, Mortillet initially saw the Aurignacian (incorporating the Perigordian), characterized by elaborate bone tools, as an early stage of the Magdalenian, but he dropped it as a separate entity by 1881; he placed the Solutrean, with its bifacially worked leaf-shaped points on flakes, between the Mousterian and the Aurignacian/Magdalenian. The importance of stratigraphy in determining the relative chronology of Upper Paleolithic subdivisions, and the restoration of the Aurignacian to its appropriate place at the beginning of the Upper Paleolithic, were not established until H. Breuil's work at the beginning of the twentieth century. Basing his conclusions on the work of D. Peyrony and others, Breuil also defined three stages within each of three Upper Paleolithic industries: Aurignacian, Solutrean, and Magdalenian. His Lower and Upper Aurignacian corresponded to the Chatelperronian and the Upper Perigordian, respectively, while his "middle" Aurignacian incorporated the type industry from Aurignac.

In 1933, Peyrony introduced refinements to Breuil's scheme, the most important of which was the separation of the Perigordian (= Breuil's Lower and Upper Aurignacian) from the Aurignacian *sensu stricto* and the development of five parallel stages for each tradition, or *phylum*. The Perigordian was distinguished by the use of backing (abrupt retouch) along one side of a blade to create a point; the Aurignacian was characterized by a series of bone-point forms. Implicit in this scheme was a model of two distinct cultural units, which shared the same terrain in southwestern France over a long period of time (ca. 15 Kyr) but did not interbreed or adopt each other's technology, except in limited instances represented by what Peyrony called *second-group* Perigordian industries (Perigordian II, Vc), with

traces of Aurignacian "admixture." Additionally, Peyrony defined the Protomagdalenian and the Protosolutrean industries, prior to the Solutrean proper, from Laugerie Haute.

While the subdivisions of the four (or five, if the Chatelperronian is separated from the Perigordian) recognized Upper Paleolithic industries became more elaborate, it gradually became apparent, through statistical approaches and further excavation, that the sequence of the Dordogne did not even apply to eastern France, let alone to other regions of Europe and southwestern Asia. In southern Europe, southwestern Asia, and northeastern Africa small-tool industries (Mode 5) become increasingly dominant after 20 Ka; in northern and eastern Europe, final Paleolithic industries reflect a greater level of economic specialization and cultural elaboration than in the west. Recently, various authors have proposed the division of the Upper Paleolithic into two major periods: Early (EUP) and Late (LUP), with a break occurring almost everywhere around the time of the glacial maximum, ca. 20–18 Ka.

Early Upper Paleolithic Industries of Europe

The earliest prismatic blade industry in Europe, an Early Aurignacian from Bacho Kiro and Temnata (Bulgaria), may date to more than 40 Ka. Just slightly younger (40–38 Ka) are similar assemblages from Hungary (Istállöskö) and northern Spain (El Castillo, Arbreda), and soon afterward (ca. 34 Ka), the Aurignacian expanded in France (Abri Pataud), southern Germany (in association with numerous carved figurines at Vogelherd and Geissenklösterle), and across Europe. The Aurignacian is the most widespread industry of the European Upper Paleolithic. It is known from most European countries south of the North European Plain and west of Belarus and Ukraine, although in the Mediterranean region Aurignacian sites are rare or absent. However, some of the apparent similarities between different regions may, in fact, be due to a common level of technological development rather than to stylistic patterns across a common cultural group. It is characterized by blade technology; a range of bone points from split-base to solid forms; a proliferation of jewelry in ivory, bone, stone, and shell; carved and incised bone and antler; heavy invasive marginal retouch; and thick scrapers and burins (gouges) created by lamellar removals. The richest sites both in density and in elaboration of bone working and carving are located in areas dominated by large gregarious herbivores (horse, mammoth, reindeer). This industry has no potential antecedents in Europe or neighboring regions but may possibly derive from the Levant or east Africa, where blades occurred widely in the later Middle Stone Age.

In several areas, the next Upper Paleolithic industries (dated to 35–33 Ka) share many characteristics with the preceding Mousterian industries of the same region. More than half of some Châtelperronian (ex-Perigordian I) assemblages consist of flake tools of Mousterian affinities, and the only skeletal remains identified with this industry to date (1999) are those of a Neanderthal (Saint-Césaire and Arcy-sur-Cure). In several sites and regions, there appears to be an al-

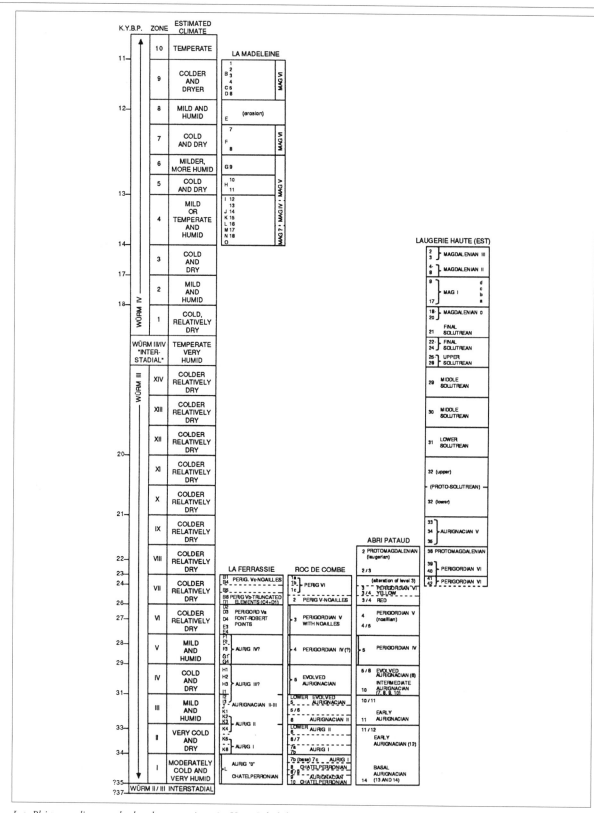

Late Pleistocene climate and cultural sequences in major Upper Paleolithic sites in southwestern France, ca. 37–11 Ka. The sequence of Aurignacian phases and the coexistence of Aurignacian and Chatelperronian ("Lower Perigordian") was first based on studies at La Ferrassie, then substantiated at Abri Pataud and Roc de Combe. Laugerie Haute provides the most complete sequence from final Gravettian ("Upper Perigordian") through middle Magdalenian, overlapping Abri Pataud below and matching La Madeleine (type locality of the Magdalenian) above. Most of these sites have been dated by radiocarbon, and correlation among them has also been proposed by Laville et al. on the basis of interpretation of local environmental indicators, as summarized at the left. Modified after Laville et al., 1980.

ternation of Aurignacian and Châtelperronian. Some authors have interpreted the latter as a Neanderthal/Mousterian copying of Aurignacian techniques. From southern Italy, an industry with similar backed knives or points in an assemblage with many flake tools (dated ca. 31 Ka) is known as the Uluzzian, from the type site of Uluzzo, near Lecce. In Hungary and the Czech and Slovak Republics, leaf-shaped points, similar to those found in later Mousterian (or Altmuhlian) sites of southern Germany, characterize an early Upper Paleolithic industry with both blade tools and Levallois technology, known as the Szeletian; a similar industry, the Jermanovician, is described from Poland. All of these early Upper Paleolithic transitional industries have yielded bone and other organic materials, worked into points, awls, and beads or pendants. The early Upper Paleolithic level at Kent's Cavern (England) also contained leaf-shaped points, although they are unlike the examples from central Europe.

Perigordian industries characterized by narrow backed points (gravettes) and associated with certain types of bone points, perforated teeth, and female figurines in stone and ivory are known from southwestern France; industries with related specific stone-tool types, termed either Perigordian or Gravettian, occur in Germany, Belgium, Spain, and Italy. To the east and north, a similar group of industries, but with a variety of different point types, known as the Eastern Gravettian (including Pavlovian, and at the early Kostenki sites), occur from Poland to Russia and south to Romania, Croatia, and Greece. As in the Aurignacian, the development of carvings (figurines), decorative items, elaborate group burials (Předmosti, Sungir), and site complexity is greatest in the areas associated with large herbivores, such as eastern Europe, with little bone working or personal ornamentation in association with Mediterranean sites (with the significant exception of the Italian Grimaldi Caves).

Late Upper Paleolithic Industries of Europe

The Weichselian glacial maximum (20–18 Ka) was marked by the abandonment of many areas of northern Europe and by the intensification of adaptations in southern Europe in the context of Solutrean industries, characterized by bifacial and unifacial leaf-shaped points and a profusion of carved and engraved images. As the climate began to moderate, regionally diverse and elaborate industries developed in Europe. In Switzerland, France, Spain, Belgium, and Germany, Magdalenian industries with highly developed bone and antler technology, including barbed harpoons, backed microblades, and, in the latest sites, geometric microliths, were widespread between ca. 17 and 12 Ka. Most of the painted caves in France and Cantabrian Spain are associated with this industrial group and probably reflect large-scale regional interactions among bands of hunters.

On the North European Plain, a group of industries characterized by backed knives (*Federmesser*) and tanged points reflect specialized reindeer hunting and are locally known as Hamburgian (Germany), Tjongerian (Low Countries), and Creswellian (England). In eastern Europe and on the Russian Plain, a variety of assemblage types with backed

points (evolved Gravettian) and other tools, such as truncation burins and geometric microliths, are associated with a proliferation of carved ivory ornaments, mammoth-bone huts of varying dimensions, and considerable evidence for long-distance trade and possibly social stratification.

In southeastern and Mediterranean Europe, on the other hand, the backed-point (Gravettian) tradition continues in the form of much smaller tools (Epigravettian), with limited evidence of elaboration in images, decorative elements, or carved bone and antler, with the significant exception of the Pyrenees region of Spain (especially Parpalló). Long-distance trade is evident, however, in the importation of obsidian from Melos to the Greek mainland (Franchthi Cave), and sites in northwestern Greece suggest seasonal movement and scheduling of resource use.

Southwestern Asia and Northeastern Africa

The Upper Paleolithic of southwestern Asia and northeastern Africa does not follow the classic western European sequence, except in the general resemblance of some of the industries (e.g., Antelian) to the widespread Aurignacian of Europe. Additionally, the earliest blade industries in both southwestern Asia and North Africa (Amudian, pre-Aurignacian) occur in the midst of, or prior to, a Middle Paleolithic sequence (Haua Fteah, Jabrud, Tabūn). Following the Middle Paleolithic in the Levant, a six-stage sequence is often recognized, based on the Mount Carmel (Israel) sites, and demonstrates a slow development from flake-blade industries with triangular leaf-shaped points and many Mousterian forms (Emiran, Stage 1 = Lower Antelian) to evolved microlithic ones (Kebaran, Stage 6). The intervening stages are known variously as Antelian 2 through 5, Aurignacian (= Antelian 3, 4 = Upper Antelian), and Athlitian (= Antelian 5). As in southeastern Europe, the final industries are microlithic and continue into the Mesolithic without a sharp break.

In eastern North Africa (e.g., Haua Fteah), an early blade industry, the Dabban (ca. 40 Ka), is succeeded by a backed-microblade (Mode 5) industry, the eastern Oranian (ca. 18–16 Ka). The sequence in the Nile Valley is more complicated and reflects overlapping influences from the blade-using cultures of western Asia and Cyrenaica and the flake and Late Stone Age industries of sub-Saharan Africa.

Upper Paleolithic Adaptations

Major innovations of Upper Paleolithic people signify an increasing ability to exploit cold environments. These included improved technologies, especially bone and antler working, but also the invention of the spear thrower, harpoon, bow and arrow, fish weir, calendar or other notations of time or seasonal change, eyed needle for tailored clothing, controlled high-temperature-hearth and ceramic technology (at Dolni Věstonice), boats (evidenced by Melian obsidian on the Greek mainland), stone lamps (Lascaux), and other items especially important in a culture dependent on animal protein for long periods of the year. Evidence of long-distance trade, large-scale ritual sites, and possible social stratification indicates the development of social mecha-

Part of the Upper Paleolithic shelter of Laugerie-Haute, where a long sequence from Perigordian through Magdalenian industries is preserved.

nisms to reduce risk in unpredictable environments. The greater density of remains and the faunal dominance of particular sites by single species may indicate increased scheduling of resource use, as well as a greater amount of mass-processing and storage against hard times (logistical behavior).

See also Abri Pataud; Africa; Africa, North; Aggregation-Dispersal; Amud Cave; Amudian; Antelian; Archaic Moderns; Asia, Eastern and Southern; Asia, Western; Athlitian; Aurignac; Aurignacian; Awl; Bacho Kiro; Badegoulian; Baradostian; Baton de Commandement; Bow and Arrow; Burin; Chatelperronian; Clothing; Creswellian; Cro-Magnon; Cueva Morin; Dabban; Diet; Dolni Věstonice; Domestication; Economy, Prehistoric; Emiran; Epigravettian; Epipaleolithic; Europe; Exotics; Fire; Flake-Blade; Gravettian; Hamburgian; Harpoon; Haua Fteah; Holocene; Homo sapiens; Howieson's Poort; Hunter-Gatherers; Ibero-Maurusian; Jabrud; Jewelry; Kebaran; Kent's Cavern; Kostenki; La Ferrassie; Lascaux; Late Paleolithic; Later Stone Age; Laugerie Sites; Le Moustier; Levallois; Magdalenian; Mal'ta; Man-Land Relationships; Mesolithic; Mezhirich; Middle Paleolithic; Modern Human Origins; Molodova; Mousterian; Musical Instruments; Neanderthals; Paleolithic; Paleolithic Calendar; Paleolithic Image; Paleolithic Lifeways; Parpalló; Pavlov; Perigordian; Pleistocene; Pre-Aurignacian; Předmosti; Protomagdalenian; Protosolutrean; Raw Materials; Ritual; Romanellian; Sagaie; Saint-Césaire; Skhūl; Solutré; Solutrean; Split-Base Bone Point; Stone-Tool Making; Sungir; Szeletian; Tabūn; Uluzzian. [A.S.B.]

Further Readings

Gamble, G. (1986) The Palaeolithic Settlement of Europe. Cambridge: Cambridge University Press.

Klein, R.G. (1969) Man and Culture in the Late Pleistocene: A Case Study. New York: Chandler.

Knecht, H., Pike-Tay, A., and White, R. (eds.) (1993) Before Lascaux: The Complex Record of the Early Upper Paleolithic. Boca Raton: CRC Press.

Laville, H., Rigaud, J.-P., and Sackett, J.R. (1980) Rock Shelters of the Périgord. New York: Academic.

Soffer, O. (1985) The Upper Paleolithic of the Central Russian Plain. Orlando: Academic.

Soffer, O. and Gamble, C. (eds.) (1990) The World at 18000 BP: Volume One, High Latitudes. London: Unwin Hyman.

Straus, L.G., Erikson, B.V., Erlandson, J.M., and Yesner, D.R. (1996) Humans at the End of the Ice Age: The Archaeology of the Pleistocene-Holocene Transition. New York, Plenum.

Wymer, J. (1982) The Palaeolithic Age. New York: St. Martin's.

Uraha

Pliocene site named after the village where an early hominin mandible, UR 501, was recovered from the Chiwondo Beds, northern Malawi. The mandible, referred to *Homo rudolfensis*, occurs within the upper part of Unit 3A near Uraha Hill, which is dated, by means of faunal correlation, to ca. 2.4 Ma. It was found in a ferruginous calcimorphic paleosol that lies

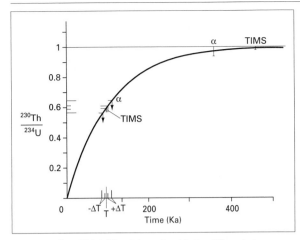

Variation of 230Th/234U activity ratio with time. The ratio in a sample is shown by a point on the x-axis. Here, for a sample with a true ratio of 0.6, are shown the error bars corresponding to alpha-spectrometric measurement (a, light line) and TIMS (heavy line). Note the corresponding errors (?T) in the ages (on the horizontal axis), and that the age errors are asymmetric. The upper age limit for the method is determined by the point at which the error bar for the Th/U ratio overlaps the infinite-age value of 1.0.

in siltstones to mudstones interbedded with sandstones displaying lenticular geometries. These deposits are assigned to a swamp-to-interchannel setting, as no evidence for open lacustrine conditions exists. Laterally (south and west), these deposits interfinger with low energetic ramp deposits and lagoonal siltstones and mudstones with pelecypods and gastropods indicating more open lacustrine conditions.

See also Africa, Southern; Chiwondo Beds; Homo rudolfensis. [T.G.B.]

Further Readings

Schrenk, F., Bromage, T.G., Betzler, C.G., Ring, U., and Juwayeyi, Y.M. (1993) Oldest *Homo* and Pliocene biogeography of the Malawi Rift. Nature 365:833–836.

Uranium-Series Dating

Age determinations based on decay of the short-lived isotopes of uranium and their daughter isotopes. The principally used system, generally known as the *thorium-uranium system* or just *thorium dating*, employs the slow decay of uranium-238 (^{238}U) to the moderately radioactive uranium-234 (^{234}U; half-life = 248,000 years), which decays, in turn, to thorium-230 (^{230}Th; half-life = 75,200 years). In most near-surface environments, uranium is soluble in groundwater while thorium is not. Therefore, chemically and biologically deposited materials at archaeological sites may initially contain some uranium but will lack radiogenic daughter ^{230}Th. After the deposit is formed, a new crop of this isotope will begin to accumulate and grow toward equilibrium with the parent ^{234}U. Thus, the age can be measured from the ^{230}Th/^{234}U ratio. The primordial isotope of thorium, ^{232}Th, serves as a control for any original thorium in the sample.

Uranium-235 (^{235}U) is the parent of another short-lived isotope, protactinium-231 (^{231}Pa; half-life = 34,300 years), which can also be used to date surficial deposits. Like

thorium, protactinium is insoluble in groundwater, and chemical or biological processes will separate it from the parent isotope during deposition in archaeological sites. The maxiumum activity of ^{231}Pa, however, is only ½ that of ^{230}Th, due to the fact that its parent ^{235}U is much less abundant, and it is, therefore, harder to detect.

Materials selected for U-series dating must meet three criteria: (1) they must have been formed at the time of interest; (2) they must have initially contained uranium but no (or very little) thorium, as is usually the case with chemically or biologically deposited materials; and (3) they must have been closed systems since deposition, neither gaining nor losing atoms except by internal radioactive conversions. Materials at archaeological sites that satisfy these criteria are listed here in order of preference for U-series dating.

Speleothems, or coalesced stalagmitic floors (also called *plancher stalagmitique*, or *flowstone*), are deposits of calcite formed in caves and rockshelters, sometimes found interstratified with archaeological strata or bone-bearing silts; they may be contaminated with detritus containing nonradiogenic (i.e., common) thorium, but they can still be dated using the isochron method.

Travertine is spring-deposited limestone, which can be deposited at intermittent habitation sites. Many travertines are very porous and tend to alter after deposition, but coarsely crystalline layers are suitable for dating.

Freshwater marls (clayey limestones) in some lake bed sequences may be associated with tools, bones, or living sites, and, although these may be highly contaminated with detritus, they are amenable to isochron dating.

Calcretes are calcitic layers, or hardpan, that form by evaporation of soil water in the subsurface *B-zone* of soils in arid and subarid regions. They are usually highly contaminated with detritus, but, if the host sediment is noncalcareous (e.g., volcanic, siliceous), isochron dating is possible.

Other types of carbonate precipitates, such as *kunkar* deposits in coastal flats, are also datable. With regard to biologically precipitated carbonate, such as the aragonite and calcite of marine shells, only corals are amenable to dating. This is because molluscs (i.e., bivalves, snails, limpets) and echinoderms (i.e., sea urchins) contain no initial uranium and absorb postmortem uranium gradually over time. In general, poor agreement has been found between uranium-series dates and carbon-14 (^{14}C) dates on corals, and coral is seldom found in archaeological contexts. Vertebrate bones and teeth also contain no initial uranium, but they may take up significant amounts soon after death during the fossilization process. Agreement between uranium-series dates and ^{14}C dates on bone is also poor, although tooth enamel appears to be better behaved.

U-series analyses are carried out by measuring the ratios ^{230}Th/^{234}U and ^{234}U/^{238}U in one of three ways. Measurement of the relative radioactivities of the unstable isotopes such as ^{230}Th with an α-particle spectrometer requires 10–30 g of sample and has a precision error of 5–10 percent of the date. Counting the number of atoms of each isotope using a thermal ionization mass spectrometer (TIMS) takes 0.1–5 g of sample and is precise to within 1 percent. Counting gamma rays emitted by each isotope requires 50–500 g of sample and is precise only within 10–20 percent. Using the TIMS method, the lower and upper dating limits of uranium-series dating are 0.5 Ka and 500 Ka, respectively, while the upper dating limit for α-spectrometry is 350 Ka.

Examples of U-series dating are numerous. At La Chaise de Vouthon (France), stalagmitic layers were dated from 240 to 70 Ka, interposed between detrital cave-filling sediments containing Paleolithic artifacts and hominid (Neanderthal) skeletal remains. At Ehringsdorf (Germany), where quarrying of travertine deposits near Weimar revealed layers containing Paleolithic artifacts and hominid remains, a U-series isochron date of 230 Ka was obtained for the lower travertine, corresponding to the interglacial of isotope Stage 7. At El Castillo Cave (Spain), a travertine layer separating Acheulean and Mousterian deposits is part of the thick detrital fill. Although badly contaminated with common Th, it gave a Th/U date of 89 ± 11 Ka, which is a minimum age for the transition from Early to Middle Paleolithic culture at this site.

See also Geochronometry; Pleistocene; Radiocarbon Dating; Radiometric Dating. [H.P.S.]

Further Readings

Schwarcz, H.P. (1992) Uranium series dating in paleoanthropology. Evol. Anthropol. 1:56–62.

Schwarcz, H.P. (1994) Uranium series dating. In R.E. Taylor and M. Aitken (eds.): Chronology of Archaeological Sites.

Schwarcz, H.P., and Blackwell, B. (1991) Archaeometry. In M. Ivanovitch and R.S. Harmon (eds.): Uranium Series Disequilibrium: Application to Environment Problems in the Earth Sciences, 2nd ed. Oxford: Oxford University Press, pp. 513–552.

Taylor, R.E. and Aitken, M.J. (eds.) (1997) Chronometric Dating in Archaeology. New York: Plenum.

Vallois, Henri Victor (1889–1981)

French anatomist and paleoanthropologist. Following his mentor, M. Boule, at the Museum National d'Histoire Naturelle in Paris, Vallois became the leading proponent during the 1940s and 1950s of the *presapiens* theory, whereby Neanderthals were seen as not ancestral to modern *Homo sapiens*. According to this viewpoint, modern humans are derivatives of a separate lineage. Vallois considered the specimens of Piltdown (England) (prior to their exposure as a forgery in 1953), Fontéchevade (France), and Swanscombe (England) to be evidence of a European presapiens lineage. More recent analyses, however, have shown that these specimens are not significantly different from other contemporaneous hominids.

See also Boule, [Pierre] Marcellin; Fontéchevade; *Homo sapiens*; Neanderthals; Piltdown; Presapiens; Swanscombe. [F.S.]

Vallonnet

Cave located near Nice at Roquebrune-Cap-Martin in southeastern France. Excavations at Vallonnet have recovered an abundant late Early Pleistocene (Biharian or final Villafranchian) fauna and pollen spectra indicating cool-temperate conditions. Against the back of the cave, Levels B and C contain ca. 10 chipped stones, identified as simple choppers and flakes, in sediments with normal magnetic polarity. The excavators equate these levels with the Jaramillo Normal Subchron, dating the site to ca. 1.0 Ma, placing it among the oldest archaeological sites in Europe, but others place the site in the Brunhes Normal Chron, less than 780 Ka. Reanalysis has suggested that the chipped-stone artifacts may, in fact, be of natural origin, resulting from flaking of the cave wall or roof.

See also Chilhac; Early Paleolithic; Europe; Soleilhac. [A.S.B., J.J.S.]

Velika Pecina

Cave in Croatia that produced a frontal bone in association with early Upper Paleolithic (Aurignacian) artifacts in 1961. This adult frontal bone has a modern form of supraorbital torus and is important as one of the oldest absolutely dated modern specimens in Europe, since the succeeding stratigraphic level has been dated at ca. 34 Ka by radiocarbon—though a much younger date has been reported.

See also Aurignacian; Europe; Homo sapiens; Upper Paleolithic. [C.B.S.]

Venosa Sites

Group of Early and Middle Paleolithic open-air and cave sites, including Notarchirico and Loreto, near the town of Venosa in southern Italy. Together with the nearby site of Cimiterio di Atella, these constitute an important record of Early Paleolithic human activity in Europe, as well as some of the earliest European evidence for Acheulean bifaces. The open-air site of Notarchirico contains 10 Early Paleolithic archaeological horizons, both with and without bifaces, interstratified with ashfalls from the nearby Monte Vulture. The earliest level, with a few bifaces, is stratified below a primary-context ashfall dated by tephra correlation to a regional event at ca. 650 Ka. This dating is confirmed by a direct thermoluminescence date on the ash. Cultural materials from Notarchirico suggest exploitation of large mammals (elephant, large bovids) at the margin of a river/lake system. A human femoral diaphysis was recovered from the uppermost horizon.

See also Acheulean; Early Paleolithic; Europe. [A.S.B.]

Further Readings

Belli, G., Belluomini, G., Cassoli, P.F., Cecchi, S., Cucarzi, M., Delitala, L., Fornaciari, G., Mallegni, F., Piperno, M., Segre, A.G., and Segre-Naldini, E. (1991) Découverte d'un femur humain acheuléen à Notarchirico (Venosa, Basilicate). L'Anthropol. 95:47–88.

Vértesszöllös

Travertine site near Budapest (Hungary) that produced hominid fossils and an Early Paleolithic stone-tool assemblage in 1964–1965. The dating of this site is problematical, with faunal remains indicating a date within a temperate stage of the "Mindel" glaciation of continental Europe (perhaps ca. 400 Ka). Uranium-series dates originally suggested a date of more than 250 Ka for the hominid-bearing levels, but more recent dating attempts place them only ca. 210–160 Ka. Archaeological levels are well preserved, with impressions of leaves and of a claimed hominid footprint. The lithic assemblages (called the *Buda industry* by the excavator, L. Vértes) feature small choppers and flake tools made on quartzite pebbles. Circular concentrations of bones ca. 50–60 cm in diameter occur in small depressions, and some of the bones exhibit traces of burning.

The hominid specimens include some teeth of a child and the occipital bone of an adult. The affinities and classification of the latter specimen have been the subject of much dispute. Although thick and fairly angulated, with a centrally developed occipital torus, the specimen is also large, with a long and curved occipital plane. The cranial capacity of the whole skull was probably more than 1,300 ml, which has led to suggestions that it is an "archaic *Homo sapiens*" fossil; but other researchers, pointing to its age, thickness, and shape, prefer to classify it as *Homo erectus*. The specimen may well derive from a population similar to that represented at Petralona (Greece) and perhaps Bilzingsleben (Germany).

See also Archaic Homo sapiens; Bilzingsleben; Buda Industry; Europe; Homo erectus; Petralona. [C.B.S., J.J.S.]

Victoriapithecinae

Subfamily of Cercopithecidae that includes the two earliest genera of Old World monkey, *Victoriapithecus* and *Prohylobates*. The oldest-known cercopithecid fossils are probably an upper molar and incompletely published canine and elbow fragments from Napak (Uganda), dated to ca. 19 Ma. About 15 jaws and isolated teeth have been described from the Kenyan locality of Buluk, dated to 17 Ma, and two teeth were recovered from deposits at Loperot of probably similar age. In North Africa, Wadi Moghara (Egypt) yielded three partial lower jaws named *Prohylobates tandyi,* and a single mandible fragment was described from near Gebel Zelten (Libya) and named *P. simonsi;* both of these localities probably date to ca. 16 Ma. However, it is from the early Middle Miocene (ca. 15 Ma) sites on Maboko Island and nearby Nyakach on Lake Victoria (Kenya) that these early monkeys are best known, from more than 800 specimens, including a cranium, a face, teeth, and fragmentary postcrania. Undescribed late victoriapithecines have been noted from the Tugen Hills (Kenya) ca. 12 Ma.

Victoriapithecines share an apparently derived mandibular symphysis structure, as well as several features that are probably conservative among cercopithecids or eucatarrhines, such as P_4 long axis slightly oblique to the molar row, small hypoconulid typically present on M_{1-2}, and incompletely bilophodont upper molars with persistent crista obliqua (unknown in *Prohylobates*). Molar crown relief is low, the trigonids short, flare moderately developed, and lower-molar bilophodonty (nearly) complete.

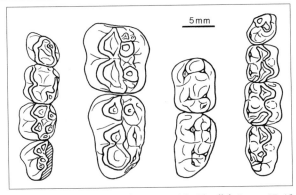

Lower dentitions of victoriapithecine cercopithecids, all dating ca. 17–15 Ma. From left to right: Prohylobates tandyi, Wadi Moghara (Egypt); P. simonsi, Gebel Zelten area (Libya); two jaws of Victoriapithecus macinnesi, Maboko Island (Kenya).

The face presents a narrow interorbital distance, a moderately long snout, strong supraorbital tori, and frontal costae (ridges) forming a trigone. These features are usually seen in the Cercopithecinae and considered derived among catarrhines by comparison to opposing states seen in pliopithecidae, Colobinae, Hylobatidae, and mosaically in other taxa. B.R. Benefit has argued that, instead, these character states should be viewed as ancestral, in part because they are present in ancient fossils, but that view is not accepted here. In fact, it may be that a special relationship to Cercopithecinae is indicated for at least some victoriapithecines.

Several authors (especially E. Delson) previously suggested a morphological dichotomy in teeth and postcranial elements (possibly indicating two species that documented the divergence between cercopithecines and colobines), but that has not been supported by the more extensive newer finds. Instead, it appears that Victoriapithecinae represents the sister taxon of all later cercopithecids, which share several derived characters that their common ancestor must have evolved after separating from the victoriapithecines. It has been suggested that this group should be ranked as a full family of Cercopithecoidea, but, pending a better understanding of the polarity of several character-state morphoclines, that suggestion is not followed here.

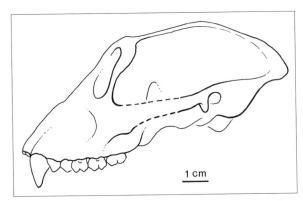

Left lateral view of male cranium of Victoriapithecus macinnesi, from the Middle Miocene (16–14.7 Ma) of Maboko Island, Kenya. Note the relatively straight facial profile and small sagittal crest. By L. Meeker from photo provided courtesy of B.R. Benefit and M.L. McCrossin.

See also Africa; Africa, East; Baringo Basin/Tugen Hills; Buluk; Catarrhini; Cercopithecidae; Cercopithecinae; Cercopithecoidea; Colobinae; Maboko; Napak; Skull; Teeth. [E.D.]

Further Readings

Benefit, B.R. (1993) The permanent dentition and phylogenetic position of *Victoriapithecus* from Maboko Island, Kenya. J. Hum. Evol. 25:83–172.

Benefit, B.R. (1999) *Victoriapithecus*: The key to Old World monkey and catarrhine origins. Evol. Anthropol. 7:155–174.

Benefit, B.R., and McCrossin, M.L. (1993) Facial anatomy of *Victoriapithecus* and its relevance to the ancestral cranial morphology of Old World monkeys and apes. Am. J. Phys. Anthropol. 92:329–370.

Delson, E. (1979) *Prohylobates* (Primates) from the Early Miocene of Libya: A new species and its implications for cercopithecid origins. Geobios 12:725–733.

Leakey, M.G. (1985) Early Miocene cercopithecids from Buluk, northern Kenya. Folia Primatol. 44:1–14.

Miller, E.R. (1999) Faunal correlation of Wadi Moghara, Egypt: Implications for the age of *Prohylobates tandyi*. J. Hum. Evol. 36:519–533.

Strasser, E., and Delson, E. (1987) Cladistic analysis of cercopithecid relationships. J. Hum. Evol. 16:81–99.

Szalay, F.S., and Delson, E. (1979) Evolutionary History of the Primates. New York: Academic.

Vindija

Cave in Croatia that since 1974 has produced a number of fragmentary Late Pleistocene fossil hominids. Those from Level G3 are Neanderthal-like and associated with a Mousterian industry that amino-acid-racemization assays date to 42.4 Ka. Some of these specimens exhibit a degree of thinning in their supraorbital tori, incipient chins, and relatively narrow nasal apertures. A date of 27 Ka has been obtained for an Aurignacian layer, and fossils from the Aurignacian and the overlying Gravettian levels are anatomically modern in morphology. Remains said to exhibit transitional (or, alternatively, indeterminate) morphology occur in Level G1, which is assigned to the Aurignacian on the basis of a split-based bone point found in the upper part of this level. Some scholars regard this attribution as questionable, suggesting the possibility of stratigraphic mixing through cryoturbation. In any event, the specimens in question are very fragmentary (some, indeed, are burnt and cutmarked), and their archaeological associations need to be further clarified.

See also Aurignacian; Europe; Gravettian; Modern Human Origins; Neanderthals. [J.J.S., C.B.S.]

Virchow, Rudolph (1821–1902)

German pathologist, anthropologist, and statesman. On receiving an M.D. degree from the Friedrich Wilhelm Institute of the University of Berlin in 1843, Virchow conducted research into pathological histology. In 1847, he assisted in the founding of the journal *Archiv für Pathologische Anatomie und Physiologie und Klinische Medizin*. In the same year, he was appointed lecturer in pathological anatomy at the University of Berlin. Nine years later, largely in recognition of his pioneering contributions to pathology, public health, and sanitary reforms, he was made full professor. In addition to his academic and medical activities, Virchow was a political activist and a member of the Prussian National Assembly and the German Reichstag, where he vigorously opposed the policies of Chancellor Otto von Bismarck. As a scientist, Virchow was a cautious empiricist. He considered that C. Darwin's theory of natural selection lacked sufficient inductive demonstration and persuaded many of his colleagues that the Feldhofer (Neanderthal) skull was merely a pathological specimen. In the late 1860s, Virchow played an active role in founding the German Anthropological Society and the Berlin Society for Anthropology, Ethnology, and Prehistory. From 1869 until his death, he was president and editor of the journal *Zeitschrift für Ethnologie*. [F.S.]

Visual-Predation Hypothesis

One of several current views on the adaptive origin of euprimates. As originally enunciated by M. Cartmill in 1974, this hypothesis maintains that the cranial hallmarks of euprimates, such as stereoscopy and orbital rings, in addition to manual grasping, are related to nocturnal and visually mediated prey detection and capture of insects. More specifically, the hypothesis states that this occurred "in the terminal branches of the lower strata of tropical forests." Arboreal small mammals of all sorts prey on insects, so undoubtedly there can be no strong arguments against such an activity in the stem euprimate lineage. But does this postulated behavior account for the taxonomic properties of the Euprimates?

The hallmarks of primate dentitions, specifically the molars of the reconstructed ancestors of euprimates, as compared to obligate insectivorous mammals, show signs of a clear shift toward a more seed- and fruit-oriented diet, a near certainty among the earliest-known euprimates. The most serious objections against the visual-predation hypothesis, however, resides in its failure to account for the totality of osteological evidence, which contains clear documentation of diagnostic attributes. The hallmarks of the euprimate common ancestor are most strikingly represented on the postcranial skeleton. These features leave little doubt about the rapid-leaping adaptations in the ancestry of this clade, particularly the importance of grasping not so much in the hands (often used for prey capture by mammals) but in the feet. The hypertrophied pedal grasping ability of these ancestors, coupled with the modified hip bone and "fast" joints of the skeleton (e.g., knee, hip, and elbow), imply a better corroborated alternative to the visual-predation hypothesis.

Based on the diagnostic grasp-leaping locomotion of the protoeuprimate, their key adaptation involved major and frequent *precise* and rapid leaping from branch to branch where they landed using grasping. The selectional consequences of this locomotor behavior (i.e., this activity becoming the selective agent, whatever the dietary regime) on the visual system and the skull are obvious. Stereoscopy is positively selected, and the nervous system must cope with three-dimensional substrate choices more rapidly than before, or else. Note, however, that postorbital rings, by themselves, are found in mammals from camels to manatees (and many others) and are related to numerous complex mechanics and selective agents, so that they do not postdict visual predation. The visual-predation hypothesis is not supported by known evidence, but the grasp-leaping hypothesis is corroborated and not contradicted by any known line of evidence.

See also Adaptation(s); Euprimates; Evolutionary Morphology; Locomotion; Primates; Skeleton; Skull; Teeth. [F.S.S.]

Wallace, Alfred Russel (1823–1913)

British naturalist. During his early career, the impecunious Wallace undertook two important collecting expeditions, the first to the jungles of the Amazon (1848–1852) and then to the Malay Archipelago (1854–1862). It was during this latter expedition that he independently formulated a theory of natural selection, which he communicated to C. Darwin in 1857. In the following year, his paper, and extracts from Darwin's letters and manuscripts, were presented under a joint authorship to the Linnaean Society (London), announcing the theory of evolution by natural selection. With regard to human evolution, Wallace, believing in a spiritual purpose behind consciousness, argued that the genus *Homo* had been shielded from the action of natural selection. Wallace also founded the science of evolutionary zoogeography.

See also Darwin, Charles Robert; Evolution. [F.S.]

Washburn, Sherwood L. (1911–)

American physical anthropologist. On completing his doctoral thesis (under the direction of E.A. Hooton) at Harvard University in 1939, Washburn began his professional career at Columbia University. After World War II, he went to the University of Chicago (1947), where he remained until 1958 when he received an appointment at the University of California, Berkeley. Washburn's writings on the "new physical anthropology" during the 1950s and early 1960s did much to heighten anthropological consciousness of changes occurring in evolutionary biology at that time. He also played a major role in determining the theoretical and methodological orientation of primate behavioral research in America during the 1960s. In this same period, he advanced an early version of the *knuckle-walking hypothesis*, proposing that the progression from brachiation to bipedalism had involved an intermediate stage similar to modern pongids.

See also Hooton, Earnest Albert. [F.S.]

Weidenreich, Franz (1873–1948)

German anatomist and paleoanthropologist. After receiving his M.D. degree from the University of Strasbourg in 1899, Weidenreich was appointed professor of anatomy there in 1904. While he was at Strasbourg his interest in primate evolution was enhanced by his association with G. Schwalbe. After World War I, Weidenreich held several academic appointments at German universities, first at Heidelberg (1919–1927) and then at Frankfurt (1928–1933), before he was obliged to leave Germany because of his Jewish ancestry. Following a short stint at the University of Chicago, he was appointed to succeed D. Black at the Peking Union Medical College in China in 1935. It was here that Weidenreich undertook a protracted study of the fossil hominid ("*Sinanthropus*") materials discovered at Zhoukoudian (China). His descriptions and interpretations of this material form an imposing series of monographs published in *Palaeontologia Sinica* between 1936 and 1943. Weidenreich is considered by proponents of the *Multiregional* view of modern human origins to be the intellectual father of their theory. With the outbreak of World War II, Weidenreich returned to the United States, where until his death he worked at the American Museum of Natural History in New York City.

See also Homo erectus; Modern Human Origins; Schwalbe, Gustav; Zhoukoudian. [F.S.]

Western Rift

The branch of the African Rift system occupied by lakes Albert and Edward, draining into the Nile, and lakes Kivu and Tanganyika, draining into the Congo. The southern segment yields Plio-Pleistocene fossils (with *Homo rudolfensis*) at Chiwondo in the satellite Rukwa Basin east of Lake Tanganyika.

Miocene and Pliocene fossil beds near Kaiso village, on the Uganda side of Lake Albert, and Pleistocene deposits in the Kazinga Channel connecting to Lake Edward, were among the first to to be described in East Africa. Recent studies led by M. Pickford and B. Senut have worked out a tuff-calibrated sequence of fossil beds along the east side of

Lake Albert, with large mammal faunas closely complementary to those of the Turkana and Victoria basins over the range of 6 to 1.0 Ma. The majority of fossils are from iron-rich swamp sediments of Late Miocene and Early Pliocene age (6–4.5 Ma), conflated in early literature as the "Kaiso fauna," with abundant gastropods and fish. Other faunas are from beds roughly coeval to basal Shungura, Laetoli, and Olduvai Bed I, e.g., at Senga. Tuffs in the Albert sequence include the Lomugol or Sagantole (3.6 Ma) at Warwire, the Lokochot or Shungura A (3.4 Ma) at Kyampanga, and the Koobi Fora (1.63 Ma) at Kagusa. No significant hominid material has been reported from the Albert rift sequence to date, but Late Pleistocene *Homo sapiens* remains at Ishango on the Zaire side of Lake Edward (Lake Rutanzige) are associated with a unique harpoon-point culture. Even earlier harpoons occur with MSA assemblages at Katanda, dating ca. 85 Ka.

See also Africa, East; Chiwondo Beds; Ishango; Katanda; Laetoli; Olduvai Gorge; Rift Valley; Senga-5; Tephrochronology; Turkana Basin. [J.A.V.C.]

Further Readings

Pickford, M., Senut, B., Poupeau, G., Brown, F., and Haileab, B. (1991) Correlation of tephra layers from the Western Rift Valley (Uganda) to the Turkana Basin (Ethiopia/Kenya) and the Gulf of Aden. C.R. Acad. Sci. Paris, ser. 2, 313:223–229.

Wilton

Later Stone Age industry of southern Africa, named after the Wilton rockshelter west of Howieson's Poort in the Cape Province (South Africa) and characterized by a microblade technology yielding small convex scrapers, backed bladelets, backed points, and segments. Also associated with the industry are ostrich-eggshell beads and fragments of containers, bone awls and arrow linkshafts, pierced marine shells, rock paintings, and, in the later stages, ceramics and iron beads. Faunal remains indicate widespread use of marine and other small-scale resources, as well as effective big-game hunting. The industry is widely distributed in both coastal and interior sites, and comparable microlithic industries with backed segments from central and East Africa have also been referred to this industry on the basis of general technological resemblance.

In southern Africa, the Wilton industry *sensu strictu* begins ca. 9 Ka and continues to the historic present in some areas, although microblade technology may be present as early as 25 Ka at Rose Cottage Cave. Microlithic industries are widespread at 18 Ka or earlier in eastern central Africa at the sites of Matupi (Zaire), Kalemba (Zambia-Nachiltufan industry), Kisese (Tanzania), Lukenya Hill (Kenya), and Buvuma Island (Uganda). During the Holocene, industries similar to the Wilton include the Zambian Wilton and the Pfupian and Matopan of Zimbabwe.

See also Africa, Southern; Bow and Arrow; Economy, Prehistoric; Howieson's Poort; Hunter-Gatherers; Later Stone Age; Mesolithic; Rose Cottage; Smithfield; Stone-Tool Making. [A.S.B.]

Wonderwerk

A cave near Kuruman (South Africa) with deposits containing Acheulean artifacts beneath Middle Stone Age levels (as is also the case at the South African sites of Montagu Cave and Cave of Hearths). Engraved stones have also been recovered from the Later Stone Age levels from ca. 10 Ka.

See also Acheulean; Africa, Southern; Cave of Hearths; Later Stone Age; Middle Stone Age. [N.T., K.S.]

Further Readings

Deacón, H.D. and Yealor, J. (1999) Human Beginnings in South Africa: Uncovering the Secrets of the Stone Age. Walnut Creek CA: AltaMira Press.

Woodward, [Sir] Arthur Smith (1864–1944)

British paleontologist. While an undergraduate at Owen's College (now Manchester University), Woodward came under the influence of the geologist W.B. Dawkins (1837–1929), who encouraged him to apply for a position in the Department of Geology (later Palaeontology) at the British Museum (Natural History) in 1882. During the next few years, Woodward spent his days cataloging the museum's collection of fossil fishes and his evenings attending classes at the University of London to complete his scientific education. Although he matriculated with honors in 1887, what prompted Woodward's promotion to assistant keeper in 1892 was the appearance of the first volumes of his *Catalogue of the Fossil Fishes in the British Museum*, which has been considered "not only as a monument of meticulous accuracy, of intense research, but also as the source of many other ichthyological publications." Equally important was his introductory textbook *Outlines of Vertebrate Palaeontology*, which had a great influence in its time on students of paleontology and zoology. By 1900, Woodward was regarded as a world authority on fossil fish. In recognition of this, he was made keeper in 1901, the same year he was elected a Fellow of the Royal Society. From 1912 onward, however, Woodward's attention was diverted from work for which he was better qualified by his involvement in the interpretation of the remains recovered from a gravel pit at Piltdown, Sussex (England), which were later shown to have been an elaborate hoax. From all indications, Woodward was not involved in the fabrication of this deception; indeed, on retiring from the museum in 1923, he continued to work at the site in a fruitless effort to gather further evidence. He received his knighthood in 1924.

See also Piltdown. [F.S.]

Wright, Sewall (1889–1988)

American geneticist. After receiving his doctorate at Harvard University in 1915, Wright worked as a geneticist for the U.S. Department of Agriculture (1915–1925) and then at the University of Chicago (1926–1954) and the University of Wisconsin (1955–1960). He is regarded as one of the founders of population genetics. He also developed a mathematical theory of evolution and formulas for evaluating the statistical consequences of various mating systems, noting that natural selection among individuals operates largely on the separate average gene effects. His genetic models, and particularly his *adaptive landscape* notion, are accepted as crucial to subsequent advances in evolutionary biological methodology.

See also Evolution; Genetics. [F.S.]

Wu, Rukang (also Woo Ju-k'ang or J.K. Woo) (1916–)

Chinese anatomist and human paleontologist. Wu received the doctoral degree in anthropology (1949) from Washington University in St. Louis, Missouri, and is senior research professor in the Palaeoanthropology Division of the Chinese Academy of Sciences' Institute of Vertebrate Palaeontology and Palaeoanthropology (Beijing). Wu is best known for his anatomical studies of fossil remains of *Lufengpithecus* and *Gigantopithecus*, as well as his thorough analyses of the series of *Homo erectus* materials from Zhoukoudian (China) in the 1960s through 1980s. He is honorary chairman of the board of directors of the Chinese Anatomy Association, a member of the Chinese Academy of Sciences, and holds concurrent professorships at Peking University (Beijing), Zhongshan University (Guangzhou), and Hong Kong University.

See also China; Gigantopithecus; Homo erectus; Jia, Lanpo; Lufengpithecus; Yang, Zhongjian; Zhoukoudian. [J.W.O.]

Further Readings

Wu, R. (1982) Recent Advances of Chinese Palaeoanthropology (Occasional Papers Series No. 2). Hong Kong: Hong Kong University Press.

Wu, R., and Xu, Q. (1985) *Ramapithecus* and *Sivapithecus* from Lufeng, China. In R. Wu and J.W. Olsen (eds.): Palaeoanthropology and Palaeolithic Archaeology in the People's Republic of China. Orlando: Academic, pp. 53–68.

X

Xiaochangliang

Chinese Early Paleolithic site located in the Nihewan Basin of northern China. Since its discovery in 1978, several thousand fresh, unabraided stone artifacts have been recovered from a 20–50-cm layer of fine, sandy sediment that appears to date to at least 780 Ka and may exceed 1.0 Ma. The artifacts, fashioned on locally available cherty silicified rock, include simple flake cores and flakes, as well as some casually retouched flakes.

See also China; Early Paleolithic; Nihewan. [J.W.O.]

Further Readings

Pope, G.G. (1993) Ancient Asia's cutting edge. Nat. Hist. 102(5):55–59.

Schick, K.D., and Dong, Z. (1993) Early Paleolithic of China and eastern Asia. Evol. Anthropol. 2:22–35.

Xihoudu

Archaeological site in southern Shanxi Province (China) that has yielded artifacts, traces of fire, and a disputably early fauna. Some Chinese workers regard it as the earliest evidence of hominid activity in China. However, the fauna, which supposedly dates to a time equivalent to the Final Villafranchian in Europe (ca. 1 Ma), contains elements that probably have been redeposited and mixed with younger elements. Both fossils and artifacts appear to be rolled and abraded. Thus, it is likely that the entire assemblage is time transgressive. The artifacts may date to the early middle Pleistocene.

See also Asia, Eastern and Southern; China. [G.G.P.]

Further Readings

Schick, K.D., and Dong, Z. (1993) Early Paleolithic of China and eastern Asia. Evol. Anthropol. 2:22–35.

Y

Yang, Zhongjian (also Yang Chung-chien or C.C. Young) (1897–1979)

Chinese vertebrate paleontologist, Quaternary geologist, and prehistoric archaeologist. Yang began his long career by working closely with P. Teilhard de Chardin and other foreign researchers on a broad range of paleontological topics, including Triassic reptiles, late Cenozoic mammals, and vertebrate assemblages associated with human fossils, particularly those of *Homo erectus* at Zhoukoudian (China).

Yang received his B.A. (1923) and Ph.D. (1927) in geology from Peking University and was affiliated with the Cenozoic Research Lab in Beijing from 1929 until 1948 (Yang was honorary director of the lab from 1940 to 1948). With his skills in German, English, Latin, and Russian, Yang was director of the Chinese Academy of Sciences' Bureau of Translation and Editing from 1949 to 1953. From 1954 until his death, he was director of the Institute of Vertebrate Palaeontology and Palaeoanthropology, the successor to the old Cenozoic Research Lab. Beginning in 1959, Yang also was director of the Beijing Natural History Museum.

See also China; Homo erectus; Jia, Lanpo; Teilhard de Chardin, Pierre; Wu, Rukang; Zhoukoudian. [J.W.O.]

Yayo

Open-air site in Chad of Early Pleistocene age based on fauna; also known as Koro-Toro. A partial hominid cranium found at Yayo, consisting of the front of the braincase and face, is now usually attributed to early *Homo* but was originally said to possess characteristics of both *Australopithecus* and *Homo*. The Yayo hominid was originally named *Tchadanthropus uxoris* by Y. Coppens.

See also Africa; Australopithecus; Australopithecus bahrelghazali Homo. [R.P.]

Yeti

Legendary "Abominable Snowman" of the Himalayas, roughly equivalent to the "Bigfoot" of North America. One suggestion is that the extinct hominoid *Gigantopithecus* still survives in the Himalayan snows; but apart from the inherent improbability of such scenarios, there is no convincing proof from either Asia or North America of the continuing existence of a large hominoid unknown to science.

See also Gigantopithecus. [I.T.]

Yuanmou

Large sedimentary basin in northern Yunnan Province, south China, known for its rich assemblage of later Neogene vertebrate fossils in fluvio-lacustrine sediments. The region was first studied in the 1930s, when it was termed the Makai Valley. In 1965, a Yuanmou Basin locality near Shangnabang yielded two human teeth (left and right upper medial incisors), ascribed to "*Homo erectus yuanmouensis*" and thought to be those of a single individual, perhaps a young adult male. Thick quartzite scrapers discovered near the hominin findspot but not in direct association with the fossils were also attributed to *H. erectus*. Cores, flakes, choppers, pointed tools, and scrapers collected in 1973 at five additional localities within a 15-km radius of Shangnabang, while not associated with hominin remains, are thought to be related to the original artifact finds at Shangnabang on the basis of their morphology and technique of manufacture.

In 1973, a large quantity of charcoal-like material was excavated from the bed containing the Yuanmou incisors, while in 1975 two blackened mammalian fossils were recovered at Shangnabang. This is thought by some to constitute evidence of the use of fire by "*H. erectus yuanmouensis*."

Dating of the Yuanmou sequence is problematic. The Yuanmou Formation consists of an almost 700-m-thick sequence of fluvio-lacustrine strata subdivisible into four main members and 28 distinct layers. In the mid-1970s, the hominin- and artifact-bearing unit was dated to 1.7 ± 0.1 Ma on the basis of coarse biostratigraphic correlation and paleomagnetic studies. Subsequent reanalyses have yielded dates for the presumed *H. erectus* stratum ranging from 1.63–1.64 Ma to only 0.5–0.6 Ma. Reexamination of the Yuanmou paleomagnetic correlations and biostratigraphy supports the much younger age. There is also some question as to whether the Yuanmou incisors were found *in situ*. In any case, even the early description of the incisors recognized a strong affinity to Zhoukoudian (China) *H. erectus* incisors, which are also shovel shaped.

In the late 1980s, more than 200 isolated teeth and a juvenile face of a hominoid were recovered from much lower in the Yuanmou sequence, at several sites in the Zhupeng area, such as Hudielangzi and Baozidongqin. The specimens were originally attributed to the new taxa *Homo orientalis* and *Ramapithecus hudiensis*, but they are now widely recognized as an Early Pliocene (or Late Miocene) hominoid that seems to show some affinities to the Ponginae but might also relate to *Lufengpithecus*. The genera *Sinopithecus* and *Dianopithecus* have also been proposed for what is probably the same or similar material. No detailed analysis has yet been published. Simple chipped-stone tools were also claimed to occur in the Pliocene levels, but these are now known to be of natural origin.

See also Asia, Eastern and Southern; China; Dryopithecinae; Homo erectus; Lufengpithecus; Ponginae; Zhoukoudian. [G.G.P., J.W.O, E.D.]

Further Readings

He, Z. (ed.) (1996) Yuanmou Hominoid Fauna. Kunming: Yunnan Science and Technology Press (in Chinese, English summary).

Olsen, J.W., and Miller-Antonio, S. (1992) The Palaeolithic in southern China. Asian Perspectives 31(2):129–160.

Wu, X., and Poirier, F.E. (1995) Human Evolution in China: A Metric Description of the Fossils and a Review of the Sites. New York: Oxford University Press.

Yunxian

Open-air site in calcareous river terrace deposits in Yunxian County, Hubei Province, China. In 1989 and 1990, two distorted human crania were discovered in nodules, along with well-preserved fossil mammals of the Middle Pleistocene *Stegodon-Ailuropoda* fauna, and core and flake tools in quartz and quartzite. The site's age has been estimated ca. 850 Ka by paleomagnetic analysis and ca. 580 ± 90 Ka by ESR.

The first cranium (EV 9001) is badly compressed vertically but has a reasonably preserved palate, dentition, and base. The second cranium (EV 9002) is also vertically compressed, but the face and anterior vault are better preserved. Both crania are evidently very large compared with other Chinese Middle Pleistocene specimens and more closely approximate cristae such as Bodo, Broken Hill, and Petralona in overall dimensions. The faces appear broad and relatively flat, with a high origin for the lower zygomaxillary border. The palates and teeth are large, but, while EV 9002 has very reduced third molars, in EV 9001 they are the largest of the molar sequence. The temporal bone in EV 9002 is relatively high, but the tympanic is very robust, and the occipital bone is highly angled, with a relatively short occipital plane. However, the occipital torus is not strongly developed. Cranial buttressing typical of Asian *Homo erectus* is also generally lacking, but no data on cranial thickness are yet available. The supraorbital torus of EV 9002 is not strongly developed laterally, and the torus is laterally retracted in superior view.

The Yunxian specimens, despite their crushed preservation, are important additions to the Chinese fossil hominid record and extend the range of morphological variation observed. They show a mixture of *H. erectus* and non-*erectus* characters, but I would disagree with T. Li and D. Etler's preferred assignment to the former species and would instead suggest provisional allocation to *Homo heidelbergensis* (= "archaic *Homo sapiens*"). The same authors have asserted that the Yunxian material provides support for multiregional evolution, but this claim seems premature without further work (and possible preparation and reconstruction work) on the specimens, as well as more detailed local and interregional comparisons. It is equally plausible that the specimens document the appearance of a new species in China that replaced *H. erectus*, and that is represented in the later fossil record by material such as Dali and Jinniushan.

See also Archaic Homo sapiens; Asia, Eastern and Southern; Bodo; China; Dali; Homo erectus; Homo heidelbergensis; Homo sapiens; Jinniushan; Kabwe; Modern Human Origins; Petralona; Stegodon-Ailuropoda Fauna. [C.B.S.]

Further Readings

Chen, T., Yang, Q., Hu, Y., Bao, W., and Li, T. (1997) ESR dating of tooth enamel from Yunxian Homo erectus site, China. Quatern. Sci. Revs. 16:455–458.

Li, T., and Etler, D. (1992) New Middle Pleistocene hominid crania from Yunxian in China. Nature 357: 404–407.

Pope G.G. (1992) The craniofacial evidence for the origin of modern humans in China. Yrbk. Phys. Anthropol. 35:243–298.

Z

Zafarraya

Cave site in southern Spain, east of Malaga, with evidence of Mousterian occupation as recently as 27 Ka. A well-preserved and typical Neanderthal lower jaw from the site is said to date from ca. 30 Ka; this date makes it, along with more fragmentary remains of similar age from Portugal's Figueira Brava, Salemas and Columbeira Caves, the latest Neanderthal fossil known.

See also Europe; Mousterian; Neanderthals. [I.T.]

Zhoukoudian

Stratified karst cave and fissure deposits ca. 45 km southwest of Beijing (China), dated from mid-Pliocene to Late Pleistocene on paleomagnetic, radiometric, and faunal evidence. The best known of the Zhoukoudian fossiliferous deposits, Locality 1, is a collapsed limestone cave sequence preserving a column of more than 40 m of stratified infilling.

The site has been known since at least the 1920s as a rich source of vertebrate fossils ("dragon bones"). Joint Chinese-Western excavations in Locality 1 between 1927 and 1937 resulted in the recovery of more than 40 individuals of what was initially referred to *Sinanthropus pekinensis* ("Peking Man") and is now included in *Homo erectus*, the largest-known sample of this taxon from a single site. Locality 1 also yielded ca. 100,000 artifacts. Artifacts have also been recovered from Localities 3, 4, 13, 15, and the much younger Upper Cave, while other localities have yielded faunal remains as old as mid-Pliocene.

The sequence at Locality 1 has been divided into 17 layers from top to bottom. Layers 1–13 have yielded evidence of early human activity in the form of hominid fossils, artifacts, and/or ash deposits, and blackened bones and rocks. All of these layers (except possibly 13) are of normal polarity; thus, the entire hominid-bearing portion of the locality has been assigned to the Brunhes Chron, younger than 780 Ka. Several kinds of radiometric evidence, including uranium-series, fission-track, and thermoluminescence dating, indicate that the hominid-bearing Locality 1 sequence can be securely dated to

460–230 Ka. R. Grün and colleagues reported new ESR analyses in 1997 which suggested a date of ca. 300 Ka for layer 3, the youngest level with *H. erectus* remains.

In 1998, S. Weiner and colleagues discussed their analysis of the burnt bones and purported ash from Layer 10, as well as sedimentology of the deposits. They determined that at least some of the blackened bones had been burned, but that no chemical residues characteristic of wood ash were identifiable. There was no support for the presence of hearths or camp fires. Instead, some of the burned and unburned bones, closely associated with stone tools, were apparently deposited under water in Layer 10 and also in the bottom of Layer 4. The burning was suggested to have been caused by natural processes, perhaps outside the cave, before deposition. The association of burned bone and stone tools suggested to Weiner and colleagues that there might have been use of fire by humans, but they were unable to prove this idea. They also indicated that rather than being a closed cavern, Zhoukoudian might have been an open fissure for at least part of its existence; this raises the possibility that at least some of the faunal remains entered the cave by natural means.

A vast collection of modified or transported stone artifacts and débitage (ca. 100,000 pieces) has been recovered from Layers 1–13 in Locality 1 and from other occupied sites at Zhoukoudian. A detailed analysis was made in 1985 by W. Bei and S. Zhang, who studied more than 17,000 artifacts from Locality 1. Nearly 90 percent were made on quartz, with few other raw materials used (e.g., ca. 2.5 percent in chert). About half of the elements studied were débitage, another 7,400 pieces were scrapers and flakes, and most of the rest were cores and "points." As has long been known, the Zhoukoudian assemblage is of Mode 1 type—there are no bifaces and no significant use of prepared-core technology or flake standardization.

L. Binford and colleagues have suggested that the Locality 1 stratigraphy is composed largely of secondary deposits that do not relate to the human occupational history of the site, if any. Furthermore, it has been suggested that the

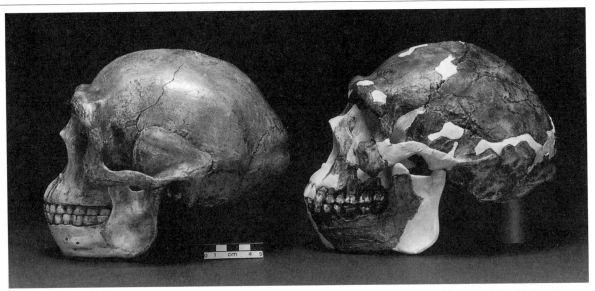

Comparison of two reconstructions of "Peking Man" skulls from Zhoukoudian. On the left is a prewar reconstruction by F. Weidenreich, based on a calotte and two fragments of maxilla and mandible, all identified as female. On the right is a recent reconstruction by G. Sawyer and I. Tattersall, based on a much larger array of pieces, identified as male, that permit an accurate reconstitution of facial anatomy.

blackened bones and rocks and thick ash lenses do not indicate human control of fire but reflect, respectively, chemical alteration and the spontaneous combustion of dung-bearing deposits in a cave environment. Carnivores have also been cited as the main taphonomic agent responsible for the accumulation of hominid and other fossils at Zhoukoudian. The latter idea, however, is viewed as speculative and ill founded by most Asian specialists familiar with the locality. In fact, a comparison of the stratigraphic sequence with paleoclimatological evidence (palynological, biostratigraphic, and chemical data) indicates that hominids were consistently present at the site during relatively moist and warm periods, as also attested by the extensive archaeological residues.

Incised bones are also present at Locality 1, but, in spite of suggestions put forward in the 1930s, there is little evidence for a bone-tool industry at Zhoukoudian. Cannibalism by *H. erectus* has often been claimed on the basis of relatively consistent damage to the skull bases, implying removal of the brain, but evidence for this is equivocal at best. Carnivores and rodents undoubtedly played some role in the modification of bone at the site. Burnt hackberry seeds and numerous specimens of large deer may also represent components of the diet of *H. erectus*, but their presence at Zhoukoudian might be due at least in part to nonhominid agencies.

Physically just above Locality 1, but far younger in age, Zhoukoudian's Upper Cave (Shandingdong) contained a number of remains of *Homo sapiens sapiens*, including three relatively complete crania and numerous postcranial bones from Layer 4. Younger burials derived from Layers 1 and 2. F. Weidenreich originally perceived three "racial types" in the three Layer 4 individuals: Eskimo, Ainu (and, indirectly, Caucasian), and Melanesian. Few modern workers support this interpretation, preferring instead to recognize the Upper Cave specimens as indicative of the range of variability in prehistoric northern Chinese populations.

Only a handful of stone artifacts are associated with the human remains in the Upper Cave, but the recovery of numerous ornaments, including a necklace of shells, fish vertebrae, and carnivore teeth, is noteworthy as one of the earliest nonutilitarian artifact groupings in China.

Carbon-14 dates obtained for the Upper Cave deposits suggest a maximum age of 18–11 Ka, although the former age derives from Layer 5 and thus predates *all* of the human fossils. The artifacts support the younger age, as they are similar (and, in one case, conjoining) from Layer 1 to Layer 4. Additionally, perforated seashells in Layer 4 suggest the likelihood of an Early Holocene date, when the sea would have been only 150 km away rather than 1,000.

The *H. erectus* specimens collected in the 1930s disappeared at the beginning of World War II when the Japanese invaded Beijing. Despite subsequent intensive efforts to locate them, the wherabouts of the fossils remains a mystery. Postwar studies have been based on the excellent casts and detailed descriptions and measurements made by Weidenreich. Chinese researchers continue to excavate periodically at Zhoukoudian, and a few new specimens of *H. erectus*, some of which fit onto casts of the prewar specimens, have been recovered as a result of post-1949 excavations.

In 1993, the Institute of Vertebrate Palaeontology and Palaeoanthropology in Beijing created the Zhoukoudian International Palaeoanthropological Research Center. This center, affiliated with the Chinese Academy of Sciences and organized by Chinese, French, and American scholars, is intended to provide a logistical base from which a new series of investigations at Zhoukoudian might stem.

See also Asia, Eastern and Southern; China; Early Paleolithic; Fire; Homo erectus; Homo sapiens; Movius' Line; Taphonomy; Weidenreich, Franz. [G.G.P., J.W.O]

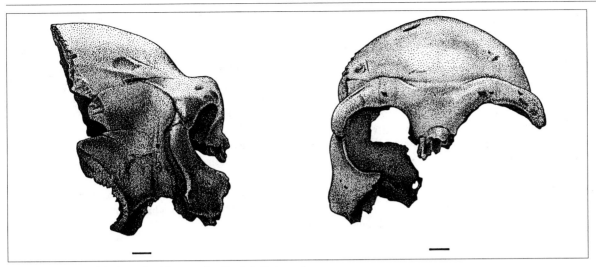

Side and front views of the fronto-facial fragment from Zuttiyeh. Scales are 1 cm.

Further Readings

Binford, L., and Ho, C.K. (1985) Taphonomy at a distance: Zhoukoudian the cave home of Beijing Man? Curr. Anthropol. 26:413–443.

Grün, R., Huang, P., Wu, X., Stringer, C.B., Thorne, A.G., and McCulloch, M. (1997) ESR analysis of teeth from the paleoanthropological site of Zhoukoudian, China. J. Hum. Evol. 32:83–91.

Kamminga, J. (1992) New interpretations of the Upper Cave, Zhoukoudian. In T. Akazawa, K. Aoki, and T. Kimura (eds.): The Evolution and Dispersal of Modern Humans in Asia. Tokyo: Hokushen-Sha, pp. 379–400.

Pei, W., and Zhang, S. (1985) A Study on the Lithic Artifacts of *Sinanthropus*. Beijing: Science Press.

Weiner, S., Xu, Q., Goldberg, P., Liu, J., and Bar-Yosef, O. (1998) Evidence for the use of fire at Zhoukoudian, China. Science 281:251–253. *See also* Wu, X. (1999) Letter to Science, and Weiner *et al.* Reply. Science 283:299.

Wu, R., and Lin, S. (1983) Peking Man. Sci. Amer. 248(3):86–94.

Wu, X., and Poirier, F.E. (1995) Human Evolution in China: A Metric Description of the Fossils and a Review of the Sites. New York: Oxford University Press.

Zooarchaeology

Study of faunal remains, including bones, teeth, horns, and shells, from archaeological sites. The studies are conducted by zoologists or by archaeologists trained in zoology and involve the collection, cleaning, sorting, identification, and measurement of faunal remains and their subsequent interpretation. The material is collected from the soil during excavation; because preservation factors favor the survival of large fragments, other methods, such as sieving and flotation, may be adopted to ensure recovery of unbiased samples. After being collected, the material is sorted into identifiable and unidentifiable pieces, and identifiable fragments are further described, when possible, by species, body part, sex and age, season of death, and the presence of butchering or eating marks. Identifications are facilitated by the use of zoology reference books and a comparative collection of modern fauna. In some cases, a zooarchaeologist may estimate the minimum number of individuals (MNI) of each species present in an assemblage, by counting the number of certain body parts for each species. The specialist may also estimate the total amount of meat available to prehistoric occupants, by multiplying the average weight of edible meat for each species by their MNI; this information can be used to reveal the duration or size of occupation.

Data derived from zooarchaeological studies are used to reconstruct past environments; ancient diets; the transition from hunting to herding; and past hunting, butchering, and meat-distribution practices. The ancient climate and local vegetation at a site may be reconstructed from the presence or absence of certain animals that have well-defined habitats (e.g., reindeer prefer a tundra environment, and fallow deer favor woodland settings) or the relative abundance and diversity of species in a faunal assemblage. The ancient diet can be reconstituted by enumerating the types and relative frequencies of animal species from a site. Faunal remains can also be used to pinpoint the fundamental prehistoric transition from hunting wild animals to herding domesticated ones. Criteria used to establish the timing and location of domestication include morphological changes in animal body size or horn shape, the sudden appearance of nonlocal species, a shift in the relative abundances of different species, a change in the age and sex composition of a faunal assemblage, and evidence of a close relationship between animals and humans (e.g., burial of an animal with a human). Faunal remains have also shed light on former hunting strategies; on meat processing, distribution, and consumption habits; and on the location and duration of these activities at an ancient settlement. The presence and location of cutmarks and/or carnivore tooth marks on faunal remains can illuminate the relationships between humans and their carnivorous competitors and suggest the prevalence of hunting vs. scavenging in food-procurement strategies.

See also Domestication; Neolithic; Paleolithic Lifeways; Taphonomy. [N.B.]

Zuttiyeh

The cave site of Mugharet-el-Zuttiyeh (Israel) was excavated between 1925 and 1926 and produced the first non-modern fossil hominid recovered in western Asia. The frontal bone and part of the upper face of the Zuttiyeh hominid were derived from the Mugharan (or Jabrudian) level of the site, which is believed to date from the late Middle Pleistocene. Recent age estimates range from 300 to 200 Ka. The fossil, therefore, clearly antedates southwestern Asian Neanderthals, such as those from Tabūn, Amud, and Kebara, as well as the archaic moderns from Qafzeh and Skhūl. It is also known as the Galilee hominid.

The Zuttiyeh specimen must have had a relatively small cranial capacity, and the supraorbital torus is quite straight and strongly developed laterally. The upper face is flat, in contrast to that of the later Neanderthals, and this has led to debate about the affinities of the specimen. Some workers believe that the Zuttiyeh fossil represents a primitive ancestral Neanderthal, in which midfacial projection had not yet evolved, while others suggest that it may be more closely related to the ancestry of the archaic moderns. Another alternative is that the specimen represents an extension out of Africa of broadly "archaic *Homo sapiens*" before the separation of the modern human lineage.

See also Amud Cave; Archaic Homo sapiens; Archaic Moderns; Asia, Western; Jabrudian; Kebara; Modern Human Origins; Neanderthals; Qafzeh; Skhūl; Tabūn. [C.B.S.]

Index